# MyEconLab www.myeconlab.com

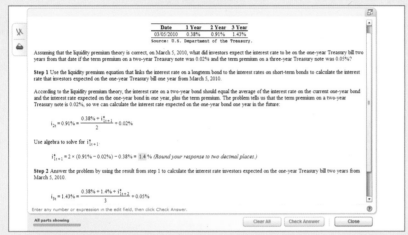

| Date | 1 Year | 2 Year | 3 Year |
|------|--------|--------|--------|
| 03/05/2010 | 0.38% | 0.91% | 1.43% |

Source: U.S. Department of the Treasury.

Assuming that the liquidity premium theory is correct, on March 5, 2010, what did investors expect the interest rate to be on the one-year Treasury bill two years from that date if the term premium on a two-year Treasury note was 0.02% and the term premium on a three-year Treasury note was 0.05%?

**Step 1** Use the liquidity premium equation that links the interest rate on a longterm bond to the interest rates on short-term bonds to calculate the interest rate that investors expected on the one-year Treasury bill one year from March 5, 2010.

According to the liquidity premium theory, the interest rate on a two-year bond should equal the average of the interest rate on the current one-year bond and the interest rate expected on the one-year bond in one year, plus the term premium. The problem tells us that the term premium on a two-year Treasury note is 0.02%, so we can calculate the interest rate expected on the one-year bond one year in the future:

$$i_{2t} = 0.91\% = \frac{0.38\% + i^e_{1t+1}}{2} + 0.02\%$$

Use algebra to solve for $i^e_{1t+1}$.

$$i^e_{1t+1} = 2 \times (0.91\% - 0.02\%) - 0.38\% = \boxed{1.4}\% \ \textit{(Round your response to two decimal places.)}$$

**Step 2** Answer the problem by using the result from step 1 to calculate the interest rate investors expected on the one-year Treasury bill two years from March 5, 2010.

$$i_{3t} = 1.43\% = \frac{0.38\% + 1.4\% + i^e_{1t+2}}{3} + 0.05\%$$

Enter any number or expression in the edit field, then click Check Answer.

All parts showing — Clear All — Check Answer — Close

**Learning Resources.** To further reinforce understanding, Study Plan and Homework problems link to additional learning resources:

- *A step-by-step Guided Solution* helps students break down a problem much the same way as an instructor would do during office hours.

- *The eText page* on which the topic of the exercise is explained promotes reading the text when further explanation is needed.

- *A graphing tool* encourages students to draw and manipulate graphs and deepen their understanding by illustrating economic relationships and ideas.

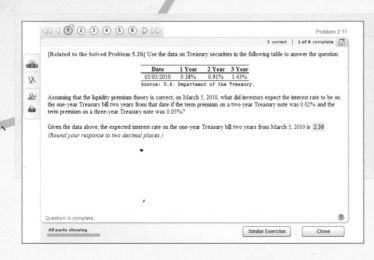

Problem 2 11

1 correct | 1 of 6 complete

[Related to the Solved Problem 5.2b] Use the data on Treasury securities in the following table to answer the question:

| Date | 1 Year | 2 Year | 3 Year |
|------|--------|--------|--------|
| 03/05/2010 | 0.38% | 0.91% | 1.43% |

Source: U.S. Department of the Treasury.

Assuming that the liquidity premium theory is correct, on March 5, 2010, what did investors expect the interest rate to be on the one-year Treasury bill two years from that date if the term premium on a two-year Treasury note was 0.02% and the term premium on a three-year Treasury note was 0.05%?

Given the data above, the expected interest rate on the one-year Treasury bill two years from March 5, 2010 is 2.36. *(Round your response to two decimal places.)*

Question is complete.

All parts showing — Similar Exercise — Close

**Unlimited Practice.** Many Study Plan and Instructor-assigned exercises contain algorithms to ensure students get as much practice as they need.

As students work through Study Plan or Homework exercises, instant feedback and tutorial resources guide them towards understanding.

# THE PEARSON SERIES IN ECONOMICS

**Abel/Bernanke/Croushore**
*Macroeconomics**

**Bade/Parkin**
*Foundations of Economics**

**Berck/Helfand**
*The Economics of the Environment*

**Bierman/Fernandez**
*Game Theory with
Economic Applications*

**Blanchard**
*Macroeconomics**

**Blau/Ferber/Winkler**
*The Economics of Women, Men and
Work*

**Boardman/Greenberg/Vining/Weimer**
*Cost-Benefit Analysis*

**Boyer**
*Principles of Transportation
Economics*

**Branson**
*Macroeconomic Theory and Policy*

**Brock/Adams**
*The Structure of American Industry*

**Bruce**
*Public Finance and the American
Economy*

**Carlton/Perloff**
*Modern Industrial Organization*

**Case/Fair/Oster**
*Principles of Economics**

**Caves/Frankel/Jones**
*World Trade and Payments:
An Introduction*

**Chapman**
*Environmental Economics:
Theory, Application, and Policy*

**Cooter/Ulen**
*Law & Economics*

**Downs**
*An Economic Theory of
Democracy*

**Ehrenberg/Smith**
*Modern Labor Economics*

**Ekelund/Ressler/Tollison**
*Economics**

**Farnham**
*Economics for Managers*

**Folland/Goodman/Stano**
*The Economics of Health and
Health Care*

**Fort**
*Sports Economics*

**Froyen**
*Macroeconomics*

**Fusfeld**
*The Age of the Economist*

**Gerber**
*International Economics**

**Gordon**
*Macroeconomics**

**Greene**
*Econometric Analysis*

**Gregory**
*Essentials of Economics*

**Gregory/Stuart**
*Russian and Soviet Economic
Performance and Structure*

**Hartwick/Olewiler**
*The Economics of Natural
Resource Use*

**Heilbroner/Milberg**
*The Making of the Economic
Society*

**Heyne/Boettke/Prychitko**
*The Economic Way of Thinking*

**Hoffman/Averett**
*Women and the Economy:
Family, Work, and Pay*

**Holt**
*Markets, Games and Strategic
Behavior*

**Hubbard/O'Brien**
*Economics**

*Money, Banking, and the Financial
System**

**Hubbard/O'Brien/Rafferty**
*Macroeconomics**

**Hughes/Cain**
*American Economic History*

**Husted/Melvin**
*International Economics*

**Jehle/Reny**
*Advanced Microeconomic Theory*

**Johnson-Lans**
*A Health Economics Primer*

**Keat/Young**
*Managerial Economics*

**Klein**
*Mathematical Methods
for Economics*

**Krugman/Obstfeld/Melitz**
*International Economics:
Theory & Policy**

**Laidler**
*The Demand for Money*

**Leeds/von Allmen**
*The Economics of Sports*

**Leeds/von Allmen/Schiming**
*Economics**

**Lipsey/Ragan/Storer**
*Economics**

**Lynn**
*Economic Development: Theory
and Practice for a Divided World*

**Miller**
*Economics Today**

*Understanding Modern
Economics*

**Miller/Benjamin**
*The Economics of Macro Issues*

**Miller/Benjamin/North**
*The Economics of Public Issues*

**Mills/Hamilton**
*Urban Economics*

**Mishkin**
*The Economics of Money,
Banking, and Financial Markets**

*The Economics of Money,
Banking, and Financial Markets,
Business School Edition**

*Macroeconomics: Policy and
Practice**

**Murray**
*Econometrics: A Modern
Introduction*

**Nafziger**
*The Economics of Developing
Countries*

**O'Sullivan/Sheffrin/Perez**
*Economics: Principles, Applications
and Tools**

**Parkin**
*Economics**

**Perloff**
*Microeconomics**

*Microeconomics: Theory and
Applications with Calculus**

**Perman/Common/McGilvray/Ma**
*Natural Resources and
Environmental Economics*

**Phelps**
*Health Economics*

**Pindyck/Rubinfeld**
*Microeconomics**

**Riddell/Shackelford/Stamos/ Schneider**
*Economics: A Tool for Critically
Understanding Society*

**Ritter/Silber/Udell**
*Principles of Money, Banking &
Financial Markets**

**Roberts**
*The Choice: A Fable of Free Trade
and Protection*

**Rohlf**
*Introduction to Economic
Reasoning*

**Ruffin/Gregory**
*Principles of Economics*

**Sargent**
*Rational Expectations and
Inflation*

**Sawyer/Sprinkle**
*International Economics*

**Scherer**
*Industry Structure, Strategy,
and Public Policy*

**Schiller**
*The Economics of Poverty and
Discrimination*

**Sherman**
*Market Regulation*

**Silberberg**
*Principles of Microeconomics*

**Stock/Watson**
*Introduction to Econometrics*

*Introduction to Econometrics,
Brief Edition*

**Studenmund**
*Using Econometrics: A
Practical Guide*

**Tietenberg/Lewis**
*Environmental and Natural
Resource Economics*

*Environmental Economics
and Policy*

**Todaro/Smith**
*Economic Development*

**Waldman**
*Microeconomics*

**Waldman/Jensen**
*Industrial Organization:
Theory and Practice*

**Weil**
*Economic Growth*

**Williamson**
*Macroeconomics*

# Economics

# Economics

**Fourth Edition**

**R. Glenn Hubbard**
Columbia University

**Anthony Patrick O'Brien**
Lehigh University

**PEARSON**

Boston   Columbus   Indianapolis   New York   San Francisco   Upper Saddle River
Amsterdam   Cape Town   Dubai   London   Madrid   Milan   Munich   Paris   Montréal   Toronto
Delhi   Mexico City   São Paulo   Sydney   Hong Kong   Seoul   Singapore   Taipei   Tokyo

Editorial Director: Sally Yagan
Editor in Chief: Donna Battista
AVP/Executive Editor: David Alexander
VP/Development Director: Stephen Deitmer
Executive Development Editor:
    Lena Buonanno
Editorial Project Manager: Lindsey Sloan
Editorial Assistant: Emily Brodeur
Marketing Director: Patrice Jones
AVP/Executive Marketing Manager:
    Lori DeShazo
Marketing Assistant: Courtney Kamauf
Senior Managing Editor: Nancy H. Fenton
Production Project Manager:
    Carla Thompson
Manufacturing Director: Evelyn Beaton
Senior Manufacturing Buyer: Carol Melville
Senior Media Buyer: Ginny Michaud

Creative Director: Christy Mahon
Senior Art Director, Cover: Jonathan Boylan
Image Manager: Rachel Youdelman
Text Permissions Project Supervisor:
    Michael Joyce
Media Director: Susan Schoenberg
Content Lead, MyEconLab: Noel Lotz
Senior Media Producer:
    Melissa Honig
Associate Production Project Manager:
    Alison Eusden
Full-Service Project Management/Interior
Design/Photo Research/Composition:
    PreMediaGlobal, Inc.
Printer/Binder: Courier, Kendallville
Cover Printer: Courier, Kendallville
Text Font: Minion

Credits and acknowledgments borrowed from other sources and reproduced, with permission, in this textbook appear on appropriate page within text (or on page C-1).

Microsoft® and Windows® are registered trademarks of the Microsoft Corporation in the U.S.A. and other countries. Screen shots and icons reprinted with permission from the Microsoft Corporation. This book is not sponsored or endorsed by or affiliated with the Microsoft Corporation.

Many of the designations by manufacturers and sellers to distinguish their products are claimed as trademarks. Where those designations appear in this book, and the publisher was aware of a trademark claim, the designations have been printed in initial caps or all caps.

**Cataloging-in-Publication Data is on file at the Library of Congress**

10 9 8 7 6 5 4 3 2 1

ISBN 13: 978-0-13-281725-7
ISBN 10: 0-13-281725-X

www.pearsonhighered.com

**For Constance, Raph, and Will**
*—R. Glenn Hubbard*

**For Cindy, Matthew, Andrew, and Daniel**
*—Anthony Patrick O'Brien*

# ABOUT THE AUTHORS

**Glenn Hubbard, policymaker, professor, and researcher.** R. Glenn Hubbard is the dean and Russell L. Carson Professor of Finance and Economics in the Graduate School of Business at Columbia University and professor of economics in Columbia's Faculty of Arts and Sciences. He is also a research associate of the National Bureau of Economic Research and a director of Automatic Data Processing, Black Rock Closed-End Funds, KKR Financial Corporation, and MetLife. He received his Ph.D. in economics from Harvard University in 1983. From 2001 to 2003, he served as chairman of the White House Council of Economic Advisers and chairman of the OECD Economy Policy Committee, and from 1991 to 1993, he was deputy assistant secretary of the U.S. Treasury Department. He currently serves as co-chair of the nonpartisan Committee on Capital Markets Regulation. Hubbard's fields of specialization are public economics, financial markets and institutions, corporate finance, macroeconomics, industrial organization, and public policy. He is the author of more than 100 articles in leading journals, including *American Economic Review, Brookings Papers on Economic Activity, Journal of Finance, Journal of Financial Economics, Journal of Money, Credit, and Banking, Journal of Political Economy, Journal of Public Economics, Quarterly Journal of Economics, RAND Journal of Economics,* and *Review of Economics and Statistics*. His research has been supported by grants from the National Science Foundation, the National Bureau of Economic Research, and numerous private foundations.

**Tony O'Brien, award-winning professor and researcher.** Anthony Patrick O'Brien is a professor of economics at Lehigh University. He received his Ph.D. from the University of California, Berkeley, in 1987. He has taught principles of economics for more than 15 years, in both large sections and small honors classes. He received the Lehigh University Award for Distinguished Teaching. He was formerly the director of the Diamond Center for Economic Education and was named a Dana Foundation Faculty Fellow and Lehigh Class of 1961 Professor of Economics. He has been a visiting professor at the University of California, Santa Barbara, and the Graduate School of Industrial Administration at Carnegie Mellon University. O'Brien's research has dealt with such issues as the evolution of the U.S. automobile industry, sources of U.S. economic competitiveness, the development of U.S. trade policy, the causes of the Great Depression, and the causes of black-white income differences. His research has been published in leading journals, including *American Economic Review, Quarterly Journal of Economics, Journal of Money, Credit, and Banking, Industrial Relations, Journal of Economic History,* and *Explorations in Economic History*. His research has been supported by grants from government agencies and private foundations. In addition to teaching and writing, O'Brien also serves on the editorial board of the *Journal of Socio-Economics*.

# BRIEF CONTENTS

# CONTENTS

*These end-of-chapter resource materials repeat in all chapters.

# PART 2: Markets in Action: Policy and Applications

# PART 6: Labor Markets, Public Choice, and the Distribution of Income

# PART 7: Macroeconomic Foundations and Long-Run Growth

# PART 8: Short-Run Fluctuations

# PART 9: Monetary and Fiscal Policy

# PART 10: The International Economy

# FLEXIBILITY CHART

The following chart helps you organize your syllabus based on your teaching preferences and objectives:

| Core | Optional | Policy |
|------|----------|--------|
| **Chapter 1:** Economics: Foundations and Models | **Chapter 1 Appendix:** Using Graphs and Formulas | |
| **Chapter 2:** Trade-offs, Comparative Advantage, and the Market System | | |
| **Chapter 3:** Where Prices Come From: The Interaction of Demand and Supply | | |
| | **Chapter 4 Appendix:** Quantitative Demand and Supply Analysis | **Chapter 4:** Economic Efficiency, Government Price Setting, and Taxes |
| | | **Chapter 5:** Externalities, Environmental Policy, and Public Goods |
| **Chapter 6:** Elasticity: The Responsiveness of Demand and Supply | | |
| | | **Chapter 7:** The Economics of Health Care |
| | **Chapter 8:** Firms, the Stock Market, and Corporate Governance | |
| | **Chapter 8 Appendix:** Tools to Analyze Firms' Financial Information | |
| **Chapter 9:** Comparative Advantage and the Gains from International Trade | | |
| | **Chapter 10:** Consumer Choice and Behavioral Economics | |
| | **Chapter 10 Appendix:** Using Indifference Curves and Budget Lines to Understand Consumer Behavior | |
| **Chapter 11:** Technology, Production, and Costs | **Chapter 11 Appendix:** Using Isoquants and Isocost Lines to Understand Production and Cost | |
| **Chapter 12:** Firms in Perfectly Competitive Markets | | |
| **Chapter 13:** Monopolistic Competition: The Competitive Model in a More Realistic Setting | | |
| **Chapter 14:** Oligopoly: Firms in Less Competitive Markets | | |
| **Chapter 15:** Monopoly and Antitrust Policy | | |
| | **Chapter 16:** Pricing Strategy | |

| Core | Optional | Policy |
|---|---|---|
| **Chapter 17:** The Markets for Labor and Other Factors of Production | | |
| | | **Chapter 18:** Public Choice, Taxes, and the Distribution of Income |
| **Chapter 19:** GDP: Measuring Total Production and Income | | |
| **Chapter 20:** Unemployment and Inflation | | |
| **Chapter 21:** Economic Growth, the Financial System, and Business Cycles | | |
| **Chapter 22:** Long-Run Economic Growth: Sources and Policies | | |
| | **Chapter 23:** Aggregate Expenditure and Output in the Short Run | |
| | **Chapter 23 Appendix:** The Algebra of Macroeconomic Equilibrium | |
| **Chapter 24:** Aggregate Demand and Aggregate Supply Analysis | | |
| | **Chapter 24 Appendix:** Macroeconomic Schools of Thought | |
| **Chapter 25:** Money, Banks, and the Federal Reserve System | | |
| | | **Chapter 26:** Monetary Policy |
| | **Chapter 27 Appendix:** A Closer Look at the Multiplier | **Chapter 27:** Fiscal Policy |
| | | **Chapter 28:** Inflation, Unemployment, and Federal Reserve Policy |
| | **Chapter 29:** Macroeconomics in an Open Economy | |
| | **Chapter 30:** The International Financial System | |
| | **Chapter 30 Appendix:** The Gold Standard and the Bretton Woods System | |

When George Lucas was asked why he made *Star Wars*, he replied, "It's the kind of movie I like to see, but no one seemed to be making them. So, I decided to make one." We realized that no one seemed to be writing the kind of textbook we wanted to use in our classes. So, after years of supplementing texts with fresh, lively, real-world examples from newspapers, magazines, Web sites, and professional journals, we decided to write an economics text that delivers complete economics coverage with many real-world business examples. Our goal was to keep our classes "widget free."

# New to the Fourth Edition

The severe economic downturn that began in 2007 with the bursting of the housing bubble was still affecting the economy in 2011. Unemployment had risen to levels not seen in decades and remained above 9 percent for more than two and a half years. The crisis in the financial system was the worst since the Great Depression of the 1930s. Policy debates intensified as Congress passed and President Barack Obama enacted the American Recovery and Reinvestment Act of 2009, the largest package of spending increases and tax cuts in history. The Federal Reserve sailed into uncharted waters as it developed new policy tools to deal with the unprecedented financial turmoil. Other long-running policy debates continued as well, as comprehensive health care legislation, looming cost increases for Social Security and Medicare, huge long-run budget deficits, environmental problems, income inequality, and changes to the tax system all received attention from economists, policymakers, and the public.

In this new edition, we help students understand recent economic events and the policy responses to them. As in the earlier editions, we place applications at the forefront of the discussion. We believe that students find the study of economics more interesting and easier to master when they see economic analysis applied to real-world issues that concern them.

Here is a summary of the changes in this fourth edition. Please see the next section, starting on the next page, for details on each of these changes:

- A new Chapter 7, "The Economics of Health Care," covers health care around the world, information problems and externalities in the market for health care, and the debate over President Obama's Patient Protection and Affordable Care Act.

- There is new coverage of the slow recovery from the recession and financial crisis of 2007–2009.

- There is new coverage of initiatives by the Federal Reserve, including quantitative easing and Operation Twist.

- There is new coverage of fiscal policy, including analysis of the debate over fiscal stimulus and the magnitude of multipliers for government spending and taxes.

- All companies in the chapter openers have been either replaced with new companies or updated with current information.

- All chapters include new *An Inside Look* newspaper articles and analyses to help students apply economic thinking to current events and policy debates.

- There are 28 new *Making the Connection* features to help students tie economic concepts to current events and policy issues.

- Figures and tables have been updated, using the latest data available.

- Many of the end-of-chapter problems have been either replaced or updated.

In this new edition, we have taken the opportunity to make many changes throughout the text, while concentrating on the key areas described in the following sections.

*Policy debates, including health care, trade, and pollution.* The number of jobs in the health care sector continues to increase. In Chapter 1, "Economics: Foundations and Models," we use the debate about whether public policy is resulting in physicians leaving private practice to introduce students to positive and normative economic analysis. In Chapter 9, "Comparative Advantage and the Gains from International Trade," we explore the "Buy American" provision in the 2009 stimulus package.

As this book goes to press, the debate continues over the consequences of the 2010 overhaul of the U.S. health care system. In Chapter 2, "Trade-offs, Comparative Advantage, and the Market System," we discuss the trade-offs involved in health care spending and the Medicare and Medicaid programs. We revisit the topic of health care in the new Chapter 7, "The Economics of Health Care," where we discuss projections of health care spending and the role of the U.S. government in the health care system. In Chapter 17, "The Markets for Labor and Other Factors of Production," we discuss whether U.S. firms are handicapped in competing with foreign firms by paying for their employees' health insurance. We return to the health care topic in Chapter 18, "Public Choice, Taxes, and the Distribution of Income," with a news article and analysis on a proposed soda tax to pay for health care.

The United States has made progress in reducing air pollution in the years since Congress passed the Clean Air Act in 1970. In Chapter 5, "Externalities, Environmental Policy, and Public Goods," we use the economic concepts of marginal cost, marginal benefit, and efficiency to discuss environmental policy, including President Barack Obama's proposed cap-and-trade policy to reduce emissions of carbon dioxide.

*The recession and financial crisis of 2007–2009 and its aftermath.* Today's students feel the effects of the slow recovery from the worst economic crisis since the Great Depression of the 1930s. The problems in the financial system in the United States and the euro zone have proven that it is important for students in both microeconomics and macroeconomics courses to understand the basics of how financial markets work and the role of government in financial regulation. In Chapter 8, "Firms, the Stock Market, and Corporate Governance," we cover the basics of the stock and bond markets, discuss why stock prices fluctuate, and examine the role of the principal–agent problem in the financial meltdown of 2007–2009. Chapter 24, "Aggregate Demand and Aggregate Supply Analysis," covers the origins of the recession and includes a new discussion of how long it takes the economy to return to potential GDP. The housing bust and subprime crisis are discussed in Chapter 25, "Money, Banks, and the Federal Reserve System," and Chapter 26,"Monetary Policy."

*New initiatives by the Federal Reserve.* During 2008, the Fed dramatically broke with precedent by setting up a number of new "lending facilities" and by participating in actions such as the purchase of Bear Stearns by JPMorgan Chase. In this new edition, we provide students with a basic background on investment banks and the process of securitization; the mortgage-backed securities market, including the roles of Fannie Mae and Freddie Mac; and the debate among economists concerning the Fed's two rounds of quantitative easing and "Operation Twist."

*Real-world company examples and newspaper articles.* As in previous editions, we open each chapter by highlighting a company to establish a real-world context for learning and to spark students' interest in economics. We have chosen new companies for some chapters and updated the information in the other chapters. As in previous editions, each chapter closes with the *An Inside Look* feature, which shows students how to apply the concepts from the chapter to the analysis of a news article. We have replaced all the *An Inside Look* features in this edition. Here is a snapshot of some of these changes:

> Chapter 3, "Where Prices Come From: The Interaction of Demand and Supply," opens with a discussion of the iPad and the tablet reader revolution. The *An Inside Look* feature presents an article and analysis of how a shortage of display screens could affect the sale of tablet readers.

Chapter 7, "The Economics of Health Care," opens with a discussion of the rising health care costs for small businesses. The *An Inside Look* feature presents an article and analysis of health care spending and the Patient Protection and Affordable Care Act of 2010.

Chapter 8, "Firms, the Stock Market, and Corporate Governance," opens with a discussion of the runaway success of the private company Facebook and how some of the company's stock is available for sale in private markets. *An Inside Look* features Internet companies that allow qualified investors a chance to buy stock in private companies.

Chapter 10, "Consumer Choice and Behavioral Economics," opens with a discussion of how aging rock star Ozzy Osbourne and teenage singing sensation Justin Bieber endorsed Best Buy's new electronics program. The *An Inside Look* feature presents an article and analysis of how endorsements from celebrities ranging from Jennifer Lopez to Charlie Sheen can help or hurt a brand.

Chapter 19, "GDP: Measuring Total Production and Income," opens with a discussion of Ford Motor Company's performance following the 2007–2009 recession. The *An Inside Look* feature presents an analysis of how uncertain economic conditions in 2011 and 2012 kept demand for automobiles below initial sales estimates

Chapter 26, "Monetary Policy," opens with a discussion of homebuilder Toll Brothers. The *An Inside Look* feature presents an analysis of the effects of "Operation Twist," the Federal Reserve's attempt to boost the economy in late 2011 by stimulating the sluggish housing market.

## Further changes to the fourth edition

The following are further changes to the fourth edition:

- This edition provides many new *Making the Connection* features, which help students tie economic concepts to current events and policy issues, as well as updated sections, figures, and tables:

  Chapter 1 opens with a new discussion of doctors in private practice and includes two new *Making the Connections*, "Does Health Insurance Give People an Incentive to Become Obese?" and "Should Medical School Be Free?"

  Chapter 2 includes a new *Making the Connection*, "A Story of the Market System in Action: How Do You Make an iPad?"

  Chapter 3 opens with discussion of the tablet computer industry and includes three new *Making the Connections*: "The Aging of the Baby Boom Generation," "Forecasting the Demand for iPads," and "Are Quiznos Sandwiches Normal Goods and Subway Sandwiches Inferior Goods?"

  Chapter 5 includes revised graphs of the economic effects of government taxes and subsidies to improve student understanding of this sometimes difficult subject, and two new *Making the Connections*: "Should the Government Tax Cigarettes and Soda?" and "Can a Cap-and-Trade System Reduce Global Warming?"

  Chapter 7 is new to this edition and covers health care around the world; information problems and externalities in the market for health care; and the Patient Protection and Affordable Care Act in the United States. The chapter contains *Making the Connections* titled "How Much Is That MRI Scan?" and "Health Exchanges, Small Businesses, and Rising Medical Costs."

  Chapter 8 has a new section on the financial crisis of 2007–2009 and two new *Making the Connections*: "The Rating Game: Is the U.S. Treasury Likely to Default on Its Bonds?" and "Are Buyers of Facebook Stock Getting a Fair Deal?"

  Chapter 9 includes two new *Making the Connections*: "Leave New York City? Risky for Financial Firms" and "Save Jobs Making Hangers . . . and Lose Jobs in Dry Cleaning."

Chapter 10 opens with a new discussion of Justin Bieber and Ozzy Osbourne and includes two new *Making the Connections*: "Why Do Firms Pay Tom Brady to Endorse Their Products?" and "What's Up with 'Fuel Surcharges'?"

Chapter 11 includes a new *Solved Problem*, "Using Long-Run Average Cost Curves to Understand Business Strategy."

Chapter 12 includes a new *Solved Problem*, "When to Pull the Plug on a Movie."

Chapter 15 has a new *Making the Connection*: "Should AT&T Have Been Allowed to Merge with T-Mobile?"

Chapter 17 opens with a new discussion of the San Diego Padres trading Adrian Gonzalez to the Red Sox and includes a new *Making the Connection*: "Does Greg Have an Easier Time Finding a Job Than Jamal?"

Chapter 20 opens with a new discussion of Bank of America's 2011 announcement to lay off 30,000 workers and includes two new *Making the Connections*: "How Unusual Was the Unemployment Situation Following the 2007–2009 Recession?" and "How Should We Categorize Unemployment at Bank of America?"

Chapter 22 includes two new *Making the Connections*: "Is Income All That Matters?" and "Will China's Standard of Living Ever Exceed That of the United States?"

Chapter 24 includes two new *Making the Connections*: "Which Components of Aggregate Demand Changed the Most during the 2007–2009 Recession?" and "How Long Does It Take to Return to Potential GDP? Economic Forecasts Following the Recession of 2007–2009."

Chapter 26 includes two new *Making* the *Connections*: "Too Low for Zero: The Fed Tries 'Quantitative Easing' and 'Operation Twist'" and "Trying to Hit a Moving Target: Making Policy with "Real-Time Data.""

Chapter 27 opens with a new discussion of the role of government in creating jobs, and includes a new section on "Fiscal Policy in Action: Did the Fiscal Stimulus Package Work?"; a new table showing competing estimates of the size of the government spending and tax multipliers; and a new *Making the Connection*: "Why Was the Recession of 2007–2009 So Severe?"

Chapter 28 opens with a new discussion of CarMax.

Chapter 30 opens with a new discussion of Airbus and includes updated information about the euro debt crisis.

- Figures and tables have been updated using the latest data available.
- Many of the end-of-chapter problems have been either replaced or updated.
- Finally, we have gone over the text literally line-by-line, tightening the discussion, rewriting unclear points, and making many other small changes. We are grateful to the many instructors and students who made suggestions for improvements in the previous edition. We have done our best to incorporate as many of those suggestions as possible.

# The Foundation:
## Contextual Learning and Modern Organization

We believe a course is a success if students can apply what they have learned in both personal and business settings and if they have developed the analytical skills to understand what they read in the media. That's why we explain economic concepts by using many real-world business examples and applications in the chapter openers, graphs, *Making the Connection* features, *An Inside Look* features, and end-of-chapter problems. This approach helps both business majors and liberal arts majors become educated consumers, voters, and citizens. In addition to our widget-free approach, we also have a modern organization and place interesting policy topics early in the book to pique student interest.

## Microeconomics

We are convinced that students learn to apply economic principles best if they are taught in a familiar context. Whether they open an art studio, do social work, trade on Wall Street, work for the government, or tend bar, students benefit from understanding the economic forces behind their work. And though business students will have many opportunities to see economic principles in action in various courses, liberal arts students may not. We therefore use many diverse real-world business and policy examples to illustrate economic concepts and to develop educated consumers, voters, and citizens:

- **A strong set of introductory chapters.** The introductory chapters provide students with a solid foundation in the basics. We emphasize the key ideas of marginal analysis and economic efficiency. In Chapter 4, "Economic Efficiency, Government Price Setting, and Taxes," we use the concepts of consumer surplus and producer surplus to measure the economic effects of price ceilings and price floors as they relate to the familiar examples of rental properties and the minimum wage. (We revisit consumer surplus and producer surplus in Chapter 9, "Comparative Advantage and the Gains from International Trade," where we discuss outsourcing and analyze government policies that affect trade; in Chapter 15, "Monopoly and Antitrust Policy," where we examine the effect of market power on economic efficiency; and in Chapter 16, "Pricing Strategy," where we examine the effect of firm pricing policy on economic efficiency.) In Chapter 8, "Firms, the Stock Market, and Corporate Governance," we provide students with a basic understanding of how firms are organized, how they raise funds, and how they provide information to investors. We also illustrate how in a market system entrepreneurs meet consumer wants and efficiently organize production.

- **Early coverage of policy issues.** To expose students to policy issues early in the course, we discuss immigration in Chapter 1, "Economics: Foundations and Models"; rent control and the minimum wage in Chapter 4, "Economic Efficiency, Government Price Setting, and Taxes"; air pollution, global warming, and whether the government should run the health care system in Chapter 5, "Externalities, Environmental Policy, and Public Goods"; government policy toward illegal drugs in Chapter 6, "Elasticity: The Responsiveness of Demand and Supply"; and health care policy in Chapter 7, "The Economics of Health Care."

- **Complete coverage of monopolistic competition.** We devote a full chapter, Chapter 13, "Monopolistic Competition: The Competitive Model in a More Realistic Setting," to monopolistic competition prior to covering oligopoly and monopoly in Chapter 14, "Oligopoly: Firms in Less Competitive Markets," and Chapter 15, "Monopoly and Antitrust Policy." Although many instructors cover monopolistic competition very briefly or dispense with it entirely, we think it is an overlooked tool for reinforcing the basic message of how markets work in a context that is much more familiar to students than are the agricultural examples that dominate other discussions of perfect competition. We use the monopolistic competition model to introduce the downward-sloping demand curve material usually introduced in a monopoly chapter. This helps students grasp the important point that nearly all firms—not just monopolies—face downward-sloping demand curves. Covering monopolistic competition directly after perfect competition also allows for the early discussion of topics such as brand management and sources of competitive success. Nevertheless, we wrote the chapter so that instructors who prefer to cover monopoly (Chapter 15, "Monopoly and Antitrust Policy") directly after perfect competition (Chapter 12, "Firms in Perfectly Competitive Markets") can do so without loss of continuity.

- **Extensive, realistic game theory coverage.** In Chapter 14, "Oligopoly: Firms in Less Competitive Markets," we use game theory to analyze competition among oligopolists. Game theory helps students understand how companies with market power make strategic decisions in many competitive situations. We use familiar companies such as Apple, Hewlett-Packard, Coca-Cola, PepsiCo, and Dell in our game theory applications.

- **Unique coverage of pricing strategy.** In Chapter 16, "Pricing Strategy," we explore how firms use pricing strategies to increase profits. Students encounter pricing strategies everywhere—when they buy a movie ticket, book a flight for spring break, or research book prices online. We use these relevant, familiar examples to illustrate how companies use strategies such as price discrimination, cost-plus pricing, and two-part tariffs.

## Macroeconomics

Students come to study macroeconomics with a strong interest in understanding events and developments in the economy. We try to capture that interest and develop students' economic intuition and understanding in this text. We present macroeconomics in a way that is modern and based in the real world of business and economic policy. And we believe we achieve this presentation without making the analysis more difficult. We avoid the recent trend of using simplified versions of intermediate models, which are often more detailed and more complex than what students need to understand the basic macroeconomic issues. Instead, we use a more realistic version of the familiar aggregate demand and aggregate supply model to analyze short-run fluctuations and monetary and fiscal policy. We also avoid the "dueling schools of thought" approach often used to teach macroeconomics at the principles level. We emphasize the many areas of macroeconomics where most economists agree. And we present throughout real business and policy situations to develop students' intuition. Here are a few highlights of our approach to macroeconomics:

- **A broad discussion of macro statistics.** Many students pay at least some attention to the financial news and know that the release of statistics by federal agencies can cause movements in stock and bond prices. A background in macroeconomic statistics helps clarify some of the policy issues encountered in later chapters. In Chapter 19, "GDP: Measuring Total Production and Income," and Chapter 20, "Unemployment and Inflation," we provide students with an understanding of the uses and potential shortcomings of the key macroeconomic statistics, without getting bogged down in the minutiae of how the statistics are constructed. So, for instance, we discuss the important differences between the payroll survey and the household survey for understanding conditions in the labor market. We explain why financial markets react more strongly to news from the payroll survey. New to this edition is a discussion of the employment–population ratio, which some economists regard as a key measure of labor market performance. Chapter 26, "Monetary Policy," discusses why the Federal Reserve prefers to measure inflation using the personal consumption expenditures price index rather than the consumer price index.

- **Early coverage of long-run topics.** We place key macroeconomic issues in their long-run context in Chapter 21, "Economic Growth, the Financial System, and Business Cycles," and Chapter 22, "Long-Run Economic Growth: Sources and Policies." Chapter 21 puts the business cycle in the context of underlying long-run growth and discusses what actually happens during the phases of the business cycle. We believe this material is important if students are to have the understanding of business cycles they will need to interpret economic events; this material is often discussed only briefly or omitted entirely in other books. We know that many instructors prefer to have a short-run orientation to their macro courses, with a strong emphasis on policy. Accordingly, we have structured Chapter 21 so that its discussion of long-run growth would be sufficient for instructors who want to move quickly to short-run analysis. Chapter 22 uses a simple neoclassical growth model to explain important growth issues. We apply the model to topics such as the decline of the Soviet economy, the surprisingly strong growth performance of Botswana, and the failure of many developing countries to sustain high growth rates. And we challenge students with the discussion "Why Isn't the Whole World Rich?"

- **A dynamic model of aggregate demand and aggregate supply.** We take a fresh approach to the standard aggregate demand and aggregate supply (*AD–AS*) model. We realize there is no good, simple alternative to using the *AD–AS* model when explaining movements in the price level and in real GDP. But we know that more instructors are dissatisfied with the *AD–AS* model than with any other aspect of the macro principles course. The key problem, of course, is that *AD–AS* is a static model that attempts to account for dynamic changes in real GDP and the price level. Our approach retains the basics of the *AD–AS* model but makes it more accurate and useful by making it more dynamic. We emphasize two points: First, changes in the position of the short-run (upward-sloping) aggregate supply curve depend mainly on the state of expectations of the inflation rate. Second, the existence of growth in the economy means that the long-run (vertical) aggregate supply curve shifts to the right every year. This "dynamic" *AD–AS* model provides students with a more accurate understanding of the causes and consequences of fluctuations in real GDP and the price level. Chapter 24, "Aggregate Demand and Aggregate Supply Analysis," includes a three-layer, full-color acetate for the key introductory dynamic *AD–AS* graph (Figure 24.8, "A Dynamic Aggregate Demand and Aggregate Supply Model," on page 813 and reproduced on the right). We created this acetate to help students see how the graph builds step by step and to help make the graph easier for instructors to present. The acetate will help instructors who want to use dynamic *AD–AS* in class but believe the model needs to be developed carefully. We introduce this model in Chapter 24 and use it to discuss monetary policy in Chapter 26, "Monetary Policy," and fiscal policy in Chapter 27, "Fiscal Policy." Instructors may safely omit the sections on the dynamic *AD–AS* model without any loss in continuity to the discussion of macroeconomic theory and policy.

- **Extensive coverage of monetary policy.** Because of the central role monetary policy plays in the economy and in students' curiosity about business and financial news, we devote two chapters—Chapters 26, "Monetary Policy," and 28, "Inflation, Unemployment, and Federal Reserve Policy"—to the topic. We emphasize the issues involved in the Fed's choice of monetary policy targets, and we include coverage of the Taylor rule. The fourth edition includes coverage of the Fed's new policies aimed at dealing with the housing crisis and its effects on financial markets.

- **Coverage of both the demand-side and supply-side effects of fiscal policy.** Our discussion of fiscal policy in Chapter 27, "Fiscal Policy," carefully distinguishes between automatic stabilizers and discretionary fiscal policy. We also provide significant coverage of the supply-side effects of fiscal policy.

- **A self-contained but thorough discussion of the Keynesian income-expenditure approach.** The Keynesian income-expenditure approach (the "45°-line diagram," or "Keynesian cross") is useful for introducing students to the short-run relationship between spending and production. Many instructors, however, prefer to omit this material.

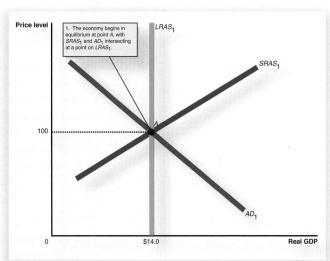

The first acetate overlay adds the shifts in the long-run and short-run aggregate supply curves.

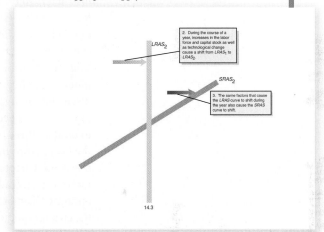

The second acetate overlay adds the shifts in the aggregate demand curve to complete the dynamic model.

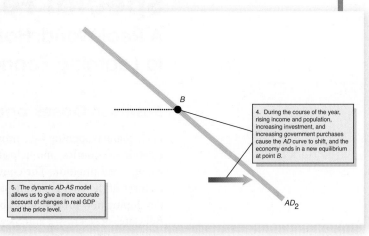

Therefore, we use the 45°-line diagram only in Chapter 23, "Aggregate Expenditure and Output in the Short Run." The discussion of monetary and fiscal policy in later chapters uses only the *AD–AS* model, making it possible to omit Chapter 23.

- **Extensive international coverage.** We include three chapters devoted to international topics: Chapter 9, "Comparative Advantage and the Gains from International Trade," Chapter 29, "Macroeconomics in an Open Economy," and Chapter 30, "The International Financial System." Having a good understanding of the international trading and financial systems is essential to understanding the macroeconomy and to satisfying students' curiosity about the economic world around them. In addition to the material in our three international chapters, we weave international comparisons into the narratives of several other chapters, including our discussion of labor market policies in Chapter 28, "Inflation, Unemployment, and Federal Reserve Policy," and central banking in Chapter 25, "Money, Banks, and the Federal Reserve System."

- **Flexible chapter organization.** Because we realize that there are a variety of approaches to teaching principles of macroeconomics, we have structured our chapters for maximum flexibility. For example, our discussion of long-run economic growth in Chapter 21, "Economic Growth, the Financial System, and Business Cycles," makes it possible for instructors to omit the more thorough discussion of these issues in Chapter 22, "Long-Run Economic Growth: Sources and Policies." Our discussion of the Keynesian 45°-line diagram is confined to Chapter 23 so that instructors who do not use this approach can proceed directly to aggregate demand and aggregate supply analysis in Chapter 24, "Aggregate Demand and Aggregate Supply Analysis." While we devote two chapters to monetary policy, the first of these—Chapter 26, "Monetary Policy"—is a self-contained discussion, so instructors may safely omit the material in Chapter 28, "Inflation, Unemployment, and Federal Reserve Policy," if they choose to. Finally, instructors may choose to omit all three of the international chapters (Chapter 9, "Comparative Advantage and the Gains from International Trade," Chapter 29, "Macroeconomics in an Open Economy," and Chapter 30, "The International Financial System"), cover just Chapter 9 on international trade; cover just Chapter 29; or cover Chapter 29 and Chapter 30 while omitting Chapter 9. Please refer to the flexibility chart on pages xxvi–xxvii to help select the chapters and order best suited to your classroom needs.

# Special Features:
## A Real-World, Hands-on Approach to Learning Economics

### Business Cases and *An Inside Look* News Articles

Each chapter-opening case provides a real-world context for learning, sparks students' interest in economics, and helps to unify the chapter. The case describes an actual company facing a real situation. The company is integrated in the narrative, graphs, and pedagogical features of the chapter. Many of the chapter openers focus on the role of entrepreneurs in developing new products and bringing them to the market. For example, Chapter 3 covers Bill Gates of Microsoft and Steve Jobs of Apple, Chapter 8 covers Mark Zuckerberg of Facebook, and Chapter 24 covers Fred Smith of FedEx. Here are a few examples of companies we explore in the chapter openers in this new edition:

- Apple (Chapter 3, "Where Prices Come From: The Interaction of Demand and Supply")
- Facebook (Chapter 8, "Firms, the Stock Market, and Corporate Governance")
- FedEx (Chapter 24, "Aggregate Demand and Aggregate Supply Analysis")

*An Inside Look* is a two-page feature that shows students how to apply the concepts from the chapter to the analysis of a news article. Select articles deal with policy issues and are titled *An Inside Look at Policy*. Articles are from sources such as the *Wall Street Journal*, the *Economist*, and *BusinessWeek*. The *An Inside Look* feature presents an excerpt from an article, analysis of the article, a graph(s), and critical thinking questions.

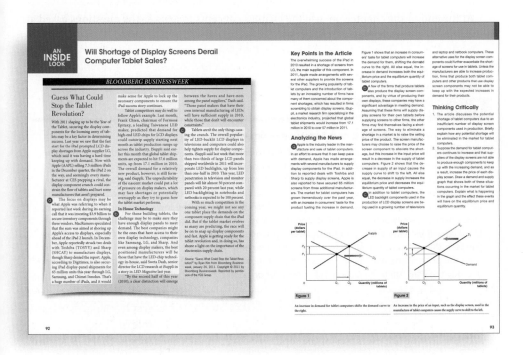

Here are some examples of the articles featured in *An Inside Look*:

- "Guess What Could Stop the Tablet Revolution?" *Bloomberg Businessweek* (Chapter 3, "Where Prices Come From: The Interaction of Demand and Supply")
- "How to Buy into Facebook Before It Goes Public," *Kiplinger* (Chapter 8, "Firms, the Stock Market, and Corporate Governance")

- "Will the Fed's New Policies Revitalize the Housing Market?" *Atlantic* (Chapter 26, "Monetary Policy")
- "Obama Proposes Additional Spending to Stimulate the Economy" *U.S. News & World Report* (Chapter 27, "Fiscal Policy")

## Economics in Your Life

After the chapter-opening real-world business case, we have added a personal dimension to the chapter opener, with a feature titled *Economics in Your Life*, which asks students to consider how economics affects their own lives. The feature piques the interest of students and emphasizes the connection between the material they are learning and their own experiences.

---

### Economics in Your Life

**Will You Buy an Apple iPad or a Samsung Galaxy Tab?**

Suppose you are considering buying a tablet computer and that you are choosing between an Apple iPad and a Samsung Galaxy Tab. Apple introduced the iPad in April 2010, and Samsung introduced the Galaxy Tab in November 2010; seven months is a long time in the world of high-tech gadgets. Apple products have become very fashionable, and if you buy an iPad, you will have access to many more applications—or "apps"—that can increase the enjoyability and productivity of your tablet. One strategy Samsung can use to overcome those advantages is to compete based on price and value. Would you choose to buy a Galaxy Tab if it had a lower price than an iPad? If your income increased, would it affect your decision about which tablet to buy? As you read the chapter, see if you can answer these questions. You can check your answers against those we provide **page 91** at the end of this chapter.

---

At the end of the chapter, we use the chapter concepts to answer the questions asked at the beginning of the chapter.

---

Continued from page 69

### Economics in Your Life

**Will You Buy an Apple iPad or a Samsung Galaxy Tab?**

At the beginning of the chapter, we asked you to consider two questions: Would you choose to buy a Samsung Galaxy Tab tablet if it had a lower price than an Apple iPad? and Would your decision be affected if your income increased? To determine the answer to the first question, you have to recognize that the iPad and the Galaxy Tab are substitutes. If you consider the two tablets to be very close substitutes, then you are likely to buy the one with the lower price. In the market, if consumers generally believe that iPad and the Galaxy Tab are close substitutes, a fall in the price of the iPad will increase the quantity of iPads demanded and decrease the demand for Galaxy Tabs. Suppose that you are currently leaning toward buying the Galaxy Tab because its price is lower than the price of the iPad. If an increase in your income would cause you to change your decision and buy the iPad, then the Galaxy Tab is an inferior good for you.

---

The following are examples of the topics we cover in the *Economics in Your Life* feature:

- Will you buy an Apple iPad or a Samsung Galaxy tablet? (Chapter 3, "Where Prices Come From: The Interaction of Demand and Supply")
- Do corporate managers act in the best interests of shareholders? (Chapter 8, "Firms, the Stock Market, and Corporate Governance.")
- Is an employer likely to cut your pay during a recession? (Chapter 24, "Aggregate Demand and Aggregate Supply Analysis")

# Solved Problems

Many students have great difficulty handling applied economics problems. We help students overcome this hurdle by including two or three worked-out problems tied to select chapter-opening learning objectives. Our goals are to keep students focused on the main ideas of each chapter and to give students a model of how to solve an economic problem by breaking it down step by step. Additional exercises in the end-of-chapter *Problems and Applications* section are tied to every *Solved Problem*. Additional *Solved Problems* appear in the Instructor's Manuals and the print Study Guides. In addition, the Test Item Files include problems tied to the *Solved Problems* in the main book.

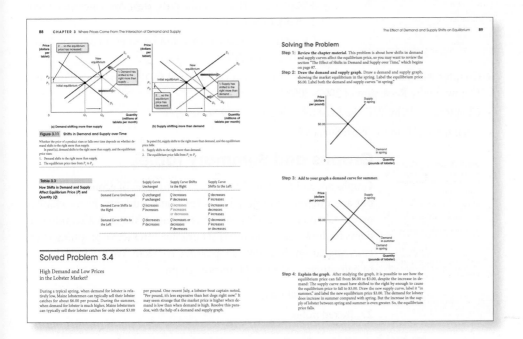

# Don't Let This Happen to You

We know from many years of teaching which concepts students find most difficult. Each chapter contains a box feature called *Don't Let This Happen to You* that alerts students to the most common pitfalls in that chapter's material. We follow up with a related question in the end-of-chapter *Problems and Applications* section.

# Making the Connection

Each chapter includes two to four *Making the Connection* features that provide real-world reinforcement of key concepts and help students learn how to interpret what they read on the Web and in newspapers. Most *Making the Connection* features use relevant, stimulating, and provocative news stories focused on businesses and policy issues. One-third of the *Making the Connection* features are new to this edition, and most others have been updated. Several *Making the Connection* features discuss health care, which remains a pressing policy issue. Each *Making the Connection* has at least one supporting end-of-chapter problem to allow students to test

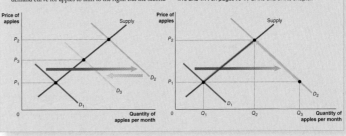

**Making the Connection** | **Forecasting the Demand for iPads**

One of the most important decisions that the managers of any large firm face is which new products to develop. A firm must devote people, time, and money to designing a new product, negotiating with suppliers, formulating a marketing campaign, and many other tasks. But any firm has only limited resources and so faces a trade-off: Resources used to develop one product will not be available to develop another product. Ultimately, the products a firm chooses to develop will be those that it believes will be the most profitable. So, to decide which products to develop, firms need to forecast the demand for those products.

We saw at the beginning of the chapter that in 2001, Bill Gates predicted that within five years, a majority of computers sold would be tablets. If Gates had been correct about the way the computer market was changing, then any computer firm that didn't develop a tablet would have run the risk of being left behind. David Sobotta, who worked at Apple for 20 years and eventually became its national sales manager, has described discussions at Apple during 2002 about whether to develop a tablet. According to Sobotta, representatives of the federal government's National Institutes of Health urged Apple to develop a tablet computer, arguing that it would be particularly useful to doctors, nurses, and hospitals. Apple's managers decided not to develop a tablet, however, because they believed the technology available at that time was too complex for the average computer user and they also believed that the demand from doctors and nurses would be small. As we saw in the chapter opener, Apple's forecast was correct. Despite Bill Gates's prediction, in 2006,

*Will the future demand for tablets such as the iPad continue to grow?*

their understanding of the topic discussed. Here are some of the new *Making the Connection* features:

- Chapter 2: " A Story of the Market System in Action: How Do You Make an iPad?"
- Chapter 3: "The Aging of the Baby Boom Generation"
- Chapter 9: "Leave New York City? Risky for Financial Firms"
- Chapter 12: "Easy Entry Makes the Long Run Pretty Short in the Apple iPhone Apps Store"
- Chapter 20: "How Should We Categorize Unemployment at Bank of America?"
- Chapter 21: "The Connection between Economic Prosperity and Health"
- Chapter 24: "How Long Does It Take to Return to Potential GDP? Economic Forecasts Following the Recession of 2007–2009"
- Chapter 27: "Why Was the Recession of 2007–2009 So Severe?"
- Chapter 30: "Can the Euro Survive?"

## Graphs and Summary Tables

Graphs are an indispensable part of a principles of economics course but are a major stumbling block for many students. Every chapter except Chapter 1 includes end-of-chapter problems that require students to draw, read, and interpret graphs. Interactive graphing exercises appear on the book's supporting Web site. We use four devices to help students read and interpret graphs:

1. Detailed captions
2. Boxed notes

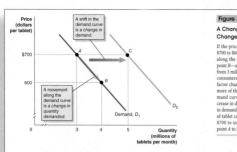

**Figure 3.3**

**A Change in Demand versus a Change in Quantity Demanded**

If the price of tablet computers falls from $700 to $600, the result will be a movement along the demand curve from point *A* to point *B*—an increase in quantity demanded from 3 million tablets to 4 million tablets. If consumers' incomes increase, or if another factor changes that makes consumers want more of the product at every price, the demand curve will shift to the right—an increase in demand. In this case, the increase in demand from $D_1$ to $D_2$ causes the quantity of tablet computers demanded at a price of $700 to increase from 3 million tablets at point *A* to 5 million tablets at point *C*.

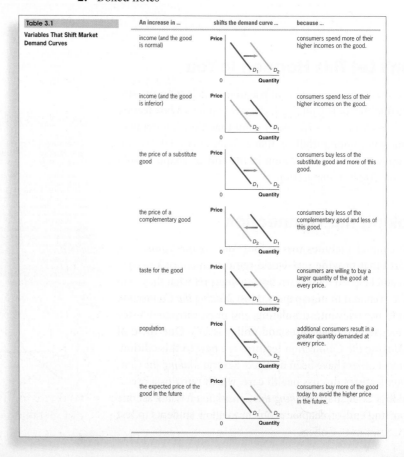

| Table 3.1 | An increase in … | shifts the demand curve … | because … |
|---|---|---|---|
| **Variables That Shift Market Demand Curves** | income (and the good is normal) | | consumers spend more of their higher incomes on the good. |
| | income (and the good is inferior) | | consumers spend less of their higher incomes on the good. |
| | the price of a substitute good | | consumers buy less of the substitute good and more of this good. |
| | the price of a complementary good | | consumers buy less of the complementary good and less of this good. |
| | taste for the good | | consumers are willing to buy a larger quantity of the good at every price. |
| | population | | additional consumers result in a greater quantity demanded at every price. |
| | the expected price of the good in the future | | consumers buy more of the good today to avoid the higher price in the future. |

3. Color-coded curves
4. Summary tables with graphs (see pages 76, 81, and 799 for examples)

## Review Questions and Problems and Applications— Grouped by Learning Objective to Improve Assessment

All the end-of-chapter material—*Summary*, *Review Questions*, and *Problems and Applications*—is grouped under learning objectives. The goals of this organization are to make it easier for instructors to assign problems based on learning objectives, both in the book and in MyEconLab, and to help students efficiently review material that they find difficult. If students have difficulty with a particular learning objective, an instructor can easily identify which end-of-chapter questions and problems support that objective and assign them as homework or discuss them in class. Every exercise in a chapter's *Problems and Applications* section is available in MyEconLab. Using MyEconLab, students can complete these and many other exercises online, get tutorial help, and receive instant feedback and assistance on exercises they answer incorrectly. Also, student learning will be enhanced by having the summary material and problems grouped together by learning objective, which will allow students to focus on the parts of the chapter they found most challenging. Each major section of the chapter, paired with a learning objective, has at least two review questions and three problems.

As in the previous editions, we include one or more end-of-chapter problems that test students' understanding of the content presented in the *Solved Problem*, *Making the Connection*, and *Don't Let This Happen to You* special features in the chapter. Instructors can cover a feature in class and assign the corresponding problem for homework. The Test Item Files also include test questions that pertain to these special features.

# Integrated Supplements

The authors and Pearson Education/Prentice Hall have worked together to integrate the text, print, and media resources to make teaching and learning easier.

MyEconLab is a unique online course management, testing, and tutorial resource.

# MyEconLab

## For the Instructor

Instructors can choose how much or how little time to spend setting up and using MyEconLab. Here is a snapshot of what instructors are saying about MyEconLab:

> "MyEconLab offers [students] a way to practice every week. They receive immediate feedback and a feeling of personal attention. As a result, my teaching has become more targeted and efficient."—Kelly Blanchard, Purdue University

> "Students tell me that offering them MyEconLab is almost like offering them individual tutors."—Jefferson Edwards, Cypress Fairbanks College

> "MyEconLab's eText is great—particularly in that it helps offset the skyrocketing cost of textbooks. Naturally, students love that."—Doug Gehrke, Moraine Valley Community College

Each chapter contains two preloaded homework exercise sets that can be used to build an individualized study plan for each student. These study plan exercises contain tutorial resources, including instant feedback, links to the appropriate learning objective in the eText, pop-up definitions from the text, learning objective summaries, and step-by-step guided solutions, where appropriate. After the initial setup of the course by the instructor, student use of these materials requires no further instructor setup. The online grade book records each student's performance and time spent on the tests and study plan and generates reports by student or by chapter.

Alternatively, instructors can fully customize MyEconLab to match their course exactly, including reading assignments, homework assignments, video assignments, current news assignments, and quizzes and tests. Assignable resources include:

- Preloaded homework exercise sets for each chapter that include the student tutorial resources mentioned above
- Preloaded quizzes for each chapter that are unique to the text and not repeated in the study plan or homework exercise sets
- Study plan problems that are similar to the end-of-chapter problems and numbered exactly like the book to make assigning homework easier
- *Economics in the News* articles that are updated weekly with appropriate exercises
- ABC News clips, which explore current economic applications and policy issues, along with exercises
- Real-Time Data Exercises continuously update with real-time data.
- **Real-Time Data** The real-time data problems are new. These problems load the latest available data from FRED, a comprehensive up-to-date data set maintained by the Federal Reserve Bank of St. Louis. The questions are graded with feedback in exactly the same way as those based on static data.
- **Experiments in MyEconLab** Experiments are a fun and engaging way to promote active learning and mastery of important economic concepts. Pearson's Experiments program is flexible and easy for instructors and students to use.
  - Single-player experiments allow your students to play against virtual players from anywhere at anytime so long as they have an Internet connection.
  - Multiplayer experiments allow you to assign and manage a real-time experiment with your class.
  - Pre- and post-questions for each experiment are available for assignment in MyEconLab.

For a complete list of available experiments, visit www.myeconlab.com

- Test Item File questions that allow you to assign quizzes or homework that will look just like your exams
- Econ Exercise Builder, which allows you to build your own customized exercises

Exercises include multiple-choice, graph drawing, and free-response items, many of which are generated algorithmically so that each time a student works them, a different variation is presented.

MyEconLab grades every problem type except essays, even problems with graphs. When working homework exercises, students receive immediate feedback, with links to additional learning tools.

### Customization and Communication

MyEconLab in MyLab/Mastering provides additional optional customization and communication tools. Instructors who teach distance-learning courses or very large lecture sections find the MyLab/Mastering format useful because they can upload course documents and assignments, customize the order of chapters, and use communication features such as Document Sharing, Chat, ClassLive, and Discussion Board.

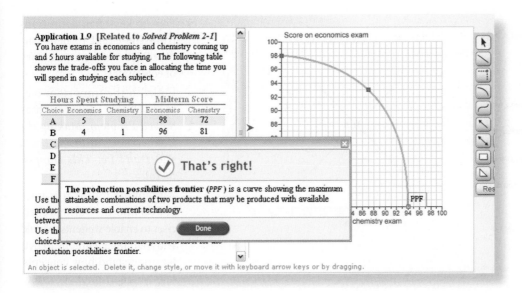

## For the Student

MyEconLab puts students in control of their learning through a collection of testing, practice, and study tools tied to the online, interactive version of the textbook and other media resources. Here is a snapshot of what students are saying about MyEconLab:

> "It was very useful because it had EVERYTHING, from practice exams to exercises to reading. Very helpful."—student, Northern Illinois University

> "I would recommend taking the quizzes on MyEconLab because it gives you a true account of whether or not you understand the material."—student, Montana Tech

> "It made me look through the book to find answers, so I did more reading."—student, Northern Illinois University

Students can study on their own, or they can complete assignments created by their instructor. In MyEconLab's structured environment, students practice what they learn, test their understanding, and pursue a personalized study plan generated from their performance on sample tests and from quizzes created by their instructors. In Homework or Study Plan mode, students have access to a wealth of tutorial features, including:

- Instant feedback on exercises that helps students understand and apply the concepts
- Links to the eText to promote reading of the text just when the student needs to revisit a concept or an explanation
- Step-by-step guided solutions that force students to break down a problem in much the same way an instructor would do during office hours
- Pop-up summaries of the appropriate learning objective to remind students of key ideas while studying

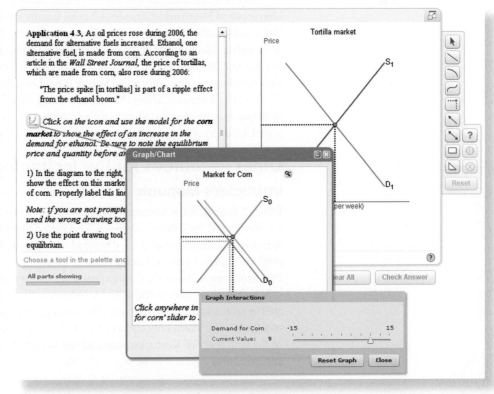

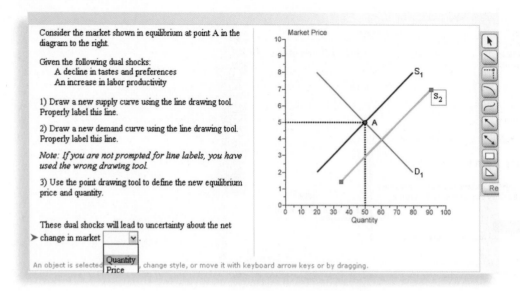

Consider the market shown in equilibrium at point A in the diagram to the right.

Given the following dual shocks:
    A decline in tastes and preferences
    An increase in labor productivity

1) Draw a new supply curve using the line drawing tool. Properly label this line.

2) Draw a new demand curve using the line drawing tool. Properly label this line.

*Note: If you are not prompted for line labels, you have used the wrong drawing tool.*

3) Use the point drawing tool to define the new equilibrium price and quantity.

These dual shocks will lead to uncertainty about the net
➤ change in market [        ⌄] .

An object is selected    Quantity    change style, or move it with keyboard arrow keys or by dragging.
                         Price

- Pop-up key term definitions from the eText to help students master the vocabulary of economics
- Links to the important features of the eText, such as *Solved Problem, Making the Connection, An Inside Look,* and *Don't Let This Happen to You*
- A graphing tool that is integrated into the various exercises to enable students to build and manipulate graphs to better understand how concepts, numbers, and graphs connect

## Additional MyEconLab Tools

MyEconLab includes the following additional features:

- **eText**—In addition to the portions of eText available as pop-ups or links, a fully searchable eText is available for students who wish to read and study in a fully electronic environment.
- **Print upgrade**—For students who wish to complete assignments in MyEconLab but read in print, Pearson offers registered MyEconLab users a loose-leaf version of the print text at a significant discount.
- **Glossary flashcards**—Every key term is available as a flashcard, allowing students to quiz themselves on vocabulary from one or more chapters at a time.
- **MySearchLab**—Research **MySearchLab** provides extensive help on the research process and four exclusive databases of credible and reliable source material, including the *New York Times,* the *Financial Times,* and peer-reviewed journals.

MyEconLab content has been created through the efforts of Chris Annala, State University of New York–Geneseo; Charles Baum, Middle Tennessee State University; Carol Dole, Jacksonville University; Sarah Ghosh, University of Scranton; Satyajit Ghosh, Universtity of Scranton; Melissa Honig, Pearson Education; Woo Jung, University of Colorado; Courtney Kamauf, Pearson Education; Chris Kauffman, University of Tennessee–Knoxville; Russell Kellogg, University of Colorado–Denver; Noel Lotz, Pearson Education; Katherine McCann, University of Delaware; Daniel Mizak, Frostburg State University; Christine Polek, University of Massachusetts–Boston; Mark Scanlan, Stephen F. Austin State University; Leonie L. Stone, State University of New York–Geneseo; and Bert G. Wheeler, Cedarville University.

## Other Resources for the Instructor

### Instructor's Manuals

Edward Scahill of the University of Scranton prepared the Instructor's Manual for *Microeconomics* and for *Macroeconomics.* The Instructor's Manuals include chapter-by-chapter summaries, learning objectives, extended examples and class exercises, teaching outlines incorporating key terms and definitions, teaching tips, topics for class discussion, new *Solved Problems,* new *Making the Connection* features, new *Economics in Your Life* scenarios, and solutions to all review questions and problems in the book. The Instructor's Manuals are available in print and for download from the Instructor's Resource Center (**www.pearsonhighered.com/hubbard**). The authors, Harry Ellis of the University of North Texas, and Robert Gillette of the University of Kentucky prepared the solutions to the end-of-chapter review questions and problems.

# Four Test Item Files

Randy Methenitis of Richland College prepared two Test Item Files for *Microeconomics* and two Test Item Files for *Macroeconomics*. Each Test Item File includes 2,000 multiple-choice, true/false, short-answer, and graphing questions. There are questions to support each key feature in the book. The Test Item Files are available in print and for download from the Instructor's Resource Center (www.pearsonhighered.com/hubbard). Test questions are annotated with the following information:

- **Difficulty:** 1 for straight recall, 2 for some analysis, 3 for complex analysis
- **Type:** multiple-choice, true/false, short-answer, essay
- **Topic:** the term or concept the question supports
- **Learning outcome**
- **AACSB** (see description that follows)
- **Page number**
- **Special feature in the main book:** chapter-opening business example, *Economics in Your Life*, *Solved Problem*, *Making the Connection*, *Don't Let This Happen to You*, and *An Inside Look*

### The Association to Advance Collegiate Schools of Business (AACSB)

The Test Item File author has connected select questions to the general knowledge and skill guidelines found in the AACSB Assurance of Learning Standards.

## What Is the AACSB?

AACSB is a not-for-profit corporation of educational institutions, corporations, and other organizations devoted to the promotion and improvement of higher education in business administration and accounting. A collegiate institution offering degrees in business administration or accounting may volunteer for AACSB accreditation review. The AACSB makes initial accreditation decisions and conducts periodic reviews to promote continuous quality improvement in management education. Pearson Education is a proud member of the AACSB and is pleased to provide advice to help you apply AACSB Assurance of Learning Standards.

### What Are AACSB Assurance of Learning Standards?

One of the criteria for AACSB accreditation is the quality of curricula. Although no specific courses are required, the AACSB expects a curriculum to include learning experiences in the following categories of Assurance of Learning Standards:

- Communication
- Ethical Reasoning
- Analytic Skills
- Use of Information Technology
- Multicultural and Diversity
- Reflective Thinking

Questions that test skills relevant to these standards are tagged with the appropriate standard. For example, a question testing the moral questions associated with externalities would receive the Ethical Reasoning tag.

### How Can Instructors Use the AACSB Tags?

Tagged questions help you measure whether students are grasping the course content that aligns with the AACSB guidelines noted above. This in turn may suggest enrichment activities or other educational experiences to help students achieve these skills.

### TestGen

The computerized TestGen package allows instructors to customize, save, and generate classroom tests. The test program permits instructors to edit, add, or delete questions from the Test Item Files; analyze test results; and organize a database of tests and student results. This software allows for extensive flexibility and ease of use. It provides many options for organizing and displaying tests, along with search and sort features. The software and the Test Item Files can be downloaded from the Instructor's Resource Center (www.pearsonhighered.com/hubbard).

### PowerPoint Lecture Presentation

Three sets of PowerPoint slides, prepared by Fernando Quijano, Dickinson State University, are available:

1. A comprehensive set of PowerPoint slides can be used by instructors for class presentations or by students for lecture preview or review. These slides include all the graphs, tables, and equations in the textbook. Two versions are available—step-by-step mode, in which you can build graphs as you would on a blackboard, and automated mode, in which you use a single click per slide.

2. A comprehensive set of PowerPoint slides have Classroom Response Systems (CRS) questions built in so that instructors can incorporate CRS "clickers" into their classroom lectures. For more information on Pearson Education's partnership with CRS, see the description below. Instructors can download these PowerPoint presentations from the Instructor's Resource Center (www.pearsonhighered.com/hubbard).

3. A student version of the PowerPoint slides is available as .pdf files. This version allows students to print the slides and bring them to class for note taking. Instructors can download these PowerPoint presentations from the Instructor's Resource Center (www.pearsonhighered.com/hubbard).

### Instructor's Resource Disk

The Instructor's Resource Disk contains all the faculty and student resources that support this text. Instructors can access and edit the Instructor's Manuals, Test Item Files, TestGen files, and PowerPoint presentations. By simply clicking a chapter, faculty can access an interactive library of resources. They can then pick and choose from the various supplements and export them to their hard drives.

### Classroom Response Systems

Classroom Response Systems (CRS) is an exciting new wireless polling technology that increases the interactivity of large and small classrooms by enabling instructors to pose questions to their students, record results, and display the results instantly. Students can answer questions easily, using compact remote-control transmitters. Pearson Education has partnerships with leading CRS providers and can show you everything you need to know about setting up and using CRS. Pearson Education will provide the classroom hardware, text-specific PowerPoint slides, software, and support, and will also show you how your students can benefit! Please contact your local Pearson Education sales representative for more information.

### Blackboard and WebCT Course Content

Pearson Education offers fully customizable course content for the Blackboard and WebCT Course Management Systems.

## Other Resources for the Student

In addition to MyEconLab, Pearson provides the following resources.

## Study Guides

Fatma Abdel-Raouf from Goldey-Beacom College prepared the Study Guide to accompany *Microeconomics*, and Jim Lee of Texas A&M University, Corpus Christi, prepared the Study Guide to accompany *Macroeconomics*, which reinforces the textbook and provides students with the following:

- Chapter summary
- Discussion of each learning objective
- Section-by-section review of the concepts presented
- Helpful study hints
- Additional *Solved Problems* to supplement those in the text
- Key terms with definitions
- A self-test, including 40 multiple-choice questions plus a number of short-answer and true/false questions, with accompanying answers and explanations

## PowerPoint Slides

For student use as a study aid or note-taking guide, PowerPoint slides, prepared by Fernando Quijano, Dickinson State University, and Shelly Tefft, can be downloaded from MyEconLab or the Instructor's Resource Center and made available to students. The slides include:

- All graphs, tables, and equations in the text
- Figures in step-by-step mode and automated modes, using a single click per graph curve
- End-of-chapter key terms with hyperlinks to relevant slides

## Instructors

CourseSmart goes beyond traditional expectations, providing instant online access to the textbooks and course materials you need, at a lower cost to students. And, even as students save money, you can save time and hassle with a digital textbook that allows you to search the most relevant content at the very moment you need it. Whether it's evaluating textbooks or creating lecture notes to help students with difficult concepts, CourseSmart can make life a little easier. See how when you visit www.coursesmart.com.

## Students

CourseSmart goes beyond traditional expectations, providing instant, online access to the textbooks and course materials students need, at lower cost. They can also search, highlight, and take notes anywhere, any time. See all the benefits to students at www.coursesmart.com.

# Consultant Board, Accuracy Review Board, and Reviewers

The guidance and recommendations of the following instructors helped us develop the revision plans for the fourth edition and the supplements package. While we could not incorporate every suggestion from every consultant board member, reviewer, or accuracy checker, we do thank each and every one of you and acknowledge that your feedback was indispensable in developing this text. We greatly appreciate your assistance in making this the best text it could be; you have helped teach a whole new generation of students about the exciting world of economics.

## Consultant Board

Sherman T. Folland, Oakland University
Robert Gillette, University of Kentucky
William Goffe, State University of New York–Oswego
Edward Scahill, University of Scranton
Stephen Snyder, University of Pittsburgh
Robert Whaples, Wake Forest University

## Accuracy Review Board

Our accuracy checkers did a particularly painstaking and thorough job of helping us proof the graphs, equations, and features of the text and the supplements. We are grateful for their time and commitment:

Fatma Abdel-Raouf, Goldey-Beacom College
Cynthia Bansak, St. Lawrence University
Kelly Hunt Blanchard, Purdue University
Harry Ellis, University of North Texas
Mark Gius, Quinnipiac University
William Goffe, State University of New York–Oswego
Anthony Gyapong, Pennsylvania State University
Randy Methenitis, Richland College
David Mitch, University of Maryland–Baltimore County
Fernando Quijano, Dickinson State University
Ratha Ramoo, Diablo Valley College
Edward Scahill, University of Scranton
Michael Stone, Quinnipiac University
Arlena Sullivan, Jones County Junior College
Julianne Treme, University of North Carolina
  –Wilmington

## Reviewers

The guidance and thoughtful recommendations of many instructors helped us develop and implement a revision plan that expanded the book's content, improved the figures, and strengthened assessment features. We extend special thanks to Edward Scahill of the University of Scranton for helping us revise the chapter openers, to Randy Methenitis of Richland College for helping us revise the *An Inside Look* feature, and to Robert Gillette of the University of Kentucky for helping us revise the end-of-chapter questions. We are grateful for the comments and many helpful suggestions received from the following reviewers:

Sindy Abadie, Southwest Tennessee Community College
Shawn Abbott, College of the Siskiyous
Bradley Andrew, Juniata College
Rita Balaban, University of North Carolina
Annette Chamberlin, National College
James D'Angelo, Xavier University
Alexander Deshkovski, North Carolina Central University
Kirk Doran, University of Notre Dame
Debbie Evercloud, University of Colorado–Denver
Lydia Gan, School of Business, University of North
  Carolina–Pembroke
Edgar Ghossoub, University of Texas at San Antonio
Scott Houser, Colorado School of Mines
Peng Huang, Ripon College
James Ibe, Morris College
Jean Kujawa, Lourdes College
Larry Landrum, Virginia Western Community College
Jim Lee, Texas A&M University–Corpus Christi
Solomon Namala, Cerritos College
Eugene Bempong Nyantakyi, West Virginia University
Curtis Price, University of Southern Indiana
Bobby Puryear, North Carolina State University
Denis Raihall, West Chester University
Robert Rycroft, University of Mary Washington
Peter Schuhmann, University of North Carolina–
  Wilmington
Abdulhamid Sukar, Cameron University
Yaqin Wang, Youngstown State University
Tara Westerhold, Western Illinois University
Anne Williams, Gateway Community College

# Previous Edition Class Testers, Accuracy Reviewers, and Consultants

## Class Testers

We are grateful to both the instructors who class-tested manuscript of the first edition and their students for providing clear-cut recommendations on how to make chapters interesting, relevant, and comprehensive:

Charles A. Bennett, Gannon University

Anne E. Bresnock, University of California–Los Angeles, and California State Polytechnic University–Pomona

Linda Childs-Leatherbury, Lincoln University, Pennsylvania

John Eastwood, Northern Arizona University

David Eaton, Murray State University

Paul Elgatian, St. Ambrose University

Patricia A. Freeman, Jackson State University

Robert Godby, University of Wyoming

Frank Gunter, Lehigh University

Ahmed Ispahani, University of LaVerne

Brendan Kennelly, Lehigh University and National University of Ireland–Galway

Ernest Massie, Franklin University

Carol McDonough, University of Massachusetts–Lowell

Shah Mehrabi, Montgomery College

Sharon Ryan, University of Missouri–Columbia

Bruce G. Webb, Gordon College

Madelyn Young, Converse College

Susan Zumas, Lehigh University

## Accuracy Review Boards

We are grateful to the following accuracy checkers of the previous editions for their hard work on the book and supplements:

Fatma Abdel-Raouf, Goldey-Beacom College

Anne Alexander, University of Wyoming

Mohammad Bajwa, Northampton Community College

Hamid Bastin, Shippensburg University

Kelly Hunt Blanchard, Purdue University

Don Bumpass, Sam Houston State University

Charles Callahan III, State University of New York–Brockport

Mark S. Chester, Reading Area Community College

Kenny Christianson, Binghamton University

Ishita Edwards, Oxnard College

Harold Elder, University of Alabama

Harry Ellis, University of North Texas

Can Erbil, Brandeis University

Marc Fusaro, Arkansas Tech University

Sarah Ghosh, University of Scranton

Robert Gillette, University of Kentucky

Maria Giuili, Diablo Valley College

Robert Godby, University of Wyoming

William L. Goffe, State University of New York–Oswego

Travis Hayes, University of Tennessee–Chattanooga

Carol Hogan, University of Michigan–Dearborn

Anisul M. Islam, University of Houston–Downtown

Aaron Jackson, Bentley College

Nancy Jianakoplos, Colorado State University

Thomas C. Kinnaman, Bucknell University

Mary K. Knudson, University of Iowa

Faik A. Koray, Louisiana State University

Stephan Kroll, California State University–Sacramento

Tony Lima, California State University–East Bay

Randy Methenitis, Richland College

Normal C. Miller, Miami University

David Mitch, University of Maryland–Baltimore County

James A. Moreno, Blinn College

Michael Potepan, San Francisco State University

Mary L. Pranzo, California State University–Fresno

Matthew Rafferty, Quinnipiac University

Jeff Reynolds, Northern Illinois University

Brian Rosario, University of California–Davis

Joseph M. Santos, South Dakota State University

Edward Scahill, University of Scranton

Mark V. Siegler, California State University–Sacramento

Rachel Small, University of Colorado–Boulder

Stephen Smith, Bakersfield College

Rajeev Sooreea, Pennsylvania State University–Altoona

Rebecca Stein, University of Pennsylvania

Ed Steinberg, New York University

Arlena Sullivan, Jones County Junior College

Wendine Thompson-Dawson, University of Utah

Robert Whaples, Wake Forest University

## Consultant Boards

We received guidance from a dedicated consultant board during the development of the previous editions at several critical junctures. We relied on the board for input on content, figure treatment, and design:

Kate Antonovics, University of California–San Diego

Robert Beekman, University of Tampa

Valerie Bencivenga, University of Texas–Austin

Kelly Blanchard, Purdue University

Susan Dadres, Southern Methodist University

Harry Ellis, Jr., University of North Texas

Robert Gillette, University of Kentucky

Robert Godby, University of Wyoming

William L. Goffe, State University of New York–Oswego

Jane S. Himarios, University of Texas–Arlington

Donn M. Johnson, Quinnipiac University

Mark Karscig, Central Missouri State University

Jenny Minier, University of Kentucky

David Mitch, University of Maryland–Baltimore County

Nicholas Noble, Miami University

Michael Potepan, San Francisco State University

Matthew Rafferty, Quinnipiac University

Helen Roberts, University of Illinois–Chicago

Robert Rosenman, Washington State University

Joseph M. Santos, South Dakota State University

Martin C. Spechler, Indiana University–Purdue University Indianapolis

Robert Whaples, Wake Forest University

Jonathan B. Wight, University of Richmond

## Reviewers

The guidance and recommendations of the following instructors helped us shape the previous editions.

ALABAMA

Doris Bennett, Jacksonville State University

Harold W. Elder, University of Alabama–Tuscaloosa

Wanda Hudson, Alabama Southern Community College

Edward Merkel, Troy University

James L. Swofford, University of Southern Alabama

ARIZONA

Doug Conway, Mesa Community College

John Eastwood, Northern Arizona University

Price Fishback, University of Arizona

ARKANSAS

Jerry Crawford, Arkansas State University

Marc Fusaro, Arkansas Tech University

Randall Kesselring, Arkansas State University

Dan Marburger, Arkansas State University

CALIFORNIA

Renatte Adler, San Diego State University

Ercument Aksoy, Los Angeles Valley College

Maneeza Aminy, Golden Gate University

Kate Antonovics, University of California–San Diego

Becca Arnold, Mesa College

Asatar Bair, City College of San Francisco

Diana Bajrami, College of Alameda

Robert Bise, Orange Coast Community College

Victor Brajer, California State University–Fullerton

Anne E. Bresnock, University of California–Los Angeles, and California State Polytechnic University–Pomona

David Brownstone, University of California–Irvine

Maureen Burton, California State Polytechnic University–Pomona

Anoshua Chaudhuri, San Francisco State University

James G. Devine, Loyola Marymount University

Jose Esteban, Palomar College

Roger Frantz, San Diego State University

Craig Gallet, California State University–Sacramento

Andrew Gill, California State University–Fullerton

Maria Giuili, Diablo Valley College

Julie Gonzalez, University of California–Santa Cruz

Lisa Grobar, California State University–Long Beach

Steve Hamilton, California State University–Fullerton

Dewey Heinsma, Mt. San Jacinto Community College

Jessica Howell, California State University–Sacramento

Greg Hunter, California State University–Pomona

John Ifcher, Santa Clara University

Ahmed Ispahani, University of LaVerne

George A. Jouganatos, California State University–Sacramento

Jonathan Kaplan, California State University–Sacramento

Leland Kempe, California State University–Fresno

Philip King, San Francisco State University

Lori Kletzer, University of California, Santa Cruz

Stephan Kroll, California State University–Sacramento

David Lang, California State University–Sacramento

Carsten Lange, California State Polytechnic University–Pomona

Don Leet, California State University–Fresno

Rose LeMont, Modesto Junior College

Tony Lima, California State University–East Bay

Solina Lindahl, California Polytechnic State University–San Luis Obispo

Roger Mack, DeAnza College

Michael Marlow, California Polytechnic State University

Kristen Monaco, California State University–Long Beach

W. Douglas Morgan, University of California, Santa Barbara

Nivedita Mukherji, Oakland University

Andrew Narwold, University of San Diego

Hanna Paulson, West Los Angeles College

Joseph M. Pogodzinksi, San Jose State University

Michael J. Potepan, San Francisco State University

Mary L. Pranzo, California State University–Fresno

Sasha Radisich, Glendale Community College

Ratha Ramoo, Diablo Valley College

Scott J. Sambucci, California State University–East Bay

Ariane Schauer, Marymount College

Frederica Shockley, California State University–Chico

Mark Siegler, California State University–Sacramento

Jonathan Silberman, Oakland University

Lisa Simon, California Polytechnic State University–San Louis Obispo

Stephen Smith, Bakersfield College

Rodney B. Swanson, University of California–Los Angeles
Martha Stuffler, Irvine Valley College
Lea Templer, College of the Canyons
Kristin A. Van Gaasbeck, California State University–Sacramento
Va Nee Van Vleck, California State University–Fresno
Michael Visser, Sonoma State University
Steven Yamarik, California State University–Long Beach
Guy Yamashiro, California State University–Long Beach
Kevin Young, Diablo Valley College
Anthony Zambelli, Cuyamaca College

COLORADO
Mohammed Akacem, Metropolitan State College of Denver
Rhonda Corman, University of Northern Colorado
Dale DeBoer, University of Colorado–Colorado Springs
Karen Gebhardt, Colorado State University
Murat Iyigun, University of Colorado at Boulder
Nancy Jianakoplos, Colorado State University
Jay Kaplan, University of Colorado–Boulder
William G. Mertens, University of Colorado–Boulder
Rachael Small, University of Colorado–Boulder
Stephen Weiler, Colorado State University

CONNECTICUT
Christopher P. Ball, Quinnipiac University
Mark Gius, Quinnipiac University
Donn M. Johnson, Quinnipiac University
Robert Martel, University of Connecticut
Judith Mills, Southern Connecticut State University
Matthew Rafferty, Quinnipiac University
Christian Zimmermann, University of Connecticut

DISTRICT OF COLUMBIA
Colleen Callahan, American University
Robert Feinberg, American University
Walter Park, American University

DELAWARE
Fatma Abdel-Raouf, Goldey-Beacom College
Ali Ataiifar, Delaware County Community College
Andrew T. Hill, University of Delaware

FLORIDA
Herman Baine, Broward Community College
Robert L. Beekman, University of Tampa
Eric P. Chiang, Florida Atlantic University
Martine Duchatelet, Barry University
Hadley Hartman, Santa Fe Community College
Richard Hawkins, University of West Florida
Brad Kamp, University of South Florida
Brian Kench, University of Tampa
Thomas McCaleb, Florida State University
Barbara A. Moore, University of Central Florida
Augustine Nelson, University of Miami
Jamie Ortiz, Florida Atlantic University
Deborah Paige, Santa Fe Community College

Robert Pennington, University of Central Florida
Bob Potter, University of Central Florida
Jerry Schwartz, Broward Community College–North
William Stronge, Florida Atlantic University
Nora Underwood, University of Central Florida
Zhiguang Wang, Florida International University
Joan Wiggenhorn, Barry University

GEORGIA
Greg Brock, Georgia Southern University
Donna Fisher, Georgia Southern University
Shelby Frost, Georgia State University
John King, Georgia Southern University
Constantin Ogloblin, Georgia Southern University
Dr. Greg Okoro, Georgia Perimeter College–Clarkston
Michael Reksulak, Georgia Southern University
Bill Yang, Georgia Southern University

IDAHO
Cynthia Hill, Idaho State University
Don Holley, Boise State University
Tesa Stegner, Idaho State University

ILLINOIS
Teshome Abebe, Eastern Illinois University
Ali Akarca, University of Illinois–Chicago
Zsolt Becsi, Southern Illinois University–Carbondale
James Bruehler, Eastern Illinois University
Louis Cain, Loyola University Chicago and Northwestern University
Rosa Lea Danielson, College of DuPage
Kevin Dunagan, Oakton Community College
Scott Gilbert, Southern Illinois University
Rajeev K. Goel, Illinois State University
David Gordon, Illinois Valley Community College
Alan Grant, Eastern Illinois University
Rik Hafer, Southern Illinois University–Edwardsville
Alice Melkumian, Western Illinois University
Christopher Mushrush, Illinois State University
Jeff Reynolds, Northern Illinois University
Helen Roberts, University of Illinois–Chicago
Thomas R. Sadler, Western Illinois University
Eric Schulz, Northwestern University
Dennis Shannon, Southwestern Illinois College
Charles Sicotte, Rock Valley Community College
Neil T. Skaggs, Illinois State University
Kevin Sylwester, Southern Illinois University–Carbondale
Wendine Thompson-Dawson, Monmouth College
Mark Witte, Northwestern University
Laurie Wolff, Southern Illinois University–Carbondale
Paula Worthington, Northwestern University

INDIANA
Kelly Blanchard, Purdue University
Cecil Bohanon, Ball State University
Thomas Gresik, University of Notre Dame

Robert B. Harris, Indiana University–Purdue University, Indianapolis

Fred Herschede, Indiana University–South Bend

John Pomery, Purdue University

Rob Rude, Ivy Tech Community College

James K. Self, Indiana University–Bloomington

Esther-Mirjam Sent, University of Notre Dame

Virginia Shingleton, Valparaiso University

Martin C. Spechler, Indiana University–Purdue University Indianapolis

Arun K. Srinivasan, Indiana University–Southeast Campus

Geetha Suresh, Purdue University–West Lafayette

IOWA

Terry Alexander, Iowa State University

Paul Elgatian, St. Ambrose University

Jennifer Fuhrman, University of Iowa

Ken McCormick, University of Northern Iowa

Andy Schuchart, Iowa Central Community College

John Solow, University of Iowa

Jonathan Warner, Dordt College

KANSAS

Guatam Bhattacharya, University of Kansas

Amanda Freeman, Kansas State University

Dipak Ghosh, Emporia State University

Alan Grant, Baker University

Wayne Oberle, St. Ambrose University

Jodi Messer Pelkowski, Wichita State University

Martin Perline, Wichita State University

Joel Potter, Kansas State University

Joshua Rosenbloom, University of Kansas

Shane Sanders, Kansas State University

Bhavneet Walia, Kansas State University

KENTUCKY

Tom Cate, Northern Kentucky University

Nan-Ting Chou, University of Louisville

David Eaton, Murray State University

Ann Eike, University of Kentucky

Robert Gillette, University of Kentucky

Barry Haworth, University of Louisville

Gail Hoyt, University of Kentucky

Donna Ingram, Eastern Kentucky University

Waithaka Iraki, Kentucky State University

Hak Youn Kim, Western Kentucky University

Martin Milkman, Murray State University

Jenny Minier, University of Kentucky

David Shideler, Murray State University

John Vahaly, University of Louisville

LOUISIANA

Lara Gardner, Southeastern Louisiana University

Jay Johnson, Southeastern Louisiana University

Faik Koray, Louisiana State University

Paul Nelson, University of Louisiana–Monroe

Sung Chul No, Southern University and A&M College

Tammy Parker, University of Louisiana–Monroe

Wesley A. Payne, Delgado Community College

Nancy Rumore, University of Louisiana at Lafayette

MARYLAND

Carey Borkoski, Anne Arundel Community College

Kathleen A. Carroll, University of Maryland–Baltimore County

Jill Caviglia-Harris, Salisbury University

Dustin Chambers, Salisbury University

Karl Einolf, Mount Saint Mary's University

Marsha Goldfarb, University of Maryland–Baltimore City

Bruce Madariaga, Montgomery College

Shah Mehrabi, Montgomery College

Gretchen Mester, Anne Arundel Community College

David Mitch, University of Maryland–Baltimore County

John Neri, University of Maryland

Henry Terrell, University of Maryland

MASSACHUSETTS

William L. Casey, Jr., Babson College

Arthur Schiller Casimir, Western New England College

Michael Enz, Western New England College

Can Erbil, Brandeis University

Lou Foglia, Suffolk University

Gerald Friedman, University of Massachusetts

Todd Idson, Boston University

Aaron Jackson, Bentley College

Russell A. Janis, University of Massachusetts–Amherst

Anthony Laramie, Merrimack College

Carol McDonough, University of Massachusetts–Lowell

William O'Brien, Worcester State College

Ahmad Saranjam, Bridgewater State College

Howard Shore, Bentley College

Janet Thomas, Bentley College

Gregory H. Wassall, Northeastern University

Bruce G. Webb, Gordon College

Gilbert Wolpe, Newbury College

Jay Zagorsky, Boston University

MICHIGAN

Eric Beckman, Delta College

Jared Boyd, Henry Ford Community College

Victor Claar, Hope College

Dr. Sonia Dalmia, Grand Valley State University

Daniel Giedeman, Grand Valley State University

Steven Hayworth, Eastern Michigan University

Gregg Heidebrink, Washtenaw Community College

Carol Hogan, University of Michigan–Dearborn

Marek Kolar, Delta College

Susan J. Linz, Michigan State University

James Luke, Lansing Community College

Ilir Miteza, University of Michigan–Dearborn

John Nader, Grand Valley State University

Norman P. Obst, Michigan State University
Laudo M. Ogura, Grand Valley State University
Robert J. Rossana, Wayne State University
Michael J. Ryan, Western Michigan University
Charles A. Stull, Kalamazoo College
Michael J. Twomey, University of Michigan–Dearborn
Mark Wheeler, Western Michigan University
Wendy Wysocki, Monroe County Community College

MINNESOTA
Mary Edwards, Saint Cloud State University
Phillip J. Grossman, Saint Cloud State University
Monica Hartman, University of St. Thomas
Matthew Hyle, Winona State University
David J. O'Hara, Metropolitan State University–Minneapolis
Kwang Woo (Ken) Park, Minnesota State University–Mankato
Artatrana Ratha, Saint Cloud State University
Ken Rebeck, Saint Cloud State University
Katherine Schmeiser, University of Minnesota

MISSISSIPPI
Becky Campbell, Mississippi State University
Randall Campbell, Mississippi State University
Patricia A. Freeman, Jackson State University
Arlena Sullivan, Jones County Junior College

MISSOURI
Chris Azevedo, University of Central Missouri
Ariel Belasen, Saint Louis University
Catherine Chambers, University of Central Missouri
Paul Chambers, University of Central Missouri
Kermit Clay, Ozarks Technical Community College
Ben Collier, Northwest Missouri State University
John R. Crooker, University of Central Missouri
Jo Durr, Southwest Missouri State University
Julie H. Gallaway, Southwest Missouri State University
Terrel Gallaway, Southwest Missouri State University
Mark Karscig, Central Missouri State University
Nicholas D. Peppes, Saint Louis Community College–Forest Park
Steven T. Petty, College of the Ozarks
Sharon Ryan, University of Missouri–Columbia
Ben Young, University of Missouri–Kansas City

MONTANA
Agnieszka Bielinska-Kwapisz, Montana State University–Bozeman
Jeff Bookwalter, University of Montana–Missoula

NEBRASKA
Allan Jenkins, University of Nebraska–Kearney
James Knudsen, Creighton University
Craig MacPhee, University of Nebraska–Lincoln
Kim Sosin, University of Nebraska–Omaha
Mark E. Wohar, University of Nebraska–Omaha

NEVADA
Bernard Malamud, University of Nevada–Las Vegas
Bill Robinson, University of Nevada–Las Vegas

NEW HAMPSHIRE
Evelyn Gick, Dartmouth College
Neil Niman, University of New Hampshire

NEW JERSEY
Len Anyanwu, Union County College
Maharuk Bhiladwalla, Rutgers University–New Brunswick
Giuliana Campanelli-Andreopoulos, William Paterson University
Gary Gigliotti, Rutgers University–New Brunswick
John Graham, Rutgers University–Newark
Berch Haroian, William Paterson University
Paul Harris, Camden County College
Jeff Rubin, Rutgers University
Henry Ryder, Gloucester County College
Donna Thompson, Brookdale Community College

NEW MEXICO
Donald Coes, University of New Mexico
Kate Krause, University of New Mexico
Curt Shepherd, University of New Mexico

NEW YORK
Seemi Ahmad, Dutchess Community College
Chris Annala, State University of New York–Geneseo
Erol Balkan, Hamilton College
John Bockino, Suffolk County Community College–Ammerman
Charles Callahan III, State University of New York–Brockport
Michael Carew, Baruch College
Sean Corcoran, New York University
Ranjit S. Dighe, City University of New York–Bronx Community College
Debra Dwyer, Stony Brook University
Glenn Gerstner, Saint John's University–Queens
Susan Glanz, Saint John's University–Queens
William L. Goffe, State University of New York–Oswego
Wayne A. Grove, LeMoyne College
Nancy Howe, Hudson Valley Community College
Christopher Inya, Monroe Community College
Ghassan Karam, Pace University
Clifford Kern, State University of New York–Binghamton
Mary Lesser, Iona College
Anna Musatti, Columbia University
Theodore Muzio, St. John's University, New York
Emre Ozsoz, Fashion Institute of Technology
Howard Ross, Baruch College
Ed Steinberg, New York University
Leonie Stone, State University of New York–Geneseo
Ganti Subrahmanyam, University of Buffalo
Jogindar S. Uppal, State University of New York–Albany
Susan Wolcott, Binghamton University

## NORTH CAROLINA

Otilia Boldea, North Carolina State University
Robert Burrus, University of North Carolina–Wilmington
Lee A. Craig, North Carolina State University
Kathleen Dorsainvil, Winston–Salem State University
Michael Goode, Central Piedmont Community College
Salih Hakeem, North Carolina Central University
Melissa Hendrickson, North Carolina State University
Haiyong Liu, East Carolina University
Kosmas Marinakis, North Carolina State University
Todd McFall, Wake Forest University
Shahriar Mostashari, Campbell University
Jonathan Phillips, North Carolina State University
Jeff Sarbaum, University of North Carolina–Greensboro
Peter Schuhmann, University of North Carolina–Wilmington
Robert Shoffner, Central Piedmont Community College
Catherine Skura, Sandhills Community College
Carol Stivender, University of North Carolina–Charlotte
Vera Tabakova, East Carolina University
Eric Taylor, Central Piedmont Community College
Hui-Kuan Tseng, University of North Carolina at Charlotte
Robert Whaples, Wake Forest University
John Whitehead, Appalachian State University
Gary W. Zinn, East Carolina University
Rick Zuber, University of North Carolina at Charlotte

## OHIO

John P. Blair, Wright State University
Bolong Cao, Ohio University–Athens
Kyongwook Choi, Ohio University
James D'Angelo, University of Cincinnati
Darlene DeVera, Miami University
Tim Fuerst, Bowling Green University
Harley Gill, Ohio State University
Leroy Gill, Ohio State University
Steven Heubeck, Ohio State University
Daniel Horton, Cleveland State University
Ernest Massie, Franklin University
Ida A. Mirzaie, Ohio State University
Jay Mutter, University of Akron
Mike Nelson, University of Akron
Nicholas Noble, Miami University
Dennis C. O'Neill, University of Cincinnati
Joseph Palardy, Youngstown State University
Charles Reichheld, Cuyahoga Community College
Teresa Riley, Youngstown State University
Rochelle Ruffer, Youngstown State University
Kate Sheppard, University of Akron
Richard Stratton, University of Akron
Albert Sumell, Youngstown State University
Steve Szheghi, Wilmington College

Melissa Thomasson, Miami University
Yaqin Wang, Youngstown State University
Bert Wheeler, Cedarville University
Kathryn Wilson, Kent State University
Sourushe Zandvakili, University of Cincinnati

## OKLAHOMA

David Hudgins, University of Oklahoma
Bill McLean, Oklahoma State University
Denny Myers, Oklahoma City Community College
Ed Price, Oklahoma State University
Abdulhamid Sukar, Cameron University

## OREGON

Bill Burrows, Lane Community College
Tom Carroll, Central Oregon Community College
Tim Duy, University of Oregon
B. Starr McMullen, Oregon State University
Ted Scheinman, Mount Hood Community College
Larry Singell, University of Oregon
Ayca Tekin-Koru, Oregon State University

## PENNSYLVANIA

Bradley Andrew, Juniata College
Mohammad Bajwa, Northampton Community College
Gustavo Barboza, Mercyhurst College
Charles A. Bennett, Gannon University
Cynthia Benzing, West Chester University
Howard Bodenhorn, Lafayette College
Milica Bookman, St. Joseph's University
Robert Brooker, Gannon University
Eric Brucker, Widener University
Linda Childs-Leatherbury, Lincoln University
Scott J. Dressler, Villanova University
Satyajit Ghosh, University of Scranton
Anthony Gyapong, Pennsylvania State University–Abington
Mehdi Haririan, Bloomsburg University
Andrew Hill, Federal Reserve Bank of Philadelphia
Steven Husted, University of Pittsburgh
James Jozefowicz, Indiana University of Pennsylvania
Stephanie Jozefowicz, Indiana University of Pennsylvania
Nicholas Karatjas, Indiana University of Pennsylvania
Mary Kelly, Villanova University
Brendan Kennelly, Lehigh University
Thomas C. Kinnaman, Bucknell University
Christopher Magee, Bucknell University
Katherine McCann, Penn State
Judy McDonald, Lehigh University
Ranganath Murthy, Bucknell University
Hong V. Nguyen, University of Scranton
Cristian Pardo, Saint Joseph's University
Iordanis Petsas, University of Scranton
Adam Renhoff, Drexel University
Nicole Sadowski, York College of Pennsylvania
Edward Scahill, University of Scranton

Ken Slaysman, York College of Pennsylvania
Rajeev Sooreea, Pennsylvania State University–Altoona
Rebecca Stein, University of Pennsylvania
Sandra Trejos, Clarion University
Peter Zaleski, Villanova University
Ann Zech, Saint Joseph's University
Lei Zhu, West Chester University of Pennsylvania
Susan Zumas, Lehigh University

RHODE ISLAND

Jongsung Kim, Bryant University
Leonard Lardaro, University of Rhode Island
Nazma Latif-Zaman, Providence College

SOUTH CAROLINA

Calvin Blackwell, College of Charleston
Ward Hooker, Orangeburg–Calhoun Technical College
Woodrow W. Hughes, Jr., Converse College
John McArthur, Wofford College
Chad Turner, Clemson University
Madelyn Young, Converse College

SOUTH DAKOTA

Joseph M. Santos, South Dakota State University
Jason Zimmerman, South Dakota State University

TENNESSEE

Sindy Abadie, Southwest Tennessee Community College
Charles Baum, Middle Tennessee State University
John Brassel, Southwest Tennessee Community College
Bichaka Fayissa, Middle Tennessee State University
Michael J. Gootzeit, University of Memphis
Travis Hayes, University of Tennessee–Chattanooga
Christopher C. Klein, Middle Tennessee State University
Leila Pratt, University of Tennessee at Chattanooga
Millicent Sites, Carson-Newman College

TEXAS

Carlos Aguilar, El Paso Community College
Rashid Al-Hmoud, Texas Tech University
William Beaty, Tarleton State University
Klaus Becker, Texas Tech University
Alex Brown, Texas A&M University
Jack A. Bucco, Austin Community College–Northridge and Saint Edward's University
Don Bumpass, Sam Houston State University
Marilyn M. Butler, Sam Houston State University
Mike Cohick, Collin County Community College
Cesar Corredor, Texas A&M University
Steven Craig, University of Houston
Patrick Crowley, Texas A&M University–Corpus Christi
Richard Croxdale, Austin Community College
Susan Dadres, Southern Methodist University
Harry Ellis, Jr., University of North Texas
Paul Emberton, Texas State University
Diego Escobari, Texas A&M University
Nicholas Feltovich, University of Houston–Main

Charles Harold Fifield, Baylor University
Mark Frank, Sam Houston State University
Richard Gosselin, Houston Community College–Central
Sheila Amin Gutierrez de Pineres, University of Texas–Dallas
Tina J. Harvell, Blinn College–Bryan Campus
James W. Henderson, Baylor University
Jane S. Himarios, University of Texas–Arlington
James Holcomb, University of Texas–El Paso
Jamal Husein, Angelo State University
Ansul Islam, University of Houston–Downtown
Karen Johnson, Baylor University
Kathy Kelly, University of Texas–Arlington
Thomas Kemp, Tarrant County College–Northwest
Jim Lee, Texas A&M University–Corpus Christi
Ronnie W. Liggett, University of Texas–Arlington
Akbar Marvasti, University of Houston–Downtown
James Mbata, Houston Community College
Kimberly Mencken, Baylor University
Randy Methenitis, Richland College
Carl Montano, Lamar University
James Moreno, Blinn College
Camille Nelson, Texas A & M University
Michael Nelson, Texas A&M University
Charles Newton, Houston Community College–Southwest College
John Pisciotta, Baylor University
Sara Saderion, Houston Community College–Southwest College
George E. Samuels, Sam Houston State University
David Schutte, Mountain View College
Ivan Tasic, Texas A&M University
David Torres, University of Texas–El Paso
Ross vanWassenhove, University of Houston
Roger Wehr, University of Texas–Arlington
Jim Wollscheid, Texas A&M University–Kingsville
J. Christopher Wreh, North Central Texas College
David W. Yoskowitz, Texas A&M University–Corpus Christi
Inske Zandvliet, Brookhaven College

UTAH

Chris Fawson, Utah State University
Lowell Glenn, Utah Valley State College
Aric Krause, Westminster College
Arden Pope, Brigham Young University

VERMONT

Nancy Brooks, University of Vermont

VIRGINIA

Lee Badgett, Virginia Military Institute
Lee A. Coppock, University of Virginia
Janelle Davenport, Hampton University
Philip Heap, James Madison University
George E. Hoffer, Virginia Commonwealth University

Oleg Korenok, Virginia Commonwealth University
Frances Lea, Germanna Community College
Carrie Meyer, George Mason University
John Min, Northern Virginia Community College
James Roberts, Tidewater Community College–Virginia Beach
Araine A. Schauer, Mary Mount College
Sarah Stafford, The College of William & Mary
Bob Subrick, James Madison University
Susanne Toney, Hampton University
Michelle Vachris, Christopher Newport University
James Wetzel, Virginia Commonwealth University
George Zestos, Christopher Newport University

WASHINGTON
Andrew Ewing, University of Washington
Stacey Jones, Seattle University
Dean Peterson, Seattle University
Robert Rosenman, Washington State University

WEST VIRGINIA
Jacqueline Agesa, Marshall University
Richard Agesa, Marshall University

WISCONSIN
Marina Karabelas, Milwaukee Area Technical College
Elizabeth Sawyer Kelly, University of Wisconsin–Madison
Pascal Ngoboka, University of Wisconsin–River Falls
Kevin Quinn, St. Norbert College
John R. Stoll, University of Wisconsin–Green Bay

WYOMING
Robert Godby, University of Wyoming

DISTRICT OF COLUMBIA
Leon Battista, American Enterprise Institute
Michael Bradley, George Washington University
Colleen M. Callahan, American University

INTERNATIONAL
Minh Quang Dao, Carleton University–Ottawa, Canada

# A Word of Thanks

Once again, we benefited greatly from the dedication and professionalism of the Pearson Economics team. Executive Editor David Alexander's energy and support were indispensable. David helped mold the presentation and provided words of encouragement whenever our energy flagged. Executive Development Editor Lena Buonanno worked tirelessly to ensure that this text was as good as it could be and to coordinate the many moving parts involved in a project of this magnitude. This new edition posed particular challenges, and we remain astonished at the amount of time, energy, and unfailing good humor she brings to this project. As we worked on the first edition, Director of Key Markets David Theisen provided invaluable insight into how best to structure a principles text. His advice helped shape nearly every chapter. We have worked with Executive Marketing Manager Lori DeShazo on three different books: principles of economics, money and banking, and intermediate macroeconomics, and we continue to be amazed at her energy and creativity in promoting the field of economics. Steve Deitmer, Director of Development, brought sound judgment to the many decisions required to create this book. Alison Eusden and Lindsey Sloan managed the extensive supplement package that accompanies the book. Carla Thompson, Kristin Ruscetta, and Jonathan Boylan turned our manuscript pages into a beautiful published book. We received excellent research assistance from Ed Timmons, Matthew Saboe, David Van Der Goes, and Jason Hockenberry. We thank Pam Smith, Elena Zeller, and Jennifer Brailsford for their careful proofreading of first- and second-round page proofs.

A good part of the burden of a project of this magnitude is borne by our families. We appreciate the patience, support, and encouragement of our wives and children.

# Economics:
## Foundations and Models

## Chapter Outline and Learning Objectives

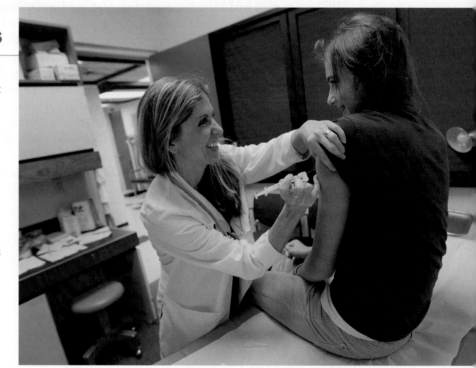

# Why Are Some Doctors Leaving Private Practice?

When you visit a doctor's office, you probably don't think of it as a small business, but that's what it is. Like other businesspeople, a doctor hires workers—nurses, physician's assistants, and receptionists—and buys or rents machinery and equipment. A doctor's income represents the profits from his or her practice, or the difference between the revenue received from patients and their health insurance plans and the costs to the doctor of wages, rent, loans, and insurance. For many years, the typical doctor operated his or her practice either alone or in partnership with other doctors. Lately, though, an increasing number of doctors have given up their practices and become salaried employees of hospitals. Although as recently as 2002 more than three times as many medical practices were owned by doctors as by hospitals, by 2008 more medical practices were owned by hospitals.

The movement of many doctors from running their own businesses to being salaried employees of hospitals is due to changes occurring within the U.S. health care system. Soaring health care costs have led many private health care insurers, as well as the federal and state governments, to reduce the payments they make to doctors in return for treating patients. President Barack Obama's package of health care changes, sometimes referred to as "Obamacare," was passed by Congress in 2010 and is being gradually phased in through 2014. The package will result in major changes in how some people will receive health insurance and how doctors will be compensated. Policymakers are also considering changes to Medicare, the federal government program that provides health care to people over age 65, because the costs of the program have been rising very rapidly. Over time, these changes have increased the amount of paperwork doctors must complete in order to be paid for treating patients. This paperwork has raised the costs doctors incur in running their practices, which makes becoming a salaried employee of a hospital more attractive.

Throughout this book, we will see that many policy issues, including changes in the U.S. medical system, involve economics. In fact, knowledge of economics can help you to better understand and analyze many policy issues.

**AN INSIDE LOOK** on **page 20** discusses how health professionals may be delaying retirement because they are concerned about their finances.

Based on Robert Kocher, M.D., and Nikhil R. Sahni, "Hospitals' Race to Employ Physicians—The Logic Behind a Money-Losing Proposition," *New England Journal of Medicine*, May 12, 2011; and Uwe E. Reinhardt, "Producing More Primary-Care Doctors," *New York Times*, June 10, 2011.

## Economics in Your Life

### Will There Be Plenty of Jobs Available in the Health Care Industry?

The U.S. Health Resources and Services Administration (HRSA) forecasts that the number of doctors in the United States will increase from about 808,000 in 2010 to 866,400 in 2020. But the HRSA also forecasts that the number of doctors needed to provide patient care will rise from about 805,000 in 2010 to 922,000 in 2020. In other words, this federal government agency forecasts that there will be a shortage of about 56,000 doctors in 2020. The U.S. Bureau of Labor Statistics projects that four of the six fastest growing occupations over the next 10 years will be in the medical field. It would seem that plenty of jobs should be available in health care during the next few years. But the availability of these jobs depends on the reliability of the forecasts. What is the basis for the forecasts on the availability of jobs in health care, and how reliable are the forecasts? As you read this chapter, see if you can answer this question. You can check your answer against the one we provide on **page 18** at the end of this chapter.

I n this book, we use economics to answer questions such as the following:

- How are the prices of goods and services determined?
- How does pollution affect the economy, and how should government policy deal with these effects?
- Why do firms engage in international trade, and how do government policies affect international trade?
- Why does government control the prices of some goods and services, and what are the effects of those controls?

Economists do not always agree on the answers to every question. In fact, as we will see, economists engage in lively debate on some issues. In addition, new problems and issues are constantly arising. So, economists are always at work developing new methods to analyze economic questions.

All the issues we discuss in this book illustrate a basic fact of life: People must make choices as they try to attain their goals. We must make choices because we live in a world of **scarcity**, which means that although our wants are unlimited, the resources available to fulfill those wants are limited. You might like to own a BMW and spend each summer in five-star European hotels, but unless Bill Gates is a close and generous relative, you probably lack the money to fulfill these dreams. Every day, you make choices as you spend your limited income on the many goods and services available. The finite amount of time you have also limits your ability to attain your goals. If you spend an hour studying for your economics midterm, you have one hour less to study for your history midterm. Firms and the government are in the same situation as you: They also must attain their goals with limited resources. **Economics** is the study of the choices consumers, business managers, and government officials make to attain their goals, given their scarce resources.

We begin this chapter by discussing three important economic ideas that we will return to many times in this book: *People are rational, people respond to incentives, and optimal decisions are made at the margin.* Then we consider the three fundamental questions that any economy must answer: *What* goods and services will be produced? *How* will the goods and services be produced? and *Who* will receive the goods and services produced? Next, we consider the role of *economic models* in analyzing economic issues. **Economic models** are simplified versions of reality used to analyze real-world economic situations. We will explore why economists use models and how they construct them. Finally, we will discuss the difference between microeconomics and macroeconomics, and we will preview some important economic terms.

**Scarcity** A situation in which unlimited wants exceed the limited resources available to fulfill those wants.

**Economics** The study of the choices people make to attain their goals, given their scarce resources.

**Economic model** A simplified version of reality used to analyze real-world economic situations.

**1.1 LEARNING** OBJECTIVE

Explain these three key economic ideas: People are rational, people respond to incentives, and optimal decisions are made at the margin.

**Market** A group of buyers and sellers of a good or service and the institution or arrangement by which they come together to trade.

# Three Key Economic Ideas

As you try to achieve your goals, whether they involve buying a new computer or finding a part-time job, you will interact with other people in *markets*. A **market** is a group of buyers and sellers of a good or service and the institution or arrangement by which they come together to trade. Most of economics involves analyzing what happens in markets. Throughout this book, as we study how people make choices and interact in markets, we will return to three important ideas:

1. People are rational.
2. People respond to economic incentives.
3. Optimal decisions are made at the margin.

## People Are Rational

Economists generally assume that people are rational. This assumption does *not* mean that economists believe everyone knows everything or always makes the "best" decision. It means that economists assume that consumers and firms use all available information as they act to achieve their goals. Rational individuals weigh the benefits and costs of each action, and they choose an action only if the benefits outweigh the costs. For example, if Microsoft charges a price of $239 for a copy of Windows, economists assume that the managers at Microsoft have estimated that a price of $239 will earn Microsoft the most profit. The managers may be wrong; perhaps a price of $265 would be more profitable, but economists assume that the managers at Microsoft have acted rationally, on the basis of the information available to them, in choosing the price. Of course, not everyone behaves rationally all the time. Still, the assumption of rational behavior is very useful in explaining most of the choices that people make.

## People Respond to Economic Incentives

Human beings act from a variety of motives, including religious belief, envy, and compassion. Economists emphasize that consumers and firms consistently respond to *economic* incentives. This fact may seem obvious, but it is often overlooked. For example, according to an article in the *Wall Street Journal*, the FBI couldn't understand why banks were not taking steps to improve security in the face of an increase in robberies: "FBI officials suggest that banks place uniformed, armed guards outside their doors and install bullet-resistant plastic, known as a 'bandit barrier,' in front of teller windows." FBI officials were surprised that few banks took their advice. But the article also reported that installing bullet-resistant plastic costs $10,000 to $20,000, and a well-trained security guard receives $50,000 per year in salary and benefits. The average loss in a bank robbery is only about $1,200. The economic incentive to banks is clear: It is less costly to put up with bank robberies than to take additional security measures. FBI agents may be surprised by how banks respond to the threat of robberies—but economists are not.

In each chapter, the *Making the Connection* feature discusses a news story or another application related to the chapter material. Read the following *Making the Connection* for a discussion of whether people respond to economic incentives even when deciding how much to eat and how much exercise to undertake.

| Making the Connection | Does Health Insurance Give People an Incentive to Become Obese? |
|---|---|

Obesity is an increasing problem in the United States. The U.S. Centers for Disease Control (CDC) defines obesity for an adult as having a body mass index (BMI) of 30 or greater. The body mass index measures a person's weight relative to the person's height. (The exact formula is: BMI = (Weight in pounds/(Height in inches)$^2$) × 703.) A BMI of 30 is equivalent to a person 5'4" being 30 pounds overweight. Obesity is related to a variety of diseases, including heart disease, stroke, diabetes, and hypertension.

The two maps below show the striking increase in obesity in the 15 years between 1994 and 2009. In 1994, in a majority of states the population was between 10 percent and 14 percent obese, and in no state was more than 20 percent of the population obese. By 2009, only in Colorado was less than 20 percent of the population obese, and in about two-thirds of the states, 25 percent or more of the population was obese, including nine states where more than 30 percent of the population was obese.

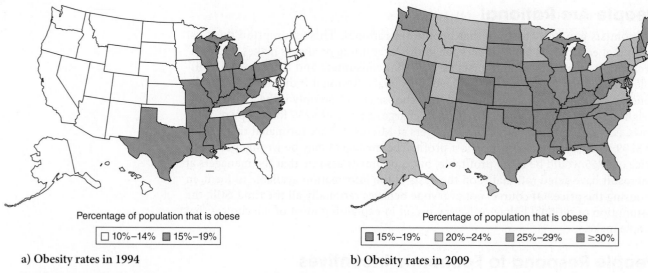

Percentage of population that is obese

☐ 10%–14%  ■ 15%–19%

**a) Obesity rates in 1994**

Percentage of population that is obese

■ 15%–19%  ☐ 20%–24%  ■ 25%–29%  ■ ≥30%

**b) Obesity rates in 2009**

Data from Centers for Disease Control and Prevention, "Behavior Risk Factor Surveillance System."

Many people who suffer from obesity have underlying medical conditions. For these people, obesity is an unfortunate medical problem that they cannot control. The fact that obesity is increasing, though, indicates that for some people obesity is the result of diet and lifestyle choices. Potential explanations for the increase in obesity include greater intake of high-calorie fast foods, insufficient exercise, and a decline in the physical activity associated with many jobs. The CDC recommends that teenagers get a minimum of 60 minutes of aerobic exercise per day, a standard that only 15 percent of high school students were meeting in 2011. In 1960, 50 percent of jobs in the United States required at least moderate physical activity. By 2010, only 20 percent of jobs did. As a result, the typical worker was burning off about 130 fewer calories per workday.

In addition to eating too much and not exercising enough, could health insurance be a cause of obesity? Obese people tend to suffer more medical problems than do people who are not overweight and so incur higher medical costs. Overweight people with health insurance that will reimburse them for only part of their medical bills or who have no health insurance must pay some or all of these higher medical bills themselves. Overweight people with health insurance that covers most of their medical bills will not suffer as large a monetary cost from being obese. In other words, by reducing some of the costs of obesity, health insurance may give people an economic incentive to gain weight. At first glance, this argument may seem implausible. Some people suffer from medical conditions that can make physical activity difficult or that can cause weight gain even with moderate eating, so they may become overweight whether they have health insurance or not. Some people are overweight due to poor eating habits, and they probably don't consider health insurance when deciding whether to have another slice of chocolate cake or to watch television instead of going to the gym. But if economists are correct about the importance of economic incentives, then we would expect that if we hold all other personal characteristics—such as age, gender, and income—constant, people with health insurance will be more likely to be overweight than people without health insurance.

Jay Bhattacharya and Kate Bundorf of Stanford University, Noemi Pace of University College London, and Neeraj Sood of the RAND Corporation, a research center, have analyzed the effects of health insurance on weight. Using a sample that followed nearly 80,000 people during the years 1989–2004, they found that after controlling for income, education, race, gender, age, and other factors, people with health insurance are significantly more likely to be overweight than are people without health insurance. Having private health insurance increased BMI by 1.3 points, and having public health insurance, such as *Medicaid*, which is a program under which the government provides health care to low-income people, increased BMI by 2.3 points. These findings suggest that people respond to economic incentives even when making decisions about what they eat and how much they exercise.

Based on Centers for Disease Control and Prevention, "Obesity Trends Among U.S. Adults Between 1985 and 2009," www.cdc.gov; Katherine M. Flegal, Margaret D. Caroll, Cynthia L. Ogden, and Lester R. Curtin, "Prevalence and Trends in Obesity Among U.S. Adults, 1999–2008," *Journal of the American Medical Association*, Vol. 303, No. 3, January 20, 2010, pp. 235–41; Jay Bhattacharya, Kate Bundorf, Noemi Pace, and Neeraj Soodin, "Does Health Insurance Make You Fat?" in Michael Grossman and Naci H. Mocan, eds., *Economic Aspects of Obesity*, (Chicago: University of Chicago Press, 2011); and Tara Parker-Pope, "Less Active at Work, Americans Have Packed on Pounds," *New York Times*, May 25, 2011.

**Your Turn:** Test your understanding by doing related problems 1.5 and 1.6 on page 22 at the end of this chapter.    MyEconLab

## Optimal Decisions Are Made at the Margin

Some decisions are "all or nothing": For instance, when an entrepreneur decides whether to open a new restaurant, she either starts the new restaurant or she doesn't. When you decide whether to enter graduate school or to take a job, you either enter graduate school or you don't. But rather than being all or nothing, most decisions in life involve doing a little more or a little less. If you are trying to decrease your spending and increase your saving, the decision is not really between saving all the money you earn or spending it all. Rather, many small choices are involved, such as whether to buy a caffè mocha at Starbucks every day or just three times per week.

Economists use the word *marginal* to mean "extra" or "additional." Should you watch another hour of TV or spend that hour studying? The *marginal benefit* (or, in symbols, *MB*) of watching more TV is the additional enjoyment you receive. The *marginal cost* (or *MC*) is the lower grade you receive from having studied a little less. Should Apple produce an additional 300,000 iPhones? Firms receive *revenue* from selling goods. Apple's marginal benefit is the additional revenue it receives from selling 300,000 more iPhones. Apple's marginal cost is the additional cost—for wages, parts, and so forth—of producing 300,000 more iPhones. *Economists reason that the optimal decision is to continue any activity up to the point where the marginal benefit equals the marginal cost—in symbols, where* MB = MC. Often we apply this rule without consciously thinking about it. Usually you will know whether the additional enjoyment from watching a television program is worth the additional cost involved in not spending that hour studying, without giving the decision a lot of thought. In business situations, however, firms often have to make careful calculations to determine, for example, whether the additional revenue received from increasing production is greater or less than the additional cost of the production. Economists refer to analysis that involves comparing marginal benefits and marginal costs as **marginal analysis**.

**Marginal analysis** Analysis that involves comparing marginal benefits and marginal costs.

In each chapter of this book, you will see the special feature *Solved Problem*. This feature will increase your understanding of the material by leading you through the steps of solving an applied economic problem. After reading the problem, you can test your understanding by working the related problems that appear at the end of the chapter and in the study guide that accompanies this book. You can also complete Solved Problems on www.myeconlab.com and receive tutorial help.

# Solved Problem 1.1

## A Doctor Makes a Decision at the Margin

A doctor is considering keeping her office open 9 hours per day rather than 8 hours. The doctor's office manager argues, "Keeping the office open an extra hour is a good idea because your practice will make a total profit of $300,000 per year when the office is open 9 hours per day." Do you agree with the office manager's reasoning? What, if any, additional information do you need to decide whether the doctor should keep her office open an additional hour per day?

## Solving the Problem

**Step 1:** **Review the chapter material.** This problem is about making decisions, so you may want to review the section "Optimal Decisions Are Made at the Margin," which begins on page 7.

**Step 2:** **Explain whether you agree with the manager's reasoning.** We have seen that any activity should be continued to the point where the marginal benefit is equal to the marginal cost. In this case, that involves a doctor continuing to keep her office open up to the point where the additional revenue she receives from seeing more patients is equal to the marginal cost of keeping her office open an additional hour. The office manager has not done a marginal analysis, so you should not agree with the manager's reasoning. The statement about the total profit of keeping the office open for 9 hours is not relevant to the decision of whether to stay open an additional hour.

**Step 3:** **Explain what additional information you need.** You will need additional information to make a correct decision. You will need to know the marginal revenue and the marginal cost of keeping the practice open an extra hour. The marginal revenue would depend on how many more patients the doctor can see in the extra hour. The marginal cost would include the additional salary to be paid to the office staff, any additional medical supplies that would be used, as well as any additional electricity or other utilities. The doctor would also need to take into account the nonmonetary cost of spending another hour working rather than spending time with her family and friends or in other leisure activities.

MyEconLab **Your Turn:** For more practice, do related problems 1.7, 1.8, and 1.9 on page 23 at the end of this chapter.

**1.2 LEARNING** OBJECTIVE

Discuss how an economy answers these questions: What goods and services will be produced? How will the goods and services be produced? Who will receive the goods and services produced?

**Trade-off** The idea that because of scarcity, producing more of one good or service means producing less of another good or service.

**Opportunity cost** The highest-valued alternative that must be given up to engage in an activity.

# The Economic Problem That Every Society Must Solve

Because we live in a world of scarcity, any society faces the *economic problem* that it has only a limited amount of economic resources—such as workers, machines, and raw materials—and so can produce only a limited amount of goods and services. Therefore, every society faces **trade-offs**: Producing more of one good or service means producing less of another good or service. In fact, the best way to measure the cost of producing a good or service is the value of what has to be given up to produce it. The **opportunity cost** of any activity—such as producing a good or service—is the highest-valued alternative that must be given up to engage in that activity. The concept of opportunity cost is very important in economics and applies to individuals as much as it does to firms or to society as a whole. Consider the example of a doctor who could receive a salary of $100,000 per year working as an employee of a hospital but decides to open his own private practice instead. In that case, the opportunity cost of the physician services he supplies to his own firm is the $100,000 he gives up by not working for the hospital, even if he does not explicitly pay himself a salary.

Trade-offs force society to make choices when answering the following three fundamental questions:

1. *What* goods and services will be produced?
2. *How* will the goods and services be produced?
3. *Who* will receive the goods and services produced?

Throughout this book, we will return to these questions many times. For now, we briefly introduce each question.

## What Goods and Services Will Be Produced?

How will society decide whether to produce more economics textbooks or more Blu-ray players? More daycare facilities or more football stadiums? Of course, "society" does not make decisions; only individuals make decisions. The answer to the question of what will be produced is determined by the choices that consumers, firms, and the government make. Every day, you help decide which goods and services firms will produce when you choose to buy an iPhone instead of a BlackBerry or a caffè mocha rather than a chai tea. Similarly, Apple must choose whether to devote its scarce resources to making more iPhones or more iPad tablet computers. The federal government must choose whether to spend more of its limited budget on breast cancer research or on repairing highways. In each case, consumers, firms, and the government face the problem of scarcity by trading off one good or service for another. And each choice made comes with an opportunity cost, measured by the value of the best alternative given up.

## How Will the Goods and Services Be Produced?

Firms choose how to produce the goods and services they sell. In many cases, firms face a trade-off between using more workers or using more machines. For example, a local service station has to choose whether to provide car repair services using more diagnostic computers and fewer auto mechanics or more auto mechanics and fewer diagnostic computers. Similarly, movie studios have to choose whether to produce animated films using highly skilled animators to draw them by hand or fewer animators and more computers. In deciding whether to move production offshore to China, firms may need to choose between a production method in the United States that uses fewer workers and more machines and a production method in China that uses more workers and fewer machines.

## Who Will Receive the Goods and Services Produced?

In the United States, who receives the goods and services produced depends largely on how income is distributed. Individuals with the highest income have the ability to buy the most goods and services. Often, people are willing to give up some of their income—and, therefore, some of their ability to purchase goods and services—by donating to charities to increase the incomes of poorer people. Each year, Americans donate about $300 billion to charity, or an average donation of $2,650 for each household in the country. An important policy question, however, is whether the government should intervene to make the distribution of income more equal. Such intervention already occurs in the United States, because people with higher incomes pay a larger fraction of their incomes in taxes and because the government makes payments to people with low incomes. There is disagreement over whether the current attempts to redistribute income are sufficient or whether there should be more or less redistribution.

## Centrally Planned Economies versus Market Economies

**Centrally planned economy** An economy in which the government decides how economic resources will be allocated.

**Market economy** An economy in which the decisions of households and firms interacting in markets allocate economic resources.

To answer the three questions—what, how, and who—societies organize their economies in two main ways. A society can have a **centrally planned economy** in which the government decides how economic resources will be allocated. Or a society can have a **market economy** in which the decisions of households and firms interacting in markets allocate economic resources.

From 1917 to 1991, the most important centrally planned economy in the world was that of the Soviet Union, which was established when Vladimir Lenin and the Communist Party staged a revolution and took over the Russian Empire. In the Soviet Union, the government decided what goods to produce, how the goods would be produced, and who would receive the goods. Government employees managed factories and stores. The objective of these managers was to follow the government's orders rather than to satisfy the wants of consumers. Centrally planned economies like that of the Soviet Union have not been successful in producing low-cost, high-quality goods and services. As a result, the standard of living of the average person in a centrally planned economy tends to be low. All centrally planned economies have also been political dictatorships. Dissatisfaction with low living standards and political repression finally led to the collapse of the Soviet Union in 1991. Today, only a few small countries, such as Cuba and North Korea, still have completely centrally planned economies.

All the high-income democracies, such as the United States, Canada, Japan, and the countries of Western Europe, have market economies. Market economies rely primarily on privately owned firms to produce goods and services and to decide how to produce them. Markets, rather than the government, determine who receives the goods and services produced. In a market economy, firms must produce goods and services that meet the wants of consumers, or the firms will go out of business. In that sense, it is ultimately consumers who decide what goods and services will be produced. Because firms in a market economy compete to offer the highest-quality products at the lowest price, they are under pressure to use the lowest-cost methods of production. For example, in the past 10 years, some U.S. firms, particularly in the electronics and furniture industries, have been under pressure to reduce their costs to meet competition from Chinese firms.

In a market economy, the income of an individual is determined by the payments he receives for what he has to sell. If he is a civil engineer, and firms are willing to pay a salary of $85,000 per year for engineers with his training and skills, that is the amount of income he will have to purchase goods and services. If the engineer also owns a house that he rents out, his income will be even higher. One of the attractive features of markets is that they reward hard work. Generally, the more extensive the training a person has received and the longer the hours the person works, the higher the person's income will be. Of course, luck—both good and bad—also plays a role here, as elsewhere in life. We can conclude that market economies respond to the question "Who receives the goods and services produced?" with the answer "Those who are most willing and able to buy them."

## The Modern "Mixed" Economy

In the nineteenth and early twentieth centuries, the U.S. government engaged in relatively little regulation of markets for goods and services. Beginning in the middle of the twentieth century, government intervention in the economy dramatically increased in the United States and other market economies. This increase was primarily caused by the high rates of unemployment and business bankruptcies during the Great Depression of the 1930s. Some government intervention was also intended to raise the incomes of the elderly, the sick, and people with limited skills. For example, in the 1930s, the United States established the Social Security system, which provides government payments to retired and disabled workers, and minimum wage legislation, which sets a floor on the wages employers can pay workers in many occupations. In more recent years, government intervention in the economy has also expanded to meet such goals as protection of the environment, the promotion of civil rights, and the provision of medical care to low-income people and the elderly.

Some economists argue that the extent of government intervention makes it no longer accurate to refer to the U.S., Canadian, Japanese, and Western European economies as pure market economies. Instead, they should be referred to as *mixed economies*. A **mixed economy** is still primarily a market economy because most economic decisions result from the interaction of buyers and sellers in markets. However, the government plays a significant role in the allocation of resources. As we will see in later chapters, economists continue to debate the role government should play in a market economy.

**Mixed economy** An economy in which most economic decisions result from the interaction of buyers and sellers in markets but in which the government plays a significant role in the allocation of resources.

One of the most important developments in the international economy in recent years has been the movement of China from being a centrally planned economy to being a more mixed economy. The Chinese economy suffered decades of economic stagnation following the takeover of the government in 1949 by Mao Zedong and the Communist Party. Although China remains a political dictatorship, production of most goods and services is now determined in the market rather than by the government. The result has been rapid economic growth that in the near future may lead to total production of goods and services in China surpassing total production in the United States.

## Efficiency and Equity

Market economies tend to be more efficient than centrally planned economies. There are two types of efficiency: *productive efficiency* and *allocative efficiency*. **Productive efficiency** occurs when a good or service is produced at the lowest possible cost. **Allocative efficiency** occurs when production is in accordance with consumer preferences. Markets tend to be efficient because they promote competition and facilitate voluntary exchange. With **voluntary exchange**, both the buyer and seller of a product are made better off by the transaction. We know that the buyer and seller are both made better off because, otherwise, the buyer would not have agreed to buy the product or the seller would not have agreed to sell it. Productive efficiency is achieved when competition among firms in markets forces the firms to produce goods and services at the lowest cost. Allocative efficiency is achieved when the combination of competition among firms and voluntary exchange between firms and consumers results in firms producing the mix of goods and services that consumers prefer most. Competition will force firms to continue producing and selling goods and services as long as the additional benefit to consumers is greater than the additional cost of production. In this way, the mix of goods and services produced will match consumer preferences.

**Productive efficiency** A situation in which a good or service is produced at the lowest possible cost.

**Allocative efficiency** A state of the economy in which production is in accordance with consumer preferences; in particular, every good or service is produced up to the point where the last unit provides a marginal benefit to society equal to the marginal cost of producing it.

**Voluntary exchange** A situation that occurs in markets when both the buyer and seller of a product are made better off by the transaction.

Although markets promote efficiency, they don't guarantee it. Inefficiency can arise from various sources. To begin with, it may take some time to achieve an efficient outcome. When Blu-ray players were introduced, for example, firms did not instantly achieve productive efficiency. It took several years for firms to discover the lowest-cost method of producing this good. As we will discuss in Chapter 4, governments sometimes reduce efficiency by interfering with voluntary exchange in markets. For example, many governments limit the imports of some goods from foreign countries. This limitation reduces efficiency by keeping goods from being produced at the lowest cost. The production of some goods damages the environment. In this case, government intervention can increase efficiency because without such intervention, firms may ignore the costs of environmental damage and thereby fail to produce the goods at the lowest possible cost.

An economically efficient outcome is not necessarily a desirable one. Many people prefer economic outcomes that they consider fair or equitable, even if those outcomes

**Equity** The fair distribution of economic benefits.

are less efficient. **Equity** is harder to define than efficiency, but it usually involves a fair distribution of economic benefits. For some people, equity involves a more equal distribution of economic benefits than would result from an emphasis on efficiency alone. For example, some people support raising taxes on people with higher incomes to provide the funds for programs that aid the poor. Although governments may increase equity by reducing the incomes of high-income people and increasing the incomes of the poor, efficiency may be reduced. People have less incentive to open new businesses, to supply labor, and to save if the government takes a significant amount of the income they earn from working or saving. The result is that fewer goods and services are produced, and less saving takes place. As this example illustrates, *there is often a trade-off between efficiency and equity*. Government policymakers often confront this trade-off.

**1.3 LEARNING** OBJECTIVE

Understand the role of models in economic analysis.

# Economic Models

Economists rely on economic theories, or models (the words *theory* and *model* are used interchangeably), to analyze real-world issues, such as those involved with health care. As mentioned earlier, economic models are simplified versions of reality. Economists are certainly not alone in relying on models: An engineer may use a computer model of a bridge to help test whether it will withstand high winds, or a biologist may make a physical model of a nucleic acid to better understand its properties. One purpose of economic models is to make economic ideas sufficiently explicit and concrete so that individuals, firms, or the government can use them to make decisions. For example, we will see in Chapter 3 that the model of demand and supply is a simplified version of how the prices of products are determined by the interactions among buyers and sellers in markets.

Economists use economic models to answer questions. For example, will the United States have a sufficient number of doctors in 2020? For a complicated question like this one, economists often use several models to examine different aspects of the issue. For example, economists at the U.S. Bureau of Labor Statistics (BLS) build models that allow them to forecast future employment in different occupations. These models allow the BLS to forecast how many doctors there are likely to be at a future date. Economists can use different models to forecast the demand for medical services. Together these models can be used to determine whether there will be a sufficient number of doctors in 2020. As mentioned on page 3, economists at the U.S. Health Resources and Services Administration (HRSA) have used models to forecast that there will be a shortage of about 56,000 doctors in 2020.

Sometimes economists use an existing model to analyze an issue, but in other cases, they must develop a new model. To develop a model, economists generally follow these steps:

1. Decide on the assumptions to use in developing the model.
2. Formulate a testable hypothesis.
3. Use economic data to test the hypothesis.
4. Revise the model if it fails to explain the economic data well.
5. Retain the revised model to help answer similar economic questions in the future.

## The Role of Assumptions in Economic Models

Any model is based on making assumptions because models have to be simplified to be useful. We cannot analyze an economic issue unless we reduce its complexity. For example, economic models make behavioral assumptions about the motives of consumers and firms. Economists assume that consumers will buy the goods and services that will maximize their well-being or their satisfaction. Similarly, economists assume that firms act to maximize their profits. These assumptions are simplifications because they do not describe the motives of every consumer and every firm. How can we know if the assumptions in a model are too simplified or too limiting? We discover this when we form hypotheses based on these assumptions and test these hypotheses using real-world information.

## Forming and Testing Hypotheses in Economic Models

An **economic variable** is something measurable that can have different values, such as the incomes of doctors. A hypothesis in an economic model is a statement that may be either correct or incorrect about an economic variable. An example of a hypothesis in an economic model is the statement that the falling incomes earned by primary care physicians—often referred to as "family doctors"—will result in a decline in the number of physicians choosing to enter primary care in the United States in 2020. An economic hypothesis is usually about a causal relationship; in this case, the hypothesis states that lower incomes cause, or lead to, fewer doctors entering primary care.

**Economic variable** Something measurable that can have different values, such as the incomes of doctors.

We have to test a hypothesis before we can accept it. To test a hypothesis, we analyze statistics on the relevant economic variables. In our primary care doctor example, we would gather statistics on the incomes of primary care physicians, the number of primary care physicians, and perhaps other variables as well. Testing a hypothesis can be tricky. For example, showing that the number of primary care physicians declined at a time when the average income of these physicians declined would not be enough to demonstrate that the decline in income *caused* the decline in the number of physicians. Just because two things are correlated—that is, they happen at the same time—does not mean that one caused the other. For example, before entering practice, a doctor spends time in a teaching hospital as a resident in his or her field. Teaching hospitals determine how many residencies they will offer in a particular field. Suppose that teaching hospitals decreased the number of residencies in primary care at the same time that the incomes of primary care physicians were declining. In that case, the declining number of residencies, rather than the declining incomes, might have caused the decline in the number of primary care physicians. Over a period of time, many economic variables change, which complicates the testing of hypotheses. In fact, when economists disagree about a hypothesis, such as the effect of falling incomes on the supply of primary care physicians, it is often because of disagreements over interpreting the statistical analysis used to test the hypothesis.

Note that hypotheses must be statements that could, in principle, turn out to be incorrect. Statements such as "Increasing the number of primary care physicians is good" or "Increasing the number of primary care physicians is bad" are value judgments rather than hypotheses because it is not possible to disprove them.

Economists accept and use an economic model if it leads to hypotheses that are confirmed by statistical analysis. In many cases, the acceptance is tentative, however, pending the gathering of new data or further statistical analysis. In fact, economists often refer to a hypothesis having been "not rejected," rather than having been "accepted," by statistical analysis. But what if statistical analysis clearly rejects a hypothesis? For example, what if a model leads to a hypothesis that declining incomes of primary care physicians will lead to a decline in the number of these physicians, but the data reject this hypothesis? In this case, the model must be reconsidered. It may be that an assumption used in the model was too simplified or too limiting. For example, perhaps the model ignored the fact that primary care physicians were moving from owning their own practices to become salaried employees of hospitals, where they would be freed from the responsibilities involved in running their own businesses. This change in how primary care physicians are employed might explain why the data rejected the hypothesis.

In 2010, the BLS analyzed the accuracy of the projections it had made in 1996 of employment levels in 2006. Some projections were quite accurate, while others were less so. For instance, the BLS had projected that 677,917 physicians and surgeons would be employed in 2006, but actual employment was only 633,292, or about 7 percent less than projected. The error with respect to physician's assistants was much larger, with the projection being that 93,485 physician's assistants would be employed in 2006, but employment was actually only 65,628, or about 30 percent less than expected. Analyzing the errors in these projections helps the BLS to improve the models it uses to make projections of occupational employment.

The process of developing models, testing hypotheses, and revising models occurs not just in economics but also in disciplines such as physics, chemistry, and biology. This process is often referred to as the *scientific method*. Economics is a *social science* because it applies the scientific method to the study of the interactions among individuals.

## Normative and Positive Analysis

**Positive analysis** Analysis concerned with what is.

**Normative analysis** Analysis concerned with what ought to be.

Throughout this book, as we build economic models and use them to answer questions, we need to bear in mind the distinction between *positive analysis* and *normative analysis*. **Positive analysis** is concerned with *what is*, and **normative analysis** is concerned with *what ought to be*. Economics is about positive analysis, which measures the costs and benefits of different courses of action.

We can use the federal government's minimum wage law to compare positive and normative analysis. In 2012, under this law, it was illegal for an employer to hire a worker at a wage less than $7.25 per hour. Without the minimum wage law, some firms and some workers would voluntarily agree to a lower wage. Because of the minimum wage law, some workers have difficulty finding jobs, and some firms end up paying more for labor than they otherwise would have. A positive analysis of the federal minimum wage law uses an economic model to estimate how many workers have lost their jobs because of the law, its effect on the costs and profits of businesses, and the gains to workers receiving the minimum wage. After economists complete this positive analysis, the decision as to whether the minimum wage law is a good idea or a bad idea is a normative one and depends on how people evaluate the trade-off involved. Supporters of the law believe that the losses to employers and to workers who are unemployed as a result of the law are more than offset by the gains to workers who receive higher wages than they would without the law. Opponents of the law believe the losses are greater than the gains. The assessment by any individual depends, in part, on that person's values and political views. The positive analysis an economist provides would play a role in the decision but can't by itself decide the issue one way or the other.

In each chapter, you will see a *Don't Let This Happen to You* box like the one on the next page. These boxes alert you to common pitfalls in thinking about economic ideas. After reading this box, test your understanding by working the related problem that appears at the end of the chapter.

## Economics as a Social Science

Because economics studies the actions of individuals, it is a social science. Economics is therefore similar to other social science disciplines, such as psychology, political science, and sociology. As a social science, economics considers human behavior—particularly decision-making behavior—in every context, not just in the context of business. Economists have studied such issues as how families decide on the number of children to have, why people have difficulty losing weight or attaining other desirable goals, and why people often ignore relevant information when making decisions. Economics also has much to contribute to questions of government policy. As we will see throughout this book, economists have played an important role in formulating government policies in areas such as the environment, health care, and poverty.

# Don't Let This Happen to You

## Don't Confuse Positive Analysis with Normative Analysis

"Economic analysis has shown that the minimum wage law is a bad idea because it causes unemployment." Is this statement accurate? As of 2012, the federal minimum wage law prevents employers from hiring workers at a wage of less than $7.25 per hour. This wage is higher than some employers are willing to pay some workers. If there were no minimum wage law, some workers who currently cannot find any firm willing to hire them at $7.25 per hour would be able to find employment at a lower wage. Therefore, positive economic analysis indicates that the minimum wage law causes unemployment (although economists disagree about how much unemployment the minimum wage causes). *But*, some of those workers who have jobs benefit from the minimum wage because they are paid a higher wage than they otherwise would be. In other words, the minimum wage law creates both losers (the workers who become unemployed and the firms that have to pay higher wages) and winners (the workers who receive higher wages).

Should we value the gains to the winners more than we value the losses to the losers? The answer to this question involves normative analysis. Positive economic analysis can show the consequences of a particular policy, but it cannot tell us whether the policy is "good" or "bad." So, the statement at the beginning of this box is inaccurate.

MyEconLab

**Your Turn:** Test your understanding by doing related problem 3.9 on page 25 at the end of this chapter.

---

## Making the Connection

## Should Medical School Be Free?

The U.S. population continues to increase, which by itself would increase the demand for medical services. In addition, though, the average age of the population is rising, and older people need more medical care than do younger people. So, over time, the number of doctors needs to increase. As mentioned at the beginning of the chapter, the Health Resources and Services Administration (HRSA) estimates that the number of doctors needed to provide patient care will rise from about 805,000 in 2010 to 922,000 in 2020.

Can we be sure that these additional doctors will be available in 2020? The HRSA forecasts that, in fact, there will be a shortage of 56,000 doctors in 2020. The bulk of that shortage is likely to be in primary care physicians, or family doctors. As we will discuss in later chapters, ordinarily we expect that when consumers want more of a product, higher wages and salaries and more job openings will attract workers to that industry. For example, during the U.S. housing boom of the mid-2000s, the number of workers in the building trades—carpenters, plumbers, roofers, and others—increased rapidly. But producing more doctors is a long process. After completing his or her undergraduate education, a doctor spends four years in medical school and then three to five years at a teaching hospital, pursuing a residency in a particular field of medicine. Apparently convinced that hospitals will not train enough doctors unless they get help, Congress contributes $10 billion per year to teaching hospitals, based on the number of residents they train.

*Should these medical students have to pay tuition?*

Recently, Peter Bach of the Sloan-Kettering Cancer Center and Robert Kocher of the Brookings Institution have proposed that medical schools should charge no tuition. They argue that nearly all students graduate from medical school owing money on student loans, with the average student owing more than $150,000. We might expect that these debts, although large, would not deter students from applying to medical school, because in 2011, the average income of physicians was more than $250,000 per year. Bach and Kocher argue, though, that the high cost of medical school has two bad outcomes: Some good students do not apply because they either do not want to be saddled with such large debts or because they are unable to borrow sufficient money, and many students avoid going into primary care—where average incomes are $190,000—in favor of specialties such as plastic surgery or anesthesiology—where average incomes are $325,000. Teaching hospitals pay doctors a salary of about $50,000 per year during their residencies. Bach and Kocher propose that hospitals continue to pay residents who pursue primary care but not pay residents who specialize. The money that hospitals would otherwise pay to these residents would be paid to medical schools instead to finance the free tuition. The plan would give residents an incentive to pursue primary care rather than to specialize. Critics of the Bach and Kocher proposal have questioned whether many students capable of being admitted to medical school actually are deterred by medical school tuition. They also question whether many residents who intend to specialize would choose primary care instead, even if specializing means they have to borrow to meet living expenses rather than paying for them with a hospital salary.

Like many other policy debates, the debate over whether changes should be made in how medical school is paid for has positive and normative elements. By gathering data and using economic models, it is possible to assess some of the quantitative claims made by each side in the debate: What role does tuition play in a student's decision about whether to attend medical school? Have tuition increases had a large effect or a small effect on the number of applications to medical school? How do changes in expected future incomes affect the decisions of medical students about which specialty to choose? These are all positive questions, so it is possible to formulate quantitative answers. Ultimately, though, this debate also has a normative element. For instance, some doctors, economists, and policymakers argue that it is important that people living in low-income or rural areas have improved access to health care, so they are willing to support policies that would redirect medical students away from specialized fields and toward primary care. Other doctors, economists, and policymakers believe that medical students who enter specialized fields make a larger contribution to society than do students who enter primary care. A disagreement of this type is unlikely to be resolved by building models and analyzing data because the issue involved is essentially normative.

In 2010, President Obama and Congress enacted the Patient Protection and Affordable Care Act, which made major changes to the U.S. health care system. The changes are being phased in through 2014. Additional changes are likely as policymakers grapple with the rapidly escalating costs of health care. Whether Congress and the president will enact policies intended to increase the number of primary care physicians remains to be seen.

Based on Suzanne Sataline and Shirley S. Wang, "Medical Schools Can't Keep Up," *Wall Street Journal*, April 12, 2010; Uwe E. Reinhardt, "Producing More Primary-Care Doctors," *New York Times*, June 10, 2011; and Peter B. Bach and Robert Kocher, "Why Medical School Should Be Free," *New York Times*, May 28, 2011.

MyEconLab **Your Turn:** Test your understanding by doing related problem 3.7 on page 25 at the end of this chapter.

---

# Microeconomics and Macroeconomics

Economic models can be used to analyze decision making in many areas. We group some of these areas together as *microeconomics* and others as *macroeconomics*. **Microeconomics** is the study of how households and firms make choices, how they interact in markets, and how the government attempts to influence their choices. Microeconomic issues include explaining how consumers react to changes in product prices and how firms decide what prices to charge for the products they sell. Microeconomics also involves policy issues, such as analyzing the most efficient way to reduce teenage smoking, analyzing the costs and benefits of approving the sale of a new prescription drug, and analyzing the most efficient way to reduce air pollution.

**Macroeconomics** is the study of the economy as a whole, including topics such as inflation, unemployment, and economic growth. Macroeconomic issues include explaining why economies experience periods of recession and increasing unemployment and why, over the long run, some economies have grown much faster than others. Macroeconomics also involves policy issues, such as whether government intervention can reduce the severity of recessions.

The division between microeconomics and macroeconomics is not hard and fast. Many economic situations have *both* a microeconomic and a macroeconomic aspect. For example, the level of total investment by firms in new machinery and equipment helps to determine how rapidly the economy grows—which is a macroeconomic issue. But to understand how much new machinery and equipment firms decide to purchase, we have to analyze the incentives individual firms face—which is a microeconomic issue.

**Microeconomics** The study of how households and firms make choices, how they interact in markets, and how the government attempts to influence their choices.

**Macroeconomics** The study of the economy as a whole, including topics such as inflation, unemployment, and economic growth.

# A Preview of Important Economic Terms

In the following chapters, you will encounter certain important terms again and again. Becoming familiar with these terms is a necessary step in learning economics. Here we provide a brief introduction to some of these terms. We will discuss them all in greater depth in later chapters:

**1.5 LEARNING** OBJECTIVE

Define important economic terms.

- *Entrepreneur.* An *entrepreneur* is someone who operates a business. In a market system, entrepreneurs decide what goods and services to produce and how to produce them. An entrepreneur starting a new business puts his or her own funds at risk. If an entrepreneur is wrong about what consumers want or about the best way to produce goods and services, the entrepreneur's funds can be lost. This is not an unusual occurrence: In the United States, about half of new businesses close within four years. Without entrepreneurs willing to assume the risk of starting and operating businesses, economic progress would be impossible in a market system.

- *Innovation.* There is a distinction between an *invention* and *innovation*. An *invention* is the development of a new good or a new process for making a good. An *innovation* is the practical application of an invention. (*Innovation* may also be used more broadly to refer to any significant improvement in a good or in the means of producing a good.) Much time often passes between the appearance of a new idea and its development for widespread use. For example, the Wright brothers first achieved self-propelled flight at Kitty Hawk, North Carolina, in 1903, but the Wright brothers' plane was very crude, and it wasn't until the introduction of the DC-3 by Douglas Aircraft in 1936 that regularly scheduled intercity airline flights became common in the United States. Similarly, the first digital electronic computer—the ENIAC—was developed in 1945, but the first IBM personal computer was not introduced until 1981, and widespread use of computers did not have a significant effect on the productivity of U.S. business until the 1990s.

- *Technology.* A firm's *technology* is the processes it uses to produce goods and services. In the economic sense, a firm's technology depends on many factors, such as the skill of its managers, the training of its workers, and the speed and efficiency of its machinery and equipment.

- *Firm, company, or business.* A *firm* is an organization that produces a good or service. Most firms produce goods or services to earn profits, but there are also nonprofit firms, such as universities and some hospitals. Economists use the terms *firm*, *company*, and *business* interchangeably.

- *Goods.* *Goods* are tangible merchandise, such as books, computers, or Blu-ray players.

- *Services.* *Services* are activities done for others, such as providing haircuts or investment advice.

- *Revenue.* A firm's *revenue* is the total amount received for selling a good or service. It is calculated by multiplying the price per unit by the number of units sold.

- *Profit.* A firm's *profit* is the difference between its revenue and its costs. Economists distinguish between *accounting profit* and *economic profit*. In calculating accounting profit, we exclude the cost of some economic resources that the firm does not pay for explicitly. In calculating economic profit, we include the opportunity cost of all resources used by the firm. When we refer to *profit* in this book, we mean economic profit. It is important not to confuse *profit* with *revenue*.

- *Household.* A *household* consists of all persons occupying a home. Households are suppliers of factors of production—particularly labor—used by firms to make goods and services. Households also demand goods and services produced by firms and governments.

- *Factors of production or economic resources.* Firms use factors of production to produce goods and services. The main factors of production are labor, capital, natural resources—including land—and entrepreneurial ability. Households earn income by supplying to firms the factors of production.

- *Capital.* The word *capital* can refer to *financial capital* or to *physical capital*. Financial capital includes stocks and bonds issued by firms, bank accounts, and holdings of money. In economics, though, *capital* refers to physical capital, which includes manufactured goods that are used to produce other goods and services. Examples of physical capital are computers, factory buildings, machine tools, warehouses, and trucks. The total amount of physical capital available in a country is referred to as the country's *capital stock*.

- *Human capital.* Human capital refers to the accumulated training and skills that workers possess. For example, college-educated workers generally have more skills and are more productive than workers who have only high school degrees.

Continued from page 3

## Economics in Your Life

### Will There Be Plenty of Jobs Available in the Health Care Industry?

At the beginning of the chapter, we posed the question "What is the basis for the forecasts on the availability of jobs in health care, and how reliable are the forecasts?" As the U.S. population increases and as the average age of the population rises, it seems likely that there will be an increase in the numbers of doctors, nurses, physician's assistants, and other health care workers. The U.S. Bureau of Labor Statistics (BLS) publishes the most widely used occupational forecasts. Economists at the BLS base these forecasts on economic models. The forecasts can be inaccurate, however. For example, in 1996, the BLS forecast that 93,485 physician's assistants would be employed in 2006, when in fact only 65,628 were. The BLS analyzes errors like these in attempting to improve its forecasts. So, it is likely that the BLS's forecasts will become more accurate over time, but it would be a mistake to expect the forecasts to be exact.

# Conclusion

Economics is a group of useful ideas about how individuals make choices. Economists have put these ideas into practice by developing economic models. Consumers, business managers, and government policymakers use these models every day to help make choices. In this book, we explore many key economic models and give examples of how to apply them in the real world.

Reading newspapers and other periodicals is an important part of understanding the current business climate and learning how to apply economic concepts to a variety of real-world events. At the end of each chapter, you will see a two-page feature titled *An Inside Look*. This feature consists of an excerpt from an article that relates to the company or economic issue introduced at the start of the chapter and also to the concepts discussed in the chapter. A summary and an analysis and supporting graphs highlight the key economic points of the article. Read *An Inside Look* on the next page to explore reasons why some health care workers are delaying retirement. Test your understanding by answering the *Thinking Critically* questions.

## AMEDNEWS.COM

## Fewer Physicians Move, a Sign of Career Caution

Physicians changed addresses at a lower rate during the last year than in the previous three years, according to a survey of 253,000 medical offices.

Each year, SK&A, an Irvine, Calif.-based Cegedim firm that specializes in health care marketing information, compiles a database of 664,600 physicians who work in medical offices. Since 2008, the firm has published a report on the "move rate," which indicates how many physicians are no longer at a given office because they moved, retired or died.

Based on survey answers between March 2010 and March 2011, the firm calculated an 11.3% move rate for its most recent report, marking another year of decline. The move rate was reported as 12.4% in 2010, 15% in 2009 and 18.2% in 2008, according to SK&A.

Experts say the move rate, though an unscientific measure, could reflect the ways in which the economy is keeping physicians from changing jobs or retiring, including financial stress, the medical liability environment and licensure laws.

Physicians "don't seem to be motivated by the factors that in the past have caused a desire to move—a big caseload, a better salary [elsewhere], or a better community with better amenities," SK&A spokesman Jack Schember said.

SK&A publishes its data for the benefit of pharmaceutical and medical equipment companies who want to sell to physicians, but the figures are one lens through which to view the economy's effect on physician practices.

Mark Doescher, MD, MSPH, director of the University of Washington Center for Health Workforce Studies, said a more stable work force could be good for areas facing a declining number of physicians and other health professionals, mainly outside major cities.

"I do think the down economy has actually caused stability in the work force, which is good for many rural locations," he said. "But when people do retire, we're going to see some difficult times ahead."

Deane Waldman, MD, a pediatric cardiologist at the University of New Mexico Children's Hospital in Albuquerque and an author who writes about the health care system, cautioned that the SK&A move rate isn't a scientific measurement of physician turnover or retirement.

But he said it makes sense that physicians would be unlikely to change jobs or retire now, given a long list of pressures: uncertainty about health system reform, declining income due to falling reimbursement rates, a constantly shifting medical liability environment, licensing regulations that make it difficult to relocate, and a shortage of physicians that makes it difficult to find someone to take over a practice.

"You add up all the uncertainty, financial losses, change in laws, and it's not surprising people are afraid to make any change at all," Dr. Waldman said.

For those who find a place to go, selling their homes might make it difficult or impossible to leave without taking a financial loss.

A report released May 19 by the Conference Board research group reinforced the difficulty many health care workers face as they reach retirement age. The health industry experienced the largest decline in retirement rates between a 2004-07 survey period and a 2009-10 survey period, according to an analysis of delayed retirement across all industries. Only 1.55% of full-time health care workers age 55 to 64 retired within 12 months of the 2009-10 study period, compared with 3.95% in 2004-07. The health care sector had the lowest rate of retirement, significantly less than the other industries studied.

The SK&A survey found that doctors in some specialties are much more likely to retire or move than their peers. Physicians specializing in aerospace medicine had the highest move rate at 27.9%, and plastic surgeons had the lowest, at 6.3%. Family physicians had an 11.4% move rate.

## Key Points in the Article

This article discusses the continued decline in the number of physicians who have changed jobs or retired over the past three years. Possible reasons for the decline include the 2007–2009 economic recession, the slow recovery from that recession, the lower insurance reimbursement rates, and the still-uncertain outcome of the reforms to the health care system. A May 2011 report by the Conference Board research group shows that the health care industry had the largest decline in retirement rates from 2004 to 2007 and again from 2009 to 2010, when the industry also had the lowest rate of retirement of all industries surveyed. This decline indicates that changes in the health care industry have many health professionals concerned about their finances as they approach retirement age.

## Analyzing the News

(a) Data compiled by the health care marketing firm SK&A indicates that the rate at which physicians have been changing jobs or retiring (the "move rate") has dropped for the fourth straight year, from a high of 18.2 percent in 2008, the first year the data were collected, to a low of 11.3 percent in 2011. According to the chapter opener on page 3, physicians had for years typically operated their practices on their own or in partnerships with other doctors, but over the past several years, a growing number of physicians have given up their private practices to become salaried hospital employees, and by 2008, more medical practices were owned by hospitals than by the doctors themselves. The figure below illustrates the data. Rising costs and financial uncertainty are thought to be one of the primary reasons that a growing number of physicians have given up private practice for hospital employment, and the "move rate" seems to indicate that a growing number of these physicians are staying put at their hospital jobs, forgoing re-entering private practice or retirement.

(b) In the 1991 movie *Doc Hollywood*, Michael J. Fox plays a Beverly Hills surgeon who, after causing a traffic accident in a rural community, is sentenced to perform community service at the local hospital. The premise behind the story reflects an ongoing trend of rural communities finding it increasingly difficult to attract medical professionals to their areas. An upside to the decline in job switching and retirement could be more workforce stability in the medical field, especially in these rural areas. Economic uncertainty has kept many of these professionals from retiring or relocating and has therefore been beneficial to the populations in these locations. The upside is likely to be temporary, though, for unlike the typical happy Hollywood ending of the big-city doctor falling in love with the small town, relocation to these areas continues to fall, so when the eventual retirement of these rural physicians ultimately occurs, doctor shortages will likely continue.

(c) Economic uncertainty, changes in health care laws, and financial concerns have been credited with being partially responsible for not only an increase in physicians giving up their private practices to become salaried hospital employees but also a decrease in the number of physicians either relocating to new jobs or retiring from their practices. This trend seems to indicate that many of those doctors who are continuing to relocate are moving to hospitals rather than new or different private practices. As long as uncertainties remain in the economy and with health care reform, it would not be surprising if physicians remained concerned about their professional and financial futures and worried that this trend will continue.

## Thinking Critically

1. One important economic idea is that people are rational. Explain how this idea relates to the decline in the "move rate" of physicians over the past three years.

2. The article states that in 2009–2010, the health care industry had the lowest retirement rate of all industries surveyed. Suppose you want to develop an economic model to analyze the relationship between the retirement rate of physicians and changes in insurance reimbursement rates. Use information from the article to explain the steps you would take to develop this model.

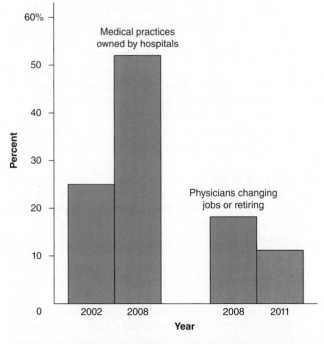

Changes in the ownership of medical practices and changes in the physician move rate.

Data from Robert Kocher, M.D., and Nikhil R. Sahni, "Hospitals' Race to Employ Physicians—The Logic Behind a Money-Losing Proposition," *New England Journal of Medicine*, May 12, 2011; and Uwe E. Reinhardt, "Producing More Primary-Care Doctors," *New York Times*, June 10, 2011. and Emily Berry, "Fewer physicians move, a sign of career caution," June 6, 2011. amednews.com.

# Chapter Summary and Problems

## Key Terms

| | | | |
|---|---|---|---|
| Allocative efficiency, p. 11 | Equity, p. 12 | Microeconomics, p. 17 | Productive efficiency, p. 11 |
| Centrally planned economy, p. 10 | Macroeconomics, p. 17 | Mixed economy, p. 11 | Scarcity, p. 4 |
| Economic model, p. 4 | Marginal analysis, p. 7 | Normative analysis, p. 14 | Trade-off, p. 8 |
| Economic variable, p. 13 | Market, p. 4 | Opportunity cost, p. 8 | Voluntary exchange, p. 11 |
| Economics, p. 4 | Market economy, p. 10 | Positive analysis, p. 14 | |

 **Three Key Economic Ideas,** pages 4–8

**1.1** LEARNING OBJECTIVE: Explain these three key economic ideas: People are rational, people respond to incentives, and optimal decisions are made at the margin.

## Summary

**Economics** is the study of the choices consumers, business managers, and government officials make to attain their goals, given their scarce resources. We must make choices because of **scarcity**, which means that although our wants are unlimited, the resources available to fulfill those wants are limited. Economists assume that people are rational in the sense that consumers and firms use all available information as they take actions intended to achieve their goals. Rational individuals weigh the benefits and costs of each action and choose an action only if the benefits outweigh the costs. Although people act from a variety of motives, ample evidence indicates that they respond to economic incentives. Economists use the word **marginal** to mean extra or additional. The optimal decision is to continue any activity up to the point where the marginal benefit equals the marginal cost.

MyEconLab    Visit **www.myeconlab.com** to complete these exercises online and get instant feedback.

## Review Questions

**1.1** Briefly discuss each of the following economic ideas: People are rational, people respond to incentives, and optimal decisions are made at the margin.

**1.2** What is scarcity? Why is scarcity central to the study of economics?

## Problems and Applications

**1.3** Bank robberies are on the rise in New Jersey, and according to the FBI, this increase has little to do with the economic downturn. The FBI claims that banks have allowed themselves to become easy targets by refusing to install clear acrylic partitions, called "bandit barriers," which separate bank tellers from the public. Of the 193 banks robbed in New Jersey in 2008, only 23 had these barriers, and of the 40 banks robbed in the first 10 weeks of 2009, only 1 had a bandit barrier. According to a special agent with the FBI, "Bandit barriers are a great deterrent. We've talked to guys who rob banks, and as soon as they see a bandit barrier,

they go find another bank." Despite this finding, many banks have been reluctant to install these barriers. Wouldn't banks have a strong incentive to install bandit barriers to deter robberies? Why, then, do so many banks not do so?

Based on Richard Cowen, "FBI: Banks Are to Blame for Rise in Robberies," *NorthJersey.com*, March 10, 2009.

**1.4** The grading system is a powerful resource for teachers. In their book *Effective Grading: A Tool for Learning and Assessment*, Barbara Walvoord and Virginia Anderson state that "teachers must manage the power and complexity of the grading system" and that "teachers must consider grading in their first deliberations about a course."

   **a.** How could the grading system a teacher uses affect the incentives of students to learn the course material?

   **b.** If teachers put too little weight in the grading scale on a certain part of the course, such as readings outside the textbook, how might students respond?

   **c.** Teachers often wish that students came to class prepared, having read the upcoming material. How could a teacher design the grading system to motivate students to come to class prepared?

Based on Barbara E. Walvoord and Virginia Johnson Anderson, *Effective Grading: A Tool for Learning and Assessment*, Jossey-Bass: San Francisco, 1998, pp. xvii–xviii.

**1.5** [Related to the Making the Connection **on page 5**] Many universities and corporations offer a health wellness program that helps their employees improve or maintain their health and get paid (a relatively small amount) for doing so. The programs vary but typically consist of employees completing a health assessment, receiving a program for healthy living, and monitoring their monthly health activities. Why would corporations and universities pay employees to take care of themselves? How does health insurance affect the incentive of employees to improve or maintain their health? How would a wellness program affect the health insurance premiums the employer pays on behalf of the employees?

**1.6** [Related to the Making the Connection **on page 5**] Jay Bhattacharya and M. Kate Bundorf of Stanford University have found evidence that people who are obese and work for firms that have employer-provided health insurance receive lower wages than people working at those firms who are not obese. At firms that do not provide health insurance, obese workers do not receive lower wages than workers who are not obese.

**a.** Why might firms that provide workers with health insurance pay a lower wage to obese workers than to workers who are not obese?

**b.** Is Bhattacharya and Bundorf's finding relevant to the question of whether health insurance provides people with an incentive to become obese? Briefly explain.

Based on Jay Bhattacharya and M. Kate Bundorf, "The Incidence of the Health Care Costs of Obesity," *Journal of Health Economics*, Vol. 28, No. 3, May 2009, pp. 649–58.

**1.7** **[Related to** Solved Problem 1.1 **on page 8]** During 2009, movie studios began to release a substantial number of films in 3-D format. To show films in this format, theater owners have to invest in 3-D equipment that costs $75,000 for each projector. Typically, theater owners can charge about $3 more for a ticket to a 3-D movie than for a movie in the conventional 2-D format. If you owned a movie theater, discuss how you would go about deciding whether to invest in 3-D equipment. How would your analysis change, given information that the proportion of total box-office spending on 3-D movies has been relatively flat since 2009?

Based on Lauren A. E. Schuker, "Can 3-D Save Hollywood?" *Wall Street Journal*, March 20, 2009; and "3D Films Struggle," *The Economist*, July 23–29, 2011.

**1.8** **[Related to** Solved Problem 1.1 **on page 8]** Two students are discussing Solved Problem 1.1:

**Joe:** "I think the key additional information you need to know in deciding whether the doctor should keep the medical practice open 9 hours per day rather than 8 hours is the amount of profit she is currently making while being open 8 hours. Then she can compare the profit earned from being open 9 hours with the profit earned from being open 8 hours. This information is more important than the additional revenue and additional cost of being open 1 more hour."

**Jill:** "Actually, Joe, knowing how much profits change when the medical practice stays open 1 more hour is exactly the same as knowing the additional revenue and the additional cost."

Briefly evaluate their arguments.

**1.9** **[Related to** Solved Problem 1.1 **on page 8]** Late in the semester, a friend tells you, "I was going to drop my psychology course so I could concentrate on my other courses, but I had already put so much time into the course that I decided not to drop it." What do you think of your friend's reasoning? Would it make a difference to your answer if your friend has to pass the psychology course at some point to graduate? Briefly explain.

**1.10** In a paper written by Bentley College economists Patricia M. Flynn and Michael A. Quinn, the authors state:

> We find evidence that Economics is a good choice of major for those aspiring to become a CEO [chief executive officer]. When adjusting for size of the pool of graduates, those with undergraduate degrees in Economics are shown to have had a greater likelihood of becoming an S&P 500 CEO than any other major.

A list of famous economics majors published by Marietta College includes business leaders Warren Buffett, Donald Trump, Ted Turner, Diane von Furstenberg, and Sam Walton, as well as former presidents George H.W. Bush, Gerald Ford, and Ronald Reagan. Why might studying economics be particularly good preparation for being the top manager of a corporation or a leader in government?

Based on Patricia M. Flynn and Michael A. Quinn, "Economics: A Good Choice of Major for Future CEOs," *Social Science Research Network*, November 28, 2006; and *Famous Economics Majors*, Marietta College, Marietta, Ohio, May 22, 2010.

---

**1.2** ## The Economic Problem That Every Society Must Solve, pages 8–12

LEARNING OBJECTIVE: Discuss how an economy answers these questions: What goods and services will be produced? How will the goods and services be produced? Who will receive the goods and services produced?

## Summary

Society faces **trade-offs**: Producing more of one good or service means producing less of another good or service. The **opportunity cost** of any activity—such as producing a good or service—is the highest-valued alternative that must be given up to engage in that activity. The choices of consumers, firms, and governments determine what goods and services will be produced. Firms choose how to produce the goods and services they sell. In the United States, who receives the goods and services produced depends largely on how income is distributed in the marketplace. In a **centrally planned economy**, most economic decisions are made by the government. In a **market economy**, most economic decisions are made by consumers and firms. Most economies, including that of the United States, are **mixed economies** in which

most economic decisions are made by consumers and firms but in which the government also plays a significant role. There are two types of efficiency: productive efficiency and allocative efficiency. **Productive efficiency** occurs when a good or service is produced at the lowest possible cost. **Allocative efficiency** occurs when production is in accordance with consumer preferences. **Voluntary exchange** is a situation that occurs in markets when both the buyer and seller of a product are made better off by the transaction. **Equity** is more difficult to define than efficiency, but it usually involves a fair distribution of economic benefits. Government policymakers often face a trade-off between equity and efficiency.

 MyEconLab    Visit **www.myeconlab.com** to complete these exercises online and get instant feedback.

## Review Questions

**2.1** Why does scarcity imply that every society and every individual face trade-offs?

**2.2** What are the three economic questions that every society must answer? Briefly discuss the differences in how centrally planned, market, and mixed economies answer these questions.

**2.3** What is the difference between productive efficiency and allocative efficiency?

**2.4** What is the difference between efficiency and equity? Why do government policymakers often face a trade-off between efficiency and equity?

## Problems and Applications

**2.5** Does Bill Gates, one of the richest people in the world, face scarcity? Does everyone? Are there any exceptions?

**2.6** In a market economy, why does a firm have a strong incentive to be productively efficient and allocatively efficient? What does the firm earn if it is productively and allocatively efficient, and what happens if it is not?

**2.7** Would you expect new and better machinery and equipment to be adopted more rapidly in a market economy or in a centrally planned economy? Briefly explain.

**2.8** Centrally planned economies have been less efficient than market economies.
  **a.** Has this difference in efficiency happened by chance, or is there some underlying reason?
  **b.** If market economies are more economically efficient than centrally planned economies, would there ever be a reason to prefer having a centrally planned economy rather than a market economy?

**2.9** Relative to a market economy, would you expect a centrally planned economy to be better at productive efficiency or allocative efficiency? Briefly explain.

**2.10** Leonard Fleck, a philosophy professor at Michigan State University, has written:

> When it comes to health care in America, we have limited resources for unlimited health care needs. We want everything contemporary medical technology can offer that will improve the length or quality of our lives as we age. But as presently healthy taxpayers, we want costs controlled.

Why is it necessary for all economic systems to limit services such as health care? How does a market system prevent people from getting as many goods and services as they want?

From Leonard Fleck, *Just Caring: Health Care Rationing and Democratic Deliberation*, (New York: Oxford University Press, 2009).

**2.11** Suppose that your local police department recovers 100 tickets to a big NASCAR race in a drug raid. Police decide to distribute the tickets to residents and announces that tickets will be given away at 10 A.M. Monday at City Hall.
  **a.** What groups of people will be most likely to try to get the tickets? Think of specific examples and then generalize.
  **b.** What is the opportunity cost of distributing the tickets this way?
  **c.** Productive efficiency occurs when a good or service (such as the distribution of tickets) is produced at the lowest possible cost. Is this an efficient way to distribute the tickets? If possible, think of a more efficient method of distributing the tickets.
  **d.** Is this an equitable way to distribute the tickets? Explain.

---

**1.3** ## Economic Models, pages 12–16

LEARNING OBJECTIVE: Understand the role of models in economic analysis.

## Summary

An **economic variable** is something measurable that can have different values, such as the wages of software programmers. Economists rely on economic models when they apply economic ideas to real-world problems. **Economic models** are simplified versions of reality used to analyze real-world economic situations. Economists accept and use an economic model if it leads to hypotheses that are confirmed by statistical analysis. In many cases, the acceptance is tentative, however, pending the gathering of new data or further statistical analysis. Economics is a *social science* because it applies the scientific method to the study of the interactions among individuals. Economics is concerned with positive analysis rather than normative analysis. **Positive analysis** is concerned with what is. **Normative analysis** is concerned with what ought to be. Because economics is based on studying the actions of individuals, it is a social science. As a social science, economics considers human behavior in every context of decision making, not just in business.

 MyEconLab Visit **www.myeconlab.com** to complete these exercises online and get instant feedback.

## Review Questions

**3.1** Why do economists use models? How are economic data used to test models?

**3.2** Describe the five steps by which economists arrive at a useful economic model.

**3.3** What is the difference between normative analysis and positive analysis? Is economics concerned mainly with normative analysis or with positive analysis? Briefly explain.

## Problems and Applications

**3.4** Do you agree with the following assertion: "The problem with economics is that it assumes that consumers and firms always make the correct decision. But we know everyone's human, and we all make mistakes."

**3.5** Suppose an economist develops an economic model and finds that "it works great in theory, but it fails in practice." What should the economist do next?

**3.6** Dr. Strangelove's theory is that the price of mushrooms is determined by the activity of subatomic particles that exist in another universe parallel to ours. When the subatomic particles are emitted in profusion, the price of mushrooms is high. When subatomic particle emissions are low, the price of mushrooms is also low. How would you go about testing Dr. Strangelove's theory? Discuss whether this theory is useful.

3.7 **[Related to the** Making the Connection **on page 15]** The *Making the Connection* explains that there are both positive and normative elements to the debate over whether medical schools should charge tuition and whether hospitals should continue to pay residents who pursue primary care but not residents who specialize. What economic statistics would be most useful in evaluating the positive elements in this debate? Assuming that these statistics are available or could be gathered, are they likely to resolve the normative issues in this debate?

3.8 **[Related to the** Chapter Opener **on page 3]** In recent years, many doctors have decided to give up running their practices as small businesses and have become salaried employees of hospitals.
   a. What important differences exist between doctors' practices and other small businesses, such as restaurants and hardware stores?
   b. How have the economic incentives for operating a private practice as opposed to becoming a salaried employee of a hospital changed over the years for doctors?

3.9 **[Related to the** Don't Let This Happen to You **on page 15]** Explain which of the following statements represent positive analysis and which represent normative analysis.

   a. A 50-cent-per-pack tax on cigarettes will lead to a 12 percent reduction in smoking by teenagers.
   b. The federal government should spend more on AIDS research.
   c. Rising paper prices will increase textbook prices.
   d. The price of coffee at Starbucks is too high.

3.10 In the United States, to receive a medical license, a doctor must complete a residency program at a hospital. Hospitals are not free to expand their residency programs in a particular medical specialty without approval from a Residency Review Committee (RRC), which is made up of physicians in that specialty. A hospital that does not abide by the rulings of the RRC runs the risk of losing its accreditation from the Accreditation Council for Graduate Medical Education (ACGME). The ACGME and the RRCs argue that this system makes it possible to ensure that residency programs do not expand to the point where they are not providing residents with high-quality training.
   a. How does this system help protect consumers?
   b. How might this system protect the financial interests of doctors more than the well-being of consumers?
   c. Briefly discuss whether you consider this system to be a good one.

   Based on Brian Palmer, "We Need More Doctors, Stat!" *Slate*, June 27, 2011; and Sean Nicholson, "*Barriers to Entering Medical Specialties*," Wharton School, September 2003.

---

**1.4**  ## Microeconomics and Macroeconomics, pages 16–17
LEARNING OBJECTIVE: Distinguish between microeconomics and macroeconomics.

## Summary

**Microeconomics** is the study of how households and firms make choices, how they interact in markets, and how the government attempts to influence their choices. **Macroeconomics** is the study of the economy as a whole, including topics such as inflation, unemployment, and economic growth.

MyEconLab    Visit **www.myeconlab.com** to complete these exercises online and get instant feedback.

## Review Question

4.1 Briefly discuss the difference between microeconomics and macroeconomics.

## Problems and Applications

4.2 Briefly explain whether each of the following is primarily a microeconomic issue or a macroeconomic issue.

   a. The effect of higher cigarette taxes on the quantity of cigarettes sold
   b. The effect of higher income taxes on the total amount of consumer spending
   c. The reasons for the economies of East Asian countries growing faster than the economies of sub-Saharan African countries
   d. The reasons for low rates of profit in the airline industry

4.3 Briefly explain whether you agree with the following assertion: "Microeconomics is concerned with things that happen in one particular place, such as the unemployment rate in one city. In contrast, macroeconomics is concerned with things that affect the country as a whole, such as how the rate of teenage smoking in the United States would be affected by an increase in the tax on cigarettes."

---

**1.5**  ## A Preview of Important Economic Terms, pages 17–19
LEARNING OBJECTIVE: Define important economic terms.

## Summary

Becoming familiar with important terms is a necessary step in learning economics. These important economic terms include

*capital, entrepreneur, factors of production, firm, goods, household, human capital, innovation, profit, revenue, services,* and *technology.*

# Appendix

## LEARNING OBJECTIVE

Review the use of graphs and formulas.

## Using Graphs and Formulas

Graphs are used to illustrate key economic ideas. Graphs appear not just in economics textbooks but also on Web sites and in newspaper and magazine articles that discuss events in business and economics. Why the heavy use of graphs? Because they serve two useful purposes: (1) They simplify economic ideas, and (2) they make the ideas more concrete so they can be applied to real-world problems. Economic and business issues can be complicated, but a graph can help cut through complications and highlight the key relationships needed to understand the issue. In that sense, a graph can be like a street map.

For example, suppose you take a bus to New York City to see the Empire State Building. After arriving at the Port Authority Bus Terminal, you will probably use a map similar to the one shown below to find your way to the Empire State Building.

Maps are very familiar to just about everyone, so we don't usually think of them as being simplified versions of reality, but they are. This map does not show much more than the streets in this part of New York City and some of the most important buildings. The names, addresses, and telephone numbers of the people who live and work in the area aren't given. Almost none of the stores and buildings those people work and live in are shown either. The map doesn't indicate which streets allow curbside parking and which don't. In fact, the map shows almost nothing about the messy reality of life in this section of New York City, except how the streets are laid out, which is the essential information you need to get from the Port Authority to the Empire State Building.

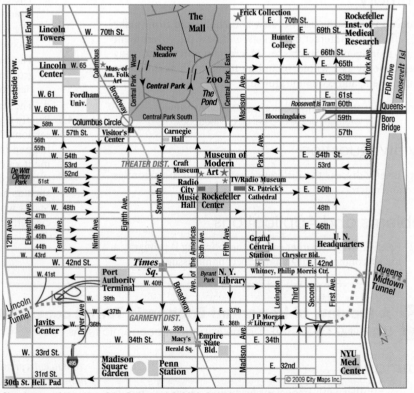

Street map of New York City. Copyright © 2011 City Maps Inc. Reprinted by permission.

Think about someone who says, "I know how to get around in the city, but I just can't figure out how to read a map." It certainly is possible to find your destination in a city without a map, but it's a lot easier with one. The same is true of using graphs in economics. It is possible to arrive at a solution to a real-world problem in economics and business without using graphs, but it is usually a lot easier if you do use them.

Often, the difficulty students have with graphs and formulas is a lack of familiarity. With practice, all the graphs and formulas in this text will become familiar to you. Once you are familiar with them, you will be able to use them to analyze problems that would otherwise seem very difficult. What follows is a brief review of how graphs and formulas are used.

## Graphs of One Variable

Figure 1A.1 displays values for *market shares* in the U.S. automobile market, using two common types of graphs. Market shares show the percentage of industry sales accounted for by different firms. In this case, the information is for groups of firms: the "Big Three"—Ford, General Motors, and Chrysler—as well as Japanese firms, European firms, and Korean firms. Panel (a) displays the information on market shares as a *bar graph*, where the market share of each group of firms is represented by the height of its bar. Panel (b) displays the same information as a *pie chart*, with the market share of each group of firms represented by the size of its slice of the pie.

Information on economic variables is also often displayed in *time-series graphs*. Time-series graphs are displayed on a coordinate grid. In a coordinate grid, we can measure the value of one variable along the vertical axis (or *y*-axis) and the value of another variable along the horizontal axis (or *x*-axis). The point where the vertical axis intersects the horizontal axis is called the *origin*. At the origin, the value of both variables is zero. The points on a coordinate grid represent values of the two variables. In Figure 1A.2, we measure the number of automobiles and trucks sold worldwide by Ford Motor Company on the vertical axis, and we measure time on the horizontal axis. In time-series

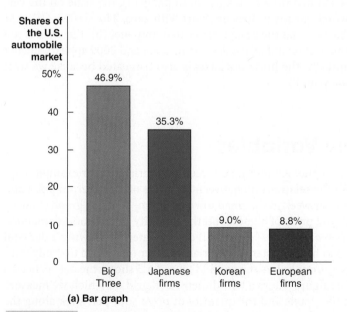

**(a) Bar graph**

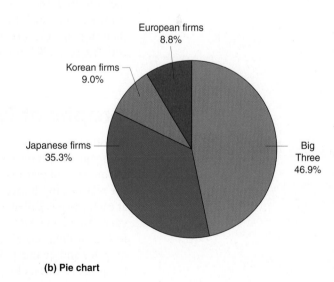

**(b) Pie chart**

**Figure 1A.1**  **Bar Graphs and Pie Charts**

Values for an economic variable are often displayed as a bar graph or as a pie chart. In this case, panel (a) shows market share data for the U.S. automobile industry as a bar graph, where the market share of each group of firms is represented by the height of its bar. Panel (b) displays the same information as a pie chart, with the market share of each group of firms represented by the size of its slice of the pie. Data from "Auto Sales," *Wall Street Journal*, July 1, 2011.

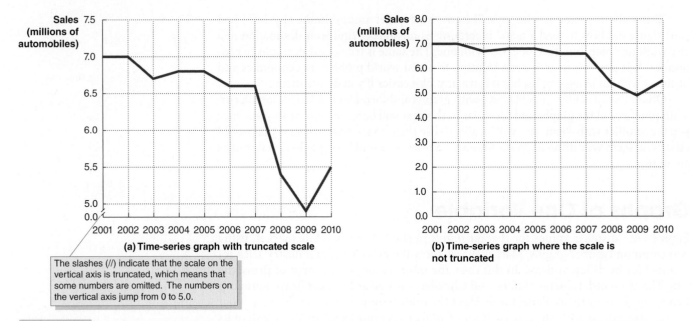

The slashes (//) indicate that the scale on the vertical axis is truncated, which means that some numbers are omitted. The numbers on the vertical axis jump from 0 to 5.0.

**Figure 1A.2** **Time-Series Graphs**

Both panels present time-series graphs of Ford Motor Company's worldwide sales during each year from 2001 to 2010. Panel (a) has a truncated scale on the vertical axis, and panel (b) does not. As a result, the fluctuations in Ford's sales appear smaller in panel (b) than in panel (a).

Data from Ford Motor Company, *Annual Report*, various years.

graphs, the height of the line at each date shows the value of the variable measured on the vertical axis. Both panels of Figure 1A.2 show Ford's worldwide sales during each year from 2001 to 2010. The difference between panel (a) and panel (b) illustrates the importance of the scale used in a time-series graph. In panel (a), the scale on the vertical axis is truncated, which means it does not start with zero. The slashes (//) near the bottom of the axis indicate that the scale is truncated. In panel (b), the scale is not truncated. In panel (b), the decline in Ford's sales during 2008 and 2009 appears smaller than in panel (a). (Technically, the horizontal axis is also truncated because we start with the year 2001, not the year 0.)

## Graphs of Two Variables

We often use graphs to show the relationship between two variables. For example, suppose you are interested in the relationship between the price of a pepperoni pizza and the quantity of pizzas sold per week in the small town of Bryan, Texas. A graph showing the relationship between the price of a good and the quantity of the good demanded at each price is called a *demand curve*. (As we will discuss later, in drawing a demand curve for a good, we have to hold constant any variables other than price that might affect the willingness of consumers to buy the good.) Figure 1A.3 shows the data collected on price and quantity. The figure shows a two-dimensional grid on which we measure the price of pizza along the *y*-axis and the quantity of pizza sold per week along the *x*-axis. Each point on the grid represents one of the price and quantity combinations listed in the table. We can connect the points to form the demand curve for pizza in Bryan, Texas. Notice that the scales on both axes in the graph are truncated. In this case, truncating the axes allows the graph to illustrate more clearly the relationship between price and quantity by excluding low prices and quantities.

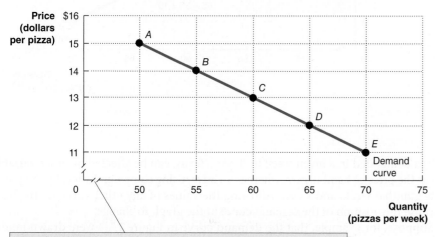

| Price (dollars per pizza) | Quantity (pizzas per week) | Points |
|---|---|---|
| $15 | 50 | A |
| 14 | 55 | B |
| 13 | 60 | C |
| 12 | 65 | D |
| 11 | 70 | E |

**Figure 1A.3**

**Plotting Price and Quantity Points in a Graph**

The figure shows a two-dimensional grid on which we measure the price of pizza along the vertical axis (or *y*-axis) and the quantity of pizza sold per week along the horizontal axis (or *x*-axis). Each point on the grid represents one of the price and quantity combinations listed in the table. By connecting the points with a line, we can better illustrate the relationship between the two variables.

As you learned in Figure 1A-2, the slashes (//) indicate that the scales on the axes are truncated, which means that numbers are omitted: On the horizontal axis numbers jump from 0 to 50, and on the vertical axis numbers jump from 0 to 11.

## Slopes of Lines

Once you have plotted the data in Figure 1A.3, you may be interested in how much the quantity of pizza sold increases as the price decreases. The *slope* of a line tells us how much the variable we are measuring on the *y*-axis changes as the variable we are measuring on the *x*-axis changes. We can use the Greek letter delta ($\Delta$) to stand for the change in a variable. The slope is sometimes referred to as the rise over the run. So, we have several ways of expressing slope:

$$\text{Slope} = \frac{\text{Change in value on the vertical axis}}{\text{Change in value on the horizontal axis}} = \frac{\Delta y}{\Delta x} = \frac{\text{Rise}}{\text{Run}}.$$

Figure 1A.4 reproduces the graph from Figure 1A.3. Because the slope of a straight line is the same at any point, we can use any two points in the figure to calculate the slope of the line. For example, when the price of pizza decreases from $14 to $12, the quantity of pizza sold increases from 55 per week to 65 per week. Therefore, the slope is:

$$\text{Slope} = \frac{\Delta \text{Price of pizza}}{\Delta \text{Quantity of pizza}} = \frac{(\$12 - \$14)}{(65 - 55)} = \frac{-2}{10} = -0.2.$$

The slope of this line gives us some insight into how responsive consumers in Bryan, Texas, are to changes in the price of pizza. The larger the value of the slope (ignoring the negative sign), the steeper the line will be, which indicates that not many additional pizzas are sold when the price falls. The smaller the value of the slope, the flatter the line will be, which indicates a greater increase in pizzas sold when the price falls.

## Taking into Account More Than Two Variables on a Graph

The demand curve graph in Figure 1A.4 shows the relationship between the price of pizza and the quantity of pizza demanded, but we know that the quantity of any good demanded depends on more than just the price of the good. For example, the quantity

## Figure 1A.4

### Calculating the Slope of a Line

We can calculate the slope of a line as the change in the value of the variable on the *y*-axis divided by the change in the value of the variable on the *x*-axis. Because the slope of a straight line is constant, we can use any two points in the figure to calculate the slope of the line. For example, when the price of pizza decreases from $14 to $12, the quantity of pizza demanded increases from 55 per week to 65 per week. So, the slope of this line equals −2 divided by 10, or −0.2.

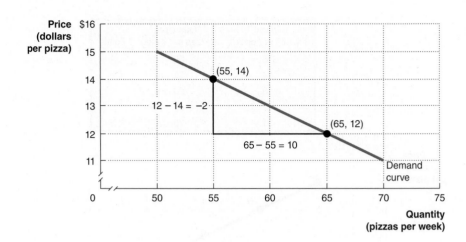

of pizza demanded in a given week in Bryan, Texas, can be affected by other variables, such as the price of hamburgers, whether an advertising campaign by local pizza parlors has begun that week, and so on. Allowing the values of any other variables to change will cause the position of the demand curve in the graph to change.

Suppose, for example, that the demand curve in Figure 1A.4 were drawn holding the price of hamburgers constant, at $1.50. If the price of hamburgers rises to $2.00, some consumers will switch from buying hamburgers to buying pizza, and more pizzas will be demanded at every price. The result on the graph will be to shift the line representing the demand curve to the right. Similarly, if the price of hamburgers falls from $1.50 to $1.00, some consumers will switch from buying pizza to buying hamburgers, and fewer pizzas will be demanded at every price. The result on the graph will be to shift the line representing the demand curve to the left.

The table in Figure 1A.5 shows the effect of a change in the price of hamburgers on the quantity of pizza demanded. For example, suppose that at first we are on the line labeled *Demand curve*₁. If the price of pizza is $14 (point *A*), an increase in the price of hamburgers from $1.50 to $2.00 increases the quantity of pizzas demanded from 55 to 60 per week (point *B*) and shifts us to *Demand curve*₂. Or, if we start on *Demand curve*₁ and the price of pizza is $12 (point *C*), a decrease in the price of hamburgers from $1.50 to $1.00 decreases the quantity of pizzas demanded from 65 to 60 per week (point *D*) and shifts us to *Demand curve*₃. By shifting the demand curve, we have taken into account the effect of changes in the value of a third variable—the price of hamburgers. We will use this technique of shifting curves to allow for the effects of additional variables many times in this book.

## Positive and Negative Relationships

We can use graphs to show the relationships between any two variables. Sometimes the relationship between the variables is *negative*, meaning that as one variable increases in value, the other variable decreases in value. This was the case with the price of pizza and the quantity of pizzas demanded. The relationship between two variables can also be *positive*, meaning that the values of both variables increase or decrease together. For example, when the level of total income—or *disposable personal income*—received by households in the United States increases, the level of total *consumption spending*, which is spending by households on goods and services, also increases. The table in Figure 1A.6 shows the values (in billions of dollars) for income and consumption spending for the years 2007–2010. The graph plots the data from the table, with disposable personal income measured along the horizontal axis and consumption spending measured along the vertical axis. Notice that the four points do not all fall exactly on the line. This is often the case with real-world data. To examine the relationship between two variables, economists often use the straight line that best fits the data.

| Quantity (pizzas per week) | | | |
|---|---|---|---|
| Price (dollars per pizza) | When the Price of Hamburgers = $1.00 | When the Price of Hamburgers = $1.50 | When the Price of Hamburgers = $2.00 |
| $15 | 45 | 50 | 55 |
| 14 | 50 | 55 | 60 |
| 13 | 55 | 60 | 65 |
| 12 | 60 | 65 | 70 |
| 11 | 65 | 70 | 75 |

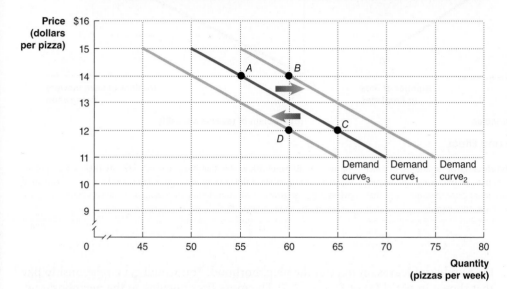

### Figure 1A.5

**Showing Three Variables on a Graph**

The demand curve for pizza shows the relationship between the price of pizzas and the quantity of pizzas demanded, *holding constant other factors that might affect the willingness of consumers to buy pizza.* If the price of pizza is $14 (point *A*), an increase in the price of hamburgers from $1.50 to $2.00 increases the quantity of pizzas demanded from 55 to 60 per week (point *B*) and shifts us to *Demand curve$_2$*. Or, if we start on *Demand curve$_1$* and the price of pizza is $12 (point *C*), a decrease in the price of hamburgers from $1.50 to $1.00 decreases the quantity of pizza demanded from 65 to 60 per week (point *D*) and shifts us to *Demand curve$_3$*.

## Determining Cause and Effect

When we graph the relationship between two variables, we often want to draw conclusions about whether changes in one variable are causing changes in the other variable. Doing so, however, can lead to incorrect conclusions. For example, suppose you graph the number of homes in a neighborhood that have a fire burning in the fireplace and

| Year | Disposable Personal Income (billions of dollars) | Consumption Spending (billions of dollars) |
|---|---|---|
| 2007 | $10,424 | $9,806 |
| 2008 | 10,953 | 10,105 |
| 2009 | 11,035 | 10,001 |
| 2010 | 11,375 | 10,349 |

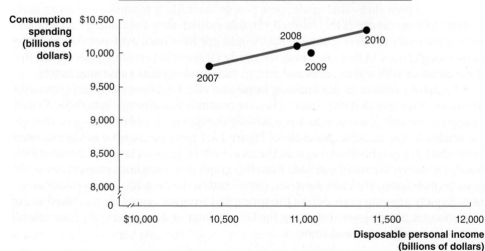

### Figure 1A.6

**Graphing the Positive Relationship between Income and Consumption**

In a positive relationship between two economic variables, as one variable increases, the other variable also increases. This figure shows the positive relationship between disposable personal income and consumption spending. As disposable personal income in the United States has increased, so has consumption spending.

Data from U.S. Department of Commerce, Bureau of Economic Analysis.

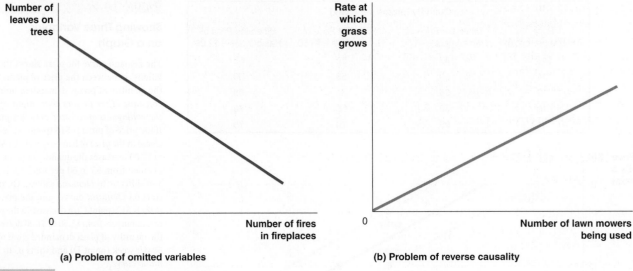

**(a) Problem of omitted variables**

**(b) Problem of reverse causality**

**Figure 1A.7** **Determining Cause and Effect**

Using graphs to draw conclusions about cause and effect can be hazardous. In panel (a), we see that there are fewer leaves on the trees in a neighborhood when many homes have fires burning in their fireplaces. We cannot draw the conclusion that the fires cause the leaves to fall because we have an *omitted variable*—the season of the year. In panel (b), we see that more lawn mowers are used in a neighborhood during times when the grass grows rapidly and fewer lawn mowers are used when the grass grows slowly. Concluding that using lawn mowers *causes* the grass to grow faster would be making the error of *reverse causality*.

the number of leaves on trees in the neighborhood. You would get a relationship like that shown in panel (a) of Figure 1A.7: The more fires burning in the neighborhood, the fewer leaves the trees have. Can we draw the conclusion from this graph that using a fireplace causes trees to lose their leaves? We know, of course, that such a conclusion would be incorrect. In spring and summer, there are relatively few fireplaces being used, and the trees are full of leaves. In the fall, as trees begin to lose their leaves, fireplaces are used more frequently. And in winter, many fireplaces are being used and many trees have lost all their leaves. The reason that the graph in Figure 1A.7 is misleading about cause and effect is that there is obviously an *omitted variable* in the analysis—the season of the year. An omitted variable is one that affects other variables, and its omission can lead to false conclusions about cause and effect.

Although in our example the omitted variable is obvious, there are many debates about cause and effect where the existence of an omitted variable has not been clear. For instance, it has been known for many years that people who smoke cigarettes suffer from higher rates of lung cancer than do nonsmokers. For some time, tobacco companies and some scientists argued that there was an omitted variable—perhaps a failure to exercise or a poor diet—that made some people more likely to smoke and more likely to develop lung cancer. If this omitted variable existed, then the finding that smokers were more likely to develop lung cancer would not have been evidence that smoking *caused* lung cancer. In this case, however, nearly all scientists eventually concluded that the omitted variable did not exist and that, in fact, smoking does cause lung cancer.

A related problem in determining cause and effect is known as *reverse causality*. The error of reverse causality occurs when we conclude that changes in variable *X* cause changes in variable *Y* when, in fact, it is actually changes in variable *Y* that cause changes in variable *X*. For example, panel (b) of Figure 1A.7 plots the number of lawn mowers being used in a neighborhood against the rate at which grass on lawns in the neighborhood is growing. We could conclude from this graph that using lawn mowers *causes* the grass to grow faster. We know, however, that in reality, the causality is in the other direction: Rapidly growing grass during the spring and summer causes the increased use of lawn mowers. Slowly growing grass in the fall or winter or during periods of low rainfall causes decreased use of lawn mowers.

Once again, in our example, the potential error of reverse causality is obvious. In many economic debates, however, cause and effect can be more difficult to determine. For example, changes in the money supply, or the total amount of money in the economy, tend to occur at the same time as changes in the total amount of income people in the economy earn. A famous debate in economics was about whether the changes in the money supply caused the changes in total income or whether the changes in total income caused the changes in the money supply. Each side in the debate accused the other side of committing the error of reverse causality.

## Are Graphs of Economic Relationships Always Straight Lines?

The graphs of relationships between two economic variables that we have drawn so far have been straight lines. The relationship between two variables is *linear* when it can be represented by a straight line. Few economic relationships are actually linear. For example, if we carefully plot data on the price of a product and the quantity demanded at each price, holding constant other variables that affect the quantity demanded, we will usually find a curved—or *nonlinear*—relationship rather than a linear relationship. In practice, however, it is often useful to approximate a nonlinear relationship with a linear relationship. If the relationship is reasonably close to being linear, the analysis is not

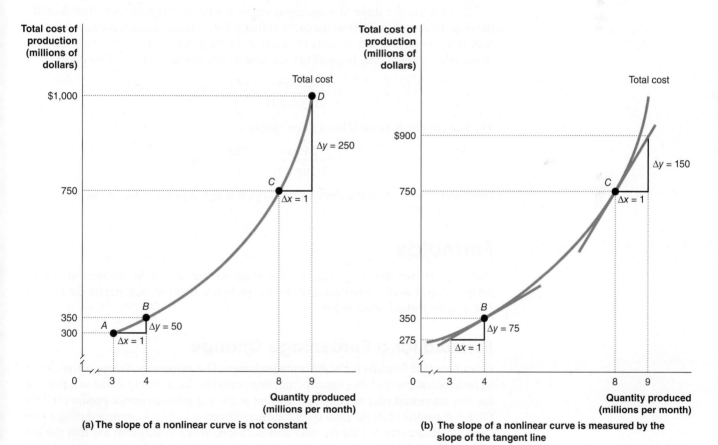

(a) The slope of a nonlinear curve is not constant

(b) The slope of a nonlinear curve is measured by the slope of the tangent line

**Figure 1A.8** The Slope of a Nonlinear Curve

The relationship between the quantity of iPhones produced and the total cost of production is curved rather than linear. In panel (a), in moving from point *A* to point *B*, the quantity produced increases by 1 million iPhones, while the total cost of production increases by $50 million. Farther up the curve, as we move from point *C* to point *D*, the change in quantity is the same—1 million iPhones—but the change in the total cost of production is now much larger: $250 million.

Because the change in the *y* variable has increased, while the change in the *x* variable has remained the same, we know that the slope has increased. In panel (b), we measure the slope of the curve at a particular point by the slope of the tangent line. The slope of the tangent line at point *B* is 75, and the slope of the tangent line at point *C* is 150.

significantly affected. In addition, it is easier to calculate the slope of a straight line, and it also is easier to calculate the area under a straight line. So, in this textbook, we often assume that the relationship between two economic variables is linear, even when we know that this assumption is not precisely correct.

## Slopes of Nonlinear Curves

In some situations, we need to take into account the nonlinear nature of an economic relationship. For example, panel (a) of Figure 1A.8 shows the hypothetical relationship between Apple's total cost of producing iPhones and the quantity of iPhones produced. The relationship is curved rather than linear. In this case, the cost of production is increasing at an increasing rate, which often happens in manufacturing. Put a different way, as we move up the curve, its slope becomes larger. (Remember that with a straight line, the slope is always constant.) To see this effect, first remember that we calculate the slope of a curve by dividing the change in the variable on the $y$-axis by the change in the variable on the $x$-axis. As we move from point $A$ to point $B$, the quantity produced increases by 1 million iPhones, while the total cost of production increases by \$50 million. Farther up the curve, as we move from point $C$ to point $D$, the change in quantity is the same— 1 million iPhones—but the change in the total cost of production is now much larger: \$250 million. Because the change in the $y$ variable has increased, while the change in the $x$ variable has remained the same, we know that the slope has increased.

To measure the slope of a nonlinear curve at a particular point, we must measure the slope of the *tangent line* to the curve at that point. A tangent line will touch the curve only at that point. We can measure the slope of the tangent line just as we would the slope of any other straight line. In panel (b), the tangent line at point $B$ has a slope equal to:

$$\frac{\Delta \text{Cost}}{\Delta \text{Quantity}} = \frac{75}{1} = 75.$$

The tangent line at point $C$ has a slope equal to:

$$\frac{\Delta \text{Cost}}{\Delta \text{Quantity}} = \frac{150}{1} = 150.$$

Once again, we see that the slope of the curve is larger at point $C$ than at point $B$.

# Formulas

We have just seen that graphs are an important economic tool. In this section, we will review several useful formulas and show how to use them to summarize data and to calculate important relationships.

## Formula for a Percentage Change

One important formula is the percentage change. The *percentage change* is the change in some economic variable, usually from one period to the next, expressed as a percentage. An important macroeconomic measure is the real gross domestic product (GDP). GDP is the value of all the final goods and services produced in a country during a year. "Real" GDP is corrected for the effects of inflation. When economists say that the U.S. economy grew 3.0 percent during 2010, they mean that real GDP was 3.0 percent higher in 2010 than it was in 2009. The formula for making this calculation is:

$$\frac{\text{GDP}_{2010} - \text{GDP}_{2009}}{\text{GDP}_{2009}} \times 100$$

or, more generally, for any two periods:

$$\text{Percentage change} = \frac{\text{Value in the second period} - \text{Value in the first period}}{\text{Value in the first period}} \times 100.$$

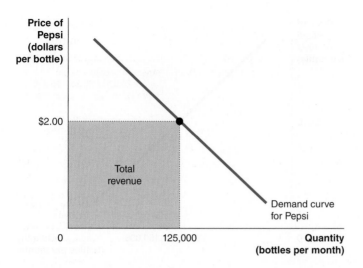

**Figure 1A.9**

**Showing a Firm's Total Revenue on a Graph**

The area of a rectangle is equal to its base multiplied by its height. Total revenue is equal to quantity multiplied by price. Here, total revenue is equal to the quantity of 125,000 bottles times the price of $2.00 per bottle, or $250,000. The area of the green-shaded rectangle shows the firm's total revenue.

In this case, real GDP was $12,703 billion in 2009 and $13,088 billion in 2010. So, the growth rate of the U.S. economy during 2010 was:

$$\left(\frac{\$13,088 - \$12,703}{\$12,703}\right) \times 100 = 2.8\%.$$

Notice that it doesn't matter that in using the formula, we ignored the fact that GDP is measured in billions of dollars. In fact, when calculating percentage changes, *the units don't matter*. The percentage increase from $12,703 billion to $13,088 billion is exactly the same as the percentage increase from $12,073 to $13,088.

## Formulas for the Areas of a Rectangle and a Triangle

Areas that form rectangles and triangles on graphs can have important economic meaning. For example, Figure 1A.9 shows the demand curve for Pepsi. Suppose that the price is currently $2.00 and that 125,000 bottles of Pepsi are sold at that price. A firm's *total revenue* is equal to the amount it receives from selling its product, or the quantity sold multiplied by the price. In this case, total revenue will equal 125,000 bottles times $2.00 per bottle, or $250,000.

The formula for the area of a rectangle is:

$$\text{Area of a rectangle} = \text{Base} \times \text{Height}.$$

In Figure 1A.9, the green-shaded rectangle also represents the firm's total revenue because its area is given by the base of 125,000 bottles multiplied by the price of $2.00 per bottle.

We will see in later chapters that areas that are triangles can also have economic significance. The formula for the area of a triangle is:

$$\text{Area of a triangle} = \frac{1}{2} \times \text{Base} \times \text{Height}.$$

The blue-shaded area in Figure 1A.10 is a triangle. The base equals 150,000 − 125,000, or 25,000. Its height equals $2.00 − $1.50, or $0.50. Therefore, its area equals 1/2 × 25,000 × $0.50, or $6,250. Notice that the blue area is a triangle only if the demand curve is a straight line, or linear. Not all demand curves are linear. However, the formula for the area of a triangle will usually still give a good approximation, even if the demand curve is not linear.

## Summary of Using Formulas

You will encounter several other formulas in this book. Whenever you must use a formula, you should follow these steps:

**1.** Make sure you understand the economic concept the formula represents.

**Figure 1A.10**

**The Area of a Triangle**

The area of a triangle is equal to 1/2 multiplied by its base multiplied by its height. The area of the blue-shaded triangle has a base equal to 150,000 − 125,000, or 25,000, and a height equal to $2.00 − $1.50, or $0.50. Therefore, its area equals 1/2 × 25,000 × $0.50, or $6,250.

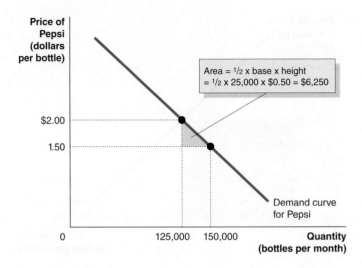

2. Make sure you are using the correct formula for the problem you are solving.
3. Make sure the number you calculate using the formula is economically reasonable. For example, if you are using a formula to calculate a firm's revenue and your answer is a negative number, you know you made a mistake somewhere.

---

**1A** **Using Graphs and Formulas,** pages 26–36

LEARNING OBJECTIVE: Review the use of graphs and formulas.

MyEconLab    Visit **www.myeconlab.com** to complete these exercises online and get instant feedback.

## Problems and Applications

**1A.1** The following table shows the relationship between the price of custard pies and the number of pies Jacob buys per week:

| Price | Quantity of Pies | Week |
|---|---|---|
| $3.00 | 6 | July 2 |
| 2.00 | 7 | July 9 |
| 5.00 | 4 | July 16 |
| 6.00 | 3 | July 23 |
| 1.00 | 8 | July 30 |
| 4.00 | 5 | August 6 |

a. Is the relationship between the price of pies and the number of pies Jacob buys a positive relationship or a negative relationship?

b. Plot the data from the table on a graph similar to Figure 1A.3 on page 29. Draw a straight line that best fits the points.

c. Calculate the slope of the line.

**1A.2** The following table gives information on the quantity of glasses of lemonade demanded on sunny and overcast days:

| Price (dollars per glass) | Quantity (glasses of lemonade per day) | Weather |
|---|---|---|
| $0.80 | 30 | Sunny |
| 0.80 | 10 | Overcast |
| 0.70 | 40 | Sunny |
| 0.70 | 20 | Overcast |
| 0.60 | 50 | Sunny |
| 0.60 | 30 | Overcast |
| 0.50 | 60 | Sunny |
| 0.50 | 40 | Overcast |

Plot the data from the table on a graph similar to Figure 1A.5 on page 31. Draw two straight lines representing the two demand curves—one for sunny days and one for overcast days.

**1A.3** Using the information in Figure 1A.2 on page 28, calculate the percentage change in auto sales from one year to the next. Between which years did sales fall at the fastest rate?

**1A.4** Real GDP in 2008 was $13,162 billion. Real GDP in 2009 was $12,703 billion. What was the percentage change in real GDP from 2008 to 2009? What do economists call the percentage change in real GDP from one year to the next?

**1A.5** Assume that the demand curve for Pepsi passes through the following two points:

| Price per Bottle of Pepsi | Number of Bottles Demanded |
| --- | --- |
| $2.50 | 100,000 |
| 1.25 | 200,000 |

**a.** Draw a graph with a linear demand curve that passes through these two points.

**b.** Show on the graph the areas representing total revenue at each price. Give the value for total revenue at each price.

**1A.6** What is the area of the blue triangle shown in the following figure?

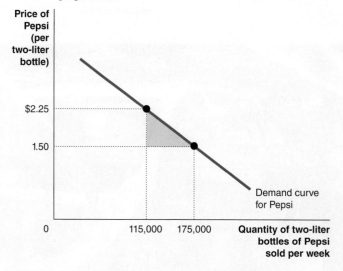

**1A.7** Calculate the slope of the total cost curve at point *A* and at point *B* in the following figure.

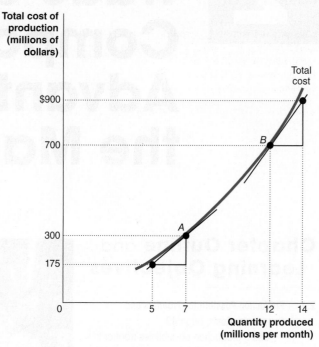

# Trade-offs, Comparative Advantage, and the Market System

## Chapter Outline and Learning Objectives

# Managers Making Choices at BMW

When you think of cars that combine fine engineering, high performance, and cutting-edge styling, you are likely to think of BMW. Founded in Germany in 1916, BMW today has 23 factories in 15 countries and worldwide sales of more than 1.5 million cars.

To compete in the automobile market, the managers of BMW must make many strategic decisions, such as whether to introduce new car models. BMW has begun selling a hydrogen-powered version of the 7-Series sedan and is also working on fuel cell–powered cars. Another strategic decision BMW's managers face is where to advertise. Although some of BMW's managers did not believe the company could sell cars in China, BMW decided to advertise heavily there. The advertising paid off: China has become the company's third-largest market, after Germany and the United States, with sales increasing by more than 85 percent in 2010 alone.

BMW's managers have also faced the strategic decision of whether to concentrate production in factories in Germany or to build new factories in overseas markets. Keeping production in Germany makes it easier for BMW's managers to supervise production and to employ German workers, who generally have high levels of technical training. By building factories in other countries, BMW can benefit from paying lower wages and can reduce political friction by producing vehicles in the same country in which it sells them. BMW opened a plant in Shenyang, in northeast China and a plant in Chennai in India. It also opened a U.S. factory in Spartanburg, South Carolina, which currently produces the X3, X5, and X6 models for sale both in the United States and worldwide.

Managers also face smaller-scale—or tactical—business decisions. For instance, in scheduling production at BMW's Spartanburg plant, managers must decide each month the quantity of X3, X5, and X6 models to produce. Like other decisions managers make, this one involves a trade-off: Producing more of one of these three models means producing fewer of the others.

**AN INSIDE LOOK** on **page 60** discusses the trade-off GM faces when deciding how to allocate resources between producing powertrains for its two electric cars—the Chevy volt and the Cadillac Converj.

Based on Christoph Rauwald, "BMW's Quarterly Profit Soars," *The Wall Street Journal*, May 4, 2011; and BMW, *Annual Report, 2010*.

## Economics in Your Life

### The Trade-offs When You Buy a Car

When you buy a car, you probably consider factors such as safety and fuel efficiency. To increase fuel efficiency, automobile manufacturers make cars small and light. Large cars absorb more of the impact of an accident than do small cars. As a result, people are usually safer driving large cars than small cars. What can we conclude from these facts about the relationship between safety and fuel efficiency? Under what circumstances would it be possible for automobile manufacturers to make cars safer and more fuel efficient? As you read the chapter, see if you can answer these questions. You can check your answers against those provided on **page 58** at the end of this chapter.

**Scarcity** A situation in which unlimited wants exceed the limited resources available to fulfill those wants.

In a market system, managers at most firms must make decisions like those made by BMW's managers. The decisions managers face reflect a key fact of economic life: *Scarcity requires trade-offs.* **Scarcity** exists because we have unlimited wants but only limited resources available to fulfill those wants. Goods and services are scarce. So, too, are the economic resources, or *factors of production*—workers, capital, natural resources, and entrepreneurial ability—used to make goods and services. Your time is scarce, which means you face trade-offs: If you spend an hour studying for an economics exam, you have one less hour to spend studying for a psychology exam or going to the movies. If your university decides to use some of its scarce budget to buy new computers for the computer labs, those funds will not be available to buy new books for the library or to resurface the student parking lot. If BMW decides to devote some of the scarce workers and machinery in its Spartanburg assembly plant to producing more X6 hybrid cars, those resources will not be available to produce more X5 SUVs.

Households and firms make many of their decisions in markets. Trade is a key activity that takes place in markets. Trade involves the decisions of millions of households and firms spread around the world. By engaging in trade, people can raise their standard of living. In this chapter, we provide an overview of how the market system coordinates the independent decisions of these millions of households and firms. We begin our analysis of the economic consequences of scarcity and the working of the market system by introducing an important economic model: the *production possibilities frontier*.

**2.1 LEARNING** OBJECTIVE

Use a production possibilities frontier to analyze opportunity costs and trade-offs.

# Production Possibilities Frontiers and Opportunity Costs

As we saw in the chapter opener, BMW operates an automobile factory in Spartanburg, South Carolina, where it assembles several car models. Because the firm's resources—workers, machinery, materials, and entrepreneurial skills—are limited, BMW faces a trade-off: Resources devoted to producing one model are not available for producing other models. Chapter 1 explained that economic models can be useful in analyzing many questions. We can use a simple model called the *production possibilities frontier* to analyze the trade-offs BMW faces in its Spartanburg plant. A **production possibilities frontier (PPF)** is a curve showing the maximum attainable combinations of two products that may be produced with available resources and current technology. In BMW's case, we simplify by assuming that the company produces only X6 hybrids and X5 SUVs at the Spartanburg plant, using workers, materials, robots, and other machinery.

**Production possibilities frontier (PPF)** A curve showing the maximum attainable combinations of two products that may be produced with available resources and current technology.

## Graphing the Production Possibilities Frontier

Figure 2.1 uses a production possibilities frontier to illustrate the trade-offs that BMW faces. The numbers from the table are plotted in the graph. The line in the graph is BMW's production possibilities frontier. If BMW uses all its resources to produce hybrids, it can produce 800 per day—point *A* at one end of the production possibilities frontier. If BMW uses all its resources to produce SUVs, it can produce 800 per day—point *E* at the other end of the production possibilities frontier. If BMW devotes resources to producing both vehicles, it could be at a point like *B*, where it produces 600 hybrids and 200 SUVs.

All the combinations either on the frontier—like *A*, *B*, *C*, *D*, and *E*—or inside the frontier—like point *F*—are *attainable* with the resources available. Combinations on the frontier are *efficient* because all available resources are being fully utilized, and the

| BMW's Production Choices at Its Spartanburg Plant | | |
|---|---|---|
| Choice | Quantity of Hybrids Produced | Quantity of SUVs Produced |
| A | 800 | 0 |
| B | 600 | 200 |
| C | 400 | 400 |
| D | 200 | 600 |
| E | 0 | 800 |

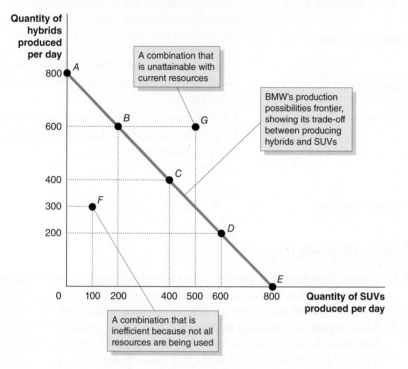

**Quantity of hybrids produced per day**

A combination that is unattainable with current resources

BMW's production possibilities frontier, showing its trade-off between producing hybrids and SUVs

A combination that is inefficient because not all resources are being used

**Quantity of SUVs produced per day**

### Figure 2.1

### BMW's Production Possibilities Frontier

BMW faces a trade-off: To build one more hybrid, it must build one less SUV. The production possibilities frontier illustrates the trade-off BMW faces. Combinations on the production possibilities frontier—like points *A*, *B*, *C*, *D*, and *E*—are *technically efficient* because the maximum output is being obtained from the available resources. Combinations inside the frontier—like point *F*—are *inefficient* because some resources are not being used. Combinations outside the frontier—like point *G*—are *unattainable* with current resources.

fewest possible resources are being used to produce a given amount of output. Combinations inside the frontier—like point *F*—are *inefficient* because maximum output is not being obtained from the available resources—perhaps because the assembly line is not operating at capacity. BMW might like to be beyond the frontier—at a point like *G*, where it would be producing 600 hybrids and 500 SUVs—but points beyond the production possibilities frontier are *unattainable*, given the firm's current resources. To produce the combination at *G*, BMW would need more machines or more workers.

Notice that if BMW is producing efficiently and is on the production possibilities frontier, the only way to produce more of one vehicle is to produce fewer of the other vehicle. Recall from Chapter 1 that the **opportunity cost** of any activity is the highest-valued alternative that must be given up to engage in that activity. For BMW, the opportunity cost of producing one more SUV is the number of hybrids the company will not be able to produce because it has shifted those resources to producing SUVs. For example, in moving from point *B* to point *C*, the opportunity cost of producing 200 more SUVs per day is the 200 fewer hybrids that can be produced.

What point on the production possibilities frontier is best? We can't tell without further information. If consumer demand for SUVs is greater than the demand for hybrids, the company is likely to choose a point closer to *E*. If demand for hybrids is greater than demand for SUVs, the company is likely to choose a point closer to *A*.

**Opportunity cost** The highest-valued alternative that must be given up to engage in an activity.

# Solved Problem 2.1

## Drawing a Production Possibilities Frontier for Rosie's Boston Bakery

Rosie's Boston Bakery specializes in cakes and pies. Rosie has 5 hours per day to devote to baking. In 1 hour, Rosie can prepare 2 pies or 1 cake.

**a.** Use the information given to complete the following table:

| | Hours Spent Making | | Quantity Made | |
|---|---|---|---|---|
| Choice | Cakes | Pies | Cakes | Pies |
| A | 5 | 0 | | |
| B | 4 | 1 | | |
| C | 3 | 2 | | |
| D | 2 | 3 | | |
| E | 1 | 4 | | |
| F | 0 | 5 | | |

**b.** Use the data in the table to draw a production possibilities frontier graph illustrating Rosie's trade-offs between making cakes and making pies. Label the vertical axis "Quantity of cakes made." Label the horizontal axis "Quantity of pies made." Make sure to label the values where Rosie's production possibilities frontier intersects the vertical and horizontal axes.

**c.** Label the points representing choice *D* and choice *E*. If Rosie is at choice *D*, what is her opportunity cost of making more pies?

## Solving the Problem

**Step 1:** **Review the chapter material.** This problem is about using production possibilities frontiers to analyze trade-offs, so you may want to review the section "Graphing the Production Possibilities Frontier," which begins on page 40.

**Step 2:** **Answer part (a) by filling in the table.** If Rosie can produce 1 cake in 1 hour, then with choice *A*, she will make 5 cakes and 0 pies. Because she can produce 2 pies in 1 hour, with choice *B*, she will make 4 cakes and 2 pies. Using similar reasoning, you can fill in the remaining cells in the table as follows:

| | Hours Spent Making | | Quantity Made | |
|---|---|---|---|---|
| Choice | Cakes | Pies | Cakes | Pies |
| A | 5 | 0 | 5 | 0 |
| B | 4 | 1 | 4 | 2 |
| C | 3 | 2 | 3 | 4 |
| D | 2 | 3 | 2 | 6 |
| E | 1 | 4 | 1 | 8 |
| F | 0 | 5 | 0 | 10 |

**Step 3:** **Answer part (b) by drawing the production possibilities frontier graph.** Using the data in the table in Step 2, you should draw a graph that looks like this:

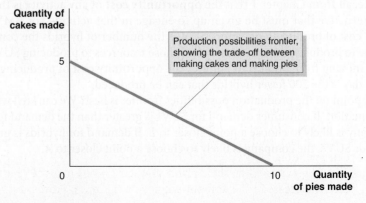

If Rosie devotes all 5 hours to making cakes, she will make 5 cakes. Therefore, her production possibilities frontier will intersect the vertical axis at 5 cakes made. If Rosie devotes all 5 hours to making pies, she will make 10 pies. Therefore, her production possibilities frontier will intersect the horizontal axis at 10 pies made.

**Step 4:** **Answer part (c) by showing choices *D* and *E* on your graph.** The points for choices *D* and *E* can be plotted using the information from the table:

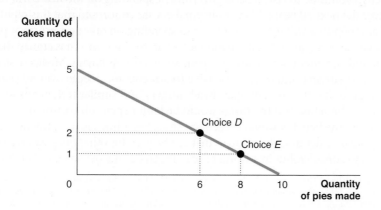

Moving from choice *D* to choice *E* increases Rosie's production of pies by 2 but lowers her production of cakes by 1. Therefore, her opportunity cost of making 2 more pies is making 1 less cake.

**Your Turn:** For more practice, do related problem 1.9 on page 63 at the end of this chapter.        MyEconLab

---

## Making the Connection

# Facing Trade-offs in Health Care Spending

Households have limited incomes. If the price of health care rises, households have to choose whether to buy less health care or spend less on other goods and services. The same is true of the federal government's spending on health care. The government provides health insurance to about 30 percent of the population through programs such as Medicare for people over age 65 and Medicaid for low-income people. If the price of health care rises, the government has to either cut back on the services provided through Medicare and Medicaid or cut spending in another part of the government's budget. (Of course, both households and the government can borrow to pay for some of their spending, but ultimately the funds they can borrow are also limited.)

About 54 percent of the population has private health insurance, often provided by an employer. When the fees doctors charge, the cost of prescription drugs, and the cost of hospital stays rise, the cost to employers of providing health insurance increases. As a result, employers will typically increase the amount they withhold from employees' paychecks to pay for the insurance. Some employers—particularly small firms—will even stop offering health insurance to their employees. In either case, the price employees pay for health care will rise. How do people respond to rising health care costs? Isn't health care a necessity that people continue to consume the same amount of, no matter how much its price increases? In fact, studies have shown that rising health care costs cause people to cut back their spending on medical services, just as people cut back their spending on other goods and services when their prices rise. One academic study indicates that for every 1 percent increase in the amount employers charge employees for insurance,

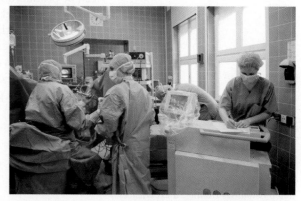

*Spending more on health care means spending less on other goods and services for both households and governments.*

164,000 people become uninsured. Of course, people without health insurance can still visit the doctor and obtain prescriptions, but they have to pay higher prices than do people with insurance. Although the consequences of being uninsured can be severe, particularly if someone develops a serious illness, economists are not surprised that higher prices for health insurance lead to less health insurance being purchased: Faced with limited incomes, people have to make choices among the goods and services they buy.

The Congressional Budget Office estimates that as the U.S. population ages and medical costs continue to rise, federal government spending on Medicare will more than double over the next 10 years. Many policymakers are concerned that this rapid increase in Medicare spending will force a reduction in spending on other government programs. Daniel Callahan, a researcher at the Hastings Center for Bioethics, has argued that policymakers should consider taking some dramatic steps, such as having Medicare stop paying for open-heart surgery and other expensive treatments for people over 80 years of age. Callahan argues that the costs of open-heart surgery and similar treatments for the very old exceed the benefits, and the funds would be better spent on treatments for younger patients, where the benefits would exceed the costs. Spending less on prolonging the lives of the very old in order to save resources that can be used for other purposes is a very painful trade-off to consider. But in a world of scarcity, trade-offs of some kind are inevitable.

Based on Daniel Callahan, "The Economic Woes of Medicare," *The New York Times*, November 13, 2008; Ezekiel J. Emanuel, "The Cost–Coverage Trade-off," *Journal of the American Medical Association*, Vol. 299, No. 8, February 27, 2008, pp. 947–949; and Congressional Budget Office, *A Preliminary Analysis of the President's Budget and an Update of CBO's Budget and Economic Outlook*, March 2009.

**MyEconLab**  **Your Turn:** Test your understanding by doing related problems 1.10, 1.11, 1.12, and 1.13 on page 63 at the end of this chapter.

## Increasing Marginal Opportunity Costs

We can use the production possibilities frontier to explore issues concerning the economy as a whole. For example, suppose we divide all the goods and services produced in the economy into just two types: military goods and civilian goods. In Figure 2.2, we let tanks represent military goods and automobiles represent civilian goods. If all the country's resources are devoted to producing military goods, 400 tanks can be produced in one year. If all resources are devoted to producing civilian goods, 500 automobiles can be produced in one year. Devoting resources to producing both goods results in the economy being at other points along the production possibilities frontier.

Notice that this production possibilities frontier is bowed outward rather than being a straight line. Because the curve is bowed out, the opportunity cost of automobiles in terms of tanks depends on where the economy currently is on the production possibilities frontier. For example, to increase automobile production from 0 to 200—moving from point *A* to point *B*—the economy has to give up only 50 tanks. But to increase

### Figure 2.2

**Increasing Marginal Opportunity Costs**

As the economy moves down the production possibilities frontier, it experiences *increasing marginal opportunity costs* because increasing automobile production by a given quantity requires larger and larger decreases in tank production. For example, to increase automobile production from 0 to 200—moving from point *A* to point *B*—the economy has to give up only 50 tanks. But to increase automobile production by another 200 vehicles—moving from point *B* to point *C*—the economy has to give up 150 tanks.

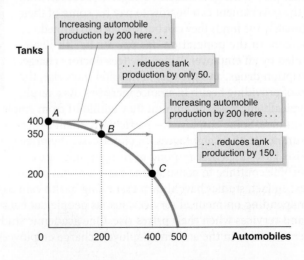

automobile production by another 200 vehicles—moving from point *B* to point *C*—the economy has to give up 150 tanks.

As the economy moves down the production possibilities frontier, it experiences *increasing marginal opportunity costs* because increasing automobile production by a given quantity requires larger and larger decreases in tank production. Increasing marginal opportunity costs occur because some workers, machines, and other resources are better suited to one use than to another. At point *A*, some resources that are well suited to producing automobiles are forced to produce tanks. Shifting these resources into producing automobiles by moving from point *A* to point *B* allows a substantial increase in automobile production, without much loss of tank production. But as the economy moves down the production possibilities frontier, more and more resources that are better suited to tank production are switched into automobile production. As a result, the increases in automobile production become increasingly smaller, while the decreases in tank production become increasingly larger. We would expect in most situations that production possibilities frontiers will be bowed outward rather than linear, as in the BMW example discussed earlier.

The idea of increasing marginal opportunity costs illustrates an important economic concept: *The more resources already devoted to an activity, the smaller the payoff to devoting additional resources to that activity.* For example, the more hours you have already spent studying economics, the smaller the increase in your test grade from each additional hour you spend—and the greater the opportunity cost of using the hour in that way. The more funds a firm has devoted to research and development during a given year, the smaller the amount of useful knowledge it receives from each additional dollar—and the greater the opportunity cost of using the funds in that way. The more funds the federal government spends cleaning up the environment during a given year, the smaller the reduction in pollution from each additional dollar—and, once again, the greater the opportunity cost of using the funds in that way.

## Economic Growth

At any given time, the total resources available to any economy are fixed. Therefore, if the United States produces more automobiles, it must produce less of something else—tanks in our example. Over time, though, the resources available to an economy may increase. For example, both the labor force and the capital stock—the amount of physical capital available in the country—may increase. The increase in the available labor force and the capital stock shifts the production possibilities frontier outward for the U.S. economy and makes it possible to produce both more automobiles and more

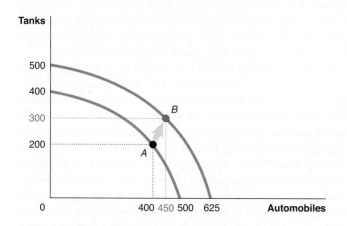

**(a) Shifting out the production possibilities frontier**

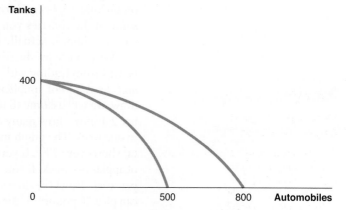

**(b) Technological change in the automobile industry**

**Figure 2.3    Economic Growth**

Panel (a) shows that as more economic resources become available and technological change occurs, the economy can move from point *A* to point *B*, producing more tanks and more automobiles. Panel (b) shows the results of technological change in the automobile industry that increases the quantity of vehicles workers can produce per year while leaving unchanged the maximum quantity of tanks that can be produced. Shifts in the production possibilities frontier represent *economic growth*.

tanks. Panel (a) of Figure 2.3 shows that the economy can move from point *A* to point *B*, producing more tanks and more automobiles.

Similarly, technological change makes it possible to produce more goods with the same number of workers and the same amount of machinery, which also shifts the production possibilities frontier outward. Technological change need not affect all sectors equally. Panel (b) of Figure 2.3 shows the results of technological change in the automobile industry that increases the quantity of automobiles workers can produce per year while leaving unchanged the quantity of tanks that can be produced.

**Economic growth** The ability of the economy to increase the production of goods and services.

Shifts in the production possibilities frontier represent **economic growth** because they allow the economy to increase the production of goods and services, which ultimately raises the standard of living. In the United States and other high-income countries, the market system has aided the process of economic growth, which over the past 200 years has greatly increased the well-being of the average person.

---

**2.2 LEARNING OBJECTIVE**

Understand comparative advantage and explain how it is the basis for trade.

**Trade** The act of buying and selling.

# Comparative Advantage and Trade

We can use the ideas of production possibilities frontiers and opportunity costs to understand the basic economic activity of *trade*. Markets are fundamentally about **trade**, which is the act of buying and selling. Sometimes we trade directly, as when children trade one baseball card for another baseball card. But often we trade indirectly: We sell our labor services as, say, an accountant, a salesperson, or a nurse for money, and then we use the money to buy goods and services. Although in these cases, trade takes place indirectly, ultimately the accountant, salesperson, or nurse is trading his or her services for food, clothing, and other goods and services. One of the great benefits of trade is that it makes it possible for people to become better off by increasing both their production and their consumption.

## Specialization and Gains from Trade

Consider the following situation: You and your neighbor both have fruit trees on your property. Initially, suppose you have only apple trees and your neighbor has only cherry trees. In this situation, if you both like apples and cherries, there is an obvious opportunity for both of you to gain from trade: You trade some of your apples for some of your neighbor's cherries, making you both better off. But what if there are apple and cherry trees growing on both of your properties? In that case, there can still be gains from trade. For example, your neighbor might be very good at picking apples, and you might be very good at picking cherries. It would make sense for your neighbor to concentrate on picking apples and for you to concentrate on picking cherries. You can then trade some of the cherries you pick for some of the apples your neighbor picks. But what if your neighbor is actually better at picking both apples and cherries than you are?

We can use production possibilities frontiers (*PPFs*) to show how your neighbor can benefit from trading with you *even though she is better than you are at picking both apples and cherries*. (For simplicity, and because it will not have any effect on the conclusions we draw, we will assume that the *PPFs* in this example are straight lines.) The table in Figure 2.4 shows how many apples and how many cherries you and your neighbor can pick in one week. The graph in the figure uses the data from the table to construct *PPFs*. Panel (a) shows your *PPF*. If you devote all your time to picking apples, you can pick 20 pounds of apples per week. If you devote all your time to picking cherries, you can pick 20 pounds per week. Panel (b) shows that if your neighbor devotes all her time to picking apples, she can pick 30 pounds. If she devotes all her time to picking cherries, she can pick 60 pounds.

The production possibilities frontiers in Figure 2.4 show how many apples and cherries you and your neighbor can consume, *without trade*. Suppose that when you don't trade with your neighbor, you pick and consume 8 pounds of apples and 12 pounds of cherries per week. This combination of apples and cherries is represented by point *A* in panel (a) of Figure 2.5. When your neighbor doesn't trade with you, she picks and consumes 9 pounds of apples and 42 pounds of cherries per week. This combination of apples and cherries is represented by point *C* in panel (b) of Figure 2.5.

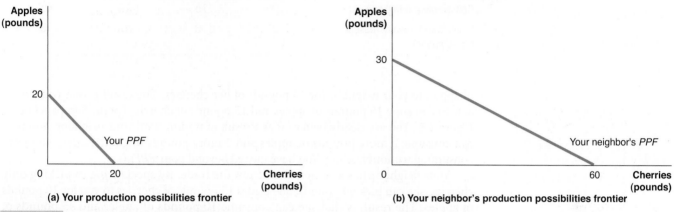

|  | You | | Your Neighbor | |
|---|---|---|---|---|
|  | Apples | Cherries | Apples | Cherries |
| Devote all time to picking apples | 20 pounds | 0 pounds | 30 pounds | 0 pounds |
| Devote all time to picking cherries | 0 pounds | 20 pounds | 0 pounds | 60 pounds |

**Figure 2.4** Production Possibilities for You and Your Neighbor, without Trade

The table in this figure shows how many pounds of apples and how many pounds of cherries you and your neighbor can each pick in one week. The graphs in the figure use the data from the table to construct production possibilities frontiers (*PPFs*) for you and your neighbor. Panel (a) shows your *PPF*. If you devote all your time to picking apples and none of your time to picking cherries, you can pick 20 pounds. If you devote all your time to picking cherries, you can pick 20 pounds. Panel (b) shows that if your neighbor devotes all her time to picking apples, she can pick 30 pounds. If she devotes all her time to picking cherries, she can pick 60 pounds.

After years of picking and consuming your own apples and cherries, suppose your neighbor comes to you one day with the following proposal: She offers to trade you 15 pounds of her cherries for 10 pounds of your apples next week. Should you accept this offer? You should accept because you will end up with more apples and more cherries to consume. To take advantage of her proposal, you should specialize in picking only apples rather than splitting your time between picking apples and picking cherries. We know this will allow you to pick 20 pounds of apples. You can trade 10 pounds

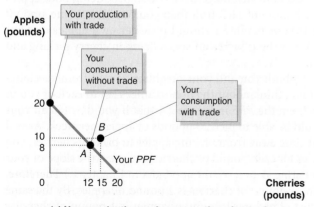

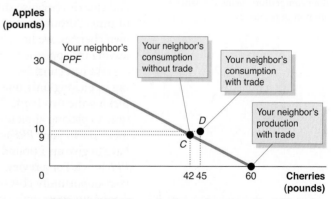

**Figure 2.5** Gains from Trade

When you don't trade with your neighbor, you pick and consume 8 pounds of apples and 12 pounds of cherries per week—point *A* in panel (a). When your neighbor doesn't trade with you, she picks and consumes 9 pounds of apples and 42 pounds of cherries per week—point *C* in panel (b). If you specialize in picking apples, you can pick 20 pounds. If your neighbor specializes in picking cherries, she can pick 60 pounds. If you trade 10 pounds of your apples for 15 pounds of your neighbor's cherries, you will be able to consume 10 pounds of apples and 15 pounds of cherries—point *B* in panel (a). Your neighbor can now consume 10 pounds of apples and 45 pounds of cherries—point *D* in panel (b). You and your neighbor are both better off as a result of the trade.

| Table 2.1 | | You | | Your Neighbor | |
|---|---|---|---|---|---|
| **A Summary of the Gains from Trade** | | Apples (in pounds) | Cherries (in pounds) | Apples (in pounds) | Cherries (in pounds) |
| | Production *and* consumption *without* trade | 8 | 12 | 9 | 42 |
| | Production *with* trade | 20 | 0 | 0 | 60 |
| | Consumption *with* trade | 10 | 15 | 10 | 45 |
| | Gains from trade (increased consumption) | 2 | 3 | 1 | 3 |

of apples to your neighbor for 15 pounds of her cherries. The result is that you will be able to consume 10 pounds of apples and 15 pounds of cherries (point *B* in panel (a) of Figure 2.5). You are clearly better off as a result of trading with your neighbor: You now can consume 2 more pounds of apples and 3 more pounds of cherries than you were consuming without trading. You have moved beyond your *PPF*!

Your neighbor has also benefited from the trade. By specializing in picking only cherries, she can pick 60 pounds. She trades 15 pounds of cherries to you for 10 pounds of apples. The result is that she can consume 10 pounds of apples and 45 pounds of cherries (point *D* in panel (b) of Figure 2.5). This is 1 more pound of apples and 3 more pounds of cherries than she was consuming before trading with you. She also has moved beyond her *PPF*. Table 2.1 summarizes the changes in production and consumption that result from your trade with your neighbor. (In this example, we chose one specific rate of trading cherries for apples—15 pounds of cherries for 10 pounds of apples. There are, however, many other rates of trading cherries for apples that would also make you and your neighbor better off.)

## Absolute Advantage versus Comparative Advantage

Perhaps the most remarkable aspect of the preceding example is that your neighbor benefits from trading with you even though she is better than you at picking both apples and cherries. **Absolute advantage** is the ability of an individual, a firm, or a country to produce more of a good or service than competitors, using the same amount of resources. Your neighbor has an absolute advantage over you in producing both apples and cherries because she can pick more of each fruit than you can in the same amount of time. Although it seems that your neighbor should pick her own apples *and* her own cherries, we have just seen that she is better off specializing in cherry picking and leaving the apple picking to you.

We can consider further why both you and your neighbor benefit from specializing in picking only one fruit. First, think about the opportunity cost to each of you of picking the two fruits. We saw from the *PPF* in Figure 2.4 that if you devoted all your time to picking apples, you would be able to pick 20 pounds of apples per week. As you move down your *PPF* and shift time away from picking apples to picking cherries, you have to give up 1 pound of apples for each pound of cherries you pick (the slope of your *PPF* is −1. For a review of calculating slopes, see the appendix to Chapter 1.) Therefore, your opportunity cost of picking 1 pound of cherries is 1 pound of apples. By the same reasoning, your opportunity cost of picking 1 pound of apples is 1 pound of cherries. Your neighbor's *PPF* has a different slope, so she faces a different trade-off: As she shifts time from picking apples to picking cherries, she has to give up 0.5 pound of apples for every 1 pound of cherries she picks (the slope of your neighbor's *PPF* is −0.5). As she shifts time from picking cherries to picking apples, she gives up 2 pounds of cherries for every 1 pound of apples she picks. Therefore, her opportunity cost of picking 1 pound of apples is 2 pounds of cherries, and her opportunity cost of picking 1 pound of cherries is 0.5 pound of apples.

**Absolute advantage** The ability of an individual, a firm, or a country to produce more of a good or service than competitors, using the same amount of resources.

| | Opportunity Cost of Picking 1 Pound of Apples | Opportunity Cost of Picking 1 Pound of Cherries | **Table 2.2** |
|---|---|---|---|
| You | 1 pound of cherries | 1 pound of apples | **Opportunity Costs of Picking Apples and Cherries** |
| Your Neighbor | 2 pounds of cherries | 0.5 pound of apples | |

Table 2.2 summarizes the opportunity costs for you and your neighbor of picking apples and cherries. Note that even though your neighbor can pick more apples in a week than you can, the *opportunity cost* of picking apples is higher for her than for you because when she picks apples, she gives up more cherries than you do. So, even though she has an absolute advantage over you in picking apples, it is more costly for her to pick apples than it is for you. The table also shows that her opportunity cost of picking cherries is lower than your opportunity cost of picking cherries. **Comparative advantage** is the ability of an individual, a firm, or a country to produce a good or service at a lower opportunity cost than competitors. In apple picking, your neighbor has an *absolute advantage* over you, but you have a *comparative advantage* over her. Your neighbor has both an absolute advantage and a comparative advantage over you in picking cherries. As we have seen, you are better off specializing in picking apples, and your neighbor is better off specializing in picking cherries.

**Comparative advantage** The ability of an individual, a firm, or a country to produce a good or service at a lower opportunity cost than competitors.

## Comparative Advantage and the Gains from Trade

We have just derived an important economic principle: *The basis for trade is comparative advantage, not absolute advantage.* The fastest apple pickers do not necessarily do much apple picking. If the fastest apple pickers have a comparative advantage in some other activity—picking cherries, playing Major League Baseball, or being industrial engineers—they are better off specializing in that other activity. Individuals, firms, and countries are better off if they specialize in producing goods and services for which they have a comparative advantage and obtain the other goods and services they need by trading. We will return to the important concept of comparative advantage in Chapter 9, which is devoted to the subject of international trade.

# Don't Let This Happen to You

### Don't Confuse Absolute Advantage and Comparative Advantage

First, make sure you know the definitions:

- **Absolute advantage.** The ability of an individual, a firm, or a country to produce more of a good or service than competitors, using the same amount of resources. In our example, your neighbor has an absolute advantage over you in both picking apples and picking cherries.
- **Comparative advantage.** The ability of an individual, a firm, or a country to produce a good or service at a lower opportunity cost than competitors. In our example, your neighbor has a comparative advantage in picking cherries, but you have a comparative advantage in picking apples.

Keep these two key points in mind:

1. It is possible to have an absolute advantage in producing a good or service without having a comparative advantage. This is the case with your neighbor picking apples.
2. It is possible to have a comparative advantage in producing a good or service without having an absolute advantage. This is the case with you picking apples.

MyEconLab

**Your Turn:** Test your understanding by doing related problem 2.5 on page 64 at the end of this chapter.

# Solved Problem 2.2

## Comparative Advantage and the Gains from Trade

Suppose that Canada and the United States both produce maple syrup and honey, which sell for the same prices in both countries. These are the combinations of the two goods that each country can produce in one day using the same amounts of capital and labor:

| Canada | | United States | |
|---|---|---|---|
| Honey (in tons) | Maple Syrup (in tons) | Honey (in tons) | Maple Syrup (in tons) |
| 0 | 60 | 0 | 50 |
| 10 | 45 | 10 | 40 |
| 20 | 30 | 20 | 30 |
| 30 | 15 | 30 | 20 |
| 40 | 0 | 40 | 10 |
| | | 50 | 0 |

**a.** Who has a comparative advantage in producing maple syrup? Who has a comparative advantage in producing honey?

**b.** Suppose that Canada is currently producing 30 tons of honey and 15 tons of maple syrup, and the United States is currently producing 10 tons of honey and 40 tons of maple syrup. Demonstrate that Canada and the United States can both be better off if they specialize in producing only one good and engage in trade.

**c.** Illustrate your answer to question (b) by drawing a *PPF* for the United States and a *PPF* for Canada. Show on your *PPF*s the combinations of honey and maple syrup produced and consumed in each country before and after trade.

## Solving the Problem

**Step 1: Review the chapter material.** This problem is about comparative advantage, so you may want to review the section "Absolute Advantage versus Comparative Advantage," which begins on page 48.

**Step 2: Answer part (a) by calculating who has a comparative advantage in each activity.** Remember that a country has a comparative advantage in producing a good if it can produce the good at the lowest opportunity cost. When Canada produces 1 more ton of honey, it produces 1.5 tons less of maple syrup. When the United States produces 1 more ton of honey, it produces 1 ton less of maple syrup. Therefore, the United States' opportunity cost of producing honey—1 ton of maple syrup—is lower than Canada's—1.5 tons of maple syrup. When Canada produces 1 more ton of maple syrup, it produces 0.67 ton less of honey. When the United States produces 1 more ton of maple syrup, it produces 1 ton less of honey. Therefore, Canada's opportunity cost of producing maple syrup—0.67 ton of honey—is lower than that of the United States—1 ton of honey. We can conclude that the United States has a comparative advantage in the production of honey and Canada has a comparative advantage in the production of maple syrup.

**Step 3: Answer part (b) by showing that specialization makes Canada and the United States better off.** We know that Canada should specialize where it has a comparative advantage, and the United States should specialize where it has a comparative advantage. If both countries specialize, Canada will produce 60 tons of maple syrup and 0 tons of honey, and the United States will produce 0 tons of maple syrup and 50 tons of honey. After both countries specialize, the United States could then trade 30 tons of honey to Canada in exchange for 40 tons of maple syrup. (Other mutually beneficial trades are possible as well.) We can summarize the results in a table:

| | Before Trade | | After Trade | |
|---|---|---|---|---|
| | Honey (in tons) | Maple Syrup (in tons) | Honey (in tons) | Maple Syrup (in tons) |
| Canada | 30 | 15 | 30 | 20 |
| United States | 10 | 40 | 20 | 40 |

The United States is better off after trade because it can consume the same amount of maple syrup and 10 more tons of honey. Canada is better off after trade because it can consume the same amount of honey and 5 more tons of maple syrup.

**Step 4:** **Answer part (c) by drawing the *PPFs*.**

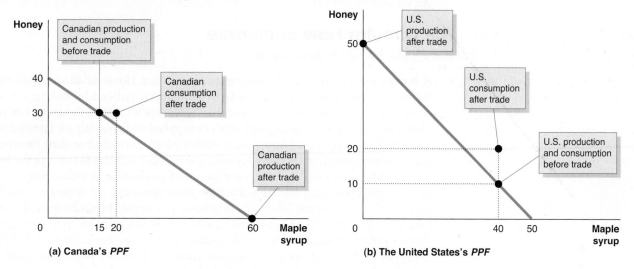

(a) Canada's *PPF*

(b) The United States's *PPF*

**Your Turn:** For more practice, do related problems 2.6 and 2.7 on page 65 at the end of this chapter.

MyEconLab

# The Market System

We have seen that households, firms, and the government face trade-offs and incur opportunity costs because resources are scarce. We have also seen that trade allows people to specialize according to their comparative advantage. By engaging in trade, people can raise their standard of living. Of course, trade in the modern world is much more complex than the examples we have considered so far. Trade today involves the decisions of millions of people around the world. But how does an economy make trade possible, and how are the decisions of these millions of people coordinated? In the United States and most other countries, trade is carried out in markets. Markets also determine the answers to the three fundamental questions discussed in Chapter 1: What goods and services will be produced? How will the goods and services be produced? and Who will receive the goods and services produced?

Recall that the definition of **market** is a group of buyers and sellers of a good or service and the institution or arrangement by which they come together to trade. Markets take many forms: They can be physical places, such as a local pizza parlor or the New York Stock Exchange, or virtual places, such as eBay. In a market, the buyers are demanders of goods or services, and the sellers are suppliers of goods or services. Households and firms interact in two types of markets: *product markets* and *factor markets*. **Product markets** are markets for goods—such as computers—and services—such as medical treatment. In product markets, households are demanders and firms are suppliers. **Factor markets** are markets for the *factors of production*. **Factors of production** are the inputs used to make goods and services. Factors of production are divided into four broad categories:

- *Labor* includes all types of work, from the part-time labor of teenagers working at McDonald's to the work of senior managers in large corporations.

- *Capital* refers to physical capital, such as computers and machine tools, that is used to produce other goods.

**Market** A group of buyers and sellers of a good or service and the institution or arrangement by which they come together to trade.

**Product market** A market for goods—such as computers—or services—such as medical treatment.

**Factor market** A market for the factors of production, such as labor, capital, natural resources, and entrepreneurial ability.

**Factors of production** The inputs used to make goods and services.

- *Natural resources* include land, water, oil, iron ore, and other raw materials (or "gifts of nature") that are used in producing goods.

- An *entrepreneur* is someone who operates a business. *Entrepreneurial ability* is the ability to bring together the other factors of production to successfully produce and sell goods and services.

## The Circular Flow of Income

Two key groups participate in markets:

- A *household* consists of all the individuals in a home. Households are suppliers of factors of production—particularly labor—employed by firms to make goods and services. Households use the income they receive from selling the factors of production to purchase the goods and services supplied by firms. We are familiar with households as suppliers of labor because most people earn most of their income by going to work, which means they are selling their labor services to firms in the labor market. But households own the other factors of production as well, either directly or indirectly, by owning the firms that have these resources. All firms are owned by households. Small firms, like a neighborhood restaurant, might be owned by one person. Large firms, like Microsoft or BMW, are owned by millions of households that own shares of stock in them. (We discuss the stock market in Chapter 8.) When firms pay profits to the people who own them, the firms are paying for using the capital and natural resources that are supplied to them by those owners. So, we can generalize by saying that in factor markets, households are suppliers and firms are demanders.

- *Firms* are suppliers of goods and services. Firms use the funds they receive from selling goods and services to buy the factors of production needed to make the goods and services.

**Circular-flow diagram** A model that illustrates how participants in markets are linked.

We can use a simple economic model called the **circular-flow diagram** to see how participants in markets are linked. Figure 2.6 shows that in factor markets, households supply labor and other factors of production in exchange for wages and other payments from firms. In product markets, households use the payments they earn in factor markets to purchase the goods and services supplied by firms. Firms produce these goods and services using the factors of production supplied by households. In the figure, the blue arrows show the flow of factors of production from households through factor markets to firms. The red arrows show the flow of goods and services from firms through product markets to households. The green arrows show the flow of funds from firms through factor markets to households and the flow of spending from households through product markets to firms.

Like all economic models, the circular-flow diagram is a simplified version of reality. For example, Figure 2.6 leaves out the important role of government in buying goods from firms and in making payments, such as Social Security or unemployment insurance payments, to households. The figure also leaves out the roles played by banks, the stock and bond markets, and other parts of the *financial system* in aiding the flow of funds from lenders to borrowers. Finally, the figure does not show that some goods and services purchased by domestic households are produced in foreign countries and some goods and services produced by domestic firms are sold to foreign households. (We explore the government, the financial system, and the international sector further in later chapters.) Despite these simplifications, the circular-flow diagram in Figure 2.6 is useful for seeing how product markets, factor markets, and their participants are linked together. One of the great wonders of the market system is that it manages to successfully coordinate the independent activities of so many households and firms.

## The Gains from Free Markets

**Free market** A market with few government restrictions on how a good or service can be produced or sold or on how a factor of production can be employed.

A **free market** exists when the government places few restrictions on how goods and services can be produced or sold or on how factors of production can be employed.

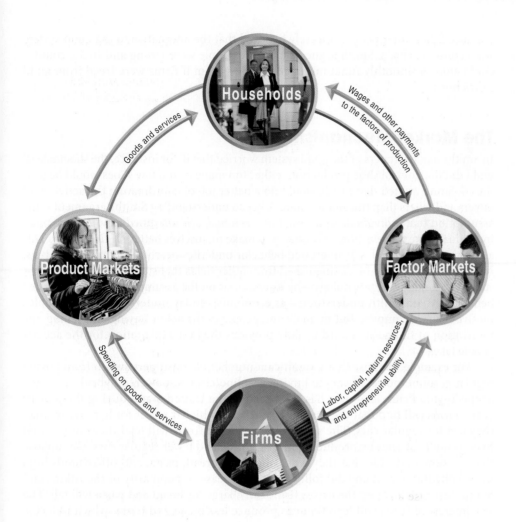

**Figure 2.6**

**The Circular-Flow Diagram**

Households and firms are linked together in a circular flow of production, income, and spending. The blue arrows show the flow of the factors of production. In factor markets, households supply labor, entrepreneurial ability, and other factors of production to firms. Firms use these factors of production to make goods and services that they supply to households in product markets. The red arrows show the flow of goods and services from firms to households. The green arrows show the flow of funds. In factor markets, households receive wages and other payments from firms in exchange for supplying the factors of production. Households use these wages and other payments to purchase goods and services from firms in product markets. Firms sell goods and services to households in product markets, and they use the funds to purchase the factors of production from households in factor markets.

Governments in all modern economies intervene more than is consistent with a fully free market. In that sense, we can think of the free market as being a benchmark against which we can judge actual economies. There are relatively few government restrictions on economic activity in the United States, Canada, the countries of Western Europe, Hong Kong, Singapore, and Estonia. So these countries come close to the free market benchmark. In countries such as Cuba and North Korea, the free market system has been rejected in favor of centrally planned economies with extensive government control over product and factor markets. Countries that come closest to the free market benchmark have been more successful than countries with centrally planned economies in providing their people with rising living standards.

The Scottish philosopher Adam Smith is considered the father of modern economics because his book *An Inquiry into the Nature and Causes of the Wealth of Nations*, published in 1776, was an early and very influential argument for the free market system. Smith was writing at a time when extensive government restrictions on markets were still common. In many parts of Europe, the *guild system* still prevailed. Under this system, governments would give guilds, or organizations of producers, the authority to control the production of a good. For example, the shoemakers' guild controlled who was allowed to produce shoes, how many shoes they could produce, and what price they could charge. In France, the cloth makers' guild even dictated the number of threads in the weave of the cloth.

Smith argued that such restrictions reduced the income, or wealth, of a country and its people by restricting the quantity of goods produced. Some people at the time supported the restrictions of the guild system because it was in their financial interest to do so. If you were a member of a guild, the restrictions served to reduce the competition you faced. But other people sincerely believed that the alternative to the guild system was economic chaos. Smith argued that these people were wrong and that a country could enjoy a smoothly functioning economic system if firms were freed from guild restrictions.

## The Market Mechanism

In Smith's day, defenders of the guild system worried that if, for instance, the shoemakers' guild did not control shoe production, either too many or too few shoes would be produced. Smith argued that prices would do a better job of coordinating the activities of buyers and sellers than the guilds could. A key to understanding Smith's argument is the assumption that *individuals usually act in a rational, self-interested way*. In particular, individuals take those actions most likely to make themselves better off financially. This assumption of rational, self-interested behavior underlies nearly all economic analysis. In fact, economics can be distinguished from other fields that study human behavior—such as sociology and psychology—by its emphasis on the assumption of self-interested behavior. Adam Smith understood—as economists today understand—that people's motives can be complex. But in analyzing people in the act of buying and selling, the motivation of financial reward usually provides the best explanation for the actions people take.

For example, suppose that a significant number of consumers switch from buying regular gasoline-powered cars to buying gasoline/electric-powered hybrid cars, such as the Toyota Prius, as in fact has happened in the United States during the past 10 years. Firms will find that they can charge relatively higher prices for hybrid cars than they can for regular cars. The self-interest of these firms will lead them to respond to consumers' wishes by producing more hybrids and fewer regular cars. Or suppose that consumers decide that they want to eat less bread, pasta, and other foods high in carbohydrates, as many did following the increase in popularity of the Atkins and South Beach diets. Then the prices firms can charge for bread and pasta will fall. The self-interest of firms will lead them to produce less bread and pasta, which in fact is what happened.

Note that for the market mechanism to work in responding to changes in consumers' wants, *prices must be flexible*. Changes in *relative prices*—that is, the price of one good or service relative to other goods or services—provides information, or a signal, to both consumers and firms. For example, in 2010, consumers worldwide increased their demand for cattle and poultry. Because corn is fed to cattle and poultry, prices for corn soared relative to prices for other crops. Many farmers in the United States received this price signal and responded by increasing the amount of corn they planted and decreasing the amount of soybeans and wheat. One Kansas farmer was quoted as saying, "It seemed to me there was $100 to $150 per acre more money in the corn than there was in the beans. That's the kind of math that a lot of guys were using." Similarly, falling prices for DVDs or music CDs in the 2000s was a signal to movie studios and record companies to devote fewer resources to these products and more resources to making movies and music available online. In the United States today, governments at the federal, state, and local levels set or regulate the price of only about 10 to 20 percent of goods and services. The prices of other goods and services are free to change as consumer wants change and as costs of production change.

In the case where consumers want more of a product, and in the case where they want less of a product, the market system responds without a guild or the government giving orders about how much to produce or what price to charge. In a famous phrase, Smith said that firms would be led by the "invisible hand" of the market to provide consumers with what they want. Firms respond *individually* to changes in prices by making decisions that *collectively* end up satisfying the wants of consumers.

| Making the Connection | # A Story of the Market System in Action: How Do You Make an iPad? |

Apple produces the iPad 2. Because Apple's headquarters is in Cupertino, California, it seems reasonable to assume that iPads are also manufactured in that state. In fact, although engineers at Apple designed the iPad, the company produces none of the components of the iPad, nor does it assemble the components into a finished product. Far from being produced entirely by one company in one place, the iPad requires the coordinated activities of thousands of workers and dozens of firms spread around the world.

Foxconn, which is based in Taiwan, assembles the iPad in factories in Shenzhen and Chengdu, China, and ships them to Apple for sale in the United States. Foxconn has announced plans to begin assembling some iPads in a new factory in Brazil by 2012. Although Foxconn does final assembly, it doesn't make any of the components and, in fact, charges Apple less than $15 for assembling each iPad.

*The market coordinates the activities of the many people spread around the world who contribute to the making of an iPad.*

The table below lists just some of the many suppliers of components for the iPad 2.

| Firm | Location of the Firm | iPad Component the Firm Supplies |
|------|----------------------|----------------------------------|
| ARM | Great Britain | Processor design |
| Broadcom | United States (California) | Touchscreen controller |
| Infineon Technologies | Germany | Semiconductors |
| LG Electronics | South Korea | Screen |
| Samsung | South Korea | Flash memory and processor |
| Texas Instruments | United States (Texas) | Touchscreen controller |

Each of these suppliers in turn relies on its own suppliers. For example, Broadcom designs the touchscreen controller for the iPad and supplies it to Apple, but it does not manufacture the components of the controller or assemble them. To manufacture the components, Broadcom relies on SilTerra, based in Malaysia; SMIC, based in mainland China; and Taiwan Semiconductor Manufacturing Corporation (TSMC) and UMC, based in Taiwan. TSMC's factories are for the most part not in Taiwan but in mainland China and Eastern Europe. To assemble the components, Broadcom uses several companies, including Amkor Technology, based in Chandler, Arizona, and STATS ChipPAC, based in Singapore.

All told, an iPad contains hundreds of parts that are designed, manufactured, and assembled by firms around the world. Many of these firms are not even aware of which other firms are also producing components for the iPad. Few of the managers of these firms have met managers of the other firms or shared knowledge of how their particular components are produced. In fact, no one person from Tim Cook, the chief executive officer of Apple, on down possesses the knowledge of how to produce all the components that are assembled into an iPad. Instead, the invisible hand of the market has led these firms to contribute their knowledge and resources to the process that ultimately results in an iPad available for sale in a store in the United States. Apple has so efficiently organized the process of producing the iPad that you can order a custom iPad with a personal engraving and have it delivered from an assembly plant in China to your doorstep in the United States in as little as three days.

Based on Andrew Rassweiler, "iPad 2 Carries Bill of Materials of $326.60, IHS iSuppli Teardown Analysis Shows," iSuppli.com, March 13, 2011; Arik Hesseldahl, "Apple iPad Components Cost At Least $259," *Bloomberg Businessweek*, April 7, 2010; and Chinmei Sung, "Foxconn Faces Limited Impact from Chengdu Fire, Analysts Say," *Bloomberg Businessweek*, May 22, 2011.

**Your Turn:** Test your understanding by doing related problems 3.8 and 3.9 on page 66 at the end of this chapter.    MyEconLab

## The Role of the Entrepreneur

**Entrepreneur** Someone who operates a business, bringing together the factors of production—labor, capital, and natural resources—to produce goods and services.

*Entrepreneurs* are central to the working of the market system. An **entrepreneur** is someone who operates a business. Entrepreneurs must first determine what goods and services they believe consumers want, and then they must decide how to produce those goods and services most profitably, using the available factors of production—labor, capital, and natural resources. Successful entrepreneurs are able to search out opportunities to provide new goods and services. Often these opportunities are created by new technology. Consumers and existing businesses typically do not at first realize that the new technology makes new products feasible. For example, even after the development of the internal combustion engine had made automobiles practicable, Henry Ford remarked, "If I had asked my customers what they wanted, they would have said a faster horse." Because consumers often cannot evaluate a new product before it exists, some of the most successful entrepreneurs, such as the late Steve Jobs of Apple, rarely use *focus groups*, or meetings with consumers in which the customers are asked what new products they would like to see. Instead, entrepreneurs think of products that consumers may not even realize they need, such as, in Jobs's case, an MP3 player—iPod—or a tablet computer—iPad.

Entrepreneurs are of great importance to the economy because they are often responsible for making new products widely available to consumers, as Henry Ford did with the automobile and Steve Jobs did with the iPod. Table 2.3 lists some of the important products entrepreneurs at small firms introduced during the twentieth century.

| **Table 2.3** | | |
| --- | --- | --- |
| **Important Products Introduced by Entrepreneurs at Small Firms** | **Product** | **Inventor** |
| | Air conditioning | William Haviland Carrier |
| | Airplane | Orville and Wilbur Wright |
| | Biomagnetic imaging | Raymond Damadian |
| | Biosynthetic insulin | Herbert Boyer |
| | DNA fingerprinting | Alec Jeffries |
| | FM radio | Edwin Howard Armstrong |
| | Helicopter | Igor Sikorsky |
| | High-resolution CAT scanner | Robert Ledley |
| | Hydraulic brake | Malcolm Lockheed |
| | Integrated circuit | Jack Kilby |
| | Microprocessor | Ted Hoff |
| | Optical scanner | Everett Franklin Lindquist |
| | Oral contraceptives | Carl Djerassi |
| | Overnight delivery service | Fred Smith |
| | Personal computer | Steve Jobs and Steve Wozniak |
| | Quick-frozen foods | Clarence Birdseye |
| | Safety razor | King Gillette |
| | Soft contact lens | Kevin Tuohy |
| | Solid fuel rocket engine | Robert Goddard |
| | Supercomputer | Seymour Cray |
| | Vacuum tube | Philo Farnsworth |
| | Zipper | Gideon Sundback |

Based on William J. Baumol, *The Microtheory of Innovative Entrepreneurship*, (Princeton, NJ: Princeton University Press, 2010) and various sources. Note that the person who first commercially developed a particular product is sometimes disputed by historians.

Entrepreneurs put their own funds at risk when they start businesses. If they are wrong about what consumers want or about the best way to produce goods and services, they can lose those funds. In fact, it is not unusual for entrepreneurs who eventually achieve great success to fail at first. For instance, early in their careers, both Henry Ford and Sakichi Toyoda, who eventually founded the Toyota Motor Corporation, started companies that quickly failed. Research by Richard Freeman of Harvard University has shown that the typical entrepreneur earns less than someone with the same education and other characteristics who is an employee at a large firm. Few entrepreneurs make the fortunes earned by Henry Ford, Steve Jobs, or Bill Gates.

Entrepreneurs make a vital contribution to economic growth through their roles in responding to consumer demand and in introducing new products. So, government policies that encourage entrepreneurship are also likely to increase economic growth and raise the standard of living. In the next section, we consider the legal framework required for a successful market in which entrepreneurs can succeed.

## The Legal Basis of a Successful Market System

In a free market, government does not restrict how firms produce and sell goods and services or how they employ factors of production. But the absence of government intervention is not enough for the market system to work well. Government has to take active steps to provide a *legal environment* that will allow the market system to succeed.

**Protection of Private Property** For the market system to work well, individuals must be willing to take risks. Someone with $250,000 can be cautious and keep it safely in a bank—or even in cash, if the person doesn't trust banks. But the market system won't work unless a significant number of people are willing to risk their funds by investing them in businesses. Investing in businesses is risky in any country. Many businesses fail every year in the United States and other high-income countries. But in high-income countries, someone who starts a new business or invests in an existing business doesn't have to worry that the government, the military, or criminal gangs might decide to seize the business or demand payments for not destroying the business. Unfortunately, in many poor countries, owners of businesses are not well protected from having their businesses seized by the government or from having their profits taken by criminals. Where these problems exist, opening a business can be extremely risky. Cash can be concealed easily, but a business is difficult to conceal and difficult to move.

**Property rights** are the rights individuals or firms have to the exclusive use of their property, including the right to buy or sell it. Property can be tangible, physical property, such as a store or factory. Property can also be intangible, such as the right to an idea. Two amendments to the U.S. Constitution guarantee property rights: The 5th Amendment states that the federal government shall not deprive any person "of life, liberty, or property, without due process of law." The 14th Amendment extends this guarantee to the actions of state governments: "No state . . . shall deprive any person of life, liberty, or property, without due process of law." Similar guarantees exist in every high-income country. Unfortunately, in many developing countries, such guarantees do not exist or are poorly enforced.

**Property rights** The rights individuals or firms have to the exclusive use of their property, including the right to buy or sell it.

In any modern economy, *intellectual property rights* are very important. Intellectual property includes books, films, software, and ideas for new products or new ways of producing products. To protect intellectual property, the federal government grants a *patent* that gives an inventor—which is often a firm—the exclusive right to produce and sell a new product for a period of 20 years from the date the patent was filed. For instance, because Microsoft has a patent on the Windows operating system, other firms cannot sell their own versions of Windows. The government grants patents to encourage firms to spend money on the research and development necessary to create new products. If other companies could freely copy Windows, Microsoft would not have spent the funds necessary to develop it. Just as a new product or a new method of making a product receives patent protection, books, films, and software receive *copyright* protection. Under U.S. law, the creator of a book, film, or piece of music has the exclusive right to use the creation during the creator's lifetime. The creator's heirs retain this exclusive right for 50 years after the death of the creator.

**Enforcement of Contracts and Property Rights** Business activity often involves someone agreeing to carry out some action in the future. For example, you may borrow $20,000 to buy a car and promise the bank—by signing a loan contract—that you will pay back the money over the next five years. Or Microsoft may sign a licensing agreement with a small technology company, agreeing to use that company's technology for a period of several years in return for a fee. Usually these agreements take the form of legal contracts. For the market system to work, businesses and individuals have to rely on these contracts being carried out. If one party to a legal contract does not fulfill its obligations—perhaps the small company had promised Microsoft exclusive use of its technology but then began licensing it to other companies—the other party can go to court to have the agreement enforced. Similarly, if property owners in the United States believe that the federal or state government has violated their rights under the 5th or 14th Amendments, they can go to court to have their rights enforced.

But going to court to enforce a contract or private property rights will be successful only if the court system is independent and judges are able to make impartial decisions on the basis of the law. In the United States and other high-income countries, the court systems have enough independence from other parts of the government and enough protection from intimidation by outside forces—such as criminal gangs—that they are able to make their decisions based on the law. In many developing countries, the court systems lack this independence and will not provide a remedy if the government violates private property rights or if a person with powerful political connections decides to violate a business contract.

If property rights are not well enforced, fewer goods and services will be produced. This reduces economic efficiency, leaving the economy inside its production possibilities frontier.

Continued from page 39

## Economics in Your Life

### The Trade-offs When You Buy a Car

At the beginning of the chapter, we asked you to think about two questions: When buying a new car, what is the relationship between safety and fuel efficiency? and Under what circumstances would it be possible for automobile manufacturers to make cars safer and more fuel efficient? To answer the first question, you have to recognize that there is a trade-off between safety and fuel efficiency. With the technology available at any particular time, an automobile manufacturer can increase fuel efficiency by making a car smaller and lighter. But driving a lighter car increases your chances of being injured if you have an accident. The trade-off between safety and fuel efficiency would look much like the relationship in Figure 2.1 on page 41. To get more of both safety and gas mileage, automobile makers would have to discover new technologies that allow them to make cars lighter and safer at the same time. Such new technologies would make points like G in Figure 2.1 attainable.

# Conclusion

We have seen that by trading in markets, people are able to specialize and pursue their comparative advantage. Trading on the basis of comparative advantage makes all participants in trade better off. The key role of markets is to facilitate trade. In fact, the market system is a very effective means of coordinating the decisions of millions of consumers, workers, and firms. At the center of the market system is the consumer. To be successful, firms must respond to the desires of consumers. These desires are communicated to firms through prices. To explore how markets work, we must study the behavior of consumers and firms. We continue this exploration of markets in Chapter 3, when we develop the model of demand and supply.

Before moving on to Chapter 3, read *An Inside Look* on the next page for a discussion of the trade-offs General Motors faces in producing its electric cars, the Chevy Volt and the Cadillac Converj.

## Managers at General Motors Approve Production of a Plug-in Cadillac

## Cadillac Reportedly to Build Chevy Volt–Based Car

Sometimes, like Lazarus, dead cars rise again.

We've learned from an inside source at General Motors, a person close to the project, that the electric Cadillac Converj luxury coupe is now back in the GM product plan.

The Converj was recently approved for production by GM product executives. It will likely launch in 2013 as a 2014 model, though it may end up with a Cadillac-style three-letter model name.

The production version will feature, says our source, "a Generation 1.5 Voltec" powertrain.

That would be an updated version of the extended-range electric powertrain from the 2011 Chevrolet Volt, possibly with better acceleration to suit the Cadillac image—but not the fully revised second-generation version that will go into production in 2015.

### Smash hit in 2009

The Converj concept car was first unveiled in January 2009 at the Detroit Auto Show. The sleek sports coupe received rave reviews, and during 2009, it was approved for production, with then-product chief Bob Lutz saying in January 2010 it had been cleared by management.

Two months later, it was killed, with Cadillac spokesman David Caldwell saying the Converj program had not reached "a point [at] which development would be occurring in earnest in any case."

Two reasons were given for ending the program almost 18 months ago: First, GM could not make a profit at the low volumes the Converj had been planned for.

Now, with the Volt essentially sold out and GM trying to boost production as fast as possible, perhaps Converj volumes can go higher, meaning each car may cost less.

Second, product planners were concerned that the greater weight and additional luxury features of a Cadillac would cut its electric range and performance—reducing its appeal, much as the Lexus HS 250h has sold in lower numbers than expected for Toyota's luxury arm.

### "All about profit"

Apparently, both concerns have been resolved. One reason for resuscitating the Converj, says our source, is that CEO Dan Akerson is "all about profit." The 2012 Volt lists at $39,990, and tops out (before dealer markup) at less than $50,000.

If some Voltec cars could be sold not for $45,000 but, say, $60,000, that might enable GM to make money on its first generation of Voltec cars. Or, perhaps more realistically, to lose less money on the technology—until a less-costly second generation can be rolled out.

And if Cadillac truly hopes to compete with the likes of Mercedes-Benz, BMW, and Audi, it needs to have one or more plug-in offerings.

All those makes have multiple plug-ins planned, from the Mercedes-Benz S-Class Plug-In Hybrid and Audi e-tron electric supercar down to the A-Class E-Cell and tiny Audi Urban Concept two-seater.

### Escalade Hybrid: hardly a halo car

But despite a plug-in hybrid concept for the XTS full-size sedan that will go on sale next spring as a 2013 model, and persistent rumors of an SRX plug-in hybrid crossover, neither of those products has been given the green light for production.

The SRX plug-in hybrid was killed in May due to inadequate range from its battery pack, which had been designed for a different and lighter vehicle. So Cadillac's sole electrified vehicle remains the 2011 Escalade Hybrid full-size sport-utility vehicle—hardly a halo car to get early adopters into their dealers, as the Volt has done for Chevy.

The Converj is not the only example of turbulence in GM's product plans over the last three years. But now that a deal has been reached to raise corporate average fuel-economy standards to 54.5 mpg by 2025, insiders hope that the GM product plan will settle down.

To reach those goals, plug-in cars will clearly become a larger portion of GM's portfolio over time.

*Source:* "Cadillac Reportedly to Build Chevy Volt-Based Car" by John Voelcker from *Green Car Reports*, August 11, 2011. Copyright © High Gear Media. Reprinted by permission from greencarreports.com.

## Key Points in the Article

This article discusses General Motors's plan to produce an electric car for its Cadillac brand with an upgrade of the powertrain technology currently in use in its Chevy Volt plug-in car. GM introduced a concept version of this Cadillac model in 2009, and after positive reviews, it was approved for production, only to be shelved two months later amid concerns about profitability and performance. High demand for the Volt and improvements to the Voltec powertrain alleviated the profitability and performance concerns, and GM again approved production of the Cadillac model, with a planned introduction in 2013. GM views production of an electric plug-in vehicle as essential for Cadillac in its effort to compete with other luxury automobile brands that have plug-in vehicles in the planning stages.

## Analyzing the News

ⓐ Based on positive reaction to the Cadillac Converj concept vehicle in 2009, GM officials approved the car for production, but concerns, including its initial limited production estimates, caused GM to reverse course and cancel its plans. Subsequently, high demand for the Volt led GM to increase production of the Voltec powertrain. This increased production of powertrains caused GM to increase its initial production estimates of the Cadillac at a potentially lower per-unit cost, again making the production version viable. If we assume that in 2009 the resources available to GM to produce its Voltec powertrain were fixed, and 10,000 could be produced, then GM must decide how to allocate those resources between producing powertrains for its Chevy and for its Cadillac. In the figure below, we illustrate the trade-off GM faces with a production possibilities frontier. In 2009, we will assume that GM was at point A, devoting 8,000 powertrains for its already-approved Volt and only 2,000 for its newly approved Converj. At point A, GM decided that the small quantity of powertrains that could be devoted to the Converj was insufficient to meet profitability goals and that the production would be better devoted entirely to the Volt, thereby moving production from point A to point B.

ⓑ When announcing that the Converj would become a production car in 2013, GM had determined that its increased production of the Voltec powertrain and the possibility of charging a higher selling price for Voltec vehicles could increase the profit potential for these vehicles. By 2013, when it expects to start selling the Converj, GM will have allocated additional resources and employed improved technology to the production of the Voltec powertrain, allowing the company to increase its production numbers. Assume that in 2013 GM is capable of producing 30,000 Voltec powertrains. This is represented in the figure below by the production possibilities frontier shifting out, allowing GM to devote more powertrains to both the Volt and the Converj. In the figure, we assume that GM will move to point C and will allocate 22,000 powertrains to production of the Volt and 8,000 to the Converj.

ⓒ GM still has reservations about approving additional electric models for its Cadillac brand, citing performance concerns for these heavier vehicles. For GM to choose to devote additional resources to address these concerns, it would need to allocate fewer resources to its current production. Companies can weigh the opportunity costs of devoting their limited resources to their various production alternatives to help determine the allocation of resources.

## Thinking Critically

1. Suppose that from 2009 to 2013, the resources GM uses to produce the Voltec powertrain remained constant, but improvements in technology allow GM in 2013 to produce the additional quantity of powertrains shown in the figure for only the Cadillac Converj but not the Chevy Volt. Draw a graph that illustrates this technology change, showing both the 2009 and new 2013 production possibilities frontiers. What is the opportunity cost of producing one powertrain for the Volt in 2009? In 2013?

2. Assume that the figure accurately represents GM's production possibilities frontiers for 2009 and 2013, and in 2013 it has customer orders for 25,000 Volts and 10,000 Converjs. Explain whether GM can fill all of these orders.

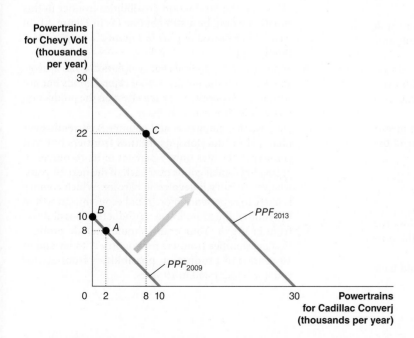

Choosing between producing a Chevy Volt and a Cadillac Converj.

# Chapter Summary and Problems

## Key Terms

Absolute advantage, p. 48

Circular-flow diagram, p. 52

Comparative advantage, p. 49

Economic growth, p. 46

Entrepreneur, p. 56

Factor market, p. 51

Factors of production, p. 51

Free market, p. 52

Market, p. 51

Opportunity cost, p. 41

Product market, p. 51

Production possibilities frontier (*PPF*), p. 40

Property rights, p. 57

Scarcity, p. 40

Trade, p. 46

 **2.1** **Production Possibilities Frontiers and Opportunity Costs,** pages 40–46

LEARNING OBJECTIVE: Use a production possibilities frontier to analyze opportunity costs and trade-offs.

## Summary

The **production possibilities frontier** (*PPF*) is a curve that shows the maximum attainable combinations of two products that may be produced with available resources. The *PPF* is used to illustrate the trade-offs that arise from **scarcity**. Points on the frontier are technically efficient. Points inside the frontier are inefficient, and points outside the frontier are unattainable. The **opportunity cost** of any activity is the highest-valued alternative that must be given up to engage in that activity. Because of increasing marginal opportunity costs, production possibilities frontiers are usually bowed out rather than straight lines. This illustrates the important economic concept that the more resources that are already devoted to any activity, the smaller the payoff from devoting additional resources to that activity is likely to be. **Economic growth** is illustrated by shifting a production possibilities frontier outward.

MyEconLab    Visit **www.myeconlab.com** to complete these exercises online and get instant feedback.

## Review Questions

1.1 What do economists mean by scarcity? Can you think of anything that is not scarce according to the economic definition?

1.2 What is a production possibilities frontier? How can we show economic efficiency on a production possibilities frontier? How can we show inefficiency? What causes a production possibilities frontier to shift outward?

1.3 What does increasing marginal opportunity costs mean? What are the implications of this idea for the shape of the production possibilities frontier?

## Problems and Applications

1.4 Draw a production possibilities frontier that shows the trade-off between the production of cotton and the production of soybeans.

a. Show the effect that a prolonged drought would have on the initial production possibilities frontier.

b. Suppose genetic modification makes soybeans resistant to insects, allowing yields to double. Show the effect of this technological change on the initial production possibilities frontier.

1.5 **[Related to the** Chapter Opener **on page 39]** One of the trade-offs BMW faces is between safety and gas mileage. For example, adding steel to a car makes it safer but also heavier, which results in lower gas mileage. Draw a hypothetical production possibilities frontier that BMW engineers face that shows this trade-off.

1.6 Suppose you win free tickets to a movie plus all you can eat at the snack bar for free. Would there be a cost to you to attend this movie? Explain.

1.7 Suppose we can divide all the goods produced by an economy into two types: consumption goods and capital goods. Capital goods, such as machinery, equipment, and computers, are goods used to produce other goods.

a. Use a production possibilities frontier graph to illustrate the trade-off to an economy between producing consumption goods and producing capital goods. Is it likely that the production possibilities frontier in this situation would be a straight line (as in Figure 2.1 on page 41) or bowed out (as in Figure 2.2 on page 44)? Briefly explain.

b. Suppose a technological change occurs that has a favorable effect on the production of capital goods but not consumption goods. Show the effect on the production possibilities frontier.

c. Suppose that country A and country B currently have identical production possibilities frontiers but that country A devotes only 5 percent of its resources to producing capital goods over each of the next 10 years, whereas country B devotes 30 percent. Which country is likely to experience more rapid economic growth in the future? Illustrate using a production possibilities frontier graph. Your graph should include production possibilities frontiers for country A today and in 10 years and production possibilities frontiers for country B today and in 10 years.

**1.8** Use the following production possibilities frontier for a country to answer the questions.

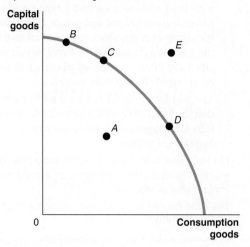

a. Which point or points are unattainable? Briefly explain why.

b. Which point or points are efficient? Briefly explain why.

c. Which point or points are inefficient? Briefly explain why.

d. At which point is the country's future growth rate likely to be the highest? Briefly explain why.

**1.9** [Related to Solved Problem 2.1 **on page 42**] You have exams in economics and chemistry coming up, and you have five hours available for studying. The following table shows the trade-offs you face in allocating the time you will spend in studying each subject:

| | Hours Spent Studying | | Midterm Score | |
| --- | --- | --- | --- | --- |
| Choice | Economics | Chemistry | Economics | Chemistry |
| A | 5 | 0 | 95 | 70 |
| B | 4 | 1 | 93 | 78 |
| C | 3 | 2 | 90 | 84 |
| D | 2 | 3 | 86 | 88 |
| E | 1 | 4 | 81 | 90 |
| F | 0 | 5 | 75 | 91 |

a. Use the data in the table to draw a production possibilities frontier graph. Label the vertical axis "Score on economics exam," and label the horizontal axis "Score on chemistry exam." Make sure to label the values where your production possibilities frontier intersects the vertical and horizontal axes.

b. Label the points representing choice C and choice D. If you are at choice C, what is your opportunity cost of increasing your chemistry score?

c. Under what circumstances would choice A be a sensible choice?

**1.10** [Related to the Making the Connection **on page 43**] Suppose the U.S. president is attempting to decide whether the federal government should spend more on research to find a cure for heart disease. He asks you, one of his economic advisors, to prepare a report discussing the relevant factors he should consider. Use the concepts of opportunity cost and trade-offs to discuss some of the main issues you would deal with in your report.

**1.11** [Related to the Making the Connection **on page 43**] Uwe Reinhardt, an economist at Princeton University, wrote the following in a column in the *New York Times*:

> [Cost-effectiveness analysis] seeks to establish which of several alternative strategies capable of achieving a given therapeutic goal is the least-cost strategy. It seems a sensible form of inquiry in a nation that is dismayed over the rising cost of health care. . . . Opponents of cost-effectiveness analysis include individuals who sincerely believe that health and life are "priceless."

Are health and life priceless? Are there any decisions you make during your everyday life that indicate whether you consider health and life to be priceless?

From Uwe E. Reinhardt, "'Cost-Effectiveness Analysis' and U.S. Health Care," *The New York Times*, March 13, 2009.

**1.12** [Related to the Making the Connection **on page 43**] Suppose that the federal government is deciding which of two cancer treatment therapies it will allow Medicare to pay for (assuming that only one treatment therapy will be funded): Therapy A, which will prolong the average life span of patients receiving the treatment by 24 months and will cost $750,000 per patient treated, and Therapy B, which will prolong the average life span of patients receiving the treatment by 20 months and will cost $25,000 per patient treated. What factors should the federal government take into consideration in making its decision?

**1.13** [Related to the Making the Connection **on page 43**] Lawrence Summers served as secretary of the treasury in the Clinton administration from 1999 to 2001 and as director of the National Economic Council in the Obama administration from 2009 to 2010. He has been quoted as giving the following moral defense of the economic approach:

> There is nothing morally unattractive about saying: We need to analyze which way of spending money on health care will produce more benefit and which less, and using our money as efficiently as we can. I don't think there is anything immoral about seeking to achieve environmental benefits at the lowest possible costs.

Would it be more ethical to reduce pollution without worrying about the cost or by taking the cost into account? Briefly explain.

From "Precepts from Professor Summers," *The Wall Street Journal*, October 17, 2002.

**1.14** In *The Wonderful Wizard of Oz* and his other books about the Land of Oz, L. Frank Baum observed that if people's wants were limited enough, most goods would not be scarce. According to Baum, this was the case in Oz:

> There were no poor people in the Land of Oz, because there was no such thing as money. . . . Each person was given freely by his neighbors whatever he required for his use, which is as much as anyone may reasonably desire. Some tilled the lands and raised great crops of grain, which was divided equally among the whole population, so that all had enough. There were many tailors and dressmakers and shoemakers and the like, who made things that any who desired them might wear. Likewise there were jewelers who made ornaments for the person, which pleased and beautified the people, and these ornaments also were free to those who asked for them. Each man and woman, no

matter what he or she produced for the good of the community, was supplied by the neighbors with food and clothing and a house and furniture and ornaments and games. If by chance the supply ever ran short, more was taken from the great storehouses of the Ruler, which were afterward filled up again when there was more of any article than people needed. . . .

> You will know, by what I have told you here, that the Land of Oz was a remarkable country. I do not suppose such an arrangement would be practical with us.

Do you agree with Baum that the economic system in Oz wouldn't work in the contemporary United States? Briefly explain why or why not.

From *The Emerald City of Oz* by L. Frank Baum, pp. 30–31. First published in 1910.

---

## 2.2 Comparative Advantage and Trade, pages 46–51

LEARNING OBJECTIVE: Understand comparative advantage and explain how it is the basis for trade.

### Summary

Fundamentally, markets are about **trade**, which is the act of buying or selling. People trade on the basis of comparative advantage. An individual, a firm, or a country has a **comparative advantage** in producing a good or service if it can produce the good or service at the lowest opportunity cost. People are usually better off specializing in the activity for which they have a comparative advantage and trading for the other goods and services they need. It is important not to confuse comparative advantage with absolute advantage. An individual, a firm, or a country has an **absolute advantage** in producing a good or service if it can produce more of that good or service using the same amount of resources. It is possible to have an absolute advantage in producing a good or service without having a comparative advantage.

 Visit **www.myeconlab.com** to complete these exercises online and get instant feedback.

### Review Questions

2.1  What is absolute advantage? What is comparative advantage? Is it possible for a country to have a comparative advantage in producing a good without also having an absolute advantage? Briefly explain.

2.2  What is the basis for trade: absolute advantage or comparative advantage? How can an individual or a country gain from specialization and trade?

### Problems and Applications

2.3  Look again at the information in Figure 2.4 on page 47. Choose a rate of trading cherries for apples different from the rate used in the text (15 pounds of cherries for 10 pounds of apples) that will allow you and your neighbor

to benefit from trading apples and cherries. Prepare a table like Table 2.1 on page 48 to illustrate your answer.

2.4  Using the same amount of resources, the United States and Canada can both produce lumberjack shirts and lumberjack boots, as shown in the following production possibilities frontiers:

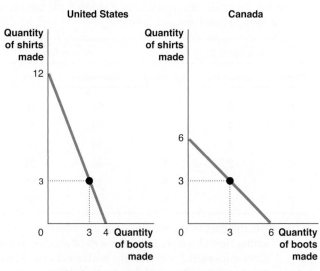

a.  Who has a comparative advantage in producing lumberjack boots? Who has a comparative advantage in producing lumberjack shirts? Explain your reasoning.

b.  Does either country have an absolute advantage in producing both goods? Explain.

c.  Suppose that both countries are currently producing three pairs of boots and three shirts. Show that both can be better off if they each specialize in producing one good and then engage in trade.

2.5  **[Related to** Don't Let This Happen to You **on page 49]** In the 1950s, the economist Bela Balassa compared 28 manufacturing industries in the United States and Britain. In every one of the 28 industries, Balassa found that the United States had an absolute advantage. In these circumstances, would there have been any gain to the United States from importing any of these products from Britain? Explain.

**2.6** [Related to Solved Problem 2.2 **on page 50**] Suppose Iran and Iraq both produce oil and olive oil, which sell for the same prices in both countries. The following table shows combinations of both goods that using the same amounts of capital and labor each country can produce in a day, measured in thousands of barrels:

| Iraq | | Iran | |
|---|---|---|---|
| Oil | Olive Oil | Oil | Olive Oil |
| 0 | 8 | 0 | 4 |
| 2 | 6 | 1 | 3 |
| 4 | 4 | 2 | 2 |
| 6 | 2 | 3 | 1 |
| 8 | 0 | 4 | 0 |

a. Who has the comparative advantage in producing oil? Explain.

b. Can these two countries gain from trading oil and olive oil? Explain.

**2.7** [Related to Solved Problem 2.2 **on page 50**] Suppose that France and Germany both produce schnitzel and wine. The following table shows combinations of the goods that each country can produce in a day:

| France | | Germany | |
|---|---|---|---|
| Wine (bottles) | Schnitzel (pounds) | Wine (bottles) | Schnitzel (pounds) |
| 0 | 8 | 0 | 15 |
| 1 | 6 | 1 | 12 |
| 2 | 4 | 2 | 9 |
| 3 | 2 | 3 | 6 |
| 4 | 0 | 4 | 3 |
| | | 5 | 0 |

a. Who has a comparative advantage in producing wine? Who has a comparative advantage in producing schnitzel?

b. Suppose that France is currently producing 1 bottle of wine and 6 pounds of schnitzel, and Germany is currently producing 3 bottles of wine and 6 pounds of schnitzel. Demonstrate that France and Germany can both be better off if they specialize in producing only one good and then engage in trade.

**2.8** Can an individual or a country produce beyond its production possibilities frontier? Can an individual or a country consume beyond its production possibilities frontier? Explain.

**2.9** If Country A can produce with the same amount of resources twice as much coffee as Country B, explain how Country B could have the comparative advantage in producing coffee.

**2.10** Imagine that the next time the Indianapolis Colts play the New England Patriots at Lucas Oil Stadium in Indianapolis, Colts star quarterback Peyton Manning has a temporary lack of judgment and plans to sell Colts memorabilia during the game because he realizes that he can sell five times more Colts products than any other player. Likewise, imagine that you are a creative and effective manager at work and that you tell your employees that during the next six months, you plan to clean the offices because you can clean five times better than the cleaning staff. What error in judgment are both Peyton and you making? Why shouldn't you do what you are better than anyone else at doing?

**2.11** Is specialization and trade between individuals and countries more about having a job or about obtaining a higher standard of living? Individually, if you go from a situation of not trading with others (you produce everything yourself) to a situation of trading with others, do you still have a job? Does your standard of living increase? Likewise, if a country goes from not trading with other countries to trading with other countries, does it still have jobs? Does its standard of living increase?

**2.12** In colonial America, the population was spread thinly over a large area, and transportation costs were very high because it was difficult to ship products by road for more than short distances. As a result, most of the free population lived on small farms, where they not only grew their own food but also usually made their own clothes and very rarely bought or sold anything for money. Explain why the incomes of these farmers were likely to rise as transportation costs fell. Use the concept of comparative advantage in your answer.

**2.13** During the 1928 presidential election campaign, Herbert Hoover, the Republican candidate, argued that the United States should import only products that could not be produced here. Do you believe that this would be a good policy? Explain.

---

**2.3** **The Market System, pages 51–58**

LEARNING OBJECTIVE: Explain the basic idea of how a market system works.

## Summary

A **market** is a group of buyers and sellers of a good or service and the institution or arrangement by which they come together to trade. **Product markets** are markets for goods and services, such as computers and medical treatment. **Factor markets** are markets for the **factors of production**, such as labor, capital, natural resources, and entrepreneurial ability. A **circular-flow diagram** shows how participants in product markets and factor markets are linked. Adam Smith argued in his 1776 book *The Wealth of Nations* that in a **free market**, where the government does not control the production of goods and services, changes in prices lead firms to produce the goods and services most desired by consumers. If consumers demand more of a good, its price will rise. Firms respond to rising prices by increasing production. If consumers demand less of a good, its price will fall. Firms respond to falling prices by producing less of a good. An **entrepreneur** is someone who operates a business. In the market system, entrepreneurs are responsible for organizing the production of goods and services. The market system will work well only if there is protection for **property rights**, which are the rights of individuals and firms to use their property.

MyEconLab    Visit **www.myeconlab.com** to complete these exercises online and get instant feedback.

## Review Questions

**3.1** What is a circular-flow diagram, and what does it demonstrate?

**3.2** What are the two main categories of participants in markets? Which participants are of greatest importance in determining what goods and services are produced?

**3.3** What is a free market? In what ways does a free market economy differ from a centrally planned economy?

**3.4** What is an entrepreneur? Why do entrepreneurs play a key role in a market system?

**3.5** Under what circumstances are firms likely to produce more of a good or service? Under what circumstances are firms likely to produce less of a good or service?

**3.6** What are private property rights? What role do they play in the working of a market system? Why are independent courts important for a well-functioning economy?

## Problems and Applications

**3.7** Identify whether each of the following transactions will take place in the factor market or in the product market and whether households or firms are supplying the good or service or demanding the good or service:

**a.** George buys a BMW X6 hybrid.

**b.** BMW increases employment at its Spartanburg plant.

**c.** George works 20 hours per week at McDonald's.

**d.** George sells land he owns to McDonald's so it can build a new restaurant.

**3.8** [Related to the Making the Connection **on page 55**] In *The Wealth of Nations*, Adam Smith wrote the following (Book I, Chapter II): "It is not from the benevolence of the butcher, the brewer, or the baker, that we expect our dinner, but from their regard to their own interest." Briefly discuss what he meant by this.

**3.9** [Related to the Making the Connection **on page 55**] According to an article in the *Wall Street Journal*, the parts contained in the BlackBerry Torch smartphone include a power management chip made by Texas Instruments (United States), a memory chip made by Samsung (South Korea), a GPS receiver made by CSR (United Kingdom), a radio frequency (RF) transceiver made by Dialog Semiconductor (Germany), an RF transceiver made by Renesas (Japan), an application and communications processor made by Marvell (United States), a video image processor made by STMicroelectronics (Switzerland), and plastic and stamped metal parts made by several firms in China. A firm in Mexico carries out final assembly of the Torch before it is shipped to BlackBerry for sale in the United

States and other countries. Is it necessary for the managers in all of these firms to know how the components of the Torch are manufactured and how the components are assembled into a smartphone? Is it necessary for the chief executive officer (CEO) of BlackBerry to know this information? Briefly explain.

Based on Jennifer Valentino-DeVries and Phred Dvorak, "Piece by Piece: The Suppliers behind the New BlackBerry Torch Smartphone." *The Wall Street Journal*, August 16, 2010.

**3.10** In many parts of Europe during the mid-1770s, governments gave guilds, or organizations of producers, the authority to control who was allowed to produce a good, the amount of the good produced, and the price charged for the good. Would you expect more competition among producers in a *guild system* or in a market system? Was the consumer or the producer at the center of the guild system, and which is at the center of the market system? How would the two systems compare over time in terms of innovation of new products and technologies?

**3.11** In a speech at the New York University Law School, Federal Reserve Chairman Ben Bernanke stated:

> Writing in the eighteenth century, Adam Smith conceived of the free-market system as an "invisible hand" that harnesses the pursuit of private interest to promote the public good. Smith's conception remains relevant today, notwithstanding the enormous increase in economic complexity since the Industrial Revolution.

Briefly explain the idea of the invisible hand. What's so important about the idea of the invisible hand?

From Ben S. Bernanke, "Financial Regulation and the Invisible Hand," speech made at the New York University Law School, New York, New York, April 11, 2007.

**3.12** Evaluate the following argument: "Adam Smith's analysis is based on a fundamental flaw: He assumes that people are motivated by self-interest. But this isn't true. I'm not selfish, and most people I know aren't selfish."

**3.13** Writing in the *New York Times*, Michael Lewis argued that "a market economy is premised on a system of incentives designed to encourage an ignoble human trait: self-interest." Do you agree that self-interest is an "ignoble human trait"? What incentives does a market system provide to encourage self-interest?

From Michael Lewis, "In Defense of the Boom," *The New York Times*, October 27, 2002.

**3.14** Some economists have been puzzled that although entrepreneurs take on the risk of losing time and money by starting new businesses, on average their incomes are lower than those of people with similar characteristics who go to work at large firms. Economist William Baumol believes part of the explanation for this puzzle may be that entrepreneurs are like people who buy lottery tickets. On average, people who don't buy lottery tickets are left with more money than people who buy tickets because lotteries take in more money than they give out. Baumol argues that "the masses of purchasers who grab up the [lottery] tickets are not irrational if they receive an adequate payment in another currency: psychic rewards."

a. What are "psychic rewards"?

b. What psychic rewards might an entrepreneur receive?

c. Do you agree with Baumol that an entrepreneur is like someone buying a lottery ticket? Briefly explain.

From William J. Baumol, *The Microtheory of Innovative Entrepreneurship*, (Princeton, NJ: Princeton University Press, 2010).

**3.15** The 2009 International Property Rights Index study states:

Data shows that countries that protect the physical and intellectual property of their people enjoy nearly nine times higher [income per person] . . . than countries ranking lowest in property rights protections. The study . . . compared the protections of physical and intellectual property to economic stability in 115 countries. . . .

How would the creation of property rights be likely to affect the economic opportunities available to citizens of those countries ranking lowest in property rights protections?

Based on Kelsey Zahourek, "Report: Property Rights Linked to Economic Security," *International Property Rights Index 2009 Report.*

# Where Prices Come From: The Interaction of Demand and Supply

## Chapter Outline and Learning Objectives

# The Tablet Computer Revolution

Bill Gates, who was then chairman of Microsoft, made a famous—but wrong!—prediction in 2001. At a computer industry trade show, he predicted that tablet computers would make up a majority of personal computer sales within five years. Microsoft had developed new software that made it possible to use a stylus to write on a laptop computer screen, and Gates hoped that consumers would respond to compact lightweight computers. But many consumers found them awkward to use and thought that the prices, at $2,000 or more, were too high. As a result, rather than making up a majority of computer sales in 2006, tablets were just 1 percent of the market.

Fast forward to 2010: After years of stating that his company would not enter the market for netbooks—or lightweight computers smaller than laptops—Apple CEO Steve Jobs introduced the iPad in April. The iPad was an immediate success, selling nearly 15 million units by the end of the year. The iPad 2, released in early 2011, experienced similarly rapid sales.

The iPad was very different from the tablet computers that had failed to win favor with consumers a few years earlier. The iPad was more awkward to use for word processing or working on spreadsheets, but it was lighter than earlier tablets, and its wireless connectivity and portability made it better for Web surfing, checking e-mail, texting, and watching videos.

Although initially Apple had the market for new-style tablets largely to itself, competitors appeared rapidly. Toshiba, Samsung, Dell, LG, Motorola, Lenovo, Amazon, and ZTE all introduced tablets running on Google's Android operating system. Research in Motion (RIM) introduced the BlackBerry Playbook, based on its operating system.

The intense competition among firms selling the new tablets is a striking example of how the market responds to changes in consumer tastes. As many consumers indicated that they would buy small tablets, firms scrambled to meet the demand for this new product. Although intense competition is not always good news for firms trying to sell products, it is a boon to consumers because it increases the available choice of products and lowers the prices consumers pay for those products.

**AN INSIDE LOOK** on **page 92** discusses how the many tablet producers are concerned about component shortages.

Based on Matt Berger and James Niccolai, "Gates Unveils Portable Tablet PC," *PC World*, November 12, 2001; Wolfgang Gruener, "240 Million Tablets: The Gazillion-Dollar Forecast Game," www.fool.com, February 6, 2011; David Pogue, "Pretty Tablet, Though Late for the Ball," *New York Times*, June 29, 2011; and Stu Woo and Yukari Iwatani Kane, "Amazon to Battle Apple iPad with Tablet," *Wall Street Journal*, July 14, 2011.

## Economics in Your Life

### Will You Buy an Apple iPad or a Samsung Galaxy Tab?

Suppose you are considering buying a tablet computer and that you are choosing between an Apple iPad and a Samsung Galaxy Tab. Apple introduced the iPad in April 2010, and Samsung introduced the Galaxy Tab in November 2010; seven months is a long time in the world of high-tech gadgets. Apple products have become very fashionable, and if you buy an iPad, you will have access to many more applications—or "apps"—that can increase the enjoyability and productivity of your tablet. One strategy Samsung can use to overcome those advantages is to compete based on price and value. Would you choose to buy a Galaxy Tab if it had a lower price than an iPad? If your income increased, would it affect your decision about which tablet to buy? As you read the chapter, see if you can answer these questions. You can check your answers against those we provide **page 91** at the end of this chapter.

I n Chapter 1, we explored how economists use models to predict human behavior. In Chapter 2, we used the model of production possibilities frontiers to analyze scarcity and trade-offs. In this chapter and the next, we explore the model of demand and supply, which is the most powerful tool in economics, and use it to explain how prices are determined.

Recall from Chapter 1 that because economic models rely on assumptions, the models are simplifications of reality. In some cases, the assumptions of the model may not seem to describe exactly the economic situation being analyzed. For example, the model of demand and supply assumes that we are analyzing a *perfectly competitive market*. In a **perfectly competitive market**, there are many buyers and sellers, all the products sold are identical, and there are no barriers to new firms entering the market. These assumptions are very restrictive and apply exactly to only a few markets, such as the markets for wheat and other agricultural products. Experience has shown, however, that the model of demand and supply can be very useful in analyzing markets where competition among sellers is intense, even if there are relatively few sellers and the products being sold are not identical. In fact, in recent studies, the model of demand and supply has been successful in analyzing markets with as few as four buyers and four sellers. In the end, the usefulness of a model depends on how well it can predict outcomes in a market. As we will see in this chapter, this model is often very useful in predicting changes in quantities and prices in many markets.

We begin considering the model of demand and supply by discussing consumers and the demand side of the market, before turning to firms and the supply side. Throughout the book we will apply this model to understand business, the economy, and economic policy.

**Perfectly competitive market** A market that meets the conditions of (1) many buyers and sellers, (2) all firms selling identical products, and (3) no barriers to new firms entering the market.

---

Discuss the variables that influence demand.

# The Demand Side of the Market

Chapter 2 explained that in a market system, consumers ultimately determine which goods and services will be produced. The most successful businesses are the ones that respond best to consumer demand. But what determines consumer demand for a product? Certainly, many factors influence the willingness of consumers to buy a particular product. For example, consumers who are considering buying a tablet computer, such as an Apple iPad or an Samsung Galaxy Tab, will make their decisions based on, among other factors, the income they have available to spend and the effectiveness of the advertising campaigns of the companies that sell tablets. The main factor in most consumer decisions, though, is the price of the product. So, it makes sense to begin with price when analyzing the decisions of consumers to buy a product. It is important to note that when we discuss demand, we are considering not what a consumer *wants* to buy but what the consumer is both willing and *able* to buy.

## Demand Schedules and Demand Curves

Tables that show the relationship between the price of a product and the quantity of the product demanded are called **demand schedules**. The table in Figure 3.1 shows the number of tablet computers consumers would be willing to buy over the course of a day at five different prices. The amount of a good or a service that a consumer is willing and able to purchase at a given price is referred to as the **quantity demanded**. The graph in Figure 3.1 plots the numbers from the table as a **demand curve**, a curve that shows the relationship between the price of a product and the quantity of the product demanded. (Note that for convenience, we made the demand curve in Figure 3.1 a straight line, or linear. There is no reason that all demand curves need to be straight lines.) The demand curve in Figure 3.1 shows the **market demand**, or the demand by all the consumers of a given good or service. The market for a product, such as restaurant meals, that is

**Demand schedule** A table that shows the relationship between the price of a product and the quantity of the product demanded.

**Quantity demanded** The amount of a good or service that a consumer is willing and able to purchase at a given price.

**Demand curve** A curve that shows the relationship between the price of a product and the quantity of the product demanded.

**Market demand** The demand by all the consumers of a given good or service.

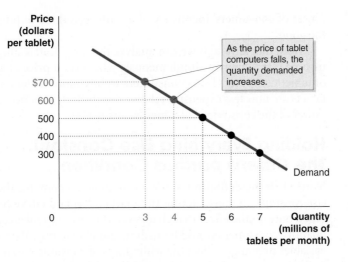

| Demand Schedule | |
|---|---|
| Price (dollars per tablet) | Quantity (millions of tablets per month) |
| $700 | 3 |
| 600 | 4 |
| 500 | 5 |
| 400 | 6 |
| 300 | 7 |

As the price of tablet computers falls, the quantity demanded increases.

### Figure 3.1

### A Demand Schedule and Demand Curve

As the price changes, consumers change the quantity of tablet computers they are willing to buy. We can show this as a *demand schedule* in a table or as a *demand curve* on a graph. The table and graph both show that as the price of tablet computers falls, the quantity demanded increases. When the price of tablet computers is $700, consumers buy 3 million tablets per month. When the price drops to $600, consumers buy 4 million tablets. Therefore, the demand curve for tablet computers is downward sloping.

purchased locally would include all the consumers in a city or a relatively small area. The market for a product that is sold internationally, such as tablet computers, would include all the consumers in the world.

The demand curve in Figure 3.1 slopes downward because consumers will buy more tablets as the price falls. When the price of a tablet is $700, consumers buy 3 million tablets per month. If the price of a tablet falls to $600, consumers buy 4 million tablets. Buyers demand a larger quantity of a product as the price falls because the product becomes less expensive relative to other products and because they can afford to buy more at a lower price.

## The Law of Demand

The inverse relationship between the price of a product and the quantity of the product demanded is called the **law of demand**: Holding everything else constant, when the price of a product falls, the quantity demanded of the product will increase, and when the price of a product rises, the quantity demanded of the product will decrease. The law of demand holds for any market demand curve. Economists have found only a very few exceptions to this law.

**Law of demand** The rule that, holding everything else constant, when the price of a product falls, the quantity demanded of the product will increase, and when the price of a product rises, the quantity demanded of the product will decrease.

## What Explains the Law of Demand?

It makes sense that consumers will buy more of a good when the price falls and less of a good when the price rises, but let's look more closely at why this is true. When the price of tablet computers falls, consumers buy a larger quantity because of the *substitution effect* and the *income effect*.

**Substitution Effect**  The **substitution effect** refers to the change in the quantity demanded of a good that results from a change in price, making the good more or less expensive *relative* to other goods that are *substitutes*. When the price of tablet computers falls, consumers will substitute buying tablet computers for buying other goods, such as laptop computers, netbook computers, or even smartphones.

**Substitution effect**  The change in the quantity demanded of a good that results from a change in price, making the good more or less expensive relative to other goods that are substitutes.

**The Income Effect**  The **income effect** of a price change refers to the change in the quantity demanded of a good that results from the effect of a change in the good's price on consumers' purchasing power. Purchasing power is the quantity of goods a consumer can buy with a fixed amount of income. When the price of a good falls, the increased purchasing power of consumers' incomes will usually lead them to purchase a larger quantity of the good. When the price of a good rises, the decreased purchasing

**Income effect**  The change in the quantity demanded of a good that results from the effect of a change in the good's price on consumers' purchasing power.

power of consumers' incomes will usually lead them to purchase a smaller quantity of the good.

Note that although we can analyze them separately, the substitution effect and the income effect happen simultaneously whenever a price changes. So, a fall in the price of tablet computers leads consumers to buy more tablet computers, both because the tablets are now less expensive relative to substitute products and because the purchasing power of the consumers' incomes has increased.

## Holding Everything Else Constant: The *Ceteris paribus* Condition

*Ceteris paribus* ("all else equal") condition The requirement that when analyzing the relationship between two variables—such as price and quantity demanded—other variables must be held constant.

Notice that the definition of the law of demand contains the phrase *holding everything else constant*. In constructing the market demand curve for tablet computers, we focused only on the effect that changes in the price of tablet computers would have on the quantity consumers would be willing and able to buy. We were holding constant other variables that might affect the willingness of consumers to buy tablets. Economists refer to the necessity of holding all variables other than price constant in constructing a demand curve as the **ceteris paribus** condition; *ceteris paribus* is Latin for "all else equal."

What would happen if we allowed a change in a variable—other than price—that might affect the willingness of consumers to buy tablet computers? Consumers would then change the quantity they demanded at each price. We can illustrate this effect by shifting the market demand curve. A shift of a demand curve is *an increase or a decrease in demand*. A movement along a demand curve is *an increase or a decrease in the quantity demanded*. As Figure 3.2 shows, we shift the demand curve to the right if consumers decide to buy more of the good at each price, and we shift the demand curve to the left if consumers decide to buy less at each price.

## Variables That Shift Market Demand

Many variables other than price can influence market demand. These five are the most important:

- Income
- Prices of related goods
- Tastes
- Population and demographics
- Expected future prices

We next discuss how changes in each of these variables affect the market demand curve.

### Figure 3.2

**Shifting the Demand Curve**

When consumers increase the quantity of a product they want to buy at a given price, the market demand curve shifts to the right, from $D_1$ to $D_2$. When consumers decrease the quantity of a product they want to buy at a given price, the demand curve shifts to the left, from $D_1$ to $D_3$.

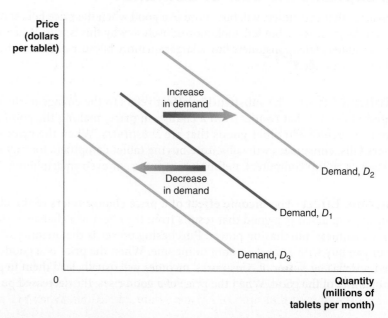

**Income**  The income that consumers have available to spend affects their willingness and ability to buy a good. Suppose that the market demand curve in Figure 3.1 on page 71 represents the willingness of consumers to buy tablet computers when average household income is $50,000. If household income rises to $52,000, the demand for tablets will increase, which we show by shifting the demand curve to the right. A good is a **normal good** when demand increases following a rise in income and decreases following a fall in income. Most goods are normal goods, but the demand for some goods falls when income rises and rises when income falls. For instance, as your income rises, you might buy less canned tuna or fewer hot dogs and buy more shrimp or prime rib. A good is an **inferior good** when demand decreases following a rise in income and increases following a fall in income. So, for you, canned tuna and hot dogs would be examples of inferior goods—not because they are of low quality but because you buy less of them as your income increases.

**Normal good**  A good for which the demand increases as income rises and decreases as income falls.

**Inferior good**  A good for which the demand increases as income falls and decreases as income rises.

| Making the Connection | ## Are Quiznos Sandwiches Normal Goods and Subway Sandwiches Inferior Goods? |
|---|---|

In recent years, as American families juggle busy schedules, they have increasingly relied on eating out rather than preparing meals at home. According to a survey by *Restaurants and Institutions* magazine, adults eat an average of nearly four meals per week outside the home. Nearly one-third of consumers frequently eat lunch away from home, and on weekdays more than 15 percent frequently eat dinner away from home, a proportion that rises to more than 35 percent on weekends.

Does this behavior change during a recession? We might expect that it would because recessions result in declining incomes, as some people lose their jobs and others are forced to work fewer hours or have their wages reduced. Dining out is more expensive than preparing meals at home, so one way to save during a recession is to cut back on restaurant meals. In fact, during the 2007–2009 recession, many restaurants had a difficult time. Particularly hard hit were "casual dining" restaurants that provide table service and serve moderately priced food. Among other restaurants, Ruby Tuesday, Olive Garden, Red Lobster, and LongHorn Steakhouse all experienced declining demand, while Bennigan's and Steak and Ale filed for bankruptcy.

*Subway experienced increased sales during 2008 and 2009, while sales of Quiznos sandwiches fell.*

However, the recession hurt some restaurants more than others. McDonald's restaurants experienced increased sales during 2008 and 2009. In the market for fast-food sandwiches, Subway reported increasing sales, while sales of Quiznos sandwiches, which are higher-priced, fell. So, Big Macs and Subway sandwiches seem to fit the economic definition of an inferior good because demand increases as income falls, while Quiznos sandwiches fit the definition of a normal good. But remember that inferior goods are not necessarily of low quality; they are just goods for which consumers increase their demand as their incomes fall.

Based on Julie Jargon and Mike Spector, "LBO, Recession Singe Quiznos," *Wall Street Journal*, July 21, 2011; Melodie Warner, "McDonald's Profit Rises 15%," *Wall Street Journal*, July 22, 2011; and "The New American Diner," *Restaurants and Institutions*, January 1, 2008.

**Your Turn:** For more practice, do related problem 1.11 on page 95 at the end of this chapter.     MyEconLab

**Prices of Related Goods**  The prices of other goods can also affect consumers' demand for a product. Goods and services that can be used for the same purpose—such as tablet computers and laptop computers—are **substitutes**. When two goods are

**Substitutes**  Goods and services that can be used for the same purpose.

substitutes, the more you buy of one, the less you will buy of the other. A decrease in the price of a substitute causes the demand curve for a good to shift to the left. An increase in the price of a substitute causes the demand curve for a good to shift to the right.

Suppose that the market demand curve in Figure 3.1 on page 71 represents the willingness and ability of consumers to buy laptop computers during a week when the average price of a laptop computer is $800. If the average price of laptops falls to $700, how will the market demand for tablets change? Consumers will demand fewer tablets at every price. We show this by shifting the demand curve for tablets to the left.

**Complements** Goods and services that are used together.

Goods and services that are used together—such as hot dogs and hot dog buns— are **complements**. When two goods are complements, the more consumers buy of one, the more they will buy of the other. A decrease in the price of a complement causes the demand curve for a good to shift to the right. An increase in the price of a complement causes the demand curve for a good to shift to the left.

Many people use applications, or "apps," on their tablet computers. So, tablets and apps are complements. Suppose the market demand curve in Figure 3.1 represents the willingness of consumers to buy tablets at a time when the average price of an app is $2.99. If the average price of apps drops to $0.99, consumers will buy more apps *and* more tablets: The demand curve for tablets will shift to the right.

**Tastes** Consumers can be influenced by an advertising campaign for a product. If Apple, Samsung, Amazon, and other firms making tablet computers begin to advertise heavily online, consumers are more likely to buy tablets at every price, and the demand curve will shift to the right. An economist would say that the advertising campaign has affected consumers' *taste* for tablet computers. Taste is a catchall category that refers to the many subjective elements that can enter into a consumer's decision to buy a product. A consumer's taste for a product can change for many reasons. Sometimes trends play a substantial role. For example, the popularity of low-carbohydrate diets caused a decline in demand for some goods, such as bread and donuts, and an increase in demand for beef. In general, when consumers' taste for a product increases, the demand curve will shift to the right, and when consumers' taste for a product decreases, the demand curve for the product will shift to the left.

**Population and Demographics** Population and demographic factors can affect the demand for a product. As the population of the United States increases, so will the number of consumers, and the demand for most products will increase. The **demographics** of a population refers to its characteristics, with respect to age, race, and gender. As the demographics of a country or region change, the demand for particular goods will increase or decrease because different categories of people tend to have different preferences for those goods. For instance, Hispanics are expected to increase from 16 percent of the U.S. population in 2010 to 29 percent in 2050. This increase will expand demand for Spanish-language books and cable television channels, among other goods and services.

**Demographics** The characteristics of a population with respect to age, race, and gender.

Making the Connection | **The Aging of the Baby Boom Generation**

The average age of the U.S. population is increasing. After World War II in 1945, the United States experienced a "baby boom," as birthrates rose and remained high through the early 1960s. Falling birthrates after 1965 mean that the baby boom generation is larger than the generation before it and the generations after it. The figure on the next page uses projections from the U.S. Census Bureau to show that as boomers age, they are increasing the fraction of the U.S. population that is older than 65.

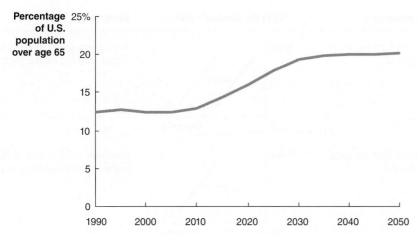

Data from U.S. Census Bureau.

What effects will the aging of the baby boom generation have on the economy? Older people have a greater demand for medical care than do younger people. So, in coming years, the demand for doctors, nurses, and hospital facilities should all increase. The increasing demand for health care is so strong that between the beginning of the 2007–2009 recession and June 2011, 1 million new jobs were created in health care—at the same time as total employment in the United States *declined* by 7 million jobs. As we mentioned in Chapter 2, the increased demand for medical care will also drive up the federal government's costs under the Medicare program, which pays part of the medical bills of people who are 65 and older.

Aging boomers will also have an effect on the housing market. Older people often "downsize" their housing by moving from large, single-family homes, whose maintenance can be difficult and expensive, to smaller homes, condominiums, or apartments. So, in coming years, the demand for large homes may decrease, while the demand for smaller homes and apartments may increase. Older people also tend to drive less often and for shorter distances than do younger drivers. So, their cars wear out more slowly and, therefore, need to be replaced less often, reducing the total demand for cars.

Based on U.S. Bureau of Labor Statistics, "Employment, Hours, and Earnings from the Current Employment Statistics Survey," July 2011; Liam Denning, "Car Makers Hit the Age Speed Bump," *Wall Street Journal*, September 18, 2010; Kendra Marr, "The Economy's Steady Pulse—Health-Care Sector Is Poised to Keep Expanding, but So Are Its Costs," *Washington Post*, June 13, 2008; and Peter Francese, "The Changing Face of the U.S. Consumer," *Advertising Age*, July 7, 2008.

**Your Turn:** For more practice, do related problems 1.12 and 1.13 on page 95 at the end of this chapter.     MyEconLab

**Expected Future Prices**  Consumers choose not only which products to buy but also when to buy them. For instance, if enough consumers become convinced that houses will be selling for lower prices in three months, the demand for houses will decrease now, as some consumers postpone their purchases to wait for the expected price decrease. Alternatively, if enough consumers become convinced that the price of houses will be higher in three months, the demand for houses will increase now, as some consumers try to beat the expected price increase.

Table 3.1 on page 76 summarizes the most important variables that cause market demand curves to shift. Note that the table shows the shift in the demand curve that results from an *increase* in each of the variables. A *decrease* in these variables would cause the demand curve to shift in the opposite direction.

## A Change in Demand versus a Change in Quantity Demanded

It is important to understand the difference between a *change in demand* and a *change in quantity demanded*. A change in demand refers to a shift of the demand curve. A shift occurs if there is a change in one of the variables, *other than the price of the product*, that

**Table 3.1**

**Variables That Shift Market Demand Curves**

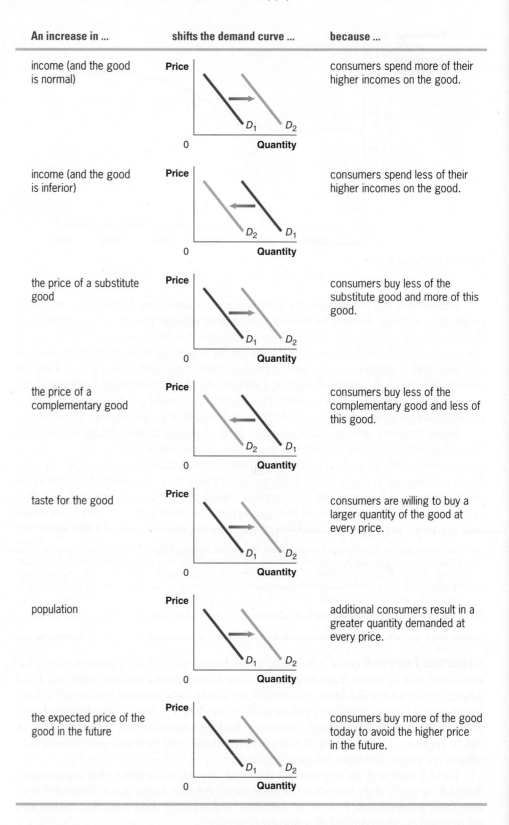

| An increase in ... | shifts the demand curve ... | because ... |
| --- | --- | --- |
| income (and the good is normal) | | consumers spend more of their higher incomes on the good. |
| income (and the good is inferior) | | consumers spend less of their higher incomes on the good. |
| the price of a substitute good | | consumers buy less of the substitute good and more of this good. |
| the price of a complementary good | | consumers buy less of the complementary good and less of this good. |
| taste for the good | | consumers are willing to buy a larger quantity of the good at every price. |
| population | | additional consumers result in a greater quantity demanded at every price. |
| the expected price of the good in the future | | consumers buy more of the good today to avoid the higher price in the future. |

affects the willingness of consumers to buy the product. A change in quantity demanded refers to a movement along the demand curve as a result of a change in the product's price. Figure 3.3 illustrates this important distinction. If the price of tablet computers falls from $700 to $600 per tablet, the result will be a movement along the demand curve from point *A* to point *B*—an increase in quantity demanded from 3 million to 4 million. If consumers' incomes increase, or if another factor changes that makes consumers want more of the product at every price, the demand curve will shift to the right—an increase

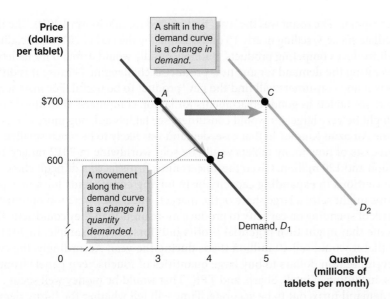

**Figure 3.3**

**A Change in Demand versus a Change in Quantity Demanded**

If the price of tablet computers falls from $700 to $600, the result will be a movement along the demand curve from point *A* to point *B*—an increase in quantity demanded from 3 million tablets to 4 million tablets. If consumers' incomes increase, or if another factor changes that makes consumers want more of the product at every price, the demand curve will shift to the right—an increase in demand. In this case, the increase in demand from $D_1$ to $D_2$ causes the quantity of tablet computers demanded at a price of $700 to increase from 3 million tablets at point *A* to 5 million tablets at point *C*.

in demand. In this case, the increase in demand from $D_1$ to $D_2$ causes the quantity of tablet computers demanded at a price of $700 to increase from 3 million at point *A* to 5 million at point *C*.

| **Making the Connection** | **Forecasting the Demand for iPads** |

One of the most important decisions that the managers of any large firm face is which new products to develop. A firm must devote people, time, and money to designing a new product, negotiating with suppliers, formulating a marketing campaign, and many other tasks. But any firm has only limited resources and so faces a trade-off: Resources used to develop one product will not be available to develop another product. Ultimately, the products a firm chooses to develop will be those that it believes will be the most profitable. So, to decide which products to develop, firms need to forecast the demand for those products.

We saw at the beginning of the chapter that in 2001, Bill Gates predicted that within five years, a majority of computers sold would be tablets. If Gates had been correct about the way the computer market was changing, then any computer firm that didn't develop a tablet would have run the risk of being left behind. David Sobotta, who worked at Apple for 20 years and eventually became its national sales manager, has described discussions at Apple during 2002 about whether to develop a tablet. According to Sobotta, representatives of the federal government's National Institutes of Health urged Apple to develop a tablet computer, arguing that it would be particularly useful to doctors, nurses, and hospitals. Apple's managers decided not to develop a tablet, however, because they believed the technology available at that time was too complex for the average computer user and they also believed that the demand from doctors and nurses would be small. As we saw in the chapter opener, Apple's forecast was correct. Despite Bill Gates's prediction, in 2006, tablets made up only 1 percent of the computer market. According to Sobotta, "Apple executives had a theory that the route to success will not be through selling thousands of relatively expensive things, but millions of very inexpensive things like iPods."

Apple continued to work on tablets, though, developing the technology to eliminate keyboards in favor of touchscreen displays. Rather than proceed immediately to building a tablet, Steve Jobs, who was then Apple's CEO, realized he could use this technology in a different way: "I thought 'My God we can build a phone out of this.'" After the technology had been successfully embodied in the iPhone, Apple and Jobs turned back to developing

*Will the future demand for tablets such as the iPad continue to grow?*

a tablet computer. The result was the iPad, first offered for sale in April 2010. The iPad was an immediate success, selling nearly 15 million units by the end of 2010 and leading other firms to introduce competing products. But how rapidly would demand for tablets grow?

Forecasting the demand for any new product is challenging because it is difficult to gauge how many consumers will find the new product to be useful. For instance, would consumers see tablets as good replacements for laptop computers? If so, the demand for tablets might be very large. Or would consumers see tablets as being more like e-readers, such as the Amazon Kindle? In that case, demand was likely to be much smaller. In mid-2011, forecasts of how many tablets would be sold worldwide in 2012 ranged between 54.8 million and 120 million. Given this uncertainty, firms faced a difficult choice: If they were too cautious in expanding capacity or in buying components for a new product, other firms might seize a large share of the market. But if they were too optimistic, they ran the risk of spending on capacity to produce more units than they could actually sell—an outcome that might turn potential profits into losses. For example, in 2011, Apple forecast that it would sell 40 million iPads during the year. Accordingly, the company spent several billion dollars to buy large quantities of touchscreen panels from manufacturers, including Wintek, Sharp, and TPK. That would be money well spent . . . if the forecast demand turns out to be accurate. Time will tell whether the future demand for tablets will be as large as Apple and other firms were forecasting it would be during 2011.

Based on Wolfgang Gruener, "240 Million Tablets: The Gazillion-Dollar Forecast Game," www.fool.com, February 6, 2011; "Apple Conference Call on Q1 2011 Financial Results," www.apple.com, January 18, 2011; David Sobotta, "What Jobs Told Me on the iPhone," *The Guardian* (London), January 3, 2007, p. 1; "Jobs Says iPad Idea Came Before iPhone," *Associated Press*, January 2, 2010; and Laura June, "The Apple Tablet: A Complete History, Supposedly," endgadget.com, January 26, 2010.

MyEconLab **Your Turn:** For more practice, do related problem 1.16 on page 95 at the end of this chapter.

do related problem 1.16 on page 95

---

**3.2 LEARNING** OBJECTIVE

Discuss the variables that influence supply.

# The Supply Side of the Market

Just as many variables influence the willingness and ability of consumers to buy a particular good or service, many variables also influence the willingness and ability of firms to sell a good or service. The most important of these variables is price. The amount of a good or service that a firm is willing and able to supply at a given price is the **quantity supplied**. Holding other variables constant, when the price of a good rises, producing the good is more profitable, and the quantity supplied will increase. When the price of a good falls, the good is less profitable, and the quantity supplied will decrease. In addition, as we saw in Chapter 2, devoting more and more resources to the production of a good results in increasing marginal costs. If, for example, Apple, Toshiba, Samsung, LG, and other firms increase production of tablet computers during a given time period, they are likely to find that the cost of producing additional tablets increases as their suppliers run existing factories for longer hours and pay higher prices for components and higher wages for workers. With higher marginal costs, firms will supply a larger quantity only if the price is higher.

**Quantity supplied** The amount of a good or service that a firm is willing and able to supply at a given price.

## Supply Schedules and Supply Curves

A **supply schedule** is a table that shows the relationship between the price of a product and the quantity of the product supplied. The table in Figure 3.4 is a supply schedule showing the quantity of tablet computers that firms would be willing to supply per month at different prices. The graph in Figure 3.4 plots the numbers from the supply schedule as a *supply curve*. A **supply curve** shows the relationship between the price of a product and the quantity of the product supplied. The supply schedule and supply curve both show that as the price of tablet computers rises, firms will increase the quantity they supply. At a price of $600 per tablet, firms will supply 6 million tablets per month. At the higher price of $700, firms will supply 7 million. (Once again, we are assuming for convenience that the supply curve is a straight line, even though not all supply curves are actually straight lines.)

**Supply schedule** A table that shows the relationship between the price of a product and the quantity of the product supplied.

**Supply curve** A curve that shows the relationship between the price of a product and the quantity of the product supplied.

| Supply Schedule | |
|---|---|
| Price (dollars per tablet) | Quantity (millions of tablets per month) |
| $700 | 7 |
| 600 | 6 |
| 500 | 5 |
| 400 | 4 |
| 300 | 3 |

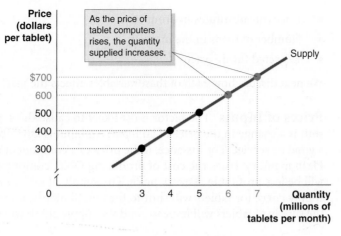

As the price of tablet computers rises, the quantity supplied increases.

**Figure 3.4**

**A Supply Schedule and Supply Curve**

As the price changes, Apple, Toshiba, Samsung, LG, and other firms producing tablet computers change the quantity they are willing to supply. We can show this as a *supply schedule* in a table or as a *supply curve* on a graph. The supply schedule and supply curve both show that as the price of tablet computers rises, firms will increase the quantity they supply. At a price of $600 per tablet, firms will supply 6 million tablets. At a price of $700, firms will supply 7 million tablets.

## The Law of Supply

The *market supply curve* in Figure 3.4 is upward sloping. We expect most supply curves to be upward sloping, according to the **law of supply**, which states that, holding everything else constant, increases in price cause increases in the quantity supplied, and decreases in price cause decreases in the quantity supplied. Notice that the definition of the law of supply—like the definition of the law of demand—contains the phrase *holding everything else constant*. If only the price of the product changes, there is a movement along the supply curve, which is *an increase or a decrease in the quantity supplied*. As Figure 3.5 shows, if any other variable that affects the willingness of firms to supply a good changes, the supply curve will shift, which is *an increase or a decrease in supply*. When firms increase the quantity of a product they want to sell at a given price, the supply curve shifts to the right. The shift from $S_1$ to $S_3$ represents *an increase in supply*. When firms decrease the quantity of a product they want to sell at a given price, the supply curve shifts to the left. The shift from $S_1$ to $S_2$ represents *a decrease in supply*.

**Law of supply** The rule that, holding everything else constant, increases in price cause increases in the quantity supplied, and decreases in price cause decreases in the quantity supplied.

## Variables That Shift Market Supply

The following are the most important variables that shift market supply:

- Prices of inputs
- Technological change

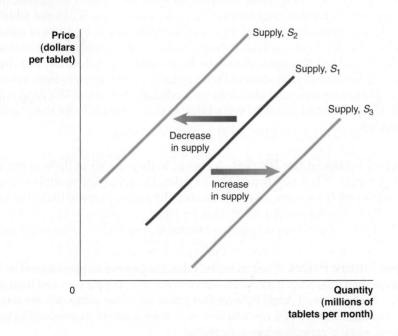

**Figure 3.5**

**Shifting the Supply Curve**

When firms increase the quantity of a product they want to sell at a given price, the supply curve shifts to the right. The shift from $S_1$ to $S_3$ represents an *increase in supply*. When firms decrease the quantity of a product they want to sell at a given price, the supply curve shifts to the left. The shift from $S_1$ to $S_2$ represents a *decrease in supply*.

- Prices of substitutes in production
- Number of firms in the market
- Expected future prices

We next discuss how each of these variables affects the market supply curve.

**Prices of Inputs** The factor most likely to cause the supply curve for a product to shift is a change in the price of an *input*. An input is anything used in the production of a good or service. For instance, if the price of a component of tablet computers, such as Flash memory, rises, the cost of producing tablet computers will increase, and tablets will be less profitable at every price. The supply of tablets will decline, and the market supply curve for tablets will shift to the left. Similarly, if the price of an input declines, the supply of tablets will increase, and the supply curve will shift to the right.

**Technological change** A positive or negative change in the ability of a firm to produce a given level of output with a given quantity of inputs.

**Technological Change** A second factor that causes a change in supply is *technological change*. **Technological change** is a positive or negative change in the ability of a firm to produce a given level of output with a given quantity of inputs. Positive technological change occurs whenever a firm is able to produce more output using the same amount of inputs. This shift will happen when the *productivity* of workers or machines increases. If a firm can produce more output with the same amount of inputs, its costs will be lower, and the good will be more profitable to produce at any given price. As a result, when positive technological change occurs, the firm will increase the quantity supplied at every price, and its supply curve will shift to the right. Normally, we expect technological change to have a positive effect on a firm's willingness to supply a product.

Negative technological change is relatively rare, although it could result from an earthquake or another natural disaster or from a war that reduces firms' ability to supply as much output with a given amount of inputs. Negative technological change will raise firms' costs, and the good will be less profitable to produce. Therefore, negative technological change will cause the market supply curve to shift to the left.

**Prices of Substitutes in Production** Firms often choose which good or service they will produce. Alternative products that a firm could produce are called *substitutes in production*. To this point, we have considered the market for all types of tablet computers. A key feature of tablet computers is whether they connect to the Internet just by Wi-Fi or by either Wi-Fi or a cellular network. Suppose we consider as separate markets tablet computers capable of only connecting to the Internet by Wi-Fi and tablet computers that can connect either by Wi-Fi or a cellular network. If the price of tablets that connect by either Wi-Fi or a cellular network increases, these tablets will become more profitable than tablets that connect only by Wi-Fi, and Apple, Toshiba, and the other firms making tablets will shift some of their productive capacity away from Wi-Fi–only models and toward models that also allow for a cellular connection. The firms will offer fewer Wi-Fi–only models for sale at every price, so the supply curve for these tablets will shift to the left.

**Number of Firms in the Market** A change in the number of firms in the market will change supply. When new firms *enter* a market, the supply curve shifts to the right, and when existing firms leave, or *exit*, a market, the supply curve shifts to the left. For instance, when Toshiba entered the market for tablet computers in July 2011 by introducing the Thrive, the market supply curve for tablet computers shifted to the right.

**Expected Future Prices** If a firm expects that the price of its product will be higher in the future than it is today, it has an incentive to decrease supply now and increase it in the future. For instance, if Apple believes that prices for tablet computers are temporarily low—perhaps because of a recession—it may store some of its production today to sell later on, when it expects prices to be higher.

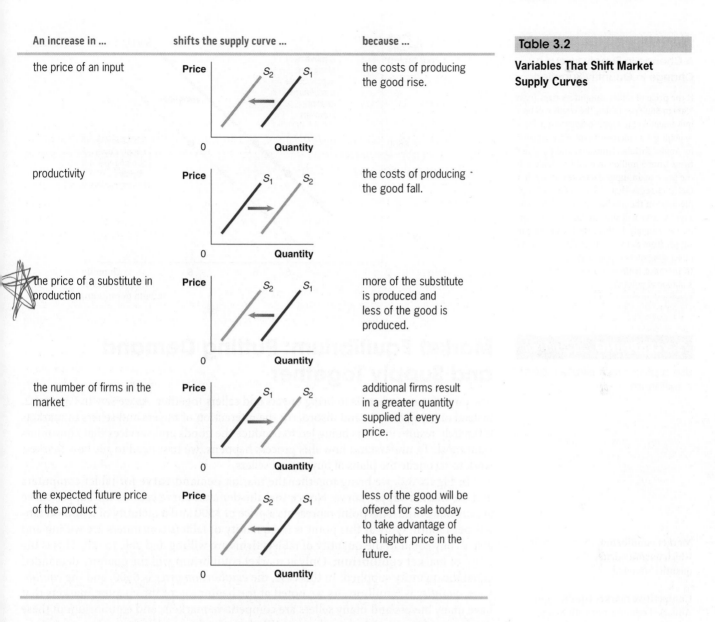

**Table 3.2**

**Variables That Shift Market Supply Curves**

| An increase in ... | shifts the supply curve ... | because ... |
| --- | --- | --- |
| the price of an input | | the costs of producing the good rise. |
| productivity | | the costs of producing the good fall. |
| the price of a substitute in production | | more of the substitute is produced and less of the good is produced. |
| the number of firms in the market | | additional firms result in a greater quantity supplied at every price. |
| the expected future price of the product | | less of the good will be offered for sale today to take advantage of the higher price in the future. |

Table 3.2 summarizes the most important variables that cause market supply curves to shift. Note that the table shows the shift in the supply curve that results from an *increase* in each of the variables. A *decrease* in these variables would cause the supply curve to shift in the opposite direction.

## A Change in Supply versus a Change in Quantity Supplied

We noted earlier the important difference between a change in demand and a change in quantity demanded. There is a similar difference between a *change in supply* and a *change in quantity supplied*. A change in supply refers to a shift of the supply curve. The supply curve will shift when there is a change in one of the variables, *other than the price of the product*, that affects the willingness of suppliers to sell the product. A change in quantity supplied refers to a movement along the supply curve as a result of a change in the product's price. Figure 3.6 illustrates this important distinction. If the price of tablet computers rises from $500 to $600 per tablet, the result will be a movement up the supply curve from point *A* to point *B*—an increase in quantity supplied from 5 million tablets to 6 million tablets. If the price of an input decreases or another factor changes that causes sellers to supply more of the product at every price, the supply curve will shift to the right—an increase in supply. In this case, the increase in supply from $S_1$ to $S_2$ causes the quantity of tablet computers supplied at a price of $600 to increase from 6 million at point *B* to 8 million at point *C*.

**Figure 3.6**

**A Change in Supply versus a Change in Quantity Supplied**

If the price of tablet computers rises from $500 to $600 per tablet, the result will be a movement up the supply curve from point *A* to point *B*—an increase in quantity supplied by Apple, Toshiba, Samsung, and the other firms from 5 million to 6 million tablets. If the price of an input decreases or another factor changes that causes sellers to supply more of the product at every price, the supply curve will shift to the right—an increase in supply. In this case, the increase in supply from $S_1$ to $S_2$ causes the quantity of tablet computers supplied at a price of $600 to increase from 6 million at point *B* to 8 million at point *C*.

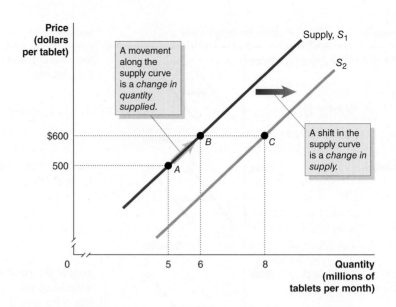

**Figure 3.6**

**A Change in Supply versus a Change in Quantity Supplied**

---

Use a graph to illustrate market equilibrium.

**Market equilibrium** A situation in which quantity demanded equals quantity supplied.

**Competitive market equilibrium** A market equilibrium with many buyers and many sellers.

# Market Equilibrium: Putting Demand and Supply Together

The purpose of markets is to bring buyers and sellers together. As we saw in Chapter 2, instead of being chaotic and disorderly, the interaction of buyers and sellers in markets ultimately results in firms being led to produce the goods and services that consumers want most. To understand how this process happens, we first need to see how markets work to reconcile the plans of buyers and sellers.

In Figure 3.7, we bring together the market demand curve for tablet computers and the market supply curve. Notice that the demand curve crosses the supply curve at only one point. This point represents a price of $500 and a quantity of 5 million tablets per month. Only at this point is the quantity of tablets consumers are willing and able to buy equal to the quantity of tablets firms are willing and able to sell. This is the point of **market equilibrium**. Only at market equilibrium will the quantity demanded equal the quantity supplied. In this case, the *equilibrium price* is $500, and the *equilibrium quantity* is 5 million. As we noted at the beginning of the chapter, markets that have many buyers and many sellers are competitive markets, and equilibrium in these markets is a **competitive market equilibrium**. In the market for tablet computers,

---

**Figure 3.7**

**Market Equilibrium**

Where the demand curve crosses the supply curve determines market equilibrium. In this case, the demand curve for tablet computers crosses the supply curve at a price of $500 and a quantity of 5 million tablets. Only at this point is the quantity of tablet computers consumers are willing to buy equal to the quantity that Apple, Amazon, Samsung, and the other firms are willing to sell: The quantity demanded is equal to the quantity supplied.

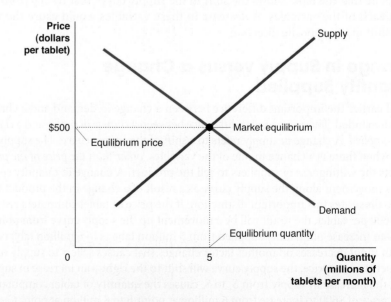

there are many buyers but only about 20 firms. Whether 20 firms is enough for our model of demand and supply to apply to this market is a matter of judgment. In this chapter, we are assuming that the market for tablet computers has enough sellers to be competitive.

## How Markets Eliminate Surpluses and Shortages

A market that is not in equilibrium moves toward equilibrium. Once a market is in equilibrium, it remains in equilibrium. To see why, consider what happens if a market is not in equilibrium. For instance, suppose that the price in the market for tablet computers was $600, rather than the equilibrium price of $500. As Figure 3.8 shows, at a price of $600, the quantity of tablets supplied would be 6 million, and the quantity of tablets demanded would be 4 million. When the quantity supplied is greater than the quantity demanded, there is a **surplus** in the market. In this case, the surplus is equal to 2 million tablets (6 million − 4 million = 2 million). When there is a surplus, firms have unsold goods piling up, which gives them an incentive to increase their sales by cutting the price. Cutting the price will simultaneously increase the quantity demanded and decrease the quantity supplied. This adjustment will reduce the surplus, but as long as the price is above $500, there will be a surplus, and downward pressure on the price will continue. Only when the price has fallen to $500 will the market be in equilibrium.

If, however, the price were $300, the quantity demanded would be 7 million, and the quantity supplied would be 3 million, as shown in Figure 3.8. When the quantity demanded is greater than the quantity supplied, there is a **shortage** in the market. In this case, the shortage is equal to 4 million tablets (7 million − 3 million = 4 million). When a shortage occurs, some consumers will be unable to buy tablet computers at the current price. In this situation, firms will realize that they can raise the price without losing sales. A higher price will simultaneously increase the quantity supplied and decrease the quantity demanded. This adjustment will reduce the shortage, but as long as the price is below $500, there will be a shortage, and upward pressure on the price will continue. Only when the price has risen to $500 will the market be in equilibrium.

At a competitive market equilibrium, all consumers willing to pay the market price will be able to buy as much of the product as they want, and all firms willing to accept the market price will be able to sell as much of the product as they want. As a result, there will be no reason for the price to change unless either the demand curve or the supply curve shifts.

**Surplus** A situation in which the quantity supplied is greater than the quantity demanded.

**Shortage** A situation in which the quantity demanded is greater than the quantity supplied.

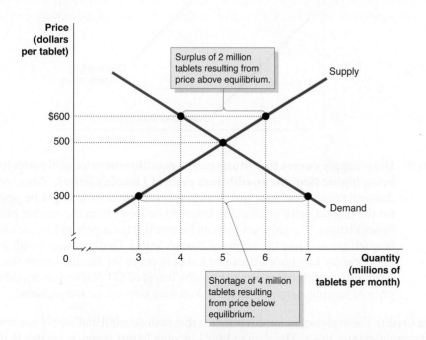

### Figure 3.8

### The Effect of Surpluses and Shortages on the Market Price

When the market price is above equilibrium, there will be a *surplus*. In the figure, a price of $600 for tablet computers results in 6 million tablets being supplied but only 4 million tablets being demanded, or a surplus of 2 million. As Apple, Toshiba, Dell, and other firms cut the price to dispose of the surplus, the price will fall to the equilibrium of $500. When the market price is below equilibrium, there will be a *shortage*. A price of $300 results in 7 million tablets being demanded but only 3 million tablets being supplied, or a shortage of 4 million tablets. As firms find that consumers who are unable to find tablet computers available for sale are willing to pay higher prices to get them, the price will rise to the equilibrium of $500.

## Demand and Supply Both Count

Keep in mind that the interaction of demand and supply determines the equilibrium price. Neither consumers nor firms can dictate what the equilibrium price will be. No firm can sell anything at any price unless it can find a willing buyer, and no consumer can buy anything at any price without finding a willing seller.

---

# Solved Problem 3.3

## Demand and Supply Both Count: A Tale of Two Letters

Which letter is likely to be worth more: one written by Abraham Lincoln or one written by his assassin, John Wilkes Booth? Lincoln is one of the greatest presidents, and many people collect anything he wrote. The demand for letters written by Lincoln surely would seem to be much greater than the demand for letters written by Booth. Yet when R. M. Smythe and Co. auctioned off on the same day

a letter written by Lincoln and a letter written by Booth, the Booth letter sold for $31,050, and the Lincoln letter sold for only $21,850. Use a demand and supply graph to explain how the Booth letter has a higher market price than the Lincoln letter, even though the demand for letters written by Lincoln is greater than the demand for letters written by Booth.

## Solving the Problem

**Step 1:** **Review the chapter material.** This problem is about prices being determined at market equilibrium, so you may want to review the section "Market Equilibrium: Putting Demand and Supply Together," which begins on page 82.

**Step 2:** **Draw demand curves that illustrate the greater demand for Lincoln's letters.** Begin by drawing two demand curves. Label one "Demand for Lincoln's letters" and the other "Demand for Booth's letters." Make sure that the Lincoln demand curve is much farther to the right than the Booth demand curve.

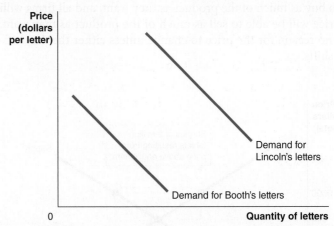

**Step 3:** **Draw supply curves that illustrate the equilibrium price of Booth's letters being higher than the equilibrium price of Lincoln's letters.** Based on the demand curves you have just drawn, think about how it might be possible for the market price of Lincoln's letters to be lower than the market price of Booth's letters. The only way this can be true is if the supply of Lincoln's letters is much greater than the supply of Booth's letters. Draw on your graph a supply curve for Lincoln's letters and a supply curve for Booth's letters that will result in an equilibrium price of Booth's letters of $31,050 and an equilibrium price of Lincoln's letters of $21,850. You have now solved the problem.

**Extra Credit:** The explanation for this puzzle is that both demand and supply count when determining market price. The demand for Lincoln's letters is much greater than the

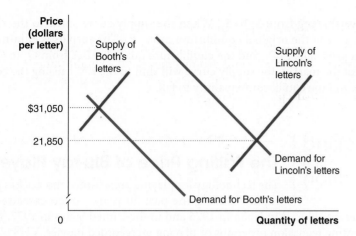

demand for Booth's letters, but the supply of Booth's letters is very small. Historians believe that only eight letters written by Booth exist today. (Note that the supply curves for letters written by Booth and by Lincoln are upward sloping, even though only a fixed number of each of these types of letters is available and, obviously, no more can be produced. The upward slope of the supply curves occurs because the higher the price, the larger the quantity of letters that will be offered for sale by people who currently own them.)

**Your Turn:** For more practice, do related problems 3.5 and 3.6 on page 97 at the end of this chapter.    MyEconLab

# The Effect of Demand and Supply Shifts on Equilibrium

We have seen that the interaction of demand and supply in markets determines the quantity of a good that is produced and the price at which it sells. We have also seen that several variables cause demand curves to shift and other variables cause supply curves to shift. As a result, demand and supply curves in most markets are constantly shifting, and the prices and quantities that represent equilibrium are constantly changing. In this section, we look at how shifts in demand and supply curves affect equilibrium price and quantity.

## The Effect of Shifts in Supply on Equilibrium

When Toshiba entered the market for tablet computers by introducing the Thrive, the market supply curve for tablet computers shifted to the right. Figure 3.9 shows the

**3.4 LEARNING** OBJECTIVE

Use demand and supply graphs to predict changes in prices and quantities.

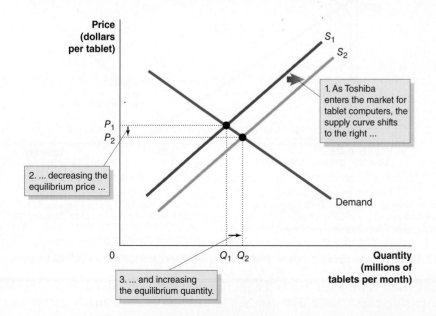

**Figure 3.9**

**The Effect of an Increase in Supply on Equilibrium**

If a firm enters a market, as Toshiba entered the market for tablet computers when it introduced the Thrive, the equilibrium price will fall, and the equilibrium quantity will rise:

1. As Toshiba enters the market for tablet computers, a larger quantity of tablets will be supplied at every price, so the market supply curve shifts to the right, from $S_1$ to $S_2$, which causes a surplus of tablets at the original price, $P_1$.

2. The equilibrium price falls from $P_1$ to $P_2$.

3. The equilibrium quantity rises from $Q_1$ to $Q_2$.

supply curve shifting from $S_1$ to $S_2$. When the supply curve shifts to the right, there will be a surplus at the original equilibrium price, $P_1$. The surplus is eliminated as the equilibrium price falls to $P_2$, and the equilibrium quantity rises from $Q_1$ to $Q_2$. If existing firms exit the market, the supply curve will shift to the left, causing the equilibrium price to rise and the equilibrium quantity to fall.

## Making the Connection | The Falling Price of Blu-ray Players

The technology for playing prerecorded movies has progressed rapidly during the past 30 years. Video cassette recorders (VCRs) were introduced in Japan in 1976 and in the United States in 1977. As the first way of recording television programs or playing prerecorded movies, VHS players were immensely popular. In 1997, though, digital video disc (DVD) players became available in the United States. DVDs could store more information than could the VHS tapes played on VCRs and could produce a crisper picture. Within a few years, sales of DVD players were greater than sales of VCRs, and by 2006 the movie studios had stopped releasing films on VHS tapes. In 2006, Blu-ray players were introduced. Because Blu-ray discs can store 25 gigabytes of data, compared with fewer than 5 gigabytes on a typical DVD, Blu-ray players can reproduce high-definition images that DVD players cannot.

When firms first began selling VCRs, DVD players, and Blu-ray players, they initially charged high prices that declined rapidly within a few years. As the figure below shows, the average price of a Blu-ray player was about $800 in May 2006, but it had declined to about $120 in December 2010. Sales of Blu-ray players rose from about 425,000 in 2006 to 11.25 million in 2010. The figure shows that the decline in price and increase in quantity resulted from a large shift to the right of the supply curve. The supply curve in 2010 was much farther to the right than the supply curve in 2006 for two reasons: First, after Samsung introduced the first Blu-ray player—at a price of $999—other firms entered the industry, increasing the quantity supplied at every price. Second, the prices of the parts used in manufacturing Blu-ray players, particularly the laser components, declined sharply. As the cost of manufacturing the players declined, the quantity supplied at every price increased.

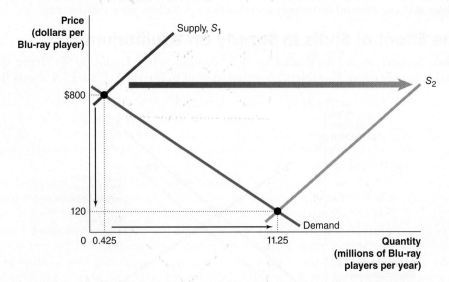

Based on Sarah McBride, "New DVD Players Resolve Battle of Formats," *Wall Street Journal*, January 4, 2007; Yukari Iwatani Kane and Miguel Bustillo, "Dreaming of a Blu Christmas," *Wall Street Journal*, December 23, 2009; and "DEG 2010 Year-End Home Entertainment Report," www.degonline.com.

MyEconLab **Your Turn:** For more practice, do related problem 4.6 on page 98 at the end of this chapter.

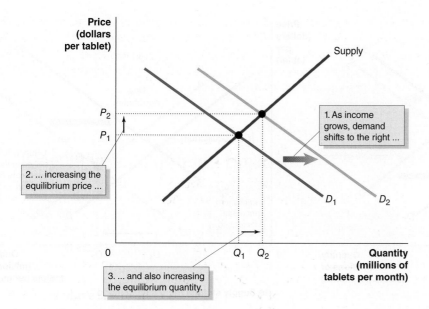

**Figure 3.10**

**The Effect of an Increase in Demand on Equilibrium**

Increases in income will cause the equilibrium price and quantity to rise:

1. Because tablet computers are a normal good, as income grows, the quantity demanded increases at every price, and the market demand curve shifts to the right, from $D_1$ to $D_2$, which causes a shortage of tablet computers at the original price, $P_1$.
2. The equilibrium price rises from $P_1$ to $P_2$.
3. The equilibrium quantity rises from $Q_1$ to $Q_2$.

## The Effect of Shifts in Demand on Equilibrium

Because tablet computers are a normal good, when incomes increase, the market demand curve for tablet computers shifts to the right. Figure 3.10 shows the effect of a demand curve shifting to the right, from $D_1$ to $D_2$. This shift causes a shortage at the original equilibrium price, $P_1$. To eliminate the shortage, the equilibrium price rises to $P_2$, and the equilibrium quantity rises from $Q_1$ to $Q_2$. In contrast, if the price of a substitute good, such as laptop computers, were to fall, the demand for tablet computers would decrease, shifting the demand curve for tablets to the left. When the demand curve shifts to the left, the equilibrium price and quantity will both decrease.

## The Effect of Shifts in Demand and Supply over Time

Whenever only demand or only supply shifts, we can easily predict the effect on equilibrium price and quantity. But what happens if *both* curves shift? For instance, in many markets, the demand curve shifts to the right over time as population and income grow. The supply curve also often shifts to the right as new firms enter the market and positive technological change occurs. Whether the equilibrium price in a market rises or falls over time depends on whether demand shifts to the right more than does supply. Panel (a) of Figure 3.11 shows that when demand shifts to the right more than supply, the equilibrium price rises. But, as panel (b) shows, when supply shifts to the right more than demand, the equilibrium price falls.

Table 3.3 summarizes all possible combinations of shifts in demand and supply over time and the effects of the shifts on equilibrium price (*P*) and quantity (*Q*). For example, the entry in red in the table shows that if the demand curve shifts to the right and the supply curve also shifts to the right, the equilibrium quantity will increase, while the equilibrium price may increase, decrease, or remain unchanged. To make sure you understand each entry in the table, draw demand and supply graphs to check whether you can reproduce the predicted changes in equilibrium price and quantity. If the entry in the table says the predicted change in equilibrium price or quantity can be either an increase or a decrease, draw two graphs similar to panels (a) and (b) of Figure 3.11, one showing the equilibrium price or quantity increasing and the other showing it decreasing. Note also that in the ambiguous cases where either price or quantity might increase or decrease, it is also possible that price or quantity might remain unchanged. Be sure you understand why this is true.

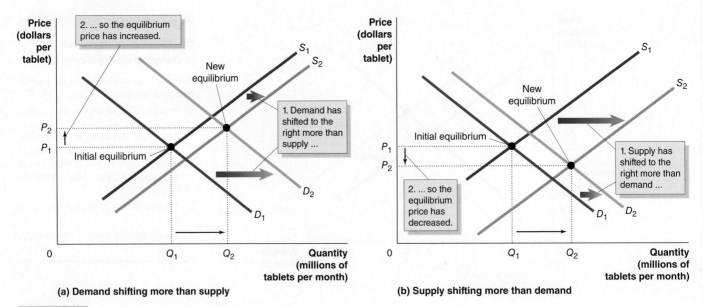

**Figure 3.11** **Shifts in Demand and Supply over Time**

Whether the price of a product rises or falls over time depends on whether demand shifts to the right more than supply.

In panel (a), demand shifts to the right more than supply, and the equilibrium price rises:

1. Demand shifts to the right more than supply.
2. The equilibrium price rises from $P_1$ to $P_2$.

In panel (b), supply shifts to the right more than demand, and the equilibrium price falls:

1. Supply shifts to the right more than demand.
2. The equilibrium price falls from $P_1$ to $P_2$.

**Table 3.3**

**How Shifts in Demand and Supply Affect Equilibrium Price (P) and Quantity (Q)**

| | Supply Curve Unchanged | Supply Curve Shifts to the Right | Supply Curve Shifts to the Left |
|---|---|---|---|
| **Demand Curve Unchanged** | Q unchanged<br>P unchanged | Q increases<br>P decreases | Q decreases<br>P increases |
| **Demand Curve Shifts to the Right** | Q increases<br>P increases | Q increases<br>P increases or decreases | Q increases or decreases<br>P increases |
| **Demand Curve Shifts to the Left** | Q decreases<br>P decreases | Q increases or decreases<br>P decreases | Q decreases<br>P increases or decreases |

# Solved Problem 3.4

## High Demand and Low Prices in the Lobster Market?

During a typical spring, when demand for lobster is relatively low, Maine lobstermen can typically sell their lobster catches for about $6.00 per pound. During the summer, when demand for lobster is much higher, Maine lobstermen can typically sell their lobster catches for only about $3.00 per pound. One recent July, a lobster-boat captain noted, "Per pound, it's less expensive than hot dogs right now." It may seem strange that the market price is higher when demand is low than when demand is high. Resolve this paradox, with the help of a demand and supply graph.

## Solving the Problem

**Step 1:** **Review the chapter material.** This problem is about how shifts in demand and supply curves affect the equilibrium price, so you may want to review the section "The Effect of Shifts in Demand and Supply over Time," which begins on page 87.

**Step 2:** **Draw the demand and supply graph.** Draw a demand and supply graph, showing the market equilibrium in the spring. Label the equilibrium price $6.00. Label both the demand and supply curves "in spring."

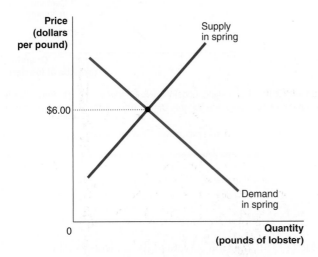

**Step 3:** **Add to your graph a demand curve for summer.**

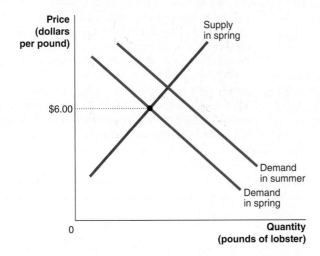

**Step 4:** **Explain the graph.** After studying the graph, it is possible to see how the equilibrium price can fall from $6.00 to $3.00, despite the increase in demand: The supply curve must have shifted to the right by enough to cause the equilibrium price to fall to $3.00. Draw the new supply curve, label it "in summer," and label the new equilibrium price $3.00. The demand for lobster does increase in summer compared with spring. But the increase in the supply of lobster between spring and summer is even greater. So, the equilibrium price falls.

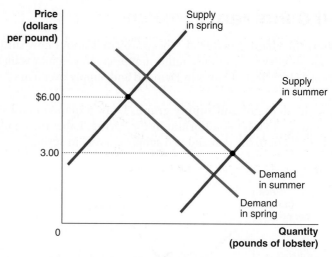

Based on Beth D'Addono, "With Prices Falling, Lobster Is No Longer a Splurge," *Philadelphia Daily News*, June 16, 2011; and Jon Birger, "Looking for a Bargain Dinner: Try Lobster," cnnmoney.com, July 18, 2009.

MyEconLab **Your Turn:** For more practice, do related problems 4.7 and 4.8 on page 98 at the end of this chapter.

# Don't Let This Happen to You

## Remember: A Change in a Good's Price Does *Not* Cause the Demand or Supply Curve to Shift

Suppose a student is asked to draw a demand and supply graph to illustrate how an increase in the price of oranges would affect the market for apples, other variables being constant. He draws the graph on the left below and explains it as follows: "Because apples and oranges are substitutes, an increase in the price of oranges will cause an initial shift to the right in the demand curve for apples, from $D_1$ to $D_2$. However, because this initial shift in the demand curve for apples results in a higher price for apples, $P_2$, consumers will find apples less desirable, and the demand curve will shift to the left, from $D_2$ to $D_3$, resulting in a final equilibrium price of $P_3$." Do you agree or disagree with the student's analysis?

You should disagree. The student has correctly understood that an increase in the price of oranges will cause the demand curve for apples to shift to the right. But the second

demand curve shift the student describes, from $D_2$ to $D_3$, will not take place. Changes in the price of a product do not result in shifts in the product's demand curve. Changes in the price of a product result only in movements along a demand curve.

The graph on the right below shows the correct analysis. The increase in the price of oranges causes the demand curve for apples to increase from $D_1$ to $D_2$. At the original price, $P_1$, the increase in demand initially results in a shortage of apples equal to $Q_3 - Q_1$. But, as we have seen, a shortage causes the price to increase until the shortage is eliminated. In this case, the price will rise to $P_2$, where the quantity demanded and the quantity supplied are both equal to $Q_2$. Notice that the increase in price causes a decrease in the *quantity demanded*, from $Q_3$ to $Q_2$, but does *not* cause a decrease in demand.

MyEconLab

**Your Turn:** Test your understanding by doing related problems 4.13 and 4.14 on pages 98–99 at the end of this chapter.

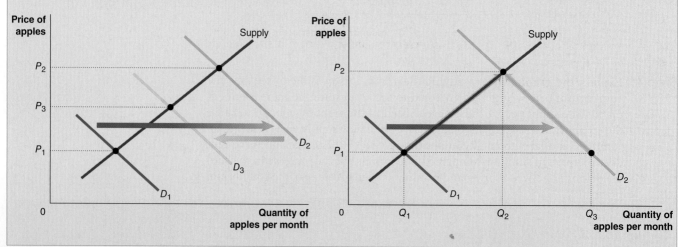

## Shifts in a Curve versus Movements along a Curve

When analyzing markets using demand and supply curves, it is important to remember that *when a shift in a demand or supply curve causes a change in equilibrium price, the change in price does not cause a further shift in demand or supply*. For instance, suppose an increase in supply causes the price of a good to fall, while everything else that affects the willingness of consumers to buy the good is constant. The result will be an increase in the quantity demanded but not an increase in demand. For demand to increase, the whole curve must shift. The point is the same for supply: If the price of the good falls but everything else that affects the willingness of sellers to supply the good is constant, the quantity supplied decreases, but the supply does not. For supply to decrease, the whole curve must shift.

Continued from page 69

## Economics in Your Life

### Will You Buy an Apple iPad or a Samsung Galaxy Tab?

At the beginning of the chapter, we asked you to consider two questions: Would you choose to buy a Samsung Galaxy Tab tablet if it had a lower price than an Apple iPad? and Would your decision be affected if your income increased? To determine the answer to the first question, you have to recognize that the iPad and the Galaxy Tab are substitutes. If you consider the two tablets to be very close substitutes, then you are likely to buy the one with the lower price. In the market, if consumers generally believe that iPad and the Galaxy Tab are close substitutes, a fall in the price of the iPad will increase the quantity of iPads demanded and decrease the demand for Galaxy Tabs. Suppose that you are currently leaning toward buying the Galaxy Tab because its price is lower than the price of the iPad. If an increase in your income would cause you to change your decision and buy the iPad, then the Galaxy Tab is an inferior good for you.

## Conclusion

The interaction of demand and supply determines market equilibrium. The model of demand and supply is a powerful tool for predicting how changes in the actions of consumers and firms will cause changes in equilibrium prices and quantities. As we have seen in this chapter, we can use the model to analyze markets that do not meet all the requirements for being perfectly competitive. As long as there is intense competition among sellers, the model of demand and supply can often successfully predict changes in prices and quantities. We will use this model in the next chapter to analyze economic efficiency and the results of government-imposed price floors and price ceilings.

Before moving on to Chapter 4, read *An Inside Look* on the next page for a discussion of how a potential shortage of LCD display screens could affect the market for tablets, such as Apple's iPad.

# Will Shortage of Display Screens Derail Computer Tablet Sales?

## *BLOOMBERG BUSINESSWEEK*

## Guess What Could Stop the Tablet Revolution?

With 2011 shaping up to be the Year of the Tablet, securing the display components for the looming army of tablets may be a key factor in determining success. Last year we saw that the fast start for the iPad prompted LCD display shortages from Apple supplier LG, which said it was having a hard time keeping up with demand. Now with Apple (AAPL) selling 7.3 million iPads in the December quarter, the iPad 2 on the way, and seemingly every manufacturer at CES prepping a rival, the display component crunch could constrain the flow of tablets and hurt some manufacturers that aren't prepared.

**(a)** The focus on displays may be what Apple was referring to when it reported last week during its earning call that it was investing $3.9 billion to secure inventory components through three vendors. MacRumors speculated that the sum was aimed at shoring up Apple's access to displays, especially ahead of the iPad 2 launch. In December, Apple reportedly struck two deals with Toshiba (TOSYY) and Sharp (SHCAY) to manufacture displays, though Sharp denied the report. Apple, according to Digitimes, is also securing iPad display-panel shipments for 65 million units this year through LG, Samsung, and Chimei Innolux. That's a huge number of iPads, and it would

make sense for Apple to lock up the necessary components to ensure the iPad success story continues.

Tablet competitors may do well to follow Apple's example. Last month, Frank Chien, chairman of Formosa Epitaxy, a leading Taiwanese LED maker, predicted that demand for high-end LED chips for LCD displays could outstrip supply starting next month as tablet production ramps up across the industry. ISuppli said earlier this month that global tablet shipments are expected to hit 57.6 million units, up from 17.1 million in 2010. The overall demand for a relatively new product, however, is still forming, said iSuppli. The unpredictability of the nascent market could put a lot of pressure on display makers, which may face shortages or potentially oversupply as they try to guess how the tablet market performs.

### In-House Technology

**(b)** For those building tablets, the challenge may be to make sure they have enough display panels to meet demand. The best companies might be the ones that have access to their own display technology, companies like Samsung, LG, and Sharp. And even among display makers, the best positioned manufacturers will be those that have the LED-chip technology in-house, said Sweta Dash, senior director for LCD research at iSuppli in a story in *LED Magazine* last year.

"By the second half of this year (2010), a clear distinction will emerge

between the haves and have-nots among the panel suppliers," Dash said. "Those panel makers that have their own internal manufacturing of LEDs will have sufficient supply in 2010, while those that don't will encounter constraints."

**(c)** Tablets aren't the only things causing the crunch. The overall popularity of LED-backlit LCD displays in televisions and computers could also help tighten supply for display components. iSuppli said last week that more than two-thirds of large LCD panels shipped worldwide in 2011 will incorporate LED backlights, up from less than one-half in 2010. This year, LED penetration in television and monitor panels will hit almost 50 percent compared with 20 percent last year, while LED backlighting in notebooks and netbooks is expected to be 100 percent.

With so much competition in the coming year, we might not see any one tablet place the demands on the component supply chain that the iPad did. But if the tablet market evolves as many are predicting, the race will be on to snap up display components and fast. Apple is getting ready for the tablet revolution and, in doing so, has shone a light on the importance of the electronics supply chain.

*Source:* "Guess What Could Stop the Tablet Revolution?" by Ryan Kim from *Bloomberg Businessweek*, January 24, 2011. Copyright © 2011 by Bloomberg Businessweek. Reprinted by permission of the YGS Group.

## Key Points in the Article

The overwhelming success of the iPad in 2010 resulted in a shortage of screens from LG, the main supplier of this component. In 2011, Apple made arrangements with several other suppliers to provide the screens for the iPad. The growing popularity of tablet computers and the introduction of tablets by an increasing number of firms have many of them concerned about the component shortages, which has resulted in firms scrambling to obtain display screens. iSuppli, a market research firm specializing in the electronics industry, projected that global tablet shipments would increase from 17.1 million in 2010 to over 57 million in 2011.

## Analyzing the News

(a) Apple is the industry leader in the manufacture and sale of tablet computers. In an effort to ensure that it can keep pace with demand, Apple has made arrangements with several manufacturers to supply display components for the iPad. In addition to reported deals with Toshiba and Sharp to supply display screens, Apple is also reported to have secured 65 million screens from three additional manufacturers. The market for tablet computers has grown tremendously over the past year, with an increase in consumers' taste for the product fueling the increase in demand.

Figure 1 shows that an increase in consumers' taste for tablet computers will increase the demand for them, shifting the demand curve to the right. All else equal, the increase in demand increases both the equilibrium price and the equilibrium quantity of tablet computers.

(b) A few of the firms that produce tablets also produce the display screen components, and by virtue of producing their own displays, these companies may have a significant advantage in meeting demand. Assuming that these firms will supply display screens for their own tablets before supplying screens to other firms, the other firms may find themselves facing a shortage of screens. The way to eliminate a shortage in a market is to raise the selling price of the product. The screen manufacturers may choose to raise the price of the screen component to alleviate the shortage, but this increase in the input price will result in a decrease in the supply of tablet computers. Figure 2 shows that the decrease in supply of an input causes the supply curve to shift to the left. All else equal, the decrease in supply increases the equilibrium price and decreases the equilibrium quantity of tablet computers.

(c) In addition to tablet computers, the LED backlight components used in the production of LCD display screens are being used in a growing number of televisions

and laptop and netbook computers. These alternative uses for the display screen components could further exacerbate the shortage of screens for use in tablets. Unless the manufacturers are able to increase production, firms that produce both tablet computers and other products that use display screen components may not be able to keep up with the expected increases in demand for their products.

## Thinking Critically

1. The article discusses the potential shortage of tablet computers due to an insufficient number of display screen components used in production. Briefly explain how any potential shortage will be eliminated in the market for tablet computers.

2. Suppose the demand for tablet computers continues to increase and that suppliers of the display screens are not able to produce enough components to keep up with the increasing demand, and as a result, increase the price of each display screen. Draw a demand and supply graph that shows both of these situations occurring in the market for tablet computers. Explain what is happening in the graph and the effect these events will have on the equilibrium price and equilibrium quantity.

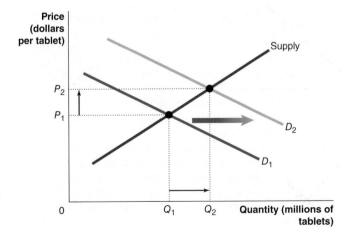

**Figure 1**

An increase in demand for tablet computers shifts the demand curve to the right.

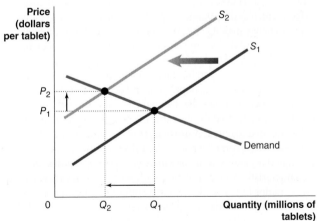

**Figure 2**

An increase in the price of an input, such as the display screen, used in the manufacture of tablet computers causes the supply curve to shift to the left.

# Chapter Summary and Problems

## Key Terms

*Ceteris paribus* ("all else equal") condition, p. 72

Competitive market equilibrium, p. 82

Complements, p. 74

Demand curve, p. 70

Demand schedule, p. 70

Demographics, p. 74

Income effect, p. 71

Inferior good, p. 73

Law of demand, p. 71

Law of supply, p. 79

Market demand, p. 70

Market equilibrium, p. 82

Normal good, p. 73

Perfectly competitive market, p. 70

Quantity demanded, p. 70

Quantity supplied, p. 78

Shortage, p. 83

Substitutes, p. 73

Substitution effect, p. 71

Supply curve, p. 78

Supply schedule, p. 78

Surplus, p. 83

Technological change, p. 80

---

**3.1**  ### The Demand Side of the Market, pages 70–78
LEARNING OBJECTIVE: Discuss the variables that influence demand.

## Summary

The model of demand and supply is the most powerful tool in economics. The model applies exactly only to **perfectly competitive markets**, where there are many buyers and sellers, all the products sold are identical, and there are no barriers to new sellers entering the market. But the model can also be useful in analyzing markets that don't meet all these requirements. The **quantity demanded** is the amount of a good or service that a consumer is willing and able to purchase at a given price. A **demand schedule** is a table that shows the relationship between the price of a product and the quantity of the product demanded. A **demand curve** is a graph that shows the relationship between the price of a good and the quantity of the good demanded. **Market demand** is the demand by all consumers of a given good or service. The **law of demand** states that *ceteris paribus*—holding everything else constant—the quantity of a product demanded increases when the price falls and decreases when the price rises. Demand curves slope downward because of the **substitution effect**, which is the change in quantity demanded that results from a price change making one good more or less expensive relative to another good, and the income effect, which is the change in quantity demanded of a good that results from the effect of a change in the good's price on consumer purchasing power. Changes in income, the prices of related goods, tastes, population and demographics, and expected future prices all cause the demand curve to shift. **Substitutes** are goods that can be used for the same purpose. **Complements** are goods that are used together. A **normal good** is a good for which demand increases as income increases. An **inferior good** is a good for which demand decreases as income increases. **Demographics** refers to the characteristics of a population with respect to age, race, and gender. A change in demand refers to a shift of the demand curve. A change in quantity demanded refers to a movement along the demand curve as a result of a change in the product's price.

 MyEconLab    Visit **www.myeconlab.com** to complete these exercises online and get instant feedback.

## Review Questions

1.1  What is a demand schedule? What is a demand curve?

1.2  What do economists mean when they use the Latin expression *ceteris paribus*?

1.3  What is the difference between a change in demand and a change in quantity demanded?

1.4  What is the law of demand? Use the substitution effect and the income effect to explain why an increase in the price of a product causes a decrease in the quantity demanded.

1.5  What are the main variables that will cause the demand curve to shift? Give an example of each.

## Problems and Applications

1.6  For each of the following pairs of products, state which are complements, which are substitutes, and which are unrelated.

    **a.**  Gasoline and electric car batteries

    **b.**  Houses and household appliances

    **c.**  UGG boots and Kindle e-readers

    **d.**  iPads and Kindle e-readers

1.7  **[Related to the** Chapter Opener **on page 69]** When tablet computers based on the Android operating system were first introduced, there were relatively few applications, or "apps," available for them. Now, there are many more apps available for Android-based tablets. Are these apps substitutes or complements for tablet computers? How has the increase in the availability of apps for Android-based tablets affected the demand for Apple iPads? Briefly explain.

1.8  State whether each of the following events will result in a movement along the demand curve for McDonald's Big Mac hamburgers or whether it will cause the curve to shift. If the demand curve shifts, indicate whether it will shift to the left or to the right and draw a graph to illustrate the shift.

    **a.**  The price of Burger King's Whopper hamburger declines.

    **b.**  McDonald's distributes coupons for $1.00 off the purchase of a Big Mac.

    **c.**  Because of a shortage of potatoes, the price of French fries increases.

    **d.**  Fast-food restaurants post nutrition warning labels.

    **e.**  The U.S. economy enters a period of rapid growth in incomes.

**1.9** Imagine that the table below shows the quantity demanded of UGG boots at five different prices in 2012 and in 2013:

| | Quantity Demanded | |
| Price | 2012 | 2013 |
| --- | --- | --- |
| $160 | 5,000 | 4,000 |
| 170 | 4,500 | 3,500 |
| 180 | 4,000 | 3,000 |
| 190 | 3,500 | 2,500 |
| 200 | 3,000 | 2,000 |

Name two different variables that could cause the quantity demanded of UGG boots to change as indicated from 2012 to 2013.

**1.10** Suppose that the curves in the graph below represent two demand curves for rib eye steaks. What would cause a movement from point *A* to point *B* on $D_1$? Name two variables that would cause a movement from point *A* to point *C*.

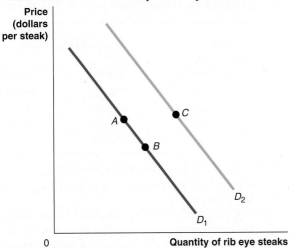

**1.11** [Related to the Making the Connection **on page 73**] A student makes the following argument:

> The chapter says that for consumers as a group, Quiznos sandwiches are normal goods, and Subway sandwiches are inferior goods. But I like the taste of Subway sandwiches better than I like the taste of Quiznos sandwiches, so for me Quiznos sandwiches are inferior goods, and Subway sandwiches are normal goods.

Do you agree with the student's reasoning? Briefly explain.

**1.12** [Related to the Making the Connection **on page 74**] Name three products whose demand is likely to increase rapidly if the following demographic groups increase at a faster rate than the population as a whole:
a. Teenagers
b. Children under age five
c. Recent immigrants

**1.13** [Related to the Making the Connection **on page 74**] Since 1979, China has had a policy that allows couples to have only one child. This policy has caused a change in the demographics of China. Between 2000 and 2010, the share of the population under age 14 decreased from 23 percent to 17 percent, and, as parents attempt to ensure that the lone child is a son, the number of newborn males relative to females has increased. How has the one-child policy changed the relative demand for goods and services in China?

Based on "China's Family Planning: Illegal Children Will Be Confiscated" and "China's Population: Only and Lonely," *The Economist*, July 21, 2011.

**1.14** Suppose the following table shows the price of a base model Toyota Prius hybrid and the quantity of Priuses sold for three years. Do these data indicate that the demand curve for Priuses is upward sloping? Explain.

| Year | Price | Quantity |
| --- | --- | --- |
| 2010 | $24,880 | 35,265 |
| 2011 | 24,550 | 33,250 |
| 2012 | 25,250 | 36,466 |

**1.15** Richard Posner is a federal court judge who also writes on economic topics. A newspaper reporter summarized Posner's views on the effect of online bookstores and e-books on the demand for books:

> Posner's [argument] is that the disappearance of bookstores is to be celebrated and not mourned, partly because e-books and online stores will reduce the cost of books and thus drive up demand for them.

Do you agree with Posner's statement, as given by the reporter? Briefly explain.

From Christopher Shea, "Judge Posner Hails the Demise of Bookstores," *Wall Street Journal*, January 13, 2011.

**1.16** [Related to the Making the Connection **on page 77**] In early 2011, financial journalist Wolfgang Gruener made the following observation about forecasts of the future demand for tablet computers:

> The conclusion can only be that the market is too young to sustain a reliable short-, mid- or long-term forecast. If you trust any number at this time, good luck with that. Only a fool would bet the farm and a business on any forecast for the tablet market right now.

Why might it be particularly difficult to forecast the demand for a new product? Which issues might make it particularly difficult to forecast the demand for tablet computers?

From Wolfgang Gruener, "240 Million Tablets: The Gazillion-Dollar Forecast Game," ConceivablyTech.com, February 6, 2011.

---

**3.2** **The Supply Side of the Market, pages 78–82**

LEARNING OBJECTIVE: Discuss the variables that influence supply.

## Summary

The **quantity supplied** is the amount of a good that a firm is willing and able to supply at a given price. A **supply schedule** is a table that shows the relationship between the price of a product and the quantity of the product supplied. A **supply curve** shows on a graph the relationship between the price of a product and the quantity of the product supplied. When the price of a product rises, producing the product is more profitable, and a greater amount will be supplied. The **law of supply** states that, holding everything else constant, the quantity of a product supplied increases when the price rises and decreases when the price falls. Changes in the prices of inputs, technology, the prices of substitutes in production, expected future prices, and the number of firms in a market all cause the supply curve to shift. **Technological change** is a positive or negative change in the ability of a firm to produce a given level of output with a given quantity of inputs. A change in supply refers to a shift of the supply curve. A change in quantity supplied refers to a movement along the supply curve as a result of a change in the product's price.

MyEconLab   Visit **www.myeconlab.com** to complete these exercises online and get instant feedback.

## Review Questions

**2.1**  What is a supply schedule? What is a supply curve?

**2.2**  What is the difference between a change in supply and a change in the quantity supplied?

**2.3**  What is the law of supply? What are the main variables that will cause a supply curve to shift? Give an example of each.

## Problems and Applications

**2.4**  Briefly explain whether each of the following statements describes a change in supply or a change in the quantity supplied:

  **a.**  To take advantage of high prices for snow shovels during a snowy winter, Alexander Shovels, Inc., decides to increase output.

  **b.**  The success of the Apple iPad leads more firms to begin producing tablet computers.

  **c.**  In the six months following the Japanese earthquake and tsunami in 2011, production of automobiles in Japan declined by 20 percent.

**2.5**  Suppose that the curves at the top of the next column represent two supply curves for rib eye steaks. What would cause a movement from point *A* to point *B* on *S₁*? Name two variables that would cause a movement from point *A* to point *C*.

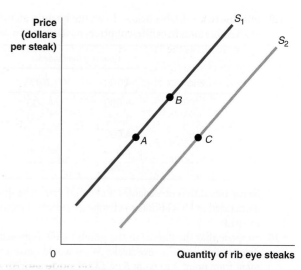

**2.6**  Suppose that the following table shows the quantity supplied of UGG boots at five different prices in 2012 and in 2013:

| Price | Quantity Supplied | |
| --- | --- | --- |
| | 2012 | 2013 |
| $160 | 300,000 | 200,000 |
| 170 | 350,000 | 250,000 |
| 180 | 400,000 | 300,000 |
| 190 | 450,000 | 350,000 |
| 200 | 500,000 | 400,000 |

Name two different variables that would cause the quantity supplied of UGG boots to change as indicated in the table from 2012 to 2013.

**2.7**  Will each firm in the tablet computer industry always supply the same quantity as every other firm at each price? What factors might cause the quantity of tablet computers supplied by different firms to be different at a particular price?

**2.8**  If the price of a good increases, is the increase in the quantity of the good supplied likely to be smaller or larger, the longer the time period being considered? Briefly explain.

---

##  3.3  Market Equilibrium: Putting Demand and Supply Together, pages 82–85

LEARNING OBJECTIVE: Use a graph to illustrate market equilibrium.

## Summary

**Market equilibrium** occurs where the demand curve intersects the supply curve. A **competitive market equilibrium** has a market equilibrium with many buyers and many sellers. Only at this point is the quantity demanded equal to the quantity supplied. Prices above equilibrium result in **surpluses**, with the quantity supplied being greater than the quantity demanded. Surpluses cause the market price to fall. Prices below equilibrium result in **shortages**, with the quantity demanded being greater than the quantity supplied. Shortages cause the market price to rise.

MyEconLab   Visit **www.myeconlab.com** to complete these exercises online and get instant feedback.

## Review Questions

**3.1**  What do economists mean by *market equilibrium*?

**3.2**  What do economists mean by a *shortage*? By a *surplus*?

**3.3**  What happens in a market if the current price is above the equilibrium price? What happens if the current price is below the equilibrium price?

## Problems and Applications

**3.4**  Briefly explain whether you agree with the following statement: "When there is a shortage of a good, consumers eventually give up trying to buy it, so the demand for the good declines, and the price falls until the market is finally in equilibrium."

**3.5** [**Related to** Solved Problem 3.3 **on page 84**] In *The Wealth of Nations*, Adam Smith discussed what has come to be known as the "diamond and water paradox":

> Nothing is more useful than water: but it will purchase scarce anything; scarce anything can be had in exchange for it. A diamond, on the contrary, has scarce any value in use; but a very great quantity of other goods may frequently be had in exchange for it.

Graph the market for diamonds and the market for water. Show how it is possible for the price of water to be much lower than the price of diamonds, even though the demand for water is much greater than the demand for diamonds.

From Adam Smith, *An Inquiry into the Nature and Causes of the Wealth of Nations*, Vol. I, (Oxford, UK: Oxford University Press, 1976 original edition, 1776).

**3.6** [**Related to** Solved Problem 3.3 **on page 84**] An article discusses the market for autographs by Mickey Mantle, the superstar centerfielder for the New York Yankees during the 1950s and 1960s: "At card shows, golf outings, charity dinners, Mr. Mantle signed his name over and over." One expert on sport autographs is quoted as saying: "He was a real good signer. . . . He is not rare." Yet the article quotes another expert as saying: "Mr. Mantle's autograph ranks No. 3 of most-popular autographs, behind Babe Ruth and Muhammad Ali." A baseball signed by Mantle is likely to sell for the relatively high price of $250 to $400. By contrast, baseballs signed by Whitey Ford, a teammate of Mantle's on the Yankees, typically sell for less than $150. Use one graph to show both the demand and supply for autographs by Whitey Ford and the demand and supply for autographs by Mickey Mantle. Show how it is possible for the price of Mantle's autographs to be higher than the price of Ford's autographs, even though the supply of Mantle autographs is larger than the supply of Ford autographs.

Based on Beth DeCarbo, "Mantle Autographs Not Rare, but Collectors Don't Care," *Wall Street Journal*, August 4, 2008.

**3.7** If a market is in equilibrium, is it necessarily true that all buyers and all sellers are satisfied with the market price? Briefly explain.

**3.8** During the summer of 2011, General Motors (GM) had trouble selling pickup trucks. According to an article in *USA Today*:

> General Motors dealers had a 122-day supply of Chevrolet Silverado and GMC Sierra pickups in June, more than 50% above what's considered optimum. . . . Behind the glut: The year started strong and makers pumped up production. Then the economy slowed faster than they cut back.

**a.** What does a glut imply about the quantity demanded of GM pickup trucks relative to the quantity supplied?

**b.** Would prices of GM pickup trucks be expected to rise or fall in the summer of 2011?

**c.** Why did the slowing economy help cause the glut of pickup trucks?

From Chris Woodyard, "Pickup Truck Glut Brings Hot Deals This Summer," *USA Today*, July 11, 2011.

---

## 3.4 The Effect of Demand and Supply Shifts on Equilibrium, pages 85–91

LEARNING OBJECTIVE: Use demand and supply graphs to predict changes in prices and quantities.

## Summary

In most markets, demand and supply curves shift frequently, causing changes in equilibrium prices and quantities. Over time, if demand increases more than supply, equilibrium price will rise. If supply increases more than demand, equilibrium price will fall.

 Visit **www.myeconlab.com** to complete these exercises online and get instant feedback.

## Review Questions

**4.1** Draw a demand and supply graph to show the effect on the equilibrium price in a market in the following two situations:
 **a.** The demand curve shifts to the right.
 **b.** The supply curve shifts to the left.

**4.2** If, over time, the demand curve for a product shifts to the right more than the supply curve does, what will happen to the equilibrium price? What will happen to the equilibrium price if the supply curve shifts to the right more than the demand curve? For each case, draw a demand and supply graph to illustrate your answer.

## Problems and Applications

**4.3** The following is from an article in the *Wall Street Journal*:

> Fuel prices tend to rise [during the summer] for a number of reasons, from the use of more expensive fuel additives in warm weather to maintenance shutdowns at refineries that tend to tighten the supply. Demand for gasoline also traditionally rises during the summer driving season as more people head out on long vacation road trips.

Draw a demand and supply graph of the market for gasoline to analyze the situation described in this article. Be sure to indicate the equilibrium price of gasoline at the beginning of summer, the equilibrium price of gasoline during summer, and any shifts in the demand curve and supply curve for gasoline.

"Is $4 per Gallon the New 'Normal' for Gas?" by Jonathan Welsh from *The Wall Street Journal*, June 11, 2011. Copyright © 2011 by *Dow Jones & Company, Inc*. Reproduced with permission of *Dow Jones & Company, Inc*.

**4.4** According to an article in the *Wall Street Journal* about the effect of increases in the demand for corn: "Farmers are likely to cut back on some crops, such as soybeans and rice, to make room for the additional corn." Use a demand and supply graph to analyze the effect on the equilibrium price of soybeans resulting from the increase in the demand for corn.

From Scott Kilman, "Corn Planting to Surge as Farmers Chase High Prices," *Wall Street Journal*, March 31, 2011.

**4.5** As oil prices rose during 2006, the demand for alternative fuels increased. Ethanol, one alternative fuel, is made from corn. According to an article in the *Wall Street Journal*, the price of tortillas, which are made from corn, also rose during 2006: "The price spike [in tortillas] is part of a ripple effect from the ethanol boom."

a. Draw a demand and supply graph for the corn market and use it to show the effect on this market of an increase in the demand for ethanol. Be sure to indicate the equilibrium price and quantity before and after the increase in the demand for ethanol.

b. Draw a demand and supply graph for the tortilla market and use it to show the effect on this market of an increase in the price of corn. Once again, be sure to indicate the equilibrium price and quantity before and after the increase in the demand for ethanol.

c. During 2009, the demand for gasoline had fallen, lowering its price. The demand for ethanol had declined as well. Ethanol producers, though, were asking the Environmental Protection Agency (EPA) to raise the allowable amount of ethanol in gasoline blends from 10 percent to 15 percent. If the EPA were to agree to this proposal, what would be the likely effect on tortilla prices?

Based on Stephen Power, "Industry Seeks to Raise Ethanol Levels in Fuel," *Wall Street Journal*, March 7, 2009; and Mark Gongloff, "Tortilla Soup," *Wall Street Journal*, January 25, 2007.

**4.6** **[Related to the** Making the Connection **on page 86]** During 2009, the demand for LCD televisions appeared to be falling. At the same time, some industry observers expected that several smaller television manufacturers might exit the market. Use a demand and supply graph to analyze the effects of these factors on the equilibrium price and quantity of LCD televisions. Clearly show on your graph the old equilibrium price and quantity and the new equilibrium price and quantity. Can you tell for certain whether the new equilibrium price will be higher or lower than the old equilibrium price? Briefly explain.

**4.7** **[Related to** Solved Problem 3.4 **on page 88]** The demand for watermelons is highest during summer and lowest during winter. Yet watermelon prices are normally lower in summer than in winter. Use a demand and supply graph to demonstrate how this is possible. Be sure to carefully label the curves in your graph and to clearly indicate the equilibrium summer price and the equilibrium winter price.

**4.8** **[Related to** Solved Problem 3.4 **on page 88]** According to one observer of the lobster market: "After Labor Day, when the vacationers have gone home, the lobstermen usually have a month or more of good fishing conditions, except for the occasional hurricane." Use a demand and supply graph to explain whether lobster prices are likely to be higher or lower during the fall than during the summer.

Based on Jay Harlow, "Lobster: An Affordable Luxury," Sallybernstein.com.

**4.9** Years ago, an apple producer argued that the United States should enact a tariff, or a tax, on imports of bananas. His reasoning was that "the enormous imports of cheap bananas into the United States tend to curtail the domestic consumption of fresh fruits produced in the United States."

a. Was the apple producer assuming that apples and bananas are substitutes or complements? Briefly explain.

b. If a tariff on bananas acts as an increase in the cost of supplying bananas in the United States, use two demand and supply graphs to show the effects of the apple producer's proposal. One graph should show the effect on the banana market in the United States, and the other graph should show the effect on the apple market in the United States. Be sure to label the change

in equilibrium price and quantity in each market and any shifts in the demand and supply curves.

From Douglas A. Irwin, *Peddling Protectionism: Smoot-Hawley and the Great Depression*, (Princeton, NJ: Princeton University Press, 2011), p. 22.

**4.10** An article in the *Wall Street Journal* noted that the demand for Internet advertising was declining at the same time that the number of Internet sites accepting advertising was increasing. After reading the article, a student argues: "From this information, we know that the price of Internet ads should fall, but we don't know whether the total quantity of Internet ads will increase or decrease." Is the student's analysis correct? Illustrate your answer with a demand and supply graph.

Based on Martin Peers, "Future Shock for Internet Ads?" *Wall Street Journal*, February 17, 2009.

**4.11** Historically, the production of many perishable foods, such as dairy products, was highly seasonal. Thus, as the supply of those products fluctuated, prices tended to fluctuate tremendously—typically by 25 to 50 percent or more—over the course of the year. One impact of mechanical refrigeration, which was commercialized on a large scale in the last decade of the nineteenth century, was that suppliers could store perishables from one season to the next. Economists have estimated that as a result of refrigerated storage, wholesale prices rose by roughly 10 percent during peak supply periods, while they fell by almost the same amount during the off season. Use a demand and supply graph for each season to illustrate how refrigeration affected the market for perishable food.

Based on Lee A. Craig, Barry Goodwin, and Thomas Grennes, "The Effect of Mechanical Refrigeration on Nutrition in the U.S.," *Social Science History*, Vol. 28, No. 2, Summer 2004, pp. 327–328.

**4.12** Briefly explain whether each of the following statements is true or false.

a. If the demand and supply for a product both increase, the equilibrium quantity of the product must also increase.

b. If the demand and supply for a product both increase, the equilibrium price of the product must also increase.

c. If the demand for a product decreases and the supply of the product increases, the equilibrium price of the product may increase or decrease, depending on whether supply or demand has shifted more.

**4.13** **[Related to the** Don't Let This Happen to You **on page 90]** A student writes the following: "Increased production leads to a lower price, which in turn increases demand." Do you agree with his reasoning? Briefly explain.

**4.14** **[Related to the** Don't Let This Happen to You **on page 90]** A student was asked to draw a demand and supply graph to illustrate the effect on the tablet computers market of a fall in the price of displays used in tablet computers, holding everything else constant. She drew the graph below and explained it as follows:

Displays are an input to tablet computers, so a fall in the price of displays will cause the supply curve for tablets to shift to the right (from $S_1$ to $S_2$). Because this shift in the supply curve results in a lower price ($P_2$), consumers will want to buy more tablets, and the demand curve will shift to the right (from $D_1$ to $D_2$). We know that more tablets will be sold, but we can't be sure whether the price of tablets will rise or fall. That depends on whether the supply curve or the demand curve has shifted farther to the right. I assume that the effect on supply is greater than the effect on demand, so I show the final equilibrium price ($P_3$) as being lower than the initial equilibrium price ($P_1$).

Explain whether you agree or disagree with the student's analysis. Be careful to explain exactly what—if anything—you find wrong with her analysis.

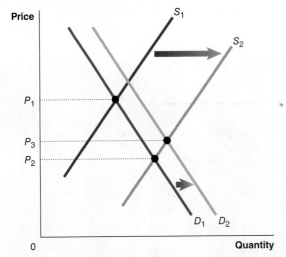

**4.15** Following are four graphs and four market scenarios, each of which would cause either a movement along the supply curve for Pepsi or a shift of the supply curve. Match each scenario with the appropriate graph.

**a.** A decrease in the supply of Coke

**b.** A drop in the average household income in the United States from $52,000 to $50,000

**c.** An improvement in soft drink bottling technology

**d.** An increase in the prices of sugar and high-fructose corn syrup

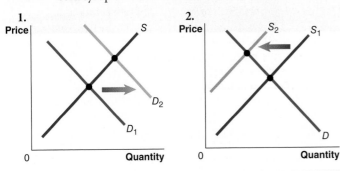

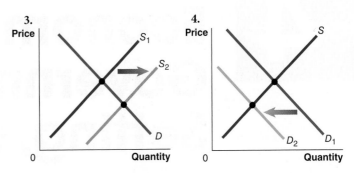

**4.16** Proposals have been made to increase government regulation of firms providing childcare services by, for instance, setting education requirements for childcare workers. Suppose that these regulations increase the quality of childcare and cause the demand for childcare services to increase. At the same time, assume that complying with the new government regulations increases the costs of firms providing childcare services. Draw a demand and supply graph to illustrate the effects of these changes in the market for childcare services. Briefly explain whether the total quantity of childcare services purchased will increase or decrease as a result of regulation.

**4.17** The following graphs show the supply and demand curves for two markets. One of the markets is for BMW automobiles, and the other is for a cancer-fighting drug, without which lung cancer patients will die. Briefly explain which graph most likely represents which market.

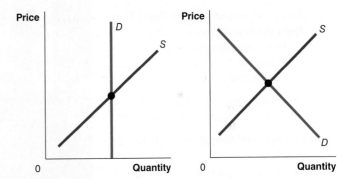

# Economic Efficiency, Government Price Setting, and Taxes

## Chapter Outline and Learning Objectives

# Should the Government Control Apartment Rents?

Robert F. Moss owns an apartment building in New York City. Unlike most other business owners, he is not free to charge the prices he would like for the service he offers. In New York, San Francisco, Los Angeles, and nearly 200 smaller cities, apartments are subject to rent control by the local government. Rent control puts a legal limit on the rent that landlords can charge for an apartment.

New York City has 2 million apartments, about half of which are subject to rent control. The other 1 million apartments have their rents determined in the market by the demand and supply for apartments. Mr. Moss's building includes apartments that are rent controlled and apartments that are not. The market-determined rents are usually far above the controlled rents. The government regulations that determine what Mr. Moss can charge for a rent-controlled apartment are very complex. The following is Mr. Moss's description:

> When [an apartment] is vacated, state rent laws entitle landlords to raise rents in three primary ways: a vacancy increase of 20 percent for a new tenant's two-year lease (a bit less for a one-year lease); one-fortieth per month of the cost of any improvements, and a "longevity bonus" for longtime residents (calculated at six-tenths of 1 percent times the tenant's last legal rent multiplied by the number of years of residency beyond eight). . . . Apartments renting for $2,000 a month are automatically deregulated if they are vacant. Occupied apartments whose rent reaches that figure can

be deregulated if the income of the tenants has been $175,000 or more for two years.

As this description shows, someone earning a living by renting out apartments in New York City has to deal with much more complex government regulation of prices than someone who owns, for instance, a McDonald's restaurant.

Tenants in rent-controlled apartments in New York are reluctant to see rent control end because rents for those apartments are much lower than rents for apartments that aren't rent controlled. Although rent control laws are intended to make housing more affordable for people with low incomes, high-income people can end up benefiting. For example, in New York City, rent control has resulted in actress Mia Farrow and television host Alistair Cooke living for many years in large apartments overlooking Central Park, while paying rents far below market levels. When the FBI arrested James "Whitey" Bulger, a former Boston crime boss, in 2011, they discovered that he had been living for more than 15 years in a rent-controlled apartment in Santa Monica.

**AN INSIDE LOOK AT POLICY** on **page 122** discusses a legal battle between Oscar-winning actress Faye Dunaway and the landlord of her rent-controlled New York City apartment.

Based on Robert F. Moss, "A Landlord's Lot Is Sometimes Not an Easy One," *New York Times*, August 3, 2003; and Lynda Gorov, "Whitey Bulger Used Rent-Controlled Apartment Since Mid-1990s, Property Manager Says," *The Boston Globe*, June 23, 2011.

## Economics in Your Life

### Does Rent Control Make It Easier for You to Find an Affordable Apartment?

Suppose you have job offers in two cities. One factor in deciding which job to accept is whether you can find an affordable apartment. If one city has rent control, are you more likely to find an affordable apartment in that city, or would you be better off looking for an apartment in a city without rent control? As you read the chapter, see if you can answer this question. You can check your answer against the one we provide on **page 121** at the end of this chapter.

W e saw in Chapter 3 that in a competitive market the price adjusts to ensure that the quantity demanded equals the quantity supplied. Stated another way, in equilibrium, every consumer willing to pay the market price is able to buy as much of the product as the consumer wants, and every firm willing to accept the market price can sell as much as it wants. Even so, consumers would naturally prefer to pay a lower price, and sellers would prefer to receive a higher price. Normally, consumers and firms have no choice but to accept the equilibrium price if they wish to participate in the market. Occasionally, however, consumers succeed in having the government impose a **price ceiling**, which is a legally determined maximum price that sellers may charge. Rent control is an example of a price ceiling. Firms also sometimes succeed in having the government impose a **price floor**, which is a legally determined minimum price that sellers may receive. In markets for farm products such as milk, the government has been setting price floors that are above the equilibrium market price since the 1930s.

Another way the government intervenes in markets is by imposing taxes. The government relies on the revenue raised from taxes to finance its operations. Unfortunately, whenever the government imposes a price ceiling, a price floor, or a tax, there are predictable negative economic consequences. It is important for government policymakers and voters to understand the negative consequences when evaluating these policies. Economists have developed the concepts of *consumer surplus*, *producer surplus*, and *economic surplus* to analyze the economic effects of price ceilings, price floors, and taxes.

**Price ceiling** A legally determined maximum price that sellers may charge.

**Price floor** A legally determined minimum price that sellers may receive.

# Consumer Surplus and Producer Surplus

Consumer surplus measures the dollar benefit consumers receive from buying goods or services in a particular market. Producer surplus measures the dollar benefit firms receive from selling goods or services in a particular market. Economic surplus in a market is the sum of consumer surplus plus producer surplus. As we will see, *when the government imposes a price ceiling or a price floor, the amount of economic surplus in a market is reduced*—in other words, price ceilings and price floors reduce the total benefit to consumers and firms from buying and selling in a market. To understand why this is true, we need to understand how consumer surplus and producer surplus are determined.

## Consumer Surplus

**Consumer surplus** is the difference between the highest price a consumer is willing to pay for a good or service and the price the consumer actually pays. For example, suppose you are in Wal-Mart, and you see a DVD of *Harry Potter and the Deathly Hallows, Part 2* on the rack. No price is indicated on the package, so you take it over to the register to check the price. As you walk to the register, you think to yourself that $18 is the highest price you would be willing to pay. At the register, you find out that the price is actually $12, so you buy the DVD. Your consumer surplus in this example is $6: the difference between the $18 you were willing to pay and the $12 you actually paid.

We can use the demand curve to measure the total consumer surplus in a market. Demand curves show the willingness of consumers to purchase a product at different prices. Consumers are willing to purchase a product up to the point where the marginal benefit of consuming a product is equal to its price. The **marginal benefit** is the additional benefit to a consumer from consuming one more unit of a good or service. As a simple example, suppose there are only four consumers in the market for chai tea: Theresa, Tom, Terri, and Tim. Because these four consumers have different tastes for tea and different incomes, the marginal benefit each of them receives

**Consumer surplus** The difference between the highest price a consumer is willing to pay for a good or service and the price the consumer actually pays.

**Marginal benefit** The additional benefit to a consumer from consuming one more unit of a good or service.

| Consumer | Highest Price Willing to Pay |
|----------|------------------------------|
| Theresa | $6 |
| Tom | 5 |
| Terri | 4 |
| Tim | 3 |

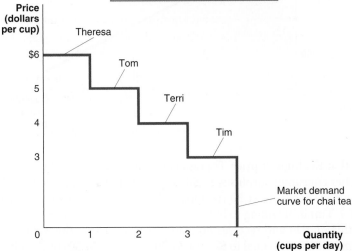

**Figure 4.1**

### Deriving the Demand Curve for Chai Tea

With four consumers in the market for chai tea, the demand curve is determined by the highest price each consumer is willing to pay. For prices above $6, no tea is sold because $6 is the highest price any consumer is willing to pay. For prices of $3 and below, every one of the four consumers is willing to buy a cup of tea.

from consuming a cup of tea will be different. Therefore, the highest price each is willing to pay for a cup of tea is also different. In Figure 4.1, the information from the table is used to construct a demand curve for chai tea. For prices above $6 per cup, no tea is sold because $6 is the highest price any of the consumers is willing to pay. At a price of $5, both Theresa and Tom are willing to buy tea, so two cups are sold. At prices of $3 and below, all four consumers are willing to buy tea, and four cups are sold.

Suppose the market price of tea is $3.50 per cup. As Figure 4.2 shows, the demand curve allows us to calculate the total consumer surplus in this market. In panel (a),

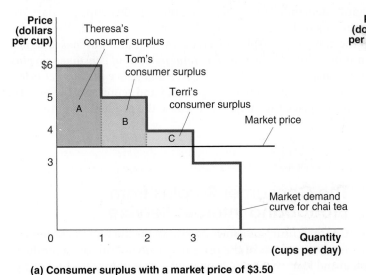

**(a) Consumer surplus with a market price of $3.50**

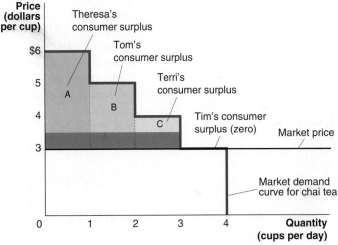

**(b) Consumer surplus with a market price of $3.00**

**Figure 4.2    Measuring Consumer Surplus**

Panel (a) shows the consumer surplus for Theresa, Tom, and Terri when the price of tea is $3.50 per cup. Theresa's consumer surplus is equal to the area of rectangle A and is the difference between the highest price she would pay—$6—and the market price of $3.50. Tom's consumer surplus is equal to the area of rectangle B, and Terri's consumer surplus is equal to the area of rectangle C. Total consumer

surplus in this market is equal to the sum of the areas of rectangles A, B, and C, or the total area below the demand curve and above the market price. In panel (b), consumer surplus increases by the shaded area as the market price declines from $3.50 to $3.00.

**Figure 4.3**

### Total Consumer Surplus in the Market for Chai Tea

The demand curve tells us that most buyers of chai tea would have been willing to pay more than the market price of $2.00. For each buyer, consumer surplus is equal to the difference between the highest price he or she is willing to pay and the market price actually paid. Therefore, the total amount of consumer surplus in the market for chai tea is equal to the area below the demand curve and above the market price. Consumer surplus represents the benefit to consumers in excess of the price they paid to purchase the product.

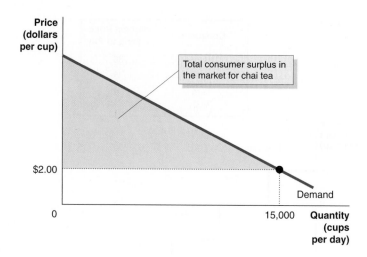

we can see that the highest price Theresa is willing to pay is $6, but because she pays only $3.50, her consumer surplus is $2.50 (shown by the area of rectangle *A*). Similarly, Tom's consumer surplus is $1.50 (rectangle *B*), and Terri's consumer surplus is $0.50 (rectangle *C*). Tim is unwilling to buy a cup of tea at a price of $3.50, so he doesn't participate in this market and receives no consumer surplus. In this simple example, the total consumer surplus is equal to $2.50 + $1.50 + $0.50 = $4.50 (or the sum of the areas of rectangles *A*, *B*, and *C*). Panel (b) shows that a lower price will increase consumer surplus. If the price of tea drops from $3.50 per cup to $3.00, Theresa, Tom, and Terri each receive $0.50 more in consumer surplus (shown by the shaded areas), so total consumer surplus in the market rises to $6.00. Tim now buys a cup of tea but doesn't receive any consumer surplus because the price is equal to the highest price he is willing to pay. In fact, Tim is indifferent between buying the cup or not—his well-being is the same either way.

The market demand curves shown in Figures 4.1 and 4.2 do not look like the smooth curves we saw in Chapter 3. This is because this example uses a small number of consumers, each consuming a single cup of tea. With many consumers, the market demand curve for chai tea will have the normal smooth shape shown in Figure 4.3. In this figure, the quantity demanded at a price of $2.00 is 15,000 cups per day. We can calculate total consumer surplus in Figure 4.3 the same way we did in Figures 4.1 and 4.2: by adding up the consumer surplus received on each unit purchased. Once again, we can draw an important conclusion: *The total amount of consumer surplus in a market is equal to the area below the demand curve and above the market price.* Consumer surplus is shown as the blue area in Figure 4.3 and represents the benefit to consumers in excess of the price they paid to purchase the product—in this case, chai tea.

|   |   |
|---|---|
| **Making the Connection** | ### The Consumer Surplus from Broadband Internet Service |

Consumer surplus allows us to measure the benefit consumers receive in excess of the price they paid to purchase a product. Recently, Shane Greenstein and Ryan McDevitt, economists at Northwestern University, estimated the consumer surplus that households receive from subscribing to broadband Internet service. To do this, they estimated the demand curve for broadband Internet service and then computed the shaded area shown in the graph on the next page.

In 2006, 47 million consumers paid an average price of $36 per month to subscribe to a broadband Internet service. The demand curve shows the marginal benefit consumers

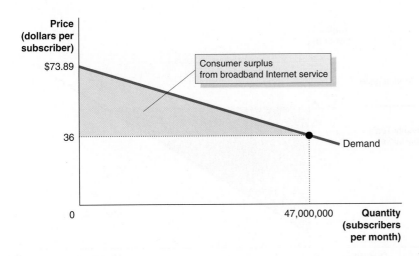

receive from subscribing to a broadband Internet service rather than using dialup or doing without access to the Internet. The area below the demand curve and above the $36 price line represents the difference between the price consumers would have paid rather than do without broadband service and the $36 they did pay. The shaded area on the graph represents the total consumer surplus in the market for broadband Internet service. Greenstein and McDevitt estimate that the value of this area is $890.5 million. This is one month's benefit to the consumers who subscribe to a broadband Internet service.

Based on Shane Greenstein and Ryan C. McDevitt, "The Broadband Bonus: Accounting for Broadband Internet's Impact on U.S. GDP," National Bureau of Economic Research Working Paper 14758, February 2009.

**Your Turn:** Test your understanding by doing related problem 1.9 on page 124 at the end of this chapter.

MyEconLab

## Producer Surplus

Just as demand curves show the willingness of consumers to buy a product at different prices, supply curves show the willingness of firms to supply a product at different prices. The willingness to supply a product depends on the cost of producing it. Firms will supply an additional unit of a product only if they receive a price equal to the additional cost of producing that unit. **Marginal cost** is the additional cost to a firm of producing one more unit of a good or service. Consider the marginal cost to the firm Heavenly Tea of producing one more cup: In this case, the marginal cost includes the ingredients to make the tea and the wages paid to the worker preparing the tea. Often, the marginal cost of producing a good increases as more of the good is produced during a given period of time. This is the key reason—as we saw in Chapter 3—that supply curves are upward sloping.

Panel (a) of Figure 4.4 shows Heavenly Tea's producer surplus. For simplicity, we show Heavenly producing only a small quantity of tea. The figure shows that Heavenly's marginal cost of producing the first cup of tea is $1.25. Its marginal cost of producing the second cup is $1.50, and so on. The marginal cost of each cup of tea is the lowest price Heavenly is willing to accept to supply that cup. The supply curve, then, is also a marginal cost curve. Suppose the market price of tea is $2.00 per cup. On the first cup of tea, the price is $0.75 higher than the lowest price Heavenly is willing to accept. **Producer surplus** is the difference between the lowest price a firm would be willing to accept for a good or service and the price it actually receives. Therefore, Heavenly's

**Marginal cost** The additional cost to a firm of producing one more unit of a good or service.

**Producer surplus** The difference between the lowest price a firm would be willing to accept for a good or service and the price it actually receives.

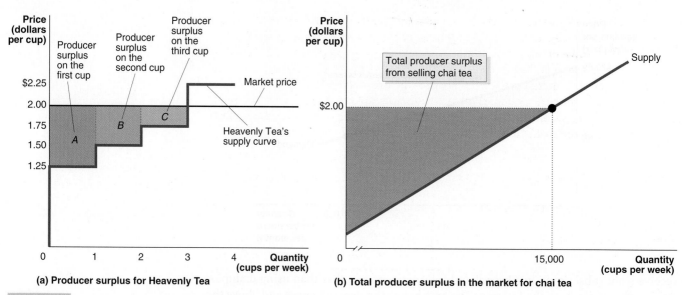

**Figure 4.4** Measuring Producer Surplus

Panel (a) shows Heavenly Tea's producer surplus. Producer surplus is the difference between the lowest price a firm would be willing to accept and the price it actually receives. The lowest price Heavenly Tea is willing to accept to supply a cup of tea is equal to its marginal cost of producing that cup. When the market price of tea is $2.00, Heavenly receives producer surplus of $0.75 on the first cup (the area of rectangle $A$), $0.50 on the second cup (rectangle $B$), and $0.25 on the third cup (rectangle $C$). In panel (b), the total amount of producer surplus tea sellers receive from selling chai tea can be calculated by adding up for the entire market the producer surplus received on each cup sold. In the figure, total producer surplus is equal to the area above the supply curve and below the market price, shown in red.

producer surplus on the first cup is $0.75 (shown by the area of rectangle $A$). Its producer surplus on the second cup is $0.50 (rectangle $B$). Its producer surplus on the third cup is $0.25 (rectangle $C$). Heavenly will not be willing to supply the fourth cup because the marginal cost of producing it is greater than the market price. Heavenly Tea's total producer surplus is equal to $0.75 + $0.50 + $0.25 = $1.50 (or the sum of rectangles $A$, $B$, and $C$). A higher price will increase producer surplus. For example, if the market price of chai tea rises from $2.00 to $2.25, Heavenly Tea's producer surplus will increase from $1.50 to $2.25. (Make sure you understand how the new level of producer surplus was calculated.)

The supply curve shown in panel (a) of Figure 4.4 does not look like the smooth curves we saw in Chapter 3 because this example uses a single firm producing only a small quantity of tea. With many firms, the market supply curve for chai tea will have the normal smooth shape shown in panel (b) of Figure 4.4. In panel (b), the quantity supplied at a price of $2.00 is 15,000 cups per day. We can calculate total producer surplus in panel (b) the same way we did in panel (a): by adding up the producer surplus received on each cup sold. Therefore, *the total amount of producer surplus in a market is equal to the area above the market supply curve and below the market price*. The total producer surplus tea sellers receive from selling chai tea is shown as the red area in panel (b) of Figure 4.4.

## What Consumer Surplus and Producer Surplus Measure

We have seen that consumer surplus measures the benefit to consumers from participating in a market, and producer surplus measures the benefit to producers from participating in a market. It is important, however, to be clear about what this means. In a sense, consumer surplus measures the *net* benefit to consumers from participating in a market rather than the *total* benefit. That is, if the price of a product were zero, the consumer surplus in a market would be all of the area under the demand curve. When the price is not zero, consumer surplus is the area below the demand curve and above the market price. So, consumer surplus in a market is equal to the total benefit received by consumers minus the total amount they must pay to buy the good or service.

Similarly, producer surplus measures the *net* benefit received by producers from participating in a market. If producers could supply a good or service at zero cost, the producer surplus in a market would be all of the area below the market price. When cost is not zero, producer surplus is the area below the market price and above the supply curve. So, producer surplus in a market is equal to the total amount firms receive from consumers minus the cost of producing the good or service.

# The Efficiency of Competitive Markets

**4.2 LEARNING** OBJECTIVE

Understand the concept of economic efficiency.

In Chapter 3, we defined a *competitive market* as a market with many buyers and many sellers. An important advantage of the market system is that it results in efficient economic outcomes. But what do we mean by *economic efficiency*? The concepts we have developed so far in this chapter give us two ways to think about the economic efficiency of competitive markets. We can think in terms of marginal benefit and marginal cost. We can also think in terms of consumer surplus and producer surplus. As we will see, these two approaches lead to the same outcome, but using both can increase our understanding of economic efficiency.

## Marginal Benefit Equals Marginal Cost in Competitive Equilibrium

Figure 4.5 again shows the market for chai tea. Recall from our discussion that the demand curve shows the marginal benefit received by consumers, and the supply curve shows the marginal cost of production. To achieve economic efficiency in this market, the marginal benefit from the last unit sold should equal the marginal cost of production. The figure shows that this equality occurs at competitive equilibrium where 15,000 cups per day are produced and marginal benefit and marginal cost are both equal to $2.00. Why is this outcome economically efficient? Because every cup of chai tea has been produced where the marginal benefit to buyers is greater than or equal to the marginal cost to producers.

Another way to see why the level of output at competitive equilibrium is efficient is to consider what the situation would be if output were at a different level. For instance, suppose that output of chai tea were 14,000 cups per day. Figure 4.5 shows that at this level of output, the marginal benefit from the last cup sold is $2.20, whereas the marginal cost is only $1.80. This level of output is not efficient because 1,000 more cups could be produced for which the additional benefit to consumers would be greater than the additional cost of production. Consumers would willingly purchase those cups, and

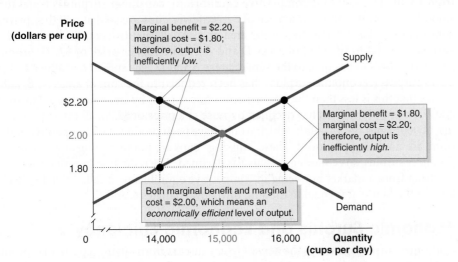

**Price (dollars per cup)**

Marginal benefit = $2.20, marginal cost = $1.80; therefore, output is inefficiently *low*.

Supply

Marginal benefit = $1.80, marginal cost = $2.20; therefore, output is inefficiently *high*.

Both marginal benefit and marginal cost = $2.00, which means an *economically efficient* level of output.

Demand

0    14,000    15,000    16,000    **Quantity (cups per day)**

**Figure 4.5**

**Marginal Benefit Equals Marginal Cost Only at Competitive Equilibrium**

In a competitive market, equilibrium occurs at a quantity of 15,000 cups and a price of $2.00 per cup, where marginal benefit equals marginal cost. This is the economically efficient level of output because every cup has been produced where the marginal benefit to buyers is greater than or equal to the marginal cost to producers.

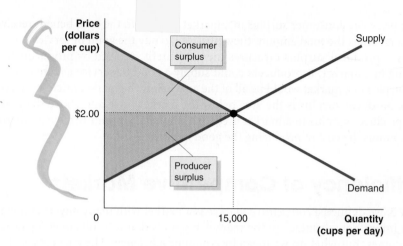

**Figure 4.6**

**Economic Surplus Equals the Sum of Consumer Surplus and Producer Surplus**

The economic surplus in a market is the sum of the blue area, representing consumer surplus, and the red area, representing producer surplus.

tea sellers would willingly supply them, making both consumers and sellers better off. Similarly, if the output of chai tea were 16,000 cups per day, the marginal cost of the 16,000th cup is $2.20, whereas the marginal benefit is only $1.80. Tea sellers would only be willing to supply this cup at a price of $2.20, which is $0.40 higher than consumers would be willing to pay. In fact, consumers would not be willing to pay the price tea sellers would need to receive for any cup beyond the 15,000th.

To summarize, we can say this: *Equilibrium in a competitive market results in the economically efficient level of output, where marginal benefit equals marginal cost.*

## Economic Surplus

**Economic surplus** The sum of consumer surplus and producer surplus.

**Economic surplus** in a market is the sum of consumer surplus and producer surplus. In a competitive market, with many buyers and sellers and no government restrictions, economic surplus is at a maximum when the market is in equilibrium. To see this, let's look one more time at the market for chai tea shown in Figure 4.6. The consumer surplus in this market is the blue area below the demand curve and above the line indicating the equilibrium price of $2.00. The producer surplus is the red area above the supply curve and below the price line.

## Deadweight Loss

**Deadweight loss** The reduction in economic surplus resulting from a market not being in competitive equilibrium.

To show that economic surplus is maximized at equilibrium, consider a situation in which the price of chai tea is *above* the equilibrium price, as shown in Figure 4.7. At a price of $2.20 per cup, the number of cups consumers are willing to buy per day drops from 15,000 to 14,000. At competitive equilibrium, consumer surplus is equal to the sum of areas A, B, and C. At a price of $2.20, fewer cups are sold at a higher price, so consumer surplus declines to just the area of A. At competitive equilibrium, producer surplus is equal to the sum of areas D and E. At the higher price of $2.20, producer surplus changes to be equal to the sum of areas B and D. The sum of consumer and producer surplus—economic surplus—has been reduced to the sum of areas A, B, and D. Notice that this is less than the original economic surplus by an amount equal to areas C and E. Economic surplus has declined because at a price of $2.20, all the cups between the 14,000th and the 15,000th, which would have been produced in competitive equilibrium, are not being produced. These "missing" cups are not providing any consumer or producer surplus, so economic surplus has declined. The reduction in economic surplus resulting from a market not being in competitive equilibrium is called the **deadweight loss**. In the figure, it is equal to the sum of yellow triangles C and E.

## Economic Surplus and Economic Efficiency

Consumer surplus measures the benefit to consumers from buying a particular product, such as chai tea. Producer surplus measures the benefit to firms from selling a particular

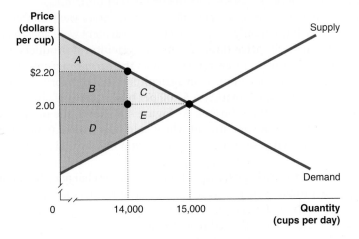

| | At Competitive Equilibrium | At a Price of $2.20 |
|---|---|---|
| Consumer Surplus | A + B + C | A |
| Producer Surplus | D + E | B + D |
| Deadweight Loss | None | C + E |

**Figure 4.7**

**When a Market Is Not in Equilibrium, There Is a Deadweight Loss**

Economic surplus is maximized when a market is in competitive equilibrium. When a market is not in equilibrium, there is a deadweight loss. When the price of chai tea is $2.20 instead of $2.00, consumer surplus declines from an amount equal to the sum of areas *A*, *B*, and *C* to just area *A*. Producer surplus increases from the sum of areas *D* and *E* to the sum of areas *B* and *D*. At competitive equilibrium, there is no deadweight loss. At a price of $2.20, there is a deadweight loss equal to the sum of areas *C* and *E*.

product. Therefore, economic surplus—which is the sum of the benefit to firms plus the benefit to consumers—is the best measure we have of the benefit to society from the production of a particular good or service. This gives us a second way of characterizing the economic efficiency of a competitive market: *Equilibrium in a competitive market results in the greatest amount of economic surplus, or total net benefit to society, from the production of a good or service.* Anything that causes the market for a good or service not to be in competitive equilibrium reduces the total benefit to society from the production of that good or service.

Now we can give a more general definition of *economic efficiency* in terms of our two approaches: **Economic efficiency** is a market outcome in which the marginal benefit to consumers of the last unit produced is equal to its marginal cost of production and in which the sum of consumer surplus and producer surplus is at a maximum.

**Economic efficiency** A market outcome in which the marginal benefit to consumers of the last unit produced is equal to its marginal cost of production and in which the sum of consumer surplus and producer surplus is at a maximum.

# Government Intervention in the Market: Price Floors and Price Ceilings

**4.3 LEARNING** OBJECTIVE

Explain the economic effect of government-imposed price floors and price ceilings.

Notice that we have *not* concluded that every *individual* is better off if a market is at competitive equilibrium. We have only concluded that economic surplus, or the *total* net benefit to society, is greatest at competitive equilibrium. Any individual producer would rather receive a higher price, and any individual consumer would rather pay a lower price, but usually producers can sell and consumers can buy only at the competitive equilibrium price.

Producers or consumers who are dissatisfied with the competitive equilibrium price can lobby the government to legally require that a different price be charged. In the United States, the government only occasionally overrides the market outcome by setting prices. When the government does intervene, it can either attempt to aid sellers by requiring that a price be above equilibrium—a price floor—or aid buyers by requiring that a price be below equilibrium—a price ceiling. To affect the market outcome, the government must set a price floor that is above the equilibrium price or set a price ceiling that is below the equilibrium price. Otherwise, the price ceiling or price floor will not be *binding* on buyers and sellers. The preceding section demonstrates that moving away from competitive equilibrium will reduce economic efficiency. We can use the concepts of consumer surplus, producer surplus, and deadweight loss to see more clearly the economic inefficiency of price floors and price ceilings.

# Price Floors: Government Policy in Agricultural Markets

The Great Depression of the 1930s was the worst economic disaster in U.S. history, affecting every sector of the U.S. economy. Many farmers were unable to sell their products or could sell them only at very low prices. Farmers were able to convince the federal government to set price floors for many agricultural products. Government intervention in agriculture—often referred to as the *farm program*—has continued ever since. To see how a price floor in an agricultural market works, suppose that the equilibrium price in the wheat market is $3.00 per bushel, but the government decides to set a price floor of $3.50 per bushel. As Figure 4.8 shows, the price of wheat rises from $3.00 to $3.50, and the quantity of wheat sold falls from 2.0 billion bushels per year to 1.8 billion. Initially, suppose that production of wheat also falls to 1.8 billion bushels.

Just as we saw in the earlier example of the market for chai tea (shown in Figure 4.7 on page 109), the producer surplus received by wheat farmers increases by an amount equal to the area of the red rectangle *A* and falls by an amount equal to the area of the yellow triangle *C*. The area of the red rectangle *A* represents a transfer from consumer surplus to producer surplus. The total fall in consumer surplus is equal to the area of the red rectangle *A* plus the area of the yellow triangle *B*. Wheat farmers benefit from this program, but consumers lose. There is also a deadweight loss equal to the areas of the yellow triangles *B* and *C*, which represents the decline in economic efficiency due to the price floor. There is a deadweight loss because the price floor has reduced the amount of economic surplus in the market for wheat. Or, looked at another way, the price floor has caused the marginal benefit of the last bushel of wheat to be greater than the marginal cost of producing it. We can conclude that a price floor reduces economic efficiency.

We assumed initially that farmers reduce their production of wheat to the amount consumers are willing to buy. In fact, as Figure 4.8 shows, a price floor will cause the quantity of wheat that farmers want to supply to increase from 2.0 billion to 2.2 billion bushels. Because the higher price also reduces the amount of wheat consumers want to buy, the result is a surplus of 0.4 billion bushels of wheat (the 2.2 billion bushels supplied minus the 1.8 billion demanded).

## Figure 4.8

### The Economic Effect of a Price Floor in the Wheat Market

If wheat farmers convince the government to impose a price floor of $3.50 per bushel, the amount of wheat sold will fall from 2.0 billion bushels per year to 1.8 billion. If we assume that farmers produce 1.8 billion bushels, producer surplus then increases by the red rectangle *A*—which is transferred from consumer surplus—and falls by the yellow triangle *C*. Consumer surplus declines by the red rectangle *A* plus the yellow triangle *B*. There is a deadweight loss equal to the yellow triangles *B* and *C*, representing the decline in economic efficiency due to the price floor. In reality, a price floor of $3.50 per bushel will cause farmers to expand their production from 2.0 billion to 2.2 billion bushels, resulting in a surplus of wheat.

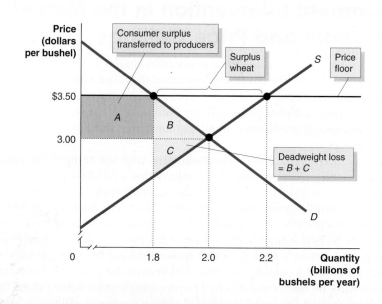

The federal government's farm programs have often resulted in large surpluses of wheat and other agricultural products. In response, the government has usually either bought the surplus food or paid farmers to restrict supply by taking some land out of cultivation. Because both of these options are expensive, Congress passed the Freedom to Farm Act of 1996. The intent of the act was to phase out price floors and government purchases of surpluses and return to a free market in agriculture. To allow farmers time to adjust, the federal government began paying farmers *subsidies*, or cash payments based on the number of acres planted. Although the subsidies were originally scheduled to be phased out, Congress has passed additional Farm Acts that have resulted in the continuation of subsidies.

| | |
|---|---|
| Making the Connection | **Price Floors in Labor Markets: The Debate over Minimum Wage Policy** |

The minimum wage may be the most controversial "price floor." Supporters see the minimum wage as a way of raising the incomes of low-skilled workers. Opponents argue that it results in fewer jobs and imposes large costs on small businesses.

Since July 2009, the national minimum wage as set by Congress has been $7.25 per hour for most occupations. It is illegal for an employer to pay less than this wage in those occupations. For most workers, the minimum wage is irrelevant because it is well below the wage employers are voluntarily willing to pay them. But for low-skilled workers—such as workers in fast-food restaurants—the minimum wage is above the wage they would otherwise receive. The following figure shows the effect of the minimum wage on employment in the market for low-skilled labor.

Without a minimum wage, the equilibrium wage would be $W_1$ and the number of workers hired would be $L_1$. With a minimum wage set above the equilibrium wage, the number of workers demanded by employers declines from $L_1$ to $L_2$, and the quantity of labor supplied increases to $L_3$, leading to a surplus of workers unable to find jobs equal to $L_3 - L_2$. The quantity of labor supplied increases because the higher wage attracts more people to work. For instance, some teenagers may decide that working after school is worthwhile at the minimum wage of $7.25 per hour but would not be worthwhile at a lower wage.

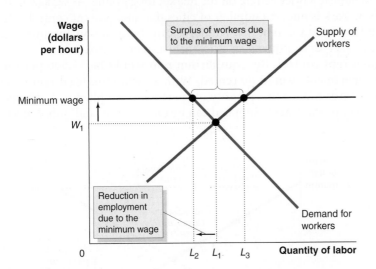

This analysis is very similar to our analysis of the wheat market in Figure 4.8. Just as a price floor in the wheat market leads to less wheat being consumed, a price floor in the labor market should lead to fewer workers being hired. Views differ sharply among economists, however, concerning how large a reduction in employment the minimum wage causes. For instance, David Card of the University of California, Berkeley, and Alan Krueger of Princeton University, who in 2011 was appointed by President Barack Obama to chair the Council of Economic Advisers, conducted a study of fast-food restaurants in New Jersey and Pennsylvania. Their study indicated that the effect of minimum wage increases on employment is very small. This study has been very controversial, however. Other economists have examined similar data and have come to the different conclusion that the minimum wage leads to a significant decrease in employment.

Whatever the extent of employment losses from the minimum wage, because it is a price floor, it will cause a deadweight loss, just as a price floor in the wheat market does. Therefore, many economists favor alternative policies for attaining the goal of raising the incomes of low-skilled workers. One policy many economists support is the *earned income tax credit*. The earned income tax credit reduces the amount of tax that low-income wage earners would otherwise pay to the federal government. Workers with very low incomes who do not owe any tax receive a payment from the government. Compared with the minimum wage, the earned income tax credit can increase the incomes of low-skilled workers without reducing employment. The earned income tax credit also places a lesser burden on the small businesses that employ many low-skilled workers, and it may cause a smaller loss of economic efficiency.

Based on David Card and Alan B. Krueger, *Myth and Measurement: The New Economics of the Minimum Wage*, (Princeton, NJ: Princeton University Press, 1995); David Neumark and William Wascher, "Minimum Wages and Employment: A Case Study of the Fast-Food Industry in New Jersey and Pennsylvania: Comment," *American Economic Review*, Vol. 90, No. 5, December 2000, pp. 1362–1396; and David Card and Alan B. Krueger, "Minimum Wages and Employment: A Case Study of the Fast-Food Industry in New Jersey and Pennsylvania: Reply," *American Economic Review*, Vol. 90, No. 5, December 2000, pp. 1397–1420.

MyEconLab    **Your Turn:** Test your understanding by doing related problem 3.12 on page 127 at the end of this chapter.

# Price Ceilings: Government Rent Control Policy in Housing Markets

Support for governments setting price floors typically comes from sellers, and support for governments setting price ceilings typically comes from consumers. For example, when there is a sharp increase in gasoline prices, there are often proposals for the government to impose a price ceiling on the market for gasoline. As we saw in the chapter opener, New York is one of a number of cities that impose rent control, which puts a ceiling on the maximum rent that landlords can charge for an apartment. Figure 4.9 shows the market for apartments in a city that has rent control.

Without rent control, the equilibrium rent would be $1,500 per month, and 2,000,000 apartments would be rented. With a maximum legal rent of $1,000 per month, landlords reduce the quantity of apartments supplied to 1,900,000. The fall in the quantity of apartments supplied can be the result of landlords converting some

## Figure 4.9

### The Economic Effect of a Rent Ceiling

Without rent control, the equilibrium rent is $1,500 per month. At that price, 2,000,000 apartments would be rented. If the government imposes a rent ceiling of $1,000, the quantity of apartments supplied falls to 1,900,000, and the quantity of apartments demanded increases to 2,100,000, resulting in a shortage of 200,000 apartments. Producer surplus equal to the area of the blue rectangle *A* is transferred from landlords to renters, and there is a deadweight loss equal to the areas of yellow triangles *B* and *C*.

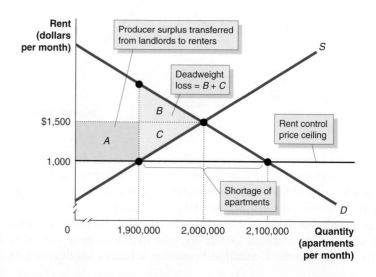

# Don't Let This Happen to You

## Don't Confuse "Scarcity" with "Shortage"

At first glance, the following statement seems correct: "There is a shortage of every good that is scarce." In everyday conversation, we describe a good as "scarce" if we have trouble finding it. For instance, if you are looking for a gift for a child, you might call the latest hot toy "scarce" if you are willing to buy it at its listed price but can't find it online or in any store. But recall from Chapter 2 that economists have a broad definition of *scarce*. In the economic sense, almost everything—except undesirable things like garbage—is

scarce. A shortage of a good occurs only if the quantity demanded is greater than the quantity supplied at the current price. Therefore, the preceding statement—"There is a shortage of every good that is scarce"—is incorrect. In fact, there is no shortage of most scarce goods.

MyEconLab

**Your Turn:** Test your understanding by doing related problem 3.15 on page 128 at the end of this chapter.

---

apartments into offices, selling some off as condominiums, or converting some small apartment buildings into single-family homes. Over time, landlords may even abandon some apartment buildings. At one time in New York City, rent control resulted in landlords abandoning whole city blocks because they were unable to cover their costs with the rents the government allowed them to charge. In London, when rent controls were applied to rooms and apartments located in a landlord's own home, the quantity of these apartments supplied dropped by 75 percent.

In Figure 4.9, with the rent ceiling of $1,000, the quantity of apartments demanded rises to 2,100,000. There is a shortage of 200,000 apartments. Consumer surplus increases by rectangle A and falls by triangle B. Rectangle A would have been part of producer surplus if rent control were not in place. With rent control, it is part of consumer surplus. Rent control causes the producer surplus received by landlords to fall by rectangle A plus triangle C. Triangles B and C represent the deadweight loss. There is a deadweight loss because rent control has reduced the amount of economic surplus in the market for apartments. Rent control has caused the marginal benefit of the last apartment rented to be greater than the marginal cost of supplying it. We can conclude that a price ceiling, such as rent control, reduces economic efficiency. The appendix to this chapter shows how we can make quantitative estimates of the deadweight loss, and it provides an example of the changes in consumer surplus and producer surplus that can result from rent control.

Renters as a group benefit from rent controls—total consumer surplus is larger—but landlords lose. Because of the deadweight loss, the total loss to landlords is greater than the gain to renters. Notice also that although renters as a group benefit, the number of renters is reduced, so some renters are made worse off by rent controls because they are unable to find an apartment at the legal rent.

## Black Markets

To this point, our analysis of rent controls is incomplete. In practice, renters may be worse off and landlords may be better off than Figure 4.9 makes it seem. We have assumed that renters and landlords actually abide by the price ceiling, but sometimes they don't. Because rent control leads to a shortage of apartments, renters who would otherwise not be able to find apartments have an incentive to offer landlords rents above the legal maximum. When governments try to control prices by setting price ceilings or price floors, buyers and sellers often find a way around the controls. The result is a **black market** where buying and selling take place at prices that violate government price regulations.

In a housing market with rent controls, the total amount of consumer surplus received by renters may be reduced and the total amount of producer surplus received by landlords may be increased if apartments are being rented at prices above the legal price ceiling.

**Black market** A market in which buying and selling take place at prices that violate government price regulations.

# Solved Problem **4.3**

## What's the Economic Effect of a Black Market for Apartments?

In many cities that have rent controls, the actual rents paid can be much higher than the legal maximum. Because rent controls cause a shortage of apartments, desperate tenants are often willing to pay landlords rents that are higher than the law allows, perhaps by writing a check for the legally allowed rent and paying an additional amount in cash. Look again at Figure 4.9 on page 112. Suppose that competition among tenants results in the black market rent rising to $2,000 per month. At this rent, tenants demand 1,900,000 apartments. Use a graph showing the market for apartments to compare this situation with the one shown in Figure 4.9. Be sure to note any differences in consumer surplus, producer surplus, and deadweight loss.

## Solving the Problem

**Step 1:** **Review the chapter material.** This problem is about price controls in the market for apartments, so you may want to review the section "Price Ceilings: Government Rent Control Policy in Housing Markets," which begins on page 112.

**Step 2:** **Draw a graph similar to Figure 4.9, with the addition of the black market price.**

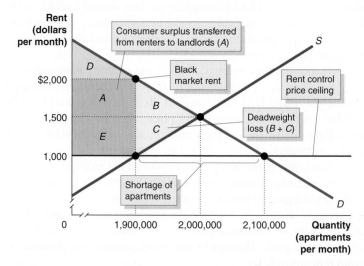

**Step 3:** **Analyze the changes from Figure 4.9.** The black market rent is now $2,000—even higher than the original competitive equilibrium rent shown in Figure 4.9. So, consumer surplus declines by an amount equal to the red rectangle *A* plus the red rectangle *E*. The remaining consumer surplus is the blue triangle *D*. Note that the rectangle *A*, which would have been part of consumer surplus without rent control, represents a transfer from renters to landlords. Compared with the situation shown in Figure 4.9, producer surplus has increased by an amount equal to rectangles *A* and *E*, and consumer surplus has declined by the same amount. Deadweight loss is equal to triangles *B* and *C*, the same as in Figure 4.9.

**Extra Credit:** This analysis leads to a surprising result: With an active black market in apartments, rent control may leave renters as a group worse off—with less consumer surplus—than if there were no rent control. There is one more possibility to consider, however. If enough landlords become convinced that they can get away with charging rents above the legal ceiling, the quantity of apartments supplied will increase. Eventually, the market could even end up at the competitive equilibrium, with an equilibrium rent of $1,500 and equilibrium quantity of 2,000,000 apartments. In that case, the rent control price ceiling becomes nonbinding, not because it was set below the equilibrium price but because it was not legally enforced.

Rent controls can also lead to an increase in racial and other types of discrimination. With rent controls, more renters are looking for apartments than there are apartments to rent. Landlords can afford to indulge their prejudices by refusing to rent to people they don't like. In cities without rent controls, landlords face more competition, which makes it more difficult to turn down tenants on the basis of irrelevant characteristics, such as race.

## The Results of Government Price Controls: Winners, Losers, and Inefficiency

When the government imposes price floors or price ceilings, three important results occur:

- Some people win.

- Some people lose.

- There is a loss of economic efficiency.

The winners with rent control are the people who are paying less for rent because they live in rent-controlled apartments. Landlords may also gain if they break the law by charging rents above the legal maximum for their rent-controlled apartments, provided that those illegal rents are higher than the competitive equilibrium rents would be. The losers from rent control are the landlords of rent-controlled apartments who abide by the law and renters who are unable to find apartments to rent at the controlled price. Rent control reduces economic efficiency because fewer apartments are rented than would be rented in a competitive market (refer again to Figure 4.9, on page 112). The resulting deadweight loss measures the decrease in economic efficiency.

## Positive and Normative Analysis of Price Ceilings and Price Floors

Are rent controls, government farm programs, and other price ceilings and price floors bad? As we saw in Chapter 1, questions of this type have no right or wrong answers. Economists are generally skeptical of government attempts to interfere with competitive market equilibrium. Economists know the role competitive markets have played in raising the average person's standard of living. They also know that too much government intervention has the potential to reduce the ability of the market system to produce similar increases in living standards in the future.

But recall from Chapter 1 the difference between positive and normative analysis. Positive analysis is concerned with *what is*, and normative analysis is concerned with *what should be*. Our analysis of rent control and of the federal farm programs in this chapter is positive analysis. We discussed the economic results of these programs. Whether these programs are desirable or undesirable is a normative question. Whether the gains to the winners more than make up for the losses to the losers and for the decline in economic efficiency is a matter of judgment and not strictly an economic question. Price ceilings and price floors continue to exist partly because people who understand their downside still believe they are good policies and therefore support them. The policies also persist because many people who support them do not understand the economic analysis in this chapter and so do not understand the drawbacks to these policies.

## The Economic Impact of Taxes

**4.4 LEARNING** OBJECTIVE

Analyze the economic impact of taxes.

Supreme Court Justice Oliver Wendell Holmes once remarked, "Taxes are what we pay for a civilized society." When the government taxes a good or service, however, it affects the market equilibrium for that good or service. Just as with a price ceiling or price floor, one result of a tax is a decline in economic efficiency. Analyzing taxes is an important part of the field of economics known as *public finance*. In this section, we will use the model of demand and supply and the concepts of consumer surplus, producer surplus, and deadweight loss to analyze the economic impact of taxes.

**Figure 4.10**

**The Effect of a Tax on the Market for Cigarettes**

Without the tax, market equilibrium occurs at point *A*. The equilibrium price of cigarettes is $4.00 per pack, and 4 billion packs of cigarettes are sold per year. A $1.00-per-pack tax on cigarettes will cause the supply curve for cigarettes to shift up by $1.00, from $S_1$ to $S_2$. The new equilibrium occurs at point *B*. The price of cigarettes will increase by $0.90, to $4.90 per pack, and the quantity sold will fall to 3.7 billion packs. The tax on cigarettes has increased the price paid by consumers from $4.00 to $4.90 per pack. Producers receive a price of $4.90 per pack (point *B*), but after paying the $1.00 tax, they are left with $3.90 (point *C*). The government will receive tax revenue equal to the green-shaded box. Some consumer surplus and some producer surplus will become tax revenue for the government, and some will become deadweight loss, shown by the yellow-shaded area.

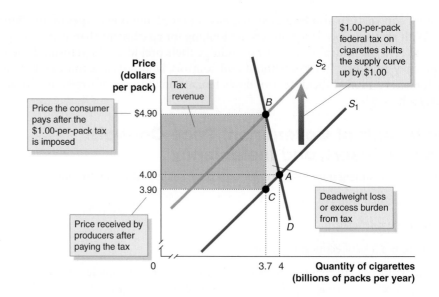

## The Effect of Taxes on Economic Efficiency

Whenever a government taxes a good or service, less of that good or service will be produced and consumed. For example, a tax on cigarettes will raise the cost of smoking and reduce the amount of smoking that takes place. We can use a demand and supply graph to illustrate this point. Figure 4.10 shows the market for cigarettes.

Without the tax, the equilibrium price of cigarettes would be $4.00 per pack, and 4 billion packs of cigarettes would be sold per year (point *A*). If the federal government requires sellers of cigarettes to pay a $1.00-per-pack tax, then their cost of selling cigarettes will increase by $1.00 per pack. This increase in costs causes the supply curve for cigarettes to shift up by $1.00 because sellers will now require a price that is $1.00 greater to supply the same quantity of cigarettes. In Figure 4.10, the supply curve shifts up by $1.00 to show the effect of the tax, and there is a new equilibrium price of $4.90 and a new equilibrium quantity of 3.7 billion packs (point *B*).

The federal government will collect tax revenue equal to the tax per pack multiplied by the number of packs sold, or $3.7 billion. The area shaded in green in Figure 4.10 represents the government's tax revenue. Consumers will pay a higher price of $4.90 per pack. Although sellers appear to be receiving a higher price per pack, once they have paid the tax, the price they receive falls from $4.00 per pack to $3.90 per pack. There is a loss of consumer surplus because consumers are paying a higher price. The price producers receive falls, so there is also a loss of producer surplus. Therefore, the tax on cigarettes has reduced *both* consumer surplus and producer surplus. Some of the reduction in consumer and producer surplus becomes tax revenue for the government. The rest of the reduction in consumer and producer surplus is equal to the deadweight loss from the tax, shown by the yellow-shaded triangle in the figure.

We can conclude that the true burden of a tax is not just the amount consumers and producers pay the government but also includes the deadweight loss. The deadweight loss from a tax is referred to as the *excess burden* of the tax. *A tax is efficient if it imposes a small excess burden relative to the tax revenue it raises.* One contribution economists make to government tax policy is to advise policymakers on which taxes are most efficient.

## Tax Incidence: Who Actually Pays a Tax?

The answer to the question "Who pays a tax?" seems obvious: Whoever is legally required to send a tax payment to the government pays the tax. But there can be an important difference between who is legally required to pay the tax and who actually *bears*

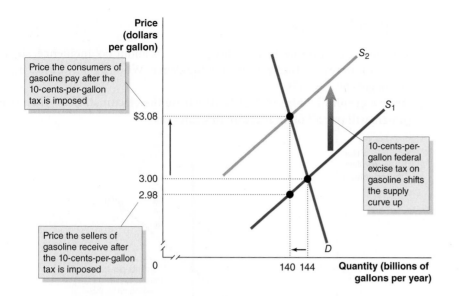

**Figure 4.11**

**The Incidence of a Tax on Gasoline**

With no tax on gasoline, the price would be $3.00 per gallon, and 144 billion gallons of gasoline would be sold each year. A 10-cents-per-gallon excise tax shifts up the supply curve from $S_1$ to $S_2$, raises the price consumers pay from $3.00 to $3.08, and lowers the price sellers receive from $3.00 to $2.98. Therefore, consumers pay 8 cents of the 10-cents-per-gallon tax on gasoline, and sellers pay 2 cents.

*the burden* of the tax. The actual division of the burden of a tax between buyers and sellers is referred to as **tax incidence**. The federal government currently levies an excise tax of 18.4 cents per gallon of gasoline sold. Gas station owners collect this tax and forward it to the federal government, but who actually bears the burden of the tax?

**Tax incidence** The actual division of the burden of a tax between buyers and sellers in a market.

**Determining Tax Incidence on a Demand and Supply Graph**  Suppose that currently the federal government does not impose a tax on gasoline. In Figure 4.11, equilibrium in the retail market for gasoline occurs at the intersection of the demand curve and supply curve, $S_1$. The equilibrium price is $3.00 per gallon, and the equilibrium quantity is 144 billion gallons. Now suppose that the federal government imposes a 10-cents-per-gallon tax. As a result of the tax, the supply curve for gasoline will shift up by 10 cents per gallon. At the new equilibrium, where the demand curve intersects the supply curve, $S_2$, the price has risen by 8 cents per gallon, from $3.00 to $3.08. Notice that only in the extremely unlikely case that demand is a vertical line will the market price rise by the full amount of the tax. Consumers are paying 8 cents more per gallon. Sellers of gasoline receive a new higher price of $3.08 per gallon, but after paying the 10-cents-per-gallon tax, they are left with $2.98 per gallon, or 2 cents less than they were receiving in the old equilibrium.

Although the sellers of gasoline are responsible for collecting the tax and sending the tax receipts to the government, they do not bear most of the burden of the tax. In this case, consumers pay 8 cents of the tax because the market price has risen by 8 cents, and sellers pay 2 cents of the tax because after sending the tax to the government, they are receiving 2 cents less per gallon of gasoline sold. Expressed in percentage terms, consumers pay 80 percent of the tax, and sellers pay 20 percent of the tax.

# Solved Problem 4.4

## When Do Consumers Pay All of a Sales Tax Increase?

A student makes the following statement: "If the federal government raises the sales tax on gasoline by $0.25, then the price of gasoline will rise by $0.25. Consumers can't get by without gasoline, so they have to pay the whole amount of any increase in the sales tax." Under what circumstances will the student's statement be true? Illustrate your answer with a graph of the market for gasoline.

## Solving the Problem

**Step 1:** **Review the chapter material.** This problem is about tax incidence, so you may want to review the section "Tax Incidence: Who Actually Pays a Tax?" that begins on page 116.

**Step 2:** **Draw a graph like Figure 4.11 to illustrate the circumstances when consumers will pay all of an increase in a sales tax.**

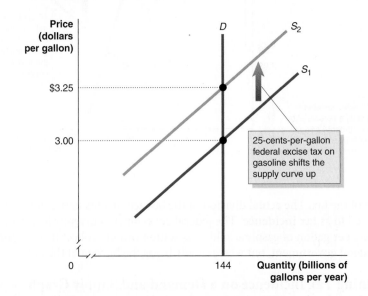

**Step 3:** **Use the graph to evaluate the statement.** The graph shows that consumers will pay all of an increase in a sales tax only if the demand curve is a vertical line. It is very unlikely that the demand for gasoline would look like this because we expect that for every good, an increase in price will cause a decrease in the quantity demanded. Because the demand curve for gasoline is not a vertical line, the statement is incorrect.

MyEconLab    **Your Turn:** For more practice, do related problem 4.7 on page 130 at the end of the chapter.

---

**Does It Make a Difference Whether the Government Collects a Tax from Buyers or Sellers?** We have already seen the important distinction between the true burden of a tax and whether buyers or sellers are legally required to pay a tax. We can reinforce this point by noting explicitly that the incidence of a tax does *not* depend on whether the government collects a tax from the buyers of a good or from the sellers. Figure 4.12 illustrates this point by showing the effect on equilibrium in the market for gasoline if a 10-cents-per-gallon tax is imposed on buyers rather than on sellers. That is, we are now assuming that instead of sellers having to collect the 10-cents-per-gallon tax at the pump, buyers are responsible for keeping track of how many gallons of gasoline they purchase and sending the tax to the government. (Of course, it would be very difficult for buyers to keep track of their purchases or for the government to check whether they were paying all of the taxes they owe. That is why the government collects the tax on gasoline from sellers.)

Figure 4.12 is similar to Figure 4.11 except that it shows the gasoline tax being imposed on buyers rather than sellers. In Figure 4.12, the supply curve does not shift because nothing has happened to change the quantity of gasoline sellers are willing to supply at any given price. The demand curve has shifted, however, because consumers now have to pay a 10-cent tax on every gallon of gasoline they buy. Therefore, at every

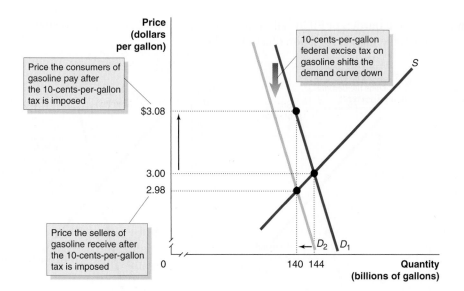

**Figure 4.12**

**The Incidence of a Tax on Gasoline Paid by Buyers**

With no tax on gasoline, the demand curve is $D_1$. If a 10-cents-per-gallon tax is imposed that consumers are responsible for paying, the demand curve shifts down by the amount of the tax, from $D_1$ to $D_2$. In the new equilibrium, consumers pay a price of $3.08 per gallon, including the tax. Producers receive $2.98 per gallon. This is the same result we saw when producers were responsible for paying the tax.

quantity, they are willing to pay a price 10 cents less than they would have without the tax. In the figure, we indicate the effect of the tax by shifting the demand curve down by 10 cents, from $D_1$ to $D_2$. Once the tax has been imposed and the demand curve has shifted down, the new equilibrium quantity of gasoline is 140 billion gallons, which is exactly the same as in Figure 4.11.

The new equilibrium price after the tax is imposed appears to be different in Figure 4.12 than in Figure 4.11, but if we include the tax, buyers will pay the same price and sellers will receive the same price in both figures. To see this, notice that in Figure 4.11, buyers pay sellers a price of $3.08 per gallon. In Figure 4.12, they pay sellers only $2.98, but they must also pay the government a tax of 10 cents per gallon. So, the total price buyers pay remains $3.08 per gallon. In Figure 4.11, sellers receive $3.08 per gallon from buyers, but after they pay the tax of 10 cents per gallon, they are left with $2.98, which is the same amount they receive in Figure 4.12.

| Making the Connection | **Is the Burden of the Social Security Tax Really Shared Equally between Workers and Firms?** |
| --- | --- |

Most people who receive paychecks have several different taxes withheld from them by their employers, who forward these taxes directly to the government. In fact, many people are shocked after getting their first job when they discover the gap between their gross pay and their net pay after taxes have been deducted. The largest tax many people of low or moderate income pay is FICA, which stands for the Federal Insurance Contributions Act. FICA funds the Social Security and Medicare programs, which provide income and health care to the elderly and disabled. FICA is sometimes referred to as the *payroll tax*. When Congress passed the act, it wanted employers and workers to equally share the burden of the tax. Currently, FICA is 15.3 percent of wages, with 7.65 percent paid by workers by being withheld from their paychecks and the other 7.65 percent paid by employers.

But does requiring workers and employers to each pay half the tax mean that the burden of the tax is also shared equally? Our discussion in this chapter shows that the answer is no. In the labor market, employers are buyers, and workers are sellers. As we saw in the example of the federal tax on gasoline, whether the tax is collected from buyers or from sellers does not affect the incidence of the tax. Most economists believe, in fact, that the burden of FICA falls almost entirely on workers. The following figure, which shows the market for labor, illustrates why.

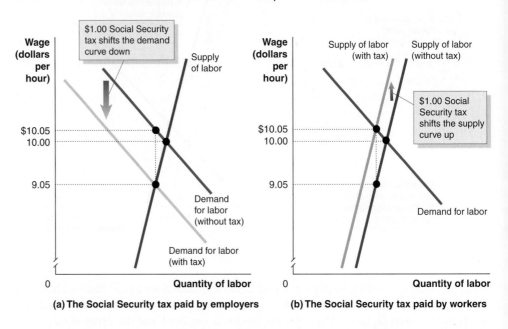

**(a) The Social Security tax paid by employers**

**(b) The Social Security tax paid by workers**

In the market for labor, the demand curve represents the quantity of labor demanded by employers at various wages, and the supply curve represents the quantity of labor supplied by workers at various wages. The intersection of the demand curve and the supply curve determines the equilibrium wage. In both panels, the equilibrium wage without a Social Security payroll tax is $10 per hour. For simplicity, let's assume that the payroll tax equals $1 per hour of work. In panel (a), we assume that employers must pay the tax. The tax causes the demand for labor curve to shift down by $1 at every quantity of labor because firms now must pay a $1 tax for every hour of labor they hire. We have drawn the supply curve for labor as being very steep because most economists believe the quantity of labor supplied by workers does not change much as the wage rate changes. Workers pay $0.95 of the tax because their wages fall from $10 before the tax to $9.05 after the tax. Firms pay only $0.05 of the tax because the amount they pay for an hour of labor increases from $10 before the tax to $10.05 after the tax. In panel (a), after the tax is imposed, the equilibrium wage declines from $10 per hour to $9.05 per hour. Firms are now paying a total of $10.05 for every hour of work they hire: $9.05 in wages to workers and $1 in tax to the government. In other words, workers have paid $0.95 of the $1 tax, and firms have paid only $0.05.

Panel (b) shows that this result is exactly the same if the tax is imposed on workers rather than on firms. In this case, the tax causes the supply curve for labor to shift up by $1 at every quantity of labor because workers must now pay a tax of $1 for every hour they work. After the tax is imposed, the equilibrium wage increases to $10.05 per hour. But workers receive only $9.05 after they have paid the $1.00 tax. Once again, workers have paid $0.95 of the $1 tax, and firms have paid only $0.05.

Although the figure presents a simplified analysis, it reflects the conclusion of most economists who have studied the incidence of FICA: Even though Congress requires employers to pay half the tax and workers to pay the other half, in fact, the burden of the tax falls almost entirely on workers. This conclusion would not be changed even if Congress revised the law to require either employers or workers to pay all of the tax. The forces of demand and supply working in the labor market, and not Congress, determine the incidence of the tax.

MyEconLab **Your Turn:** Test your understanding by doing related problems 4.8 and 4.9 on page 130 at the end of this chapter.

Continued from page 101

## Economics in Your Life

**Does Rent Control Make It Easier for You to Find an Affordable Apartment?**

At the beginning of the chapter, we posed the following question: If you have two job offers in different cities, one with rent control and one without, will you be more likely to find an affordable apartment in the city with rent control? In answering the question, this chapter has shown that although rent control can keep rents lower than they might otherwise be, it can also lead to a permanent shortage of apartments. You may have to search for a long time to find a suitable apartment, and landlords may even ask you to give them payments "under the table," which would make your actual rent higher than the controlled rent. Finding an apartment in a city without rent control should be much easier, although the rent may be higher.

# Conclusion

The model of demand and supply introduced in Chapter 3 showed that markets free from government intervention eliminate surpluses and shortages and do a good job of responding to the wants of consumers. We have seen in this chapter that both consumers and firms sometimes try to use the government to change market outcomes in their favor. The concepts of consumer and producer surplus and deadweight loss allow us to measure the benefits consumers and producers receive from competitive market equilibrium. These concepts also allow us to measure the effects of government price floors and price ceilings and the economic impact of taxes.

Read *An Inside Look at Policy* on the next page for an example of how celebrity Faye Dunaway and her son have financially benefited from rent-control laws in New York City.

# ... and the Rent-Controlled Apartment Goes to ... Actress Faye Dunaway!

## NEW YORK TIMES

## For Faye Dunaway, Real-Life Role in Housing Court

She was a brazen bank robber in "Bonnie and Clyde," the mysterious Evelyn Mulwray in "Chinatown" and a scheming television executive in "Network," for which she won an Oscar.

Now Faye Dunaway is a defendant in case No. 76667/11 in Manhattan housing court, just another rent-stabilized tenant facing eviction.

In a lawsuit filed Tuesday, her landlord claims that Ms. Dunaway, who pays $1,048.72 a month for a one-bedroom walk-up apartment in a century-old tenement building on East 78th Street, does not actually live there, but rather lives in California. The suit also names her son, Liam Dunaway O'Neill, whose father is the photographer Terry O'Neill, as a subtenant in the apartment.

As proof, the landlord, unnamed in court papers, states that Ms. Dunaway owns a home in West Hollywood, and has her voter and automobile registrations there. The suit also cites three moving violations she received in California from May 2009 to December 2010.

Rent stabilization rules require tenants to live in the apartment they are renting as a primary residence, not as a second home. Ms. Dunaway, 70, does not appear to be living glamorously. The home in California is a nice but not flashy house on which she still carries a mortgage, according to the lawsuit. Her car is a 2007 Toyota Corolla.

Ms. Dunaway is one of the many celebrities who have fought to keep rent-regulated apartments in New York over the years. But Ms. Dunaway's current apartment is also a vast departure from the 20th-floor apartment she inhabited at the Eldorado earlier in her career. . . .

If Ms. Dunaway leaves, the landlord is likely to get far more rent. According to rental data tracked by the brokerage Citi Habitats, one-bedroom walk-up apartments on the Upper East Side currently rent for an average of $2,318 a month.

Ms. Dunaway rented her current apartment on the Upper East Side on Aug. 1, 1994, in a six-story yellow brick building with fire escapes in the front. The name next to the outdoor buzzer reads "F. Dunaway." The building's hallway floors are green linoleum. Its cream walls are chipped, and pink marble steps lead up to her third-floor unit. Her front door is painted aquamarine and has the names "Dunaway/ONeill" and "PT Bascom" listed by the black doorbell. There is a simple brown doormat with black trim. No one answered the door on Tuesday afternoon.

Ms. Dunaway had problems in the past with her landlord, who filed a notice in 2009 in Civil Court in Manhattan for nonpayment of rent. That case appeared to have been resolved, and she signed a lease in April 2009 to remain in her apartment until July 31, 2011.

Court papers show that the landlord investigated earlier this year to determine where she actually lived and contacted Ms. Dunaway in March with its findings. The landlord asked her to leave when her lease expired on July 31.

Neighbors said that while they had seen Ms. Dunaway in the past, they had not seen her much lately. Keith Cohen, owner of Orwasher's Bakery near Ms. Dunaway's apartment, said that employees had told him when he arrived in 2007 that Ms. Dunaway lived nearby, but that he had never seen her.

Rosane Franco, manager of the nearby Tiny Doll House shop, said she had seen Ms. Dunaway a few times in the past two years, but that the last time was "many months ago."

The occupant of an apartment next door, who would not give her name, said through her door, "I've never met her."

Ms. Dunaway's Twitter feed shows no mention of her being in New York recently. Her son, Mr. O'Neill, has written on his Twitter feed, "I live in LA."

Ms. Dunaway is scheduled for a hearing in Civil Court on Aug. 11 at 2 P.M.

If she departs, it may not have much effect on her sleepy block between First and Second Avenues.

"She's not that glamorous person everybody saw in the movies," Ms. Franco said. "We were surprised that she lived here in the first place."

## Key Points in the Article

In July 2011, Oscar-winning actress Faye Dunaway found herself embroiled in a legal battle as the defendant in a lawsuit filed by the landlord of her rent-controlled New York City apartment. According to the lawsuit, Dunaway faced eviction from her apartment based on the landlord's claim that she had violated the New York rent stabilization rule that requires the apartment be the primary residence of the tenant. Dunaway first moved into the apartment in 1994, and as recently as 2009 renewed her lease through July 2011. Following an investigation, the landlord concluded that Dunaway's primary residence is actually in Los Angeles, and based on these findings, asked her to leave the apartment when the lease expired on July 31. Dunaway's refusal to leave prompted the landlord to file the lawsuit in Manhattan housing court following the expiration of her lease.

## Analyzing the News

ⓐ According to her landlord, Dunaway's monthly rent on the rent-controlled apartment is $1,048.72. Rent-controlled apartments generally rent for an amount below what the equilibrium price would be were the market not subject to this government-set price. Rent control not only reduces the potential revenue that could be received by landlords if the market were not

regulated, but also results in a shortage of apartments.

ⓑ In the case of Dunaway's apartment, the controlled rent is apparently significantly below the amount that could be charged in an unregulated market. Rental data show that in the same neighborhood, apartments of a similar size and layout rent for an average of $2,318 per month, more than double the rent Dunaway is paying. The figure below shows an example of rent control in the New York City apartment market, using the average rent of $2,318 as the equilibrium price. At the rent-controlled price of $1,048.72, a shortage of apartments will exist, represented by the distance from $Q_1$ to $Q_2$. The shortage indicates that more people will want to rent apartments at the rent controlled price than there will be apartments available for rent. It is understandable why Dunaway's landlord would like to take advantage of the primary residency restriction in the New York rent stabilization rules and have her evicted from the apartment. As described in the chapter opener, current rent control laws in New York are quite complex, but landlords can raise the rent on vacant apartments, and apartments renting for $2,000 a month are automatically deregulated if they are vacant. Based on these laws, the monthly revenue the landlord could receive by renting this apartment to a new tenant would definitely increase.

ⓒ Dunaway's landlord filed a legal notice against her for nonpayment of rent in 2009, so this is not the first time the two parties have engaged in legal wrangling. That issue was apparently resolved, but this time the landlord definitely seems to want Dunaway out and is using the residency restriction as the means. Neighborhood residents have stated that they have not seen Dunaway much lately, supporting the landlord's claim that the New York apartment is not the actor's primary residence. No matter what methods landlords use in an attempt to reclaim rent-controlled apartments, if their efforts are successful, they will be able to increase their revenues so long as demand remains strong for these properties.

## Thinking Critically About Policy

1. One consequence of rent control is a shortage of apartments, which is shown in the figure. Suppose rent control also leads to a reduction in the supply of affordable apartments. Use the figure on this page to illustrate the effects of a reduction in supply, and explain what will happen to the shortage of apartments.

2. One reason some economists are critical of rent control laws is that they create a deadweight loss. Using the figure on this page, identify the area representing the deadweight loss. What causes the deadweight loss? What would the supply curve have to look like for the deadweight loss to equal zero?

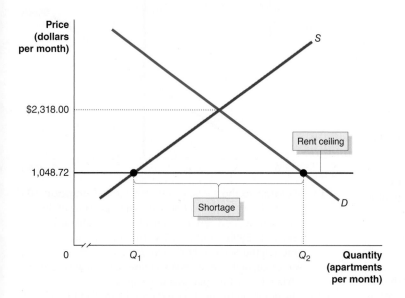

The effect of rent control laws on the supply of affordable apartments.

# Chapter Summary and Problems

## Key Terms

 **Consumer Surplus and Producer Surplus, pages 102–107**

LEARNING OBJECTIVE: Distinguish between the concepts of consumer surplus and producer surplus.

## Summary

Although most prices are determined by demand and supply in markets, the government sometimes imposes *price ceilings* and *price floors*. A **price ceiling** is a legally determined maximum price that sellers may charge. A **price floor** is a legally determined minimum price that sellers may receive. Economists analyze the effects of price ceilings and price floors using *consumer surplus* and *producer surplus*. **Marginal benefit** is the additional benefit to a consumer from consuming one more unit of a good or service. The demand curve is also a marginal benefit curve. **Consumer surplus** is the difference between the highest price a consumer is willing to pay for a good or service and the price the consumer actually pays. The total amount of consumer surplus in a market is equal to the area below the demand curve and above the market price. **Marginal cost** is the additional cost to a firm of producing one more unit of a good or service. The supply curve is also a marginal cost curve. **Producer surplus** is the difference between the lowest price a firm is willing to accept for a good or service and the price it actually receives. The total amount of producer surplus in a market is equal to the area above the supply curve and below the market price.

MyEconLab   Visit **www.myeconlab.com** to complete these exercises online and get instant feedback.

## Review Questions

1.1 What is marginal benefit? Why is the demand curve referred to as a marginal benefit curve?

1.2 What is marginal cost? Why is the supply curve referred to as a marginal cost curve?

1.3 What is consumer surplus? How does consumer surplus change as the equilibrium price of a good rises or falls?

1.4 What is producer surplus? How does producer surplus change as the equilibrium price of a good rises or falls?

## Problems and Applications

1.5 Suppose that a frost in Florida reduces the size of the orange crop, which causes the supply curve for oranges to shift to the left. Briefly explain whether consumer surplus will increase or decrease and whether producer surplus will increase or decrease. Use a demand and supply graph to illustrate your answers.

1.6 A student makes the following argument: "When a market is in equilibrium, there is no consumer surplus. We know this because in equilibrium, the market price is equal to the price consumers are willing to pay for the good." Briefly explain whether you agree with the student's argument.

1.7 How does consumer surplus differ from the total benefit consumers receive from purchasing products? Similarly, how does producer surplus differ from the total revenue that firms receive from selling products? Under what special case will consumer surplus equal the total benefit consumers receive from consuming a product? Under what special case will producer surplus equal the total revenue firms receive from selling a product?

1.8 The following graph illustrates the market for a breast cancer–fighting drug, without which breast cancer patients cannot survive. What is the consumer surplus in this market? How does it differ from the consumer surplus in the markets you have studied up to this point?

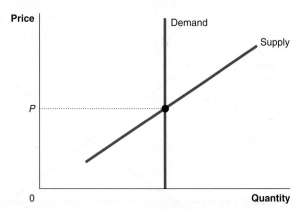

1.9 [**Related to the** Making the Connection **on page 104**] The *Making the Connection* states that the value of the area representing consumer surplus from broadband Internet service is $890.5 million. Use the information from the graph in the *Making the Connection* to show how this value was calculated. (For a review of how to calculate the area of a triangle, see the appendix to Chapter 1.)

1.10 The graph on the next page shows the market for tickets to a concert that will be held in a local arena that seats 15,000 people. What is the producer surplus in this market? How does it differ from the producer surplus in the markets you have studied up to this point?

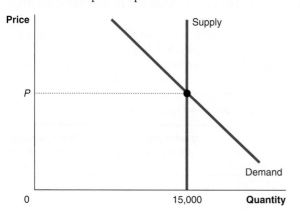

1.11 A study estimates that the total consumer surplus gained by people participating in auctions on eBay in a recent year was $7 billion. Is it likely that the total consumer surplus for the items bought in these auctions was higher or lower than it would have been if consumers had purchased these items for fixed prices in retail stores?

Based on Ravi Bapna, Wolfgang Jank, and Galit Shmueli, "Consumer Surplus in Online Auctions," *Information Systems Research*, Vol. 19, No. 4, December 2008, pp. 400–416.

1.12 Movies, songs, and books are covered by copyrights, which allow the creators of these works to keep other people from reproducing them without permission. Many people, though, violate copyright laws by using file-sharing services that allow them to download copies of songs and movies at a zero price.
  a. Does file sharing increase the consumer surplus from consuming existing songs and movies? Draw a demand curve to illustrate your answer. The demand curve should indicate the price when file sharing is not possible, the zero price with file sharing, and the amount of consumer surplus with and without file sharing.
  b. What are the likely effects of file sharing in the long run? Is file sharing likely to increase the total consumer surplus from consuming songs and movies in the long run? Briefly explain.

Based on Joel Waldfogel, "Bye, Bye, Miss American Pie? The Supply of New Recorded Music Since Napster," National Bureau of Economic Research Working Paper 16882, March 2011.

---

## 4.2 The Efficiency of Competitive Markets, pages 107–109

LEARNING OBJECTIVE: Understand the concept of economic efficiency.

## Summary

Equilibrium in a competitive market is **economically efficient**. **Economic surplus** is the sum of consumer surplus and producer surplus. Economic efficiency is a market outcome in which the marginal benefit to consumers from the last unit produced is equal to the marginal cost of production and where the sum of consumer surplus and producer surplus is at a maximum. When the market price is above or below the equilibrium price, there is a reduction in economic surplus. The reduction in economic surplus resulting from a market not being in competitive equilibrium is called the **deadweight loss**.

 MyEconLab    Visit **www.myeconlab.com** to complete these exercises online and get instant feedback.

## Review Questions

2.1 Define *economic surplus* and *deadweight loss*.
2.2 What is economic efficiency? Why do economists define *efficiency* in this way?

## Problems and Applications

2.3 Briefly explain whether you agree with the following statement: "A lower price in a market always increases economic efficiency in that market."
2.4 Briefly explain whether you agree with the following statement: "If at the current quantity marginal benefit is greater than marginal cost, there will be a deadweight loss in the

market. However, there is no deadweight loss when marginal cost is greater than marginal benefit."
2.5 Using a demand and supply graph, illustrate and briefly explain the effect on consumer surplus and producer surplus of a price below the equilibrium price. Show any deadweight loss on your graph.
2.6 Briefly explain whether you agree with the following statement: "If consumer surplus in a market increases, producer surplus must decrease."
2.7 Does an increase in economic surplus in a market always mean that economic efficiency in the market has increased? Briefly explain.
2.8 Using the graph below, explain why economic surplus would be smaller if $Q_1$ or $Q_3$ were the quantity produced than if $Q_2$ is the quantity produced.

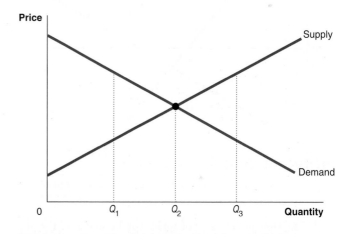

**4.3** **Government Intervention in the Market: Price Floors and Price Ceilings, pages 109–115**

LEARNING OBJECTIVE: Explain the economic effect of government-imposed price floors and price ceilings.

## Summary

Producers or consumers who are dissatisfied with the market out-come can attempt to convince the government to impose price floors or price ceilings. Price floors usually increase producer surplus, decrease consumer surplus, and cause a deadweight loss. Price ceilings usually increase consumer surplus, reduce producer surplus, and cause a deadweight loss. The results of the government imposing price ceilings and price floors are that some people win, some people lose, and a loss of economic efficiency occurs. Price ceilings and price floors can lead to a **black market**, where buying and selling take place at prices that violate government price regulations. Positive analysis is concerned with what is, and normative analysis is concerned with what should be. Positive analysis shows that price ceilings and price floors cause dead-weight losses. Whether these policies are desirable or undesirable, though, is a normative question.

 MyEconLab   Visit **www.myeconlab.com** to complete these exercises online and get instant feedback.

## Review Questions

**3.1** Why do some consumers tend to favor price controls while others tend to oppose them?

**3.2** Do producers tend to favor price floors or price ceilings? Why?

**3.3** What is a black market? Under what circumstances do black markets arise?

**3.4** Can economic analysis provide a final answer to the question of whether the government should intervene in markets by imposing price ceilings and price floors? Briefly explain.

## Problems and Applications

**3.5** The graph below shows the market for apples. Assume that the government has imposed a price floor of $10 per crate.

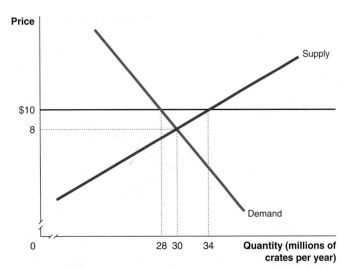

a.   How many crates of apples will be sold after the price floor has been imposed?

b.   Will there be a shortage or a surplus? If there is a shortage or a surplus, how large will it be?

c.   Will apple producers benefit from the price floor? If so, explain how they will benefit.

**3.6** Use the information on the kumquat market in the table to answer the following questions:

| Price (per Crate) | Quantity Demanded (Millions of Crates per Year) | Quantity Supplied (Millions of Crates per Year) |
|---|---|---|
| $10 | 120 | 20 |
| 15 | 110 | 60 |
| 20 | 100 | 100 |
| 25 | 90 | 140 |
| 30 | 80 | 180 |
| 35 | 70 | 220 |

a.   What are the equilibrium price and quantity? How much revenue do kumquat producers receive when the market is in equilibrium? Draw a graph showing the market equilibrium and the area representing the revenue received by kumquat producers.

b.   Suppose the federal government decides to impose a price floor of $30 per crate. Now how many crates of kumquats will consumers purchase? How much revenue will kumquat producers receive? Assume that the government does not purchase any surplus kumquats. On your graph from question (a), show the price floor, the change in the quantity of kumquats purchased, and the revenue received by kumquat producers after the price floor is imposed.

c.   Suppose the government imposes a price floor of $30 per crate and purchases any surplus kumquats from producers. Now how much revenue will kumquat producers receive? How much will the government spend on purchasing surplus kumquats? On your graph from question (a), show the area representing the amount the government spends to purchase the surplus kumquats.

**3.7** Suppose that the government sets a price floor for milk that is above the competitive equilibrium price.

a.   Draw a graph showing this situation. Be sure your graph shows the competitive equilibrium price, the price floor, the quantity that would be sold in competitive equilibrium, and the quantity that would be sold with the price floor.

b.   Compare the economic surplus in this market when there is a price floor and when there is no price floor.

**3.8** A newspaper headline reads: "State Officials Take on Pricing Regulations to Try to Provide Better, Dependable Income to Dairy Farmers." Is providing dependable income to dairy farmers a good policy goal for government officials? How are government officials likely to try to achieve this goal using pricing regulations? Should government officials use regulations to try to provide dependable incomes to every business in the country?

Based on Tim Darragh, "Thirsty for More Milk," *Morning Call*, (Allentown, PA) July 12, 2010.

**3.9** During 2007, the Venezuelan government allowed consumers to buy only a limited quantity of sugar. The government also imposed a ceiling on the price of sugar. As a result, both the quantity of sugar consumed and the market price of sugar were below the competitive equilibrium price and quantity. Draw a graph to illustrate this situation. On your graph, be sure to indicate the areas representing consumer surplus, producer surplus, and deadweight loss.

**3.10** Refer to problem 3.9. An article in the *New York Times* contained the following (Hugo Chávez is the president of Venezuela):

> José Vielma Mora, the chief of Seniat, the government's tax agency, oversaw a raid this month on a warehouse here where officials seized about 165 tons of sugar. Mr. Vielma said the raid exposed hoarding by vendors who were unwilling to sell the sugar at official prices. He and other officials in Mr. Chávez's government have repeatedly blamed the shortages on producers, intermediaries and grocers.

Do you agree that the shortages in the Venezuelan sugar market are the fault of "producers, intermediaries and grocers"? Briefly explain.

From Simon Romero, "Chavez Threatens to Jail Price Control Violators," *New York Times*, February 17, 2007.

**3.11** To drive a taxi legally in New York City, you must have a medallion issued by the city government. City officials have issued only 13,200 medallions. Let's assume that this puts an absolute limit on the number of taxi rides that can be supplied in New York City on any day because no one breaks the law by driving a taxi without a medallion. Let's also assume that each taxi can provide 6 trips per day. In that case, the supply of taxi rides is fixed at 79,200 (or 6 rides per taxi × 13,200 taxis). We show this in the following graph, with a vertical line at this quantity. *Assume that there are no government controls on the prices that drivers can charge for rides.* Use the graph below to answer the following questions.

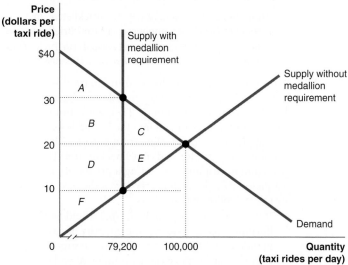

**a.** What would the equilibrium price and quantity be in this market if there were no medallion requirement?

**b.** What are the price and quantity with the medallion requirement?

**c.** Indicate on the graph the areas representing consumer surplus and producer surplus if there were no

medallion requirement. Calculate the values of consumer and producer surplus.

**d.** Indicate on the graph the areas representing consumer surplus, producer surplus, and deadweight loss with the medallion requirement. Calculate the values of consumer surplus, producer surplus, and deadweight loss.

**e.** In 2011, the state of New York allowed New York City to sell 1,500 new taxi medallions. Assuming that each of the new taxis can also provide 6 rides per day, what is the new quantity of taxi rides per day? On the graph, show the effects of the new medallions on consumer surplus, producer surplus, and deadweight loss. You do not have to calculate the values.

Based on Jeremy Smerd, "Taxi Plan Breakthrough in Albany," www .crainsnewyork.com, June 24, 2011.

**3.12** **[Related to the** Making the Connection **on page 111]** Some economists studying the effects of the minimum wage law have found that it tends to reduce the employment of black teenagers relative to white teenagers. Does the graph in the *Making the Connection* help you understand why black teenagers may have been disproportionately affected by the minimum wage law? Briefly explain.

**3.13** **[Related to the** Chapter Opener **on page 101]** Writing in the *New York Times*, economist Paul Krugman commented on an article he read that concerned the trials of people who were searching for apartments in San Francisco. Krugman recounted the story's "tales of would-be renters, pounding the pavements, of dozens of desperate applicants arriving at a newly offered apartment, trying to impress the landlord with their credentials. And yet there was something . . . missing . . . two words I knew had to be part of the story." What two words do you think were missing from the story?

Based on Paul Krugman, "Reckonings; A Rent Affair," *New York Times*, June 7, 2000.

**3.14** **[Related to** Solved Problem 4.3 **on page 114]** Use the information on the market for apartments in Bay City in the table to answer the following questions:

| Rent | Quantity Demanded | Quantity Supplied |
|---|---|---|
| $500 | 375,000 | 225,000 |
| 600 | 350,000 | 250,000 |
| 700 | 325,000 | 275,000 |
| 800 | 300,000 | 300,000 |
| 900 | 275,000 | 325,000 |
| 1,000 | 250,000 | 350,000 |

**a.** In the absence of rent control, what is the equilibrium rent, and what is the equilibrium quantity of apartments rented? Draw a demand and supply graph of the market for apartments to illustrate your answer. In equilibrium, will there be any renters who are unable to find an apartment to rent or any landlords who are unable to find a renter for an apartment?

**b.** Suppose the government sets a ceiling on rents of $600 per month. What is the quantity of apartments demanded, and what is the quantity of apartments supplied?

**c.** Assume that all landlords abide by the law. Use a demand and supply graph to illustrate the effect of this price ceiling on the market for apartments. Be sure to indicate on your graph each of the following: (i) the area representing consumer surplus after the price ceiling has been imposed, (ii) the area representing producer surplus after the price ceiling has been imposed, and (iii) the area representing the deadweight loss after the ceiling has been imposed.

   d. Assume that the quantity of apartments supplied is the same as you determined in (b). But now assume that landlords ignore the law and rent this quantity of apartments for the highest rent they can get. Briefly explain what this rent will be.

**3.15** [Related to the Don't Let This Happen to You on page 113] Briefly explain whether you agree or disagree with the following statement: "If there is a shortage of a good, it must be scarce, but there is not a shortage of every scarce good."

**3.16** A student makes the following argument:

> A price floor reduces the amount of a product that consumers buy because it keeps the price above the competitive market equilibrium. A price ceiling, on the other hand, increases the amount of a product that consumers buy because it keeps the price below the competitive market equilibrium.

Do you agree with the student's reasoning? Use a demand and supply graph to illustrate your answer.

**3.17** University towns with major football programs experience an increase in demand for hotel rooms during home football weekends. Hotel management responds to the increase in demand by increasing the price they charge for a room. Periodically, there is an outcry against the higher prices and accusations of "price gouging."

   a. Draw a demand and supply graph of the market for hotel rooms in Boostertown for weekends with home football games and another graph for weekends without home football games. If the Boostertown city council passes a law stating that prices for rooms are not allowed to rise, what would happen to the market for hotel rooms during home football game weekends? Show your answer on your graph.

   b. If the prices of hotel rooms are not allowed to increase, what will be the effect on out-of-town football fans?

   c. How might the city council's law affect the supply of hotel rooms over time? Briefly explain.

   d. University towns are not the only places that face peak and non-peak "seasons." Can you think of other locations that face a large increase in demand for hotel rooms during particular times of the year? Why do we typically not see laws limiting the prices hotels can charge during peak seasons?

**3.18** An advocate of medical care system reform makes the following argument:

> The 15,000 kidneys that are transplanted in the United States each year are received for free from organ donors. Despite this, because of hospital and doctor fees, the average price of a kidney transplant is $250,000. As a result, only rich people or people with very good health insurance can afford these transplants. The government should put a ceiling of $100,000 on the price of kidney transplants. That way, middle-income people will be able

to afford them, the demand for kidney transplants will increase, and more kidney transplants will take place.

Do you agree with the advocate's reasoning? Use a demand and supply graph to illustrate your answer.

**3.19** [Related to the Chapter Opener on page 101] The cities of Peabody and Woburn are 5 miles apart. Woburn enacts a rent control law that puts a ceiling on rents well below their competitive market value. Predict the effect of this law on the competitive equilibrium rent in Peabody, which does not have a rent control law. Illustrate your answer with a demand and supply graph.

**3.20** [Related to the Chapter Opener on page 101] The competitive equilibrium rent in the city of Lowell is currently $1,000 per month. The government decides to enact rent control and to establish a price ceiling for apartments of $750 per month. Briefly explain whether rent control is likely to make each of the following people better or worse off:

   a. Someone currently renting an apartment in Lowell

   b. Someone who will be moving to Lowell next year and who intends to rent an apartment

   c. A landlord who intends to abide by the rent control law

   d. A landlord who intends to ignore the law and illegally charge the highest rent possible for his apartments

**3.21** [Related to the Chapter Opener on page 101] The following newspaper article describes a journalist's experience renting an apartment about thirteen years ago:

> . . . [A] lawyer suggested that I withhold my rent because my landlord had consistently failed to provide adequate heat, and my building was infested with mice and roaches. When the landlord took me to court for not paying rent, . . . . I won an abatement and did not have to pay any rent for six months.
>
> [I didn't realize] that allowing the landlord to take me to Housing Court would make it almost impossible for me to rent another apartment. . . anywhere in the United States.

Is it more likely that a tenant will be "blacklisted" in a city with rent control or one without rent control? Briefly explain.

Based Susan Lippman, "Blacklist Blues: Landlords Use Dodgy Database to Fend Off Feisty Tenants," *The Indypendent*, December 12, 2008.

**3.22** Suppose that initially the gasoline market is in equilibrium, at a price of $3.00 per gallon and a quantity of 45 million gallons per month. Then a war in the Middle East disrupts imports of oil into the United States, shifting the supply curve for gasoline from $S_1$ to $S_2$. The price of gasoline begins to rise, and consumers protest. The federal government responds by setting a price ceiling of $3.00 per gallon. Use the graph at the top of the next column to answer the following questions.

   a. If there were no price ceiling, what would be the equilibrium price of gasoline, the quantity of gasoline demanded, and the quantity of gasoline supplied? Now assume that the price ceiling is imposed and that there is no black market in gasoline. What are the price of gasoline, the quantity of gasoline demanded, and the quantity of gasoline supplied? How large is the shortage of gasoline?

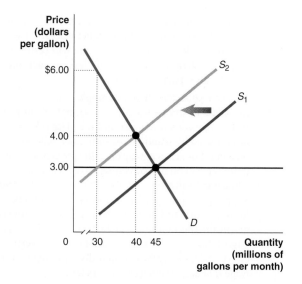

b. Assume that the price ceiling is imposed, and there is no black market in gasoline. Show on the graph the areas representing consumer surplus, producer surplus, and deadweight loss.

c. Now assume that there is a black market, and the price of gasoline rises to the maximum that consumers are willing to pay for the amount supplied by producers at $3.00 per gallon. Show on the graph the areas representing producer surplus, consumer surplus, and deadweight loss.

d. Are consumers made better off with the price ceiling than without it? Briefly explain.

3.23 An editorial in the *Economist* magazine discusses the fact that in most countries—including the United States—it is illegal for individuals to buy or sell body parts, such as kidneys.

a. Draw a demand and supply graph for the market for kidneys. Show on your graph the legal maximum price of zero and indicate the quantity of kidneys supplied at this price. (*Hint:* Because we know that some kidneys are donated, the quantity supplied will not be zero.)

b. The editorial argues that buying and selling kidneys should be legalized:

> With proper regulation, a kidney market would be a big improvement over the current sorry state of affairs. Sellers could be checked for disease and drug use, and cared for after operations. . . . Buyers would get better kidneys, faster. Both sellers and buyers would do better than in the illegal market, where much of the money goes to middlemen.

Do you agree with this argument? Should the government treat kidneys like other goods and allow the market to determine the price?

From "Psst, Wanna Buy a Kidney?" *The Economist*, November 18, 2006, p. 15.

---

 **4.4**

## The Economic Impact of Taxes, pages 115–120

LEARNING OBJECTIVE: Analyze the economic impact of taxes.

## Summary

Most taxes result in a loss of consumer surplus, a loss of producer surplus, and a deadweight loss. The true burden of a tax is not just the amount paid to government by consumers and producers but also includes the deadweight loss. The deadweight loss from a tax is the excess burden of the tax. **Tax incidence** is the actual division of the burden of a tax. In most cases, consumers and firms share the burden of a tax levied on a good or service.

MyEconLab   Visit **www.myeconlab.com** to complete these exercises online and get instant feedback.

## Review Questions

4.1 What is meant by *tax incidence*?

4.2 What do economists mean by an *efficient tax*?

4.3 Does who is legally responsible for paying a tax—buyers or sellers—make a difference in the amount of tax each pays? Briefly explain.

## Problems and Applications

4.4 Suppose the current equilibrium price of a quarter-pound hamburger is $5, and 10 million quarter-pound hamburgers are sold per month. After the federal government imposes a tax of $0.50 per hamburger, the equilibrium price of hamburgers rises to $5.20, and the equilibrium quantity falls to 9 million. Illustrate this situation with a demand and supply graph. Be sure your graph shows the equilibrium price before and after the tax, the equilibrium quantity before and after the tax, and the areas representing consumer surplus after the tax, producer surplus after the tax, tax revenue collected by the government, and deadweight loss.

4.5 Use the graph of the market for cigarettes below to answer the following questions.

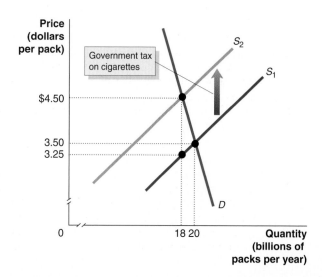

a. According to the graph, how much is the government tax on cigarettes?

b. What price do producers receive after paying the tax?

c. How much tax revenue does the government collect?

4.6 Consider the graph of the market for cigarettes in problem 4.5, where it is assumed that the government collects the tax from the producers of cigarettes.

a. How would the graph be different if the tax were collected from the buyers of cigarettes?

b. What would be the new equilibrium price that buyers pay producers of cigarettes?

c. Including the tax, what would be the total amount that cigarette buyers pay per pack?

4.7 **[Related to** Solved Problem 4.4 **on page 117]** Suppose the federal government decides to levy a sales tax on pizza of $1.00 per pie. Briefly explain whether you agree with the following statement, made by a representative of the pizza industry:

> The pizza industry is very competitive. As a result, pizza sellers will have to pay the whole tax because they are unable to pass any of it on to consumers in the form of higher prices. Therefore, a sales tax of $1.00 per pie will result in pizza sellers receiving $1.00 less on each pie sold, after paying the tax.

Illustrate your answer with a graph.

4.8 **[Related to the** Making the Connection **on page 119]** If the price consumers pay and the price sellers receive are not affected by whether consumers or sellers collect a tax on a good or service, why does the government usually require sellers and not consumers to collect a tax?

4.9 **[Related to the** Making the Connection **on page 119]** Suppose the government imposes a payroll tax of $1 per hour of work and collects the tax from employers. Use a graph for the market for labor to show the effect of the payroll tax, assuming the special case of a vertical supply curve of labor. By how much does the new equilibrium wage that employers pay workers fall?

# Appendix

## Quantitative Demand and Supply Analysis

**LEARNING** OBJECTIVE

Use quantitative demand and supply analysis.

Graphs help us understand economic change *qualitatively*. For instance, a demand and supply graph can tell us that if household incomes rise, the demand curve for a normal good will shift to the right, and its price will rise. Often, though, economists, business managers, and policymakers want to know more than the qualitative direction of change; they want a *quantitative estimate* of the size of the change.

In this chapter, we carried out a qualitative analysis of rent controls. We saw that imposing rent controls involves a trade-off: Renters as a group gain, but landlords lose, and the market for apartments becomes less efficient, as shown by the deadweight loss. To better evaluate rent controls, we need to know more than just that these gains and losses exist; we need to know how large they are. A quantitative analysis of rent controls will tell us how large the gains and losses are.

## Demand and Supply Equations

The first step in a quantitative analysis is to supplement our use of demand and supply curves with demand and supply *equations*. We noted briefly in Chapter 3 that economists often statistically estimate equations for demand curves. Supply curves can also be statistically estimated. For example, suppose that economists have estimated that the demand for apartments in New York City is:

$$Q^D = 3,000,000 - 1,000P$$

and the supply of apartments is:

$$Q^S = -450,000 + 1,300P.$$

We have used $Q^D$ for the quantity of apartments demanded per month, $Q^S$ for the quantity of apartments supplied per month, and $P$ for the apartment rent, in dollars per month. In reality, both the quantity of apartments demanded and the quantity of apartments supplied will depend on more than just the rental price of apartments in New York City. For instance, the demand for apartments in New York City will also depend on the average incomes of families in the New York area and on the rents of apartments in surrounding cities. For simplicity, we will ignore these other factors.

With no government intervention, we know that at competitive market equilibrium, the quantity demanded must equal the quantity supplied, or:

$$Q^D = Q^S.$$

We can use this equation, which is called an *equilibrium condition*, to solve for the equilibrium monthly apartment rent by setting the quantity demanded from the demand equation equal to the quantity supplied from the supply equation:

$$3,000,000, - 1,000P = -450,000 + 1,300P$$
$$3,450,000 = 2,300P$$
$$P = \frac{3,450,000}{2,300} = \$1,500.$$

### Graphing Supply and Demand Equations

After statistically estimating supply and demand equations, we can use the equations to draw supply and demand curves. In this case, the equilibrium rent for apartments is $1,500 per month, and the equilibrium quantity of apartments rented is 1,500,000. The supply equation tells us that at a rent of $346, the quantity of apartments supplied will be zero. The demand equation tells us that at a rent of $3,000, the quantity of apartments demanded will be zero. The areas representing consumer surplus and producer surplus are also indicated on the graph.

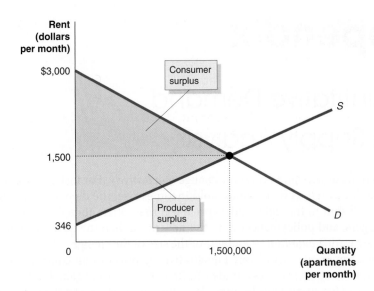

We can then substitute this price back into either the supply equation or the demand equation to find the equilibrium quantity of apartments rented:

$$Q^D = 3,000,000 - 1,000P = 3,000,000 - 1,000(1,500) = 1,500,000$$

$$Q^S = -450,000 + 1,300P = -450,000 + 1,300(1,500) = 1,500,000.$$

Figure 4A.1 illustrates the information from these equations in a graph. The figure shows the values for rent when the quantity supplied is zero and when the quantity demanded is zero. These values can be calculated from the demand equation and the supply equation by setting $Q^D$ and $Q^S$ equal to zero and solving for price:

$$Q^D = 0 = 3,000,000 - 1,000P$$

$$P = \frac{3,000,000}{1,000} = \$3,000$$

and:

$$Q^S = 0 = -450,000 + 1,300P$$

$$P = \frac{-450,000}{-1,300} = \$346.15.$$

## Calculating Consumer Surplus and Producer Surplus

Figure 4A.1 shows consumer surplus and producer surplus in this market. Recall that the sum of consumer surplus and producer surplus equals the net benefit that renters and landlords receive from participating in the market for apartments. We can use the values from the demand and supply equations to calculate the value of consumer surplus and producer surplus. Remember that consumer surplus is the area below the demand curve and above the line representing market price. Notice that this area forms a right triangle because the demand curve is a straight line—it is *linear*. As we noted in the appendix to Chapter 1, the area of a triangle is equal to ½ × Base × Height. In this case, the area is:

$$\tfrac{1}{2} \times (1,500,000) \times (3,000 - 1,500) = \$1,125,000,000.$$

So, this calculation tells us that the consumer surplus in the market for rental apartments in New York City would be about $1.125 billion.

We can calculate producer surplus in a similar way. Remember that producer surplus is the area above the supply curve and below the line representing market price.

Because our supply curve is also a straight line, producer surplus in the figure is equal to the area of the right triangle:

$$\tfrac{1}{2} \times 1,500,000 \times (1,500 - 346) = \$865,500,000.$$

This calculation tells us that the producer surplus in the market for rental apartments in New York City is about $865.5 million.

We can use this same type of analysis to measure the impact of rent control on consumer surplus, producer surplus, and economic efficiency. For instance, suppose the city imposes a rent ceiling of $1,000 per month. Figure 4A.2 can help guide us as we measure the impact.

First, we can calculate the quantity of apartments that will actually be rented by substituting the rent ceiling of $1,000 into the supply equation:

$$Q^S = -450,000 + (1,300 \times 1,000) = 850,000.$$

We also need to know the price on the demand curve when the quantity of apartments is 850,000. We can do this by substituting 850,000 for quantity in the demand equation and solving for price:

$$850,000 = 3,000,000 - 1,000P$$

$$P = \frac{-2,150,000}{-1,000} = \$2,150.$$

Compared with its value in competitive equilibrium, consumer surplus has been reduced by a value equal to the area of the yellow triangle $B$ but increased by a value equal to the area of the blue rectangle $A$. The area of the yellow triangle $B$ is:

$$\tfrac{1}{2} \times (1,500,000 - 850,000) \times (2,150 - 1,500) = \$211,250,000,$$

and the area of the blue rectangle $A$ is Base × Height, or:

$$(\$1,500 - \$1,000) \times (850,000) = \$425,000,000.$$

The value of consumer surplus in competitive equilibrium was $1,125,000,000. As a result of the rent ceiling, it will be increased to:

$$(\$1,125,000,000 + \$425,000,000) - \$211,250,000 = \$1,338,750,000.$$

Compared with its value in competitive equilibrium, producer surplus has been reduced by a value equal to the area of the yellow triangle $C$ plus a value equal to the area of the blue rectangle. The area of the yellow triangle $C$ is:

$$\tfrac{1}{2} \times (1,500,000 - 850,000) \times (1,500 - 1,000) = \$162,500,000.$$

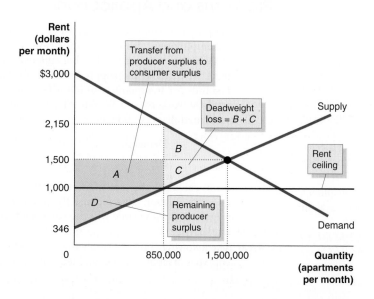

**Figure 4A.2**

**Calculating the Economic Effect of Rent Controls**

Once we have estimated equations for the demand and supply of rental housing, a diagram can guide our numerical estimates of the economic effects of rent control. Consumer surplus falls by an amount equal to the area of the yellow triangle $B$ and increases by an amount equal to the area of the blue rectangle $A$. The difference between the values of these two areas is $213,750,000. Producer surplus falls by an amount equal to the area of the blue rectangle $A$ plus the area of the yellow triangle $C$. The value of these two areas is $587,500,000. The remaining producer surplus is equal to the area of triangle $D$, or $278,000,000. Deadweight loss is equal to the area of triangle $B$ plus the area of triangle $C$, or $373,750,000.

We have already calculated the area of the blue rectangle *A* as $425,000,000. The value of producer surplus in competitive equilibrium was $865,500,000. As a result of the rent ceiling, it will be reduced to:

$$\$865,500,000 - \$162,500,000 - \$425,000,000 = \$278,000,000.$$

The loss of economic efficiency, as measured by the deadweight loss, is equal to the value represented by the areas of the yellow triangles *B* and *C*, or:

$$\$211,250,000 + \$162,500,000 = \$373,750,000.$$

The following table summarizes the results of the analysis (the values are in millions of dollars):

| Consumer Surplus | | Producer Surplus | | Deadweight Loss | |
|---|---|---|---|---|---|
| Competitive Equilibrium | Rent Control | Competitive Equilibrium | Rent Control | Competitive Equilibrium | Rent Control |
| $1,125 | $1,338.75 | $865.50 | $278 | $0 | $373.75 |

Qualitatively, we know that imposing rent control will make consumers better off, make landlords worse off, and decrease economic efficiency. The advantage of the analysis we have just gone through is that it puts dollar values on the qualitative results. We can now see how much consumers have gained, how much landlords have lost, and how great the decline in economic efficiency has been. Sometimes the quantitative results can be surprising. Notice, for instance, that after the imposition of rent control, the deadweight loss is actually greater than the remaining producer surplus.

Economists often study issues where the qualitative results of actions are apparent, even to non-economists. You don't have to be an economist to understand who wins and who loses from rent control or that if a company cuts the price of its product, its sales will increase. Business managers, policymakers, and the general public do, however, need economists to measure quantitatively the effects of different actions—including policies such as rent control—so that they can better assess the results of these actions.

---

| **4A** | **Quantitative Demand and Supply Analysis**, pages 131–134 |
|---|---|
| | LEARNING OBJECTIVE: Use quantitative demand and supply analysis. |

## Review Questions

**4A.1** In a linear demand equation, what economic information is conveyed by the intercept on the price axis? Similarly, what economic information is conveyed by the intercept on the price axis in a linear supply equation?

**4A.2** Suppose you were assigned the task of choosing a price that maximizes economic surplus in a market. What price would you choose? Why?

**4A.3** Consumer surplus is used as a measure of a consumer's net benefit from purchasing a good or service. Explain why consumer surplus is a measure of net benefit.

**4A.4** Why would economists use the term *deadweight loss* to describe the impact on consumer surplus and producer surplus from a price control?

## Problems and Applications

**4A.5** Suppose that you have been hired to analyze the impact on employment from the imposition of a minimum wage in the labor market. Further suppose that you estimate the demand and supply functions for labor, where *L* stands for the quantity of labor (measured in thousands of workers) and *W* stands for the wage rate (measured in dollars per hour):

Demand:    $L^D = 100 - 4W$

Supply:    $L^S = 6W$

First, calculate the free market equilibrium wage and quantity of labor. Now suppose the proposed minimum wage is $12. How large will the surplus of labor in this market be?

**4A.6** The following graphs illustrate the markets for two different types of labor. Suppose an identical minimum wage is imposed in both markets. In which market will the minimum wage have the largest impact on employment? Why?

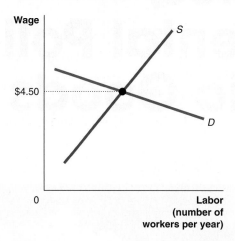

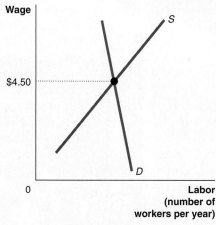

**4A.7** Suppose that you are the vice president of operations of a manufacturing firm that sells an industrial lubricant in a competitive market. Further suppose that your economist gives you the following demand and supply functions:

$$\text{Demand: } Q^D = 45 - 2P$$
$$\text{Supply: } Q^S = -15 + P$$

What is the consumer surplus in this market? What is the producer surplus?

**4A.8** The following graph shows a market in which a price floor of $3.00 per unit has been imposed. Calculate the values of each of the following:

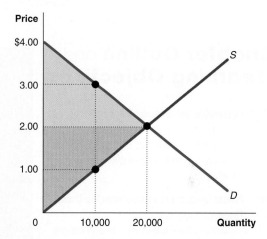

a. The deadweight loss
b. The transfer of producer surplus to consumers or the transfer of consumer surplus to producers
c. Producer surplus after the price floor is imposed
d. Consumer surplus after the price floor is imposed

**4A.9** Construct a table like the one in this appendix on page 134, but assume that the rent ceiling is $1,200 rather than $1,000.

# Externalities, Environmental Policy, and Public Goods

## Chapter Outline and Learning Objectives

# Can Government Policies Help Protect the Environment?

Pollution is a part of economic life. Consumers create air pollution by burning gasoline to power their cars and by burning natural gas to heat their homes. Firms create air pollution when they produce electricity, pesticides, or plastics, among other products. Utilities produce sulfur dioxide when they burn coal to generate electricity. Sulfur dioxide contributes to acid rain, which can damage trees, crops, and buildings. The burning of fossil fuels generates carbon dioxide and other greenhouse gases that can increase global warming.

Government policies to reduce pollution have proven to be controversial. In 2011, New Jersey Governor Chris Christie announced that he would pull the state out of the Regional Greenhouse Gas Initiative (RGGI), a coalition of 10 states that agreed to reduce their emissions of carbon dioxide by 10 percent by 2018. Christie argued, "The whole system is not working as it was intended to work. It is a failure." RGGI requires electric power plants that burn fossil fuels in 10 northeastern states to buy pollution permits for the carbon they emit. The permits are sold in auctions. If the cost of reducing emissions for a power plant is lower than the cost of its permits, the owner can sell permits to another plant that would have a higher cost to reduce its emissions. RGGI is an example of a *cap-and-trade program*.

In the past, Congress often ordered firms to use particular methods to reduce pollution, but many economists are critical of this approach—known as *command and control*—because some companies can reduce their emissions at a lower cost if they are allowed to choose the method. Many economists argue that a more efficient way to reduce pollution is through a *market-based approach*, such as RGGI, that relies on economic incentives rather than on administrative rules.

The U.S. Environmental Protection Agency (EPA) plans to implement New Source Performance Standards (NSPS) for air pollution that would affect the entire nation. As of late 2011, the EPA had yet to spell out the regulations under which NSPS would operate, but some economists and business leaders worried that it might lead to a command-and-control program that would shut down coal-fired power plants and raise electricity prices more than a market-based program would. Thomas Fanning, the head of Southern Company, an electric utility based in Atlanta, Georgia, said his company would need to spend up to $4.1 billion over three years to comply with proposed EPA rules—costs that would increase his customers' electricity prices by 25 percent.

As we will see in this chapter, economic analysis can play a significant role in evaluating the effects of environmental policies.

**AN INSIDE LOOK AT POLICY** on **page 162** discusses arguments for and against the stricter air-quality standard proposed by the Environmental Protection Agency.

Based on Juliet Eilperin, "New Jersey Gov. Chris Christie Pulls Out of Greenhouse Gas Effort," *Washington Post*, May 26, 2011; and Gabriel Nelson, "States, Utilities Ask EPA to Boost Regional Cap-And-Trade Plans," April 19, 2011.

## Economics in Your Life

### What's the "Best" Level of Pollution?

Policymakers debate alternative approaches for achieving the goal of reducing carbon dioxide emissions. But how do we know the "best" level of carbon emissions? If carbon dioxide emissions hurt the environment, should the government take action to eliminate them completely? As you read the chapter, see if you can answer these questions. You can check your answers against those we provide on **page 161** at the end of this chapter.

**Externality** A benefit or cost that affects someone who is not directly involved in the production or consumption of a good or service.

Pollution is just one example of an *externality*. An **externality** is a benefit or cost that affects someone who is not directly involved in the production or consumption of a good or service. In the case of air pollution, there is a *negative externality* because, for example, people with asthma may bear a cost even though they were not involved in the buying or selling of the electricity that caused the pollution. *Positive externalities* are also possible. For instance, medical research can provide a positive externality because people who are not directly involved in producing it or paying for it can benefit. A competitive market usually does a good job of producing the economically efficient amount of a good or service. This may not be true, though, if there is an externality in the market. When there is a negative externality, the market may produce a quantity of the good that is greater than the efficient amount. When there is a positive externality, the market may produce a quantity that is less than the efficient amount. In Chapter 4, we saw that government interventions in the economy—such as price floors on agricultural products or price ceilings on rents—can reduce economic efficiency. But when there are externalities, government intervention may actually increase economic efficiency and enhance the well-being of society. The way in which government intervenes is important, however. Economists can help policymakers ensure that government programs are as efficient as possible.

In this chapter, we explore how best to deal with the problem of pollution and other externalities. We also look at *public goods*, which are goods that may not be produced at all unless the government produces them.

**5.1 LEARNING** OBJECTIVE

Identify examples of positive and negative externalities and use graphs to show how externalities affect economic efficiency.

# Externalities and Economic Efficiency

When you consume a Big Mac, only you benefit, but when you consume a college education, other people also benefit. College-educated people are less likely to commit crimes and, by being better-informed voters, they are more likely to contribute to better government policies. So, although you capture most of the benefits of your college education, you do not capture all of them.

When you buy a Big Mac, the price you pay covers all of McDonald's costs of producing the Big Mac. When you buy electricity from a utility that burns coal and generates acid rain, the price you pay for the electricity does not cover the cost of the damage caused by the acid rain.

So, there is a *positive externality* in the production of college educations because people who do not pay for college educations will nonetheless benefit from them. There is a *negative externality* in the generation of electricity because, for example, people with homes on a lake from which fish and wildlife have disappeared because of acid rain have incurred a cost, even though they might not have bought their electricity from the polluting utility.

## The Effect of Externalities

**Private cost** The cost borne by the producer of a good or service.

**Social cost** The total cost of producing a good or service, including both the private cost and any external cost.

**Private benefit** The benefit received by the consumer of a good or service.

**Social benefit** The total benefit from consuming a good or service, including both the private benefit and any external benefit.

Externalities interfere with the *economic efficiency* of a market equilibrium. We saw in Chapter 4 that a competitive market achieves economic efficiency by maximizing the sum of consumer surplus and producer surplus. *But that result holds only if there are no externalities in production or consumption.* An externality causes a difference between the *private cost* of production and the *social cost*, or the *private benefit* from consumption and the *social benefit*. The **private cost** is the cost borne by the producer of a good or service. The **social cost** is the total cost of producing a good or service, and it is equal to the private cost plus any external cost, such as the cost of pollution. Unless there is an externality, the private cost and the social cost are equal. The **private benefit** is the benefit received by the consumer of a good or service. The **social benefit** is the total benefit from consuming a good or service, and it is equal to the private benefit plus any external benefit, such as the benefit to others resulting from

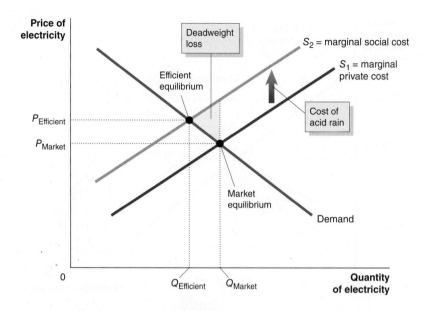

**Figure 5.1**

**The Effect of Pollution on Economic Efficiency**

Because utilities do not bear the cost of acid rain, they produce electricity beyond the economically efficient level. Supply curve $S_1$ represents just the marginal private cost that the utility has to pay. Supply curve $S_2$ represents the marginal social cost, which includes the costs to those affected by acid rain. The figure shows that if the supply curve were $S_2$, rather than $S_1$, market equilibrium would occur at price $P_{Efficient}$ and quantity $Q_{Efficient}$, the economically efficient level of output. But when the supply curve is $S_1$, the market equilibrium occurs at price $P_{Market}$ and quantity $Q_{Market}$, where there is a deadweight loss equal to the area of the yellow triangle. Because of the deadweight loss, this equilibrium is not efficient.

your college education. Unless there is an externality, the private benefit and the social benefit are equal.

## How a Negative Externality in Production Reduces Economic Efficiency

Consider how a negative externality in production affects economic efficiency. In Chapters 3 and 4, we assumed that the producer of a good or service must bear all the costs of production. We now know that this observation is not always true. In producing electricity, private costs are borne by the utility, but some external costs of pollution are borne by people who are not customers of the utility. The social cost of producing electricity is the sum of the private cost plus the external cost. Figure 5.1 shows the effect on the market for electricity of a negative externality in production.

$S_1$ is the market supply curve and represents only the private costs that utilities have to bear in generating electricity. As we saw in Chapter 4, firms will supply an additional unit of a good or service only if they receive a price equal to the additional cost of producing that unit, so a supply curve represents the *marginal cost* of producing a good or service. If utilities also had to bear the cost of pollution, the supply curve would be $S_2$, which represents the true marginal social cost of generating electricity. The equilibrium with price $P_{Efficient}$ and quantity $Q_{Efficient}$ is efficient. The equilibrium with price $P_{Market}$ and quantity $Q_{Market}$ is not efficient. To see why, remember from Chapter 4 that an equilibrium is economically efficient if economic surplus—which is the sum of consumer surplus plus producer surplus—is at a maximum. When economic surplus is at a maximum, the net benefit to society from the production of the good or service is at a maximum. With an equilibrium quantity of $Q_{Efficient}$, economic surplus is at a maximum, so this equilibrium is efficient. But with an equilibrium quantity of $Q_{Market}$, economic surplus is reduced by the deadweight loss, shown in Figure 5.1 by the yellow triangle, and the equilibrium is not efficient. The deadweight loss occurs because the supply curve is above the demand curve for the production of the units of electricity between $Q_{Efficient}$ and $Q_{Market}$. That is, the additional cost—including the external cost—of producing these units is greater than the marginal benefit to consumers, as represented by the demand curve. In other words, because of the cost of the pollution, economic efficiency would be improved if less electricity were produced.

We can conclude the following: *When there is a negative externality in producing a good or service, too much of the good or service will be produced at market equilibrium.*

## How a Positive Externality in Consumption Reduces Economic Efficiency

We have seen that a negative externality interferes with achieving economic efficiency. The same holds true for a positive externality. In Chapters 3 and 4, we assumed that the demand curve represents all the benefits that come from consuming a good. But

### Figure 5.2

### The Effect of a Positive Externality on Economic Efficiency

People who do not consume college educations can still benefit from them. As a result, the marginal social benefit from a college education is greater than the marginal private benefit to college students. Because only the marginal private benefit is represented in the market demand curve $D_1$, the quantity of college educations produced, $Q_{Market}$, is too low. If the market demand curve were $D_2$ instead of $D_1$, the level of college educations produced would be $Q_{Efficient}$, which is the efficient level. At the market equilibrium of $Q_{Market}$, there is a deadweight loss equal to the area of the yellow triangle.

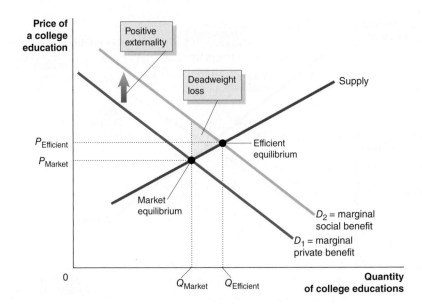

we have seen that a college education generates benefits that are not captured by the student receiving the education and so are not included in the market demand curve for college educations. Figure 5.2 shows the effect of a positive externality in consumption on the market for college educations.

If students receiving a college education could capture all its benefits, the demand curve would be $D_2$, which represents the marginal social benefits. The actual demand curve is $D_1$, however, which represents only the marginal private benefits received by students. The efficient equilibrium would come at price $P_{Efficient}$ and quantity $Q_{Efficient}$. At this equilibrium, economic surplus is maximized. The market equilibrium, at price $P_{Market}$ and quantity $Q_{Market}$, will not be efficient because the demand curve is above the supply curve for production of the units between $Q_{Market}$ and $Q_{Efficient}$. That is, the marginal benefit—including the external benefit—for producing these units is greater than the marginal cost. As a result, there is a deadweight loss equal to the area of the yellow triangle. Because of the positive externality, economic efficiency would be improved if more college educations were produced. We can conclude the following: *When there is a positive externality in consuming a good or service, too little of the good or service will be produced at market equilibrium.*

## Externalities and Market Failure

We have seen that because of externalities, the efficient level of output may not occur in either the market for electricity or the market for college educations. These are examples of **market failure**: situations in which the market fails to produce the efficient level of output. Later, we will discuss possible solutions to problems of externalities. But first we need to consider why externalities occur.

**Market failure** A situation in which the market fails to produce the efficient level of output.

## What Causes Externalities?

We saw in Chapter 2 that governments need to guarantee *property rights* in order for a market system to function well. **Property rights** refers to the rights individuals or businesses have to the exclusive use of their property, including the right to buy or sell it. Property can be tangible, physical property, such as a store or factory. Property can also be intangible, such as the right to an idea. Most of the time, the U.S. government and the governments of other high-income countries do a good job of enforcing property rights, but in certain situations, property rights do not exist or cannot be legally enforced.

Consider the following situation: Lee owns land that includes a lake. A paper company wants to lease some of Lee's land to build a paper mill. The paper mill will discharge

**Property rights** The rights individuals or businesses have to the exclusive use of their property, including the right to buy or sell it.

pollutants into Lee's lake. Because Lee owns the lake, he can charge the paper company the cost of cleaning up the pollutants. The result is that the cost of the pollution is a private cost to the paper company and is included in the price of the paper it sells. There is no external-ity, the efficient level of paper is produced, and there is no market failure.

Now suppose that the paper company builds its paper mill on privately owned land on the banks of a lake that is owned by the state. In the absence of any government regulations, the company will be free to discharge pollutants into the lake. The cost of the pollution will be external to the company because it doesn't have to pay the cost of cleaning it up. More than the economically efficient level of paper will be produced, and a market failure will occur. Or, suppose that Lee owns the lake, but the pollution is caused by acid rain generated by an electric utility hundreds of miles away. The law does not allow Lee to charge the electric utility for the damage caused by the acid rain. Even though someone is damaging Lee's property, the law does not allow him to enforce his property rights in this situation. Once again, there is an externality, and the market failure will result in too much electricity being produced.

Similarly, if you buy a house, the government will protect your right to exclusive use of that house. No one else can use the house without your permission. Because of your property rights in the house, your private benefit from the house and the social benefit are the same. When you buy a college education, however, other people are, in effect, able to benefit from your college education. You have no property right that will enable you to prevent them from benefiting or to charge them for the benefits they receive. As a result, there is a positive externality, and the market failure will result in too few college educations being supplied.

We can conclude the following: *Externalities and market failures result from incomplete property rights or from the difficulty of enforcing property rights in certain situations.*

# Private Solutions to Externalities: The Coase Theorem

**5.2 LEARNING** OBJECTIVE

Discuss the Coase theorem and explain how private bargaining can lead to economic efficiency in a market with an externality.

As noted at the beginning of this chapter, government intervention may actually increase economic efficiency and enhance the well-being of society when externalities are present. It is also possible, however, for people to find private solutions to the problem of externalities.

Can the market cure market failure? In an influential article written in 1960, Ronald Coase of the University of Chicago, winner of the 1991 Nobel Prize in Economics, ar-gued that under some circumstances, private solutions to the problem of externalities will occur. To understand Coase's argument, it is important to recognize that completely eliminating an externality usually is not economically efficient. Consider pollution, for example. There is, in fact, an *economically efficient level of pollution reduction*. At first, this seems paradoxical. Pollution is bad, and you might think the efficient amount of a bad thing is zero. But it isn't zero.

## The Economically Efficient Level of Pollution Reduction

Chapter 1 introduced the important idea that the optimal decision is to continue any ac-tivity up to the point where the marginal benefit equals the marginal cost. This applies to reducing pollution just as much as it does to other activities. Sulfur dioxide emissions contribute to smog and acid rain. As sulfur dioxide emissions—or any other type of pollution—decline, society benefits: Fewer trees die, fewer buildings are damaged, and fewer people suffer breathing problems. But a key point is that the additional benefit—that is, the *marginal benefit*—received from eliminating another ton of sulfur dioxide declines as sulfur dioxide emissions are reduced. To see why this is true, consider what happens with no reduction in sulfur dioxide emissions. In this situation, many smoggy days will occur in the cities of the Midwest and Northeast. Even healthy people may experience breathing problems. As sulfur dioxide emissions are reduced, the number of smoggy days will fall, and healthy people will no longer experience breathing problems.

Eventually, if emissions of sulfur dioxide fall to low levels, even people with asthma will no longer be affected. Further reductions in sulfur dioxide will have little additional benefit. The same will be true of the other benefits from reducing sulfur dioxide emissions: As the reductions increase, the additional benefits from fewer buildings and trees being damaged and lakes polluted will decline.

|  |  |
|---|---|
| Making<br>the<br>Connection | ### The Clean Air Act: How a Government Policy Reduced Infant Mortality |

The following bar graphs show that the United States has made tremendous progress in reducing air pollution since Congress passed the Clean Air Act in 1970: Total emissions of the six main air pollutants have fallen by more than half. Over the same period, real U.S. gross domestic product—which measures the value, corrected for inflation, of all the final goods and services produced in the country—almost tripled, energy consumption increased by half, and the number of miles traveled by all vehicles doubled.

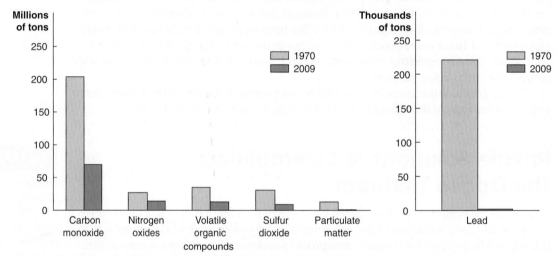

Data from U.S. Environmental Protection Agency, "Air Trends," March 10, 2010.

As we have seen, when levels of pollution are high, the marginal benefit of reducing pollution is also high. We would expect, then, that the benefit of reducing air pollution in 1970 was much higher than the benefit from a proportional reduction in air pollution would be today, when the level of pollution is much lower. Kenneth Y. Chay of Brown University and Michael Greenstone of MIT have shown that the benefits from the air pollution reductions that occurred in the period immediately after passage of the Clean Air Act were indeed high. Chay and Greenstone argue that the exposure of pregnant women to high levels of air pollution can be damaging to their unborn children, possibly by retarding lung functioning. This damage would increase the chance that the infant would die in the first weeks after being born. In the two years following passage of the Clean Air Act, there was a sharp reduction in air pollution and also a reduction in infant mortality. The decline in infant mortality was mainly due to a reduction in deaths within one month of birth. Of course, other factors also may have been responsible for the decline in infant mortality, but Chay and Greenstone use statistical analysis to isolate the effect of the decline in air pollution. They conclude that "1,300 fewer infants died in 1972 than would have in the absence of the Clean Air Act."

Based on Kenneth Y. Chay and Michael Greenstone, "Air Quality, Infant Mortality, and the Clean Air Act of 1970," National Bureau of Economic Research Working Paper 10053, October 2003.

MyEconLab **Your Turn:** Test your understanding by doing related problem 2.8 on page 166 at the end of this chapter.

What about the marginal cost to electric utilities of reducing pollution? To reduce sulfur dioxide emissions, utilities have to switch from burning high-sulfur coal to burning more costly fuel, or they have to install pollution control devices, such as scrubbers. As the level of pollution falls, further reductions become increasingly costly. Reducing emissions or other types of pollution to very low levels can require complex and expensive new technologies. For example, Arthur Fraas, formerly of the federal Office of Management and Budget, and Vincent Munley, of Lehigh University, have shown that the marginal cost of removing 97 percent of pollutants from municipal wastewater is more than twice as high as the marginal cost of removing 95 percent.

The *net benefit* to society from reducing pollution is equal to the difference between the benefit of reducing pollution and the cost. To maximize the net benefit to society, sulfur dioxide emissions—or any other type of pollution—should be reduced up to the point where the marginal benefit from another ton of reduction is equal to the marginal cost. Figure 5.3 illustrates this point.

In Figure 5.3, we measure *reductions* in sulfur dioxide emissions on the horizontal axis. We measure the marginal benefit and marginal cost in dollars from eliminating another ton of sulfur dioxide emissions on the vertical axis. As reductions in pollution increase, the marginal benefit declines and the marginal cost increases. The economically efficient amount of pollution reduction occurs where the marginal benefit equals the marginal cost. The figure shows that in this case, the economically efficient reduction of sulfur dioxide emissions is 8.5 million tons per year. In a program begun in 1990, this is the amount of reduction Congress decided should occur by 2010. At that level of emission reduction, the marginal benefit and the marginal cost of the last ton of sulfur dioxide emissions eliminated are both $200 per ton. Suppose instead that the emissions target was only 7.0 million tons. The figure shows that, at that level of reduction, the last ton of reduction has added $250 to the benefits received by society, but it has added only $175 to the costs of utilities. There has been a net benefit to society from this ton of pollution reduction of $75. In fact, the figure shows a net benefit to society from pollution reduction for every ton from 7.0 million to 8.5 million. Only when sulfur dioxide

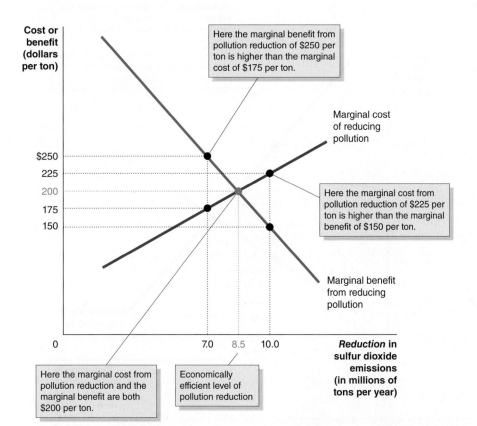

**Figure 5.3**

**The Marginal Benefit from Pollution Reduction Should Equal the Marginal Cost**

If the reduction of sulfur dioxide emissions is at 7.0 million tons per year, the marginal benefit of $250 per ton is greater than the marginal cost of $175 per ton. Further reductions in emissions will increase the net benefit to society. If the reduction of sulfur dioxide emissions is at 10.0 million tons, the marginal cost of $225 per ton is greater than the marginal benefit of $150 per ton. An increase in sulfur dioxide emissions will increase the net benefit to society. Only when the reduction is at 8.5 million tons is the marginal benefit equal to the marginal cost. This level is the economically efficient level of pollution reduction.

emissions are reduced by 8.5 million tons per year will marginal benefit fall enough and marginal cost rise enough that the two are equal.

Now suppose Congress had set the target for sulfur dioxide emissions reduction at 10 million tons per year. Figure 5.3 shows that the marginal benefit at that level of reduction has fallen to only $150 per ton and the marginal cost has risen to $225 per ton. The last ton of reduction has actually *reduced* the net benefit to society by $75 per ton. In fact, every ton of reduction beyond 8.5 million reduces the net benefit to society.

To summarize: If the marginal benefit of reducing sulfur dioxide emissions is greater than the marginal cost, further reductions will make society better off. But if the marginal cost of reducing sulfur dioxide emissions is greater than the marginal benefit, reducing sulfur dioxide emissions will actually make society worse off.

## The Basis for Private Solutions to Externalities

In arguing that private solutions to the problem of externalities were possible, Ronald Coase emphasized that when more than the optimal level of pollution is occurring, the benefits from reducing the pollution to the optimal level are greater than the costs. Figure 5.4 illustrates this point.

The marginal benefit curve shows the additional benefit from each reduction in a ton of sulfur dioxide emissions. The area under the marginal benefit curve between the two emission levels is the *total* benefit received from reducing emissions from one level to another. For instance, in Figure 5.4, the total benefit from increasing the reduction in sulfur dioxide emissions from 7.0 million tons to 8.5 million tons is the sum of the areas of A and B. The marginal cost curve shows the additional cost from each reduction in a ton of emissions. The *total* cost of reducing emissions from one level to another is the

### Figure 5.4

**The Benefits of Reducing Pollution to the Optimal Level Are Greater than the Costs**

Increasing the reduction in sulfur dioxide emissions from 7.0 million tons to 8.5 million tons results in total benefits equal to the sum of the areas A and B under the marginal benefits curve. The total cost of this decrease in pollution is equal to the area B under the marginal cost curve. The total benefits are greater than the total costs by an amount equal to the area of triangle A. Because the total benefits from reducing pollution are greater than the total costs, it's possible for those receiving the benefits to arrive at a private agreement with polluters to pay them to reduce pollution.

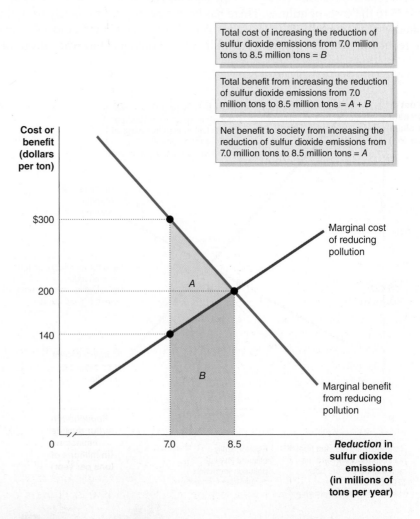

# Don't Let This Happen to You

## Remember That It's the *Net* Benefit That Counts

Why would we not want to *completely* eliminate anything unpleasant? As long as any person suffers any unpleasant consequences from air pollution, the marginal benefit of reducing air pollution will be positive. So, removing every particle of air pollution results in the largest *total* benefit to society. But removing every particle of air pollution is not optimal for the same reason that it is not optimal to remove every particle of dirt or dust from a room when cleaning it. The cost of cleaning your room is not just the price of the cleaning products but also the opportunity cost of your time. The more time you devote to cleaning your room, the less time you have for other activities. As you devote more

and more additional hours to cleaning your room, the alternative activities you have to give up are likely to increase in value, raising the opportunity cost of cleaning: Cleaning instead of watching TV may not be too costly, but cleaning instead of eating any meals or getting any sleep is very costly. Optimally, you should eliminate dirt in your room up to the point where the marginal benefit of the last dirt removed equals the marginal cost of removing it. Society should take the same approach to air pollution. The result is the largest *net* benefit to society.

MyEconLab

**Your Turn:** Test your understanding by doing related problem 2.9 on page 166 at the end of this chapter.

---

area under the marginal cost curve between the two emissions levels. The total cost from increasing the reduction in emissions from 7.0 million tons to 8.5 million tons is the area *B*. The net benefit from reducing emissions is the difference between the total cost and the total benefit, which is equal to the area of triangle *A*.

In Figure 5.4, the benefits from further reductions in sulfur dioxide emissions are much greater than the costs. In the appendix to Chapter 1, we reviewed the formula for calculating the area of a triangle, which is ½ × Base × Height, and the formula for the area of a rectangle, which is Base × Height. Using these formulas, we can calculate the value of the total benefits from the reduction in emissions and the value of the total costs. The value of the benefits (*A* + *B*) is $375 million. The value of the costs (*B*) is $255 million. If the people who would benefit from a reduction in pollution could get together, they could offer to pay the electric utilities $255 million to reduce the pollution to the optimal level. After making the payment, they would still be left with a net benefit of $120 million. In other words, a private agreement to reduce pollution to the optimal level is possible, without any government intervention.

## Making the Connection

### The Fable of the Bees

Apple trees must be pollinated by bees in order to bear fruit. Bees need the nectar from apple trees (or other plants) to produce honey. In an important article published in the early 1950s, the British economist James Meade, winner of the 1977 Nobel Prize in Economics, argued that there were positive externalities in both apple growing and beekeeping. The more apple trees growers planted, the more honey would be produced in the hives of local beekeepers. And the more hives beekeepers kept, the larger the apple crops in neighboring apple orchards. Meade assumed that beekeepers were not being compensated by apple growers for the pollination services they were providing to apple growers and that apple growers were not being compensated by beekeepers for the use of their nectar in honey making. Therefore, he concluded that unless the government intervened, the market would not supply enough apple trees and beehives.

*Some apple growers and beekeepers make private arrangements to arrive at an economically efficient outcome.*

Steven Cheung of the University of Washington showed, however, that government intervention was not necessary because beekeepers and apple growers had long since arrived at private agreements. In fact, in Washington State, farmers with fruit orchards had been renting beehives to pollinate their trees since at least as early as 1917. According to Cheung, "Pollination contracts usually include stipulations regarding the number and strength of the [bee] colonies, the rental fee per hive, the time of delivery and removal of hives, the protection of bees from pesticide sprays, and the strategic placing of hives."

Today, honeybees pollinate more than $14 billion worth of crops annually, from blueberries in Maine all the way to almonds in California. Increasing demand for almonds has expanded the crop in California until it now stretches for 300 miles, across 580,000 acres, producing 80 percent of the world's almonds. Currently, about 1.4 million beehives are required to pollinate the California almond crop. Beehives are shipped into the state in February and March to pollinate the almond trees, and then they are shipped to Oregon and Washington to pollinate the cherry, pear, and apple orchards in those states during April and May.

Based on J. E. Meade, "External Economies and Diseconomies in a Competitive Situation," *Economic Journal*, Vol. 62, March 1952, pp. 54–67; Steven N. S. Cheung, "The Fable of the Bees: An Economic Investigation," *Journal of Law and Economics*, Vol. 16, 1973, pp. 11–33; and "Vitamin Bee: A New Attempt to Save the Most Vital Workers in the Orchards," *Economist*, March 4, 2010.

MyEconLab  **Your Turn:** Test your understanding by doing related problem 2.11 on page 166 at the end of this chapter.

## Do Property Rights Matter?

In discussing the bargaining between the electric utilities and the people suffering the effects of the utilities' pollution, we assumed that the electric utilities were not legally liable for the damage they were causing. In other words, the victims of pollution could not legally enforce the right of their property not to be damaged, so they would have to pay the utilities to reduce the pollution. But would it make any difference if the utilities were legally liable for the damages? Surprisingly, as Coase was the first to point out, it does not matter for the amount of pollution reduction. The only difference would be that now the electric utilities would have to pay the victims of pollution for the right to pollute rather than the victims having to pay the utilities to reduce pollution. Because the marginal benefits and marginal costs of pollution reduction would not change, the bargaining should still result in the efficient level of pollution reduction—in this case, 8.5 million tons.

In the absence of the utilities being legally liable, the victims of pollution have an incentive to pay the utilities to reduce pollution up to the point where the marginal benefit of the last ton of reduction is equal to the marginal cost. If the utilities are legally liable, they have an incentive to pay the victims of pollution to allow them to pollute up to the same point.

## The Problem of Transactions Costs

**Transactions costs** The costs in time and other resources that parties incur in the process of agreeing to and carrying out an exchange of goods or services.

Unfortunately, there are frequently practical difficulties that interfere with a private solution to the problem of externalities. In cases of pollution, for example, there are often both many polluters and many people suffering from the negative effects of pollution. Bringing together all those suffering from pollution with all those causing the pollution and negotiating an agreement often fails due to *transactions costs*. **Transactions costs** are the costs in time and other resources that parties incur in the process of agreeing to and carrying out an exchange of goods or services. In this case, the transactions costs would include the time and other costs of negotiating an agreement, drawing up a binding contract, purchasing insurance, and monitoring the agreement. Unfortunately, when many people are involved, the transactions costs are often higher than the net benefits from reducing the externality. In that case, the cost of transacting ends up exceeding the gain from the transaction, and a private solution to an externality problem is not feasible.

## The Coase Theorem

**Coase theorem** The argument of economist Ronald Coase that if transactions costs are low, private bargaining will result in an efficient solution to the problem of externalities.

Coase's argument that private solutions to the problem of externalities are possible is summed up in the **Coase theorem**: *If transactions costs are low, private bargaining will result in an efficient solution to the problem of externalities*. We have seen the basis for the

Coase theorem in the preceding example of pollution by electric utilities: Because the benefits from reducing an externality are often greater than the costs, private bargaining can lead to an efficient outcome. But we have also seen that this outcome will occur only if transactions costs are low, and in the case of pollution, they usually are not. In general, private bargaining is most likely to reach an efficient outcome if the number of parties bargaining is small.

In practice, we must add a couple of other qualifications to the Coase theorem. In addition to low transactions costs, private solutions to the problem of externalities will occur only if all parties to the agreement have full information about the costs and benefits associated with the externality, and all parties must be willing to accept a reasonable agreement. For example, if those suffering from the effects of pollution do not have information on the costs of reducing pollution, it is unlikely that the parties can reach an agreement. Unreasonable demands can also hinder an agreement. For instance, in the example of pollution by electric utilities, we saw that the total benefit of reducing sulfur dioxide emissions was $375 million. Even if transactions costs are very low, if the utilities insist on being paid more than $375 million to reduce emissions, no agreement will be reached because the amount paid exceeds the value of the reduction to those suffering from the emissions.

# Government Policies to Deal with Externalities

When private solutions to externalities are not feasible, how should the government intervene? The first economist to analyze market failure systematically was A. C. Pigou, a British economist at Cambridge University. Pigou argued that to deal with a negative externality in production, the government should impose a tax equal to the cost of the externality. The effect of such a tax is shown in Figure 5.5, which reproduces the negative externality from acid rain shown in Figure 5.1 on page 139.

By imposing a tax on the production of electricity equal to the cost of acid rain, the government will cause electric utilities to *internalize* the externality. As a consequence, the cost of the acid rain will become a private cost borne by the utilities, and the supply curve for electricity will shift from $S_1$ to $S_2$. The result will be a decrease in the equilibrium output of electricity from $Q_{Market}$ to the efficient level, $Q_{Efficient}$. The price consumers pay for electricity will rise from $P_{Market}$—which does not include the cost of acid rain—to $P_{Efficient}$—which does include the cost. Producers will receive a price $P$, which is equal to $P_{Efficient}$ minus the amount of the tax.

**5.3 LEARNING** OBJECTIVE

Analyze government policies to achieve economic efficiency in a market with an externality.

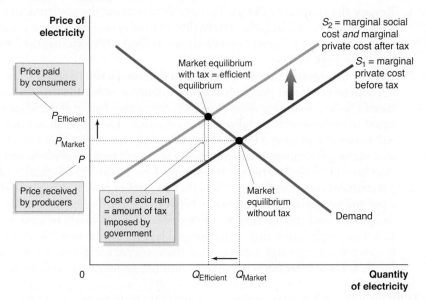

**Figure 5.5**

**When There Is a Negative Externality, a Tax Can Lead to the Efficient Level of Output**

Because utilities do not bear the cost of acid rain, they produce electricity beyond the economically efficient level. If the government imposes a tax equal to the cost of acid rain, the utilities will internalize the externality. As a consequence, the supply curve will shift up, from $S_1$ to $S_2$. The market equilibrium quantity changes from $Q_{Market}$, where an inefficiently high level of electricity is produced, to $Q_{Efficient}$, the economically efficient equilibrium quantity. The price of electricity will rise from $P_{Market}$—which does not include the cost of acid rain—to $P_{Efficient}$—which does include the cost. Consumers pay the price $P_{Efficient}$, while producers receive a price $P$, which is equal to $P_{Efficient}$ minus the amount of the tax.

# Solved Problem 5.3

## Using a Tax to Deal with a Negative Externality

Companies that produce toilet paper bleach the paper to make it white. Some paper plants discharge the bleach into rivers and lakes, causing substantial environmental damage. Suppose the following graph illustrates the situation in the toilet paper market.

Explain how the federal government can use a tax on toilet paper to bring about the efficient level of production. What should the value of the tax be?

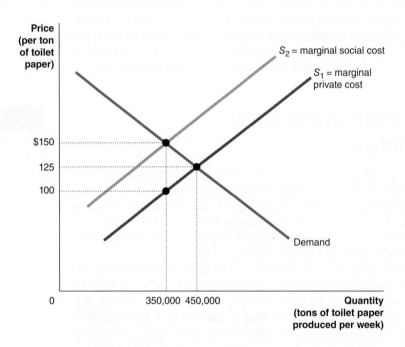

## Solving the Problem

**Step 1:** **Review the chapter material.** This problem is about the government using a tax to deal with a negative externality in production, so you may want to review the section "Government Policies to Deal with Externalities," which begins on page 147.

**Step 2:** **Use the information from the graph to determine the necessary tax.** The efficient level of toilet paper production will occur where the marginal social benefit from consuming toilet paper, as represented by the demand curve, is equal to the marginal social cost of production. The graph shows that this will occur at a price of $150 per ton and production of 350,000 tons. In the absence of government intervention, the price will be $125 per ton, and production will be 450,000 tons. It is tempting—but incorrect!—to think that the government could bring about the efficient level of production by imposing a per-ton tax equal to the difference between the price when production is at its optimal level and the current market price. But this would be a tax of only $25. The graph shows that at the optimal level of production, the difference between the marginal private cost and the marginal social cost is $50. Therefore, a tax of $50 per ton is required to shift the supply curve up from $S_1$ to $S_2$.

MyEconLab   **Your Turn:** For more practice, do related problem 3.8 on page 167 at the end of this chapter.

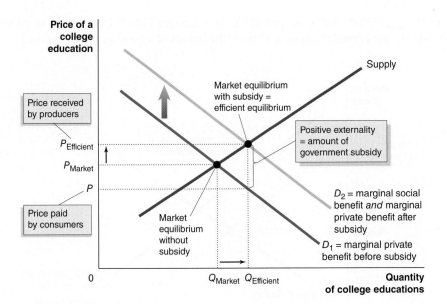

**Price of a college education**

Price received by producers

$P_{\text{Efficient}}$

$P_{\text{Market}}$

$P$

Price paid by consumers

Supply

Market equilibrium with subsidy = efficient equilibrium

Positive externality = amount of government subsidy

$D_2$ = marginal social benefit *and* marginal private benefit after subsidy

$D_1$ = marginal private benefit before subsidy

Market equilibrium without subsidy

0     $Q_{\text{Market}}$   $Q_{\text{Efficient}}$     **Quantity of college educations**

### Figure 5.6

**When There Is a Positive Externality, a Subsidy Can Bring about the Efficient Level of Output**

People who do not consume college educations can benefit from them. As a result, the social benefit from a college education is greater than the private benefit to college students. If the government pays a subsidy equal to the external benefit, students will internalize the externality. The subsidy will cause the demand curve to shift up, from $D_1$ to $D_2$. As a result, the market equilibrium quantity will shift from $Q_{\text{Market}}$, where an inefficiently low level of college educations is supplied, to $Q_{\text{Efficient}}$, the economically efficient equilibrium quantity.

Producers receive the price $P_{\text{Efficient}}$, while consumers pay a price $P$, which is equal to $P_{\text{Efficient}}$ minus the amount of the subsidy.

Pigou also argued that the government can deal with a positive externality in consumption by giving consumers a subsidy, or payment, equal to the value of the externality. The effect of the subsidy is shown in Figure 5.6, which reproduces the positive externality from college education shown in Figure 5.2 on page 140.

By paying college students a subsidy equal to the external benefit from a college education, the government will cause students to *internalize* the externality. That is, the external benefit from a college education will become a private benefit received by college students, and the demand curve for college educations will shift from $D_1$ to $D_2$. The equilibrium number of college educations supplied will increase from $Q_{\text{Market}}$ to the efficient level, $Q_{\text{Efficient}}$. Producers receive the price $P_{\text{Efficient}}$, while consumers pay a price $P$, which is equal to $P_{\text{Efficient}}$ minus the amount of the subsidy. In fact, the government does heavily subsidize college educations. All states have government-operated universities that charge tuitions well below the cost of providing the education. The state and federal governments also provide students with grants and low-interest loans that subsidize college educations. The economic justification for these programs is that college educations provide an external benefit to society.

| Making the Connection | ### Should the Government Tax Cigarettes and Soda? |
|---|---|

Typically, governments use Pigouvian taxes to deal with negative externalities in *production*. Governments also impose taxes—sometimes called "sin taxes"—on products such as cigarettes and liquor. Some policymakers have argued that these products generate negative externalities in *consumption*, so a tax on them can increase economic efficiency. Recently, several cities have considered taxing sweetened soda, on the grounds that these sodas cause a negative externality by raising medical costs. Just as governments can deal with a positive externality in consumption by giving consumers a subsidy, they can deal with a negative externality by imposing a tax. The effect of a tax on soda is shown in the figure on the next page. By imposing a tax on soda, the government will cause consumers to internalize the externality. That is, the external cost to drinking soda will become a private cost paid by consumers. Because consumers now have to pay a tax on soda, at every quantity they are willing to pay less than they would have without the tax, so the demand curve for soda will shift down by the amount of the tax, from $D_1$ to $D_2$. The equilibrium quantity of sodas consumed will decrease from $Q_{\text{Market}}$ to the efficient level, $Q_{Efficient}$. (Note that as we saw in Chapter 4, pages 118–119, we get the same result whether the government imposes a tax on the buyers of a good or on the sellers.)

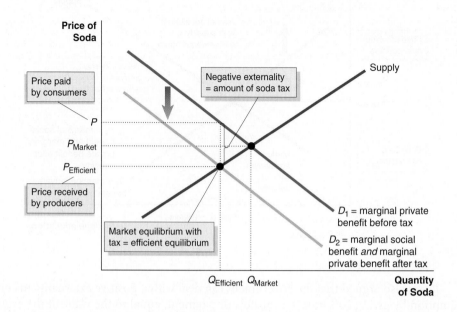

But do people actually cause a negative externality by smoking and drinking sweetened sodas? It might seem that they don't because consumers of cigarettes and sodas bear the costs of any health problems they experience. In fact, though, the higher medical expenses from treating the complications of cigarette smoking or obesity are not paid for entirely by the smokers or soda drinkers. A smoker who receives health insurance through his employer may increase the costs of that insurance, which will be paid for by all of the workers at the firm. Similarly, someone who is over 65 and is part of the federal government's Medicare program has his or her health care paid for partly by taxpayers. The costs of medical care that are not paid for by smokers or soda drinkers would appear to represent a negative externality.

There is a complication to this conclusion, however: Smokers and people who are obese tend to die early. This tragic outcome means that smokers and the obese may have been paying taxes to help pay for Social Security and Medicare benefits that they will never receive. They may also have made payments into company and public employee pension plans and purchased long-term care insurance, but they may not have lived long enough to receive many pension payments or to have spent time in a nursing home. So, there are offsetting effects: While alive, smokers and obese people may impose costs on others who bear the expense of their higher medical costs, but because they are likely to die early, they provide a financial gain to recipients of Social Security, Medicare, company and public employee pension plans, and purchasers of long-term care insurance. W. Kip Viscusi of Vanderbilt University has studied the case of tobacco smoking and concluded that the external costs and benefits roughly offset each other, meaning that there doesn't appear to be a significant negative externality from smoking. Studies of obesity have arrived at somewhat conflicting results: A study of obesity in the Netherlands found that the cost savings from premature death offset the additional lifetime medical costs of obese people. But another study on U.S. data found that obesity did lead to a net increase in lifetime medical costs, even taking into account the shorter average life spans of obese people.

There may also be costs to smoking and obesity beyond additional medical costs. Smokers may inflict costs on others because of secondhand smoke or because smoking during pregnancy can lead to low birth weights and other health problems for babies. Airlines have noted that they spend more on fuel costs because of the increasing weight of passengers.

In the end, economists and policymakers continue to debate whether the government should use taxes to deal with negative externalities in consumption.

Based on David Leonhardt, "The Battle Over Taxing Soda," *New York Times*, May 18, 2010; W. Kip Viscusi, "Cigarette Taxation and the Social Consequences of Smoking," in James Poterba, ed., *Tax Policy and the Economy*, Vol. 9, Cambridge: MIT Press, 1995; Pieter H. M. van Baal, et al., "Lifetime Medical Costs of Obesity: Prevention No Cure for Increasing Health Expenditure," *PLoS Medicine*, Vol. 5, No. 2, February 2008, pp. 242–249; Pierre-Carl Michaud, "Understanding the Economic Consequences of Shifting Trends in Population Health," National Bureau of Economic Research Working Paper 15231, August 2009; and "Feds Say Obesity Epidemic Hurts Airlines by Increasing Fuel Costs," *Associated Press*, November 5, 2004.

**Your Turn:** Test your understanding by doing related problem 3.9 on page 167 at the end of this chapter.                    MyEconLab

---

Because Pigou was the first economist to propose using government taxes and subsidies to deal with externalities, they are sometimes referred to as **Pigovian taxes and subsidies**. Note that a Pigovian tax eliminates deadweight loss and improves economic efficiency. This situation is the opposite of the one we saw in Chapter 4, in which we discussed how most taxes reduce consumer surplus and producer surplus and create a deadweight loss. In fact, one reason that economists support Pigovian taxes as a way to deal with negative externalities is that the government can use the revenues raised by Pigovian taxes to lower other taxes that reduce economic efficiency. For instance, the Canadian province of British Columbia has enacted a Pigovian tax on emissions of carbon dioxide and uses the revenue raised to reduce personal income taxes.

**Pigovian taxes and subsidies**
Government taxes and subsidies intended to bring about an efficient level of output in the presence of externalities.

## Command-and-Control versus Market-Based Approaches

Although the federal government has sometimes used taxes and subsidies to deal with externalities, in dealing with pollution, it has traditionally used a *command-and-control approach* with firms that pollute. A **command-and-control approach** to reducing pollution involves the government imposing quantitative limits on the amount of pollution firms are allowed to generate or requiring firms to install specific pollution control devices. For example, in the 1980s, the federal government required auto manufacturers such as Ford and General Motors to install catalytic converters to reduce auto emissions on all new automobiles.

**Command-and-control approach**
An approach that involves the government imposing quantitative limits on the amount of pollution firms are allowed to emit or requiring firms to install specific pollution control devices.

Congress could have used direct pollution controls to deal with the problem of acid rain. To achieve its objective of a reduction of 8.5 million tons per year in sulfur dioxide emissions by 2010, Congress could have required every utility to reduce sulfur dioxide emissions by the same specified amount. However, this approach would not have been an economically efficient solution to the problem because utilities can have very different costs of reducing sulfur dioxide emissions. Some utilities that already use low-sulfur coal can reduce emissions further only at a high cost. Other utilities, particularly those in the Midwest, are able to reduce emissions at a lower cost.

Congress decided to use a market-based approach to reducing sulfur dioxide emissions by setting up a cap-and-trade system of tradable emissions allowances. The federal government gave utilities allowances equal to the total amount of allowable sulfur dioxide emissions. The utilities were then free to buy and sell the allowances. An active market where the allowances can be bought and sold is conducted on the Chicago Mercantile Exchange. Utilities that could reduce emissions at low cost have done so and have sold their allowances. Utilities that could only reduce emissions at high cost have bought allowances. Using tradable emissions allowances to reduce acid rain has been a great success and has made it possible for utilities to meet Congress's emissions goal at a much lower cost than expected. Just before Congress enacted the allowances program in 1990, the Edison Electric Institute estimated that the cost to utilities of complying with the program would be $7.4 billion by 2010. By 1994, the federal government's General Accounting Office estimated that the cost would be less than $2 billion. In practice, the cost appears likely to be almost 90 percent less than the initial estimate, or only about $870 *million*.

## Are Tradable Emissions Allowances Licenses to Pollute?

Some environmentalists have criticized tradable emissions allowances, labeling them "licenses to pollute." They argue that just as the government does not issue licenses to rob banks or to drive drunk, it should not issue licenses to pollute. But this criticism ignores one of the central lessons of economics: Resources are scarce, and trade-offs exist. Resources that are spent on reducing one type of pollution are not available to reduce other types of pollution or for any other use. Because reducing acid rain using tradable emissions allowances has cost utilities $870 million, rather than $7.4 billion, as originally estimated, society has saved more than $6.5 billion per year.

<table>
<tr><td>Making<br>the<br>Connection</td><td>

## Can a Cap-and-Trade System Reduce Global Warming?

In the past 35 years, the global surface temperature has increased about 0.75 degree Fahrenheit (or 0.40 degree Centigrade) compared with the average for the period between 1951 and 1980. The following

</td></tr>
</table>

grade) compared with the average for the period between 1951 and 1980. The following graph shows changes in temperature over the years since 1880.

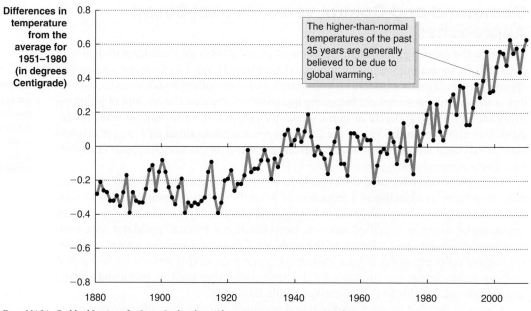

From NASA, Goddard Institute for Space Studies, http://data.giss.nasa.gov/gistemp/graphs/.

Over the centuries, global temperatures have gone through many long periods of warming and cooling. Nevertheless, many scientists are convinced that the recent warming trend is not part of the natural fluctuations in temperature but is instead primarily due to the burning of fossil fuels, such as coal, natural gas, and petroleum. Burning these fuels releases carbon dioxide, which accumulates in the atmosphere as a "greenhouse gas." Greenhouse gases cause some of the heat released from the earth to be reflected back, increasing temperatures. Annual emissions of carbon dioxide have increased from about 50 million metric tons of carbon in 1850 to 1,600 million metric tons in 1950 and to nearly 8,500 million metric tons in 2008.

If greenhouse gases continue to accumulate in the atmosphere, according to some estimates global temperatures could increase by 3 degrees Fahrenheit or more during the next 100 years. Such an increase in temperature could lead to significant changes in climate, which might result in more hurricanes and other violent weather conditions, disrupt farming in many parts of the world, and lead to increases in sea levels, which could lead to flooding in coastal areas.

Although most economists and policymakers agree that emitting carbon dioxide results in a significant negative externality, there has been a long and heated debate over which policies should be adopted. Part of the debate arises from disagreements over how rapidly global warming is likely to occur and what the economic cost will be. In addition, carbon dioxide emissions are a global problem; sharp reductions in carbon dioxide emissions only in the United States and Europe, for instance, would not be enough to eliminate global warming. But coordinating policy across countries has proven difficult. Finally, policymakers and economists debate the relative effectiveness of different policies.

Several approaches to reducing carbon dioxide emissions have been used. As mentioned earlier, the Canadian province of British Columbia has introduced a Pigovian tax on carbon dioxide emissions. Cap-and-trade policies, similar to the one used successfully in the United States to reduce sulfur dioxide emissions, have also been tried. In 2005, 24 countries in the European Union set up a cap-and-trade system called the European Union Emissions Trading Scheme. Under this program, each country issues emission allowances that can be freely traded over time. Although carbon dioxide emissions rose slightly during the first few years of the plan, over time, as the number of emission allowances is reduced, emissions should decline. In 2009, President Barack Obama proposed a cap-and-trade system for the United States that would result in gradually reducing carbon dioxide emissions to their 1990 level by 2020 and to 80 percent below their 1990 level by 2050. However, Congress failed to approve the plan. As we saw in the chapter opener, beginning in 2005, several states in the Northeast established a cap-and-trade program, with the goal of reducing carbon dioxide emissions from power plants by 10 percent by 2018. Beginning in 2008, power plants in the states participating in the program were required to buy emissions permits, which made the program the first in the United States to limit greenhouse gas emissions. Critics questioned the effectiveness of a plan limited to one region and, as we have seen, in 2011, New Jersey Governor Christie withdrew his state from the program. The federal government intends to regulate greenhouse gas emissions under the Environmental Protection Agency's (EPA's) New Source Performance Standards. As of late 2011, the details of the EPA's new program had not been announced.

The debate over which policies to use in reducing carbon dioxide emissions will likely continue for many years.

Based on Gabriel Nelson, "Wrapped Up in Politics, Granddaddy of Cap-And-Trade Plans Has an Uncertain Future," *New York Times*, July 19, 2011; Juliet Eilperin, "New Jersey Gov. Chris Christie Pulls Out of Greenhouse Gas Effort," *Washington Post*, May 26, 2011; "Cap-and-Trade's Last Hurrah," *Economist*, May 18, 2010; and Tom Boden, Gregg Marland, and Bob Andres, "Global Carbon Dioxide Emissions from Fossil-Fuel Burning, Cement Manufacture, and Gas Flaring: 1751-2008," Carbon Dioxide Information Analysis Center, Oak Ridge National Laboratory, June 10, 2011.

**Your Turn:** Test your understanding by doing related problem 3.14 on page 168 at the end of this chapter.

MyEconLab

**5.4 LEARNING** OBJECTIVE

Explain how goods can be categorized on the basis of whether they are rival or excludable and use graphs to illustrate the efficient quantities of public goods and common resources.

# Four Categories of Goods

We can explore further the question of when the market is likely to succeed in supplying the efficient quantity of a good by understanding that goods differ on the basis of whether their consumption is *rival* and *excludable*. **Rivalry** occurs when one person's consuming a unit of a good means no one else can consume it. If you consume a Big

**Rivalry** The situation that occurs when one person's consuming a unit of a good means no one else can consume it.

**Excludability** The situation in which anyone who does not pay for a good cannot consume it.

**Private good** A good that is both rival and excludable.

**Public good** A good that is both nonrival and nonexcludable.

**Free riding** Benefiting from a good without paying for it.

**Common resource** A good that is rival but not excludable.

Mac, for example, no one else can consume it. **Excludability** means that anyone who does not pay for a good cannot consume it. If you don't pay for a Big Mac, MacDonald's can exclude you from consuming it. The consumption of a Big Mac is therefore rival and excludable. The consumption of some goods, however, can be either *nonrival* or *nonexcludable*. Nonrival means that one person's consumption does not interfere with another person's consumption. Nonexcludable means that it is impossible to exclude others from consuming the good, whether they have paid for it or not. Figure 5.7 shows four possible categories into which goods can fall.

We next consider each of the four categories:

1. *Private goods.* A good that is both rival and excludable is a **private good**. Food, clothing, haircuts, and many other goods and services fall into this category. One person's consuming a unit of these goods precludes other people from consuming that unit, and no one can consume these goods without buying them. Although we didn't state it explicitly, when we analyzed the demand and supply for goods and services in Chapter 3, we assumed that the goods and services were all private goods.

2. *Public goods.* A **public good** is both nonrival and nonexcludable. Public goods are often, although not always, supplied by a government rather than by private firms. The classic example of a public good is national defense. Your consuming national defense does not interfere with your neighbor's consuming it, so consumption is nonrival. You also cannot be excluded from consuming it, whether you pay for it or not. No private firm would be willing to supply national defense because everyone can consume national defense without paying for it. The behavior of consumers in this situation is referred to as *free riding*. **Free riding** involves individuals benefiting from a good—in this case, the provision of national defense—without paying for it.

3. *Quasi-public goods.* Some goods are excludable but not rival. An example is cable television. People who do not pay for cable television do not receive it, but one person's watching it doesn't affect other people's watching it. The same is true of a toll road. Anyone who doesn't pay the toll doesn't get on the road, but one person using the road doesn't interfere with someone else using the road (unless so many people are using the road that it becomes congested). Goods that fall into this category are called *quasi-public goods*.

4. *Common resources.* If a good is rival but not excludable, it is a **common resource**. Forest land in many poor countries is a common resource. If one person cuts down a tree, no one else can use the tree. But if no one has a property right to the forest, no one can be excluded from using it. As we will discuss in more detail later, people often overuse common resources.

We discussed the demand and supply for private goods in Chapter 3. For the remainder of this chapter, we focus on the categories of public goods and common resources. To determine the optimal quantity of a public good, we have to modify the demand and supply analysis of Chapter 3 to take into account that a public good is both nonrival and nonexcludable.

**Figure 5.7**

**Four Categories of Goods**

Goods and services can be divided into four categories on the basis of whether people can be excluded from consuming them and whether they are rival in consumption. A good or service is rival in consumption if one person consuming a unit of a good means that another person cannot consume that unit.

|  | Excludable | Nonexcludable |
|---|---|---|
| **Rival** | **Private Goods** *Examples:* Big Macs Running shoes | **Common Resources** *Examples:* Tuna in the ocean Public pasture land |
| **Nonrival** | **Quasi-Public Goods** *Examples:* Cable TV Toll road | **Public Goods** *Examples:* National defense Court system |

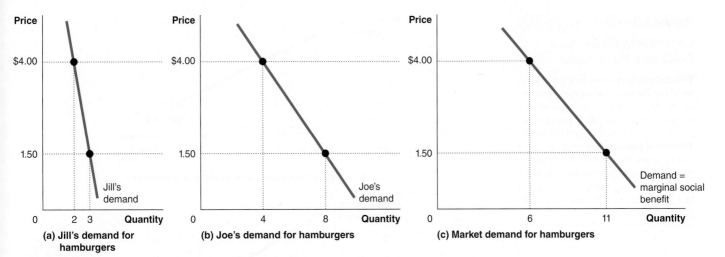

**Figure 5.8** Constructing the Market Demand Curve for a Private Good

The market demand curve for private goods is determined by adding horizontally the quantity of the good demanded at each price by each consumer. For instance, in panel (a), Jill demands 2 hamburgers when the price is $4.00, and in panel (b), Joe demands 4 hamburgers when the price is $4.00. So, a quantity of 6 hamburgers and a price of $4.00 is a point on the market demand curve in panel (c).

# The Demand for a Public Good

We can determine the market demand curve for a good or service by adding up the quantity of the good demanded by each consumer at each price. To keep things simple, let's consider the case of a market with only two consumers. Figure 5.8 shows that the market demand curve for hamburgers depends on the individual demand curves of Jill and Joe.

At a price of $4.00, Jill demands 2 hamburgers per week and Joe demands 4. Adding horizontally, the combination of a price of $4.00 per hamburger and a quantity demanded of 6 hamburgers will be a point on the market demand curve for hamburgers. Similarly, adding horizontally at a price of $1.50, we have a price of $1.50 and a quantity demanded of 11 as another point on the market demand curve. A consumer's demand curve for a good represents the marginal benefit the consumer receives from the good, so when we add together the consumers' demand curves, we not only have the market demand curve but also the marginal social benefit curve for this good, assuming that there is no externality in consumption.

How can we find the demand curve or marginal social benefit curve for a public good? Once again, for simplicity, assume that Jill and Joe are the only consumers. Unlike with a private good, where Jill and Joe can end up consuming different quantities, with a public good, they will consume *the same quantity*. Suppose that Jill owns a service station on an isolated rural road, and Joe owns a car dealership next door. These are the only two businesses around for miles. Both Jill and Joe are afraid that unless they hire a security guard at night, their businesses may be burgled. Like national defense, the services of a security guard are in this case a public good: Once hired, the guard will be able to protect both businesses, so the good is nonrival. It also will not be possible to exclude either business from being protected, so the good is nonexcludable.

To arrive at a demand curve for a public good, we don't add quantities at each price, as with a private good. Instead, we add the price each consumer is willing to pay for each quantity of the public good. This value represents the total dollar amount consumers as a group would be willing to pay for that quantity of the public good. Put another way, to find the demand curve, or marginal social benefit curve, for a private good, we add the demand curves of individual consumers horizontally; for public goods, we add individual demand curves vertically. Figure 5.9 shows how the marginal social benefit curve for security guard services depends on the individual demand curves of Jill and Joe.

**Figure 5.9**

**Constructing the Demand Curve for a Public Good**

To find the demand curve for a public good, we add up the price at which each consumer is willing to purchase each quantity of the good. In panel (a), Jill is willing to pay $8 per hour for a security guard to provide 10 hours of protection. In panel (b), Joe is willing to pay $10 for that level of protection. Therefore, in panel (c), the price of $18 per hour and the quantity of 10 hours will be a point on the demand curve for security guard services.

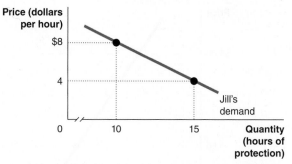

**(a) Jill's demand for security guard services**

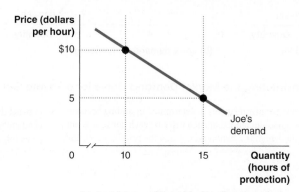

**(b) Joe's demand for security guard services**

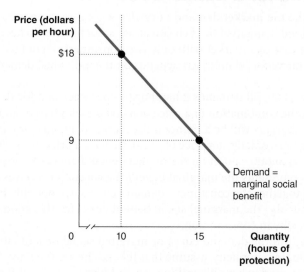

**(c) Total demand for security guard services**

The figure shows that Jill is willing to pay $8 per hour for the guard to provide 10 hours of protection per night. Joe would suffer a greater loss from a burglary, so he is willing to pay $10 per hour for the same amount of protection. Adding the dollar amount that each is willing to pay gives us a price of $18 per hour and a quantity of 10 hours as a point on the marginal social benefit curve for security guard services. The figure also shows that because Jill is willing to spend $4 per hour for 15 hours of guard services and Joe is willing to pay $5, a price of $9 per hour and a quantity of 15 hours is another point on the marginal social benefit curve for security guard services.

## The Optimal Quantity of a Public Good

We know that to achieve economic efficiency, a good or service should be produced up to the point where the sum of consumer surplus and producer surplus is maximized, or, alternatively, where the marginal social cost equals the marginal social

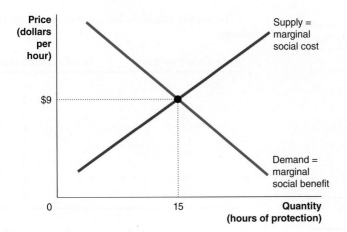

**Figure 5.10**

**The Optimal Quantity of a Public Good**

The optimal quantity of a public good is produced where the sum of consumer surplus and producer surplus is maximized, which occurs where the demand curve intersects the supply curve. In this case, the optimal quantity of security guard services is 15 hours, at a price of $9 per hour.

benefit. Therefore, the optimal quantity of security guard services—or any other public good—will occur where the marginal social benefit curve intersects the supply curve. As with private goods, in the absence of an externality in production, the supply curve represents the marginal social cost of supplying the good. Figure 5.10 shows that the optimal quantity of security guard services supplied is 15 hours, at a price of $9 per hour.

Will the market provide the economically efficient quantity of security guard services? One difficulty is that the individual preferences of consumers, as shown by their demand curves, are not revealed in this market. This difficulty does not arise with private goods because consumers must reveal their preferences in order to purchase private goods. If the market price of Big Macs is $4.00, Joe either reveals that he is willing to pay that much by buying it or he does without it. In our example, neither Jill nor Joe can be excluded from consuming the services provided by a security guard once either hires one, and, therefore, neither has an incentive to reveal her or his preferences. In this case, though, with only two consumers, it is likely that private bargaining will result in an efficient quantity of the public good. This outcome is not likely for a public good—such as national defense—that is supplied by the government to millions of consumers.

Governments sometimes use *cost–benefit analysis* to determine what quantity of a public good should be supplied. For example, before building a dam on a river, the federal government will attempt to weigh the costs against the benefits. The costs include the opportunity cost of other projects the government cannot carry out if it builds the dam. The benefits include improved flood control or new recreational opportunities on the lake formed by the dam. However, for many public goods, including national defense, the government does not use a formal cost–benefit analysis. Instead, the quantity of national defense supplied is determined by a political process involving Congress and the president. Even here, of course, Congress and the president realize that trade-offs are involved: The more resources used for national defense, the fewer resources available for other public goods or for private goods.

# Solved Problem 5.4

## Determining the Optimal Level of Public Goods

Suppose, once again, that Jill and Joe run businesses that are next door to each other on an isolated road and both are in need of the services of a security guard. Their demand schedules for security guard services are as follows:

### Joe

| Price (dollars per hour) | Quantity (hours of protection) |
| --- | --- |
| $20 | 0 |
| 18 | 1 |
| 16 | 2 |
| 14 | 3 |
| 12 | 4 |
| 10 | 5 |
| 8 | 6 |
| 6 | 7 |
| 4 | 8 |
| 2 | 9 |

### Jill

| Price (dollars per hour) | Quantity (hours of protection) |
| --- | --- |
| $20 | 1 |
| 18 | 2 |
| 16 | 3 |
| 14 | 4 |
| 12 | 5 |
| 10 | 6 |
| 8 | 7 |
| 6 | 8 |
| 4 | 9 |
| 2 | 10 |

The supply schedule for security guard services is as follows:

| Price (dollars per hour) | Quantity (hours of protection) |
| --- | --- |
| $8 | 1 |
| 10 | 2 |
| 12 | 3 |
| 14 | 4 |
| 16 | 5 |
| 18 | 6 |
| 20 | 7 |
| 22 | 8 |
| 24 | 9 |

**a.** Draw a graph that shows the optimal level of security guard services. Be sure to label the curves on the graph.

**b.** Briefly explain why 8 hours of security guard protection is not an optimal quantity.

## Solving the Problem

**Step 1:** **Review the chapter material.** This problem is about determining the optimal level of public goods, so you may want to review the section "The Optimal Quantity of a Public Good," which begins on page 156.

**Step 2:** **Begin by deriving the demand curve or marginal social benefit curve for security guard services.** To calculate the marginal social benefit of guard services, we need to add the prices that Jill and Joe are willing to pay at each quantity:

### Demand or Marginal Social Benefit

| Price (dollars per hour) | Quantity (hours of protection) |
| --- | --- |
| $38 | 1 |
| 34 | 2 |
| 30 | 3 |
| 26 | 4 |
| 22 | 5 |
| 18 | 6 |
| 14 | 7 |
| 10 | 8 |
| 6 | 9 |

**Step 3:** **Answer part (a) by plotting the demand (marginal social benefit) and supply (marginal social cost) curves.** The graph shows that the optimal level of security guard services is 6 hours.

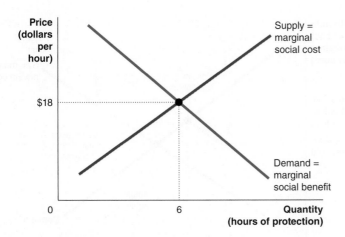

**Step 4:    Answer part (b) by explaining why 8 hours of security guard protection is not an optimal quantity.** For each hour beyond 6, the supply curve is above the demand curve. Therefore, the marginal social benefit received will be less than the marginal social cost of supplying these hours. This results in a dead-weight loss and a reduction in economic surplus.

**Your Turn:** For more practice, do related problem 4.4 on page 168 at the end of this chapter.                MyEconLab

# Common Resources

In England during the Middle Ages, each village had an area of pasture, known as a *commons*, on which any family in the village was allowed to graze its cows or sheep without charge. Of course, the grass one family's cow ate was not available for another family's cow, so consumption was rival. But every family in the village had the right to use the commons, so it was nonexcludable. Without some type of restraint on usage, the commons would be overgrazed. To see why, consider the economic incentives facing a family that was thinking of buying another cow and grazing it on the commons. The family would gain the benefits from increased milk production, but adding another cow to the commons would create a negative externality by reducing the amount of grass available for the cows of other families. Because this family—and the other families in the village—did not take this negative externality into account when deciding whether to add another cow to the commons, too many cows would be added. The grass on the commons would eventually be depleted, and no family's cow would get enough to eat.

**The Tragedy of the Commons**    The tendency for a common resource to be over-used is called the **tragedy of the commons**. The forests in many poor countries are a modern example. When a family chops down a tree in a public forest, it takes into account the benefits of gaining firewood or wood for building, but it does not take into account the costs of deforestation. Haiti, for example, was once heavily forested. Today, 80 percent of the country's forests have been cut down, primarily to be burned to create charcoal, which is used for heating and cooking. Because the mountains no longer have tree roots to hold the soil, heavy rains lead to devastating floods. The following is from a newspaper account of tree cutting in Haiti:

**Tragedy of the commons** The tendency for a common resource to be overused.

> "No Tree Cutting" signs hang over the park entrance, but without money and manpower, there is no way to enforce that. Loggers make nightly journeys, hacking away at trees until they fall. The next day, they're on a truck out. Days later, they've been chopped up, burned and packaged in white bags offered for sale by soot-covered women. "This is the only way I can feed my four kids," said Vena Verone, one of the vendors. "I've heard about the floods and deforestation that caused them, but there's nothing I can do about that."

## Figure 5.11

### Overuse of a Common Resource

For a common resource such as wood from a forest, the efficient level of use, $Q_{Efficient}$, is determined by the intersection of the demand curve—which represents the marginal benefit received by consumers—and $S_2$, which represents the marginal social cost of cutting the wood. Because each individual tree cutter ignores the external cost, the equilibrium quantity of wood cut is $Q_{Actual}$, which is greater than the efficient quantity. At the actual equilibrium level of output, there is a deadweight loss, as shown by the yellow triangle.

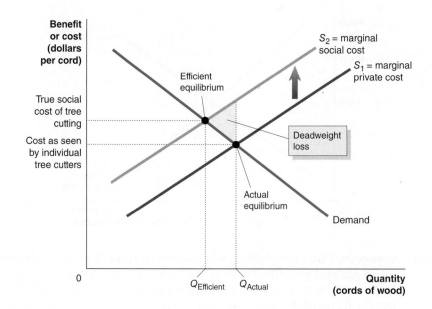

Figure 5.11 shows that with a common resource such as wood from a forest, the efficient level of use, $Q_{Efficient}$, is determined by the intersection of the demand curve—which represents the marginal social benefit received by consumers—and $S_2$, which represents the marginal social cost of cutting the wood. As in our discussion of negative externalities, the social cost is equal to the private cost of cutting the wood plus the external cost. In this case, the external cost represents the fact that the more wood each person cuts, the less wood there is available for others and the greater the deforestation, which increases the chances of floods. Because each individual tree cutter ignores the external cost, the equilibrium quantity of wood cut is $Q_{Actual}$, which is greater than the efficient quantity. At the actual equilibrium level of output, there is a deadweight loss, as shown in Figure 5.11 by the yellow triangle.

**Is There a Way Out of the Tragedy of the Commons?** Notice that our discussion of the tragedy of the commons is very similar to our earlier discussion of negative externalities. The source of the tragedy of the commons is the same as the source of negative externalities: lack of clearly defined and enforced property rights. For instance, suppose that instead of being held as a collective resource, a piece of pastureland is owned by one person. That person will take into account the effect of adding another cow on the food available to cows already using the pasture. As a result, the optimal number of cows will be placed on the pasture. Over the years, most of the commons lands in England were converted to private property. Most of the forest land in Haiti and other developing countries is actually the property of the government. The failure of the government to protect the forests against trespassers or convert them to private property is the key to their overuse.

In some situations, though, enforcing property rights is not feasible. An example is the oceans. Because no country owns the oceans beyond its own coastal waters, the fish and other resources of the ocean will remain a common resource. In situations in which enforcing property rights is not feasible, two types of solutions to the tragedy of the commons are possible. If the geographic area involved is limited and the number of people involved is small, access to the commons can be restricted through community norms and laws. If the geographic area or the number of people involved is large, legal restrictions on access to the commons are required. As an example of the first type of solution, the tragedy of the commons was avoided in the Middle Ages by traditional limits on the number of animals each family was allowed to put on the common pasture. Although these traditions were not formal laws, they were usually enforced adequately by social pressure.

With the second type of solution, the government imposes restrictions on access to the common resources. These restrictions can take several different forms, of which taxes, quotas, and tradable permits are the most common. By setting a tax equal to the external cost, governments can ensure that the efficient quantity of a resource is used. Quotas, or legal limits, on the quantity of the resource that can be taken during a given time period have been used in the United States to limit access to pools of oil that are beneath property owned by many different persons. The governments of Canada, New Zealand, and Iceland have used a system of tradable permits to restrict access to ocean fisheries. Under this system, a total allowable catch (TAC) limits the number of fish that fishermen can catch during a season. The fishermen are then assigned permits called individual transferable quotas (ITQs) that are equal to the total allowable catch. This system operates like the tradable emissions allowances described earlier in this chapter. The fishermen are free to use the ITQs or to sell them, which ensures that the fishermen with the lowest costs use the ITQs. The use of ITQs has sometimes proven controversial, which has limited their use in managing fisheries along the coastal United States. Critics argue that allowing trading of ITQs can result in their concentration in the hands of a relatively few large commercial fishing firms. Such a concentration may, though, be economically efficient if these firms have lower costs than smaller, family-based firms.

Continued from page 137

## Economics in Your Life

### What's the "Best" Level of Pollution?

At the beginning of the chapter, we asked you to think about what the "best" level of carbon emissions is. Conceptually, this is a straightforward question to answer: The efficient level of carbon emissions is the level for which the marginal benefit of reducing carbon emissions exactly equals the marginal cost of reducing carbon emissions. In practice, however, this is a very difficult question to answer. Scientists disagree about how much carbon emissions are contributing to climate change and what the damage from climate change will be. In addition, the cost of reducing carbon emissions depends on the method of reduction used. As a result, neither the marginal cost curve nor the marginal benefit curve for reducing carbon emissions is known with certainty. This uncertainty makes it difficult for policymakers to determine the economically efficient level of carbon emissions and is the source of much of the current debate. In any case, economists agree that the total cost of *completely* eliminating carbon emissions is much greater than the total benefit.

# Conclusion

In Chapter 4, we saw that government intervention in the economy can reduce economic efficiency. In this chapter, however, we have seen that the government plays an indispensable role in the economy when the absence of well-defined and enforceable property rights keeps the market from operating efficiently. For instance, because no one has a property right for clean air, in the absence of government intervention, firms will produce too great a quantity of products that generate air pollution. We have also seen that public goods are nonrival and nonexcludable and are, therefore, often supplied directly by the government.

Read *An Inside Look at Policy* on the next page for a discussion of reactions to the new proposed ozone emission standards from the Environmental Protection Agency.

# Pros and Cons of Tougher Air Pollution Regulations

## WALL STREET JOURNAL

## Business Blasts Ozone Limits: Trade Groups Warn White House That New EPA Curbs Would Choke Off Growth

Business groups are stepping up pressure on the Obama administration to stop the Environmental Protection Agency from enacting tougher limits on smog-forming ozone, saying a new rule pending White House approval would damp the fragile economic recovery.

(a) EPA administrator Lisa Jackson is pushing back, with encouragement from environmental and medical groups, stressing the threat smog poses to public health and likening some of the groups' warnings to predictions in the 1990s that tighter limits on ozone would lead to the banning of fireworks and backyard barbecues. The EPA says tightening the standard could save as many as 12,000 lives a year and generate as much as $100 billion annually in health benefits by 2020, by reducing spending on health problems associated with excessive ozone, such as asthma and bronchitis.

A White House spokesman said that President Barack Obama supported a standard "guided by science and the law" and that in implementing a standard "we will do so in a way that maximizes flexibility to ensure it does not impede our economic recovery in any way."

The ozone issue presents the White House with a difficult choice between angering environmentalists, many of whom cheered Mr. Obama's election in 2008 but have voiced disappointment with some of his policies, and vexing the business community—and opening itself to further Republican attacks on the president's regulatory policies as the election campaign gets under way. Business groups are casting the proposal as a threat to jobs, a sensitive issue with unemployment above 9%, and sense that Ms. Jackson, who in the case of ozone faces no court mandate, is vulnerable.

(b) In recent days, the heads of more than half a dozen trade associations . . . have met with Ms. Jackson to try to persuade her not to go forward with a proposal to set the nation's air-quality standard for ozone at 60 to 70 parts per billion. In 2008, the George W. Bush administration tightened the ozone standard to 75 ppb, where it stands now, from 84 ppb.

The new constraint would be expensive. The EPA says a standard of 60 ppb could cost the economy as much as $90 billion annually by 2020. The costs could include new emissions controls that businesses might have to install; higher electricity prices as power plants switched to cleaner-burning but costlier fuels; and more frequent auto inspections. Business groups say the costs could be significantly higher because the proposal assumes the use of certain technologies that have yet to be developed.

Local governments deemed out of compliance with federal air-quality standards must come up with plans for achieving compliance or risk the loss of federal highway dollars. Business groups say new and expanding businesses would be required to install new pollution controls to avoid any emission increases, and some would either hold off on investing or shift their operations elsewhere, including outside the U.S.

(c) The chairman of the Business Roundtable's Regulatory Reform Working Group, Dow Chemical Co. CEO Andrew Liveris, has also appealed to White House Chief of Staff Bill Daley, telling him in an open letter last week that whatever standard the administration picks would be prohibitively expensive and could "seriously impede economic expansion." Just last month, Mr. Obama announced that Mr. Liveris would lead a joint effort by industry, universities and the federal government to help reposition the U.S. as a leader in cutting-edge manufacturing. . . .

The American Lung Association wrote in its own letter to Mr. Daley on Monday that "following the advice of the [Business] Roundtable will lead to unnecessary illness and death and is not in compliance with the law." The group noted that the EPA's proposal is consistent with the recommendation of a 23-member panel of scientists who advised the agency on the issue after reviewing more than 1,700 studies. . . .

*Source:* "Business Blasts Ozone Limits: Trade Groups Warn White House That New EPA Curbs Would Choke Off Growth," by Stephen Power from *Wall Street Journal*, July 21, 2011. Copyright © 2011 by Dow Jones & Company, Inc. Reproduced with permission of Dow Jones & Company, Inc.

## Key Points in the Article

The Environmental Protection Agency (EPA) is proposing a stricter air-quality standard for ozone emissions of 60 to 70 parts per billion (ppb), down from the current standard of 75 ppb. Environmental and medical groups are encouraging the EPA to move forward with the new regulation, citing the health benefits from the lower limit, including fewer deaths and reduced future spending on pollution-related illnesses. Business groups are fighting the stricter regulations, arguing that the costs to implement them would be prohibitively expensive to both businesses and households and have the potential of threatening the job market and seriously impeding economic recovery.

## Analyzing the News

**a** Implementing the stricter air-quality standards proposed by the EPA can be viewed as an effort to reduce a negative externality. Environmental and medical organizations argue that the more stringent ozone regulations would reduce smog levels across the country, which they claim would generate significant health benefits by reducing spending on ozone-related illnesses by as much as $100 billion annually by 2020. A negative externality in production, such as air pollution, reduces economic efficiency because the producers do not bear all the external costs of the pollution. This type of externality results in a greater than efficient quantity of the good

being produced and a lower than efficient market price. By increasing the pollution standards, firms would bear more of the external cost of production, and this would result in a more economically efficient output and a higher selling price.

**b** Although the EPA has noted the potential savings in health care spending, the agency also acknowledges that an ozone standard of 60 ppb could cost the economy as much as $90 billion annually by 2020. Business groups say that the costs could be even higher. Under the proposal, businesses may have to invest in new emissions controls to meet the higher standard, and households and businesses would likely pay higher electricity prices since power providers would be required to switch to cleaner and higher-priced fuels. If the EPA does implement the new standards by imposing quantitative limits on the amount of smog-forming ozone firms are allowed to emit, the EPA would be using a command-and-control approach to deal with this negative externality. Firms would be required to meet the new pollution standard, and for many this would require additional investment in pollution-reduction equipment. The figure below shows how pollution affects economic efficiency. With the implementation of new pollution regulations, firms would bear more of the external cost of pollution, so $S_1$ would shift up toward $S_2$, narrowing the gap between the marginal private cost and the marginal social cost. The quantity being produced would decline

and the price would increase, with each moving closer to the efficient equilibrium.

**c** With business groups claiming that the new pollution regulations will be prohibitively expensive and that they could significantly hinder economic recovery, and health and environmental groups claiming that not implementing the new limits would result in unnecessary illness and death, the Obama administration is caught in a difficult political position. Whatever the outcome, the debate over additional government regulation of the environment will no doubt continue well into the future.

## Thinking Critically About Policy

1. The article indicates that the EPA is considering a command-and-control approach to reducing ozone emissions. Explain why this approach may not be the most economically efficient solution to the pollution problem.

2. Suppose the government decided to impose a "smog tax" in order to reduce ozone to its economically efficient level. Draw a graph that shows how a smog tax could result in an efficient equilibrium quantity of the goods that generate smog. Make sure to identify the cost of the smog, the amount of the tax, the market and efficient prices and quantities, and the prices received by the producers and paid by consumers with and without the tax.

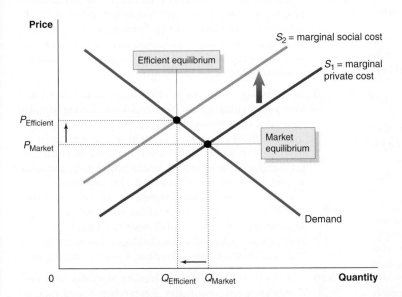

With the implementation of new pollution regulations, producers would bear more of the external cost of pollution.

# Chapter Summary and Problems

## Key Terms

Coase theorem, p. 146

Command-and-control approach, p. 151

Common resource, p. 154

Excludability, p. 154

Externality, p. 138

Free riding, p. 154

Market failure, p. 140

Pigovian taxes and subsidies, p. 151

Private benefit, p. 138

Private cost, p. 138

Private good, p. 154

Property rights, p. 140

Public good, p. 154

Rivalry, p. 154

Social benefit, p. 138

Social cost, p. 138

Tragedy of the commons, p. 159

Transactions costs, p. 146

 **5.1** **Externalities and Economic Efficiency, pages 138–141**

LEARNING OBJECTIVE: Identify examples of positive and negative externalities and use graphs to show how externalities affect economic efficiency.

## Summary

An **externality** is a benefit or cost to parties who are not involved in a transaction. Pollution and other externalities in production cause a difference between the **private cost** borne by the producer of a good or service and the **social cost**, which includes any external cost, such as the cost of pollution. An externality in consumption causes a difference between the **private benefit** received by the consumer and the **social benefit**, which includes any external benefit. If externalities exist in production or consumption, the market will not produce the optimal level of a good or service. This outcome is referred to as **market failure**. Externalities arise when property rights do not exist or cannot be legally enforced. **Property rights** are the rights individuals or businesses have to the exclusive use of their property, including the right to buy or sell it.

MyEconLab   Visit www.myeconlab.com to complete these exercises online and get instant feedback.

## Review Questions

1.1  What is an externality? Give an example of a positive externality, and give an example of a negative externality.

1.2  When will the private cost of producing a good differ from the social cost? Give an example. When will the private benefit from consuming a good differ from the social benefit? Give an example.

1.3  What is economic efficiency? How do externalities affect the economic efficiency of a market equilibrium?

1.4  What is market failure? When is market failure likely to arise?

1.5  Briefly explain the relationship between property rights and the existence of externalities.

## Problems and Applications

1.6  The chapter states that your consuming a Big Mac does not create an externality. But suppose you arrive at your favorite McDonald's at lunchtime and get in a long line to be served. By the time you reach the counter, there are 10 people in line behind you. Because you decided to have a Big Mac for lunch—instead of, say, a pizza—each of those 10 people must wait in line an additional 2 minutes. Is it still correct to say that your consuming a Big Mac creates no externalities? Might there be a justification here for the government to intervene in the market for Big Macs? Briefly explain.

1.7  A neighbor's barking dog can be both a positive externality and a negative externality. Under what circumstances would the barking dog serve as a positive externality? Under what circumstances would the barking dog be a negative externality?

1.8  Yellowstone National Park is in bear country. The National Park Service, at its Yellowstone Web site, states the following about camping and hiking in bear country:

> Do not leave packs containing food unattended, even for a few minutes. Allowing a bear to obtain human food even once often results in the bear becoming aggressive about obtaining such food in the future. Aggressive bears present a threat to human safety and eventually must be destroyed or removed from the park. Please obey the law and do not allow bears or other wildlife to obtain human food.

What negative externality does obtaining human food pose for the bear? What negative externality does the bear's obtaining human food pose for future campers and hikers?

From National Park Service, Yellowstone National Park, "Backcountry Camping and Hiking," http://www.nps.gov/yell/planyourvisit/backcountryhiking.htm, August 9, 2011.

1.9  John Cassidy, a writer for the *New Yorker* magazine, wrote a blog post arguing against New York City's having installed bike lanes. Cassidy complained that the bike lanes had eliminated traffic lanes on some streets as well as some on-street parking. A writer for the *Economist* magazine disputed Cassidy's argument by writing: "I hate to belabour the point, but driving, as it turns out, is associated with a number of negative externalities." What externalities are associated with driving? How do these externalities affect the debate over whether big cities should install more bike lanes?

Based on John Cassidy, "Battle of the Bike Lanes," *New Yorker*, March 8, 2011; and "The World Is His Parking Spot," *Economist*, March 9, 2011.

1.10  In a study at a large state university, students were randomly assigned roommates. Researchers found that, on average, males assigned to roommates who reported drinking alcohol in the year before entering college had GPAs one-quarter point lower than those assigned to non-drinking roommates. For males who drank frequently before college, being assigned to a roommate who also drank frequently before college reduced their GPAs by two-thirds of a point. Draw a graph showing the price of alcohol and the quantity of alcohol consumption on college campuses. Include in the graph the demand for drinking and the private and social costs of drinking. Label any deadweight loss that arises in this market.

Based on Michael Kremer and Dan M. Levy, "Peer Effects and Alcohol Use Among College Students," *Journal of Economic Perspectives*, Vol. 22, No. 3, Summer 2008, pp. 189–206.

**1.11** Tom and Jacob are college students. Each of them will probably get married later and have two or three children. Each knows that if he studies more in college, he'll get a better job and earn more money than if he doesn't study. Earning more will enable them to spend more on their future families—things like orthodontia, nice clothes, admission to expensive colleges, and travel. Tom thinks about the potential benefits to his potential children when he decides how much studying to do. Jacob doesn't.
  **a.** What type of externality arises from studying?
  **b.** Draw a graph showing this externality, contrasting the responses of Tom and Jacob. Who studies more? Who acts more efficiently? Why?

**1.12** The following information regarding cable television is from the Federal Communications Commission (FCC) Web site:

> In general, a cable television operator has the right to select the channels and services that are available on its cable system. With the exception of certain channels like local broadcast television channels which are required to be carried by federal law, the cable operator has broad discretion in choosing which channels will be available and how those channels will be packaged and marketed to subscribers. . . . With the exception of programming that is required to be carried on the basic tier, the cable operator and the entity that owns the channel or programming service negotiate the terms

and conditions for carriage on the cable system. Terms may include whether the channel or service will be offered in a package with other programming or whether the channel or service will be offered on a per-channel or pay-per-view basis.

Suppose you are a fan of *The Daily Show* with Jon Stewart and *The Colbert Report*, both on the Comedy Central cable channel, but the only way you can get Comedy Central from your local cable provider is to subscribe to a package that includes 30 other channels. Is there an externality involved here? If so, is it an externality in production or consumption, and is it positive or negative? If there is an externality, discuss possible solutions.

From Consumer and Government Affairs Bureau, "Choosing Cable Channels," www.fcc.gov/cgb/consumerfacts/cablechannels.html, November 6, 2008

**1.13** In an article in the agriculture magazine *Choices*, Oregon State University economist JunJie Wu made the following observation about the conversion of farmland to urban development:

> Land use provides many economic and social benefits, but often comes at a substantial cost to the environment. Although most economic costs are figured into land use decisions, most environmental externalities are not. These environmental "externalities" cause a divergence between private and social costs for some land uses, leading to an inefficient land allocation. For example, developers may not bear all the environmental and infrastructural costs generated by their projects. Such "market failures" provide a justification for private conservation efforts and public land use planning and regulation.

What does the author mean by *market failures* and *inefficient land allocation*? Explain why the author describes inefficient land allocation as a market failure. Illustrate your argument with a graph showing the market for land to be used for urban development.

From JunJie Wu, "Land Use Changes: Economic, Social, and Environmental Impacts," *Choices*, Vol. 23, No. 4, Fourth Quarter 2008, pp. 6–10.

---

**5.2** | **Private Solutions to Externalities: The Coase Theorem,** pages 141–147
LEARNING OBJECTIVE: Discuss the Coase theorem and explain how private bargaining can lead to economic efficiency in a market with an externality.

## Summary

Externalities and market failures result from incomplete property rights or from the difficulty of enforcing property rights in certain situations. When an externality exists, and the efficient quantity of a good is not being produced, the total cost of reducing the externality is usually less than the total benefit. According to the **Coase theorem**, if **transactions costs** are low, private bargaining will result in an efficient solution to the problem of externalities.

## Review Questions

**2.1** What do economists mean by "an economically efficient level of pollution"?

**2.2** What is the Coase theorem? Why do the parties involved in an externality have an incentive to reach an efficient solution?

**2.3** What are transactions costs? When are we likely to see private solutions to the problem of externalities?

## Problems and Applications

**2.4** Is it ever possible for an *increase* in pollution to make society better off? Briefly explain, using a graph like Figure 5.3 on page 143.

**2.5** If the marginal cost of reducing a certain type of pollution is zero, should all that type of pollution be eliminated? Briefly explain.

**2.6** Discuss the factors that determine the marginal cost of reducing crime. Discuss the factors that determine the marginal benefit of reducing crime. Would it be economically efficient to reduce the amount of crime to zero? Briefly explain.

**2.7** In discussing the reduction of air pollution in the developing world, Richard Fuller of the Blacksmith Institute, an environmental organization, observed, "It's the 90/10 rule. To do 90 percent of the work only costs 10 percent of the money. It's the last 10 percent of the cleanup that costs 90 percent of the money." Why should it be any more costly to clean up the last 10 percent of polluted air than to clean up the first 90 percent? What trade-offs would be involved in cleaning up the final 10 percent?

Based on Tiffany M. Luck, "The World's Dirtiest Cities," *Forbes*, February 28, 2008.

**2.8** **[Related to the** Making the Connection **on page 142]** In the first years following the passage of the Clean Air Act in 1970, air pollution declined sharply, and there were important health benefits, including a decline in infant mortality. Should the government take action to reduce air pollution further? How should government go about deciding this question?

**2.9** **[Related to the** Don't Let This Happen to You **on page 145]** Briefly explain whether you agree or disagree with the following statement: "Sulfur dioxide emissions cause acid rain and breathing difficulties for people with respiratory problems. The total benefit to society is greatest if we completely eliminate sulfur dioxide emissions. Therefore, the economically efficient level of emissions is zero."

**2.10** According to the Coase theorem, why would a steel plant that creates air pollution agree to curtail production (and therefore pollution) if it were not legally liable for the damage the pollution was causing? Must the property right to clean air be assigned to the victims of air pollution to get the steel plant to reduce pollution?

**2.11** **[Related to the** Making the Connection **on page 145]** We know that owners of apple orchards and owners of beehives are able to negotiate private agreements. Is it likely that as a result of these private agreements, the market supplies the efficient quantities of apple trees and beehives? Are there any real-world difficulties that might stand in the way of achieving this efficient outcome?

---

**5.3** **Government Policies to Deal with Externalities,** pages 147–153

LEARNING OBJECTIVE: Analyze government policies to achieve economic efficiency in a market with an externality.

## Summary

When private solutions to externalities are unworkable, the government sometimes intervenes. One way to deal with a negative externality in production is to impose a tax equal to the cost of the externality. The tax causes the producer of the good to internalize the externality. The government can deal with a positive externality in consumption by giving consumers a subsidy, or payment, equal to the value of the externality. Government taxes and subsidies intended to bring about an efficient level of output in the presence of externalities are called **Pigovian taxes and subsidies**. Although the federal government has sometimes used subsidies and taxes to deal with externalities, in dealing with pollution it has more often used a command-and-control approach. A **command-and-control approach** involves the government imposing quantitative limits on the amount of pollution allowed or requiring firms to install specific pollution control devices. Direct pollution controls of this type are not economically efficient, however. As a result, Congress decided to use a system of tradable emissions allowances to reduce sulfur dioxide emissions.

 MyEconLab Visit **www.myeconlab.com** to complete these exercises online and get instant feedback.

## Review Questions

**3.1** What is a Pigovian tax? At what level must a Pigovian tax be set to achieve efficiency?

**3.2** What does it mean for a producer or consumer to internalize an externality? What would cause a producer or consumer to internalize an externality?

**3.3** Why do most economists prefer tradable emissions allowances to the command-and-control approach to pollution?

## Problems and Applications

**3.4** The federal government's nutrition guidelines urge adults to eat at least five cups of fruits and vegetables each day. Does consuming fruits and vegetables have a positive externality? Should the government subsidize the consumption of fruits and vegetables? Briefly explain.

**3.5** Many antibiotics that once were effective in eliminating infections no longer are because bacteria have evolved to become resistant to them. Some bacteria are now resistant to all but one or two existing antibiotics. Some policymakers have argued that pharmaceutical companies should receive subsidies for developing new antibiotics. A newspaper article states:

> While the notion of directly subsidizing drug companies may be politically unpopular in many quarters, proponents say it is necessary to bridge the gap between the high value that new antibiotics have for society and the low returns they provide to drug companies.

Is there a positive externality in the production of antibiotics? Should firms producing every good where there is a gap between the value of the good to society and the profit to the firms making the good receive subsidies? Briefly explain.

From Andrew Pollack, "Antibiotics Research Subsidies Weighed by U.S.," *New York Times*, November 5, 2010.

**3.6** Draw a graph showing the deadweight loss from a negative externality in production and illustrate how a Pigovian tax eliminates the deadweight loss. Draw another graph showing the deadweight loss from a positive externality in consumption and illustrate how a Pigovian subsidy eliminates the deadweight loss. Briefly explain how the Pigovian tax and subsidy eliminate the deadweight loss.

**3.7** Writing in the *New York Times*, Michael Lewis argued: "Good new technologies are a bit like good new roads: Their social benefits far exceed what any one person or company can get paid for creating them." Does this observation justify the government subsidizing the production of new technologies? If so, how might the government do this?

From Michael Lewis, "In Defense of the Boom," *New York Times*, October 27, 2002.

**3.8** **[Related to** Solved Problem 5.3 **on page 148]** The fumes from dry cleaners can contribute to air pollution. Suppose the following graph illustrates the situation in the dry cleaning market:

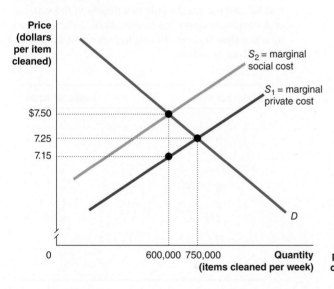

a. Explain how a government can use a tax on dry cleaning to bring about the efficient level of production. What should the value of the tax be?

b. How large is the deadweight loss (in dollars) from excessive dry cleaning, according to the figure?

**3.9** **[Related to the** Making the Connection **on page 149]** Draw a graph for the market for sweetened soda and assume that consumption of sweetened soda causes a negative externality by raising medical costs. Draw both the actual demand curve representing the marginal private benefits and the demand curve representing the marginal social benefit. Show the deadweight loss caused by the externality.

a. Should the government prohibit consumption of sweetened soda if it causes a negative externality by raising medical costs?

b. How could the government get drinkers of sweetened soda to incorporate in their consumption decisions the cost they impose by raising medical costs?

**3.10** In 2007, Governor Deval Patrick of Massachusetts proposed that criminals would have to pay a "safety fee" to the government. The size of the fee would be based on the seriousness of the crime (that is, the fee would be larger for more serious crimes).

a. Is there an economically efficient amount of crime? Briefly explain.

b. Briefly explain whether the "safety fee" is a Pigovian tax of the type discussed in this chapter.

Based on Michael Levenson, "Patrick Proposes New Fee on Criminals," *Boston Globe*, January 14, 2007.

**3.11** In a paper written for the Harvard Project on International Climate Agreements, the authors state that while a majority of developed nations are enacting significant regulations to mitigate climate change, "Developing countries typically place greater priority on economic development than on environmental protection, despite being vulnerable to the potential adverse effects of continued warming." Recall the definition of *normal goods* given in Chapter 3. Is environmental protection a normal good? If so, is there any connection between this fact and the observation of the authors of the above statement? Briefly explain. How do the marginal cost and marginal benefit of environmental protection change with economic development?

Based on Daniel S. Hall, Michael A. Levi, William A. Pizer, and Takahiro Ueno, "Policies for Developing Country Engagement," Discussion Paper 08-15, Harvard Project on International Climate Agreements, Belfer Center for Science and International Affairs, Harvard Kennedy School, October 2008.

**3.12** The following graph illustrates the situation in the dry cleaning market. In contrast to problem 3.8, the marginal social cost of the pollution rises as the quantity of items cleaned per week increases. In addition, there are two demand curves, one for a smaller city, $D_S$, and the other for a larger city, $D_L$.

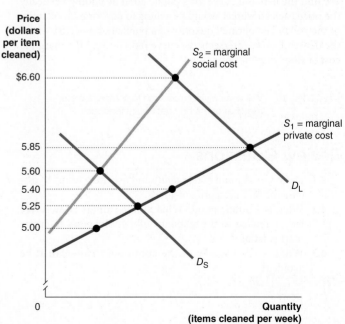

a. Explain why the marginal social cost curve has a different slope than the marginal private cost curve.

b. What tax per item cleaned will achieve economic efficiency in the smaller city? In the larger city? Explain why the efficient tax is different in the two cities.

**3.13** **[Related to the** Chapter Opener **on page 137]** According to an article on the position of managers of power plants on the EPA's proposed new air-quality regulations, "Some of them [managers] are willing to accept tougher air pollution limits than EPA has established, so long as they get certainty on deadlines and get to avoid more onerous command-and-control rules."

a. What are command-and-control rules? Why would power plant managers find them to be onerous?

b. What alternative to command-and-control rules might power plant managers favor? Briefly explain.

Based on Gabriel Nelson, "Wrapped Up in Politics, Granddaddy of Cap-And-Trade Plans Has an Uncertain Future," *New York Times*, July 19, 2011.

**3.14** **[Related to the** Making the Connection **on page 152]** As discussed in this chapter, a system of tradable permits was very successful in efficiently reducing emissions of sulfur dioxide in the United States. Why have some economists proposed a similar system of tradable permits to reduce carbon dioxide emissions? Briefly discuss similarities and differences between the problem of reducing sulfur dioxide emissions and the problem of reducing carbon dioxide emissions.

---

| **5.4** | **Four Categories of Goods,** pages 153–161 |
|---|---|

LEARNING OBJECTIVE: Explain how goods can be categorized on the basis of whether they are rival or excludable and use graphs to illustrate the efficient quantities of public goods and common resources.

## Summary

There are four categories of goods: private goods, public goods, quasi-public goods, and common resources. **Private goods** are both rival and excludable. **Rivalry** means that when one person consumes a unit of a good, no one else can consume that unit. **Excludability** means that anyone who does not pay for a good cannot consume it. **Public goods** are both nonrival and nonexcludable. Private firms are usually not willing to supply public goods because of free riding. **Free riding** involves benefiting from a good without paying for it. Quasi-public goods are excludable but not rival. **Common resources** are rival but not excludable. The **tragedy of the commons** refers to the tendency for a common resource to be overused. The tragedy of the commons results from a lack of clearly defined and enforced property rights. We find the market demand curve for a private good by adding the quantity of the good demanded by each consumer at each price. We find the demand curve for a public good by adding vertically the price each consumer would be willing to pay for each quantity of the good. The optimal quantity of a public good occurs where the demand curve intersects the curve representing the marginal cost of supplying the good.

 Visit **www.myeconlab.com** to complete these exercises online and get instant feedback.

## Review Questions

**4.1** Define *rivalry* and *excludability* and use these terms to discuss the four categories of goods.

**4.2** What is a public good? What is free riding? How is free riding related to the tendency of a public good to create market failure?

**4.3** What is the tragedy of the commons? How can it be avoided?

## Problems and Applications

**4.4** **[Related to** Solved Problem 5.4 **on page 157]** Suppose that Jill and Joe are the only two people in the small town of Andover. Andover has land available to build a park of no more than 9 acres. Jill and Joe's demand schedules for the park are as follows:

| Joe | |
|---|---|
| Price per Acre | Number of Acres |
| $10 | 0 |
| 9 | 1 |
| 8 | 2 |
| 7 | 3 |
| 6 | 4 |
| 5 | 5 |
| 4 | 6 |
| 3 | 7 |
| 2 | 8 |
| 1 | 9 |

| Jill | |
|---|---|
| Price per Acre | Number of Acres |
| $15 | 0 |
| 14 | 1 |
| 13 | 2 |
| 12 | 3 |
| 11 | 4 |
| 10 | 5 |
| 9 | 6 |
| 8 | 7 |
| 7 | 8 |
| 6 | 9 |

The supply curve is as follows:

| Price | Number of Acres |
|-------|-----------------|
| $11   | 1               |
| 13    | 2               |
| 15    | 3               |
| 17    | 4               |
| 19    | 5               |
| 21    | 6               |
| 23    | 7               |
| 25    | 8               |
| 27    | 9               |

    **a.** Draw a graph showing the optimal size of the park. Be sure to label the curves on the graph.

    **b.** Briefly explain why a park of 2 acres is not optimal.

**4.5** Commercial whaling has been described as a modern example of the tragedy of the commons. Briefly explain whether you agree or disagree.

**4.6** Nancy Folbre, an economist at the University of Massachusetts, Amherst, argued: "We must take responsibility for governing the commons—not just the quaint old-fashioned village green, but things that cannot easily be privatized—[such as] clean air." Do you agree that clean air is like a common pasture in England in the Middle Ages? Briefly explain.

From Nancy Folbre, "Taking Responsibility for the Commons," *New York Times*, February 26, 2009.

**4.7** The more frequently bacteria are exposed to antibiotics, the more quickly the bacteria will develop resistance to the antibiotics. An article from MayoClinic.com includes the following statement regarding the responsibility of antibiotic users:

> Antibiotic resistance is a pressing, global health problem. Nearly all significant bacterial infections in the world are becoming resistant to commonly used antibiotics. When you abuse antibiotics, the resistant microorganisms that you help create can become widely established, causing new and hard-to-treat infections. That's why the decisions you make about antibiotic use—unlike almost any other medicine you take—extend far beyond your reach. Responsible antibiotic use protects the health of your family, neighbors and ultimately the global community.

Briefly discuss in what sense antibiotics can be considered a common resource.

Based on Mayo Clinic staff, "Antibiotics: Use Them Wisely," MayoClinic.com, February 13, 2008.

**4.8** Put each of these goods or services into one of the boxes in Figure 5.7 on page 154. That is, categorize them as private goods, public goods, quasi-public goods, or common resources.

    **a.** A television broadcast of the World Series

    **b.** Home mail delivery

    **c.** Education in a public school

    **d.** Education in a private school

    **e.** Hiking in a park surrounded by a fence

    **f.** Hiking in a park not surrounded by a fence

    **g.** An apple

**4.9** Explain whether you agree or disagree with the following statement:

> Providing health care is obviously a public good. If one person becomes ill and doesn't receive treatment, that person may infect many other people. If many people become ill, then the output of the economy will be negatively affected. Therefore, providing health care is a public good that should be supplied by the government.

**4.10** Deer-hunting clubs in southeast Virginia impose a fine on anyone harvesting a buck with antlers below a certain size on land where those clubs have exclusive rights to hunt. The hunt clubs, however, do not impose a fine for harvesting a buck with small antlers on land where several clubs have the right to hunt. Why would the hunt clubs treat the harvesting of bucks on the two lands differently?

**4.11** In the early 1800s, more than 60 million American bison (commonly known as the buffalo) roamed the Great Plains. By the late 1800s, the buffalo was nearly extinct. Considering the four categories of goods discussed in the chapter, why might it be that hunters nearly killed buffalo to extinction but not cattle?

**4.12** William Easterly in *The White Man's Burden* shares the following account by New York University Professor Leonard Wantchekon of how Professor Wantchekon's village in Benin, Africa, managed the local fishing pond when he was growing up:

> To open the fishing season, elders performed ritual tests at Amlé, a lake fifteen kilometers from the village. If the fish were large enough, fishing was allowed for two or three days. If they were too small, all fishing was forbidden, and anyone who secretly fished the lake at this time was outcast, excluded from the formal and informal groups that formed the village's social structure. Those who committed this breach of trust were often shunned by the whole community; no one would speak to the offender, or even acknowledge his existence for a year or more.

What economic problem were the village elders trying to prevent? Do you think their solution would have worked?

From William Easterly, *The White Man's Burden: Why the West's Efforts to Aid the Rest Have Done so much Ill and so Little Good*, (New York: Pengiun Books, 2006), p. 94.

# Elasticity:
## The Responsiveness of Demand and Supply

## Chapter Outline and Learning Objectives

# Do People Respond to Changes in the Price of Gasoline?

Some people have argued that consumers don't vary the quantity of gas they buy as the price changes because the number of miles they need to drive to get to work or school or to run errands is roughly constant. During the spring and summer of 2011, however, as the price of gasoline soared close to $4.00 per gallon in many parts of the country, consumers certainly responded. For instance, during May 2011, when the average price of gasoline was $3.76, U.S. consumers bought about 5 percent less gasoline than they had bought during May 2010, when the average price of gasoline had been $2.79 per gallon. According to Dennis Jacobe, chief economist of Gallup, a public opinion poll firm, "At $4 a gallon, you get people who might have money to spend, but with the amount gasoline costs, they start to cut back in response to the price. At $4 a gallon . . . they make fewer trips."

Consumers were finding many ways to cut back the quantity of gasoline they purchased. Some people moved closer to where they worked to reduce the miles they had to commute. In San Francisco, the number of cars crossing the Golden Gate Bridge declined, as commuters switched to using busses and ferries. Car dealers reported that sales of smaller, more fuel-efficient cars were increasing compared with sales of SUVs and other less fuel-efficient vehicles.

All businesses have a strong interest in knowing how much less they will sell as prices rise. Governments are also interested in knowing how consumers will react if the price of a product such as gasoline increases following a tax increase. In this chapter, we will explore what determines the responsiveness of the quantity demanded and the quantity supplied to changes in the market price.

**AN INSIDE LOOK** on **page 196** discusses how higher gas prices in 2011 affected the spending of households and firms.

Based on Ron Scherer, "Gas Prices Nearing the Point Where Americans Cut Back," *Christian Science Monitor*, April 18, 2011; Motoko Rich and Stephanie Clifford, "In Consumer Behavior, Signs of Gas Price Pinch," *New York Times*, May 17, 2011; and data on gasoline prices and consumption from the U.S. Energy Information Administration.

## Economics in Your Life

### How Much Do Gas Prices Matter to You?

What factors would make you more or less responsive to price when purchasing gasoline? Have you responded differently to price changes during different periods of your life? Why do consumers seem to respond more to changes in gas prices at a particular service station but seem less sensitive when gas prices rise or fall at all service stations? As you read the chapter, see if you can answer these questions. You can check your answers against those we provide on **page 194** at the end of this chapter.

**W**hether you are managing a service station, a bookstore, or a coffee shop, you need to know how an increase or a decrease in the price of your products will affect the quantity consumers are willing to buy. We saw in Chapter 3 that cutting the price of a good increases the quantity demanded and that raising the price reduces the quantity demanded. But the critical question is this: *How much* will the quantity demanded change as a result of a price increase or decrease? Economists use the concept of **elasticity** to measure how one economic variable—such as the quantity demanded—responds to changes in another economic variable—such as the price. For example, the responsiveness of the quantity demanded of a good to changes in its price is called the *price elasticity of demand*. Knowing the price elasticity of demand allows you to compute the effect of a price change on the quantity demanded.

**Elasticity** A measure of how much one economic variable responds to changes in another economic variable.

We also saw in Chapter 3 that the quantity of a good that consumers demand depends not just on the price of the good but also on consumer income and on the prices of related goods. As a manager, you would also be interested in measuring the responsiveness of demand to these other factors. As we will see, we can use the concept of elasticity here as well. We are also interested in the responsiveness of the quantity supplied of a good to changes in its price, which is called the *price elasticity of supply*.

Elasticity is an important concept not just for business managers but for policymakers as well. If the government wants to discourage teenage smoking, it can raise the price of cigarettes by increasing the tax on them. If we know the price elasticity of demand for cigarettes, we can calculate how many fewer packs of cigarettes will be demanded at a higher price. In this chapter, we will also see how policymakers use the concept of elasticity.

**6.1 LEARNING OBJECTIVE**

Define price elasticity of demand and understand how to measure it.

# The Price Elasticity of Demand and Its Measurement

We know from the law of demand that when the price of a product falls, the quantity demanded of the product increases. But the law of demand tells firms only that the demand curves for their products slope downward. More useful is a measure of the responsiveness of the quantity demanded to a change in price. This measure is called the **price elasticity of demand**.

**Price elasticity of demand** The responsiveness of the quantity demanded to a change in price, measured by dividing the percentage change in the quantity demanded of a product by the percentage change in the product's price.

## Measuring the Price Elasticity of Demand

We might measure the price elasticity of demand by using the slope of the demand curve because the slope of the demand curve tells us how much quantity changes as price changes. Using the slope of the demand curve to measure price elasticity has a drawback, however: The measurement of slope is sensitive to the units chosen for quantity and price. For example, suppose a $1 per gallon decrease in the price of gasoline leads to an increase in the quantity demanded from 10.1 million gallons to 10.2 million gallons per day. The change in quantity is 0.1 million gallons, and the change in price is $-$1, so the slope is $0.1/-1 = -0.1$. But if we measure price in cents, rather than dollars, the slope is $0.1/-100 = -0.001$. If we measure price in dollars and gallons in thousands, instead of millions, the slope is $100/-1 = -100$. Clearly, the value we compute for the slope can change dramatically, depending on the units we use for quantity and price.

To avoid this confusion over units, economists use *percentage changes* when measuring the price elasticity of demand. Percentage changes are not dependent on units of measurement. (For a review of calculating percentage changes, see the appendix to Chapter 1.) No matter what units we use to measure the quantity of gasoline, 10 percent more gasoline is 10 percent more gasoline. Therefore, the price elasticity of demand is measured by dividing the percentage change in the quantity demanded by the percentage change in the price. Or:

$$\text{Price elasticity of demand} = \frac{\text{Percentage change in quantity demanded}}{\text{Percentage change in price}}.$$

It's important to remember that *the price elasticity of demand is not the same as the slope of the demand curve.*

If we calculate the price elasticity of demand for a price cut, the percentage change in price will be negative, and the percentage change in quantity demanded will be positive. Similarly, if we calculate the price elasticity of demand for a price increase, the percentage change in price will be positive, and the percentage change in quantity demanded will be negative. Therefore, the price elasticity of demand is always negative. In comparing elasticities, though, we are usually interested in their relative size. So, we often drop the minus sign and compare their *absolute values*. In other words, although $-3$ is actually a smaller number than $-2$, a price elasticity of $-3$ is larger than a price elasticity of $-2$.

## Elastic Demand and Inelastic Demand

If the quantity demanded is very responsive to changes in price, the percentage change in quantity demanded will be *greater* than the percentage change in price, and the price elasticity of demand will be greater than 1 in absolute value. In this case, demand is **elastic**. For example, if a 10 percent decrease in the price of bagels results in a 20 percent increase in the quantity of bagels demanded, then:

$$\text{Price elasticity of demand} = \frac{20\%}{-10\%} = -2,$$

and we can conclude that the demand for bagels is elastic.

When the quantity demanded is not very responsive to price, however, the percentage change in quantity demanded will be *less* than the percentage change in price, and the price elasticity of demand will be less than 1 in absolute value. In this case, demand is **inelastic**. For example, if a 10 percent decrease in the price of wheat results in a 5 percent increase in the quantity of wheat demanded, then:

$$\text{Price elasticity of demand} = \frac{5\%}{-10\%} = -0.5,$$

and we can conclude that the demand for wheat is inelastic.

In the special case in which the percentage change in the quantity demanded is equal to the percentage change in price, the price elasticity of demand equals $-1$ (or 1 in absolute value). In this case, demand is **unit elastic**.

## An Example of Computing Price Elasticities

Suppose you own a service station, and you are trying to decide whether to cut the price you are charging for a gallon of gas. You are currently at point *A* in Figure 6.1: selling 1,000 gallons per day at a price of $4.00 per gallon. How many more gallons you will sell by cutting the price to $3.70 depends on the price elasticity of demand for gasoline at your service station. Let's consider two possibilities: If $D_1$ is the demand curve for gasoline at your station, your sales will increase to 1,200 gallons per day, point *B*. But if $D_2$ is your demand curve, your sales will increase only to 1,050 gallons per day, point *C*. We might expect—correctly, as we will see—that between these points, demand curve $D_1$ is *elastic*, and demand curve $D_2$ is *inelastic*.

To confirm that $D_1$ is elastic between these points and that $D_2$ is inelastic, we need to calculate the price elasticity of demand for each curve. In calculating price elasticity between two points on a demand curve, though, we run into a problem because we get a different value for price increases than for price decreases. For example, suppose we calculate the price elasticity for $D_1$ as the price is cut from $4.00 to $3.70.

**Elastic demand**  Demand is elastic when the percentage change in quantity demanded is *greater* than the percentage change in price, so the price elasticity is *greater* than 1 in absolute value.

**Inelastic demand**  Demand is inelastic when the percentage change in quantity demanded is *less* than the percentage change in price, so the price elasticity is *less* than 1 in absolute value.

**Unit-elastic demand**  Demand is unit elastic when the percentage change in quantity demanded is *equal to* the percentage change in price, so the price elasticity is equal to 1 in absolute value.

**Elastic and Inelastic Demand**

Along $D_1$, cutting the price from $4.00 to $3.70 increases the number of gallons sold from 1,000 per day to 1,200 per day, so demand is elastic between point $A$ and point $B$. Along $D_2$, cutting the price from $4.00 to $3.70 increases the number of gallons sold from 1,000 per day only to 1,050 per day, so demand is inelastic between point $A$ and point $C$.

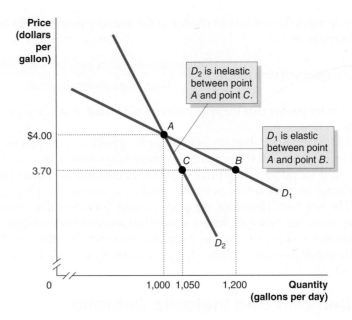

This reduction is a 7.5 percent price cut that increases the quantity demanded from 1,000 gallons to 1,200 gallons, or by 20 percent. Therefore, the price elasticity of demand between points $A$ and $B$ is $20/-7.5 = -2.7$. Now let's calculate the price elasticity for $D_1$ as the price is *increased* from $3.70 to $4.00. This is an 8.1 percent price increase that decreases the quantity demanded from 1,200 gallons to 1,000 gallons, or by 16.7 percent. So, now our measure of the price elasticity of demand between points $A$ and $B$ is $-16.7/8.1 = -2.1$. It can be confusing to have different values for the price elasticity of demand between the same two points on the same demand curve. As we will see in the next section, to avoid this confusion, economists often use a particular formula when calculating elasticities.

## The Midpoint Formula

We can use the *midpoint formula* to ensure that we have only one value of the price elasticity of demand between the same two points on a demand curve. The midpoint formula uses the *average* of the initial and final quantities and the initial and final prices. If $Q_1$ and $P_1$ are the initial quantity and price and $Q_2$ and $P_2$ are the final quantity and price, the midpoint formula is:

$$\text{Price elasticity of demand} = \frac{(Q_2 - Q_1)}{\left(\dfrac{Q_1 + Q_2}{2}\right)} \div \frac{(P_2 - P_1)}{\left(\dfrac{P_1 + P_2}{2}\right)}.$$

The midpoint formula may seem challenging at first, but the numerator is just the change in quantity divided by the average of the initial and final quantities, and the denominator is just the change in price divided by the average of the initial and final prices.

Let's apply the formula to calculating the price elasticity of $D_1$ in Figure 6.1. Between point $A$ and point $B$ on $D_1$, the change in quantity is 200, and the average of the two quantities is 1,100. Therefore, there is an 18.2 percent change in quantity. The change in price is $-$0.30, and the average of the two prices is $3.85. Therefore, there is a $-7.8$ percent change in price. So, the price elasticity of demand is $18.2/-7.8 = -2.3$. Notice these three results from calculating the price elasticity of demand using the midpoint formula: First, as we suspected from examining Figure 6.1, demand curve $D_1$ is elastic between points $A$ and $B$. Second, our value for the price elasticity calculated using the midpoint formula is between the two values we calculated earlier. Third, the midpoint formula will give us the same value whether we are moving from the higher price to the lower price or from the lower price to the higher price.

We can also use the midpoint formula to calculate the elasticity of demand between point $A$ and point $C$ on $D_2$. In this case, there is a 4.9 percent change in quantity and a $-7.8$ percent change in price. So, the elasticity of demand is $4.9/-7.8 = -0.6$. Once again, as we suspected, demand curve $D_2$ is price inelastic between points $A$ and $C$.

# Solved Problem 6.1

## Calculating the Price Elasticity of Demand

Suppose you own a service station, and you are currently selling gasoline for $3.50 per gallon. At this price you can sell 2,000 gallons per day. You are considering cutting the price to $3.30 to attract drivers who have been buying their gas at competing stations. The graph below shows two possible increases in the quantity sold as a result of your price cut. Use the information in the graph to calculate the price elasticity between these two prices on each of the demand curves. Use the midpoint formula in your calculations. State whether each demand curve is elastic or inelastic between these two prices.

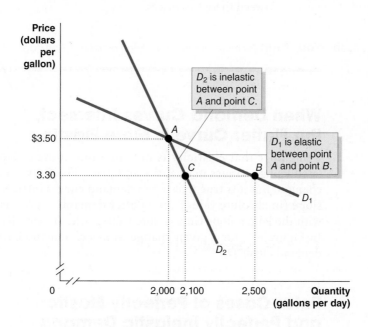

## Solving the Problem

**Step 1:** **Review the chapter material.** This problem requires calculating the price elasticity of demand, so you may want to review the material in the section "The Midpoint Formula," which begins on page 174.

**Step 2:** **To begin using the midpoint formula, calculate the average quantity and the average price for demand curve $D_1$.**

$$\text{Average quantity} = \frac{2,000 + 2,500}{2} = 2,250$$

$$\text{Average price} = \frac{\$3.50 + \$3.30}{2} = \$3.40$$

**Step 3:** **Now calculate the percentage change in the quantity demanded and the percentage change in price for demand curve $D_1$.**

$$\text{Percentage change in quantity demanded} = \frac{2,500 - 2,000}{2,250} \times 100 = 22.2\%$$

$$\text{Percentage change in price} = \frac{\$3.30 - \$3.50}{\$3.40} \times 100 = -5.9\%$$

**Step 4:** **Divide the percentage change in the quantity demanded by the percentage change in price to arrive at the price elasticity for demand curve $D_1$.**

$$\text{Price elasticity of demand} = \frac{22.2\%}{-5.9\%} = -3.8$$

Because the elasticity is greater than 1 in absolute value, $D_1$ is price *elastic* between these two prices.

**Step 5:** **Calculate the price elasticity of demand curve $D_2$ between these two prices.**

$$\text{Percentage change in quantity demanded} = \frac{2,100 - 2,000}{2,050} \times 100 = 4.9\%$$

$$\text{Percentage change in price} = \frac{\$3.30 - \$3.50}{\$3.40} \times 100 = -5.9\%$$

$$\text{Price elasticity of demand} = \frac{4.9\%}{-5.9\%} = -0.8$$

Because the elasticity is less than 1 in absolute value, $D_2$ is price *inelastic* between these two prices.

MyEconLab **Your Turn:** For more practice, do related problem 1.7 on page 198 at the end of this chapter.

## When Demand Curves Intersect, the Flatter Curve Is More Elastic

Remember that elasticity is not the same thing as slope. While slope is calculated using changes in quantity and price, elasticity is calculated using percentage changes. But it *is* true that if two demand curves intersect, the one with the smaller slope (in absolute value)—the flatter demand curve—is more elastic, and the one with the larger slope (in absolute value)—the steeper demand curve—is less elastic. In Figure 6.1, for a given change in price, demand curve $D_1$ is more elastic than demand curve $D_2$.

## Polar Cases of Perfectly Elastic and Perfectly Inelastic Demand

**Perfectly inelastic demand** The case where the quantity demanded is completely unresponsive to price and the price elasticity of demand equals zero.

Although they do not occur frequently, you should be aware of the extreme, or polar, cases of price elasticity. If a demand curve is a vertical line, it is **perfectly inelastic**. In this case, the quantity demanded is completely unresponsive to price, and the price elasticity of demand equals zero. No matter how much price may increase or decrease, the quantity remains the same. For only a very few products will the quantity demanded be completely unresponsive to the price, making the demand curve a vertical line. The drug insulin is an example. Some diabetics must take a certain amount of insulin each day. If the price of insulin declines, it will not affect the required dose and thus will not increase the quantity demanded. Similarly, a price increase will not affect the required dose or decrease the quantity demanded. (Of course, some diabetics who need it will not be able to afford insulin at a higher price. If so, even in this case, the demand curve may not be completely vertical and, therefore, not perfectly inelastic.)

**Perfectly elastic demand** The case where the quantity demanded is infinitely responsive to price, and the price elasticity of demand equals infinity.

If a demand curve is a horizontal line, it is **perfectly elastic**. In this case, the quantity demanded is infinitely responsive to price, and the price elasticity of demand equals infinity. If a demand curve is perfectly elastic, an increase in price causes the quantity demanded to fall to zero. Once again, perfectly elastic demand curves are rare, and it is important not to confuse *elastic* with *perfectly elastic*. Table 6.1 summarizes the different price elasticities of demand.

| If demand is... | then the absolute value of price elasticity is... |
|---|---|
| elastic | greater than 1 |
| inelastic | less than 1 |
| unit-elastic | equal to 1 |
| perfectly elastic | equal to infinity |
| perfectly inelastic | equal to 0 |

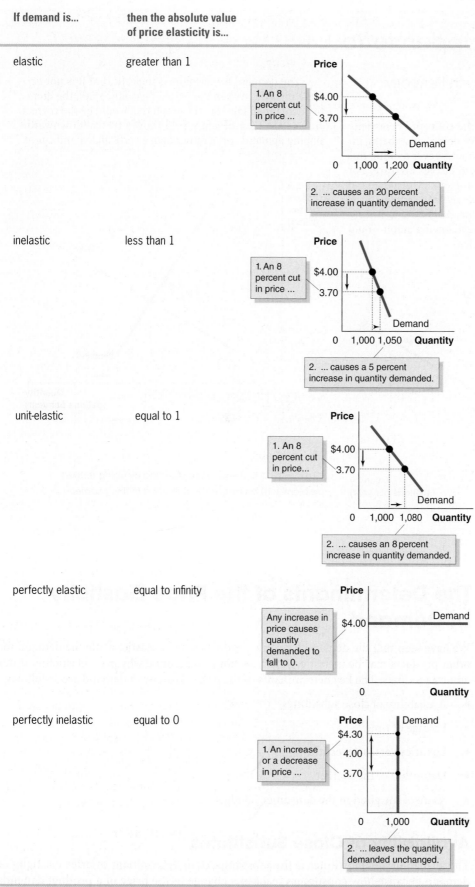

**Table 6.1**

**Summary of the Price Elasticity of Demand**

*Note:* The percentage changes shown in the boxes in the graphs were calculated using the midpoint formula, given on page 174, and are rounded to the nearest whole number.

# Don't Let This Happen to You

## Don't Confuse Inelastic with Perfectly Inelastic

You may be tempted to simplify the concept of elasticity by assuming that any demand curve described as being inelastic is *perfectly* inelastic. You should never assume this because perfectly inelastic demand curves are rare. For example, consider the following problem: "Use a demand and supply graph to show how a decrease in supply affects the equilibrium quantity of gasoline. Assume that the demand for gasoline is inelastic." The following graph would be an *incorrect* answer to this problem.

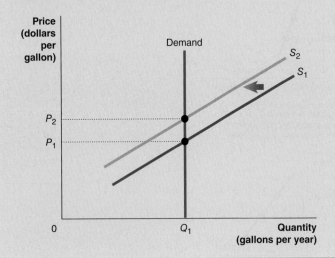

The demand for gasoline is inelastic, but it is not *perfectly* inelastic. When the price of gasoline rises, the quantity demanded falls. So, the graph that would be the correct answer to this problem would show a typical downward-sloping demand curve rather than a vertical demand curve.

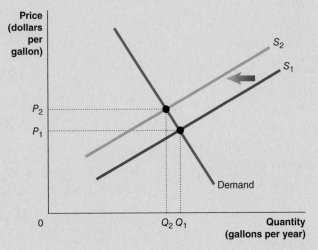

MyEconLab

**Your Turn:** Test your understanding by doing related problem 1.10 on page 199 at the end of this chapter.

---

**6.2 LEARNING** OBJECTIVE

Understand the determinants of the price elasticity of demand.

# The Determinants of the Price Elasticity of Demand

We have seen that the demand for some products may be elastic, while the demand for other products may be inelastic. In this section, we examine why price elasticities differ among products. The key determinants of the price elasticity of demand are as follows:

- Availability of close substitutes
- Passage of time
- Luxuries versus necessities
- Definition of the market
- Share of the good in the consumer's budget

## Availability of Close Substitutes

The availability of substitutes is the most important determinant of price elasticity of demand because how consumers react to a change in the price of a product depends on what alternatives they have. When the price of gasoline rises, consumers have few alternatives, so the quantity demanded falls only a little. But if the price of pizza rises, consumers have many alternative foods they can eat instead, so the quantity demanded is likely to fall substantially. In fact, a key constraint on a firm's pricing policies is how many close substitutes exist for its product. In general, *if a product has more substitutes available, it will have more elastic demand. If a product has fewer substitutes available, it will have less elastic demand.*

## Passage of Time

It usually takes consumers some time to adjust their buying habits when prices change. If the price of chicken falls, for example, it takes a while before consumers decide to change from eating chicken for dinner once per week to eating it twice per week. If the price of gasoline increases, it also takes a while for consumers to decide to begin taking public transportation, to buy more fuel-efficient cars, or to find new jobs closer to where they live. *The more time that passes, the more elastic the demand for a product becomes.*

## Luxuries versus Necessities

Goods that are luxuries usually have more elastic demand curves than goods that are necessities. For example, the demand for bread is inelastic because bread is a necessity, and the quantity that people buy is not very dependent on its price. Tickets to a concert are a luxury, so the demand for concert tickets is much more elastic than the demand for bread. *The demand curve for a luxury is more elastic than the demand curve for a necessity.*

## Definition of the Market

In a narrowly defined market, consumers have more substitutes available. For example, if you own a service station and raise the price you charge for gasoline, many of your customers will switch to buying from a competitor. So, the demand for gasoline at one particular station is likely to be elastic. The demand for gasoline as a product, on the other hand, is inelastic because consumers have few alternatives (in the short run) to buying it. *The more narrowly we define a market, the more elastic demand will be.*

## Share of a Good in a Consumer's Budget

Goods that take only a small fraction of a consumer's budget tend to have less elastic demand than goods that take a large fraction. For example, most people buy table salt infrequently and in relatively small quantities. The share of the average consumer's budget that is spent on salt is very low. As a result, even a doubling of the price of salt is likely to result in only a small decline in the quantity of salt demanded. "Big-ticket items," such as houses, cars, and furniture, take up a larger share in the average consumer's budget. Increases in the prices of these goods are likely to result in significant declines in quantity demanded. In general, *the demand for a good will be more elastic the larger the share of the good in the average consumer's budget.*

## Some Estimated Price Elasticities of Demand

Table 6.2 shows some estimated short-run price elasticities of demand. It's important to remember that estimates of the price elasticities of different goods can vary, depending on the data used and the time period over which the estimates were made. The results

| Table 6.2 | |
|---|---|

**Estimated Real-World Price Elasticities of Demand**

| Product | Estimated Elasticity | Product | Estimated Elasticity |
|---|---|---|---|
| Books (Barnes & Noble) | −4.00 | Bread | −0.40 |
| Books (Amazon) | −0.60 | Water (residential use) | −0.38 |
| DVDs (Amazon) | −3.10 | Chicken | −0.37 |
| Post Raisin Bran | −2.50 | Cocaine | −0.28 |
| Automobiles | −1.95 | Cigarettes | −0.25 |
| Tide (liquid detergent) | −3.92 | Beer | −0.23 |
| Coca-Cola | −1.22 | Residential natural gas | −0.09 |
| Grapes | −1.18 | Gasoline | −0.06 |
| Restaurant meals | −0.67 | Milk | −0.04 |
| Health insurance (low-income households) | −0.65 | Sugar | −0.04 |

Based on Kelly D. Brownell and Thomas R. Frieden, "Ounces of Prevention—The Public Policy Case for Taxes on Sugared Beverages," *New England Journal of Medicine*, April 30, 2009; Sheila M. Olmstead and Robert N. Stavins, "Comparing Price and Non-Price Approaches to Urban Water Conservation," Resources for the Future, Discussion paper 08-22, June 2008; Jonathan E. Hughes, Christopher R. Knittel, and Daniel Sperling, "Evidence of a Shift in the Short-Run Price Elasticity of Gasoline Demand," Research Report UCD-ITS-RR-06-16 (University of California, Davis: Institute of Transportation Studies, 2006); Robert P. Trost, Frederick Joutz, David Shin, and Bruce McDonwell, "Using Shrinkage Estimators to Obtain Regional Short-Run and Long-Run Price Elasticities of Residential Natural Gas Demand in the U.S." George Washington University Working Paper, March 13, 2009; Lesley Chiou, "Empirical Analysis of Competition between Wal-Mart and Other Retail Channels", *Journal of Economics and Management Strategy*, forthcoming; Judith Chevalier, and Austan Goolsbee, "Price Competition Online: Amazon versus Barnes and Noble", *Quantitative Marketing and Economics*, Vol. 1, no. 2, June, 2003; Henry Saffer and Frank Chaloupka, "The Demand for Illicit Drugs," *Economic Inquiry*, Vol. 37, No. 3, July 1999; "Response to Increases in Cigarette Prices by Race/Ethnicity, Income, and Age Groups—United States, 1976–1993," *Morbidity and Mortality Weekly Report*, July 31, 1998; James Wetzel and George Hoffer, "Consumer Demand for Automobiles: A Disaggregated Market Approach," *Journal of Consumer Research*, Vol. 9, No. 2, September 1982; Jerry A. Hausman, "The Price Elasticity of Demand for Breakfast Cereal," in Timothy F. Bresnahan and Robert J. Gordon, eds., *The Economics of New Goods*, Chicago: University of Chicago Press, 1997; X. M. Gao, Eric J. Wailes, and Gail L. Cramer, "A Microeconometric Model Analysis of U.S. Consumer Demand for Alcoholic Beverages," *Applied Economics*, January 1995; and U.S. Department of Agriculture, Economic Research Service.

given in the table are consistent with our discussion of the determinants of price elasticity. Goods for which there are few substitutes, such as cigarettes, gasoline, and health insurance, are price inelastic, as are broadly defined goods, such as bread or beer. Particular brands of products, such as Coca-Cola, Tide, or Post Raisin Bran, are price elastic. (This point is discussed further in the *Making the Connection* on the price elasticity of breakfast cereal.)

The table shows that the demand for books or DVDs bought from a particular retailer is typically price elastic. Note, though, that demand for books from Amazon is inelastic, which indicates that consumers do not consider ordering from other online sites to be good substitutes for ordering from Amazon.

An increase in the price of grapes will lead some consumers to substitute other fruits, so demand for grapes is price elastic. Similarly, an increase in the price of new automobiles will lead some consumers to buy used automobiles or to continue driving their current cars, so demand for automobiles is also price elastic. The demand for necessities, such as natural gas and water, is also price inelastic.

<table>
<tr><td>Making<br>the<br>Connection</td><td>**The Price Elasticity of Demand<br>for Breakfast Cereal**</td></tr>
</table>

MIT economist Jerry Hausman has estimated the price elasticity of demand for breakfast cereal. He divided breakfast cereals into three categories: children's cereals, such as Trix and Froot Loops; adult cereals, such as Special K and Grape-Nuts; and family cereals, such as Corn Flakes and Raisin Bran. Some of the results of his estimates are given in the following table:

| Cereal | Price Elasticity of Demand |
| --- | :---: |
| Post Raisin Bran | −2.5 |
| All family breakfast cereals | −1.8 |
| All types of breakfast cereals | −0.9 |

Data from Jerry A. Hausman, "Valuation of New Goods under Perfect and Imperfect Competition," in Timothy F. Bresnahan and Robert J. Gordon, eds., *The Economics of New Goods*, (Chicago: University of Chicago Press, 1997), p. 226.

Just as we would expect, the price elasticity for a particular brand of raisin bran was larger in absolute value than the elasticity for all family cereals, and the elasticity for all family cereals was larger than the elasticity for all types of breakfast cereals. If Post increases the price of its Raisin Bran by 10 percent, sales will decline by 25 percent, as many consumers switch to another brand of raisin bran. If the prices of all family breakfast cereals rise by 10 percent, sales will decline by 18 percent, as consumers switch to child or adult cereals. In both of these cases, demand is elastic. But if the prices of all types of breakfast cereals rise by 10 percent, sales will decline by only 9 percent. Demand for all breakfast cereals is inelastic.

Based on Jerry A. Hausman, "Valuation of New Goods under Perfect and Imperfect Competition," in Timothy F. Bresnahan and Robert J. Gordon, eds., *The Economics of New Goods*, (Chicago: University of Chicago Press, 1997).

**Your Turn:** Test your understanding by doing related problem 2.4 on page 199 at the end of this chapter.

MyEconLab

# The Relationship between Price Elasticity of Demand and Total Revenue

**6.3 LEARNING** OBJECTIVE

Understand the relationship between the price elasticity of demand and total revenue.

**Total revenue** The total amount of funds received by a seller of a good or service, calculated by multiplying price per unit by the number of units sold.

A firm is interested in price elasticity because it allows the firm to calculate how changes in price will affect its **total revenue**, which is the total amount of funds it receives from selling a good or service. Total revenue is calculated by multiplying price per unit by the number of units sold. When demand is inelastic, price and total revenue move in the same direction: An increase in price raises total revenue, and a decrease in price reduces total revenue. When demand is elastic, price and total revenue move inversely: An increase in price reduces total revenue, and a decrease in price raises total revenue.

To understand the relationship between price elasticity and total revenue, consider Figure 6.2. Panel (a) shows a demand curve for gasoline (as in Figure 6.1 on page 174). This demand curve is inelastic between point $A$ and point $B$. The total revenue received by the service station owner at point $A$ equals the price of $4.00 multiplied by the 1,000 gallons sold, or $4,000. This amount equals the areas of the rectangles $C$ and $D$ in the figure because together the rectangles have a height of $4.00 and a base of 1,000 gallons. Because this demand curve is inelastic between point $A$ and point $B$ (it was demand curve $D_2$ in Figure 6.1), cutting the price to $3.70 (point $B$) reduces total revenue. The

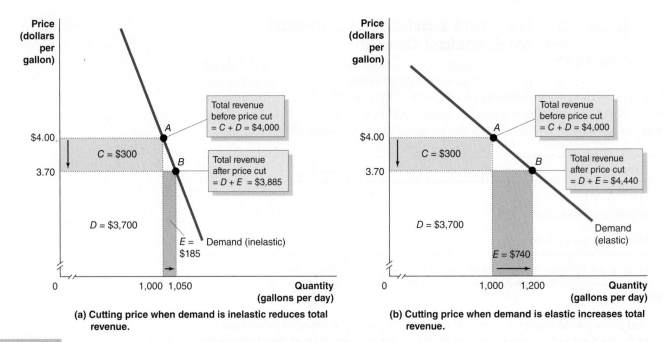

**Figure 6.2** The Relationship between Price Elasticity and Total Revenue

When demand is inelastic, a cut in price will decrease total revenue. In panel (a), at point *A*, the price is $4.00, 1,000 gallons are sold, and total revenue received by the service station equals $4.00 × 1,000 gallons, or $4,000. At point *B*, cutting the price to $3.70 increases the quantity demanded to 1,050 gallons, but the fall in price more than offsets the increase in quantity. As a result, revenue falls to $3.70

× 1,050 gallons, or $3,885. When demand is elastic, a cut in the price will increase total revenue. In panel (b), at point *A*, the area of rectangles *C* and *D* is still equal to $4,000. But at point *B*, the area of rectangles *D* and *E* is equal to $3.70 × 1,200 gallons, or $4,440. In this case, the increase in the quantity demanded is large enough to offset the fall in price, so total revenue increases.

new total revenue is shown by the areas of rectangles *D* and *E* and is equal to $3.70 multiplied by 1,050 gallons, or $3,885. Total revenue falls because the increase in the quantity demanded is not large enough to make up for the decrease in price. As a result, the $185 increase in revenue gained as a result of the price cut—dark-green rectangle *E*—is less than the $300 in revenue lost—light-green rectangle *C*.

Panel (b) of Figure 6.2 shows a demand curve that is elastic between point *A* and point *B*. (It was demand curve $D_1$ in Figure 6.1.) In this case, cutting the price increases total revenue. At point *A*, the areas of rectangles *C* and *D* are still equal to $4,000, but at point *B*, the areas of rectangles *D* and *E* are equal to $3.70 multiplied by 1,200 gallons, or $4,440. Here, total revenue rises because the increase in the quantity demanded is large enough to offset the lower price. As a result, the $740 increase in revenue gained as a result of the price cut—dark-green rectangle *E*—is greater than the $300 in revenue lost—light-green rectangle *C*.

The third, less common possibility is that demand is unit elastic. In that case, a small change in price is exactly offset by a proportional change in quantity demanded, leaving revenue unaffected. Therefore, when demand is unit elastic, neither a decrease in price nor an increase in price affects revenue. Table 6.3 summarizes the relationship between price elasticity and revenue.

## Elasticity and Revenue with a Linear Demand Curve

Along most demand curves, elasticity is not constant at every point. For example, a straight-line, or linear, demand curve for gasoline is shown in panel (a) of Figure 6.3. (For simplicity, the quantities used are small.) The numbers from the table are plotted in the graphs. The demand curve shows that when the price drops by $1 per gallon, consumers always respond by buying 2 more gallons per day. When the price is high and the quantity demanded is low, demand is elastic. Demand is elastic because a $1 drop in price is a smaller percentage change when the price is high, and an increase of 2 gallons is a larger percentage change when the quantity of gasoline purchased is small. By similar reasoning, we can see why demand is inelastic when the price is low and the quantity demanded is high.

| If demand is ... | then ... | because ... |
|---|---|---|
| elastic | an increase in price reduces revenue | the decrease in quantity demanded is proportionally *greater* than the increase in price. |
| elastic | a decrease in price increases revenue | the increase in quantity demanded is proportionally *greater* than the decrease in price. |
| inelastic | an increase in price increases revenue | the decrease in quantity demanded is proportionally *smaller* than the increase in price. |
| inelastic | a decrease in price reduces revenue | the increase in quantity demanded is proportionally *smaller* than the decrease in price. |
| unit elastic | an increase in price does not affect revenue | the decrease in quantity demanded is proportionally *the same as* the increase in price. |
| unit elastic | a decrease in price does not affect revenue | the increase in quantity demanded is proportionally *the same as* the decrease in price. |

**Table 6.3**

**The Relationship between Price Elasticity and Revenue**

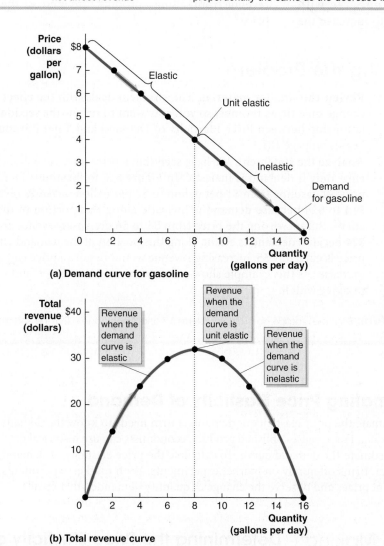

| Price | Quantity Demanded | Total Revenue |
|---|---|---|
| $8 | 0 | $0 |
| 7 | 2 | 14 |
| 6 | 4 | 24 |
| 5 | 6 | 30 |
| 4 | 8 | 32 |
| 3 | 10 | 30 |
| 2 | 12 | 24 |
| 1 | 14 | 14 |
| 0 | 16 | 0 |

(a) Demand curve for gasoline

(b) Total revenue curve

**Figure 6.3    Elasticity Is Not Constant Along a Linear Demand Curve**

The data from the table are plotted in the graphs. Panel (a) shows that as we move down the demand curve for gasoline, the price elasticity of demand declines. In other words, at higher prices, demand is elastic, and at lower prices, demand is inelastic. Panel (b) shows that as the quantity of gasoline purchased increases from 0, revenue will increase until it reaches a maximum of $32 when 8 gallons are purchased. As purchases increase beyond 8 gallons, revenue falls because demand is inelastic on this portion of the demand curve.

Panel (a) in Figure 6.3 shows that when price is between $8 and $4 and quantity demanded is between 0 and 8 gallons, demand is elastic. Panel (b) shows that over this same range, total revenue will increase as price falls. For example, in panel (a), as price falls from $7 to $6, quantity demanded increases from 2 to 4, and in panel (b), total revenue increases from $14 to $24. Similarly, when price is between $4 and 0 and quantity demanded is between 8 and 16, demand is inelastic. Over this same range, total revenue will decrease as price falls. For example, as price falls from $3 to $2 and quantity demanded increases from 10 to 12, total revenue decreases from $30 to $24.

# Solved Problem 6.3

## Price and Revenue Don't Always Move in the Same Direction

Briefly explain whether you agree or disagree with the following statement: "The only way to increase the revenue from selling a product is to increase the product's price."

### Solving the Problem

**Step 1:** **Review the chapter material.** This problem deals with the effect of a price change on a firm's revenue, so you may want to review the section "The Relationship between Price Elasticity of Demand and Total Revenue," which begins on page 181.

**Step 2:** **Analyze the statement.** We have seen that a price increase will increase revenue only if demand is inelastic. In Figure 6.3, for example, increasing the price of gasoline from $1 per gallon to $2 per gallon *increases* revenue from $14 to $24 because demand is inelastic along this portion of the demand curve. But increasing the price from $5 to $6 *decreases* revenue from $30 to $24 because demand is elastic along this portion of the demand curve. If the price is currently $5, increasing revenue would require a price *cut*, not a price increase. As this example shows, the statement is incorrect, and you should disagree with it.

MyEconLab **Your Turn:** For more practice, do related problems 3.7 and 3.8 on page 200 at the end of this chapter.

## Estimating Price Elasticity of Demand

To estimate the price elasticity of demand, a firm needs to know the demand curve for its product. For a well-established product, economists can use historical data to statistically estimate the demand curve. To calculate the price elasticity of demand for a new product, firms often rely on market experiments. With market experiments, firms try different prices and observe the change in quantity demanded that results.

Making
the
Connection

## Determining the Price Elasticity of Demand through Market Experiments

Firms usually have a good idea of the price elasticity of demand for products that have been on the market for at least a few years. For new products, however, firms often experiment with different prices to determine the price elasticity. For example, Apple introduced the first-generation iPhone in June 2007, at a price of $599. But demand for the iPhone was more elastic than Apple had expected, and when sales failed to reach Apple's projections, the company cut the price to $399 just two months later. Similarly, when 3D televisions were introduced into the U.S. market in early 2010, Sony and other manufacturers believed that sales would be strong despite prices being several hundred dollars higher than for other high-end ultra-thin televisions. Once again, though, demand turned out to be more elastic than expected, and by December firms were cutting prices 40 percent or more in an effort to increase revenue.

*The price elasticity of demand for 3D televisions was higher than Sony had expected.*

Since electronic books (e-books) became popular after Amazon introduced the Kindle e-reader, firms have experimented with different prices in trying to determine the relevant price elasticity. Amazon had originally priced most best selling e-books at $9.99, but when Apple introduced the iPad in 2010, Apple negotiated contracts with publishers that raised prices for e-books. Amazon and Barnes & Noble eventually signed similar contracts, and the prices for best selling e-books rose from $9.99 to $12.99 or $14.99. Publishers hoped that a low price elasticity of demand for e-books would result in the price increase leading to higher revenues. Many buyers, however, claimed that rather than pay higher prices, they would go back to reading printed books. Joel Waldfogel, an economist at the University of Pennsylvania, raised the possibility that the higher prices might lead some readers to illegally download pirated e-books, in violation of the publishers' copyrights. Although piracy has been a problem with music and movies, it had not yet been a problem with books. Waldfogel argued that, "I would be scared to death about a culture of piracy taking hold. I wouldn't mess around with price increases." Whether the demand for e-books turns out to be elastic or inelastic may depend on how many readers consider printed books or pirated e-books to be close substitutes for legally downloaded e-books.

Based on Daisuke Wakabayashi and Miguel Bustillo, "TV Makers Can't Hold Line on 3-D Prices," *Wall Street Journal*, December 20, 2010; Motoko Rich and Brad Stone, "Cost of an e-Book Will Be Going Up," *New York Times*, February 11, 2010; and Kate Hafner and Brad Stone, "iPhone Owners Crying Foul Over Price Cut," *New York Times*, September 7, 2007.

**Your Turn:** Test your understanding by doing related problem 3.12 on page 201 at the end of this chapter.     MyEconLab

---

# Other Demand Elasticities

Elasticity is an important concept in economics because it allows us to quantify the responsiveness of one economic variable to changes in another economic variable. In addition to price elasticity, two other demand elasticities are important: *cross-price elasticity of demand* and *income elasticity of demand*.

## Cross-Price Elasticity of Demand

Suppose you work at Apple, and you need to predict the effect of an increase in the price of Samsung's Galaxy Tab on the quantity of iPads demanded, holding other factors constant. You can do this by calculating the **cross-price elasticity of demand**, which is the percentage change in the quantity of iPads demanded divided by the percentage change in the price of Galaxy Tabs—or, in general:

$$\text{Cross-price elasticity of demand} = \frac{\text{Percentage change in quantity demanded of one good}}{\text{Percentage change in price of another good}}.$$

**6.4 LEARNING OBJECTIVE**

Define cross-price elasticity of demand and income elasticity of demand and understand their determinants and how they are measured.

**Cross-price elasticity of demand**
The percentage change in quantity demanded of one good divided by the percentage change in the price of another good.

**Table 6.4**

**Summary of Cross-Price Elasticity of Demand**

| If the products are ... | then the cross-price elasticity of demand will be ... | Example |
| --- | --- | --- |
| substitutes | positive. | Two brands of tablet computers |
| complements | negative. | Tablet computers and applications downloaded from online stores |
| unrelated | zero. | Tablet computers and peanut butter |

The cross-price elasticity of demand is positive or negative, depending on whether the two products are substitutes or complements. Recall that substitutes are products that can be used for the same purpose, such as two brands of tablet computers. Complements are products that are used together, such as tablet computers and applications that can be downloaded from online stores. An increase in the price of a substitute will lead to an increase in quantity demanded, so the cross-price elasticity of demand will be positive. An increase in the price of a complement will lead to a decrease in the quantity demanded, so the cross-price elasticity of demand will be negative. Of course, if the two products are unrelated—such as tablet computers and peanut butter—the cross-price elasticity of demand will be zero. Table 6.4 summarizes the key points concerning the cross-price elasticity of demand.

Cross-price elasticity of demand is important to firm managers because it allows them to measure whether products sold by other firms are close substitutes for their products. For example, Pepsi-Cola and Coca-Cola spend heavily on advertising with the hope of convincing consumers that each cola tastes better than its rival. How can these firms tell whether or not their advertising campaigns have been effective? One way is by seeing whether the cross-price elasticity of demand has changed. If, for instance, Coca-Cola has a successful advertising campaign, then when it increases the price of Coke, the percentage increase in sales of Pepsi should be smaller. In other words, the value of the cross-price elasticity of demand should have declined.

## Income Elasticity of Demand

**Income elasticity of demand** A measure of the responsiveness of quantity demanded to changes in income, measured by the percentage change in quantity demanded divided by the percentage change in income.

The **income elasticity of demand** measures the responsiveness of quantity demanded to changes in income. It is calculated as follows:

$$\text{Income elasticity of demand} = \frac{\text{Percentage change in quantity demanded}}{\text{Percentage change in income}}.$$

As we saw in Chapter 3, if the quantity demanded of a good increases as income increases, then the good is a *normal good*. Normal goods are often further subdivided into *luxuries* and *necessities*. A good is a luxury if the quantity demanded is very responsive to changes in income, so that a 10 percent increase in income results in more than a 10 percent increase in quantity demanded. Expensive jewelry and vacation homes are examples of luxuries. A good is a necessity if the quantity demanded is not very responsive to changes in income, so that a 10 percent increase in income results in less than a 10 percent increase in quantity demanded. Food and clothing are examples of necessities. A good is *inferior* if the quantity demanded falls when income increases. Ground beef with a high fat content is an example of an inferior good. We should note that *normal good*, *inferior good*, *necessity*, and *luxury* are just labels economists use for

**Table 6.5**

**Summary of Income Elasticity of Demand**

| If the income elasticity of demand is ... | then the good is ... | Example |
|---|---|---|
| positive but less than 1 | normal and a necessity. | Bread |
| positive and greater than 1 | normal and a luxury. | Caviar |
| negative | inferior. | High-fat meat |

goods with different income elasticities; the labels are not intended to be value judgments about the worth of these goods.

Because most goods are normal goods, during periods of economic expansion, when consumer income is rising, most firms can expect—holding other factors constant—that the quantity demanded of their products will increase. Sellers of luxuries can expect particularly large increases. During recessions, falling consumer income can cause firms to experience increases in demand for inferior goods. For example, the demand for bus trips increases as consumers cut back on air travel, and supermarkets find that the demand for hamburger increases relative to the demand for steak. Table 6.5 summarizes the key points about the income elasticity of demand.

## Making the Connection | Price Elasticity, Cross-Price Elasticity, and Income Elasticity in the Market for Alcoholic Beverages

Many public policy issues are related to the consumption of alcoholic beverages. These issues include underage drinking, drunk driving, and the possible beneficial effects of red wine in lowering the risk of heart disease. X. M. Gao, an economist who works at American Express, and two colleagues have estimated statistically the following elasticities. (*Spirits* refers to all beverages that contain alcohol, other than beer and wine.)

| | |
|---|---|
| Price elasticity of demand for beer | −0.23 |
| Cross-price elasticity of demand between beer and wine | 0.31 |
| Cross-price elasticity of demand between beer and spirits | 0.15 |
| Income elasticity of demand for beer | −0.09 |
| Income elasticity of demand for wine | 5.03 |
| Income elasticity of demand for spirits | 1.21 |

The demand for beer is inelastic. A 10 percent increase in the price of beer will result in a 2.3 percent decline in the quantity of beer demanded. Not surprisingly, both wine and spirits are substitutes for beer. A 10 percent increase in the price of wine will result in a 3.1 percent *increase* in the quantity of beer demanded. A 10 percent increase in income will result in a little less than a 1 percent *decline* in the quantity of beer demanded. So, beer is an inferior good. Both wine and spirits are categorized as luxuries because their income elasticities are greater than 1.

Based on X. M. Gao, Eric J. Wailes, and Gail L. Cramer, "A Microeconometric Model Analysis of U.S. Consumer Demand for Alcoholic Beverages," *Applied Economics*, January 1995.

**Your Turn:** Test your understanding by doing related problem 4.8 on page 202 at the end of this chapter.    MyEconLab

**6.5 LEARNING** OBJECTIVE

Use price elasticity and income elasticity to analyze economic issues.

# Using Elasticity to Analyze the Disappearing Family Farm

The concepts of price elasticity and income elasticity can help us understand many economic issues. For example, some people are concerned that the family farm is becoming an endangered species in the United States. Although food production continues to grow rapidly, the number of farms and the number of farmers continue to dwindle. In 1950, the United States was home to more than 5 million farms, and more than 23 million people lived on farms. By 2011, only about 2 million farms remained, and fewer than 3 million people lived on them. In Chapter 4, we discussed several federal government programs designed to aid farmers. Many of these programs have been aimed at helping small, family-operated farms, but rapid growth in farm production, combined with low price and income elasticities for most food products, has made family farming difficult in the United States.

Productivity measures the ability of firms to produce goods and services with a given amount of economic inputs, such as workers, machines, and land. Productivity has grown very rapidly in U.S. agriculture. In 1950, the average U.S. wheat farmer harvested about 17 bushels from each acre of wheat planted. By 2011, because of the development of superior strains of wheat and improvements in farming techniques, the average American wheat farmer harvested 45 bushels per acre. So, even though the total number of acres devoted to growing wheat declined from about 62 million to about 56 million, total wheat production rose from about 1.0 billion bushels to about 2.2 billion.

Unfortunately for U.S. farmers, this increase in wheat production resulted in a substantial decline in wheat prices. Two key factors explain this decline: (1) The demand for wheat is inelastic, and (2) the income elasticity of demand for wheat is low. Even though the U.S. population has increased greatly since 1950 and the income of the average American is much higher than it was in 1950, the demand for wheat has increased only moderately. For all of the additional wheat to be sold, the price has had to decline. Because the demand for wheat is inelastic, the price decline has been substantial. Figure 6.4 illustrates these points.

A large shift in supply, a small shift in demand, and an inelastic demand curve combined to drive down the price of wheat from $18.56 per bushel in 1950 to $5.70 per bushel in 2011. (The 1950 price is measured in terms of prices in 2011, to adjust for the general increase in prices since 1950.) With low prices, only the most efficiently run farms have been able to remain profitable. Small family-run farms have found it difficult to survive, and many of these farms have disappeared. The markets for most

## Figure 6.4

**Elasticity and the Disappearing Family Farm**

In 1950, U.S. farmers produced 1.0 billion bushels of wheat at a price of $18.56 per bushel. Over the next 60 years, rapid increases in farm productivity caused a large shift to the right in the supply curve for wheat. The income elasticity of demand for wheat is low, so the demand for wheat increased relatively little over this period. Because the demand for wheat is also inelastic, the large shift in the supply curve and the small shift in the demand curve resulted in a sharp decline in the price of wheat, from $18.56 per bushel in 1950 to $5.70 per bushel in 2011.

Data from United States Department of Agriculture, *Wheat Yearbook Tables*, July 21, 2011.

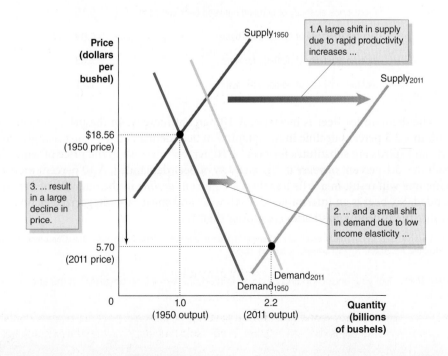

other food products are similar to the market for wheat. They are characterized by rapid output growth and low income and price elasticities. The result is the paradox of American farming: ever more abundant and cheaper food, supplied by fewer and fewer farms. American consumers have benefited, but most family farmers have not.

---

# Solved Problem 6.5

## Using Price Elasticity to Analyze a Policy of Taxing Gasoline

In Chapter 5, we saw that if the consumption of a product results in a negative externality, taxing the product may improve economic efficiency. Some economists and policymakers argue that driving cars and trucks involves a negative externality because burning gasoline increases emissions of greenhouse gases and contributes to the congestion that clogs many highways in and around big cities. Some economists have suggested substantially increasing the federal excise tax on gasoline, which in 2011 was 18.5 cents per gallon. How much the tax would cause consumption to fall and how much revenue the tax would raise depend on the price elasticity of demand. Suppose that the price of gasoline is currently $4.00 per gallon, the quantity of gasoline demanded is 140 billion gallons per year, the price elasticity of demand for gasoline is $-0.06$, and the federal government decides to increase the excise tax on gasoline by $1.00 per gallon. We saw in Chapter 4 that the price of a product will not rise by the full amount of a tax increase unless the demand for the product is perfectly inelastic. In this case, suppose that the price of gasoline increases by $0.80 per gallon after the $1.00 excise tax is imposed.

a. What is the new quantity of gasoline demanded after the tax is imposed? How effective would a gas tax be in reducing consumption of gasoline in the short run?

b. How much revenue does the federal government receive from the tax?

## Solving the Problem

**Step 1:** **Review the chapter material.** This problem deals with applications of the price elasticity of demand formula, so you may want to review the section "Measuring the Price Elasticity of Demand," which begins on page 172.

**Step 2:** **Answer the first question in part (a) using the formula for the price elasticity of demand to calculate the new quantity demanded.**

$$\text{Price elasticity of demand} = \frac{\text{Percentage change in quantity demanded}}{\text{Percentage change in price}}.$$

We can plug into the midpoint formula the values given for the price elasticity, the original price of $4.00, and the new price of $4.80 $(= \$4.00 + \$0.80)$:

$$-0.06 = \frac{\text{Percentage change in quantity demanded}}{\left(\dfrac{(\$4.80 - \$4.00)}{\dfrac{\$4.00 + \$4.80}{2}}\right)}.$$

Or, rearranging and writing out the expression for the percentage change in quantity demanded:

$$-0.011 = \frac{(Q_2 - 140\,\text{billion})}{\left(\dfrac{140\,\text{billion} + Q_2}{2}\right)}.$$

Solving for $Q_2$, the new quantity demanded:

$$Q_2 = 138.5\,\text{billion gallons}.$$

**Step 3:** **Answer the second question in part (a).** Because the price elasticity of demand for gasoline is so low—$-0.06$—even a substantial increase in the gasoline tax of

$1.00 per gallon would reduce gasoline consumption by only a small amount: from 140 billion gallons of gasoline per year to 138.5 billion gallons. Note, though, that price elasticities typically increase over time. Economists estimate that the long-run price elasticity of gasoline is in the range of −0.40 to −0.60, so in the long run, the decline in the consumption of gasoline would be larger.

**Step 4:** **Calculate the revenue earned by the federal government to answer part (b).** The federal government would collect an amount equal to the tax per gallon multiplied by the number of gallons sold: $1 per gallon × 138.5 billion gallons = $138.5 billion.

**Extra Credit:** The amount of tax as calculated in Step 4 is substantial: about 15 percent of all the revenue the federal government raised from the personal income tax in 2010. It is also much larger than the roughly $25 billion the federal government received in 2011 from the existing 18.5-cents-per-gallon gasoline tax. We can conclude that raising the federal excise tax on gasoline would be a good way to raise revenue for the federal government, but, at least in the short run, increasing the tax would not greatly reduce the quantity of gasoline consumed. Notice that if the demand for gasoline were elastic, this result would be reversed: The quantity of gasoline consumed would decline much more, but so would the revenue that the federal government would receive from the tax increase.

MyEconLab   **Your Turn:** For more practice, do related problems 5.2 and 5.3 on page 202 at the end of this chapter.

---

**6.6 LEARNING** OBJECTIVE

Define price elasticity of supply and understand its main determinants and how it is measured.

# The Price Elasticity of Supply and Its Measurement

We can use the concept of elasticity to measure the responsiveness of firms to a change in price, just as we used it to measure the responsiveness of consumers. We know from the law of supply that when the price of a product increases, the quantity supplied increases. To measure how much the quantity supplied increases when price increases, we use the *price elasticity of supply*.

## Measuring the Price Elasticity of Supply

**price elasticity of supply** The responsiveness of the quantity supplied to a change in price, measured by dividing the percentage change in the quantity supplied of a product by the percentage change in the product's price.

Just as with the price elasticity of demand, we calculate the **price elasticity of supply** by using percentage changes:

$$\text{Price elasticity of supply} = \frac{\text{Percentage change in quantity supplied}}{\text{Percentage change in price}}.$$

Notice that because supply curves are upward sloping, the price elasticity of supply will be a positive number. We categorize the price elasticity of supply the same way we categorized the price elasticity of demand: If the price elasticity of supply is less than 1, then supply is *inelastic*. For example, the price elasticity of supply of gasoline from U.S. oil refineries is about 0.20, and so it is inelastic; a 10 percent increase in the price of gasoline will result in only a 2 percent increase in the quantity supplied. If the price elasticity of supply is greater than 1, then supply is *elastic*. If the price elasticity of supply is equal to 1, the supply is *unit elastic*. As with other elasticity calculations, when we calculate the price elasticity of supply, we hold constant the values of other factors.

## Determinants of the Price Elasticity of Supply

Whether supply is elastic or inelastic depends on the ability and willingness of firms to alter the quantity they produce as price increases. Often, firms have difficulty increasing the quantity of the product they supply during any short period of time. For example, a pizza parlor cannot produce more pizzas on any one night than is possible using the ingredients on hand. Within a day or two, it can buy more ingredients, and within a few months, it can hire more cooks and install additional ovens. As a result, the supply curve for pizza and most other products will be inelastic if we measure it over a short period of time, but the supply curve will be increasingly elastic the longer the period of time over which we measure it. Products that require resources that are themselves in fixed supply are an exception to this rule. For example, a French winery may rely on a particular variety of grape. If all the land on which that grape can be grown is already planted in vineyards, then the supply of that wine will be inelastic even over a long period.

| Making the Connection | ## Why Are Oil Prices So Unstable? |
|---|---|

Bringing oil to market is a long process. Oil companies hire geologists to locate fields for exploratory oil well drilling. If significant amounts of oil are present, the company begins full-scale development of the field. The process from exploration to pumping significant amounts of oil can take years. This long process is why the price elasticity of supply for oil is very low.

During the period from 2003 to mid-2008, the worldwide demand for oil increased rapidly as India, China, and some other developing countries increased both their manufacturing production and their use of automobiles. As the graph below shows, when supply is inelastic, an increase in demand can cause a large increase in price. The shift in the demand curve from $D_1$ to $D_2$ causes the equilibrium quantity of oil to increase only by 5 percent, from 80 million barrels per day to 84 million, but the equilibrium price rises by 75 percent, from $80 per barrel to $140 per barrel.

The world oil market is heavily influenced by the Organization of the Petroleum Exporting Countries (OPEC). OPEC has 11 members, including Saudi Arabia, Kuwait, Iran, Venezuela, and Nigeria. Together OPEC members own 75 percent of the world's proven oil reserves. Periodically, OPEC has attempted to force up the price of oil by reducing the quantity of oil its members supply. As we will discuss further in Chapter 14, since the 1970s, OPEC's attempts to reduce the quantity of oil on world markets have been successful only sporadically. As a result, the supply curve for oil shifts fairly frequently. Combined with the low price elasticities of oil supply and demand, these shifts in supply have caused the price of oil to fluctuate significantly over the past 30 years, from as low as $10 per barrel to more than $140 per barrel.

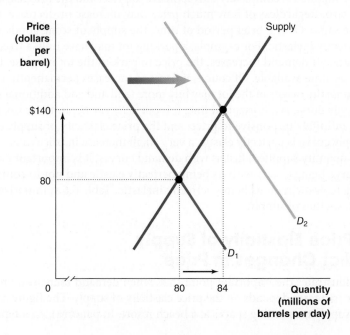

Beginning in mid-2008, the financial crisis that had begun in the United States had spread to other countries, resulting in a severe recession. As production and incomes fell during the recession, the worldwide demand for oil declined sharply. Over the space of a few months, the equilibrium price of oil fell from $140 per barrel to $40 per barrel. As the graph below shows, once again, the extent of the price change reflected not only the size of the decline in demand but also oil's low price elasticity of supply.

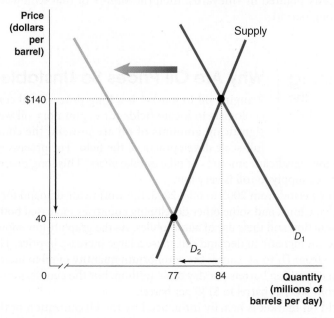

MyEconLab **Your Turn:** Test your understanding by doing related problem 6.3 on page 203 at the end of this chapter.

## Polar Cases of Perfectly Elastic and Perfectly Inelastic Supply

Although it occurs infrequently, it is possible for supply to fall into one of the polar cases of price elasticity. If a supply curve is a vertical line, it is *perfectly inelastic*. In this case, the quantity supplied is completely unresponsive to price, and the price elasticity of supply equals zero. Regardless of how much price may increase or decrease, the quantity remains the same. Over a brief period of time, the supply of some goods and services may be perfectly inelastic. For example, a parking lot may have only a fixed number of parking spaces. If demand increases, the price to park in the lot may rise, but no more spaces will become available. Of course, if demand increases permanently, over a longer period of time, the owner of the lot may buy more land and add additional spaces.

If a supply curve is a horizontal line, it is *perfectly elastic*. In this case, the quantity supplied is infinitely responsive to price, and the price elasticity of supply equals infinity. If a supply curve is perfectly elastic, a very small increase in price causes a very large increase in quantity supplied. Just as with demand curves, it is important not to confuse a supply curve being elastic with its being perfectly elastic and not to confuse a supply curve being inelastic with its being perfectly inelastic. Table 6.6 summarizes the different price elasticities of supply.

## Using Price Elasticity of Supply to Predict Changes in Price

Figure 6.5 illustrates the important point that, when demand increases, the amount by which price increases depends on the price elasticity of supply. The figure shows the demand and supply for parking spaces at a beach resort. In panel (a), on a typical summer

| If supply is ... | then the value of price elasticity is... | | |
|---|---|---|---|
| elastic | greater than 1 | | |
| inelastic | less than 1 | | |
| unit-elastic | equal to 1 | | |
| perfectly elastic | equal to infinity | | |
| perfectly inelastic | equal to 0 | | |

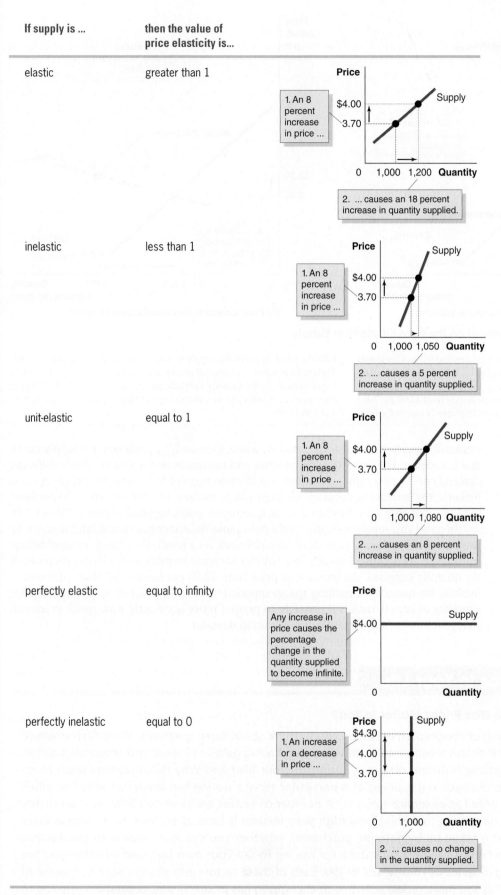

**Table 6.6**

**Summary of the Price Elasticity of Supply**

*Note*: The percentage increases shown in the boxes in the graphs were calculated using the midpoint formula, given on page 174.)

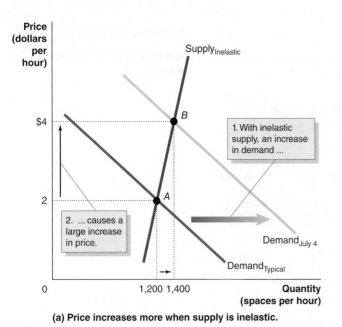

(a) Price increases more when supply is inelastic.

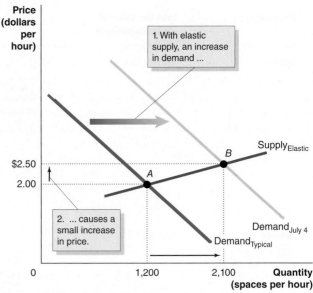

(b) Price increases less when supply is elastic.

**Figure 6.5** **Changes in Price Depend on the Price Elasticity of Supply**

In panel (a), Demand$_{Typical}$ represents the typical demand for parking spaces on a summer weekend at a beach resort. Demand$_{July\ 4}$ represents demand on the Fourth of July. Because supply is inelastic, the shift in equilibrium from point A to point B results in a large increase in price—from $2.00 per hour to $4.00—but only a small increase in the quantity of spaces supplied—from

1,200 to 1,400. In panel (b), supply is elastic. As a result, the change in equilibrium from point A to point B results in a smaller increase in price and a larger increase in the quantity supplied. An increase in price from $2.00 per hour to $2.50 is sufficient to increase the quantity of parking supplied from 1,200 to 2,100.

weekend, equilibrium occurs at point A, where Demand$_{Typical}$ intersects a supply curve that is inelastic. The increase in demand for parking spaces on the Fourth of July shifts the demand curve to the right, moving the equilibrium to point B. Because the supply curve is inelastic, the increase in demand results in a large increase in price—from $2.00 per hour to $4.00—but only a small increase in the quantity of spaces supplied—from 1,200 to 1,400.

In panel (b), supply is elastic, perhaps because the resort has vacant land that can be used for parking during periods of high demand. As a result, the change in equilibrium from point A to point B results in a smaller increase in price and a larger increase in the quantity supplied. An increase in price from $2.00 per hour to $2.50 is sufficient to increase the quantity of parking spaces supplied from 1,200 to 2,100. Knowing the price elasticity of supply makes it possible to predict more accurately how much price will change following an increase or a decrease in demand.

Continued from page 171

## Economics in Your Life

### How Much Do Gas Prices Matter to You?

At the beginning of the chapter, we asked you to think about three questions: What factors would make you more or less sensitive to price when purchasing gasoline? Have you responded differently to price changes during different periods of your life? and Why do consumers seem to respond more to changes in gas prices at a particular service station but seem less sensitive when gas prices rise or fall at all service stations? A number of factors are likely to affect your sensitivity to changes in gas prices, including how high your income is (and, therefore, how large a share of your budget is taken up by gasoline purchases), whether you live in an area with good public transportation (which can be a substitute for having to use your own car), and whether you live within walking distance of your school or job. Each of these factors may change over the course of your life, making you more or less sensitive to changes in gas prices. Finally, consumers respond to changes in the price of gas at a particular service station because gas at other service stations is a good substitute. But there are presently few good substitutes for gasoline as a product.

# Conclusion

In this chapter, we have explored the important concept of elasticity. Table 6.7 summarizes the various elasticities we discussed. Computing elasticities is important in economics because it allows us to measure how one variable changes in response to changes in another variable. For example, by calculating the price elasticity of demand for its product, a firm can make a quantitative estimate of the effect of a price change on the revenue it receives. Similarly, by calculating the price elasticity of demand for cigarettes, the government can better estimate the effect of an increase in cigarette taxes on smoking.

Before going further in analyzing how firms decide on the prices to charge and the quantities to produce, we need to look at how firms are organized. We do this in the next chapter. Read *An Inside Look* on the next page for a discussion of the effect of higher gas prices on consumer and business spending.

**Table 6.7**

**Summary of Elasticities**

### Price Elasticity of Demand

Formula: $\dfrac{\text{Percentage change in quantity demanded}}{\text{Percentage change in price}}$

Midpoint Formula: $\dfrac{(Q_2 - Q_1)}{\left(\dfrac{Q_2 + Q_1}{2}\right)} \div \dfrac{(P_2 - P_1)}{\left(\dfrac{P_1 + P_2}{2}\right)}$

|  | Absolute Value of Price Elasticity | Effect on Total Revenue of an Increase in Price |
|---|---|---|
| Elastic | Greater than 1 | Total revenue falls |
| Inelastic | Less than 1 | Total revenue rises |
| Unit elastic | Equal to 1 | Total revenue unchanged |

### Cross-Price Elasticity of Demand

Formula: $\dfrac{\text{Percentage change in quantity demanded of one good}}{\text{Percentage change in price of another good}}$

| Types of Products | Value of Cross-Price Elasticity |
|---|---|
| Substitutes | Positive |
| Complements | Negative |
| Unrelated | Zero |

### Income Elasticity of Demand

Formula: $\dfrac{\text{Percentage change in quantity demanded}}{\text{Percentage change in income}}$

| Types of Products | Value of Income Elasticity |
|---|---|
| Normal and a necessity | Positive but less than 1 |
| Normal and a luxury | Positive and greater than 1 |
| Inferior | Negative |

### Price Elasticity of Supply

Formula: $\dfrac{\text{Percentage change in quantity supplied}}{\text{Percentage change in price}}$

|  | Value of Price Elasticity |
|---|---|
| Elastic | Greater than 1 |
| Inelastic | Less than 1 |
| Unit elastic | Equal to 1 |

# Gasoline Price Increases Change Consumer Spending Patterns, May Stall Recovery

## WASHINGTON POST

## $4-a-Gallon Gas Fueling Fears for Recovery

Gasoline prices are soaring toward $4 a gallon, a threshold that some analysts say will damage the fragile economic recovery and crimp consumer spending just as families are planning their summer vacations.

Higher prices saddle businesses with higher transportation costs, causing them to either swallow them or pass them along to already strapped customers. As gasoline costs go up, consumers are left with less money to spend elsewhere. And there is evidence that the hike at the pump is beginning to push drivers off the road.

Gasoline prices, which are approaching record levels, "are going to have a very profound effect on the economy," said Peter Morici, an economist at the University of Maryland.

D.C. resident Amber Sutton, who drives 25 miles each way to her job in Woodbridge, said rising gasoline prices have caused her to cut back on restaurants and other entertainment.

"I already was spending a ton on gas," she said. "But now it's absolutely ridiculous. . . ."

Prices have risen so high, so fast that some market analysts predicted a sell-off in the short term. That sentiment sent crude oil prices tumbling Tuesday for the second consecutive day, dragging stock markets down about 1 percent, as evidence grew that escalating prices are beginning to threaten the global economic recovery.

But Morici and other economists say the pullback may only provide temporary relief at the pump and that higher prices could be here to stay.

Gasoline prices peaked in July 2008, when a gallon of regular sold for an average of $4.11 nationally. Some analysts fear prices could again approach that level in the near future, since demand for gasoline generally rises in the warm-weather months.

Nearly three-quarters of Americans says higher prices could slow their spending in other areas in the months ahead, according to a Deloitte survey of consumers' spending intentions. . . .

Already, motorists are cutting back on driving because of the increasing prices. "We are seeing some deterioration in U.S. motor gasoline demand . . . as pump prices near $3.75 a gallon," which is when demand got soft in 2008, said David Greely, an analyst at Goldman Sachs. "As the market moves to higher prices, the likelihood that you're going to weaken demand increases."

Bill Simon, chief executive of Wal-Mart U.S., said recently that the retailer sees fewer customers when gas prices begin to rise, because its mammoth stores are typically farther away than local grocery and convenience stores.

But as the spike continues, customers begin consolidating shopping trips and are more likely to visit just Wal-Mart instead of a handful of smaller retailers, Simon said. "We know that gas prices are going to continue to challenge people."

New reports from Goldman Sachs and the International Energy Agency were the triggers for Tuesday's $3.67-a-barrel drop in the price on the New York Mercantile Exchange, where a barrel of the U.S. benchmark West Texas Intermediate closed at $106.25.

Oil prices above $100 will hurt the recovery, the IEA report said. "Economic impacts from high prices are never instantaneous, and often take months to materialize, but preliminary data for early 2011 already show signs of oil demand slowdown," the IEA report said. "Unfortunately, the surest remedy for high prices may ultimately prove to be high prices themselves."

Fears of continued Middle East unrest and the possibility that supply disruptions could spread beyond Libya have driven up the price of Brent crude, another key oil benchmark that is used by about two-thirds of the world, from $100 a barrel in mid-February to $125 a barrel last Friday, a level not seen since May of the record-setting 2008. Yet inventories and spare production capacity are bigger this year than they were then, Goldman noted. . . .

## Key Points in the Article

Rapidly increasing prices for crude oil during the first quarter of 2011 translated into higher prices at the gas pump. Businesses with higher transportation costs must either absorb these higher prices or pass them along to customers in the form of higher product prices. For households, higher gas prices have resulted in a reduction in driving as well as a shift in spending patterns. As gas prices have risen, consumers have cut back on other forms of spending because they are using a larger portion of their budgets for fuel expenses. Analysts are concerned that the higher costs to businesses and cuts in consumer spending could be detrimental to the economic recovery, and the overall effect of the higher gas prices may take months to become evident in the economy.

## Analyzing the News

**a** The demand for gasoline is inelastic, so when price increases by a certain percentage, the quantity demanded will decrease by a smaller percentage. Therefore, as the price of gasoline increases, a larger portion of the average consumer's budget will be devoted to purchasing gasoline, even though the quantity demanded will decrease. The article indicates that as gasoline prices increase, consumers are not only cutting back on driving, but they also have less money to spend on other products. This illustrates the inelasticity of demand for gasoline because the reduction in driving represents the decrease in quantity

demanded, and spending less on other goods represents consumers devoting more of their budget to gasoline purchases.

**b** A survey of planned consumer spending indicates that nearly 75 percent of American consumers may reduce spending on other products if gas prices continue to rise. Also likely is a change in the demand for gasoline. As time passes, if increasing gas prices persist, consumers will be better able to adjust their lifestyles to a point where they do not need to purchase as much gasoline as they used to. This change could materialize in several ways, including people moving closer to work or public transportation; people telecommuting for their jobs; and people purchasing more fuel-efficient vehicles. The more time that passes, the more elastic the demand for a product becomes. The figure below illustrates the effect of price elasticity increasing over time. Suppose that initially the price of gasoline is $3.00 per gallon, and $Q_1$ gallons of gasoline are being purchased. If the price of gasoline increases to $5.00 per gallon, then at first consumers will move up the demand curve, $D_{\text{Short run}}$, and the quantity of gasoline demanded will decline to $Q_2$. But if high gasoline prices persist, the demand for gasoline will become more elastic ($D_{\text{Long run}}$). As demand becomes more elastic over the longer time period, the quantity of gasoline demanded will decline further, to $Q_3$.

**c** It can take time for households and firms to respond fully to a rise in gasoline prices. Businesses may try holding off on raising prices due to increases in transportation cost but may ultimately find it in their best interest to raise prices. Households

may have to initially cut back on other purchases, but as time passes, they may also be able to decrease their dependence on gasoline. The ultimate effect of a rise in gasoline prices is difficult to predict. The unpredictability of prices by itself has the potential of slowing the economy down, which indicates how important changes in gasoline prices can be for an economy.

## Thinking Critically

1. Joe Ferris owns Joe's Gas-and-Go service station. Joe reads a newspaper article in which an economist describes the demand for gasoline as price inelastic. Remembering his principles of economics course from college, Joe comes to the following conclusion: "Because the demand for gasoline is inelastic, if I increase the price I charge, I will lose a few customers, but the price increase will more than compensate for the fact that I will be selling a smaller quantity of gasoline. Therefore, the revenue I earn from gasoline sales will increase." Briefly explain whether you agree with Joe's reasoning.

2. Suppose that initially the only sellers of gasoline in a town are conventional service stations. Then Wal-Mart and Costco decide to begin selling gasoline. They install service islands near their stores and sell gasoline for lower prices than the conventional service stations. What effect do these new gasoline sellers have on the demand curves faced by the conventional service stations?

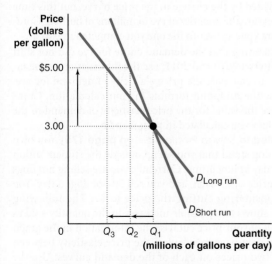

The demand for gasoline becomes more elastic over time.

# Chapter Summary and Problems

## Key Terms

Cross-price elasticity of demand, p. 185

Elastic demand, p. 173

Elasticity, p. 172

Income elasticity of demand, p. 186

Inelastic demand, p. 173

Perfectly elastic demand, p. 176

Perfectly inelastic demand, p. 176

Price elasticity of demand, p. 172

Price elasticity of supply, p. 190

Total revenue, p. 181

Unit-elastic demand, p. 173

---

**6.1** **Price Elasticity of Demand and Its Measurement, pages 172–178**

LEARNING OBJECTIVE: Define price elasticity of demand and understand how to measure it.

## Summary

**Elasticity** measures how much one economic variable responds to changes in another economic variable. The **price elasticity of demand** measures how responsive quantity demanded is to changes in price. The price elasticity of demand is equal to the percentage change in quantity demanded divided by the percentage change in price. If the quantity demanded changes more than proportionally when price changes, the price elasticity of demand is greater than 1 in absolute value, and demand is **elastic**. If the quantity demanded changes less than proportionally when price changes, the price elasticity of demand is less than 1 in absolute value, and demand is **inelastic**. If the quantity demanded changes proportionally when price changes, the price elasticity of demand is equal to 1 in absolute value, and demand is **unit elastic**. **Perfectly inelastic demand** curves are vertical lines, and **perfectly elastic demand** curves are horizontal lines. Relatively few products have perfectly elastic or perfectly inelastic demand curves.

MyEconLab    Visit **www.myeconlab.com** to complete these exercises online and get instant feedback.

## Review Questions

**1.1** Write the formula for the price elasticity of demand. Why isn't elasticity just measured by the slope of the demand curve?

**1.2** If a 10 percent increase in the price of Cheerios causes a 25 percent reduction in the number of boxes of Cheerios demanded, what is the price elasticity of demand for Cheerios? Is the demand for Cheerios elastic or inelastic?

**1.3** What is the midpoint method for calculating price elasticity of demand? How else can you calculate the price elasticity of demand? What is the advantage of the midpoint method?

**1.4** Draw a graph of a perfectly inelastic demand curve. Think of a product that would have a perfectly inelastic demand curve. Explain why demand for this product would be perfectly inelastic.

## Problems and Applications

**1.5** In the 2010 holiday season, Steve Richardson decided to cut the prices of his hand-crafted wooden puzzles to increase sales. According to a newspaper account, "the number of orders at Stave Puzzles Inc., his Norwich, Vt., business, hasn't been enough to offset the price cuts." Is the demand for these puzzles elastic or inelastic? Briefly explain.

Based on Emily Maltby, "In Season of Big Discounts, Small Shops Suffer," *Wall Street Journal*, November 24, 2010.

**1.6** The following table gives data on the price of rye and the number of bushels of rye sold in 2010 and 2011:

| Year | Price (dollars per bushel) | Quantity (bushels) |
|------|---------------------------|--------------------|
| 2010 | $3.00 | 8 million |
| 2011 | 2.00 | 12 million |

a. Calculate the change in the quantity of rye demanded divided by the change in the price of rye. Measure the quantity of rye in bushels.

b. Calculate the change in the quantity of rye demanded divided by the change in the price of rye, but this time measure the quantity of rye in millions of bushels. Compare your answer to the one you computed in part a.

c. Assuming that the demand curve for rye did not shift between 2010 and 2011, use the information in the table to calculate the price elasticity of demand for rye. Use the midpoint formula in your calculation. Compare the value for the price elasticity of demand to the values you calculated in parts a and b.

**1.7** **[Related to** Solved Problem 6.1 **on page 175]** You own a hot dog stand that you set up outside the student union every day at lunchtime. Currently, you are selling hot dogs for a price of $3 each, and you sell 30 hot dogs a day. You are considering cutting the price to $2. The following graph shows two possible increases in the quantity sold as a result of your price cut. Use the information in the graph on the next page to calculate the price elasticity between these two prices on each of the demand curves. Use the midpoint formula to calculate the price elasticities.

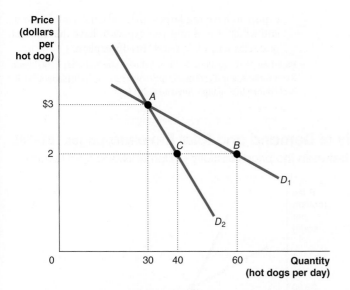

**1.8** In the fall of 2006, Pace University in New York raised its annual tuition from $24,751 to $29,454. Freshman enrollment declined from 1,469 in the fall of 2005 to 1,131 in the fall of 2006. Assuming that the demand curve for places in the freshman class at Pace did not shift between 2005 and 2006, use this information to calculate the price elasticity of demand. Use the midpoint formula in your calculation. Is the demand for places in Pace's freshman class elastic or inelastic? Did the total amount of tuition Pace received from its freshman class rise or fall in 2006 compared with 2005?

Based on Karen W. Arenson, "At Universities, Plum Post at Top Is Now Shaky," *New York Times*, January 9, 2007.

**1.9** In 1916, the Ford Motor Company sold 500,000 Model T Fords at a price of $440 each. Henry Ford believed that he could increase sales of the Model T by 1,000 cars for every dollar he cut the price. Use this information to calculate the price elasticity of demand for Model T Fords. Use the midpoint formula in your calculation.

**1.10** **[Related to the** Don't Let This Happen to You **on page 178]** The publisher of a magazine gives his staff the following information:

| Current price | $2.00 per issue |
| --- | --- |
| Current sales | 150,000 copies per month |
| Current total costs | $450,000 per month |

He tells the staff, "Our costs are currently $150,000 more than our revenues each month. I propose to eliminate this problem by raising the price of the magazine to $3.00 per issue. This will result in our revenue being exactly equal to our cost." Do you agree with the publisher's analysis? Explain. (*Hint:* Remember that a firm's revenue is equal to the price of the product multiplied by the quantity sold.)

---

**6.2** | ## The Determinants of the Price Elasticity of Demand, pages 178–181

LEARNING OBJECTIVE: Understand the determinants of the price elasticity of demand.

## Summary

The main determinants of the price elasticity of demand for a product are the availability of close substitutes, the passage of time, whether the good is a necessity or a luxury, how narrowly the market for the good is defined, and the share of the good in the consumer's budget.

MyEconLab  Visit www.myeconlab.com to complete these exercises online and get instant feedback.

## Review Questions

**2.1** Is the demand for most agricultural products elastic or inelastic? Why?

**2.2** What are the key determinants of the price elasticity of demand for a product? Which determinant is the most important?

## Problems and Applications

**2.3** Briefly explain whether the demand for each of the following products is likely to be elastic or inelastic.
  **a.** Milk
  **b.** Frozen cheese pizza
  **c.** Cola
  **d.** Prescription medicine

**2.4** **[Related to the** Making the Connection **on page 181]** One study found that the price elasticity of demand for soda is −0.78, while the price elasticity of demand for Coca-Cola is −1.22. Coca-Cola is a type of soda, so why isn't its price elasticity the same as the price elasticity for soda as a product?

Based on Kelly D. Brownell and Thomas R. Frieden, "Ounces of Prevention—The Public Policy Case for Taxes on Sugared Beverages," *New England Journal of Medicine*, April 30, 2009, pp. 1805–1808.

**2.5** The price elasticity of demand in the United States for crude oil has been estimated to be −0.061 in the short run and −0.453 in the long run. Why would the demand for crude oil be more price elastic in the long run than in the short run?

Based on John C. B. Cooper, "Price Elasticity of Demand for Crude Oil: Estimate for 23 Countries," *OPEC Review*, March, 2003, pp. 1–8.

**2.6** According to an article in the *Wall Street Journal*, in 1999, when the average price of a gallon of gasoline was $1.19, the average household spent 4.0 percent of its income on gasoline. In 2008, when the average price of gasoline had risen to $4.06 per gallon, the average household spent 11.5 percent of its income on gasoline. During which year was the price elasticity of gasoline likely to have been higher? Briefly explain.

Based on WJS Staff "Income vs. Gas Prices, an Update," *Wall Street Journal*, August 4, 2008.

**2.7** The entrance fee into Yellowstone National Park in northwestern Wyoming is "$25 for a private, noncommercial vehicle; $20 for each snowmobile or motorcycle; or $12 for each visitor 16 and older entering by foot, bike, ski, etc." The fee provides the visitor with a seven-day entrance permit into Yellowstone and nearby Grand Teton National Park.

a. Would you expect the demand for entry into Yellowstone National Park for visitors in private, noncommercial vehicles to be elastic or inelastic? Briefly explain.
b. Of the three ways to enter the park—in a private, noncommercial vehicle; on a snowmobile or motorcycle; and by foot, bike, or ski—which way would you

expect to have the largest price elasticity of demand, and which way would you expect to have the smallest price elasticity of demand? Briefly explain.

Based on National Park Service, Yellowstone National Park, "Fees, Reservations, and Permits," http://www.nps.gov/yell/planyourvisit/backcountryhiking.htm, August 16, 2011.

---

**6.3**  **The Relationship between Price Elasticity of Demand and Total Revenue,** pages 181–185

LEARNING OBJECTIVE: Understand the relationship between the price elasticity of demand and total revenue.

## Summary

**Total revenue** is the total amount of funds received by a seller of a good or service. When demand is inelastic, a decrease in price reduces total revenue, and an increase in price increases total revenue. When demand is elastic, a decrease in price increases total revenue, and an increase in price decreases total revenue. When demand is unit elastic, an increase or a decrease in price leaves total revenue unchanged.

MyEconLab   Visit **www.myeconlab.com** to complete these exercises online and get instant feedback.

## Review Questions

3.1  If the demand for orange juice is inelastic, will an increase in the price of orange juice increase or decrease the revenue received by orange juice sellers?
3.2  The price of organic apples falls, and apple growers find that their revenue increases. Is the demand for organic apples elastic or inelastic?

## Problems and Applications

3.3  Economists' estimates of price elasticities can differ somewhat, depending on the time period and on the markets in which the price and quantity data used in the estimates were gathered. An article in the *New York Times* contained the following statement from the Centers for Disease Control and Prevention: "A 10 percent increase in the price of cigarettes reduces consumption by 3 percent to 5 percent." Given this information, compute the range of price elasticity of demand for cigarettes. Explain whether the demand for cigarettes is elastic, inelastic, or unit elastic. If cigarette manufacturers raise prices, will their revenue increase or decrease? Briefly explain.

Based on Shaila Dewan, "States Look at Tobacco to Balance the Budget," *New York Times*, March 20, 2009.

3.4  According to an article in the *New York Times*, in 2011 the Port Authority of New York and New Jersey was planning to increase the tolls on the bridges and tunnels crossing the Hudson River by as much as 50 percent. According to the article, "Revenue from the . . . higher tolls would raise an additional $720 million for the agency. . . ." Is the Port Authority assuming that the demand for using bridges and tunnels crossing the Hudson is elastic or inelastic? Why might the Port Authority be reasonably confident in this assumption?

Based on Michael M. Grynbaum, "Port Authority Seeks Big Tool Increase," *New York Times*, August 5, 2011.

3.5  Use the graph at the top of the next column for Yolanda's Frozen Yogurt Stand to answer the questions.
a. Use the midpoint formula to calculate the price elasticity of demand for $D_1$ between point $A$ and point $C$ and

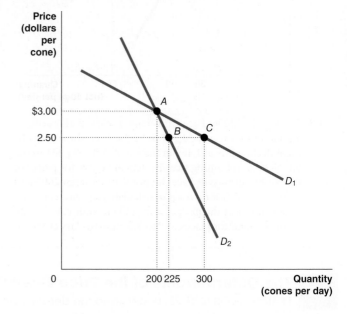

the price elasticity of demand for $D_2$ between point $A$ and point $B$. Which demand curve is more elastic, $D_1$ or $D_2$? Briefly explain.
b. Suppose Yolanda is initially selling 200 cones per day at a price of $3.00 per cone. If she cuts her price to $2.50 per cone and her demand curve is $D_1$, what will be the change in her revenue? What will be the change in her revenue if her demand curve is $D_2$?

3.6  A sportswriter makes the following observation: "The Yankees slashed some ticket prices. . . . Only the Yankees know exactly how much money this will cost them, but it makes sense that they're working to fill the empty seats around home plate." Is this sportswriter correct that the Yankees will lose money if they cut ticket prices? Briefly explain.

Based on Buster Olney, "Steroids Talk Kept Alive By More Than Just Media," Espn.com, April 29, 2009.

3.7  **[Related to** Solved Problem 6.3 **on page 184]** Briefly explain whether you agree or disagree with Manager 2's reasoning:
*Manager 1:* "The only way we can increase the revenue we receive from selling our frozen pizzas is by cutting the price."
*Manager 2:* "Cutting the price of a product never increases the amount of revenue you receive. If we want to increase revenue, we have to increase price."

3.8  **[Related to** Solved Problem 6.3 **on page 184]** If a firm increases the price of its product and its total revenue increases, will further increases in its price necessarily lead to further increases in its total revenue? Briefly explain.

3.9  Consider the following description of a pricing decision by an academic book publisher:

A publisher may have issued a monograph several years ago, when both costs and book prices were lower, and priced it at $19.95. The book is still selling reasonably well and would continue to do so even at $29.95. Why not, then, raise the price? The only danger is miscalculation: By raising the price you may reduce sales to the point where you make less money overall, even while making more per copy.

Assume that the situation described in the last sentence happens. What does this tell us about the price elasticity of demand for that book? Briefly explain.

From Beth Luey, *Handbook for Academic Authors*, Fifth Edition, (Cambridge, UK: Cambridge University Press, 2010), p. 220.

**3.10** In November 2008, parking rates were increased substantially for the "Big Blue Deck" at Detroit's Metro Airport. According to an article in a local newspaper, "In December, . . . after parking rates jumped from $10 to $16 a day . . . fewer cars used the Big Blue Deck compared to the previous year. . . . Still, the move at the North Terminal structure brought in about $61,000 more than the previous December." Use the information in the following table to calculate the price elasticity of demand for parking spaces at the Big Blue Deck, using the midpoint formula. Assume that nothing happened between December 2007 and December 2008 to shift the demand curve for parking places. Be sure to state whether demand is elastic or inelastic.

| Month | Rate | Revenue |
|---|---|---|
| December 2007 | $10 | $1,387,000 |
| December 2008 | 16 | 1,448,000 |

Based on Mary Francis Masson, "Metro Airport Parking Rate Hikes Worry Employees," *Detroit Free Press*, February 14, 2009; and Tanveer Ali, "Parking Dips; Revenue Soars," *Detroit News*, February 13, 2009.

**3.11** The Delaware River Joint Toll Bridge Commission increased the toll on the bridges on Route 22 and Interstate 78 from New Jersey to Pennsylvania from $0.50 to $1.00. Use the information in the following table to answer the questions. (Assume that besides the toll change, nothing occurred during the months that would affect consumer demand.)

| | Number of Vehicles Crossing the Bridge | | |
|---|---|---|---|
| Month | Toll | Route 22 Bridge | Interstate 78 Bridge |
| November | $0.50 | 519,337 | 728,022 |
| December | 1.00 | 433,691 | 656,257 |

a. Calculate the price elasticity of demand for each bridge, using the midpoint formula.
b. How much total revenue did the commission collect from these bridges in November? How much did it collect in December? Relate your answer to your answer in part a.

Based on Garrett Therolf, "Frugal Drivers Flood Free Bridge," *The Morning Call*, January 20, 2003.

**3.12** **[Related to the** Making the Connection **on page 184]** A publisher was quoted as saying the following about the pricing of e-books: "We may introduce [an e-book] at $14.95 for a year and then move the book to $9.99 when we would have put out the trade paperback edition. I suspect you're going to see a fair amount of experimentation." Why would issuing a paperback version of a book affect the price a publisher would charge for an e-book? Why would publishers be experimenting with the prices of e-books?

From Motoko Rich and Brad Stone, "Cost of an e-Book Will Be Going Up," *New York Times*, February 11, 2010.

---

**6.4** **Other Demand Elasticities,** pages 185–187

LEARNING OBJECTIVE: Define cross-price elasticity of demand and income elasticity of demand and understand their determinants and how they are measured.

## Summary

In addition to the elasticities already discussed, other important demand elasticities are the **cross-price elasticity of demand**, which is equal to the percentage change in quantity demanded of one good divided by the percentage change in the price of another good, and the **income elasticity of demand**, which is equal to the percentage change in the quantity demanded divided by the percentage change in income.

 MyEconLab   Visit **www.myeconlab.com** to complete these exercises online and get instant feedback.

## Review Questions

**4.1** Define the *cross-price elasticity of demand*. What does it mean if the cross-price elasticity of demand is negative? What does it mean if the cross-price elasticity of demand is positive?

**4.2** Define the *income elasticity of demand*. Use income elasticity to distinguish a normal good from an inferior good. Is it possible to tell from the income elasticity of demand whether a product is a luxury good or a necessity good?

## Problems and Applications

**4.3** When lettuce prices doubled, from about $1.50 per head to about $3.00, the reaction of one consumer was quoted in a newspaper article: "I will not buy [lettuce] when it's $3 a head," she said, adding that other green vegetables can fill in for lettuce. "If bread were $5 a loaf we'd still have to buy it. But lettuce is not that important in our family."

a. For this consumer's household, which product has the higher price elasticity of demand: bread or lettuce? Briefly explain.
b. Is the cross-price elasticity of demand between lettuce and other green vegetables positive or negative for this consumer? Briefly explain.

Based on Justin Bachman, "Sorry, Romaine Only," *Associated Press*, March 29, 2002.

**4.4** In the graph on the next page, the demand for hot dog buns has shifted outward because the price of hot dogs has fallen from $2.20 to $1.80 per package. Calculate the cross-price elasticity of demand between hot dogs and hot dog buns.

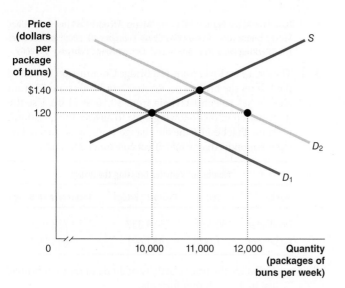

Sales of traditional S.U.V.'s are down more than 25 percent this year. In April, for example, sales of G.M.'s Chevrolet Tahoe fell 35 percent. Full-size pickup sales have fallen more than 15 percent this year, with Ford's industry-leading F-Series pickup dropping 27 percent in April alone.

Sales of traditional S.U.V.'s are down more than 25 percent this year. In April, for example, sales of G.M.'s Chevrolet Tahoe fell 35 percent. Full-size pickup sales have fallen more than 15 percent this year, with Ford's industry-leading F-Series pickup dropping 27 percent in April alone.

a. Is the cross-price elasticity of demand between gasoline and high-mileage subcompact cars positive or negative? Is the cross-price elasticity of demand between gasoline and low-mileage SUVs and full-size pickups positive or negative? Briefly explain.

b. How can we best think of the relationships among gasoline, subcompact cars, and SUVs? Briefly discuss which can be thought of as substitutes and which can be thought of as complements.

Based on Bill Vlasic, "As Gas Costs Soar, Buyers Flock to Small Cars," *New York Times*, May 2, 2008.

4.7 Rank the following four goods from lowest income elasticity of demand to highest income elasticity of demand. Briefly explain your ranking.
a. Bread
b. Pepsi
c. Mercedes-Benz automobiles
d. Laptop computers

4.8 **[Related to the** Making the Connection **on page 187]** Is the cross-price elasticity of demand between wine and spirits likely to be positive or negative? Can you think of reasons why the income elasticity of demand for wine is so much higher than the income elasticity of demand for spirits?

4.9 Consider firms selling three goods—one firm sells a good with an income elasticity of demand less than zero, one firm sells a good with an income elasticity of demand greater than zero but less than one, and one firm sells a good with an income elasticity of demand greater than one. In a recession, which firm is likely to see its sales decline the most? Which firm is likely to see its sales increase the most? Briefly explain.

4.5 Are the cross-price elasticities of demand between the following pairs of products likely to be positive or negative? Briefly explain.
a. Iced coffee and iced tea
b. French fries and ketchup
c. Steak and chicken
d. Blu-ray players and Blu-ray discs

4.6 **[Related to** Chapter Opener **on page 171]** During the spring of 2008, gasoline prices increased sharply in the United States. According to a newspaper article, rising gas prices had the following impact in the car market:

Sales of Toyota's subcompact Yaris increased 46 percent, and Honda's tiny Fit had a record month. Ford's compact Focus model jumped 32 percent in April from a year earlier. All those models are rated at more than 30 miles per gallon for highway driving. . . .

---

| 6.5 | **Using Elasticity to Analyze the Disappearing Family Farm**, pages 188–190 |
|---|---|
| | LEARNING OBJECTIVE: Use price elasticity and income elasticity to analyze economic issues. |

## Summary

Price elasticity and income elasticity can be used to analyze many economic issues. One example is the disappearance of the family farm in the United States. Because the income elasticity of demand for food is low, the demand for food has not increased proportionally as incomes in the United States have grown. As farmers have become more productive, they have increased the supply of most foods. Because the price elasticity of demand for food is low, increasing supply has resulted in continually falling food prices.

 MyEconLab    Visit **www.myeconlab.com** to complete these exercises online and get instant feedback.

## Review Questions

5.1 The demand for agricultural products is inelastic, and the income elasticity of demand for agricultural products is low. How do these facts help explain the decline of the family farm in the United States?

## Problems and Applications

5.2 **[Related to** Solved Problem 6.5 **on page 189]** According to a study by the U.S. Centers for Disease Control and Prevention, the price elasticity of demand for cigarettes is −0.25. Americans purchase about 360 billion cigarettes each year.
a. If the federal tax on cigarettes were increased enough to cause a 50 percent increase in the price of cigarettes, what would be the effect on the quantity of cigarettes demanded?
b. Is raising the tax on cigarettes a more effective way to reduce smoking if the demand for cigarettes is elastic or if it is inelastic? Briefly explain.

Based on "Response to Increases in Cigarette Prices by Race/Ethnicity, Income, and Age Groups—United States, 1976–1993," *Morbidity and Mortality Weekly Report*, July 31, 1998.

5.3 **[Related to** Solved Problem 6.5 **on page 189]** Suppose that the long-run price elasticity of demand for gasoline is −0.55. Assume that the price of gasoline is currently $4.00 per gallon, the quantity of gasoline is 140 billion gallons per year, and the federal government decides to increase the excise tax on gasoline by $1.00 per gallon. Suppose that in the long run the price of gasoline increases by $0.70 per gallon after the $1.00 excise tax is imposed.

   **a.** What is the new quantity of gasoline demanded after the tax is imposed? How effective would a gas tax be in reducing consumption of gasoline in the long run?

   **b.** How much does the federal government receive from the tax?

   **c.** Compare your answers to those in Solved Problem 6.5 on page 189.

**5.4** Corruption has been a significant problem in Iraq. Opening and running a business in Iraq usually requires paying multiple bribes to government officials. We can think of there being a demand and supply for bribes, with the curves having the usual shapes: The demand for bribes will be downward sloping because the smaller the bribe, the more business owners will be willing to pay it. The supply of bribes will be upward sloping because the larger the bribe, the more government officials will be willing to run the risk of breaking the law by accepting the bribe. Suppose that the Iraqi government introduces a new policy to reduce corruption that raises the cost to officials of accepting bribes—perhaps by increasing the jail term for accepting a bribe. As a result, the supply curve for bribes will shift to the left. If we measure the burden on the economy from corruption by the total value of the bribes paid, what must be true of the demand for bribes if the government policy is to be effective? Illustrate your answer with a demand and supply graph. Be sure to show on your graph the areas representing the burden of corruption before and after the government policy is enacted.

  Based on Frank Gunter, "Corruption in Iraq: Poor Data, Questionable Policies," Working Paper, March 2009.

**5.5** The head of the United Kumquat Growers Association makes the following statement:

> The federal government is considering implementing a price floor in the market for kumquats. The government will not be able to buy any surplus kumquats produced at the price floor or to pay us any other subsidy. Because the demand for kumquats is elastic, I believe this program will make us worse off, and I say we should oppose it.

  Explain whether you agree or disagree with this reasoning.

**5.6** Review the concept of economic efficiency from Chapter 4 before answering the following question: Will there be a greater loss of economic efficiency from a price ceiling when demand is elastic or inelastic? Illustrate your answer with a demand and supply graph.

---

## 6.6   The Price Elasticity of Supply and Its Measurement, pages 190–194

LEARNING OBJECTIVE: Define price elasticity of supply and understand its main determinants and how it is measured.

## Summary

The **price elasticity of supply** is equal to the percentage change in quantity supplied divided by the percentage change in price. The supply curves for most goods are inelastic over a short period of time, but they become increasingly elastic over longer periods of time. Perfectly inelastic supply curves are vertical lines, and perfectly elastic supply curves are horizontal lines. Relatively few products have perfectly elastic or perfectly inelastic supply curves.

 Visit **www.myeconlab.com** to complete these exercises online and get instant feedback.

## Review Questions

**6.1** Write the formula for the price elasticity of supply. If an increase of 10 percent in the price of frozen pizzas results in a 9 percent increase in the quantity of frozen pizzas supplied, what is the price elasticity of supply for frozen pizzas? Is the supply of pizzas elastic or inelastic?

**6.2** What is the main determinant of the price elasticity of supply?

## Problems and Applications

**6.3** [Related to the Making the Connection **on page 191**] Refer again to the first graph in the *Making the Connection* on page 191. Suppose that demand had stayed at the level indicated in the graph, with the equilibrium price of oil remaining at $140 per barrel. Over long periods of time, high oil prices lead to greater increases in the quantity of oil supplied. In other words, the price elasticity of supply for oil increases. This happens because higher prices provide an economic incentive to recover oil from more costly sources, such as under the oceans, from tar sands, or at greater depths in the earth. If the supply of oil becomes more elastic, explain how the increase in demand shown in the figure will result in a lower equilibrium price than $140 per barrel and a higher equilibrium quantity than 84 million barrels per day. Illustrate your answer with a demand and supply graph.

**6.4** Use the midpoint formula for calculating elasticity to calculate the price elasticity of supply between point *A* and point *B* for each panel of Figure 6.5 on page 194.

**6.5** Briefly explain whether you agree with the following statement: "The longer the period of time following an increase in the demand for apples, the greater the increase in the equilibrium quantity of apples and the smaller the increase in the equilibrium price."

**6.6** Consider an increase in the demand for petroleum engineers in the United States. How would the supply of these engineers respond in the short run and in the long run? Conversely, consider a decrease in demand for lawyers. How would the supply of lawyers respond in the short run and in the long run?

**6.7** On most days, the price of a rose is $1, and 8,000 roses are purchased. On Valentine's Day, the price of a rose jumps to $2, and 30,000 roses are purchased.

   **a.** Draw a demand and supply graph that shows why the price jumps.

   **b.** Based on this information, what do we know about the price elasticity of demand for roses? What do we know about the price elasticity of supply for roses? Calculate values for the price elasticity of demand and the price elasticity of supply or explain why you can't calculate these values.

## Chapter Outline and Learning Objectives

# Small Businesses Feel the Pinch of Escalating Health Care Costs

Elizabeth Crowell and her husband, Robert Wilson, own two antique stores in Brooklyn, New York. Like other small business owners, they face various challenges as they compete with the many similar stores in their area. But in 2011, Elizabeth and Robert were most concerned with paying Empire Blue Cross for health insurance for their family and their employees. In 2010, the premium—the payment a firm or an individual makes to buy health insurance—increased by 20 percent, and in 2011, the premium increased by 25 percent. Elizabeth said that: "It's the only cost in my business that's unmanageable. . . . If you have a cost to a business that jumps 20% to 25% a year, it's unsustainable."

Elizabeth and Robert were not alone in worrying about escalating health care costs. For several decades, health care spending has been steadily increasing as a fraction of gross domestic product (GDP), which is the value of the total production of goods and services in the economy. Health care spending increased from 5.2 percent of GDP in 1960 to 17.5 percent in 2011, an upward trend that is expected to continue. The federal government provides medical insurance to people aged 65 and older under the Medicare program, and the federal and state governments provide medical insurance to low-income people under the Medicaid program. The U.S. Congressional Budget Office projects that Medicare and Medicaid spending will increase from 5.6 percent of GDP in 2011 to nearly 12 percent in 2050. If governments do not reduce spending on these programs, they will have to sharply increase taxes or reduce spending on other programs.

In 2010, President Obama and Congress enacted the Patient Protection and Affordable Care Act, which made major changes to the U.S. health care system. The changes are being phased in through 2014. Included in the act is a provision for each state to set up health insurance exchanges to make health insurance less expensive for small businesses and individuals by allowing them to enter an insurance pool where both healthy and sick people will be in the same insurance plan and pay the same insurance premium. In 2011, economists and policymakers debated whether the health insurance exchanges would succeed in lowering health care premiums for small businesses and individuals.

**AN INSIDE LOOK AT POLICY** on **page 230** discusses government projections of future health care costs.

Based on Judith Messina, "Small Businesses Wary on Health Insurance Exchange," www.crainsnewyork.com, June 12, 2011; Celia Barbour, "The Ultimate Recyclers," *New York Times*, October 21, 2007; "Antique and Gift Store Owner Sold on Affordable Care Act," www.smallbusinessmajority.org; U.S. Center for Medicare and Medicaid Studies, "National Health Expenditure Data;" and U.S. Congressional Budget Office, "CBO's 2011 Long-Term Budget Outlook," June 2011.

## Economics in Your Life

### Why Is It Difficult for People Who Are Seriously Ill to Buy Health Insurance?

If you become ill and don't have health insurance, you are likely to be stuck paying large medical bills. Even a brief stay in a hospital can result in a bill of thousands of dollars. You may conclude that people with chronic illnesses are most likely to buy health insurance to help reduce their medical bills. But if you are chronically ill and don't currently have health insurance, buying it can be very difficult. Usually, people who demand a service can easily find a provider of that service. So, why is it difficult for people who are seriously ill to buy health insurance? As you read the chapter, see if you can answer this question. You can check your answer against the one we provide on **page 229** at the end of this chapter.

**Health care** The goods and services, such as prescription drugs and consultations with a doctor, that are intended to maintain or improve a person's health.

Health care refers to the goods and services, such as prescription drugs and consultations with a doctor, that are intended to maintain or improve a person's health. Improvements in health care are an important part of the tremendous increase in living standards people in the United States and other high-income countries have experienced over the past 100 years. Health care has seen rapid technological change with new products, such as MRI units and other diagnostic equipment; prescription drugs to treat cancer, high blood pressure, and AIDS; vaccinations for meningitis; and new surgical techniques, such as cardiac catheterizations for treatment of heart disease.

Health care is provided through markets, just as are most other goods and services such as hamburgers or haircuts. So, we can apply the tools of economic analysis we used in previous chapters to health care. But the market for health care has interesting features that make it different from other markets. In the United States, the doctors and hospitals that supply most health care are primarily private firms, but the government also provides some health care services directly through the Veterans Health Administration, which is part of the U.S. Department of Veterans Affairs. The government also provides health care indirectly through the *Medicare* and *Medicaid* programs. In addition to having a large government role, the market for health care differs from most markets in other ways. Most importantly, the typical consumer of health care doesn't pay its full price. Most people either have private medical insurance—most often provided through their employer—or they are enrolled in the Medicare or Medicaid programs. Consumers who have insurance make different decisions about the quantity of health care they wish to consume than they would if they were paying the full cost of the services they receive. As we will see, to analyze the market for health care we will need to use economic tools beyond those introduced in previous chapters. We begin our analysis of health care with an overview of health care around the world.

**7.1 LEARNING** OBJECTIVE

Discuss trends in U.S. health over time.

# The Improving Health of People in the United States

Two hundred years ago, the whole world was very poor by modern standards. Today, the average person in high-income countries has a standard of living well beyond what even the richest people in the past could have dreamed of. One aspect of this higher standard of living is the improved health the average person enjoys. For example, in the late 1700s, England had the highest level of income per person of any large country. But the average person in England had a short life span and suffered from diseases, such as cholera, yellow fever, dysentery, and smallpox, that have disappeared from high-income countries today. The average life expectancy at birth was only 38 years, and 30 percent of the population died before reaching the age of 30. Even people who survived to age 20 could only expect to live an average of 34 more years. In 2011, the average life expectancy at birth in the United Kingdom and other high-income countries was around 80 years. People in eighteenth century England were also short by modern standards. The average height of an adult male was 5 feet, 5 inches compared with 5 feet, 9 inches today.

In this section, we discuss the health of the average person in the United States. In section 7.2, we discuss the health of people in other countries.

## Changes over Time in U.S. Health

When economists measure changes over time in the standard of living in a country, they usually look first at increases in income per person. Changes in the health of the average person, though, are also an important indicator of changes in well-being and, therefore,

| Variable | 1850 | 2011 |
|---|---|---|
| Life expectancy at birth | 38.3 years | 78.4 years |
| Average height (adult males) | 5'7" | 5'9" |
| Infant mortality (death of a person aged one year or less) | 228.9 per 1,000 live births | 6.1 per 1,000 live births |

**Table 7.1**

**Health in the United States, 1850 and 2011**

*Note:* The data on heights for 1850 include only native-born white and black citizens. The data on heights for 2011 were gathered in 2003–2006.

Based on Susan B. Carter, et al., eds., *Historical Statistics of the United States: Millennium Edition*; U.S. National Center for Health Statistics, *Anthropometric Reference Data for Children and Adults: United States*, 2003–2006, October 22, 2008; U.S. Central Intelligence Agency, *World Factbook*.

changes in the standard of living. The health of the average person in the United States improved significantly during the nineteenth and twentieth centuries, and, by and large, it continues to improve today.

Table 7.1 compares some indicators of health in the United States in 1850 and 2011. Individuals in the United States today are taller, they live much longer, and they are much less likely to die in the first months of life than was true 150 years ago.

## The Rise and Fall and Rise of American Heights

A person's height relies partly on genetics—that is, tall parents tend to have tall children—but also on a person's *nutritional status*. Nutritional status depends on a person's food intake relative to the work the person has to perform, whether the person is able to remain warm in cold weather, and the diseases to which the person is exposed. Over time, people in high-income countries have, on average, become taller, just as people in high-income countries today are taller than people in low-income countries. Height, then, can be used as a measure of health and well-being in situations when other direct measures may not be available.

Take the case of the United States: Figure 7.1 shows changes in the average height of adult males born in the given years in the United States between 1710–1970, measured in centimeters. The trend has been upward, except for the period from 1830–1890, when the average adult male became about two inches shorter. This decline in height did not occur because incomes were falling during these years and people had to reduce their food purchases. Quite the opposite: The income of the average person in the United States was almost three times greater in 1890 than it had been in 1830. Instead, the nutritional status of the average person deteriorated as people moved from farms to cities. At that time, a lack of refrigeration made distributing meat and dairy products difficult in cities, so many people did not consume enough protein. More importantly, U.S. cities were very unhealthy places in the late nineteenth century. Most cities lacked basic sanitation, including sewers, clean drinking water, and regular garbage removal. People often dumped garbage into the streets and left it to rot. Not surprisingly, cities suffered from periodic epidemics of diseases such as cholera, dysentery, scarlet fever, diphtheria, and yellow fever that are largely unknown in the modern United States. The widespread acceptance in the late nineteenth century that diseases were caused by bacteria helped lead to the *public health movement* in the late nineteenth and early twentieth centuries, which eventually brought sewers, clean drinking water, and regular garbage removal to all U.S. cities. The improvement in sanitary conditions in cities and improvements in food distribution caused the increases in height that began around 1890. So, changes in the height of the average American over time can give us insight into health and well-being that we could not obtain by looking only at income.

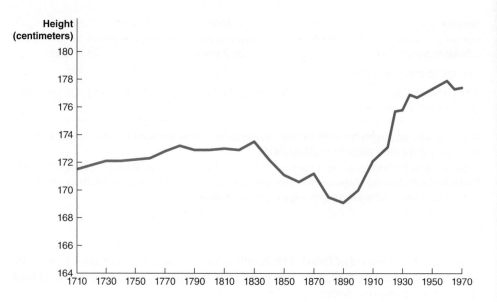

**Figure 7.1**

**The Average Height of Adult Males in the United States, 1710–1970**

The average height of adult males has increased over time in the United States, with the exception of the period from 1830 to 1890, when the average male born in those years lost 2 inches in height in part due to limited distribution of food, particularly protein, and poor sanitation in cities.

*Note:* Values are for native-born adult males.

Data from "The Average Height of Adult Males in the United States, 1710–1970" from *Historical Statistics of the United States: Millennium Edition*, Series Bd653 (Cambridge University Press, 2003); and Centers for Disease Control and Prevention.

# Reasons for Long-Run Improvements in U.S. Health

Apart from the temporary setback in the mid-nineteenth century, the health of people in the United States has steadily improved, with heights and life expectancies increasing and death rates decreasing. Panel (a) of Figure 7.2 shows the increase in life expectancy from 1900 to 2009 and the decline in the mortality rate, or death rate, measured as deaths per 100,000 people for the same years. Note that the mortality rate is "age adjusted," which means that it is not affected by changes in the age structure of the population. Life expectancy at birth in the United States increased from 47.3 years in 1900 to 78.2 years in 2009. Panel (b) in Figure 7.2 shows for recent years the change in the overall mortality rate of the U.S. population, measured as deaths per 100,000 people, and the age-adjusted mortality rates for several diseases. The overall mortality

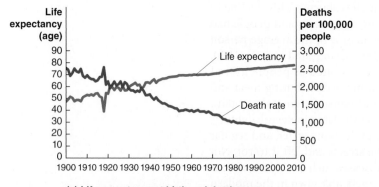

**(a) Life expectancy at birth and death rate per 100,000 people in the United States**

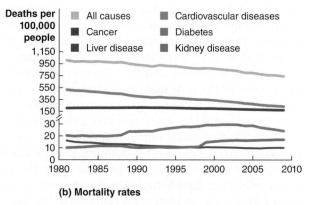

**(b) Mortality rates**

**Figure 7.2** **The Improving Health of the U.S. Population**

Since 1900, life expectancy in the United States has increased and mortality rates have decreased. Since 1981, there have been significant decreases in rates of death due to cancer, cardiovascular diseases, and diseases of the liver. Rates of death due to kidney disease and diabetes have increased as obesity have increased slightly. Note that in panel (a), the increase in mortality and decrease in life expectancy in 1918 are due to the severe influenza epidemic of that year.

Data from [Panel (a)]: Susan B. Carter et al., eds., *Historical Statistics of the United States: Millennium Edition*, Series Ab644; and Centers for Disease Control and Prevention, National Vital Statistics Reports, various issues; [Panel (b)]: "Age-Adjusted Mortality per 100,000 by Underlying and Multiple Cause, Ages 181: US, 1981–2009"; Centers for Disease Control and Prevention, National Center for Health Statistics, "VitalStats: Mortality," www.cdc.gov/nchs/vitalstats.htm.

rate decreased by more than 25 percent between 1981 and 2009. Over this same period, deaths from cancer, from cardiovascular disease, such as heart attacks and strokes, and from diseases of the liver all declined substantially. Deaths from diabetes and from kidney disease both increased slightly during this period, largely due to the effects of increasing obesity. The overall decline in death rates in the United States since 1981, was due to changes in lifestyle, particularly a decline in smoking, and advances in new diagnostic equipment, new prescription drugs, and new surgical techniques.

What explains the long-run increases in life expectancy and declines in death rates? We have already seen that improvements in sanitation and in the distribution of food during the late nineteenth and early twentieth centuries led to better health during that period. Nobel Laureate Robert Fogel of the University of Chicago and Roderick Floud of Gresham College, along with coauthors, have described a process by which better health makes it possible for people to work harder as they become taller, stronger, and more resistant to disease. Working harder raises a country's total income, making it possible for the country to afford better sanitation, more food, and a better system for distributing the food. In effect, improving health shifts out a country's production possibilities frontier. Higher incomes also allow the country to devote more resources to research and development, including medical research.

# Health Care around the World

**7.2 LEARNING** OBJECTIVE

Compare the health care systems and health care outcomes in the United States and other countries.

In the United States, most health care is provided by private firms, either through doctors' practices or hospitals. The main exception is the care the government provides through the network of hospitals operated by the federal government's Veterans Administration, although some cities also own and operate hospitals. Governments in most countries outside of the United States have a more substantial direct role in paying for or providing health care. Policymakers and economists debate the effects of greater government involvement in the health care system on health outcomes such as life expectancy, infant mortality, and successful treatment of diseases.

## The U.S. Health Care System

One important difference among health care systems in different countries is how people pay for the health care they receive. Most people in the United States have *health insurance* that helps them to pay their medical bills. **Health insurance** is a contract under which a buyer agrees to make payments, or *premiums*, in exchange for the provider's agreeing to pay some or all of the buyer's medical bills. Figure 7.3 shows the sources of health insurance in the United States in 2009. About 54 percent of people have private health insurance. Most people who have private health insurance receive it through their employer. In 2010, about 99 percent of firms employing more than 200 workers and

**Health insurance** A contract under which a buyer agrees to make payments, or *premiums*, in exchange for the provider's agreeing to pay some or all of the buyer's medical bills.

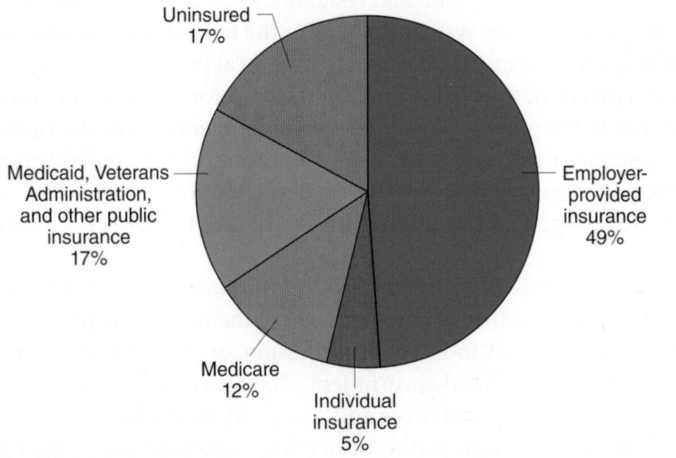

**Figure 7.3**

**Sources of Health Insurance in the United States, 2009**

A majority of people in the United States live in households that have private health insurance (provided by an employer or purchased directly). Government programs insure about 29 percent of the population.
Data from Kaiser Commission on Medicaid and the Uninsured; the Urban Institute; and the U.S. Bureau of the Census.

Pie chart labels: Uninsured 17%; Medicaid, Veterans Administration, and other public insurance 17%; Employer-provided insurance 49%; Medicare 12%; Individual insurance 5%.

**Fee-for-service** A system under which doctors and hospitals receive a separate payment for each service that they provide.

about 68 percent of firms employing between 3 and 199 workers offered health insurance as a fringe benefit (that is, a type of non-wage compensation) to their employees. Private health insurance companies can be either not-for-profit firms, such as some of the Blue Cross and Blue Shield organizations, or for-profit firms, such as Aetna and John Hancock, which typically also sell other types of insurance. Private health insurance firms sell *group plans* to employers to cover all of their employees or individual plans directly to the public. Some health insurance plans reimburse doctors and hospitals on a **fee-for-service** basis, which means that doctors and hospitals receive a payment for each service they provide. Other health insurance plans are organized as *health maintenance organizations (HMOs)*, which typically reimburse doctors mainly by paying a flat fee per patient, rather than paying a fee for each individual office visit or other service provided.

In 2009, 29 percent of people received health insurance either through Medicare, Medicaid, the Veterans Administration, or through some other government program. Seventeen percent of people were not covered by health insurance in 2009. Many people lack health insurance because their incomes are low, and they believe they cannot afford to buy private health insurance. Some low-income people either do not qualify for Medicaid or they choose not to participate in that program. About two-thirds of the uninsured live in families where at least one member has a job. These individuals either were not offered health insurance through their employers or chose not to purchase it. Some young people opt out of employer-provided health insurance because they are healthy and do not believe that the cost of the premium their employer charges for the insurance is worth the benefit of having the insurance. In 2009, 57 percent of the uninsured were younger than 34. Although 99 percent of firms with 200 or more employees offer health insurance to their employees, only about 63 percent of employees accept the coverage. The remaining employees are either covered by a spouse's policy or have decided to go uninsured because they do not want to pay the premium for the insurance. The uninsured must pay for their own medical bills *out-of-pocket*, with money from their own income, just as they pay their other bills, or receive care from doctors or hospitals either free or below the normal price. As we will see, addressing the problems of the uninsured was one of the motivations for the federal government's health care legislation enacted in 2010.

## The Health Care Systems of Canada, Japan, and the United Kingdom

In many countries, such as Canada, Japan, and the United Kingdom, the government either supplies health care directly by operating hospitals and employing doctors and nurses, or pays for most health care expenses, even if hospitals are not government owned and doctors are not government employees. In this section, we look briefly at the health care system in several countries.

**Single-payer health care system** A system, such as the one in Canada, in which the government provides health insurance to all of the country's residents.

**Canada** Canada has a **single-payer health care system** in which the government provides *national health insurance* to all Canadian residents. Each of the 10 Canadian provinces has its own system, although each system must meet the federal government's requirement of covering 100 percent of all medically necessary medical procedures. Individuals pay nothing for doctor's visits or hospital stays; instead they pay for medical care indirectly through the taxes they pay to the provincial and federal governments. As in the United States, most doctors and hospitals are private businesses, but unlike in the United States, doctors and hospitals are required to accept the fees that are set by the government. Also as in the United States, doctors and hospitals are typically reimbursed on a fee-for-service basis.

**Japan** Japan has a system of *universal health insurance* under which every resident of the country is required to either (a) enroll in one of the many non-profit health insurance societies that are organized by industry or profession, or (b) enroll in the health insurance program provided by the national government. The system is funded by a combination of premiums paid by employees and firms and a payroll tax similar to the tax that funds the Medicare program in the United States. Unlike the Canadian system, the Japanese system requires substantial *co-payments* under which patients pay as much as 30 percent of their medical bills, while health insurance pays for the rest. Japanese health insurance does not pay for most preventive care, such as annual physical exams, or for medical expenses connected with pregnancies, unless complications result. Health insurance in the United States and Canada typically does cover these expenses. As in the United States, most doctors in Japan do not work for the government and there are many privately owned hospitals. The number of government-run hospitals, though, is greater than in the United States.

**The United Kingdom** In the United Kingdom the government, through the National Health Service (NHS), owns nearly all hospitals and directly employs nearly all doctors. This is unlike in the United States, Canada, and Japan, where the government employs relatively few doctors and owns relatively few hospitals. Because there is only a small system of private insurance and private hospitals in the United Kingdom, its health care system is often referred to as **socialized medicine**. With 1.7 million employees, the NHS is the largest government-run health care system in the world. Apart from a small co-payment for prescriptions, the NHS supplies health care services without charge to patients, receiving its funding from income taxes. The NHS concentrates on preventive care and care for acute conditions. Elective care—such as hip replacements or reconstructive surgery following a mastectomy—is a low priority. The NHS's goals result in waiting lists for elective procedures that can be very long, with patients sometimes waiting a year or more for a procedure that would available in a few weeks or less in the United States. To avoid the waiting lists, more than 10 percent of the population also has private health insurance, frequently provided by employers, which the insured use to pay for elective procedures. The NHS essentially trades off broader coverage for longer waiting times and performing fewer procedures, particularly non-emergency surgeries.

**Socialized medicine** A health care system under which the government owns most of the hospitals and employs most of the doctors.

## Comparing Health Care Outcomes around the World

We have seen that the way health care systems are organized varies significantly across countries. Health care outcomes and the amounts countries spend on health care are also quite different. As Figure 7.4 shows, typically, the higher the level of income per person in a country, the higher the level of spending per person on health care. This is not surprising, because health care is a *normal good*. As we saw in Chapter 3, as income increases, so does spending on normal goods. The line in the figure shows the average relationship between income per person and health care spending per person. The dots for most countries are fairly close to the line, but note that the dot representing the United States is significantly above the line. Being well above the line indicates that health care spending

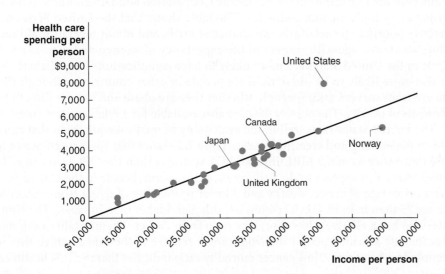

**Figure 7.4**

**Levels of Income per Person and Spending per Person on Health Care, 2009**

The United States is well above the line showing the average relationship between income per person and health care spending per person, which indicates that the United States spends more per person on health care than do other countries, even taking into account the relatively high levels of income in the United States.

*Note:* Income per person is measured as real GDP per person.

Data from the Organization for Economic Co-operation and Development, *OECD Health Data 2011*, June 2011.

**Table 7.2**    Health Outcomes in High-Income Countries

| Health Care Outcome | United States | Canada | Japan | United Kingdom | OECD average |
|---|---|---|---|---|---|
| **Life Expectancy** | | | | | |
| Life expectancy at birth | 78.2 years | 80.7 years | 83.0 years | 80.4 years | 79.3 years |
| Male life expectancy at age 65 | 17.3 years | 18.1 years | 18.2 years | 18.1 years | 17.1 years |
| Female life expectancy at age 65 | 20.0 years | 21.3 years | 24.0 years | 20.8 years | 20.4 years |
| Infant mortality (deaths per 1,000 live births) | 6.5 | 5.1 | 2.6 | 4.7 | 4.7 |
| **Health Problems** | | | | | |
| Obesity (percentage of the population self-reported) | 27.7% | 16.5% | n/a | n/a | 15.5% |
| Diabetes hospital admissions per 100,000 population | 57 | 23 | n/a | 32 | 21 |
| **Diagnostic Equipment** | | | | | |
| MRI units and CT scanners per 1,000,000 population | 60.2 | 19.4 | n/a | n/a | 27.2 |
| **Cancer** | | | | | |
| Deaths from cancer per 100,000 population | 104.1 | 113.3 | 94.8 | 115.8 | 114.7 |
| Risk of dying of cancer before age 75 | 11.2% | 11.8% | 9.7% | 11.9% | 12.0% |
| Mortality ratio for cancer | 39.5% | 40.4% | 52.3% | 47.6% | 48.1% |

*Note:* The data for the first six rows are the most recent available, typically 2009. For cancer, the data are for 2008, and the last column presents data for the 27 countries in the European Union rather than for the OECD. Cancer mortality rates are age adjusted, which means they are not affected by differences in age structure across countries. n/a means that there are no data available.

Data from the Organization for Economic Cooperation and Development, *OECD Health Data 2011*; J. Ferlay, H.R. Shin, F. Bray, D. Forman, C. Mathers, and D.M. Parkin, *Globocan 2008* v1.2, Cancer Incidence and Mortality Worldwide: IARC CancerBase No. 10, Lyon, France: International Agency for Research on Cancer, 2010, http://globocan.iarc.fr; and Mark Pearson, "Why Does the United States Spend So Much More Than other Countries?" Written Statement of Mark Pearson, Head, Health Division, OECD, to Senate Special Committee on Aging, September 30, 2009.

per person in the United States is higher than in other countries, even taking into account the relatively high income levels in the United States. Later in this chapter, we will discuss explanations for the high levels of health care spending in the United States.

Have the high levels of spending on health care in the United States resulted in better health outcomes? Are people in the United States healthier, and do they have their medical problems addressed more rapidly than do people in the other countries? Table 7.2 compares several health care outcomes for the countries that are members of the Organization for Economic Cooperation and Development (OECD), a group of 34 high-income countries. The table shows that the United States does relatively poorly in terms of life expectancy at birth, and infant mortality, although it does about average with respect to life expectancy of women and men at age 65. People in the United States are more likely to have complications from diabetes and are also more likely to be obese than are people in other countries, although these data are from surveys asking people whether they are obese and are not direct measurements of obesity. The obesity data are also available for a relatively few countries.

The United States rates well in the availability of medical equipment that can be used in diagnosing and treating illness. Table 7.2 shows that the United States has more than twice as many MRI units and CT scanners than the OECD average. The United States also appears to do well in cancer treatment. People in the United States have a lower rate of cancer deaths and a lower probability of dying from cancer before age 75 than in most OECD countries, although higher than in Japan. The United States also has a relatively low mortality ratio from cancer. The mortality ratio measures the rate at which people die from cancer relative to the rate at which they are diagnosed with cancer. A low cancer mortality ratio indicates that the U.S. health care system does a relatively good job of reducing the death rate among people diagnosed with cancer.

How useful are cross-country comparisons of health care outcomes in measuring the effectiveness of different health care systems? Health economists and other researchers disagree strongly about the answer to this question. We can consider some of the difficulties in making cross-country comparisons in health care outcomes:

- *Data problems.* Countries do not always collect data on diseases and other health problems in the same way. So, there are not enough consistent data available to compare health care outcomes for more than a few diseases.

- *Problems with measuring health care delivery.* The easiest outcomes to measure are deaths because a specific event has occurred. So, measures of life expectancy, infant mortality, and mortality rates from some diseases, such as cancer, are available across countries. But much of health care involves care of injuries, simple surgical procedures, writing pharmaceutical prescriptions, and other activities where outcomes are difficult to measure. For example, although the United Kingdom does well in many of the measures shown in Table 7.2, patients there have long waiting times for elective surgical procedures that can be arranged much more quickly in some other countries, including the United States. Measuring the cost of these waiting times to patients is difficult, however.

- *Problems with distinguishing health care effectiveness from lifestyle choices.* Health care outcomes depend partly on the effectiveness of doctors and hospitals in delivering medical services. But they also depend on the choices of individuals. So, for example, in the United States the high rates of obesity and hospitalizations for diabetes—which can be a complication of obesity—may be caused more by the decisions individuals make about diet and exercise than by the effectiveness of the U.S. health care system.

- *Problems with determining consumer preferences.* In most markets, we can assume that the quantities and prices we observe reflect the interactions of the preferences of consumers (demand) with the costs to firms of producing goods and services (supply). Given their incomes and their preferences, consumers compare the prices of different goods and services when making their buying decisions. The prices firms charge represent the costs of providing the good or service. In the market for health care, however, the government plays the dominant role in supplying the service in most countries other than the United States, so the cost of the service is not fully represented in its price, which in some countries is zero. Even in countries where consumers must pay for medical services, the prices they pay usually do not represent the cost of providing the service. In the United States, for instance, consumers with private health insurance typically pay only 10 percent to 20 percent of the price as a co-payment. For these reasons, it is difficult to determine whether some countries do a better job than others in providing health care services whose cost and effectiveness are consistent with consumer preferences.

# Information Problems and Externalities in the Market for Health Care

The market for health care is significantly affected by the problem of **asymmetric information**, which occurs when one party to an economic transaction has less information than the other party. Understanding the concept of asymmetric information can help us analyze the actions of buyers and sellers of health care and health care insurance and the actions of the government in the health care market. The consequences of asymmetric information may be easier to understand if we first consider its effect on the market for used automobiles, which was the market in which economists first began to carefully study the problem of asymmetric information.

**7.3 LEARNING** OBJECTIVE

Discuss how information problems and externalities affect the market for health care.

**Asymmetric information** A situation in which one party to an economic transaction has less information than the other party.

## Adverse Selection and the Market for "Lemons"

Nobel Laureate George Akerlof, of the University of California, Berkeley, pointed out that the seller of a used car will always have more information on the true condition of the car than will potential buyers. A car that has been poorly maintained—by, for instance, not having its oil changed regularly—may have damage that even a trained mechanic would have difficulty detecting.

If potential buyers of used cars know that they will have difficulty separating the good used cars from the bad used cars, or "lemons," they will take this into account in the prices they are willing to pay. Consider the following simple example: Suppose that half of the 2010 Volkswagen Jettas offered for sale have been well maintained and are good, reliable used cars. The other half have been poorly maintained and are lemons that will be unreliable. Suppose that potential buyers of 2010 Jettas would be willing to pay $10,000 for a reliable one but only $5,000 for an unreliable one. The sellers know how well they have maintained their cars and whether they are reliable, but the buyers do not have this information and so have no way of telling the reliable cars from the unreliable ones.

In this situation, buyers will generally offer a price somewhere between the price they would be willing to pay for a good car and the price they would be willing to pay for a lemon. In this case, with a 50–50 chance of buying a good car or a lemon, buyers might offer $7,500, which is halfway between the price they would pay if they knew for certain the car was a good one and the price they would pay if they knew it was a lemon.

Unfortunately for used car buyers, a major glitch arises at this point. From the buyers' perspective, given that they don't know whether any particular car offered for sale is a good car or a lemon, an offer of $7,500 seems reasonable. But the sellers do know whether the cars they are offering are good cars or lemons. To a seller of a good car, an offer of $7,500 is $2,500 below the true value of the car, and the seller will be reluctant to sell. But to a seller of a lemon, an offer of $7,500 is $2,500 above the true value of the car, and the seller will be quite happy to sell. As sellers of lemons take advantage of knowing more about the cars they are selling than buyers do, the used car market will fall victim to **adverse selection**: Most used cars offered for sale will be lemons. In other words, because of asymmetric information, the market has selected adversely the cars that will be offered for sale. Notice as well that the problem of adverse selection reduces the total quantity of used cars bought and sold in the market because few good cars are offered for sale.

**Adverse selection** The situation in which one party to a transaction takes advantage of knowing more than the other party to the transaction.

## Asymmetric Information in the Market for Health Insurance

Asymmetric information problems are particularly severe in the markets for all types of insurance, including health care insurance. To understand this point, first consider how insurance works. Insurance companies provide the service of *risk pooling* when they sell policies to households. For example, if you own a $150,000 house but do not have a fire insurance policy, a fire that destroys your house can be a financial catastrophe. But an insurance company can pool the risk of your house burning down by selling fire insurance policies to you and thousands of other homeowners. Homeowners are willing to pay the certain cost represented by the premium they pay for insurance in return for eliminating the uncertain—but potentially very large—cost should their house burn down. Notice that for the insurance company to cover all of its costs, the total amount it receives in premiums must be greater than the amount it pays out in claims to policyholders. To survive, insurance companies have to predict accurately the amount they are likely to pay out to policyholders. For instance, if an insurance company predicts that the houses of only 2 percent of policyholders will burn down during a year when 5 percent of houses actually burn down, the company will suffer losses. On the other hand, if the company predicts that 8 percent of houses will burn down when only 5 percent actually do, the company will have charged premiums that are too high. A company that charges premiums that are too high will lose customers to other companies and may eventually be driven out of business.

**Adverse Selection in the Market for Health Insurance**  One obstacle to health insurance companies accurately predicting the number of claims policyholders will make is that buyers of health insurance policies always know more about the state of their health—and, therefore, how likely they are to submit medical bills for payment—than will the insurance companies. In other words, insurance companies face an adverse selection problem because sick people are more likely to want health insurance than are healthy people. If insurance companies have trouble determining who is healthy and who is sick, they will end up setting their premiums too low and will fail to cover their costs. An insurance company that finds that the premiums it is charging are too low to cover the costs of the claims being submitted faces a problem. The company might try to increase the premiums it charges, but this runs the risk of making the adverse selection problem worse. If premiums rise, then younger, healthier people who rarely visit the doctor or have to be hospitalized may respond to the increase in premiums by dropping their insurance. The insurance company will then find its adverse selection problem has been made worse because its policyholders will be less healthy on average than they were before the premium increase. The situation is similar to that facing a used car buyer who knows that adverse selection is a problem in the used car market and decides to compensate for it by lowering the price he is willing to pay for a car. The lower price will reduce the number of sellers of good cars willing to sell to him, making his adverse selection problem worse.

One controversial way to deal with the problem of adverse selection is to require individuals to buy health insurance. Most states require drivers to buy automobile insurance, so that both high-risk and low-risk drivers will carry insurance. The Patient Protection and Affordable Care Act (PPACA) passed in 2010 requires that beginning in 2014 residents of the United States must carry insurance or pay a fine. This provision of the law is known as the *individual mandate*. We discuss it further later in the chapter.

**Moral Hazard in the Market for Health Insurance**  The insurance market is subject to a second consequence of asymmetric information. **Moral hazard** refers to actions people take after they have entered into a transaction that make the other party to the transaction worse off. Moral hazard in the insurance market occurs when people change their behavior after becoming insured. For example, once a firm has taken out a fire insurance policy on a warehouse, it might be reluctant to install an expensive sprinkler system. Similarly, someone with health insurance may visit the doctor for treatment of a cold or other minor illness, when he would not do so without the insurance. Or someone with health insurance might engage in risky activities, such as riding a motorcycle, that she would avoid if she lacked insurance.

> **Moral hazard** The actions people take after they have entered into a transaction that make the other party to the transaction worse off.

One way to think about the basic moral hazard problem with insurance is to note that normally there are two parties to an economic transaction: the buyer and the seller. The insurance company becomes a third party to the purchase of medical services because the insurance company, rather than the patient, pays for some or all of the service. For this reason, economists refer to traditional health insurance as a *third-party payer* system. The third-party payer system means that consumers of health care do not pay a price that reflects the full cost of providing the service. This lower price leads consumers to use more health care than they otherwise would.

Third-party payer health insurance can also lead to another consequence of moral hazard known as the *principal–agent problem* because doctors may be led to take actions that are not necessarily in the best interests of their patients, such as prescribing unnecessary tests or other treatments. The **principal–agent problem** results from agents—in this case, doctors—pursuing their own interests rather than the interests of the principals—in this case, patients—who hired them. If patients had to pay the full price of lab tests, MRI scans, and other procedures, they would be more likely to question whether the procedures were really necessary. Because health insurance pays most of the bill for these procedures, patients are more likely to accept them. Note that the fee-for-service aspect of most health insurance can make the principal–agent problem worse because doctors and hospitals are paid for each service performed,

> **Principal–agent problem** A problem caused by agents pursuing their own interests rather than the interests of the principals who hired them.

## Don't Let This Happen to You

### Don't Confuse Adverse Selection with Moral Hazard

The two key consequences of asymmetric information are adverse selection and moral hazard. It is easy to get these concepts mixed up. One way to keep the concepts straight is to remember that adverse selection refers to what happens at the time of entering into the transaction. An example would be an insurance company that sells a life insurance policy to a terminally ill person because the company lacks full information on the person's health. Moral hazard refers

to what happens after entering into the transaction. For example, a nonsmoker buys a life insurance policy and then starts smoking four packs of cigarettes a day. (It may help to remember that *a* comes before *m* in the alphabet just as *a*dverse selection comes before *m*oral hazard.)

MyEconLab

**Your Turn:** Test your understanding by doing related problem 3.9 on page 234 at the end of this chapter.

whether or not the service was effective. Many doctors argue that the increasing number of medical procedures is not the result of third-party payer health insurance. Instead the increase reflects the improved effectiveness of the procedures in diagnosing illness and the tendency of some doctors to practice "defensive medicine" because they fear that if they fail to diagnose an illness, a patient may file a malpractice lawsuit against them.

**How Insurance Companies Deal with Adverse Selection and Moral Hazard**
Insurance companies can take steps to reduce adverse selection and moral hazard problems. For example, insurance companies can use deductibles and coinsurance to reduce moral hazard. A deductible requires the policyholder to pay a certain dollar amount of a claim. With coinsurance, the insurance company pays only a percentage of any claim. Suppose you have a health insurance policy with a $200 deductible and 20 percent coinsurance, and you have a medical bill of $1,000. You must pay the first $200 of the bill and 20 percent of the remaining $800. Deductibles and coinsurance make the policies less attractive to people who intend to file many claims, thereby reducing the adverse selection problem. Deductibles and coinsurance also provide policyholders with an incentive to avoid filing claims, thereby reducing the moral hazard problem. Notice, though, that deductibles and coinsurance reduce, but do not eliminate, adverse selection and moral hazard. People who anticipate having large medical bills will still have a greater incentive than healthy people to buy insurance, and people with health insurance are still more likely to file claims than are people without health insurance.

To reduce the problem of adverse selection, someone applying for an individual health insurance policy is usually required to submit his or her medical records to the insurance company. Insurance companies usually also carry out their own medical examinations. Companies have often limited coverage of *pre-existing conditions*, which are medical problems, such as heart disease or cancer, that the buyer already has before purchasing the insurance. The limits that health insurance companies placed on pre-existing conditions typically lasted for one or two years or, occasionally, were permanent. Limits on pre-existing conditions have been very common in health insurance policies for individuals, but were also sometimes included in group policies, such as the policies companies sell to businesses providing coverage to their employees. Exclusions and limits on coverage of pre-existing conditions have been controversial. Critics argue that by excluding coverage of pre-existing conditions, insurance companies were forcing people with serious illnesses to pay the entire amount of what might be very large medical bills or to go without medical care. Some people with chronic or terminal illnesses found it impossible to buy an individual health insurance policy. The insurance companies argue that if they do not exclude coverage of pre-existing conditions, then adverse selection problems might make it difficult to offer any health insurance policies or might force the companies to charge premiums that are so high as to cause relatively healthy people to not renew their policies, which would make adverse selection problems worse. To some extent, the debate over coverage of pre-existing conditions is a normative one. Ordinarily, in a market system, people who cannot afford a good or service must do without it. Many people, though, are reluctant to see people not have access to health insurance because they cannot afford it. As we will discuss in the next section, the Patient Protection and Affordable Care Act passed by Congress in 2010 included significant restrictions on the ability of insurance companies to limit coverage of pre-existing conditions.

# Solved Problem 7.3

## Dealing with Adverse Selection

Private health insurance that has deductibles and co-payments can generate a lot of paper work for patients: insurance companies send patients statements indicating how much they owe doctors, doctors send bills asking for payment, and disagreements arise over which treatments are eligible for insurance. In 2011, the company Off Your Desk was offering consumers a service that would handle all the paperwork involved with health insurance for a fee of $65 per month. A newspaper article on the service noted that: "Still, the service does have an adverse selection problem. . . ."

**a.** What adverse selection problem does the firm face? Be sure to define adverse selection in your answer.

**b.** How might the firm attempt to deal with this adverse selection problem?

## Solving the Problem

**Step 1:** **Review the chapter material.** This problem is about adverse selection, so you may want to review the section "Adverse Selection in the Market for Health Insurance," which appears on page 215, and the section "How Insurance Companies Deal with Problems of Adverse Selection and Moral Hazard," which begins on page 216.

**Step 2:** **Answer part a by defining adverse selection and explaining how the concept applies in this example.** Adverse selection is the situation in which one party to a transaction takes advantage of knowing more than the other party to the transaction. In this example, Off Your Desk runs the risk of attracting a disproportionate number of customers who have extensive paperwork needs that will cost the company more than $65 per month to process.

**Step 3:** **Answer part b by explaining how the firm might deal with the problem of adverse selection.** The firm has strategies available: It could restrict its service to only covering bills its customers receive after they sign up. This strategy would reduce adverse selection by limiting the attractiveness of the service to customers who already had complicated billing questions that they needed help with and that would be likely to cost more than $65 per month to resolve. The strategy would be similar to health insurance plans that exclude coverage of patients' pre-existing conditions. The firm could also put a limit on the number of bills that it would process for the flat fee of $65. That strategy would avoid attracting customers who anticipate having many bills. In fact, Off Your Desk uses both strategies: It does not cover bills customers received before signing up for the service, and it will only cover the paperwork involved with 10 medical claims over a three-month period.

Based on Jennifer Saranow Schultz, "Outsourcing Insurance Paperwork," *New York Times*, January 19, 2011.

**Your Turn:** For more practice, do related problem 3.11 on page 234 at the end of this chapter.     MyEconLab

## Externalities in the Market for Health Care

For most goods and services, we assume that the consumer receives all the benefits from consuming the good and that the firm producing the good bears all of the costs of production. Some goods or services, though, involve an *externality*, which is a benefit or cost that affects someone who is not directly involved in the production or consumption of a good or service. For example, if a utility burns coal to produce electricity, the result will be air pollution, which causes a *negative externality* because people with asthma or other breathing problems may bear a cost even though they were not involved in buying or selling the electricity that caused the pollution. College education may result in a *positive externality* because college-educated people are less likely to commit crimes and, by being better-informed voters, more likely to contribute to better government policies. So, although you receive most of the benefits of your college education, other people also receive some of the benefits.

Externalities interfere with the economic efficiency of a market equilibrium. We saw in Chapter 4 that a competitive market achieves economic efficiency by maximizing the sum of consumer surplus and producer surplus. But when there is a negative externality in production, as with air pollution, the market will produce more than the efficient quantity. When there is a positive externality in consumption, as with college educations, the market will produce less than the efficient quantity. (A more complete discussion of externalities appears in Chapter 5, "Externalities, Environmental Policy, and Public Goods.")

Are there externalities involved with medicine and health care? There are several aspects of health care that many economists believe involve externalities. For example, anyone vaccinated against a communicable disease protects not just himself or herself but also reduces the chances that people who have not been vaccinated will contract the disease. There is some debate over whether obesity may involve a negative externality. People who are obese are more likely to suffer from heart disease, diabetes, or other medical problems. Obesity may involve an externality because people who are *not* obese may pay for some of the health care costs obese people incur.

Economists and policymakers debate whether the existence of externalities requires significant government involvement in health care.

| Making the Connection | Should the Government Run the Health Care System? |
|---|---|

During the debate over President Barack Obama's health care plan during 2009 and 2010, some members of Congress proposed expanding the federal government's role in health care by adopting a system similar to the single-payer system used in Canada under which the government would provide health care to all residents of the United States. What role the federal government should play in health care remains a controversial public policy issue.

Economists categorize goods on the basis of whether they are *rival* and *excludable*. Rivalry occurs when one person's consuming a unit of a good means no one else can consume it. If you consume a taco, for example, no one else can consume it. Excludability means that anyone who does not pay for a good cannot consume it. If you don't pay for a taco, for example, Taco Bell can exclude you from consuming it. A *public good* is both nonrival and nonexcludable. Public goods are often, although not always, supplied by a government rather than by private firms. The classic example of a public good is national defense. Your consuming national defense does not interfere with your neighbor's consuming it, so consumption is nonrivalrous. You also cannot be excluded from consuming it, whether you pay for it or not. No private firm would be willing to supply national defense because everyone can consume national defense without paying for it.

Is health care a public good that government should supply—or, at least, pay for? Is it a private good, like furniture, clothing, or computers, that private firms should supply and consumers should pay for without government aid? Should private firms supply most health care, subject to some government regulation? Economists differ in their answers to these questions because the delivery of health care involves a number of complex issues, but we can consider briefly some of the most important points. Because public goods are both nonrivalrous and nonexcludable, health care does not qualify as a public good under the usual definition. More than one person cannot simultaneously consume the same surgical operation, for example. And someone who will not pay for an operation can be excluded from consuming it. (Most states require hospitals to treat patients who are too poor to pay for treatment, and many doctors will treat poor people at a reduced price. But because there is nothing in the nature of health care that keeps people who do not pay for it from being excluded from consuming it, health care does not fit the definition of a public good.)

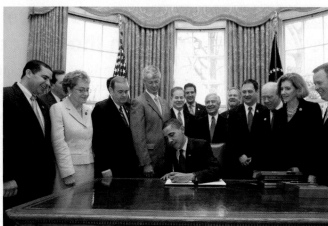

*Congress passed, and President Obama signed, the Patient Protection and Affordable Care Act in 2010.*

There are aspects of the delivery of health care that have convinced some economists that government intervention is justified, however. For example, consuming certain types of health care generates positive externalities. Being vaccinated against a communicable disease, such as influenza or meningitis, not only reduces the chance that the person vaccinated will catch the disease but also reduces the probability that an epidemic of the disease will occur. Therefore, the market may supply an inefficiently small quantity of vaccinations unless vaccinations receive a government subsidy.

Information problems can also be important in the market for private health insurance. Consumers as buyers of health insurance often know much more about the state of their health than do the companies selling health insurance. This information problem may raise costs to insurance companies when the pool of people being insured is small, making insurance companies less willing to offer health insurance to consumers the companies suspect may file too many claims. Economists debate how important information problems are in health care markets and whether government intervention is required to reduce them.

Many economists believe that market-based solutions are the best approach to improving the health care system. As we saw in Table 7.2 on page 212, the United States has a mixed record with respect to health care outcomes. The United States is, however, a world leader in innovation in medical technology and prescription drugs. The market-oriented approach to reforming health care starts with the goal of improving health care outcomes while preserving incentives for U.S. firms to continue with innovations in medical screening equipment, surgical procedures, and prescription drugs. Presently, markets are delivering inaccurate signals to consumers because when buying health care, unlike when buying most other goods and services, consumers pay a price well below the true cost of providing the service. Under current tax laws, individuals do not pay taxes on health insurance benefits they receive from their employers, and this encourages them to want very generous coverage that reduces incentives to control costs. As we will discuss later in the chapter, market-based approaches to health care reform attempt to address these issues.

It remains an open question whether the U.S. health care system will continue to move toward greater government intervention, which is the approach adopted in most other countries, or whether market-based reforms will be implemented. Because health care is so important to consumers and because health care spending looms so large in the U.S. economy, the role of the government in the health care system is likely to be the subject of intense debate for some time to come.

**Your Turn:** Test your understanding by doing related problems 3.13 and 3.14 on page 234 at the end of this chapter.    MyEconLab

**7.4 LEARNING** OBJECTIVE

Explain the major issues involved in the debate over health care policy in the United States.

# The Debate over Health Care Policy in the United States

Shortly after taking office in January 2009, President Barack Obama proposed far-reaching changes in the U.S. health care system. The result was the Patient Protection and Affordable Care Act (PPACA), which Congress passed in March 2010. The act was controversial, with every Republican member of Congress and 34 Democratic members of Congress voting against it. Economists vigorously debated its likely effects on health care and the economy. In the next section, we explore the issue of rising health care costs, which played an important role in the health care debate, before discussing the details of the PPACA and the debate over the legislation's effect.

## The Rising Cost of Health Care

Figure 7.5 illustrates a key fact underlying the debate over health care policy in the United States: Health care's share of gross domestic product, which is the total value of output in the economy, is increasing. Panel (a) shows that spending on health care was less than 6 percent of GDP in 1965, but had risen to about 17.5 percent in 2011, and was projected to rise to about 19.5 percent in 2019. In other words, an increasing percentage of total production in the United States is being devoted to health care. Panel (b) shows increases in health care spending per person in the United States and 10 other high-income countries. Spending on health care has grown faster in the United States than in other countries.

Does it matter that spending on health care is an increasing share of total spending and output in the U.S. economy? The shares of different products in total spending change frequently. For instance, in the United States, the shares of spending on cell

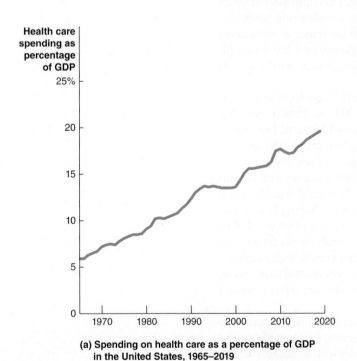

**(a) Spending on health care as a percentage of GDP in the United States, 1965–2019**

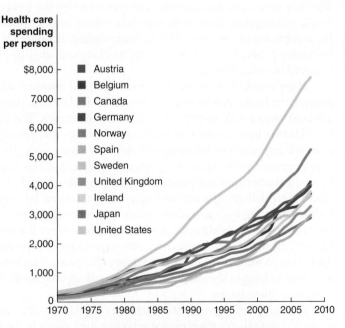

**(b) Health care spending per person, 1970–2008**

**Figure 7.5** **Spending on Health Care around the World**

Panel (a) shows that health care spending has been a rising percentage of GDP in the United States. Health care spending rose from less than 6 percent of GDP in 1965 to about 17.5 percent in 2011, and it is projected to rise to about 19.5 percent in 2019. Panel (b) shows that health care spending per person has been growing faster in the United States than in other high-income countries.

Data from [Panel (a)]: U.S. Department of Health and Human Services, Centers for Medicare and Medicaid Services; panel (b): Organization for Economic Cooperation and Development, *OECD Health Data 2011*, June 2011.

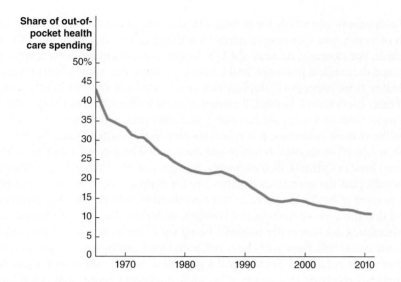

**Figure 7.6**

**The Declining Share of Out-of-Pocket Health Care Spending**

Out-of-pocket spending on health care has declined sharply as a fraction of all health care spending.
Data from U.S. Department of Health and Human Services, Centers for Medicare and Medicaid Services.

phones or LCD televisions were much greater in 2012 than in 2000. Spending on food as a share of total spending has been declining for decades. Economists interpret these changes as reflecting consumers' preferences—consumers choose to devote relatively more of their incomes to spending on cell phones and relatively less to spending on food. As we have seen, though, most people pay for health care by relying on third-party payers, such as employer-provided health insurance or government-provided Medicare or Medicaid. Out-of-pocket spending, spending on health care that consumers pay out of their own incomes rather than through health insurance, has been declining.

Figure 7.6 shows that out-of-pocket spending on health care as a percentage of all spending on health care has steadily declined since 1965. In 1965, 45 percent of all health care spending was out-of-pocket, while in 2011, only 11 percent was. As a result, in recent years, consumers of health care have been directly paying for only a small fraction of the true cost of providing health care, with third-party payers picking up the remainder. As average incomes rise, consumers might be expected to spend a rising share of the increase on health care. But because consumers do not pay the full cost of increases in health care spending, they may not be willing to buy as much health care as they currently receive if they had to pay the full price.

Because the federal and state governments in the United States pay for just over half of health care spending through Medicare, Medicaid, and other programs, increases in health care spending can cause problems for government budgets. The Medicare and Medicaid programs began in 1965. By 2010, spending on these programs had grown to 5.5 percent of GDP. That percentage is expected to more than double over the next 40 years unless health care costs begin to grow at a slower rate. In 2011, the federal government was struggling to find ways to pay for the projected increases in Medicare and Medicaid without severely cutting other federal spending or sharply raising taxes.

# Explaining Rapid Increases in Health Care Spending

In this section we briefly discuss some reasons economists believe that health care spending has been increasing rapidly in the United States. We start by reviewing explanations that are sometimes offered by policymakers and journalists, but that are unlikely to account for most of the increases in health care costs.

### Factors That Do Not Explain Sustained Increases in Health Care Spending

The two panels of Figure 7.5 show that spending on health care has been growing faster than the economy as a whole for at least the past several decades. Explaining the rapid growth of health care spending requires identifying factors that have more than a one-time effect. For example, because the U.S. health care system relies on many independent hospitals, medical practices, and insurance companies, some observers argue that it generates more paperwork, duplication, and waste than systems in other countries. Even if this observation is correct, it cannot account for health care's rising share of GDP unless paperwork and waste are *increasing* year after year, which seems unlikely.

Unlike in most countries, it is relatively easy in the United States for patients who have been injured by medical errors to sue doctors and hospitals for damages. The Congressional Budget Office (CBO) estimates, though, that the payments to settle malpractice lawsuits plus the premiums doctors pay for malpractice insurance amount to less than 1 percent of health care costs. Other economists believe the CBO estimate is too low and that the costs of malpractice lawsuits, including the costs of unnecessary tests and procedures doctors order to avoid being sued, are as much as 7 percent of total health care costs. Still, these costs have not been significantly increasing over time.

Somewhere between 1 percent and 4 percent of health care costs are due to uninsured patients receiving treatments at hospital emergency rooms that could have been provided less expensively in doctors' offices. But once again, this cost has not been increasing rapidly enough to account for much of the increase in health care as a percentage of GDP.

**"Cost Disease" in the Health Care Sector** Some economists argue that health care suffers from a problem often encountered in service industries. In some sectors of the economy, particularly manufacturing and the production of goods, *productivity*, or the amount of output each worker can produce in a given period, increases steadily. These increases in productivity occur because over time firms provide workers with more machinery and equipment, including computers, with which to work, and because technological progress results in improvements in machinery and equipment and other parts of the production process. As workers produce more goods, firms are able to pay them higher wages. In service-producing industries, though, increasing output per worker is more difficult. In education, for instance, computers and the Internet have been useful, but most of education still involves a teacher standing in front of a classroom of students. Increasing the number of students per teacher year after year is not feasible. The same is true of medicine, where MRI units, CT scanners, and other medical technology have improved diagnosis and treatment, but most medicine still requires a face-to-face meeting between a doctor and a patient. As wages rise in industries in which productivity is increasing rapidly, service industries in which productivity is increasing less rapidly must match these wage increases or lose workers. Because increases in wages are not offset by increases in productivity in service industries, the cost to firms of supplying services increases.

William Baumol of New York University has labeled the tendency for low productivity in service industries to lead to higher costs in those industries as "the cost disease of the service sector." There is good reason to think that health care suffers from this cost disease because growth in labor productivity in health care has been less than half as fast as labor productivity growth in the economy as a whole. This slow growth in productivity can help explain why the cost of health care has been rising so rapidly, thereby increasing health care's share of total spending and output.

**The Aging of the Population and Advances in Medical Technology** As people age, they increase their spending on health care. Firms continue to develop new prescription drugs and new medical equipment that typically have higher costs than the drugs and equipment they replace. The aging of the U.S. population and the introduction of higher cost drugs and medical equipment interact to drive up spending on the federal government's Medicare program and on health care generally. Many newly introduced drugs and diagnostic tools are used disproportionately by people over age 65. Partly as a result, health care spending on people over age 65 is six times greater than spending on people aged 18 to 24 and four times greater than on people aged 25 to 44.

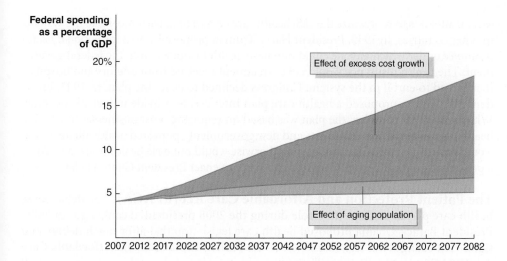

**Figure 7.7**

**Reasons for Rising Federal Spending on Medicare and Medicaid**

Although the aging of the U.S. population will increase federal government spending on the Medicare and Medicaid programs, increases in the cost of providing health care will have a larger effect on government spending on these programs.
Data from U.S. Congressional Budget Office, *Long-Term Outlook for Health Care Spending*, Washington, DC: U.S. Government Printing Office, November 2007.

In 2010, there were 47 million people receiving Medicare, and that number is expected to grow to 80 million by 2030. As we have seen, even in the absence of the development of new drugs and other medical technology, low rates of productivity in the health care sector could be expected to drive up costs. In fact, as Figure 7.7 illustrates, the CBO estimates that most of the increase in federal spending on the Medicare and Medicaid programs will be due to increases in the cost of providing health care, rather than to the aging of the population. In the figure, "effect of excess cost growth" refers to the extent to which health care costs per person grow faster than GDP per person. So, the combination of an aging population and increases in the cost of providing health care are an important reason why health care spending is an increasing percentage of GDP.

**Distorted Economic Incentives** As we noted earlier, some part of the increase in health care spending shown in Figure 7.5 on page 220 represents consumers choosing to allocate more of their incomes to health care as their incomes rise. But as we have also seen, consumers usually pay less than the true cost of medical treatment because a third party—typically, an insurance company or the government—often pays most of the bill. For example, consumers who have health insurance provided by their employers usually pay only a small amount—perhaps $20—for a visit to a doctor's office, when the true cost of the visit might be $80 or $90. The result is that consumers demand a larger quantity of health care services than they would if they paid a price that better represented the cost of providing the services. Doctors and other health care providers also have a reduced incentive to control costs because they know that an insurance company will pick up most of the bill.

In some important ways, health insurance is different from other types of insurance. As we discussed earlier, the basic idea of insurance is that the risk of an unpredictable, high-cost event—a house fire or a serious car accident—is pooled among the many consumers who buy insurance. Health insurance, though, also typically covers many planned expenses, such as routine checkups, annual physicals, vaccinations, and other low-cost events, such as treatment for minor illnesses. By disguising the true cost of these routine expenses, health insurance encourages overuse of health care services.

We discuss further the role of economic incentives in health care in the next section.

# The Debate over Health Care Policy

As we have seen, the United States has been unusual among high-income countries in relying on private health insurance—largely from firms—to provide health care coverage to the majority of the population. Most other high-income countries either provide health care directly, as the United Kingdom does, through government-owned hospitals and government-employed doctors, or they provide health insurance to all residents, as Canada does, without directly employing doctors or owning hospitals. There have been several attempts to reorganize the U.S. health care system to make it more like the systems in other countries. In 1945, President Harry Truman proposed a plan for *national health insurance* under which anyone could purchase health insurance from the federal government. The health insurance would cover treatment received from doctors and hospitals that agreed to enroll in the system. Congress declined to enact the plan. In 1993, President Bill Clinton proposed a health care plan intended to provide universal coverage. While somewhat complex, the plan was based on requiring most businesses to provide health insurance to their employees and new government-sponsored health alliances that would ensure coverage for anyone who otherwise would not have health insurance. After a prolonged political debate, Congress chose not to enact President Clinton's plan.

**The Patient Protection and Affordable Care Act (PPACA)**  The debate over health care played an important role during the 2008 presidential campaign. In 2009, President Barack Obama proposed health care legislation that after much debate and significant changes was signed into law as the **Patient Protection and Affordable Care Act (PPACA)** in March 2010. The act was long and complex, taking up over 20,000 pages and touching nearly every aspect of health care in the United States. Here is a summary of only the act's main provisions:

**Patient Protection and Affordable Care Act (PPACA)**  Health care reform legislation passed by Congress and signed by President Barack Obama in 2010.

- *Individual mandate*  The act required that, with limited exceptions, every resident of the United States have health insurance that meets certain basic requirements. Beginning in 2014, individuals who do not acquire health insurance will be subject to a fine. The fine will rise over time, reaching $895 per person or 2.5 percent of income, whichever is greater, by 2018.

- *State health exchanges*  Beginning in 2014, each state is to establish an Affordable Insurance Exchange. Separate exchanges are to be established for individuals and small businesses with fewer than 50 employees. The exchanges will be run by a state government agency or by a non-profit firm and will offer health insurance policies that meet certain specified requirements. The intention is that private insurance companies will compete by offering policies on the exchanges to individuals and small businesses. Low-income individuals and small businesses with 25 or fewer employees will be eligible for tax credits to offset the costs of buying health insurance.

- *Employer mandate*  Beginning in 2014, every firm with more than 200 employees must offer health insurance to its employees and must automatically enroll them in the plan. Firms with more than 50 employees must offer health insurance or pay a fee of $3,000 to the federal government for every employee who receives a tax credit from the federal government for obtaining health insurance through a health exchange.

- *Regulation of health insurance*  Insurance companies are required to participate in a high-risk pool that will insure individuals with pre-existing medical conditions who have been unable to buy health insurance for at least six months. All individual and group policies must provide coverage for dependent children up to age 26. Beginning in 2014, lifetime dollar maximums on coverage are prohibited. Limits are also placed on the size of deductibles and on the waiting period before coverage becomes effective.

- *Medicare and Medicaid*  Eligibility for Medicaid was expanded to persons with incomes up to 400 percent of the federal poverty line; in 2011, the federal poverty line was an annual income of $10,890 for an individual. In an attempt to control increases in health care costs, an Independent Payment Advisory Board (IPAB) was established with the power to reduce Medicare payments for prescription drugs and for the use of diagnostic equipment and other technology if Medicare spending exceeds certain levels. Some Medicare reimbursements to hospitals and doctors were reduced.

- *Taxes*  Several new taxes will help fund the program. Beginning in 2013, workers earning more than $200,000 will have their share of the Medicare payroll tax increase from 1.45 percent to a 2.35 percent, and investors who earn more than $200,000 will pay a new 3.8 percent tax on their investment income. Beginning in 2018, a tax will be imposed on employer-provided health insurance plans that have a value above $10,200 for an individual or $27,500 for a family. Pharmaceutical firms, health insurance firms, and firms producing medical devices will also pay new taxes.

The PPACA is scheduled to be fully implemented by 2019 at which point more than 30 million additional individuals are expected to have health care coverage. The Congressional Budget Office (CBO) has estimated that the law will increase federal government spending by about $938 billion over 10 years. The CBO estimates that the additional taxes and fees enacted under the law will raise over $1 trillion, which would be enough to pay for the plan and reduce the federal government's budget deficit by more than $100 billion over 10 years. Many economists have disputed this estimate, arguing that the law's new spending will increase the deficit.

**The Debate over the PPACA** Any law as far-reaching and complex as the PPACA is bound to draw criticism. As noted earlier in the chapter, the congressional debate over the law was highly partisan with every Republican ultimately voting against it and all Democrats in the Senate and all but 34 Democrats in the House voting in favor of it. Critics of the act can be divided into two broad groups: Those who argue that health care reform should involve a greater movement toward a system similar to the European, Canadian, and Japanese systems, and those who argue that health care reform should include more market-based changes.

As we discussed in the *Making the Connection* on page 218, some economists and policymakers believe that information problems and externalities in the market for health care are sufficiently large that the government should either provide health care directly through government-owned hospitals and government-employed doctors or pay for health care through national health insurance, sometimes referred to as a *single-payer system*. Although the PPACA significantly increased the federal government's involvement in the health care system, it stopped short of the degree of government involvement that exists in the Canadian, Japanese, or European systems. Critics in favor of moving toward greater government involvement typically argue that doing so would reduce the paperwork and waste caused by the current system or the system as it will be under PPACA. They argue that the current Medicare system—which is essentially a single-payer system for people over age 65—has proved to have lower administrative costs than have private health insurance companies. Supporters of greater government involvement in the health care system have also argued that the Canadian and European systems have had lower levels of health care spending per person and lower rates of increase in total health care spending, while providing good health care outcomes.

**Market-based reforms** of health care involve changing the market for health care so that it becomes more like the markets for other goods and services. As in other markets, the prices consumers pay and suppliers receive would do a better job of conveying information on consumer demand and supplier costs. The expectation is that increased competition among doctors, hospitals, pharmaceutical companies, and other providers of health care would reduce costs and increase economic efficiency. Economists who support market-based reforms as the best approach to improving the health care system were disappointed that the PPACA did not adopt this approach. Currently, markets are delivering inaccurate signals to consumers because when buying health care, unlike when buying most other goods and services, consumers pay a price well below the true cost of providing the service.

**Market-based reforms** Changes in the market for health care that would make it more like the markets for other goods and services.

## Making the Connection

### How Much Is That MRI Scan?

Magnetic Resonance Imaging (MRI) units play an important role in modern medicine. First introduced in the early 1980s, MRI units allow doctors to see inside the body's soft tissues to identify tumors, torn muscles, and other medical problems.

As we noted earlier, MRI units are more widely available in the United States than in most other countries. We would normally expect that when a product is widely available, competition among firms results in the price of the product being about the same everywhere. Customers would not buy a bestselling book from Amazon.com if the price was 50 percent higher than on BarnesandNoble.com.

Does competition equalize the prices of medical services? The data in the table below indicates that the prices of abdominal MRI scans vary widely. In most cities in the United States, the most expensive MRI scan has a price that is more than double the least expensive scan. Two reporters looking at prices for shoulder MRI scans in Pensacola, Florida, found that Sacred Heart Hospital was charging $800 for a shoulder MRI scan, while Pensacola Open MRI & Imaging, a private firm located less than one mile away, was charging $450 for the same scan. Pensacola Open MRI & Imaging was actually using newer MRI units that give higher resolution images, so they were charging less for a better service.

| City | Highest price | Lowest price | Difference |
|---|---|---|---|
| New York, New York | $9,300 | $2,400 | $6,900 |
| Orlando, Florida | 6,800 | 2,250 | 4,550 |
| Dallas, Texas | 6,500 | 2,100 | 4,400 |
| San Francisco, California | 7,200 | 2,850 | 4,350 |
| Chicago, Illinois | 6,100 | 2,100 | 4,000 |
| Omaha, Nebraska | 5,700 | 2,000 | 3,700 |
| Baton Rouge, Louisiana | 5,600 | 2,025 | 3,575 |
| Atlanta, Georgia | 5,500 | 2,100 | 3,400 |
| Lexington, Kentucky | 5,100 | 2,000 | 3,100 |
| Charlotte, North Carolina | 4,500 | 2,100 | 2,400 |

How can some providers of medical services charge hundreds or thousands of dollars more than competitors and remain in business? The answer is that most patients are unconcerned about prices because they do not pay them or pay only a fraction of them. Patients typically rely on doctors to refer them to a facility for an MRI scan or other procedure and make little or no effort to determine the price the facility charges. A goal of market-based reforms of the health care system is to give patients an incentive to pay more attention to the prices of medical services.

Based on Caitlin Kenney, "Shopping for an MRI," npr.org, November 6, 2009; MRI prices from newchoicehealth.com, August 21, 2011.

MyEconLab **Your Turn:** Test your understanding by doing related problem 4.10 and on page 235 at the end of this chapter.

Supporters of market-based reforms note that employees have to pay federal income and payroll taxes on the wages their employers pay them, but in most circumstances they do not pay taxes on the value of the health insurance their employers provide them. This feature of the tax laws encourages employees to want very generous health care coverage; in fact, if offered the choice between a $1,000 salary increase or increased health care coverage that was worth $1,000, many people would choose the increased health care coverage because it would be tax free (although someone who was young and healthy and did not expect to have medical bills would probably still choose the increase in salary). The size of this tax break is quite substantial—more than $250 billion in 2011. But individuals typically get no tax break when buying an individual health insurance policy or when they spend money on health care out-of-pocket.[1] Some economists have proposed making the tax treatment of employer-provided health insurance the same as the tax treatment of individually purchased health insurance and out-of-pocket health care spending. They argue that this change could, potentially, significantly reduce spending on health care without reducing the effectiveness of the health care received. Such tax law changes would make it more likely that employer-provided health insurance would focus on large medical bills—such as those resulting from hospitalizations—while consumers would pay prices closer to the costs of providing routine medical care. John Cogan of the Hoover Institution, R. Glenn Hubbard of Columbia University, and Daniel Kessler of Stanford estimate that repealing the tax preference for employer-provided health insurance would reduce spending by people enrolled in these programs by 33 percent.

Currently, the U.S. health care system is a world leader in innovation in medical technology and prescription drugs. About two-thirds of pharmaceutical patents are issued to U.S. firms and about two-thirds of research on new medicines is carried out in the United States. One goal of market-based reforms would be to ensure that U.S. firms continue with innovations in medical screening equipment, surgical procedures, and prescription drugs. Executives of U.S. pharmaceutical firms have voiced concern over whether aspects of PPACA will affect their ability to profitably bring new prescription drugs to market. In particular, managers at these firms worry that the new Independent Payment Advisory Board might reduce the payments Medicare would make for new prescription drugs.

Both critics of the PPACA who favor greater government involvement in health care and those who favor market reforms raise questions about the act's individual mandate. The individual mandate requires every U.S. resident to have health insurance. The mandate was considered necessary because otherwise healthy people might avoid buying insurance until they become ill. Because insurance companies would not be allowed to deny coverage for pre-existing conditions, they would end up paying large medical bills for people who had not been paying premiums to support the system while they were healthy. There were questions, though, about whether the requirement to buy health insurance would be enforceable. Although people who do not buy insurance are subject to fines under the act, there was no mechanism set up to collect the fines if people refused to pay them voluntarily.

## Making the Connection | Health Exchanges, Small Businesses, and Rising Medical Costs

We saw at the beginning of the chapter that for many small businesses, the cost of providing health insurance to their employees has become a heavy burden. A key provision of the PPACA was intended to address this problem. As noted earlier, by 2014, every state is obligated to set up an Affordable Insurance Exchange. Each exchange must operate a Small Business Health Options Program (SHOP) where private insurance companies will offer small firms health insurance plans that the firms can purchase for their workers. Small firms with up to 100 employees will be eligible to purchase health insurance through their state's SHOP. In addition, firms with fewer than 25 employees will receive a tax credit to offset up to 50 percent of the cost of providing health insurance to their workers.

The plan is intended to get over one of the key disadvantages small firms face when buying health insurance: limited risk pooling. When an insurance company sells health insurance to a large firm, the risk of illness and large medical bills is spread across many employees. Adverse selection problems are also reduced when a plan covers a large number of workers. When a firm employs only a few workers, as is the case with the New York antique store we discussed in the chapter opener, a single illness

---

[1]Individuals receive a deduction on their federal income tax only if their medical expenses are greater than 7.5 percent of their income. Only a relatively small number of individuals have expenses high enough to make use of that deduction. The threshold is being raised under the PPACA to 10 percent.

*Will the Small Business Health Options Program (SHOP) help small businesses keep health insurance costs down?*

can cause an insurance company to make payments far above the premiums it has received from the firm. Typically, the insurance company will then substantially raise the premiums the firm will pay. Even if none of the employees of a firm becomes ill, insurance companies concerned about adverse selection problems may raise premiums substantially over time. The owners of the antique store had to pay premium increases of more than 20 percent per year. Under the SHOP plan, a small firm's employees would be pooled with the employees of other small firms and premiums could differ across firms only on the basis of the age of the employees and whether the employees smoke. The federal government has given the states significant flexibility in designing the exchanges.

Will SHOP provide a solution to the difficulties small firms encounter in providing health insurance for their employees? Initially, the New York antique store owner was optimistic: "In the short run, the tax credits definitely give me money to potentially hire another employee. . . . I'm hopeful we'll see other benefits, especially all of the savings from the exchanges, in the long run." It is difficult to say how effective the exchanges will be, however, because they will not begin operating until 2014, and as of 2011 many states had not yet announced the rules under which their exchanges would operate. The failure of a health insurance exchange that the state of California ran from 1993 to 2006 shows one potential problem. Firms with relatively healthy workers found that they could buy health insurance more cheaply outside of the exchange. As they left the exchange, insurers needed to raise rates to cover the remaining pool of companies with less healthy workers. Higher rates led more firms to withdraw until finally the exchange collapsed. This process is sometimes referred to as an *adverse selection death spiral*. To succeed, the new health exchanges need to avoid this spiral.

The federal government hopes that the exchanges will improve the choices available to small businesses by requiring that insurance companies meet guidelines for the types of insurance they offer and the information they provide to these businesses. Supporters of the exchanges also hope that they will reduce administrative costs, which will allow insurance companies to offer plans with lower premiums. Some economists and policymakers, however, argue that by increasing the number of people covered by health insurance the exchanges were likely to increase the demand for medical services, further driving up their costs. If health care costs rise as a result, the exchanges would have to pass the costs along to businesses in the form of higher insurance premiums.

As of 2011, the health exchanges, as well as other aspects of the PPACA, were subject to lawsuits from states that claimed that the act violated the U.S. Constitution. Some members of Congress were also attempting to amend the act before it went fully into effect in 2014. The outcome of these political debates could potentially alter how the health exchanges would be run.

Based on "Affordable Insurance Exchanges: Choices, Competition and Clout for Small Businesses," healthcare.gov, July 11, 2011; Judith Messina, "Health Care Reform for Small Business: This Is Going to Hurt," *Crain's New York Business*, 2010; and Kaiser Family Foundation, "Establishing Health Insurance Exchanges: An Update on State Efforts," July 2011; "Antique and Gift Store Owner Sold on Affordable Care Act," www.smallbusinessmajority.org; and Michael Sanerino, "California Offers Lessons on Insurance Exchanges," *Wall Street Journal*, August 3, 2009.

MyEconLab **Your Turn:** Test your understanding by doing related problem 4.12 on page 235 at the end of this chapter.

Continued from page 205

## Economics in Your Life

### Why Is It Difficult for People Who Are Seriously Ill to Buy Health Insurance?

At the beginning of this chapter, we asked: Why is it difficult for people who are seriously ill to buy health insurance? Someone who is seriously ill can face frighteningly large medical bills. It is natural that such a person would like to purchase health insurance to help pay those bills. Unfortunately, insurance works best when it involves risk pooling for people who face an uncertain and high-cost event, such as their house burning down or being diagnosed with cancer. Insurance companies are naturally reluctant to provide insurance to someone who is already seriously ill because the premiums they receive from the person are certain to be less than the person's medical bills—which the insurance company will have to pay. In order to remain in business, insurance companies will either not insure people with preexisting medical conditions or will insure them only after a waiting period of perhaps years. The Patient Protection and Affordable Care Act (PPACA), which became law in 2010, attempts to make it easier for people with preexisting conditions to buy health insurance. Under the act, each state will run a health exchange that will offer individual health insurance policies to individuals who cannot be excluded because of preexisting conditions and who will pay premiums that can vary only by the buyer's age and whether the buyer is a smoker. Economists and policymakers debate whether the act will be effective.

## Conclusion

In this chapter, we have seen that economic analysis can provide important insights into the market for health care. As with many other policy issues, though, economic analysis can help inform the debate, but cannot resolve it. Because health care is so important to consumers and because health care spending looms so large in the U.S. economy, the role of the government in the health care system is likely to be the subject of intense debate for years to come.

Before moving on to Chapter 8, read *An Inside Look at Policy* on the next page for a discussion of health care spending and the Patient Protection and Affordable Care Act.

# Health Care Spending Expected to Increase 70 Percent by End of Decade

## ASSOCIATED PRESS

## U.S. Health Care Tab to Hit $4.6T in 2020

The nation's health care tab is on track to hit $4.6 trillion in 2020, accounting for about $1 of every $5 in the economy, government number crunchers estimate in a report out Thursday.

(a) How much is that? Including government and private money, health care spending in 2020 will average $13,710 for every man, woman and child, says Medicare's Office of the Actuary.

By comparison, U.S. health care spending this year is projected to top $2.7 trillion, or about $8,650 per capita, roughly $1 of $6 in the economy. Most of that spending is for care for the sickest people.

The report from Medicare economists and statisticians is an annual barometer of a trend that many experts say is unsustainable but doesn't seem to be slowing down. A political compromise over the nation's debt and deficits might succeed in tapping the brakes on health care, but polarized lawmakers have been unable to deliver a deal.

(b) The analysis found that President Barack Obama's health care overhaul would only be a modest contributor to growing costs, even though an additional 30 million people who would be otherwise uninsured stand to gain coverage.

The main reasons that health care spending keeps growing faster than the economy are the high cost of medical innovations and an aging society that consumes increasing levels of service.

Many of the newly insured people under the health care law will be younger and healthier. As a result, they are expected to use more doctor visits and prescription drugs and relatively less of pricey hospital care. Health care spending will jump by 8 percent in 2014, when the law's coverage expansion kicks in. But over the 2010–2020 period covered by the estimate, the average yearly growth in health care spending will be only 0.1 percentage point higher than without Obama's overhaul.

Part of the reason for that optimistic prognosis is that cuts and cost controls in the health care law start to bite down late in the decade. However, the same nonpartisan Medicare experts who produced Thursday's estimate have previously questioned whether that austerity will be politically sustainable if hospitals and other providers start going out of business as a result. The actuary's office is responsible for long-range cost estimates.

The report found that health care spending in 2010 grew at a historically low rate of 3.9 percent, partly because of the sluggish economy. That will change as the economy shakes off the lingering effects of the recession.

(c) Government, already the dominant player because of Medicare and Medicaid, will become even more important. By 2020, federal, state and local government health care spending will account for just under half the total tab, up from 45 percent currently. As the health care law's coverage expansion takes effect, "health care financing is anticipated to further shift toward governments," the report said.

Estimates from previous years had projected that the government share would already be at the 50 percent mark, but the actuary's office changed its method for making the complex calculations. Under the previous approach, some private payments such as worker's compensation insurance had been counted in the government column. Technical accuracy—not political pressure—was behind that change, said Stephen Heffler, one of the experts who worked on the estimates.

Separately, another new report finds that the United States continues to spend far more on health care than other economically developed countries. The study by the Commonwealth Fund found that U.S. health care spending per person in 2008 was more than double the median—or midpoint—for other leading economies. Although survival rates for some cancers were higher in the U.S., the report found that quality of care overall was not markedly better.

## Key Points in the Article

Government analysts predict that the cost of health care will reach $4.6 trillion in 2020, an average of $13,710 per person. The total cost in 2011 is expected to exceed $2.7 trillion, or about $8,650 per person. The high costs of medical innovation and an aging population are cited as the primary reasons for the rapid increase in health care costs. The implementation of health care reform is expected to contribute only modestly to this increase, with the government's share of spending rising from 45 percent to just under 50 percent of the total cost. A majority of this increase will be for Medicare and Medicaid payments, with the health care overhaul expected to account for an increase of only one-tenth of one percent. A number of analysts believe the continued increases in health care costs are unsustainable for the economy.

## Analyzing the News

(a) Spending on health care in the United States is increasing at a rapid pace, and it is expected to be roughly 20 percent of GDP by 2020. This means that one-fifth of total production in the United States will be devoted to health care, compared to one-twentieth in the mid-1960s. While health care spending as a percentage of GDP has been steadily growing, the percentage of this spending that is being paid directly by consumers has been steadily declining. The figure below shows both the increase in health

care spending as a percentage of GDP and the decrease in out-of-pocket health care spending by consumers as a percentage of all health care spending in the United States since 1965. These data show that while increasing amounts of production are being devoted to health care, consumers are directly paying a smaller and smaller percentage of the cost. The declining out-of-pocket spending, and subsequent increasing percentage of third-party payouts, is often cited as one of the reasons for the overall increase in health care spending.

(b) The rapid increase in health care spending is thought by many to be unsustainable without increases in taxes or decreases in other areas of spending. In 2009, President Obama proposed sweeping changes for the U.S. health care system, and the following year, he signed the Patient Protection and Affordable Care Act (PPACA) into law. There has been much debate as to whether this health care overhaul package will increase or decrease overall spending on health care, but an analysis by Medicare officials claims that the PPACA will result in only a 0.1 percent additional increase in annual health care spending over the next decade. If this projection is accurate, the PPACA will not significantly contribute to the continued increases in health care spending.

(c) One of the biggest concerns over the rise in health care spending in the United States is the government's increasingly large share of the overall cost. Due

primarily to Medicare and Medicaid, federal, state, and local governments already account for 45 percent of the nation's annual health care spending, and with the passage of the PPACA, this share is expected to rise to nearly 50 percent by 2020. If the current rate of increase in spending is truly unsustainable and the government will be responsible for a larger share of these increasing costs, major changes to government spending or taxes will need to be implemented to get health care costs under control. This will no doubt continue to be a topic of heated debate in Washington in years to come.

## Thinking Critically about Policy

1. Under the Patient Protection and Affordable Care Act (PPACA), every resident of the United States will be required to have health insurance, so up to 30 million people who would otherwise be uninsured will potentially have insurance coverage. Explain the effect that this increase in the number of insured people may have on the adverse selection problem and the moral hazard problem in the market for health insurance. How might this change affect total spending on health care?

2. Analysts and policymakers have described rapid increases in health care spending as unsustainable for the economy. In what sense are these increases unsustainable?

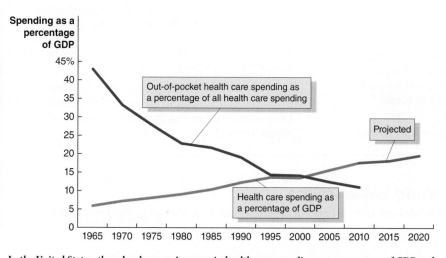

In the United States, there has been an increase in health care spending as a percentage of GDP and a decrease in out-of-pocket health care spending by consumers since 1965.

# Chapter Summary and Problems

## Key Terms

Adverse selection, p. 214

Asymmetric information, p. 213

Fee-for-service, p. 210

Health care, p. 206

Health insurance, p. 209

Market-based reforms, p. 225

Moral hazard, p. 215

Patient Protection and Afford-able Care Act (PPACA), p. 224

Principal–agent problem, p. 215

Single-payer health care system, p. 210

Socialized medicine, p. 211

---

**7.1** **The Improving Health of People in the United States,** pages 206–209

LEARNING OBJECTIVE: Discuss trends in U.S. health over time.

### Summary

**Health care** refers to goods and services, such as prescription drugs and consultations with a doctor, that are intended to maintain or improve health. Over time, the health of people in most countries has improved. In the United States, as a result of improving health, life expectancy has increased, death rates have decreased, infant mortality has decreased, and the average person has become taller.

 Visit **www.myeconlab.com** to complete these exercises online and get instant feedback.

### Review Questions

1.1 Briefly discuss the ways in which the market for health care is different from and the ways in which it is similar to the markets for other goods and services.

1.2 Briefly describe changes over time in the health of the average person in the United States.

1.3 How can changes over time in the average height of the people in a country be a measure of the country's living standards?

1.4 How can improvements in health increase a country's total income? How can increases in a country's total income improve health?

### Problems and Applications

1.5 Consider the following statement: "To some economists, nutritional status—measured for example by heights—suffers as a measure of living standards because height is not normally seen . . . as something that can be bought."
   a. What is meant by "nutritional status"?
   b. Is income per person the only good measure of living standards? Briefly explain.

c. Why might nutritional status be used as a measure of living standards? Does it matter that it isn't possible to buy a greater height? Briefly explain.

From Roderick Floud, et al., *The Changing Body: Health, Nutrition, and Human Development in the Western World Since 1700*, (Cambridge: Cambridge University Press, 2011), p. 13.

1.6 In what sense have improvements in the health of the average American caused the U.S. production possibilities frontier to shift out? Panel (a) in Figure 7.2 on page 208 indicates that life expectancy in the United States declined between 1916 and 1918. What effect did this decline in life expectancy likely have on the U.S. production possibilities frontier? Briefly explain.

1.7 In *The Elusive Quest for Growth*, William Easterly describes the bottom poor in Malawi as "the stunted poor, with thin bodies, short stature . . . , who experience frequent illnesses and a severe lack of food." He reports that "In the poorest nations like Burundi, Madagascar, and Uganda, nearly half of all children under the age of three are abnormally short because of nutritional deficiency."
   a. Why do a "severe lack of food" and "nutritional deficiency" have anything to do with adults being of short stature and children being abnormally short?
   b. Easterly states, "Poverty is not just low GDP; it is dying babies, starving children . . ." How could rising GDP per capita decrease the number of dying babies?

Based on William Easterly, *The Elusive Quest for Growth: Economists' Adventures and Misadventures in the Tropics*, (Cambridge: The MIT Press, 2001), p. 11 and 14–15.

1.8 How was the public health movement in the United States in the late nineteenth and early twentieth centuries like a technological advance to the country's production possibilities frontier?

---

**7.2** **Health Care Around the World,** pages 209–213

LEARNING OBJECTIVE: Compare the health care systems and health care outcomes in the United States and other countries.

### Summary

**Health insurance** is a contract under which a buyer agrees to make payments, or premiums, in exchange for the provider's agreeing to pay some or all of the buyer's medical bills. A majority of people

in the United States live in households that have private health insurance, which they typically obtain through an employer. Other people have health insurance through the government's Medicare and Medicaid programs. In 2009, about 17 percent of people in the United States lacked health insurance. Many health insurance plans operate on a **fee-for-service** basis under which doctors and hospitals receive a payment for each service they provide. Most countries outside of the United States have greater government involvement in their health care systems. Canada has a **single-payer health care system**, in which the government provides national health insurance to all Canadian residents. In the United Kingdom, the government owns most hospitals and employs most doctors, and the health care system is referred to as **socialized medicine**. The United States spends more per person on health care than do other high-income countries. The United States has lower life expectancy, higher infant mortality, and a greater incidence of obesity than do other high-income countries. The United States has more medical technology per person and has lower mortality rates for people diagnosed with cancer than do other high-income countries. Various problems make it difficult to compare health care outcomes across countries.

MyEconLab  Visit www.myeconlab.com to complete these exercises online and get instant feedback.

## Review Questions

**2.1** Define the following terms:
  **a.** Health insurance
  **b.** Fee-for-service
  **c.** Single-payer health care system
  **d.** Socialized medicine
**2.2** What are the main sources of health insurance in the United States?
**2.3** Briefly compare the health care systems in Canada, Japan, and the United Kingdom with the health care system in the United States.

**2.4** What is meant by the phrase "health care outcome"? How do health care outcomes in the United States compare with those of other high-income countries? What problems arise in attempting to compare health care outcomes across countries?

## Problems and Applications

**2.5** If health care is a normal good, would we expect that spending on health care would increase or decrease over time? Briefly explain.
**2.6** Why do comparisons in health care outcomes across countries often concentrate on measures such as life expectancy and infant mortality? Are there other measures of the quality of health care systems? Briefly explain.
**2.7** Two health care analysts argue that in the United States, "we have arrived at a moment where we are making little headway in defeating various kinds of diseases. Instead, our main achievements today consist of devising ways to marginally extend the lives of the very sick."
  **a.** Should "marginally extend[ing] the lives of the very sick" be an important goal of a health care system? What other goals should have a higher priority? (*Note:* This question is basically a normative one without a definitive correct or incorrect answer. You are being asked to consider what the goals of a health care system *should be.*)
  **b.** Would it be possible to measure how successful the health care systems of different countries are in extending the lives of the very sick? If so, how might it be done?
  From David Brooks, "Death and Budgets," *New York Times*, July 14, 2011.

---

**7.3** **Information Problems and Externalities in the Market for Health Care,** pages 213–219
LEARNING OBJECTIVE: Discuss how information problems and externalities affect the market for health care.

## Summary

The market for health care is affected by the problem of **asymmetric information**, which occurs when one party to an economic transaction has less information than the other party. **Adverse selection**, the situation in which one party to a transaction takes advantage of knowing more than the other party to the transaction, is a problem for firms selling health insurance policies because it results in less healthy people being more likely to buy insurance than are healthier people. **Moral hazard**, actions people take after they have entered into a transaction that make the other party to the transaction worse off, is also a problem for insurance companies because once people have health insurance they are likely to make more visits to their doctors and in other ways increase their use of medical services. Moral hazard can also involve a **principal–agent problem** in which doctors may order more lab tests, MRI scans, and other procedures than they would if their patients lacked health insurance. Insurance companies use deductibles, copayments, and restrictions on coverage of patients with preexisting conditions to reduce the problems of adverse selection and moral hazard. There may be externalities involved with medicine and health care because, for example,

people who are vaccinated against influenza or other diseases may not receive all of the benefits from having been vaccinated and people who become obese may not bear all of the costs from their obesity.

MyEconLab  Visit www.myeconlab.com to complete these exercises online and get instant feedback.

## Review Questions

**3.1** Define the following terms:
  **a.** Asymmetric information
  **b.** Adverse selection
  **c.** Moral hazard
  **d.** Principal–agent problem
**3.2** What are the asymmetric information problems in the market for health insurance?
**3.3** How do health insurance companies deal with asymmetric information problems?
**3.4** What is an externality? Are there externalities in the market for health care? Briefly explain.

## Problems and Applications

**3.5** Suppose you see a 2006 Volkswagen Jetta GLS Turbo Sedan advertised in the campus newspaper for $10,000. If you knew the car was reliable, you would be willing to pay $12,000 for it. If you knew the car was unreliable, you would only be willing to pay $8,000 for it. Under what circumstances should you buy the car?

**3.6** What is the "lemons problem"? Is there a lemons problem with health insurance? Briefly explain.

**3.7** Michael Kinsley, a political columnist, observes, "The idea of insurance is to share the risks of bad outcomes." In what sense does insurance involve sharing risks? How does the problem of adverse selection affect the ability of insurance to provide the benefit of sharing risk?

From Michael Kinsley, "Congress on Drugs," *Slate*, August 1, 2002.

**3.8** Under the Social Security retirement system, the federal government collects a tax on most people's wage income and makes payments to retired workers above a certain age who are covered by the system. (The age to receive full Social Security retirement benefits varies based on the year the worker was born.) The Social Security retirement system is sometimes referred to as a program of social insurance. Is Social Security an insurance program in the same sense as a health insurance policy that a company provides to its workers? Briefly explain.

**3.9** **[Related to the** Don't Let This Happen to You **on page 216]** Briefly explain whether you agree with the following statement: "The reluctance of healthy young adults to buy medical insurance creates a moral hazard problem for insurance companies."

**3.10** A newspaper editorial observes:

Doctors complain that high malpractice awards drive up their insurance premiums and that they are forced to practice "defensive medicine," ordering unnecessary tests and procedures to protect themselves from possible lawsuits.

Is there another economic explanation for why doctors may end up ordering unnecessary tests and other medical procedures? Briefly explain.

From "Medicaid and the N.Y. Budget: A Bad Deal on Malpractice," *New York Times*, March 12, 2011.

**3.11** **[Related to** Solved Problem 7.3 **on page 217]** An article in the *Economist* magazine argues that the real problem with health insurance is:

The healthy people who decide not to buy insurance out of rational self-interest, and who turn out to be right. By not buying insurance, those (largely young) healthy people will be failing to subsidize the people insurance is meant for: the ones who end up getting sick.

a. Why is it rational for healthy people not to buy health insurance?

b. Do you agree that health insurance is meant for people who end up getting sick?

c. Why is the situation described here a problem for a system of health insurance? If it is a problem, suggest possible solutions.

From "Romney on Health Care: To Boldly Go Where He Had Already Been Before," *Economist*, May 13, 2011.

**3.12** An article in the *Economist* magazine contains the following description of the "classic adverse selection spiral": "because [health insurance] premiums go higher, healthy people become even less likely to buy insurance, which drives premiums higher yet, and so on until the whole thing winks out. . . ." Why does an adverse selection spiral develop? What steps can insurance companies take to avoid it?

From "Romney on Health Care: To Boldly Go Where He Had Already Been Before," *Economist*, May 13, 2011.

**3.13** **[Related to the** Making the Connection **on page 218]** Is health care a public good? Briefly explain. Why does the government directly provide health care in some countries, such as the United Kingdom, but not in others?

**3.14** **[Related to the** Making the Connection **on page 218]** Explain whether you agree with the following statement:

Providing health care is obviously a public good. If one person becomes ill and doesn't receive treatment, that person may infect many other people. If many people become ill, then the output of the economy will be negatively affected. Therefore, providing health care is a public good that should be supplied by the government.

---

  **The Debate over Health Care Policy in the United States, pages 220–228**

LEARNING OBJECTIVE: Explain the major issues involved in the debate over health care policy in the United States.

## Summary

In March 2010, Congress passed the Patient Protection and Affordable Care Act (PPACA), which significantly reorganized the U.S. health care system. Spending on health care in the United States has been growing rapidly as a percentage of GDP, and spending per person on health care has been growing more rapidly than in other high-income countries. Third-party payers, such as employer-provided health insurance and the Medicare and Medicaid programs, have financed an increasing fraction of health care spending, while out-of-pocket payments have sharply declined as a fraction of total health care spending. Several explanations have been offered for the rapid increase in health care spending in the United States: Slow rates of growth of labor productivity in health care may be driving up costs, the U.S. population is becoming older, medical technology and new prescription drugs have higher costs, and the tax system and the reliance on third-party payers have distorted the economic incentives of consumers and suppliers of health care. The PPACA has several important provisions: (1) an individual mandate that requires every resident of the United States to obtain health insurance or be fined; (2) the establishment of health exchanges that will be run by the state governments and provide a means for individuals and small businesses to purchase health insurance; (3) an employer mandate that requires every firm with more than 200 employees to offer health insurance to them; (4) increased regulation of health insurance companies; (5) expansion of eligibility for Medicaid and the establishment of the Independent Payment Advisory Board, which has the power to reduce Medicare payments for prescription drugs and for the use of diagnostic equipment and other technology if Medicare spending exceeds certain levels; and (6) increased taxes on workers with incomes above $200,000. Some critics of the PPACA argue that it does not go far enough in increasing government involvement in the health care system, while other critics argue that health care reform should rely more heavily on **market-based reforms**, which involve changing the market for health care so that it becomes more like the markets for other goods and services.

**MyEconLab** Visit **www.myeconlab.com** to complete these exercises online and get instant feedback.

## Review Questions

**4.1** What is the Patient Protection and Affordable Care Act (PPACA)? Briefly list its major provisions.

**4.2** In the United States, what has been the trend in health care spending as a percentage of GDP? Compare the increases in health care spending per person in the United States with the increases in health care spending per person in other high-income countries. What implications do current trends in health care spending have for the growth of federal government spending in the United States?

**4.3** Briefly discuss how economists explain the rapid increases in health care spending.

**4.4** What arguments do economists and policymakers make who believe that the federal government should have a larger role in the health care system criticize the PPACA?

**4.5** What arguments do economists and policymakers make who believe that market-based reforms are the key to improving the health care system criticize the PPACA?

## Problems and Applications

**4.6** Figure 7.7 on page 223 shows that the Congressional Budget Office forecasts that only about 10 percent of the PPACA-related increase in spending on Medicare as a percentage of GDP will be due to the aging of the population. What factors explain the other 90 percent of the increase?

**4.7** Some economists and policymakers have argued that one way to control federal government spending on Medicare is to have a board of experts decide whether new medical technologies are worth their higher costs. If the board decides that they are *not* worth the costs, Medicare would not pay for them. Other economists and policymakers argue that the costs to beneficiaries should more closely represent the costs of providing medical services. This result might be attained by raising premiums, deductibles, and copayments or by "means testing," which would limit the Medicare benefits high-income individuals receive. Political columnist David Brooks has summarized these two ways to restrain the growth of spending on Medicare: "From the top, a body of experts can be empowered to make rationing decisions. . . . Alternatively, at the bottom, costs can be shifted to beneficiaries with premium supports to help them handle the burden."

**a.** What are "rationing decisions"? How would these decisions restrain the growth of Medicare spending?

**b.** How would shifting the costs of Medicare to beneficiaries restrain the growth of Medicare spending? What does Brooks mean by "premium supports"?

**c.** Should Congress and the president be concerned about the growth of Medicare spending? If so, which of these approaches should they adopt or is there a third approach that might be better? (*Note:* This last question is normative and has no definitive answer. It is intended to lead you to consider possible approaches to the Medicare program.)

Based on David Brooks, "The Missing Fifth," *New York Times*, May 9, 2011.

**4.8** Ross Douthat, a political columnist, offers the following observations about the Medicare program:

Certainly telling seniors to buy all their own health care is a complete political (and ethical) non-starter. But telling seniors to pay for more of their own health care—well, it's hard to see how else we can hope to reduce Medicare's fiscal burden.

**a.** What does Douthat mean by Medicare's "fiscal burden"?

**b.** How could the government change the Medicare program so that seniors would pay for more of their own health care? How would this change restrain growth in the spending on Medicare? How would this change affect very low-income seniors?

Based on Ross Douthat, "We're All Rationers," *New York Times*, May 19, 2011.

**4.9** Nobel Laureate Robert Fogel of the University of Chicago has argued, "Expenditures on healthcare are driven by demand, which is spurred by income and by advances in biotechnology that make health interventions increasingly effective."

**a.** If Fogel is correct, should policymakers be concerned by projected increases in health care spending as a percentage of GDP?

**b.** What objections do some economists raise to Fogel's analysis of what is driving increases in spending on health care?

Based on Robert Fogel, "Forecasting the Cost of U.S. Healthcare," *The American*, September 3, 2009.

**4.10** **[Related to the** Making the Connection **on page 225]** How can providers of some medical services charge hundreds or thousands of dollars more than competitors and remain in business? Why don't patients go to the providers that charge the lower price for the same medical service?

**4.11** **[Related to the** Chapter Opener **on page 205]** Why do small firms face more of a problem with risk pooling when buying insurance than do large firms?

**4.12** **[Related to the** Making the Connection **on page 227]** How are the state insurance exchanges with the Small Business Health Option Program (SHOP) intended to help small businesses with their problem of limited risk pooling when buying health insurance for their employees? What is the adverse selection death spiral that led to the collapse of the health insurance exchange run by the state of California from 1993 to 2006?

CHAPTER

# 8

# Firms, the Stock Market, and Corporate Governance

## Chapter Outline and Learning Objectives

# How Can You Buy a Piece of Facebook?

When Mark Zuckerberg started Facebook in 2004, he was a sophomore in college. Just 5 years later, Facebook had 150 million users. By contrast, it took cell phone companies 15 years to reach 150 million users and 7 years for Apple's iPod to reach that many users. Zuckerberg started Facebook because he believed that people were less interested in meeting new friends online—the assumption built into other sites—than they were in finding a better way of staying in touch with the friends they already had. On Facebook, pages would typically be visible only to people the user had linked to, or "friended," which helped to reduce the problem of fake identities that plagued other sites.

Any business experiencing the runaway success of Facebook quickly develops a need to raise money to finance its expansion. Some businesses raise the funds they need by borrowing from banks. Large firms, as Facebook has become, have the ability to sell stocks and bonds to investors in financial markets. By selling stock, a firm trades partial ownership of the firm in exchange for the funds needed for growth and expansion. Firms that sell stock that is traded in financial markets such as the New York Stock Exchange are called *public firms*, whereas firms that do not sell stock are called *private firms*.

In late 2011, Facebook remained a private firm. However, a small number of its shares are available for sale on private markets but not on public financial markets. Companies such as Facebook often issue shares to their founders, some of their employees, and some private investors. Under federal regulations, holders of these shares can sell them under certain conditions. In mid-2011, stock in Facebook was selling for about $35 per share, which made the total value of the firm about $80 billion.

Because the buying and selling of stock in Facebook was not being done on the public financial markets, the firm was not subject to the usual federal regulations that apply to public firms. Some economists and policymakers argued that the result was less protection for investors. As we will see in this chapter, financial markets are crucial to the health of the economy, and how financial markets should be regulated is an important policy issue.

**AN INSIDE LOOK** on **page 256** discusses how two new Internet companies allow qualified investors a chance to buy stock in private companies.

Based on Shayndi Raice, "Is Facebook Worth $100 Billion?" *Wall Street Journal*, July 14, 2011; Sarah Morgan, "How to Buy Shares of Facebook," *Wall Street Journal*, January 5, 2011; Jessi Hempel, "How Facebook Is Taking Over Our Lives," *Fortune*, March 11, 2009.

## Economics in Your Life

### Do Corporate Managers Act in the Best Interests of Shareholders?

Although stockholders legally own corporations, managers often have a great deal of freedom in deciding how corporations are run. As a result, managers can make decisions, such as spending money on large corporate headquarters or decorating their offices with expensive paintings, that are in their interests but not in the interests of the shareholders. If managers make decisions that waste money and lower the profits of a firm, the price of the firm's stock will fall, which hurts the investors who own the stock. Suppose you own stock in a corporation. Why is it difficult to get the managers to act in your interests rather than in their own? Given this problem, should you ever take on the risk of buying stock? As you read the chapter, see if you can answer these questions. You can check your answers against those we provide on **page 255** at the end of this chapter.

I n this chapter, we look at firms: how they are organized, how they raise funds, and the information they provide to investors. As we have discussed in earlier chapters, firms in a market system are responsible for organizing the factors of production to produce goods and services. Firms are the vehicles entrepreneurs use to earn profits. To succeed, entrepreneurs must meet consumers' wants by producing new or better goods and services or by finding ways of producing existing goods and services at a lower cost so they can be sold at a lower price. Entrepreneurs also need access to sufficient funds, and they must be able to efficiently organize production. As the typical firm in many industries has become larger over the past 100 years, the task of efficiently organizing production has become more difficult. In the final section of this chapter, we look at problems of corporate governance that have occurred in recent years. We also look at the steps firms and the government have taken to avoid similar problems in the future.

## Types of Firms

**8.1 LEARNING** OBJECTIVE

Categorize the major types of firms in the United States.

**Sole proprietorship** A firm owned by a single individual and not organized as a corporation.

**Partnership** A firm owned jointly by two or more persons and not organized as a corporation.

**Corporation** A legal form of business that provides owners with protection from losing more than their investment should the business fail.

**Asset** Anything of value owned by a person or a firm.

**Limited liability** The legal provision that shields owners of a corporation from losing more than they have invested in the firm.

In studying a market economy, it is important to understand the basics of how firms operate. In the United States, there are three legal categories of firms: *sole proprietorships*, *partnerships*, and *corporations*. A **sole proprietorship** is a firm owned by a single individual. Although most sole proprietorships are small, some employ many workers and earn large profits. **Partnerships** are firms owned jointly by two or more—sometimes many—persons. Most law and accounting firms are partnerships. Some of them can be quite large. For instance, in 2011, the Baker & McKenzie law firm based in Chicago had 1,350 partners. Most large firms, though, are organized as *corporations*. A **corporation** is a legal form of business that provides owners with protection from losing more than their investment should the business fail.

### Who Is Liable? Limited and Unlimited Liability

A key distinction among the three types of firms is that the owners of sole proprietorships and partnerships have unlimited liability. Unlimited liability means there is no legal distinction between the personal assets of the owners of the firm and the assets of the firm. An **asset** is anything of value owned by a person or a firm. If a sole proprietorship or a partnership owes a lot of money to the firm's suppliers or employees, the suppliers and employees have a legal right to sue the firm for payment, even if this requires the firm's owners to sell some of their personal assets, such as stocks or bonds. In other words, with sole proprietorships and partnerships, the owners are not legally distinct from the firms they own.

It may only seem fair that the owners of a firm be responsible for a firm's debts. But early in the nineteenth century, it became clear to many state legislatures in the United States that unlimited liability was a significant problem for any firm that was attempting to raise funds from large numbers of investors. An investor might be interested in making a relatively small investment in a firm but be unwilling to become a partner in the firm, for fear of placing at risk all of his or her personal assets if the firm were to fail. To get around this problem, state legislatures began to pass *general incorporation laws*, which allowed firms to be organized as corporations. Under the corporate form of business, the owners of a firm have **limited liability**, which means that if the firm fails, the owners can never lose more than the amount they have invested in the firm. The personal assets of the owners of the firm are not affected by the failure of the firm. In fact, in the eyes of the law, a corporation is a legal "person," separate from its owners. Limited liability has made it possible for corporations to raise funds by issuing shares of stock to large numbers of investors. For example, if you buy a share of Google stock, you are a part owner of the firm, but even if Google were to go bankrupt, you would not be personally responsible

| | Sole Proprietorship | Partnership | Corporation |
|---|---|---|---|
| Advantages | • Control by owner<br>• No layers of management | • Ability to share work<br>• Ability to share risks | • Limited personal liability<br>• Greater ability to raise funds |
| Disadvantages | • Unlimited personal liability<br>• Limited ability to raise funds | • Unlimited personal liability<br>• Limited ability to raise funds | • Costly to organize<br>• Possible double taxation of income |

**Table 8.1**

**Differences among Business Organizations**

for any of Google's debts. Therefore, you could not lose more than the amount you paid for the stock.

Organizing a firm as a corporation also has some disadvantages. In the United States, corporate profits are taxed twice—once at the corporate level and again when investors receive a share of corporate profits. Corporations generally are larger than sole proprietorships and partnerships and are therefore more difficult to organize and run. Table 8.1 reviews the advantages and disadvantages of different forms of business organization.

## Corporations Earn the Majority of Revenue and Profits

Figure 8.1 gives basic statistics on the three types of business organizations. Panel (a) shows that almost three-quarters of all firms are sole proprietorships. Panels (b) and (c) show that although only 18 percent of all firms are corporations, corporations account for a large majority of the revenue and profits earned by all firms. *Profit* is the difference between revenue and the total cost to a firm of producing the goods and services it offers for sale.

There are more than 5.8 million corporations in the United States, but only 35,000 have annual revenues of more than $50 million. We can think of these 35,000 firms—including Microsoft, McDonald's, and Google—as representing "big business." These large firms earn 84 percent of the total profits of all corporations in the United States.

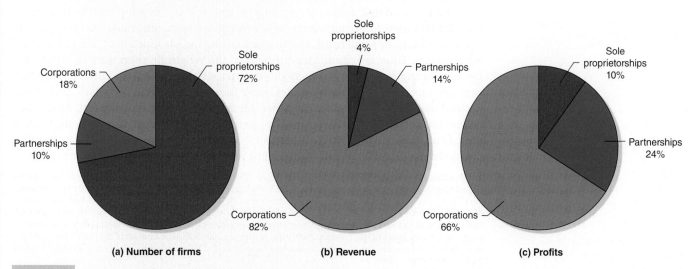

(a) Number of firms   (b) Revenue   (c) Profits

**Figure 8.1**   **Business Organizations: Sole Proprietorships, Partnerships, and Corporations**

The three types of firms in the United States are sole proprietorships, partnerships, and corporations. Panel (a) shows that only 18 percent of all firms are corporations. Yet, as panels (b) and (c) show, corporations account for a large majority of the total revenue and profits earned by all firms.

Data from U.S. Census Bureau, *The 2011 Statistical Abstract of the United States.*

| Making<br>the<br>Connection | **How Important Are Small Businesses to the U.S. Economy?** |
|---|---|

We have seen that although a large majority of all firms are sole proprietorships, they account for only a small fraction of total revenues and profits earned by all firms. And while 85 percent of all firms employ fewer than 20 workers, fewer than 20 percent of all workers are employed by these firms.

Does this mean that small businesses are unimportant to the U.S. economy?

To the contrary, most economists would argue that small firms are vital to the health of the economy. Starting a small firm provides an entrepreneur with a vehicle for bringing a new product or process to market. Locating the funding to start a small firm is often difficult, though, because a new firm lacks a record of operating profitably, so banks and other lenders are worried that the firm won't be able to pay back borrowed money. As a result, more than 80 percent of small firms are started using funds provided by the founders and their families, by credit cards, or by loans taken out against the value of the founders' homes. While anyone starting a new firm hopes to become successful, perhaps even wealthy, the act of founding a company can also provide employment opportunities for workers and new goods and services for consumers. In a typical year, more than 600,000 new firms open in the United States, and of these, more than 95 percent employ fewer than 20 workers. In a typical year, new small firms create 3.3 million jobs; 40 percent of all new jobs are created by small firms, and in some years more than half are. Strikingly, more than 85 percent of all jobs created by new firms are created by small firms.

*In a typical year, 40 percent of new jobs are created by small firms.*

Although, on average, jobs at small firms pay lower wages than jobs at large firms and are less likely to provide fringe benefits, such as health insurance and retirement accounts, workers at small firms tend to be younger and, in fact, the first job for many workers is often with a small firm. Small firms are also less likely to lay off workers during a recession than are large firms.

Entrepreneurs founding small firms have been the source of many of the most important new goods and services available to consumers. This is true even though large firms spend much more on research and development than do small firms. Some economists have argued that although spending on research and development by large firms often leads to important improvements in existing products, innovative new products are often introduced by small firms. For instance, during the late nineteenth and early twentieth centuries, Thomas Edison, Henry Ford, and the Wright Brothers were all responsible for introducing important products shortly after starting what were initially very small firms. In more recent years, Bill Gates, Steve Jobs, Michael Dell, and Mark Zuckerberg decided that the best way to develop their ideas was by founding Microsoft, Apple, Dell Computer, and Facebook rather than by going to work for large corporations. Each of these firms began with a handful of employees, and the key products and processes they pioneered were developed long before they evolved into the large firms they are today.

Based on David Neumark, Brandon Wall, and Junfu Zhang, "Do Small Businesses Create More Jobs? New Evidence for the United States from the National Establishment Time Series," *Review of Economics and Statistics*, Vol. 93, No. 1, February 2011, pp. 16-29; Conor Dougherty and Pui-Wing Tam, "Start-Ups Chase Cash as Funds Trickle Back," *Wall Street Journal*, April 1, 2010; Amar Bhidé, *The Origins and Evolution of New Businesses*, New York: Oxford University Press, 2003; Giuseppe Moscarini and Fabien Postel-Vinay, "Large Employers Are More Cyclically Sensitive," National Bureau of Economic Research, Working Paper 14740, February 2009; data are from the 2009 Statistical Abstract of the United States, the U.S. Small Business Administration, and the U.S. Bureau of Labor Statistics. National Bureau of Economic Research Working Paper 13818, February 2008.

MyEconLab **Your Turn:** Test your understanding by doing related problem 1.8 on page 258 at the end of this chapter.

# The Structure of Corporations and the Principal–Agent Problem

Because large corporations account for most sales and profits in the economy, it is important to know how they are managed. Most large corporations have a similar management structure. The way in which a corporation is structured and the effect that structure has on the corporation's behavior is referred to as **corporate governance**.

## Corporate Structure and Corporate Governance

Corporations are legally owned by their *shareholders*, the owners of the corporation's stock. Unlike with a sole proprietorship, a corporation's shareholders, although they are the firm's owners, do not manage the firm directly. Instead, they elect a *board of directors* to represent their interests. The board of directors appoints a *chief executive officer* (CEO) to run the day-to-day operations of the corporation. Sometimes the board of directors also appoints other members of *top management*, such as the *chief financial officer* (CFO). At other times, the CEO appoints other members of top management. Members of top management, including the CEO and CFO, often serve on the board of directors. Members of management serving on the board of directors are referred to as *inside directors*. Members of the board of directors who do not have a direct management role in the firm are referred to as *outside directors*. The outside directors are intended to act as checks on the decisions of top managers, but the distinction between an outside director and an inside director is not always clear. For example, the CEO of a firm that sells a good or service to a large corporation may sit on the board of directors of that corporation. Although technically an outside director, this person may be reluctant to oppose the top managers because they have the power to stop purchasing from his or her firm. In some instances, top managers have effectively controlled their firms' boards of directors.

Unlike the owners of family businesses or private firms such as Facebook, the top management of a large corporation does not generally own a large share of the firm's stock, so large corporations have a **separation of ownership from control**. Although the shareholders actually own the firm, top management controls the firm's day-to-day operations. Because top managers do not own the entire firm, they may decrease the firm's profits by spending money to purchase private jets or schedule management meetings at luxurious resorts. Economists refer to the conflict between the interests of shareholders and the interests of top management as a **principal–agent problem**.[1] This problem occurs when agents—in this case, a firm's top management—pursue their own interests rather than the interests of the principal who hired them—in this case, the shareholders of the corporation. To reduce the effect of the principal–agent problem, many boards of directors in the 1990s began to tie the salaries of top managers to the profits of the firm or to the price of the firm's stock. They hoped this would give top managers an incentive to make the firm as profitable as possible, thereby benefiting its shareholders. Sometimes, though, top managers would take steps that increased the profits of the firm in the short run—and the salaries and bonuses of the top managers—but that actually reduced the profits of the firm in the long run.

Describe the typical management structure of corporations and understand the concepts of separation of ownership from control and the principal–agent problem.

**Corporate governance** The way in which a corporation is structured and the effect that structure has on the corporation's behavior.

**Separation of ownership from control** A situation in a corporation in which the top management, rather than the shareholders, control day-to-day operations.

**Principal–agent problem** A problem caused by an agent pursuing his own interests rather than the interests of the principal who hired him.

---

[1]In Chapter 7, we saw that the principal–agent problem arises from moral hazard that can occur because of asymmetric information. In this case, the asymmetric information involves top managers knowing more about how the firm is actually run than do the firm's shareholders.

# Solved Problem 8.2

## Does the Principal–Agent Problem Apply to the Relationship between Managers and Employees?

Briefly explain whether you agree with the following argument:

> The principal–agent problem applies not just to the relationship between shareholders and top managers. It

also applies to the relationship between managers and workers. Just as shareholders have trouble monitoring whether top managers are earning as much profit as possible, managers have trouble monitoring whether employees are working as hard as possible.

### Solving the Problem

**Step 1:** **Review the chapter material.** This problem concerns the principal–agent problem, so you may want to review the section "Corporate Structure and Corporate Governance" on page 241.

**Step 2:** **Evaluate the argument.** You should agree with the argument. A corporation's shareholders have difficulty monitoring the activities of top managers. In practice, they attempt to do so indirectly through the corporation's board of directors. But the firm's top managers may influence—or even control—the firm's board of directors. Even if top managers do not control a board of directors, it may be difficult for the board to know whether actions managers take—such as opening a branch office in Paris—will increase the profitability of the firm or just increase the enjoyment of the top managers.

To answer the problem, we must extend this analysis to the relationship between managers and workers: Managers would like employees to work as hard as possible. Employees would often rather not work hard, particularly if they do not see a direct financial reward for doing so. Managers can have trouble monitoring whether employees are working hard or goofing off. (Is that employee in his cubicle diligently staring at a computer screen because he is hard at work on a report or because he is surfing the Web for sports scores or posting to his Facebook page?) So, the principal–agent problem does apply to the relationship between managers and employees.

**Extra Credit:** Boards of directors try to reduce the principal–agent problem by designing compensation policies for top managers that give them financial incentives to increase profits. Similarly, managers try to reduce the principal–agent problem by designing compensation policies that give workers an incentive to work harder. For example, some manufacturers pay factory workers on the basis of how much they produce rather than on the basis of how many hours they work.

MyEconLab **Your Turn:** For more practice, do related problems 2.7 and 2.8 on page 259 at the end of this chapter.

---

**8.3 LEARNING** OBJECTIVE

Explain how firms raise the funds they need to operate and expand.

# How Firms Raise Funds

Owners and managers of firms try to earn a profit. To earn a profit, a firm must raise funds to pay for its operations, including paying its employees and buying or renting computers and other machinery and equipment. Indeed, a central challenge for anyone running a firm, whether that person is a sole proprietor or a top manager of a large corporation, is raising the funds needed to operate and expand the business. Suppose you decide to open an online social networking site, using $100,000 you have saved in a bank.

You use the $100,000 to rent a building for your firm, to buy computers, and to pay other start-up expenses. Your firm is a great success, and you decide to expand by moving to a larger building and buying more computers. As the owner of a small business, you can raise the funds for this expansion in three ways:

1. If you are making a profit, you could reinvest the profits back into your firm. Profits that are reinvested in a firm rather than taken out of a firm and paid to the firm's owners are *retained earnings*.
2. You could raise funds by recruiting additional owners to invest in the firm. This arrangement would increase the firm's *financial capital*.
3. Finally, you could borrow the funds from relatives, friends, or a bank.

The managers of a large public firm have some additional ways to raise funds, as we will see in the next section.

## Sources of External Funds

Unless firms rely on retained earnings, they have to raise the *external funds* they need from others who have funds available to invest. It is the role of an economy's *financial system* to transfer funds from savers to borrowers—directly through financial markets or indirectly through financial intermediaries such as banks.

Most firms raise external funds in two ways. The first way relies on financial intermediaries such as banks and is called **indirect finance**. If you put $1,000 in a checking account or a savings account, or if you put money in a $1,000 certificate of deposit (CD), the bank will loan most of those funds to borrowers. The bank will combine your funds with those of other depositors and, for example, make a $100,000 loan to a local business. Small businesses rely heavily on bank loans as their primary source of external funds.

A second way for firms to acquire external funds is through *financial markets*. Raising funds in these markets, such as the New York Stock Exchange on Wall Street in New York, is called **direct finance**. Direct finance usually takes the form of the borrower selling the lender a *financial security*. A financial security is a document—sometimes in electronic form—that states the terms under which the funds have passed from the buyer of the security (who is lending funds) to the borrower. *Bonds* and *stocks* are the two main types of financial securities. Typically, only large corporations are able to sell bonds and stocks on financial markets. Investors are generally unwilling to buy securities issued by small and medium-sized firms because the investors lack sufficient information on the financial health of smaller firms.

**Bonds** **Bonds** are financial securities that represent promises to repay a fixed amount of funds. When General Electric (GE) sells a bond to raise funds, it promises to pay the purchaser of the bond an interest payment each year for the term of the bond, as well as a final payment of the amount of the loan, or the *principal*, at the end of the term. GE may need to raise many millions of dollars to build a factory, but each individual bond has a principal, or *face value*, of $1,000, which is the amount each bond purchaser is lending GE. So, GE must sell many bonds to raise all the funds it needs. Suppose GE promises it will pay interest of $60 per year to anyone who buys one of its bonds. The interest payments on a bond are referred to as **coupon payments**. The **interest rate** is the cost of borrowing funds, usually expressed as a percentage of the amount borrowed. If we express the coupon as a percentage of the face value of the bond, we find the interest rate on the bond, called the *coupon rate*. In this case, the interest rate is:

$$\frac{\$60}{\$1,000} = 0.06, \text{ or } 6\%$$

Many bonds that corporations issue have terms, or *maturities*, of 30 years. In this example, if you bought a bond from GE, GE would pay you $60 per year for 30 years, and at the end of the thirtieth year, GE would repay the $1,000 principal to you.

The interest rate that a borrower selling a bond has to pay depends on how likely bond buyers—investors—think that the bond seller is to default, or not make the

**Indirect finance** A flow of funds from savers to borrowers through financial intermediaries such as banks. Intermediaries raise funds from savers to lend to firms (and other borrowers).

**Direct finance** A flow of funds from savers to firms through financial markets, such as the New York Stock Exchange.

**Bond** A financial security that represents a promise to repay a fixed amount of funds.

**Coupon payment** An interest payment on a bond.

**Interest rate** The cost of borrowing funds, usually expressed as a percentage of the amount borrowed.

promised coupon or principal payments. The higher the *default risk* on a bond, the higher the interest rate. For example, investors see the federal government as being very unlikely to default on its bonds, so federal government bonds pay a lower interest rate than do bonds of a firm such as GE. In turn, GE pays a lower interest rate on its bonds than does a corporation that investors believe is not as likely to make its bond payments.

| Making the Connection | **The Rating Game: Is the U.S. Treasury Likely to Default on Its Bonds?** |
|---|---|

Federal regulations require that before they can sell bonds to investors, firms and governments must first have bonds rated by one of the credit rating agencies. The three largest rating agencies are Moody's Investors Service, Standard & Poor's Corporation, and Fitch Ratings. These private firms rate bonds by giving them letter grades—AAA or Aaa being the highest—that reflect the probability that the firm or government will be able to make the payments on the bond. The following table shows the ratings:

| | Moody's Investors Service | Standard & Poor's (S&P) | Fitch Ratings | Meaning of the Ratings |
|---|---|---|---|---|
| Investment-grade bonds | Aaa | AAA | AAA | Highest credit quality |
| | Aa | AA | AA | Very high credit quality |
| | A | A | A | High credit quality |
| | Baa | BBB | BBB | Good credit quality |
| Non-investment-grade bonds | Ba | BB | BB | Speculative |
| | B | B | B | Highly speculative |
| | Caa | CCC | CCC | Substantial default risk |
| | Ca | CC | CC | Very high levels of default risk |
| | C | C | C | Exceptionally high levels of default risk |
| | — | D | D | Default |

*Note:* The entries in the "Meaning of the Ratings" column are slightly modified from those that Fitch uses. The other two rating agencies have similar descriptions. For each rating from Aa to Caa, Moody's adds a numerical modifier of 1, 2, or 3. The rating Aa1 is higher than the rating Aa2, and the rating Aa2 is higher than the rating Aa3. Similarly, Standard & Poor's and Fitch Ratings add a plus (+) or minus (−) sign. The rating AA+ is higher than the rating AA, and the rating AA is higher than the rating AA−.

Source: *Money, Banking, and the Financial System* 1st edition by R. Glenn Hubbard and Anthony P. O'Brien. Copyright © 2012 by Pearson Education, Inc. Reprinted and Electronically reproduced by permission of Pearson Education, Inc., Upper Saddle River, New Jersey.

Investors can use the ratings in deciding how much risk they are willing to take on when buying a bond. Generally, the lower the rating, the higher the interest rate an investor will receive, but also the higher the risk that the issuer of the bond will default.

The ratings agencies charge firms and governments—rather than investors—for their services. This arrangement raises the question of whether rating agencies face a conflict of interest. Because firms issuing bonds can choose which of the agencies to hire to rate their bonds, the agencies may have an incentive to give higher ratings than might be justified in order to keep the firms' business. During the housing boom of the mid-2000s, some financial firms issued *mortgage-backed bonds*. These bonds were similar to regular corporate bonds except that the interest payments came from mortgage loans people had taken out to buy houses. The money from those mortgage payments was passed along to investors who had bought the mortgage-backed bonds. The rating agencies gave many of these bonds AAA ratings, even though when housing prices began to decline in 2006, the issuers of many of these bonds defaulted on them. Some economists and policymakers believe the rating agencies provided the high ratings primarily to ensure that the firms that issued them would continue to hire them.

Standard & Poor's (S&P) became involved in another controversy in August 2011, when it downgraded U.S. Treasury bonds from AAA to AA+. This was the first time since the rating agencies had begun rating Treasury bonds that any of them had given Treasury bonds less than a AAA rating. The reason for the rating downgrade was the state of the federal government's budget deficit. Whenever the federal government runs a budget deficit, the Treasury must borrow an amount equal to the deficit by issuing bonds. In 2011, the federal government was spending much more than it was collecting in taxes, resulting in a large budget deficit. The budget deficit reflected the lower tax receipts and increased government spending resulting from the 2007–2009 economic recession. But forecasts from the U.S. Congressional Budget Office indicated that even after the effects of the recession had disappeared, large budget deficits would remain because spending on Social Security, Medicare, Medicaid, and other government programs were expected to increase faster than tax revenues. When prolonged negotiations between President Barack Obama and Congress failed to make much of a dent in the problem, S&P announced the rating downgrade. In the days following the announcement, interest rates on Treasury bonds actually fell rather than rising, as might have been expected if investors had believed that a default was possible.

So, is it likely that the U.S. Treasury will default on its bonds? S&P argued that while a default is still unlikely, the continuing large deficits increased the chance that someday the Treasury might not make the interest payments on its bonds. Like the Ghost of Christmas Yet to Come in Charles Dickens's *A Christmas Carol*, S&P was giving a warning of something that might happen rather than something that necessarily must happen.

Based on Tom Lauricella, Matt Phillips and Serena Ng, "Markets Brace for Downgrade's Toll," *Wall Street Journal*, August 8, 2011; and Andrew Ross Sorkin, "S.E.C. Urges Changes to Ratings-Agency Rules," *New York Times*, August, 29, 2010.

**Your Turn:** Test your understanding by doing related problem 3.8 on page 260 at the end of this chapter.

MyEconLab

---

**Stocks** When you buy a newly issued bond from a firm, you are lending funds to that firm. When you buy **stock** issued by a firm, you are actually buying part ownership of the firm. When a corporation sells stock, it is doing the same thing the owner of a small business does when she takes on a partner: The firm is increasing its financial capital by bringing additional owners into the firm. Any individual shareholder usually owns only a small fraction of the total shares of stock issued by a corporation.

A shareholder is entitled to a share of the corporation's profits, if there are any. Corporations generally keep some of their profits—known as retained earnings—to finance future expansion. The remaining profits are paid to shareholders as **dividends**. Investors hope that a firm will earn economic profits by using its retained earnings to grow, causing the firm's share price to rise, and providing a *capital gain* for investors. If a corporation is unable to make a profit, it usually does not pay a dividend. Under the law, corporations must make payments on any debt they have before making payments to their owners. That is, a corporation must make promised payments to bondholders before it can make any dividend payments to shareholders. In addition, when firms sell stock, they acquire from investors an open-ended commitment of funds to the firm.

Unlike bonds, stocks do not have a maturity date, so the firm is not obliged to return the investor's funds at any particular date.

**Stock** A financial security that represents partial ownership of a firm.

**Dividends** Payments by a corporation to its shareholders.

## Stock and Bond Markets Provide Capital— and Information

The original purchasers of stocks and bonds may resell them to other investors. In fact, most of the buying and selling of stocks and bonds that takes place each day involves investors reselling existing stocks and bonds to each other rather than corporations selling new stocks and bonds to investors. The buyers and sellers of stocks and bonds together make up the *stock and bond markets*. There is no single place where stocks and bonds are bought and sold. Some trading of stocks and bonds takes place in buildings known as *exchanges*, such as the New York Stock Exchange or the Tokyo Stock Exchange. In the United States, the stocks and bonds of the largest corporations are traded on the New York Stock Exchange. The development of computer technology has spread the trading of stocks and bonds outside exchanges to *securities dealers* linked by computers. These dealers comprise the *over-the-counter market*. The stocks of many computer and other high-technology firms—including Apple, Google, and Microsoft—are traded in the most important of the over-the-counter markets, the *National Association of Securities Dealers Automated Quotations* system, which is referred to by its acronym, NASDAQ.

Shares of stock represent claims on the profits of the firms that issue them. Therefore, as the fortunes of the firms change and they earn more or less profit, the prices of the stock the firms have issued should also change. Similarly, bonds represent claims to receive coupon payments and one final payment of principal. Therefore, a particular bond that was issued in the past may have its price go up or down, depending on whether the coupon payments being offered on newly issued bonds are higher or lower than on existing bonds. If you hold a bond with a coupon of $40 per year, and newly issued bonds have coupons of $50 per year, the price of your bond will fall because it is less attractive to investors. The price of a bond will also be affected by changes in default risk, or the investors' perceptions of the issuing firm's ability to make the coupon payments. For example, if investors begin to believe that a firm may soon go out of business and stop making coupon payments to its bondholders, the price of the firm's bonds will fall to very low levels.

Changes in the value of a firm's stocks and bonds offer important information for a firm's managers, as well as for investors. An increase in the stock price means that investors are more optimistic about the firm's profit prospects, and the firm's managers might want to expand the firm's operations as a result. By contrast, a decrease in the firm's stock price indicates that investors are less optimistic about the firms' profit

# Don't Let This Happen to You

### When Google Shares Change Hands, Google Doesn't Get the Money

Google is a popular investment, with investors buying and selling shares often as their views about the value of the firm shift. That's great for Google, right? Think of all that money flowing into Google's coffers as shares change hands and the stock price goes up. *Wrong.* Google raises funds in a primary market, but shares change hands in a secondary market. Those trades don't put money into Google's hands, but they do give important information to the firm's managers. Let's see why.

*Primary markets* are those in which newly issued claims are sold to initial buyers by the issuer. Businesses can raise funds in a primary financial market in two ways—by borrowing (selling bonds) or by selling shares of stock—which result in different types of claims on the borrowing firm's future income. Although you may hear about the stock market fluctuations every day in news updates, bonds actually account for more of the funds raised by borrowers. The total value of bonds in the United States is typically about twice the value of stocks.

In *secondary markets*, stocks and bonds that have already been issued are sold by one investor to another. If

Google sells shares to the public, it is turning to a primary market for new funds. Once Google shares are issued, investors trade the shares in the secondary market. Google does not receive any new funds when Google shares are traded on secondary markets. The initial seller of a stock or bond raises funds from a lender only in the primary market. Secondary markets convey information to firms' managers and to investors by determining the price of stocks and bonds. For example, a major increase in Google's stock price conveys the market's good feelings about the firm, and the firm may decide to raise funds to expand. So, secondary markets are valuable sources of information for corporations that are considering raising funds.

Primary and secondary markets are both important, but they play different roles. As an investor, you principally trade stocks and bonds in a secondary market. As a corporate manager, you may help decide how to raise new funds to expand the firm where you work.

MyEconLab

**Your Turn:** Test your understanding by doing related problem 3.12 on page 260 at the end of this chapter.

prospects, so management may want to shrink the firm's operations. Likewise, changes in the value of the firm's bonds imply changes in the cost of external funds to finance the firm's investment in research and development or in new factories. A higher bond price indicates a lower cost of new external funds, while a lower bond price indicates a higher cost of new external funds.

## Why Do Stock Prices Fluctuate So Much?

The performance of the U.S. stock market is often measured using *stock market indexes*. Stock market indexes are averages of stock prices with the value of the index set equal to 100 in a particular year, called the *base year*. Because the stock indexes are intended to show movements in prices from one year to the next, rather than the actual dollar values of the underlying stocks, the year chosen for the base year is unimportant. Figure 8.2 shows movements from January 1995 to September 2011 in the three most widely followed stock indexes:

- The Dow Jones Industrial Average, which is an index of the stock prices of 30 large U.S. corporations.

- The S&P 500, which is an index prepared by Standard & Poor's Corporation and includes the stock prices of 500 large U.S. firms.

- The NASDAQ Composite Index, which includes the stock prices of the more than 4,000 firms whose shares are traded in the NASDAQ stock market. NASDAQ is an "over-the-counter" market, meaning that buying and selling on NASDAQ is carried out between dealers who are linked together by computer. The listings on NASDAQ are dominated by high-tech firms such as Apple, Microsoft, and Google.

As we have seen, ownership of a firm's stock represents a claim on the firm's profits. So, the larger the firm's profits are, the higher its stock price will be. When the overall economy is expanding, incomes, employment, and spending will all increase, as will corporate profits. When the economy is in a recession, incomes, employment, and spending will fall, as will corporate profits. We would expect that stock prices will rise when the economy is expanding and fall when the economy is in recession. We see this pattern reflected in the three stock market indexes in Figure 8.2. All three indexes follow a roughly similar pattern: Increases in stock prices during the economic expansion of the late 1990s, declines after the "dot-com crash" of 2000 and the recession of 2001, increases from late 2001 to late 2007, declines as the U.S. economy entered a recession at the end of 2007, and then increases beginning in early 2009.

The stock prices of many early Internet companies soared in the late 1990s, as some analysts made what turned out to be overly optimistic predictions about how rapidly

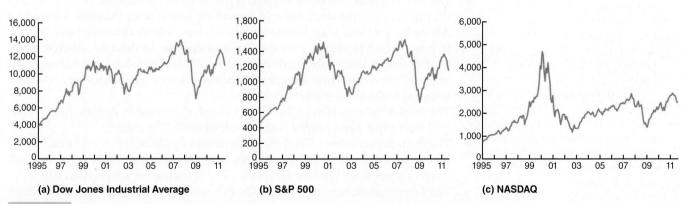

(a) Dow Jones Industrial Average    (b) S&P 500    (c) NASDAQ

**Figure 8.2**    Movements in Stock Market Indexes, January 1995 to September 2011

The performance of the U.S. stock market is often measured by market indexes, which are averages of stock prices. The three most important indexes are the Dow Jones Industrial Average, the S&P 500, and the NASDAQ. During the period from 1995 to 2011, the three indexes followed similar patterns, rising when the U.S. economy was expanding and falling when the economy was in recession.

online retailing would grow. In 2000, when investors came to believe that many dot-coms would never be profitable, their stock prices crashed. Because the NASDAQ is dominated by high-tech stocks, it experienced greater swings during the dot-com boom and bust of the late 1990s and early 2000s than did the other two indexes. The sharp declines in all three indexes beginning in late 2007 reflected the severity of the recession that began in December of that year. The severity of the recession was due in part to problems with financial firms, which we will discuss later in this chapter.

| Making the Connection | ## Following Abercrombie & Fitch's Stock Price in the Financial Pages |
|---|---|

If you read the online stock listings on the *Wall Street Journal's* web site or on another site, you will notice that the listings pack into a small space a lot of information about what happened to stocks during the previous day's trading. The figure on the next page reproduces a small portion of the listings from the *Wall Street Journal* from August 9, 2011, for stocks listed on the New York Stock Exchange. The listings provide information on the buying and selling of the stock of five firms during the previous day. Let's focus on the highlighted listing for Abercrombie & Fitch, the clothing store, and examine the information in each column:

- The first column gives the name of the company.
- The second column gives the firm's "ticker" symbol (ANF), which you may have seen scrolling along the bottom of the screen on cable financial news channels.
- The third column (Open) gives the price (in dollars) of the stock at the time that trading began, which is 9:30 A.M. on the New York Stock Exchange. Abercrombie & Fitch opened for trading at a price of $67.85.
- The fourth column (High) and the fifth column (Low) give the highest price and the lowest price the stock sold for during the day.
- The sixth column (Close) gives the price the stock sold for the last time it was traded before the close of trading (4:00 P.M.), which in this case was $61.05.
- The seventh column (Net Chg) gives the amount by which the closing price changed from the closing price the day before. In this case, the price of Abercrombie & Fitch's stock had fallen by $9.25 per share from its closing price the day before. Changes in Abercrombie & Fitch's stock price give the firm's managers a signal that they may want to expand or contract the firm's operations.
- The eighth column (%Chg) gives the change in the price in percentage terms rather than in dollar terms.
- The ninth column (Vol) gives the number of shares of stock traded on the previous day.
- The tenth column (52 Week High) and the eleventh column (52 Week Low) give the highest price the stock has sold for and the lowest price the stock has sold for during the previous year. These numbers tell how *volatile* the stock price is—that is, how much it fluctuates over the course of the year. In this case, Abercrombie's stock had been quite volatile, rising as high as $78.25 per share and falling as low as $33.97 per share. These large fluctuations in price are an indication of how risky investing in the stock market can be.
- The twelfth column (Div) gives the dividend, expressed in dollars. In this case, 0.70 means that Abercrombie paid a dividend of $0.70 per share.
- The thirteenth column (Yield) gives the *dividend yield*, which is calculated by dividing the dividend by the *closing price* of the stock—that is, the price at which Abercrombie's stock last sold before the close of trading on the previous day.
- The fourteenth column (PE) gives the *P-E ratio* (or *price–earnings ratio*), which is calculated by dividing the price of the firm's stock by its earnings per share. (Remember that because firms retain some earnings, earnings per share is not necessarily the same as dividends per share.) Abercrombie's P-E ratio was 37, meaning that its price per share was 37 times its earnings per share. So, you would have to pay $37 to buy $1 of Abercrombie & Fitch's earnings.

- The final column (Year-To-Date %Chg) gives the percentage change in the price of the stock from the beginning of the year to the previous day. In this case, the price of Abercrombie's stock had fallen by 5.9 percent since the beginning of 2011.

| | Symbol | Open | High | Low | Close | Net Chg | %Chg | Vol | 52 Week High | 52 Week Low | Div | Yield | PE | Year-To-Date %Chg |
|---|---|---|---|---|---|---|---|---|---|---|---|---|---|---|
| ABB ADS | ABB | 20.60 | 20.89 | 19.59 | 19.59 | -2.00 | -9.26 | 7,134,463 | 27.58 | 18.53 | 0.64 | 3.3 | 16 | -12.7 |
| ABBOTT LABORATORIES | ABT | 49.30 | 50.13 | 47.56 | 48.06 | -2.17 | -4.32 | 18,398,789 | 54.24 | 45.07 | 1.92 | 4.0 | 17 | 0.3 |
| ABERCROMBIE & FITCH CO. | ANF | 67.85 | 68.93 | 58.84 | 61.05 | -9.25 | -13.16 | 6,891,113 | 78.25 | 33.97 | 0.70 | 1.15 | 37 | -5.9 |
| ABITIBIBOWATER | ABH | 16.11 | 16.18 | 15.58 | 15.72 | -0.96 | -5.76 | 1,703,003 | 30.54 | 15.58 | ... | ... | ... | -33.6 |
| ABM INDUSTRIES | ABM | 19.79 | 20.72 | 17.29 | 17.29 | -3.34 | -16.19 | 1,762,427 | 27.14 | 17.29 | 0.56 | 3.2 | 16 | -34.26 |

Source: "Abercrombie and Fitch Stock History" from *The Wall Street Journal*. Copyright © 2011 by *Dow Jones & Company, Inc*. Reproduced with permission of *Dow Jones & Company, Inc.*

**Your Turn:** Test your understanding by doing related problems 3.13 and 3.14 on pages 260–261 at the end of this chapter.

MyEconLab

# Using Financial Statements to Evaluate a Corporation

**8.4 LEARNING** OBJECTIVE

Understand the information provided in corporations' financial statements.

To raise funds, a firm's managers must persuade banks or buyers of its stocks or bonds that it will be profitable. Before a firm can sell new issues of stocks or bonds, it must first provide investors and financial regulators with information about its finances. To borrow from a bank or another financial intermediary, the firm must disclose financial information to the lender as well.

In most high-income countries, government agencies require firms to disclose specific financial information to the public before they are allowed to sell securities such as stocks or bonds in financial markets. In the United States, the Securities and Exchange Commission requires publicly owned firms to report their performance in financial statements prepared using standard accounting methods, often referred to as *generally accepted accounting principles*. Such disclosure reduces information costs, but it doesn't eliminate them—for two reasons. First, some firms may be too young to have much information for potential investors to evaluate. Second, managers may try to present the required information in the best possible light so that investors will overvalue their securities.

Private firms also collect information on business borrowers and sell the information to lenders and investors. If the information-gathering firm does a good job, lenders and investors purchasing the information will be better able to judge the quality of borrowing firms. Firms specializing in information—including Moody's Investors Service, Standard & Poor's Corporation, Value Line, and Dun & Bradstreet—collect information from businesses and sell it to subscribers. Buyers include individual investors, libraries, and financial intermediaries. You can find some of these publications in your college library or through online information services.

What kind of information do investors and firm managers need? A firm must answer three basic questions: What to produce? How to produce it? and What price to charge? To answer these questions, a firm's managers need two pieces of information: The first is

**Liability** Anything owed by a person or a firm.

the firm's revenues and costs, and the second is the value of the property and other assets the firm owns and the firm's debts, or other **liabilities**, that it owes to other persons and firms. Potential investors in the firm also need this information to decide whether to buy the firm's stocks or bonds. This information is contained in the firm's *financial statements*, principally its income statement and balance sheet, which we discuss next.

## The Income Statement

**Income statement** A financial statement that sums up a firm's revenues, costs, and profit over a period of time.

A firm's **income statement** sums up its revenues, costs, and profit over a period of time. Corporations issue annual income statements, although the 12-month *fiscal year* covered may be different from the calendar year to better represent the seasonal pattern of the business. We explore income statements in greater detail in the appendix to this chapter.

**Getting to Accounting Profit** An income statement shows a firm's revenue, costs, and profit for the firm's fiscal year. To determine profitability, the income statement starts with the firm's revenue and subtracts its operating expenses and taxes paid. The remainder, *net income*, is the **accounting profit** of the firm.

**Accounting profit** A firm's net income, measured as revenue minus operating expenses and taxes paid.

**. . . And Economic Profit** Accounting profit provides information on a firm's current net income, measured according to accepted accounting standards. Accounting profit is not, however, the ideal measure of a firm's profits because it neglects some of the firm's costs. By taking into account all costs, *economic profit* provides a better indication than accounting profit of how successful a firm is. Firms making an economic profit will remain in business and may even expand. Firms making an *economic loss* are unlikely to remain in business in the long run. To understand how economic profit is calculated, remember that economists always measure cost as *opportunity cost*. The **opportunity cost** of any activity is the highest-valued alternative that must be given up to engage in that activity. Costs are either *explicit* or *implicit*. When a firm spends money, an **explicit cost** results. If a firm incurs an opportunity cost but does not spend money, an **implicit cost** results. For example, firms incur an explicit labor cost when they pay wages to employees. Firms have many other explicit costs as well, such as the cost of the electricity used to light their buildings or the costs of advertising or insurance.

**Opportunity cost** The highest-valued alternative that must be given up to engage in an activity.

**Explicit cost** A cost that involves spending money.

**Implicit cost** A nonmonetary opportunity cost.

Some costs are implicit, however. The most important of these is the opportunity cost to investors of the funds they have invested in the firm. Economists use the term *nominal rate of return* to refer to the minimum amount that investors must earn on the funds they invest in a firm, expressed as a percentage of the amount invested. If a firm fails to provide investors with at least a normal rate of return, it will not be able to remain in business over the long run because investors will not continue to invest their funds in the firm. For example, Bethlehem Steel was once the second-leading producer of steel in the United States and a very profitable firm, with stock that sold for more than $50 per share. By 2002, investors became convinced that the firm's uncompetitive labor costs in world markets meant that the firm would never be able to provide investors with a normal rate of return. Many investors expected that the firm would eventually have to declare bankruptcy, and as a result, the price of Bethlehem Steel's stock plummeted to $1 per share. Shortly thereafter, the firm declared bankruptcy, and its remaining assets were sold off to a competing steel firm. The return (in dollars) that investors require to continue investing in a firm is a true cost to the firm and should be subtracted from the firm's revenues to calculate its profits.

The necessary rate of return that investors must receive to continue investing in a firm varies from firm to firm. If the investment is risky—as would be the case with a biotechnology start-up—investors may require a high rate of return to compensate them for the risk. Investors in firms in more established industries, such as electric utilities, may require lower rates of return. The exact rate of return investors require to invest in any particular firm is difficult to calculate, which also makes it difficult for an accountant to include the return as a cost on an income statement. Firms have other implicit costs besides the return investors require that can also be difficult to calculate. As a result, the rules of accounting generally require that only explicit costs be included in the firm's financial records. *Economic costs* include both explicit costs *and* implicit costs. **Economic profit** is equal to a firm's revenues minus its economic costs. Because accounting profit excludes some implicit costs, it is larger than economic profit.

**Economic profit** A firm's revenues minus all of its implicit and explicit costs.

## The Balance Sheet

A firm's **balance sheet** sums up its financial position on a particular day, usually the end of a quarter or year. Recall that an asset is anything of value that a firm owns, and a liability is a debt or an obligation owed by a firm. Subtracting the value of a firm's liabilities from the value of its assets leaves its *net worth*. We can think of the net worth as what the firm's owners would be left with if the firm were closed, its assets were sold, and its liabilities were paid off. Investors can determine a firm's net worth by inspecting its balance sheet. We analyze a balance sheet in more detail in the appendix to this chapter, which begins on page 263.

**Balance sheet** A financial statement that sums up a firm's financial position on a particular day, usually the end of a quarter or year.

# Corporate Governance Policy and the Financial Crisis of 2007–2009

**8.5 LEARNING** OBJECTIVE

Discuss the role that corporate governance problems may have played in the financial crisis of 2007–2009.

A firm's financial statements provide important information on the firm's ability to create value for investors and the economy. Accurate and easy-to-understand financial statements are inputs to decisions by the firm's managers and by investors. Indeed, the information in accounting statements helps guide resource allocation in the economy.

Firms disclose financial statements in periodic filings to the federal government and in *annual reports* to shareholders. An investor is more likely to buy a firm's stock if the firm's income statement shows a large after-tax profit and if its balance sheet shows a large net worth. The top management of a firm has at least two reasons to attract investors and keep the firm's stock price high. First, a higher stock price increases the funds the firm can raise when it sells a given amount of stock. Second, to reduce the principal–agent problem, boards of directors often tie the salaries of top managers to the firm's stock price or to the profitability of the firm.

Top managers clearly have an incentive to maximize the profits reported on the income statement and the net worth reported on the balance sheet. If top managers make good decisions, the firm's profits will be high, and the firm's assets will be large relative to its liabilities. Problems that surfaced during the early 2000s, however, revealed that some top managers have inflated profits and hidden liabilities that should have been listed on their balance sheets. At other firms, managers took on more risk than they disclosed to investors. We will explore recent problems with corporate governance, and the government's reaction to these problems, by discussing the accounting scandals of the early 2000s and problems that many financial firms encountered during 2007–2009.

## The Accounting Scandals of the Early 2000s

In the early 2000s, the top managers of several large and well-known firms, including Enron, an energy trading firm, and WorldCom, a telecommunications firm, were shown to have falsified their firms' financial statements in order to mislead investors about how profitable the firms actually were. Several top managers were sentenced to long jail terms, and some of the firms, including Enron, went out of business.

How was it possible for corporations such as Enron and WorldCom to falsify their financial statements? The federal government regulates how financial statements are prepared, but this regulation cannot by itself guarantee the accuracy of the statements. All firms that issue stock to the public have certified public accountants *audit* their financial statements. Unfortunately, as the Enron and WorldCom scandals revealed, top managers who are determined to deceive investors about the true financial condition of their firms can also deceive outside auditors.

To guard against future scandals, new federal legislation was enacted in 2002. The landmark *Sarbanes-Oxley Act of 2002* requires that CEOs personally certify the accuracy of financial statements. The Sarbanes-Oxley Act also requires that financial analysts and auditors disclose whether any conflicts of interest might exist that would limit their independence in evaluating a firm's financial condition. On balance, most observers acknowledge that the Sarbanes-Oxley Act increased confidence in the U.S. corporate governance system. However, as we will discuss in the next section, problems during 2007–2009 at financial firms again raised questions of whether corporations were adequately disclosing information to investors.

## The Financial Crisis of 2007–2009

Beginning in 2007 and lasting into 2009, the U.S. economy suffered the worst financial crisis since the Great Depression of the 1930s. At the heart of the crisis was a problem in the market for home mortgages. When people buy houses, they typically borrow the money by taking out a mortgage loan from a bank or another financial institution. The house they are buying is pledged as collateral for the loan, meaning that the bank can take possession of the house and sell it if the borrower defaults by failing to make the payments on the loan.

For many years, the bank or other financial institution granting a mortgage would keep the loan until the borrower had paid it off. Beginning in the 1970s, financial institutions began *securitizing* some mortgage loans, which means that groups of mortgages were bundled together and sold to investors. These *mortgage-backed securities* are very similar to bonds in that the investor who buys one receives regular interest payments, which in this case come from the payments being made on the original mortgage loans. At first, the securitization process was carried out by the Federal National Mortgage Association ("Fannie Mae") and the Federal Home Loan Mortgage Corporation ("Freddie Mac"), which Congress had established to help increase the volume of lending in the home mortgage market. Fannie Mae and Freddie Mac would buy mortgages granted to credit-worthy borrowers and bundle them into securities that were then sold to investors.

Beginning in the 1990s, private financial firms, primarily investment banks, started to securitize mortgages. By the early 2000s, many mortgages were being granted by banks and other financial institutions to "subprime" borrowers, who are borrowers whose credit histories include failures to make payments on bills, and "Alt-A" borrowers, who failed to document that their incomes were high enough to afford their mortgage payments. Both subprime and Alt-A borrowers were more likely to default on loans than were conventional borrowers. Fueled by the ease of obtaining a mortgage, housing prices in the United States soared before beginning a sharp downturn in mid-2006. By 2007, many borrowers—particularly subprime and Alt-A borrowers—began to default on their mortgages. This was bad news for anyone owning mortgage-backed securities because the value of these securities depended on steady payments being made on the underlying mortgages. As prices of these securities plunged, many financial institutions suffered heavy losses, and some of the largest of them remained in business only because they received aid from the federal government.

During the financial crisis, many investors complained that they weren't aware of the riskiness of some of the assets—particularly mortgage-backed securities—on the balance sheets of financial firms. Some observers believed that the managers of many financial firms had intentionally misled investors about the riskiness of these assets. Others argued that the managers themselves had not understood how risky the assets were. In the fall of 2008, Fannie Mae and Freddie Mac were brought under direct control of the government. As the crisis passed, in July 2010, Congress overhauled regulation of the financial system with the passage of the **Wall Street Reform and Consumer Protection Act**, referred to as the Dodd-Frank Act. Among its provisions, the act created the Consumer Financial Protection Bureau, housed in the Federal Reserve, to write rules intended to protect consumers in their borrowing and investing activities. The act also established the Financial Stability Oversight Council, which includes representatives from all the major federal financial regulatory bodies, including the SEC and the Federal Reserve. The council is intended to identify and act on risks to the financial system. Economists are divided in their opinions about whether the Dodd-Frank Act would significantly reduce the risk of future financial crises.

**Wall Street Reform and Consumer Protection Act (Dodd-Frank Act)** Legislation passed during 2010 that was intended to reform regulation of the financial system.

# Did Principal–Agent Problems Help Bring on the Financial Crisis?

As we have seen, the process of securitizing mortgages played an important role in the financial crisis of 2007–2009. Beginning in the 1990s, private investment banks began to securitize mortgages. Unlike commercial banks, whose main activities are accepting deposits and making loans, investment banks had traditionally concentrated on providing advice to corporations on selling new stocks and bonds and on *underwriting* the issuance of stocks and bonds by guaranteeing a price to the firm selling them. Investment banking is considered more risky than commercial banking because investment banks can suffer heavy losses on underwriting. To address this greater risk, Congress passed the Glass-Steagall Act in 1933. The act prevented financial firms from being both commercial banks and investment banks.

Some economists and policymakers argued that Glass-Steagall reduced competition for investment banking services by prohibiting commercial banks from offering these services. Congress repealed the Glass-Steagall Act in 1999, after which some commercial banks began engaging in investment banking. Many of the largest, best-known investment banks, such as Lehman Brothers, Bear Stearns, Goldman Sachs, Merrill Lynch, and Morgan Stanley, remained exclusively investment banks. The mortgage-backed securities originated by the investment banks were mostly sold to investors, but some were retained as investments by these firms. As a result, when the prices of these securities declined beginning in 2007, the investment banks suffered heavy losses. Lehman Brothers was forced to declare bankruptcy, Merrill Lynch and Bear Stearns were sold to commercial banks in deals arranged by the U.S. government, and Goldman Sachs and Morgan Stanley became bank holding companies, which allowed them to engage in commercial banking activity. With these developments, the era of the large Wall Street investment bank came to an end.

Why did the investment banks take on so much risk by originating securities backed by mortgages granted to borrowers who had a high likelihood of defaulting on the loans? Michael Lewis, a financial journalist and former Wall Street bond salesman, has argued that a key reason was a change in how the investment banks were organized. Traditionally, Wall Street investment banks had been organized as partnerships, but by 2000 they had all converted to being publicly traded corporations. As we have seen, in a partnership the funds of the relatively small group of owners are put directly at risk, and the principal–agent problem is reduced because there is little separation of ownership from control. With a publicly traded corporation, on the other hand, the principal–agent problem can be severe. Lewis argues:

> No investment bank owned by its employees would have . . . bought and held $50 billion in [exotic mortgage-backed securities]. . . . or even allow [these securities] to be sold to its customers. The hoped-for short-term gain would not have justified the long-term hit.

Issues of corporate governance will clearly continue to be a concern for economists, policymakers, and investors.

---

**Making the Connection** | ## Are Buyers of Facebook Stock Getting a Fair Deal?

Many technology firms, including Facebook, turn to *venture capital firms* for funds. These firms raise funds from investors and use the funds to make investments in small start-up firms. A venture capital firm frequently takes a large ownership stake in a start-up firm, often placing its own employees on the board of directors or even having them serve as managers. These steps can reduce principal–agent problems because the venture capital firm has a greater ability to closely monitor the managers. The firm's managers will probably be attentive to

*Was buying stock in Facebook a good investment?*

the wishes of a large investor because having a large investor sell its stake in the firm may make it difficult to raise funds from new investors.

Several venture capital funds, including Accel Partners, invested in Facebook. If a start-up firm becomes successful, then it will typically become a public firm by issuing stock. The first issue of stock by a firm is called an *initial public offering (IPO)*. The IPO makes it possible for the venture capital firm to easily sell its ownership share of the firm to other investors. In the case of Facebook, though, CEO Mark Zuckerberg was reluctant to allow an IPO because he wanted to keep the company private rather than bring in many additional investors, which could reduce his control of the firm. The lack of an IPO meant that Accel, other venture capital firms, and Facebook employees who had received stock could not easily "cash out" by selling their shares. As we saw at the beginning of the chapter, though, it is possible for private firms to sell a limited amount of stock. These sales don't take place on the New York Stock Exchange or NASDAQ but are arranged by firms such as SharesPost and SecondMarket, which match up sellers of stock in private firms with buyers. These sales are sometimes called *private placements*, and the market for shares of private firms is sometimes referred to as the *shadow market* to distinguish it from the stock markets on which shares of public firms are traded. Trading in private-company shares has been increasing rapidly; it doubled from 2009 to 2010 and was expected to grow by 50 percent during 2011.

Only so-called accredited investors are eligible to buy shares of private firms. An investor is accredited if he or she has an income of $200,000 or more for at least the previous two years or has a net worth of $1 million. A private company cannot have more than 499 individual shareholders. Because the Securities and Exchange Commission (SEC) assumes that accredited investors are experienced and sophisticated, the market for shares of private firms is not closely regulated. In particular, private firms do not have to disclose their financial statements, such as their income statements and balance sheets, as public firms do. Some economists and policymakers, though, worry that there is potential for sellers of shares in a private firm to take advantage of buyers because the insiders selling the shares have information about the firm's financial statements that the investors do not. For instance, in mid-2011, stock in Facebook was selling for about $35 per share, which would make the total value of the firm about $80 billion. Was Facebook really worth that much? It was difficult to tell because the firm did not have to make public its revenue or profits.

As the SEC considered changing the regulations governing the sale of shares in private firms, it faced conflicting pressures. Some economists and policymakers wanted the SEC to require private firms to disclose more information to potential investors. Others argued that the SEC should relax some of the existing regulations to make it easier for start-ups to raise funds without having to meet all of the requirements to become a publicly traded firm. In late 2011, it was unclear which way the SEC would move, although it did appear to be favoring a proposal to raise the limit on the number of shareholders allowed in a private firm.

Based on Shayndi Raice, "Is Facebook Worth $100 Billion?" *Wall Street Journal*, July 14, 2011; Pui-Wing Tam, "As Web IPOs Hit, Few Share the Spoils," *Wall Street Journal*, July 8, 2011; Miguel Helft, "Facebook Deal Offers Freedom From Scrutiny," *New York Times*, January 3, 2011; Jean Eaglesham, "U.S. Eyes New Stock Rules," *Wall Street Journal*, April 6, 2011; and Michael Hickins, "Investor Criticizes 'Shadow Market,'" *Wall Street Journal*, March 17, 2011.

MyEconLab  **Your Turn:** Test your understanding by doing related problem 5.7 on page 262 at the end of this chapter.

Continued from page 237

## Economics in Your Life

### Do Corporate Managers Act in the Best Interests of Shareholders?

At the beginning of the chapter, we asked you to consider two questions: Why is it difficult to get the managers of a firm to act in your interests rather than in their own? and Given this problem, should you ever take on the risk of buying stock? The reason managers may not act in shareholders' interest is that in large corporations there is separation of ownership from control: The shareholders own the firm, but the top managers actually control it. This results in the principal–agent problem discussed in the chapter. The principal–agent problem clearly adds to the risk you would face by buying stock rather than doing something safe with your money, such as putting it in the bank. But the rewards to owning stock can also be substantial, potentially earning you far more over the long run than a bank account. Buying the stock of well-known firms, such as Google, that are closely followed by Wall Street investment analysts helps to reduce the principal–agent problem. It is less likely that the managers of these firms will take actions that are clearly not in the best interests of shareholders because the managers' actions are difficult to conceal. Buying the stock of large, well-known firms certainly does not completely eliminate the risk from the principal–agent problem, however. Enron, WorldCom, and some of the other firms that were involved in the scandals discussed in this chapter were all well known and closely followed by Wall Street analysts, as were the large financial firms that ran into difficulties during the financial crisis of 2007–2009, but their stock turned out to be very poor investments.

## Conclusion

In a market system, firms make independent decisions about which goods and services to produce, how to produce them, and what prices to charge. In modern high-income countries, such as the United States, large corporations account for a majority of the sales and profits earned by firms. Generally, the managers of these corporations do a good job of representing the interests of stockholders while providing the goods and services demanded by consumers. As the business scandals of the early 2000s and the problems with financial firms in 2007–2009 showed, however, the principal–agent problem can sometimes become severe. Economists debate the costs and benefits of regulations proposed to address these problems.

An *Inside Look* on the next page discusses how the Web sites SecondMarket and SharesPost help qualified investors buy shares of private companies.

## KIPLINGER

## How to Buy Into Facebook Before It Goes Public

Goldman Sachs caused a stir in early January when word broke that it would invest $450 million in Facebook. Even more intriguing, though, was the news that Goldman would create a fund through which its clients could buy some $1.5 billion worth of shares in the fast-growing, privately held social-networking company.

(a) But you don't have to be a well-heeled Goldman client to get in on Facebook or other hot, privately held companies before they go public. Two Web sites—SharesPost.com and SecondMarket.com—provide electronic platforms that allow qualified investors to buy shares from company insiders and employees who want to cash out before a company goes public. By offering a way to enter an area previously open only to Wall Street's elite, "we democratize the opportunity to invest in private company stocks," says David Weir, chief executive of SharesPost.

(b) Since 2004, SecondMarket, a registered brokerage, has been offering a marketplace for alternative investments, such as asset-backed securities, mortgage securities and limited-partnership interests. Last year, $400 million worth of transactions closed on SecondMarket, up from $100 million in 2009. At present, 40 private stock issues trade on the platform, with Facebook, Twitter and LinkedIn the most active.

SharesPost, founded in June 2009, is not a brokerage but works with brokers to manage transactions. Currently, it lists 150 privately held companies, with the total number of buy and sell orders available (not actual trades) worth roughly $400 million.

**Why would you want to invest in a nonpublic company?** You could become an insider before a firm goes public, presumably at a much higher price than you paid for your shares. Facebook is at the center of attention because of its extraordinary growth and the perception that its initial public offering could be as successful as that of Google (symbol GOOG). Facebook hasn't yet announced plans for an IPO, but many market watchers expect the Palo Alto, Cal., company to go public next year. . . .

(c) Signing up with the secondary-market services is as easy as joining Facebook; actually getting to trade is another matter. Neither outfit requires clients to pony up $2 million or more and hold the shares until 2013, as Goldman is stipulating for its Facebook offering. However, both companies require clients to be accredited investors. According to the Securities and Exchange Commission, this means investors must have enough knowledge and experience to evaluate an investment's risks and be able to bear them, and they must have a net worth of at least $1 million or income exceeding $200,000 per year for the preceding two years. After the company verifies your information, a process that typically takes 48 hours, you're ready to trade. In addition, once you make a purchase, both SharesPost and SecondMarket require you to hold the shares for at least one year.

Privately held stocks don't trade quickly, or even every day. Typically, the seller sets a price, but buyers and sellers can—and do—haggle. And agreeing to a price doesn't mean the trade will actually go through. Mark Murphy, a spokesman for Second-Market, says companies have the right of first refusal. So even if the seller accepts the deal, his or her company has 30 days to check you out to determine if they want you as a shareholder. If not, the company can deny the trade and buy the shares from the seller itself. If a trade goes through, you can expect to pay a commission of 2% to 5% of the size of the transaction. Murphy says the typical SecondMarket transaction is about $2 million. SharesPost says its transactions range from $10,000 to millions of dollars.

## Key Points in the Article

When Goldman Sachs invested in Facebook in 2011, it also offered some of its best clients a chance to purchase shares in the company. In addition to companies such as Goldman Sachs, two relatively new companies, SecondMarket and SharesPost, offer qualified investors the chance to purchase private company stock from company insiders and employees who want to sell their personal shares. These new firms give investors an opportunity to purchase stock before a company goes public. Signing up with SecondMarket and SharesPost is a relatively quick process, but both companies require their clients to meet the qualifications of the Securities and Exchange Commission's (SEC's) definition of an accredited investor.

## Analyzing the News

**a** Some companies are publicly traded, and others are privately held. Most large corporations are owned by stockholders, who through boards of directors have the right to hire or fire top managers. Publicly traded companies sell stock as a way to raise funds. Some large corporations, such as Facebook, are privately held. With a private company, upper management has more control of the company than if the company were publicly traded, but the company must look to alternatives such as taking on private investors to raise capital. In 2011, Facebook turned to investment banking firm Goldman Sachs, which invested $450 million in the social networking company. Goldman Sachs then offered an opportunity to some of its best clients to purchase shares in Facebook. Private offerings to top clients are one of the few ways investors can buy into private companies. Two Web sites, however, are now offering investors the opportunity to buy shares of private companies from company insiders and employees, opening the door a little wider to investment in private companies.

**b** SecondMarket and SharesPost are two Web sites that list for sale shares in privately held companies. Offerings are limited to a total of 190 private stocks but include well-known companies such as Facebook and Twitter. The figure below shows that these numbers are tiny compared to the roughly 15,000 publicly traded companies represented by the New York Stock Exchange, NASDAQ, and stocks traded over-the-counter. The chapter discusses the principal–agent problem, which normally does not occur in privately held companies where the founder and majority shareholder typically runs the company. Management and ownership are one and the same, so they do not have differing interests. When private companies take on investors, ownership interests can start to vary from those of management, and the principal–agent problem can become a reality. With shares of privately held companies now being offered to a wider variety of investors, the principal–agent problem has the potential of becoming more significant.

**c** Because privately held companies are not legally required to release financial statements, these investments have the potential of being quite risky. Both SecondMarket and SharesPost abide by SEC guidelines for accredited investors and require investors to meet qualifications, which include experience in evaluating an investment's risk and having a minimum net worth of $1 million or having annual income of at least $200,000 over the preceding two years. Both companies also require purchased shares to be held for at least one year, so these opportunities are designed for serious, knowledgeable investors and not for casual investors.

## Thinking Critically

1. Explain why purchasing shares of a privately held company such as Facebook could be much more risky for investors than purchasing shares of a publicly traded company.

2. In January 2011, Goldman Sachs announced it would invest $450 million in Facebook. An executive at Facebook who knew when this deal would be announced could have made money quickly by buying Goldman Sachs stock and selling it at a higher price a few days later. (Goldman Sachs stock went up almost $7 a share over a seven-day period surrounding the investment.) Such "insider trading" is illegal, however. Do you think that insider trading should be illegal? Are there benefits to other investors or to the economy as a whole associated with insider trading? Are there problems associated with insider trading?

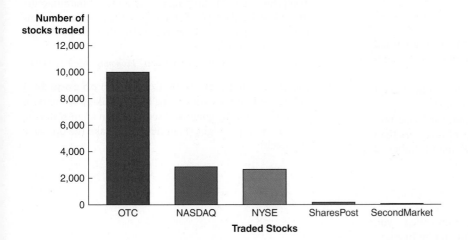

SecondMarket and SharesPost offer 190 private stocks, which is a small number compared with the number of stock that are publicly traded.

# Chapter Summary and Problems

## Key Terms

Accounting profit, p. 250

Asset, p. 238

Balance sheet, p. 251

Bond, p. 243

Corporate governance, p. 241

Corporation, p. 238

Coupon payment, p. 243

Direct finance, p. 243

Dividends, p. 245

Economic profit, p. 251

Explicit cost, p. 250

Implicit cost, p. 250

Income statement, p. 250

Indirect finance, p. 243

Interest rate, p. 243

Liability, p. 250

Limited liability, p. 238

Opportunity cost, p. 250

Partnership, p. 238

Principal–agent problem, p. 241

Separation of ownership from control, p. 241

Sole proprietorship, p. 238

Stock, p. 245

Wall Street Reform and Consumer Protection Act (Dodd-Frank Act), p. 252

---

**8.1** | **Types of Firms, pages 238–240**

LEARNING OBJECTIVE: Categorize the major types of firms in the United States.

## Summary

There are three types of firms: A **sole proprietorship** is a firm owned by a single individual and not organized as a corporation. A **partnership** is a firm owned jointly by two or more persons and not organized as a corporation. A **corporation** is a legal form of business that provides the owners with limited liability. An **asset** is anything of value owned by a person or a firm. The owners of sole proprietorships and partners have unlimited liability, which means there is no legal distinction between the personal assets of the owners of the business and the assets of the business. The owners of corporations have **limited liability**, which means they can never lose more than their investment in the firm. Although only 20 percent of firms are corporations, they account for the majority of revenue and profit earned by all firms.

 **MyEconLab** Visit **www.myeconlab.com** to complete these exercises online and get instant feedback.

## Review Questions

**1.1** What are the three major types of firms in the United States? Briefly discuss the most important characteristics of each type.

**1.2** What is limited liability? Why does the government grant limited liability to the owners of corporations?

**1.3** Why is limited liability more important for firms trying to raise funds from a large number of investors than for firms trying to raise funds from a small number of investors?

## Problems and Applications

**1.4** Suppose that shortly after graduating from college, you decide to start your own business. Will you be likely to organize the business as a sole proprietorship, a partnership, or a corporation? Explain your reasoning.

**1.5** How would the establishment of limited liability for the owners of corporations affect the production possibilities frontier of a country over time?

**1.6** Evaluate the following argument:

> I would like to invest in the stock market, but I think that buying shares of stock in a corporation is too risky. Suppose I buy $10,000 of General Electric stock, and the company ends up going bankrupt. Because as a stockholder I'm part owner of the company, I might be responsible for paying hundreds of thousands of dollars of the company's debts.

**1.7** According to an article in the *Economist* magazine, historian David Faure has argued that the Chinese economy failed to grow rapidly during the nineteenth century because "family-run companies . . . could not raise sufficient capital to exploit the large-scale opportunities tied to the rise of the steam engine, notably railways and (with limited exceptions) global shipping and automated manufacturing." How did the United States solve the problem of firms raising enough funds to operate railroads and other large-scale businesses?

Based on "The PCCW Buy-out in Court," *Economist*, April 21, 2009.

**1.8** **[Related to the** Making the Connection **on page 240]** Why might large existing firms be more likely to focus on improving existing goods and services than on introducing new ones? Why might small new firms take the opposite approach?

| 8.2 | **The Structure of Corporations and the Principal–Agent Problem,** pages 241–242 |
| --- | --- |

LEARNING OBJECTIVE: Describe the typical management structure of corporations and understand the concepts of separation of ownership from control and the principal–agent problem.

## Summary

**Corporate governance** refers to the way in which a corporation is structured and the impact a corporation's structure has on the firm's behavior. Most corporations have a similar management structure: The shareholders elect a board of directors that appoints the corporation's top managers, such as the chief executive officer (CEO). Because the top management often does not own a large fraction of the stock in the corporation, large corporations have a **separation of ownership from control**. Because top managers have less incentive to increase the corporation's profits than to increase their own salaries and their own enjoyment, corporations can suffer from the **principal–agent problem**. The principal–agent problem exists when the principals—in this case, the shareholders of the corporation—have difficulty getting the agent—the corporation's top management—to carry out their wishes.

MyEconLab    Visit **www.myeconlab.com** to complete these exercises online and get instant feedback.

## Review Questions

**2.1** What does it mean to say that there is a separation of ownership from control in large corporations?

**2.2** How is the separation of ownership from control related to the principal–agent problem?

**2.3** Why is it important for a board of directors to have outside directors, as opposed to only inside directors?

## Problems and Applications

**2.4** The principal–agent problem arises almost everywhere in the business world, and it also crops up even closer to home. Discuss the principal–agent problem that exists in the college classroom. Who is the principal? Who is the agent? What potential conflicts in objectives are there between this principal and this agent?

**2.5** The principal–agent problem in a public corporation between ownership and top management results from asymmetric information. What information, if known, would prevent this principal–agent problem?

**2.6** Sales personnel, whether selling life insurance, automobiles, or magazine subscriptions, typically get paid on commission instead of a straight hourly wage. How does paying a commission help solve the principal–agent problem between the owner of a business and the sales force?

**2.7** **[Related to** Solved Problem 8.2 **on page 242]** Briefly explain whether you agree with the following argument: "The separation of ownership from control in large corporations and the principal–agent problem mean that top managers can work short days, take long vacations, and otherwise slack off."

**2.8** **[Related to** Solved Problem 8.2 **on page 242]** The members of many corporate boards of directors have to be reelected by the firm's stockholders every year. Some corporations, though, have staggered elections for their boards of directors, with only one-half or one-third of the members being up for election each year. According to an article in the *Economist* magazine, studies have found that firms that have staggered elections for their boards of directors are less profitable than similar firms where all members of the boards of directors are elected each year. Provide a possible explanation for this finding.

Based on "A Different Class," *Economist*, February 18, 2011.

**2.9** An article in *BusinessWeek* states that members of boards of directors believe that, in general, the compensation of CEOs is too high. However, most board members believe that the compensation of the CEO of their firm is appropriate. The article concludes: "Given this and that they work for the CEO, it is not surprising that boards continue to support high levels of CEO compensation." How does this statement relate to the principal–agent problem?

Based on "Fixing Executive Compensation Excesses," by Edward E. Lawler from *BusinessWeek*, February 5, 2009.

| 8.3 | **How Firms Raise Funds,** pages 242–249 |
| --- | --- |

LEARNING OBJECTIVE: Explain how firms raise the funds they need to operate and expand.

## Summary

Firms rely on retained earnings—which are profits retained by the firm and not paid out to the firm's owners—or on using the savings of households for the funds they need to operate and expand. With **direct finance**, the savings of households flow directly to businesses when investors buy **stocks** and **bonds** in financial markets. With **indirect finance**, savings flow indirectly to businesses when households deposit money in saving and checking accounts in banks and the banks lend these funds to businesses. Federal, state, and local governments also sell bonds in financial markets, and households also borrow funds from banks. When a firm sells a bond, it is borrowing money from the buyer of the bond. The firm makes a **coupon payment** to the buyer of the bond. The **interest rate** is the cost of borrowing funds, usually expressed as a percentage of the amount borrowed. When a firm sells stock, it is selling part ownership of the firm to the buyer of the stock. **Dividends** are payments by a corporation to its shareholders. The original purchasers of stocks and bonds may resell them in stock and bond markets, such as the New York Stock Exchange. The performance of the U.S. stock market is often measured using stock market indexes. The three most widely followed stock indexes are the Dow Jones Industrial Average, the S&P 500, and the NASDAQ Composite Index.

MyEconLab    Visit **www.myeconlab.com** to complete these exercises online and get instant feedback.

## Review Questions

**3.1** What is the difference between direct finance and indirect finance? If you borrow money from a bank to buy a new car, are you using direct finance or indirect finance?

**3.2** Why is a bond considered to be a loan but a share of stock is not? Why do corporations issue both bonds and shares of stock?

**3.3** How do the stock and bond markets provide information to businesses? Why do stock and bond prices change over time?

## Problems and Applications

**3.4** Suppose that a firm in which you have invested is losing money. Would you rather own the firm's stock or the firm's bonds? Explain.

**3.5** Suppose you originally invested in a firm when it was small and unprofitable. Now the firm has grown to be large and profitable. Would you be better off if you had bought the firm's stock or the firm's bonds? Explain.

**3.6** If you deposit $20,000 in a savings account at a bank, you might earn 1 percent interest per year. Someone who borrows $20,000 from a bank to buy a new car might have to pay an interest rate of 6 percent per year on the loan. Knowing this, why don't you just lend your money directly to the car buyer, cutting out the bank?

**3.7** **[Related to the** Chapter Opener **on page 237]** The owners of Facebook have had several opportunities to sell the company to larger firms or to make the firm a public corporation by selling stock. In 2009, the value of Facebook was estimated to be somewhere between $2 billion and $5 billion. So, selling Facebook or making it a public corporation would make Mark Zuckerberg and its other owners very wealthy. In those circumstances, why might a firm such as Facebook choose to remain a private company?

Based on Felix Salmon, "Facebook Eyes Additional Funding," Reuters. com, April 30, 2009.

**3.8** **[Related to the** Making the Connection **on page 244]** The following is from an article in the *Wall Street Journal*:

> Moody's Investors Service. . . . said it was cutting Japan's government bond rating to Aa3 from Aa2, citing "large budget deficits and the build-up in Japanese government debt since the 2009 global recession."

**a.** Moody's downgraded Japan's government debt from Aa2 to Aa3. What is Moody's top bond rating?

**b.** Why would "large budget deficits and the build-up in Japanese government debt" be a reason to downgrade Japan's debt rating?

"Moody's Downgrades Japan Debt, But Offers A Stable Outlook," by William Sposato from *Wall Street Journal*, August 24, 2011. Copyright © 2011 by Dow Jones & Company, Inc.. Reproduced with permission of Dow Jones & Company, Inc.

**3.9** What effect would the following events be likely to have on the price of Google's stock?

**a.** A competitor launches a search engine that's just as good as Google's.

**b.** The corporate income tax is abolished.

**c.** Google's board of directors becomes dominated by close friends and relatives of its top management.

**d.** The price of wireless Internet connections unexpectedly drops, so more and more people use the Internet.

**e.** Google announces a huge profit of $1 billion, but everybody anticipated that Google would earn a huge profit of $1 billion.

**3.10** The French government issues bonds with 50-year maturities. Would such bonds be purchased only by very young investors who expect to still be alive when the bond matures? Briefly explain.

**3.11** The following appeared in an article in the *Wall Street Journal* about the bond market in high-income (or "developed") countries (that is, the United States and countries in Europe) and the emerging-market countries (that is, Latin American and Asian countries):

> "In the developed markets, it's been about analyzing the business cycle, and in emerging markets, it's been about solvency," says David Rolley, the co-manager of the Loomis Sayles Global Bond fund. "Now it's not. You have to do both for both." . . . It could ultimately mean that developed economies, the U.S. included, could face extra penalties for the perceived, even if ever-so-slight, risk that they may not repay their debts.

**a.** What does it mean to say that the emerging markets have been about "solvency"?

**b.** What are the "extra penalties" the developed economies could face from the increase in perceived risk?

From Matthieu Wirz and Matt Phillips, "Sea Change in Map of Global Risk," *Wall Street Journal*, August 1, 2011.

**3.12** **[Related to the** Don't Let This Happen to You **on page 246]** Briefly explain whether you agree or disagree with the following statement: "The total value of the shares of Microsoft stock traded on the NASDAQ last week was $250 million, so the firm actually received more revenue from stock sales than from selling software."

**3.13** **[Related to the** Making the Connection **on page 248]** Loans from banks are the most important external source of funds to businesses because most businesses are too small to borrow in financial markets by issuing stocks or bonds. Most investors are reluctant to buy the stocks or bonds of small businesses because of the difficulty of gathering accurate information on the financial strength and

# Appendix

## Tools to Analyze Firms' Financial Information

**LEARNING** OBJECTIVE

Understand the concept of present value and the information contained on a firm's income statement and balance sheet.

As we saw in the chapter, modern business firms are not just "black boxes" transforming inputs into output. Most business revenues and profits are earned by large corporations. Unlike founder-dominated firms, the typical large corporation is run by managers who generally do not own a controlling interest in the firm. Large firms raise funds from outside investors, and outside investors seek information on firms and the assurance that the managers of firms will act in the interests of the investors.

This chapter shows how corporations raise funds by issuing stocks and bonds. This appendix provides more detail to support that discussion. We begin by analyzing *present value* as a key concept in determining the prices of financial securities. We then provide greater information on *financial statements* issued by corporations, using Google as an example.

## Using Present Value to Make Investment Decisions

Firms raise funds by selling equity (stock) and debt (bonds and loans) to investors and lenders. If you own shares of stock or a bond, you will receive payments in the form of dividends or coupons over a number of years. Most people value funds they already have more highly than funds they will receive some time in the future. For example, you would probably not trade $1,000 you already have for $1,000 you will not receive for one year. The longer you have to wait to receive a payment, the less value it will have for you. One thousand dollars you will not receive for two years is worth less to you than $1,000 you will receive after one year. The value you give today to money you will receive in the future is called the future payment's **present value**. The present value of $1,000 you will receive in one year will be less than $1,000.

Why is this true? Why is the $1,000 you will not receive for one year less valuable to you than the $1,000 you already have? The most important reason is that if you have $1,000 today, you can use that $1,000 today. You can buy goods and services with the money and receive enjoyment from them. The $1,000 you receive in one year does not have direct use to you now.

Also, prices will likely rise during the year you are waiting to receive your $1,000. So, when you finally do receive the $1,000 in one year, you will not be able to buy as much with it as you could with $1,000 today. Finally, there is some risk that you will not receive the $1,000 in one year. The risk may be very great if an unreliable friend borrows $1,000 from you and vaguely promises to pay you back in one year. The risk may be very small if you lend money to the federal government by buying a U.S. Treasury bond. In either case, though, there is at least some risk that you will not receive the funds promised.

When someone lends money, the lender expects to be paid back both the amount of the loan and some additional interest. Say that you decide that you are willing to lend your $1,000 today if you are paid back $1,100 one year from now. In this case, you are charging $100/$1,000 = 0.10, or 10 percent interest on the funds you have loaned. Economists would say that you value $1,000 today as equivalent to the $1,100 to be received one year in the future.

**Present value** The value in today's dollars of funds to be paid or received in the future.

Notice that $1,100 can be written as $1,000 $(1 + 0.10)$. That is, the value of money received in the future is equal to the value of money in the present multiplied by 1 plus the interest rate, with the interest rate expressed as a decimal. Or:

$$\$1,100 = \$1,000(1 + 0.10).$$

Notice, also, that if we divide both sides by $(1 + 0.10)$, we can rewrite this formula as:

$$\$1,000 = \frac{\$1,100}{(1 + 0.10)}.$$

The rewritten formula states that the present value is equal to the future value to be received in one year divided by 1 plus the interest rate. This formula is important because you can use it to convert any amount to be received in one year into its present value. Writing the formula generally, we have:

$$\text{Present value} = \frac{\text{Future value}_1}{(1 + i)}.$$

The present value of funds to be received in one year—Future value$_1$—can be calculated by dividing the amount of those funds to be received by 1 plus the interest rate. With an interest rate of 10 percent, the present value of $1,000,000 to be received one year from now is:

$$\frac{\$1,000,000}{(1 + 0.10)} = \$909,090.91.$$

This method is a useful way of calculating the value today of funds that will be received in one year. But financial securities such as stocks and bonds involve promises to pay funds over many years. Therefore, it would be even more useful if we could expand this formula to calculate the present value of funds to be received more than one year in the future.

This expansion is easy to do. Go back to the original example, where we assumed you were willing to loan out your $1,000 for one year, provided that you received 10 percent interest. Suppose you are asked to lend the funds for two years and that you are promised 10 percent interest per year for each year of the loan. That is, you are lending $1,000, which at 10 percent interest will grow to $1,100 after one year, and you are agreeing to loan that $1,100 out for a second year at 10 percent interest. So, after two years, you will be paid back $1,100 $(1 + 0.10)$, or $1,210. Or:

$$\$1,210 = \$1,000(1 + 0.10)(1 + 0.10),$$

or:

$$\$1,210 = \$1,000(1 + 0.10)^2.$$

This formula can also be rewritten as:

$$\$1,000 = \frac{\$1,210}{(1 + 0.10)^2}.$$

To put this formula in words, the $1,210 you receive two years from now has a present value equal to $1,210 divided by the quantity 1 plus the interest rate squared. If you agree to lend out your $1,000 for three years at 10 percent interest, you will receive:

$$\$1,331 = \$1,000(1 + 0.10)^3.$$

Notice, again, that:

$$\$1,000 = \frac{\$1,331}{(1 + 0.10)^3}.$$

You can probably see a pattern here. We can generalize the concept to say that the present value of funds to be received $n$ years in the future—whether $n$ is 1, 20, or 85 does not matter—equals the amount of the funds to be received divided by the quantity 1 plus the interest rate raised to the $n$th power. For instance, with an interest rate of 10 percent, the value of \$1,000,000 to be received 25 years in the future is:

$$\text{Present value} = \frac{\$1,000,000}{(1 + 0.10)^{25}} = \$92,296.$$

Or, more generally:

$$\text{Present value} = \frac{\text{Future value}_n}{(1 + i)^n}$$

where Future value$_n$ represents funds that will be received in $n$ years.

# Solved Problem 8A.1

## How to Receive Your Contest Winnings

Suppose you win a contest and are given the choice of the following prizes:

**Prize 1:** \$50,000 to be received right away, with four additional payments of \$50,000 to be received each year for the next four years

**Prize 2:** \$175,000 to be received right away

Explain which prize you would choose and the basis for your decision.

## Solving the Problem

**Step 1: Review the material.** This problem involves applying the concept of present value, so you may want to review the section "Using Present Value to Make Investment Decisions," which begins on page 263.

**Step 2: Explain the basis for choosing the prize.** Unless you need cash immediately, you should choose the prize with the highest present value.

**Step 3: Calculate the present value of each prize.** Prize 2 consists of one payment of \$175,000 received right away, so its present value is \$175,000. Prize 1 consists of five payments spread out over time. To find the present value of the prize, we must find the present value of each of these payments and add them together. To calculate present value, we must use an interest rate. Let's assume an interest rate of 10 percent. In that case, the present value of Prize 1 is:

$$\$50,000 + \frac{\$50,000}{(1 + 0.10)} + \frac{\$50,000}{(1 + 0.10)^2} + \frac{\$50,000}{(1 + 0.10)^3} + \frac{\$50,000}{(1 + 0.10)^4} =$$

$$\$50,000 + \$45,454.55 + \$41,322.31 + \$37,565.74 + \$34,150.67 = \$208,493.$$

**Step 4: State your conclusion.** Prize 1 has the greater present value, so you should choose it rather than Prize 2.

**Your Turn:** For more practice, do related problems 8A.6, 8A.7, 8A.8, and 8A.9 on page 270 at the end of this appendix.    MyEconLab

# Using Present Value to Calculate Bond Prices

Anyone who buys a financial asset, such as shares of stock or a bond, is really buying a promise to receive certain payments—dividends in the case of shares of stock or coupons in the case of a bond. The price investors are willing to pay for a financial asset should be equal to the value of the payments they will receive as a result of owning the asset. Because most of the coupon or dividend payments will be received in the future, it is their present value that matters. Put another way, we have the following important idea: *The price of a financial asset should be equal to the present value of the payments to be received from owning that asset.*

Let's consider an example. Suppose that in 1982, General Electric issued a bond with an $80 coupon that will mature in 2012. It is now 2010, and that bond has been bought and sold by investors many times. You are considering buying it. If you buy the bond, you will receive two years of coupon payments plus a final payment of the bond's principal, or face value, of $1,000. Suppose, once again, that you need an interest rate of 10 percent to invest your funds. If the bond has a coupon of $80, the present value of the payments you receive from owning the bond—and, therefore, the present value of the bond—will be:

$$\text{Present value} = \frac{\$80}{(1 + 0.10)} + \frac{\$80}{(1 + 0.10)^2} + \frac{\$1,000}{(1 + 0.10)^2} = \$965.29.$$

That is, the present value of the bond will equal the present value of the three payments you will receive during the two years you own the bond. You should, therefore, be willing to pay $965.29 to own this bond and have the right to receive these payments from GE. This process of calculating present values of future payments is used to determine bond prices, with one qualification: The relevant interest rate used by investors in the bond market to calculate the present value and, therefore, the price of an existing bond is usually the coupon rate on comparable newly issued bonds. Therefore, the general formula for the price of a bond is:

$$\text{Bond price} = \frac{\text{Coupon}_1}{(1 + i)} + \frac{\text{Coupon}_2}{(1 + i)^2} + \dots + \frac{\text{Coupon}_n}{(1 + i)^n} + \frac{\text{Face value}}{(1 + i)^n},$$

where $\text{Coupon}_1$ is the coupon payment to be received after one year, $\text{Coupon}_2$ is the coupon payment to be received after two years, up to $\text{Coupon}_n$, which is the coupon payment received in the year the bond matures. The ellipsis takes the place of the coupon payments—if any—received between the second year and the year when the bond matures. Face value is the amount that will be received when the bond matures. The interest rate on comparable newly issued bonds is $i$.

## Using Present Value to Calculate Stock Prices

When you own a firm's stock, you are legally entitled to your share of the firm's profits. Remember that the profits a firm pays out to its shareholders are referred to as *dividends*. The price of a share of stock should be equal to the present value of the dividends investors expect to receive as a result of owning that stock. Therefore, the general formula for the price of a stock is:

$$\text{Stock price} = \frac{\text{Dividend}_1}{(1 + i)} + \frac{\text{Dividend}_2}{(1 + i)^2} + \dots$$

Notice that this formula looks very similar to the one we used to calculate the price of a bond, with a couple important differences. First, unlike a bond, stock has no maturity date, so we have to calculate the present value of an infinite number of dividend payments. At first, it may seem that the stock's price must be infinite as well, but remember that dollars you don't receive for many years are worth very little today. For instance, a dividend payment of $10 that will be received 40 years in the future is worth only a little more than $0.20 today at a 10 percent interest rate. The second difference between the stock price formula and the bond price formula is that whereas the coupon payments you receive from owning the bond are known with certainty—they are written on the bond and cannot be changed—you don't know for sure what the dividend payments from owning a stock will be. How large a dividend payment you will receive depends on how profitable the company will be in the future.

Although it is possible to forecast the future profitability of a company, this cannot be done with perfect accuracy. To emphasize this point, some economists rewrite the basic stock price formula by adding a superscript $e$ to each dividend term to emphasize that these are *expected* dividend payments. Because the future profitability of companies is often very difficult to forecast, it is not surprising that differences of opinion exist over what the price of a particular stock should be. Some investors will be very optimistic about the future profitability of a company and will, therefore, believe that the company's stock should have a high price. Other investors might be very pessimistic and believe that the company's stock should have a low price.

## A Simple Formula for Calculating Stock Prices

It is possible to simplify the formula for determining the price of a stock, if we assume that dividends will grow at a constant rate:

$$\text{Stock price} = \frac{\text{Dividend}}{(i - \text{Growth rate})}.$$

In this equation, Dividend is the dividend expected to be received one year from now, and Growth rate is the rate at which those dividends are expected to grow. If a company pays a dividend of $1 per share to be received one year from now and Growth rate is 10 percent, the company is expected to pay a dividend of $1.10 the following year, $1.21 the year after that, and so on.

Now suppose that IBM will pay a dividend of $5 per share at the end of year, the consensus of investors is that these dividends will increase at a rate of 5 percent per year for the indefinite future, and the interest rate is 10 percent. Then the price of IBM's stock should be:

$$\text{Stock price} = \frac{\$5.00}{(0.10 - 0.05)} = \$100.00.$$

Particularly during the years 1999 and 2000, there was much discussion of whether the high prices of many Internet stocks—such as the stock of Amazon.com—were justified, given that many of these companies had not made any profit yet and so had not paid any dividends. Is there any way that a rational investor would pay a high price for the stock of a company currently not earning profits? The formula for determining stock prices shows that it is possible, provided that the investor's assumptions are optimistic enough! For example, during 1999, one stock analyst predicted that Amazon.com would soon be earning $10 per share of stock. That is, Amazon.com's total earnings divided by the number of shares of its stock outstanding would be $10. Suppose Amazon.com pays out that $10 in dividends and that the $10 will grow rapidly over the years, by, say, 7 percent per year. Then our formula indicates that the price of Amazon.com stock should be:

$$\text{Stock price} = \frac{\$10.00}{(0.10 - 0.07)} = \$333.33.$$

If you are sufficiently optimistic about the future prospects of a company, a high stock price can be justified even if the company is not currently earning a profit. But investors in growth stocks must be careful. Suppose investors believe that growth prospects for Amazon are only 4 percent per year instead of 7 percent because the firm turns out not to be as profitable as initially believed. Then our formula indicates that the price of Amazon.com stock should be:

$$\text{Stock price} = \frac{\$10.00}{(0.10 - 0.04)} = \$166.67.$$

This price is only half the price determined assuming a more optimistic growth rate. Hence investors use information about a firm's profitability and growth prospects to determine what the firm is worth.

# Going Deeper into Financial Statements

Corporations disclose substantial information about their business operations and financial position to actual and potential investors. Some of this information meets the demands of participants in financial markets and of information-collection agencies, such as Moody's Investors Service, which develops credit ratings that help investors judge how risky corporate bonds are. Other information meets the requirements of the U.S. Securities and Exchange Commission.

Key sources of information about a corporation's profitability and financial position are its principal financial statements—the *income statement* and the *balance sheet*. These important information sources were first introduced in the chapter. In the following section we go into more detail, using recent data for Google as an example.

## Analyzing Income Statements

As discussed in the chapter, a firm's income statement summarizes its revenues, costs, and profit over a period of time. Figure 8A.1 shows Google's income statement for 2010.

Google's income statement presents the results of the company's operations during the year. Listed first are the revenues it earned, largely from selling advertising on its Web site, from January 1, 2010, to December 31, 2010: $29,321 million. Listed next are Google's operating expenses, the most important of which is its *cost of revenue*—which is commonly known as *cost of sales* or *cost of goods sold*: $10,417 million. Cost of revenue is the direct cost of producing the products sold, including in this case the salaries of the computer programmers Google hires to write the software for its Web site. Google also has substantial costs for researching and developing its products ($3,762 million) and for advertising and marketing them ($2,799 million). General and administrative expenses ($1,962 million) include costs such as the salaries of top managers.

The difference between a firm's revenue and its costs is its profit. Profit shows up in several forms on an income statement. A firm's *operating income* is the difference between its revenue and its operating expenses. Most corporations, including Google, also have investments, such as government and corporate bonds, that normally generate some income for them. In this case, Google earned $415 million on its investments, which

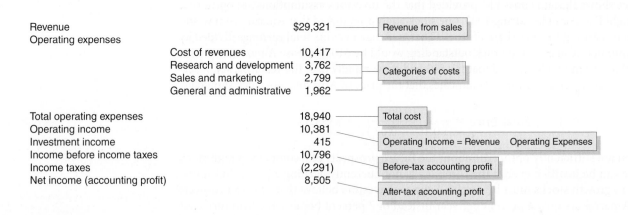

Note: All numbers are in millions of dollars.

**Figure 8A.1** **Google's Income Statement for 2010**

Google's income statement shows the company's revenue, costs, and profit for 2010. The difference between its revenue ($29,321 million) and its operating expenses ($18,940 million) is its operating income ($10,381 million). Most corporations also have investments, such as government or corporate bonds, that generate some income for them. In this case, Google earned $415 million, giving the firm an income before taxes of $10,796 million. After paying taxes of $2,291 million, Google was left with a net income, or accounting profit, of $8,505 million for the year.

Data from Google Inc. (2010) 10-K Annual Report. SEC EDGAR website www.sec.gov/edgar.shtml.

increased its *income before taxes* to $10,796 million. The federal government taxes the profits of corporations. During 2010, Google paid $2,291 million—or about 21 percent of its profits—in taxes. *Net income* after taxes was $8,505 million. The net income that firms report on their income statements is referred to as their after-tax *accounting profit*.

# Analyzing Balance Sheets

As discussed in the chapter, while a firm's income statement reports the firm's activities for a period of time, a firm's balance sheet summarizes its financial position on a particular day, usually the end of a quarter or year. To understand how a balance sheet is organized, first recall that an asset is anything of value that the firm owns, and a liability is a debt or an obligation that the firm owes. Subtracting the value of a firm's liabilities from the value of its assets leaves its *net worth*. Because a corporation's stockholders are its owners, net worth is often listed as **stockholders' equity** on a balance sheet. Using these definitions, we can state the balance sheet equation (also called the basic accounting equation) as follows:

$$\text{Assets} - \text{Liabilities} = \text{Stockholders Equity},$$

or:

$$\text{Assets} = \text{Liabilities} + \text{Stockholders Equity}.$$

This formula tells us that the value of a firm's assets must equal the value of its liabilities plus the value of stockholders' equity. An important accounting rule dating back to the beginning of modern bookkeeping in fifteenth-century Italy holds that balance sheets should list assets on the left side and liabilities and net worth, or stockholders' equity, on the right side. Notice that this means that *the value of the left side of the balance sheet must always equal the value of the right side.* Figure 8A.2 shows Google's balance sheet as of December 31, 2010.

A couple of the entries on the asset side of the balance sheet may be unfamiliar: *Current assets* are assets that the firm could convert into cash quickly, such as the balance in its checking account or its accounts receivable, which is money currently owed to the firm for products that have been delivered but not yet paid for. *Goodwill* represents the difference between the purchase price of a company and the market value of its assets. It represents the ability of a business to earn an economic profit from its assets. For example, if you buy a restaurant that is located on a busy intersection and you employ a chef with a reputation for preparing delicious food, you may pay more than the market value of the tables, chairs, ovens, and other assets. This additional amount you pay will be entered on the asset side of your balance sheet as goodwill.

*Current liabilities* are short-term debts such as accounts payable, which is money owed to suppliers for goods received but not yet paid for, or bank loans that will be paid back in less than one year. Long-term bank loans and the value of outstanding corporate bonds are *long-term liabilities*.

**Stockholders' equity** The difference between the value of a corporation's assets and the value of its liabilities; also known as *net worth*.

| Assets | | Liabilities and Stockholders' Equity | |
|---|---|---|---|
| Current Assets | $41,562 | Current Liabilities | $9,996 |
| Property and Equipment | 7,759 | Long-term Liabilities | 1,614 |
| Investments | 523 | Total Liabilities | 11,610 |
| Goodwill | 6,256 | Stockholders' Equity | 46,241 |
| Other long-term assets | 1,751 | | |
| Total Assets | 57,851 | Total liabilities and stockholders' equity | 57,851 |

Note: All values are in millions of dollars.

**Figure 8A.2**

**Google's Balance Sheet as of December 31, 2010**

Corporations list their assets on the left of their balance sheets and their liabilities on the right. The difference between the value of a firm's assets and the value of its liabilities equals the net worth of the firm, or stockholders' equity. Stockholders' equity is listed on the right side of the balance sheet. Therefore, the value of the left side of the balance sheet must always equal the value of the right side.
Data from Google Inc. (2010) 10-K Annual Report. SEC EDGAR website www.sec.gov/edgar.shtml.

## Key Terms

Present value, p. 263
Stockholders' equity, p. 269

 **Tools to Analyze Firms' Financial Information,** pages 263–269
**LEARNING OBJECTIVE:** Understand the concept of present value and the information contained on a firm's income statement and balance sheet.

MyEconLab   Visit www.myeconlab.com to complete these exercises online and get instant feedback.

## Review Questions

**8A.1** Why is money you receive at some future date worth less to you than money you receive today? If the interest rate rises, what effect does this have on the present value of payments you receive in the future?

**8A.2** Give the formula for calculating the present value of a bond that will pay a coupon of $100 per year for 10 years and that has a face value of $1,000.

**8A.3** Compare the formula for calculating the present value of the payments you will receive from owning a bond to the formula for calculating the present value of the payments you will receive from owning a stock. What are the key similarities? What are the key differences?

**8A.4** How is operating income calculated? How does operating income differ from net income? How does net income differ from accounting profit?

**8A.5** What is the key difference between a firm's income statement and its balance sheet? What is listed on the left side of a balance sheet? What is listed on the right side?

## Problems and Applications

**8A.6** **[Related to** Solved Problem 8A.1 **on page 265]**
If the interest rate is 10 percent, what is the present value of a bond that matures in two years, pays $85 one year from now, and pays $1,085 two years from now?

**8A.7** **[Related to** Solved Problem 8A.1 **on page 265]**
Before the 2008 season, the New York Yankees signed second baseman Robinson Cano to a contract that would pay him the following amounts: $3 million for the 2008 season, $6 million for the 2009 season, $9 million for the 2010 season, and $10 million for the 2011 season, with an option for $14 million for the 2012 season and an option for $15 million for the 2013 season. Assume that Cano plays all six seasons for the Yankees and that he receives each of his six seasonal salaries as a lump-sum payment at the end of the season and he receives his 2008 salary one year after he signs the contract.
  **a.** Some newspaper reports described Cano as having signed a $57 million contract with the Yankees. Do you agree that $57 million was the value of this contract? Briefly explain.

  **b.** What was the present value of Cano's contract at the time he signed it (assuming an interest rate of 10 percent)?
  **c.** If you use an interest rate of 5 percent, what was the present value of Cano's contract?

Based on Joel Sherman, "Robinson Cano Deal Final," *New York Post,* January 8, 2008.

**8A.8** **[Related to** Solved Problem 8A.1 **on page 265]**
A winner of the Pennsylvania Lottery was given the choice of receiving $18 million at once or $1,440,000 per year for 25 years.
  **a.** If the winner had opted for the 25 annual payments, how much in total would she have received?
  **b.** At an interest rate of 10 percent, what would be the present value of the 25 payments?
  **c.** At an interest rate of 5 percent, what would be the present value of the 25 payments?
  **d.** What interest rate would make the present value of the 25 payments equal to the one payment of $18 million? (This question is difficult and requires the use of a financial calculator or a spreadsheet. *Hint:* If you are familiar with the Excel spreadsheet program, use the RATE function. You can answer parts b and c by using the Excel NPV [Net Present Value] function.)

**8A.9** **[Related to** Solved Problem 8A.1 **on page 265]**
Before the start of the 2000 baseball season, the New York Mets decided they didn't want Bobby Bonilla playing for them any longer. But Bonilla had a contract with the Mets for the 2000 season that would have obliged the Mets to pay him $5.9 million. When the Mets released Bonilla, he agreed to take the following payments in lieu of the $5.9 million the Mets would have paid him in the year 2000: He would receive 25 equal payments of $1,193,248.20 each July 1 from 2011 to 2035. If you were Bobby Bonilla, which would you rather have had, the lump-sum $5.9 million or the 25 payments beginning in 2011? Explain the basis for your decision.

**8A.10** Suppose that eLake, an online auction site, is paying a dividend of $2 per share. You expect this dividend to grow 2 percent per year, and the interest rate is 10 percent. What is the most you would be willing to pay for a share of stock in eLake? If the interest rate is 5 percent, what is the most you would be willing to pay? When interest rates in the economy decline, would you expect stock prices in general to rise or fall? Explain.

**8A.11** Suppose you buy the bond of a large corporation at a time when the inflation rate is very low. If the inflation rate increases during the time you hold the bond, what is likely to happen to the price of the bond?

**8A.12** Use the information in the following table for calendar year 2010 to prepare an income statement for McDonald's Corporation's. Be sure to include entries for operating income and net income.

| | |
|---|---|
| Revenue from company restaurants | $16,233 million |
| Revenue from franchised restaurants | 7,841 million |
| Cost of operating company-owned restaurants | 13,060 million |
| Income taxes | 2,054 million |
| Interest expense | 451 million |
| General and administrative cost | 2,333 million |
| Cost of restaurant leases | 1,378 million |

Data from McDonalds Corp. (2010) 10-K Annual Report. SEC EDGAR (www.sec.gov/edgar.shtml).

**8A.13** Use the information in the following table on the financial situation of Starbucks Corporation as of October 3, 2010, to prepare a balance sheet for the firm. Be sure to include an entry for stockholders' equity.

| | |
|---|---|
| Current assets | $2,756 million |
| Current liabilities | 1,779 million |
| Property and equipment | 2,417 million |
| Long-term liabilities | 925 million |
| Goodwill | 262 million |
| Other assets | 951 million |

Data from Starbucks Corp. (2010) 10-K Annual Report. SEC EDGAR (www.sec.gov/edgar.shtml).

**8A.14** The *current ratio* is equal to a firm's current assets divided by its current liabilities. Use the information in Figure 8A.2 on page 269 to calculate Google's current ratio on December 31, 2010. Investors generally prefer that a firm's current ratio be greater than 1.5. What problems might a firm encounter if the value of its current assets is low relative to the value of its current liabilities?

# Comparative Advantage and the Gains from International Trade

## Chapter Outline and Learning Objectives

# Does the Federal Government's "Buy American" Policy Help U.S. Firms?

In response to the economic recession of 2007–2009, Congress and President Barack Obama passed the American Recovery and Reinvestment Act of 2009, a bill that included tax cuts and increased government spending, particularly on infrastructure such as bridges and roads. The bill included a "Buy American" provision that required all manufactured goods bought with these funds to be made in the United States. The intention was to increase the number of jobs the bill would create by preventing foreign companies from participating in the new spending projects.

Some U.S. firms, though, were opposed to the Buy American provision. These firms had two concerns: First, they were afraid that foreign governments would retaliate. Canada and China in particular, protested before the bill was passed that the United States had signed international agreements in which it had promised not to impose new barriers to foreign companies selling in the United States. Once the bill passed, retaliation did take place. China passed a similar bill that increased infrastructure spending, while specifying that only Chinese firms could participate. Illinois-based Caterpillar, which makes bulldozers and other construction equipment, and other U.S. firms were excluded. One executive at Caterpillar was quoted as saying, "The so-called Buy American amendment is really an anti-export provision."

U.S. firms were also concerned because in the modern business world, foreign-based firms often buy from U.S. suppliers, and U.S. suppliers often buy from foreign firms. As one executive for General Electric put it, "The supply chains are so integrated, it is crazy to try to impose a Buy American provision. Some components cross the border four or five times."

Are Buy American provisions and other attempts to protect U.S. firms from foreign competition good ideas? As we will see in this chapter, these policies create winners—the firms that are sheltered from foreign competition—but they also create losers—U.S. firms that rely on exports to foreign countries, as well as U.S. consumers and taxpayers who must pay higher prices for goods that could have been purchased at lower prices from foreign companies.

**AN INSIDE LOOK** on **page 298** examines a federal lawsuit against Home Depot, alleging that the company violated the Buy American provision.

Based on Keith Bradsher, "Pentagon Must 'Buy American,' Barring Chinese Solar Panels," *New York Times*, January 9, 2011; Peter Fritsch and Corey Boles, "How 'Buy American' Can Hurt U.S. Firms," *Wall Street Journal*, September 17, 2009; and Mark Drajem, "GE, Caterpillar Fight 'Buy American' Rule in Stimulus," Bloomberg.com, January 22, 2009.

## Economics in Your Life

### Have You Heard of the "Buy American" Provision?

Politicians often support restrictions on trade to convince people to vote for them. The workers in the industries these restrictions protect are likely to vote for the politicians because the workers think trade restrictions will protect their jobs. But most people are not workers in industries protected from foreign competition by trade restrictions. Many people work for firms, such as Caterpillar, that sell goods in foreign markets. These workers risk losing their jobs if foreign countries retaliate against U.S. attempts to reduce imported goods. How, then, did some U.S. companies convince Congress to include the Buy American provision in the American Recovery and Reinvestment Act of 2009, and why have relatively few people even heard of this provision? As you read the chapter, see if you can answer these questions. You can check your answers against those we provide on **page 297** at the end of this chapter.

Trade is simply the act of buying or selling. Is there a difference between trade that takes place within a country and international trade? Within the United States, domestic trade makes it possible for consumers in Ohio to eat salmon caught in Alaska and for consumers in Montana to drive cars built in Michigan or Kentucky. Similarly, international trade makes it possible for consumers in the United States to drink wine from France and use Blu-ray players from Japan. But one significant difference between domestic trade and international trade is that international trade is more controversial. At one time, nearly all the televisions, shoes, clothing, and toys bought in the United States were also produced in the United States. Today, firms in other countries produce most of these goods. This shift has benefited U.S. consumers because foreign-made goods have lower prices or higher quality than the U.S.-made goods they have replaced. But at the same time, many U.S. firms that produced these goods have gone out of business, and their workers have had to find other jobs. Not surprisingly, opinion polls show that many Americans favor reducing international trade because they believe doing so will preserve jobs in the United States. But is this belief accurate?

We can use the tools of demand and supply developed in Chapter 3 to analyze markets for internationally traded goods and services. We saw in Chapter 2 that trade in general—whether within a country or between countries—is based on the principle of comparative advantage. In this chapter, we look more closely at the role of comparative advantage in international trade. We also use the concepts of consumer surplus, producer surplus, and deadweight loss from Chapter 4 to analyze government policies that interfere with trade. With this background, we can return to the political debate over whether the United States benefits from international trade. We begin by looking at how large a role international trade plays in the U.S. economy.

## 9.1 LEARNING OBJECTIVE

Discuss the role of international trade in the U.S. economy.

# The United States in the International Economy

International trade has grown tremendously over the past 50 years. The increase in trade is the result of the falling costs of shipping products around the world, the spread of inexpensive and reliable communications, and changes in government policies. Firms can use large container ships to send their products across oceans at low cost. Businesspeople today can travel to Europe or Asia, using fast, inexpensive, and reliable air transportation. The Internet, cell phones, and text messaging allow managers to communicate instantaneously and at a very low cost with customers and suppliers around the world. These and other improvements in transportation and communication have created an integrated global marketplace that earlier generations of businesspeople could only dream of.

**Tariff** A tax imposed by a government on imports.

**Imports** Goods and services bought domestically but produced in other countries.

**Exports** Goods and services produced domestically but sold in other countries.

Over the past 50 years, many governments have changed policies to facilitate international trade. For example, tariff rates have fallen. A **tariff** is a tax imposed by a government on *imports* of a good into a country. **Imports** are goods and services bought domestically but produced in other countries. In the 1930s, the United States charged an average tariff rate above 50 percent. Today, the rate is less than 2 percent. In North America, most tariffs between Canada, Mexico, and the United States were eliminated following the passage of the North American Free Trade Agreement (NAFTA) in 1994. Twenty-seven countries in Europe have formed the European Union, which has eliminated all tariffs among member countries, greatly increasing both imports and **exports**, which are goods and services produced domestically but sold in other countries.

## The Importance of Trade to the U.S. Economy

U.S. consumers buy increasing quantities of goods and services produced in other countries. At the same time, U.S. businesses sell increasing quantities of goods and services to consumers in other countries. Figure 9.1 shows that since 1970, both exports and imports have been steadily increasing as a fraction of U.S. gross domestic product (GDP).

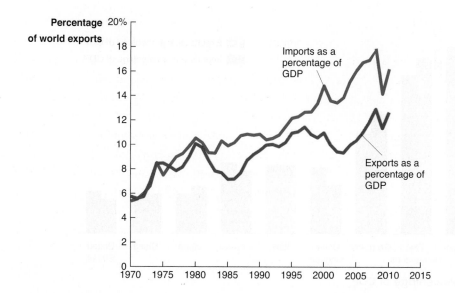

**Figure 9.1**

**International Trade Is of Increasing Importance to the United States**

Exports and imports of goods and services as a percentage of total production—measured by GDP—show the importance of international trade to an economy. Since 1970, both imports and exports have been steadily rising as a fraction of U.S. GDP.

Data from the U.S. Department of Commerce, Bureau of Economic Analysis.

Recall that GDP is the value of all the final goods and services produced in a country during a year. In 1970, exports and imports were both less than 6 percent of GDP. In 2010, exports were about 13 percent of GDP, and imports were about 16 percent.

Not all sectors of the U.S. economy are affected equally by international trade. For example, although it's difficult to import or export some services, such as haircuts and appendectomies, a large percentage of U.S. agricultural production is exported. Each year, the United States exports about 50 percent of its wheat and rice crops and 20 percent of its corn crop.

Many U.S. manufacturing industries also depend on trade. About 20 percent of U.S. manufacturing jobs depend directly or indirectly on exports. In some industries, such as computers, the products these workers make are directly exported. In other industries, such as steel, the products are used to make other products, such as bulldozers or machine tools, that are then exported. In all, about two-thirds of U.S. manufacturing industries depend on exports for at least 10 percent of jobs.

## U.S. International Trade in a World Context

The United States is the largest exporter in the world, as Figure 9.2 illustrates. Six of the other seven leading exporting countries are also high-income countries. Although China is still a relatively low-income country, the rapid growth of the Chinese economy over the past 30 years has resulted in its becoming the third-largest exporter.

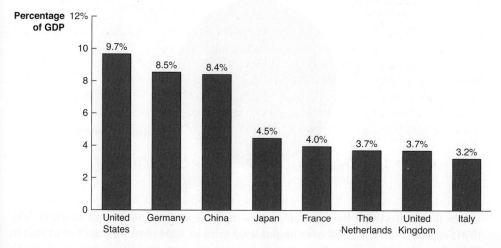

**Figure 9.2**

**The Eight Leading Exporting Countries, 2010**

The United States is the leading exporting country, accounting for 9.7 percent of total world exports. The values are the shares of total world exports of merchandise and commercial services.

Data from World Trade Organization, *International Trade Statistics*, 2010.

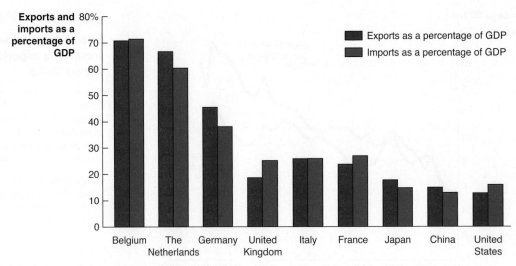

**Figure 9.3** International Trade as a Percentage of GDP

International trade is still less important to the United States than to most other countries.
Data from Organization for Economic Cooperation and Development, *Country Statistical Profile*, 2011.

Figure 9.3 shows that international trade is less important to the United States than to many other countries, with imports and exports being smaller percentages of GDP. In some smaller countries, such as Belgium and the Netherlands, imports and exports make up more than half of GDP. In the larger European economies, imports and exports make up one-quarter to one-half of GDP.

**Making the Connection**

## How Caterpillar Depends on International Trade

We saw in the chapter opener that Caterpillar, Inc., was opposed to the Buy American provision in the American Recovery and Reinvestment Act. Jim Owens, Caterpillar's CEO, argued, "We need to avoid things like . . . 'Buy American.' . . . If we turn inward, it sends a terrible signal to the rest of the world, and I'm concerned that other countries will adopt even more protectionist measures for their countries." Owens had cause to be concerned because, as the graph below shows, in 2010, 68 percent of Caterpillar sales were outside North America. This dependence on exports made Caterpillar vulnerable to foreign governments responding to the Buy American provision by restricting exports from the United States.

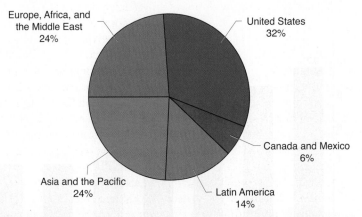

In fact, Caterpillar has become increasingly dependent on foreign markets. The firm's exports rose from just over half of total sales in 2004 to more than two-thirds in 2010. Because Caterpillar sells earth-moving and other construction equipment, it was severely affected by the decline in the U.S. housing market that began in 2006. Although sales in the United States declined by more than half between 2006 and 2008, increases in exports were enough to make 2008 a record sales year for Caterpillar. By 2009, however, the slowdown in the world economy had begun to affect the company, and sales declined 37 percent. Sales rose by 31 percent in 2010, but the increase came largely from higher sales outside of the United States.

Although Caterpillar now sells more outside the United States than inside, it still remains a major employer in the United States. At the end of 2010, Caterpillar employed more than 41,000 workers in 278 offices and factories in the United States. In addition, Caterpillar dealers in the United States employed more than 50,000 people. Thousands of other workers are employed at the many U.S. firms that supply Caterpillar with parts and components for its products. Problems at Caterpillar result in problems in the U.S. communities where the company and its suppliers are located. Caterpillar employs more than 20,000 people in the area around its headquarters in Peoria, Illinois. When sales declines led to layoffs in early 2009, the local real estate market, local stores and businesses, and the tax revenues of local governments were all affected. Like many U.S. firms that depend on exports, Caterpillar and its employees are vulnerable to disruptions in world trade caused by foreign retaliation against U.S. exports or other political problems.

Based on Geoff Colvin, "Caterpillar Is Absolutely Crushing It," *Fortune*, May 12, 2011; Steve Tarter, "Cat Raises the Possibility of Leaving Illinois," *Journal Star*, March 25, 2011; Steven Gray, "Caterpillar Layoffs: How They're Playing in Peoria," *Time*, January 29, 2009; and Caterpillar, 2010 *Annual Report*.

**Your Turn:** Test your understanding by doing related problem 1.7 on page 300 at the end of this chapter.

MyEconLab

# Comparative Advantage in International Trade

**9.2 LEARNING** OBJECTIVE

Understand the difference between comparative advantage and absolute advantage in international trade.

Why have businesses around the world increasingly looked for markets in other countries? Why have consumers increasingly purchased goods and services made in other countries? People trade for one reason: Trade makes them better off. Whenever a buyer and seller agree to a sale, they must both believe they are better off; otherwise, there would be no sale. This outcome must hold whether the buyer and seller live in the same city or in different countries. As we will see, governments are more likely to interfere with international trade than they are with domestic trade, but the reasons for the interference are more political than economic.

## A Brief Review of Comparative Advantage

In Chapter 2, we discussed the key economic concept of *comparative advantage*. **Comparative advantage** is the ability of an individual, a firm, or a country to produce a good or service at a lower opportunity cost than competitors. Recall that **opportunity cost** is the highest-valued alternative that must be given up to engage in an activity. People, firms, and countries specialize in economic activities in which they have a comparative advantage. In trading, we benefit from the comparative advantage of other people (or firms or countries), and they benefit from our comparative advantage.

A good way to think of comparative advantage is to recall the example in Chapter 2 of you and your neighbor picking fruit. Your neighbor is better at picking both apples and cherries than you are. Why, then, doesn't your neighbor pick both types of fruit? Because the opportunity cost to your neighbor of picking her own apples is very high: She is a particularly skilled cherry picker, and every hour spent picking apples is an hour taken away from picking cherries. You can pick apples at a much lower opportunity cost than your neighbor, so you have a comparative advantage in picking apples. Your neighbor can pick cherries at a much lower opportunity cost than you can, so she has a comparative advantage in picking cherries. Your neighbor is better off specializing in picking cherries, and you are better off specializing in picking apples. You can then trade some of your apples for some of your neighbor's cherries, and both of you will end up with more of each fruit.

**Comparative advantage** The ability of an individual, a firm, or a country to produce a good or service at a lower opportunity cost than competitors.

**Opportunity cost** The highest-valued alternative that must be given up to engage in an activity.

**Table 9.1**

**An Example of Japanese Workers Being More Productive Than American Workers**

| | Output per Hour of Work | |
|---|---|---|
| | Cell Phones | Tablet Computers |
| Japan | 12 | 6 |
| United States | 2 | 4 |

# Comparative Advantage in International Trade

The principle of comparative advantage can explain why people pursue different occupations. It can also explain why countries produce different goods and services. International trade involves many countries importing and exporting many different goods and services. Countries are better off if they specialize in producing the goods for which they have a comparative advantage. They can then trade for the goods for which other countries have a comparative advantage.

We can illustrate why specializing on the basis of comparative advantage makes countries better off with a simple example involving just two countries and two products. Suppose the United States and Japan produce only cell phones and tablet computers, like Apple's iPad or Samsung's Galaxy Tab. Assume that each country uses only labor to produce each good and that Japanese and U.S. cell phones and tablet computers are exactly the same. Table 9.1 shows how much each country can produce of each good with one hour of labor.

Notice that Japanese workers are more productive than U.S. workers in making both goods. In one hour of work, Japanese workers can make six times as many cell phones and one and one-half times as many tablet computers as U.S. workers. Japan has an *absolute advantage* over the United States in producing both goods. **Absolute advantage** is the ability to produce more of a good or service than competitors when using the same amount of resources. In this case, Japan can produce more of both goods using the same amount of labor as the United States.

It might seem at first that Japan has nothing to gain from trading with the United States because it has an absolute advantage in producing both goods. However, Japan should specialize and produce only cell phones and obtain the tablet computers it needs by exporting cell phones to the United States in exchange for tablet computers. The reason that Japan benefits from trade is that although it has an *absolute advantage* in the production of both goods, it has a *comparative advantage* only in the production of cell phones. The United States has a comparative advantage in the production of tablet computers.

If it seems contrary to common sense that Japan should import tablet computers from the United States even though Japan can produce more tablets per hour of work, think about the opportunity cost to each country of producing each good. If Japan wants to produce more tablet computers, it has to switch labor away from cell phone production. Every hour of labor switched from producing cell phones to producing tablet computers increases tablet computer production by 6 and reduces cell phone production by 12. Japan has to give up 12 cell phones for every 6 tablet computers it produces. Therefore, the opportunity cost to Japan of producing one more tablet computer is 12/6, or 2 cell phones.

If the United States switches one hour of labor from cell phones to tablet computers, production of cell phones falls by 2, and production of tablet computers rises by 4. Therefore, the opportunity cost to the United States of producing one more tablet computer is 2/4, or 0.5 cell phone. The United States has a lower opportunity cost of producing tablet

**Absolute advantage** The ability to produce more of a good or service than competitors when using the same amount of resources.

**Table 9.2**

**The Opportunity Costs of Producing Cell Phones and Tablet Computers**

The table shows the opportunity cost each country faces in producing cell phones and tablet computers. For example, the entry in the first row and second column shows that Japan must give up 2 cell phones for every tablet computer it produces.

| | Opportunity Costs | |
|---|---|---|
| | Cell Phones | Tablet Computers |
| **Japan** | 0.5 tablet computer | 2 cell phones |
| **United States** | 2 tablet computers | 0.5 cell phone |

| | Production and Consumption | |
|---|---|---|
| | Cell Phones | Tablet Computers |
| Japan | 9,000 | 1,500 |
| United States | 1,500 | 1,000 |

computers and, therefore, has a comparative advantage in making this product. By similar reasoning, we can see that Japan has a comparative advantage in producing cell phones. Table 9.2 summarizes the opportunity cost each country faces in producing these goods.

# How Countries Gain from International Trade

Can Japan really gain from producing only cell phones and trading with the United States for tablet computers? To see that it can, assume at first that Japan and the United States do not trade with each other. A situation in which a country does not trade with other countries is called **autarky**. Assume that in autarky, each country has 1,000 hours of labor available to produce the two goods, and each country produces the quantities of the two goods shown in Table 9.3. Because there is no trade, these quantities also represent consumption of the two goods in each country.

## Increasing Consumption through Trade

Suppose now that Japan and the United States begin to trade with each other. The **terms of trade** is the ratio at which a country can trade its exports for imports from other countries. For simplicity, let's assume that the terms of trade end up with Japan and the United States being willing to trade one cell phone for one tablet computer.

Once trade has begun, the United States and Japan can exchange tablet computers for cell phones or cell phones for tablet computers. For example, if Japan specializes by using all 1,000 available hours of labor to produce cell phones, it will be able to produce 12,000. It then could export 1,500 cell phones to the United States in exchange for 1,500 tablet computers. (Remember that we are assuming that the terms of trade are one cell phone for one tablet computer.) Japan ends up with 10,500 cell phones and 1,500 tablet computers. Compared with the situation before trade, Japan has the same number of tablet computers but 1,500 more cell phones. If the United States specializes in producing tablet computers, it will be able to produce 4,000. It could then export 1,500 tablet computers to Japan in exchange for 1,500 cell phones. The United States ends up with 2,500 tablet computers and 1,500 cell phones. Compared with the situation before trade, the United States has the same number of cell phones but 1,500 more tablet computers. Trade has allowed both countries to increase the quantities of goods consumed. Table 9.4 summarizes the gains from trade for the United States and Japan.

By trading, Japan and the United States are able to consume more than they could without trade. This outcome is possible because world production of both goods increases after trade. (In this example, our "world" consists of just the United States and Japan.)

Why does total production of cell phones and tablet computers increase when the United States specializes in producing tablet computers and Japan specializes in producing cell phones? A domestic analogy helps to answer this question: If a company shifts production from an old factory to a more efficient modern factory, its output will increase. In effect, the same thing happens in our example. Producing tablet computers in Japan and cell phones in the United States is inefficient. Shifting production to the more efficient country—the one with the comparative advantage—increases total production. The key point is this: *Countries gain from specializing in producing goods in which they have a comparative advantage and trading for goods in which other countries have a comparative advantage.*

**Autarky** A situation in which a country does not trade with other countries.

**Terms of trade** The ratio at which a country can trade its exports for imports from other countries.

**Table 9.4**

**Gains from Trade for Japan and the United States**

### Without Trade

**Production and Consumption**

|  | Cell Phones | Tablet Computers |
|---|---|---|
| **Japan** | 9,000 | 1,500 |
| **United States** | 1,500 | 1,000 |

### With Trade

| | Production with Trade | | Trade | | Consumption with Trade | |
|---|---|---|---|---|---|---|
| | Cell Phones | Tablet Computers | Cell Phones | Tablet Computers | Cell Phones | Tablet Computers |
| **Japan** | 12,000 | 0 | **Export** 1,500 | **Import** 1,500 | 10,500 | 1,500 |
| **United States** | 0 | 4,000 | **Import** 1,500 | **Export** 1,500 | 1,500 | 2,500 |

With trade, the United States and Japan specialize in the good they have a comparative advantage in producing . . .

. . . and export some of that good in exchange for the good the other country has a comparative advantage in producing.

### Gains from Trade

**Increased Consumption**

| | |
|---|---|
| **Japan** | 1,500 Cell Phones |
| **United States** | 1,500 Tablet Computers |

The increased consumption made possible by trade represents the gains from trade.

# Solved Problem 9.3

## The Gains from Trade

The first discussion of comparative advantage appears in *On the Principles of Political Economy and Taxation*, a book written by David Ricardo in 1817. Ricardo provided a famous example of the gains from trade, using wine and cloth production in Portugal and England. The following table is adapted from Ricardo's example, with cloth measured in sheets and wine measured in kegs:

| | Output per Year of Labor | |
|---|---|---|
| | Cloth | Wine |
| Portugal | 100 | 150 |
| England | 90 | 60 |

a. Explain which country has an absolute advantage in the production of each good.
b. Explain which country has a comparative advantage in the production of each good.

c. Suppose that Portugal and England currently do not trade with each other. Each country has 1,000 workers, so each has 1,000 years of labor time to use producing cloth and wine, and the countries are currently producing the amounts of each good shown in the following table:

| | Cloth | Wine |
|---|---|---|
| Portugal | 18,000 | 123,000 |
| England | 63,000 | 18,000 |

Show that Portugal and England can both gain from trade. Assume that the terms of trade are that one sheet of cloth can be traded for one keg of wine.

## Solving the Problem

**Step 1:**  **Review the chapter material.** This problem is about absolute and comparative advantage and the gains from trade, so you may want to review the section "Comparative Advantage in International Trade," which begins on page 278, and the section "How Countries Gain from International Trade," which begins on page 279.

**Step 2:** **Answer part a. by determining which country has an absolute advantage.** Remember that a country has an absolute advantage over another country when it can produce more of a good using the same resources. The first table in the problem shows that Portugal can produce more cloth *and* more wine with one year's worth of labor than can England. Thus, Portugal has an absolute advantage in the production of both goods and, therefore, England does not have an absolute advantage in the production of either good.

**Step 3:** **Answer part b. by determining which country has a comparative advantage.** A country has a comparative advantage when it can produce a good at a lower opportunity cost. To produce 100 sheets of cloth, Portugal must give up producing 150 kegs of wine. Therefore, the opportunity cost to Portugal of producing 1 sheet of cloth is 150/100, or 1.5 kegs of wine. England has to give up producing 60 kegs of wine to produce 90 sheets of cloth, so its opportunity cost of producing 1 sheet of cloth is 60/90, or 0.67 keg of wine. The opportunity costs of producing wine can be calculated in the same way. The following table shows the opportunity cost to Portugal and England of producing each good.

| | Opportunity Costs | |
|---|---|---|
| | Cloth | Wine |
| Portugal | 1.5 kegs of wine | 0.67 sheet of cloth |
| England | 0.67 keg of wine | 1.5 sheets of cloth |

Portugal has a comparative advantage in wine because its opportunity cost is lower. England has a comparative advantage in cloth because its opportunity cost is lower.

**Step 4:** **Answer part c. by showing that both countries can benefit from trade.** By now it should be clear that both countries will be better off if they specialize where they have a comparative advantage and trade for the other product. The following table is very similar to Table 9.4 and shows one example of trade making both countries better off. (To test your understanding, construct another example.)

**Without Trade**

| | Production and Consumption | |
|---|---|---|
| | Cloth | Wine |
| Portugal | 18,000 | 123,000 |
| England | 63,000 | 18,000 |

**With Trade**

| | Production with Trade | | Trade | | Consumption with Trade | |
|---|---|---|---|---|---|---|
| | Cloth | Wine | Cloth | Wine | Cloth | Wine |
| Portugal | 0 | 150,000 | Import 18,000 | Export 18,000 | 18,000 | 132,000 |
| England | 90,000 | 0 | Export 18,000 | Import 18,000 | 72,000 | 18,000 |

**Gains from Trade**

| | Increased Consumption |
|---|---|
| Portugal | 9,000 wine |
| England | 9,000 cloth |

**Your Turn:** For more practice, do related problems 3.5 and 3.6 on page 302 at the end of this chapter.   MyEconLab

## Why Don't We See Complete Specialization?

In our example of two countries producing only two products, each country specializes in producing one of the goods. In the real world, many goods and services are produced in more than one country. For example, the United States, Japan, Germany, Canada, Mexico, India, China, and other countries produce automobiles. We do not see complete specialization in the real world for three main reasons:

- *Not all goods and services are traded internationally.* Even if, for example, Japan had a comparative advantage in the production of medical services, it would be difficult for Japan to specialize in producing medical services and then export them. There is no easy way for U.S. patients who need appendectomies to receive them from surgeons in Japan.

- *Production of most goods involves increasing opportunity costs.* Recall from Chapter 2 that production of most goods involves increasing opportunity costs. So, in our example, if the United States devotes more workers to producing tablet computers, the opportunity cost of producing more tablet computers will increase. At some point, the opportunity cost of producing tablet computers in the United States may rise to the level of the opportunity cost of producing tablet computers in Japan. When that happens, international trade will no longer push the United States further toward specialization. The same will be true of Japan: Increasing opportunity cost will cause Japan to stop short of complete specialization in producing cell phones.

- *Tastes for products differ.* Most products are *differentiated*. Cell phones, tablet computers, cars, and televisions—to name just a few products—come with a wide variety of features. When buying automobiles, some people look for reliability and fuel efficiency, others look for room to carry seven passengers, and still others want styling and high performance. So, some car buyers prefer Toyota Prius hybrids, some prefer Chevy Suburbans, and others prefer BMWs. As a result, Japan, the United States, and Germany may each have a comparative advantage in producing different types of automobiles.

## Does Anyone Lose as a Result of International Trade?

In our cell phone and tablet computer example, consumption increases in both the United States and Japan as a result of trade. Everyone gains, and no one loses. Or do

## Don't Let This Happen to You

### Remember That Trade Creates Both Winners and Losers

The following statement is from a Federal Reserve publication: "Trade is a win–win situation for all countries that participate." People sometimes interpret statements like this to mean that there are no losers from international trade. But notice that the statement refers to *countries*, not individuals. When countries participate in trade, they make their consumers better off by increasing the quantity of goods and services available to them. As we have seen, however, expanding trade eliminates the jobs of workers employed at companies that are less efficient than foreign companies. Trade also creates new jobs at companies that export to foreign markets. It may be difficult, though, for workers who lose their jobs because of trade to easily find others. That is

why in the United States, the federal government uses the Trade Adjustment Assistance program to provide funds for workers who have lost their jobs due to international trade. Qualified unemployed workers can use these funds to pay for retraining, for searching for new jobs, or for relocating to areas where new jobs are available. This program—and similar programs in other countries—recognizes that there are losers from international trade as well as winners.

Based on Federal Reserve Bank of Dallas, "International Trade and the Economy," www.dallasfed.org/educate/everyday/ev7.html.

MyEconLab

**Your Turn:** Test your understanding by doing related problem 3.12 on page 303 at the end of this chapter.

they? In our example, we referred repeatedly to "Japan" or the "United States" producing cell phones or tablet computers. But countries do not produce goods—firms do. In a world without trade, there would be cell phone and tablet computer firms in both Japan and the United States. In a world with trade, there would be only Japanese cell phone firms and U.S. tablet computer firms. Japanese tablet computer firms and U.S. cell phone firms would close. Overall, total employment would not change, and production would increase as a result of trade. Nevertheless, the owners of Japanese tablet computer firms, the owners of U.S. cell phone firms, and the people who work for them are worse off as a result of trade. The losers from trade are likely to do their best to convince the Japanese and U.S. governments to interfere with trade by barring imports of the competing products from the other country or by imposing high tariffs on them.

## Where Does Comparative Advantage Come From?

Among the main sources of comparative advantage are the following:

- *Climate and natural resources.* This source of comparative advantage is the most obvious. Because of geology, Saudi Arabia has a comparative advantage in the production of oil. Because of climate and soil conditions, Costa Rica has a comparative advantage in the production of bananas, and the United States has a comparative advantage in the production of wheat.

- *Relative abundance of labor and capital.* Some countries, such as the United States, have many highly skilled workers and a great deal of machinery. Other countries, such as China, have many unskilled workers and relatively little machinery. As a result, the United States has a comparative advantage in the production of goods that require highly skilled workers or sophisticated machinery to manufacture, such as aircraft, semiconductors, and computer software. China has a comparative advantage in the production of goods, such as tools, clothing, and children's toys, that require unskilled workers and small amounts of simple machinery.

- *Technology.* Broadly defined, *technology* is the process firms use to turn inputs into goods and services. At any given time, firms in different countries do not all have access to the same technologies. In part, this difference is the result of past investments countries have made in supporting higher education or in providing support for research and development. Some countries are strong in *product technologies*, which involve the ability to develop new products. For example, firms in the United States have pioneered the development of such products as radios, televisions, digital computers, airliners, medical equipment, and many prescription drugs. Other countries are strong in *process technologies*, which involve the ability to improve the processes used to make existing products. For example, Japanese-based firms, such as Toyota and Honda, have succeeded by greatly improving the processes for designing and manufacturing automobiles.

- *External economies.* It is difficult to explain the location of some industries on the basis of climate, natural resources, the relative abundance of labor and capital, or technology. For example, why does southern California have a comparative advantage in making movies or Switzerland in making watches or New York in providing financial services? The answer is that once an industry becomes established in an area, firms that locate in that area gain advantages over firms located elsewhere. The advantages include the availability of skilled workers, the opportunity to interact with other firms in the same industry, and proximity to suppliers. These advantages result in lower costs to firms located in the area. Because these lower costs result from increases in the size of the industry in an area, economists refer to them as **external economies**.

**External economies** Reductions in a firm's costs that result from an increase in the size of an industry.

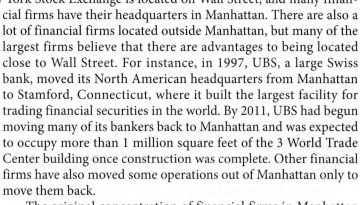

**Making the Connection**

## Leave New York City? Risky for Financial Firms

The name "Wall Street" is shorthand for the whole U.S. financial system of banks, brokerage houses, and other financial firms. Wall Street is also, of course, an actual street in the New York City borough of Manhattan. The New York Stock Exchange is located on Wall Street, and many financial firms have their headquarters in Manhattan. There are also a lot of financial firms located outside Manhattan, but many of the largest firms believe that there are advantages to being located close to Wall Street. For instance, in 1997, UBS, a large Swiss bank, moved its North American headquarters from Manhattan to Stamford, Connecticut, where it built the largest facility for trading financial securities in the world. By 2011, UBS had begun moving many of its bankers back to Manhattan and was expected to occupy more than 1 million square feet of the 3 World Trade Center building once construction was complete. Other financial firms have also moved some operations out of Manhattan only to move them back.

*Financial firms benefit from the external economies of being located in New York City.*

The original concentration of financial firms in Manhattan was something of a historical accident. In colonial times and up through the early nineteenth century, Philadelphia and Boston were at least close rivals to New York City as business and financial centers. In fact, Philadelphia had both a larger population than New York and was the headquarters of the federal government's first two central banks. New York City received a boost in its rivalry with other cities when the Erie Canal was completed in upstate New York in 1825. The canal resulted in crops and other raw materials being shipped to New York City rather than to other ports. This inflow led to the development of banking, insurance, and other financial firms. Coupled with the gradual increase in trading on the New Stock Exchange, the increase in business resulting from the completion of the canal established New York City as the leading financial center in the country.

But the Erie Canal has long since ceased to operate, and most stock trading takes place electronically rather than on the floor of the New York Stock Exchange. So, why has New York continued to see a high concentration of financial firms, with some firms that temporarily left deciding to return? The answer is that financial firms benefit from the external economies of being located in New York City. Even in the Internet age, many financial deals are still conducted face-to-face, so not having a physical presence in Manhattan puts a firm at a disadvantage. Many people pursuing careers in finance also want to be physically located in Manhattan because that is where most of the highest-paying financial jobs are. Firms that have moved out of Manhattan have had more difficulty attracting and retaining the most productive workers. In addition, Manhattan also has a large concentration of firms that provide support services, such as software programming for running financial firms' computer systems.

Large financial firms located outside Manhattan, particularly those that heavily trade securities or attempt to make deals that involve mergers between firms, may have higher costs than firms located in Manhattan. Having many financial firms originally located in Manhattan was a historical accident, but external economies gave the area a comparative advantage in providing financial services once the industry began to grow there.

Based on Brett Philbin, "UBS Shifts Staff to New York," *Wall Street Journal*, July 13, 2011; and Charles V. Bagli, "Regretting Move, Bank May Return to Manhattan," *New York Times*, June 8, 2011.

MyEconLab **Your Turn:** Test your understanding by doing related problem 3.13 on page 303 at the end of this chapter.

## Comparative Advantage over Time: The Rise and Fall—and Rise—of the U.S. Consumer Electronics Industry

A country may develop a comparative advantage in the production of a good, and then, as time passes and circumstances change, the country may lose its comparative advantage in producing that good and develop a comparative advantage in producing other goods. For several decades, the United States had a comparative advantage in the production of consumer electronic goods, such as televisions, radios, and stereos. The comparative advantage of the United States in these products was based on having developed most of the underlying technology, having the most modern factories, and having a skilled and experienced workforce. Gradually, however, other countries, particularly Japan, gained access to the technology, built modern factories, and developed skilled workforces. As mentioned earlier, Japanese firms have excelled in process technologies, which involve the ability to improve the processes used to make existing products. By the 1970s and 1980s, Japanese firms were able to produce many consumer electronic goods more cheaply and with higher quality than could U.S. firms. Japanese firms Sony, Panasonic, and Pioneer replaced U.S. firms Magnavox, Zenith, and RCA as world leaders in consumer electronics.

By 2011, however, as the technology underlying consumer electronics had evolved, comparative advantage had shifted again, and several U.S. firms had surged ahead of their Japanese competitors. For example, Apple had developed the iPod, iPhone, and iPad; Linksys, a division of Cisco Systems, took the lead in home wireless networking technology; and TiVo pioneered the digital video recorder (DVR). As pictures and music converted to digital data, process technologies became less important than the ability to design and develop new products. These new consumer electronic products required skills similar to those in computer design and software writing, where the United States had long maintained a comparative advantage.

Once a country has lost its comparative advantage in producing a good, its income will be higher and its economy will be more efficient if it switches from producing the good to importing it, as the United States did when it switched from producing televisions to importing them. As we will see in the next section, however, there is often political pressure on governments to attempt to preserve industries that have lost their comparative advantage.

## Government Policies That Restrict International Trade

**9.4 LEARNING** OBJECTIVE

Analyze the economic effects of government policies that restrict international trade.

**Free trade** Trade between countries that is without government restrictions.

**Free trade**, or trade between countries that is without government restrictions, makes consumers better off. We can expand on this idea by using the concepts of consumer surplus and producer surplus from Chapter 4. Figure 9.4 shows the market in the United States for the bio-fuel ethanol, which can be used as a substitute for gasoline. The figure shows the situation of autarky, where the United States does not trade with other countries. The equilibrium price of ethanol is $2.00 per gallon, and the equilibrium quantity is 6.0 billion gallons per year. The blue area represents consumer surplus, and the red area represents producer surplus.

Now suppose that the United States begins importing ethanol from Brazil and other countries that produce ethanol for $1.00 per gallon. Because the world market for ethanol is large, we will assume that the United States can buy as much ethanol as it wants without causing the *world price* of $1.00 per gallon to rise. Therefore, once imports of ethanol are permitted into the United States, U.S. firms will not be able to sell ethanol at prices higher than the world price of $1.00, and the U.S. price will become equal to the world price.

Figure 9.5 shows the result of allowing imports of ethanol into the United States. With the price lowered from $2.00 to $1.00, U.S. consumers increase their purchases

**Figure 9.4**

**The U.S. Market for Ethanol under Autarky**

This figure shows the market for ethanol in the United States, assuming autarky, where the United States does not trade with other countries. The equilibrium price of ethanol is $2.00 per gallon, and the equilibrium quantity is 6.0 billion gallons per year. The blue area represents consumer surplus, and the red area represents producer surplus.

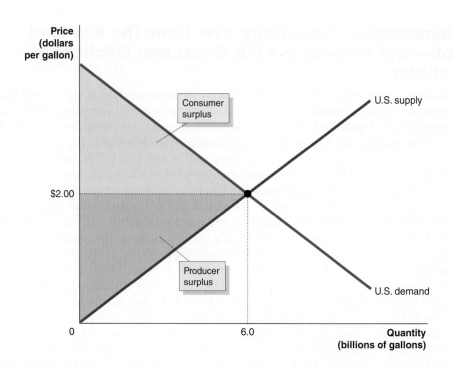

from 6.0 billion gallons to 9.0 billion gallons. Equilibrium moves from point *F* to point *G*. In the new equilibrium, U.S. producers have reduced the quantity of ethanol they supply from 6.0 billion gallons to 3.0 billion gallons. Imports will equal 6.0 billion gallons, which is the difference between U.S. consumption and U.S. production.

Under autarky, consumer surplus would be area *A* in Figure 9.5. With imports, the reduction in price increases consumer surplus, so it is now equal to the sum of areas *A*, *B*, *C*, and *D*. Although the lower price increases consumer surplus, it reduces producer surplus. Under autarky, producer surplus was equal to the sum of the areas *B* and *E*.

**Figure 9.5**

**The Effect of Imports on the U.S. Ethanol Market**

When imports are allowed into the United States, the price of ethanol falls from $2.00 to $1.00. U.S. consumers increase their purchases from 6.0 billion gallons to 9.0 billion gallons. Equilibrium moves from point *F* to point *G*. U.S. producers reduce the quantity of ethanol they supply from 6.0 billion gallons to 3.0 billion gallons. Imports equal 6.0 billion gallons, which is the difference between U.S. consumption and U.S. production. Consumer surplus equals the areas *A*, *B*, *C*, and *D*. Producer surplus equals the area *E*.

| | Under Autarky | With Imports |
|---|---|---|
| Consumer Surplus | A | A + B + C + D |
| Producer Surplus | B + E | E |
| Economic Surplus | A + B + E | A + B + C + D + E |

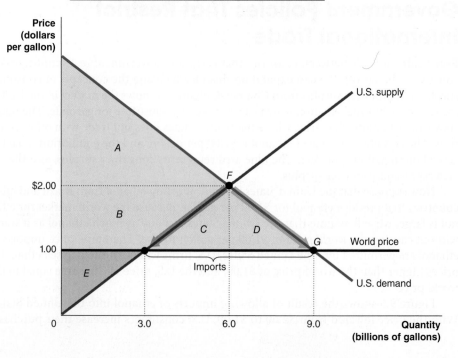

With imports, producer surplus is equal to only area *E*. Recall that economic surplus equals the sum of consumer surplus and producer surplus. Moving from autarky to allowing imports increases economic surplus in the United States by an amount equal to the sum of areas *C* and *D*.

We can conclude that international trade helps consumers but hurts firms that are less efficient than foreign competitors. As a result, these firms and their workers are often strong supporters of government policies that restrict trade. These policies usually take one of two forms: *tariffs* or *quotas* and *voluntary export restraints*.

## Tariffs

The most common interferences with trade are *tariffs*, which are taxes imposed by a government on goods imported into a country. Like any other tax, a tariff increases the cost of selling a good. Figure 9.6 shows the effect of a tariff of $0.50 per gallon on ethanol imports into the United States. The $0.50 tariff raises the price of ethanol in the United States from the world price of $1.00 per gallon to $1.50 per gallon. At this higher price, U.S. ethanol producers increase the quantity they supply from 3.0 billion gallons to 4.5 billion gallons. U.S. consumers, though, cut back their purchases of ethanol from 9.0 billion gallons to 7.5 billion gallons. Imports decline from 6.0 billion gallons (9.0 billion − 3.0 billion) to 3.0 billion gallons (7.5 billion − 4.5 billion). Equilibrium moves from point *G* to point *H*.

By raising the price of ethanol from $1.00 to $1.50, the tariff reduces consumer surplus by the sum of areas *A*, *T*, *C*, and *D*. Area *A* is the increase in producer surplus from the higher price. The government collects tariff revenue equal to the tariff of $0.50 per gallon multiplied by the 3.0 billion gallons imported. Area *T* represents the government's tariff revenue. Areas *C* and *D* represent losses to U.S. consumers that are not captured by anyone. These areas are deadweight loss and represent the decline in economic efficiency resulting from the ethanol tariff. Area *C* shows the effect on U.S. consumers of being forced to buy from U.S. producers who are less efficient than foreign producers, and area *D* shows the effect of U.S. consumers buying less ethanol than they would have at the world price. As a result of the tariff, economic surplus has been reduced by the sum of areas *C* and *D*.

We can conclude that the tariff succeeds in helping U.S. ethanol producers but hurts U.S. consumers and the efficiency of the U.S. economy.

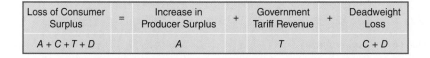

| Loss of Consumer Surplus | = | Increase in Producer Surplus | + | Government Tariff Revenue | + | Deadweight Loss |
|---|---|---|---|---|---|---|
| *A* + *C* + *T* + *D* | | *A* | | *T* | | *C* + *D* |

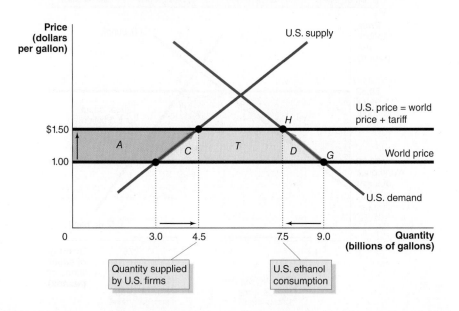

**Figure 9.6**

**The Effects of a Tariff on Ethanol**

Without a tariff on ethanol, U.S. producers will sell 3.0 billion gallons of ethanol, U.S. consumers will purchase 9.0 billion gallons, and imports will be 6.0 billion gallons. The U.S. price will equal the world price of $1.00 per gallon. The $0.50-per-gallon tariff raises the price of ethanol in the United States to $1.50 per gallon, and U.S. producers increase the quantity they supply to 4.5 billion gallons. U.S. consumers reduce their purchases to 7.5 billion gallons. Equilibrium moves from point *G* to point *H*. The ethanol tariff causes a loss of consumer surplus equal to the area *A* + *C* + *T* + *D*. The area *A* is the increase in producer surplus due to the higher price. The area *T* is the government's tariff revenue. The areas *C* and *D* represent deadweight loss.

**Quota** A numerical limit a government imposes on the quantity of a good that can be imported into the country.

**Voluntary export restraint (VER)** An agreement negotiated between two countries that places a numerical limit on the quantity of a good that can be imported by one country from the other country.

## Quotas and Voluntary Export Restraints

A **quota** is a numerical limit on the quantity of a good that can be imported, and it has an effect similar to that of a tariff. A quota is imposed by the government of the importing country. A **voluntary export restraint (VER)** is an agreement negotiated between two countries that places a numerical limit on the quantity of a good that can be imported by one country from the other country. In the early 1980s, the United States and Japan negotiated a VER that limited the quantity of automobiles the United States would import from Japan. The Japanese government agreed to the VER primarily because it was afraid that if it did not, the United States would impose a tariff or quota on imports of Japanese automobiles. Quotas and VERs have similar economic effects.

The main purpose of most tariffs and quotas is to reduce the foreign competition that domestic firms face. For many years, Congress has imposed a quota on sugar imports to protect U.S. sugar producers. Figure 9.7 shows the actual statistics for the U.S. sugar market in 2010. The effect of a quota is very similar to the effect of a tariff. By limiting imports, a quota forces the domestic price of a good above the world price. In this case, the sugar quota limits sugar imports to 5.3 billion pounds (shown by the bracket in Figure 9.7), forcing the U.S. price of sugar up to $0.53 per pound, or $0.25 higher than the world price of $0.28 per pound. The U.S. price is above the world price because the quota keeps foreign sugar producers from selling the additional sugar in the United States that would drive the price down to the world price. At a price of $0.53 per pound, U.S. producers increase the quantity of sugar they supply from the 4.7 billion pounds they would supply at the world price to 15.9 billion pounds, and U.S. consumers cut back their purchases of sugar from the 27.5 billion pounds they would purchase at the world price to the 21.2 billion pounds they are willing to purchase at the higher U.S. price. If there were no import quota, equilibrium would be at the world price (point *E*), but with the quota equilibrium is at the U.S. price (point *F*).

## Measuring the Economic Effect of the Sugar Quota

We can use the concepts of consumer surplus, producer surplus, and deadweight loss to measure the economic impact of the sugar quota. Without a sugar quota, the world price of $0.28 per pound would also be the U.S. price. In Figure 9.7, without a sugar

**Figure 9.7**

**The Economic Effect of the U.S. Sugar Quota**

Without a sugar quota, U.S. sugar producers would have sold 4.7 billion pounds of sugar, U.S. consumers would have purchased 27.5 billion pounds of sugar, and imports would have been 22.8 billion pounds. The U.S. price would have equaled the world price of $0.28 per pound. Because the sugar quota limits imports to 5.3 billion pounds (the bracket in the graph), the price of sugar in the United States rises to $0.53 per pound, and U.S. producers supply 15.9 billion pounds. U.S. consumers purchase 21.2 billion pounds rather than the 27.5 billion pounds they would purchase at the world price. Without the import quota, equilibrium would be at point *E*; with the quota, equilibrium is at point *F*. The sugar quota causes a loss of consumer surplus equal to the area *A* + *B* + *C* + *D*. The area *A* is the gain to U.S. sugar producers. The area *B* is the gain to foreign sugar producers. The areas *C* and *D* represent deadweight loss. The total loss to U.S. consumers in 2010 was $6.08 billion.

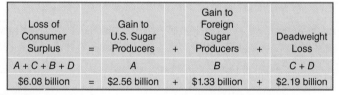

| Loss of Consumer Surplus | = | Gain to U.S. Sugar Producers | + | Gain to Foreign Sugar Producers | + | Deadweight Loss |
|---|---|---|---|---|---|---|
| *A* + *C* + *B* + *D* | | *A* | | *B* | | *C* + *D* |
| $6.08 billion | = | $2.56 billion | + | $1.33 billion | + | $2.19 billion |

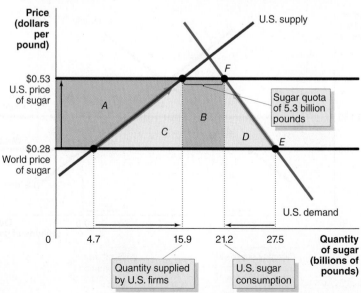

quota, consumer surplus would equal the area above the $0.28 price line and below the demand curve. The sugar quota causes the U.S. price to rise to $0.53 and reduces consumer surplus by the area $A + B + C + D$. Without a sugar quota, producer surplus received by U.S. sugar producers would be equal to the area below the $0.28 price line and above the supply curve. The higher U.S. price resulting from the sugar quota increases the producer surplus of U.S. sugar producers by an amount equal to area $A$.

A foreign producer must have a license from the U.S. government to import sugar under the quota system. Therefore, a foreign sugar producer that is lucky enough to have an import license also benefits from the quota because it is able to sell sugar in the U.S. market at $0.53 per pound instead of $0.28 per pound. The gain to foreign sugar producers is area $B$. Areas $A$ and $B$ represent transfers from U.S. consumers of sugar to U.S. and foreign producers of sugar. Areas $C$ and $D$ represent losses to U.S. consumers that are not captured by anyone. These areas are deadweight loss and represent the decline in economic efficiency resulting from the sugar quota. Area $C$ shows the effect of U.S. consumers being forced to buy from U.S. producers that are less efficient than foreign producers, and area $D$ shows the effect of U.S. consumers buying less sugar than they would have at the world price.

Figure 9.7 provides enough information to calculate the dollar value of each of the four areas. The table in the figure shows the results of these calculations. The total loss to consumers from the sugar quota was $6.08 billion in 2010. About 42 percent of the loss to consumers, or $2.56 billion, was gained by U.S. sugar producers as increased producer surplus. About 22 percent, or $1.33 billion, was gained by foreign sugar producers as increased producer surplus, and about 36 percent, or $2.19 billion, was a deadweight loss to the U.S. economy. The U.S. International Trade Commission estimates that eliminating the sugar quota would result in the loss of about 3,000 jobs in the U.S. sugar industry. The cost to U.S. consumers of saving these jobs is equal to $6.08 billion/3,000, or about $2,026,667 per job. In fact, this cost is an underestimate because eliminating the sugar quota would result in new jobs being created, particularly in the candy industry. Over the years, several U.S. candy companies—including the makers of Life Savers and Star Brite mints—have moved factories to other countries to escape the effects of the sugar quota.

# Solved Problem 9.4

## Measuring the Economic Effect of a Quota

Suppose that the United States currently both produces and imports apples. The U.S. government then decides to restrict international trade in apples by imposing a quota that allows imports of only 4 million boxes of apples into the United States each year. The figure shows the results of imposing the quota.

Fill in the following table, using the prices, quantities, and letters in the figure:

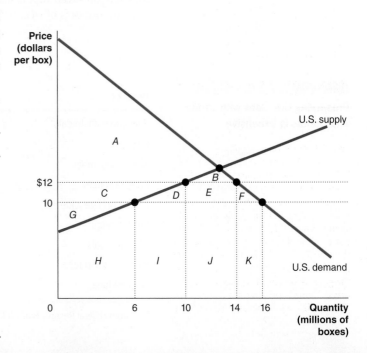

| | Without Quota | With Quota |
|---|---|---|
| World price of apples | | |
| U.S. price of apples | | |
| Quantity supplied by U.S. firms | | |
| Quantity demanded by U.S. consumers | | |
| Quantity imported | | |
| Area of consumer surplus | | |
| Area of producer surplus | | |
| Area of deadweight loss | | |

# Solving the Problem

**Step 1:** **Review the chapter material.** This problem is about measuring the economic effects of a quota, so you may want to review the section "Quotas and Voluntary Export Restraints," and "Measuring the Economic Effect of the Sugar Quota," which begin on page 288.

**Step 2:** **Fill in the table.** After studying Figure 9.7, you should be able to fill in the table. Remember that consumer surplus is the area below the demand curve and above the market price:

|  | Without Quota | With Quota |
|---|---|---|
| World price of apples | $10 | $10 |
| U.S. price of apples | $10 | $12 |
| Quantity supplied by U.S. firms | 6 million boxes | 10 million boxes |
| Quantity demanded by U.S. consumers | 16 million boxes | 14 million boxes |
| Quantity imported | 10 million boxes | 4 million boxes |
| Area of consumer surplus | $A + B + C + D + E + F$ | $A + B$ |
| Area of domestic producer surplus | $G$ | $G + C$ |
| Area of deadweight loss | No deadweight loss | $D + F$ |

MyEconLab **Your Turn:** For more practice, do related problem 4.14 on page 305 at the end of this chapter.

# The High Cost of Preserving Jobs with Tariffs and Quotas

The sugar quota is not alone in imposing a high cost on U.S. consumers to save jobs at U.S. firms. Table 9.5 shows, for several industries, the costs tariffs and quotas impose on U.S. consumers per year for each job saved.

Many countries besides the United States also use tariffs and quotas to try to protect jobs. Table 9.6 shows the cost to Japanese consumers per year for each job saved as a result of tariffs and quotas in the listed industries. Note the staggering cost of $51 million for each job saved that is imposed on Japanese consumers by their government's restrictions on imports of rice.

**Table 9.5**

**Preserving U.S. Jobs with Tariffs and Quotas Is Expensive**

| Product | Number of Jobs Saved | Cost to Consumers per Year for Each Job Saved |
|---|---|---|
| Benzenoid chemicals | 216 | $1,376,435 |
| Luggage | 226 | 1,285,078 |
| Softwood lumber | 605 | 1,044,271 |
| Dairy products | 2,378 | 685,323 |
| Frozen orange juice | 609 | 635,103 |
| Ball bearings | 146 | 603,368 |
| Machine tools | 1,556 | 479,452 |
| Women's handbags | 773 | 263,535 |
| Canned tuna | 390 | 257,640 |

Data from Federal Reserve Bank of Dallas, 2002 *Annual Report*, Exhibit 11.

| Product | Cost to Consumers per Year for Each Job Saved |
|---|---|
| Rice | $51,233,000 |
| Natural gas | 27,987,000 |
| Gasoline | 6,329,000 |
| Paper | 3,813,000 |
| Beef, pork, and poultry | 1,933,000 |
| Cosmetics | 1,778,000 |
| Radio and television sets | 915,000 |

**Table 9.6**

**Preserving Japanese Jobs with Tariffs and Quotas Is Also Expensive**

"Preserving Japanese Jobs with Tariffs and Quotas Is Also Expensive" by Yoko Sazabami, Shujiro Urata, and Hiroki Kawai from *Measuring the Cost of Protection in Japan.* Copyright © 1995 by the Institute for International Economics. Reprinted by permission.

Just as the sugar quota costs jobs in the candy industry, other tariffs and quotas cost jobs outside the industries immediately affected. For example, in 1991, the United States imposed tariffs on flat-panel displays used in laptop computers. This was good news for U.S. producers of these displays but bad news for companies producing laptop computers. Toshiba, Sharp, and Apple all closed their U.S. laptop production facilities and moved production overseas. In fact, whenever one industry receives tariff or quota protection, jobs are lost in other domestic industries.

## Making the Connection

### Save Jobs Making Hangers ... and Lose Jobs in Dry Cleaning

When supporters of tariffs and quotas argue that these interferences with trade save jobs, they are referring to jobs in the industry protected by the tariffs and quotas. We have seen that a tariff or quota makes it easier for domestic firms to compete against foreign firms that may have lower costs. More production by domestic firms means more employment at those firms, thereby saving jobs in that industry. But as we have also seen, other industries can see their costs rise as a result of the tariff or quota, causing firms in these industries to raise prices. Higher prices will reduce the quantity demanded resulting in lower production and fewer jobs in those industries.

This is just what happened when the United States raised the tariff on wire garment hangers imported from China. Under trade agreements signed with other countries, the United States is allowed to impose tariffs on imports if foreign firms are selling products in the United States at below their production cost. The U.S. International Trade Commission (ITC) determined that Chinese firms had, in fact, been selling wire garment hangers in the United States at below the firms' production cost and so imposed a tariff on imports of the hangers. Dry cleaners in the United States use a lot of wire hangers, so the tariff sharply increased the cleaners' costs. For example, a dry cleaner in East Harlem in New York City found that the price of a box of 500 hangers rose from $17.50 to $40. The dry cleaner uses 4,000 hangers per week, so his costs rose by $180 per week, or by $9,360 per year. The dry cleaning industry is made up of thousands of mostly small firms and is highly competitive. Small dry cleaners had difficulty absorbing the increased cost. The owner of the East Harlem dry cleaner was quoted as saying, "We can't do this business any more."

At the time the tariff was imposed, the dry cleaning industry employed 221,230 workers. Over the following two years, employment declined by about 17,000 workers, although not all of this decline was due to the increase in the cost of hangers. The ITC

*A tariff on hangers increased the cost of doing business for U.S. dry cleaners.*

estimated that the tariff would save about 300 jobs in U.S. factories producing wire hangers, and it would raise the average cost per dry cleaner by about $4,000 per year. At the time the tariff was imposed, there were about 30,000 dry cleaners in the United States, so the total cost of the tariff was about $120,000,000. The cost each year per job saved was about $120,000,000/300 = $400,000. At the time, the typical worker making wire hangers was earning about $31,000 per year.

As dry cleaners, their employees, and consumers buying wire hangers found out, tariffs can be both an expensive and ineffective way to attempt to preserve jobs.

Based on Jennifer Bleyer, "Dry Cleaners Feel an Ill Wind from China," *New York Times*, April 27, 2008; Gigi Douban, "Costs Up, So Dry Cleaners Want Their Hangers Back,'" npr.org, May 8, 2008; U.S. International Trade Commission, *Steel Wire Garment Hangers from China: Investigation No. 731-TA-1123 (Final)*, Publication 4034, September 2008; and U.S. Bureau of Labor Statistics, *Occupational Employment Statistics*, May 17, 2011.

MyEconLab **Your Turn:** Test your understanding by doing related problem 4.15 on page 305 at the end of this chapter.

## Gains from Unilateral Elimination of Tariffs and Quotas

Some politicians argue that eliminating U.S. tariffs and quotas would help the U.S. economy only if other countries eliminated their tariffs and quotas in exchange. It is easier to gain political support for reducing or eliminating tariffs or quotas if it is done as part of an agreement with other countries that involves their eliminating some of their tariffs or quotas. But as the example of the sugar quota shows, *the U.S. economy would gain from the elimination of tariffs and quotas even if other countries did not reduce their tariffs and quotas.*

## Other Barriers to Trade

In addition to tariffs and quotas, governments sometimes erect other barriers to trade. For example, all governments require that imports meet certain health and safety requirements. Sometimes, however, governments use these requirements to shield domestic firms from foreign competition. This can be true when a government imposes stricter health and safety requirements on imported goods than on goods produced by domestic firms.

Many governments also restrict imports of certain products on national security grounds. The argument is that in time of war, a country should not be dependent on imports of critical war materials. Once again, these restrictions are sometimes used more to protect domestic companies from competition than to protect national security. For example, for years, the U.S. government would buy military uniforms only from U.S. manufacturers, even though uniforms are not a critical war material.

**9.5 LEARNING** OBJECTIVE

Evaluate the arguments over trade policies and globalization.

# The Arguments over Trade Policies and Globalization

The argument over whether the U.S. government should regulate international trade dates back to the early days of the country. One particularly controversial attempt to restrict trade took place during the Great Depression of the 1930s. At that time, the United States and other countries attempted to help domestic firms by raising tariffs on foreign imports. The United States started the process by passing the Smoot-Hawley Tariff in 1930, which raised average tariff rates to more than 50 percent. As other countries retaliated by raising their tariffs, international trade collapsed.

By the end of World War II in 1945, government officials in the United States and Europe were looking for a way to reduce tariffs and revive international trade. To help achieve this goal, they set up the General Agreement on Tariffs and Trade (GATT) in 1948. Countries that joined GATT agreed not to impose new tariffs or import quotas. In addition, a series of *multilateral negotiations*, called *trade rounds*, took place, in which countries agreed to reduce tariffs from the very high levels of the 1930s.

In the 1940s, most international trade was in goods, and the GATT agreement covered only goods. In the following decades, trade in services and in products incorporating *intellectual property*, such as software programs and movies, grew in importance. Many GATT members pressed for a new agreement that would cover services and intellectual property, as well as goods. A new agreement was negotiated, and in January 1995, GATT was replaced by the **World Trade Organization (WTO)**, headquartered in Geneva, Switzerland. More than 150 countries are currently members of the WTO.

**World Trade Organization (WTO)** An international organization that oversees international trade agreements.

## Why Do Some People Oppose the World Trade Organization?

During the years immediately after World War II, many low-income, or developing, countries enacted high tariffs and restricted investment by foreign companies. When these policies failed to produce much economic growth, many of these countries decided during the 1980s to become more open to foreign trade and investment. This process became known as **globalization**. Most developing countries joined the WTO and began to follow its policies.

**Globalization** The process of countries becoming more open to foreign trade and investment.

During the 1990s, opposition to globalization began to increase. In 1999, this opposition took a violent turn at a meeting of the WTO in Seattle, Washington. A large number of protestors assembled in Seattle to meet the WTO delegates. Protests started peacefully but quickly became violent. Protesters looted stores and burned cars, and many delegates were unable to leave their hotel rooms. Similar incidents have occurred at most WTO meetings in the years since.

Why would attempts to reduce trade barriers with the objective of increasing income around the world cause such a furious reaction? The opposition to the WTO comes from three sources. First, some opponents are specifically against the globalization process that began in the 1980s and became widespread in the 1990s. Second, other opponents have the same motivation as the supporters of tariffs in the 1930s—to erect trade barriers to protect domestic firms from foreign competition. Third, some critics of the WTO support globalization in principle but believe that the WTO favors the interests of the high-income countries at the expense of the low-income countries. Let's look more closely at the sources of opposition to the WTO.

**Anti-globalization** Many of those who protest at WTO meetings distrust globalization. Some believe that free trade and foreign investment destroy the distinctive cultures of many countries. As developing countries began to open their economies to imports from the United States and other high-income countries, these imports of food, clothing, movies, and other goods began to replace the equivalent local products. So, a teenager in Thailand might be sitting in a McDonald's restaurant, wearing Levi's jeans and a Ralph Lauren shirt, listening to a recording by Lady Gaga on his iPod, before downloading *The Dark Knight Rises* to his iPad. Globalization has increased the variety of products available to consumers in developing countries, but some people argue that this is too high a price to pay for what they see as damage to local cultures.

Globalization has also allowed multinational corporations to relocate factories from high-income countries to low-income countries. These new factories in Indonesia, Malaysia, Pakistan, and other countries pay much lower wages than are paid in the United States, Europe, and Japan and often do not meet the environmental or safety regulations that are imposed in high-income countries. Some factories use child labor, which is illegal in high-income countries. Some people have argued that firms with factories in developing countries should pay workers wages as high as those paid in high-income countries. They also believe these firms should abide by the health, safety, and environmental regulations that exist in the high-income countries.

The governments of most developing countries have resisted these proposals. They argue that when the currently rich countries were poor, they also lacked environmental or safety standards, and their workers were paid low wages. They argue that it is easier for rich countries to afford high wages and environmental and safety regulations than it is for poor countries. They also point out that many jobs that seem to have very low wages based on the standards of high-income countries are often better than the alternatives available to workers in low-income countries.

| Making the Connection | The Unintended Consequences of Banning Goods Made with Child Labor |
|---|---|

In many developing countries, such as Indonesia, Thailand, and Peru, children as young as seven or eight work 10 or more hours a day. Reports of very young workers laboring long hours, producing goods for export, have upset many people in high-income countries. In the United States, boycotts have been organized against stores that stock goods made in developing countries with child labor. Many people assume that if child workers in developing countries weren't working in factories making clothing, toys, and other products, they would be in school, as are children in high-income countries.

*Would eliminating child labor, such as stitching soccer balls, improve the quality of children's lives?*

In fact, children in developing countries usually have few good alternatives to work. Schooling is frequently available for only a few months each year, and even children who attend school rarely do so for more than a few years. Poor families are often unable to afford even the small costs of sending their children to school. Families may rely on the earnings of very young children to survive, as poor families once did in the United States, Europe, and Japan. There is substantial evidence that as incomes begin to rise in poor countries, families rely less on child labor. The United States eventually outlawed child labor, but not until 1938. In developing countries where child labor is common today, jobs producing export goods are usually better paying and less hazardous than the alternatives.

As preparations began in France for the 1998 World Cup, there were protests that Baden Sports—the main supplier of soccer balls—was purchasing the balls from suppliers in Pakistan that used child workers. France decided to ban all use of soccer balls made by child workers. Bowing to this pressure, Baden Sports moved production from Pakistan, where the balls were hand-stitched by child workers, to China, where the balls were machine-stitched by adult workers in factories. There was some criticism of the boycott of hand-stitched soccer balls at the time. In a broad study of child labor, three economists argued:

> Of the array of possible employment in which impoverished children might engage, soccer ball stitching is probably one of the most benign. . . . [In Pakistan] children generally work alongside other family members in the home or in small workshops. . . . Nor are the children exposed to toxic chemicals, hazardous tools or brutal working conditions. Rather, the only serious criticism concerns the length of the typical child stitcher's work-day and the impact on formal education.

In fact, the alternatives to soccer ball stitching for child workers in Pakistan turned out to be extremely grim. According to Keith Maskus, an economist at the University of Colorado and the World Bank, a "large proportion" of the children who lost their jobs stitching soccer balls ended up begging or in prostitution.

Based on Tom Wright, "Pakistan Defends Its Soccer Industry," *Wall Street Journal*, April 26, 2010; Drusilla K. Brown, Alan V. Deardorff, and Robert M. Stern, "U.S. Trade and Other Policy Options to Deter Foreign Exploitation of Child Labor," in Magnus Blomstrom and Linda S. Goldberg, eds., *Topics in Empirical International Economics: A Festchrift in Honor of Bob Lispey*, (Chicago: University of Chicago Press, 2001); Tomas Larsson, *The Race to the Top: The Real Story of*

*Globalization*, (Washington, DC: Cato Institute, 2001), p. 48; and Eric V. Edmonds and Nina Pavcnik, "Child Labor in the Global Economy," *Journal of Economic Perspectives*, Vol. 19, No. 1, Winter 2005, pp. 199–220.

**Your Turn:** Test your understanding by doing related problem 5.5 on page 306 at the end of this chapter.                    MyEconLab

### "Old-Fashioned" Protectionism

The anti-globalization argument against free trade and the WTO is relatively new. Another argument against free trade, called *protectionism*, has been around for centuries. **Protectionism** is the use of trade barriers to shield domestic firms from foreign competition. For as long as international trade has existed, governments have attempted to restrict it to protect domestic firms. As we saw with the analysis of the sugar quota, protectionism causes losses to consumers and eliminates jobs in the domestic industries that buy the protected product. In addition, by reducing the ability of countries to produce according to comparative advantage, protectionism reduces incomes.

> **Protectionism** The use of trade barriers to shield domestic firms from foreign competition.

Why, then, does protectionism attract support? Protectionism is usually justified on the basis of one of the following arguments:

- *Saving jobs.* Supporters of protectionism argue that free trade reduces employment by driving domestic firms out of business. It is true that when more-efficient foreign firms drive less-efficient domestic firms out of business, jobs are lost, but jobs are also lost when more-efficient domestic firms drive less-efficient domestic firms out of business. These job losses are rarely permanent. In the U.S. economy, jobs are lost and new jobs are created continually. No economic study has ever found a long-term connection between the total number of jobs available and the level of tariff protection for domestic industries. In addition, trade restrictions destroy jobs in some industries at the same time that they preserve jobs in others. The U.S. sugar quota may have saved jobs in the U.S. sugar industry, but it has also destroyed jobs in the U.S. candy industry.

- *Protecting high wages.* Some people worry that firms in high-income countries will have to start paying much lower wages to compete with firms in developing countries. This fear is misplaced, however, because free trade actually raises living standards by increasing economic efficiency. When a country practices protectionism and produces goods and services it could obtain more inexpensively from other countries, it reduces its standard of living. The United States could ban imports of coffee and begin growing it domestically. But this would entail a very high opportunity cost because coffee could only be grown in the continental United States in greenhouses and would require large amounts of labor and equipment. The coffee would have to sell for a very high price to cover these costs. Suppose the United States did ban coffee imports: Eliminating the ban at some future time would eliminate the jobs of U.S. coffee workers, but the standard of living in the United States would rise as coffee prices declined and labor, machinery, and other resources moved out of coffee production and into production of goods and services for which the United States has a comparative advantage.

- *Protecting infant industries.* It is possible that firms in a country may have a comparative advantage in producing a good, but because the country begins production of the good later than other countries, its firms initially have higher costs. In producing some goods and services, substantial "learning by doing" occurs. As workers and firms produce more of the good or service, they gain experience and become more productive. Over time, costs and prices will fall. As the firms in the "infant industry" gain experience, their costs will fall, and they will be able to compete successfully with foreign producers. Under free trade, however, they may not get a chance. The established foreign producers can sell the product at a lower price and drive domestic producers out of business before they gain enough experience to compete. To economists, this is the most persuasive of the protectionist arguments. It has a significant drawback, however. Tariffs used to protect an infant industry eliminate the need for the firms in the industry to become productive enough to compete with foreign firms. After World War II, the governments of many developing countries used the "infant industry" argument to justify high tariff rates. Unfortunately, most of their infant industries never grew up, and they continued for years as inefficient drains on their economies.

- *Protecting national security.* As already discussed, a country should not rely on other countries for goods that are critical to its military defense. For example, the United States would probably not want to import all its jet fighter engines from China. The definition of which goods are critical to military defense is a slippery one, however. In fact, it is rare for an industry to ask for protection without raising the issue of national security, even if its products have mainly nonmilitary uses.

## Dumping

**Dumping** Selling a product for a price below its cost of production.

In recent years, the United States has extended protection to some domestic industries by using a provision in the WTO agreement that allows governments to impose tariffs in the case of *dumping*. **Dumping** is selling a product for a price below its cost of production. Although allowable under the WTO agreement, using tariffs to offset the effects of dumping is very controversial.

In practice, it is difficult to determine whether foreign companies are dumping goods because the true production costs of a good are not easy for foreign governments to calculate. As a result, the WTO allows countries to determine that dumping has occurred if a product is exported for a lower price than it sells for on the home market. There is a problem with this approach, however. Often there are good business reasons for a firm to sell a product for different prices to different consumers. For example, the airlines charge business travelers higher ticket prices than leisure travelers. Firms also use "loss leaders"—products that are sold below cost, or even given away free—when introducing a new product or, in the case of retailing, to attract customers who will also buy full-price products. For example, during the holiday season, Wal-Mart sometimes offers toys at prices below what they pay to buy them from manufacturers. It's unclear why these normal business practices should be unacceptable when used in international trade.

## Positive versus Normative Analysis (Once Again)

Economists emphasize the burden on the economy imposed by tariffs, quotas, and other government restrictions on free trade. Does it follow that these interferences are bad? Remember from Chapter 1 the distinction between *positive analysis* and *normative analysis*. Positive analysis concerns what *is*. Normative analysis concerns what *ought to be*. Measuring the effect of the sugar quota on the U.S. economy is an example of positive analysis. Asserting that the sugar quota is bad public policy and should be eliminated is normative analysis. The sugar quota—like all other interferences with trade—makes some people better off and some people worse off, and it reduces total income and consumption. Whether increasing the profits of U.S. sugar companies and the number of workers they employ justifies the costs imposed on consumers and the reduction in economic efficiency is a normative question.

Most economists do not support interferences with trade, such as the sugar quota. Few people become economists if they don't believe that markets should usually be as free as possible. But the opposite view is certainly intellectually respectable. It is possible for someone to understand the costs of tariffs and quotas but still believe that tariffs and quotas are a good idea, perhaps because they believe unrestricted free trade would cause too much disruption to the economy.

The success of industries in getting the government to erect barriers to foreign competition depends partly on some members of the public knowing the costs of trade barriers but supporting them anyway. However, two other factors are also at work:

1. The costs tariffs and quotas impose on consumers are large in total but relatively small per person. For example, the sugar quota imposes a total burden of about $6.08 billion per year on consumers. Spread across 310 million Americans, the burden is less than $20 per person: too little for most people to worry about, even if they know the burden exists.
2. The jobs lost to foreign competition are easy to identify, but the jobs created by foreign trade are less easy to identify.

In other words, the industries that benefit from tariffs and quotas benefit a lot—for example, the sugar quota increases the profits of U.S. sugar producers by $2.28 billion—whereas each consumer loses relatively little. This concentration of benefits and widely spread burdens makes it easy to understand why members of Congress receive strong pressure from some industries to enact tariffs and quotas and relatively little pressure from the general public to reduce them.

Continued from page 273

## Economics in Your Life

### Have You Heard of the "Buy American" Provision?

At the beginning of the chapter, we asked you to consider how some U.S. companies convinced Congress to include the Buy American provision in the American Recovery and Reinvestment Act and why relatively few people have heard of this provision. In the chapter, we saw that trade restrictions tend to preserve relatively few jobs in the protected industries, while leading to job losses in other industries and costing consumers billions per year in higher prices. This might seem to increase the mystery of why Congress enacted the Buy American provision. We have also seen, though, that *per person*, the burden of specific trade restrictions can be small. The sugar quota, for instance, imposes a per-person cost on consumers of only about $19 per year. Not many people will take the trouble of writing a letter to their member of Congress or otherwise make their views known in the hope of saving $19 per year. In fact, few people will even spend the time to become aware that a specific trade restriction exists. So, if before you read this chapter you had never heard of the Buy American provision, you are certainly not alone.

## Conclusion

There are few issues economists agree upon more than the economic benefits of free trade. However, there are few political issues as controversial as government policy toward trade. Many people who would be reluctant to see the government interfere with domestic trade are quite willing to see it interfere with international trade. The damage high tariffs inflicted on the world economy during the 1930s shows what can happen when governments around the world abandon free trade. Whether future episodes of that type can be avoided is by no means certain.

Read *An Inside Look at Policy* on the next page for a discussion of a legal dispute between Home Depot and the government in connection with the Buy American provision.

# Did Home Depot Knowingly Defy the "Buy American" Policy?

## ABC NEWS

## Home Depot Accused of Violating Buy American Act

Home Depot is the target of a lawsuit for allegedly selling goods manufactured in China and other prohibited countries to U.S. government agencies in violation of the Buy American Act, according to court documents.

The suit was filed in 2008 by two employees of another government contractor and alleges that "Home Depot had major sourcing operations in China for many years," as well as India, and that the company knew that certain brands and products were to be excluded from sale to U.S. government agencies because they were not compliant with the Trade Agreements Act.

The suit also says, "Home Depot affirmatively misrepresented to federal government customers that its GSA-scheduled contract 'covered everything in our store.'"

GSA is the federal General Services Administration, which supplies products for U.S. government offices.

The Buy American Act and Trade Agreements Act work together to promote the purchase of U.S. goods or goods manufactured in countries when it serves the nation's economic interest.

The Atlanta-based home improvement retailer, with more than 2,200 locations in four countries (including China), denies the allegations.

"We would never knowingly sell prohibited goods under any circumstances, and we have been cooperating with the government to provide requested information," Home Depot spokesman Ron wrote in a statement. "We believe the plaintiffs have an inaccurate view of the facts, so we look forward to presenting our side of this case as the process moves forward."

The plaintiffs' attorney, Paul D. Scott, said, "We're looking forward to having our day in court and having a jury of American citizens decide what they think of this case."

The U.S. Department of Justice had no comment about the allegations.

The Great Depression–era Buy American Act of 1933 was intended to produce jobs and keep the economy afloat.

"It's faulty logic to think that's going to benefit the United States to favor U.S. products if the government could buy foreign made products for lower prices," Stephen Bronars, senior economist with Welch Consulting, said.

"The view that if you do something yourself you're going to have closer to full employment ignores [the fact that] if you can get something more cheaply, it frees up resources you can allocate to something else."

But some disagree. This view "ignores the effect of trade on jobs and ignores the effect of trade on business," Robert E. Scott of the Economic Policy Institute said. "Globalization: Everybody wins except for most of us. That is in fact what happened."

While the Home Depot fends off the suit, the company continues to offer government buyers a look at how "Federal Dollars Go Farther at the Home Depot."

According to Scott's research, Americans lost 2.4 million jobs from 2001 to 2008 because U.S. multinational corporations outsourced production companies to China.

"It's not in the interest of the United States," Scott said. "It has hurt us as producer of goods. It has hurt wages and it has hurt GDP," Scott said.

"I tend to think that U.S. companies are increasingly outsourcing production and I think that has hurt the American economy," said Scott, who views the Buy American Act as a net benefit to the U.S. economy.

## Key Points in the Article

A lawsuit filed against Home Depot, alleged that the Atlanta-based home improvement company knowingly violated the Buy American provision of the American Recovery and Reinvestment Act of 2009 by selling to U.S. government agencies products prohibited by the legislation. A spokesman for Home Depot denied the allegations, claiming that the company would never intentionally sell prohibited goods and that the plaintiffs in the lawsuit had misinterpreted the facts surrounding the case.

## Analyzing the News

(a) Part of the American Recovery and Reinvestment Act of 2009, the Buy American provision required that all manufactured goods purchased with funds authorized under the act be made in the United States. In 1979, the United States passed the Trade Agreements Act, which mandates that the government only purchase end products valued over a specific dollar amount if they are made in the United States or come from a list of designated countries, unless the desired product is not available from these countries. Some view the Buy American provision as a partner of the Trade Agreements Act in the promotion of U.S. produced goods. The Home Depot case is not the first filed against a major U.S. corporation for violating the Buy American provi-

sion. The table below lists several major companies that made settlement payments to the U.S. government following litigation for allegedly violating the Buy American provision or the Trade Agreements Act.

| Company | Settlement | Date |
| --- | --- | --- |
| Fastenal | $6.25 million | 2011 |
| Corporate Express Office Products | 5.02 million | 2006 |
| Staples | 7.4 million | 2005 |
| Office Depot | 4.75 million | 2005 |
| Office Max | 9.72 million | 2005 |
| Invacare | 2.6 million | 1998 |

(b) Critics of the Buy American provision argue that paying more for U.S.-produced products when lower-priced products are available from other countries misallocates resources and drives up the costs of some projects being funded with federal money. Because the total amount of spending under the American Recovery and Reinvestment Act of 2009 was fixed, the more costly each project was, the fewer projects that would be funded. The Buy American provision was intended to increase employment in the United States, but if resources are being misallocated and, as a result, fewer projects can be funded, the number of new jobs created would be reduced.

(c) Proponents of the Buy American provision believe that the provision does, indeed, create jobs and benefit American businesses and workers.

The figure shows the effect of the Buy American provision on the steel market in the United States. (For simplicity, we assume that there are no barriers to foreign steel producers selling to the United States, apart from the Buy American provision. We also assume that the figure represents the whole market for steel in the United States, not just the market for steel to be used in projects funded by the American Recovery and Reinvestment Act of 2009.) In the absence of the Buy American provision, the price of steel in the United States is $P_1$, which is both the U.S. price and the world price. By limiting the amount of steel that can be imported into the United States, the Buy American provision raises the price of steel in the United States to $P_2$, which is above the world price, and equilibrium moves from point $A$ to point $B$. U.S. consumption of steel falls from $Q_4$ to $Q_3$, the quantity of steel supplied by U.S. steel producers increases from $Q_1$ to $Q_2$, and imports of foreign steel decline from $Q_4 - Q_1$ to $Q_3 - Q_2$. U.S. steel companies—and their workers—gain from the provision, as do foreign steel companies still able to sell in the United States because they receive a price higher than the world price. However, U.S. consumers—and taxpayers—lose because they must now pay a price above the world price.

## Thinking Critically about Policy

1. The Buy American provision, as well as tariffs and quotas on foreign imports, are intended to save jobs in the United States. Do they, in fact, save jobs? Do you support these trade restrictions? Briefly explain.
2. Consumers lose when the government interferes with trade as it did with the Buy American provision. Why, then, does Congress enact such legislation?

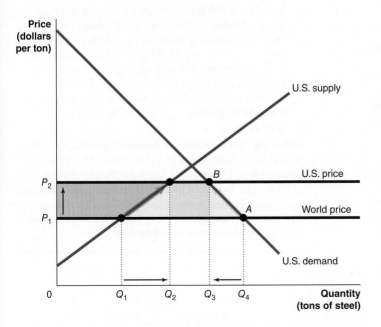

The effect of the "Buy American" provision on the steel market in the United States.

# Chapter Summary and Problems

## Key Terms

Absolute advantage, p. 278

Autarky, p. 279

Comparative advantage, p. 277

Dumping, p. 296

Exports, p. 274

External economies, p. 283

Free trade, p. 285

Globalization, p. 293

Imports, p. 274

Opportunity cost, p. 277

Protectionism, p. 295

Quota, p. 288

Tariff, p. 274

Terms of trade, p. 279

Voluntary export restraint (VER), p. 288

World Trade Organization (WTO), p. 293

---

**9.1** **The United States in the International Economy, pages 274–277**
LEARNING OBJECTIVE: Discuss the role of international trade in the U.S. economy.

## Summary

International trade has been increasing in recent decades, in part because of reductions in *tariffs* and other barriers to trade. A **tariff** is a tax imposed by a government on imports. The quantity of goods and services the United States imports and exports has been continually increasing. **Imports** are goods and services bought domestically but produced in other countries. **Exports** are goods and services produced domestically and sold to other countries. Today, the United States is the leading exporting country in the world, and about 20 percent of U.S. manufacturing jobs depend on exports.

MyEconLab    Visit **www.myeconlab.com** to complete these exercises online and get instant feedback.

## Review Questions

1.1 Briefly explain whether the value of U.S. exports is typically larger or smaller than the value of U.S. imports.

1.2 Are imports and exports a smaller or larger fraction of GDP than they were 40 years ago?

1.3 Briefly explain whether you agree with the following statement: "International trade is more important to the U.S. economy than to most other economies."

## Problems and Applications

1.4 If the United States were to stop trading goods and services with other countries, which U.S. industries would be likely to see their sales decline the most? Briefly explain.

1.5 Briefly explain whether you agree with the following statement: "Japan has always been much more heavily involved in international trade than are most other nations. In fact, today Japan exports a larger fraction of its GDP than Germany, Great Britain, or the United States."

1.6 Why might a smaller country, such as the Netherlands, be more likely to import and export larger fractions of its GDP than would a larger country, such as China or the United States?

1.7 **[Related to the** Making the Connection **on page 276]** Douglas Irwin, a professor of economics at Dartmouth College, wrote the following in a column in the *New York Times*:

> General Electric and Caterpillar have opposed the Buy American provision because they fear it will hurt their ability to win contracts abroad. . . . Once we get through the current economic mess, China, India and other countries are likely to continue their large investments in building projects. If such countries also adopt our preferences for domestic producers, then America will be at a competitive disadvantage in bidding for those contracts.

What are "preferences for domestic producers"? Why would these preferences put U.S. firms at a "competitive disadvantage"? Why might having difficulty making sales in China and India be a particular problem for Caterpillar?

"If We Buy American, No One Else Will", by Douglas A. Irwin from *New York Times*, January 31, 2009. Copyright © 2009 by Douglas A. Irwin. Reprinted by permission of the author.

## **Comparative Advantage in International Trade, pages 277–279**

**9.2**

LEARNING OBJECTIVE: Understand the difference between comparative advantage and absolute advantage in international trade.

## Summary

**Comparative advantage** is the ability of an individual, a business, or a country to produce a good or service at the lowest **opportunity cost**. **Absolute advantage** is the ability to produce more of a good or service than competitors when using the same amount of resources. Countries trade on the basis of comparative advantage, not on the basis of absolute advantage.

## Review Questions

**2.1** What is the difference between absolute advantage and comparative advantage? Will a country always be an exporter of a good where it has an absolute advantage in production? Briefly explain.

**2.2** A WTO publication calls comparative advantage "arguably the single most powerful insight in economics." What is comparative advantage? What makes it such a powerful insight?

Based on World Trade Organization, "Understanding the WTO," www.wto.org/english/thewto_e/whatis_e/tif_e/fact3_e.htm.

## Problems and Applications

**2.3** Why do the goods that countries import and export change over time? Use the concept of comparative advantage in your answer.

**2.4** In a newspaper column, Frank Wolak, a professor of economics at Stanford, referred to "the economic forces that lead to most children's toys being developed in the United States and mass-produced in China and other developing countries." What economic forces is he referring to? If a U.S. company develops a toy, why is a Chinese company likely to end up manufacturing the toy?

Source: Frank A. Wolak, "Our Comparative Advantage," *New York Times*, January 19, 2011.

**2.5** Briefly explain whether you agree with the following argument: "Unfortunately, Bolivia does not have a comparative advantage with respect to the United States in the production of any good or service." (*Hint:* You do not need any specific information about the economies of Bolivia or the United States to be able to answer this question.)

**2.6** The following table shows for Greece and Italy the hourly output per worker measured as quarts of olive oil and pounds of pasta:

| | Output per Hour of Work | |
|---|---|---|
| | Olive Oil | Pasta |
| Greece | 4 | 2 |
| Italy | 4 | 8 |

Calculate the opportunity cost of producing olive oil and pasta in both Greece and in Italy.

**2.7** In January 2008, the Bank of France published a report, stating that in 2006, hourly labor productivity in the United States was higher than the productivity in Japan. If U.S. workers can produce more goods and services per hour than Japanese workers, why does the United States continue to import from Japan some products it could produce at home?

Based on Gilbert Cette, Yusuf Kocoglu, and Jacques Mairesse, "A Comparison of Productivity in France, Japan, The United Kingdom and the United States over the Past Century," Banque de France, January 8, 2008.

**2.8** Patrick J. Buchanan, a former presidential candidate, argued in his book on the global economy that there is a flaw in David Ricardo's theory of comparative advantage:

> Classical free trade theory fails the test of common sense. According to Ricardo's law of comparative advantage . . . if America makes better computers and textiles than China does, but our advantage in computers is greater than our advantage in textiles, we should (1) focus on computers, (2) let China make textiles, and (3) trade U.S. computers for Chinese textiles. . . .

> The doctrine begs a question. If Americans are more efficient than Chinese in making clothes . . . why surrender the more efficient American industry? Why shift to a reliance on a Chinese textile industry that will take years to catch up to where American factories are today?

Do you agree with Buchanan's argument? Briefly explain.

From Patrick J. Buchanan, *The Great Betrayal: How American Sovereignty and Social Justice Are Being Sacrificed to the Gods of the Global Economy*, (Boston: Little, Brown & Company), 1998, p. 66.

**2.9** In a 2007 debate among Democratic presidential candidates, Barack Obama made the following statement: "Well, look, people don't want a cheaper T-shirt if they're losing a job in the process." What did Obama mean by the phrase "losing a job in the process"? Using the economic concept of comparative advantage, explain under what circumstances it would make sense for the United States to produce all of the T-shirts purchased in the United States. Do you agree with Obama's statement? Briefly explain.

Based on James Pethokoukis, "Democratic Debate Spawns Weird Economics," *U.S. News & World Report*, August 8, 2007.

## 9.3 How Countries Gain from International Trade, pages 279–285

LEARNING OBJECTIVE: Explain how countries gain from international trade.

## Summary

**Autarky** is a situation in which a country does not trade with other countries. The **terms of trade** is the ratio at which a country can trade its exports for imports from other countries. When a country specializes in producing goods where it has a comparative advantage and trades for the other goods it needs, the country will have a higher level of income and consumption. We do not see complete specialization in production for three reasons: Not all goods and services are traded internationally, production of most goods involves increasing opportunity costs, and tastes for products differ across countries. Although the population of a country as a whole benefits from trade, companies—and their workers—that are unable to compete with lower-cost foreign producers lose. Among the main sources of comparative advantage are climate and natural resources, relative abundance of labor and capital, technology, and external economies. **External economies** are reductions in a firm's costs that result from an increase in the size of an industry. A country may develop a comparative advantage in the production of a good, and then as time passes and circumstances change, the country may lose its comparative advantage in producing that good and develop a comparative advantage in producing other goods.

MyEconLab   Visit www.myeconlab.com to complete these exercises online and get instant feedback.

## Review Questions

3.1 Briefly explain how international trade increases a country's consumption.

3.2 What is meant by a country specializing in the production of a good? Is it typical for countries to be completely specialized? Briefly explain.

3.3 What are the main sources of comparative advantage?

3.4 Does everyone gain from international trade? If not, explain which groups lose.

## Problems and Applications

3.5 **[Related to** Solved Problem 9.3 **on page 280]** The following table shows the hourly output per worker in two industries in Chile and Argentina:

| | Output per Hour of Work | |
|---|---|---|
| | Hats | Beer |
| Chile | 8 | 6 |
| Argentina | 1 | 2 |

a. Explain which country has an absolute advantage in the production of hats and which country has an absolute advantage in the production of beer.

b. Explain which country has a comparative advantage in the production of hats and which country has a comparative advantage in the production of beer.

c. Suppose that Chile and Argentina currently do not trade with each other. Each has 1,000 hours of labor to use producing hats and beer, and the countries are currently producing the amounts of each good shown in the following table:

| | Hats | Beer |
|---|---|---|
| Chile | 7,200 | 600 |
| Argentina | 600 | 800 |

Using this information, give a numerical example of how Chile and Argentina can both gain from trade. Assume that after trading begins, one hat can be exchanged for one barrel of beer.

3.6 **[Related to** Solved Problem 9.3 **on page 280]** A political commentator makes the following statement:

The idea that international trade should be based on the comparative advantage of each country is fine for rich countries like the United States and Japan. Rich countries have educated workers and large quantities of machinery and equipment. These advantages allow them to produce every product more efficiently than poor countries can. Poor countries like Kenya and Bolivia have nothing to gain from international trade based on comparative advantage.

Do you agree with this argument? Briefly explain.

3.7 Briefly explain whether you agree with the following statement: "Most countries exhaust their comparative advantage in producing a good or service before they reach complete specialization."

3.8 Is free trade likely to benefit a large, populous country more than a small country with fewer people? Briefly explain.

3.9 An article in the *New Yorker* magazine states, "the main burden of trade-related job losses and wage declines has fallen on middle- and lower-income Americans. But . . . the very people who suffer most from free trade are often, paradoxically, among its biggest beneficiaries." Explain how it is possible that middle- and lower-income Americans are both the biggest losers and at the same time the biggest winners from free trade.

Based on James Surowiecki, "The Free-Trade Paradox," *New Yorker*, May 26, 2008.

3.10 Hal Varian, an economist at the University of California, Berkeley, has made two observations about international trade:

a. Trade allows a country "to produce more with less."

b. There is little doubt who wins [from trade] in the long run: consumers.

Briefly explain whether you agree with either or both of these observations.

Based on Hal R. Varian, "The Mixed Bag of Productivity," *New York Times*, October 23, 2003.

**3.11** Imagine that the graph below shows Tanzania's production possibilities frontier for cashew nuts and mangoes. Assume that the output per hour of work is 8 bushels of cashew nuts or 2 bushels of mangoes, and that Tanzania has 1,000 hours of labor. Without trade, Tanzania evenly splits its labor hours between cashews and mangoes and produces and consumes at point *A*.

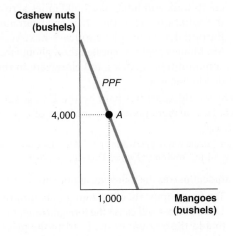

**a.** Suppose Tanzania opens trade with Kenya, and Kenya's output per hour of work is 1 bushel of cashew nuts or 1 bushel of mangoes. Having the comparative advantage, Tanzania completely specializes in cashew nuts. How many bushels of cashew nuts can Tanzania produce? Denote this point on the graph as point *B*.

**b.** Suppose Tanzania keeps 5,000 bushels of cashew nuts and exports the remaining 3,000 bushels. If the terms of trade are 1 bushel of mangoes for 2 bushels of cashew nuts, how many bushels of mangoes will Tanzania get in exchange? Denote on the graph the quantity of cashew nuts and mangoes that Tanzania consumes with trade and label this point as point *C*. How does point *C* with trade compare to point *A* without trade?

**c.** With trade, is Tanzania producing on its production possibilities frontier? With trade, is Tanzania consuming on its production possibilities frontier?

**3.12** [Related to the Don't Let This Happen to You **on page 282**] In 2011, President Barack Obama described a trade agreement reached with the government of Colombia as a "'win-win' for both our countries." Is everyone in both countries likely to win from the agreement? Briefly explain.

Based on Kent Klein, "Obama: Free Trade Agreement a 'Win-Win' for US, Colombia," Voice of America (voanews.com), accessed April 7, 2011.

**3.13** [Related to the Making the Connection **on page 284**] Explain why there are advantages to a movie studio operating in southern California, rather than in, say, Florida.

---

<table><tr><td>**9.4**</td><td>

## Government Policies That Restrict International Trade, pages 285–292
LEARNING OBJECTIVE: Analyze the economic effects of government policies that restrict international trade.
</td></tr></table>

## Summary

**Free trade** is trade between countries without government restrictions. Government policies that interfere with trade usually take the form of *tariffs*, *quotas*, or *voluntary export restraints* (VERs). A **tariff** is a tax imposed by a government on imports. A **quota** is a numeric limit imposed by a government on the quantity of a good that can be imported into the country. A **voluntary export restraint (VER)** is an agreement negotiated between two countries that places a numerical limit on the quantity of a good that can be imported by one country from the other country. The federal government's sugar quota costs U.S. consumers $6.08 billion per year, or about $2,026,667 per year for each job saved in the sugar industry. Saving jobs by using tariffs and quotas is often very expensive.

 Visit **www.myeconlab.com** to complete these exercises online and get instant feedback.

## Review Questions

**4.1** What is a tariff? What is a quota? Give an example, other than a quota, of a non-tariff barrier to trade.

**4.2** Who gains and who loses when a country imposes a tariff or a quota on imports of a good?

## Problems and Applications

**4.3** In a public opinion poll, 47 percent of people responding believed that free trade hurts the U.S. economy, while only 23 percent believed that it helps the economy. (The remaining people were uncertain about the effects of free trade or believed that it did not make much difference.) What is "free trade"? Do you believe it helps or hurts the economy? (Be sure to define what you mean by "helps" or "hurts.") Why do you think that more Americans appear to believe that free trade hurts the economy than believe that it helps the economy?

Based on Gallup Poll, February 2–5, 2011, www.pollingreport.com/trade.

**4.4** The G20 is a group of central bankers and finance ministers from 19 countries and the European Union who have a common goal of promoting global economic stability. In a letter to the editor of the *New York Times*, Victor K. Fung, the chairman of the International Chamber of Commerce, comments on the 2009 G20 summit in London: "While global leaders promise to fight protectionism when they gather at summit meetings, they must also resist intense pressure back home to adopt populist policies that will most certainly protract the recession." What does Fung mean by "fighting protectionism"? What does he mean by "populist policies"? How might populist trade policies extend a period of high unemployment and low production, such as the 2007–2009 recession?

Based on Victor K. Fung, "Resist Protectionism," Letter to the Editor, *New York Times*, March 30, 2009.

**4.5** Political commentator B. Bruce-Briggs once wrote the following in the *Wall Street Journal*: "This is not to say that the case for international free trade is invalid; it is just irrelevant. It is an 'if only everybody . . .' argument. . . . In the real world almost everybody sees benefits in economic nationalism." What do you think he means by "economic nationalism"? Do you agree that a country benefits from free trade only if every other country also practices free trade? Briefly explain.

Based on B. Bruce-Biggs, "The Coming Overthrow of Free Trade," *Wall Street Journal*, February 24, 1983, p. 28.

**4.6** Two U.S. senators made the following argument against allowing free trade: "Fewer and fewer Americans support our government's trade policy. They see a shrinking middle class, lost jobs and exploding trade deficits. Yet supporters of free trade continue to push for more of the same—more job-killing trade agreements." Do you agree with these senators that reducing barriers to trade reduces the number of jobs available to workers in the United States? Briefly explain.

Based on Byron Dorgan and Sherrod Brown, "How Free Trade Hurts," *Washington Post*, December 23, 2006, p. A21.

**4.7** The United States produces beef and also imports beef from other countries.

**a.** Draw a graph showing the demand and supply of beef in the United States. Assume that the United States can import as much as it wants at the world price of beef without causing the world price of beef to increase. Be sure to indicate on the graph the quantity of beef imported.

**b.** Now show on your graph the effect of the United States imposing a tariff on beef. Be sure to indicate on your graph the quantity of beef sold by U.S. producers before and after the tariff is imposed, the quantity of beef imported before and after the tariff, and the price of beef in the United States before and after the tariff.

**c.** Discuss who benefits and who loses when the United States imposes a tariff on beef.

**4.8** **[Related to the** Chapter Opener **on page 273]** Which U.S. firms are most likely to be unfavorably affected by a provision which states that only U.S. firms can participate in programs financed by federal spending?

**4.9** When Congress was considering a bill to impose quotas on imports of textiles, shoes, and other products, the late Milton Friedman, a Nobel Prize–winning economist, made the following comment: "The consumer will be forced to spend several extra dollars to subsidize the producers [of these goods] by one dollar. A straight handout would be far cheaper." Why would a quota result in consumers paying much more than domestic producers receive? Where do the other dollars go? What does Friedman mean by a "straight handout"? Why would this be cheaper than a quota?

Based on Milton Friedman, "Free Trade," *Newsweek Magazine*, August 27, 1970.

**4.10** The United States has about 9,000 rice farmers. In 2006, these rice farmers received $780 million in subsidy payments from the U.S. government (or nearly $87,000 per farmer). These payments result in U.S. farmers producing much more rice than they otherwise would, a substantial amount of which is exported. According to an article in the *Wall Street Journal*, Kpalagim Mome, a farmer in the African country of Ghana, can no longer find buyers in Ghana for his rice:

> "We can't sell our rice anymore. It gets worse every year," Mr. Mome says. . . . Years of economic hardship have driven three of his brothers to walk and hitchhike 2,000 miles across the Sahara to reach the Mediterranean and Europe. His sister plans to leave next year. Mr. Mome's plight is repeated throughout farm communities in Africa and elsewhere in the developing world.

Why would subsidies paid by the U.S. government to U.S. rice farmers reduce the incomes of rice farmers in Africa?

From Juliane von Reppert-Bismarck, "How Trade Barriers Keep Africans Adrift," *Wall Street Journal*, December 27, 2006.

**4.11** A student makes the following argument:

> Tariffs on imports of foreign goods into the United States will cause the foreign companies to add the amount of the tariff to the prices they charge in the United States for those goods. Instead of putting a tariff on imported goods, we should ban importing them. Banning imported goods is better than putting tariffs on them because U.S. producers benefit from the reduced competition, and U.S. consumers don't have to pay the higher prices caused by tariffs.

Briefly explain whether you agree with the student's reasoning.

**4.12** Suppose China decides to pay large subsidies to any Chinese company that exports goods or services to the United States. As a result, these companies are able to sell products in the United States at far below their cost of production. In addition, China decides to bar all imports from the United States. The dollars that the United States pays to import Chinese goods are left in banks in China. Will this strategy raise or lower the standard of living in China? Will it raise or lower the standard of living in the United States? Briefly explain. Be sure to provide a definition of "standard of living" in your answer.

**4.13** According to an editorial in the *Washington Post*: "Sugar protectionism is a burden on consumers and a job-killer."

**a.** In what sense does the United States practice "sugar protectionism"?

**b.** In what way is sugar protectionism a burden on consumers? In what way is it a job-killer?

**c.** If sugar protectionism has the bad effects stated in the editorial, why don't Congress and the president eliminate it?

Based on "Sourball," *Washington Post*, March 22, 2010.

**4.14** **[Related to** Solved Problem 9.4 **on page 289]** Suppose that the United States currently both produces kumquats and imports them. The U.S. government then decides to restrict international trade in kumquats by imposing a quota that allows imports of only 6 million pounds of kumquats into the United States each year. The figure shows the results of imposing the quota.

Fill in the table in the next column using the letters in the figure:

| | Without Quota | With Quota |
|---|---|---|
| World price of kumquats | _____ | _____ |
| U.S. price of kumquats | _____ | _____ |
| Quantity supplied by U.S. firms | _____ | _____ |
| Quantity demanded | _____ | _____ |
| Quantity imported | _____ | _____ |
| Area of consumer surplus | _____ | _____ |
| Area of domestic producer surplus | _____ | _____ |
| Area of deadweight loss | _____ | _____ |

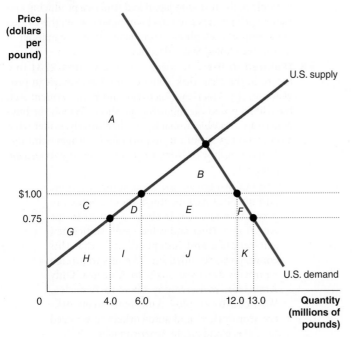

**4.15** **[Related to the** Making the Connection **on page 291]** An economic analysis of a proposal to impose a quota on steel imports into the United States indicated that the quota would save 3,700 jobs in the steel industry but cost about 35,000 jobs in other U.S. industries. Why would a quota on steel imports cause employment to fall in other industries? Which other industries are likely to be most affected?

Based on Study cited in Douglas A. Irwin, *Free Trade Under Fire*, (Princeton, NJ: Princeton University Press, 2002), p. 82.

---

**9.5** | **The Arguments over Trade Policies and Globalization,** pages 292–297

LEARNING OBJECTIVE: Evaluate the arguments over trade policies and globalization.

## Summary

The **World Trade Organization (WTO)** is an international organization that enforces international trade agreements. The WTO has promoted **globalization**, the process of countries becoming more open to foreign trade and investment. Some critics of the WTO argue that globalization has damaged local cultures around the world. Other critics oppose the WTO because they believe in **protectionism**, which is the use of trade barriers to shield domestic firms from foreign competition. The WTO allows countries to use tariffs in cases of **dumping**, when an imported product is sold for a price below its cost of production. Economists can point out the burden imposed on the economy by tariffs, quotas, and other government interferences with free trade. But whether these policies should be used is a normative decision.

## Review Questions

**5.1** What events led to the General Agreement on Tariffs and Trade (GATT)? Why did the WTO eventually replace GATT?

**5.2** What is globalization? Why are some people opposed to globalization?

**5.3** What is protectionism? Who benefits and who loses from protectionist policies? What are the main arguments people use to justify protectionism?

**5.4** What is dumping? Who benefits and who loses from dumping? What problems arise when anti-dumping laws are implemented?

# Problems and Applications

**5.5 [Related to the** Making the Connection **on page 294]**
The following excerpt is from a newspaper story on President Bill Clinton's proposal to create a group within the Word Trade Organization (WTO) responsible for developing labor standards. The story was published just before the 1999 WTO meeting in Seattle that ended in rioting:

> [President Clinton proposed that] core labor standards . . . become "part of every trade agreement. And ultimately I would favor a system in which sanctions would come for violating any provision of a trade agreement. . . ." But the new U.S. stand is sure to meet massive resistance from developing countries, which make up more than 100 of the 135 countries in the WTO. They are not interested in adopting tougher U.S. labor standards.

What did Clinton mean by "core labor standards"? Why would developing countries resist adopting these standards?

From Terence Hunt, "Salute to Trade's Benefits Turns into 'Kind of Circus,'" *Associated Press*, December 2, 1999.

**5.6** Steven Landsburg, an economist at the University of Rochester, wrote the following in an article in the *New York Times*:

> Free trade is not only about the right of American consumers to buy at the cheapest possible price; it's also about the right of foreign producers to earn a living. Steelworkers in West Virginia struggle hard to make ends meet. So do steelworkers in South Korea. To protect one at the expense of the other, solely because of where they happened to be born, is a moral outrage.

How does the U.S. government protect steelworkers in West Virginia at the expense of steelworkers in South Korea? Is Landsburg making a positive or a normative statement? A few days later, Tom Redburn published an article disagreeing with Landsburg:

> It is not some evil character flaw to care more about the welfare of people nearby than about that of those far away—it's human nature. And it is morally—and economically—defensible. . . . A society that ignores the consequences of economic disruption on those among its citizens who come out at the short end of the stick is not only heartless, it also undermines its own cohesion and adaptability.

Which of the two arguments do you find most convincing?

Based on Steven E. Landsburg, "Who Cares if the Playing Field Is Level?" *The New York Times*, June 13, 2001; and Tom Redburn, "Economic View: Of Politics, Free Markets, and Tending to Society," *The New York Times*, June 17, 2001.

**5.7** Suppose you are explaining the benefits of free trade and someone states, "I don't understand all the principles of comparative advantage and gains from trade. I just know that if I buy something produced in America, I create a job for an American, and if I buy something produced in Brazil, I create a job for a Brazilian." Do you agree with this statement? When the United States imports products in which it does not have a comparative advantage, does that mean that there are fewer jobs in the United States? In the example in the text with Japan and America producing and trading cell phones and tablet computers, when the United States imports cell phones from Japan, does the number of jobs in the United States decline?

**5.8 [Related to the** Chapter Opener **on page 273]** In a forum in the *New York Times* on the Buy American provision in the American Recovery and Reinvestment Act, the editors posed the following question: "Why is the buy-American idea objectionable, or, alternatively, under what circumstances should it be promoted?" Roger Simmermaker, the author of *How Americans Can Buy American*, responded:

> The buy-American provision in the economic stimulus bill isn't as much about a return to protectionism as it is about a return to the American virtues and values—self-sufficiency, self-reliance and independence—that this country was founded on. Workers in foreign countries don't pay taxes to America. Only American workers pay taxes to America. We need to employ American steelworkers, ironworkers and autoworkers so we need to . . . keep and create American jobs.

Burton Folsom Jr., a professor at Hillsdale College, offered an opposing view:

> "Slap a tariff on China and save American jobs," the protectionists say. This tempting line of reasoning is flawed for two reasons. First, if Americans pay more for, say, American-made shoes or shirts, then they have less to spend for other things they might need—they are simply subsidizing inefficient local producers. And those American manufacturers, who are protected from foreign competitors, have little incentive to innovate and cut prices. Second, if we refuse to buy China's imports, China will refuse to buy our exports, including our first-rate computers and iPods. Our export market collapses.

Which of the two arguments do you find the most convincing?

From "That 'Buy American' Provision" series. *New York Times*, February 11, 2009. Reprinted with kind permission from Roger Simmermaker and Burton Folsom, Jr.

**5.9** President George W. Bush and President Barack Obama had trouble getting Congress to ratify free trade agreements the United States had negotiated with South Korea, Colombia, and Panama. According to an article in the *New York Times*, "When the Democrats controlled Congress, they resisted the trade agreements because they feared they would harm American workers." Is it likely that trade agreements that reduce tariffs and quotas will harm American workers? Briefly explain.

Based on Mark Drajem, "Obama to Pursue Trade Deals, Avoid Turning 'Inward,'" Bloomberg.com, April 23, 2009.

**5.10** The following appeared in an article in *BusinessWeek* that argued against free trade: "The U.S. is currently in a precarious position. In addition to geopolitical threats, we face a severe economic shock. We have already lost trillions of dollars and millions of jobs to foreigners." If a country engages in free trade, is the total number of jobs in the country likely to decline? Briefly explain.

Based on Vladimir Masch, "A Radical Plan to Manage Globalization," *BusinessWeek*, February 14, 2007.

## Chapter Outline and Learning Objectives

# Can Justin Bieber and Ozzy Osbourne Get You to Shop at Best Buy?

Managers at Best Buy had an idea they believed people would love: The company would buy any cell phone or other electronic product back from their customers, within two years of purchase, and allow them to upgrade to a newer model. To announce this Buy Back program, Best Buy ran a new commercial during the 2011 Super Bowl, an opportunity to reach over 110 million viewers. This commercial featured an unlikely pair of celebrities: aging rock star Ozzie Osborne and teenage singing sensation Justin Bieber. Although many Best Buy customers are old enough to be the 16-year-old Bieber's parents, demand for mobile and technology-related products was growing more than the demand for televisions and stereos that had fueled Best Buy's past growth. The retailer was anxious to change its image. "Justin Bieber is the biggest star out there . . . " explained marketing chief Drew Panayiotou. "He . . . represents something important to the brand message."

In 2010, *Forbes* magazine ranked Justin Bieber as the third-most-powerful entertainment personality in 2010, just behind Lady Gaga and Oprah Winfrey, and ahead of Taylor Swift, Simon Cowell, and LeBron James. Do celebrity endorsements affect consumer behavior? When asked in surveys, many consumers claim that celebrity endorsements don't influence their buying decisions.

Marc Babej, an authority on marketing strategy, argues that survey responses are unreliable because advertisements appeal to the subconscious as well as the conscious mind. To be successful, Babej believes that celebrity endorsements must be relevant to the advertised product:

> In . . . image-driven consumer categories such as fashion, perfume or liquor, celebrity endorsements can be credible. For sporting goods, endorsement by an athlete can work wonders. . . . But in [other] categories . . . a celebrity endorser isn't likely to have much of a positive impact . . . [because] movie stars or athletes aren't considered authorities in these areas.

Will Justin Bieber's endorsement increase Best Buy's sales of cell phones? In this chapter, we will examine how consumers make decisions about which products to buy. Firms must understand consumer behavior to determine what strategies are likely to be most effective in selling their products.

**AN INSIDE LOOK** on **page 332** discusses whether endorsements from celebrities ranging from Jennifer Lopez to Charlie Sheen can help or hurt a brand.

Based on Marc E. Babej, "Poll: Celebrity Endorsements Don't Work . . . Don't Tell Angelina," *Forbes*, June 14, 2011; Amanda Massa, "Justin Bieber Leads List Of Celebrity 100 Newcomers," forbes.com, May 18, 2011; and Bruce Horovitz, "Justin Bieber . . . and Ozzy? . . . to Star in Best Buy Super Bowl Ad," *USA Today*, January 27, 2011.

## Economics in Your Life

### Do You Make Rational Decisions?

Economists generally assume that people make decisions in a rational, consistent way. But are people actually as rational as economists assume? Consider the following situation: You bought a concert ticket for $75, which is the most you were willing to pay. While you are in line to enter the concert hall, someone offers you $90 for the ticket. Would you sell the ticket? Would an economist think it is rational to sell the ticket? As you read the chapter, see if you can answer these questions. You can check your answers against those we provide **on page 331** at the end of this chapter.

W e begin this chapter by exploring how consumers make decisions. In Chapter 1, we saw that economists usually assume that people act in a rational, self-interested way. In explaining consumer behavior, this means economists believe consumers make choices that will leave them as satisfied as possible, given their *tastes*, their *incomes*, and the *prices* of the goods and services available to them. We will see how the downward-sloping demand curves we encountered in Chapters 3 through 5 result from the economic model of consumer behavior. We will also explore how in certain situations, knowing which decision is the best one can be difficult. In these cases, economic reasoning provides a powerful tool for consumers to improve their decision making. Finally, we will see that *experimental economics* has shown that factors such as social pressure and notions of fairness can affect consumer behavior. We will look at how businesses take these factors into account when setting prices. In the appendix to this chapter, we extend the analysis by using indifference curves and budget lines to understand consumer behavior.

# Utility and Consumer Decision Making

We saw in Chapter 3 that the model of demand and supply is a powerful tool for analyzing how prices and quantities are determined. We also saw that, according to the *law of demand*, whenever the price of a good falls, the quantity demanded increases. In this section, we will show how the economic model of consumer behavior leads to the law of demand.

## The Economic Model of Consumer Behavior in a Nutshell

Imagine walking through a shopping mall, trying to decide how to spend your clothing budget. If you had an unlimited budget, your decision would be easy: Just buy as much of everything as you want. Given that you have a limited budget, what do you do? Economists assume that consumers act so as to make themselves as well off as possible. Therefore, you should choose the one combination of clothes that makes you as well off as possible from among those combinations that you can afford. Stated more generally, the economic model of consumer behavior predicts that consumers will choose to buy the combination of goods and services that makes them as well off as possible from among all the combinations that their budgets allow them to buy.

This prediction may seem obvious and not particularly useful. But as we explore the implication of this prediction, we will see that it leads to conclusions that are useful but not obvious.

## Utility

How much satisfaction you receive from consuming a particular combination of goods and services depends on your tastes or preferences. There is an old saying—"There's no accounting for tastes"—and economists don't try to. If you buy a can of Red Bull energy drink instead of a can of Monster Energy, even though Monster Energy has a lower price, you must receive more enjoyment or satisfaction from drinking Red Bull. Economists refer to the enjoyment or satisfaction people receive from consuming goods and services as **utility**. So we can say that the goal of a consumer is to spend available income so as to maximize utility. But utility is a difficult concept to measure because there is no way of knowing exactly how much enjoyment or satisfaction someone receives from consuming a product. Similarly, it is not possible to compare utility across consumers. There is no way of knowing for sure whether Jill receives more or less satisfaction than Jack from drinking a can of Red Bull.

Two hundred years ago, economists hoped to measure utility in units called *utils*. The util would be an objective measure in the same way that temperature is: If it is

**Utility** The enjoyment or satisfaction people receive from consuming goods and services.

70 degrees in New York and 70 degrees in Los Angeles, it is just as warm in both cities. These economists wanted to say that if Jack's utility from drinking a can of Red Bull is 10 utils and Jill's utility is 5 utils, then Jack receives exactly twice the satisfaction from drinking a can of Red Bull as Jill does. In fact, it is *not* possible to measure utility across people. It turns out that none of the important conclusions of the economic model of consumer behavior depend on utility being directly measurable (a point we demonstrate in the appendix to this chapter). Nevertheless, the economic model of consumer behavior is easier to understand if we assume that utility is something directly measurable, like temperature.

## The Principle of Diminishing Marginal Utility

To make the model of consumer behavior more concrete, let's see how a consumer makes decisions in a case involving just two products: pepperoni pizza and Coke. To begin, consider how the utility you receive from consuming a good changes with the quantity of the good you consume. For example, suppose that you have just arrived at a Super Bowl party, where the hosts are serving pepperoni pizza, and you are very hungry. In this situation, you are likely to receive quite a lot of enjoyment, or utility, from consuming the first slice of pizza. Suppose this satisfaction is measurable and is equal to 20 units of utility, or *utils*. After eating the first slice, you decide to have a second slice. Because you are no longer as hungry, the satisfaction you receive from eating the second slice of pizza is less than the satisfaction you received from eating the first slice. Consuming the second slice increases your utility by only an *additional* 16 utils, which raises your *total* utility from eating the 2 slices to 36 utils. If you continue eating slices, each additional slice gives you less and less additional satisfaction.

The table in Figure 10.1 shows the relationship between the number of slices of pizza you consume while watching the Super Bowl and the amount of utility you receive. The second column in the table shows the total utility you receive from eating a particular number of slices. The third column shows the additional utility, or **marginal utility (MU)**, you receive from consuming one additional slice. (Remember that in economics, *marginal* means *additional*.) For example, as you increase your consumption from 2 slices to 3 slices, your total utility increases from 36 to 46, so your marginal utility from consuming the third slice is 10 utils. As the table shows, by the time you eat the fifth slice of pizza that evening, your marginal utility is very low: only 2 utils. If you were to eat a sixth slice, you would become slightly ill, and your marginal utility would actually be a *negative* 3 utils.

**Marginal utility (MU)** The change in total utility a person receives from consuming one additional unit of a good or service.

Figure 10.1 also plots the numbers from the table as graphs. Panel (a) shows how your total utility rises as you eat the first 5 slices of pizza and then falls as you eat the sixth slice. Panel (b) shows how your marginal utility declines with each additional slice you eat and finally becomes negative when you eat the sixth slice. The height of the marginal utility line at any quantity of pizza in panel (b) represents the change in utility as a result of consuming that additional slice. For example, the change in utility as a result of consuming 4 slices instead of 3 is 6 utils, so the height of the marginal utility line in panel (b) is 6 utils.

The relationship illustrated in Figure 10.1 between consuming additional units of a product during a period of time and the marginal utility received from consuming each additional unit is referred to as the **law of diminishing marginal utility**. For nearly every good or service, the more you consume during a period of time, the less you increase your total satisfaction from each additional unit you consume.

**Law of diminishing marginal utility** The principle that consumers experience diminishing additional satisfaction as they consume more of a good or service during a given period of time.

## The Rule of Equal Marginal Utility per Dollar Spent

The key challenge for consumers is to decide how to allocate their limited incomes among all the products they wish to buy. Every consumer has to make trade-offs: If you have $100 to spend on entertainment for the month, then the more movies you buy online, the fewer movies you can see in the theater. Economists refer to the limited amount of income you have available to spend on goods and services as your **budget constraint**. The principle of diminishing marginal utility helps us understand how consumers can best spend their limited incomes on the products available to them.

**Budget constraint** The limited amount of income available to consumers to spend on goods and services.

### Figure 10.1

**Total and Marginal Utility from Eating Pizza on Super Bowl Sunday**

The table shows that for the first 5 slices of pizza, the more you eat, the more your total satisfaction, or utility, increases. If you eat a sixth slice, you start to feel ill from eating too much pizza, and your total utility falls. Each additional slice increases your utility by less than the previous slice, so your marginal utility from each slice is less than the one before. Panel (a) shows your total utility rising as you eat the first 5 slices and falling with the sixth slice. Panel (b) shows your marginal utility falling with each additional slice you eat and becoming negative with the sixth slice. The height of the marginal utility line at any quantity of pizza in panel (b) represents the change in utility as a result of consuming that additional slice. For example, the change in utility as a result of consuming 4 slices instead of 3 is 6 utils, so the height of the marginal utility line in panel (b) for the fourth slice is 6 utils.

| Number of Slices | Total Utility from Eating Pizza | Marginal Utility from the Last Slice Eaten |
|---|---|---|
| 0 | 0 | -- |
| 1 | 20 | 20 |
| 2 | 36 | 16 |
| 3 | 46 | 10 |
| 4 | 52 | 6 |
| 5 | 54 | 2 |
| 6 | 51 | -3 |

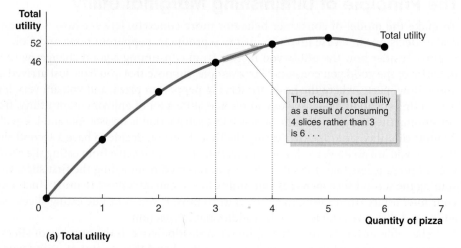

**(a) Total utility**

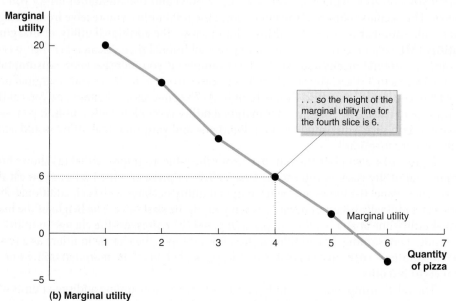

**(b) Marginal utility**

Suppose you attend a Super Bowl party at a restaurant, and you have $10 to spend on refreshments. Pizza is selling for $2 per slice, and Coke is selling for $1 per cup. Table 10.1 shows the relationship between the amount of pizza you eat, the amount of Coke you drink, and the amount of satisfaction, or utility, you receive. The values for pizza are repeated from the table in Figure 10.1. The values for Coke also follow the principle of diminishing marginal utility.

How many slices of pizza and how many cups of Coke do you buy if you want to maximize your utility? If you did not have a budget constraint, you would buy 5 slices of pizza and 5 cups of Coke because that would give you total utility of 107 (54 + 53), which is the maximum utility you can achieve. Eating another slice of pizza or drinking another cup of Coke during the evening would lower your utility. Unfortunately, you do have a budget constraint: You have only $10 to spend. To buy 5 slices of pizza (at $2 per slice) and 5 cups of Coke (at $1 per cup), you would need $15.

| Number of Slices of Pizza | Total Utility from Eating Pizza | Marginal Utility from the Last Slice | Number of Cups of Coke | Total Utility from Drinking Coke | Marginal Utility from the Last Cup |
|---|---|---|---|---|---|
| 0 | 0 | — | 0 | 0 | — |
| 1 | 20 | 20 | 1 | 20 | 20 |
| 2 | 36 | 16 | 2 | 35 | 15 |
| 3 | 46 | 10 | 3 | 45 | 10 |
| 4 | 52 | 6 | 4 | 50 | 5 |
| 5 | 54 | 2 | 5 | 53 | 3 |
| 6 | 51 | −3 | 6 | 52 | −1 |

**Table 10.1**

**Total Utility and Marginal Utility from Eating Pizza and Drinking Coke**

To select the best way to spend your $10, remember this key economic principle: *Optimal decisions are made at the margin.* That is, most of the time, economic decision makers—consumers, firms, and the government—are faced with decisions about whether to do a little more of one thing or a little more of an alternative. In this case, you are choosing to consume a little more pizza or a little more Coke. BMW chooses to manufacture more hybrid cars or more SUVs in its South Carolina factory. Congress and the president choose to spend more for research on heart disease or more for research on breast cancer. Everyone faces a budget constraint, and everyone faces trade-offs.

The key to making the best consumption decision is to maximize utility by following the *rule of equal marginal utility per dollar spent.* As you decide how to spend your income, you should buy pizza and Coke up to the point where the last slice of pizza purchased and the last cup of Coke purchased give you equal increases in utility *per dollar.* By doing this, you will have maximized your total utility.

It is important to remember that to follow this rule, you must equalize your marginal utility per dollar spent, *not* your marginal utility from each good. Buying season tickets for your favorite NFL team or for the symphony or buying a BMW may give you a lot more satisfaction than drinking a cup of Coke, but the NFL tickets may well give you less satisfaction *per dollar spent.* To decide how many slices of pizza and how many cups of Coke to buy, you must convert the values for marginal utility in Table 10.1 into marginal utility per dollar. You can do this by dividing marginal utility by the price of each good, as shown in Table 10.2.

In column (3), we calculate marginal utility per dollar spent on pizza. Because the price of pizza is $2 per slice, the marginal utility per dollar from eating 1 slice of pizza equals 20 divided by $2, or 10 utils per dollar. Similarly, we show in column (6) that because the price of Coke is $1 per cup, the marginal utility per dollar from drinking 1 cup of Coke equals 20 divided by $1, or 20 utils per dollar. To maximize the total utility you receive, you must make sure that the utility per dollar of pizza for the last slice of pizza is equal to the utility per dollar of Coke for the last cup of Coke. Table 10.2 shows that there are three combinations of slices of pizza and cups of Coke where marginal utility per

| (1) Slices of Pizza | (2) Marginal Utility ($MU_{Pizza}$) | (3) Marginal Utility per Dollar $\left(\dfrac{MU_{Pizza}}{P_{Pizza}}\right)$ | (4) Cups of Coke | (5) Marginal Utility ($MU_{Coke}$) | (6) Marginal Utility per Dollar $\left(\dfrac{MU_{Coke}}{P_{Coke}}\right)$ |
|---|---|---|---|---|---|
| 1 | 20 | 10 | 1 | 20 | 20 |
| 2 | 16 | 8 | 2 | 15 | 15 |
| 3 | 10 | 5 | 3 | 10 | 10 |
| 4 | 6 | 3 | 4 | 5 | 5 |
| 5 | 2 | 1 | 5 | 3 | 3 |
| 6 | −3 | −1.5 | 6 | −1 | −1 |

**Table 10.2**

**Converting Marginal Utility to Marginal Utility per Dollar**

| Table 10.3 | Combinations of Pizza and Coke with Equal Marginal Utilities per Dollar | Marginal Utility per Dollar (*MU/P*) | Total Spending | Total Utility |
|---|---|---|---|---|
| **Equalizing Marginal Utility per Dollar Spent** | 1 slice of pizza and 3 cups of Coke | 10 | $2 + $3 = $5 | 20 + 45 = 65 |
| | 3 slices of pizza and 4 cups of Coke | 5 | $6 + $4 = $10 | 46 + 50 = 96 |
| | 4 slices of pizza and 5 cups of Coke | 3 | $8 + $5 = $13 | 52 + 53 = 105 |

dollar is equalized. Table 10.3 lists the combinations, the total amount of money needed to buy each combination, and the total utility received from consuming each combination.

If you buy 4 slices of pizza, the last slice gives you 3 utils per dollar. If you buy 5 cups of Coke, the last cup also gives you 3 utils per dollar, so you have equalized your marginal utility per dollar. Unfortunately, as the third column in the table shows, to buy 4 slices and 5 cups, you would need $13, and you have only $10. You could also equalize your marginal utility per dollar by buying 1 slice and 3 cups, but that would cost just $5, leaving you with $5 to spend. Only when you buy 3 slices and 4 cups have you equalized your marginal utility per dollar and spent neither more nor less than the $10 available.

We can summarize the two conditions for maximizing utility:

1. $\dfrac{MU_{Pizza}}{P_{Pizza}} = \dfrac{MU_{Coke}}{P_{Coke}}$

2. Spending on pizza + Spending on Coke = Amount available to be spent

The first condition shows that the marginal utility per dollar spent must be the same for both goods. The second condition is the budget constraint, which states that total spending on both goods must equal the amount available to be spent. Of course, these conditions for maximizing utility apply not just to pizza and Coke but to any two pairs of goods.

# Solved Problem 10.1

## Finding the Optimal Level of Consumption

The following table shows Lee's utility from consuming ice cream cones and cans of Lime Fizz soda:

| Number of Ice Cream Cones | Total Utility from Ice Cream Cones | Marginal Utility from Last Cone | Number of Cans of Lime Fizz | Total Utility from Cans of Lime Fizz | Marginal Utility from Last Can |
|---|---|---|---|---|---|
| 0 | 0 | — | 0 | 0 | — |
| 1 | 30 | 30 | 1 | 40 | 40 |
| 2 | 55 | 25 | 2 | 75 | 35 |
| 3 | 75 | 20 | 3 | 101 | 26 |
| 4 | 90 | 15 | 4 | 119 | 18 |
| 5 | 100 | 10 | 5 | 134 | 15 |
| 6 | 105 | 5 | 6 | 141 | 7 |

a. Ed inspects this table and concludes, "Lee's optimal choice would be to consume 4 ice cream cones and 5 cans of Lime Fizz because with that combination, his marginal utility from ice cream cones is equal to his marginal utility from Lime Fizz." Do you agree with Ed's reasoning? Briefly explain.

b. Suppose that Lee has an unlimited budget to spend on ice cream cones and cans of Lime Fizz. Under these circumstances, how many ice cream cones and how many cans of Lime Fizz will he consume? (Assume that Lee cannot consume more than 6 ice cream cones or 6 cans of Lime Fizz.)

c.  Suppose that Lee has $7 per week to spend on ice cream cones and Lime Fizz. The price of an ice cream cone is $2, and the price of a can of Lime Fizz is $1. If Lee wants to maximize his utility, how many ice cream cones and how many cans of Lime Fizz should he buy?

## Solving the Problem

**Step 1:** **Review the chapter material.** This problem involves finding the optimal consumption of two goods, so you may want to review the section "The Rule of Equal Marginal Utility per Dollar Spent," which begins on page 311.

**Step 2:** **Answer part a. by analyzing Ed's reasoning.** Ed's reasoning is incorrect. To maximize utility, Lee needs to equalize marginal utility per dollar for the two goods.

**Step 3:** **Answer part b. by determining how Lee would maximize utility with an unlimited budget.** With an unlimited budget, consumers maximize utility by continuing to buy each good as long as their utility is increasing. In this case, Lee will maximize utility by buying 6 ice cream cones and 6 cans of Lime Fizz, given that we are assuming he can't buy more than 6 units of either good.

**Step 4:** **Answer part c. by determining Lee's optimal combination of ice cream cones and cans of Lime Fizz.** Lee will maximize his utility if he spends his $7 per week so that the marginal utility of ice cream cones divided by the price of ice cream cones is equal to the marginal utility of Lime Fizz divided by the price of Lime Fizz. We can use the following table to solve this part of the problem:

| Quantity | Ice Cream Cones MU | Ice Cream Cones $\frac{MU}{P}$ | Cans of Lime Fizz MU | Cans of Lime Fizz $\frac{MU}{P}$ |
|---|---|---|---|---|
| 1 | 30 | 15 | 40 | 40 |
| 2 | 25 | 12.5 | 35 | 35 |
| 3 | 20 | 10 | 26 | 26 |
| 4 | 15 | 7.5 | 18 | 18 |
| 5 | 10 | 5 | 15 | 15 |
| 6 | 5 | 2.5 | 7 | 7 |

Lee will maximize his utility by buying 1 ice cream cone and 5 cans of Lime Fizz. At this combination, the marginal utility of each good divided by its price equals 15. He has also spent all of his $7.

**Your Turn:** For more practice, do related problems 1.8 and 1.9 on pages 334–335 at the end of this chapter.  MyEconLab

## What If the Rule of Equal Marginal Utility per Dollar Does Not Hold?

The idea of getting the maximum utility by equalizing the ratio of marginal utility to price for the goods you are buying can be difficult to grasp, so it is worth thinking about in another way. Suppose that instead of buying 3 slices of pizza and 4 cups of Coke, you buy 4 slices and 2 cups. Four slices and 2 cups cost $10, so you would meet your budget constraint by spending all the money available to you, but would you have gotten the maximum amount of utility? No, you wouldn't have. From the information in Table 10.1 on page 313, we can list the additional utility per dollar you are getting from the last slice and the last cup and the total utility from consuming 4 slices and 2 cups:

Marginal utility per dollar for the fourth slice of pizza = 3 utils per dollar

Marginal utility per dollar for the second cup of Coke = 15 utils per dollar

Total utility from 4 slices of pizza and 2 cups of Coke = 87 utils

# Don't Let This Happen to You

## Equalize Marginal Utilities *per Dollar*

Consider the information in the following table, which gives Harry's utility from buying CDs and DVDs:

**Harry's Utility from Buying CDs and DVDs**

| Quantity of CDs | Total Utility from CDs | Marginal Utility from Last CD | Quantity of DVDs | Total Utility from DVDs | Marginal Utility from Last DVD |
|---|---|---|---|---|---|
| 0 | 0 | — | 0 | 0 | — |
| 1 | 50 | 50 | 1 | 60 | 60 |
| 2 | 85 | 35 | 2 | 105 | 45 |
| 3 | 110 | 25 | 3 | 145 | 40 |
| 4 | 130 | 20 | 4 | 175 | 30 |
| 5 | 140 | 10 | 5 | 195 | 20 |
| 6 | 145 | 5 | 6 | 210 | 15 |

Can you determine from this information the optimal combination of CDs and DVDs for Harry? It is very tempting to say that Harry should buy 4 CDs and 5 DVDs because his marginal utility from CDs is equal to his marginal utility from DVDs with that combination. In fact, we can't be sure this is the best combination because we are lacking some critical information: Harry's budget constraint—how much he has available to spend on CDs and DVDs—and the prices of CDs and DVDs.

Let's say that Harry has $100 to spend this month, the price of a CD is $10, and the price of a DVD is $20. Using the information from the first table, we can now calculate Harry's marginal utility per dollar for both goods, as shown in the following table:

**Harry's Marginal Utility and Marginal Utility per Dollar from Buying CDs and DVDs**

| Quantity of CDs | Marginal Utility from Last CD $(MU_{CD})$ | Marginal Utility per Dollar $\left(\dfrac{MU_{CD}}{P_{CD}}\right)$ | Quantity of DVDs | Marginal Utility from Last DVD $(MU_{DVD})$ | Marginal Utility per Dollar $\left(\dfrac{MU_{DVD}}{P_{DVD}}\right)$ |
|---|---|---|---|---|---|
| 1 | 50 | 5 | 1 | 60 | 3 |
| 2 | 35 | 3.5 | 2 | 45 | 2.25 |
| 3 | 25 | 2.5 | 3 | 40 | 2 |
| 4 | 20 | 2 | 4 | 30 | 1.5 |
| 5 | 10 | 1 | 5 | 20 | 1 |
| 6 | 5 | 0.5 | 6 | 15 | 0.75 |

Harry's marginal utility per dollar is the same for two combinations of CDs and DVDs, as shown in the following table:

| Combinations of CDs and DVDs with Equal Marginal Utilities per Dollar | Marginal Utility per Dollar $(MU/P)$ | Total Spending | Total Utility |
|---|---|---|---|
| 5 CDs and 5 DVDs | 1 | $50 + $100 = $150 | 140 + 195 = 335 |
| 4 CDs and 3 DVDs | 2 | $40 + $60 = $100 | 130 + 145 = 275 |

Unfortunately, 5 CDs and 5 DVDs would cost Harry $150, and he has only $100. The best Harry can do is to buy 4 CDs and 3 DVDs. This combination provides him with the maximum amount of utility attainable, given his budget constraint.

The key point, which we also saw in Solved Problem 10.1, is that consumers maximize their utility when they equalize marginal utility *per dollar* for every good they buy, not when they equalize marginal utility.

MyEconLab

**Your Turn:** Test your understanding by doing related problem 1.11 on page 335 at the end of this chapter.

Obviously, the marginal utilities per dollar are not equal. The last cup of Coke gave you considerably more satisfaction per dollar than did the last slice of pizza. You could raise your total utility by buying less pizza and more Coke. Buying 1 less slice of pizza frees up $2 that will allow you to buy 2 more cups of Coke. Eating 1 less slice of pizza reduces your utility by 6 utils, but drinking 2 additional cups of Coke raises your utility by 15 utils (make sure you see this), for a net increase of 9. You end up equalizing your marginal utility per dollar (5 utils per dollar for both the last slice and the last cup) and raising your total utility from 87 utils to 96 utils.

## The Income Effect and Substitution Effect of a Price Change

We can use the rule of equal marginal utility per dollar to analyze how consumers adjust their buying decisions when a price changes. Suppose you are back at the restaurant for the Super Bowl party, but this time the price of pizza is $1.50 per slice, rather than $2. You still have $10 to spend on pizza and Coke.

When the price of pizza was $2 per slice and the price of Coke was $1 per cup, your optimal choice was to consume 3 slices of pizza and 4 cups of Coke. The fall in the price of pizza to $1.50 per slice has two effects on the quantity of pizza you consume: the *income effect* and the *substitution effect*. First, consider the income effect. When the price of a good falls, you have more purchasing power. In our example, 3 slices of pizza and 4 cups of Coke now cost a total of only $8.50 instead of $10.00. An increase in purchasing power is essentially the same thing as an increase in income. The change in the quantity of pizza you will demand because of this increase in purchasing power—holding all other factors constant—is the **income effect** of the price change. Recall from Chapter 3 that if a product is a *normal good*, a consumer increases the quantity demanded as the consumer's income rises, but if a product is an *inferior good*, a consumer decreases the quantity demanded as the consumer's income rises. So, if we assume that for you pizza is a normal good, the income effect of a fall in price causes you to consume more pizza. If pizza were an inferior good for you, the income effect of a fall in the price would have caused you to consume less pizza.

> **Income effect** The change in the quantity demanded of a good that results from the effect of a change in price on consumer purchasing power, holding all other factors constant.

The second effect of the price change is the substitution effect. When the price of pizza falls, pizza becomes cheaper *relative* to Coke, and the marginal utility per dollar for each slice of pizza you consume increases. If we hold constant the effect of the price change on your purchasing power and just focus on the effect of the price being lower relative to the price of the other good, we have isolated the **substitution effect** of the price change. The lower price of pizza relative to the price of Coke has lowered the *opportunity cost* to you of consuming pizza because now you have to give up less Coke to consume the same quantity of pizza. Therefore, the substitution effect from the fall in the price of pizza relative to the price of Coke causes you to eat more pizza and drink less Coke. In this case, both the income effect and the substitution effect of the fall in price cause you to eat more pizza. If the price of pizza had risen, both the income effect and the substitution effect would have caused you to eat less pizza. Table 10.4 summarizes the effect of a price change on the quantity demanded.

> **Substitution effect** The change in the quantity demanded of a good that results from a change in price making the good more or less expensive relative to other goods, holding constant the effect of the price change on consumer purchasing power.

We can use Table 10.5 to determine the effect of the fall in the price of pizza on your optimal consumption. Table 10.5 has the same information as Table 10.2, with one

| When price ... | consumer purchasing power ... | The income effect causes quantity demanded to ... | The substitution effect causes the opportunity cost of consuming a good to ... |
|---|---|---|---|
| decreases, | increases. | increase, if a normal good, and decrease, if an inferior good. | decrease when the price decreases, which causes the quantity of the good demanded to increase. |
| increases, | decreases. | decrease, if a normal good, and increase, if an inferior good. | increase when the price increases, which causes the quantity of the good demanded to decrease. |

**Table 10.4**

**Income Effect and Substitution Effect of a Price Change**

**Table 10.5**

**Adjusting Optimal Consumption to a Lower Price of Pizza**

| Number of Slices of Pizza | Marginal Utility from Last Slice ($MU_{Pizza}$) | Marginal Utility per Dollar $\left(\dfrac{MU_{Pizza}}{P_{Pizza}}\right)$ | Number of Cups of Coke | Marginal Utility from Last Cup ($MU_{Coke}$) | Marginal Utility per Dollar $\left(\dfrac{MU_{Coke}}{P_{Coke}}\right)$ |
|---|---|---|---|---|---|
| 1 | 20 | 13.33 | 1 | 20 | 20 |
| 2 | 16 | 10.67 | 2 | 15 | 15 |
| 3 | 10 | 6.67 | 3 | 10 | 10 |
| 4 | 6 | 4 | 4 | 5 | 5 |
| 5 | 2 | 1.33 | 5 | 3 | 3 |
| 6 | –3 | — | 6 | –1 | — |

change: The marginal utility per dollar from eating pizza has been changed to reflect the new lower price of $1.50 per slice. Examining the table, we can see that the fall in the price of pizza will result in your eating 1 more slice of pizza, so your optimal consumption now becomes 4 slices of pizza and 4 cups of Coke. You will be spending all of your $10, and the last dollar you spend on pizza will provide you with about the same marginal utility per dollar as the last dollar you spend on Coke. You will not be receiving exactly the same marginal utility per dollar spent on the two products. As Table 10.5 shows, the last slice of pizza gives you 4 utils per dollar, and the last cup of Coke gives you 5 utils per dollar. But this is as close as you can come to equalizing marginal utility per dollar for the two products, unless you can buy a fraction of a slice of pizza or a fraction of a cup of Coke.

# Where Demand Curves Come From

We saw in Chapter 3 that, according to the *law of demand*, whenever the price of a product falls, the quantity demanded increases. Now that we have covered the concepts of total utility, marginal utility, and the budget constraint, we can look more closely at why the law of demand holds.

In our example of optimal consumption of pizza and Coke at the Super Bowl party, we found the following:

Price of pizza $=$ $2 per slice $\Rightarrow$ Quantity of pizza demanded $=$ 3 slices

Price of pizza $=$ $1.50 per slice $\Rightarrow$ Quantity of pizza demanded $=$ 4 slices

In panel (a) of Figure 10.2, we plot the two points showing the optimal number of pizza slices you choose to consume at each price. In panel (b) of Figure 10.2, we draw a line connecting the two points. This downward-sloping line represents your demand curve for pizza. We could find more points on the line by changing the price of pizza and using the information in Table 10.2 to find the new optimal number of slices of pizza you would demand at each price.

To this point in this chapter, we have been looking at an individual demand curve. As we saw in Chapter 3, however, economists are typically interested in market demand curves. We can construct the market demand curve from the individual demand curves for all the consumers in the market. To keep things simple, let's assume that there are only three consumers in the market for pizza: you, David, and Lori. The table in Figure 10.3 shows the individual demand schedules for the three consumers. Because consumers differ in their incomes and their preferences for products, we would not expect every consumer to demand the same quantity of a given product at each price. The final column gives the market demand, which is simply the sum of the quantities demanded by each of the three consumers at each price. For example, at a price of $1.50 per slice, your quantity demanded is 4 slices, David's quantity demanded is

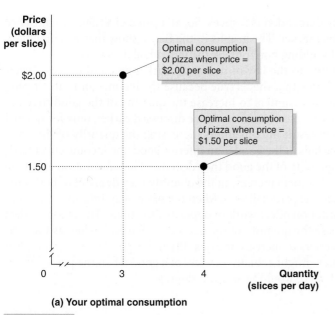

**Figure 10.2**    Deriving the Demand Curve for Pizza

A consumer responds optimally to a fall in the price of a product by consuming more of that product. In panel (a), the price of pizza falls from $2 per slice to $1.50, and the optimal quantity of slices consumed rises from 3 to 4. When we graph this result in panel (b), we have the consumer's demand curve

| | Quantity (slices per day) | | | |
|---|---|---|---|---|
| Price (dollars per slice) | You | David | Lori | Market |
| $2.50 | 2 | 4 | 1 | 7 |
| 2.00 | 3 | 5 | 3 | 11 |
| 1.50 | 4 | 6 | 5 | 15 |
| 1.00 | 5 | 7 | 7 | 19 |
| 0.50 | 6 | 8 | 9 | 23 |

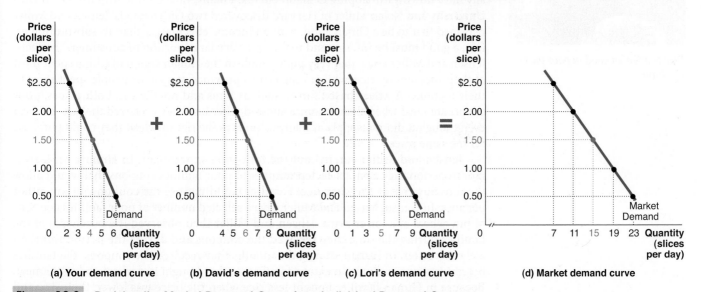

**Figure 10.3**    Deriving the Market Demand Curve from Individual Demand Curves

The table shows that the total quantity demanded in a market is the sum of the quantities demanded by each buyer. We can find the market demand curve by adding horizontally the individual demand curves in panels (a), (b), and (c). For instance, at a price of $1.50, your quantity demanded is 4 slices, David's quantity demanded is 6 slices, and Lori's quantity demanded is 5 slices. Therefore, panel (d) shows that a price of $1.50 and a quantity demanded of 15 is a point on the market demand curve.

6 slices, and Lori's quantity demanded is 5 slices. So, at a price of $1.50, a quantity of 15 slices is demanded in the market. The graphs in the figure show that we can obtain the market demand curve by adding horizontally the individual demand curves.

Remember that according to the law of demand, market demand curves always slope downward. We now know that this is true because the income and substitution effects of a fall in price cause consumers to increase the quantity of the good they demand. There is a complicating factor, however. As we discussed earlier, only for normal goods will the income effect result in consumers increasing the quantity of the good they demand when the price falls. If the good is an inferior good, the income effect leads consumers to *decrease* the quantity of the good they demand. The substitution effect, on the other hand, results in consumers increasing the quantity they demand of both normal and inferior goods when the price falls. So, when the price of an inferior good falls, the income effect and substitution effect work in opposite directions: The income effect causes consumers to decrease the quantity of the good they demand, whereas the substitution effect causes consumers to increase the quantity of the good they demand. Is it possible, then, that consumers might actually buy less of a good when the price falls? If this happened, the demand curve would be upward sloping.

*Rice is a Giffen good in poor parts of China.*

## Making the Connection | Are There Any Upward-Sloping Demand Curves in the Real World?

For a demand curve to be upward sloping, the good would have to be an inferior good and the income effect would have to be larger than the substitution effect. Economists have understood the conditions for an upward-sloping demand curve since the possibility was first discussed by the British economist Alfred Marshall in the 1890s. Marshall wrote that his friend, Sir Robert Giffen, had told him that when the price of bread rose, very poor people in British cities would actually buy more bread rather than less. Since that time, goods with upward-sloping demand curves have been referred to as *Giffen goods*.

For more than a century, finding an actual Giffen good proved impossible. A close examination of the data showed that Giffen had been mistaken and that poor people in British cities bought less bread when prices rose, so their demand curves were downward sloping. Other possible candidates for being Giffen goods were also found to actually have downward-sloping demand curves. Finally, in 2006 Robert Jensen of Brown University and Nolan Miller of Harvard discovered two Giffen goods. Jensen and Miller reasoned that to be a Giffen good, with an income effect larger than its substitution effect, a good must be inferior and make up a very large portion of consumers' budgets. Jensen and Miller knew that very poor people in the Hunan region of China spent most of their incomes on rice, while in the Gansu province, very poor people spent most of their income on wheat-based foods, such as buns and noodles. In both places, poor people ate meat when their incomes allowed it because they preferred the taste of meat even though it did not supply as many calories as the rice or wheat they could purchase for the same price.

Jensen and Miller carried out the following experiment: In Hunan, for a five-month period they gave a selected number of poor families coupons that would allow them to buy rice at a lower price. Families could not use the coupons for any other purpose. In Gansu, Jensen and Miller gave a selected number of poor families coupons to buy wheat at a lower price. Jensen and Miller then observed the purchases of the families during the time they received the coupons and during the period immediately thereafter. In Hunan, during the months they received the coupons, the families bought less rice and more meat, and in Gansu, they bought less wheat and more meat. Because in Hunan families bought less rice when the price was lower, their demand curves for rice were upward sloping. Similarly, in Gansu, families bought less wheat when the price was lower, so their demand curves for wheat were upward sloping. After more than a century of searching, economists had finally discovered examples of a Giffen good.

Based on Robert T. Jensen and Nolan H. Miller, "Giffen Behavior and Subsistence Consumption," *American Economic Review*, Vol. 98, No. 4, September 2008, pp. 1553–1577.

**Your Turn:** Test your understanding by doing related problem 2.9 on pages 335–336 at the end of this chapter.

MyEconLab

# Social Influences on Decision Making

**10.3 LEARNING** OBJECTIVE

Explain how social influences can affect consumption choices.

Sociologists and anthropologists have argued that social factors such as culture, customs, and religion are very important in explaining the choices consumers make. Economists have traditionally seen such factors as being relatively unimportant, if they take them into consideration at all. Recently, however, some economists have begun to study how social factors influence consumer choice.

For example, people seem to receive more utility from consuming goods they believe are popular. As the economists Gary Becker and Kevin Murphy put it:

> The utility from drugs, crime, going bowling, owning a Rolex watch, voting Democratic, dressing informally at work, or keeping a neat lawn depends on whether friends and neighbors take drugs, commit crimes, go bowling, own Rolex watches, vote Democratic, dress informally, or keep their lawns neat.

This reasoning can help to explain why one restaurant is packed, while another restaurant that serves essentially the same food and has similar décor has many fewer customers. Consumers decide which restaurant to go to partly on the basis of food and décor but also on the basis of the restaurant's popularity. People receive utility from being seen eating at a popular restaurant because they believe it makes them appear knowledgeable and fashionable. Whenever consumption takes place publicly, many consumers base their purchasing decisions on what other consumers are buying. Examples of public consumption include eating in restaurants, attending sporting events, wearing clothes or jewelry, and driving cars. In all these cases, the decision to buy a product depends partly on the characteristics of the product and partly on how many other people are buying the product.

## The Effects of Celebrity Endorsements

In many cases, it is not just the number of people who use a product that makes it desirable but the types of people who use it. If consumers believe that media stars or professional athletes use a product, demand for the product will often increase. This may be partly because consumers believe public figures are particularly knowledgeable about products: "Justin Bieber probably knows more about cell phones and other electronics than I do, so I'll buy these products at Best Buy because he does." But many consumers also feel more fashionable and closer to famous people if they use the same products. These considerations help to explain why companies such as Best Buy are willing to pay millions of dollars to have celebrities endorse their products. Some companies, such as Coca-Cola, have been using celebrities in their advertising for decades.

*Are you more likely to purchase a product based on Tom Brady's endorsement?*

Making the Connection | **Why Do Firms Pay Tom Brady to Endorse Their Products?**

Tom Brady is one of the biggest stars in the National Football League (NFL). As the quarterback of the New England Patri-

ots, he led his team to three Super Bowl championships between 2001 and 2010 and was twice named the Most Valuable Player in the NFL. Judging by television ratings and news coverage, the NFL is by far the most popular sports league in the United States, so it may not be surprising that companies have lined up to have Brady endorse their products. His endorsements include Glaceau Smartwater, Stetson cologne, Movado watches,

UGG boots for men, and Audi automobiles. Under Armour was so eager to have him endorse their sportswear that they gave him part ownership of the company in exchange for his endorsement. Brady makes at least $4 million per year from his endorsements.

Tom Brady is a great football player, but should consumers care what products he uses? There seems little doubt that consumers care what products Brady uses, but why do they care? It might be that they believe Brady has better information than they do about the products he endorses. The average football fan might believe that if Brady endorses Under Armour sportswear, maybe Under Armour makes better sportswear. But it seems more likely that people buy products associated with Tom Brady or other celebrities because using these products makes them feel closer to the celebrity endorser or because it makes them appear to be fashionable.

Based on Steve Schaefer, "Tom Brady, Under Armour Shareholder," forbes.com, November 11, 2010.

MyEconLab **Your Turn:** Test your understanding by doing related problem 3.10 on page 336 at the end of this chapter.

## Network Externalities

Technology can play a role in explaining why consumers buy products that many other consumers are already buying. There is a **network externality** in the consumption of a product if the usefulness of the product increases with the number of consumers who use it. For example, if you owned the only phone in the world, it would not be very useful. The usefulness of phones increases as the number of people who own them increases. Similarly, your willingness to buy an Apple iPad depends in part on the number of other people who own iPads. The more people who own iPads, the more applications, or apps, other firms will produce for the iPad, and the more novels, textbooks, newspapers, and magazines publishers will make available for downloading to the iPad, and, therefore, the more useful an iPad is to you.

> **Network externality** A situation in which the usefulness of a product increases with the number of consumers who use it.

Some economists have suggested the possibility that network externalities may have a significant downside because they might result in consumers buying products that contain inferior technologies. This outcome could occur because network externalities can create significant *switching costs* related to changing products: When a product becomes established, consumers may find it too costly to switch to a new product that contains a better technology. The selection of products may be *path dependent*. This means that because of switching costs, the technology that was first available may have advantages over better technologies that were developed later. In other words, the path along which the economy has developed in the past is important.

One example of path dependence and the use of an inferior technology is the QWERTY order of the letters along the top row of most computer keyboards. This order became widely used when manual typewriters were developed in the late nineteenth century. The metal keys on manual typewriters would stick together if a user typed too fast, and the QWERTY keyboard was designed to slow down typists and minimize the problem of the keys sticking together. With computers, the problem that QWERTY was developed to solve no longer exists, so keyboards could be changed to have letters in a more efficient layout. But because the overwhelming majority of people have learned to use keyboards with the QWERTY layout, there might be significant costs to them if they had to switch, even if a new layout ultimately made them faster typists.

Other products that supposedly embodied inferior technologies are VHS video recorders—supposedly inferior to Sony Betamax recorders—and the Windows computer operating system—supposedly inferior to the Macintosh operating system. Some economists have argued that because of path dependence and switching costs, network externalities can result in *market failures*. As we saw in Chapter 5, a market failure is a situation in which the market fails to produce the efficient level of output. If network externalities result in market failure, government intervention in these markets might improve economic efficiency. Many economists are skeptical, however, that network externalities really do lead to consumers being locked into products with inferior technologies.

In particular, economists Stan Leibowitz of the University of Texas, Dallas and Stephen Margolis of North Carolina State University have argued that, in practice, the gains from using a superior technology are larger than the losses due to switching costs. After carefully studying the cases of the QWERTY keyboard, VHS video recorders, and the Windows computer operating system, they have concluded that there is no good evidence that the alternative technologies were actually superior. The implications of network externalities for economic efficiency remain controversial among economists.

## Does Fairness Matter?

If people were only interested in making themselves as well off as possible in a material sense, they would not be concerned with fairness. There is a great deal of evidence, however, that people like to be treated fairly and that they usually attempt to treat others fairly, even if doing so makes them worse off financially. Tipping servers in restaurants is an example. In the United States, diners in restaurants typically add 15 to 20 percent to their food bills as tips to their servers. Tips are not *required*, but most people see it as very unfair not to tip, unless the service has been exceptionally bad. You could argue that people leave tips not to be fair but because they are afraid that if they don't leave a tip, the next time they visit the restaurant they will receive poor service. Studies have shown, however, that most people leave tips at restaurants even while on vacation or in other circumstances where they are unlikely to visit the restaurant again.

There are many other examples where people willingly part with money when they are not required to do so and when they receive nothing material in return. The most obvious example is making donations to charity. Apparently, donating money to charity or leaving tips in restaurants that they will never visit again gives people more utility than they would receive from keeping the money and spending it on themselves.

### A Test of Fairness in the Economic Laboratory: The Ultimatum Game Experiment
Economists have used experiments to increase their understanding of the role that fairness plays in consumer decision making. *Experimental economics* has been widely used during the past two decades, and a number of experimental economics laboratories exist in the United States and Europe. Economists Maurice Allais, Reinhard Selten, and Vernon Smith were awarded the Nobel Prize in Economics in part because of their contributions to experimental economics. Experiments make it possible to focus on a single aspect of consumer behavior. The *ultimatum game*, first popularized by Werner Güth of the Max Planck Institute of Economics, is an experiment that tests whether fairness is important in consumer decision making. Various economists have conducted the ultimatum game experiment under slightly different conditions, but with generally the same result. In this game, a group of volunteers—often college students—are divided into pairs. One member of each pair is the "allocator," and the other member of the pair is the "recipient."

Each pair is given an amount of money, say $20. The allocator decides how much of the $20 each member of the pair will get. There are no restrictions on how the allocator divides up the money. He or she could keep it all, give it all to the recipient, or anything in between. The recipient must then decide whether to accept the allocation or reject it. If the recipient decides to accept the allocation, each member of the pair gets to keep his or her share. If the recipient decides to reject the allocation, both members of the pair receive nothing.

If neither the allocator nor the recipient cares about fairness, optimal play in the ultimatum game is straightforward: The allocator should propose a division of the money in which the allocator receives $19.99 and the recipient receives $0.01. The allocator has maximized his or her gain. The recipient should accept the division because the alternative is to reject the division and receive nothing at all: Even a penny is better than nothing.

In fact, when the ultimatum game experiment is carried out, both allocators and recipients act as if fairness is important. Allocators usually offer recipients at least a 40 percent share of the money, and recipients almost always reject offers of less than a 10 percent share. Why do allocators offer recipients more than a negligible amount? It might be that allocators do not care about fairness but fear that recipients do care and will reject offers they consider unfair. This possibility was tested in an experiment known as the *dictator game* carried out by Daniel Kahneman (a psychologist who shared the Nobel Prize in Economics), Jack Knetsch, and Richard Thaler, using students at Cornell University. In this experiment, the allocators were given only two possible divisions of $20: either $18 for themselves and $2 for the recipient or an even division of $10 for themselves and $10 for the recipient. One important difference from the ultimatum game was that *the recipient was not allowed to reject the division*. Of the 161 allocators, 122 chose the even division of the $20. Because there was no possibility of the $18/$2 split being rejected, the allocators must have chosen the even split because they valued acting fairly.

Why would recipients in the ultimatum game ever reject any division of the money in which they receive even a very small amount, given that even a small amount of money is better than nothing? Apparently, most people value fairness enough that they will refuse to participate in transactions they consider unfair, even if they are worse off financially as a result.

**Are the Results of Economic Experiments Reliable?** Because economists have conducted the ultimatum game and the dictator game many times in different countries using different groups of people, most economists believe that the results of the game provide strong evidence that people value fairness. Recently, however, some economists have begun to question this conclusion. To begin with, the experimental situation is artificial, so results obtained from experiments may not hold up in the real world. Although allocators in the dictatorship game give money to the other player, whose identity is not known to the allocator, in the real world people rarely just hand money to strangers. So, it is possible that the fairness observed in the experiments may be the result of people wanting to avoid appearing selfish rather than people valuing fairness. For instance, in the ultimatum game, anyone who kept $19.99 and gave the other person only $0.01 might be afraid of appearing selfish in the eyes of the economist conducting the experiment. Particularly because the dollar amounts involved in the experiment are small, wanting to please the person conducting the experiment may be the main motive behind the choices made.

John List of the University of Chicago has carried out variations of the dictator game. When he gave every player $5 and followed the usual procedure of having half the players act as dictators in dividing up the $5, he found the usual result, with 71 percent of dictators allocating some money to the other player. But when he gave the dictator the choice of either giving money to the other player or *taking* up to $5 from the other player, only 10 percent of dictators gave the other player any money, and more than half the dictators took money from the other player. When List asked players to work for 30 minutes at a simple task to earn the $5 before playing the game, two-thirds of the dictators neither gave anything nor took anything from the other player. This last result may indicate that the source of the money being allocated matters.

List's results do not completely reverse the usual interpretation of the results of the ultimatum and dictator games. They do show, however, that the results of those games are not as clear-cut as many economists had thought. They also show that the details of an economic experiment can have a significant effect on its results.

**Business Implications of Fairness** If consumers value fairness, how does this affect firms? One consequence is that firms will sometimes not raise prices of goods and services, even when there is a large increase in demand, because they are afraid their customers will consider the price increases unfair and may buy elsewhere.

Consider several examples where it seems that businesses could increase their profits by raising prices. In April 2011, the dance rock band LCD played a concert at New York's Madison Square Garden. The tickets were priced at $50 each. Demand for the tickets was so large, however, that tickets sold online for as much as $2,500 each. Why didn't the band, or the concert promoter, charge more than $50 for the tickets? Each year, many more people would like to buy tickets to see the Super Bowl than there are tickets for them to buy at the price the National Football League charges. Why doesn't the National Football League raise prices? The restaurant Next opened in Chicago in 2011. Rather than use normal pricing, the restaurant sold tickets that entitled the buyer to a dinner, including drinks and tip. The restaurant sold the tickets for $45 to $75, depending on the dinner chosen. The tickets were resold online for prices from $500 to $3,000. Why didn't Next increase its ticket prices?

In each of these cases, it appears that a firm could increase its profits by raising prices. The seller would be selling the same quantity—of seats at a concert or in a football stadium or meals in a restaurant—at a higher price, so profits should increase. Economists have provided two explanations for why firms sometimes do not raise prices in these situations. Gary Becker, who was awarded the Nobel Prize in Economics, has suggested that the products involved—concerts, football games, or restaurant meals—are all products that buyers consume together with other buyers. In those situations, the amount consumers wish to buy may be related to how much of the product other people are consuming. People like to consume, and be seen consuming, a popular product. If rock bands, the NFL, and popular restaurants increased their prices enough to equate the quantity of tickets demanded with the quantity supplied, they might find that they had also eliminated their popularity.

Daniel Kahneman, Jack Knetsch, and Richard Thaler have offered another explanation for why firms don't always raise prices when doing so would seem to increase their profits. In surveys of consumers, these researchers found that most people considered it fair for firms to raise their prices following an increase in costs but unfair to raise prices following an increase in demand. For example, Kahneman, Knetsch, and Thaler conducted a survey in which people were asked their opinion of the following situation: "A hardware store has been selling snow shovels for $15. The morning after a large snowstorm, the store raises the price to $20." Eighty-two percent of those surveyed responded that they considered the hardware store's actions to be unfair. Kahneman, Knetsch, and Thaler have concluded that firms may sometimes not raise their prices even when the quantity demanded of their product is greater than the quantity supplied out of fear that in the long run, they will lose customers who believe the price increases were unfair.

In analyzing the pricing of Super Bowl tickets, economist Alan Krueger of Princeton University provided some support for Kahneman, Knetsch, and Thaler's explanation of why companies do not always raise prices when the quantity demanded is greater than the quantity supplied. In 2011, the NFL charged $1,200 for the best seats and $600 for most of the rest. Many of these tickets were resold online for as much as $5,000 each. Krueger decided to survey football fans attending the Super Bowl to see if their views could help explain why the NFL didn't charge higher prices for the tickets. When asked whether it would "be fair for the NFL to raise the [price of tickets] to $1,500 if that is still less than the amount most people are willing to pay for tickets," 92 percent of the fans surveyed answered "no." Even 83 percent of the fans who had paid more than $1,500 for their tickets answered "no." Krueger concluded that whatever the NFL might gain in the short run from raising ticket prices, it would more than lose in the long run by alienating football fans.

These explanations for why firms don't always raise prices to a level that would equate the quantity demanded with the quantity supplied share the same basic idea: Sometimes firms will give up some profits in the short run to keep their customers happy and increase their profits in the long run.

| Making the Connection | ## What's Up with "Fuel Surcharges"? |
|---|---|

Ordinarily, when firms present their customers with a bill, they don't itemize the costs of producing the good or service: Restaurants don't list on their menus the costs of the lettuce and tomatoes in a salad, and automobile companies don't list on their window price stickers the prices they paid their suppliers for the transmission or the tires. As oil prices began to rise in 2008, however, a number of companies began adding a line for "fuel surcharge" to their bills. For instance, Waste Management, the largest waste removal firm in the United States, includes a line for a fuel surcharge on its bills even though it doesn't itemize any other costs. The same is true for FedEx and UPS. Most major airlines do so as well. For example, in mid-2011, every airline flight from New York to London included a fuel surcharge of $362.

An article in the *Wall Street Journal* noted that although airlines had raised the fuel surcharge four times during the first half of 2011, they failed to cut the surcharge as oil prices dropped by 20 percent between April and August. The mystery of why the price of airline tickets didn't fall as oil prices fell can be solved by considering why the airlines started itemizing a fuel surcharge to begin with. As the research of Daniel Kahneman, Jack Knetsch, and Richard Thaler has shown, consumers see it as fair for firms to raise prices after an increase in costs. By explicitly including a fuel surcharge in their prices, the airlines—and other firms that followed this practice—were able to increase prices without consumers seeing the increases as being unfair.

We know from Chapter 3, though, that the prices of airline tickets and other goods and services are determined by the interaction of demand and supply. The decline in oil prices reduced the airlines' costs, thereby shifting the supply curve for airline tickets to the right. As the U.S. economy continued to recover from the recession of 2007–2009, the demand for airline tickets increased during the summer of 2011, shifting the demand curve to the right. As a result, the price of most airline tickets did not decline as oil prices declined. The figure below illustrates this point by showing the price of tickets remaining at $P_1$ despite the shifts in the demand and supply curves. In fact, on some airline routes, ticket prices actually increased slightly during these months.

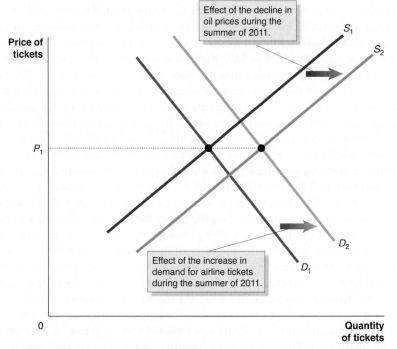

Prices are determined by *all* of the factors that affect demand and supply. Airlines and other firms began singling out fuel costs in their prices only because they knew that doing so would make consumers believe that the price increases were fair.

Based on Timothy W. Martin and Jennifer Levitz, "Oil Falls, but Surcharges Stay Aloft," *Wall Street Journal*, August 11, 2011; and Daniel Kahneman, Jack Knetsch, and Richard Thaler, "Fairness as a Constraint on Profit Seeking: Entitlements in the Market," *American Economic Review*, Vol. 76, No. 4, September 1986, pp. 728-741.

MyEconLab    **Your Turn:** Test your understanding by doing related problems 3.12 and 3.13 on page 337 at the end of this chapter.

---

**10.4 LEARNING** OBJECTIVE

Describe the behavioral economics approach to understanding decision making.

# Behavioral Economics: Do People Make Their Choices Rationally?

When economists say that consumers and firms are behaving "rationally," they mean that consumers and firms are taking actions that are appropriate to reach their goals, given the information available to them. In recent years, some economists have begun studying situations in which people do not appear to be making choices that are economically rational. This new area of economics is called **behavioral economics**. Why might consumers or businesses not act rationally? The most obvious reason would be that they do not realize that their actions are inconsistent with their goals. As we discussed in Chapter 1, one of the objectives of economics is to suggest ways to make better decisions. In this section, we discuss ways in which consumers can improve their decisions by avoiding some common pitfalls.

**Behavioral economics** The study of situations in which people make choices that do not appear to be economically rational.

Consumers commonly commit the following three mistakes when making decisions:

1. They take into account monetary costs but ignore nonmonetary opportunity costs.
2. They fail to ignore sunk costs.
3. They are unrealistic about their future behavior.

## Ignoring Nonmonetary Opportunity Costs

Remember from Chapter 2 that the **opportunity cost** of any activity is the highest-valued alternative that must be given up to engage in that activity. For example, if you own something you could sell, using it yourself involves an opportunity cost. It is often difficult for people to think of opportunity costs in these terms.

**Opportunity cost** The highest-valued alternative that must be given up to engage in an activity.

Consider the following example: Some of the fans at the Super Bowl participated in a lottery run by the National Football League that allowed the winners to purchase tickets at their face value, which was either $325 or $400, depending on where in the stadium the seats were located. Alan Krueger surveyed the lottery winners, asking them two questions:

*Question 1:* If you had not won the lottery, would you have been willing to pay $3,000 for your ticket?

*Question 2:* If after winning your ticket (and before arriving in Florida for the Super Bowl) someone had offered you $3,000 for your ticket, would you have sold it?

In answer to the first question, 94 percent said that if they had not won the lottery, they would not have paid $3,000 for a ticket. In answer to the second question, 92 percent said they would not have sold their ticket for $3,000. But these answers are contradictory! If someone offers you $3,000 for your ticket, then by using the ticket rather than selling it, you incur an opportunity cost of $3,000. There really is a $3,000 cost involved in using that ticket, even though you do not pay $3,000 in cash. The two alternatives—either paying $3,000 or not receiving $3,000—amount to exactly the same thing.

If the ticket is really not worth $3,000 to you, you should sell it. If it is worth $3,000 to you, you should be willing to pay $3,000 in cash to buy it. Not being willing to sell a ticket you already own for $3,000 while at the same time not being willing to buy a ticket for $3,000 if you didn't already own one is inconsistent behavior. The inconsistency comes from a failure to take into account nonmonetary opportunity costs. Behavioral economists believe this inconsistency is caused by the **endowment effect**, which is the tendency of people to be unwilling to sell a good they already own even if they are offered a price that is greater than the price they would be willing to pay to buy the good if they didn't already own it.

**Endowment effect** The tendency of people to be unwilling to sell a good they already own even if they are offered a price that is greater than the price they would be willing to pay to buy the good if they didn't already own it.

The failure to take into account opportunity costs is a very common error in decision making. Suppose, for example, that a friend is in a hurry to have his room cleaned—it's the Friday before parents' weekend—and he offers you $50 to do it for him. You turn him down and spend the time cleaning your own room, even though you know somebody down the hall who would be willing to clean your room for $20. Leave aside complicating details—the guy who asked you to clean his room is a real slob, or you don't want the person who offered to clean your room for $20 to go through your stuff—and you should see the point we are making. The opportunity cost of cleaning your own room is $50—the amount your friend offered to pay you to clean his room. It is inconsistent to turn down an offer from someone else to clean your room for $20 when you are doing it for yourself at a cost of $50. The key point here is this: *Nonmonetary opportunity costs are just as real as monetary costs and should be taken into account when making decisions.*

There are many examples of businesses taking advantage of the tendency of consumers to ignore nonmonetary costs. For example, some firms sell products with mail-in rebates. Rather than have a mail-in rebate of $10, why not just cut the price by $10?

Companies are relying on the fact that not mailing in a rebate form once you have already paid for a product is a nonmonetary opportunity cost rather than a direct monetary cost. In fact, only a small percentage of customers actually mail in rebates.

## Failing to Ignore Sunk Costs

**Sunk cost** A cost that has already been paid and cannot be recovered.

A **sunk cost** is a cost that has already been paid and cannot be recovered. Once you have paid money and can't get it back, you should ignore that money in any later decisions you make. Consider the following two situations:

*Situation 1:* You bought a ticket to a play for $75. The ticket is nonrefundable and must be used on Tuesday night, which is the only night the play will be performed. On Monday, a friend calls and invites you to a local comedy club to see a comedian you both like who is appearing only on Tuesday night. Your friend offers to pay the cost of going to the club.
*Situation 2:* It's Monday night, and you are about to buy a ticket for the Tuesday night performance of the same play as in situation 1. As you are leaving to buy the ticket, your friend calls and invites you to the comedy club.

Would your decision to go to the play or to the comedy club be different in situation 1 than in situation 2? Most people would say that in situation 1, they would go to the play, because otherwise they would lose the $75 they had paid for the ticket. In fact, though, the $75 is "lost" no matter what you do because the ticket is not refundable. The only real issue for you to decide is whether you would prefer to see the play or prefer to go with your friend to the comedy club. If you would prefer to go to the club, the fact that you have already paid $75 for the ticket to the play is irrelevant. Your decision should be the same in situation 1 as in situation 2.

Psychologists Daniel Kahneman and Amos Tversky explored the tendency of consumers to not ignore sunk costs by asking two samples of people the following questions:

*Question 1:* One sample of people was asked: "Imagine that you have decided to see a play and have paid the admission price of $10 per ticket. As you enter the theater, you discover that you have lost the ticket. The seat was not marked, and the ticket cannot be recovered. Would you pay $10 for another ticket?" Of those asked, 46 percent answered "yes," and 54 percent answered "no."
*Question 2:* A different sample of people was asked: "Imagine that you have decided to see a play where admission is $10 per ticket. As you enter the theater, you discover that you have lost a $10 bill. Would you still pay $10 for a ticket to the play?" Of those asked, 88 percent answered "yes," and 12 percent answered "no."

The situations presented in the two questions are actually the same and should have received the same fraction of yes and no responses. Many people, though, have trouble seeing that in question 1, when deciding whether to see the play, they should ignore the $10 already paid for a ticket because it is a sunk cost.

## Making the Connection | A Blogger Who Understands the Importance of Ignoring Sunk Costs

In recent years, many people have started blogs—or, "Web logs"—where they record their thoughts on politics, sports, their favorite hobbies, or anything else that interests them. Some bloggers can spend hours a day writing up their latest ideas and providing links to relevant material on the Web. A few blogs become so successful that they attract paid advertising and earn their owners a good income. Arnold Kim began blogging about Apple products in 2000, during his fourth year of medical school. He continued blogging on his site, MacRumors.com, over the next eight years, while pursuing a medical career as a nephrologist—a doctor who treats kidney problems.

By 2008, Kim's site had become very successful, attracting 4.4 million people and more than 40 million page views each month. Kim was earning more than $100,000 per year from paid advertising by companies such as Verizon, Audible.com, and CDW.

*Would you give up being a surgeon to start your own blog?*

But the tasks of compiling rumors about new Apple products, keeping an Apple buying guide up to date, and monitoring multiple discussion boards on the site became more than he could handle as a part-time job. Kim enjoyed working on the Web site and believed that ultimately it could earn him more than he was earning as a doctor. Still, he hesitated to abandon his medical career because he had invested nearly $200,000 in his education.

But the $200,000, as well as the years he had spent in medical school, completing a residency in internal medicine, and completing a fellowship in nephrology, were sunk costs. Kim realized that he needed to ignore these sunk costs in order to make a rational decision about whether to continue in medicine or to become a full-time blogger. After calculating that he would make more from his Web site than from his medical career—and taking into account that by working from home he could spend more time with his young daughter—he decided to blog full time. He was quoted as saying, "on paper it was an easy decision." By mid-2011, MacRumors.com was being viewed by more than 9 million people per month, and Kim's income had risen above what he would have made as a doctor.

Knowing that it is rational to ignore sunk costs can be important in making key decisions in life.

Based on Brian X. Chen, "Arnold Kim Celebrates 10 Years as Apple Rumor King," wired.com, February 23, 2010; Brian Stelter, "My Son, the Blogger: An M.D. Trades Medicine for Apple Rumors," *New York Times*, July 21, 2008; Dan Frommer, "Nephrologist to Mac Blogger: The Unlikely Career Path of MacRumors' Arnold Kim," businessinsider.com, July 13, 2008; and "Macrumors Traffic," quantcast.com, August 23, 2011.

**Your Turn:** Test your understanding by doing related problems 4.7, 4.8, and 4.9 on pages 337–338 at the end of this chapter.                MyEconLab

## Being Unrealistic about Future Behavior

Studies have shown that a majority of adults in the United States are overweight. Why do many people choose to eat too much? One possibility is that they receive more utility from eating too much than they would from being thin. A more likely explanation, however, is that many people eat a lot today because they expect to eat less tomorrow. But they never do eat less, and so they end up overweight. (Of course, some people also suffer from medical problems that lead to weight gain.) Similarly, some people continue smoking today because they expect to be able to give it up sometime in the future. Unfortunately, for many people that time never comes, and they suffer the health consequences of prolonged smoking. In both these cases, people are overvaluing the utility from current choices—eating chocolate cake or smoking—and undervaluing the utility to be received in the future from being thin or not getting lung cancer.

Economists who have studied this question argue that many people have preferences that are not consistent over time. In the long run, you would like to be thin or give up smoking or achieve some other goal, but each day, you make decisions (such as to eat too much or to smoke) that are not consistent with this long-run goal. If you are unrealistic about your future behavior, you underestimate the costs of choices—such as overeating or smoking—that you make today. A key way of avoiding this problem is to be realistic about your future behavior.

## Making the Connection | Why Don't Students Study More?

Government statistics show that students who do well in college earn at least $10,000 more per year than students who fail to graduate or who graduate with low grades. So, over the course of a career of 40 years or more, students who do well in college will have earned upward of $400,000 more than students who failed to graduate or who received low grades. Most colleges advise that students study at least two hours outside class for every hour they spend in class. Surveys show that students often ignore this advice.

If the opportunity cost of not studying is so high, why do many students choose to study relatively little? Some students have work or family commitments that limit the amount of

*If the payoff to studying is so high, why don't students study more?*

time they can study. But many other students study less than they would if they were more realistic about their future behavior. On any given night, a student has to choose between studying and other activities—such as watching television, going to a movie, or going to a party—that may seem to provide higher utility in the short run. Many students choose one of these activities over studying because they expect to study tomorrow or the next day, but tomorrow they face the same choices and make similar decisions. As a result, they do not study enough to meet their long-run goal of graduating with high grades. If they were more realistic about their future behavior, they would not make the mistake of overvaluing the utility from activities such as watching television or partying because they would realize that those activities can endanger their long-run goal of graduating with honors.

MyEconLab **Your Turn:** Test your understanding by doing related problems 4.10 and 4.11 on page 338 at the end of this chapter.

# Solved Problem 10.4

## How Do You Get People to Save More of Their Income?

Under 401(k) retirement plans, firms can send some of a worker's pay to a mutual fund or other investment, where its returns will accumulate tax free until the worker retires. Partly because of research by behavioral economists into what determines people's saving behavior, Congress included in the Pension Protection Act of 2006 a provision that made it easier for companies to automatically enroll employees in a 401(k) plan. As a result, participation rates in 401(k) plans at large companies increased from 67 percent to 85 percent.

a. Why would more people participate in a retirement plan when they are automatically enrolled than when they have to fill out a form to enroll?

b. One unintended consequence of the change in the law was a decline in the saving rate among employees in 401(k) plans. Most plans automatically enrolled employees at a saving rate of 3 percent of their salary. One study indicated, though, that 40 percent of employees would have enrolled at a higher saving rate if they hadn't been automatically enrolled at the 3 percent rate. Why wouldn't employees enrolled at the 3 percent rate who wanted to save at a higher rate simply tell their employers that they wanted to save at a higher rate (which is easy to do under the plans)?

Based on Anne Tergesen, "401K Law Suppresses Saving for Retirement," *Wall Street Journal*, July 7, 2011.

## Solving the Problem

**Step 1: Review the chapter material.** This problem is about people not always being realistic about their future behavior, so you may want to review the section "Being Unrealistic about Future Behavior," which begins on page 329.

**Step 2: Use your understanding of consumer decision making to answer part a.** Some people appear to have acted irrationally by not taking the minor action of filling out a form to enroll in a retirement plan when they would voluntarily stay in the plan if automatically enrolled. Here is one possible explanation for this puzzle that is consistent with what we have seen about many people being unrealistic about their future behavior: Some people spend money today that they should be saving for retirement because they expect to increase their saving in the future. If people who act in this way are not automatically enrolled in a plan, they are unlikely to take the steps to enroll because they expect—possibly unrealistically—that in the future they will enroll or save money for retirement in other ways. However, if they are automatically enrolled, then taking the step of opting out of the plan would make it more obvious to themselves that they are behaving in a way that is inconsistent with their long-term goal of saving for retirement. So, once automatically enrolled, most people choose to stay enrolled, even if they would not have taken the necessary action to enroll themselves.

**Step 3:** **Answer part b. by explaining why some employees don't raise their saving rate above the default rate of 3 percent.** The answer here is similar to the answer to part a. Presumably, people who would have chosen a saving rate of 5 percent or 10 percent if they had not been automatically enrolled at 3 percent intend to raise their saving rate in the future. Some may actually do so, but for others the fact that they are at least saving something may disguise the fact that they are spending too much in the present and saving too little to meet their long-run saving goals.

**Your Turn:** For more practice, do related problems 4.12 and 4.13 on page 338 at the end of this chapter.                                                                                    MyEconLab

Taking into account nonmonetary opportunity costs, ignoring sunk costs, and being more realistic about future behavior are three ways in which consumers are able to improve the decisions they make.

Continued from page 309

## Economics in Your Life

**Do You Make Rational Decisions?**

At the beginning of the chapter, we asked you to consider a situation in which you had paid $75 for a concert ticket, which is the most you would be willing to pay. Just before you enter the concert hall, someone offers you $90 for the ticket. We posed two questions: Would you sell the ticket? and Would an economist think it is rational to sell the ticket? If you answered that you would sell, then your answer is rational in the sense in which economists use the term. The cost of going to see the concert is what you have to give up for the ticket. Initially, the cost was just $75—the dollar price of the ticket. This amount was also the most you were willing to pay. However, once someone offers you $90 for the ticket, the cost of seeing the concert rises to $90. The reason the cost of the concert is now $90 is that once you turn down an offer of $90 for the ticket, you have incurred a nonmonetary opportunity cost of $90 if you use the ticket yourself. The endowment effect explains why some people would not sell the ticket. People seem to value things that they have more than things that they do not have. Therefore, a concert ticket you already own may be worth more to you than a concert ticket you have yet to purchase. Behavioral economists study situations like this where people make choices that do not appear to be economically rational.

# Conclusion

In a market system, consumers are in the driver's seat. Goods are produced only if consumers want them to be. Therefore, how consumers make their decisions is an important area for economists to study. Economists expect that consumers will spend their incomes so that the last dollar spent on each good provides them with equal additional amounts of satisfaction, or utility. In practice, there are significant social influences on consumer decision making, particularly when a good or service is consumed in public. Fairness also seems to be an important consideration for most consumers. Finally, many consumers could improve the decisions they make if they would take into account nonmonetary opportunity costs and ignore sunk costs.

In this chapter, we studied consumers' choices. In the next several chapters, we will study firms' choices. Before moving on to the next chapter, read *An Inside Look* on the next page for a discussion of how celebrity endorsements affect the demand of products—for good and bad.

# Findings Are Mixed on the Success of Celebrity Endorsements

*YAHOO! ADVERTISING BLOG*

## Do Celebrity Endorsements Help or Hurt a Brand?

In these celebrity-obsessed times, does the presence of a big-name endorser boost the effectiveness of advertising? Some recent research delivers a mixed, but largely positive, verdict.

(a) A report this month from the Nielsen Co. examined viewer response to commercials that aired during the Academy Awards telecast on February 27, and it found that celeb endorsements garnered four of the top 10 places in the brand-recall standings. Of these, the strongest rating went to a spot for Best Buy, featuring not one but two celebrities: Ozzy Osbourne and Justin Bieber.

Right behind the Best Buy spot in the rankings was a commercial for Gillette's Venus razor, starring Jennifer Lopez and her legs. Also in Nielsen's brand-recall Top 10 were Celine Dion singing for the American Cancer society, and Adrien Brody crooning on behalf of Stella Artois.

In its report of the findings, Nielsen noted that the Best Buy and Stella Artois spots scored much better on Oscar night than they did when making their debut on this year's Super Bowl telecast, which might indicate that viewers who already are intent on gazing at celebs are more receptive to them when they appear during a commercial break.

### More Proof

Celebrity endorsements also got a thumbs-up in a study released last month by GfK MRI's Starch Advertising Research. It found that print ads get higher readership scores when they featured a celeb. "On average, the ads that contained a celebrity endorser produced 9.4 percent higher consumer readership than ads without a celebrity endorser," said Starch's report of its findings. . . .

### On the Other Hand . . .

(b) While the Starch and Nielsen studies found consumers responding positively to celeb-endorsement advertising, a report released in January by Ace Metrix offered a dissenting voice where TV spots are concerned. (Ace specializes in gauging the effectiveness of TV advertising.) Analyzing viewer response to 2,600 commercials that aired between September and December 2010, the research firm found that celeb-centered commercials on average "do not perform any better than non-celebrity ads, and in some cases they perform much worse. . . . Over and over again, our analysis illustrated that celebrity ads performed either below average or merely equaled it."

Part of the problem is that celebrities "are often polarizing." The report cited Sarah Jessica Parker as an example of this, with respect to cosmetics advertising: "Some women believe Sarah Jessica Parker is beautiful, but others do not—the eye-of-the-beholder issue."

Like them or not, celebrity endorsements are all the more ubiquitous these days, thanks to social media. A company called Ad.ly has made a business of running celebrity endorsements via Twitter and, more recently, Facebook. . . .

(c) Whatever the medium in which celebrity endorsements appear, the vagaries of celeb behavior pose a risk for brands that employ big-name endorsers. As Starch notes in the analysis of its findings, "the downside of using celebrity endorsers has been in stark relief in the past few years" due to celebrity scandals. (The report gives Tiger Woods, Brett Favre and Charlie Sheen dishonorable mentions in this context.)

But do consumers hold it against a brand when its celeb endorser strays from the straight and narrow? An AdweekMedia/Harris Poll examined that question last year and found relatively few people inclined to engage in such guilt by association.

Seventy-four percent of that survey's respondents said it wouldn't affect how they feel about a brand if an endorser were involved in a scandal, vs. 22 percent saying they'd feel worse about the brand. And let us not forget that some people relish a good scandal. That may account for the six percent of men and three percent of women who said they "feel better" about a brand when its endorser has been caught in a scandal. Among respondents in the 18–34 age bracket, the "feel better" vote rose to double digits, at 11 percent.

*Source:* "Do Celebrity Endorsements Help or Hurt a Brand? Are companies 'winning' when they hire celebs to shill, and what happens when their spokesperson goes off the deep end?" by Mark Dolliver. *Yahoo! Advertising Blog,* March 10, 2011. Reprinted with permission.

## Key Points in the Article

In February 2011, the Nielsen Company surveyed viewers to determine what they remembered about commercials that aired during the Academy Awards telecast. The survey found that in terms of brand recall, 4 of the top 10 advertisements used celebrity endorsers. In a May 2011 study, celebrity endorsements were also found to be effective in print advertising, with ads featuring a celebrity receiving an average of 9.4 percent more readership than those without a celebrity endorsement. Ace Metrix reported a different finding in an analysis of viewer response to TV commercials airing from September to December 2010. This report found that ads featuring celebrity endorsements performed no better, and often worse, than non-celebrity ads. Celebrity endorsements may also pose a risk to companies if the endorsing celebrity falls out of public favor due to being involved in a scandal. But an AdweekMedia/Harris Poll found that almost three-fourths of the respondents would not feel differently about a brand if the brand's celebrity endorser became involved in a scandal.

## Analyzing the News

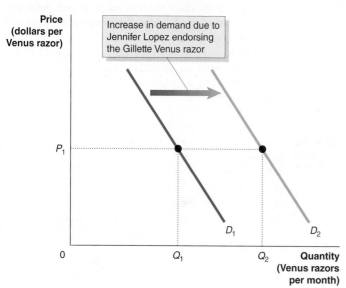 The Nielsen study found that during the Academy Awards broadcast, celebrity-endorsed products fared well, taking 4 of the top 10 slots for consumer recall of advertisements. One of those ads featured Jennifer Lopez endorsing the Gillette Venus razor. A celebrity of Lopez's stature can command huge fees to endorse a product, so Gillette must believe that consumers' taste for its Venus razor will significantly increase due to hiring Lopez for its ads.

We saw in Chapter 3 that when consumers' taste for a product increases, the demand curve shifts to the right. The figure below shows that if the endorsement by Jennifer Lopez is successful, the demand curve for the Venus razor shifts from $D_1$ to $D_2$. The increase in demand allows Gillette to sell more Venus razors at every price. For example, at a price of $P_1$, it could sell $Q_1$ Venus razors without the endorsement from Lopez, but $Q_2$ Venus razors with the endorsement.

**(b)** Whereas the Nielsen and Starch reports indicate a positive reaction by consumers to celebrity-endorsed products, a study by Ace Metrix found that television advertising featuring celebrity endorsers fared no better, and sometimes worse, than ads without a celebrity endorsement. The chapter notes two reasons celebrity endorsements attract customers: Consumers perceive the celebrity as particularly knowledgeable about the product, and some consumers feel fashionable and closer to celebrities if they use the same products. These considerations help explain why some companies are willing to pay considerable sums to have celebrities endorse their products, but the Ace Metrix study indicates that these large payouts may not reap the desired benefits.

**(c)** Celebrity endorsements can backfire if the celebrity gets caught up in a scandal. Although an AdweekMedia/Harris Poll found that only 22 percent of respondents would feel worse about a brand if its celebrity endorser were involved in a scandal and 74 percent would be indifferent, with the millions of dollars that are spent hiring celebrities to endorse products, it is understandable why companies may be very selective in their choice of celebrity endorsers.

## Thinking Critically

1. Celebrity endorsements may be rewarding to firms, but they can also be risky. By hiring Jennifer Lopez to endorse the Venus razor, Gillette tied the image of the razor to Lopez's image in the minds of the public. What do you think would happen to the demand curve for the Venus razor if Jennifer Lopez were to get involved in an embarrassing scandal?

2. Gillette presumably paid Jennifer Lopez a considerable amount to endorse the Venus razor. Should a firm whose celebrity endorser was just arrested make a decision about whether to cancel its ad campaign based on the amount of money it has already spent on making the ads? Briefly explain.

When successful, a celebrity endorsement can shift the demand curve for a product to the right, from $D_1$ to $D_2$.

# Chapter Summary and Problems

## Key Terms

Behavioral economics, p. 327

Budget constraint, p. 311

Endowment effect, p. 327

Income effect, p. 317

Law of diminishing marginal utility, p. 311

Marginal utility (*MU*), p. 311

Network externality, p. 322

Opportunity cost, p. 327

Substitution effect, p. 317

Sunk cost, p. 328

Utility, p. 310

 **10.1** **Utility and Consumer Decision Making,** pages 310–318

LEARNING OBJECTIVE: Define utility and explain how consumers choose goods and services to maximize their utility.

## Summary

**Utility** is the enjoyment or satisfaction that people receive from consuming goods and services. The goal of a consumer is to spend available income so as to maximize utility. **Marginal utility** is the change in total utility a person receives from consuming one additional unit of a good or service. The **law of diminishing marginal utility** states that consumers receive diminishing additional satisfaction as they consume more of a good or service during a given period of time. The **budget constraint** is the amount of income consumers have available to spend on goods and services. To maximize utility, consumers should make sure they spend their income so that the last dollar spent on each product gives them the same marginal utility. The **income effect** is the change in the quantity demanded of a good that results from the effect of a change in the price on consumer purchasing power. The **substitution effect** is the change in the quantity demanded of a good that results from a change in price making the good more or less expensive relative to other goods, holding constant the effect of the price change on consumer purchasing power.

MyEconLab    Visit **www.myeconlab.com** to complete these exercises online and get instant feedback.

## Review Questions

**1.1** What is the economic definition of *utility*? Is utility measurable?

**1.2** What is the definition of *marginal utility*? What is the law of diminishing marginal utility? Why is marginal utility more useful than total utility in consumer decision making?

**1.3** What is meant by a consumer's *budget constraint*? What is the rule of equal marginal utility per dollar spent?

**1.4** How does a change in the price of a product cause both a substitution effect and an income effect?

## Problems and Applications

**1.5** Does the law of diminishing marginal utility hold true in every situation? Is it possible to think of goods for which consuming additional units, at least initially, will result in increasing marginal utility?

**1.6** If consumers should allocate their income so that the last dollar spent on every product gives them the same amount of additional utility, how should they decide the amount of their income to save?

**1.7** You have six hours to study for two exams tomorrow. The following table shows the relationship between hours of study and test scores:

| Economics | | Psychology | |
|---|---|---|---|
| **Hours** | **Score** | **Hours** | **Score** |
| 0 | 54 | 0 | 54 |
| 1 | 62 | 1 | 60 |
| 2 | 69 | 2 | 65 |
| 3 | 75 | 3 | 69 |
| 4 | 80 | 4 | 72 |
| 5 | 84 | 5 | 74 |
| 6 | 87 | 6 | 75 |

a. Use the rule for determining optimal purchases to decide how many hours you should study each subject. Treat each point on an exam as 1 unit of utility and assume that you consider an extra point on an economics exam to have the same value as an extra point on a psychology exam.

b. Now suppose that you are a psychology major and that you value each point you earn on a psychology exam as being worth three times as much as each point you earn on an economics exam. Now how many hours will you study each subject?

**1.8** **[Related to** Solved Problem 10.1 **on page 314]** Joe has $16 to spend on Twinkies and Ho-Hos. Twinkies have a price of $1 per pack, and Ho-Hos have a price of $2 per pack. Use the information in the graphs below to

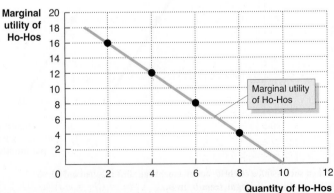

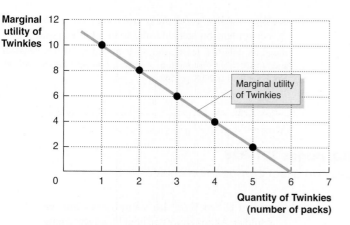

Marginal utility of Twinkies

Quantity of Twinkies (number of packs)

| | Price | Quantity | Total Utility | Marginal Utility of Last Unit |
|---|---|---|---|---|
| Apples | $0.50 | 50 | 1,000 | 20 |
| Oranges | $0.75 | 40 | 500 | 30 |

determine the number of Twinkies packs and the number of Ho-Hos packs Joe should buy to maximize his utility. Briefly explain your reasoning.

**1.9** **[Related to** Solved Problem 10.1 **on page 314]** Joe has $55 to spend on apples and oranges. Given the information in the following table, is Joe maximizing utility? Briefly explain.

**1.10** Suppose the price of a bag of Frito's corn chips declines from $0.69 to $0.59. Which is likely to be larger: the income effect or the substitution effect? Briefly explain.

**1.11** **[Related to the** Don't Let This Happen to You **on page 316]** Mary is buying corn chips and soda. She has 4 bags of corn chips and 5 bottles of soda in her shopping cart. The marginal utility of the fourth bag of corn chips is 10, and the marginal utility of the fifth bottle of soda is also 10. Is Mary maximizing utility? Briefly explain.

**1.12** When the price of pizza falls in the Super Bowl example on pages 317–318, both the income effect and the substitution effect cause you to want to consume more pizza. If pizza were an inferior good, how would the analysis be changed? In this case, is it possible that a lower price for pizza might lead you to buy less pizza? Briefly explain.

---

 **10.2** | **Where Demand Curves Come From, pages 318–321**

LEARNING OBJECTIVE: Use the concept of utility to explain the law of demand.

## Summary

When the price of a good declines, the ratio of the marginal utility to price rises. This leads consumers to buy more of that good. As a result, whenever the price of a product falls, the quantity demanded increases. We saw in Chapter 1 that this is known as the *law of demand*. The market demand curve can be constructed from the individual demand curves for all the consumers in the market.

MyEconLab    Visit **www.myeconlab.com** to complete these exercises online and get instant feedback.

## Review Questions

**2.1** Explain how a downward-sloping demand curve results from consumers adjusting their consumption choices to changes in price.

**2.2** How is the market demand curve derived from consumers' individual demand curves?

**2.3** What would need to be true for a demand curve to be upward sloping?

## Problems and Applications

**2.4** Considering only the income effect, if the price of an inferior good declines, would a consumer want to buy a larger quantity or a smaller quantity of the good? Does this mean that the demand curves for inferior goods should slope upward? Briefly explain.

**2.5** The chapter states that "when the price of an inferior good falls, the income effect and substitution effect work in opposite directions." Explain what this statement means.

**2.6** Suppose the market for ice cream cones is made up of three consumers: Josh, Jon, and Tim. Use the information in the following table to construct the market demand curve for ice cream cones. Show the information in a table and in a graph.

| | Josh | Jon | Tim |
|---|---|---|---|
| Price | Quantity Demanded (cones per week) | Quantity Demanded (cones per week) | Quantity Demanded (cones per week) |
| $1.75 | 2 | 1 | 0 |
| 1.50 | 4 | 3 | 2 |
| 1.25 | 6 | 4 | 3 |
| 1.00 | 7 | 6 | 4 |
| 0.75 | 9 | 7 | 5 |

**2.7** Suppose the wage you are being paid doubles. Is there an income and substitution effect involved in your decision about how many hours you choose to work? If so, what is being substituted for what?

**2.8** Assume two goods: pizza and Coke. Along an individual's demand curve for pizza, as the price of pizza falls, does the marginal utility per dollar spent on pizza always equal the marginal utility per dollar spent on Coke? In other words, does the rule of equal marginal utility per dollar spent hold as the price changes and you move up or down the demand curve? How can the rule hold given that the price of pizza changes along the demand curve? If you need help to answer this problem, look back at the discussion of Figure 10.2 on page 319 on deriving the demand curve for pizza.

**2.9** **[Related to the** Making the Connection **on page 320]** In studying the consumption of very poor families in China, Robert Jensen and Nolan Miller found that in both Hunan and Gansu "Giffen behavior is most likely to be found among a range of households that are poor (but not too poor or too rich)."

**a.** What do Jensen and Miller mean by "Giffen behavior"?

**b.** Why would the poorest of the poor be less likely than people with slightly higher incomes to exhibit this behavior?

**c.** Why must a good make up a very large portion of consumers' budgets in order to be a Giffen good?

Based on Robert T. Jensen and Nolan H. Miller, "Giffen Behavior and Subsistence Consumption," *American Economic Review*, Vol. 98, No. 4, September 2008, p. 1569 .

---

## 10.3 Social Influences on Decision Making, pages 321–326

LEARNING OBJECTIVE: Explain how social influences can affect consumption choices.

## Summary

Social factors can have an effect on consumption. For example, the amount of utility people receive from consuming a good often depends on how many other people they know who also consume the good. There is a **network externality** in the consumption of a product if the usefulness of the product increases with the number of consumers who use it. There is also evidence that people like to be treated fairly and that they usually attempt to treat others fairly, even if doing so makes them worse off financially. This result has been demonstrated in laboratory experiments, such as the ultimatum game. When firms set prices, they take into account consumers' preference for fairness. For example, hardware stores often do not increase the price of snow shovels to take advantage of a temporary increase in demand following a snowstorm.

MyEconLab    Visit **www.myeconlab.com** to complete these exercises online and get instant feedback.

## Review Questions

**3.1** In which of the following situations are social influences on consumer decision making likely to be greater: choosing a restaurant for dinner or choosing a brand of toothpaste to buy? Briefly explain.

**3.2** Why do consumers pay attention to celebrity endorsements of products?

**3.3** What are network externalities? For what types of products are network externalities likely to be important? What is path dependence?

**3.4** What is the ultimatum game? What insight does this game provide into consumer decision making?

**3.5** How does the fact that consumers apparently value fairness affect the pricing decisions that businesses make?

## Problems and Applications

**3.6** Which of the following products are most likely to have significant network externalities? Explain.
  **a.** Tablet computers
  **b.** Dog food
  **c.** Board games
  **d.** LCD televisions
  **e.** 3D televisions

**3.7** Speaking about a recent trip to Switzerland, Daniel Hamermesh made the following comment in the *New York Times*:

> A waste of time! After arriving at our hotel in Switzerland at 7 P.M., my wife and I had both hoped to work on our computers—but we couldn't. Although we had bought universal plug adapters (which convert American plugs to European, Australian, and English outlets), it turns out that Switzerland has its own unique three-prong plug. Why? This kind of plug adapter is not sold with standard adapter sets. Why does Switzerland renounce the network externalities that would come with using standard European plugs with their standard 220-volt electricity?

How is Switzerland "renouncing network externalities" by not using standard European plugs?

From "If Switzerland Would Only Change Its Plugs" by Daniel Hamermesh, from the *Freakonomics Blog*, September 23, 2008. Copyright © 2008 by Daniel Hamermesh. Reprinted with permission of the author.

**3.8** **[Related to the** Chapter Opener **on page 309]** In a 2011 survey of 1,500 people, Snoopy was found to be the most appealing celebrity endorser. The beagle from the popular *Peanuts* comic strip appeared in commercials for the insurance company MetLife. What advantages and disadvantages are there in using Snoopy, rather than a real person, to endorse a product?

Based on Jeff Bercovici, "America's Most Loved Spokespersons," *Forbes*, March 14, 2011.

**3.9** **[Related to the** Chapter Opener **on page 309]** When asked, most survey respondents claim that celebrity endorsements do not influence their buying decisions. Marketing strategist Marc Babej has argued that these survey responses are unreliable because advertisements appeal to the subconscious as well as the conscious mind. Explain what Babej means by this.

Based on Marc E. Babej, " Poll: Celebrity Endorsements Don't Work . . . Don't Tell Angelina." *Forbes*, June 14, 2011.

**3.10** **[Related to the** Making the Connection **on page 321]** Tom Brady is a star NFL quarterback who knows more than most consumers about football and football-related products. However, he does not necessarily know more than consumers about Stetson cologne, Movado watches, and Audi automobiles. Consider the model of utility-maximizing behavior described in this chapter. For Stetson's use of Tom Brady as a celebrity endorser to make economic sense, how must Brady's endorsement affect the marginal utility that at least some consumers receive from using Stetson cologne? What will this do to the demand curve for that cologne?

**3.11** Las Vegas is one of the most popular tourist destinations in the United States. In November 2008, the Rio Hotel and Casino in Las Vegas dropped the price of its breakfast buffet to $5.99

for local residents, while keeping the regular price of $14.99 for nonlocals. When setting the price for a meal, why would it matter to the restaurant if the customer is a local resident?

Based on: *Las Vegas Advisor*, November, 2008.

**3.12** **[Related to the** Making the Connection **on page 325]** Suppose that Lady Gaga can sell out a concert at Madison Square Garden with tickets priced at $85 each. Lady Gaga's manager estimates that the singer could still sell out the Garden at $150 per ticket. Why might Lady Gaga and her manager want to keep the ticket price at $85?

**3.13** **[Related to the** Making the Connection **on page 325]** Suppose that *The Amazing Spider-Man* comes out, and hundreds of people arrive at a theater and discover that the movie is already sold out. Meanwhile, the theater is also showing a boring movie in its third week of release in a mostly empty theater. Why would this firm charge the same $7.50 for a ticket to either movie, when the quantity of tickets demanded is much greater than the quantity supplied for one movie, and the quantity of tickets demanded is much less than the quantity supplied for the other?

---

  **Behavioral Economics: Do People Make Their Choices Rationally?** pages 326–331

Describe the behavioral economics approach to understanding decision making.

## Summary

**Behavioral economics** is the study of situations in which people act in ways that are not economically rational. **Opportunity cost** is the highest-valued alternative that must be given up to engage in an activity. People would improve their decision making if they took into account nonmonetary opportunity costs. People sometimes ignore nonmonetary opportunity costs because of the **endowment effect**— the tendency of people to be unwilling to sell something they already own even if they are offered a price that is greater than the price they would be willing to pay to buy the good if they didn't already own it. People would also improve their decision making if they ignored *sunk costs*. A **sunk cost** is a cost that has already been paid and cannot be recovered. Finally, people would improve their decision making if they were more realistic about their future behavior.

MyEconLab    Visit **www.myeconlab.com** to complete these exercises online and get instant feedback.

## Review Questions

**4.1** What does it mean to be economically rational?

**4.2** Define *behavioral economics*. What are the three common mistakes that consumers often make? Give an example of each mistake.

## Problems and Applications

**4.3** Suppose your little brother tells you on Tuesday that one of his friends offered him $80 for his Albert Pujols rookie baseball card, but your brother decides not to sell the card. On Wednesday, your brother loses the card. Your parents feel sorry for him and give him $80 to make up the loss. Instead of buying another Albert Pujols card with the money (which we will assume he could have done), your brother uses the money to buy an iPod shuffle. Explain your brother's actions by using the concepts in this chapter.

**4.4** Richard Thaler, an economist at the University of Chicago, is the person who first used the term *endowment effect* to describe placing a higher value on something already owned than would be placed on the object if not currently owned. According to an article in the *Economist*:

Dr. Thaler, who recently had some expensive bottles of wine stolen, observes that he is "now

confronted with precisely one of my own experiments: these are bottles I wasn't planning to sell and now I'm going to get a cheque from an insurance company and most of these bottles I will not buy. I'm a good enough economist to know there's a bit of an inconsistency there."

Based on Thaler's statement, how do his stolen bottles of wine illustrate the endowment effect, and why does he make the statement: "I'm a good enough economist to know there's a bit of an inconsistency there"?

From "It's mine, I tell you," *The Economist*, June 19, 2008.

**4.5** Suppose that you are a big fan of the Harry Potter books. You would love to own a copy of the very first printing of the first book, but unfortunately you can't find it for sale for less than $5,000. You are willing to pay at most $200 for a copy, but can't find one at that price until one day in a used bookstore you see a copy selling for $10, which you immediately buy. Are you being irrational if you keep the copy rather than sell it?

**4.6** Someone who owns a townhouse wrote to a real estate advice columnist to ask whether he should sell his townhouse or wait and sell it in the future when he hoped that prices would be higher. The columnist replied: "Ask yourself: would you buy this townhouse today as an investment? Because every day you don't sell it, you're buying it." Do you agree with the columnist? In what sense are you buying something if you don't sell it? Should the owner's decision about whether or not to sell depend on what price he originally paid for the townhouse?

Source: Edith Lane, "Contract Exclusion OK?" (Allentown, PA) *Morning Call*, May 22, 2011.

**4.7** **[Related to the** Making the Connection **on page 328]** Rob Neyer is a baseball writer for sbnation.com. He has described attending a Red Sox game at Fenway Park in Boston and having a seat in the sun on a hot, humid day: "Granted, I could have moved under the overhang and enjoyed today's contest from a nice, cool, shady seat. But when you paid forty-five dollars for a ticket in the fourth row, it's tough to move back to the twenty-fourth [row]." Evaluate Neyer's reasoning.

Based on Rob Neyer, *Feeding the Green Monster*, (New York: iPublish. com, 2001), p. 50.

**4.8** **[Related to the** Making the Connection **on page 328]** After owning a used car for two years, you start having problems with it. You take it into the shop, and a mechanic tells you that repairs will cost $4,000. What factors will you take into account in deciding whether to have the repairs done or to junk the car and buy another one? Will the price you paid for the car be one of those factors? Briefly explain.

**4.9** **[Related to the** Making the Connection **on page 328]** The following excerpt is from a letter sent to a financial advice columnist: "My wife and I are trying to decide how to invest a $250,000 windfall. She wants to pay off our $114,000 mortgage, but I'm not eager to do that because we refinanced only nine months ago, paying $3,000 in fees and costs." Briefly discuss what effect the $3,000 refinancing cost should have on this couple's investment decision.

Based on Liz Pulliam, *Los Angeles Times* advice column, March 24, 2004.

**4.10** **[Related to the** Making the Connection **on page 328]** In a blog posting on msn.com, J. D. Roth recalls his desire to get in better physical condition:

> I paid about $100 (nonrefundable, nontransferable) to sign up for the Portland Marathon. . . . At the end of May, however, I hurt myself. . . . Eventually I decided that maybe I could walk the marathon. I'd paid $100 for it, and I wasn't going to let that money go to waste.

Was Roth's reasoning flawed?

From "The Sunk-Cost Fallacy Revisited" by J.D. Roth, November 3, 2008. From www.getrichslowly.org. Reprinted with permission.

**4.11** **[Related to the** Making the Connection **on page 329]** Briefly explain whether you agree with the following statement: "If people were more realistic about their future behavior, the demand curve for potato chips would shift to the left."

**4.12** **[Related to** Solved Problem 10.4 **on page 330]** In an article in the *Quarterly Journal of Economics*, Ted O'Donoghue and Matthew Rabin make the following observation: "People have self-control problems caused by a tendency to pursue immediate gratification in a way that their 'long-run selves' do not appreciate." What do they mean by a person's "long-run self"? Give two examples of people pursuing immediate gratification that their long-run selves would not appreciate.

Based on Ted O'Donoghue and Matthew Rabin, "Choice and Procrastination," *Quarterly Journal of Economics*, February 2001, pp. 125–126.

**4.13** **[Related to** Solved Problem 10.4 **on page 330]** Data from health clubs show that members who choose a contract with a flat monthly fee over $70 attend, on average, 4.8 times per month. They pay a price per expected visit of more than $14, even though a $10-per-visit fee is also available. Why would these consumers choose a monthly contract when they lose money on it?

# Appendix

## Using Indifference Curves and Budget Lines to Understand Consumer Behavior

### Consumer Preferences

In this chapter, we analyzed consumer behavior, using the assumption that satisfaction, or *utility*, is measurable in utils. Although this assumption made our analysis easier to understand, it is unrealistic. In this appendix we use the more realistic assumption that consumers are able to *rank* different combinations of goods and services in terms of how much utility they provide. For example, a consumer is able to determine whether he or she prefers 2 slices of pizza and 1 can of Coke or 1 slice of pizza and 2 cans of Coke, even if the consumer is unsure exactly how much utility he or she would receive from consuming these goods. This approach has the advantage of allowing us to actually draw a map of a consumer's preferences.

To begin with, suppose that a consumer is presented with the following alternatives, or *consumption bundles*:

| Consumption Bundle A | Consumption Bundle B |
| --- | --- |
| 2 slices of pizza and 1 can of Coke | 1 slice of pizza and 2 cans of Coke |

We assume that the consumer will always be able to decide which of the following is true:

- The consumer prefers bundle A to bundle B.
- The consumer prefers bundle B to bundle A.
- The consumer is indifferent between bundle A and bundle B. That is, the consumer would be equally happy to receive either bundle, so we can say the consumer receives equal utility from the two bundles.

For consistency, we also assume that the consumer's preferences are *transitive*. For example, if a consumer prefers pepperoni pizza to mushroom pizza and prefers mushroom pizza to anchovy pizza, the consumer must prefer pepperoni pizza to anchovy pizza.

### Indifference Curves

Given the assumptions in the preceding section, we can draw a map of a consumer's preferences by using indifference curves. An **indifference curve** shows combinations of consumption bundles that give the consumer the same utility. In reality, consumers choose among consumption bundles containing many goods and services, but to make the discussion easier to follow, we will assume that only two goods are involved. Nothing important would change if we expanded the discussion to include many goods instead of just two.

The table in Figure 10A.1 gives Dave's preferences for pizza and Coke. The graph plots the information from the table. Every possible combination of pizza and Coke will have an indifference curve passing through it, although in the figure we have shown only four of Dave's indifference curves. Dave is indifferent among all the consumption bundles that are on the same indifference curve. So, he is indifferent among bundles $E$, $B$, and $F$ because they all lie on indifference curve $I_3$. Even though Dave has 4 fewer cans of Coke with bundle $B$ than with bundle $E$, the additional slice of pizza he has in bundle $B$ means he has the same amount of utility at both points.

**Indifference curve** A curve that shows the combinations of consumption bundles that give the consumer the same utility.

## Figure 10A.1

### Plotting Dave's Preferences for Pizza and Coke

Every possible combination of pizza and Coke will have an indifference curve passing through it, although in the graph we show just four of Dave's indifference curves. Dave is indifferent among all the consumption bundles that are on the same indifference curve. So, he is indifferent among bundles $E$, $B$, and $F$ because they all lie on indifference curve $I_3$. Moving to the upper right in the graph increases the quantities of both goods available for Dave to consume. Therefore, the further to the upper right the indifference curve is, the greater the utility Dave receives.

| Consumption Bundle | Slices of Pizza | Cans of Coke |
|---|---|---|
| A | 1 | 2 |
| B | 3 | 4 |
| C | 4 | 5 |
| D | 1 | 6 |
| E | 2 | 8 |
| F | 5 | 2 |

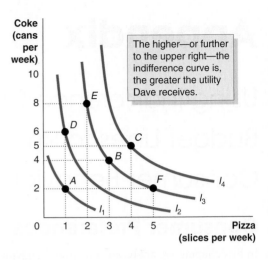

Even without looking at Dave's indifference curves, we know he will prefer consumption bundle $D$ to consumption bundle $A$ because in $D$ he receives the same quantity of pizza as in $A$ but 4 additional cans of Coke. But we need to know Dave's preferences, as shown by his indifference curves, to know how he will rank bundle $B$ and bundle $D$. Bundle $D$ contains more Coke but less pizza than bundle $B$, so Dave's ranking will depend on how much pizza he would be willing to give up to receive more Coke. The higher the indifference curve—that is, the further to the upper right on the graph—the greater the amounts of both goods that are available for Dave to consume and the greater his utility. In other words, Dave receives more utility from the consumption bundles on indifference curve $I_2$ than from the consumption bundles on indifference curve $I_1$, more utility from the bundles on $I_3$ than from the bundles on $I_2$, and so on.

## The Slope of an Indifference Curve

Remember that the slope of a curve is the ratio of the change in the variable on the vertical axis to the change in the variable on the horizontal axis. Along an indifference curve, the slope tells us the rate at which the consumer is willing to trade off one product for another while keeping the consumer's utility constant. Economists call this rate the **marginal rate of substitution (*MRS*)**.

We expect that the *MRS* will change as we move down an indifference curve. In Figure 10A.1, at a point like $E$ on indifference curve $I_3$, Dave's indifference curve is relatively steep. As we move down the curve, it becomes less steep, until it becomes relatively flat at a point like $F$. This is the usual shape of indifference curves: They are bowed in, or convex. A consumption bundle like $E$ contains a lot of Coke and not much pizza. We would expect that Dave could give up a significant quantity of Coke for a smaller quantity of additional pizza and still have the same level of utility. Thus, the *MRS* will be high. As we move down the indifference curve, Dave moves to bundles, like $B$ and $F$, that have more pizza and less Coke. As a result, Dave is willing to trade less Coke for pizza, and the *MRS* declines.

## Can Indifference Curves Ever Cross?

Remember that we assume that consumers have transitive preferences. That is, if Dave prefers consumption bundle $X$ to consumption bundle $Y$ and he prefers consumption bundle $Y$ to consumption bundle $Z$, he must prefer bundle $X$ to bundle $Z$. If indifference curves cross, this assumption is violated. To understand why, look at Figure 10A.2, which shows two of Dave's indifference curves crossing.

Because bundle $X$ and bundle $Z$ are both on indifference curve $I_1$, Dave must be indifferent between them. Similarly, because bundle $X$ and bundle $Y$ are on indifference curve $I_2$, Dave must be indifferent between them. The assumption of transitivity means that Dave should also be indifferent between bundle $Z$ and bundle $Y$. We know that this is not true, however, because bundle $Y$ contains more pizza and more Coke than bundle $Z$. So, Dave will definitely prefer bundle $Y$ to bundle $Z$, which violates the assumption of transitivity. Therefore, none of Dave's indifference curves can cross.

**Marginal rate of substitution (*MRS*)** The rate at which a consumer would be willing to trade off one good for another.

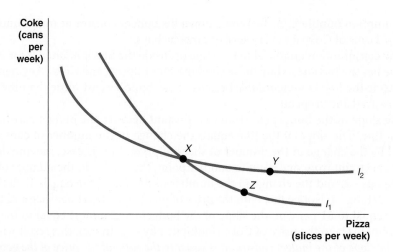

**Figure 10A.2**

**Indifference Curves Cannot Cross**

Because bundle $X$ and bundle $Z$ are both on indifference curve $I_1$, Dave must be indifferent between them. Similarly, because bundle $X$ and bundle $Y$ are on indifference curve $I_2$, Dave must be indifferent between them. The assumption of transitivity means that Dave should also be indifferent between bundle $Z$ and bundle $Y$. We know that this is not true, however, because bundle $Y$ contains more pizza and more Coke than bundle $Z$. So Dave will definitely prefer bundle $Y$ to bundle $Z$, which violates the assumption of transitivity. *Therefore, none of Dave's indifference curves can cross.*

# The Budget Constraint

Remember that a consumer's *budget constraint* is the amount of income he or she has available to spend on goods and services. Suppose that Dave has $10 per week to spend on pizza and Coke. The table in Figure 10A.3 shows the combinations that he can afford to buy if the price of pizza is $2 per slice and the price of Coke is $1 per can. As you can see, all the points lie on a straight line. This line represents Dave's budget constraint. The line intersects the vertical axis at the maximum number of cans of Coke Dave can afford to buy with $10, which is consumption bundle $G$. The line intersects the horizontal axis at the maximum number of slices of pizza Dave can afford to buy with $10, which

| Combinations of Pizza and Coke Dave Can Buy with $10 | | | |
| --- | --- | --- | --- |
| Consumption Bundle | Slices of Pizza | Cans of Coke | Total Spending |
| G | 0 | 10 | $10.00 |
| H | 1 | 8 | 10.00 |
| I | 2 | 6 | 10.00 |
| J | 3 | 4 | 10.00 |
| K | 4 | 2 | 10.00 |
| L | 5 | 0 | 10.00 |

**Figure 10A.3**

**Dave's Budget Constraint**

Dave's budget constraint shows the combinations of slices of pizza and cans of Coke he can buy with $10. The price of Coke is $1 per can, so if he spends all of his $10 on Coke, he can buy 10 cans (bundle $G$). The price of pizza is $2 per slice, so if he spends all of his $10 on pizza, he can buy 5 slices (bundle $L$). As he moves down his budget constraint from bundle $G$, he gives up 2 cans of Coke for every slice of pizza he buys. Any consumption bundles along the line or inside the line are affordable. Any bundles that lie outside the line are unaffordable.

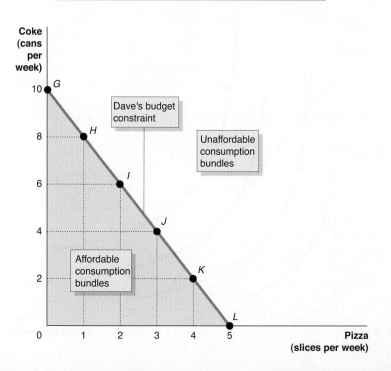

is consumption bundle *L*. As he moves down his budget constraint from bundle *G*, he gives up 2 cans of Coke for every slice of pizza he buys.

Any consumption bundle along the line or inside the line is *affordable* for Dave because he has the income to buy those combinations of pizza and Coke. Any bundle that lies outside the line is *unaffordable* because those bundles cost more than the income Dave has available to spend.

The slope of the budget constraint is constant because the budget constraint is a straight line. The slope of the line equals the change in the number of cans of Coke divided by the change in the number of slices of pizza. In this case, moving down the budget constraint from one point to another point, the change in the number of cans of Coke equals –2, and the change in the number of slices of pizza equals 1, so the slope equals –2/1, or –2. Notice that with the price of pizza equal to $2 per slice and the price of Coke equal to $1 per can, the slope of the budget constraint is equal to the ratio of the price of pizza to the price of Coke (multiplied by –1). In fact, this result will always hold: *The slope of the budget constraint is equal to the ratio of the price of the good on the horizontal axis divided by the price of the good on the vertical axis multiplied by –1.*

## Choosing the Optimal Consumption of Pizza and Coke

Dave would like to be on the highest possible indifference curve because higher indifference curves represent more pizza and more Coke. But Dave can only buy the bundles that lie on or inside his budget constraint. In other words, *to maximize utility, a consumer needs to be on the highest indifference curve, given his budget constraint.*

Figure 10A.4 plots the consumption bundles from Figure 10A.1 along with the budget constraint from Figure 10A.3. The figure also shows the indifference curves that pass through each consumption bundle. In Figure 10A.4, the highest indifference curve shown is $I_4$. Unfortunately, Dave lacks the income to purchase consumption bundles—such as *C*—that lie on $I_4$. He has the income to purchase bundles such as *A* and *D*, but he can do better. If he consumes bundle *B*, he will be on the highest indifference curve he can reach, given his budget constraint of $10. The resulting combination of 3 slices of pizza and 4 cans of Coke represents optimal consumption of pizza and Coke, given

**Figure 10A.4**

**Finding Optimal Consumption**

Dave would like to be on the highest possible indifference curve, but he cannot reach indifference curves such as $I_4$ that are outside his budget constraint. Dave's optimal combination of slices of pizza and cans of Coke is at point *B*, where his budget constraint just touches—or is *tangent* to—the highest indifference curve he can reach. At point *B*, he buys 3 slices of pizza and 4 cans of Coke.

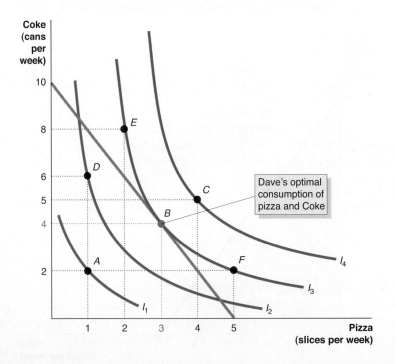

Dave's preferences and given his budget constraint. Notice that at point *B*, Dave's budget constraint just touches—or is *tangent to*—$I_3$. In fact, bundle *B* is the only bundle on $I_3$ that Dave is able to purchase for $10.

| Making the Connection | ## Dell Determines the Optimal Mix of Products |
|---|---|

Consumers have different preferences, which helps explain why many firms offer products with a variety of characteristics. For example, Dell sells laptop computers with different screen sizes, processor speeds, hard drive sizes, graphics cards, and so on. We can use the model of consumer choice to analyze a simplified version of the situation Dell faces in deciding which features to offer consumers.

Assume that consumers have $1,000 each to spend on laptops and that they are concerned with only two laptop characteristics: screen size and processor speed. Because larger screens and faster processors increase Dell's cost of producing laptops, consumers face a trade-off: The larger the screen, the slower the processor speed. Consumers in panel (a) of the figure prefer screen size to processor speed. For this group, the point of tangency between a typical consumer's indifference curve and the budget constraint shows an optimal choice of a 17-inch screen and a 2.0-gigahertz processor. Consumers in panel (b) prefer processor speed to screen size. For this group, the point of tangency between a typical consumer's indifference curve and the budget constraint shows an optimal choice of a 13-inch screen and 3.4-gigahertz processor.

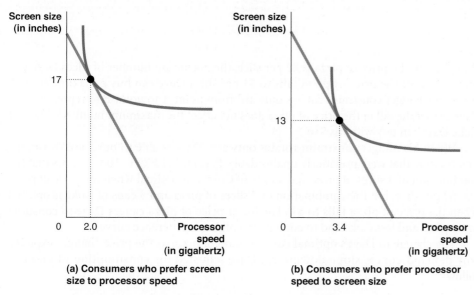

(a) Consumers who prefer screen size to processor speed

(b) Consumers who prefer processor speed to screen size

Companies such as Dell use surveys and other means to gather information about consumer preferences. With knowledge of consumers' preferences and data on the costs of producing different laptop components, Dell can determine the mix of components to offer consumers.

**Your Turn:** Test your understanding by doing related problem 10A.8 on page 351 at the end of this appendix.

MyEconLab

# Deriving the Demand Curve

Suppose the price of pizza falls from $2 per slice to $1 per slice. How will this affect Dave's decision about which combination of pizza and Coke is optimal? First, notice what happens to Dave's budget constraint when the price of pizza falls. As Figure 10A.5

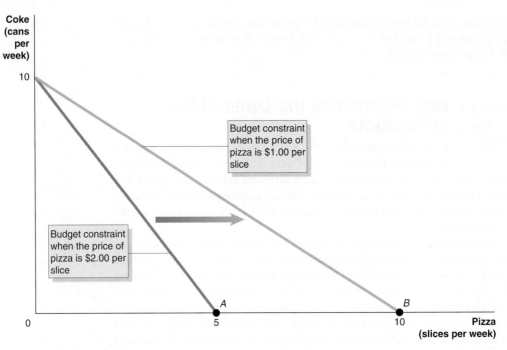

**Figure 10A.5** How a Price Decrease Affects the Budget Constraint

A fall in the price of pizza from $2 per slice to $1 per slice increases the maximum number of slices Dave can buy with $10 from 5 to 10. The budget constraint rotates outward from point *A* to point *B* to show the effect of the price decrease.

shows, when the price of pizza is $2 per slice, the maximum number of slices Dave can buy is 5. After the price of pizza falls to $1 per slice, Dave can buy a maximum of 10 slices. His budget constraint rotates outward from point *A* to point *B* to represent this. (Notice that the fall in the price of pizza does not affect the maximum number of cans of Coke Dave can buy with his $10.)

When his budget constraint rotates outward, Dave is able to purchase consumption bundles that were previously unaffordable. Panel (a) of Figure 10A.6 shows that the combination of 3 slices of pizza and 4 cans of Coke was optimal when the price of pizza was $2 per slice, but the combination of 7 slices of pizza and 3 cans of Coke is optimal when the price of pizza falls to $1. The lower price of pizza causes Dave to consume more pizza and less Coke and to end up on a higher indifference curve.

The change in Dave's optimal consumption of pizza as the price changes explains why demand curves slope downward. Dave adjusted his consumption of pizza as follows:

Price of pizza = $2 per slice ⇒ Quantity of pizza demanded = 3 slices

Price of pizza = $1 per slice ⇒ Quantity of pizza demanded = 7 slices

In panel (b) of Figure 10A.6, we plot the two points of optimal consumption and draw a line to connect the points. This downward-sloping line is Dave's demand curve for pizza. We could find more points on the demand curve by changing the price of pizza and finding the new optimal number of slices of pizza Dave would demand.

Remember that according to the law of demand, demand curves always slope downward. We have just shown that the law of demand results from the optimal adjustment by consumers to changes in prices. A fall in the price of a good will rotate *outward* the budget constraint and make it possible for a consumer to reach higher indifference curves. As a result, the consumer will increase the quantity of the good demanded. An increase in price will rotate *inward* the budget constraint and force the consumer to a lower indifference curve. As a result, the consumer will decrease the quantity of the good demanded.

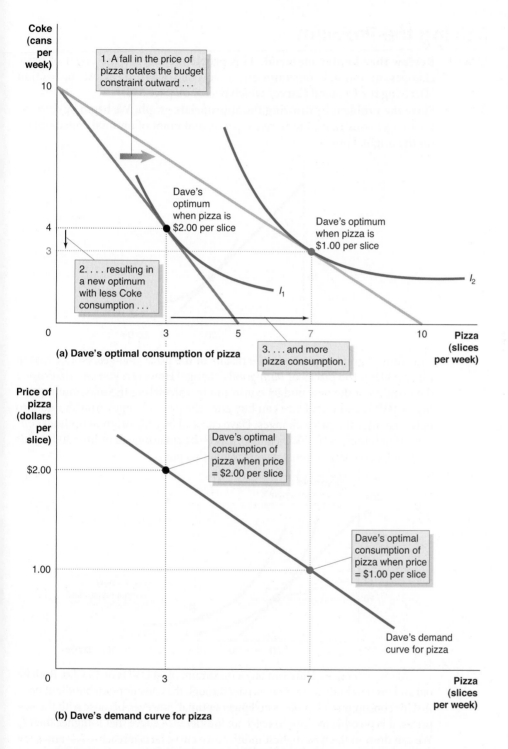

**(a) Dave's optimal consumption of pizza**

**(b) Dave's demand curve for pizza**

### Figure 10A.6

#### How a Price Change Affects Optimal Consumption

In panel (a), a fall in the price of pizza results in Dave's consuming less Coke and more pizza.

1.  A fall in the price of pizza rotates the budget constraint outward because Dave can now buy more pizza with his $10.
2.  In the new optimum on indifference curve $I_2$, Dave changes the quantities he consumes of both goods. His consumption of Coke falls from 4 cans to 3 cans.
3.  In the new optimum, Dave's consumption of pizza increases from 3 slices to 7 slices.

In panel (b) Dave responds optimally to the fall in the price of pizza from $2 per slice to $1, by increasing the quantity of slices he consumes from 3 slices to 7 slices. When we graph this result, we have Dave's demand curve for pizza.

# Solved Problem 10A.1

## When Does a Price Change Make a Consumer Better Off?

Dave has $300 to spend each month on DVDs and CDs. DVDs and CDs both currently have a price of $10, and Dave is maximizing his utility by buying 20 DVDs and 10 CDs. Suppose Dave still has $300 to spend, but the price of a CD rises to $20, while the price of a DVD drops to $5. Is Dave better or worse off than he was before the price change? Use a budget constraint–indifference curve graph to illustrate your answer.

## Solving the Problem

**Step 1:** **Review the chapter material.** This problem concerns the effect of price changes on optimal consumption, so you may want to review the section "Deriving the Demand Curve," which begins on page 343.

**Step 2:** **Slove the problem by drawing the appropriate graph.** We begin by drawing the budget constraint, indifference curve, and point of optimal consumption for the original prices:

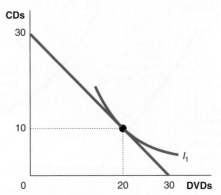

Now draw a graph that shows the results of the price changes. Notice that in this problem, the prices of *both* goods change. However, you can determine the position of the new budget constraint by calculating the maximum quantity of DVDs and CDs Dave can buy after the price changes. You should also note that after the price changes, Dave can still buy his original optimal consumption bundle—20 DVDs and 10 CDs—by spending all of his $300, so his new budget constraint must pass through this point.

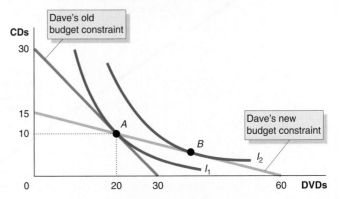

At the new prices, Dave can buy a maximum of 60 DVDs or 15 CDs. Both his old and his new budget constraints pass through the consumption bundle at point *A*. This consumption bundle is no longer optimal, however, because with the new prices, it is possible for him to reach an indifference curve that is higher than $I_1$. We can draw in the new highest indifference curve he can reach—$I_2$—and show the new optimal consumption bundle—point *B*:

Because Dave can now reach a higher indifference curve, we can conclude that he is better off as a result of the price change.

MyEconLab **Your Turn:** For more practice, do related problem 10A.10 on page 351 at the end of this appendix.

## The Income Effect and the Substitution Effect of a Price Change

We saw in this chapter that a price change has two effects on the quantity of a good consumed: the *income effect* and the *substitution effect*. The income effect is the change in the quantity demanded of a good that results from the effect of a change in price on

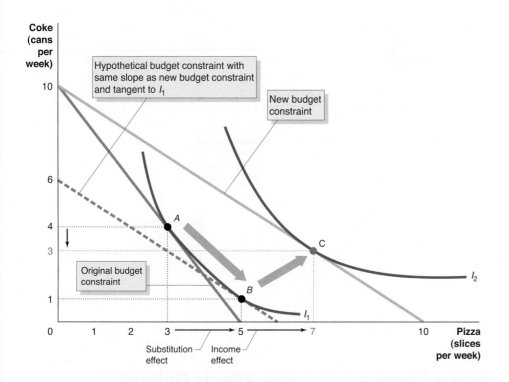

**Figure 10A.7**

**Income and Substitution Effects
of a Price Change**

Following a decline in the price of pizza, Dave's optimal consumption of pizza increases from 3 slices (point $A$) per week to 7 slices per week (point $C$). We can think of this movement from point $A$ to point $C$ as taking place in two steps: The movement from point $A$ to point $B$ along indifference curve $I_1$ represents the substitution effect, and the movement from point $B$ to point $C$ represents the income effect. Dave increases his consumption of pizza from 3 slices per week to 5 slices per week because of the substitution effect of a fall in the price of pizza and from 5 slices per week to 7 slices per week because of the income effect.

consumer purchasing power, holding all other factors constant. The substitution effect is the change in the quantity demanded of a good that results from a change in price making the good more or less expensive relative to other goods, holding constant the effect of the price change on consumer purchasing power. We can use indifference curves and budget constraints to analyze these two effects more exactly.

Figure 10A.7 illustrates the same situation as Figure 10A.6: The price of pizza has fallen from $2 per slice to $1 per slice, and Dave's budget constraint has rotated outward. As before, Dave's optimal consumption of pizza increases from 3 slices (point $A$ in Figure 10A.7) per week to 7 slices per week (point $C$). We can think of this movement from point $A$ to point $C$ as taking place in two steps: The movement from point $A$ to point $B$ represents the substitution effect, and the movement from point $B$ to point $C$ represents the income effect. To isolate the substitution effect, we have to hold constant the effect of the price change on Dave's income. We do this by changing the price of pizza relative to the price of Coke *but at the same time holding his utility constant by keeping Dave on the same indifference curve.* In Figure 10A.7, in moving from point $A$ to point $B$, Dave remains on indifference curve $I_1$. Point $A$ is a point of tangency between $I_1$ and Dave's original budget constraint. Point $B$ is a point of tangency between $I_1$ and a new, *hypothetical* budget constraint that has a slope equal to the new ratio of the price of pizza to the price of Coke. At point $B$, Dave has increased his consumption of pizza from 3 slices to 5 slices. Because we are still on indifference curve $I_1$, we know that this increase is Dave's response only to the change in the relative price of pizza and, therefore, that the increase represents the substitution effect of the fall in the price of pizza.

At point $B$, Dave has not spent all his income. Remember that the fall in the price of pizza has increased Dave's purchasing power. In Figure 10A.7, we illustrate the additional pizza Dave consumes because of the income effect of increased purchasing power by the movement from point $B$ to point $C$. Notice that in moving from point $B$ to point $C$, the price of pizza relative to the price of Coke is constant because the slope of the new budget constraint is the same as the slope of the hypothetical budget constraint that is tangent to $I_1$ at point $B$.

We can conclude that Dave increases his consumption of pizza from 3 slices per week to 5 slices per week because of the substitution effect of a fall in the price of pizza and from 5 slices per week to 7 slices per week because of the income effect. Recall from our discussion of income and substitution effects in this chapter that the income effect of a price decline causes consumers to buy more of a normal good and less of an inferior good. Because the income effect causes Dave to increase his consumption of pizza, pizza must be a normal good for him.

## Figure 10A.8

**How a Change in Income Affects the Budget Constraint**

When the income Dave has to spend on pizza and Coke increases from $10 to $20, his budget constraint shifts outward. With $10, Dave could buy a maximum of 5 slices of pizza or 10 cans of Coke. With $20, he can buy a maximum of 10 slices of pizza or 20 cans of Coke.

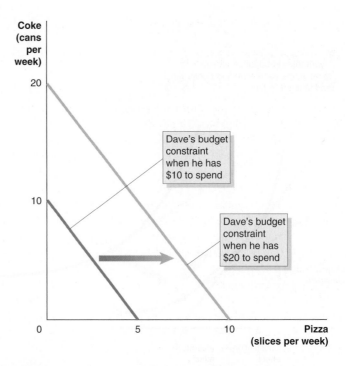

# How a Change in Income Affects Optimal Consumption

Suppose that the price of pizza remains at $2 per slice, but the income Dave has to spend on pizza and Coke increases from $10 to $20. Figure 10A.8 shows how this affects his budget constraint. With an income of $10, Dave could buy a maximum of 5 slices of pizza or 10 cans of Coke. With an income of $20, he can buy 10 slices of pizza or 20 cans of Coke. The additional income allows Dave to increase his consumption of both pizza and Coke and to move to a higher indifference curve. Figure 10A.9 shows Dave's new optimum. Dave is able to increase his consumption of pizza from 3 slices per week to 7 and his consumption of Coke from 4 cans per week to 6.

## Figure 10A.9

**How a Change in Income Affects Optimal Consumption**

An increase in income leads Dave to consume more Coke and more pizza.

1. An increase in income shifts Dave's budget constraint outward because he can now buy more of both goods.
2. In the new optimum on indifference curve $I_2$, Dave changes the quantities he consumes of both goods. His consumption of Coke increases from 4 cans to 6 cans.
3. In the new optimum, Dave's consumption of pizza increases from 3 slices to 7 slices.

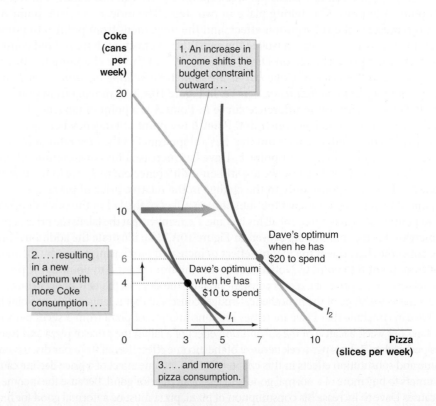

# The Slope of the Indifference Curve, the Slope of the Budget Line, and the Rule of Equal Marginal Utility per Dollar Spent

In this chapter, we saw that consumers maximize utility when they consume each good up to the point where the marginal utility per dollar spent is the same for every good. This condition seems different from the one we stated earlier in this appendix that to maximize utility, a consumer needs to be on the highest indifference curve, given his budget constraint. In fact, though, the two conditions are equivalent. To see this, begin by looking at Figure 10A.10, which again combines Dave's indifference curve and budget constraint. Remember that at the point of optimal consumption, the indifference curve and the budget constraint are tangent, so they have the same slope. Therefore, *at the point of optimal consumption, the marginal rate of substitution* (MRS) *is equal to the ratio of the price of the product on the horizontal axis to the price of the product on the vertical axis.*

The slope of the indifference curve tells us the rate at which a consumer is *willing* to trade off one good for the other. The slope of the budget constraint tells us the rate at which a consumer is *able* to trade off one good for the other. Only at the point of optimal consumption is the rate at which a consumer is willing to trade off one good for the other equal to the rate at which he can trade off one good for the other.

## The Rule of Equal Marginal Utility per Dollar Spent Revisited

Recall from this chapter the *rule of equal marginal utility per dollar*, which states that to maximize utility, consumers should spend their income so that the last dollar spent on each product gives them the same marginal utility. We can use our indifference curve and budget constraint analysis to see why this rule holds. When we move from one point on an indifference curve to another, we end up with more of one product and less of the other product but the same amount of utility. For example, as Dave moves down an indifference curve, he consumes less Coke and more pizza, but he has the same amount of utility.

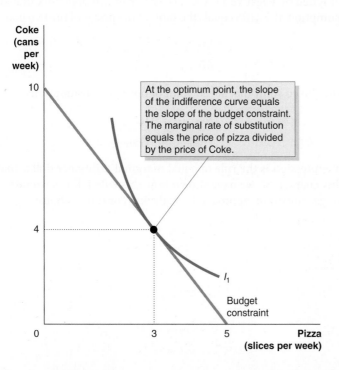

At the optimum point, the slope of the indifference curve equals the slope of the budget constraint. The marginal rate of substitution equals the price of pizza divided by the price of Coke.

**Figure 10A.10**

**At the Optimum Point, the Slopes of the Indifference Curve and Budget Constraint Are the Same**

At the point of optimal consumption, the marginal rate of substitution is equal to the ratio of the price of the product on the horizontal axis to the price of the product on the vertical axis.

Remember that marginal utility ($MU$) tells us how much additional utility a consumer gains (or loses) from consuming more (or less) of a good. So when Dave consumes less Coke by moving down an indifference curve, he loses utility equal to:

$$- \text{Change in the quantity of Coke} \times MU_{Coke}$$

but he consumes more pizza, so he gains utility equal to:

$$\text{Change in the quantity of pizza} \times MU_{Pizza}.$$

We know that the gain in utility from the additional pizza is equal to the loss from the smaller quantity of Coke because Dave's total utility remains the same along an indifference curve. Therefore, we can write:

$$- (\text{Change in the quantity of Coke} \times MU_{Coke}) = (\text{Change in the quantity of pizza} \times MU_{Pizza}).$$

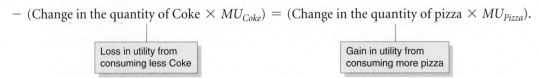

Loss in utility from consuming less Coke

Gain in utility from consuming more pizza

If we rearrange terms, we have:

$$\frac{- \text{Change in the quantity of Coke}}{\text{Change in the quantity of pizza}} = \frac{MU_{Pizza}}{MU_{Coke}}.$$

Because the expression:

$$\frac{- \text{Change in the quantity of Coke}}{\text{Change in the quantity of pizza}}$$

is the slope of the indifference curve, it is equal to the marginal rate of substitution (multiplied by negative 1). So, we can write:

$$\frac{- \text{Change in the quantity of Coke}}{\text{Change in the quantity of pizza}} = MRS = \frac{MU_{Pizza}}{MU_{Coke}}.$$

The slope of Dave's budget constraint equals the price of pizza divided by the price of Coke (multiplied by negative 1). We saw earlier in this appendix that at the point of optimal consumption, the $MRS$ equals the ratio of the prices of the two goods. Therefore:

$$\frac{MU_{Pizza}}{MU_{Coke}} = \frac{P_{Pizza}}{P_{Coke}}.$$

We can rewrite this to show that at the point of optimal consumption:

$$\frac{MU_{Pizza}}{P_{Pizza}} = \frac{MU_{Coke}}{P_{Coke}}.$$

This last expression is the rule of equal marginal utility per dollar that we first developed in this chapter. So we have shown how this rule follows from the indifference curve and budget constraint approach to analyzing consumer choice.

## Key Terms

Indifference curve, p. 339

Marginal rate of substitution (*MRS*), p. 340

 **10A** **Using Indifference Curves and Budget Lines to Understand Consumer Behavior, pages 339–350**

LEARNING OBJECTIVE: Use indifference curves and budget lines to understand consumer behavior.

MyEconLab  Visit **www.myeconlab.com** to complete these exercises online and get instant feedback.

## Review Questions

**10A.1** What are the two assumptions economists make about consumer preferences?

**10A.2** What is an indifference curve? What is a budget constraint?

**10A.3** How do consumers choose the optimal consumption bundle?

## Problems and Applications

**10A.4** Jacob receives an allowance of $5 per week. He spends all his allowance on ice cream cones and cans of Lemon Fizz soda.
   a. If the price of ice cream cones is $0.50 per cone and the price of Lemon Fizz is $1 per can, draw a graph showing Jacob's budget constraint. Be sure to indicate on the graph the maximum number of ice cream cones and the maximum number of cans of Lemon Fizz that Jacob can buy.
   b. Jacob buys 8 cones and 1 can of Lemon Fizz. Draw an indifference curve representing Jacob's choice, assuming that he has chosen the optimal combination.
   c. Suppose that the price of ice cream cones rises to $1 per cone. Draw Jacob's new budget constraint and his new optimal consumption of ice cream cones and Lemon Fizz.

**10A.5** Suppose that Jacob's allowance in problem 10A.4 climbs from $5 per week to $10 per week.
   a. Show how the increased allowance alters Jacob's budget constraint.
   b. Draw a set of indifference curves showing how Jacob's choice of cones and Lemon Fizz changes when his allowance increases. Assume that both goods are normal.
   c. Draw a set of indifference curves showing how Jacob's choice of cones and Lemon Fizz changes when his allowance increases. Assume that Lemon Fizz is normal but cones are inferior.

**10A.6** Suppose that Calvin considers Pepsi and Coke to be perfect substitutes. They taste the same to him, and he gets exactly the same amount of enjoyment from drinking a can of Pepsi or a can of Coke.
   a. Will Calvin's indifference curves showing his trade-off between Pepsi and Coke have the same curvature as the indifference curves drawn in the figures in this appendix? Briefly explain.
   b. How will Calvin decide whether to buy Pepsi or to buy Coke?

**10A.7** In the following budget constraint–indifference curve graph, Nikki has $200 to spend on blouses and skirts.

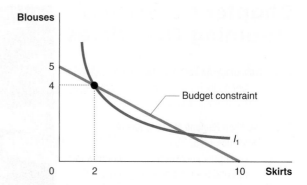

   a. What is the price of blouses? What is the price of skirts?
   b. Is Nikki making the optimum choice if she buys 4 blouses and 2 skirts? Explain how you know this.

**10A.8** [Related to the Making the Connection **on page 343**] Marilou and Hunter both purchase milk and doughnuts at the same Quik Mart. They have different tastes for milk and doughnuts and different incomes. They both buy some milk and some doughnuts, but they buy considerably different quantities of the two goods. Can we conclude that their marginal rate of substitution between milk and doughnuts is the same? Draw a graph showing their budget constraints and indifference curves and explain.

**10A.9** Sunsweet decides that prune juice has a bad image, so it launches a slick advertising campaign to convince young people that prune juice is very hip. The company hires Eminem, Jay-Z, and Trick Daddy to endorse its product. The campaign works! Prune juice sales soar, even though Sunsweet hasn't cut the price. Draw a budget constraint and indifference curve diagram with Sunsweet prune juice on one axis and other drinks on the other axis and show how the celebrity endorsements have changed things.

**10A.10** [Related to Solved Problem 10A.1 **on page 345**] Dave has $300 to spend each month on DVDs and CDs. DVDs and CDs both currently have a price of $10, and Dave is maximizing his utility by buying 20 DVDs and 10 CDs. Suppose Dave still has $300 to spend, but the price of a DVD rises to $12, while the price of a CD drops to $6. Is Dave better or worse off than he was before the price change? Use a budget constraint–indifference curve graph to illustrate your answer.

# Technology, Production, and Costs

## Chapter Outline and Learning Objectives

# Sony Uses a Cost Curve to Determine the Prices of Radios

Technological change leads to new products and lower production costs. As a firm's costs change, how does the firm adjust the price it charges? This is an important question that we will explore in the next few chapters, and it is a question that Sony Corporation, the Japanese electronics giant, must answer every day. Sony manufactures computers, televisions, and game consoles, among other products.

Sony's early success resulted from the vision and energy of two young entrepreneurs, Akio Morita and Masaru Ibuka. In 1953, Sony purchased a license that allowed it to use transistor technology developed in the United States at Bell Laboratories. Sony used the technology to develop a transistor radio that was far smaller than any other radio then available. In 1955, Akio Morita arrived in New York, hoping to convince one of the U.S. department store chains to carry the Sony radios.

Morita offered to sell one department store chain 5,000 radios at a price of $29.95 each. If the chain wanted more than 5,000 radios, the price would change. As Morita described it years later:

> I sat down and drew a curve that looked something like a lopsided letter U. The price for five thousand would be our regular price. That would be the beginning of the curve. For ten thousand there would be a discount, and that was at the bottom of the curve. For thirty thousand the price would begin to climb. For fifty thousand the price per unit would be higher than for five thousand, and for one hundred thousand units the price per unit would have to be much higher than for the first five thousand.

Morita offered prices that followed a U shape because Sony's cost per unit, or *average cost*, of manufacturing the radios had the same shape. Curves that show the relationship between the level of output and per-unit cost are called *average total cost curves*. Average total cost curves typically have the U shape of Morita's curve. As we explore the relationship between production and costs in this chapter, we will see why average total cost curves have this shape.

**AN INSIDE LOOK AT POLICY** on **page 374** discusses a loan guarantee the U.S. Department of Energy made to a company that manufactures solar panels.

From Akio Morita, with Edwin M. Reingold and Mitsuko Shimomura, *Made in Japan: Akio Morita and Sony,* (New York: Signet Books, 1986), p. 94.

## Economics in Your Life

### Using Cost Concepts in Your Own Business

Suppose that you have the opportunity to open a store that sells recliners. You learn that you can purchase the recliners from the manufacturer for $300 each. Bob's Big Chairs is an existing store that is the same size your new store will be. Bob's sells the same recliners you plan to sell and also buys them from the manufacturer for $300 each. Your plan is to sell the recliners for a price of $500. After studying how Bob's is operated, you find that Bob's is selling more recliners per month than you expect to be able to sell and that it is selling them for $450. You wonder how Bob's makes a profit at the lower price. Are there any reasons to expect that because Bob's sells more recliners per month, its costs will be lower than your store's costs? You can check your answer against the one we provide on **page 372** at the end of this chapter.

I n Chapter 10, we looked behind the demand curve to better understand consumer decision making. In this chapter, we look behind the supply curve to better understand firm decision making. Earlier chapters showed that supply curves are upward sloping because marginal cost increases as firms increase the quantity of a good that they supply. In this chapter, we look more closely at why this is true. In the appendix to this chapter, we extend the analysis by using isoquants and isocost lines to understand the relationship between production and costs. Once we have a good understanding of production and cost, we can proceed in the following chapters to understand how firms decide what level of output to produce and what price to charge.

**11.1 LEARNING** OBJECTIVE

Define technology and give examples of technological change.

**Technology** The processes a firm uses to turn inputs into outputs of goods and services.

**Technological change** A change in the ability of a firm to produce a given level of output with a given quantity of inputs.

# Technology: An Economic Definition

The basic activity of a firm is to use *inputs*, such as workers, machines, and natural resources, to produce *outputs* of goods and services. A pizza parlor, for example, uses inputs such as pizza dough, pizza sauce, cooks, and ovens to produce pizza. A firm's **technology** is the processes it uses to turn inputs into outputs of goods and services. Notice that this economic definition of technology is broader than the everyday definition. When we use the word *technology* in everyday language, we usually refer only to the development of new products. In the economic sense, a firm's technology depends on many factors, such as the skills of its managers, the training of its workers, and the speed and efficiency of its machinery and equipment. The technology of pizza production, for example, includes not only the capacity of the pizza ovens and how quickly they bake the pizza but also how quickly the cooks can prepare the pizza for baking, how well the manager motivates the workers, and how well the manager has arranged the facilities to allow the cooks to quickly prepare the pizzas and get them in the ovens.

Whenever a firm experiences positive **technological change**, it is able to produce more output using the same inputs or the same output using fewer inputs. Positive technological change can come from many sources. A firm's managers may rearrange the factory floor or the layout of a retail store in order to increase production and sales. The firm's workers may go through a training program. The firm may install faster or more reliable machinery or equipment. It is also possible for a firm to experience negative technological change. If a firm hires less-skilled workers or if a hurricane damages its facilities, the quantity of output it can produce from a given quantity of inputs may decline.

<table>
<tr><td>Making<br>the<br>Connection</td><td>**Improving Inventory Control at Wal-Mart**</td></tr>
</table>

Inventories are goods that have been produced but not yet sold. For a retailer such as Wal-Mart, inventories at any point in time include the goods on the store shelves as well as goods in warehouses. Inventories are an input into Wal-Mart's output of goods sold to consumers. Having money tied up in holding inventories is costly, so firms have an incentive to hold as few inventories as possible and to *turn over* their inventories as rapidly as possible by ensuring that goods do not remain on the shelves long. Holding too few inventories, however, results in *stockouts*—that is, sales being lost because the goods consumers want to buy are not on the shelf.

Improvements in inventory control meet the economic definition of positive technological change because they allow firms to produce the same output with fewer inputs. In recent years, many firms have adopted *just-in-time* inventory systems in which firms accept shipments from suppliers as close as possible to the time they will be needed. The just-in-time system was pioneered by Toyota, which used it to reduce the inventories of parts in its automobile assembly plants. Wal-Mart has been a pioneer in using similar inventory control systems in its stores.

Wal-Mart actively manages its *supply chain*, which stretches from the manufacturers of the goods it sells to its retail stores. Entrepreneur Sam Walton, the company founder, built a series of distribution centers spread across the country to supply goods to the retail stores. As goods are sold in the stores, this *point-of-sale* information is sent electronically to the firm's distribution centers to help managers determine what products will be shipped to each store. Depending on a store's location relative to a distribution center, managers can use Wal-Mart's trucks to ship goods overnight. This distribution system allows Wal-Mart to minimize its inventory holdings without running the risk of many stockouts occurring. Because Wal-Mart sells 15 percent to 25 percent of all the toothpaste, disposable diapers, dog food, and many other products sold in the United States, it has been able to involve many manufacturers closely in its supply chain. For example, a company such as Procter & Gamble, which is one of the world's largest manufacturers of toothpaste, laundry detergent, toilet paper, and other products, receives Wal-Mart's point-of-sale and inventory information electronically. Procter & Gamble uses that information to help determine its production schedules and the quantities it should ship to Wal-Mart's distribution centers.

Technological change has been a key to Wal-Mart's becoming one of the largest firms in the world, with 2.1 million employees and revenue of nearly $420 billion in 2011.

*Better inventory controls have helped Wal-Mart and other firms to reduce their costs.*

**Your Turn:** Test your understanding by doing related problem 1.5 on page 376 at the end of this chapter.

MyEconLab

---

# The Short Run and the Long Run in Economics

**11.2 LEARNING** OBJECTIVE

Distinguish between the economic short run and the economic long run.

When firms analyze the relationship between their level of production and their costs, they separate the time period involved into the short run and the long run. In the **short run**, at least one of the firm's inputs is fixed. In particular, in the short run, the firm's technology and the size of its physical plant—its factory, store, or office—are both fixed, while the number of workers the firm hires is variable. In the **long run**, the firm is able to vary all its inputs and can adopt new technology and increase or decrease the size of its physical plant. Of course, the actual length of calendar time in the short run will be different from firm to firm. A pizza parlor may be able to increase its physical plant by adding another pizza oven and some tables and chairs in just a few weeks. BMW, in contrast, may take more than a year to increase the capacity of one of its automobile assembly plants by installing new equipment.

**Short run** The period of time during which at least one of a firm's inputs is fixed.

**Long run** The period of time in which a firm can vary all its inputs, adopt new technology, and increase or decrease the size of its physical plant.

## The Difference between Fixed Costs and Variable Costs

**Total cost** is the cost of all the inputs a firm uses in production. We have just seen that in the short run, some inputs are fixed and others are variable. The costs of the fixed inputs are *fixed costs*, and the costs of the variable inputs are *variable costs*. We can also think of **variable costs** as the costs that change as output changes. Similarly, **fixed costs** are costs that remain constant as output changes. A typical firm's variable costs include its labor costs, raw material costs, and costs of electricity and other utilities. Typical fixed costs include lease payments for factory or retail space, payments for fire insurance, and payments for newspaper and television advertising. All of a firm's costs are either fixed or variable, so we can state the following:

**Total cost** The cost of all the inputs a firm uses in production.

**Variable costs** Costs that change as output changes.

**Fixed costs** Costs that remain constant as output changes.

Total cost = Fixed cost + Variable cost

or, using symbols:

$$TC = FC + VC.$$

*The wages of these workers are a variable cost to the publishers who employ them.*

## Making the Connection

### Fixed Costs in the Publishing Industry

An editor at Cambridge University Press gives the following estimates of the annual fixed cost for a medium-size academic book publisher:

| Cost | Amount |
| --- | --- |
| Salaries and benefits | $625,000 |
| Rent | 75,000 |
| Utilities | 20,000 |
| Supplies | 6,000 |
| Postage | 5,000 |
| Travel | 9,000 |
| Subscriptions, etc. | 5,000 |
| Miscellaneous | 5,000 |
| Total | $750,000 |

Academic book publishers hire editors, designers, and production and marketing managers who help prepare books for publication. Because these employees work on several books simultaneously, the number of people the company hires does not go up and down with the quantity of books the company publishes during any particular year. Publishing companies therefore consider the salaries and benefits of people in these job categories to be fixed costs.

In contrast, for a company that *prints* books, the quantity of workers varies with the quantity of books printed. The wages and benefits of the workers operating the printing presses, for example, would be a variable cost.

The other costs listed in the table above are typical of fixed costs at many firms.

*Handbook for Academic Authors*, 5th edition by Beth Lucy. Copyright © 2010 by Cambridge University Press. Reprinted by permission.

MyEconLab **Your Turn:** Test your understanding by doing related problems 2.6, 2.7, and 2.8 on page 377 at the end of this chapter.

## Implicit Costs versus Explicit Costs

**Opportunity cost** The highest-valued alternative that must be given up to engage in an activity.

**Explicit cost** A cost that involves spending money.

**Implicit cost** A nonmonetary opportunity cost.

It is important to remember that economists always measure costs as *opportunity costs*. The **opportunity cost** of any activity is the highest-valued alternative that must be given up to engage in that activity. As we saw in Chapter 8, costs are either *explicit* or *implicit*. When a firm spends money, it incurs an **explicit cost**. When a firm experiences a non-monetary opportunity cost, it incurs an **implicit cost**.

For example, suppose that Jill Johnson owns a pizza restaurant. In operating her store, Jill has explicit costs, such as the wages she pays her workers and the payments she makes for rent and electricity. But some of Jill's most important costs are implicit. Before opening her own restaurant, Jill earned a salary of $30,000 per year managing a restaurant for someone else. To start her restaurant, Jill quit her job, withdrew $50,000 from her bank account—where it earned her interest of $3,000 per year—and used the funds to equip her restaurant with tables, chairs, a cash register, and other equipment. To open her own business, Jill had to give up the $30,000 salary and the $3,000 in interest. This $33,000 is an implicit cost because it does not represent payments that Jill has to make. Nevertheless, giving up this $33,000 per year is a real cost to Jill. In addition, during the course of the year, the $50,000 worth of tables, chairs, and other physical capital in Jill's store will lose some of its value due partly to wear and tear and partly to better furniture, cash registers, and so forth becoming available. *Economic depreciation* is the difference between what Jill paid for her capital at the beginning of the year and what she could sell

| | | |
|---|---|---:|
| Pizza dough, tomato sauce, and other ingredients | | $20,000 |
| Wages | | 48,000 |
| Interest payments on loan to buy pizza ovens | | 10,000 |
| Electricity | | 6,000 |
| Lease payment for store | | 24,000 |
| Forgone salary | | 30,000 |
| Forgone interest | | 3,000 |
| Economic depreciation | | 10,000 |
| Total | | $151,000 |

**Table 11.1**

**Jill Johnson's Costs per Year**

the capital for at the end of the year. If Jill could sell the capital for $40,000 at the end of the year, then the $10,000 in economic depreciation represents another implicit cost. (Note that the whole $50,000 she spent on the capital is not a cost because she still has the equipment at the end of the year, although it is now worth only $40,000.)

Table 11.1 lists Jill's costs. The entries in red are explicit costs, and the entries in blue are implicit costs. As we saw in Chapter 8, the rules of accounting generally require that only explicit costs be used for purposes of keeping the company's financial records and for paying taxes. Therefore, explicit costs are sometimes called *accounting costs*. *Economic costs* include both accounting costs and implicit costs.

# The Production Function

Let's look at the relationship between the level of production and costs in the short run for Jill Johnson's restaurant. To keep things simpler than in the more realistic situation in Table 11.1, let's assume that Jill uses only labor—workers—and one type of capital—pizza ovens—to produce a single good: pizzas. Many firms use more than two inputs and produce more than one good, but it is easier to understand the relationship between output and cost by focusing on the case of a firm using only two inputs and producing only one good. In the short run, Jill doesn't have time to build a larger restaurant, install additional pizza ovens, or redesign the layout of her restaurant. So, in the short run, she can increase or decrease the quantity of pizzas she produces only by increasing or decreasing the quantity of workers she employs.

The first three columns of Table 11.2 show the relationship between the quantity of workers and ovens Jill uses per week and the quantity of pizzas she can produce. The relationship between the inputs employed by a firm and the maximum output it can produce with those inputs is called the firm's **production function**. Because a firm's technology is the processes it uses to turn inputs into output, the production function

**Production function** The relationship between the inputs employed by a firm and the maximum output it can produce with those inputs.

**Table 11.2** **Short-Run Production and Cost at Jill Johnson's Restaurant**

| Quantity of Workers | Quantity of Pizza Ovens | Quantity of Pizzas per Week | Cost of Pizza Ovens (Fixed Cost) | Cost of Workers (Variable Cost) | Total Cost of Pizzas per Week | Cost per Pizza (Average Total Cost) |
|---|---|---|---|---|---|---|
| 0 | 2 | 0 | $800 | $0 | $800 | — |
| 1 | 2 | 200 | 800 | 650 | 1,450 | $7.25 |
| 2 | 2 | 450 | 800 | 1,300 | 2,100 | 4.67 |
| 3 | 2 | 550 | 800 | 1,950 | 2,750 | 5.00 |
| 4 | 2 | 600 | 800 | 2,600 | 3,400 | 5.67 |
| 5 | 2 | 625 | 800 | 3,250 | 4,050 | 6.48 |
| 6 | 2 | 640 | 800 | 3,900 | 4,700 | 7.34 |

represents the firm's technology. In this case, Table 11.2 shows Jill's *short-run* production function because we are assuming that the time period is too short for Jill to increase or decrease the quantity of ovens she is using.

## A First Look at the Relationship between Production and Cost

Table 11.2 shows Jill Johnson's costs. We can determine the total cost of producing a given quantity of pizzas if we know how many workers and ovens are required to produce that quantity of pizzas and what Jill has to pay for those workers and pizzas. Suppose Jill has taken out a bank loan to buy two pizza ovens. The cost of the loan is $800 per week. Therefore, her fixed costs are $800 per week. If Jill pays $650 per week to each worker, her variable costs depend on how many workers she hires. In the short run, Jill can increase the quantity of pizzas she produces only by hiring more workers. Table 11.2 shows that if she hires 1 worker, she produces 200 pizzas during the week; if she hires 2 workers, she produces 450 pizzas; and so on. For a particular week, Jill's total cost of producing pizzas is equal to the $800 she pays on the loan for the ovens plus the amount she pays to hire workers. If Jill decides to hire 4 workers and produce 600 pizzas, her total cost is $3,400: $800 to lease the ovens and $2,600 to hire the workers. Her cost per pizza is equal to her total cost of producing pizzas divided by the quantity of pizzas produced. If she produces 600 pizzas at a total cost of $3,400, her cost per pizza, or *average total cost*, is $3,400/600 = $5.67. A firm's **average total cost** is always equal to its total cost divided by the quantity of output produced.

**Average total cost** Total cost divided by the quantity of output produced.

Panel (a) of Figure 11.1 uses the numbers in the next-to-last column of Table 11.2 to graph Jill's total cost. Panel (b) uses the numbers in the last column to graph her average total cost. Notice in panel (b) that Jill's average cost has roughly the same U shape as the average cost curve we saw Akio Morita describe for Sony transistor radios at the beginning of this chapter. As production increases from low levels, average total cost falls.

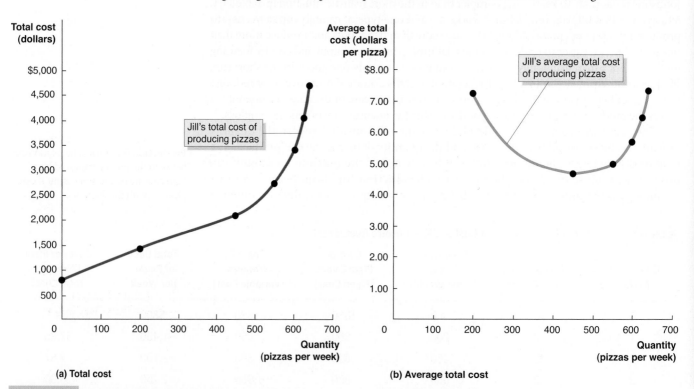

(a) Total cost

(b) Average total cost

**Figure 11.1** Graphing Total Cost and Average Total Cost at Jill Johnson's Restaurant

We can use the information from Table 11.2 to graph the relationship between the quantity of pizzas Jill produces and her total cost and average total cost. Panel (a) shows that total cost increases as the level of production increases. In panel (b), we see that the average total cost is roughly U shaped: As production increases from low levels, average total cost falls before rising at higher levels of production. To understand why average total cost has this shape, we must look more closely at the technology of producing pizzas, as shown by the production function.

Average total cost then becomes fairly flat, before rising at higher levels of production. To understand why average total cost has this U shape, we first need to look more closely at the technology of producing pizzas, as shown by the production function for Jill's restaurant. Then we need to look at how this technology determines the relationship between production and cost.

# The Marginal Product of Labor and the Average Product of Labor

**11.3 LEARNING** OBJECTIVE

Understand the relationship between the marginal product of labor and the average product of labor.

To better understand the choices Jill faces, given the technology available to her, think first about what happens if she hires only one worker. That one worker will have to perform several different activities, including taking orders from customers, baking the pizzas, bringing the pizzas to the customers' tables, and ringing up sales on the cash register. If Jill hires two workers, some of these activities can be divided up: One worker could take the orders and ring up the sales, and one worker could bake the pizzas. With such a division of tasks, Jill will find that hiring two workers actually allows her to produce more than twice as many pizzas as she could produce with just one worker.

The additional output a firm produces as a result of hiring one more worker is called the **marginal product of labor**. We can calculate the marginal product of labor by determining how much total output increases as each additional worker is hired. We do this for Jill's restaurant in Table 11.3.

**Marginal product of labor** The additional output a firm produces as a result of hiring one more worker.

When Jill hires only 1 worker, she produces 200 pizzas per week. When she hires 2 workers, she produces 450 pizzas per week. Hiring the second worker increases her production by 250 pizzas per week. So, the marginal product of labor for the first worker is 200 pizzas. For the second worker, the marginal product of labor rises to 250 pizzas. This increase in marginal product results from the *division of labor* and from *specialization*. By dividing the tasks to be performed—the division of labor—Jill reduces the time workers lose moving from one activity to the next. She also allows them to become more specialized at their tasks. For example, a worker who concentrates on baking pizzas will become skilled at doing so quickly and efficiently.

## The Law of Diminishing Returns

In the short run, the quantity of pizza ovens Jill leases is fixed, so as she hires more workers, the marginal product of labor eventually begins to decline. This happens because at some point, Jill uses up all the gains from the division of labor and from specialization and starts to experience the effects of the **law of diminishing returns**. This law states that adding more of a variable input, such as labor, to the same amount of a fixed input, such as capital, will eventually cause the marginal product of the variable input to decline. For Jill, the marginal product of labor begins to decline when she hires the third worker. Hiring three workers raises the quantity of pizzas she produces from

**Law of diminishing returns** The principle that, at some point, adding more of a variable input, such as labor, to the same amount of a fixed input, such as capital, will cause the marginal product of the variable input to decline.

**Table 11.3**

**The Marginal Product of Labor at Jill Johnson's Restaurant**

| Quantity of Workers | Quantity of Pizza Ovens | Quantity of Pizzas | Marginal Product of Labor |
|---|---|---|---|
| 0 | 2 | 0 | — |
| 1 | 2 | 200 | 200 |
| 2 | 2 | 450 | 250 |
| 3 | 2 | 550 | 100 |
| 4 | 2 | 600 | 50 |
| 5 | 2 | 625 | 25 |
| 6 | 2 | 640 | 15 |

450 per week to 550. But the increase in the quantity of pizzas—100—is less than the increase when she hired the second worker—250.

If Jill kept adding more and more workers to the same quantity of pizza ovens, eventually workers would begin to get in each other's way, and the marginal product of labor would actually become negative. When the marginal product is negative, the level of total output declines. No firm would actually hire so many workers as to experience a negative marginal product of labor and falling total output.

## Graphing Production

Panel (a) in Figure 11.2 shows the relationship between the quantity of workers Jill hires and her total output of pizzas, using the numbers from Table 11.3. Panel (b) shows the marginal product of labor. In panel (a), output increases as more workers are hired, but the increase in output does not occur at a constant rate. Because of specialization and

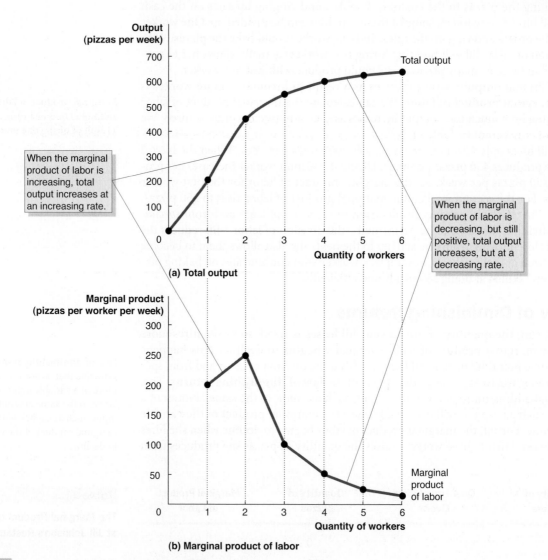

When the marginal product of labor is increasing, total output increases at an increasing rate.

When the marginal product of labor is decreasing, but still positive, total output increases, but at a decreasing rate.

**(a) Total output**

**(b) Marginal product of labor**

**Figure 11.2** Total Output and the Marginal Product of Labor

In panel (a), output increases as more workers are hired, but the increase in output does not occur at a constant rate. Because of specialization and the division of labor, output at first increases at an increasing rate, with each additional worker hired causing production to increase by a *greater* amount than did the hiring of the previous worker. After the third worker has been hired, hiring more workers while keeping the number of pizza ovens constant results in diminishing returns. When the point of diminishing returns is reached, production increases at a decreasing rate. Each additional worker hired after the third worker causes production to increase by a *smaller* amount than did the hiring of the previous worker. In panel (b), the *marginal product of labor* is the additional output produced as a result of hiring one more worker. The marginal product of labor rises initially because of the effects of specialization and division of labor, and then it falls due to the effects of diminishing returns.

the division of labor, output at first increases at an increasing rate, with each additional worker hired causing production to increase by a *greater* amount than did the hiring of the previous worker. But after the second worker has been hired, hiring more workers while keeping the quantity of ovens constant results in diminishing returns. When the point of diminishing returns is reached, production increases at a decreasing rate. Each additional worker hired after the second worker causes production to increase by a *smaller* amount than did the hiring of the previous worker. In panel (b), the marginal product of labor curve rises initially because of the effects of specialization and division of labor, and then it falls due to the effects of diminishing returns.

| Making the Connection | Adam Smith's Famous Account of the Division of Labor in a Pin Factory |
| --- | --- |

In *The Wealth of Nations*, Adam Smith uses production in a pin factory as an example of the gains in output resulting from the division of labor. The following is an excerpt from his account of how pin making was divided into a series of tasks:

> One man draws out the wire, another straightens it, a third cuts it, a fourth points it, a fifth grinds it at the top for receiving the head; to make the head requires two or three distinct operations; to put it on is a [distinct operation], to whiten the pins is another; it is even a trade by itself to put them into the paper; and the important business of making a pin is, in this manner, divided into eighteen distinct operations.

Because the labor of pin making was divided up in this way, the average worker was able to produce about 4,800 pins per day. Smith speculated that a single worker using the pin-making machinery alone would make only about 20 pins per day. This lesson from more than 225 years ago, showing the tremendous gains from division of labor and specialization, remains relevant to most business situations today.

*The gains from division of labor and specialization are as important to firms today as they were in the eighteenth century, when Adam Smith first discussed them.*

From Adam Smith, *An Inquiry into the Nature and Causes of the Wealth of Nations*, Vol. I, (Oxford, UK: Oxford University Press, 1976. original edition, 1776), pp. 14–15.

**Your Turn:** Test your understanding by doing related problem 3.7 on page 378 at the end of this chapter.

MyEconLab

## The Relationship between Marginal Product and Average Product

The marginal product of labor tells us how much total output changes as the quantity of workers hired changes. We can also calculate how many pizzas workers produce on average. The **average product of labor** is the total output produced by a firm divided by the quantity of workers. For example, using the numbers in Table 11.3 on page 359, if Jill hires 4 workers to produce 600 pizzas, the average product of labor is $600/4 = 150$.

We can state the relationship between the marginal and average products of labor this way: *The average product of labor is the average of the marginal products of labor.* For example, the numbers from Table 11.3 show that the marginal product of the first worker Jill hires is 200, the marginal product of the second worker is 250, and the marginal product of the third worker is 100. Therefore, the average product of labor for three workers is 183.3:

**Average product of labor** The total output produced by a firm divided by the quantity of workers.

$$183.3 = (200 + 250 + 100) / 3$$

| Average product of labor for three workers | Marginal product of labor of first worker | Marginal product of labor of second worker | Marginal product of labor of third worker |
| --- | --- | --- | --- |

By taking the average of the marginal products of the first three workers, we have the average product of the three workers.

Whenever the marginal product of labor is greater than the average product of labor, the average product of labor must be increasing. This statement is true for the same reason that a person 6 feet, 2 inches tall entering a room where the average height is 5 feet, 9 inches raises the average height of people in the room. Whenever the marginal product of labor is less than the average product of labor, the average product of labor must be decreasing. The marginal product of labor equals the average product of labor for the quantity of workers where the average product of labor is at its maximum.

## An Example of Marginal and Average Values: College Grades

The relationship between the marginal product of labor and the average product of labor is the same as the relationship between the marginal and average values of any variable. To see this more clearly, think about the familiar relationship between a student's grade point average (GPA) in one semester and his overall, or cumulative, GPA. The table in Figure 11.3 shows Paul's college grades for each semester, beginning with fall 2012. The graph in

### Figure 11.3

### Marginal and Average GPAs

The relationship between marginal and average values for a variable can be illustrated using GPAs. We can calculate the GPA Paul earns in a particular semester (his "marginal GPA"), and we can calculate his cumulative GPA for all the semesters he has completed so far (his "average GPA"). Paul's GPA is only 1.50 in the fall semester of his first year. In each following semester through the fall of his junior year, his GPA for the semester increases—raising his cumulative GPA. In Paul's junior year, even though his semester GPA declines from fall to spring, his cumulative GPA rises. Only in the fall of his senior year, when his semester GPA drops below his cumulative GPA, does his cumulative GPA decline.

| | Semester GPA (marginal GPA) | Cumulative GPA (average GPA) |
|---|---|---|
| *Freshman year* | | |
| Fall | 1.50 | 1.50 |
| Spring | 2.00 | 1.75 |
| *Sophomore year* | | |
| Fall | 2.20 | 1.90 |
| Spring | 3.00 | 2.18 |
| *Junior year* | | |
| Fall | 3.20 | 2.38 |
| Spring | 3.00 | 2.48 |
| *Senior year* | | |
| Fall | 2.40 | 2.47 |
| Spring | 2.00 | 2.41 |

Average GPA continues to rise, although marginal GPA falls.

With the marginal GPA below the average, the average GPA falls.

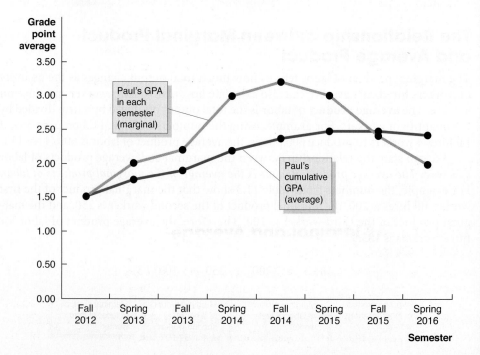

Figure 11.3 plots the grades from the table. Just as each additional worker hired adds to a firm's total production, each additional semester adds to Paul's total grade point average. We can calculate what each individual worker hired adds to total production (marginal product), and we can calculate the average production of the workers hired so far (average product).

Similarly, we can calculate the GPA Paul earns in a particular semester (his "marginal GPA"), and we can calculate his cumulative GPA for all the semesters he has completed so far (his "average GPA"). As the table shows, Paul gets off to a weak start in the fall semester of his first year, earning only a 1.50 GPA. In each subsequent semester through the fall of his junior year, his GPA for the semester increases from the previous semester—raising his cumulative GPA. As the graph shows, however, his cumulative GPA does not increase as rapidly as his semester-by-semester GPA because his cumulative GPA is held back by the low GPAs of his first few semesters. Notice that in Paul's junior year, even though his semester GPA declines from fall to spring, his cumulative GPA rises. Only in the fall of his senior year, when his semester GPA drops below his cumulative GPA, does his cumulative GPA decline.

# The Relationship between Short-Run Production and Short-Run Cost

**11.4 LEARNING** OBJECTIVE

Explain and illustrate the relationship between marginal cost and average total cost.

We have seen that technology determines the values of the marginal product of labor and the average product of labor. In turn, the marginal and average products of labor affect the firm's costs. Keep in mind that the relationships we are discussing are *short-run* relationships: We are assuming that the time period is too short for the firm to change its technology or the size of its physical plant.

At the beginning of this chapter, we saw how Akio Morita used an average total cost curve to determine the price of radios. The average total cost curve Morita used and the average total cost curve in panel (b) of Figure 11.1 on page 358 for Jill Johnson's restaurant both have a U shape. As we will soon see, the U shape of the average total cost curve is determined by the shape of the curve that shows the relationship between *marginal cost* and the level of production.

## Marginal Cost

As we saw in Chapter 1, one of the key ideas in economics is that optimal decisions are made at the margin. Consumers, firms, and government officials usually make decisions about doing a little more or a little less. As Jill Johnson considers whether to hire additional workers to produce additional pizzas, she needs to consider how much she will add to her total cost by producing the additional pizzas. **Marginal cost** is the change in a firm's total cost from producing one more unit of a good or service. We can calculate marginal cost for a particular increase in output by dividing the change in total cost by the change in output. We can express this idea mathematically (remembering that the Greek letter delta, Δ, means "change in"):

**Marginal cost**  The change in a firm's total cost from producing one more unit of a good or service.

$$MC = \frac{\Delta TC}{\Delta Q}.$$

In the table in Figure 11.4, we use this equation to calculate Jill's marginal cost of producing pizzas. The other values in the table are from Table 11.2 on page 357 and Table 11.3 on page 359.

## Why Are the Marginal and Average Cost Curves U Shaped?

Notice in the graph in Figure 11.4 that Jill's marginal cost of producing pizzas declines at first and then increases, giving the marginal cost curve a U shape. The table in Figure 11.4 also shows the marginal product of labor. This table helps us understand the important relationship between the marginal product of labor and the marginal cost of production: The marginal product of labor is *rising* for the first two workers, but the

**Figure 11.4**

**Jill Johnson's Marginal Cost and Average Total Cost of Producing Pizzas**

We can use the information in the table to calculate Jill's marginal cost and average total cost of producing pizzas. For the first two workers hired, the marginal product of labor is increasing. This increase causes the marginal cost of production to fall. For the last four workers hired, the marginal product of labor is falling. This causes the marginal cost of production to increase. Therefore, the marginal cost curve falls and then rises—that is, has a U shape—because the marginal product of labor rises and then falls. As long as marginal cost is below average total cost, average total cost will be falling. When marginal cost is above average total cost, average total cost will be rising. The relationship between marginal cost and average total cost explains why the average total cost curve also has a U shape.

| Quantity of Workers | Quantity of Pizzas | Marginal Product of Labor | Total Cost of Pizzas | Marginal Cost of Pizzas | Average Total Cost of Pizzas |
|---|---|---|---|---|---|
| 0 | 0 | — | $800 | — | — |
| 1 | 200 | 200 | 1,450 | $3.25 | $7.25 |
| 2 | 450 | 250 | 2,100 | 2.60 | 4.67 |
| 3 | 550 | 100 | 2,750 | 6.50 | 5.00 |
| 4 | 600 | 50 | 3,400 | 13.00 | 5.67 |
| 5 | 625 | 25 | 4,050 | 26.00 | 6.48 |
| 6 | 640 | 15 | 4,700 | 43.33 | 7.34 |

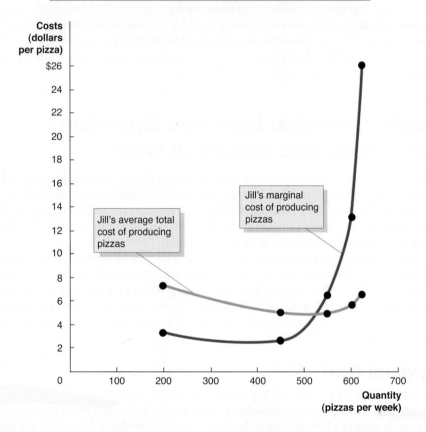

marginal cost of the pizzas produced by these workers is *falling*. The marginal product of labor is *falling* for the last four workers, but the marginal cost of pizzas produced by these workers is *rising*. To summarize this point: *When the marginal product of labor is rising, the marginal cost of output is falling. When the marginal product of labor is falling, the marginal cost of production is rising.*

One way to understand why this point is true is first to notice that the only additional cost to Jill from producing more pizzas is the additional wages she pays to hire more workers. She pays each new worker the same $650 per week. So the marginal cost of the additional pizzas each worker makes depends on that worker's additional output, or marginal product. As long as the additional output from each new worker is rising, the marginal cost of that output is falling. When the additional output from each new worker is falling, the marginal cost of that output is rising. *We can conclude that the marginal cost of production falls and then rises—forming a U shape—because the marginal product of labor rises and then falls.*

The relationship between marginal cost and average total cost follows the usual relationship between marginal and average values. As long as marginal cost is below average total cost, average total cost falls. When marginal cost is above average total cost, average total cost rises. Marginal cost equals average total cost when average total cost is at its lowest point. Therefore, the average total cost curve has a U shape because the marginal cost curve has a U shape.

# Solved Problem 11.4

## Calculating Marginal Cost and Average Cost

Santiago Delgado owns a copier store. He leases two copy machines for which he pays $12.50 each per day. He cannot increase the number of machines he leases without giving the office machine company six weeks' notice. He can hire as many workers as he wants, at a cost of $50 per day per worker. These are the only two inputs he uses to produce copies.

a. Fill in the remaining columns in the table below by using the definitions of costs.
b. Draw the average cost curve and marginal cost curve for Santiago's store. Do these curves have the expected shape? Briefly explain.

| Quantity of Workers | Quantity of Copies per Day | Fixed Cost | Variable Cost | Total Cost | Average Total Cost | Marginal Cost |
|---|---|---|---|---|---|---|
| 0 | 0 | | | | | |
| 1 | 625 | | | | | |
| 2 | 1,325 | | | | | |
| 3 | 2,200 | | | | | |
| 4 | 2,600 | | | | | |
| 5 | 2,900 | | | | | |
| 6 | 3,100 | | | | | |

## Solving the Problem

**Step 1:** **Review the chapter material.** This problem requires you to understand definitions of costs, so you may want to review the section "The Difference between Fixed Costs and Variable Costs" on page 355, and the section "Why Are the Marginal and Average Cost Curves U Shaped?" which begins on page 363.

**Step 2:** **Answer part a. by using the definitions of costs.** Santiago's fixed costs are the costs he pays to lease the copy machines. He uses two copy machines and pays $12.50 each to lease them, so his fixed cost is $25. Santiago's variable costs are the costs he pays to hire workers. He pays $50 per worker per day. His total cost is the sum of his fixed cost and his variable cost. His average total cost is his total cost divided by the quantity of copies he produces that day. His marginal cost is the change in total cost divided by the change in output. So, for example, his marginal cost of producing 1,325 copies per day, rather than 625 copies, is:

$$MC = (\$125 - \$75)/(1,325 - 625) = \$0.07.$$

| Quantity of Workers | Quantity of Copies per Day | Fixed Cost | Variable Cost | Total Cost | Average Total Cost | Marginal Cost |
|---|---|---|---|---|---|---|
| 0 | 0 | $25 | $0 | $25 | — | — |
| 1 | 625 | 25 | 50 | 75 | $0.12 | $0.08 |
| 2 | 1,325 | 25 | 100 | 125 | 0.09 | 0.07 |
| 3 | 2,200 | 25 | 150 | 175 | 0.08 | 0.06 |
| 4 | 2,600 | 25 | 200 | 225 | 0.09 | 0.13 |
| 5 | 2,900 | 25 | 250 | 275 | 0.09 | 0.17 |
| 6 | 3,100 | 25 | 300 | 325 | 0.10 | 0.25 |

**Step 3:** **Answer part b. by drawing the average total cost and marginal cost curves for Santiago's store and by explaining whether they have the usual shape.** You can use the numbers from the table to draw your graph:

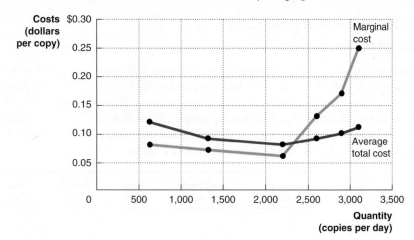

We expect average total cost and marginal cost curves to have a U shape, which Santiago's cost curves do. Both cost curves fall and then rise in the same way as the cost curves in Figure 11.4 on page 364.

MyEconLab **Your Turn:** For more practice, do related problem 4.6 on page 378 at the end of this chapter.

**11.5 LEARNING** OBJECTIVE

Graph average total cost, average variable cost, average fixed cost, and marginal cost.

**Average fixed cost** Fixed cost divided by the quantity of output produced.

**Average variable cost** Variable cost divided by the quantity of output produced.

# Graphing Cost Curves

We have seen that we calculate average total cost by dividing total cost by the quantity of output produced. Similarly, we can calculate **average fixed cost** by dividing fixed cost by the quantity of output produced. And we can calculate **average variable cost** by dividing variable cost by the quantity of output produced. Or, mathematically, with $Q$ being the level of output, we have:

$$\text{Average total cost} = ATC = \frac{TC}{Q}$$

$$\text{Average fixed cost} = AFC = \frac{FC}{Q}$$

$$\text{Average variable cost} = AVC = \frac{VC}{Q}.$$

Finally, notice that average total cost is the sum of average fixed cost plus average variable cost:

$$ATC = AFC + AVC.$$

The only fixed cost Jill incurs in operating her restaurant is the $800 per week she pays on the bank loan for her pizza ovens. Her variable costs are the wages she pays her workers. The table and graph in Figure 11.5 show Jill's costs.

We will use graphs like the one in Figure 11.5 in the next several chapters to analyze how firms decide the level of output to produce and the price to charge. Before going further, be sure you understand the following three key facts about Figure 11.5:

1. The marginal cost (*MC*), average total cost (*ATC*), and average variable cost (*AVC*) curves are all U shaped, and the marginal cost curve intersects the average variable

| Quantity of Workers | Quantity of Ovens | Quantity of Pizzas | Cost of Ovens (fixed cost) | Cost of Workers (variable cost) | Total Cost of Pizzas | ATC | AFC | AVC | MC |
|---|---|---|---|---|---|---|---|---|---|
| 0 | 2 | 0 | $800 | $0 | $800 | — | — | — | — |
| 1 | 2 | 200 | 800 | 650 | 1,450 | $7.25 | $4.00 | $3.25 | $3.25 |
| 2 | 2 | 450 | 800 | 1,300 | 2,100 | 4.67 | 1.78 | 2.89 | 2.60 |
| 3 | 2 | 550 | 800 | 1,950 | 2,750 | 5.00 | 1.45 | 3.54 | 6.50 |
| 4 | 2 | 600 | 800 | 2,600 | 3,400 | 5.67 | 1.33 | 4.33 | 13.00 |
| 5 | 2 | 625 | 800 | 3,250 | 4,050 | 6.48 | 1.28 | 5.20 | 26.00 |
| 6 | 2 | 640 | 800 | 3,900 | 4,700 | 7.34 | 1.25 | 6.09 | 43.33 |

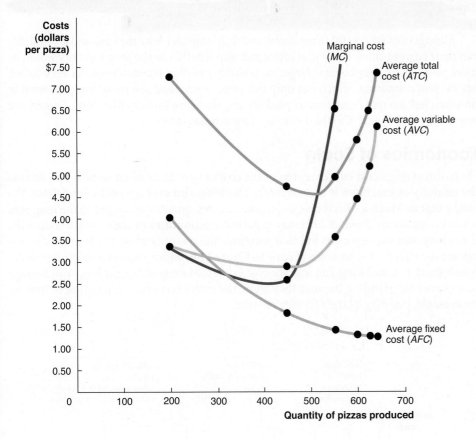

## Figure 11.5

### Costs at Jill Johnson's Restaurant

Jill's costs of making pizzas are shown in the table and plotted in the graph. Notice three important facts about the graph: (1) The marginal cost (*MC*), average total cost (*ATC*), and average variable cost (*AVC*) curves are all U shaped, and the marginal cost curve intersects both the average variable cost curve and average total cost curve at their minimum points. (2) As output increases, average fixed cost (*AFC*) gets smaller and smaller. (3) As output increases, the difference between average total cost and average variable cost decreases. Make sure you can explain why each of these three facts is true. You should spend time becoming familiar with this graph because it is one of the most important graphs in microeconomics.

cost curve and average total cost curve at their minimum points. When marginal cost is less than either average variable cost or average total cost, it causes them to decrease. When marginal cost is above average variable cost or average total cost, it causes them to increase. Therefore, when marginal cost equals average variable cost or average total cost, they must be at their minimum points.

2. As output increases, average fixed cost gets smaller and smaller. This happens because in calculating average fixed cost, we are dividing something that gets larger and larger—output—into something that remains constant—fixed cost. Firms often refer to this process of lowering average fixed cost by selling more output as "spreading the overhead" (where "overhead" refers to fixed costs).

3. As output increases, the difference between average total cost and average variable cost decreases. This happens because the difference between average total cost and average variable cost is average fixed cost, which gets smaller as output increases.

**11.6 LEARNING** OBJECTIVE

Understand how firms use the long-run average cost curve in their planning.

# Costs in the Long Run

The distinction between fixed cost and variable cost that we just discussed applies to the short run but *not* to the long run. For example, in the short run, Jill Johnson has fixed costs of $800 per week because she signed a loan agreement with a bank when she bought her pizza ovens. In the long run, the cost of purchasing more pizza ovens becomes variable because Jill can choose whether to expand her business by buying more ovens. The same would be true of any other fixed costs a company like Jill's might have. Once a company has purchased a fire insurance policy, the cost of the policy is fixed. But when the policy expires, the company must decide whether to renew it, and the cost becomes variable. The important point here is this: *In the long run, all costs are variable. There are no fixed costs in the long run.* In other words, in the long run, total cost equals variable cost, and average total cost equals average variable cost.

Managers of successful firms simultaneously consider how they can most profitably run their current store, factory, or office and also whether in the long run they would be more profitable if they became larger or, possibly, smaller. Jill must consider how to run her current restaurant, which has only two pizza ovens, and she must also plan what to do when her current bank loan is paid off and the lease on her store ends. Should she buy more pizza ovens? Should she lease a larger restaurant?

## Economies of Scale

**Long-run average cost curve** A curve that shows the lowest cost at which a firm is able to produce a given quantity of output in the long run, when no inputs are fixed.

**Economies of scale** The situation when a firm's long-run average costs fall as it increases the quantity of output it produces.

Short-run average cost curves represent the costs a firm faces when some input, such as the quantity of machines it uses, is fixed. The **long-run average cost curve** shows the lowest cost at which a firm is able to produce a given quantity of output in the long run, when no inputs are fixed. A firm may experience **economies of scale**, which means the firm's long-run average costs fall as it increases the quantity of output it produces. We can see the effects of economies of scale in Figure 11.6, which shows the relationship between short-run and long-run average cost curves. Managers can use long-run average cost curves for planning because they show the effect on cost of expanding output by, for example, building a larger factory or store.

## Figure 11.6

**The Relationship between Short-Run Average Cost and Long-Run Average Cost**

If a small bookstore expects to sell only 1,000 books per month, then it will be able to sell that quantity of books at the lowest average cost of $22 per book if it builds the small store represented by the *ATC* curve on the left of the figure. A larger bookstore will be able to sell 20,000 books per month at a lower cost of $18 per book. A bookstore selling 20,000 books per month and a bookstore selling 40,000 books per month will experience constant returns to scale and have the same average cost. A bookstore selling 20,000 books per month will have reached minimum efficient scale. Very large bookstores will experience diseconomies of scale, and their average costs will rise as sales increase beyond 40,000 books per month.

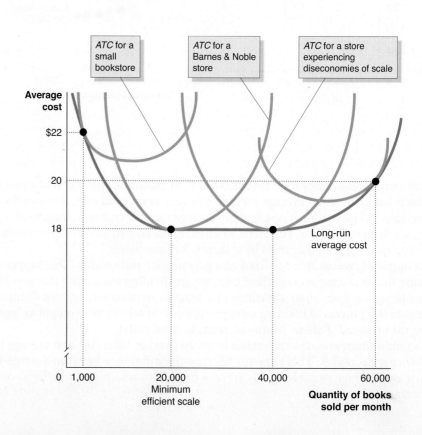

# Long-Run Average Cost Curves for Bookstores

Figure 11.6 shows long-run average cost in the retail bookstore industry. If a small bookstore expects to sell only 1,000 books per month, then it will be able to sell that quantity of books at the lowest average cost of $22 per book if it builds the small store represented by the *ATC* curve on the left of the figure. A much larger bookstore, such as one run by a national chain like Barnes & Noble, will be able to sell 20,000 books per month at a lower average cost of $18 per book. This decline in average cost from $22 to $18 represents the economies of scale that exist in bookselling. Why would the larger bookstore have lower average costs? One important reason is that the Barnes & Noble store is selling 20 times as many books per month as the small store but might need only six times as many workers. This saving in labor cost would reduce Barnes & Noble's average cost of selling books.

Firms may experience economies of scale for several reasons. First, as in the case of Barnes & Noble, the firm's technology may make it possible to increase production with a smaller proportional increase in at least one input. Second, both workers and managers can become more specialized, enabling them to become more productive, as output expands. Third, large firms, like Barnes & Noble, Wal-Mart, and General Motors, may be able to purchase inputs at lower costs than smaller competitors. In fact, as Wal-Mart expanded, its bargaining power with its suppliers increased, and its average costs fell. Finally, as a firm expands, it may be able to borrow money at a lower interest rate, thereby lowering its costs.

Economies of scale do not continue forever. The long-run average cost curve in most industries has a flat segment that often stretches over a substantial range of output. As Figure 11.6 shows, a bookstore selling 20,000 books per month and a bookstore selling 40,000 books per month have the same average cost. Over this range of output, firms in the industry experience **constant returns to scale**. As these firms increase their output, they have to increase their inputs, such as the size of the store and the quantity of workers, proportionally. The level of output at which all economies of scale are exhausted is known as **minimum efficient scale**. A bookstore selling 20,000 books per month has reached minimum efficient scale.

Very large bookstores experience increasing average costs as managers begin to have difficulty coordinating the operation of the store. Figure 11.6 shows that for sales above 40,000 books per month, firms in the industry experience **diseconomies of scale**. Firms in the auto industry can also experience diseconomies of scale. For instance, Toyota found that as it expanded production at its Georgetown, Kentucky, plant and its plants in China, its managers had difficulty keeping average cost from rising. The president of Toyota's Georgetown plant was quoted as saying, "Demand for . . . high volumes saps your energy. Over a period of time, it eroded our focus . . . [and] thinned out the expertise and knowledge we painstakingly built up over the years." One analysis of the problems Toyota faced in expanding production concluded: "It is the kind of paradox many highly successful companies face: Getting bigger doesn't always mean getting better."

**Constant returns to scale** The situation in which a firm's long-run average costs remain unchanged as it increases output.

**Minimum efficient scale** The level of output at which all economies of scale are exhausted.

**Diseconomies of scale** The situation in which a firm's long-run average costs rise as the firm increases output.

# Solved Problem 11.6

## Using Long-Run Average Cost Curves to Understand Business Strategy

In 2011, the port of Rotterdam in the Netherlands was in the process of expanding its capacity from 9.7 million containers processed per year to 18.2 million containers processed per year. An article in the *Wall Street Journal* described the port as attempting to "provide economies of scale to shippers." Shippers using the port expected that the fees charged to process their containers would decline following the expansion.

**a.** What does it mean to say that expanding the size of the port will "provide economies of scale to shippers"?

**b.** Use a long-run average total cost curve to explain why the expansion of the port might result in lower fees to shippers.

## Solving the Problem

**Step 1:** **Review the chapter material.** This problem is about the long-run average cost curve, so you may want to review the material in the section "Costs in the Long Run," which begins on page 368.

**Step 2:** **Answer part a by explaining what it means for the port to "provide economies of scale to shippers."** If by expanding, the port of Rotterdam will lower its average cost of processing a shipping container, then the port was operating at less than minimum efficient scale. In that case, the expansion of the port would provide economies of scale to shippers by lowering the average cost of processing a container.

**Step 3:** **Draw a long-run average cost graph for the port.** The problem provides us with enough information to draw the following graph:

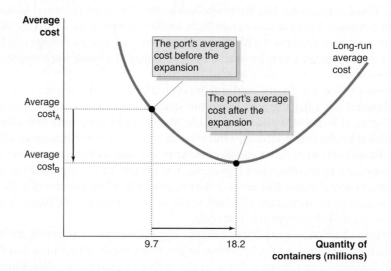

**Step 4:** **Use your graph to explain why the expansion of the port might result in lower fees to shippers.** Before the expansion, the port was below minimum efficient scale and was processing 9.7 million containers per year, at an average cost of Average cost$_A$. By expanding, the port can move to the minimum efficient scale of 18.2 million containers per year, and average cost falls to Average cost$_B$. (We can't be sure whether the expansion will actually take the port to minimum efficient scale, but it seems likely that the engineers and economists advising the port's managers would suggest an expansion that would raise capacity to that level.) With lower costs, the port may reduce the fees that they charge shippers, which is what shippers were expecting.

Based on John W. Miller, "For Port Expansion, It's Full Speed Ahead," *Wall Street Journal*, October 26, 2010.

MyEconLab **Your Turn:** For more practice, do related problems 6.7, 6.8, 6.9, and 6.10 on page 381 at the end of this chapter.

Over time, most firms in an industry will build factories or stores that are at least as large as the minimum efficient scale but not so large that diseconomies of scale occur. In the bookstore industry, stores will sell between 20,000 and 40,000 books per month. However, firms often do not know the exact shape of their long-run average cost curves. As a result, they may mistakenly build factories or stores that are either too large or too small.

## Making the Connection | The Colossal River Rouge: Diseconomies of Scale at Ford Motor Company

*Was Ford's River Rouge plant too big?*

When Henry Ford started the Ford Motor Company in 1903, automobile companies produced cars in small workshops, using highly skilled workers. Ford introduced two new ideas that allowed him to take advantage of economies of scale. First, Ford used identical—or, interchangeable—parts so that unskilled workers could assemble the cars. Second, instead of having groups of workers moving from one stationary automobile to the next, he had the workers remain stationary, while the automobiles moved along an assembly line. Ford built a large factory at Highland Park, outside Detroit, where he used these ideas to produce the famous Model T at an average cost well below what his competitors could match using older production methods in smaller factories.

Ford believed that he could produce automobiles at an even lower average cost by building a still larger plant along the River Rouge in Dearborn, Michigan. Unfortunately, Ford's River Rouge plant was too large and suffered from diseconomies of scale. Ford's managers had great difficulty coordinating the production of automobiles in such a large plant. The following description of the River Rouge comes from a biography of Ford by Allan Nevins and Frank Ernest Hill:

> A total of 93 separate structures stood on the [River Rouge] site. . . . Railroad trackage covered 93 miles, conveyors 27 [miles]. About 75,000 men worked in the great plant. A force of 5000 did nothing but keep it clean, wearing out 5000 mops and 3000 brooms a month, and using 86 tons of soap on the floors, walls, and 330 acres of windows. The Rouge was an industrial city, immense, concentrated, packed with power. . . . By its very massiveness and complexity, it denied men at the top contact with and understanding of those beneath, and gave those beneath a sense of being lost in inexorable immensity and power.

Beginning in 1927, Ford produced the Model A—its only car model at that time—at the River Rouge plant. Ford failed to achieve economies of scale and actually *lost money* on each of the four Model A body styles.

Ford could not raise the price of the Model A to make it profitable because at a higher price, the car could not compete with similar models produced by competitors such as General Motors and Chrysler. He eventually reduced the cost of making the Model A by constructing smaller factories spread out across the country. These smaller factories produced the Model A at a lower average cost than was possible at the River Rouge plant.

From Allan Nevins and Frank Ernest Hill, *Ford: Expansion and Challenge*, 1915–1933, (New York: Scribner, 1957), pp. 293, 295.

**Your Turn:** Test your understanding by doing related problems 6.11 and 6.12 on page 382 at the end of this chapter.    MyEconLab

# Don't Let This Happen to You

## Don't Confuse Diminishing Returns with Diseconomies of Scale

The concepts of diminishing returns and diseconomies of scale may seem similar, but, in fact, they are unrelated. Diminishing returns applies only to the short run, when at least one of the firm's inputs, such as the quantity of machinery it uses, is fixed. The law of diminishing returns tells us that in the short run, hiring more workers will, at some point, result in less additional output. Diminishing returns explains why marginal cost curves eventually slope upward. Diseconomies of scale apply only in the long run, when the firm is free to vary all its inputs, can adopt new technology, and can vary the amount of machinery it uses and the size of its facility. Diseconomies of scale explain why long-run average cost curves eventually slope upward.

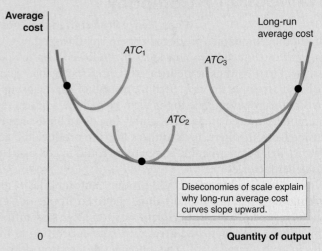

**MyEconLab**

**Your Turn:** Test your understanding by doing related problem 6.14 on page 382 at the end of this chapter.

---

Continued from page 353

## Economics in Your Life

### Using Cost Concepts in Your Own Business

At the beginning of the chapter, we asked you to suppose that you are about to open a store to sell recliners. Both you and a competing store, Bob's Big Chairs, can buy recliners from the manufacturer for $300 each. But because Bob's sells more recliners per month than you expect to be able to sell, his costs per recliner are lower than yours. We asked you to think about why this might be true. In this chapter, we have seen that firms often experience declining average costs as the quantity they sell increases. A key reason Bob's average costs might be lower than yours has to do with fixed costs. Because your store is the same size as Bob's store, you may be paying about the same amount to lease the store space. You may also be paying about the same amounts for utilities, insurance, and advertising. All these are fixed costs because they do not change as the quantity of recliners you sell changes. Because Bob's fixed costs are the same as yours, but he is selling more recliners, his average fixed costs are lower than yours, and, therefore, so are his average total costs. With lower average total costs, he can sell his recliners for a lower price than you do and still make a profit.

# Conclusion

In this chapter, we discussed the relationship between a firm's technology, production, and costs. In the discussion, we encountered a number of definitions of costs. Because we will use these definitions in later chapters, it is useful to bring them together in Table 11.4 for you to review.

We have seen the important relationship between a firm's level of production and its costs. Just as this information was vital to Akio Morita in deciding what price to charge for his transistor radios, so it remains vital today to all firms as they attempt to decide the optimal level of production and the optimal prices to charge for their products. We will explore this point further in Chapter 12. Before moving on to that chapter, read *An Inside Look at Policy* on the next page to see how federal subsidies have helped a technology firm lower production costs for solar panels.

**Table 11.4**

**A Summary of Definitions of Cost**

| Term | Definition | Symbols and Equations |
|------|-----------|----------------------|
| Total cost | The cost of all the inputs used by a firm, or fixed cost plus variable cost | $TC$ |
| Fixed costs | Costs that remain constant as a firm's level of output changes | $FC$ |
| Variable costs | Costs that change as the firm's level of output changes | $VC$ |
| Marginal cost | An increase in total cost resulting from producing another unit of output | $MC = \dfrac{\Delta TC}{\Delta Q}$ |
| Average total cost | Total cost divided by the quantity of output produced | $ATC = \dfrac{TC}{Q}$ |
| Average fixed cost | Fixed cost divided by the quantity of output produced | $AFC = \dfrac{FC}{Q}$ |
| Average variable cost | Variable cost divided by the quantity of output produced | $AVC = \dfrac{VC}{Q}$ |
| Implicit cost | A nonmonetary opportunity cost | — |
| Explicit cost | A cost that involves spending money | — |

# New Technology Could Lower the Cost of Solar Panels

## CHRISTIAN SCIENCE MONITOR

## US boosts 'game-changer' solar technology in bid for global market share

Solar power as cheap as coal, that's the holy grail of the solar power industry.

It's an elusive goal that has more than a few skeptics saying solar—no matter how much advocates pump it—will always remain the energy source of the future, and not the present.

"They're always just five years off no matter what year it is, in order to justify continued subsidies," said a Wall Street Journal editorial last July, referring to photovoltaic and other renewable energy sources. Solar is "a speculative and immature technology that costs far more than ordinary power."

But the US Department of Energy isn't buying that—just the opposite. In the past two years the Energy Department has offered over $12 billion in loan guarantees for 16 solar projects—about two thirds of the recipients are power plants, the rest are solar manufacturers—with stimulus funds from the 2009 American Recovery and Reinvestment Act.

Friday the DOE once again hammered home its view that solar's promise is real, with a $150 million loan guarantee to 1366 Technologies, a Lexington, Mass.-based solar wafer manufacturing company that has a great new technology—but no manufacturing plant. Now it will.

"This project is a game-changer that could dramatically lower the cost of photovoltaic solar cells," said Energy Secretary Steven Chu. "As global demand for solar cells increase, this kind of technology will help the US increase its market share."

For 1366 Technologies—the company is named for the amount of energy in watts that strikes the earth's atmosphere per square meter—the DOE's vote of confidence is a big deal. The company, started in 2007 on the idea of MIT professor Emanuel Sachs, will now finally be able to demonstrate in production a technology that company officials say could vault the US to technological leadership in the manufacturing of solar cells.

Using an innovative process, the company plans to cast silicon wafers for solar panels directly from the molten output of an industrial furnace—rather than cut ingots of pure silicon with a special saw. That change alone saves fully half of the high-cost silicon usually wasted in that process. In addition, the company has figured out how to coat its wafers with materials that boost their efficiency.

"With this loan, 1366 will realize its goal to make solar energy as cheap as coal while helping the US to reclaim a key part of the silicon supply chain and restore the nation's dominance in photovoltaics," Frank van Mierlo, 1366's president, said in a statement.

Part of the plan is not only to manufacture the photovoltaic cells more efficiently but also to produce at least a three percentage point gain in the solar cells' output. Their goal is to reduce the cost of manufacturing a photovoltaic cell to less than $1 per watt.

With the federal loan guarantee, the company is already scouting for a site for its first production plant, which it hopes will be manufacturing 200 megawatts of wafers annually by 2013. Right on the heels of that, it plans to build another facility capable of producing a 1,000 megawatts of wafers per year.

Solar power advocates say there are signs that the industry is on track to be competitive, though costs still need to be cut.

"There's tremendous progress being made in the solar power industry with costs of photovoltaics coming down dramatically," says Robert Margolis, a senior energy analyst for the National Renewable Energy Laboratory. "Solar module [panel] prices are dropping rapidly this year—about 10–20 percent already this year—and expected to continue dropping rapidly."

For solar power to compete without subsidies with coal, the Department of Energy says, the installed cost of solar energy modules needs to drop another 75 percent.

At the current rates of declining cost, the DOE and others project, solar will be competitive with coal in 2020.

At that point, the DOE website says, there will be "rapid, large-scale adoption of solar electricity across the United States . . . ."

## Key Points in the Article

A company called 1366 Technologies has developed new technologies to manufacture solar cells. A loan guarantee from the U.S. Department of Energy will allow 1366 Technologies to build a plant where it can produce photovoltaic solar cells and increase its share of the global solar energy market. The solar power industry is becoming more competitive as costs decline, but costs must fall even further for the industry to compete with more traditional energy sources without government subsidies.

## Analyzing the News

**a** Many countries are advocating the use of alternative energy sources, but the relatively high cost of the inputs needed, such as solar panels, has been an obstacle. When a product with a new technology is introduced, companies often initially charge high selling prices in an attempt to recoup what were probably high development costs. The high selling prices often limit sales to a small number of customers, and the low production numbers can make it difficult for a company to realize economies of scale. This is precisely what occurred when solar panels were first introduced to the market. In the figure below, we see that the average total cost of producing solar panels is high because

the initial quantity produced by the manufacturer is relatively low. The manufacturer can lower its average total cost ($ATC_A$ to $ATC_B$) by increasing production ($Q_A$ to $Q_B$), but it will likely have to decrease the selling price to be able to sell the higher production quantity. Solar panel manufacturers are taking a risk by increasing production in an attempt to realize economies of scale because they have no guarantee of being able to charge a price that is low enough to sell the higher quantity and still high enough to be profitable.

**b** Massachusetts-based 1366 Technologies has developed technologies to significantly decrease the cost of producing the photovoltaic cells used in the production of solar panels and to also increase their efficiency. The company believes these advances will result in more powerful solar panels being produced at a lower cost than those currently available in the market. This company would realize economies of scale by increasing production to lower its average total cost and charging a price low enough to sell the larger quantity.

**c** Federal subsidies have helped to lower production costs for solar power industries in the United States and have allowed domestic manufacturers to become more competitive in the global market, but solar advocates acknowledge that costs need to continue to fall. As costs decline, the market

for solar energy products should be further stimulated as more consumers and businesses become willing to use solar power to meet all or part of their energy needs. According to the Department of Energy, the installed cost of solar energy panels needs to fall by an additional 75 percent before solar power can compete without subsidies against electricity generated by coal.

## Thinking Critically

1. Suppose that 1366 Technologies can produce 200,000 solar wafers per year at lowest average total cost if it builds a 10,000 square foot factory. Also suppose that the firm can produce 400,000 solar wafers per year at lowest average total cost if it builds a 15,000 square foot factory. Draw a graph showing the average total cost curves representing these two factories. In drawing the graph, assume that 1366 Technologies experiences economies of scale over this range of output.

2. 1366 Technologies is the first manufacturer to cast silicon wafers for solar panels directly from the molten output of an industrial furnace. How might being the first in the market to use this technology be an advantage to 1366 Technologies? How might it be a risk?

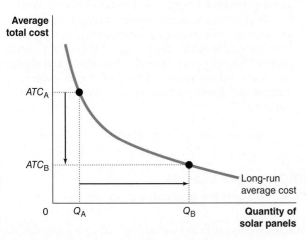

A manufacturer of solar panels can lower its average total cost by increasing production.

# Chapter Summary and Problems

## Key Terms

Average fixed cost, p. 366

Average product of labor, p. 361

Average total cost, p. 358

Average variable cost, p. 366

Constant returns to scale, p. 369

Diseconomies of scale, p. 369

Economies of scale, p. 368

Explicit cost, p. 356

Fixed costs, p. 355

Implicit cost, p. 356

Law of diminishing returns, p. 359

Long run, p. 355

Long-run average cost curve, p. 368

Marginal cost, p. 363

Marginal product of labor, p. 359

Minimum efficient scale, p. 369

Opportunity cost, p. 356

Production function, p. 357

Short run, p. 355

Technological change, p. 354

Technology, p. 354

Total cost, p. 355

Variable costs, p. 355

---

**11.1**  **Technology: An Economic Definition, pages 354–355**
LEARNING OBJECTIVE: Define technology and give examples of technological change.

### Summary

The basic activity of a firm is to use inputs, such as workers, machines, and natural resources, to produce goods and services. The firm's **technology** is the processes it uses to turn inputs into goods and services. **Technological change** refers to a change in the ability of a firm to produce a given level of output with a given quantity of inputs.

 Visit **www.myeconlab.com** to complete these exercises online and get instant feedback.

### Review Questions

**1.1** What is the difference between technology and technological change?

**1.2** Is it possible for technological change to be negative? If so, give an example.

### Problems and Applications

**1.3** Briefly explain whether you agree with the following observation: "Technological change refers only to the introduction of new products, so it is not relevant to the operations of most firms."

**1.4** Which of the following are examples of a firm experiencing positive technological change?
   **a.** A fall in oil prices leads United Airlines to lower its ticket prices.
   **b.** A training program makes a firm's workers more productive.
   **c.** An exercise program makes a firm's workers more healthy and productive.
   **d.** A firm cuts its workforce and is able to maintain its initial level of output.
   **e.** A firm rearranges the layout of its factory and finds that by using its initial set of inputs, it can produce exactly as much as before.

**1.5** **[Related to the** Making the Connection **on page 354]** The 7-Eleven chain of convenience stores in Japan reorganized its system for supplying its stores with food. This led to a sharp reduction in the number of trucks the company had to use, while increasing the amount of fresh food on store shelves. Someone discussing 7-Eleven's new system argues, "This is not an example of technological change because it did not require the use of new machinery or equipment." Briefly explain whether you agree with this argument.

---

**11.2**  **The Short Run and the Long Run in Economics, pages 355–359**
LEARNING OBJECTIVE: Distinguish between the economic short run and the economic long run.

### Summary

In the **short run**, a firm's technology and the size of its factory, store, or office are fixed. In the **long run**, a firm is able to adopt new technology and to increase or decrease the size of its physical plant. **Total cost** is the cost of all the inputs a firm uses in production. **Variable costs** are costs that change as output changes. **Fixed costs** are costs that remain constant as output changes. **Opportunity cost** is the highest-valued alternative that must be given up to engage in an activity. An **explicit cost** is a cost that involves spending money. An **implicit cost** is a nonmonetary opportunity cost. The relationship between the inputs employed by a firm and the maximum output it can produce with those inputs is called the firm's **production function**.

 Visit **www.myeconlab.com** to complete these exercises online and get instant feedback.

### Review Questions

**2.1** What is the difference between the short run and the long run? Is the amount of time that separates the short run from the long run the same for every firm?

**2.2** Distinguish between a firm's fixed cost and variable cost and give an example of each.

**2.3** What are implicit costs? How are they different from explicit costs?

**2.4** What is the production function? What does the short-run production function hold constant?

## Problems and Applications

**2.5** An article in *BusinessWeek* discussed Apple's cost to produce the iPod shuffle: "All told, the cost of the shuffle's components, the headphones, and the packaging it ships in comes to $21.77 . . . That's about 28% of the device's retail price [of $79]." Can we conclude from this information that Apple is making a profit of about $57 per shuffle? Briefly explain.

Based on Arik Hesseldahl, "Deconstructing Apple's Tiny iPod Shuffle," *BusinessWeek*, April 13, 2009.

**2.6** **[Related to the** Making the Connection **on page 356]** Many firms consider their wage costs to be variable costs. Why do publishers usually consider their wage and salary costs to be fixed costs? Are the costs of utilities always fixed, are they always variable, or can they be both? Briefly explain.

**2.7** **[Related to the** Making the Connection **on page 356]** For Jill Johnson's pizza restaurant, explain whether each of the following is a fixed cost or a variable cost:
  **a.** The payment she makes on her fire insurance policy
  **b.** The payment she makes to buy pizza dough
  **c.** The wages she pays her workers
  **d.** The lease payment she makes to the landlord who owns the building where her store is located
  **e.** The $300-per-month payment she makes to her local newspaper for running her weekly advertisements

**2.8** **[Related to the** Making the Connection **on page 356]** The *Statistical Abstract of the United States* is published each year by the U.S. Census Bureau. It provides a summary of business, economic, social, and political statistics. It is available for free online, and a printed copy can also be purchased from the U.S. Government Printing Office for $39. Because government documents are not copyrighted, anyone can print copies of the *Statistical Abstract* and sell them. Each year, one or two companies typically will print and sell copies for a significantly lower price than the Government Printing Office does. The copies of the *Statistical Abstract* that these companies sell are usually identical to those sold by the government, except for having different covers. How can these companies sell the same book for a lower price than the government and still cover their costs?

**2.9** Suppose that Bill owns an automobile collision repair shop. The table below shows how the quantity of cars Bill can repair per month depends on the number of workers that he hires. Assume that he pays each worker $4,000 per month and his fixed cost is $6,000 per month. Using the information provided, complete the table.

| Quantity of Workers | Quantity of Cars per Month | Fixed Cost | Variable Cost | Total Cost | Average Total Cost |
|---|---|---|---|---|---|
| 0 | 0 | $6,000 | | | — |
| 1 | 20 | | | | |
| 2 | 30 | | | | |
| 3 | 40 | | | | |
| 4 | 50 | | | | |
| 5 | 55 | | | | |

**2.10** In 2008, Clay Bennett, the owner of the then Seattle Supersonics NBA basketball team (now the Oklahoma City Thunder), estimated that if the team remained in Seattle, he would suffer a loss of about $63 million over the following two seasons. If the team were allowed to move to Oklahoma City, he estimated that he would earn a profit of $19 million. What was the opportunity cost to Bennett of his team playing in Seattle rather than Oklahoma City? Briefly explain.

Based on Jim Brunner, "New Details Emerge from Sonics Owner's Combative Deposition," *Seattle Times*, June 7, 2008.

**2.11** Suppose Jill Johnson operates her pizza restaurant in a building she owns in the center of the city. Similar buildings in the neighborhood rent for $4,000 per month. Jill is considering selling her building and renting space in the suburbs for $3,000 per month. Jill decides not to make the move. She reasons, "I would like to have a restaurant in the suburbs, but I pay no rent for my restaurant now, and I don't want to see my costs rise by $3,000 per month." Evaluate Jill's reasoning.

**2.12** When the DuPont chemical company first attempted to enter the paint business, it was not successful. According to a company report, in one year it "lost nearly $500,000 in actual cash in addition to an expected return on investment of nearly $500,000, which made a total loss of income to the company of nearly a million." Why did this report include as part of the company's loss the amount it had expected to earn—but didn't—on its investment in manufacturing paint?

From Alfred D. Chandler, Jr., Thomas K. McCraw, and Richard Tedlow, *Management Past and Present*, © 2000 Cengage Learning, Inc. Reproduced by permission. www.cengage.com/permissions.

---

**11.3** **The Marginal Product of Labor and the Average Product of Labor,** pages 359–363

LEARNING OBJECTIVE: Understand the relationship between the marginal product of labor and the average product of labor.

## Summary

The **marginal product of labor** is the additional output produced by a firm as a result of hiring one more worker. Specialization and division of labor cause the marginal product of labor to rise for the first few workers hired. Eventually, the **law of diminishing returns** causes the marginal product of labor to decline. The **average product of labor** is the total amount of output produced by a firm divided by the quantity of workers hired. When the marginal product of labor is greater than the average product of labor, the average product of labor increases. When the marginal product of labor is less than the average product of labor, the average product of labor decreases.

## Review Questions

3.1 Draw a graph that shows the usual relationship between the marginal product of labor and the average product of labor. Why do the marginal product of labor and the average product of labor have the shapes you drew?

3.2 How do specialization and division of labor typically affect the marginal product of labor?

3.3 What is the law of diminishing returns? Does it apply in the long run?

## Problems and Applications

3.4 Fill in the missing values in the following table:

| Quantity of Workers | Total Output | Marginal Product of Labor | Average Product of Labor |
|---|---|---|---|
| 0 | 0 | | |
| 1 | 400 | | |
| 2 | 900 | | |
| 3 | 1,500 | | |
| 4 | 1,900 | | |
| 5 | 2,200 | | |
| 6 | 2,400 | | |
| 7 | 2,300 | | |

3.5 Use the numbers from problem 3.4 to draw one graph that shows how total output increases with the quantity of workers hired and a second graph that shows the marginal product of labor and the average product of labor.

3.6 A student looks at the data in Table 11.3 on page 359 and draws this conclusion:

> The marginal product of labor is increasing for the first two workers hired, and then it declines for the next four workers. I guess each of the first two workers must have been hard workers. Then Jill must have had to settle for increasingly poor workers.

Do you agree with the student's analysis? Briefly explain.

3.7 **[Related to the** Making the Connection **on page 361]** Briefly explain whether you agree with the following argument:

> Adam Smith's idea of the gains to firms from the division of labor makes a lot of sense when the good being manufactured is something complex like automobiles or computers, but it doesn't apply in the manufacturing of less complex goods or in other sectors of the economy, such as retail sales.

3.8 Sally looks at her college transcript and says to you, "How is this possible? My grade point average for this semester's courses is higher than my grade point average for last semester's courses, but my cumulative grade point average still went down from last semester to this semester." Explain to Sally how this is possible.

3.9 Is it possible for a firm to experience a technological change that would increase the marginal product of labor while leaving the average product of labor unchanged? Explain.

---

 **11.4**   **The Relationship between Short-Run Production and Short-Run Cost,** pages 363–366

LEARNING OBJECTIVE: Explain and illustrate the relationship between marginal cost and average total cost.

## Summary

The **marginal cost** of production is the increase in total cost resulting from producing another unit of output. The marginal cost curve has a U shape because when the marginal product of labor is rising, the marginal cost of output is falling, and when the marginal product of labor is falling, the marginal cost of output is rising. When marginal cost is less than average total cost, average total cost falls. When marginal cost is greater than average total cost, average total cost rises. Therefore, average total cost also has a U shape.

## Review Questions

4.1 What is the difference between the average cost of production and marginal cost of production?

4.2 If the marginal product of labor is rising, is the marginal cost of production rising or falling? Briefly explain.

4.3 Explain why the marginal cost curve intersects the average total cost curve at the level of output where average total cost is at a minimum.

## Problems and Applications

4.4 Is it possible for average total cost to be decreasing over a range of output where marginal cost is increasing? Briefly explain.

4.5 Suppose a firm has no fixed costs, so all its costs are variable, even in the short run.
   a. If the firm's marginal costs are continually increasing (that is, marginal cost is increasing from the first unit of output produced), will the firm's average total cost curve have a U shape?
   b. If the firm's marginal costs are $5 at every level of output, what shape will the firm's average total cost have?

4.6 **[Related to** Solved Problem 11.4 **on page 365]** Santiago Delgado owns a copier store. He leases two copy machines for which he pays $20 each per day. He cannot increase the number of machines he leases without giving the office machine company six weeks' notice. He can hire as many workers as he wants, at a cost of $40 per day per worker. These are the only two inputs he uses to produce copies.

a. Fill in the remaining columns in the table below.

b. Draw the average total cost curve and marginal cost curve for Santiago's store. Do these curves have the expected shape? Briefly explain.

| Quantity of Workers | Quantity of Copies per Day | Fixed Cost | Variable Cost | Total Cost | Average Total Cost | Marginal Cost |
|---|---|---|---|---|---|---|
| 0 | 0 | | | | | |
| 1 | 600 | | | | | |
| 2 | 1,100 | | | | | |
| 3 | 1,500 | | | | | |
| 4 | 1,800 | | | | | |
| 5 | 2,000 | | | | | |
| 6 | 2,100 | | | | | |

**4.7** Is Jill Johnson correct when she says the following: "I am currently producing 10,000 pizzas per month at a total cost of $50,000.00. If I produce 10,001 pizzas, my total cost will rise to $50,011.00. Therefore, my marginal cost of producing pizzas must be increasing." Draw a graph to illustrate your answer.

**4.8** Is Jill Johnson correct when she says the following: "I am currently producing 20,000 pizzas per month at a total cost of $75,000. If I produce 20,001 pizzas, my total cost will rise to $75,002. Therefore, my marginal cost of producing pizzas must be increasing." Illustrate your answer with a graph.

**4.9** (This problem is somewhat advanced.) Using symbols, we can write that the marginal product of labor is equal to $\Delta Q/\Delta L$. Marginal cost is equal to $\Delta TC/\Delta Q$. Because fixed costs by definition don't change, marginal cost is also equal to $\Delta VC/\Delta Q$. If Jill Johnson's only variable cost ($VC$) is labor cost, then her variable cost is just the wage multiplied by the quantity of workers hired, or $wL$.

a. If the wage Jill pays is constant, then what is $\Delta VC$ in terms of $w$ and $L$?

b. Use your answer to question a. and the expressions given above for the marginal product of labor and the marginal cost of output to find an expression for marginal cost, $\Delta TC/\Delta Q$, in terms of the wage, $w$, and the marginal product of labor, $\Delta Q/\Delta L$.

c. Use your answer to question b. to determine Jill's marginal cost of producing pizzas if the wage is $750 per week and the marginal product of labor is 150 pizzas. If the wage falls to $600 per week and the marginal product of labor is unchanged, what happens to Jill's marginal cost? If the wage is unchanged at $750 per week and the marginal product of labor rises to 250 pizzas, what happens to Jill's marginal cost?

---

**11.5** ## Graphing Cost Curves, pages 366–367

LEARNING OBJECTIVE: Graph average total cost, average variable cost, average fixed cost, and marginal cost.

## Summary

**Average fixed cost** is equal to fixed cost divided by the level of output. **Average variable cost** is equal to variable cost divided by the level of output. Figure 11.5 on page 367 shows the relationship among marginal cost, average total cost, average variable cost, and average fixed cost. It is one of the most important graphs in microeconomics.

 MyEconLab    Visit **www.myeconlab.com** to complete these exercises online and get instant feedback.

## Review Questions

**5.1** As the level of output increases, what happens to the value of average fixed cost?

**5.2** As the level of output increases, what happens to the difference between the value of average total cost and average variable cost?

## Problems and Applications

**5.3** Suppose the total cost of producing 10,000 tennis balls is $30,000, and the fixed cost is $10,000.

a. What is the variable cost?

b. When output is 10,000, what are the average variable cost and the average fixed cost?

c. Assuming that the cost curves have the usual shape, is the dollar difference between the average total cost and the average variable cost greater when the output is 10,000 tennis balls or when the output is 30,000 tennis balls? Explain.

**5.4** One description of the costs of operating a railroad makes the following observation: "The fixed . . . expenses which attach to the operation of railroads . . . are in the nature of a tax upon the business of the road; the smaller the [amount of] business, the larger the tax." Briefly explain why fixed costs are like a tax. In what sense is this tax smaller when the amount of business is larger?

From Alfred D. Chandler, Jr., Thomas K. McCraw, and Richard Tedlow, *Management Past and Present*, © 2000 Cengage Learning, Inc. Reproduced by permission. www.cengage.com/permissions.

**5.5** In the ancient world, a book could be produced either on a scroll or as a codex, which was made of folded sheets glued together, something like a modern book. One scholar has estimated the following variable costs (in Greek drachmas) of the two methods:

| | Scroll | Codex |
|---|---|---|
| Cost of writing (wage of a scribe) | 11.33 drachmas | 11.33 drachmas |
| Cost of paper | 16.50 drachmas | 9.25 drachmas |

Another scholar points out that a significant fixed cost was involved in producing a codex:

> In order to copy a codex . . . the amount of text and the layout of each page had to be carefully calculated in advance to determine the exact number of sheets . . . needed. No doubt, this is more time-consuming and calls for more experimentation than the production of a scroll would. But for the next copy, these calculations would be used again.

a. Suppose that the fixed cost of preparing a codex was 58 drachmas and that there was no similar fixed cost for a scroll. Would an ancient book publisher who intended to sell 5 copies of a book be likely to publish it as a scroll or as a codex? What if he intended to sell 10 copies? Briefly explain.

b. Although most books were published as scrolls in the first century A.D., by the third century, most were published as codices. Considering only the factors mentioned in this problem, explain why this change may have taken place.

Based on T. C. Skeat, "The Length of the Standard Papyrus Roll and the Cost-Advantage of the Codex," *Zeitschrift fur Pspyrologie and Epigraphik*, (Germany: Rudolph Habelt, 1982), p. 175; and David Trobisch, *The First Edition of the New Testament*, (New York: Oxford University Press, 2000), p. 73.

**5.6** Use the information in the graph below to find the values for the following at an output level of 1,000.

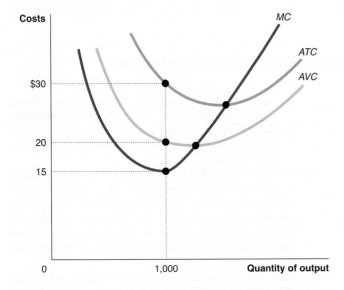

a. Marginal cost
b. Total cost
c. Variable cost
d. Fixed cost

**5.7** List the errors in the following graph. Carefully explain why the curves drawn this way are wrong. In other words, why can't these curves be as they are shown in the graph?

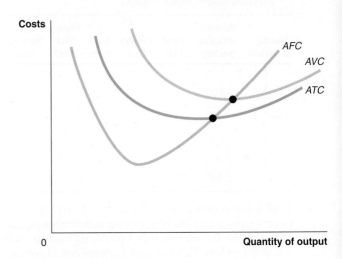

**5.8** Explain how the events listed in a. through d. would affect the following costs at Southwest Airlines:

1. Marginal cost
2. Average variable cost
3. Average fixed cost
4. Average total cost

a. Southwest signs a new contract with the Transport Workers Union that requires the airline to increase wages for its flight attendants.

b. The federal government starts to levy a $20-per-passenger carbon emissions tax on all commercial air travel.

c. Southwest decides on an across-the-board 10 percent cut in executive salaries.

d. Southwest decides to double its television advertising budget.

---

**11.6** ## Costs in the Long Run, pages 368–372

LEARNING OBJECTIVE: Understand how firms use the long-run average cost curve in their planning.

## Summary

The **long-run average cost curve** shows the lowest cost at which a firm is able to produce a given level of output in the long run. For many firms, the long-run average cost curve falls as output expands because of **economies of scale. Minimum efficient scale** is the level of output at which all economies of scale have been exhausted. After economies of scale have been exhausted, firms experience **constant returns to scale**, where their long-run average cost curve is flat. At high levels of output, the long-run average cost curve turns up as the firm experiences **diseconomies of scale**.

MyEconLab  Visit **www.myeconlab.com** to complete these exercises online and get instant feedback.

## Review Questions

**6.1** What is the difference between total cost and variable cost in the long run?

**6.2** What is minimum efficient scale? What is likely to happen in the long run to firms that do not reach minimum efficient scale?

**6.3** What are economies of scale? What are four reasons that firms may experience economies of scale?

**6.4** What are diseconomies of scale? What is the main reason that a firm eventually encounters diseconomies of scale as it keeps increasing the size of its store or factory?

**6.5** Why can short-run average cost never be less than long-run average cost for a given level of output?

## Problems and Applications

**6.6** Factories for producing computer chips are called "fabs." As the semiconductors used in computer chips have become smaller and smaller, the machines necessary to make them have become more and more expensive. According to an article in the *Economist* magazine:

> To reach the economies of scale needed to make such investments pay, chipmakers must build bigger fabs. . . . In 1966 a new fab cost $14 million. By 1995 the price had risen to $1.5 billion. Today, says Intel, the cost of a leading-edge fab exceeds $6 billion.

Why would the rising costs of chipmaking machines lead chipmaking companies, such as Intel, to build larger factories?
From "The Semiconductor Industry: Under New Management," *Economist*, April 2, 2009.

**6.7** **[Related to** Solved Problem 11.6 **on page 369]** Suppose that Jill Johnson has to choose between building a smaller restaurant and a larger restaurant. In the following graph, the relationship between costs and output for the smaller restaurant is represented by the curve $ATC_1$, and the relationship between costs and output for the larger restaurant is represented by the curve $ATC_2$.

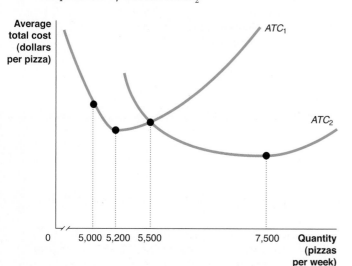

a. If Jill expects to produce 5,100 pizzas per week, should she build a smaller restaurant or a larger restaurant? Briefly explain.

b. If Jill expects to produce 6,000 pizzas per week, should she build a smaller restaurant or a larger restaurant? Briefly explain.

c. A student asks, "If the average cost of producing pizzas is lower in the larger restaurant when Jill produces 7,500 pizzas per week, why isn't it also lower when Jill produces 5,200 pizzas per week?" Give a brief answer to the student's question.

**6.8** **[Related to** Solved Problem 11.6 **on page 369]** Consider the following description of U.S. manufacturing in the late nineteenth century:

> When . . . Standard Oil . . . reorganized its refinery capacity in 1883 and concentrated almost two-fifths of the nation's refinery production in three huge refineries, the unit cost dropped from 1.5 cents a gallon to 0.5 cents. A comparable concentration of two-fifths of the nation's output of textiles or shoes in three plants would have been impossible, and in any case would have brought huge diseconomies of scale and consequently higher prices.

a. Use this information to draw a long-run average cost curve for an oil-refining firm and a long-run average cost curve for a firm manufacturing shoes.

b. Is it likely that there were more oil refineries or more shoe factories in the United States in the late nineteenth century? Briefly explain.

c. Why would concentrating two-fifths of total shoe output in three factories have led to higher shoe prices?

From Alfred D. Chandler, Jr., Thomas K. McCraw, and Richard Tedlow, *Management Past and Present*, © 2000 Cengage Learning, Inc. Reproduced by permission. www.cengage.com/permissions.

**6.9** **[Related to** Solved Problem 11.6 **on page 369]** An account of the difficulties of Japanese mobile phone manufacturers argues that these firms made a mistake by concentrating on selling in high-income countries while making little effort to sell in low-income countries:

> The main growth in the wireless industry overall is in emerging markets, which need cheap phones. The world's top three makers—Nokia, Samsung and Motorola—focus on this segment. . . . Japanese firms are caught in a vicious circle: because they are not selling to poor countries, their volume stays low, which keeps prices high, which makes selling to poor countries infeasible.

Why would the price of Japanese mobile phones be high because Japanese firms are producing these phones in low volumes? Use a graph like Figure 11.6 on page 368 to illustrate your answer.
Based on "Dropped Call: Why Japan lost the mobile-phone wars," *Economist*, March 7, 2008.

**6.10** **[Related to** Solved Problem 11.6 **on page 369]** At one point, Time Warner and the Walt Disney Company discussed merging their news operations. Time Warner owns Cable News Network (CNN), and Disney owns ABC News. After analyzing the situation, the companies decided that a combined news operation would have higher average costs than either CNN or ABC News had separately. Use a long-run average cost curve graph to illustrate why the companies did not merge their news operations.
Based on Martin Peers and Joe Flint, "AOL Calls Off CNN–ABC Deal, Seeing Operating Difficulties," *Wall Street Journal*, February 14, 2003.

**6.11** **[Related to the** Making the Connection **on page 371]** Suppose that Henry Ford had continued to experience economies of scale, no matter how large an automobile factory he built. Discuss what the implications of this would have been for the automobile industry.

**6.12** **[Related to the** Making the Connection **on page 371]** According to one account of the problems DuPont had in entering the paint business, "the du Ponts had assumed that large volume would bring profits through lowering unit costs." In fact, according to one company report, "The more paint and varnish we sold, the more money we lost." Draw an average cost curve graph that shows the relationship between paint output and the average cost DuPont expected. Draw another graph that explains the result that the more paint the company sold, the more money it lost.

From Alfred D. Chandler, Jr., Thomas K. McCraw, and Richard Tedlow, *Management Past and Present*, © 2000 Cengage Learning, Inc. Reproduced by permission. www.cengage.com/permissions.

**6.13** Online booksellers have captured a very large portion of the retail book market over the past several years. Companies that have a large online presence, such as Amazon and Barnes & Noble, now dominate this market. Over the past 15 years, the number of independent "bricks and mortar" bookstores has fallen from more than 4,500 to about 1,500. Briefly explain what role costs may have played in explaining the large decline in independent booksellers.

Based on Alex Beam, "Where Have All the Bookstores Gone?" *New York Times*, February 20, 2009.

**6.14** **[Related to the** Don't Let This Happen to You **on page 372]** Explain whether you agree with the following statement:

"Henry Ford expected to be able to produce cars at a lower average cost at his River Rouge plant. Unfortunately, because of diminishing returns, his costs were actually higher."

**6.15** **[Related to the** Chapter Opener **on page 353]** Review the discussion at the beginning of the chapter about Akio Morita selling transistor radios in the United States. Suppose that Morita had become convinced that Sony would be able to sell more than 75,000 transistor radios each year in the United States. What steps would he have taken?

**6.16** TIAA-CREF is a retirement system for people who work at colleges and universities. For some years, TIAA-CREF also offered long-term care insurance to its customers before deciding to sell that business to MetLife, a large insurance company. TIAA-CREF's chairman and chief executive officer explained the decision this way:

> In recent years, the long-term care insurance market has experienced significant consolidation. A few large insurance companies now own most of the business. MetLife has 428,000 policies, for example—nearly 10 times the number we have—and can achieve economies of scale that we can't. Over time, we would have had difficulty holding down premium rates.

Briefly explain what economies of scale have to do with the premiums (that is, the prices buyers have to pay for insurance policies) that insurance companies can charge for their policies.

From "Long-Term Care Sale in Best Interest of Policyholders," *Advance*, Spring 2004, p. 6.

# Appendix

## Using Isoquants and Isocost Lines to Understand Production and Cost

**LEARNING** OBJECTIVE

Use isoquants and isocost lines to understand production and cost.

## Isoquants

In this chapter, we studied the important relationship between a firm's level of production and its costs. In this appendix, we will look more closely at how firms choose the combination of inputs to produce a given level of output. Firms usually have a choice about how they will produce their output. For example, Jill Johnson is able to produce 5,000 pizzas per week by using 10 workers and 2 ovens or by using 6 workers and 3 ovens. We will see that firms search for the *cost-minimizing* combination of inputs that will allow them to produce a given level of output. The cost-minimizing combination of inputs depends on two factors: technology—which determines how much output a firm receives from employing a given quantity of inputs—and input prices—which determine the total cost of each combination of inputs.

## An Isoquant Graph

We begin by graphing the levels of output that Jill can produce using different combinations of two inputs: labor—the quantity of workers she hires per week—and capital—the quantity of ovens she uses per week. In reality, of course, Jill uses more than just these two inputs to produce pizzas, but nothing important would change if we expanded the discussion to include many inputs instead of just two. Figure 11A.1 measures capital along the vertical axis and labor along the horizontal axis. The curves in the graph are **isoquants**, which show all the combinations of two inputs, in this case capital and labor, that will produce the same level of output.

The isoquant labeled $Q = 5,000$ shows all the combinations of workers and ovens that enable Jill to produce that quantity of pizzas per week. For example, at point $A$, she produces 5,000 pizzas using 6 workers and 3 ovens, and at point $B$, she produces the same output using 10 workers and 2 ovens. With more workers and ovens, she can

> **Isoquant** A curve that shows all the combinations of two inputs, such as capital and labor, that will produce the same level of output.

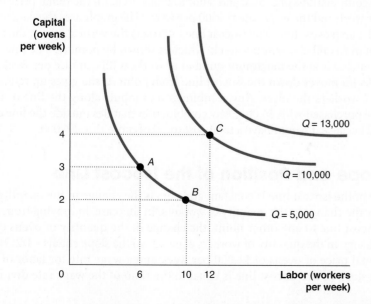

**Capital (ovens per week)**

**Labor (workers per week)**

### Figure 11A.1

#### Isoquants

Isoquants show all the combinations of two inputs, in this case capital and labor, that will produce the same level of output. For example, the isoquant labeled $Q = 5,000$ shows all the combinations of ovens and workers that enable Jill to produce that quantity of pizzas per week. At point $A$, she produces 5,000 pizzas using 3 ovens and 6 workers, and at point $B$, she produces the same output using 2 ovens and 10 workers. With more ovens and workers, she can move to a higher isoquant. For example, with 4 ovens and 12 workers, she can produce at point $C$ on the isoquant $Q = 10,000$. With even more ovens and workers, she could move to the isoquant $Q = 13,000$.

move to a higher isoquant. For example, with 12 workers and 4 ovens, she can produce at point *C* on the isoquant *Q* = 10,000. With even more workers and ovens, she could move to the isoquant *Q* = 13,000. The higher the isoquant—that is, the further to the upper right on the graph—the more output the firm produces. Although we have shown only three isoquants in this graph, there is, in fact, an isoquant for every level of output.

## The Slope of an Isoquant

Remember that the slope of a curve is the ratio of the change in the variable on the vertical axis to the change in the variable on the horizontal axis. Along an isoquant, the slope tells us the rate at which a firm is able to substitute one input for another while keeping the level of output constant. This rate is called the **marginal rate of technical substitution (*MRTS*)**.

**Marginal rate of technical substitution (*MRTS*)** The rate at which a firm is able to substitute one input for another while keeping the level of output constant.

We expect that the *MRTS* will change as we move down an isoquant. In Figure 11A.1, at a point like *A* on isoquant *Q* = 5,000, the isoquant is relatively steep. As we move down the curve, it becomes less steep at a point like *B*. This shape is the usual one for isoquants: They are bowed in, or convex. The reason isoquants have this shape is that as we move down the curve, we continue to substitute labor for capital. As the firm produces the same quantity of output using less capital, the additional labor it needs increases because of diminishing returns. Remember from the chapter that, as a consequence of diminishing returns, for a given decline in capital, increasing amounts of labor are necessary to produce the same level of output. Because the *MRTS* is equal to the change in capital divided by the change in labor, it will become smaller (in absolute value) as we move down an isoquant.

# Isocost Lines

A firm wants to produce a given quantity of output at the lowest possible cost. We can show the relationship between the quantity of inputs used and the firm's total cost by using an *isocost* line. An **isocost line** shows all the combinations of two inputs, such as capital and labor, that have the same total cost.

**Isocost line** All the combinations of two inputs, such as capital and labor, that have the same total cost.

## Graphing the Isocost Line

Suppose that Jill has $6,000 per week to spend on capital and labor. Suppose, to simplify the analysis, that Jill can rent pizza ovens by the week. The table in Figure 11A.2 shows the combinations of capital and labor available to her if the rental price of ovens is $1,000 per week and the wage rate is $500 per week. The graph uses the data in the table to construct an isocost line. The isocost line intersects the vertical axis at the maximum number of ovens Jill can rent per week, which is shown by point *A*. The line intersects the horizontal axis at the maximum number of workers Jill can hire per week, which is point *G*. As Jill moves down the isocost line from point *A*, she gives up renting 1 oven for every 2 workers she hires. Any combination of inputs along the line or inside the line can be purchased with $6,000. Any combination that lies outside the line cannot be purchased because it would have a total cost to Jill of more than $6,000.

## The Slope and Position of the Isocost Line

The slope of the isocost line is constant and equals the change in the quantity of ovens divided by the change in the quantity of workers. In this case, in moving from any point on the isocost line to any other point, the change in the quantity of ovens equals −1, and the change in the quantity of workers equals 2, so the slope equals −1/2. Notice that with a rental price of ovens of $1,000 per week and a wage rate for labor of $500 per week, the slope of the isocost line is equal to the ratio of the wage rate divided by the

| Combinations of Workers and Ovens with a Total Cost of $6,000 | | | |
|---|---|---|---|
| Point | Ovens | Workers | Total Cost |
| A | 6 | 0 | (6 x $1,000) + (0 x $500)  = $6,000 |
| B | 5 | 2 | (5 x $1,000) + (2 x $500)  =  6,000 |
| C | 4 | 4 | (4 x $1,000) + (4 x $500)  =  6,000 |
| D | 3 | 6 | (3 x $1,000) + (6 x $500)  =  6,000 |
| E | 2 | 8 | (2 x $1,000) + (8 x $500)  =  6,000 |
| F | 1 | 10 | (1 x $1,000) + (10 x $500) =  6,000 |
| G | 0 | 12 | (0 x $1,000) + (12 x $500) =  6,000 |

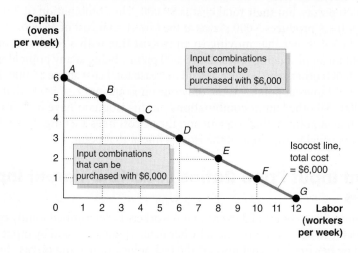

### Figure 11A.2

### An Isocost Line

The isocost line shows the combinations of inputs with a total cost of $6,000. The rental price of ovens is $1,000 per week, so if Jill spends the whole $6,000 on ovens, she can rent 6 ovens (point A). The wage rate is $500 per week, so if Jill spends the whole $6,000 on workers, she can hire 12 workers. As she moves down the isocost line, she gives up renting 1 oven for every 2 workers she hires. Any combinations of inputs along the line or inside the line can be purchased with $6,000. Any combinations that lie outside the line cannot be purchased with $6,000.

rental price of capital, multiplied by $-1$: $-\$500/\$1,000 = -1/2$. In fact, this result will always hold, whatever inputs are involved and whatever their prices may be: *The slope of the isocost line is equal to the ratio of the price of the input on the horizontal axis divided by the price of the input on the vertical axis multiplied by $-1$.*

The position of the isocost line depends on the level of total cost. Higher levels of total cost shift the isocost line outward, and lower levels of total cost shift the isocost line inward. This can be seen in Figure 11A.3, which shows isocost lines for total costs of $3,000, $6,000, and $9,000. We have shown only three isocost lines in the graph, but there is, in fact, a different isocost line for each level of total cost.

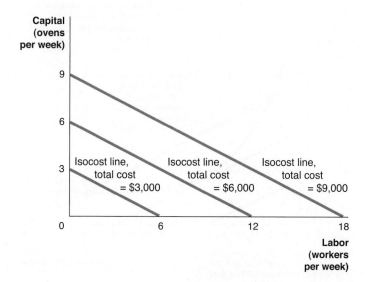

### Figure 11A.3

### The Position of the Isocost Line

The position of the isocost line depends on the level of total cost. As total cost increases from $3,000 to $6,000 to $9,000 per week, the isocost line shifts outward. For each isocost line shown, the rental price of ovens is $1,000 per week, and the wage rate is $500 per week.

# Choosing the Cost-Minimizing Combination of Capital and Labor

Suppose Jill wants to produce 5,000 pizzas per week. Figure 11A.1 shows that there are many combinations of ovens and workers that will allow Jill to produce this level of output. There is only one combination of ovens and workers, however, that will allow her to produce 5,000 pizzas *at the lowest total cost*. Figure 11A.4 shows the isoquant $Q = 5,000$ along with three isocost lines. Point $B$ is the lowest-cost combination of inputs shown in the graph, but this combination of 1 oven and 4 workers will produce fewer than the 5,000 pizzas needed. Points $C$ and $D$ are combinations of ovens and workers that will produce 5,000 pizzas, but their total cost is $9,000. The combination of 3 ovens and 6 workers at point $A$ produces 5,000 pizzas at the lowest total cost of $6,000.

Figure 11A.4 shows that moving to an isocost line with a total cost of less than $6,000 would mean producing fewer than 5,000 pizzas. Being at any point along the isoquant $Q = 5,000$ other than point $A$ would increase total cost above $6,000. In fact, the combination of inputs at point $A$ is the only one on isoquant $Q = 5,000$ that has a total cost of $6,000. All other input combinations on this isoquant have higher total costs. Notice also that at point $A$, the isoquant and the isocost lines are tangent, so the slope of the isoquant is equal to the slope of the isocost line at that point.

## Different Input Price Ratios Lead to Different Input Choices

Jill's cost-minimizing choice of 3 ovens and 6 workers is determined jointly by the technology available to her—as represented by her firm's isoquants—and by input prices—as represented by her firm's isocost lines. If the technology of making pizzas changes, perhaps because new ovens are developed, her isoquants will be affected, and her choice of inputs may change. If her isoquants remain unchanged but input prices change, then her choice of inputs may also change. This fact can explain why firms in different countries that face different input prices may produce the same good using different combinations of capital and labor, even though they have the same technology available.

For example, suppose that in China, pizza ovens are higher priced and labor is lower priced than in the United States. In our example, Jill Johnson pays $1,000 per week to rent pizza ovens and $500 per week to hire workers. Suppose a businessperson in China must pay a price of $1,500 per week to rent the identical pizza ovens but can hire Chinese workers who are as productive as U.S. workers at a wage of $300 per week.

### Figure 11A.4

**Choosing Capital and Labor to Minimize Total Cost**

Jill wants to produce 5,000 pizzas per week at the lowest total cost. Point $B$ is the lowest-cost combination of inputs shown in the graph, but this combination of 1 oven and 4 workers will produce fewer than the 5,000 pizzas needed. Points $C$ and $D$ are combinations of ovens and workers that will produce 5,000 pizzas, but their total cost is $9,000. The combination of 3 ovens and 6 workers at point $A$ produces 5,000 pizzas at the lowest total cost of $6,000.

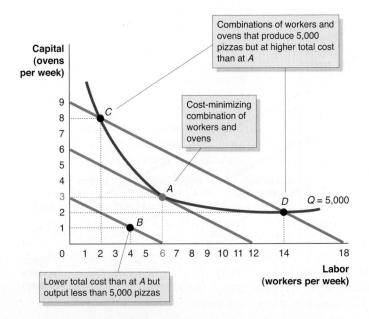

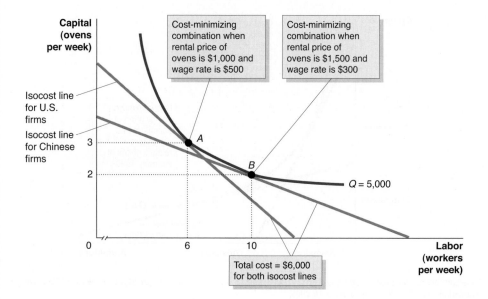

Capital (ovens per week)

Cost-minimizing combination when rental price of ovens is $1,000 and wage rate is $500

Cost-minimizing combination when rental price of ovens is $1,500 and wage rate is $300

Isocost line for U.S. firms

Isocost line for Chinese firms

$Q = 5,000$

Total cost = $6,000 for both isocost lines

Labor (workers per week)

**Figure 11A.5**

**Changing Input Prices Affects the Cost-Minimizing Input Choice**

As the graph shows, the input combination at point *A*, which was optimal for Jill, is not optimal for a businessperson in China. Using the input combination at point *A* would cost businesspeople in China more than $6,000. Instead, the Chinese isocost line is tangent to the isoquant at point *B*, where the input combination is 2 ovens and 10 workers. Because ovens cost more in China but workers cost less, a Chinese firm will use fewer ovens and more workers than a U.S. firm, even if it has the same technology as the U.S. firm.

Figure 11A.5 shows how the cost-minimizing input combination for the businessperson in China differs from Jill's.

Remember that the slope of the isocost line equals the wage rate divided by the rental price of capital multiplied by −1. The slope of the isocost line that Jill and other U.S. firms face is −$500/$1,000, or −1/2. Firms in China, however, face an isocost line with a slope of −$300/$1,500, or −1/5. As Figure 11A.5 shows, the input combination at point *A*, which was optimal for Jill, is not optimal for a firm in China. Using the input combination at point *A* would cost a firm in China more than $6,000. Instead, the Chinese isocost line is tangent to the isoquant at point *B*, where the input combination is 2 ovens and 10 workers. This result makes sense: Because ovens cost more in China, but workers cost less, a Chinese firm will use fewer ovens and more workers than a U.S. firm, even if it has the same technology as the U.S. firm.

## Making the Connection | The Changing Input Mix in Walt Disney Film Animation

The inputs used to make feature-length animated films have changed dramatically in the past 15 years. Prior to the early 1990s, the Walt Disney Company dominated the market for animated films. Disney's films were produced using hundreds of animators drawing most of the film by hand. Each film would contain as many as 170,000 individual drawings. Then, two developments dramatically affected how animated films are produced. First, in 1994, Disney had a huge hit with *The Lion King*, which cost only $50 million but earned the company more than $1 billion in profit. As a result of this success, Disney and other film studios began to produce more animated films, increasing the demand for animators and more than doubling their salaries. The second development came in 1995, when Pixar Animation Studios released the film *Toy Story*. This was the first successful feature-length film produced using computers, with no hand-drawn animation. In the following years, technological advance continued to reduce the cost of the computers and software necessary to produce an animated film.

As a result of these two developments, the price of capital—computers and software—fell relative to the price of labor—animators. As the figure shows, the change in the price of computers relative to animators changed the slope of the isocost line and resulted in film studios now producing animated films using many more computers and many fewer animators than in the early 1990s. In 2006, Disney bought Pixar, and within a few years, all the major film studios had converted to computer animation, now referred to as CGI animation, although a few hand-drawn films, such as Disney's film *Winnie the Pooh* released in 2011, continued to be produced.

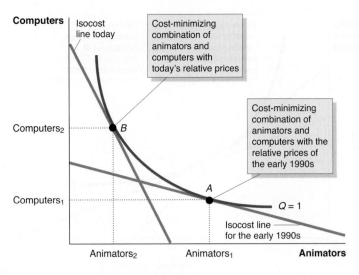

Based on "Magic Restored," *Economist*, April 17, 2008; and Laura M. Holson, "Disney Moves Away from Hand-Drawn Animation," *New York Times*, September 18, 2005.

MyEconLab **Your Turn:** Test your understanding by doing related problem 11A.8 on page 392 at the end of this appendix.

---

## Another Look at Cost Minimization

In Chapter 9, we saw that consumers maximize utility when they consume each good up to the point where the marginal utility per dollar spent is the same for every good. We can derive a very similar cost-minimization rule for firms. Remember that at the point of cost minimization, the isoquant and the isocost line are tangent, so they have the same slope. Therefore, *at the point of cost minimization, the marginal rate of technical substitution* (MRTS) *is equal to the wage rate divided by the rental price of capital.*

The slope of the isoquant tells us the rate at which a firm is able to substitute labor for capital, *given existing technology*. The slope of the isocost line tells us the rate at which a firm is able to substitute labor for capital, *given current input prices*. Only at the point of cost minimization are these two rates the same.

When we move from one point on an isoquant to another, we end up using more of one input and less of the other input, but the level of output remains the same. For example, as Jill moves down an isoquant, she uses fewer ovens and more workers but produces the same quantity of pizzas. In this chapter, we defined the *marginal product of labor* ($MP_L$) as the additional output produced by a firm as a result of hiring one more worker. Similarly, we can define the *marginal product of capital* ($MP_K$) as the additional output produced by a firm as a result of using one more machine. So, when Jill uses fewer ovens by moving down an isoquant, she loses output equal to:

$$-\text{Change in the quantity of ovens} \times MP_K.$$

But she uses more workers, so she gains output equal to:

$$\text{Change in the quantity of workers} \times MP_L.$$

We know that the gain in output from the additional workers is equal to the loss from the smaller quantity of ovens because total output remains the same along an isoquant. Therefore, we can write:

$$-\text{Change in the quantity of ovens} \times MP_K = \text{Change in the quantity of workers} \times MP_L.$$

Loss in output from using fewer ovens

Gain in output from using more workers

If we rearrange terms, we have the following:

$$\frac{-\text{Change in the quantity of ovens}}{\text{Change in the quantity of workers}} = \frac{MP_L}{MP_K}.$$

Because

$$\frac{-\text{Change in the quantity of ovens}}{\text{Change in the quantity of workers}}$$

is the slope of the isoquant, it is equal to the marginal rate of technical substitution (multiplied by negative 1). So, we can write:

$$\frac{-\text{Change in the quantity of ovens}}{\text{Change in the quantity of workers}} = MRTS = \frac{MP_L}{MP_K}.$$

The slope of the isocost line equals the wage rate ($w$) divided by the rental price of capital ($r$). We saw earlier in this appendix that at the point of cost minimization, the MRTS equals the ratio of the prices of the two inputs. Therefore:

$$\frac{MP_L}{MP_K} = \frac{w}{r}.$$

We can rewrite this to show that at the point of cost minimization:

$$\frac{MP_L}{w} = \frac{MP_K}{r}.$$

This last expression tells us that to minimize cost for a given level of output, a firm should hire inputs up to the point where the last dollar spent on each input results in the same increase in output. If this equality did not hold, a firm could lower its costs by using more of one input and less of the other. For example, if the left side of the equation were greater than the right side, a firm could rent fewer ovens, hire more workers, and produce the same output at lower cost.

# Solved Problem 11A.1

## Determining the Optimal Combination of Inputs

Consider the information in the following table for Jill Johnson's restaurant.

| | |
|---|---|
| Marginal product of capital | 3,000 pizzas per oven |
| Marginal product of labor | 1,200 pizzas per worker |
| Wage rate | $300 per week |
| Rental price of ovens | $600 per week |

Briefly explain whether Jill is minimizing costs. If she is not minimizing costs, explain whether she should rent more ovens and hire fewer workers or rent fewer ovens and hire more workers.

## Solving the Problem

**Step 1:** **Review the chapter material.** This problem is about determining the optimal choice of inputs by comparing the ratios of the marginal products of inputs to their prices, so you may want to review the section "Another Look at Cost Minimization," which begins on page 388.

**Step 2:** **Compute the ratios of marginal product to input price to determine whether Jill is minimizing costs.** If Jill is minimizing costs, the following relationship should hold:

$$\frac{MP_L}{w} = \frac{MP_K}{r}.$$

In this case, we have

$$MP_L = 1,200$$
$$MP_K = 3,000$$
$$w = \$300$$
$$r = \$600.$$

So

$$\frac{MP_L}{w} = \frac{1,200}{\$300} = 4 \text{ pizzas per dollar, and } \frac{MP_K}{r} = \frac{3,000}{\$600} = 5 \text{ pizzas per dollar.}$$

Because the two ratios are not equal, Jill is not minimizing cost.

**Step 3:** **Determine how Jill should change the mix of inputs she uses.** Jill produces more pizzas per dollar from the last oven than from the last worker. This indicates that she has too many workers and too few ovens. Therefore, to minimize cost, Jill should use more ovens and hire fewer workers.

MyEconLab **Your Turn:** For more practice, do related problems 11A.6 and 11A.7 on page 392 at the end of this appendix.

---

*Did new rules keep the Carolina Panthers from paying Cam Newton too much?*

Making the Connection

## Do National Football League Teams Behave Efficiently?

In the National Football League (NFL), the "salary cap" is the maximum amount each team can spend in a year on salaries for football players. Each year's salary cap results from negotiations between the league and the union representing the players. To achieve efficiency, an NFL team should distribute salaries among players so as to maximize the level of output—in this case, winning football games—given the constant level of cost represented by the salary cap. (Notice that maximizing the level of output for a given level of cost is equivalent to minimizing cost for a given level of output. To see why, think about the situation in which an isocost line is tangent to an isoquant. At the point of tangency, the firm has simultaneously minimized the cost of producing the level of output represented by the isoquant and maximized the output produced at the level of cost represented by the isocost line.)

In distributing salaries, teams should equalize the marginal productivity of players, as represented by their contribution to winning games to the salaries paid. Just as a firm may not use a machine that has a very high marginal product if its rental price is very high, a football team may not want to hire a superstar player if the salary the team would need to pay is too high.

Economists Cade Massey, of Duke University, and Richard Thaler, of the University of Chicago, have analyzed whether NFL teams distribute their salaries efficiently. NFL teams obtain their players either by signing free agents—who are players whose contracts with other teams have expired—or by signing players chosen in the annual draft of eligible college players. The college draft consists of seven rounds, with the teams with the worst records the previous year choosing first. Massey and Thaler find that, in fact, NFL teams do not allocate salaries efficiently. In particular, the players chosen with the first few picks of the first round of the draft tend to be paid salaries that are much higher relative to their marginal products than are players taken later in the first round. A typical team with a high draft pick would increase its ability to win football games at the constant cost represented by the salary cap if it traded for lower draft picks. Why do NFL teams apparently make the error of not efficiently distributing salaries? Massey and Thaler argue that general managers of NFL teams tend to be overconfident in their ability to forecast how well a college player is likely to perform in the NFL.

General managers of NFL teams are not alone in suffering from overconfidence. Studies have shown that, in general, people tend to overestimate their ability to forecast an uncertain outcome. Because NFL teams tend to overestimate the future marginal productivity of high draft picks, they pay them salaries that are inefficiently high compared to salaries other draft picks receive. NFL teams were aware that they were probably overpaying high draft picks. In 2011, they negotiated a new contract with the NFL Players Union that limited the salaries that drafted players could receive.

This example shows that the concepts developed in this chapter provide powerful tools for analyzing whether firms are operating efficiently.

Based on Cade Massey and Richard Thaler, "The Loser's Curse: Overconfidence vs. Market Efficiency in the National Football Leaguedraft," National Bureau of Economic Research Working Paper 11270, April 8, 2010.

**Your Turn:** Test your understanding by doing related problem 11A.14 on page 393 at the end of this appendix.       MyEconLab

# The Expansion Path

We can use isoquants and isocost lines to examine what happens as a firm expands its level of output. Figure 11A.6 shows three isoquants for a firm that produces bookcases. The isocost lines are drawn under the assumption that the machines used in producing bookcases can be rented for $100 per day and the wage rate is $25 per day. The point where each isoquant is tangent to an isocost line determines the cost-minimizing combination of capital and labor for producing that level of output. For example, 10 machines and 40 workers is the cost-minimizing combination of inputs for producing 50 bookcases per day. The cost-minimizing points *A*, *B*, and *C* lie along the firm's **expansion path**, which is a curve that shows the cost-minimizing combination of inputs for every level of output.

An important point to note is that the expansion path represents the least-cost combination of inputs to produce a given level of output *in the long run*, when the firm is able to vary the levels of all of its inputs. We know, though, that in the short run, at least one input is fixed. We can use Figure 11A.6 to show that as the firm expands in the short run, its costs will be higher than in the long run. For example, suppose that the firm is currently at point *B*, using 15 machines and 60 workers to produce 75 bookcases per day. The firm wants to expand its output to 100 bookcases per day, but in the short run, it is unable to increase the quantity of machines it uses. Therefore, to expand output, it must hire more workers. The figure shows that in the short run, to produce 100 bookcases per day using 15 machines, the lowest costs it can attain are at point *D*, where it employs 110 workers. With a rental price of machines of $100 per day and a wage rate of $25 per day, in the short run, the firm will have total costs of $4,250 to produce 100 bookcases per day. In the long run, though, the firm can increase the number of machines it uses from 15 to 20 and reduce the number of workers from 110 to 80. This

**Expansion path**  A curve that shows a firm's cost-minimizing combination of inputs for every level of output.

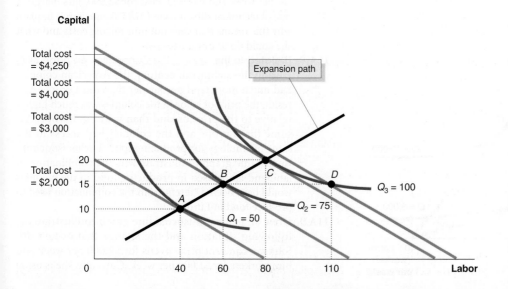

### Figure 11A.6

#### The Expansion Path

The tangency points *A*, *B*, and *C* lie along the firm's expansion path, which is a curve that shows the cost-minimizing combination of inputs for every level of output. In the short run, when the quantity of machines is fixed, the firm can expand output from 75 bookcases per day to 100 bookcases per day at the lowest cost only by moving from point *B* to point *D* and increasing the number of workers from 60 to 110. In the long run, when it can increase the quantity of machines it uses, the firm can move from point *D* to point *C*, thereby reducing its total costs of producing 100 bookcases per day from $4,250 to $4,000.

change allows it to move from point $D$ to point $C$ on its expansion path and to lower its total costs of producing 100 bookcases per day from $4,250 to $4,000. The firm's minimum total costs of production are lower in the long run than in the short run.

## Key Terms

Expansion path, p,. 391
Isocost line, p. 384

Isoquant, p. 383
Marginal rate of technical substitution (*MRTS*), p. 384

### 11A   Using Isoquants and Isocost Lines to Understand Production and Cost, pages 383–392

LEARNING OBJECTIVE: Use isoquants and isocost lines to understand production and cost.

MyEconLab   Visit **www.myeconlab.com** to complete these exercises online and get instant feedback.

## Review Questions

**11A.1** What is an isoquant? What is the slope of an isoquant?

**11A.2** What is an isocost line? What is the slope of an isocost line?

**11A.3** How do firms choose the optimal combination of inputs?

## Problems and Applications

**11A.4** Draw an isoquant–isocost line graph to illustrate the following situation: Jill Johnson can rent pizza ovens for $400 per week and hire workers for $200 per week. She is currently using 5 ovens and 10 workers to produce 20,000 pizzas per week and has total costs of $4,000. Make sure to label your graph to show the cost-minimizing input combination and the maximum quantity of labor and capital she can use with total costs of $4,000.

**11A.5** Use the following graph to answer the questions.

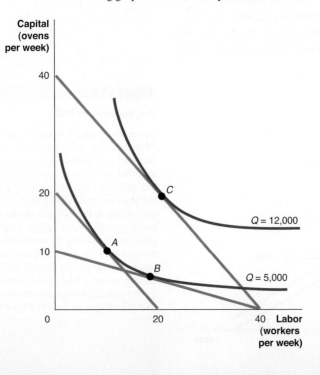

**a.** If the wage rate and the rental price of ovens are both $100 and total cost is $2,000, is the cost-minimizing point $A$, $B$, or $C$? Briefly explain.

**b.** If the wage rate is $25, the rental price of ovens is $100, and total cost is $1,000, is the cost-minimizing point $A$, $B$, or $C$? Briefly explain.

**c.** If the wage rate and the rental price of ovens are both $100 and total cost is $4,000, is the cost-minimizing point $A$, $B$, or $C$? Briefly explain.

**11A.6** **[Related to** Solved Problem 11A.1 **on page 389]** Consider the information in the following table for Jill Johnson's restaurant:

| | |
|---|---|
| Marginal product of capital | 4,000 |
| Marginal product of labor | 100 |
| Wage rate | $10 |
| Rental price of pizza ovens | $500 |

Briefly explain whether Jill is minimizing costs. If she is not minimizing costs, explain whether she should rent more ovens and hire fewer workers or rent fewer ovens and hire more workers.

**11A.7** **[Related to** Solved Problem 11A.1 **on page 389]** Draw an isoquant–isocost line graph to illustrate the following situation: Jill Johnson can rent pizza ovens for $200 per week and hire workers for $100 per week. Currently, she is using 5 ovens and 10 workers to produce 20,000 pizzas per week and has total costs of $2,000. Jill's marginal rate of technical substitution (*MRTS*) equals −1. Explain why this means that she's not minimizing costs and what she could do to minimize costs.

**11A.8** **[Related to the** Making the Connection **on page 387]** During the eighteenth century, the American colonies had much more land per farmer than did Europe. As a result, the price of labor in the colonies was much higher relative to the price of land than it was in Europe. Assume that Europe and the colonies had access to the same technology for producing food. Use an isoquant–isocost line graph to illustrate why the combination of land and labor used in producing food in the colonies would have been different from the combination used to produce food in Europe.

**11A.9** Draw an isoquant–isocost line graph to illustrate the following situation and the change that occurs: Jill Johnson can rent pizza ovens for $2,000 per week and hire workers for $1,000 per week. Currently, she is using

5 ovens and 10 workers to produce 20,000 pizzas per week and has total costs of $20,000. Then Jill reorganizes the way things are done in her business and achieves positive technological change.

**11A.10** Use the following graph to answer the following questions about Jill Johnson's isoquant curve.

**a.** Which combination of inputs yields more output: combination *A* (3 ovens and 2 workers) or combination *B* (2 ovens and 3 workers)?

**b.** What will determine whether Jill selects *A*, *B*, or some other point along this isoquant curve?

**c.** Is the marginal rate of technical substitution (*MRTS*) greater at point *A* or point *B*?

**11A.11** Draw an isoquant–isocost line graph to illustrate the following situation: Jill Johnson can rent pizza ovens for $2,000 per week and hire workers for $1,000 per week. She can minimize the cost of producing 20,000 pizzas per week by using 5 ovens and 10 workers, at a total cost of $20,000. She can minimize the cost of producing 45,000 pizzas per week by using 10 ovens and 20 workers, at a total cost of $40,000. She can minimize the cost of producing 60,000 pizzas per week by using 15 ovens and 30 workers, at a total cost of $60,000. Draw Jill's long-run average cost curve and discuss its economies of scale and diseconomies of scale.

**11A.12** In Brazil, a grove of oranges is picked using 20 workers, ladders, and baskets. In Florida, a grove of oranges is picked using 1 worker and a machine that shakes the oranges off the trees and scoops up the fallen oranges. Using an isoquant–isocost line graph, illustrate why these two different methods are used to pick the same number of oranges per day in these two locations.

**11A.13** Jill Johnson is minimizing the costs of producing pizzas. The rental price of one of her ovens is $2,000 per week, and the wage rate is $600 per week. The marginal product of capital in her business is 12,000 pizzas. What must be the marginal product of her workers?

**11A.14** **[Related to the** Making the Connection **on page 390]** If Cade Massey and Richard Thaler are correct, should the team that has the first pick in the draft keep the pick or trade it to another team for a lower pick? Briefly explain. Does the 2011 agreement that limits the salaries of drafted players affect your answer?

# Firms in Perfectly Competitive Markets

## Chapter Outline and Learning Objectives

# Perfect Competition in Farmers' Markets

In recent years, the demand for healthier foods has increased. Sales of organically grown food have increased at a rate of 20 percent per year. Many people have also begun buying their fruits and vegetables at farmers' markets. At these markets, local farmers come together at a fairground, a city plaza, or some other open space to sell their produce directly to consumers. The advantage to farmers is that they can receive a higher price than they would if they sold their produce to supermarkets. Many consumers prefer to buy from farmers' markets because they believe the produce is fresher, of higher quality, and healthier or because they want to support local farmers.

Because the profits have been higher, increasing numbers of farmers have begun participating in farmers' markets. In 2005, there were 4,093 farmers' markets in the United States. By 2011, the number had increased to 7,175. The additional supply of produce, though, has forced down prices and reduced farmers' profits. One farmer was quoted as saying: "You have a certain amount of demand, and the more you spread out the demand, you're making less."

Many farmers have found that the profits they earn from selling in farmers' markets is no longer higher than what they earn selling to supermarkets.

The process of new firms entering a profitable market and driving down prices and profits is not unique to agriculture. Throughout the economy, entrepreneurs are continually introducing new products or new ways of selling products, which—when successful—enable them to earn economic profits in the short run. But in the long run, competition among firms forces prices to the level where they just cover the costs of production. This process of competition is at the heart of the market system and is the focus of this chapter.

**AN INSIDE LOOK** on **page 422** discusses the steady decline in production and sales of organic food in the United Kingdom after 2008.

Based on Katie Zezima, "As Farmers' Markets Go Mainstream, Some Fear a Glut," *New York Times*, August 20, 2011; and Steve Martinez, et al., *Local Food Systems: Concepts, Impacts, and Issues*, U.S. Department of Agriculture Economic Research Report Number 97, May 2010.

## Economics in Your Life

### Are You an Entrepreneur?

Were you an entrepreneur during your high school years? Perhaps you didn't have your own store, but you may have worked as a babysitter, or perhaps you mowed lawns for families in your neighborhood. While you may not think of these jobs as being small businesses, that is exactly what they are. How did you decide what price to charge for your services? You may have wanted to charge $25 per hour to babysit or mow lawns, but you probably charged much less. As you read the chapter, think about the competitive situation you faced as a teenage entrepreneur and try to determine why the prices received by most people who babysit and mow lawns are so low. You can check your answers against those we provide on **page 420** at the end of this chapter.

armers' markets are an example of a *perfectly competitive* industry. Firms in perfectly competitive industries are unable to control the prices of the products they sell and are unable to earn an economic profit in the long run for two main reasons: Firms in these industries sell identical products, and it is easy for new firms to enter these industries. Studying how perfectly competitive industries operate is the best way to understand how markets answer the fundamental economic questions discussed in Chapter 1:

- What goods and services will be produced?

- How will the goods and services be produced?

- Who will receive the goods and services produced?

In fact, though, most industries are not perfectly competitive. In most industries, firms do *not* produce identical products, and in some industries, it may be difficult for new firms to enter. There are thousands of industries in the United States. Although in some ways each industry is unique, industries share enough similarities that economists group them into four market structures. In particular, any industry has three key characteristics:

1. The number of firms in the industry
2. The similarity of the good or service produced by the firms in the industry
3. The ease with which new firms can enter the industry

Economists use these characteristics to classify industries into the four market structures listed in Table 12.1.

Many industries, including restaurants, clothing stores, and other retailers, have a large number of firms selling products that are differentiated, rather than identical, and fall into the category of *monopolistic competition*. Some industries, such as computers and automobiles, have only a few firms and are *oligopolies*. Finally, a few industries, such as the delivery of first-class mail by the U.S. Postal Service, have only one firm and are *monopolies*. After discussing perfect competition in this chapter, we will devote a chapter to each of these other market structures.

**Table 12.1** **The Four Market Structures**

| | Market Structure | | | |
|---|---|---|---|---|
| Characteristic | Perfect Competition | Monopolistic Competition | Oligopoly | Monopoly |
| Number of firms | Many | Many | Few | One |
| Type of product | Identical | Differentiated | Identical or differentiated | Unique |
| Ease of entry | High | High | Low | Entry blocked |
| Examples of industries | • Growing wheat<br>• Growing apples | • Clothing stores<br>• Restaurants | • Manufacturing computers<br>• Manufacturing automobiles | • First-class mail delivery<br>• Tap water |

# Perfectly Competitive Markets

Why are firms in a **perfectly competitive market** unable to control the prices of the goods they sell, and why are the owners of these firms unable to earn economic profit in the long run? We can begin our analysis by listing the three conditions that make a market perfectly competitive:

1. There must be many buyers and many firms, all of which are small relative to the market.
2. The products sold by all firms in the market must be identical.
3. There must be no barriers to new firms entering the market.

**12.1 LEARNING** OBJECTIVE

Explain what a perfectly competitive market is and why a perfect competitor faces a horizontal demand curve.

**Perfectly competitive market** A market that meets the conditions of (1) many buyers and sellers, (2) all firms selling identical products, and (3) no barriers to new firms entering the market.

All three of these conditions hold in markets for agricultural products. For example, no single consumer or producer of apples buys or sells more than a tiny fraction of the total apple crop. The apples sold by each apple grower are identical, and there are no barriers to a new firm entering the apple market by purchasing land and planting apple trees. As we will see, it is the existence of many firms, all selling the same good, that keeps any single apple farmer from affecting the price of apples.

Although the market for apples meets the conditions for perfect competition, the markets for most goods and services do not. In particular, the second and third conditions are very restrictive. In most markets that have many buyers and sellers, firms do not sell identical products. For example, not all restaurant meals are the same, nor is all women's clothing the same. In Chapter 13, we will explore the common situation of monopolistic competition where many firms are selling similar but not identical products. In Chapters 14 and 15, we will analyze industries that are oligopolies or monopolies, where it is difficult for new firms to enter. In this chapter, we concentrate on perfectly competitive markets so we can use them as a benchmark to analyze how firms behave when facing the maximum possible competition.

## A Perfectly Competitive Firm Cannot Affect the Market Price

Prices in perfectly competitive markets are determined by the interaction of demand and supply for the good or service. The actions of any single consumer or any single firm have no effect on the market price. Consumers and firms have to accept the market price if they want to buy and sell in a perfectly competitive market.

Because a firm in a perfectly competitive market is very small relative to the market and because it is selling exactly the same product as every other firm, it can sell as much as it wants without having to lower its price. But if a perfectly competitive firm tries to raise its price, it won't sell anything at all because consumers will switch to buying the product from the firm's competitors. Therefore, the firm will be a **price taker** and will have to charge the same price as every other firm in the market. Although we don't usually think of firms as being too small to affect the market price, consumers are often in the position of being price takers. For instance, suppose your local supermarket is selling bread for $1.50 per loaf. You can load up your shopping cart with 10 loaves of bread, and the supermarket will gladly sell them all to you for $1.50 per loaf. But if you go to the cashier and offer to buy the bread for $1.49 per loaf, he or she will not sell it to you at that price. As a buyer, you are too small relative to the bread market to have any effect on the equilibrium price. Whether you leave the supermarket and buy no bread or you buy 10 loaves, you are unable to change the market price of bread by even 1 cent.

The situation you face as a bread buyer is the same one a wheat farmer faces as a wheat seller. In 2011, about 150,000 farmers grew wheat in the United States. The market price of wheat is determined not by any individual wheat farmer but by the interaction in the wheat market of all the buyers and all the sellers. If any one wheat farmer has the best crop the farmer has ever had, or if any one wheat farmer stops growing wheat altogether, the market price of wheat will not be affected *because the market supply curve for wheat will not shift by enough to change the equilibrium price by even 1 cent.*

**Price taker** A buyer or seller that is unable to affect the market price.

### Figure 12.1

**A Perfectly Competitive Firm Faces a Horizontal Demand Curve**

A firm in a perfectly competitive market is selling exactly the same product as many other firms. Therefore, it can sell as much as it wants at the current market price, but it cannot sell anything at all if it raises the price by even 1 cent. As a result, the demand curve for a perfectly competitive firm's output is a horizontal line. In the figure, whether the wheat farmer sells 6,000 bushels per year or 15,000 bushels has no effect on the market price of $4.

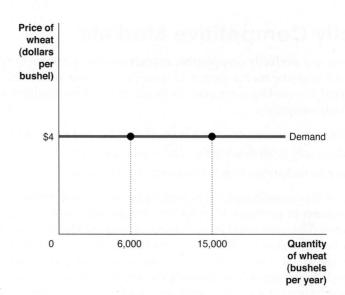

## The Demand Curve for the Output of a Perfectly Competitive Firm

Suppose Bill Parker grows wheat on a 250-acre farm in Washington State. Farmer Parker is selling wheat in a perfectly competitive market, so he is a price taker. Because he can sell as much wheat as he chooses at the market price—but can't sell any wheat at all at a higher price—the demand curve for his wheat has an unusual shape: It is horizontal, as shown in Figure 12.1. With a horizontal demand curve, Farmer Parker must accept the market price, which in this case is $4 per bushel. Whether Farmer Parker sells 6,000 bushels per year or 15,000 has no effect on the market price.

The demand curve for Farmer Parker's wheat is very different from the market demand curve for wheat. Panel (a) of Figure 12.2 shows the market for wheat. The demand curve in panel (a) is the *market demand curve for wheat* and has the normal

## Don't Let This Happen to You

### Don't Confuse the Demand Curve for Farmer Parker's Wheat with the Market Demand Curve for Wheat

The demand curve for wheat has the normal downward-sloping shape. If the price of wheat goes up, the quantity of wheat demanded goes down, and if the price of wheat goes down, the quantity of wheat demanded goes up. But the demand curve for the output of a single wheat farmer is *not* downward sloping: It is a horizontal line. If an individual wheat farmer tries to increase the price he charges for his wheat, the quantity demanded falls to zero because buyers will purchase from one of the other 150,000 wheat farmers. But any one farmer can sell as much wheat as the farmer can produce without needing to cut the price. Both of these things are true because

each wheat farmer is very small relative to the overall market for wheat.

When we draw graphs of the wheat market, we usually show the market equilibrium quantity in millions or billions of bushels. When we draw graphs of the demand for wheat produced by one farmer, we usually show the quantity produced in smaller units, such as thousands of bushels. It is important to remember this difference in scale when interpreting these graphs.

Finally, it is not just wheat farmers who have horizontal demand curves for their products; any firm in a perfectly competitive market faces a horizontal demand curve.

MyEconLab

**Your Turn:** Test your understanding by doing related problem 1.6 on page 424 at the end of this chapter.

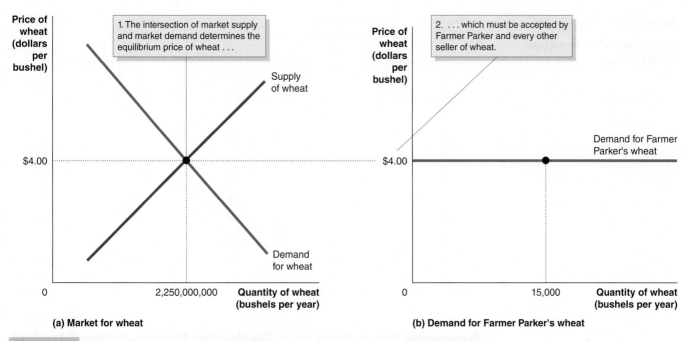

**Figure 12.2** The Market Demand for Wheat versus the Demand for One Farmer's Wheat

In a perfectly competitive market, price is determined by the intersection of market demand and market supply. In panel (a), the demand and supply curves for wheat intersect at a price of $4 per bushel. An individual wheat farmer like Farmer Parker cannot affect the market price for wheat. Therefore, as panel (b) shows, the demand curve for Farmer Parker's wheat is a horizontal line.

To understand this figure, it is important to notice that the scales on the horizontal axes in the two panels are very different. In panel (a), the equilibrium quantity of wheat is 2.25 *billion* bushels, and in panel (b), Farmer Parker is producing only 15,000 bushels of wheat.

downward slope we are familiar with from the market demand curves in Chapter 3. Panel (b) of Figure 12.2 shows the demand curve for Farmer Parker's wheat, which is a horizontal line. By viewing these graphs side by side, you can see that the price Farmer Parker receives for his wheat in panel (b) is determined by the interaction of all sellers and all buyers of wheat in the wheat market in panel (a). Keep in mind, however, that the scales on the horizontal axes in the two panels are very different. In panel (a), the equilibrium quantity of wheat is 2.25 *billion* bushels. In panel (b), Farmer Parker is producing only 15,000 bushels, or less than 0.001 percent of market output. We need to use different scales in the two panels so we can display both of them on one page. Keep in mind this key point: Farmer Parker's output of wheat is very small relative to the total market output.

# How a Firm Maximizes Profit in a Perfectly Competitive Market

We have seen that Farmer Parker cannot control the price of his wheat. In this situation, how does he decide how much wheat to produce? We assume that Farmer Parker's objective is to maximize profit. This is a reasonable assumption for most firms, most of the time. Remember that **profit** is the difference between total revenue (*TR*) and total cost (*TC*):

$$\text{Profit} = TR - TC.$$

To maximize his profit, Farmer Parker should produce the quantity of wheat where the difference between the total revenue he receives and his total cost is as large as possible.

**12.2 LEARNING** OBJECTIVE

Explain how a firm maximizes profit in a perfectly competitive market.

**Profit** Total revenue minus total cost.

| | Number of Bushels (Q) | Market Price (per bushel) (P) | Total Revenue (TR) | Average Revenue (AR) | Marginal Revenue (MR) |
|---|---|---|---|---|---|
| **Table 12.2** | 0 | $4 | $0 | — | — |
| | 1 | 4 | 4 | $4 | $4 |
| **Farmer Parker's Revenue from Wheat Farming** | 2 | 4 | 8 | 4 | 4 |
| | 3 | 4 | 12 | 4 | 4 |
| | 4 | 4 | 16 | 4 | 4 |
| | 5 | 4 | 20 | 4 | 4 |
| | 6 | 4 | 24 | 4 | 4 |
| | 7 | 4 | 28 | 4 | 4 |
| | 8 | 4 | 32 | 4 | 4 |
| | 9 | 4 | 36 | 4 | 4 |
| | 10 | 4 | 40 | 4 | 4 |

## Revenue for a Firm in a Perfectly Competitive Market

To understand how Farmer Parker maximizes profits, let's first consider his revenue. To keep the numbers simple, we will assume that he owns a very small farm and produces at most 10 bushels of wheat per year. Table 12.2 shows the revenue Farmer Parker will earn from selling various quantities of wheat if the market price for wheat is $4.

The third column in Table 12.2 shows that Farmer Parker's *total revenue* rises by $4 for every additional bushel he sells because he can sell as many bushels as he wants at the market price of $4 per bushel. The fourth and fifth columns in the table show Farmer Parker's *average revenue* and *marginal revenue* from selling wheat. His **average revenue** (AR) is his total revenue divided by the quantity of bushels he sells. For example, if he sells 5 bushels for a total of $20, his average revenue is $20/5 = 4$. Notice that his average revenue is also equal to the market price of $4. In fact, for any level of output, a firm's average revenue is always equal to the market price. This equality holds because total revenue equals price times quantity ($TR = P \times Q$), and average revenue equals total revenue divided by quantity ($AR = TR/Q$). So, $AR = TR/Q = (P \times Q)/Q = P$.

Farmer Parker's **marginal revenue** (MR) is the change in his total revenue from selling one more bushel:

$$\text{Marginal revenue} = \frac{\text{Change in total revenue}}{\text{Change in quantity}}, \text{ or } MR = \frac{\Delta TR}{\Delta Q}.$$

Because for each additional bushel sold, Farmer Parker always adds $4 to his total revenue, his marginal revenue is $4. Farmer Parker's marginal revenue is $4 per bushel because he is selling wheat in a perfectly competitive market and can sell as much as he wants at the market price. In fact, Farmer Parker's marginal revenue and average revenue are both equal to the market price. This is an important point: *For a firm in a perfectly competitive market, price is equal to both average revenue and marginal revenue.*

**Average revenue (AR)** Total revenue divided by the quantity of the product sold.

**Marginal revenue (MR)** The change in total revenue from selling one more unit of a product.

## Determining the Profit-Maximizing Level of Output

To determine how Farmer Parker can maximize profit, we have to consider his costs as well as his revenue. A wheat farmer has many costs, including the cost of seed and fertilizer, as well as the wages of farm workers. In Table 12.3, we bring together the revenue data from Table 12.2 with cost data for Farmer Parker's farm. Recall from Chapter 10 that a firm's *marginal cost* is the increase in total cost resulting from producing another unit of output.

| Quantity (bushels) (Q) | Total Revenue (TR) | Total Cost (TC) | Profit (TR − TC) | Marginal Revenue (MR) | Marginal Cost (MC) |
|---|---|---|---|---|---|
| 0 | $0.00 | $2.00 | −$2.00 | — | — |
| 1 | 4.00 | 5.00 | −1.00 | $4.00 | $3.00 |
| 2 | 8.00 | 7.00 | 1.00 | 4.00 | 2.00 |
| 3 | 12.00 | 8.50 | 3.50 | 4.00 | 1.50 |
| 4 | 16.00 | 10.50 | 5.50 | 4.00 | 2.00 |
| 5 | 20.00 | 13.00 | 7.00 | 4.00 | 2.50 |
| 6 | 24.00 | 16.50 | 7.50 | 4.00 | 3.50 |
| 7 | 28.00 | 21.50 | 6.50 | 4.00 | 5.00 |
| 8 | 32.00 | 28.50 | 3.50 | 4.00 | 7.00 |
| 9 | 36.00 | 38.00 | −2.00 | 4.00 | 9.50 |
| 10 | 40.00 | 50.50 | −10.50 | 4.00 | 12.50 |

**Table 12.3**

**Farmer Parker's Profits from Wheat Farming**

We calculate profit in the fourth column by subtracting total cost in the third column from total revenue in the second column. The fourth column shows that as long as Farmer Parker produces between 2 and 8 bushels of wheat, he will earn a profit. His maximum profit is $7.50, which he will earn by producing 6 bushels of wheat. Because Farmer Parker wants to maximize his profits, we would expect him to produce 6 bushels of wheat. Producing more than 6 bushels reduces his profit. For example, if he produces 7 bushels of wheat, his profit will decline from $7.50 to $6.50. The values for marginal cost given in the last column of the table help us understand why Farmer Parker's profits will decline if he produces more than 6 bushels of wheat: After the sixth bushel of wheat, rising marginal cost causes Farmer Parker's profits to fall.

In fact, comparing the marginal cost and marginal revenue at each level of output is an alternative method of calculating Farmer Parker's profits. We illustrate the two methods of calculating profits in Figure 12.3. We show the total revenue and total cost approach in panel (a) and the marginal revenue and marginal cost approach in panel (b). Total revenue is a straight line on the graph in panel (a) because total revenue increases at a constant rate of $4 for each additional bushel sold. Farmer Parker's profits are maximized when the vertical distance between the line representing total revenue and the total cost curve is as large as possible. Just as we saw in Table 12.3, his maximum profit occurs at an output of 6 bushels.

The last two columns of Table 12.3 show the marginal revenue (MR) Farmer Parker receives from selling another bushel of wheat and his marginal cost (MC) of producing another bushel of wheat. Panel (b) of Figure 12.3 is a graph of Farmer Parker's marginal revenue and marginal cost. Because marginal revenue is always equal to $4, it is a horizontal line at the market price. We have already seen that the demand curve for a perfectly competitive firm is also a horizontal line at the market price. *Therefore, the marginal revenue curve for a perfectly competitive firm is the same as its demand curve.* Farmer Parker's marginal cost of producing wheat first falls and then rises, following the usual pattern we discussed in Chapter 11.

We know from panel (a) that profit is at a maximum at 6 bushels of wheat. In panel (b), profit is also at a maximum at 6 bushels of wheat. To understand why profit is maximized at the level of output where marginal revenue equals marginal cost, remember a key economic principle that we discussed in Chapter 1: *Optimal decisions are made at the margin.* Firms use this principle to decide the quantity of a good to produce. For example, in deciding how much wheat to produce, Farmer Parker needs to compare the marginal revenue he earns from selling another bushel of wheat to the marginal cost of producing that bushel. The difference between the marginal revenue and the marginal

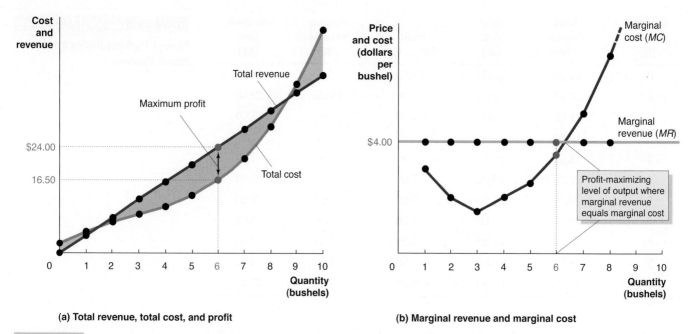

**(a) Total revenue, total cost, and profit**

**(b) Marginal revenue and marginal cost**

**Figure 12.3** **The Profit-Maximizing Level of Output**

In panel (a), Farmer Parker maximizes his profit where the vertical distance between total revenue and total cost is the largest. This happens at an output of 6 bushels. Panel (b) shows that Farmer Parker's marginal revenue (*MR*) is equal to a constant $4 per bushel. Farmer Parker maximizes profits by producing wheat up to the point where the marginal revenue of the last bushel produced is equal to its marginal cost, or *MR* = *MC*. In this case, at no level of output

does marginal revenue exactly equal marginal cost. The closest Farmer Parker can come is to produce 6 bushels of wheat. He will not want to continue to produce once marginal cost is greater than marginal revenue because that would reduce his profits. Panels (a) and (b) show alternative ways of thinking about how Farmer Parker can determine the profit-maximizing quantity of wheat to produce.

cost is the additional profit (or loss) from producing one more bushel. As long as marginal revenue is greater than marginal cost, Farmer Parker's profits are increasing, and he will want to expand production. For example, he will not stop producing at 5 bushels of wheat because producing and selling the sixth bushel adds $4.00 to his revenue but only $3.50 to his cost, so his profit increases by $0.50. He wants to continue producing until the marginal revenue he receives from selling another bushel is equal to the marginal cost of producing it. At that level of output, he will make no *additional* profit by selling another bushel, so he will have maximized his profits.

By inspecting Table 12.3 on page 401, we can see that there is no level of output at which marginal revenue exactly equals marginal cost. The closest Farmer Parker can come is to produce 6 bushels of wheat. He will not want to produce additional wheat once marginal cost is greater than marginal revenue because that would reduce his profits. For example, the seventh bushel of wheat adds $5.00 to his cost but only $4.00 to his revenue, so producing the seventh bushel *reduces* his profit by $1.00.

From the information in Table 12.3 and Figure 12.3, we can draw the following conclusions:

1. The profit-maximizing level of output is where the difference between total revenue and total cost is the greatest.

2. The profit-maximizing level of output is also where marginal revenue equals marginal cost, or *MR* = *MC*.

Both of these conclusions are true for any firm, whether or not it is in a perfectly competitive industry. We can draw one other conclusion about profit maximization that is true only of firms in perfectly competitive industries: For a firm in a perfectly competitive industry, price is equal to marginal revenue, or *P* = *MR*. So, we can restate the *MR* = *MC* condition as *P* = *MC*.

# Illustrating Profit or Loss on the Cost Curve Graph

We have seen that profit is the difference between total revenue and total cost. We can also express profit in terms of *average total cost* (*ATC*). This allows us to show profit on the cost curve graph we developed in Chapter 10.

To begin, we need to work through several steps to determine the relationship between profit and average total cost. Because profit is equal to total revenue minus total cost (*TC*) and total revenue is price times quantity, we can write the following:

$$\text{Profit} = (P \times Q) - TC.$$

If we divide both sides of this equation by *Q*, we have

$$\frac{\text{Profit}}{Q} = \frac{(P \times Q)}{Q} - \frac{TC}{Q}$$

or

$$\frac{\text{Profit}}{Q} = P - ATC,$$

because *TC*/*Q* equals *ATC*. This equation tells us that profit per unit (or average profit) equals price minus average total cost. Finally, we obtain the equation for the relationship between total profit and average total cost by multiplying again by *Q*:

$$\text{Profit} = (P - ATC) \times Q.$$

This equation tells us that a firm's total profit is equal to the quantity produced multiplied by the difference between price and average total cost.

## Showing a Profit on the Graph

Figure 12.4 shows the relationship between a firm's average total cost and its marginal cost that we discussed in Chapter 10. In this figure, we also show the firm's marginal revenue curve (which is the same as its demand curve) and the area representing total profit. Using the relationship between profit and average total cost that we just determined, we can say that the area representing total profit has a height equal to $(P - ATC)$ and a base equal to $Q$. This area is shown by the green-shaded rectangle.

**12.3 LEARNING** OBJECTIVE

Use graphs to show a firm's profit or loss.

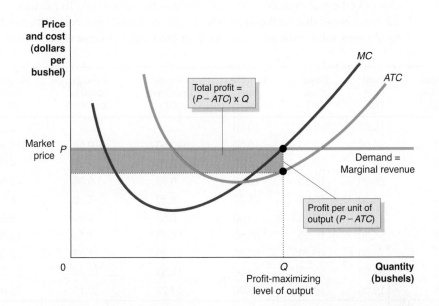

0                    *Q*            **Quantity**
          Profit-maximizing   **(bushels)**
          level of output

**Figure 12.4**

**The Area of Maximum Profit**

A firm maximizes profit at the level of output at which marginal revenue equals marginal cost. The difference between price and average total cost equals profit per unit of output. Total profit equals profit per unit multiplied by the number of units produced. Total profit is represented by the area of the green-shaded rectangle, which has a height equal to $(P - ATC)$ and a width equal to $Q$.

# Solved Problem 12.3

## Determining Profit-Maximizing Price and Quantity

Suppose that Andy sells basketballs in the perfectly competitive basketball market. His output per day and his costs are as follows:

| Output per Day | Total Cost |
|----------------|------------|
| 0 | $10.00 |
| 1 | 20.50 |
| 2 | 24.50 |
| 3 | 28.50 |
| 4 | 34.00 |
| 5 | 43.00 |
| 6 | 55.50 |
| 7 | 72.00 |
| 8 | 93.00 |
| 9 | 119.00 |

a. Suppose the current equilibrium price in the basketball market is $12.50. To maximize profit, how many basketballs will Andy produce, what price will he charge, and how much profit (or loss) will he make? Draw a graph to illustrate your answer. Your graph should be labeled clearly and should include Andy's demand, ATC, AVC, MC, and MR curves; the price he is charging; the quantity he is producing; and the area representing his profit (or loss).

b. Suppose the equilibrium price of basketballs falls to $6.00. Now how many basketballs will Andy produce, what price will he charge, and how much profit (or loss) will he make? Draw a graph to illustrate this situation, using the instructions in part a.

## Solving the Problem

**Step 1: Review the chapter material.** This problem is about using cost curve graphs to analyze perfectly competitive firms, so you may want to review the section "Illustrating Profit or Loss on the Cost Curve Graph" on page 403.

**Step 2: Calculate Andy's marginal cost, average total cost, and average variable cost.** To maximize profit, Andy will produce the level of output where marginal revenue is equal to marginal cost. We can calculate marginal cost from the information given in the table. We can also calculate average total cost and average variable cost in order to draw the required graph. Average total cost (ATC) equals total cost (TC) divided by the level of output (Q). Average variable cost (AVC) equals variable cost (VC) divided by output (Q). To calculate variable cost, recall that total cost equals variable cost plus fixed cost. When output equals zero, total cost equals fixed cost. In this case, fixed cost equals $10.00.

| Output per Day (Q) | Total Cost (TC) | Fixed Cost (FC) | Variable Cost (VC) | Average Total Cost (ATC) | Average Variable Cost (AVC) | Marginal Cost (MC) |
|---|---|---|---|---|---|---|
| 0 | $10.00 | $10.00 | $0.00 | — | — | — |
| 1 | 20.50 | 10.00 | 10.50 | $20.50 | $10.50 | $10.50 |
| 2 | 24.50 | 10.00 | 14.50 | 12.25 | 7.25 | 4.00 |
| 3 | 28.00 | 10.00 | 18.00 | 9.33 | 6.00 | 3.50 |
| 4 | 34.00 | 10.00 | 24.00 | 8.50 | 6.00 | 6.00 |
| 5 | 43.00 | 10.00 | 33.00 | 8.60 | 6.60 | 9.00 |
| 6 | 55.50 | 10.00 | 45.50 | 9.25 | 7.58 | 12.50 |
| 7 | 72.00 | 10.00 | 62.00 | 10.29 | 8.86 | 16.50 |
| 8 | 93.00 | 10.00 | 83.00 | 11.63 | 10.38 | 21.00 |
| 9 | 119.00 | 10.00 | 109.00 | 13.22 | 12.11 | 26.00 |

**Step 3:** Use the information from the table in Step 2 to calculate how many basketballs Andy will produce, what price he will charge, and how much profit he will earn if the market price of basketballs is $12.50. Andy's marginal revenue is equal to the market price of $12.50. Marginal revenue equals marginal cost when Andy produces 6 basketballs per day. So, Andy will produce 6 basketballs per day and charge a price of $12.50 per basketball. Andy's profits are equal to his total revenue minus his total costs. His total revenue equals the 6 basketballs he sells multiplied by the $12.50 price, or $75.00. So, his profit equals: $75.00 − $55.50 = $19.50.

**Step 4:** Use the information from the table in Step 2 to illustrate your answer to part a. with a graph.

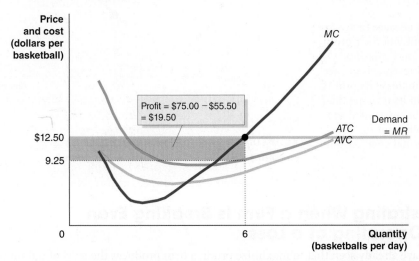

**Step 5:** Calculate how many basketballs Andy will produce, what price he will charge, and how much profit he will earn when the market price of basketballs is $6.00. Referring to the table in Step 2, we can see that marginal revenue equals marginal cost when Andy produces 4 basketballs per day. He charges the market price of $6.00 per basketball. His total revenue is only $24.00, while his total costs are $34.00, so he will have a loss of $10.00. (Can we be sure that Andy will continue to produce even though he is operating at a loss? We answer this question in the next section.)

**Step 6:** Illustrate your answer to part b. with a graph.

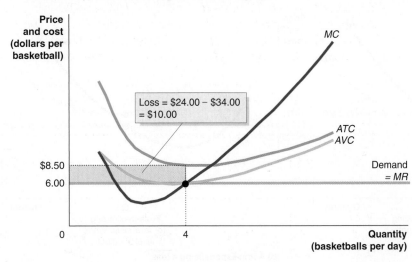

**Your Turn:** For more practice, do related problems 3.3 and 3.4 on pages 425 and 426 at the end    MyEconLab
of this chapter.

# Don't Let This Happen to You

## Remember That Firms Maximize Their Total Profit, Not Their Profit per Unit

A student examines the following graph and argues, "I believe that a firm will want to produce at $Q_1$, not $Q_2$. At $Q_1$, the distance between price and average total cost is the greatest. Therefore, at $Q_1$, the firm will be maximizing its profits per unit." Briefly explain whether you agree with the student's argument.

The student's argument is incorrect because firms are interested in maximizing their *total* profit, not their profit per unit. We know that profit are not maximized at $Q_1$ because at that level of output, marginal revenue is greater than marginal cost. A firm can always increase its profits by producing any unit that adds more to its revenue than it does to its costs. Only when the firm has expanded production to $Q_2$ will it have produced every unit for which marginal revenue is greater than marginal cost. At that point, it will have maximized profit.

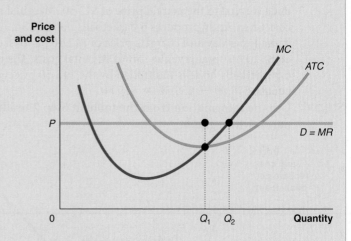

MyEconLab

**Your Turn:** Test your understanding by doing related problem 3.5 on page 426 at the end of this chapter.

## Illustrating When a Firm Is Breaking Even or Operating at a Loss

We have already seen that to maximize profit, a firm produces the level of output where marginal revenue equals marginal cost. But will the firm actually make a profit at that level of output? It depends on the relationship of price to average total cost. There are three possibilities:

1. $P > ATC$, which means the firm makes a profit
2. $P = ATC$, which means the firm *breaks even* (its total cost equals its total revenue)
3. $P < ATC$, which means the firm experiences a loss

Figure 12.4 on page 403 shows the first possibility, where the firm makes a profit. Panels (a) and (b) of Figure 12.5 show the situations where a firm breaks even or experiences losses.

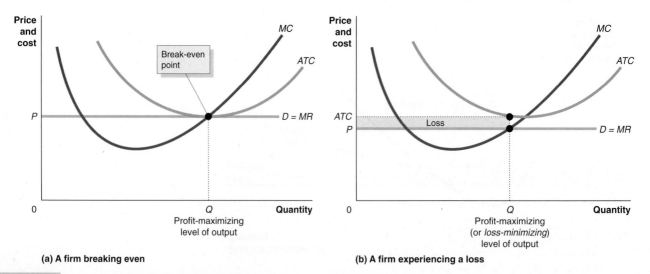

**(a) A firm breaking even**

**(b) A firm experiencing a loss**

**Figure 12.5** **A Firm Breaking Even and a Firm Experiencing a Loss**

In panel (a), price equals average total cost, and the firm breaks even because its total revenue will be equal to its total cost. In this situation, the firm makes zero economic profit. In panel (b), price is below average total cost,

and the firm experiences a loss. The loss is represented by the area of the red-shaded rectangle, which has a height equal to $(ATC - P)$ and a width equal to $Q$.

In panel (a) of Figure 12.5, at the level of output at which $MR = MC$, price is equal to average total cost. Therefore, total revenue is equal to total cost, and the firm will break even, making zero economic profit. In panel (b), at the level of output at which $MR = MC$, price is less than average total cost. Therefore, total revenue is less than total cost, and the firm has losses. In this case, maximizing profit amounts to *minimizing* loss.

## Making the Connection

### Losing Money in the Medical Screening Industry

In a market system, a good or service becomes available to consumers only if an entrepreneur brings the product to market. Thousands of new businesses open every week in the United States. Each new business represents an entrepreneur risking his or her funds, trying to earn a profit by offering a good or service to consumers. Of course, there are no guarantees of success, and many new businesses experience losses rather than earn the profits their owners hoped for.

In the early 2000s, technological advances reduced the price of computed tomography (CT) scanning equipment. For years, doctors and hospitals have prescribed CT scans to diagnose patients showing symptoms of heart disease, cancer, and other disorders. The declining price of CT scanning equipment convinced many entrepreneurs that it would be profitable to offer preventive body scans to apparently healthy people. The idea was that the scans would provide early detection of diseases before the customers had begun experiencing symptoms. Unfortunately, the new firms offering this service ran into several difficulties: First, because the CT scan was a voluntary procedure, it was not covered under most medical insurance plans. Second, very few consumers used the service more than once, so there was almost no repeat business. Finally, as with any other medical test, some false positives occurred, where the scan appeared to detect a problem that did not actually exist. Negative publicity from people who had expensive additional—and unnecessary—medical procedures as a result of false-positive CT scans also hurt these new businesses.

As a result of these problems, the demand for CT scans was less than most of these entrepreneurs had expected, and the new businesses operated at a loss. For example, the owner of California HeartScan would have broken even if the market price had been $495 per heart scan, but he suffered losses because the actual market price was only $250. The following graphs show the owner's situation:

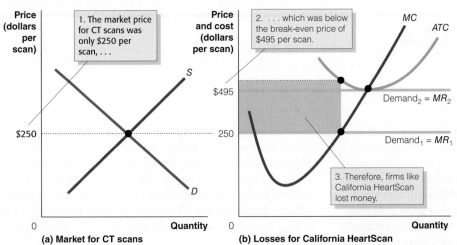

**(a) Market for CT scans**

**(b) Losses for California HeartScan**

Why didn't California HeartScan and other medical clinics just raise the price to the level they needed to break even? We have already seen that any firm that tries to raise the price it charges above the market price loses customers to competing firms. By fall 2003, many scanning businesses began to close. Most of the entrepreneurs who had started those businesses lost their investments.

Based on Patricia Callahan, "Scanning for Trouble," *Wall Street Journal*, September 11, 2003.

**Your Turn:** Test your understanding by doing related problem 3.7 on page 426 at the end of this chapter.

MyEconLab

# Deciding Whether to Produce or to Shut Down in the Short Run

In panel (b) of Figure 12.5 on page 406, we assumed that the firm would continue to produce even though it was operating at a loss. In fact, in the short run, a firm experiencing a loss has two choices:

1. Continue to produce
2. Stop production by shutting down temporarily

In many cases, a firm experiencing a loss will consider stopping production temporarily. Even during a temporary shutdown, however, a firm must still pay its fixed costs. For example, if the firm has signed a lease for its building, the landlord will expect to receive a monthly rent payment, even if the firm is not producing anything that month. Therefore, if a firm does not produce, it will suffer a loss equal to its fixed costs. This loss is the maximum the firm will accept. The firm will shut down if producing would cause it to lose an amount greater than its fixed costs.

A firm can reduce its loss below the amount of its total fixed cost by continuing to produce, provided that the total revenue it receives is greater than its variable cost. A firm can use the revenue over and above variable cost to cover part of its fixed cost. In this case, a firm will have a smaller loss by continuing to produce than if it shut down.

In analyzing the firm's decision to shut down, we are assuming that its fixed costs are *sunk costs*. Remember from Chapter 10 that a **sunk cost** is a cost that has already been paid and cannot be recovered. We assume, as is usually the case, that the firm cannot recover its fixed costs by shutting down. For example, if a farmer has taken out a loan to buy land, the farmer is legally required to make the monthly loan payment whether he grows any wheat that season or not. The farmer has to spend those funds and cannot get them back, *so the farmer should treat his sunk costs as irrelevant to his decision making.* For any firm, whether total revenue is greater or less than *variable costs* is the key to deciding whether to shut down. As long as a firm's total revenue is greater than its variable costs, it should continue to produce no matter how large or small its fixed costs are.

**Sunk cost** A cost that has already been paid and cannot be recovered.

---

# Solved Problem 12.4

## When to Pull the Plug on a Movie

When Walt Disney released the film *Mars Needs Moms*, directed by Robert Zemeckis, in March 2011, it did very poorly at the box office. Worldwide, it earned less than $40 million in revenue, even though it cost $175 million to make. A year before the film was released, Disney executives watched the parts of the film that were complete. They were disappointed in what they saw and immediately stopped production on Robert Zemeckis's next film. They

did not, however, stop production on *Mars Needs Moms*, on which the company had already spent $100 million. In March 2010, at the time the executives became concerned about the quality of the film, how should Disney have decided whether to finish *Mars Needs Moms* and release it? What role should the $100 million Disney executives had already spent on the film have played in their decision?

### Solving the Problem

**Step 1:** **Review the chapter material.** This problem is about the role of sunk costs in business decision making, so you may want to review the section "Deciding Whether to Produce or to Shut Down in the Short Run," which begins above on this page.

**Step 2:** **Use your knowledge of the role of sunk costs in decisions about whether to shut down to answer the question.** In this case, Disney was not considering whether to shut down the company but whether to shut down this particular film. By March 2010, Disney had already invested $100 million in *Mars Needs Moms*. It is tempting to argue that unless Disney completed the film, the $100 million would be lost. It is important to see, though, that the $100 million was a sunk cost: Whether Disney shut down the film or finished it and released it to theaters, the company would not be able to get that $100 million back. Therefore, the $100 million was irrelevant to Disney's decision. Instead, Disney should have made the decision based on comparing the additional cost of completing and releasing the film to the revenue the film was expected to earn. In other words, Disney should have completed the film if marginal revenue was expected to be greater than marginal cost, and it should have shut down the film if marginal cost were expected to be greater than marginal revenue.

Although Disney knew the marginal cost of completing and releasing the film, it had to estimate the marginal revenue based on its forecasts of ticket sales and later sales of DVDs and streaming video. Disney decided to finish the film. The flim cost an additional $75 million to complete, but it earned only about $39 million at the box office. With hindsight, Disney made the wrong decision, but the company may have overestimated ticket sales or expected sales of DVDs and streaming video to offset poor results at the box office.

Based on Brooks Barnes, "Many Culprits in Fall of a Family Film," *New York Times*, March 14, 2011; revenue and cost data from boxofficemojo.com.

**Your Turn:** Test your understanding by doing related problems 4.8 and 4.9 on page 427 at the end of this chapter.

MyEconLab

---

One option not available to a firm with losses in a perfectly competitive market is to raise its price. If the firm did raise its price, it would lose all its customers, and its sales would drop to zero. For example, in a recent year, the price of wheat in the United States was $3.16 per bushel. At that price, the typical U.S. wheat farmer lost $9,500. At a price of about $4.25 per bushel, the typical wheat farmer would have broken even. But any wheat farmer who tried to raise his price to $4.25 per bushel would have seen his sales quickly disappear because buyers could purchase all the wheat they wanted at $3.16 per bushel from the thousands of other wheat farmers.

## The Supply Curve of a Firm in the Short Run

Remember that the supply curve for a firm tells us how many units of a product the firm is willing to sell at any given price. Notice that the marginal cost curve for a firm in a perfectly competitive market tells us the same thing. The firm will produce at the level of output where $MR = MC$. Because price equals marginal revenue for a firm in a perfectly competitive market, the firm will produce where $P = MC$. For any given price, we can determine from the marginal cost curve the quantity of output the firm will supply. *Therefore, a perfectly competitive firm's marginal cost curve also is its supply curve.* There is, however, an important qualification to this fact. We have seen that if a firm is experiencing a loss, it will shut down if its total revenue is less than its variable cost:

$$\text{Total revenue} < \text{Variable cost},$$

or, in symbols:

$$(P \times Q) < VC.$$

## Figure 12.6

### The Firm's Short-Run Supply Curve

The firm will produce at the level of output at which $MR = MC$. Because price equals marginal revenue for a firm in a perfectly competitive market, the firm will produce where $P = MC$. For any given price, we can determine the quantity of output the firm will supply from the marginal cost curve. In other words, the marginal cost curve is the firm's supply curve. But remember that the firm will shut down if the price falls below average variable cost. The marginal cost curve crosses the average variable cost at the firm's shutdown point. This point occurs at output level $Q_{SD}$. For prices below $P_{MIN}$, the supply curve is a vertical line along the price axis, which shows that the firm will supply zero output at those prices. The red line in the figure is the firm's short-run supply curve.

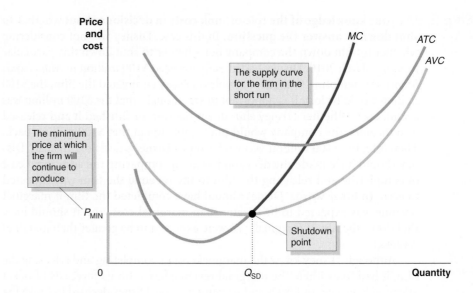

**Shutdown point** The minimum point on a firm's average variable cost curve; if the price falls below this point, the firm shuts down production in the short run.

If we divide both sides by $Q$, we have the result that the firm will shut down if

$$P < AVC.$$

If the price drops below average variable cost, the firm will have a smaller loss if it shuts down and produces no output. *So, the firm's marginal cost curve is its supply curve only for prices at or above average variable cost.* The red line in Figure 12.6 shows the supply curve for the firm in the short run.

Recall that the marginal cost curve intersects the average variable cost where the average variable cost curve is at its minimum point. Therefore, the firm's supply curve is its marginal cost curve above the minimum point of the average variable cost curve. For prices below minimum average variable cost ($P_{MIN}$), the firm will shut down, and its output will fall to zero. The minimum point on the average variable cost curve is called the **shutdown point**, and it occurs in Figure 12.6 at output level $Q_{SD}$.

## The Market Supply Curve in a Perfectly Competitive Industry

We saw in Chapter 10 that the market demand curve is determined by adding up the quantity demanded by each consumer in the market at each price. Similarly, the market supply curve is determined by adding up the quantity supplied by each firm in the market at each price. Each firm's marginal cost curve tells us how much that firm will supply at each price. So, the market supply curve can be derived directly from the marginal cost curves of the firms in the market. Panel (a) of Figure 12.7 shows the marginal cost curve for one wheat farmer. At a price of $4, this wheat farmer supplies 15,000 bushels of wheat. If every wheat farmer supplies the same amount of wheat at this price and if there are 150,000 wheat farmers, the total amount of wheat supplied at a price of $4 will be

15,000 bushels per farmer $\times$ 150,000 farms = 2.25 billion bushels of wheat.

Panel (b) shows a price of $4 and a quantity of 2.25 billion bushels as a point on the market supply curve for wheat. In reality, of course, not all wheat farms are alike. Some wheat farms supply more at the market price than the typical farm; other wheat farms supply less. The key point is that we can derive the market supply curve by adding up the quantity that each firm in the market is willing and able to supply at each price.

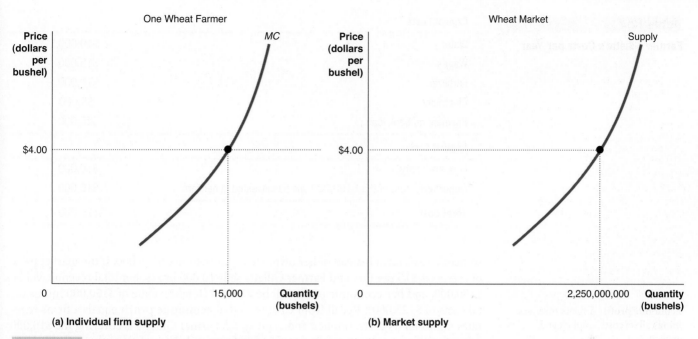

**Figure 12.7**    **Firm Supply and Market Supply**

We can derive the market supply curve by adding up the quantity that each firm in the market is willing to supply at each price. In panel (a), one wheat farmer is willing to supply 15,000 bushels of wheat at a price of $4 per bushel. If every wheat farmer supplies the same amount of wheat at this price and if there are 150,000 wheat farmers, the total amount of wheat supplied at a price of $4 will equal 15,000 bushels per farmer × 150,000 farmers = 2.25 billion bushels of wheat. This is one point on the market supply curve for wheat shown in panel (b). We can find the other points on the market supply curve by determining how much wheat each farmer is willing to supply at each price.

# "If Everyone Can Do It, You Can't Make Money at It": The Entry and Exit of Firms in the Long Run

**12.5 LEARNING** OBJECTIVE

Explain how entry and exit ensure that perfectly competitive firms earn zero economic profit in the long run.

In the long run, unless a firm can cover all its costs, it will shut down and exit the industry. In a market system, firms continually enter and exit industries. In this section, we will see how profits and losses provide signals to firms that lead to entry and exit.

## Economic Profit and the Entry or Exit Decision

To begin, let's look more closely at how economists characterize the profits earned by the owners of a firm. Suppose Sacha Gillette decides to start her own business. After considering her interests and preparing a business plan, she decides to start a vegetable farm rather than open a restaurant or gift shop. After 10 years of effort, Sacha has saved $100,000 and borrowed another $900,000 from a bank. With these funds, she has bought the land and farm equipment necessary to start her farm. She intends to sell the carrots she grows in a local farmers' market. As we saw in Chapter 11, when someone invests her own funds in her firm, the opportunity cost to the firm is the return the funds would have earned in their best alternative use. If Farmer Gillette could have earned a 10 percent return on her $100,000 in savings in their best alternative use—which might have been, for example, to buy a small restaurant—then her carrot business incurs a $10,000 opportunity cost. We can also think of this $10,000 as being the minimum amount that Farmer Gillette needs to earn on her $100,000 investment in her farm to remain in the industry in the long run.

Table 12.4 lists Farmer Gillette's costs. In addition to her explicit costs, we assume that she has two implicit costs: the $10,000 that represents the opportunity cost of the funds she invested in her farm and the $30,000 salary she could have earned managing

**Table 12.4**

**Farmer Gillette's Costs per Year**

| Explicit Costs | |
|---|---:|
| Water | $10,000 |
| Wages | $15,000 |
| Fertilizer | $10,000 |
| Electricity | $5,000 |
| Payment on bank loan | $45,000 |
| **Implicit Costs** | |
| Forgone salary | $30,000 |
| Opportunity cost of the $100,000 she has invested in her farm | $10,000 |
| **Total cost** | **$125,000** |

**Economic profit** A firm's revenues minus all its costs, implicit and explicit.

someone else's farm instead of her own. Her total costs are $125,000. If the market price of carrots is $15 per box and Farmer Gillette sells 10,000 boxes, her total revenue will be $150,000, and her economic profit will be $25,000 (total revenue of $150,000 minus total costs of $125,000). Recall from Chapter 8 that **economic profit** equals a firm's revenues minus all its costs, implicit and explicit. So, Farmer Gillette is covering the $10,000 opportunity cost of the funds invested in her firm, and she is also earning an additional $25,000 in economic profit.

**Economic Profit Leads to Entry of New Firms** Unfortunately, Farmer Gillette is unlikely to earn an economic profit for very long. Suppose other farmers are just breaking even by selling their carrots to supermarkets. In that case, they will have an incentive to switch to selling at farmers' markets so they can begin earning an economic profit. As we saw in the chapter opener, in recent years, many small farmers have begun to sell in farmers' markets, in the hope of earning higher profits. Remember that the more firms there are in an industry, the farther to the right the market supply curve is. Panel (a) of Figure 12.8 shows that as more farmers begin selling carrots in farmers' markets, the market supply curve shifts to the right. Farmers will continue entering the market until the market supply curve has shifted from $S_1$ to $S_2$.

With the supply curve at $S_2$, the market price will have fallen to $10 per box. Panel (b) shows the effect on Farmer Gillette, whom we assume has the same costs as other carrot farmers. As the market price falls from $15 to $10 per box, Farmer Gillette's demand curve shifts down, from $D_1$ to $D_2$. In the new equilibrium, Farmer Gillette is selling 8,000 boxes, at a price of $10 per box. She and the other carrot farmers are no longer earning any economic profit. They are just breaking even, and the return on their investment is just covering the opportunity cost of these funds. New farmers will stop entering the market for selling carrots in farmers' markets because the rate of return is no better than they can earn by selling their carrots elsewhere.

Will Farmer Gillette continue to sell carrots at farmers' markets even though she is just breaking even? She will because selling carrots at farmers' markets earns her as high a return on her investment as she could earn elsewhere. It may seem strange that new firms will continue to enter a market until all economic profits are eliminated and that established firms remain in a market despite not earning any economic profit. But it seems strange only because we are used to thinking in terms of accounting profits rather than *economic* profits. Remember that accounting rules generally require that only explicit costs be included on a firm's financial statements. The opportunity cost of the funds Farmer Gillette invested in her firm—$10,000—and her forgone salary—$30,000—are economic costs, but neither of them is an accounting cost. So, although an accountant would see Farmer Gillette as earning a profit of $40,000, an economist would see her as just breaking even. Farmer Gillette must pay attention to her accounting profit when preparing her financial statements and when paying her income tax. But because economic profit takes into account all her costs, it gives a more accurate indication of the financial health of her farm.

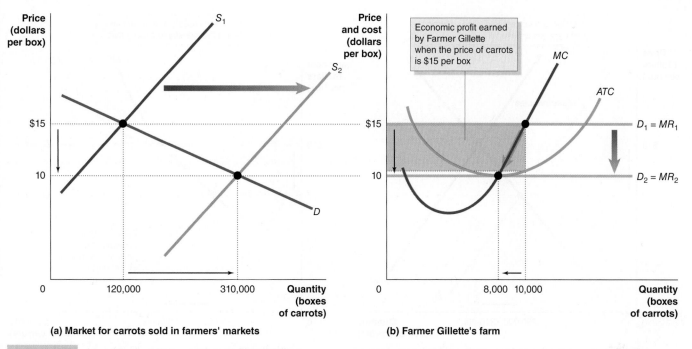

**Figure 12.8    The Effect of Entry on Economic Profits**

We assume that Farmer Gillette's costs are the same as the costs of other carrot farmers. Initially, she and other farmers selling carrots in farmers' markets are able to charge $15 per box and earn an economic profit. Farmer Gillette's economic profit is represented by the area of the green box. Panel (a) shows that as other farmers begin to sell carrots in farmers' markets, the market supply curve shifts to the right, from $S_1$ to $S_2$, and the market price drops to $10 per

box. Panel (b) shows that the falling price causes Farmer Gillette's demand curve to shift down from $D_1$ to $D_2$, and she reduces her output from 10,000 boxes to 8,000. At the new market price of $10 per box, carrot growers are just breaking even: Their total revenue is equal to their total cost, and their economic profit is zero. Notice the difference in scale between the graph in panel (a) and the graph in panel (b).

**Economic Losses Lead to Exit of Firms**  Suppose some consumers decide that there are no important benefits from locally grown produce sold at farmers' markets, and they switch back to buying their produce in supermarkets. Panel (a) of Figure 12.9 shows that the demand curve for carrots sold in farmers' markets will shift to the left, from $D_1$ to $D_2$, and the market price will fall from $10 per box to $7. Panel (b) shows that as the price falls, a farmer, like Sacha Gillette, will move down her marginal cost curve to a lower level of output. At the lower level of output and lower price, she will be suffering an **economic loss** because she will not cover all her costs. As long as price is above average variable cost, she will continue to produce in the short run, even when suffering losses. But in the long run, firms will exit an industry if they are unable to cover all their costs. In this case, some farmers will switch back to selling carrots to supermarkets rather than selling them in farmers' markets.

> **Economic loss**  The situation in which a firm's total revenue is less than its total cost, including all implicit costs.

Panel (c) of Figure 12.9 shows that as firms exit from selling at farmers' markets, the market supply curve shifts to the left. Firms will continue to exit, and the supply curve will continue to shift to the left until the price has risen back to $10 and the market supply curve is at $S_2$. Panel (d) shows that when the price is back to $10, the remaining firms in the industry will be breaking even.

## Long-Run Equilibrium in a Perfectly Competitive Market

We have seen that economic profits attract firms to enter an industry. The entry of firms forces down the market price until the typical firm is breaking even. Economic losses cause firms to exit an industry. The exit of firms forces up the equilibrium market price until the typical firm is breaking even. This process of entry and exit results in *long-run competitive equilibrium*. In **long-run competitive equilibrium**, entry and exit have resulted in the typical firm breaking even. We saw in Chapter 11 that in the

> **Long-run competitive equilibrium**  The situation in which the entry and exit of firms has resulted in the typical firm breaking even.

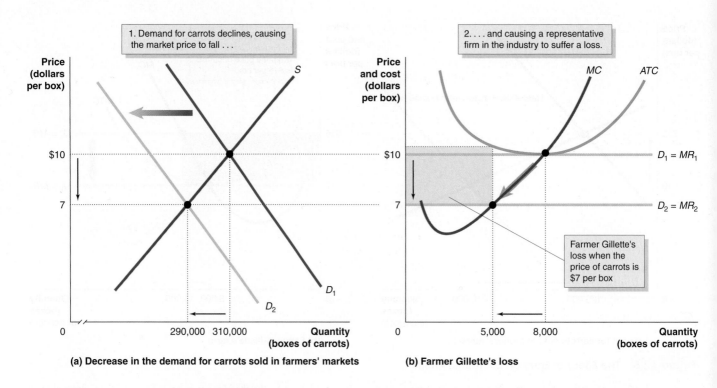

**(a) Decrease in the demand for carrots sold in farmers' markets**

**(b) Farmer Gillette's loss**

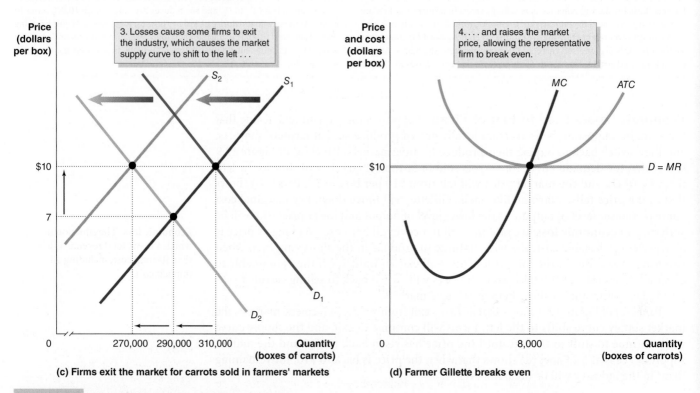

**(c) Firms exit the market for carrots sold in farmers' markets**

**(d) Farmer Gillette breaks even**

---

**Figure 12.9** **The Effect of Exit on Economic Losses**

When the price of carrots is $10 per box, Farmer Gillette and other farmers are breaking even. A total quantity of 310,000 boxes is sold in the market. Farmer Gillette sells 8,000 boxes. Panel (a) shows a decline in the demand for carrots sold in farmers' markets from $D_1$ to $D_2$ that reduces the market price to $7 per box. Panel (b) shows that the falling price causes Farmer Gillette's demand curve to shift down from $D_1$ to $D_2$ and her output to fall from 8,000 to 5,000 boxes. At a market price of $7 per box, farmers have economic losses,

represented by the area of the red box. As a result, some farmers will exit the market, which shifts the market supply curve to the left. Panel (c) shows that exit continues until the supply curve has shifted from $S_1$ to $S_2$ and the market price has risen from $7 back to $10. Panel (d) shows that with the price back at $10, Farmer Gillette will break even. In the new market equilibrium in panel (c), total sales of carrots in farmers' markets have fallen from 310,000 to 270,000 boxes.

long run firms can also vary their scale by becoming larger or smaller. The *long-run average cost curve* shows the lowest cost at which a firm is able to produce a given quantity of output in the long run. So, we would expect that in the long run, competition drives the market price to the minimum point on the typical firm's long-run average cost curve.

The long run in selling produce in farmers' markets appears to be several years, which is the amount of time it takes for new farmers' markets to be organized and for farmers to make the investment necessary to sell directly to consumers. As we discussed in the chapter opener, the number of farmers' markets operating in the United States had increased from 4,093 in 2005 to 7,175 in 2011. By 2011, some farmers had begun to exit the market because the prices they were receiving were lower than they could get by selling their produce elsewhere. In Oregon, 32 of 62 farmers' markets that had opened in recent years have since closed.

Firms in perfectly competitive markets are in a constant struggle to stay one step ahead of their competitors. They are always looking for new ways to provide a product, such as selling carrots in farmers' markets. It is possible for firms to find ways to earn an economic profit for a while, but competition typically competes those profits away in just a few years. This observation is not restricted to agriculture. In any perfectly competitive market, an opportunity to make economic profits never lasts long. As Sharon Oster, an economist at Yale University, has put it, "If everyone can do it, you can't make money at it."

## The Long-Run Supply Curve in a Perfectly Competitive Market

If the typical farmer selling carrots in a farmers' market breaks even at a price of $10 per box, in the long run, the market price will always return to this level. If an increase in demand causes the market price to rise above $10, farmers will be earning economic profits. These profits will attract additional farmers into the market, and the market supply curve will shift to the right until the price is back to $10. Panel (a) in Figure 12.10 illustrates the long-run effect of an increase in demand. An increase in demand from $D_1$ to $D_2$ causes the market price to temporarily rise from $10 per box to $15. At this price, farmers are making economic profits selling carrots at farmers' markets, but these profits attract entry of new farmers. The result is an increase in supply from $S_1$ to $S_2$, which forces the price back down to $10 per box and eliminates the economic profits.

Similarly, if a decrease in demand causes the market price to fall below $10, farmers will experience economic losses. These losses will cause some farmers to exit the market, the supply curve will shift to the left, and the price will return to $10. Panel (b) in Figure 12.10 illustrates the long-run effect of a decrease in demand. A decrease in demand from $D_1$ to $D_2$ causes the market price to fall temporarily from $10 per box to $7. At this price, farmers are suffering economic losses, but these losses cause some farmers to exit the market for organic apples. The result is a decrease in supply from $S_1$ to $S_2$, which forces the price back up to $10 per box and eliminates the losses.

The **long-run supply curve** shows the relationship in the long run between market price and the quantity supplied. In the long run, the price will be $10 per box, no matter how many boxes of carrots are produced. So, as Figure 12.10 shows, the long-run supply curve ($S_{LR}$) is a horizontal line at a price of $10. Remember that the reason the price returns to $10 in the long run is that this is the price at which the typical firm in the industry just breaks even. The typical firm breaks even at this price because it is at the minimum point on the firm's average total cost curve. We can draw the important conclusion that *in the long run, a perfectly competitive market will supply whatever amount of a good consumers demand at a price determined by the minimum point on the typical firm's average total cost curve.*

Because the position of the long-run supply curve is determined by the minimum point on the typical firm's average total cost curve, anything that raises or lowers the

**Long-run supply curve** A curve that shows the relationship in the long run between market price and the quantity supplied.

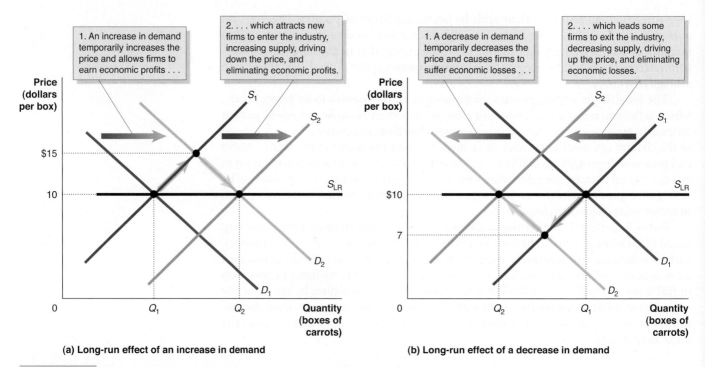

(a) Long-run effect of an increase in demand

(b) Long-run effect of a decrease in demand

**Figure 12.10** The Long-Run Supply Curve in a Perfectly Competitive Industry

Panel (a) shows that an increase in demand for carrots sold in farmers' markets will lead to a temporary increase in price from $10 to $15 per box, as the market demand curve shifts to the right, from $D_1$ to $D_2$. The entry of new firms shifts the market supply curve to the right, from $S_1$ to $S_2$, which will cause the price to fall back to its long-run level of $10. Panel (b) shows that a decrease in demand will lead to a temporary decrease in price from $10 to $7 per box, as the market

demand curve shifts to the left, from $D_1$ to $D_2$. The exit of firms shifts the market supply curve to the left, from $S_1$ to $S_2$, which causes the price to rise back to its long-run level of $10. The long-run supply curve ($S_{LR}$) shows the relationship between market price and the quantity supplied in the long run. In this case, the long-run supply curve is a horizontal line.

costs of the typical firm in the long run will cause the long-run supply curve to shift. For example, if a new disease infects carrots and the costs of treating the disease adds $2 per box to every farmers' cost of producing carrots, the long-run supply curve will shift up by $2.

*Economic profits are rapidly competed away in the iTunes apps store.*

| Making the Connection | In the Apple iPhone Apps Store, Easy Entry Makes the Long Run Pretty Short |

Apple introduced the first version of the iPhone in June 2007. Although popular, the original iPhone had some drawbacks, including a slow connection to the Internet and an inability to run any applications except those written by Apple. The iPhone 3G, released in July 2008, could connect to the Internet more quickly and easily, had a faster processor, and had a larger capacity. But perhaps most importantly, with the release of the iPhone 3G, Apple announced that a section of its immensely popular iTunes music and video store would be devoted to applications (or "apps") for the iPhone. Independent software programmers would write these iPhone apps. Apple would approve the apps and make them available in the iTunes app store in exchange for receiving 30 percent of the purchase price. Major software companies, as well as individuals writing their first software programs, have posted games, calendars, dictionaries, and many other types of apps to the iTunes store.

Apple sold more than 3 million iPhones within a month of launching the iPhone 3G. Demand for apps from the iTunes store soared along with sales of the iPhone. Ethan Nicholas, who in August 2008 was a programmer at Sun Microsystems but had never written a game before, decided to teach himself the coding language used in iPhone apps. His game, iShoot, with an initial price of $4.99, was a great success. Within one week of posting to iTunes, enough people had downloaded iShoot to earn Nicholas $200,000. At the end of five months, he had earned $800,000.

But could Nicholas's success last? As we have seen, when firms earn economic profits in a market, other firms have a strong economic incentive to enter that market. This is exactly what happened with iPhone apps, and by April 2009, more than 25,000 apps were available in the iTunes store. The cost of entering this market was very small. Anyone with the programming skills and the available time could write an app and have it posted in the store. As a result of this enhanced competition, the ability to get rich quick with a killer app was quickly fading. As an article in the *New York Times* put it: "The chances of hitting the iPhone jackpot keep getting slimmer: the Apple store is already crowded with look-alike games . . . and fresh inventory keeps arriving daily. Many of the simple but clever concepts that sell briskly . . . are already taken."

To try to maintain sales, Ethan Nicholas was forced to drop the price of iShoot from $4.99 in October 2008 to $2.99 in April 2009 to $1.99 in May 2009, and finally to $0.99 in September 2010. But his profits from the game continued to decline. In a competitive market, earning an economic profit in the long run is extremely difficult. And the ease of entering the market for iPhone apps has made the long run pretty short.

Based on Jenna Wortham, "The iPhone Gold Rush," *New York Times*, April 5, 2009; and Bruce X. Chen, "Coder's Half-Million-Dollar Baby Proves iPhone Gold Rush Is Still On," wired.com, February 12, 2009.

**Your Turn:** Test your understanding by doing related problem 5.9 on page 428 at the end of this chapter.      MyEconLab

## Increasing-Cost and Decreasing-Cost Industries

Any industry in which the typical firm's average costs do not change as the industry expands production will have a horizontal long-run supply curve, like the one in Figure 12.10. Industries, like the carrot industry, where this holds true are called *constant-cost industries*. It's possible, however, for the typical firm's average costs to change as an industry expands.

For example, if an input used in producing a good is available in only limited quantities, the cost of the input will rise as the industry expands. If only a limited amount of land is available on which to grow the grapes to make a certain variety of wine, an increase in demand for wine made from these grapes will result in competition for the land and will drive up its price. As a result, more of the wine will be produced in the long run only if the price rises to cover the higher average costs of the typical firm. In this case, the long-run supply curve will slope upward. Industries with upward-sloping long-run supply curves are called *increasing-cost industries*.

Finally, in some cases, the typical firm's costs may fall as the industry expands. Suppose that someone invents a new microwave that uses as an input a specialized memory chip that is currently produced only in small quantities. If demand for the microwave increases, firms that produce microwaves will increase their orders for the memory chip. We saw in Chapter 11 that if there are economies of scale in producing a good, its average cost will decline as output increases. If there are economies of scale in producing this memory chip, the average cost of producing it will fall, and competition will result in its price falling as well. This price decline, in turn, will lower the average cost of producing the new microwave. In the long run, competition will force the price of the microwave to fall to the level of the new lower average cost of the typical firm. In this case, the long-run supply curve will slope downward. Industries with downward-sloping long-run supply curves are called *decreasing-cost industries*.

**12.6 LEARNING** OBJECTIVE

Explain how perfect competition leads to economic efficiency.

# Perfect Competition and Efficiency

Notice how powerful consumers are in a market system. If consumers want more locally grown carrots, the market will supply them. This happens not because a government bureaucrat in Washington, DC, or an official in a carrot growers' association gives orders. The additional carrots are produced because an increase in demand results in higher prices and a higher rate of return from selling at farmers' markets. Carrot growers, trying to get the highest possible return on their investments, begin to switch from selling to supermarkets to selling at farmers' markets. If consumers lose their taste for locally grown carrots and demand falls, the process works in reverse.

## Productive Efficiency

**Productive efficiency** The situation in which a good or service is produced at the lowest possible cost.

In a market system, consumers get as many carrots as they want, produced at the lowest average cost possible. The forces of competition will drive the market price to the minimum average cost of the typical firm. **Productive efficiency** refers to the situation in which a good or service is produced at the lowest possible cost. As we have seen, perfect competition results in productive efficiency.

The managers of every firm strive to earn an economic profit by reducing costs. But in a perfectly competitive market, other firms quickly copy ways of reducing costs. Therefore, in the long run, only the consumer benefits from cost reductions.

# Solved Problem 12.6

## How Productive Efficiency Benefits Consumers

Writing in the *New York Times* on the technology boom of the late 1990s, Michael Lewis argued, "The sad truth, for investors, seems to be that most of the benefits of new technologies are passed right through to consumers free of charge."

a. What do you think Lewis means by the benefits of new technology being "passed right through to consumers free of charge"? Use a graph like Figure 12.8 on page 413 to illustrate your answer.
b. Explain why this result is a "sad truth" for investors.

## Solving the Problem

**Step 1:** **Review the chapter material.** This problem is about perfect competition and efficiency, so you may want to review the section "Perfect Competition and Efficiency," which begins above.

**Step 2:** **Use the concepts from this chapter to explain what Lewis means.** By "new technologies," Lewis means new products—such as smart phones or LED television sets—or lower-cost ways of producing existing products. In either case, new technologies will allow firms to earn economic profits for a while, but these profits will lead new firms to enter the market in the long run.

**Step 3:** **Use a graph like Figure 12.8 on page 413 to illustrate why the benefits of new technologies are "passed right through to consumers free of charge."** Figure 12.8 shows the situation in which a firm is making economic profits in the short run but has these profits eliminated by entry in the long run. We can draw a similar graph to analyze what happens in the long run in the market for LED televisions.

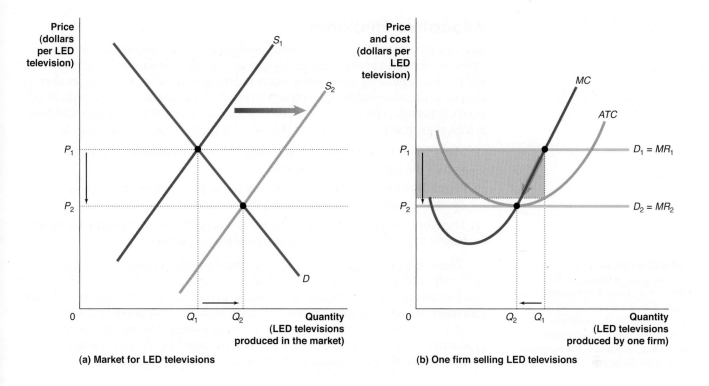

**(a) Market for LED televisions**

**(b) One firm selling LED televisions**

When LED televisions were first introduced, prices were high, and only a few firms were in the market. Panel (a) shows that the initial equilibrium price in the market for LED televisions is $P_1$. Panel (b) shows that at this price, the typical firm in the industry is earning an economic profit, which is shown by the green-shaded box. The economic profit attracts new firms into the industry. This entry shifts the market supply curve from $S_1$ to $S_2$ in panel (a) and lowers the equilibrium price from $P_1$ to $P_2$. Panel (b) shows that at the new market price, $P_2$, the typical firm is breaking even. Therefore, LED televisions are being produced at the lowest possible cost, and productive efficiency is achieved. Consumers receive the new technology "free of charge" in the sense that they only have to pay a price equal to the lowest possible cost of production.

**Step 4:** **Answer part b. by explaining why the result in part a. is a "sad truth" for investors.** We have seen in answering part a. that in the long run, firms only break even on their investment in producing high-technology goods. That result implies that investors in these firms are also unlikely to earn an economic profit in the long run.

**Extra Credit:** Lewis is using a key result from this chapter: In the long run, entry of new firms competes away economic profits. We should notice that, strictly speaking, the high-technology industries Lewis is discussing are not perfectly competitive. Smart phones or LED televisions, for instance, are not identical, and each smart phone company produces a quantity large enough to affect the market price. However, as we will see in Chapter 13, these deviations from perfect competition do not change the important conclusion that the entry of new firms benefits consumers by forcing prices down to the level of average cost. In fact, the price of LED televisions dropped by more than 35 percent within three years of their first becoming widely available.

Based on Michael Lewis, "In Defense of the Boom," *New York Times*, October 27, 2002.

**Your Turn:** For more practice, do related problems 6.5, 6.6, and 6.7 on page 429 at the end of this chapter.  MyEconLab

## Allocative Efficiency

Not only do perfectly competitive firms produce goods and services at the lowest possible cost, they also produce the goods and services that consumers value most. Firms will produce a good up to the point where the marginal cost of producing another unit is equal to the marginal benefit consumers receive from consuming that unit. In other words, firms will supply all those goods that provide consumers with a marginal benefit at least as great as the marginal cost of producing them. We know this is true because:

1. The price of a good represents the marginal benefit consumers receive from consuming the last unit of the good sold.

2. Perfectly competitive firms produce up to the point where the price of the good equals the marginal cost of producing the last unit.

3. Therefore, firms produce up to the point where the last unit provides a marginal benefit to consumers equal to the marginal cost of producing it.

**Allocative efficiency** A state of the economy in which production represents consumer preferences; in particular, every good or service is produced up to the point where the last unit provides a marginal benefit to consumers equal to the marginal cost of producing it.

These statements are another way of saying that entrepreneurs in a market system efficiently *allocate* labor, machinery, and other inputs to produce the goods and services that best satisfy consumer wants. In this sense, perfect competition achieves **allocative efficiency**. As we will explore in the next few chapters, many goods and services sold in the U.S. economy are not produced in perfectly competitive markets. Nevertheless, productive efficiency and allocative efficiency are useful benchmarks against which to compare the actual performance of the economy.

Continued from page 395

## Economics in Your Life

### Are You an Entrepreneur?

At the beginning of the chapter, we asked you to think about why you can charge only a relatively low price for performing services such as babysitting or lawn mowing. In the chapter, we saw that firms selling products in competitive markets can't charge prices higher than those being charged by competing firms. The market for babysitting and lawn mowing is very competitive. In most neighborhoods, there are many teenagers willing to supply these services. The price you can charge for babysitting may not be worth your while at age 20 but is enough to cover the opportunity cost of a 14-year-old eager to enter the market. (Or, as we put it in Table 12.1 on page 396, the ease of entry into babysitting and lawn mowing is high.) So, in your career as a teenage entrepreneur, you may have become familiar with one of the lessons of this chapter: A firm in a competitive market has no control over price.

## Conclusion

The competitive forces of the market impose relentless pressure on firms to produce new and better goods and services at the lowest possible cost. Firms that fail to adequately anticipate changes in consumer tastes or that fail to adopt the latest and most efficient technology do not survive in the long run. In the nineteenth century, the biologist Charles Darwin developed a theory of evolution based on the idea of the "survival of the fittest." Only those plants and animals that are best able to adapt to the demands of their environment are able to survive. Darwin first realized the important role that the struggle for existence plays in the natural world after reading early nineteenth-century economists' descriptions of the role it plays in the economic world. Just as "survival of the fittest" is the rule in nature, so it is in the economic world.

At the start of this chapter, we saw that there are four market structures: perfect competition, monopolistic competition, oligopoly, and monopoly. Now that we have studied perfect competition, in the following chapters we move on to the other three market structures. Before turning to those chapters, read *An Inside Look* on the next page for a discussion of the reasons for the decline in organic farming in the United Kingdom.

## GUARDIAN.CO.UK

## Farmers Turn Away from Organic as Sales Drop

Farmers have begun to turn away from organic food production in the face of waning interest from the big supermarkets.

The amount of land being converted to organic cultivation across the UK has dropped by two-thirds since 2007, according to statistics released by the Department for Environment, Food and Rural Affairs, as falling sales of organic products mean fewer farmers are seeing a reason to change.

(a) Sales of organic products fell by 5.9% in the UK last year, according to the Soil Association, from £1.8bn in 2009 to £1.7bn. That continued a decline from record sales of £2.1bn in 2008, and came amid rising food prices. The amount of organic poultry being produced has also fallen steadily.

But many farmers who have gone organic were defiant after publication of the latest figures, arguing that switching to greener methods has drastically cut their costs and that consumer interest is still strong, particularly when farmers can use sales routes other than big supermarket chains.

"There might be lots of farmers who think they can't afford to go organic, because they think the market is restricted, but if they looked into it they would find it can be cost-effective," said Ian Noble, who represents a 12-farm cooperative in south Devon growing organic vegetables. With little or no costs for fertilisers and pesticides, and—at least on smaller farms—most animals fed on grass rather than expensive grain, organic farmers can make savings at a time of high commodity prices. Adrian Dolby, of Barrington Park, said cutting input prices was one of his key reasons for putting 7,000 acres under organic cultivation in 2005.

"If we hadn't gone organic, we would have gone out of business," added Tom Rigby, who farms 160 acres near Warrington, most of it given over to pasture. "We are a small dairy farm and small dairy farmers are going bankrupt every day. I decided that if I was going to go bankrupt, I would rather do it in the way I wanted."

Rigby knows of larger producers that have quit organic methods, such as some bigger dairy farms that found their margins squeezed even on premium organic milk as they needed to import increasingly expensive feed. His smaller grass-fed herd avoids this problem, and his organically cultivated vegetables will be sold to Manchester University.

(b) Oliver Dowding, an organic farmer near Wincanton in Somerset for more than 20 years, blamed waning interest among farmers on the numbers who entered organic cultivation several years ago, attracted by government grants to convert their land and the offers of subsidies, and who have since reverted to conventional farming as the financial support has dried up. This is a widespread view among organic farmers, and seems borne out by figures from Scotland which show a massive decline in the acreage under organic production since the early 2000s.

Last year, across the UK, only 51,000 hectares were in "conversion"—the process farmers need to go through to have their land and practices certified as organic. That is less than half the amount of land in conversion in 2009, itself down markedly from the 2007 peak of 158,000 hectares....

(c) For livestock farmers, the picture is mixed. The number of cattle reared organically has risen steadily, to more than 350,000 last year. But despite widespread publicity by food campaigners on the claimed benefits of choosing free range or organic eggs and chickens, more than half a million fewer organic chickens, turkeys and other poultry were produced in the UK last year.

Amid falling sales overall, some specialists are thriving. Abel & Cole, the organic box scheme, expects a 40% increase in sales this year. Keith Abel attributes this to the same reason he believes organic sales have fallen overall—because the big supermarkets have taken organic products off the shelves to make room for cheaper non-organic goods. "It is a self-fulfilling prophecy: they take them off the shelves, and they sell less," he said. "But that's great news for me."

## Key Points in the Article

Since reaching a peak in 2008, organic food production and sales in the United Kingdom have steadily fallen, as has the amount of land farmers have converted to organic cultivation. The recession has been cited as a reason for the drop in sales, with large supermarkets cutting back on their organic selections. With sales numbers declining, many farmers have found it more difficult to justify the added expense of converting to organic production. Some farmers who had switched to organic when the British government was subsidizing conversion and production have since gone back to conventional methods now that subsidies have declined. While organic produce sales have declined in the United Kingdom, organic livestock sales have been mixed, with cattle production on the rise but poultry production falling.

## Analyzing the News

**(a)** Organic products usually command a higher price than their non-organic counterparts, and up until 2008, the demand for organic food was increasing in the United Kingdom. The potential for higher profits attracted many farmers to the organic market as demand was increasing.

However, the recession coupled with rising food prices had a negative effect on the market for organic food, and sales have declined each year since 2008. The decline in sales is due to a decrease in the overall demand for organic products. Figure 1 shows the market for organically grown corn. The decrease in demand is illustrated as a shift from $D_1$ to $D_2$, where both the equilibrium quantity and equilibrium market price decline.

**(b)** With sales falling, fewer farmers are converting to organic production, and some of those who had switched to organic are now reverting to conventional farming methods. The chapter notes that some firms exit a market when they experience economic losses. The decrease in demand in Figure 1 causes the price to decrease from $P_1$ to $P_2$. This decrease in price causes the individual farmer's demand curve to shift from $D_1$ to $D_2$ in Figure 2. The price per bushel decreases, and the farmer reduces production from $q_1$ to $q_2$. At the lower market price of $P_2$, the farmer has an economic loss represented by the area of the shaded box. Some farmers suffering losses will choose to exit the market.

**(c)** While organic produce and poultry farmers have been experiencing

declining sales in the United Kingdom, organic cattle production has continued to rise to keep pace with growing sales. As long as demand continues to increase and organic cattle producers make an economic profit, more producers will have the incentive to enter the market. If the demand starts to decrease, though, as it did in other organic markets, we would expect to eventually see producers of organic cattle begin to exit this market as well.

## Thinking Critically

1. The article states that due to declining product demand, farmers are converting from organic production back to conventional methods. Show what will happen in Figure 1 as some farmers exit the organic market, and show how this change will affect the farmer represented by Figure 2.

2. The article indicates that in addition to the decline in demand, the end of government grants and subsidies has contributed to the number of farmers leaving the organic market. How would government grants and subsidies affect this market?

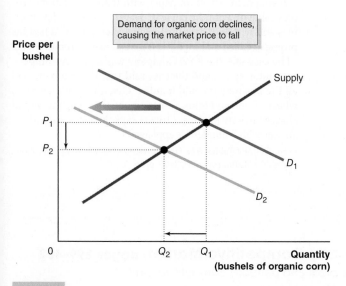

**Figure 1**

The market for organically grown corn.

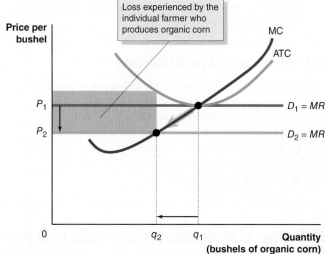

**Figure 2**

An individual farmer suffering an economic loss in the organic corn market.

# Chapter Summary and Problems

## Key Terms

Allocative efficiency, p. 420

Average revenue (*AR*), p. 400

Economic loss, p. 413

Economic profit, p. 412

Long-run competitive
equilibrium, p. 413

Long-run supply curve, p. 415

Marginal revenue (*MR*), p. 400

Perfectly competitive market,
p. 397

Price taker, p. 397

Productive efficiency, p. 418

Profit, p. 399

Shutdown point, p. 410

Sunk cost, p. 408

 **12.1** **Perfectly Competitive Markets, pages 397–399**
LEARNING OBJECTIVE: Explain what a perfectly competitive market is and why a perfect competitor faces
a horizontal demand curve.

### Summary

A **perfectly competitive market** must have many buyers and sellers, firms must be producing identical products, and there must be no barriers to entry of new firms. The demand curve for a good or service produced in a perfectly competitive market is downward sloping, but the demand curve for the output of one firm in a perfectly competitive market is a horizontal line at the market price. Firms in perfectly competitive markets are **price takers** and see their sales drop to zero if they attempt to charge more than the market price.

MyEconLab Visit **www.myeconlab.com** to complete these
exercises online and get instant feedback.

### Review Questions

**1.1** What are the three conditions for a market to be perfectly competitive?

**1.2** What is a price taker? When are firms likely to be price takers?

**1.3** Draw a graph showing the market demand and supply for corn and the demand for the corn produced by one corn farmer. Be sure to indicate the market price and the price received by the corn farmer.

### Problems and Applications

**1.4** Explain whether each of the following is a perfectly competitive market. For each market that is not perfectly competitive, explain why it is not.
   **a.** Corn farming
   **b.** Retail bookselling
   **c.** Automobile manufacturing
   **d.** New home construction

**1.5** Why are consumers usually price takers when they buy most goods and services, while relatively few firms are price takers?

**1.6** [**Related to the** Don't Let This Happen to You **on page 398**] Explain whether you agree or disagree with the following remark:

> According to the model of perfectly competitive markets, the demand for wheat should be a horizontal line. But this can't be true: When the price of wheat rises, the quantity of wheat demanded falls, and when the price of wheat falls, the quantity of wheat demanded rises. Therefore, the demand for wheat is not a horizontal line.

**1.7** The financial writer Andrew Tobias described an incident that occurred when he was a student at the Harvard Business School: Each student in the class was given large amounts of information about a particular firm and asked to determine a pricing strategy for the firm. Most of the students spent hours preparing their answers and came to class carrying many sheets of paper with their calculations. Tobias came up with the correct answer after just a few minutes and without having made any calculations. When his professor called on him in class for an answer, Tobias stated, "The case said the XYZ Company was in a very competitive industry . . . and the case said that the company had all the business it could handle." Given this information, what price do you think Tobias argued the company should charge? Briefly explain. (Tobias says the class greeted his answer with "thunderous applause.")
From Andrew Tobias, *The Only Investment Guide You'll Ever Need*, Houghton Mifflin Harcourt, 2005, pp. 6–8.

 **12.2** **How a Firm Maximizes Profit in a Perfectly Competitive Market, pages 399–402**
LEARNING OBJECTIVE: Explain how a firm maximizes profit in a perfectly competitive market.

### Summary

**Profit** is the difference between total revenue (*TR*) and total cost (*TC*). **Average revenue** (*AR*) is total revenue divided by the quantity of the product sold. A firm maximizes profit by producing the level of output where the difference between revenue and cost is the greatest. This is the same level of output where marginal revenue is equal to marginal cost. **Marginal revenue** (*MR*) is the change in total revenue from selling one more unit.

## Review Questions

**2.1** Explain why it is true that for a firm in a perfectly competitive market, $P = MR = AR$.

**2.2** Explain why if the difference between $TR$ and $TC$ is at its maximum positive value, then $MR$ must equal $MC$.

**2.3** Explain why it is true that for a firm in a perfectly competitive market, the profit-maximizing condition $MR = MC$ is equivalent to the condition $P = MC$.

## Problems and Applications

**2.4** A student argues: "To maximize profit, a firm should produce the quantity where the difference between marginal revenue and marginal cost is the greatest. If a firm produces more than this quantity, then the profit made on each additional unit will be falling." Briefly explain whether you agree with this reasoning.

**2.5** Why don't firms maximize revenue rather than profit? If a firm decided to maximize revenue, would it be likely to produce a smaller or larger quantity than if it were maximizing profit? Briefly explain.

**2.6** Refer to Table 12.2 on page 400 and Table 12.3 on page 401. Suppose the price of wheat rises to $7.00 per bushel. How many bushels of wheat will Farmer Parker produce, and how much profit will he make? Briefly explain.

**2.7** Refer to Table 12.2 and Table 12.3. Suppose that the marginal cost of wheat is $0.50 higher for every bushel of wheat produced. For example, the marginal cost of producing the eighth bushel of wheat is now $7.50. Assume that the price of wheat remains $4 per bushel. Will this increase in marginal cost change the profit-maximizing level of production for Farmer Parker? Briefly explain. How much profit will Farmer Parker make now?

**2.8** In Table 12.3, what are Farmer Parker's fixed costs? Suppose that his fixed costs increase by $1. Will this increase in fixed cost change the profit-maximizing level of production for Farmer Parker? Briefly explain. How much profit will Farmer Parker make now?

---

<table>
<tr><td>**12.3**</td><td></td></tr>
</table>

## Illustrating Profit or Loss on the Cost Curve Graph, pages 403–407

LEARNING OBJECTIVE: Use graphs to show a firm's profit or loss.

## Summary

From the definitions of profit and average total cost, we can develop the following expression for the relationship between total profit and average total cost: Profit $= (P - ATC) \times Q$. Using this expression, we can determine the area showing profit or loss on a cost-curve graph: The area of profit or loss is a box with a height equal to price minus average total cost (for profit) or average total cost minus price (for loss) and a base equal to the quantity of output.

## Review Questions

**3.1** Draw a graph showing a firm in a perfectly competitive market that is making a profit. Be sure your graph includes the firm's demand curve, marginal revenue curve, marginal cost curve, average total cost curve, and average variable cost curve and make sure to indicate the area representing the firm's profits.

**3.2** Draw a graph showing a firm in a perfectly competitive market that is operating at a loss. Be sure your graph includes the firm's demand curve, marginal revenue curve, marginal cost curve, average total cost curve, and average variable cost curve and make sure to indicate the area representing the firm's losses.

## Problems and Applications

**3.3** **[Related to** Solved Problem 12.3 **on page 404]** Frances sells earrings in the perfectly competitive earrings market. Her output per day and her costs are as follows:

| Output per Day | Total Cost |
|:---:|:---:|
| 0 | $1.00 |
| 1 | 2.50 |
| 2 | 3.50 |
| 3 | 4.20 |
| 4 | 4.50 |
| 5 | 5.20 |
| 6 | 6.80 |
| 7 | 8.70 |
| 8 | 10.70 |
| 9 | 13.00 |

a. If the current equilibrium price in the earrings market is $1.80, how many earrings will Frances produce, what price will she charge, and how much profit (or loss) will she make? Draw a graph to illustrate your answer. Your graph should be clearly labeled and should include Frances's demand, $ATC$, $AVC$, $MC$, and $MR$ curves; the price she is charging; the quantity she is producing; and the area representing her profit (or loss).

b. Suppose the equilibrium price of earrings falls to $1.00. Now how many earrings will Frances produce, what price will she charge, and how much profit (or loss) will she make? Show your work. Draw a graph to illustrate this situation, using the instructions in part a.

c. Suppose the equilibrium price of earrings falls to $0.25. Now how many earrings will Frances produce, what price will she charge, and how much profit (or loss) will she make?

**3.4** **[Related to** Solved Problem 12.3 **on page 404]** Review Solved Problem 12.3 and then answer the following: Suppose the equilibrium price of basketballs falls to $2.50. Now how many basketballs will Andy produce? What price will he charge? How much profit (or loss) will he make?

**3.5** **[Related to the** Don't Let This Happen to You **on page 406]** A student examines the following graph and argues, "I believe that a firm will want to produce at $Q_1$, not $Q_2$. At $Q_1$, the distance between price and marginal cost is the greatest. Therefore, at $Q_1$, the firm will be maximizing its profit." Briefly explain whether you agree with the student's argument.

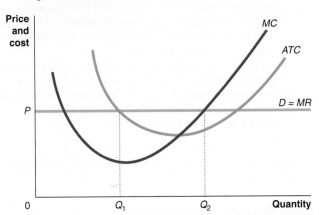

**3.6** CarMax, a nationwide retailer of used cars, announced that its total profit for the fourth quarter of 2008 fell by 10 percent, or $26.8 million, compared to the fourth quarter of 2007. At the same time, its profit per used car increased by $325. If the profit per used car increased, how could total profits fall? Illustrate your answer with a graph. Be sure to indicate profit per used car and total profit on the graph.

Based on Suzanne Ashe, "CarMax Sales Down, Net Profits Up," *CNET*, April 2, 2009.

**3.7** **[Related to the** Making the Connection **on page 407]** Suppose the medical screening firms had run an effective advertising campaign that convinced a large number of people that yearly CT scans were critical for good health. How would this have changed the fortunes of these firms? Illustrate your answer with a graph showing the situation for a representative firm in the industry. Be sure your graph includes the firm's demand curve, marginal revenue curve, marginal cost curve, and average total cost curve.

---

## 12.4 | Deciding Whether to Produce or to Shut Down in the Short Run, pages 408–411

LEARNING OBJECTIVE: Explain why firms may shut down temporarily.

### Summary

In deciding whether to shut down or produce during a given period, a firm should ignore its *sunk costs*. A **sunk cost** is a cost that has already been paid and that cannot be recovered. In the short run, a firm continues to produce as long as its price is at least equal to its average variable cost. A perfectly competitive firm's **shutdown point** is the minimum point on the firm's average variable cost curve. If price falls below average variable cost, the firm shuts down in the short run. For prices above the shutdown point, a perfectly competitive firm's marginal cost curve is also its supply curve.

MyEconLab    Visit www.myeconlab.com to complete these exercises online and get instant feedback.

### Review Questions

**4.1** What is the difference between a firm's shutdown point in the short run and in the long run? Why are firms willing to accept losses in the short run but not in the long run?

**4.2** What is the relationship between a perfectly competitive firm's marginal cost curve and its supply curve?

**4.3** How is the market supply curve derived from the supply curves of individual firms?

### Problems and Applications

**4.4** Edward Scahill produces table lamps in the perfectly competitive desk lamp market.

**a.** Fill in the missing values in the following table:

| Output per Week | Total Cost | AFC | AVC | ATC | MC |
|---|---|---|---|---|---|
| 0 | $100 | | | | |
| 1 | 150 | | | | |
| 2 | 175 | | | | |
| 3 | 190 | | | | |
| 4 | 210 | | | | |
| 5 | 240 | | | | |
| 6 | 280 | | | | |
| 7 | 330 | | | | |
| 8 | 390 | | | | |
| 9 | 460 | | | | |
| 10 | 540 | | | | |

**b.** Suppose the equilibrium price in the desk lamp market is $50. How many table lamps should Scahill produce, and how much profit will he make?

**c.** If next week the equilibrium price of desk lamps drops to $30, should Scahill shut down? Explain.

**4.5** Matthew Rafferty produces hiking boots in the perfectly competitive hiking boot market.

a. Fill in the missing values in the following table:

| Output per Week | Total Cost | AFC | AVC | ATC | MC |
|---|---|---|---|---|---|
| 0 | $100.00 | | | | |
| 1 | 155.70 | | | | |
| 2 | 205.60 | | | | |
| 3 | 253.90 | | | | |
| 4 | 304.80 | | | | |
| 5 | 362.50 | | | | |
| 6 | 431.20 | | | | |
| 7 | 515.10 | | | | |
| 8 | 618.40 | | | | |
| 9 | 745.30 | | | | |
| 10 | 900.00 | | | | |

b. Suppose the equilibrium price in the hiking boot market is $100. How many boots should Rafferty produce, what price should he charge, and how much profit will he make?

c. If next week the equilibrium price of boots drops to $65, how many boots should Rafferty produce, what price should he charge, and how much profit (or loss) will he make?

d. If the equilibrium price of boots falls to $50, how many boots should Rafferty produce, what price should he charge, and how much profit (or loss) will he make?

**4.6** The following graph represents the situation of a perfectly competitive firm:

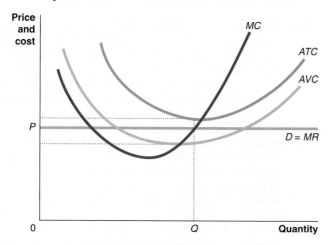

Indicate on the graph the areas that represent the following:

a. Total cost

b. Total revenue

c. Variable cost

d. Profit or loss

Briefly explain whether the firm will continue to produce in the short run.

**4.7** A report issued by the University of Illinois predicted large cost increases for inputs, including fertilizer, seed, insurance, and utilities, for soybean growers in 2009. According to the report, "Significantly higher costs will occur in 2009, leading to higher break-even prices for . . . soybeans." Draw a graph showing a farm earning a profit from soybean production before the increase in input costs. Draw a second graph showing when this same farm would shut down following the increase in input costs.

Based on Gary Schnitkey, "Dramatic Increases in Corn and Soybean Costs in 2009," Farmdoc FEFO 08-13, University of Illinois at Urbana-Champaign, July 11, 2008.

**4.8** **[Related to** Solved Problem 12.4 **on page 408]** Suppose you decide to open a copy store. You rent store space (signing a one-year lease to do so), and you take out a loan at a local bank and use the money to purchase 10 copiers. Six months later, a large chain opens a copy store two blocks away from yours. As a result, the revenue you receive from your copy store, while sufficient to cover the wages of your employees and the costs of paper and utilities, doesn't cover all your rent and the interest and repayment costs on the loan you took out to purchase the copiers. Should you continue operating your business?

**4.9** **[Related to** Solved Problem 12.4 **on page 408]** An article in the *Wall Street Journal* discussed problems some shopping malls were having retaining stores. According to the article, some stores that were currently losing money were considering not "sticking around once their leases expire." If the owner of a store that leases space in a mall is suffering a loss at that location, why wouldn't the owner close the store right away rather than wait until the lease expires?

Based on Kris Hudson and Vanessa O'Connell, "Recession Turns Malls into Ghost Towns," *Wall Street Journal*, May 22, 2009.

 **12.5**

# "If Everyone Can Do It, You Can't Make Money at It": The Entry and Exit of Firms in the Long Run, pages 411–417

LEARNING OBJECTIVE: Explain how entry and exit ensure that perfectly competitive firms earn zero economic profit in the long run.

## Summary

**Economic profit** is a firm's revenues minus all its costs, implicit and explicit. **Economic loss** is the situation in which a firm's total revenue is less than its total cost, including all implicit costs. If firms make economic profits in the short run, new firms enter the industry until the market price has fallen enough to wipe out the profits. If firms make economic losses, firms exit the industry until the market price has risen enough to wipe out the losses. **Long-run competitive equilibrium** is the situation in which the entry and exit of firms has resulted in the typical firm breaking even. The **long-run supply curve** shows the relationship between market price and the quantity supplied.

MyEconLab Visit **www.myeconlab.com** to complete these exercises online and get instant feedback.

## Review Questions

**5.1** When are firms likely to enter an industry? When are they likely to exit an industry?

**5.2** Would a firm earning zero economic profit continue to produce, even in the long run?

**5.3** Discuss the shape of the long-run supply curve in a perfectly competitive market. Suppose that a perfectly competitive market is initially at long-run equilibrium and then there is a permanent decrease in the demand for the product. Draw a graph showing how the market adjusts in the long run.

## Problems and Applications

**5.4** Suppose an assistant professor of economics is earning a salary of $75,000 per year. One day she quits her job, sells $100,000 worth of bonds that had been earning 5 percent per year, and uses the funds to open a bookstore. At the end of the year, she shows an accounting profit of $90,000 on her income tax return. What is her economic profit?

**5.5** Why does the entry of firms into an industry decrease the economic profits of the existing firms? Why does the exit of firms from an industry increase the economic profits of the existing firms?

**5.6** Consider the following statement: "The products for which demand is the greatest will also be the products that are most profitable to produce." Briefly explain whether you agree with this statement.

**5.7** In panel (b) of Figure 12.9 on page 414, Sacha Gillette reduces her output from 8,000 to 5,000 boxes of carrots when the price falls to $7. At this price and this output level, she is operating at a loss. Why doesn't she just continue charging the original $10 and continue producing 8,000 boxes of carrots?

**5.8** For a given decrease in demand, will more firms exit a constant-cost industry or an increasing-cost industry? Briefly explain.

**5.9** **[Related to the** Making the Connection **on page 416]** Ethan Nicholas developed his first game while still working as a programmer for Sun Microsystems. After his first game was a success, he quit Sun to form his own company—with himself as the only employee. How did Nicholas's quitting Sun to work full time for himself affect the cost to him of developing games?

Based on Jenna Wortham, "The iPhone Gold Rush," *New York Times*, April 5, 2009.

**5.10** A student in a principles of economics course makes the following remark:

> The economic model of perfectly competitive markets is fine in theory but not very realistic. It predicts that in the long run, a firm in a perfectly competitive market will earn no profits. No firm in the real world would stay in business if it earned zero profits.

Do you agree with this remark?

**5.11** In July 2011, National Public Radio ran a story about the new gold rush. It reported:

> The price of gold in the international market is steadily rising: more than fivefold in the past decade alone. It's currently selling for about $1,500 an ounce, paving the way for a new gold rush. Ten old mines have reopened in remote mountain and desert areas of the American West over the past decade.

The story also reported about twenty-first-century mining techniques. It stated:

> This is not 19th century gold mining—no pick axes or panning here. This dirt (after being blasted with dynamite) has a low concentration of gold, which is sprayed with a cyanide solution so the gold particles can be separated from the carbon, a process known as heap leaching.

**a.** The new gold rush is not just in the United States. It is also in Australia, Africa, Asia, and elsewhere. Why are so many firms around the globe mining for gold?

**b.** For a given demand for gold, over time what will the entry of all these firms into gold mining do to the price of gold and the economic profits from gold mining?

Based on Ruxandra Guidi, "Mining Companies On Quest To Cash In On Gold," National Public Radio, July 7, 2011; Jeanne Baron, "Gold Fever Draws African Farmers From Fields," National Public Radio, July 2, 2011; "China Mining Company, Zijin Mining Group to Expand Gold Mines Exploration in Australia," *Mining Exploration News*, August 2, 2011; "Sixteen New Firms to Prospect for Gold in Turkey's Kaz Mountains," *Hurriyet Daily News*, August 22, 2011.

**5.12** Suppose that the laptop computer industry is perfectly competitive and that the firms that assemble laptops do not also make the displays, or screens. Suppose that the laptop display industry is also perfectly competitive. Finally, suppose that because the demand for laptop displays is currently relatively small, firms in the laptop display industry have not been able to take advantage of all the economies of scale in laptop display production. Use a graph of the laptop computer market to illustrate the long-run effects on equilibrium price and quantity in the laptop computer market of a substantial and sustained increase in the demand for laptop computers. Use another graph to show the effect on the cost curves of a typical firm in the laptop computer industry. Briefly explain your graphs. Do your graphs indicate that the laptop computer industry is a constant-cost industry, an increasing-cost industry, or a decreasing-cost industry?

**5.13** **[Related to the** Chapter Opener **on page 395]** If in the long run vegetable growers who sell in farmers' markets make no greater rate of return on their investment than vegetable growers who sell to supermarkets, why did a significant number of vegetable growers switch from selling to supermarkets to selling in farmers' markets in the first place?

| 12.6 | **Perfect Competition and Efficiency,** pages 418–421 |

LEARNING OBJECTIVE: Explain how perfect competition leads to economic efficiency.

## Summary

Perfect competition results in **productive efficiency**, which means that goods and services are produced at the lowest possible cost. Perfect competition also results in **allocative efficiency**, which means the goods and services are produced up to the point where the last unit provides a marginal benefit to consumers equal to the marginal cost of producing it.

MyEconLab   Visit **www.myeconlab.com** to complete these exercises online and get instant feedback.

## Review Questions

6.1 Why are consumers so powerful in a market system?

6.2 What is meant by allocative efficiency? What is meant by productive efficiency? Briefly discuss the difference between these two concepts.

6.3 How does perfect competition lead to allocative and productive efficiency?

## Problems and Applications

6.4 The chapter states, "Firms will supply all those goods that provide consumers with a marginal benefit at least as great as the marginal cost of producing them." A student objects to this statement, arguing, "I doubt that firms will really do this. After all, firms are in business to make a profit; they don't care about what is best for consumers." Evaluate the student's argument.

6.5 **[Related to** Solved Problem 12.6 **on page 418]** Discuss the following statement: "In a perfectly competitive market, in the long run consumers benefit from reductions in costs, but firms don't." Don't firms also benefit from cost reductions because they are able to earn greater profits?

6.6 **[Related to** Solved Problem 12.6 **on page 418]** Suppose you read the following item in a newspaper article, under the headline "Price Gouging Alleged in Pencil Market":

> Consumer advocacy groups charged at a press conference yesterday that there is widespread price gouging in the sale of pencils. They released a study showing that whereas the average retail price of pencils was $1.00, the average cost

of producing pencils was only $0.50. "Pencils can be produced without complicated machinery or highly skilled workers, so there is no justification for companies charging a price that is twice what it costs them to produce the product. Pencils are too important in the life of every American for us to tolerate this sort of price gouging any longer," said George Grommet, chief spokesperson for the consumer groups. The consumer groups advocate passage of a law that would allow companies selling pencils to charge a price no more than 20 percent greater than their average cost of production.

Do you believe such a law would be advisable in a situation like this? Explain.

6.7 **[Related to** Solved Problem 12.6 **on page 418]** In 2011, Sony announced that it had lost money selling televisions for the seventh straight year. Given the strong consumer demand for plasma, LCD, and LED television sets, shouldn't Sony have been able to raise prices to earn a profit? Briefly explain.

Based on Daisuke Wakabayashi, "Sony Predicts $1 Billion Loss," *Wall Street Journal*, November 3, 2011.

6.8 Although New York State is second only to Washington State in production of apples, its production has been declining during the past 20 years. The decline has been particularly steep in counties close to New York City. In 1985, there were more than 11,000 acres of apple orchards in Ulster County, which is 75 miles north of New York City. Today, only about 6,000 acres remain. As it became difficult for apple growers in the county to compete with lower-cost producers elsewhere, the resources these entrepreneurs were using to produce apples—particularly land—became more valuable in other uses. Many farmers sold their land to housing developers. Suppose a nutritionist develops a revolutionary new diet that involves eating 10 apples per day. The new diet becomes wildly popular. What effect is the new diet likely to have on the number of apple orchards within 100 miles of New York City? What effect is the diet likely to have on housing prices in New York City?

Based on Lisa W. Foderaro, "Plenty of Apples, but a Possible Shortage of Immigrant Pickers," *New York Times*, August 21, 2007.

# Monopolistic Competition:
## The Competitive Model in a More Realistic Setting

## Chapter Outline and Learning Objectives

# Starbucks: The Limits to Growth through Product Differentiation

Like many other large firms, Starbucks started small. In 1971, entrepreneurs Gordon Bowker, Gerald Baldwin, and Zev Siegl opened the first Starbucks in Seattle, Washington. Current CEO Howard Schultz joined the company 10 years later. Schultz realized that many consumers wanted a coffeehouse where they could sit, relax, read, chat, and drink higher-quality coffee than was typically served in diners or donut shops. Designing Starbucks coffeehouses to provide this experience was the key to his success. But it was not difficult for other coffeehouses to copy the Starbucks approach.

By 2009, fierce competition and a weak economy led Starbucks to close hundreds of stores and cut prices as it tried to overcome the impression that it was the "home of the $4 coffee." Starbucks became profitable once more in 2010, partly due to expansion of its overseas markets. Schultz realizes that his company faces a constant challenge to stay ahead of its competitors and satisfy its customers: "I feel it's so important to remind us all of how fleeting success . . . can be."

In Chapter 12, we discussed the situation of firms in perfectly competitive markets. These markets share three key characteristics:

1. There are many firms.
2. All firms sell identical products.
3. There are no barriers to new firms entering the industry.

The market Starbucks competes in shares two of these characteristics: There are many coffeehouses, and the barriers to entering the market are very low. But the coffee at Starbucks is not identical to what competing coffeehouses offer. Selling coffee in coffeehouses is not like selling wheat: The products that Starbucks and its competitors sell are *differentiated* rather than identical. So, the coffeehouse market is *monopolistically competitive* rather than perfectly competitive. As we will see, most monopolistically competitive firms are unable to earn economic profits in the long run.

**AN INSIDE LOOK** on **page 450** describes how Starbucks acquired a juice maker to expand into areas outside the coffee business.

Based on Claire Cain Miller, "A Changed Starbucks. A Changed C.E.O.," *New York Times*, March 12, 2011.

## Economics in Your Life

### Opening Your Own Restaurant

After you graduate, you plan to realize your dream of opening your own Italian restaurant. You are confident that many people will enjoy the pasta prepared with your grandmother's secret sauce. Although your hometown already has three Italian restaurants, you are convinced that you can enter this market and make a profit.

You have many choices to make in operating your restaurant. Will it be "family style," with sturdy but inexpensive furniture, where families with small—and noisy!—children will feel welcome, or will it be more elegant, with nice furniture, tablecloths, and candles? Will you offer a full menu or concentrate on pasta dishes that use your grandmother's secret sauce? These and other choices you make will distinguish your restaurant from competitors. What's likely to happen in the restaurant market in your hometown after you open? How successful are you likely to be? See if you can answer these questions as you read this chapter. You can check your answers against those we provide on **page 448** at the end of this chapter.

**Monopolistic competition** A market structure in which barriers to entry are low and many firms compete by selling similar, but not identical, products.

M any markets in the U.S. economy are similar to the coffeehouse market: They have many buyers and sellers, and the barriers to entry are low, but the goods and services offered for sale are differentiated rather than identical. Examples of these markets include consumer electronics stores, restaurants, movie theaters, supermarkets, and manufacturing men's and women's clothing. In fact, the majority of the firms you patronize are competing in **monopolistically competitive** markets.

In Chapter 12, we saw how perfect competition benefits consumers and results in economic efficiency. Will these same desirable outcomes also hold for monopolistically competitive markets? This question is important because monopolistically competitive markets are common.

**13.1 LEARNING** OBJECTIVE

Explain why a monopolistically competitive firm has downward-sloping demand and marginal revenue curves.

# Demand and Marginal Revenue for a Firm in a Monopolistically Competitive Market

If the Starbucks coffeehouse located a mile from where you live raises the price of a caffè latte from $3.00 to $3.25, it will lose some, but not all, of its customers. Some customers will switch to buying their coffee at another store, but other customers will be willing to pay the higher price for a variety of reasons: This store may be closer to them, or they may prefer Starbucks caffè lattes to similar coffees at competing stores. Because changing the price affects the quantity of caffè lattes sold, a Starbucks store will face a downward-sloping demand curve rather than the horizontal demand curve that a wheat farmer faces.

## The Demand Curve for a Monopolistically Competitive Firm

Figure 13.1 shows how a change in price affects the quantity of caffè lattes Starbucks sells. The increase in the price from $3.00 to $3.25 decreases the quantity of caffè lattes sold from 3,000 per week to 2,400 per week.

## Marginal Revenue for a Firm with a Downward-Sloping Demand Curve

Recall from Chapter 12 that for a firm in a perfectly competitive market, the demand curve and the marginal revenue curve are the same. A perfectly competitive firm faces a horizontal demand curve and does not have to cut the price to sell a larger quantity. A monopolistically competitive firm, on the other hand, must cut the price to sell more, so its marginal revenue curve will slope downward and will be below its demand curve.

The data in Table 13.1 illustrate this point. To keep the numbers simple, let's assume that your local Starbucks coffeehouse is very small and sells at most 10 caffè lattes per

## Figure 13.1

### The Downward-Sloping Demand for Caffè Lattes at a Starbucks

If a Starbucks increases the price of caffè lattes, it will lose some, but not all, of its customers. In this case, raising the price from $3.00 to $3.25 reduces the quantity of caffè lattes sold from 3,000 to 2,400. Therefore, unlike a perfect competitor, a Starbucks coffeehouse faces a downward-sloping demand curve.

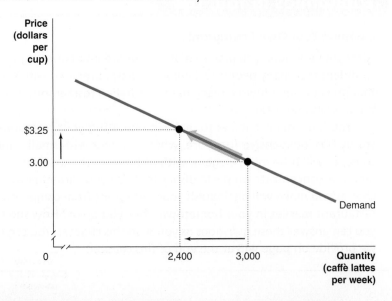

| Caffè Lattes Sold per Week (Q) | Price (P) | Total Revenue (TR = P × Q) | Average Revenue $\left(AR = \dfrac{TR}{Q}\right)$ | Marginal Revenue $\left(MR = \dfrac{\Delta TR}{\Delta Q}\right)$ |
|---|---|---|---|---|
| 0 | $6.00 | $0.00 | — | — |
| 1 | 5.50 | 5.50 | $5.50 | $5.50 |
| 2 | 5.00 | 10.00 | 5.00 | 4.50 |
| 3 | 4.50 | 13.50 | 4.50 | 3.50 |
| 4 | 4.00 | 16.00 | 4.00 | 2.50 |
| 5 | 3.50 | 17.50 | 3.50 | 1.50 |
| 6 | 3.00 | 18.00 | 3.00 | 0.50 |
| 7 | 2.50 | 17.50 | 2.50 | −0.50 |
| 8 | 2.00 | 16.00 | 2.00 | −1.50 |
| 9 | 1.50 | 13.50 | 1.50 | −2.50 |
| 10 | 1.00 | 10.00 | 1.00 | −3.50 |

**Table 13.1**

**Demand and Marginal Revenue at a Starbucks**

week. If Starbucks charges a price of $6.00 or more, all of its potential customers will buy their coffee somewhere else. If it charges $5.50, it will sell 1 caffè latte per week. For each additional $0.50 Starbucks reduces the price, it increases the number of caffè lattes it sells by 1. The third column in the table shows how the firm's *total revenue* changes as it sells more caffè lattes. The fourth column shows the firm's revenue per unit, or its *average revenue*. Average revenue is equal to total revenue divided by quantity. Because total revenue equals price multiplied by quantity, dividing by quantity leaves just price. Therefore, *average revenue is always equal to price*. This result will be true for firms selling in any of the four market structures we discussed in Chapter 12.

The last column shows the firm's marginal revenue, or the amount that total revenue changes as the firm sells 1 more caffè latte. For a perfectly competitive firm, the additional revenue received from selling 1 more unit is just equal to the price. That will not be true for Starbucks because to sell another caffè latte, it has to reduce the price. When the firm cuts the price by $0.50, one good thing and one bad thing happen:

- **The good thing.** It sells 1 more caffè latte; we can call this the *output effect*.
- **The bad thing.** It receives $0.50 less for each caffè latte that it could have sold at the higher price; we can call this the *price effect*.

Figure 13.2 illustrates what happens when the firm cuts the price from $3.50 to $3.00. Selling the sixth caffè latte adds the $3.00 price to the firm's revenue; this is the

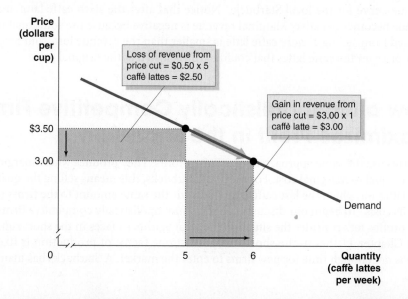

**Figure 13.2**

**How a Price Cut Affects a Firm's Revenue**

If a local Starbucks reduces the price of a caffè latte from $3.50 to $3.00, the number of caffè lattes it sells per week will increase from 5 to 6. Its marginal revenue from selling the sixth caffè latte will be $0.50, which is equal to the $3.00 additional revenue from selling 1 more caffè latte (the area of the green box) minus the $2.50 loss in revenue from selling the first 5 caffè lattes for $0.50 less each (the area of the red box).

## Figure 13.3

### The Demand and Marginal Revenue Curves for a Monopolistically Competitive Firm

Any firm that has the ability to affect the price of the product it sells will have a marginal revenue curve that is below its demand curve. We plot the data from Table 13.1 to create the demand and marginal revenue curves. After the sixth caffè latte, marginal revenue becomes negative because the additional revenue received from selling 1 more caffè latte is smaller than the revenue lost from receiving a lower price on the caffè lattes that could have been sold at the original price.

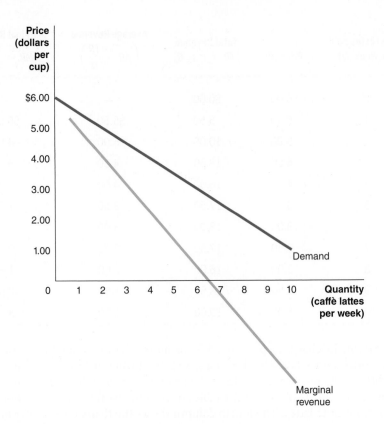

output effect. But Starbucks now receives a price of $3.00, rather than $3.50, on the first 5 caffè lattes sold; this is the price effect. As a result of the price effect, the firm's revenue on these 5 caffè lattes is $2.50 less than it would have been if the price had remained at $3.50. So, the firm has gained $3.00 in revenue on the sixth caffè latte and lost $2.50 in revenue on the first 5 caffè lattes, for a net change in revenue of $0.50. Marginal revenue is the change in total revenue from selling 1 more unit. Therefore, the marginal revenue of the sixth caffè latte is $0.50. Notice that the marginal revenue of the sixth unit is far below its price of $3.00. In fact, for each additional caffè latte Starbucks sells, marginal revenue will be less than price. There is an important general point: *Every firm that has the ability to affect the price of the good or service it sells will have a marginal revenue curve that is below its demand curve.* Only firms in perfectly competitive markets, which can sell as many units as they want at the market price, have marginal revenue curves that are the same as their demand curves.

Figure 13.3 shows the relationship between the demand curve and the marginal revenue curve for the local Starbucks. Notice that after the sixth caffè latte, marginal revenue becomes negative. Marginal revenue is negative because the additional revenue received from selling 1 more caffè latte is smaller than the revenue lost from receiving a lower price on the caffè lattes that could have been sold at the original price.

**13.2 LEARNING** OBJECTIVE

Explain how a monopolistically competitive firm maximizes profit in the short run.

# How a Monopolistically Competitive Firm Maximizes Profit in the Short Run

All firms use the same approach to maximize profits: They produce where marginal revenue is equal to marginal cost. For the local Starbucks, this means selling the quantity of caffè lattes for which the last caffè latte sold adds the same amount to the firm's revenue as to its costs. To begin our discussion of how monopolistically competitive firms maximize profits, let's consider the situation the local Starbucks faces in the short run. Recall from Chapter 11 that in the short run, at least one factor of production is fixed, and there is not enough time for new firms to enter the market. A Starbucks has many costs, including the cost of purchasing the ingredients for its caffè lattes and other coffees, the electricity it uses, and the wages of its employees. Recall that a firm's *marginal cost* is the increase in total cost resulting from producing another unit of output. We have seen that for many firms, marginal cost has a U shape. We will assume that the marginal cost curve for this Starbucks has the usual shape.

In the table in Figure 13.4, we bring together for this Starbucks the revenue data from Table 13.1 with the firm's cost data. The graphs in Figure 13.4 plot the data from the table. In panel (a), we see how Starbucks can determine its profit-maximizing quantity and price. As long as the marginal cost of selling 1 more caffè latte is less than the marginal revenue, the firm should sell additional caffè lattes. For example, increasing the quantity of caffè lattes sold from 3 per week to 4 per week increases marginal cost

| Caffè Lattes Sold per Week (Q) | Price (P) | Total Revenue (TR) | Marginal Revenue (MR) | Total Cost (TC) | Marginal Cost (MC) | Average Total Cost (ATC) | Profit |
|---|---|---|---|---|---|---|---|
| 0 | $6.00 | $0.00 | — | $5.00 | — | — | -$5.00 |
| 1 | 5.50 | 5.50 | $5.50 | 8.00 | $3.00 | $8.00 | -2.50 |
| 2 | 5.00 | 10.00 | 4.50 | 9.50 | 1.50 | 4.75 | 0.50 |
| 3 | 4.50 | 13.50 | 3.50 | 10.00 | 0.50 | 3.33 | 3.50 |
| 4 | 4.00 | 16.00 | 2.50 | 11.00 | 1.00 | 2.75 | 5.00 |
| 5 | 3.50 | 17.50 | 1.50 | 12.50 | 1.50 | 2.50 | 5.00 |
| 6 | 3.00 | 18.00 | 0.50 | 14.50 | 2.00 | 2.42 | 3.50 |
| 7 | 2.50 | 17.50 | -0.50 | 17.00 | 2.50 | 2.43 | 0.50 |
| 8 | 2.00 | 16.00 | -1.50 | 20.00 | 3.00 | 2.50 | -4.00 |
| 9 | 1.50 | 13.50 | -2.50 | 23.50 | 3.50 | 2.61 | -10.00 |
| 10 | 1.00 | 10.00 | -3.50 | 27.50 | 4.00 | 2.75 | -17.50 |

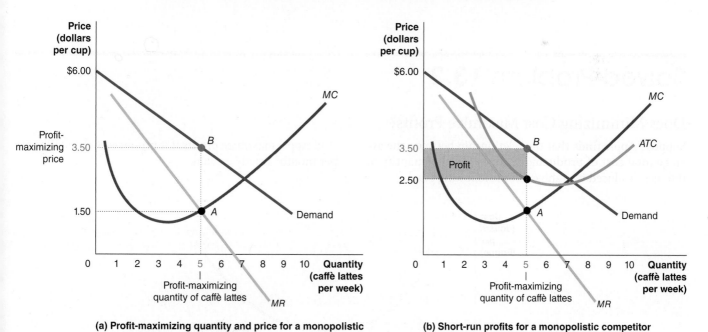

(a) **Profit-maximizing quantity and price for a monopolistic competitor**

(b) **Short-run profits for a monopolistic competitor**

**Figure 13.4**   Maximizing Profit in a Monopolistically Competitive Market

To maximize profit, a Starbucks coffeehouse wants to sell caffè lattes up to the point where the marginal revenue from selling the last caffè latte is just equal to the marginal cost. As the table shows, this happens with the fifth caffè latte—point *A* in panel (a)—which adds $1.50 to the firm's costs and $1.50 to its revenues. The firm then uses the demand curve to find the price that will lead

consumers to buy this quantity of caffè lattes (point *B*). In panel (b), the green box represents the firm's profits. The box has a height equal to $1.00, which is the $3.50 price minus the average total cost of $2.50, and it has a base equal to the quantity of 5 caffè lattes. So, this Starbucks's profit equals $1 × 5 = $5.00.

by $1.00 but increases marginal revenue by $2.50. So, the firm's profits are increased by $1.50 as a result of selling the fourth caffè latte.

As Starbucks sells more caffè lattes, rising marginal cost eventually equals marginal revenue, and the firm sells the profit-maximizing quantity of caffè lattes. Marginal cost equals marginal revenue with the fifth caffè latte, which adds $1.50 to the firm's costs and $1.50 to its revenues—point *A* in panel (a) of Figure 13.4. The demand curve tells us the price at which the firm is able to sell 5 caffè lattes per week. In Figure 13.4, if we draw a vertical line from 5 caffè lattes up to the demand curve, we can see that the price at which the firm can sell 5 caffè lattes per week is $3.50 (point *B*). We can conclude that for Starbucks, the profit-maximizing quantity is 5 caffè lattes, and the profit-maximizing price is $3.50. If the firm sells more than 5 caffè lattes per week, its profits fall. For example, selling a sixth caffè latte adds $2.00 to its costs and only $0.50 to its revenues. So, its profit would fall from $5.00 to $3.50.

Panel (b) adds the average total cost curve for Starbucks. The panel shows that the average total cost of selling 5 caffè lattes is $2.50. Recall from Chapter 12 that:

$$\text{Profit} = (P - ATC) \times Q.$$

In this case, profit = ($3.50 − $2.50) × 5 = $5.00. The green box in panel (b) shows the amount of profit. The box has a base equal to *Q* and a height equal to (*P* − *ATC*), so its area equals profit.

Notice that, unlike a perfectly competitive firm, which produces where *P* = *MC*, a monopolistically competitive firm produces where *P* > *MC*. In this case, Starbucks is charging a price of $3.50, although marginal cost is $1.50. For a perfectly competitive firm, price equals marginal revenue, *P* = *MR*. Therefore, to fulfill the *MR* = *MC* condition for profit maximization, a perfectly competitive firm will produce where *P* = *MC*. Because *P* > *MR* for a monopolistically competitive firm—which results from the marginal revenue curve being below the demand curve—a monopolistically competitive firm will maximize profits where *P* > *MC*.

# Solved Problem 13.2

### Does Minimizing Cost Maximize Profits?

Suppose Apple finds that the relationship between the average total cost of producing iPhones and the quantity of iPhones produced is as shown in the following graph.

Will Apple maximize profits if it produces 800,000 iPhones per month? Briefly explain.

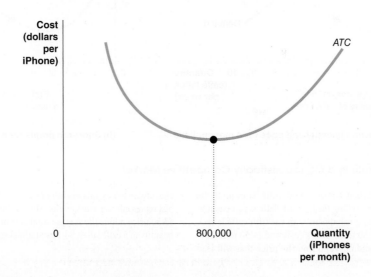

# Solving the Problem

**Step 1:** **Review the chapter material.** This problem is about how monopolistically competitive firms maximize profits, so you may want to review the section "How a Monopolistically Competitive Firm Maximizes Profits in the Short Run," which begins on page 434.

**Step 2:** **Discuss the relationship between minimizing costs and maximizing profits.** Firms often talk about the steps they take to reduce costs. The figure shows that by producing 800,000 iPhones per month, Apple will minimize its average cost of production. But remember that minimizing cost is not the firm's ultimate goal; the firm's ultimate goal is to maximize profits. Depending on demand, a firm may maximize profits by producing a quantity that is either larger or smaller than the quantity that would minimize average total cost.

**Step 3:** **Draw a graph that shows Apple maximizing profit at a quantity where average cost is not minimized.** Note that in the graph, average cost reaches a minimum at a quantity of 800,000, but profits are maximized at a quantity of 600,000.

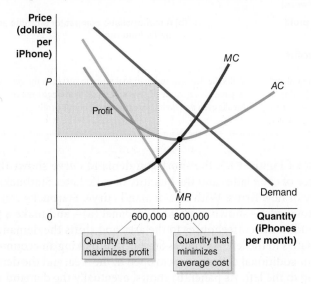

**Your Turn:** For more practice, do related problem 2.6 on page 453 at the end of this chapter.

MyEconLab

# What Happens to Profits in the Long Run?

**13.3 LEARNING** OBJECTIVE

Analyze the situation of a monopolistically competitive firm in the long run.

Remember that a firm makes an economic profit when its total revenue is greater than all of its costs, including the opportunity cost of the funds invested in the firm by its owners. Because cost curves include the owners' opportunity costs, the Starbucks coffeehouse represented in Figure 13.4 on page 435 is making an economic profit. This economic profit gives entrepreneurs an incentive to enter this market and establish new firms. If a Starbucks is earning an economic profit selling caffè lattes, new coffeehouses are likely to open in the same area.

## How Does the Entry of New Firms Affect the Profits of Existing Firms?

As new coffeehouses open near a local Starbucks, the firm's demand curve will shift to the left. The demand curve will shift because the Starbucks will sell fewer caffè lattes at each price when there are additional coffeehouses in the area selling similar drinks. The demand curve will also become more elastic because consumers have additional coffeehouses from which to buy coffee, so the Starbucks will lose more sales if it raises its prices. Figure 13.5 shows how the demand curve for the local Starbucks shifts as new firms enter its market.

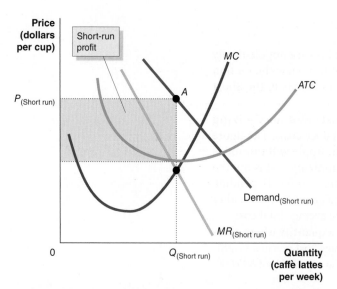

**(a) A monopolistic competitor may earn a short-run profit**

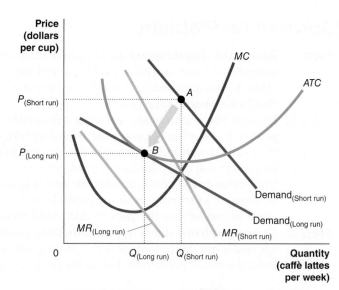

**(b) A monopolistic competitor's profits are eliminated in the long run**

**Figure 13.5** **How Entry of New Firms Eliminates Profits**

Panel (a) shows that in the short run, the local Starbucks faces the demand and marginal revenue curves labeled "Short run." With this demand curve, Starbucks can charge a price above average total cost (point *A*) and make a profit, shown by the green rectangle. But this profit attracts new firms to enter the market, which

shifts the demand and marginal revenue curves to the curves labeled "Long run" in panel (b). Because price is now equal to average total cost (point *B*), Starbucks breaks even and no longer earns an economic profit.

In panel (a) of Figure 13.5, the short-run demand curve shows the relationship between the price of caffè lattes and the quantity of caffè lattes Starbucks sells per week before the entry of new firms. With this demand curve, Starbucks can charge a price above average total cost—shown as point *A* in panel (a)—and make a profit. But this profit attracts additional coffeehouses to the area and shifts the demand curve for the Starbucks caffè lattes to the left. As long as Starbucks is making an economic profit, there is an incentive for additional coffeehouses to open in the area, and the demand curve will continue shifting to the left. As panel (b) shows, eventually the demand curve will have shifted to the point where it is just touching—or tangent to—the average total cost curve.

In the long run, at the point at which the demand curve is tangent to the average cost curve, price is equal to average total cost (point *B*), the firm is breaking even, and it no longer earns an economic profit. In the long run, the demand curve is also more elastic because the more coffeehouses there are in the area, the more sales Starbucks will lose to other coffeehouses if it raises its price.

# Don't Let This Happen to You

## Don't Confuse Zero Economic Profit with Zero Accounting Profit

Remember that economists count the opportunity cost of the owner's investment in a firm as a cost. For example, suppose you invest $200,000 opening a pizza parlor, and the return you could earn on those funds each year in a similar investment—such as opening a sandwich shop—is 10 percent. Therefore, the annual opportunity cost of investing the funds in your own business is 10 percent of $200,000, or $20,000. This $20,000 is part of your profit

in the accounting sense, and you would have to pay taxes on it. But in an economic sense, the $20,000 is a cost. In long-run equilibrium, we would expect that entry of new firms would keep you from earning more than 10 percent on your investment. So, you would end up breaking even and earning zero economic profit, even though you were earning an accounting profit of $20,000.

MyEconLab

**Your Turn:** Test your understanding by doing related problem 3.6 on page 455 at the end of this chapter.

Of course, it is possible that a monopolistically competitive firm will suffer an economic loss in the short run. As a consequence, the owners of the firm will not be covering the opportunity cost of their investment. We expect that, in the long run, firms will exit an industry if they are suffering economic losses. If firms exit, the demand curve for the output of a remaining firm will shift to the right. This process will continue until the representative firm in the industry is able to charge a price equal to its average cost and break even. Therefore, in the long run, monopolistically competitive firms will experience neither economic profits nor economic losses. Table 13.2 summarizes the short run and the long run for a monopolistically competitive firm.

**Table 13.2**    The Short Run and the Long Run for a Monopolistically Competitive Firm

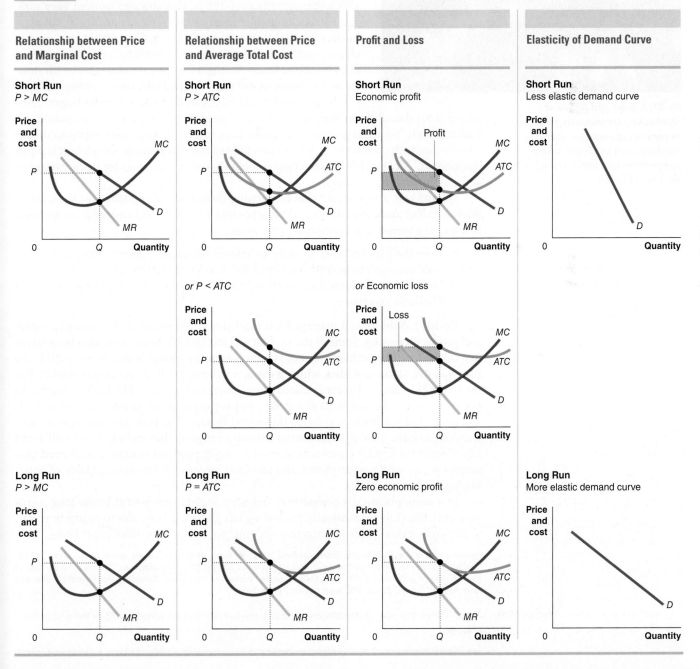

| Making the Connection | **The Rise and Decline and Rise of Starbucks** |
|---|---|

In the spring of 2009, an article from Bloomberg News summed up the situation that Starbucks was in: "After more than a decade of sensational buzz, Starbucks is struggling nationwide as it faces slowing sales growth and increased competition." The initial success and later struggles of Starbucks are a familiar pattern for firms in monopolistically competitive markets.

When Starbucks began rapidly expanding, CEO Howard Schultz knew that fresh-brewed coffee was widely available in restaurants, diners, and donut shops. He believed, though, that he had a strategy that would differentiate Starbucks from competitors: Starbucks would offer a European espresso bar atmosphere, with large, comfortable chairs, music playing, and groups of friends dropping in and out during the day. From the mid-1990s through the mid-2000s, this strategy worked very well, and Starbucks opened nearly 17,000 stores worldwide. But Starbucks's profitability attracted competitors. Other nationwide chains, such as Caribou Coffee and Diedrich Coffee, and regional chains, such as Dunn Brothers Coffee, provided stores with similar atmospheres, as did many individually owned coffeehouses.

*By 2011, sales and profits at Starbucks were increasing due in part to expansion in overseas markets, such as China, where competition was not as strong as in the United States.*

In addition, McDonald's and Dunkin' Donuts began competing more directly with Starbucks. Dunkin' Donuts began building more upscale restaurants with "rounded granite-style coffee bars where workers make espresso drinks face-to-face with customers . . . while a carefully selected pop-music soundtrack is piped throughout." McDonald's began selling espresso-based coffee drinks for prices considerably below those at Starbucks.

Schultz was also worried that in opening thousands of coffeehouses worldwide, Starbucks had made the customer experience less distinctive and easier for competitors to copy. In a memo sent to employees, he wrote:

> Over the past ten years, in order to achieve the growth, development, and scale necessary to go from less than 1,000 stores to 13,000 stores . . . we have had to make a series of decisions that . . . have led to the watering down of the Starbucks experience.

By 2011, Schultz had managed a remarkable turnaround, with Starbucks's sales and profits increasing. Some of the success was attributable to an expansion in overseas markets, where competition was not as strong as in the United States. In early 2011, the firm had 450 stores in China, which it expects will eventually be its largest market. But the firm's U.S. stores also experienced strong increases in sales. The highest Starbucks per-store sales had come in 2006, but the company expected to set a new record in 2011. The revival of Starbucks was based on several factors: The firm gave customers more freedom to customize drinks, started a loyalty program that included free refills and other perks for regular customers, started a mobile payment system that allowed customers to pay with a smartphone, and provided stores with machines capable of brewing higher-quality coffees.

In a monopolistically competitive industry, maintaining profits in the long run is very difficult. Only by constantly innovating has Starbucks been able to return to profitability after several years of struggling with intense competition from other firms.

Based on John Kell and Julie Jargon, "Starbucks Posts 34% Profit Jump," *Wall Street Journal*, July 29, 2011; Lauren Pollock, "Starbucks Adds Division Focused on Asia," *Wall Street Journal*, July 11, 2011; John Jannarone, "Starbucks Savors Taste of Success," *Wall Street Journal*, July 5, 2011; Andrew Harrer, "Starbucks Corporation," Bloomberg News, April 13, 2009; and Janet Adamy, "Brewing Battle," *Wall Street Journal*, April 8, 2006.

MyEconLab **Your Turn:** Test your understanding by doing related problem 3.8 on page 455 at the end of this chapter.

# Is Zero Economic Profit Inevitable in the Long Run?

The economic analysis of the long run shows the effects of market forces over time. Owners of monopolistically competitive firms, of course, do not have to passively accept this long-run result. The key to earning economic profits is either to sell a differentiated product or to find a way of producing an existing product at a lower cost. If a monopolistically competitive firm selling a differentiated product is earning profits, these profits will attract the entry of additional firms, and the entry of those firms will eventually eliminate the firm's profits. If a firm introduces new technology that allows it to sell a good or service at a lower cost, competing firms will eventually be able to duplicate that technology and eliminate the firm's profits. *But this result holds only if the firm stands still and fails to find new ways of differentiating its product or fails to find new ways of lowering the cost of producing its product.* Starbucks had great initial success, had difficulty maintaining its profitability against the entry of new firms, and then found its way back to profitability by introducing new products and improving its customers' experience through a loyalty program and other innovations. Firms continually struggle to find new ways of differentiating their products as they try to stay one step ahead of other firms that are attempting to copy their success.

The owner of a competitive firm is in a position like that of Ebenezer Scrooge in Charles Dickens's *A Christmas Carol*. When the Ghost of Christmas Yet to Come shows Scrooge visions of his own death, he asks the ghost, "Are these the shadows of the things that Will be, or are they shadows of things that May be, only?" The shadow of the end of their profits haunts owners of every firm. Firms try to avoid losing profits by reducing costs, by improving their products, or by convincing consumers that their products are indeed different from what competitors offer. To stay one step ahead of its competitors, a firm has to offer consumers goods or services that they perceive to have greater *value* than those competing firms offer. Value can take the form of product differentiation that makes the good or service more suited to consumers' preferences, or it can take the form of a lower price.

# Solved Problem 13.3

## Can It Be Profitable to Be the High-Price Seller?

During the year ending in March 2011, hhgregg, an appliance and electronics retailer with stores in the Eastern states, reported that its profits had risen 23 percent. During the same period, Best Buy's profits declined by 3 percent. Best Buy is much larger than hhgregg, so it is able to buy its appliances, televisions, and other goods from manufacturers at a low price. Because hhgregg must pay higher prices to manufacturers, it must charge higher prices to consumers. How is hhgregg able to succeed in competition with Best Buy, Wal-Mart, Amazon, and other big retailers, despite charging high prices?

According to an article in the *Wall Street Journal*: "hhgregg's commissioned sales staff is an advantage over national chains with young, lower-paid hourly workers that tend to stay for shorter periods." hhgregg's CEO was quoted as saying: "We have sales people that have been with us 10 to 20 years, and customers who come in and ask for them by name."

Use this information to explain how an hhgregg store might be more profitable than a similar Best Buy store, despite the fact that the hhgregg store charges higher prices. Use a graph for hhgregg and a graph for Best Buy to illustrate your answer.

## Solving the Problem

**Step 1:** **Review the chapter material.** This problem is about how a monopolistically competitive firm maximizes profits and about how firms attempt to earn economic profits in the long run, so you may want to review the section "How a Monopolistically Competitive Firm Maximizes Profits in the Short Run," which begins on page 434, and the section "Is Zero Economic Profit Inevitable in the Long Run?" on page 441.

Step 2: **Explain how hhgregg can remain profitable despite its high costs.** If an hhgregg store has higher costs than a comparable Best Buy store, it can have greater profits only if the demand for its goods is higher. According to the *Wall Street Journal* article, hhgregg has differentiated itself from the competition, particularly from large chain stores such as Best Buy, by offering better customer service. By having salespeople who are more knowledgeable and more experienced than the salespeople hired by competitors, hhgregg has attracted consumers who need help in buying televisions and appliances. The higher demand from these consumers must be enough to offset hhgregg's higher costs.

Step 3: **Draw graphs to illustrate your argument.** For simplicity, the graphs here assume that televisions are the product being sold. Panel (a) shows the situation for hhgregg, and panel (b) shows the situation for Best Buy. The graphs show that the hhgregg store has both greater demand and higher costs than the Best Buy store. Because the greater demand more than offsets the higher costs, the hhgregg store makes a larger profit.

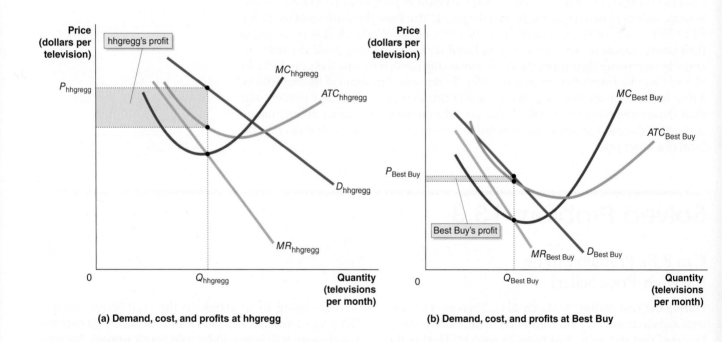

(a) Demand, cost, and profits at hhgregg

(b) Demand, cost, and profits at Best Buy

**Extra Credit:** As we have seen, firms constantly search for means of differentiating themselves from their competitors. Often, differentiation works for a while but then breaks down as competitors copy the strategy. Providing excellent customer service is more difficult to copy because it can take years to assemble an experienced sales staff and to acquire a reputation for excellent service. In fact, Best Buy, Wal-Mart, and other large chains may not want to compete for customers who are willing to pay a higher price in exchange for more help from the sales staff. In the *Wall Street Journal* article, a spokesperson for Wal-Mart was quoted as saying: "With electronics data so readily available online today, many customers come to us looking for a particular brand or item, knowledge in hand, and may not want or feel comfortable shopping with a salesperson." If the larger firms do not compete on service, smaller firms, such as hhgregg, will have an easier time defending their market niche. For consumers in that niche, hhgregg may charge higher prices, but it still provides these consumers with greater value.

Profit data from *Wall Street Journal; Scott Tilghman*, "Hhgregg Could Get a Leg Up," Barron's, June 2, 2011; and Miguel Bustillo, "Small Electronics Chains Thrive in Downturn," *Wall Street Journal*, May 27, 2009.

**Your Turn:** Test your understanding by doing related problem 3.9 on page 455 at the end of this chapter.

MyEconLab

# Comparing Monopolistic Competition and Perfect Competition

**13.4 LEARNING** OBJECTIVE

Compare the efficiency of monopolistic competition and perfect competition.

We have seen that monopolistic competition and perfect competition share the characteristic that in long-run equilibrium, firms earn zero economic profits. As Figure 13.6 shows, however, there are two important differences between long-run equilibrium in the two markets:

- Monopolistically competitive firms charge a price greater than marginal cost.

- Monopolistically competitive firms do not produce at minimum average total cost.

## Excess Capacity under Monopolistic Competition

Recall that a firm in a perfectly competitive market faces a perfectly elastic demand curve that is also its marginal revenue curve. Therefore, the firm maximizes profit by producing where price equals marginal cost. As panel (a) of Figure 13.6 shows, in long-run equilibrium, a perfectly competitive firm produces at the minimum point of its average total cost curve.

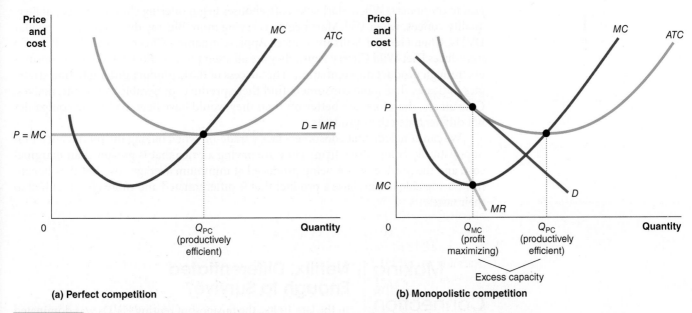

**(a) Perfect competition**

**(b) Monopolistic competition**

**Figure 13.6    Comparing Long-Run Equilibrium under Perfect Competition and Monopolistic Competition**

In panel (a), a perfectly competitive firm in long-run equilibrium produces at $Q_{PC}$, where price equals marginal cost, and average total cost is at a minimum. The perfectly competitive firm is both allocatively efficient and productively efficient. In panel (b), a monopolistically competitive firm produces at $Q_{MC}$, where price is greater than marginal cost, and average total cost is not at a minimum. As

a result, the monopolistically competitive firm is neither allocatively efficient nor productively efficient. The monopolistically competitive firm has excess capacity equal to the difference between its profit-maximizing level of output and the productively efficient level of output.

Panel (b) of Figure 13.6 shows that the profit-maximizing level of output for a monopolistically competitive firm comes at a level of output where price is greater than marginal cost, and the firm is not at the minimum point of its average total cost curve. A monopolistically competitive firm has *excess capacity*: If it increased its output, it could produce at a lower average cost.

## Is Monopolistic Competition Inefficient?

In Chapter 12, we discussed productive efficiency and allocative efficiency. *Productive efficiency* refers to the situation where a good is produced at the lowest possible cost. *Allocative efficiency* refers to the situation where every good or service is produced up to the point where the last unit provides a marginal benefit to consumers equal to the marginal cost of producing it. For productive efficiency to hold, firms must produce at the minimum point of average total cost. For allocative efficiency to hold, firms must charge a price equal to marginal cost. In a perfectly competitive market, both productive efficiency and allocative efficiency are achieved, but in a monopolistically competitive market, neither is achieved. Does it matter? Economists have debated whether monopolistically competitive markets being neither productively nor allocatively efficient results in a significant loss of well-being to society in these markets compared with perfectly competitive markets.

## How Consumers Benefit from Monopolistic Competition

Looking again at Figure 13.6, you can see that the only difference between the monopolistically competitive firm and the perfectly competitive firm is that the demand curve for the monopolistically competitive firm slopes downward, whereas the demand curve for the perfectly competitive firm is a horizontal line. The demand curve for the monopolistically competitive firm slopes downward because the good or service the firm is selling is differentiated from the goods or services being sold by competing firms. The perfectly competitive firm is selling a good or service identical to those being sold by its competitors. A key point to remember is that *firms differentiate their products to appeal to consumers.* When Starbucks coffeehouses begin offering slower-brewed, higher-quality coffees, when Wal-Mart begins carrying more Blu-ray discs and fewer regular DVDs, when General Mills introduces Apple-Cinnamon Cheerios, or when PepsiCo introduces Diet Wild Cherry Pepsi, they are all attempting to attract and retain consumers through product differentiation. The success of these product differentiation strategies indicates that some consumers find these products preferable to the alternatives. Consumers, therefore, are better off than they would have been had these companies not differentiated their products.

We can conclude that consumers face a trade-off when buying the product of a monopolistically competitive firm: They are paying a price that is greater than marginal cost, and the product is not being produced at minimum average cost, but they benefit from being able to purchase a product that is differentiated and more closely suited to their tastes.

Making the Connection | **Netflix: Differentiated Enough to Survive?**

In the late 1990s, the business of renting DVDs was dominated by specialized chain stores such as Blockbuster and Hollywood Video. Some customers were dissatisfied with these stores, however, for two main reasons: (1) After driving to the store, the customer might find that the movie he or she was hoping to rent was unavailable, and (2) unless the movie was returned on time, the customer would have to pay a late fee that might end up being higher than the price of the movie.

In 1997, Reed Hastings had just sold his start-up software firm for $750 million . . . and he was stuck with a late fee of $40 for having failed to return a copy of *Apollo 13* on time. He decided to start Netflix as a mail-order DVD rental company. For a flat monthly fee, subscribers could rent a given number of DVDs, with no late fees. Netflix was an immediate success; by 2003, it had 1 million subscribers. But Netflix faced a challenge: Many consumers were switching from renting or buying DVDs to downloading movies or streaming them from the Internet. In 2007, Netflix began offering unlimited streaming of videos in its subscription packages. Because the firm had made agreements with several movie studios and cable channels, its broad selection of films made its streaming service a hit. By 2011, Netflix had more than 25 million subscribers and profits of more than $150 million.

*By 2011, Netflix had more than 25 million subscribers and profits of more than $150 million.*

But would Netflix be able to fight off the many competitors it faces in the business of streaming movies? In the DVD rental business, Netflix had advantages that were hard to duplicate, including a national system of warehouses that allowed it to often deliver a DVD the day after a customer ordered it, and an efficient system of processing a returned DVD and mailing out the next DVD in the customer's queue. As a result of these advantages, Wal-Mart, Blockbuster, and other firms were unsuccessful in entering the business of renting DVDs by mail. But some analysts did not believe that Netflix had similar advantages in streaming movies. Many other firms were entering, or had already entered, the business of streaming movies, including Apple, Google, Amazon, Hulu (owned by Disney and News Corp.), and cable companies such as Comcast. These firms were familiar to consumers, were experts in the technology of streaming video, and had access to large selections of movie and television programs. Netflix also upset some consumers in 2011 when it increased by 60 percent the price of a subscription to both receive DVDs by mail and to stream videos. In late 2011, Netflix announced that it expected to suffer losses for a period during 2012 before returning to profitability. It remains to be seen whether Netflix can regain its profitability in the face of intense competition.

Based on Nick Wingfield, "Netflix Warns Price Rise Will Clip Growth," *Wall Street Journal*, July 26, 2011; Matt Phillips, "Netflix: Why One Investor Bets It Gets Crushed," *Wall Street Journal*, December 16, 2010; Reed Hastings and Amy Zipkin, "Out of Africa, Onto the Web," *New York Times*, December 17, 2006; and Reed Hastings and Patrick J. Sauer, "How I Did It: Reed Hastings, Netflix," *Inc.*, December 1, 2005.

**Your Turn:** Test your understanding by doing related problem 4.8 on page 456 at the end of this chapter.

MyEconLab

# How Marketing Differentiates Products

Firms can differentiate their products through marketing. **Marketing** refers to all the activities necessary for a firm to sell a product to a consumer. Marketing includes activities such as determining which product to produce, designing the product, advertising the product, deciding how to distribute the product—for example, in retail stores or through a Web site—and monitoring how changes in consumer tastes are affecting the market for the product. Peter F. Drucker, a leading business strategist, described marketing as follows: "It is the whole business seen from the point of view of its final result, that is, from the consumer's point of view. . . . True marketing . . . does not ask, 'What do we want to sell?' It asks, 'What does the consumer want to buy?' "

As we have seen, for monopolistically competitive firms to earn economic profits and defend those profits from competitors, they must differentiate their products. Firms use two marketing tools to differentiate their products: brand management and advertising.

**13.5 LEARNING** OBJECTIVE

Define marketing and explain how firms use marketing to differentiate their products.

**Marketing** All the activities necessary for a firm to sell a product to a consumer.

**Brand management** The actions of a firm intended to maintain the differentiation of a product over time.

## Brand Management

Once a firm has succeeded in differentiating its product, it must try to maintain that differentiation over time through **brand management**. As we have seen, whenever a firm successfully introduces a new product or a significantly different version of an old product, it earns economic profits in the short run. But the success of the firm inspires competitors to copy the new or improved product and, in the long run, the firm's economic profits will be competed away. Firms use brand management to postpone the time when they will no longer be able to earn economic profits.

## Advertising

An innovative advertising campaign can make even long-established and familiar products, such as Coke or McDonald's Big Mac hamburgers, seem more desirable than competing products. When a firm advertises a product, it is trying to shift the demand curve for the product to the right and to make it more inelastic. If the firm is successful, it will sell more of the product at every price, and it will be able to increase the price it charges without losing as many customers. Of course, advertising also increases a firm's costs. If the increase in revenue that results from the advertising is greater than the increase in costs, the firm's profits will rise.

## Defending a Brand Name

Once a firm has established a successful brand name, it has a strong incentive to defend it. A firm can apply for a *trademark*, which grants legal protection against other firms using its product's name.

One threat to a trademarked name is the possibility that it will become so widely used for a type of product that it will no longer be associated with the product of a specific company. Courts in the United States have ruled that when this happens, a firm is no longer entitled to legal protection of the brand name. For example, "aspirin," "escalator," and "thermos" were originally all brand names of the products of particular firms, but each became so widely used to refer to a type of product that none remains a legally protected brand name. Firms spend substantial amounts of money trying to make sure that this does not happen to them. Coca-Cola, for example, employs people to travel to restaurants around the country and order a "Coke" with their meal. If the restaurant serves Pepsi or some other cola, rather than Coke, Coca-Cola's legal department sends the restaurant a letter reminding them that "Coke" is a trademarked name and not a generic name for any cola. Similarly, Xerox Corporation spends money on advertising to remind the public that "Xerox" is not a generic term for making photocopies.

Legally enforcing trademarks can be difficult. Estimates are that each year, U.S. firms lose hundreds of billions of dollars in sales worldwide as a result of unauthorized use of their trademarked brand names. U.S. firms often find it difficult to enforce their trademarks in the courts of some foreign countries, although recent international agreements have increased the legal protections for trademarks.

Firms that sell their products through franchises rather than through company-owned stores encounter the problem that if a franchisee does not run his or her business well, the firm's brand may be damaged. Automobile firms send "roadmen" to visit their dealers to make sure the dealerships are clean and well maintained and that the service departments employ competent mechanics and are well equipped with spare parts. Similarly, McDonald's sends employees from corporate headquarters to visit McDonald's franchises to make sure the bathrooms are clean and the French fries are hot.

**13.6 LEARNING** OBJECTIVE

Identify the key factors that determine a firm's success.

## What Makes a Firm Successful?

A firm's owners and managers control some of the factors that make a firm successful and allow it to earn economic profits. The most important of these are the firm's ability to differentiate its product and to produce it at a lower average cost than competing firms. A firm that successfully does these things creates *value* for its customers.

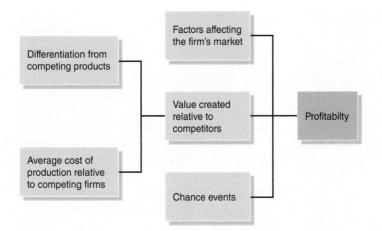

**Figure 13.7**

**What Makes a Firm Successful?**

The factors under a firm's control—the ability to differentiate its product and the ability to produce it at lower cost—combine with the factors beyond its control to determine the firm's profitability.

Adapted from Figure 13.3 in David Besanko, David Dranove, Mark Shanley, and Scott Schaefer, *The Economics of Strategy*, 5th ed., New York: John Wiley & Sons, Inc., 2009.

Consumers will buy a product if they believe it meets a need not met by competing products or if its price is below that of competitors.

Some factors that affect a firm's profitability are not directly under the firm's control. Certain factors will affect all the firms in a market. For example, rising prices for jet fuel will reduce the profitability of all airlines. If consumers decide that rather than buy DVDs, they would prefer to download or stream movies from Netflix, iTunes, or Amazon, the profitability of all stores selling DVDs will be reduced.

Sheer chance also plays a role in business, as it does in all other aspects of life. A struggling McDonald's franchise may see profits increase dramatically after the county unexpectedly decides to build a new road nearby. Many businesses in New York City, including restaurants, hotels, and theaters, experienced a marked drop in customers and profits following the September 11, 2001, terrorist attacks. Figure 13.7 illustrates the important point that factors within the firm's control and factors outside the firm's control interact to determine the firm's profitability.

## Making the Connection | Is Being the First Firm in the Market a Key to Success?

Some business analysts argue that the first firm to enter a market can have important *first-mover advantages*. By being the first to sell a particular good, a firm may find its name closely associated with the good in the public's mind, as, for instance, Amazon is closely associated with ordering books online or eBay is associated with online auctions. This close association may make it more difficult for new firms to enter the market and compete against the first mover.

Surprisingly, though, recent research has shown that the first firm to enter a market often does *not* have a long-lived advantage over later entrants. Consider, for instance, the market for pens. Until the 1940s, the only pens available were fountain pens that had to be refilled frequently from an ink bottle and used ink that dried slowly and smeared easily. In October 1945, entrepreneur Milton Reynolds introduced the first ballpoint pen, which never needed to be refilled. When it went on sale at Gimbel's department store in New York City, it was an instant success. Although the pen had a price of $12.00—the equivalent of about $135.00 at today's prices—hundreds of thousands were sold, and Milton Reynolds became a millionaire. Unfortunately, it didn't last. Although Reynolds had guaranteed that his pen would write for two years—later raised to five years—in fact, the pen often leaked and frequently stopped writing after only limited use. Sales began to collapse, the flood of pens returned under the company's guarantee wiped out its profits, and within a few years, Reynolds International Pen Company stopped selling pens in the United States. By the late 1960s, firms such as Bic, selling inexpensive—but reliable—ballpoint pens, dominated the market.

*Although not first to market, Bic ultimately was more successful than the firm that pioneered ballpoint pens.*

What happened to the Reynolds International Pen Company turns out to be more the rule than the exception. For example, Apple's iPod was not the first digital music player to appear on the U.S. market. Both Seahan's MPMan and Diamond's PMP300 were released in the United States in 1998, three years before the iPod. Similarly, although Hewlett-Packard currently dominates the market for laser printers, with a market share of more than 50 percent, it did not invent the laser printer. Xerox invented the laser printer, and IBM sold the first commercial laser printers. Nor was Procter & Gamble the first firm to sell disposable diapers when it introduced Pampers in 1961. Microsoft's Internet Explorer was not the first Web browser: Before Internet Explorer, there was Netscape; before Netscape, there was Mosaic; and before Mosaic, there were several other Web browsers that for a time looked as if they might dominate the market. In all these cases, the firms that were first to introduce a product ultimately lost out to latecomers who did a better job of providing consumers with products that were more reliable, less expensive, more convenient, or otherwise provided greater value.

Based on Steven P. Schnaars, *Managing Imitation Strategies: How Late Entrants Seize Markets from Pioneers*, (New York: The Free Press), 1994; and Gerard J. Tellis and Peter N. Golder, *Will and Vision: How Latecomers Grow to Dominate Markets*, (Los Angeles: Figueroa Press), 2002.

**MyEconLab** **Your Turn:** Test your understanding by doing related problem 6.6 on page 457 at the end of this chapter.

Continued from page 431

## Economics in Your Life

### Opening Your Own Restaurant

At the beginning of the chapter, we asked you to think about how successful you are likely to be in opening an Italian restaurant in your hometown. As you learned in this chapter, if your restaurant is successful, other people are likely to open competing restaurants, and all your economic profits will eventually disappear. This occurs because economic profits attract entry of new firms into a market. The new restaurants will sell Italian food, but it won't be exactly like your Italian food—after all, they don't have your grandmother's secret sauce recipe! Each restaurant will have its own ideas on how best to appeal to people who like Italian food. Unless your food is very different from your competitors' food—or your service is much better—in the long run you will be unable to charge prices high enough to allow you to earn an economic profit.

In a monopolistically competitive market, free entry will reduce prices and lead to zero economic profits in the long run. In addition to lowering prices, competition benefits consumers by leading firms to offer somewhat different versions of the same product; for example, two Italian restaurants will rarely be exactly alike.

## Conclusion

In this chapter, we have applied many of the ideas about competition we developed in Chapter 12 to the more common market structure of monopolistic competition. We have seen that these ideas apply to monopolistically competitive markets, just as they do to perfectly competitive markets. At the end of Chapter 12, we concluded that "The competitive forces of the market impose relentless pressure on firms to produce new and better goods and services at the lowest possible cost. Firms that fail to adequately anticipate changes in consumer tastes or that fail to adopt the latest and most efficient production technology do not survive in the long run." These conclusions are as true for coffeehouses and firms in other monopolistically competitive markets as they are for wheat farmers and carrot growers.

In Chapters 14 and 15, we discuss the remaining market structures: oligopoly and monopoly. Before moving on to those chapters, read *An Inside Look* on the next page for a discussion of how Starbucks began expanding into the juice business in 2011.

# Starbucks Expands Into Juice Business

## ASSOCIATED PRESS

(a) Starbucks Corp. hopes to do for juice what it's done for coffee.

The Seattle-based company that changed the way Americans drink their cup of Joe said Thursday that it acquired by juice maker Evolution Fresh Inc. for $30 million as part of a larger effort to move beyond just offering coffee.

Starbucks said it plans to "reinvent" the $1.6 billion super-premium juice segment with its purchase of Evolution, which is based in San Bernardino, Calif. The company plans to open a new chain of health and wellness stores in the coming year that will carry Evolution products such as juices and simple foods. Details are still thin on the new chain, but Starbucks described it as a retail model that has never been seen before.

"We are not just acquiring a juice company," said Starbucks CEO Howard Schultz. "We are using this acquisition to position ourselves, in a broad way, to build a multibillion health and wellness business over time."

(b) The move is the latest by Starbucks to broaden its business as consumers demand healthier products and it faces growing competition from the likes of McDonald's Corp. and Dunkin' Brands Group Inc.'s Dunkin' Donuts chain. Starbucks has rolled out lower-calorie and lower-fat food options and sugar-free syrups and switched from whole milk to 2 percent milk as the default in its drinks.

It's also is selling more products, like Seattle's Best coffee and Via instant coffee, through grocery stores and other retailers.

Starbucks, which estimates that at some point in the future its consumer products business will rival the size of its café business, said more than a year ago that it would be looking for acquisition candidates. Its last acquisition in 2008 was of The Coffee Equipment Co., which makes the high-end Clover coffee brewing system.

Evolution, started by the founder of Naked Juice, is a logical choice for the chain as it seeks to offer healthier options. Evolution, which makes fresh fruit and vegetable juices, has products that are sold at Whole Foods, Safeway, Costco and other retailers on the West Coast.

Evolution is one of the few larger juice companies that still cracks, peels, presses and squeezes its own fruits and vegetables rather than using pureed or powdered ingredients. It also uses a process called high-pressure pasteurization to make the juice without heating it. Starbucks sees these methods as a competitive edge over juice makers such as Odwalla or Naked Juice, which it currently carries in its stores, as it allows the juice maker it to keep a higher nutritional quality in the juice while maintaining the taste.

(c) Starbucks did not disclose how many stores the new chain carrying Evolution products will have or where the locations would be. But the company said the chain will launch on the West Coast and be roughly the size of a traditional Starbucks café. Starbucks also plans to upgrade some of its existing stores to make room for the Evolution products and distribute Evolution's products to other retailers.

Schultz said the company will launch a "full court press" to build the Evolution brand in the coming year, including more details on its new stores. Schultz also dismissed analyst concerns that it might follow in the footsteps of the Jamba Juice chain, which has struggled with soft sales as consumers have cut back on extras like blended fruit drinks. He said Starbucks will be creating an entirely different type of store.

"We understand the beverage business better than anyone else," Schultz told investors Thursday. "We are replicating the understanding we have about beverage capability and adding the theater and romance (of our coffee stores)."

Starbucks did not change its earnings forecast based on the acquisition. It expects Evolution will operate at a moderate loss in the 2012 fiscal year and breakeven in 2013....

*Source:* "Starbucks acquires juice business for $30M" by Sarah Skidmore from *The Associated Press*, November 10, 2011. Copyright © 2011 by the Associated Press. Reprinted by permission of the YGS Group.

# Key Points in the Article

With its purchase of Evolution Fresh, Inc., Starbucks is planning to open a chain of health and wellness stores in 2012 in response to increasing consumer demand for healthier products. While not revealing the number or exact locations of the new stores, the company did say that the first stores will be on the West Coast and will be roughly the size of traditional Starbucks coffeehouses. The juice products will also be made available in some existing Starbucks locations as well as other retail outlets. Starbucks projects its Evolution brand to experience moderate losses in 2012 before breaking even in 2013.

## Analyzing the News

(a) Facing increased competition in the coffeehouse market, Starbucks has shifted its focus to international expansion, consumer products, and, most recently, the premium juice business. With the acquisition of Evolution, Starbucks plans to open a new chain of health and wellness stores, a market segment it sees as having strong growth potential. If Starbucks is able to capture a significant share of the premium juice market with its new chain, the company has the potential of earning economic profits in this market segment in the short run. Figure 1 represents a Starbucks health and wellness store earning a short-run economic profit. As

long as Starbucks encounters limited competition in the premium juice market, its stores have the potential to earn short-run economic profits. Economic profits will attract competition to the market, and we would expect to eventually see the same result in the premium juice market as in the premium coffee market, with economic profits dropping to zero in the long run.

(b) Due in part to increased competition from companies like McDonalds and Dunkin' Donuts, Starbucks began closing stores in 2008. The increased competition in the coffee business is one reason why Starbucks has decided to expand into other areas. Figure 2 assumes that prior to 2008, an existing Starbucks coffeehouse is earning an economic profit from selling $Q_1$ cups of coffee and charging a price of $P_1$ dollars. The profit-maximizing quantity is found where the marginal revenue curve, $MR_1$, intersects the marginal cost curve, $MC$. The price is determined by point $A$ on the demand curve, $D_1$. The firm earns an economic profit equal to the shaded area. Other firms entering the market for premium coffees reduces the demand for Starbucks coffee. The demand and marginal revenue curves for Starbucks shift to the left, from $D_1$ to $D_2$ and $MR_1$ to $MR_2$. The profit-maximizing level of output is now $Q_2$, where $MR_2$ intersects $MC$, and the new profit-maximizing price is $P_2$. At point $E$, the firm is earning zero economic profit.

(c) While offering few details on its expansion plans for the new chain, Starbucks CEO Howard Shultz did announce that it will begin with locations on the West Coast and that Evolution products will not be limited to just the new stores. Schultz also emphasized that the new business will be an entirely new type of store, and will not follow the model of competitor Jamba Juice, which had been struggling to earn an economic profit.

## Thinking Critically

1. Suppose that the federal government required a license to open a new coffeehouse (existing coffeehouses would not require a license) and that the number of licenses was limited. How would this requirement affect the equilibrium price and quantity in the coffeehouse market? Who would gain from this requirement and who would lose?

2. Suppose that Starbucks is successful with its chain of health and wellness stores and attracts a significant number of customers from other coffee and juice retailers. How might these other retailers respond to this change in tastes?

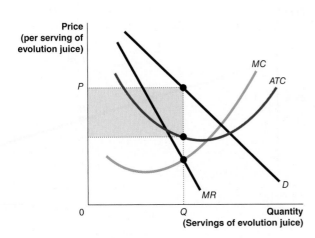

**Figure 1**

A new chain with short-run economic profit.

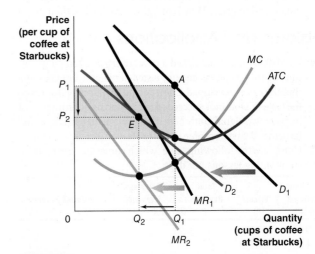

**Figure 2**

The effect of entry on price, quantity, and profit.

# Chapter Summary and Problems

## Key Terms

Brand management, p. 446                Marketing, p. 445                Monopolistic competition, p. 432

 **13.1** **Demand and Marginal Revenue for a Firm in a Monopolistically Competitive Market**, pages 432–434

LEARNING OBJECTIVE: Explain why a monopolistically competitive firm has downward-sloping demand and marginal revenue curves.

## Summary

A firm competing in a **monopolistically competitive** market sells a differentiated product. Therefore, unlike a firm in a perfectly competitive market, it faces a downward-sloping demand curve. When a monopolistically competitive firm cuts the price of its product, it sells more units but must accept a lower price on the units it could have sold at the higher price. As a result, its marginal revenue curve is downward sloping. Every firm that has the ability to affect the price of the good or service it sells will have a marginal revenue curve that is below its demand curve.

**MyEconLab**    Visit **www.myeconlab.com** to complete these exercises online and get instant feedback.

## Review Questions

**1.1** What are the most important differences between perfectly competitive markets and monopolistically competitive markets? Give two examples of products sold in perfectly competitive markets and two examples of products sold in monopolistically competitive markets.

**1.2** Why does a local McDonald's face a downward-sloping demand curve for its Quarter Pounder? If McDonald's raises the price of Quarter Pounders above the prices charged by other fast-food restaurants, won't it lose all its customers?

**1.3** With a downward-sloping demand curve, why is average revenue equal to price? Why is marginal revenue less than price?

## Problems and Applications

**1.4** In 2010, Domino's launched a new advertising campaign admitting that its pizzas had not tasted very good, but claiming that they had developed a new recipe that greatly improved the taste. If Domino's succeeded in convincing consumers that its pizza was significantly better than competing pizzas, would its demand curve become flatter or steeper? Briefly explain.

**1.5** Complete the following table, which shows the demand for snow skiing lessons per day:

| Snow Skiing Lessons per Day (Q) | Price (P) | Total Revenue (TR = P × Q) | Average Revenue (AR = TR/Q) | Marginal Revenue (MR = ΔTR/ΔQ) |
|---|---|---|---|---|
| 0 | $80.00 | | | |
| 1 | 75.00 | | | |
| 2 | 70.00 | | | |
| 3 | 65.00 | | | |
| 4 | 60.00 | | | |
| 5 | 55.00 | | | |
| 6 | 50.00 | | | |
| 7 | 45.00 | | | |
| 8 | 40.00 | | | |

**1.6** A student makes the following argument:

> When a firm sells another unit of a good, the additional revenue the firm receives is equal to the price: If the price is $10, the additional revenue is also $10. Therefore, this chapter is incorrect when it says that marginal revenue is less than price for a monopolistically competitive firm.

Briefly explain whether you agree with this argument.

**1.7** There are many wheat farms in the world, and there are also many Starbucks coffeehouses. Why, then, does a Starbucks coffeehouse face a downward-sloping demand curve, while a wheat farmer faces a horizontal demand curve?

**1.8** Is it possible for marginal revenue to be negative for a firm selling in a perfectly competitive market? Is it possible for marginal revenue to be negative for a firm selling in a monopolistically competitive market? Briefly explain.

**1.9** In the figure below, consider the marginal revenue of the eleventh unit sold. When the firm cuts the price from $5.00 to $4.75 to sell the eleventh unit, what area in the graph denotes the output effect, and what is the dollar value of the output effect? What area in the graph denotes the price effect, and what is the dollar value of the price effect? What is the marginal revenue of the eleventh unit?

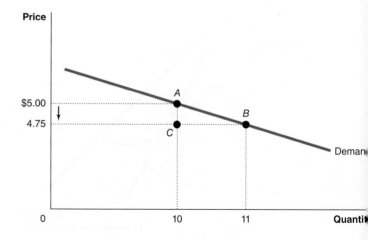

**1.10** Sally runs a vegetable stand. She is selling 100 pounds of heirloom tomatoes per week, at a price of $3.75 per pound. If she lowers the price to $3.70, she will sell 101 pounds of heirloom tomatoes. What is the marginal revenue of the 101st pound of heirloom tomatoes?

<table>
<tr><td>**13.2**</td><td>

## How a Monopolistically Competitive Firm Maximizes Profit in the Short Run, pages 434–437

</td></tr>
</table>

LEARNING OBJECTIVE: Explain how a monopolistically competitive firm maximizes profit in the short run.

## Summary

A monopolistically competitive firm maximizes profits at the level of output where marginal revenue equals marginal cost. Price equals marginal revenue for a perfectly competitive firm, but price is greater than marginal revenue for a monopolistically competitive firm. Therefore, unlike a perfectly competitive firm, which produces where $P = MC$, a monopolistically competitive firm produces where $P > MC$.

MyEconLab   Visit **www.myeconlab.com** to complete these exercises online and get instant feedback.

## Review Questions

**2.1** Why doesn't a monopolistically competitive firm produce where $P = MC$, as a perfectly competitive firm does?

**2.2** Stephen runs a pet salon. He is currently grooming 125 dogs per week. If instead of grooming 125 dogs, he grooms 126 dogs, he will add $68.50 to his costs and $60.00 to his revenues. What will be the effect on his profit of grooming 126 dogs instead of 125 dogs?

**2.3** If Daniel sells 350 Big Macs at a price of $3.25 each, and his average cost of producing 350 Big Macs is $3.00 each, what is his profit?

**2.4** Should a monopolistically competitive firm take into account its fixed costs when deciding how much to produce? Briefly explain.

## Problems and Applications

**2.5** Maria manages a bakery, that specializes in ciabatta bread, and has the following information on demand and costs:

| Ciabatta Bread Sold per Hour ($Q$) | Price ($P$) | Total Cost ($TC$) |
|---|---|---|
| 0 | $6.00 | $3.00 |
| 1 | 5.50 | 7.00 |
| 2 | 5.00 | 10.00 |
| 3 | 4.50 | 12.50 |
| 4 | 4.00 | 14.50 |
| 5 | 3.50 | 16.00 |
| 6 | 3.00 | 17.00 |
| 7 | 2.50 | 18.50 |
| 8 | 2.00 | 21.00 |

a. To maximize profit, how many loaves of ciabatta bread should Maria sell per hour, what price should she charge, and how much profit will she make?

b. What is the marginal revenue received by selling the profit-maximizing quantity of ciabatta bread? What is the marginal cost of producing the profit-maximizing quantity of ciabatta bread?

**2.6** **[Related to** Solved Problem 13.2 **on page 436]** Suppose a firm producing table lamps has the following costs:

| Quantity | Average Total Cost |
|---|---|
| 1,000 | $15.00 |
| 2,000 | 9.75 |
| 3,000 | 8.25 |
| 4,000 | 7.50 |
| 5,000 | 7.75 |
| 6,000 | 8.50 |
| 7,000 | 9.75 |
| 8,000 | 10.50 |
| 9,000 | 12.00 |

Ben and Jerry are managers at the company, and they have this discussion:

**Ben:** We should produce 4,000 lamps per month because that will minimize our average costs.

**Jerry:** But shouldn't we maximize profits rather than minimize costs? To maximize profits, don't we need to take demand into account?

**Ben:** Don't worry. By minimizing average costs, we will be maximizing profits. Demand will determine how high the price we can charge will be, but it won't affect our profit-maximizing quantity.

Evaluate the discussion between the two managers.

**2.7** According to an article in *USA Today*, American Airlines lost $436 million in the first quarter of 2011 compared with a loss of $69 million in the previous quarter. The article states, "Revenue rose 9.2%, to $5.53 billion, as passenger traffic improved modestly and fares rose since December."

a. Briefly explain how it is possible for a firm's revenue to increase at the same time that its profit decreases.

b. Use a graph to illustrate your answer to part a.

Based on David Koenig , "American Airlines Posts Huge Q1 Loss on Fuel Costs," *USA Today*, April 20, 2011.

**2.8** During the last three months of 2008, clothing retailer J. Crew cut the prices of many of its products. During that period, its profits per item of clothing declined, and it suffered a loss of $13.5 million. Does this information show that J. Crew's decision to cut prices was not a profit-maximizing strategy? Briefly explain.

Based on John Kell, "Markdowns Weigh on J. Crew," *Wall Street Journal*, March 11, 2009.

**2.9** William Germano previously served as the vice president and publishing director at the Routledge publishing company. He once gave the following description of how a publisher might deal with an unexpected increase in the cost of publishing a book:

It's often asked why the publisher can't simply raise the price [if costs increase]. . . . It's likely that the editor [is already] . . . charging as much as the market will bear. . . . In other words, you might be willing to pay $50.00 for a . . . book on the Brooklyn Bridge, but if . . . production costs [increase] by 25 percent, you might think $62.50 is too much to pay, though that would be what the publisher needs to charge. And indeed the publisher may determine that $50.00 is this book's ceiling—the most you would pay before deciding to rent a movie instead.

a. According to what you have learned in this chapter, how do firms adjust the price of a good when there is an increase in cost? Use a graph to illustrate your answer.

b. Does the model of monopolistic competition seem to fit Germano's description? If a publisher does not raise the price of a book following an increase in its production cost, what will be the result?

c. How would the elasticity of demand for published books affect the ability of the publishing company to raise book prices when costs increase?

From William Germano, *Getting It Published: A Guide to Scholars and Anyone Else Serious about Serious Books*, 2nd edition, Chicago: University of Chicago Press, 2008, p. 107.

2.10 In 1916, Ford Motor Company produced 500,000 Model T Fords, at a price of $440 each. The company made a profit of $60 million that year. Henry Ford told a newspaper reporter that he intended to reduce the price of the Model T to $360, and he expected to sell 800,000 cars at that price. Ford said, "Less profit on each car, but more cars, more employment of labor, and in the end we get all the total profit we ought to make."

a. Did Ford expect the total revenue he received from selling Model Ts to rise or fall following the price cut?

b. Use the information given above to calculate the price elasticity of demand for Model Ts. Use the midpoint formula to make your calculation. See Chapter 6, page 174, if you need a refresher on the midpoint formula.

c. What would the average total cost of producing 800,000 Model Ts have to be for Ford to make as much profit selling 800,000 Model Ts as it made selling 500,000 Model Ts? Is this smaller or larger than the average total cost of producing 500,000 Model Ts?

d. Assume that Ford would make the same total profit when selling 800,000 cars as when selling 500,000 cars. Was Henry Ford correct in saying he would make less profit per car when selling 800,000 cars than when selling 500,000 cars?

---

## 13.3 | What Happens to Profits in the Long Run? pages 437–443

LEARNING OBJECTIVE: Analyze the situation of a monopolistically competitive firm in the long run.

## Summary

If a monopolistically competitive firm is earning economic profits in the short run, entry of new firms will eliminate those profits in the long run. If a monopolistically competitive firm is suffering economic losses in the short run, exit of existing firms will eliminate those losses in the long run. Monopolistically competitive firms continually struggle to find new ways of differentiating their products as they try to stay one step ahead of other firms that are attempting to copy their success.

 Visit **www.myeconlab.com** to complete these exercises online and get instant feedback.

## Review Questions

3.1 What effect does the entry of new firms have on the economic profits of existing firms?

3.2 Why does the entry of new firms cause the demand curve of an existing firm in a monopolistically competitive market to shift to the left and to become more elastic?

3.3 What is the difference between zero accounting profit and zero economic profit?

3.4 Is it possible for a monopolistically competitive firm to continue to earn economic profits as new firms enter the market?

## Problems and Applications

3.5 Suppose Angelica opens a small store near campus, selling beef brisket sandwiches. Use the graph in the next column, which shows the demand and cost for Angelica's beef brisket sandwiches, to answer the questions that follow.

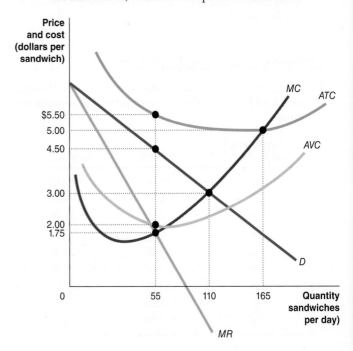

a. If Angelica wants to maximize profits, how many beef brisket sandwiches should she sell per day, and what price should she charge? Briefly explain your answer.

b. How much economic profit (or loss) is Angelica making? Briefly explain.

c. Is Angelica likely to continue selling this number of beef brisket sandwiches in the long run? Briefly explain.

**3.6** [Related to the Don't Let This Happen to You **on page 438**] A student remarks:

> If firms in a monopolistically competitive industry are earning economic profits, new firms will enter the industry. Eventually, a representative firm will find that its demand curve has shifted to the left, until it is just tangent to its average cost curve and it is earning zero profit. Because firms are earning zero profit at that point, some firms will leave the industry, and the representative firm will find that its demand curve will shift to the right. In long-run equilibrium, price will be above average total cost by just enough so that each firm is just breaking even.

Briefly explain whether you agree with this analysis.

**3.7** A columnist for the *Wall Street Journal* made the following observation: "The [oil] refining business is just too competitive, which is great for consumers, but not shareholders." Briefly explain why the high level of competition in the oil refining industry is good for consumers but bad for the shareholders who own these firms.

Based on James B. Stewart, "Coping with the Inevitable: The Losers in Your Portfolio," *Wall Street Journal*, December 3, 2008.

**3.8** [Related to the Making the Connection **on page 440**] As McDonald's began to increase its competition with Starbucks, Starbucks attempted to fight back with a new advertising campaign. According to an article in the *Wall Street Journal*, one ad proclaimed: "If your coffee isn't perfect, we'll make it over. If it's still not perfect make sure you're in a Starbucks." Starbucks CEO Howard Schultz explained the purpose of the campaign: "We don't want the public to be misled that all coffee is equal, because it's not." Why would it be a problem for Starbucks if consumers came to believe that "all coffee is equal"? How might Starbucks convince consumers that all coffee is not equal?

Based on Julie Jargon, "New Ads Will Stir Up Coffee Wars," *Wall Street Journal*, May 4, 2009.

**3.9** [Related to Solved Problem 13.3 **on page 441**] hhgregg has been successful in retailing appliances and electronics by combining high prices with excellent customer service. In late 2008, Saks Fifth Avenue tried a new strategy in retailing luxury clothing. Saks decided to slash prices on designer clothing by 70 percent just before the beginning of the holiday sales season. According to an article in the *Wall Street Journal*, "Saks's risky price-cut strategy was to be one of the first to discount deeply, rather than one of the last." According to the article:

> Saks's maneuver marked an open abandonment of the longstanding unwritten pact between retailers and designers. . . . Those old rules boiled down to this: Leave the goods at full price at least two months, and don't do markdowns until the very end of the season.

Is Saks's strategy of becoming the low-priced luxury clothing retailer likely to succeed? Contrast Saks's strategy with the strategy of hhgregg in terms of how likely the two strategies are to be successful over the long run.

Based on Vanessa O'Connell and Rachel Dodes, "Saks Upends Luxury Market With Strategy to Slash Prices," *Wall Street Journal*, February 9, 2009.

**3.10** Michael Korda was, for many years, editor-in-chief at the Simon & Schuster book publishing company. He has written about the many books that have become bestsellers by promising to give readers financial advice that will make them wealthy, by, for example, buying and selling real estate. Korda is skeptical about the usefulness of the advice in these books because "I have yet to meet anybody who got rich by buying a book, though quite a few people got rich by writing one." On the basis of the analysis in this chapter, discuss why it may be very difficult to become rich by following the advice found in a book.

Based on Michael Korda, *Making the List: A Cultural History of the American Bestseller, 1900–1999*, (New York: Barnes & Noble Books, 2001), p. 168.

**3.11** [Related to the Chapter Opener **on page 431**] John Quelch, a marketing professor at the Harvard Business School, commented on the situation facing Starbucks: "Starbucks is fundamentally selling an experience, but by no means is coffee the only part of the experience." Why might Starbucks have problems if selling coffee were the only part of the Starbucks "experience"?

Based on Sarah Skidmore, "Starbucks Gives Logo a New Look," Associated Press, January 5, 2011.

**3.12** In 2011, some Starbucks stores in New York City began putting metal plates over electric outlets to limit the time people could sit at tables using laptop computers. A spokesman for Starbucks stated that individual stores could make the decision whether to cover up power outlets. Why might some Starbucks cover up the outlets while others leave them uncovered?

Based on Emily Maltby, "Should Coffee Shop Owners Limit Laptop Usage?" *Wall Street Journal*, August 4, 2011.

**3.13** The *Wall Street Journal* reported that Western European brewers such as Heineken, Carlsberg, and Anheuser-Busch InBev are increasing their production and marketing of nonalcoholic beer. The article quotes a Carlsberg executive for new-product development as saying:

> Nonalcoholic beer is a largely unexploited opportunity for big brewers. It is quite a natural move when you see that the overall beer market [in Western Europe is] going down. So, of course, we're battling for market share.

The article further states that "brewers are hoping to capitalize on health consciousness" and that "recent brewing advances are helping improve the taste of nonalcoholic beers."

a. In what sense is nonalcoholic beer an "unexploited opportunity" for big brewers?

b. Are the brewers responding to consumer desires, or are brewers exploiting consumers? Briefly explain.

c. How will the "recent brewing advances" that improve taste affect the market for nonalcoholic beer?

Based on Ilan Brat, "Taking the Buzz Out of Beer," *Wall Street Journal*, August 30, 2011.

**13.4** **Comparing Monopolistic Competition and Perfect Competition,** pages 443–445

LEARNING OBJECTIVE: Compare the efficiency of monopolistic competition and perfect competition.

## Summary

Perfectly competitive firms produce where price equals marginal cost and at minimum average total cost. Perfectly competitive firms achieve both allocative and productive efficiency. Monopolistically competitive firms produce where price is greater than marginal cost and above minimum average total cost. Monopolistically competitive firms do not achieve either allocative or productive efficiency. Consumers face a trade-off when buying the product of a monopolistically competitive firm: They are paying a price that is greater than marginal cost, and the product is not being produced at minimum average cost, but they benefit from being able to purchase a product that is differentiated and more closely suited to their tastes.

MyEconLab Visit **www.myeconlab.com** to complete these exercises online and get instant feedback.

## Review Questions

**4.1** What are the differences between the long-run equilibrium of a perfectly competitive firm and the long-run equilibrium of a monopolistically competitive firm?

**4.2** Why is a monopolistically competitive firm not productively efficient? In what sense does a monopolistically competitive firm have excess capacity?

**4.3** Why is a monopolistically competitive firm not allocatively efficient?

**4.4** Does the fact that monopolistically competitive markets are not allocatively or productively efficient mean that there is a significant loss in economic well-being to society in these markets? In your answer, be sure to define what you mean by "economic well-being."

## Problems and Applications

**4.5** A student makes the following comment:

> I can understand why a perfectly competitive firm will not earn profits in the long run because a perfectly competitive firm charges a price equal to marginal cost. But a monopolistically competitive firm can charge a price greater than marginal cost, so why can't it continue to earn profits in the long run?

How would you answer this question?

**4.6** Consider the following graph:

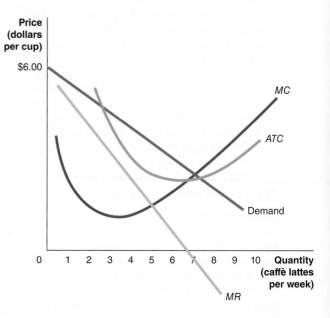

a. Is it possible to say whether this firm is a perfectly competitive firm or a monopolistically competitive firm? If so, explain how you are able to make this determination.

b. Does the graph show a short-run equilibrium or a long-run equilibrium? Briefly explain.

c. What quantity on the graph represents long-run equilibrium if the firm is perfectly competitive?

**4.7** Before the fall of Communism, most basic consumer products in Eastern Europe and the Soviet Union were standardized. For example, government-run stores would offer for sale only one type of bar soap or one type of toothpaste. Soviet economists often argued that this system of standardizing basic consumer products avoided the waste associated with the differentiated goods and services produced in Western Europe and the United States. Do you agree with this argument?

**4.8** **[Related to the** Making the Connection **on page 444]** How will the entry of firms such as Apple, Google, Amazon, Hulu, and Comcast into the business of streaming movies affect Netflix? Why do some analysts question whether Netflix can survive against these competitors? To survive, what must Netflix do?

 **13.5** **How Marketing Differentiates Products,** pages 445–446

LEARNING OBJECTIVE: Define marketing and explain how firms use marketing to differentiate their products.

## Summary

**Marketing** refers to all the activities necessary for a firm to sell a product to a consumer. Firms use two marketing tools to differentiate their products: brand management and advertising. **Brand management** refers to the actions of a firm intended to maintain the differentiation of a product over time. When a firm has established a successful brand name, it has a strong incentive to defend it. A firm can apply for a *trademark*, which grants legal protection against other firms using its product's name.

MyEconLab Visit **www.myeconlab.com** to complete these exercises online and get instant feedback.

## Review Questions

**5.1** Define *marketing*. Is marketing just another name for advertising?

**5.2** Why are many companies so concerned about brand management?

# Problems and Applications

**5.3** Draw a graph that shows the impact on a firm's profits when it increases spending on advertising and the increased advertising has *no* effect on the demand for the firm's product.

**5.4** A skeptic says, "Marketing research and brand management are redundant. If a company wants to find out what customers want, it should simply look at what they're already buying." Do you agree with this comment? Explain.

**5.5** The National Football League (NFL) has a trademark on the name "Super Bowl" for its championship game. Advertisers can use the words Super Bowl in their advertising only if they pay the NFL a fee. Many companies attempt to get around this trademark by using the phrase "the big game" in their advertising. For example, a few days before the Super Bowl, a consumer electronics store might have an advertisement with the phrase "Watch the big game on a new LED TV." In 2007, the National Football League considered legal action to have the phrase "the big game" included in its Super Bowl trademark.

    **a.** Why does the government allow firms to trademark their products?

    **b.** Would consumers gain or lose if the NFL were allowed to trademark the phrase "the big game"? Briefly explain.

Based on Craig S. Mende, "On Watching 'The Big Game,'" *Forbes*, February 1, 2008.

**5.6** Some companies have done a poor job protecting the images of their products. For example, Hormel's Spam brand name is widely ridiculed and is associated with annoying commercial messages received via e-mail. Think of other cases of companies failing to protect their brand names. What can companies do about the situation now? Should the companies re-brand their products?

---

## 13.6 | What Makes a Firm Successful? pages 446–449

LEARNING OBJECTIVE: Identify the key factors that determine a firm's success.

## Summary

A firm's owners and managers control some of the factors that determine the profitability of the firm. Other factors affect all the firms in the market or are the result of chance, so they are not under the control of the firm's owners. The interactions between factors the firm controls and factors it does not control determine its profitability.

 Visit www.myeconlab.com to complete these exercises online and get instant feedback.

## Review Questions

**6.1** What are the key factors that determine the profitability of a firm in a monopolistically competitive market?

**6.2** How might a monopolistically competitive firm continually earn economic profit greater than zero?

## Problems and Applications

**6.3** According to an article in the *Wall Street Journal*:

> In early January last year, after a disappointing Christmas season and amid worries about competition from discount retailers, Zale Corp. decided to shake things up: The self-proclaimed jeweler to Middle America was going to chase upscale customers. . . . The move was a disaster. The Irving, Texas, retailer lost many of its traditional customers without winning the new ones it coveted.

Why would a firm like Zale abandon one market niche for another market niche? We know that in this case the move was not successful. Can you think of other cases where such a move has been successful?

From Ann Zimmerman and Kris Hudson, "Chasing Upscale Customers Tarnishes Mass-Market Jeweler," *Wall Street Journal*, June 26, 2006. p. A1.

**6.4** 7-Eleven, Inc., operates more than 20,000 convenience stores worldwide. Edward Moneypenny, 7-Eleven's chief financial officer, was asked to name the biggest risk the company faced. He replied, "I would say that the biggest risk that 7-Eleven faces, like all retailers, is competition . . . because that is something that you've got to be aware of in this business." In what sense is competition a "risk" to a business? Why would a company in the retail business need to be particularly aware of competition?

Based on Company Report, "CEO Interview: Edward Moneypenny—7-Eleven, Inc.," The Wall Street Transcript Corporation.

**6.5** In 2006, Wal-Mart closed its stores in South Korea and Germany. According to an article in the *New York Times*:

> Wal-Mart's most successful markets, like Mexico, are those in which it started big. There, the company bought the country's largest and best-run retail chain, Cifra, and has never looked back. This year, Wal-Mart is spending more than $1 billion in Mexico to open 120 new stores.

What advantages does Wal-Mart gain from buying large retail chains, as it did in Mexico, rather than small chains, as it did in its unsuccessful attempts to enter the South Korean and German markets?

Based on Mark Landler and Michael Barbaro, "Wal-Mart Finds That Its Formula Doesn't Fit Every Culture," *New York Times*, August 2, 2006.

**6.6** [Related to the Making the Connection on page 447] A firm that is first to market with a new product frequently discovers that there are design flaws or problems with the product that were not anticipated. For example, the ballpoint pens made by the Reynolds International Pen Company often leaked. What effect do these problems have on the innovating firm, and how do these unexpected problems open up possibilities for other firms to enter the market?

**6.7** An article in the *New York Times* notes that in buying mutual fund shares, "Investors have . . . [a] problem . . . : determining whether good returns come from skill or luck." Is it ever easy to determine whether a firm making economic profits is doing so because of the skills of the firm's managers or because of luck? Briefly explain.

From Jeff Brown, "Hedge Funds? Only If You Like Lots of Risk," *New York Times*, August 6, 2009.

## **Chapter Outline** and **Learning Objectives**

# Competition in the Computer Market

Many of the largest corporations in the United States began as small businesses. In 1975, Bill Gates and Paul Allen founded Microsoft Corporation in Albuquerque, New Mexico, with themselves as the only employees. Steve Jobs and Steve Wozniak formed Apple in 1976, working at first out of Jobs's garage. Jobs and Wozniak were following in the tradition of William Hewlett and David Packard, who founded what became the Hewlett-Packard (H-P) company in a garage in Palo Alto, California, in the 1930s. Michael Dell started the Dell computer company in 1984, from his dorm room at the University of Texas. Sam Walton, founder of Wal-Mart, bought his first store in 1945, with $20,000 borrowed from his father-in-law.

When each of these firms was founded, their industries included many more firms than they do now. Today, in the software and computer industries, fewer than 10 firms account for the great majority of sales. Wal-Mart accounts for a large share of several segments of retail sales.

An industry with only a few firms is an *oligopoly*. In an oligopoly, a firm's profitability depends on its interactions with other firms. In these industries, firms must develop *business strategies*, which involve not just deciding what price to charge and how many units to produce but also how much to advertise, which new technologies to

adopt, how to manage relations with suppliers, and which new markets to enter.

Apple has introduced a number of electronic products, including the iPod, iPhone, and iPad. In 2008, Apple introduced the MacBook Air, a very thin and very light laptop computer intended to fill a market niche for students, business travelers, and others needing very lightweight laptops. The MacBook Air posed a challenge to other computer firms: Should they develop models to compete with the MacBook Air or be content to continue producing conventional laptops and desktops? In 2011, Samsung introduced the Series 9 notebook and Dell introduced the XPS 15z laptop, both intended to compete with Apple's MacBook Air. Because there are relatively few firms competing in an oligopolistic industry such as the computer industry, firms must continually react to each other's actions or risk losing significant sales. In this chapter, we focus on strategic interactions among firms.

**AN INSIDE LOOK** on **page 478** discusses how Intel produced the Ultrabook to respond to consumer demand.

Based on Justin Sheck and Ben Worthen, "Dell Inc. Lowers Its Sights for Gadgets, Consumers," *Wall Street Journal*, May 23, 2011; Doug Aamoth, "Samsung Takes on the MacBook Air," www.techland.time.com, April 28, 2011; and Jared Newman, "Dell's MacBook Air Rival Coming Soon," www.techland.time.com, May 23, 2011.

## Economics in Your Life

### Why Can't You Find a Cheap PlayStation 3?

You and your roommates have just moved into a great apartment and decide to treat yourselves to a PlayStation 3 320GB game system—provided that you can find one at a relatively low price. First you check Amazon and find a price of $349.99. Then you check Best Buy, and the price there is also $349.99. Then you check Target; $349.99 again! Finally, you check Wal-Mart, and you find a lower price: $349.*96*, a whopping discount of $0.03. Why isn't one of these big retailers willing to charge a lower price? What happened to price competition? As you read the chapter, see if you can answer these questions. You can check your answers against those we provide on **page 477** at the end of this chapter.

In Chapters 12 and 13, we studied perfectly competitive and monopolistically competitive industries. Our analysis focused on the determination of a firm's profit-maximizing price and quantity. We concluded that firms maximize profit by producing where marginal revenue equals marginal cost. To determine marginal revenue and marginal cost, we used graphs that included the firm's demand, marginal revenue, and marginal cost curves. In this chapter, we will study oligopoly, a market structure in which a small number of interdependent firms compete. In analyzing oligopoly, we cannot rely on the same types of graphs we used in analyzing perfect competition and monopolistic competition for two reasons.

First, we need to use economic models that allow us to analyze the more complex business strategies of large oligopoly firms. These strategies involve more than choosing the profit-maximizing price and output. Second, even in determining the profit-maximizing price and output for an oligopoly firm, demand curves and cost curves are not as useful as in the cases of perfect competition and monopolistic competition. We are able to draw the demand curves for competitive firms by assuming that the prices these firms charge have no effect on the prices other firms in their industries charge. This assumption is realistic when each firm is small relative to the market. It is not a realistic assumption, however, for firms that are as large relative to their markets as Microsoft, Apple, or Wal-Mart.

When large firms cut their prices, their rivals in the industry often—but not always—respond by also cutting their prices. Because we don't know for sure how other firms will respond to a price change, we don't know the quantity an oligopolist will sell at a particular price. In other words, it is difficult to know what an oligopolist's demand curve will look like. As we have seen, a firm's marginal revenue curve depends on its demand curve. If we don't know what an oligopolist's demand curve looks like, we also don't know what its marginal revenue curve looks like. Because we don't know marginal revenue, we can't calculate the profit-maximizing level of output and the profit-maximizing price the way we do for competitive firms.

The approach we use to analyze competition among oligopolists is called *game theory*. Game theory can be used to analyze any situation in which groups or individuals interact. In the context of economic analysis, game theory is the study of the decisions of firms in industries where the profits of each firm depend on its interactions with other firms. It has been applied to strategies for nuclear war, for international trade negotiations, and for political campaigns, among many other examples. In this chapter, we use game theory to analyze the business strategies of large firms.

**Oligopoly** A market structure in which a small number of interdependent firms compete.

# Oligopoly and Barriers to Entry

An **oligopoly** is an industry with only a few firms. This market structure lies between the competitive industries we studied in Chapters 12 and 13, which have many firms, and the monopolies we will study in Chapter 15, which have only a single firm. One measure of the extent of competition in an industry is the *concentration ratio*. Every five years, the U.S. Bureau of the Census publishes four-firm concentration ratios that state the fraction of each industry's sales accounted for by its four largest firms. Most economists believe that a four-firm concentration ratio greater than 40 percent indicates that an industry is an oligopoly.

The concentration ratio has some flaws as a measure of the extent of competition in an industry. For example, concentration ratios do not include the goods and services that foreign firms export to the United States. In addition, concentration ratios are calculated for the national market, even though the competition in some industries, such as restaurants or college bookstores, is mainly local. Finally, competition sometimes exists between firms in different industries. For example, Wal-Mart is included in the discount department stores industry but also competes with firms in the supermarket

| Retail Trade | | Manufacturing | |
|---|---|---|---|
| Industry | Four-Firm Concentration Ratio | Industry | Four-Firm Concentration Ratio |
| Discount department stores | 97% | Cigarettes | 98% |
| Warehouse clubs and supercenters | 94% | Beer | 90% |
| College bookstores | 75% | Computers | 87% |
| Hobby, toy, and game stores | 72% | Aircraft | 81% |
| Radio, television, and other electronic stores | 70% | Breakfast cereal | 80% |
| Athletic footwear stores | 68% | Dog and cat food | 71% |
| Pharmacies and drugstores | 63% | Automobiles | 68% |

**Table 14.1**

**Examples of Oligopolies in Retail Trade and Manufacturing**

Data from U.S. Census Bureau, *Concentration Ratios*, 2007.

industry and the retail toy store industry. As we will see in Chapter 15, some economists prefer another measure of competition, known as the *Herfindahl-Hirschman Index*. Despite their shortcomings, concentration ratios can be useful in providing a general idea of the extent of competition in an industry.

Table 14.1 lists examples of oligopolies in manufacturing and retail trade. Notice that the computer industry is highly concentrated. The four largest firms—Hewlett-Packard, Dell, Acer, and Apple—sell 87 percent of all the desktops and laptops sold in the United States.

## Barriers to Entry

Why do oligopolies exist? Why aren't there many more firms in the computer industry, the discount department store industry, or the beer industry? Recall that new firms will enter industries where existing firms are earning economic profits. But new firms often have difficulty entering an oligopoly. Anything that keeps new firms from entering an industry in which firms are earning economic profits is called a **barrier to entry**. Three barriers to entry are economies of scale, ownership of a key input, and government-imposed barriers.

**Barrier to entry** Anything that keeps new firms from entering an industry in which firms are earning economic profits.

**Economies of Scale**   The most important barrier to entry is economies of scale. In Chapter 11, we saw that **economies of scale** exist when a firm's long-run average costs fall as it increases output. The greater the economies of scale, the smaller the number of firms that will be in the industry. Figure 14.1 illustrates this point.

If economies of scale are relatively unimportant in the industry, the typical firm's long-run average cost curve (*LRAC*) will reach a minimum at a level of output ($Q_1$ in Figure 14.1) that is a small fraction of total industry sales. The industry will have room for a large number of firms and will be competitive. If economies of scale are significant, the typical firm will not reach the minimum point on its long-run average cost curve ($Q_2$ in Figure 14.1) until it has produced a large fraction of industry sales. Then the industry will have room for only a few firms and will be an oligopoly.

Economies of scale can explain why there is much more competition in the restaurant industry than in the computer industry. Because very large restaurants do not have lower average costs than smaller restaurants, the restaurant industry has room for many firms. In contrast, large computer firms such as Apple have much lower average costs than small computer firms, partly because large firms can spread the high fixed costs of producing computers—including very large research and development costs—over a much larger quantity of computers.

**Economies of scale** The situation when a firm's long-run average costs fall as the firm increases output.

**Figure 14.1**

**Economies of Scale Help Determine the Extent of Competition in an Industry**

An industry will be competitive if the minimum point on the typical firm's long-run average cost curve ($LRAC_1$) occurs at a level of output that is a small fraction of total industry sales, such as $Q_1$. The industry will be an oligopoly if the minimum point comes at a level of output that is a large fraction of industry sales, such as $Q_2$.

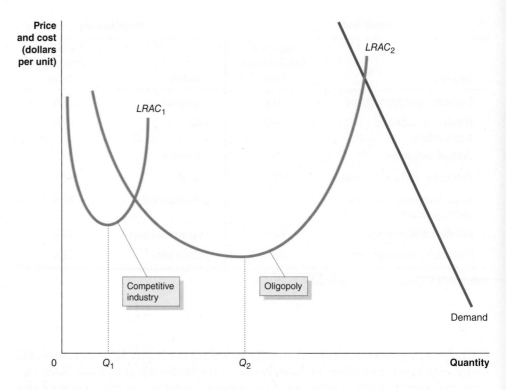

**Ownership of a Key Input** If production of a good requires a particular input, then control of that input can be a barrier to entry. For many years, the Aluminum Company of America (Alcoa) controlled most of the world's supply of high-quality bauxite, the mineral needed to produce aluminum. The only way other companies could enter the industry to compete with Alcoa was to recycle aluminum. The De Beers Company of South Africa was able to block competition in the diamond market by controlling the output of most of the world's diamond mines. Until the 1990s, Ocean Spray had very little competition in the market for fresh and frozen cranberries because it controlled almost the entire supply of cranberries. Even today, the company controls about 80 percent of the cranberry crop.

**Government-Imposed Barriers** Firms sometimes try to convince the government to impose barriers to entry. Many large firms employ *lobbyists* to convince state legislators and members of Congress to pass laws favorable to the economic interests of the firms. There are tens of thousands of lobbyists in Washington, DC, alone. Top lobbyists command annual salaries of $300,000 or more, which indicates the value firms place on their activities. Examples of government-imposed barriers to entry are patents, licensing requirements, and barriers to international trade.

A **patent** gives a firm the exclusive right to a new product for a period of 20 years from the date the patent is filed with the government. Governments use patents to encourage firms to carry out research and development of new and better products and better ways of producing existing products. Output and living standards increase faster when firms devote resources to research and development, but a firm that spends money to develop a new product may not earn much profit if other firms can copy the product. For example, the pharmaceutical company Merck spends more than $3 billion per year on developing new prescription drugs. If rival companies could freely produce these new drugs as soon as Merck developed them, most of the firm's investment would be wasted. Because Merck can patent a new drug, the firm can charge higher prices during the years the patent is in force and make an economic profit on its successful innovation.

Governments also restrict competition through *occupational licensing*. The United States currently has about 500 occupational licensing laws. For example, doctors and dentists in every state need licenses to practice. The justification for the laws is to protect the public from incompetent practitioners, but by restricting the number of people who can enter the licensed professions, the laws also raise prices. Studies have shown

**Patent** The exclusive right to a product for a period of 20 years from the date the patent is filed with the government.

that states that make it harder to earn a dentist's license have prices for dental services that are about 15 percent higher than in other states. Similarly, states that require a license for out-of-state firms to sell contact lenses have higher prices for contact lenses. When state licenses are required for occupations such as hair braiding, which was done several years ago in California, restricting competition is the main result.

Governments also impose barriers to entering some industries by imposing tariffs and quotas on foreign competition. As we saw in Chapter 9, a *tariff* is a tax on imports, and a *quota* limits the quantity of a good that can be imported into a country. A quota on foreign sugar imports severely limits competition in the U.S. sugar market. As a result, U.S. sugar companies can charge prices that are more than twice as high as prices companies outside the United States charge.

In summary, to earn economic profits, all firms would like to charge a price well above average cost, but earning economic profits attracts new firms to enter the industry. Eventually, the increased competition forces price down to average cost, and firms just break even. In an oligopoly, barriers to entry prevent—or at least slow down—entry, which allows firms to earn economic profits over a longer period.

# Using Game Theory to Analyze Oligopoly

**14.2 LEARNING** OBJECTIVE

Use game theory to analyze the strategies of oligopolistic firms.

As we noted at the beginning of the chapter, economists analyze oligopolies by using *game theory*, which was developed during the 1940s by the mathematician John von Neumann and the economist Oskar Morgenstern. **Game theory** is the study of how people make decisions in situations in which attaining their goals depends on their interactions with others. In oligopolies, the interactions among firms are crucial in determining profitability because the firms are large relative to the market.

In all games—whether poker, chess, or Monopoly—the interactions among the players are crucial in determining the outcome. In addition, games share three key characteristics:

**Game theory** The study of how people make decisions in situations in which attaining their goals depends on their interactions with others; in economics, the study of the decisions of firms in industries where the profits of a firm depend on its interactions with other firms.

1. *Rules* that determine what actions are allowable
2. *Strategies* that players employ to attain their objectives in the game
3. *Payoffs* that are the results of the interactions among the players' strategies

In business situations, the rules of the "game" include not just laws that a firm must obey but also other matters beyond a firm's control—at least in the short run—such as its production function. A **business strategy** is a set of actions that a firm takes to achieve a goal, such as maximizing profits. The *payoffs* are the profits a firm earns as a result of how its strategies interact with the strategies of other firms. The best way to understand the game theory approach is to look at an example.

**Business strategy** Actions that a firm takes to achieve a goal, such as maximizing profits.

## A Duopoly Game: Price Competition between Two Firms

In this simple example, we use game theory to analyze price competition in a *duopoly*—an oligopoly with two firms. Suppose we ignore the other firms in the industry and assume that Apple and Dell are the only two firms producing desktop computers. Let's focus on their sales of basic desktop computers, such as Apple's iMac or Dell's Inspiron All-in-One. The managers of the two firms have to decide whether to charge $1,200 or $1,000 for their computers. Which price will be more profitable depends on the price the other firm charges. The decision regarding what price to charge is an example of a business strategy. In Figure 14.2, we organize the possible outcomes that result from the actions of the two firms into a **payoff matrix**, which is a table that shows the payoffs that each firm earns from every combination of strategies by the firms.

**Payoff matrix** A table that shows the payoffs that each firm earns from every combination of strategies by the firms.

Apple's profits are shown in red, and Dell's profits are shown in blue. If Apple and Dell both charge $1,200 for their computers, each firm will make a profit of $10 million per month. If Apple charges the lower price of $1,000, while Dell charges $1,200, Apple will gain many of Dell's customers. Apple's profits will be $15 million, and Dell's will be only $5 million. Similarly, if Dell charges $1,000 while Apple is charging $1,200,

## Figure 14.2

### A Duopoly Game

Dell's profits are in blue, and Apple's profits are in red. Dell and Apple would each make profits of $10 million per month on sales of desktop computers if they both charged $1,200. However, each firm has an incentive to undercut the other by charging a lower price. If both firms charged $1,000, they would each make a profit of only $7.5 million per month.

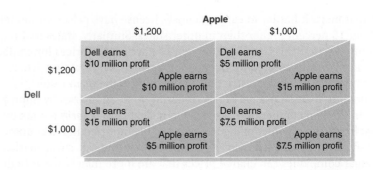

**Collusion**  An agreement among firms to charge the same price or otherwise not to compete.

**Dominant strategy**  A strategy that is the best for a firm, no matter what strategies other firms use.

**Nash equilibrium**  A situation in which each firm chooses the best strategy, given the strategies chosen by other firms.

**Cooperative equilibrium**  An equilibrium in a game in which players cooperate to increase their mutual payoff.

**Noncooperative equilibrium**  An equilibrium in a game in which players do not cooperate but pursue their own self-interest.

**Prisoner's dilemma**  A game in which pursuing dominant strategies results in noncooperation that leaves everyone worse off.

Apple's profits will be only $5 million while Dell's profits will be $15 million. If both firms charge $1,000, each will earn profits of $7.5 million per month.

Clearly, the firms will be better off if they both charge $1,200 for their computers. But will they both charge this price? One possibility is that Apple's managers and Dell's managers will get together and *collude* by agreeing to charge the higher price. **Collusion** is an agreement among firms to charge the same price or otherwise not to compete. Unfortunately for Apple and Dell—but fortunately for their customers—collusion is against the law in the United States. The government can fine companies that collude and send the managers involved to prison.

Apple's managers can't legally discuss their pricing decision with Dell's managers, so they have to predict what the other managers will do. Suppose Apple's managers are convinced that Dell's managers will charge $1,200 for their computers. In this case, Apple's managers will definitely charge $1,000 because that will increase Apple's profit from $10 million to $15 million. But suppose that, instead, Apple's managers are convinced that Dell's managers will charge $1,000. Then Apple's managers also definitely will charge $1,000 because that will increase their profit from $5 million to $7.5 million. In fact, regardless of which price Dell's managers decide to charge, Apple's managers are better off charging $1,000. So, we know that Apple's managers will choose a price of $1,000 for Apple computers.

Now consider the situation of Dell's managers. They are in the same position as Apple's managers, so we can expect them to make the same decision to charge $1,000 for their computers. In this situation, both firms have a *dominant strategy*. A **dominant strategy** is the best strategy for a firm, no matter what strategies other firms use. The result is an equilibrium where both firms charge $1,000 for their computers. This situation is an equilibrium because each firm is maximizing profits, *given the price chosen by the other firm*. In other words, neither firm can increase its profits by changing its price, given the price chosen by the other firm. An equilibrium where each firm chooses the best strategy, given the strategies chosen by other firms, is called a **Nash equilibrium**, named after Nobel Laureate John Nash of Princeton University, a pioneer in the development of game theory.

## Firm Behavior and the Prisoner's Dilemma

Notice that the equilibrium in Figure 14.2 is not very satisfactory for either firm. The firms earn $7.5 million in profit each month by charging $1,000, but they could have earned $10 million in profit if they had both charged $1,200. By "cooperating" and charging the higher price, they would have achieved a *cooperative equilibrium*. In a **cooperative equilibrium**, players cooperate to increase their mutual payoff. We have seen, though, that the outcome of this game is likely to be a **noncooperative equilibrium**, in which each firm pursues its own self-interest.

A situation like this, in which pursuing dominant strategies results in noncooperation that leaves everyone worse off, is called a **prisoner's dilemma**. The game gets its name from the problem faced by two suspects the police arrest for a crime. If the police lack other evidence, they may separate the suspects and offer each a reduced prison sentence in exchange for confessing to the crime and testifying against the other suspect. Because each suspect has a dominant strategy to confess to the crime, they will both confess and serve a jail term, even though they would have gone free if they had both remained silent.

# Don't Let This Happen to You

## Don't Misunderstand Why Each Firm Ends Up Charging a Price of $1,000

It is tempting to think that Apple and Dell would each charge $1,000 rather than $1,200 for their computers because each is afraid that the other firm will charge $1,000. In fact, fear of being undercut by the other firm's charging a lower price is not the key to understanding each firm's pricing strategy. Notice that charging $1,000 is the most profitable strategy for each firm, no matter which price the other firm decides to charge. For example, even if

Apple's managers somehow knew for sure that Dell's managers intended to charge $1,200, Apple would still charge $1,000 because its profits would be $15 million instead of $10 million. Dell's managers are in the same situation. That is why charging $1,000 is a dominant strategy for both firms.

MyEconLab

**Your Turn:** Test your understanding by doing related problem 2.14 on page 483 at the end of the chapter.

# Solved Problem 14.2

## Is Advertising a Prisoner's Dilemma for Coca-Cola and Pepsi?

Coca-Cola and Pepsi both advertise aggressively, but would they be better off if they didn't? Their commercials are usually not designed to convey new information about their products. Instead, they are designed to capture each other's customers. Construct a payoff matrix using the following hypothetical information:

- If neither firm advertises, Coca-Cola and Pepsi both earn profits of $750 million per year.

- If both firms advertise, Coca-Cola and Pepsi both earn profits of $500 million per year.

- If Coca-Cola advertises and Pepsi doesn't, Coca-Cola earns profits of $900 million and Pepsi earns profits of $400 million.

- If Pepsi advertises and Coca-Cola doesn't, Pepsi earns profits of $900 million and Coca-Cola earns profits of $400 million.

  **a.** If Coca-Cola wants to maximize profit, will it advertise? Briefly explain.

  **b.** If Pepsi wants to maximize profit, will it advertise? Briefly explain.

  **c.** Is there a Nash equilibrium to this advertising game? If so, what is it?

## Solving the Problem

**Step 1:** **Review the chapter material.** This problem uses payoff matrixes to analyze a business situation, so you may want to review the section "A Duopoly Game: Price Competition between Two Firms," which begins on page 463.

**Step 2:** **Construct the payoff matrix.**

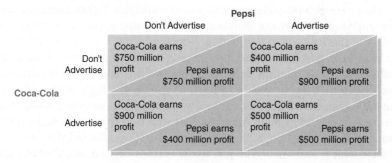

Step 3: **Answer part a. by showing that Coca-Cola has a dominant strategy of advertising.** If Pepsi doesn't advertise, then Coca-Cola will make $900 million if it advertises but only $750 million if it doesn't. If Pepsi advertises, then Coca-Cola will make $500 million if it advertises but only $400 million if it doesn't. Therefore, advertising is a dominant strategy for Coca-Cola.

Step 4: **Answer part b. by showing that Pepsi has a dominant strategy of advertising.** Pepsi is in the same position as Coca-Cola, so it also has a dominant strategy of advertising.

Step 5: **Answer part c. by showing that there is a Nash equilibrium for this game.** Both firms advertising is a Nash equilibrium. Given that Pepsi is advertising, Coca-Cola's best strategy is to advertise. Given that Coca-Cola is advertising, Pepsi's best strategy is to advertise. Therefore, advertising is the optimal decision for both firms, *given the decision by the other firm*.

**Extra Credit:** This is another example of the prisoner's dilemma game. Coca-Cola and Pepsi would be more profitable if they both refrained from advertising, thereby saving the enormous expense of television and radio commercials and newspaper and magazine ads. Each firm's dominant strategy is to advertise, however, so they end up in an equilibrium where both advertise, and their profits are reduced.

MyEconLab **Your Turn:** For more practice, do related problems 2.11, 2.12, and 2.13 on pages 482–483 at the end of this chapter.

---

Making the Connection | **Is There a Dominant Strategy for Bidding on eBay?**

An auction is a game in which bidders compete to buy a product. The payoff in winning an auction is equal to the difference between the subjective value you place on the product being auctioned and the amount of the winning bid. On the online auction site eBay, more than 200 million items valued at more than $10 billion are auctioned each year.

eBay is run as a *second-price auction*, where the winning bidder pays an amount equal to the bid of the second-highest bidder. If the high bidder on a DVD of *The Dark Knight Rises* bids $12, and the second bidder bids $8, the high bidder wins the auction and pays $8. It may seem that your best strategy when bidding on eBay is to place a bid well below the subjective value you place on the item in the hope of winning it at a low price. In fact, bidders on eBay have a dominant strategy of entering a bid equal to the maximum value they place on the item. For instance, suppose you are looking for a present for your parents' anniversary. They are U2 fans, and someone is auctioning a pair of U2 concert tickets. If the maximum value you place on the tickets is $200, that should be your bid. To see why, consider the results of strategies of bidding more or less than $200.

*On eBay, bidding the maximum value you place on an item is a dominant strategy.*

There are two possible outcomes of the auction: Either someone else bids more than you do, or you are the high bidder. First, suppose you bid $200 but someone else bids more than you do. If you had bid less than $200, you would still have lost. If you had bid more than $200, you might have been the high bidder, but because your bid would be for more than the value you place on the tickets, you would have a negative payoff. Second, suppose you bid $200 and you are the high bidder. If you had bid less than $200, you would have risked losing the tickets to someone whose bid you would have beaten by bidding $200. You would be worse off than if you had bid $200 and won. If you had bid more than $200, you would not have affected the price you ended up paying—which, remember, is equal to the second-highest bid. Therefore, a strategy of bidding $200—the maximum value you place on the tickets—dominates bidding more or less than $200.

Even though making your first bid your highest bid is a dominant strategy on eBay, many bidders don't use it. After an auction is over, a link leads to a Web page showing all the bids. In many auctions, the same bidder bids several times, showing that the bidder had not understood his or her dominant strategy.

**Your Turn:** Test your understanding by doing related problem 2.15 on page 483 at the end of this chapter.

MyEconLab

## Can Firms Escape the Prisoner's Dilemma?

Although the prisoner's dilemma game seems to show that cooperative behavior always breaks down, we know it doesn't. People often cooperate to achieve their goals, and firms find ways to cooperate by not competing on price. The reason the basic prisoner's dilemma story is not always applicable is that it assumes the game will be played only once. Most business situations, however, are repeated over and over. For example, consider the following situation: Suppose that in a small town, the only place to buy a PlayStation 3 game console is from either the local Target store or the local Wal-Mart store. (For simplicity, we will ignore the possibility of consumers buying the PlayStation 3 online.) We will assume that the managers will charge either $400 or $300 for the PlayStation. Panel (a) of Figure 14.3 shows the payoff matrix. Examining the matrix shows that, just as with Apple and Dell pricing computers, each manager has an incentive to charge the lower price. Once again, the firms appear caught in a prisoner's dilemma. But the managers will not play this game only once because each month they will decide again what price they will charge for the PlayStation 3. In the language of game theory, the managers are playing a *repeated game*. In a repeated game, the losses from

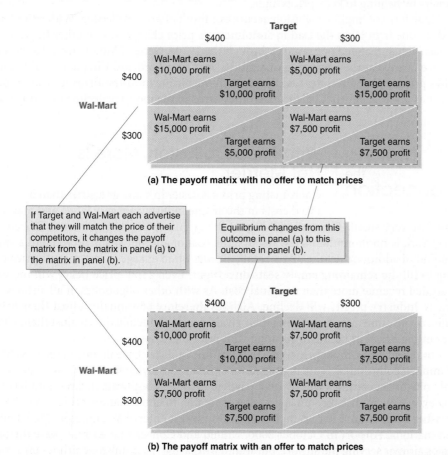

(a) The payoff matrix with no offer to match prices

If Target and Wal-Mart each advertise that they will match the price of their competitors, it changes the payoff matrix from the matrix in panel (a) to the matrix in panel (b).

Equilibrium changes from this outcome in panel (a) to this outcome in panel (b).

(b) The payoff matrix with an offer to match prices

### Figure 14.3

**Changing the Payoff Matrix in a Repeated Game**

Wal-Mart and Target can change the payoff matrix for selling PlayStation 3 game consoles by advertising that each will match its competitor's price. This retaliation strategy provides a signal that one store charging a lower price will be met automatically by the other store charging a lower price. In the payoff matrix in panel (a), there is no matching offer, and each store benefits if it charges $300 when the other charges $400. In the payoff matrix in panel (b), with the matching offer, the companies have only two choices: They can charge $400 and receive a profit of $10,000 per month, or they can charge $300 and receive a profit of $7,500 per month. The equilibrium shifts from the prisoner's dilemma result of both stores charging the low price and receiving low profits to both stores charging the high price and receiving high profits.

not cooperating are greater than in a game played once, and players can also employ *retaliation strategies* against those who don't cooperate. As a result, we are more likely to see cooperative behavior.

Panel (a) of Figure 14.3 shows that Wal-Mart and Target are earning $2,500 less per month by both charging $300 instead of $400 for the PlayStation 3. Every month that passes with both stores charging $300 increases the total amount lost: Two years of charging $300 will cause each to lose $60,000 in profit. This lost profit increases the incentive for the store managers to cooperate by *implicitly* colluding. Remember that *explicit* collusion—such as the managers meeting and agreeing to charge $400—is illegal. But if the managers can find a way to signal each other that they will charge $400, they may be within the law.

Suppose, for example, that Wal-Mart and Target both advertise that they will match the lowest price offered by any competitor—in our simple example, they are each other's only competitor. These advertisements are signals to each other that they intend to charge $400 for the PlayStation. The signal is clear because each store knows that if it charges $300, the other store will automatically retaliate by also lowering its price to $300. The offer to match prices is a good *enforcement mechanism* because it guarantees that if either store fails to cooperate and charges the lower price, the competing store will automatically punish that store by also charging the lower price. As Figure 14.3 shows, the stores have changed the payoff matrix they face.

With the original payoff matrix in panel (a), there is no matching offer, and each store makes more profit if it charges $300 when the other charges $400. The matching offer changes the payoff matrix to that shown in panel (b). Now the stores can charge $400 and receive a profit of $10,000 per month, or they can charge $300 and receive a profit of $7,500 per month. The equilibrium shifts from the prisoner's dilemma result of both stores charging the low price and receiving low profits to a result where both stores charge the high price and receive high profits. An offer to match competitors' prices might seem to benefit consumers, but game theory shows that it actually may hurt consumers by helping to keep prices high.

One form of implicit collusion occurs as a result of *price leadership*. With **price leadership**, one firm takes the lead in announcing a price change, which other firms in the industry then match. For example, through the 1970s, General Motors would announce a price change at the beginning of a model year, and Ford and Chrysler would match GM's price change. In some cases, such as in the airline industry, firms have attempted to act as price leaders but failed when other firms in the industry declined to cooperate.

**Price leadership** A form of implicit collusion in which one firm in an oligopoly announces a price change and the other firms in the industry match the change.

## Making the Connection | With Price Collusion, More Is Not Merrier

Coordinating prices is easier in some industries than in others. Fixed costs in the airline industry are very large, and marginal costs are very small. The marginal cost of flying one more passenger from Chicago to New York is no more than a few dollars: the cost of another snack served and a small amount of additional jet fuel. As a result, airlines often engage in last-minute price cutting to fill the remaining empty seats on a flight. Even a low-price ticket will increase marginal revenue more than marginal cost. As with other oligopolies, if all airlines cut prices, industry profits will decline. Airlines therefore continually adjust their prices while at the same time monitoring their rivals' prices and retaliating against them either for cutting prices or failing to go along with price increases.

In recent years, though, mergers in the airline industry have increased the possibility of implicit collusion by reducing the number of airlines flying between two cities. Often only one or two airlines will fly on a particular route. Southwest Airlines and JetBlue, however, have undertaken an aggressive campaign to enter many airports, thereby increasing competition. For example, before Southwest entered Washington, DC's Dulles International Airport in October 2006, United and Continental Airlines were the only major airlines serving the airport. But would increasing the number of airlines on a route from two to three have much effect on the ability of the airlines to engage in price collusion? Austan Goolsbee and Chad Syverson of the University of Chicago studied the effects of Southwest's entering airline markets over an 11-year period. They found that when Southwest begins flying a particular route, ticket prices drop by an average of 29 percent. These price declines are an indication that airlines may have been practicing implicit price collusion before Southwest's entry into the market. Perhaps surprisingly, Goolsbee and Syverson found that more than half of the price decline actually occurred after it became likely that Southwest would enter a market but *before* Southwest actually began flying planes on the route. One possibility is that airlines already in the market lowered prices to keep frequent flyers from switching to Southwest.

*When JetBlue enters a market, other airlines often cut their ticket prices.*

JetBlue has had a similar effect on airline fares. For example, when JetBlue entered the Chicago-to-New York market in 2006, United and American, which had previously dominated the route, slashed fares by 65 percent, to $108 for a round-trip ticket. In the following years, the airlines had trouble reestablishing the implicit price collusion they had practiced before JetBlue entered: In September 2011, a round trip ticket from Chicago to New York had a price of $106 on United and American, and $101 dollars on JetBlue.

In the airline industry, it apparently doesn't take much competition to greatly reduce opportunities for price collusion.

Based on Austan Goolsbee and Chad Syverson, "How Do Incumbents Respond to the Threat Of Entry? Evidence from the Major Airlines," *Quarterly Journal of Economics*, Vol. 123, No. 4, November 2008, pp. 1611-1633; Julie Johnson, "Rude Welcome Awaits JetBlue," *Chicago Tribune*, November 6, 2006; and route pricing data from orbitz.com.

**Your Turn:** Test your understanding by doing related problems 2.16, 2.17, and 2.18 on page 483 at the end of this chapter.     MyEconLab

## Cartels: The Case of OPEC

In the United States, firms cannot legally meet to agree on what prices to charge and how much to produce. But suppose they could. Would this be enough to guarantee that their collusion would be successful? The example of the Organization of the Petroleum Exporting Countries (OPEC) indicates that the answer to this question is "no." OPEC has 12 members, including Saudi Arabia, Kuwait, and other Arab countries, as well as Iran, Venezuela, Nigeria, and Indonesia. Together, these countries own 75 percent of the world's proven oil reserves, although they pump a smaller share of the total oil sold each year. OPEC operates as a **cartel**, which is a group of firms that collude by agreeing to restrict output to increase prices and profits. The members of OPEC meet periodically and agree on quotas, which are quantities of oil that each country agrees to produce. The quotas are intended to reduce oil production well below the competitive level in order to force up the price of oil and increase the profits of member countries.

**Cartel** A group of firms that collude by agreeing to restrict output to increase prices and profits.

Figure 14.4 shows oil prices from 1972 to mid-2011. The blue line shows the price of a barrel of oil in each year. Prices in general have risen since 1972, which has reduced the amount of goods and services that consumers can purchase with a dollar. The red line corrects for general price increases by measuring oil prices in terms of the dollar's purchasing power in 2011. The figure shows that OPEC had considerable success in raising the price of oil during the mid-1970s and early 1980s, although political unrest in the Middle East and other factors also affected the price of oil during these years. Oil prices, which had been below $3 per barrel in 1972, rose to more than $39 per barrel in 1980, which was more than $100 measured in dollars of 2011 purchasing power. The figure also shows that OPEC has had difficulty sustaining the high prices of 1980 in later years, although oil prices rose sharply between 2004 and mid-2008, in part due to increasing demand from China and India.

### Figure 14.4

#### Oil Prices, 1972 to mid-2011

The blue line shows the price of a barrel of oil in each year. The red line measures the price of a barrel of oil in terms of the purchasing power of the dollar in 2011. By reducing oil production, OPEC was able to raise the world price of oil in the mid-1970s and early 1980s. Sustaining high prices has been difficult over the long run, however, because OPEC members often exceed their output quotas.

Data from Federal Reserve Bank of St. Louis.

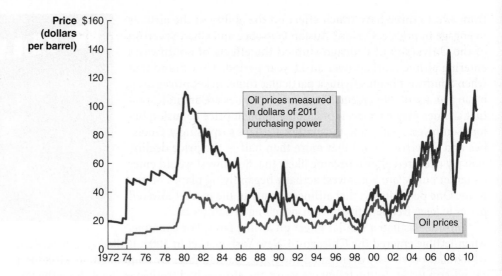

Game theory helps us understand why oil prices have fluctuated. If every member of OPEC cooperates and produces the low output level dictated by its quota, prices will be high, and the cartel will earn large profits. Once the price has been driven up, however, each member has an incentive to stop cooperating and to earn even higher profits by increasing output beyond its quota. But if no country sticks to its quota, total oil output will increase, and profits will decline. In other words, OPEC is caught in a prisoner's dilemma.

If the members of OPEC always exceeded their production quotas, the cartel would have no effect on world oil prices. In fact, the members of OPEC periodically meet and assign new quotas that, at least for a while, enable them to restrict output enough to raise prices. Two factors explain OPEC's occasional success at behaving as a cartel. First, the members of OPEC are participating in a repeated game. As we have seen, this increases the likelihood of a cooperative outcome. Second, Saudi Arabia has far larger oil reserves than any other member of OPEC. Therefore, it has the most to gain from high oil prices and a greater incentive to cooperate. To see this, consider the payoff matrix shown in Figure 14.5. To keep things simple, let's assume that OPEC has only two members: Saudi Arabia and Nigeria. In Figure 14.5, "Low Output" corresponds to cooperating with the OPEC-assigned output quota, and "High Output" corresponds to producing at maximum capacity. The payoff matrix shows the profits received per day by each country.

We can see that Saudi Arabia has a strong incentive to cooperate and maintain its low output quota. By keeping output low, Saudi Arabia can by itself significantly raise the world price of oil, increasing its own profits as well as those of other members of OPEC. Therefore, Saudi Arabia has a dominant strategy of cooperating with the quota and producing a low output. Nigeria, however, cannot by itself have much effect on the price of oil. Therefore, Nigeria has a dominant strategy of not cooperating and instead producing a high output. The equilibrium of this game will occur with Saudi Arabia producing a low output and Nigeria producing a high output. In fact, OPEC often operates in just this way. Saudi Arabia will cooperate with the quota, while the other

### Figure 14.5

#### The OPEC Cartel with Unequal Members

Because Saudi Arabia can produce much more oil than Nigeria, its output decisions have a much larger effect on the price of oil. In the figure, Low Output corresponds to cooperating with the OPEC-assigned output quota, and High Output corresponds to producing at maximum capacity. Saudi Arabia has a dominant strategy to cooperate and produce a low output. Nigeria, however, has a dominant strategy not to cooperate and instead produce a high output. Therefore, the equilibrium of this game will occur with Saudi Arabia producing a low output and Nigeria producing a high output.

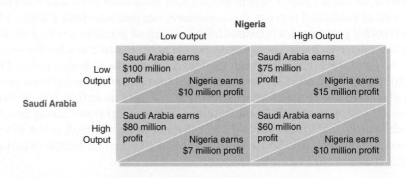

11 members produce at capacity. Because this is a repeated game, however, Saudi Arabia will occasionally produce more oil than its quota to intentionally drive down the price and retaliate against the other members for not cooperating.

# Sequential Games and Business Strategy

**14.3 LEARNING** OBJECTIVE

Use sequential games to analyze business strategies.

We have been analyzing games in which both players move simultaneously. In many business situations, however, one firm will act first, and then other firms will respond. These situations can be analyzed using *sequential games*. We will use sequential games to analyze two business strategies: deterring entry and bargaining between firms. To keep things simple, we consider situations that involve only two firms.

## Deterring Entry

We saw earlier that barriers to entry are a key to firms continuing to earn economic profits. Can firms create barriers to deter new firms from entering an industry? Some recent research in game theory has focused on this question. To take a simple example, suppose once again that Apple and Dell are the only makers of very thin and very light laptop computers. Apple has been successfully selling its MacBook Air laptops since 2008. As we saw in the chapter opener, in 2011, Dell finally decided to enter the market for very thin, very light laptops with the XPS 15z laptop. One factor firms consider in pricing a new product is the effect different prices have on the likelihood that competitors will enter the market. A high price might lead to high profits if other firms do not enter the market, but if a high price attracts entry from other firms, it might actually result in lower profits. A low price, by deterring entry, might lead to higher profits. Assume that managers at Apple have developed a very thin, very light laptop before Dell has and are considering what price to charge. To break even by covering the opportunity cost of the funds involved, laptops must provide a minimum rate of return of 15 percent on Apple's investment. If Apple has the market for this type of laptop to itself and charges a price of $800, it will earn economic profits by receiving a return of 20 percent. If Apple charges a price of $1,000 and has the market to itself, it will receive a higher return of 30 percent.

It seems clear that Apple should charge $1,000 for its laptops, but the managers are worried that Dell might also begin selling this type of laptop. If Apple charges $800 and Dell enters the market, Apple and Dell will divide up the market, and both will earn only 5 percent on their investments, which is below the 15 percent return necessary to break even. If Apple charges $1,000 and Dell enters, although the market will still be divided, the higher price means that each firm will earn 16 percent on its investment.

Apple and Dell are playing a sequential game, because Apple makes the first move—deciding what price to charge—and Dell responds. We can analyze a sequential game by using a *decision tree*, like the one shown in Figure 14.6. The boxes in the figure represent *decision nodes*, which are points where the firms must make the decisions contained in the boxes. At the left, Apple makes the initial decision of what price to charge, and then Dell responds by either entering the market or not. The decisions made are shown beside the arrows. The *terminal nodes,* in green at the right side of the figure, show the resulting rates of return.

Let's start with Apple's initial decision. If Apple charges $1,000, then the arrow directs us to the upper red decision node for Dell. If Dell decides to enter, it will earn a 16 percent rate of return on its investment, which represents an economic profit because it is above the opportunity cost of the funds involved. If Dell doesn't enter, Apple will earn 30 percent, and Dell will not earn anything in this market (indicated by the dash). Apple's managers can conclude that if they charge $1,000 for their laptops, Dell will enter the very thin, very light laptop market, and both firms will earn 16 percent on their investments.

If Apple decides to charge $800, then the arrow directs us to the lower red decision node for Dell. If Dell decides to enter, it will earn only a 5 percent rate of return. If it doesn't enter, Apple will earn 20 percent, and Dell will not earn anything in this market. Apple's managers can conclude that if they charge $800, Dell will not enter, and Apple will earn 20 percent on its investment.

**Figure 14.6**

**The Decision Tree for an Entry Game**

Apple earns its highest return if it charges $1,000 for its very thin, very light laptop and Dell does not enter the market. But at that price, Dell will enter the market, and Apple will earn only 16 percent. If Apple charges $800, Dell will not enter because Dell will suffer an economic loss by receiving only a 5 percent return on its investment. Therefore, Apple's best decision is to deter Dell's entry by charging $800. Apple will earn an economic profit by receiving a 20 percent return on its investment. Note that the dashes(—) indicate the situation where Dell does not enter the market and so makes no investment and receives no return.

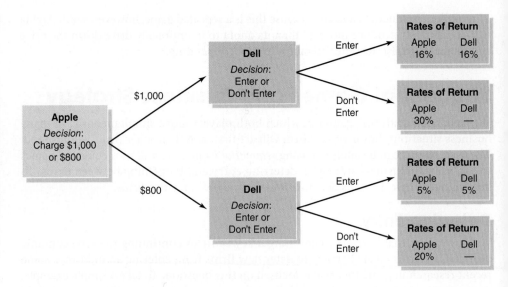

This analysis should lead Apple's managers to conclude that they can charge $1,000 and earn 16 percent—because Dell will enter—or they can charge $800 and earn 20 percent by deterring Dell's entry. Using a decision tree helps Apple's managers to make the correct choice and charge $800 to deter Dell's entry into this market. Note that our discussion is simplified because we are ignoring other characteristics, apart from price, on which the firms also compete. In practice, Apple charged a relatively high price for MacBook Air, which caused Dell to enter the market with the lower-priced XPS 15z. Apple's managers believed that the MacBook Air's features would remain attractive to consumers, despite the XPS 15z having a lower price. Time will tell whether Apple made the correct decision by not charging a low enough price to deter Dell's entry.

# Solved Problem 14.3

## Is Deterring Entry Always a Good Idea?

Like any other business strategy, deterring entry is a good idea only if it has a higher payoff than alternative strategies. Use the following decision tree to decide whether Apple should deter Dell from entering the market for very thin, very light laptops. Assume that each firm must earn a 15 percent return on its investment to break even.

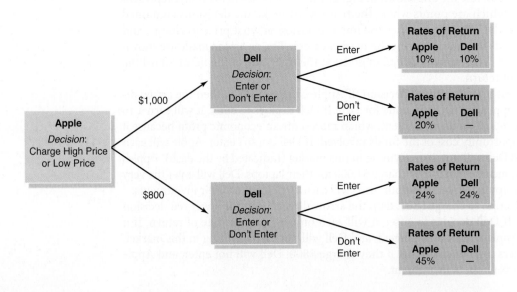

# Solving the Problem

**Step 1:** **Review the chapter material.** This problem is about sequential games, so you may want to review the section "Deterring Entry," which begins on page 471.

**Step 2:** **Determine how Dell will respond to Apple's decision.** If Apple charges $1,000 for its very thin, very light laptops, Dell will not enter the market because the return on its investment represents an economic loss. If Apple charges $800, Dell will enter because it will earn a return that represents an economic profit.

**Step 3:** **Given how Dell will react, determine which strategy maximizes profits for Apple.** If Apple charges $1,000, it will have deterred Dell's entry, and the rate of return on its investment will be 20 percent. If Apple charges $800, Dell will enter, but because these low prices will substantially increase the market for these laptops, Apple will actually earn a higher return of 24 percent, splitting the market with Dell at a lower price than it would have earned having the whole market to itself at a high price.

**Step 4:** **State your conclusion.** Like any other business strategy, deterrence is worth pursuing only if the payoff is higher than for other strategies. In this case, expanding the market for very thin, very light laptops by charging a lower price has a higher payoff for Apple, even given that Dell will enter the market.

**Your Turn:** For more practice, do related problem 3.3 on page 484 at the end of this chapter.     MyEconLab

# Bargaining

The success of many firms depends on how well they bargain with other firms. For example, firms often must bargain with their suppliers over the prices they pay for inputs. Suppose that TruImage is a small firm that has developed software that improves how pictures from a digital camera are displayed on computer screens. TruImage currently sells its software only on its Web site and earns profits of $2 million per year. Dell informs TruImage that it is considering installing the software on every new computer Dell sells. Dell expects to sell more computers at a higher price if it can install TruImage's software on its computers. The two firms begin bargaining over what price Dell will pay TruImage for its software.

The decision tree in Figure 14.7 illustrates this bargaining game. At the left, Dell makes the initial decision about what price to offer TruImage for its software, and then TruImage responds by either accepting or rejecting the contract offer. First, suppose that Dell offers TruImage a contract price of $30 per copy for its software. If TruImage

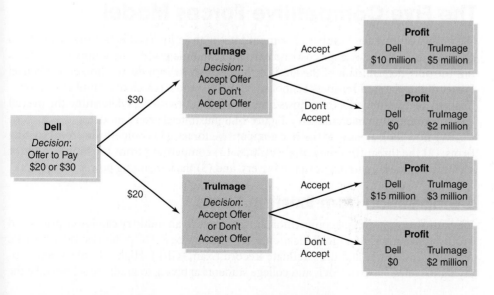

**Figure 14.7**

**The Decision Tree for a Bargaining Game**

Dell earns the highest profit if it offers a contract price of $20 per copy and TruImage accepts the contract. TruImage earns the highest profit if Dell offers it a contract of $30 per copy and it accepts the contract. TruImage may attempt to bargain by threatening to reject a $20-per-copy contract. But Dell knows this threat is not credible because once Dell has offered a $20-per-copy contract, TruImage's profits are higher if it accepts the contract than if it rejects it.

accepts this contract, its profits will be $5 million per year, and Dell will earn $10 million in additional profits. If TruImage rejects the contract, its profits will be the $2 million per year it earns selling its software on its Web site, and Dell will earn zero additional profits.

Now, suppose Dell offers TruImage a contract price of $20 per copy. If TruImage accepts this contract, its profits will be $3 million per year, and Dell will earn $15 million in additional profits. If TruImage rejects this contract, its profits will be the $2 million it earns selling its software on its Web site, and Dell will earn zero additional profits. Clearly, for Dell, a contract price of $20 per copy is more profitable, while for TruImage, a contract price of $30 per copy is more profitable.

Suppose TruImage attempts to obtain a favorable outcome from the bargaining by telling Dell that it will reject a $20-per-copy contract price. If Dell believes this threat, then it will offer TruImage a $30-per-copy contract price because Dell is better off with the $10 million profit that will result from TruImage's accepting the contract than with the zero profits Dell will earn if TruImage rejects the $20-per-copy contract price. This result is a Nash equilibrium because neither firm can increase its profits by changing its choice—*provided that Dell believes TruImage's threat.* But is TruImage's threat credible? Once Dell has offered TruImage the $20 contract price, TruImage's choices are to accept the contract and earn $3 million or reject the contract and earn only $2 million. Because rejecting the contract reduces TruImage's profits, TruImage's threat to reject the contract is not credible, and Dell should ignore it.

As a result, we would expect Dell to use the strategy of offering TruImage a $20-per-copy contract price and TruImage to use the strategy of accepting the contract. Dell will earn additional profits of $15 million per year, and TruImage will earn profits of $3 million per year. This outcome is called a *subgame-perfect equilibrium.* A subgame-perfect equilibrium is a Nash equilibrium in which no player can make himself or herself better off by changing his decision at any decision node. In our simple bargaining game, each player has only one decision to make. As we have seen, Dell's profits are highest if it offers the $20-per-copy contract price, and TruImage's profits are highest if it accepts the contract. Typically, in sequential games of this type, there is only one subgame-perfect equilibrium.

Managers use decision trees like those in Figures 14.6 and 14.7 in business planning because they provide a systematic way of thinking through the implications of a strategy and of predicting the reactions of rivals. We can see the benefits of decision trees in the simple examples considered here. In the first example, Apple's managers can conclude that charging a low price is more profitable than charging a high price. In the second example, Dell's managers can conclude that TruImage's threat to reject a $20-per-copy contract is not credible.

Use the five competitive forces model to analyze competition in an industry.

# The Five Competitive Forces Model

We have seen that the number of competitors in an industry affects a firm's ability to charge a price above average cost and earn an economic profit. The number of firms is not the only determinant of the level of competition in an industry, however. Michael Porter of the Harvard Business School has drawn on the research of a number of economists to develop a model that shows how five competitive forces determine the overall level of competition in an industry. Figure 14.8 illustrates Porter's model.

We now look at each of the five competitive forces: (1) competition from existing firms, (2) the threat from potential entrants, (3) competition from substitute goods or services, (4) the bargaining power of buyers, and (5) the bargaining power of suppliers.

## Competition from Existing Firms

We have already seen that competition among firms in an industry can lower prices and profits. As another example, Educational Testing Service (ETS) produces the Scholastic Aptitude Test (SAT) and the Graduate Record Exam (GRE). High school students applying to college take the SAT, and college students applying to graduate school take the

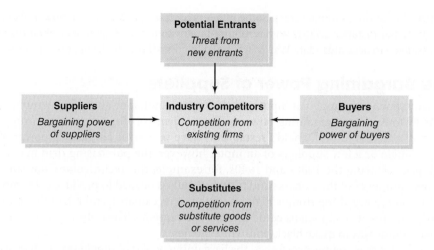

**Figure 14.8**

**The Five Competitive Forces Model**

Michael Porter's model identifies five forces that determine the level of competition in an industry: (1) competition from existing firms, (2) the threat from new entrants, (3) competition from substitute goods or services, (4) the bargaining power of buyers, and (5) the bargaining power of suppliers. Source: Reprinted with the permission of The Free Press, a Division of Simon & Schuster Adult Publishing Group, from Michael E. Porter, *Competitive Strategy: Techniques for Analyzing Industries and Competitors.* Copyright © 1980, 1998 by The Free Press. All rights reserved.

GRE. In 2011, ETS charged a price of $49 to take the SAT, and it charged $160 to take the GRE. Part of the explanation for this large price difference is that ETS faces competition in the market for tests given to high school students applying to college, where the SAT competes with the ACT Assessment, produced by ACT, Inc. But there is no competition for the GRE test. As we saw earlier in this chapter, when there are only a few firms in a market, it is easier for them to implicitly collude and to charge a price close to the monopoly price. In this case, however, competition from a single firm was enough to cause ETS to keep the price of the SAT near the competitive level.

Competition in the form of advertising, better customer service, or longer warranties can also reduce profits by raising costs. For example, online booksellers Amazon.com, BarnesandNoble.com, and Buy.com have competed by offering low-cost—or free—shipping, by increasing their customer service staffs, and by building more warehouses to provide faster deliveries. These activities have raised the booksellers' costs and reduced their profits.

## The Threat from Potential Entrants

Firms face competition from companies that currently are not in the market but might enter. We have already seen how actions taken to deter entry can reduce profits. In our hypothetical example in the previous section, Apple charged a lower price and earned less profit to deter Dell's entry. Business managers often take actions aimed at deterring entry. Some of these actions include advertising to create product loyalty, introducing new products—such as slightly different cereals or toothpastes—to fill market niches, and setting lower prices to keep profits at a level that makes entry less attractive.

## Competition from Substitute Goods or Services

Firms are always vulnerable to competitors introducing a new product that fills a consumer need better than their current product does. Consider the encyclopedia business. For decades, many parents bought expensive and bulky encyclopedias for their children attending high school or college. By the 1990s, computer software companies were offering electronic encyclopedias that sold for a small fraction of the price of printed encyclopedias. Encyclopedia Britannica and the other encyclopedia publishers responded by cutting prices and launching advertising campaigns aimed at showing the superiority of printed encyclopedias. Still, profits continued to decline, and by the end of the 1990s, most printed encyclopedias had disappeared.

## The Bargaining Power of Buyers

If buyers have enough bargaining power, they can insist on lower prices, higher-quality products, or additional services. Automobile companies, for example, have significant bargaining power in the tire market, which tends to lower tire prices and limit the profitability of tire manufacturers. Some retailers have significant buying power over their suppliers. For instance, Wal-Mart has required many of its suppliers to alter their distribution systems to accommodate Wal-Mart's need to control the stocks of goods in its stores.

## The Bargaining Power of Suppliers

If many firms can supply an input and the input is not specialized, the suppliers are unlikely to have the bargaining power to limit a firm's profits. For instance, suppliers of paper napkins to McDonald's restaurants have very little bargaining power. With only a single or a few suppliers of an input, however, the purchasing firm may face a high price. During the 1930s and 1940s, for example, the Technicolor Company was the only producer of the cameras and film that studios needed to produce color movies. Technicolor charged the studios high prices to use its cameras, and it had the power to insist that only its technicians could operate the cameras. The only alternative for the movie studios was to make black-and-white movies.

As with other competitive forces, the bargaining power of suppliers can change over time. For instance, when IBM chose Microsoft to supply the operating system for its personal computers, Microsoft was a small company with very limited bargaining power. As Microsoft's Windows operating system became standard in more than 90 percent of personal computers, this large market share increased Microsoft's bargaining power.

| Making the Connection | Can We Predict Which Firms Will Continue to Be Successful? |
|---|---|

For years, economists and business strategists believed that market structure was the most important factor in explaining the ability of some firms to continue earning economic profits. For example, most economists argued that during the first few decades after World War II, steel companies in the United States earned economic profits because barriers to entry were high, there were few firms in the industry, and competition among firms was low. In contrast, restaurants were seen as less profitable because barriers to entry were low and the industry was intensely competitive. One problem with this approach to analyzing the profitability of firms is that it does not explain how firms in the same industry can have very different levels of profit.

Today, economists and business strategists put greater emphasis on the characteristics of individual firms and the strategies their managers use to continue to earn economic profits. This approach helps explain why Nucor continues to be a profitable steel company while Bethlehem Steel, at one time the second-largest steel producer in the United States, was forced into bankruptcy. It also explains why Dell, which began as a small company Michael Dell ran from his dorm room at the University of Texas, went on to become extremely profitable and an industry leader, while other computer companies have disappeared.

*Although its business strategy had once been widely admired, Circuit City declared bankruptcy in 2009.*

Is it possible to draw general conclusions about which business strategies are likely to be successful in the future? A number of business analysts have tried to identify strategies that have made firms successful and have recommended those strategies to other firms. Although books with these recommendations are often bestsellers, they have a mixed record in identifying winning strategies. For instance, in 1982, Thomas J. Peters and Robert H. Waterman, Jr., published *In Search of Excellence: Lessons from America's Best-Run Companies.* The book was favorably reviewed by business magazines and sold more than 3 million copies. Peters and Waterman identified 43 companies that were the best at using eight key strategies to "stay on top of the heap." But just two years after the book was published, an article in *BusinessWeek* pointed out that 14 of the 43 companies were experiencing significant financial difficulties. The article noted: "It comes as a shock that so many companies have fallen from grace so quickly—and it also raises some questions. Were these companies so excellent in the first place?"

In 2002, Jim Collins published *Good to Great: Why Some Companies Make the Leap . . . and Others Don't*, with the goal of determining how companies can "achieve enduring greatness." Although this book also sold 3 million copies, not all of the 11 "great companies" it identified were able to remain successful. For instance, Circuit City was forced to file for bankruptcy in 2009, and Fannie Mae avoided bankruptcy only after the federal government largely took it over in 2008.

These two books, and many others like them, provide useful analyses of the business strategies of successful firms. That many of the firms highlighted in these books are unable to sustain their success, though, should not be surprising. Many successful strategies can be copied—and, often, improved on—by competitors. Even in oligopolies, competition can quickly erode profits and even turn a successful firm into an unsuccessful one. It remains difficult to predict which currently successful firms will maintain their success.

Based on Thomas J. Peters and Robert H. Waterman, Jr., *In Search of Excellence: Lessons from America's Best-Run Companies*, (New York: HarperCollins Publishers, 1982); Jim Collins, *Good to Great: Why Some Companies Make the Leap . . . and Others Don't*, (New York: HarperCollins Publishers, 2001); "Who's Excellent Now?" *BusinessWeek*, November 5, 1984; and Steven D. Leavitt, "From Good to Great . . . to Below Average," *New York Times*, July 28, 2008.

**Your Turn:** Test your understanding by doing related problem 4.5 on page 485 at the end of this chapter.          MyEconLab

---

**Continued from page 459**

## Economics in Your Life

### Why Can't You Find a Cheap PlayStation 3?

At the beginning of this chapter, we asked you to consider why the price of the PlayStation 3 320GB game system is almost the same at every large retailer, from Amazon to Wal-Mart. Why don't these retailers seem to compete on price for this type of product? In this chapter, we have seen that if big retailers were engaged in a one-time game of pricing PlayStations, they would be in a prisoner's dilemma and would probably all charge a low price. However, we have also seen that pricing PlayStations is actually a repeated game because the retailers will be selling the game system in competition over a long period of time. In this situation, it is more likely that the retailers will arrive at a cooperative equilibrium, in which they will all charge a high price; this is good news for the profits of the retailers but bad news for consumers! This is one of many insights that game theory provides into the business strategies of oligopolists.

---

## Conclusion

Firms are locked in a never-ending struggle to earn economic profits. As noted in the two preceding chapters, competition erodes economic profits. Even in the oligopolies discussed in this chapter, firms have difficulty earning economic profits in the long run. We have seen that firms attempt to avoid the effects of competition in various ways. For example, they can stake out a secure niche in the market, they can engage in implicit collusion with competing firms, or they can attempt to have the government impose barriers to entry. *An Inside Look* on the next page discusses how Intel produced a new processing chip to remain profitable in the market for laptop computers.

# Can Intel's "Ultrabook" Compete with Apple's MacBook Air?

## ASSOCIATED PRESS

## Intel Taps into New Computing at Taiwan Show

Intel Corp. is touting a hybrid laptop 0.8 inches (20 mm) thick with sleek tablet computing features and ultra-sharp visual images that it hopes will create a market bridging traditional PCs and new devices.

The laptop also represents what the U.S. technology giant promises its latest generation of processors will be able to deliver by 2012, when they power new computers produced by companies like Taiwan's AsusTek Computer Inc.

(a) "Computing is taking many forms," Intel executive vice president Sean Maloney said Tuesday at the opening of Taipei's Computex, the world's second-largest computing show.

He said that by the end of 2012, Intel aims to shift 40 percent of consumer laptops to its "Ultrabook" model, a new category of thin and light mobile computers.

Like many other tech companies, Intel is under immense pressure from Apple Inc., whose iPhones and iPads have swept through global markets with the force of a hurricane and show no signs of slowing.

(b) Maloney described the Ultrabook as a laptop-tablet hybrid, featuring touch screens and instant log on, all with a price of less than $1,000.

The projected thickness of the new Intel-powered device would make it the sleekest laptop in the marketplace after Apple's MacBook Air 15 model, which ranges from .11 to .68 inches.

The devices will be based on Intel's "Ivy Bridge," a new generation of chips made with 22 nanometer manufacturing technology and the 3-D transistor the company unveiled early in May. It is slated to be on the market by 2012, Intel said.

The new transistor, with increased density, will make more powerful computing devices, it said.

(c) Also by 2012, a new Intel chip designed for tablets and smartphones, named "Medfield," will be launched. It will give the mobile devices longer use-time, advanced imaging and more power efficiency, the company said.

Intel general manager for the Asia-Pacific region Navin Shenoy acknowledged the market is experiencing significant changes with "the explosion of smartphones and tablets."

"The industry is in constant change," he said. "We're more and more like the fashion industry. Nothing sticks forever."

"We win when we go after and create new markets," he said.

AsusTek is among the Taiwanese computer makers which have pledged to collaborate with Intel.

With the advent of tablets, "the whole industry is reshuffling, including the microprocessors and including operating systems," said AsusTek Chairman Jonney Shih.

"The boundaries between notebooks, tablets and smartphones are blurring," he told a news conference Monday. Laptops "have to evolve quickly to respond" and become "ultra-thin, ultra-light and ultra-responsive."

Also at Computex, Google Inc. pushed its Chromebook notebook, which is based on its web-browsing-oriented Chrome operating system—an up-and-coming rival in a field long dominated by Microsoft Corp.

Google is partnering with Intel and has engaged South Korea's Samsung Electronics Co. and Taiwan's Acer Inc. to produce the Chromebooks, set to go on sale in June.

Google's Senior Vice President Sundar Pichai said the company has set up a center in Taipei to try to bring more manufacturing partners on-board, but declined to give specifics on his expectations for Chromebook's market share.

"Today my only goal is to make sure we deliver Chromebooks and make customers happy," he said. "That's the only criteria. Focus on quality of experience for consumers rather than quantity."

Source: "Intel taps into new computing at Taiwan show," by Annie Huang from the Associated Press, May 31, 2011. Copyright © 2011 by the Associated Press. Reproduced with permission of the YGS Group.

# Key Points in the Article

U.S.-based Intel Corp. introduced new products at Taiwan's Computex computer show: (1) the "Ultrabook," a laptop–tablet hybrid that is 0.8 inches thick and features a touchscreen, excellent image quality, and an updated processor, and (2) a new processing chip for use in tablets and smartphones. Intel noted that to remain successful, it must quickly adapt to the growth and constant changes in the industry. One of Intel's main competitors is Apple, whose MacBook Air, iPhone, and iPad have been highly successful and profitable products. With its new offerings, scheduled to be available in 2012, Intel is positioning itself to compete with Apple with what it believes are better and more advanced products.

## Analyzing the News

**(a)** When a market is an oligopoly, each firm must take into account the actions of its competitors. With the Ultrabook, Intel expects to compete with firms such as Apple. This means Intel has to account for the likelihood that its rivals will choose to develop models with features similar to those of the Ultrabook. Intel plans to convert 40 percent of consumer laptops to this new model.

**(b)** Intel announced that its Ultrabook will be priced under $1,000. In an oligopoly market, a firm's profits depend not only on the price it chooses but on the price its rivals choose. The figures below illustrate the competition between Intel and Apple, using two possible scenarios. In both figures, we assume that Intel has decided to sell its Ultrabook for $999, and Apple must then decide whether it should also develop a new, comparable computer for the same price. We assume that each company needs a 15 percent return on its investment in these computers to break even. In Figure 1, if Apple decides to develop a new model, both companies will earn a 20 percent return. If Apple decides not to compete with the new Intel model, Intel will earn 30 percent and Apple will earn nothing in this market. Because 20 percent is higher than the minimum 15 percent required return, we can conclude that Apple will enter the market and both firms will earn a 20 percent return.

But suppose that Intel determines that its position relative to Apple is that shown in Figure 2. If Apple enters this market, both Apple and Intel will earn 10 percent returns. If Apple does not enter the market, Intel will earn a 30 percent return. Because 10 percent is below the required return of 15 percent, Apple will not enter the market. In this case, it turns out that whether Figure 1 or Figure 2 more accurately describes the situation in this market is not important for Intel's initial decision to sell the Ultrabook. Whether Apple enters the market or not, Intel will still earn a return greater than 15 percent. Therefore, Intel should sell the Ultrabook.

**(c)** Oligopoly firms often try to introduce new products to fill consumer needs better than existing products can, which is what Intel is attempting to do with the Ultrabook. Intel realizes that the computer market changes quickly, and the company must adapt to these rapid changes by introducing new and better products to remain competitive, relevant, and profitable.

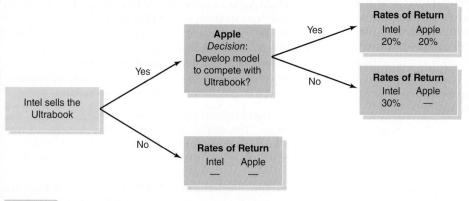

## Figure 1

Apple should develop a model to compete with the Ultrabook

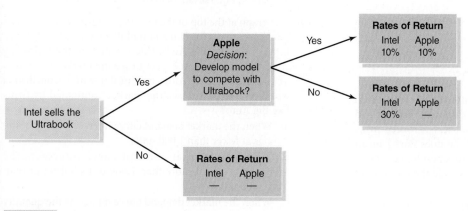

## Figure 2

Apple should not develop a model to compete with the Ultrabook

## Thinking Critically

1. Intel is hoping that its strategy to develop the Ultrabook will increase its share of the laptop computer market. What risks does the company face that could defeat its strategy?
2. Apply the five competitive forces model to Intel. Cite one example of each of the competitive forces that Intel faces.

# Chapter Summary and Problems

## Key Terms

Barrier to entry, p. 461

Business strategy, p. 463

Cartel, p. 469

Collusion, p. 464

Cooperative equilibrium, p. 464

Dominant strategy, p. 464

Economies of scale, p. 461

Game theory, p. 463

Nash equilibrium, p. 464

Noncooperative equilibrium, p. 464

Oligopoly, p. 460

Patent, p. 462

Payoff matrix, p. 463

Price leadership, p. 468

Prisoner's dilemma, p. 464

---

**14.1** **Oligopoly and Barriers to Entry, pages 460–463**

LEARNING OBJECTIVE: Show how barriers to entry explain the existence of oligopolies.

## Summary

An **oligopoly** is a market structure in which a small number of interdependent firms compete. **Barriers to entry** keep new firms from entering an industry. The three most important barriers to entry are economies of scale, ownership of a key input, and government barriers. Economies of scale are the most important barrier to entry. **Economies of scale** exist when a firm's long-run average costs fall as it increases output. Government barriers include patents, licensing, and barriers to international trade. A **patent** is the exclusive right to a product for a period of 20 years from the date the patent is filed with the government.

 MyEconLab    Visit www.myeconlab.com to complete these exercises online and get instant feedback.

## Review Questions

1.1  What is an oligopoly? Give three examples of oligopolistic industries in the United States.

1.2  What do barriers to entry have to do with the extent of competition in an industry? What are the most important barriers to entry?

1.3  Give an example of a government-imposed barrier to entry. Why would a government be willing to erect barriers to entering an industry?

1.4  What is a patent? If a patent serves as a barrier to entry, why do governments issue patents?

## Problems and Applications

1.5  Michael Porter has argued, "The intensity of competition in an industry is neither a matter of coincidence nor bad luck. Rather, competition in an industry is rooted in its underlying economic structure." What does Porter mean by "economic structure"? What factors besides economic structure might be expected to determine the intensity of competition in an industry?

Based on Michael Porter, Competitive *Strategy: Techniques for Analyzing Industries and Competitors*, (New York: The Free Press), 1980, p. 3.

1.6  In 2009, some analysts of the smartphone industry argued that Apple would be likely to offer a variety of iPhones, each with different features. One observer objected to this argument, though, arguing, "Selling models differentiated by hardware seems unlikely. Different iPhones with very different physical specs could have far-reaching implications for Apple's production methods, volumes and costs." How would Apple's costs be affected by offering different iPhones with "very different specs"? How would this change in costs be likely to affect the prices Apple charged for the iPhone? How would this change in costs be likely to affect the ability of other firms to compete against the iPhone?

Based on James Sherwood, "Apple to Look to Software to Differentiate Multiple iPhone Models," www.reghardware.co.uk, May 18, 2009.

1.7  Thomas McCraw, a professor at Harvard Business School, wrote, "Throughout American history, entrepreneurs have tried, sometimes desperately, to create big businesses out of naturally small-scale operations. It has not worked." What advantage would entrepreneurs expect to gain from creating "big businesses"? Why would entrepreneurs fail to create big businesses with "naturally small-scale operations"? Illustrate your answer with a graph showing long-run average costs.

Based on Thomas K. McCraw, ed., *Creating Modern Capitalism*, (Cambridge, MA: Harvard University Press), 1997, p. 323.

1.8  The graph at the top of the next page illustrates the average total cost curves for two automobile manufacturing firms: Little Auto and Big Auto. Under which of the following conditions would you expect to see the market composed of firms like Little Auto, and under which conditions would you expect to see the market dominated by firms like Big Auto?

a. When the market demand curve intersects the quantity axis at fewer than 1,000 units

b. When the market demand curve intersects the quantity axis at more than 1,000 units but fewer than 10,000 units

c. When the market demand curve intersects the quantity axis at more than 10,000 units

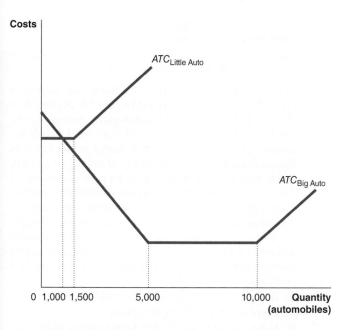

**1.9** The following graph contains two long-run average cost curves. Briefly explain which cost curve would most likely be associated with an oligopoly and which would most likely be associated with a perfectly competitive industry.

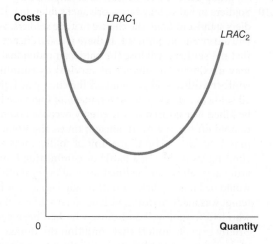

**1.10** Alfred Chandler, who was a professor at Harvard Business School, observed, "Imagine the diseconomies of scale—the great increase in unit costs—that would result from placing close to one-fourth of the world's production of shoes, or textiles, or lumber into three factories or mills!" The shoe, textiles, and lumber industries are very competitive, with many firms producing each of these products. Briefly explain how Chandler's observation helps explain why these industries are competitive.

From Alfred D. Chandler, Jr., "The Emergence of Managerial Capitalism," in Alfred D. Chandler, Jr., and Richard S. Tedlow, *The Coming of Managerial Capitalism*, (New York: Irwin), 1985, p. 406.

**1.11** A historical account of the development of the cotton textile industry in England argued:

> The cotton textile industry was shaped by ruthless competition. Rapid growth in demand, low barriers to entry, frequent technological innovations, and a high rate of firm bankruptcy all combined to form an environment in which . . . oligopolistic competition became almost impossible.

Explain how each of the factors described here would contribute to making oligopolistic competition in the cotton textile industry very difficult.

Based on Thomas K. McCraw, ed., *Creating Modern Capitalism*, (Cambridge, MA: Harvard University Press), 1997, p. 61-62.

---

**14.2** **Using Game Theory to Analyze Oligopoly, pages 463–471**

LEARNING OBJECTIVE: Use game theory to analyze the strategies of oligopolistic firms.

## Summary

Because an oligopoly has only a few firms, interactions among those firms are particularly important. **Game theory** is the study of how people make decisions in situations in which attaining their goals depends on their interactions with others; in economics, it is the study of the decisions of firms in industries where the profits of each firm depend on its interactions with other firms. A **business strategy** refers to actions taken by a firm to achieve a goal, such as maximizing profits. Oligopoly games can be illustrated with a **payoff matrix**, which is a table that shows the payoffs that each firm earns from every combination of strategies

by the firms. One possible outcome in oligopoly is **collusion**, which is an agreement among firms to charge the same price or otherwise not to compete. A **cartel** is a group of firms that collude by agreeing to restrict output to increase prices and profits. In a **cooperative equilibrium**, firms cooperate to increase their mutual payoff. In a **noncooperative equilibrium**, firms do not cooperate but pursue their own self-interest. A **dominant strategy** is a strategy that is the best for a firm, no matter what strategies other firms use. A **Nash equilibrium** is a situation in which each firm chooses the best strategy, given the strategies chosen by other firms. A situation in which pursuing dominant strategies results in noncooperation that leaves everyone worse off is called a **prisoner's dilemma**. Because many business situations are repeated games, firms may end up implicitly colluding to keep prices high. With **price leadership**, one firm takes the lead in announcing a price change, which is then matched by the other firms in the industry.

MyEconLab    Visit www.myeconlab.com to complete these exercises online and get instant feedback.

## Review Questions

**2.1** Give brief definitions of the following concepts:
 a. Game theory
 b. Cooperative equilibrium
 c. Noncooperative equilibrium
 d. Dominant strategy
 e. Nash equilibrium

**2.2** Why do economists refer to the methodology for analyzing oligopolies as game theory?

**2.3** Why do economists refer to the pricing strategies of oligopoly firms as a prisoner's dilemma game?

**2.4** What is the difference between explicit collusion and implicit collusion? Give an example of each.

**2.5** How is the result of the prisoner's dilemma changed in a repeated game?

## Problems and Applications

**2.6** Bob and Tom are two criminals who have been arrested for burglary. The police put Tom and Bob in separate cells. They offer to let Bob go free if he confesses to the crime and testifies against Tom. Bob also is told that he will serve a 15-year sentence if he remains silent while Tom confesses. If Bob confesses and Tom also confesses, they will each serve a 10-year sentence. Separately, the police make the same offer to Tom. Assume that Bob and Tom know that if they both remain silent, the police have only enough evidence to convict them of a lesser crime, and they will both serve 3-year sentences.
 a. Use the information provided to write a payoff matrix for Bob and Tom.
 b. Does Bob have a dominant strategy? If so, what is it?
 c. Does Tom have a dominant strategy? If so, what is it?
 d. What sentences do Bob and Tom serve? How might they have avoided this outcome?

**2.7** Explain how collusion makes firms better off. Given the incentives to collude, briefly explain why every industry doesn't become a cartel.

**2.8** Under "early decision" college admission plans, students apply to a college in the fall and, if they are accepted, they must enroll in that college. According to an article in *BusinessWeek*, Yale president Richard Levin argues that early decision plans put too much pressure on students to decide early in their senior years which college to attend. Levin has proposed abolishing early decision plans. But the author of the article is doubtful that this will succeed because "as long as some big-name schools offer early admissions, the others feel they must, too, or lose out on the best talent." Do you agree with this conclusion? How can game theory help analyze this situation?

Based on William C. Symonds, "Commentary: Second Thoughts on Early Decision," *BusinessWeek*, March 11, 2002.

**2.9** Baseball players who hit the most home runs *relative to other players* usually receive the highest pay. Beginning in the mid-1990s, the typical baseball player became significantly stronger and more muscular. As one baseball announcer put it, "The players of 20 years ago look like stick figures compared with the players of today." As a result, the average number of home runs hit each year increased dramatically. Some of the increased strength that baseball players gained came from more weight training and better conditioning and diet. As some players admitted, though, some of the increased strength came from taking steroids and other illegal drugs. Taking steroids can significantly increase the risk of developing cancer and other medical problems.
 a. In these circumstances, are baseball players in a prisoner's dilemma? Carefully explain.
 b. Major League Baseball has begun testing players for steroids and fining and suspending players who are caught using steriods (or other illegal muscle-building drugs). Has this testing made baseball players as a group better off or worse off? Briefly explain.

**2.10** Soldiers in battle may face a prisoner's dilemma. If all soldiers stand and fight, the chance that the soldiers, as a unit, will survive is maximized. If there is a significant chance that the soldiers will lose the battle, an individual soldier may maximize his chance of survival by running away while the other soldiers hold off the enemy by fighting. If all soldiers run away, however, many of them are likely to be killed or captured by the enemy because no one is left to hold off the enemy. In ancient times, the Roman army practiced "decimation." If a unit of soldiers was guilty of running away during a battle or committing other cowardly acts, all would be lined up, and every tenth soldier would be killed by being run through with a sword. No attempt was made to distinguish between soldiers in the unit who had fought well and those who had been cowardly. Briefly explain under what condition the Roman system of decimation was likely to have solved the prisoner's dilemma of soldiers running away in battle.

**2.11** [**Related to** Solved Problem 14.2 **on page 465**] Would a ban on advertising beer on television be likely to increase or decrease the profits of beer companies? Briefly explain.

**2.12** [**Related to** Solved Problem 14.2 **on page 465**] Beginning in 2003, the U.S. government spent billions of dollars rebuilding the infrastructure damaged by the war in Iraq. Much of the work was carried out by construction and engineering firms that had to bid for the business. Suppose, hypothetically, that only two companies—Bechtel and Halliburton—enter the bidding and that each firm is deciding whether to bid either $4 billion or $5 billion. (Remember that in this type of bidding, the winning bid is the *low* bid because the bid represents the amount the government will have to pay to have the work done.) Each firm will have costs of $2.5 billion to do the work. If they both make the same bid, they will both be hired and will split the work and the profits. If one makes a low bid and one makes a high bid, only the low bidder will be hired, and it will receive all the profits. The result is the following payoff matrix.

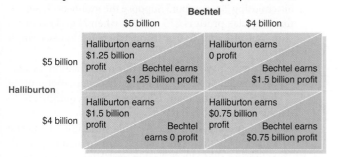

**Bechtel**

| | $5 billion | $4 billion |
|---|---|---|
| Halliburton $5 billion | Halliburton earns $1.25 billion profit / Bechtel earns $1.25 billion profit | Halliburton earns 0 profit / Bechtel earns $1.5 billion profit |
| Halliburton $4 billion | Halliburton earns $1.5 billion profit / Bechtel earns 0 profit | Halliburton earns $0.75 billion profit / Bechtel earns $0.75 billion profit |

a. Is there a Nash equilibrium in this game? Briefly explain.

b. How might the situation be changed if the two companies expect to be bidding on many similar projects in future years?

**2.13** [Related to Solved Problem 14.2 **on page 465**] Radio frequency identification (RFID) tracking tags may ultimately replace bar codes. With this system, a radio signal automatically records the arrival of a product in a warehouse, its shipment to a store, and its purchase by the consumer. Suppose that Wal-Mart and Target are independently deciding whether to stick with bar codes or switch to RFID tags to monitor the flow of products. Because many suppliers sell to both Wal-Mart and Target, it is much less costly for suppliers to use one system or the other rather than to use both. The following payoff matrix shows the profits per year for each company resulting from the interaction of their strategies.

**Target**

| | Bar codes | RFID tags |
|---|---|---|
| Wal-Mart Bar codes | Wal-Mart earns $4 billion / Target earns $3 billion | Wal-Mart earns $1 billion / Target earns $2 billion |
| Wal-Mart RFID tags | Wal-Mart earns $3 billion / Target earns $1 billion | Wal-Mart earns $2 billion / Target earns $4 billion |

a. Briefly explain whether Wal-Mart has a dominant strategy.

b. Briefly explain whether Target has a dominant strategy.

c. Briefly explain whether there is a Nash equilibrium in this game.

**2.14** [Related to the Don't Let This Happen to You **on page 465**] A student argues, "The prisoner's dilemma game is unrealistic. Each player's strategy is based on the assumption that the other player won't cooperate. But if each player assumes that the other player *will* cooperate, the 'dilemma' disappears." Briefly explain whether you agree with this argument.

**2.15** [Related to the Making the Connection **on page 466**] We made the argument that a bidder on an eBay auction has a dominant strategy of bidding only once, with that bid being the maximum the bidder would be willing to pay.

a. Is it possible that a bidder might receive useful information during the auction, particularly from the dollar amounts other bidders are bidding? If so, how does that change a bidder's optimal strategy?

b. Many people recommend the practice of "sniping," or placing your bid at the last second before the auction

ends. Is there a connection between sniping and your answer to part a?

**2.16** [Related to the Making the Connection **on page 468**] The following appeared in an article in the *Wall Street Journal*: "Last week, true to discount roots dating to 1971, Southwest [Airlines] launched a summer fare sale on domestic flights, with one-way prices as low as $49. As in the past, major competitors were forced to follow suit." Why would other airlines be "forced" to follow Southwest's fare decrease? Does your answer change if you learn that this fare decrease took place during an economic recession, when incomes and the demand for airline travel were falling? Briefly explain.

Based on Mike Esterl, "Southwest Airlines CEO Flies Uncharted Skies," *Wall Street Journal*, March 25, 2009.

**2.17** [Related to the Making the Connection **on page 468**] Airlines often find themselves in price wars. Consider the following game: Delta and United are the only two airlines flying the route from Houston to Omaha. Each firm has two strategies: Charge a high price or charge a low price.

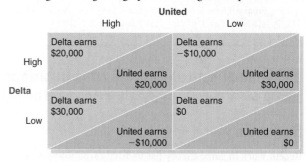

**United**

| | High | Low |
|---|---|---|
| Delta High | Delta earns $20,000 / United earns $20,000 | Delta earns −$10,000 / United earns $30,000 |
| Delta Low | Delta earns $30,000 / United earns −$10,000 | Delta earns $0 / United earns $0 |

a. What (if any) is the dominant strategy for each firm?

b. Is this game a prisoner's dilemma?

c. How could repeated playing of the game change the strategy each firm uses?

**2.18** [Related to the Making the Connection **on page 468**] Until the late 1990s, airlines would post proposed changes in ticket prices on computer reservation systems several days before the new ticket prices went into effect. Then the federal government took action to end this practice. Now airlines can post prices on their reservation systems only for tickets that are immediately available for sale. Why would the federal government object to the old system of posting prices before they went into effect?

Based on Scott McCartney, "Airfare Wars Show Why Deals Arrive and Depart," *Wall Street Journal*, March 19, 2002.

**2.19** Finding dominant strategies is often a very effective way of analyzing a game. Consider the following game: Microsoft and Apple are the two firms in the market for operating systems. Each firm has two strategies: Charge a high price or charge a low price.

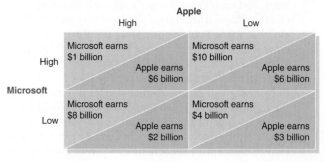

**Apple**

| | High | Low |
|---|---|---|
| Microsoft High | Microsoft earns $1 billion / Apple earns $6 billion | Microsoft earns $10 billion / Apple earns $6 billion |
| Microsoft Low | Microsoft earns $8 billion / Apple earns $2 billion | Microsoft earns $4 billion / Apple earns $3 billion |

a. What (if any) is the dominant strategy for each firm?

b. Is there a Nash equilibrium? Briefly explain.

**2.20** DemandTec is a firm that provides software to retailers, such as department stores, that allow the firms to make better decisions about when to increase or cut prices, given changes in demand, changes in costs, and other factors. DemandTec and firms selling similar software have allowed smaller retailers to adopt pricing strategies that had long been used by larger retailers, such as Wal-Mart. According to an article in the *Wall Street Journal,* use of this software has reduced the amount of price cutting that retail firms engage in following a fall in demand. Is a decline in price cutting good news for consumers? Good news for the firms involved? Good news for both? Briefly explain.

Based on John Jannarone, "Fashioning a Retail Stock Rally," *Wall Street Journal,* July 8, 2011.

**2.21** A newspaper article referred to Saudi Arabia as "the cartel's enforcer and enabler." What cartel was the article referring to? In what way is Saudi Arabia an enabler and an enforcer?

From Andrew E. Kramer, "Russia Cashes In on Anxiety Over Supply of Middle East Oil," *New York Times,* March 7, 2011.

**2.22** Refer to Figure 14.5 on page 470. Consider the entries in the row of the payoff matrix that correspond to Saudi Arabia choosing "low output." Suppose the numbers change so that Nigeria's profit is $15 million when Nigeria chooses "low output" and $10 million when it chooses "high output."

a. Create the payoff matrix for this new situation, assuming that Saudi Arabia and Nigeria choose their output levels simultaneously. Is there a Nash equilibrium to this game? If so, what is it?

b. Draw the decision tree for this situation (using the values from the payoff matrix you created in part a), assuming that Saudi Arabia and Nigeria make their decisions sequentially: First, Saudi Arabia chooses its output level, and then Nigeria responds by choosing its output level. Is there a Nash equilibrium in this game? If so, what is it?

c. Compare your answers to parts a. and b. Briefly explain the reason for any differences in the outcomes of these two games.

---

## Sequential Games and Business Strategy, pages 471–474

LEARNING OBJECTIVE: Use sequential games to analyze business strategies.

## Summary

Recent work in game theory has focused on actions firms can take to deter the entry of new firms into an industry. Deterring entry can be analyzed using a sequential game, where first one firm makes a decision and then another firm reacts to that decision. Sequential games can be illustrated using decision trees.

MyEconLab    Visit **www.myeconlab.com** to complete these exercises online and get instant feedback.

## Review Questions

**3.1** What is a sequential game?

**3.2** How are decision trees used to analyze sequential games?

## Problems and Applications

**3.3** [**Related to** Solved Problem 14.3 **on page 472**] Bradford is a small town that currently has no fast-food restaurants. McDonald's and Burger King are both considering entering this market. Burger King will wait until McDonald's has made its decision before deciding whether to enter. McDonald's will choose between building a large store and building a small store. Once McDonald's has made its decision about the size of the store it will build, Burger King will decide whether to enter this market. Use the following decision tree to decide the optimal strategy for each company. Does your answer depend on the rate of return that owners of fast-food restaurants must earn on their investments in order to break even? Briefly explain.

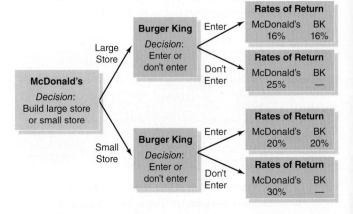

**3.4** [**Related to the** Chapter Opener **on page 459**] This chapter describes how firms can create barriers to deter firms from entering an industry:

> One factor firms consider in pricing a new product is the effect different prices have on the likelihood that competitors will enter the market. A high price might lead to high profits if other firms do not enter the market, but if a high price attracts entry from other firms, it might actually result in lower profits. A low price, by deterring entry, might lead to higher profits.

In response to the profits Apple earned from the iPad, other companies, including Dell, Motorola, Research in Motion (makers of BlackBerry cell phones), and Samsung developed their own tablets. Did Apple make a mistake in not selling its iPads at lower prices in order to prevent other firms from entering the market for tablets?

From "Tablet War Is an Apple Rout," *Wall Street Journal,* August 12, 2011.

**3.5** Suppose that in the situation shown in Figure 14.7 on page 473, TruImage's profits are $1.5 million if the firm accepts Dell's contract offer of $20 per copy. Now will Dell offer TruImage a contract of $20 per copy or a contract of $30 per copy? Briefly explain.

---

## **14.4** The Five Competitive Forces Model, pages pages 474–477
LEARNING OBJECTIVE: Use the five competitive forces model to analyze competition in an industry.

### Summary

Michael Porter of Harvard Business School argues that the state of competition in an industry is determined by five competitive forces: the degree of competition among existing firms, the threat from new entrants, competition from substitute goods or services, the bargaining power of buyers, and the bargaining power of suppliers.

 MyEconLab    Visit **www.myeconlab.com** to complete these exercises online and get instant feedback.

### Review Questions

**4.1** List the competitive forces in the five competitive forces model.

**4.2** Does the strength of each of the five competitive forces remain constant over time? Briefly explain.

### Problems and Applications

**4.3** Michael Porter argued that in many industries, "strategies converge and competition becomes a series of races down identical paths that no one can win." Briefly explain whether firms in these industries will likely earn economic profits.
Based on Michael E. Porter, "What Is Strategy?" *Harvard Business Review*, November–December 1996, p. 64.

**4.4** According to an article in the *New York Times*:

On Tuesday, Google will release a free Web browser called Chrome that the company said would challenge Microsoft's Internet Explorer, as well as the Firefox browser.

The browser is a universal doorway to the Internet, and the use of Internet software and services is rapidly growing. Increasingly, the browser is also the doorway to the Web on cellphones and other mobile devices, widening the utility of the Web and Web advertising. Google, analysts say, cannot let Microsoft's dominant share of the browser market go without a direct challenge.

John Lilly, chief executive of the Mozilla Corporation, which manages the Firefox project, said that Google's action would put "more competitive pressure on us to keep coming up with great browser technology."

a. What does the article mean by "competitive pressure"? Which of the five competitive forces is the article referring to?

b. In the long run, will the company that first incorporates new innovations in its browser technology earn economic profits? Which group is likely to benefit the most from these innovations: the browser companies or consumers?
Based on Steve Lohr, "Microsoft Faces New Browser Foe in Google," *New York Times*, September 1, 2008.

**4.5** **[Related to the** Making the Connection **on page 476]** In the preface to the 2004 reprint of *In Search of Excellence*, Thomas Peters and Robert Waterman wrote: "Our main detractors point to the decline of some of the companies we featured. They miss the point . . . . We weren't writing *Forever Excellent*, just as it would be absurd to expect any great athlete not to age." Is the analogy the authors make between great firms and great athletes a good one? Should we expect firms to become less successful as they age, just as athletes do?
Based on Thomas Peters and Robert H. Waterman, Jr., "Authors' Note: Excellence 2003," from *In Search of Excellence: Lessons from America's Best-Run Companies*, [New York: HarperCollins, 2004 (original edition 1982)].

**4.6** In a forum posting on the Web site www.startupnation.com, a contributor made the following comment regarding the advice in the business strategy book *Blue Ocean Strategy*: "The key message for me was don't try to look like, taste like, act like the competition." Briefly explain what this person meant by "look like, taste like, act like the competition." Briefly discuss whether the strategy of "look like, taste like, act like the competition" ever makes sense.
Based on "As a Small Business Owner, What Kind of Book Would You Like to Read?" "Coffee Talk" Forum, www.startupnation.com, April 25, 2007.

**4.7** The market for electronic readers consists of relatively few firms, including Amazon, Sony, and Plastic Logic. In an interview, Walter Mossberg of the *Wall Street Journal* asked Rich Archuleta, CEO of Plastic Logic, what price the company would be charging for a new electronic reader that it was developing, aimed at business users. Archuleta declined to give a specific price, saying instead, "The market sets pricing. We don't set pricing." But Plastic Logic is competing in an oligopolistic industry, so shouldn't the firm, not the market, be setting the price? Explain why Archuleta made this statement.
Based on "Plastic Logic Shows New E-Book Reader," *Wall Street Journal*, May 27, 2009.

## Chapter Outline and Learning Objectives

# Is Cable Television a Monopoly?

Today, most people can hardly imagine life without cable television. The first cable systems were established in the 1940s, in cities that were too small to support broadcast stations. In the early years, the cable industry grew slowly because the technology did not exist to rebroadcast the signals of distant stations, so cable systems offered just a few channels. By 1970, only about 7 percent of households had cable television. In addition, the Federal Communications Commission (FCC)—the U.S. government agency that regulates the television industry—placed restrictions on both rebroadcasting the signals of distant stations and the fees that cable systems could charge for "premium channels" that would show movies or sporting events. In the late 1970s, two key developments occurred: First, satellite relay technology made it feasible for local cable systems to receive signals relayed by satellite from distant broadcast stations. Second, Congress loosened regulations on rebroadcasting distant stations and charging for premium channels, which allowed cable networks such as Home Box Office (HBO) and Showtime to develop.

A firm needs a license from the city government to enter a local cable television market. Until 2008, Time Warner Cable was the only provider of cable TV in the Manhattan borough of New York City; Time Warner had a *monopoly*. Few firms in the United States are monopolies because usually in a market system, whenever a firm earns economic profits, other firms will enter its market. Therefore, it is very difficult for a firm to remain the only provider of a good or service. In this chapter, we will develop an economic model of monopoly that can help analyze how cable systems in some cities and other firms that lack competition in their markets affect the economy.

**AN INSIDE LOOK AT POLICY** on **page 510** discusses the entry of Verizon into the market for cable TV in upstate New York to compete with Time Warner Cable.

## Economics in Your Life

### Why Can't I Watch the NFL Network?

Are you a fan of the National Football League? Would you like to see more NFL-related programming on television? If so, you're not alone. The NFL concluded that there was so much demand for more football programming that it began its own football network, the NFL Network.

Unfortunately for many football fans, the NFL Network is not available to many households that have cable television, including, as of August 2011, Time Warner Cable that serves the majority of cable customers in New York, the largest television market in the United States. Why are some of the largest cable TV systems unwilling to include the NFL Network in their channel lineups? Why are some systems requiring customers who want the NFL Network to upgrade to more expensive channel packages? As you read this chapter, see if you can answer these questions. You can check your answers against those we provide on **page 508** at the end of this chapter.

A
lthough few firms are monopolies, the economic model of monopoly can be quite useful. As we saw in Chapter 12, even though perfectly competitive markets are rare, this market model provides a benchmark for how a firm acts in the most competitive situation possible: when it is in an industry with many firms that all supply the same product. Monopoly provides a benchmark for the other extreme, where a firm is the only one in its market and, therefore, faces no competition from other firms supplying its product. The monopoly model is also useful in analyzing situations in which firms agree to *collude*, or not compete, and act together as if they were a monopoly. As we will discuss in this chapter, collusion is illegal in the United States, but it occasionally happens.

Monopolies pose a dilemma for the government. Should the government allow monopolies to exist? Are there circumstances in which the government should actually promote the existence of monopolies? Should the government regulate the prices monopolies charge? If so, will such price regulation increase economic efficiency? In this chapter, we will explore these public policy issues.

Define *monopoly*.

**Monopoly** A firm that is the only seller of a good or service that does not have a close substitute.

## Is Any Firm Ever Really a Monopoly?

A **monopoly** is a firm that is the only seller of a good or service that does not have a close substitute. Because substitutes of some kind exist for just about every product, can any firm really be a monopoly? The answer is "yes," provided that the substitutes are not "close" substitutes. But how do we decide whether a substitute is a close substitute? A narrow definition of monopoly that some economists use is that a firm has a monopoly if it can ignore the actions of all other firms. In other words, other firms must not be producing close substitutes if the monopolist can ignore the other firms' prices. For example, candles are a substitute for electric lights, but your local electric company can ignore candle prices because however low the price of candles becomes, almost no customers will give up using electric lights and switch to candles. Therefore, your local electric company is clearly a monopoly.

Many economists, however, use a broader definition of *monopoly*. For example, suppose Donn Johnson owns the only pizza parlor in a small town. (We will consider later the question of *why* a market may have only a single firm.) Does Donn have a monopoly? Substitutes for pizza certainly exist. If the price of pizza is too high, people will switch to hamburgers or fried chicken or some other food instead. People do not have to eat at Donn's or starve. Donn is in competition with the local McDonald's and KFC, among other firms. So, Donn does not meet the narrow definition of a monopoly. But many economists would still argue that it is useful to think of Donn as having a monopoly.

Although hamburgers and fried chicken are substitutes for pizza, competition from firms selling them is not enough to keep Donn from earning economic profits. We saw in Chapter 12 that when firms earn economic profits, we can expect new firms to enter the industry, and in the long run, the economic profits are competed away. Donn's profits will not be competed away as long as he is the *only* seller of pizza. Using the broader definition, Donn has a monopoly because there are no other firms selling a substitute close enough that his economic profits are competed away in the long run.

## Making the Connection | Is Google a Monopoly?

As we will discuss later in this chapter, the federal government can take legal action against a firm under the *antitrust laws* if the government believes that the firm has created a monopoly. In mid-2011, the U.S. Federal Trade Commission (FTC) indicated that it was investigating whether Google had violated the antitrust laws. The European Union, which is an organization of 27 European countries, has similar rules against firms forming monopolies. The European Commission enforces these rules. In early 2011,

Microsoft filed a complaint with the European Commission that Google was using its dominant position as an Internet search engine to exclude competitors.

But is Google a monopoly? Clearly, Google is not the only Internet search option available. For example, Yahoo! has for a number of years operated a search engine, Microsoft operates the Bing search engine, and there are a number of smaller search engines. Critics point out, though, that Google has a dominant market share of 70 percent in the United States and 90 percent in Europe. Can the other search engines effectively compete with Google? Microsoft argues that Google has taken steps to create an effective monopoly:

*Google has a dominant market share in the United States and in Europe. Can other search engines effectively compete?*

> [Google] understands as well as anyone that search engines depend upon the openness of the Web in order to function properly. . . . Unfortunately, Google has engaged in a broadening pattern of walling off access to content and data that competitors need to provide search results to consumers and to attract advertisers.

Microsoft was particularly concerned that Google was limiting the access of other search engines to YouTube, which Google owns: "Without proper access to YouTube, Bing and other search engines cannot stand with Google on an equal footing in returning search results with links to YouTube videos and that, of course, drives more users away from competitors and to Google." Microsoft also complained that Google was limiting the access of other search engines to many of the books that Google had scanned and made available on the Web.

Google, naturally, takes a different view of its position. The company argues that its dominant market share is due to the higher quality of its search engine, not any attempts the company has made to reduce the access of other search engines to online content. In a response to the FTC investigation, Google noted, "We want [users of search engines] to stay with us because we're innovating and making our products better—not because [they are] locked in."

As we have seen, many economists consider a firm to have a monopoly if other firms are unable to compete away its profits in the long run. The debate over whether other search engines can compete with Google or whether it is effectively a monopoly is likely to continue.

Based on Thomas Catan, "FTC to Serve Google with Subpoenas in Broad Antitrust Probe," *Wall Street Journal*, June 23, 2011; Miguel Helft, "Google Confirms F.T.C. Antitrust Inquiry," *New York Times*, June 24, 2011; Amit Singhal, "Supporting Choice, Ensuring Economic Opportunity," googleblog.blogspot.com, June 24, 2011; David Goldman, "Microsoft Accuses Google of Antitrust Violations," money.cnn.com, March 31, 2011; and Brad Smith, "Adding Our Voice to Concerns about Search in Europe," blogs.technet.com, March 31, 2011.

**Your Turn:** Test your understanding by doing related problems 1.7 and 1.8 on page 512 at the end of this chapter.                   MyEconLab

# Where Do Monopolies Come From?

Because monopolies do not face competition, every firm would like to have a monopoly. But to have a monopoly, barriers to entering the market must be so high that no other firms can enter. *Barriers to entry* may be high enough to keep out competing firms for four main reasons:

1. A government blocks the entry of more than one firm into a market.
2. One firm has control of a key resource necessary to produce a good.
3. There are important *network externalities* in supplying the good or service.
4. Economies of scale are so large that one firm has a *natural monopoly*.

**15.2 LEARNING** OBJECTIVE

Explain the four main reasons monopolies arise.

## Government Action Blocks Entry

As we will discuss later in this chapter, governments ordinarily try to promote competition in markets, but sometimes governments take action to block entry into a market. In the United States, governments block entry in two main ways:

1. By granting a *patent* or *copyright* to an individual or a firm, giving it the exclusive right to produce a product
2. By granting a firm a *public franchise*, making it the exclusive legal provider of a good or service

**Patent** The exclusive right to a product for a period of 20 years from the date the patent is filed with the government.

**Patents and Copyrights** The U.S. government grants patents to firms that develop new products or new ways of making existing products. A **patent** gives a firm the exclusive right to a new product for a period of 20 years from the date the patent is filed with the government. Because Microsoft has a patent on the Windows operating system, other firms cannot sell their own versions of Windows. The government grants patents to encourage firms to spend money on the research and development necessary to create new products. If other firms could have freely copied Windows, Microsoft would have been unlikely to spend the money necessary to develop it. Sometimes a firm is able to maintain a monopoly in the production of a good without patent protection, provided that it can keep secret how the product is made.

Patent protection is of vital importance to pharmaceutical firms as they develop new prescription drugs. Pharmaceutical firms start research and development work on a new prescription drug an average of 12 years before the drug is available for sale. A firm applies for a patent about 10 years before it begins to sell the product. The average 10-year delay between the government granting a patent and the firm actually selling the drug is due to the federal Food and Drug Administration's requirements that the firm demonstrate that the drug is both safe and effective. Therefore, during the period before the drug can be sold, the firm will have substantial costs to develop and test the drug. If the drug does not successfully make it to market, the firm will have a substantial loss.

Once a drug is available for sale, the profits the firm earns from the drug will increase throughout the period of patent protection—which is usually about 10 years—as the drug becomes more widely known to doctors and patients. After the patent has expired, other firms are free to legally produce chemically identical drugs called *generic drugs*. Gradually, competition from generic drugs will eliminate the profits the original firm had been earning. For example, when patent protection expired for Glucophage, a diabetes drug manufactured by Bristol-Myers Squibb, sales of the drug declined by more than $1.5 billion in the first year due to competition from 12 generic versions of the drug produced by other firms. When the patent expired on Prozac, an antidepressant drug manufactured by Eli Lilly, sales dropped by more than 80 percent. Most economic profits from selling a prescription drug are eliminated 20 years after the drug is first offered for sale.

Making the Connection | ## The End of the Christmas Plant Monopoly

In December, the poinsettia plant seems to be almost everywhere, decorating stores, restaurants, and houses. Although it may seem strange that anyone can have a monopoly on the production of a plant, for many years the Paul Ecke Ranch in Encinitas, California, had a monopoly on poinsettias.

The poinsettia is a wildflower native to Mexico. It was almost unknown in the United States before Albert Ecke, a German immigrant, began selling it in the early twentieth century at his flower stand in Hollywood, California. Unlike almost every other flowering plant, the poinsettia blossoms in the winter. This timing, along with the plant's striking red and green colors, makes the poinsettia ideal for Christmas decorating.

Albert Ecke's son, Paul, discovered that by grafting together two varieties of poinsettias, it was possible to have multiple branches grow from one stem. The result was a plant that had more leaves and was much more colorful than conventional poinsettias. Paul Ecke did not attempt to patent his new technique for growing poinsettias. But because the Ecke family kept the technique secret for decades, it was able to maintain a monopoly on the commercial production of the plants. Unfortunately for the Ecke family—but fortunately for consumers—a university researcher discovered the technique and published it in an academic journal.

New firms quickly entered the industry, and the price of poinsettias plummeted. Soon consumers could purchase them for as little as three for $10. At those prices, the Ecke family's firm was unable to earn economic profits. Eventually, Paul Ecke III, the owner of the firm, decided to give up commercial production of poinsettias on his family's ranch. He sold off more than half the firm's land to fund new state-of-the-art greenhouses and research into new varieties of plants that he hoped would earn the firm economic profits once again.

Based on Adam Kaye, "Ecke Farming Out His Poinsettia Crop," *North County Times*, November 18, 2007; Cynthia Crosen, "Holiday's Ubiquitous Houseplant," *Wall Street Journal*, December 19, 2000; and Mike Freeman and David E. Graham, "Ecke Ranch Plans to Sell Most of Its Remaining Land," *San Diego Union-Tribune*, December 11, 2003.

**Your Turn:** Test your understanding by doing related problem 2.10 on page 513 at the end of this chapter.

*At one time, the Ecke family had a monopoly on growing poinsettias, but many new firms entered the industry.*

MyEconLab

---

Just as the government grants a new product patent protection, it grants books, films, and pieces of music **copyright** protection. U.S. law grants the creator of a book, film, or piece of music the exclusive right to use the creation during the creator's lifetime. The creator's heirs retain this exclusive right for 70 years after the creator's death. In effect, copyrights create monopolies for the copyrighted items. Without copyrights, individuals and firms would be less likely to invest in creating new books, films, and software.

> **Copyright** A government-granted exclusive right to produce and sell a creation.

**Public Franchises**  In some cases, the government grants a firm a **public franchise** that allows it to be the only legal provider of a good or service. For example, state and local governments often designate one company as the sole provider of electricity, natural gas, or water.

> **Public franchise** A government designation that a firm is the only legal provider of a good or service.

Occasionally, a government may decide to provide certain services directly to consumers through a *public enterprise*. This is much more common in Europe than in the United States. For example, the governments in most European countries own the railroad systems. In the United States, many city governments provide water and sewage service themselves rather than rely on private firms.

## Control of a Key Resource

Another way for a firm to become a monopoly is by controlling a key resource. This happens infrequently because most resources, including raw materials such as oil or iron ore, are widely available from a variety of suppliers. There are, however, a few prominent examples of monopolies based on control of a key resource, such as the Aluminum Company of America (Alcoa) and the International Nickel Company of Canada.

For many years until the 1940s, Alcoa either owned or had long-term contracts to buy nearly all of the available bauxite, the mineral needed to produce aluminum. Without access to bauxite, competing firms had to use recycled aluminum, which limited the amount of aluminum they could produce. Similarly, the International Nickel Company of Canada controlled more than 90 percent of available nickel supplies. Competition in the nickel market increased when the Petsamo nickel fields in northern Russia were developed after World War II.

In the United States, a key resource for a professional sports team is a large stadium. The teams that make up the major professional sports leagues—Major League Baseball, the National Football League, and the National Basketball Association—usually either own or have long-term leases with the stadiums in major cities. Control of these stadiums is a major barrier to new professional baseball, football, or basketball leagues forming.

| Making the Connection | Are Diamond Profits Forever? The De Beers Diamond Monopoly |

*De Beers promoted the sentimental value of diamonds as a way to maintain its position in the diamond market.*

The most famous monopoly based on control of a raw material is the De Beers diamond mining and marketing company of South Africa. Before the 1860s, diamonds were extremely rare. Only a few pounds of diamonds were produced each year, primarily from Brazil and India. Then in 1870, enormous deposits of diamonds were discovered along the Orange River in South Africa. It became possible to produce thousands of pounds of diamonds per year, and the owners of the new mines feared that the price of diamonds would plummet. To avoid financial disaster, the mine owners decided in 1888 to merge and form De Beers Consolidated Mines, Ltd.

De Beers became one of the most profitable and longest-lived monopolies in history. The company has carefully controlled the supply of diamonds to keep prices high. As new diamond deposits were discovered in Russia and Zaire, De Beers was able to maintain prices by buying most of the new supplies.

Because diamonds are rarely destroyed, De Beers has always worried about competition from the resale of stones. Heavily promoting diamond engagement and wedding rings with the slogan "A Diamond Is Forever" was a way around this problem. Because engagement and wedding rings have great sentimental value, they are seldom resold, even by the heirs of the original recipients. De Beers advertising has been successful even in some countries, such as Japan, that have had no custom of giving diamond engagement rings. As the populations in De Beers's key markets age, its advertising in recent years has focused on middle-aged men presenting diamond rings to their wives as symbols of financial success and continuing love and on professional women buying "right-hand rings" for themselves.

Over the years, competition has gradually increased in the diamond business. By 2000, De Beers directly controlled only about 40 percent of world diamond production. The company became concerned about the amount it was spending to buy diamonds from other sources to keep them off the market. It decided to abandon its strategy of attempting to control the worldwide supply of diamonds and to concentrate instead on differentiating its diamonds by relying on its name recognition. Each De Beers diamond is now marked with a microscopic brand—a "Forevermark"—to reassure consumers of its high quality. Other firms, such as BHP Billiton, which owns mines in northern Canada, have followed suit by branding their diamonds. Whether consumers will pay attention to brands on diamonds remains to be seen, although through 2011, the branding strategy had helped De Beers to maintain a 35 to 40 percent share of the diamond market.

Based on William J. Holstein, "De Beers Reworks Its Image as Rivals Multiply," *New York Times*, December 12, 2008; Edward Jay Epstein, "Have You Ever Tried to Sell a Diamond?" *Atlantic Monthly*, February 1982; and Donna J. Bergenstock, Mary E. Deily, and Larry W. Taylor, "A Cartel's Response to Cheating: An Empirical Investigation of the De Beers Diamond Empire," *Southern Economic Journal*, Vol. 73, No. 1, July 2006, pp. 173–189.

MyEconLab    **Your Turn:** Test your understanding by doing related problem 2.11 on page 513 at the end of this chapter.

## Network Externalities

**Network externalities** A situation in which the usefulness of a product increases with the number of consumers who use it.

There are **network externalities** in the consumption of a product if its usefulness increases with the number of people who use it. If you owned the only HD televison in the world, for example, it would not be very valuable because firms would not have an incentive to develop HD programming. The more HD televisions there are in use, the more valuable they become to consumers.

Some economists argue that network externalities can serve as barriers to entry. For example, in the early 1980s, Microsoft gained an advantage over other software companies by developing MS-DOS, the operating system for the first IBM personal computers. Because IBM sold more computers than any other company, software developers wrote many application programs for MS-DOS. The more people who used MS-DOS–based programs, the greater the value to a consumer of using an MS-DOS–based program. By the 1990s, Microsoft had replaced MS-DOS with Windows. Today, Windows has an 85 percent share in the market for personal computer operating systems, with Apple's operating system having a 10 percent share, and other operating systems, including the open-source Linux system, having shares of about 1 percent or less. If another firm introduced a new operating system, some economists argue that relatively few people would use it initially, and few applications would run on it, which would limit the operating system's value to other consumers.

eBay was the first Internet site to attract a significant number of people to its online auctions. Once a large number of people began to use eBay to buy and sell collectibles, antiques, and many other products, it became a more valuable place to buy and sell. Yahoo.com, Amazon.com, and other Internet sites eventually started online auctions, but they had difficulty attracting buyers and sellers. On eBay, a buyer expects to find more sellers, and a seller expects to find more potential buyers than on Amazon or other auction sites.

As these examples show, from a firm's point of view, network externalities can set off a *virtuous cycle*: If a firm can attract enough customers initially, it can attract additional customers because the value of its product has been increased by more people using it, which attracts even more customers, and so on. With products such as computer operating systems and online auctions, it might be difficult for new firms to enter the market and compete away the profits being earned by the first firm in the market.

Economists engage in considerable debate, however, about the extent to which network externalities are important barriers to entry in the business world. Some economists argue that Microsoft and eBay have dominant positions primarily because they are efficient in offering products that satisfy consumer preferences rather than because of the effects of network externalities. In this view, the advantages existing firms gain from network externalities would not be enough to protect them from competing firms offering better products. In other words, a firm entering the operating system market with a program better than Windows or a firm offering an Internet auction site better than eBay would be successful despite the effects of network externalities. (We discussed this point in more detail in Chapter 10.) In fact, the market shares of both Windows and eBay have been slowly declining in recent years.

## Natural Monopoly

We saw in Chapter 10 that economies of scale exist when a firm's long-run average costs fall as it increases the quantity of output it produces. A **natural monopoly** occurs when economies of scale are so large that one firm can supply the entire market at a lower average total cost than two or more firms. In that case, there is really "room" in the market for only one firm.

**Natural monopoly** A situation in which economies of scale are so large that one firm can supply the entire market at a lower average total cost than can two or more firms.

Figure 15.1 shows the average total cost curve for a firm producing electricity and the total demand for electricity in the firm's market. Notice that the average total cost curve is still falling when it crosses the demand curve at point *A*. If the firm is a monopoly and produces 30 billion kilowatt-hours of electricity per year, its average total cost of production will be $0.04 per kilowatt-hour. Suppose instead that two firms are in the market, each producing half of the market output, or 15 billion kilowatt-hours per year. Assume that each firm has the same average total cost curve. The figure shows that producing 15 billion kilowatt-hours would move each firm back up its average cost curve so that the average cost of producing electricity would rise to $0.06 per kilowatt-hour (point *B*). In this case, if one of the firms expands production, it will move down the average total cost curve. With lower average costs, it will be able to offer electricity at a lower price than the other firm can offer. Eventually, the other firm will be driven out

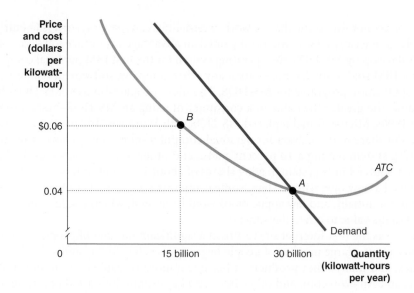

**Figure 15.1**

**Average Total Cost Curve for a Natural Monopoly**

With a natural monopoly, the average total cost curve is still falling when it crosses the demand curve (point *A*). If only one firm is producing electric power in the market, and it produces where the average cost curve intersects the demand curve, average total cost will equal $0.04 per kilowatt-hour of electricity produced. If the market is divided between two firms, each producing 15 billion kilowatt-hours, the average cost of producing electricity rises to $0.06 per kilowatt-hour (point *B*). In this case, if one firm expands production, it can move down the average total cost curve, lower its price, and drive the other firm out of business.

of business, and the remaining firm will have a monopoly. Because a monopoly would develop automatically—or *naturally*—in this market, it is a natural monopoly.

Natural monopolies are most likely to occur in markets where fixed costs are very large relative to variable costs. For example, a firm that produces electricity must make a substantial investment in machinery and equipment necessary to generate the electricity and in the wires and cables necessary to distribute it. Once the initial investment has been made, however, the marginal cost of producing another kilowatt-hour of electricity is relatively small.

# Solved Problem 15.2

## Is the OpenTable Web Site a Natural Monopoly?

OpenTable is a Web site and smartphone application that allows people to make restaurant reservations online. OpenTable charges participating restaurants a fee for each reservation. As business writer James Stewart wrote in the *Wall Street Journal*, "You simply go to the site, choose your neighborhood, enter your requested date, time and number of diners, and OpenTable shows all available restaurants with specific times available." Stewart argued that the site is a natural monopoly because "users are attracted to the site with the largest number of listings, and restaurants are attracted to the site with the largest number of users."

a. Assuming that Stewart is correct, draw a graph showing the market for online restaurant reservation sites. Be sure that the graph contains the demand for online restaurant reservations and OpenTable's average total cost curve. Explain why OpenTable would have lower average costs than would a new site that enters the market to compete against it.

b. Does the number of years OpenTable has been operating affect how you evaluate Stewart's claim that the business is a natural monopoly? Briefly explain.

### Solving the Problem

**Step 1:** **Review the chapter material.** This problem is about natural monopoly, so you may want to review the section "Natural Monopoly," which begins on page 493.

**Step 2:** **Answer part a. by drawing a natural monopoly graph and explaining why OpenTable would have lower average costs than new entrants to the market.** If Stewart is correct that OpenTable is actually a natural monopoly, the relationship between market demand and its average total costs should look like Figure 15.1.

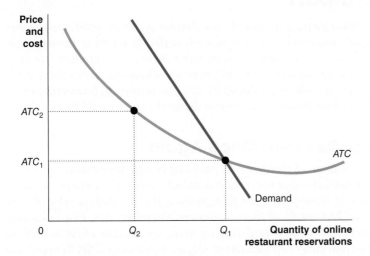

Make sure your average total cost curve is still declining when it crosses the demand curve. As shown in the figure, the market for online reservations is a natural monopoly because if one firm can supply $Q_1$ online reservations at an average total cost of $ATC_1$, then dividing the business equally between two firms each supplying $Q_2$ online reservations would raise average total cost to $ATC_2$.

OpenTable's fixed costs for servers, software programming, and marketing are very large relative to its variable costs. OpenTable's marginal cost of accommodating one more visitor to its site will be extremely small. Therefore, economies of scale in this market are likely to be so large that a firm that enters and attracts a small number of visitors to its site will have much higher average costs than OpenTable.

**Step 3:** **Answer part b. by discussing whether how long OpenTable has been in business is relevant to assessing whether it is a natural monopoly.** If a firm is a natural monopoly, it is unlikely that firms will be able to successfully enter its market. But a firm that is the first to enter a new market may not initially attract competitors. It can take time for potential competitors to decide whether it would be profitable to enter an industry, particularly an industry that might require a substantial initial investment. The longer OpenTable continues to operate without significant competition, the more likely it is that the firm actually is a natural monopoly.

OpenTable began operating in San Francisco in 1999, and it had expanded nationwide by 2003. One restaurant owner was quoted as saying, "All restaurants have to [participate with OpenTable], whether you like it or not. There's no way around it. At this point, there's no other technology or easy solution for making Web reservations." This statement indicates that restaurant owners see OpenTable as effectively having a monopoly.

**Extra Credit:** Keep in mind that competition is not good for its own sake. It is good because it can lead to lower costs, lower prices, and better products. In certain markets, however, cost conditions are such that competition is likely to lead to higher costs and higher prices. These markets are natural monopolies that are best served by one firm. Time will tell whether advances in technology or innovative marketing will make it possible for other firms to successfully compete with OpenTable.

Based on James B. Stewart, "What's New on the Menu: Hot IPO with Rare Quality," *Wall Street Journal*, May 27, 2009; and Katie Hafner, "Restaurant Reservations Go Online," *New York Times*, June 18, 2007.

**Your Turn:** For more practice, do related problem 2.12 on page 513 at the end of this chapter.    MyEconLab

# How Does a Monopoly Choose Price and Output?

Like every other firm, a monopoly maximizes profit by producing where marginal revenue equals marginal cost. A monopoly differs from other firms in that *a monopoly's demand curve is the same as the demand curve for the product*. We emphasized in Chapter 12 that the market demand curve for wheat was very different from the demand curve for the wheat produced by any one farmer. If, however, one farmer had a monopoly on wheat production, the two demand curves would be exactly the same.

## Marginal Revenue Once Again

Recall from Chapter 12 that firms in perfectly competitive markets—such as a farmer in the wheat market—face horizontal demand curves. They are *price takers*. All other firms, including monopolies, are *price makers*. If price makers raise their prices, they will lose some, but not all, of their customers. Therefore, they face a downward-sloping demand curve and a downward-sloping marginal revenue curve as well. Let's review why a firm's marginal revenue curve slopes downward if its demand curve slopes downward.

Remember that when a firm cuts the price of a product, one good thing happens, and one bad thing happens:

- *The good thing.* It sells more units of the product.

- *The bad thing.* It receives less revenue from each unit than it would have received at the higher price.

For example, consider the table in Figure 15.2, which shows the demand curve for Time Warner Cable's basic cable package. For simplicity, we assume that the market has only 10 potential subscribers instead of the millions it actually has. If Time Warner charges a price of $60 per month, it won't have any subscribers. If it charges a price of $57, it sells 1 subscription. At $54, it sells 2 subscriptions, and so on. Time Warner's total revenue is equal to the number of subscriptions sold per month multiplied by the price. The firm's average revenue—or revenue per subscription sold—is equal to its total revenue divided by the quantity of subscriptions sold. Time Warner is particularly interested in marginal revenue because marginal revenue tells the firm how much its revenue will increase if it cuts the price to sell one more subscription.

Notice that Time Warner's marginal revenue is less than the price for every subscription sold after the first subscription. To see why, think about what happens if Time Warner cuts the price of its basic cable package from $42 to $39, which increases its subscriptions sold from 6 to 7. Time Warner increases its revenue by the $39 it receives for the seventh subscription. But it also loses revenue of $3 per subscription on the first 6 subscriptions because it could have sold them at the old price of $42. So, its marginal revenue on the seventh subscription is $39 − $18 = $21, which is the value shown in the table. The graph in Figure 15.2 plots Time Warner's demand and marginal revenue curves, based on the information in the table.

## Profit Maximization for a Monopolist

Figure 15.3 shows how Time Warner combines the information on demand and marginal revenue with information on average and marginal costs to decide how many subscriptions to sell and what price to charge. We assume that the firm's marginal cost and average total cost curves have the usual U shapes we encountered in Chapters 11 and 12. In panel (a), we see how Time Warner can calculate its profit-maximizing quantity and price. As long as the marginal cost of selling one more subscription is less than the marginal revenue, the firm should sell additional subscriptions because it is adding to its profits. As Time Warner sells more cable subscriptions, rising marginal cost will eventually equal

| Subscribers per Month (Q) | Price (P) | Total Revenue (TR = P x Q) | Average Revenue (AR = TR/Q) | Marginal Revenue (MR = ΔTR/ΔQ) |
|---|---|---|---|---|
| 0 | $60 | $0 | – | – |
| 1 | 57 | 57 | $57 | $57 |
| 2 | 54 | 108 | 54 | 51 |
| 3 | 51 | 153 | 51 | 45 |
| 4 | 48 | 192 | 48 | 39 |
| 5 | 45 | 225 | 45 | 33 |
| 6 | 42 | 252 | 42 | 27 |
| 7 | 39 | 273 | 39 | 21 |
| 8 | 36 | 288 | 36 | 15 |
| 9 | 33 | 297 | 33 | 9 |
| 10 | 30 | 300 | 30 | 3 |

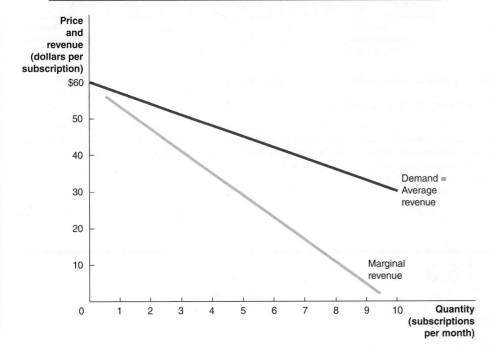

### Figure 15.2

### Calculating a Monopoly's Revenue

Time Warner Cable faces a downward-sloping demand curve for subscriptions to basic cable. To sell more subscriptions, it must cut the price. When this happens, it gains revenue from selling more subscriptions but loses revenue from selling at a lower price the subscriptions that it could have sold at a higher price. The firm's marginal revenue is the change in revenue from selling another subscription. We can calculate marginal revenue by subtracting the revenue lost as a result of a price cut from the revenue gained. The table shows that Time Warner's marginal revenue is less than the price for every subscription sold after the first subscription. Therefore, Time Warner's marginal revenue curve will be below its demand curve.

marginal revenue, and the firm will be selling the profit-maximizing quantity of subscriptions. This happens with the sixth subscription, which adds $27 to the firm's costs and $27 to its revenues—point *A* in panel (a) of Figure 15.3. The demand curve tells us that Time Warner can sell 6 subscriptions for a price of $42 per month. We can conclude that Time Warner's profit-maximizing quantity of subscriptions is 6, and its profit-maximizing price is $42.

Panel (b) shows that the average total cost of 6 subscriptions is $30 and that Time Warner can sell 6 subscriptions at a price of $42 per month (point *B* on the demand curve). Time Warner is making a profit of $12 per subscription—the price of $42 minus the average cost of $30. Its total profit is $72 (6 subscriptions × $12 profit per subscription), which is shown by the area of the green-shaded rectangle in the figure. We could also have calculated Time Warner's total profit as the difference between its total revenue and its total cost. Its total revenue from selling 6 subscriptions is $252. Its total cost equals its average cost multiplied by the number of subscriptions sold, or $30 × 6 = $180. So, its profit is $252 − $180 = $72.

It's important to note that even though Time Warner is earning economic profits, new firms will *not* enter the market. Because Time Warner has a monopoly, it will not face competition from other cable operators. Therefore, if other factors remain unchanged, Time Warner will be able to continue to earn economic profits, even in the long run.

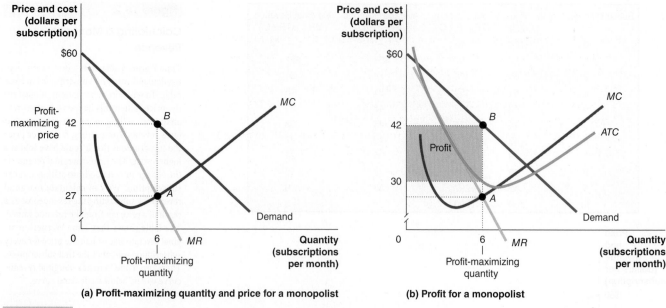

**(a) Profit-maximizing quantity and price for a monopolist**

**(b) Profit for a monopolist**

**Figure 15.3** **Profit-Maximizing Price and Output for a Monopoly**

Panel (a) shows that to maximize profit, Time Warner should sell subscriptions up to the point where the marginal revenue from selling the last subscription equals its marginal cost (point A). In this case, the marginal revenue from selling the sixth subscription and the marginal cost are both $27. Time Warner maximizes profit by selling 6 subscriptions per month and charging a price of $42 (point B). In panel (b),

the green box represents Time Warner's profit. The box has a height equal to $12, which is the price of $42 minus the average total cost of $30, and a base equal to the quantity of 6 cable subscriptions. Time Warner's profit therefore equals $12 × 6 = $72.

# Solved Problem 15.3

## Finding the Profit-Maximizing Price and Output for a Monopolist

Suppose that Comcast has a cable monopoly in Philadelphia. The following table gives Comcast's demand and costs per

month for subscriptions to basic cable (for simplicity, we once again keep the number of subscribers artificially small):

| Price | Quantity | Total Revenue | Marginal Revenue $\left( MR = \dfrac{\Delta TR}{\Delta Q} \right)$ | Total Cost | Marginal Cost $\left( MC = \dfrac{\Delta TC}{\Delta Q} \right)$ |
|---|---|---|---|---|---|
| $27 | 3 | | | $56 | |
| 26 | 4 | | | 73 | |
| 25 | 5 | | | 91 | |
| 24 | 6 | | | 110 | |
| 23 | 7 | | | 130 | |
| 22 | 8 | | | 151 | |

a. Fill in the missing values in the table.
b. If Comcast wants to maximize profits, what price should it charge, and how many cable subscriptions per month should it sell? How much profit will Comcast make? Briefly explain.

c. Suppose the local government imposes a $25-per-month tax on cable companies. Now what price should Comcast charge, how many subscriptions should it sell, and what will its profits be?

# Solving the Problem

**Step 1:** **Review the chapter material.** This problem is about finding the profit-maximizing quantity and price for a monopolist, so you may want to review the section "Profit Maximization for a Monopolist," which begins on page 496.

**Step 2:** **Answer part a. by filling in the missing values in the table.** Remember that to calculate marginal revenue and marginal cost, you must divide the change in total revenue or total cost by the change in quantity.

We don't have enough information from the table to fill in the values for marginal revenue and marginal cost in the first row.

| Price | Quantity | Total Revenue | Marginal Revenue $\left( MR = \dfrac{\Delta TR}{\Delta Q} \right)$ | Total Cost | Marginal Cost $\left( MC = \dfrac{\Delta TC}{\Delta Q} \right)$ |
|---|---|---|---|---|---|
| $27 | 3 | $81 | — | $56 | — |
| 26 | 4 | 104 | $23 | 73 | $17 |
| 25 | 5 | 125 | 21 | 91 | 18 |
| 24 | 6 | 144 | 19 | 110 | 19 |
| 23 | 7 | 161 | 17 | 130 | 20 |
| 22 | 8 | 176 | 15 | 151 | 21 |

**Step 3:** **Answer part b. by determining the profit-maximizing quantity and price.** We know that Comcast will maximize profits by selling subscriptions up to the point where marginal cost equals marginal revenue. In this case, that means selling 6 subscriptions per month. From the information in the first two columns, we know Comcast can sell 6 subscriptions at a price of $24 each. Comcast's profits are equal to the difference between its total revenue and its total cost: Profit = $144 − $110 = $34 per month.

**Step 4:** **Answer part c. by analyzing the impact of the tax.** This tax is a fixed cost to Comcast because it is a flat $25, no matter how many subscriptions it sells. Because the tax doesn't affect Comcast's marginal revenue or marginal cost, the profit-maximizing level of output has not changed. So, Comcast will still sell 6 subscriptions per month at a price of $24, but its profits will fall by the amount of the tax, from $34 per month to $9.

**Your Turn:** For more practice, do related problems 3.4 and 3.5 on page 514 at the end of this chapter. MyEconLab

---

# Don't Let This Happen to You

## Don't Assume That Charging a Higher Price Is Always More Profitable for a Monopolist

In answering part c. of Solved Problem 15.3, it's tempting to argue that Comcast should increase its price to make up for the tax. After all, Comcast is a monopolist, so why can't it just pass along the tax to its customers? The reason it can't is that Comcast, like any other monopolist, must pay attention to demand. Comcast is not interested in charging high prices for the sake of charging high prices; it is interested in maximizing profits. Charging a price of $1,000 for a basic cable subscription sounds nice, but if no one will buy at that price, Comcast would hardly be maximizing profits.

To look at it another way, before the tax is imposed, Comcast has already determined that $24 is the price that will maximize its profits. After the tax is imposed, it must determine whether $24 is still the profit-maximizing price. Because the tax has not affected Comcast's marginal revenue or marginal cost (or had any effect on consumer demand), $24 is still the profit-maximizing price, and Comcast should continue to charge it. The tax reduces Comcast's profits but doesn't cause it to increase the price of cable subscriptions.

MyEconLab

**Your Turn:** Test your understanding by doing related problem 3.8 on page 514 at the end of this chapter.

**15.4 LEARNING** OBJECTIVE

Use a graph to illustrate how a monopoly affects economic efficiency.

# Does Monopoly Reduce Economic Efficiency?

We saw in Chapter 12 that a perfectly competitive market is economically efficient. How would economic efficiency be affected if instead of being perfectly competitive, a market were a monopoly? In Chapter 4, we developed the idea of *economic surplus*. Economic surplus provides a way of characterizing the economic efficiency of a perfectly competitive market: *Equilibrium in a perfectly competitive market results in the greatest amount of economic surplus, or total benefit to society, from the production of a good or service.* What happens to economic surplus under a monopoly? We can begin the analysis by considering the hypothetical case of what would happen if the market for tablet computers begins as perfectly competitive and then becomes a monopoly.

## Comparing Monopoly and Perfect Competition

Panel (a) in Figure 15.4 illustrates the situation if the market for tablet computers is perfectly competitive. Price and quantity are determined by the intersection of the demand and supply curves. Remember that none of the individual firms in a perfectly competitive industry has any control over price. Each firm must accept the price determined by the market. Panel (b) shows what happens if the tablet computer industry becomes a monopoly. We know that the monopoly will maximize profits by producing where marginal revenue equals marginal cost. To do this, the monopoly reduces the quantity of tablets that would have been produced if the industry were perfectly competitive and increases the price. Panel (b) illustrates an important conclusion: *A monopoly will produce less and charge a higher price than would a perfectly competitive industry producing the same good.*

## Measuring the Efficiency Losses from Monopoly

Figure 15.5 uses panel (b) from Figure 15.4 to illustrate how monopoly affects consumers, producers, and the efficiency of the economy. Recall from Chapter 4 that *consumer*

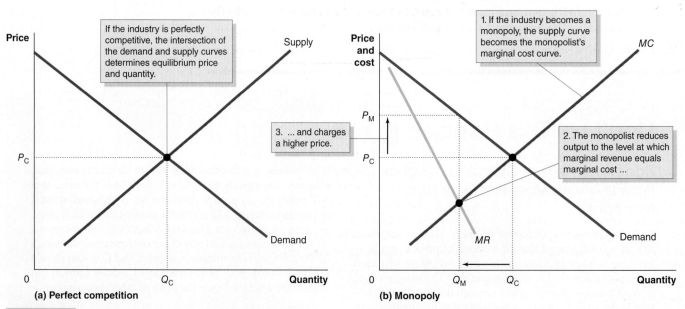

**Figure 15.4**   **What Happens If a Perfectly Competitive Industry Becomes a Monopoly?**

In panel (a), the market for tablet computers is perfectly competitive, and price and quantity are determined by the intersection of the demand and supply curves. In panel (b), the perfectly competitive tablet computer industry becomes a monopoly. As a result:

1. The industry supply curve becomes the monopolist's marginal cost curve.
2. The monopolist reduces output to where marginal revenue equals marginal cost, $Q_M$.
3. The monopolist raises the price from $P_C$ to $P_M$.

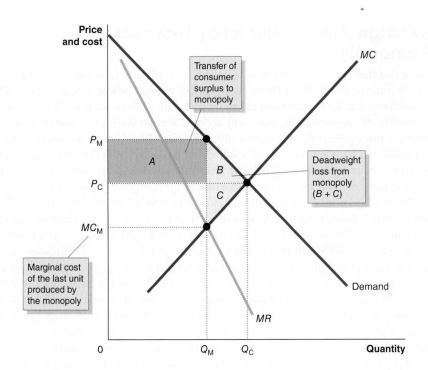

**Figure 15.5**

**The Inefficiency of Monopoly**

A monopoly charges a higher price, $P_M$, and produces a smaller quantity, $Q_M$, than a perfectly competitive industry, which charges price $P_C$ and produces $Q_C$. The higher price reduces consumer surplus by the area equal to the rectangle $A$ and the triangle $B$. Some of the reduction in consumer surplus is captured by the monopoly as producer surplus, and some becomes deadweight loss, which is the area equal to triangles $B$ and $C$.

*surplus* measures the net benefit received by consumers from purchasing a good or service. We measure consumer surplus as the area below the demand curve and above the market price. The higher the price, the smaller the consumer surplus. Because a monopoly raises the market price, it reduces consumer surplus. In Figure 15.5, the loss of consumer surplus is equal to rectangle $A$ plus triangle $B$. Remember that *producer surplus* measures the net benefit to producers from selling a good or service. We measure producer surplus as the area above the supply curve and below the market price. The increase in price due to monopoly increases producer surplus by an amount equal to rectangle $A$ and reduces it by an amount equal to triangle $C$. Because rectangle $A$ is larger than triangle $C$, we know that a monopoly increases producer surplus compared with perfect competition.

Economic surplus is equal to the sum of consumer surplus plus producer surplus. By increasing price and reducing the quantity produced, the monopolist has reduced economic surplus by an amount equal to the areas of triangles $B$ and $C$. This reduction in economic surplus is called *deadweight loss* and represents the loss of economic efficiency due to monopoly.

The best way to understand how a monopoly causes a loss of economic efficiency is to recall that price is equal to marginal cost in a perfectly competitive market. As a result, a consumer in a perfectly competitive market is always able to buy a good if she is willing to pay a price equal to the marginal cost of producing it. As Figure 15.5 shows, the monopolist stops producing at a point where the price is well above marginal cost. Consumers are unable to buy some units of the good for which they would be willing to pay a price greater than the marginal cost of producing them. Why doesn't the monopolist produce this additional output? Because the monopolist's profits are greater if it restricts output and forces up the price. A monopoly produces the profit-maximizing level of output but fails to produce the efficient level of output from the point of view of society.

We can summarize the effects of monopoly as follows:

1. Monopoly causes a reduction in consumer surplus.
2. Monopoly causes an increase in producer surplus.
3. Monopoly causes a deadweight loss, which represents a reduction in economic efficiency.

# How Large Are the Efficiency Losses Due to Monopoly?

**Market power** The ability of a firm to charge a price greater than marginal cost.

We know that there are relatively few monopolies, so the loss of economic efficiency due to monopoly must be small. Many firms, though, have **market power**, which is the ability of a firm to charge a price greater than marginal cost. The analysis we just completed shows that some loss of economic efficiency will occur whenever a firm has market power and can charge a price greater than marginal cost, even if the firm is not a monopoly. The only firms that do *not* have market power are firms in perfectly competitive markets, which must charge a price equal to marginal cost. Because few markets are perfectly competitive, *some loss of economic efficiency occurs in the market for nearly every good or service.*

Is the total loss of economic efficiency due to market power large or small? It is possible to put a dollar value on the loss of economic efficiency by estimating for every industry the size of the deadweight loss triangle, as in Figure 15.5. The first economist to do this was Arnold Harberger of the University of Chicago. His estimates—largely confirmed by later researchers—indicated that the total loss of economic efficiency in the U.S. economy due to market power is small. According to his estimates, if every industry in the economy were perfectly competitive, so that price were equal to marginal cost in every market, the gain in economic efficiency would equal less than 1 percent of the value of total production in the United States, or about $480 per person.

The loss of economic efficiency is this small primarily because true monopolies are very rare. In most industries, competition keeps price much closer to marginal cost than would be the case in a monopoly. The closer price is to marginal cost, the smaller the size of the deadweight loss.

# Market Power and Technological Change

Some economists have raised the possibility that the economy may actually benefit from firms having market power. This argument is most closely identified with Joseph Schumpeter, an Austrian economist who spent many years as a professor of economics at Harvard. Schumpeter argued that economic progress depends on technological change in the form of new products. For example, the replacement of horse-drawn carriages by automobiles, the replacement of ice boxes by refrigerators, and the replacement of mechanical calculators by electronic computers all represent technological changes that significantly raised living standards. In Schumpeter's view, new products unleash a "gale of creative destruction" that drives older products—and, often, the firms that produced them—out of the market. Schumpeter was not concerned that firms with market power would charge higher prices than perfectly competitive firms:

> It is not that kind of [price] competition which counts but the competition from the new commodity, the new technology, the new source of supply, the new type of organization . . . competition which commands a decisive cost or quality advantage and which strikes not at the margins of the profits and outputs of the existing firms but at their foundations and their very lives.

Economists who support Schumpeter's view argue that the introduction of new products requires firms to spend funds on research and development. It is possible for firms to raise this money by borrowing from investors or from banks. But investors and banks are usually skeptical of ideas for new products that have not yet passed the test of consumer acceptance in the market. As a result, firms are often forced to rely on their profits to finance the research and development needed for new products. Because firms with market power are more likely to earn economic profits than are perfectly competitive firms, they are also more likely to carry out research and development and introduce new products. In this view, the higher prices firms with market power charge are unimportant compared with the benefits from the new products these firms introduce to the market.

Some economists disagree with Schumpeter's views. These economists point to the number of new products developed by smaller firms, including, for example, Steve Jobs and Steve Wozniak inventing the first Apple computer in Jobs's garage, and Larry Page and Sergey Brin inventing the Google search engine as graduate students at Stanford. As we will see in the next section, government policymakers continue to struggle with the issue of whether, on balance, large firms with market power are good or bad for the economy.

# Government Policy toward Monopoly

Because monopolies reduce consumer surplus and economic efficiency, most governments have policies that regulate their behavior. Recall from Chapter 14 that **collusion** refers to an agreement among firms to charge the same price or otherwise not to compete. In the United States, *antitrust laws* are designed to prevent monopolies and collusion. Governments also regulate firms that are natural monopolies, often by controlling the prices they charge.

## Antitrust Laws and Antitrust Enforcement

The first important law regulating monopolies in the United States was the Sherman Act, which Congress passed in 1890 to promote competition and prevent the formation of monopolies. Section 1 of the Sherman Act outlaws "every contract, combination in the form of trust or otherwise, or conspiracy in restraint of trade." Section 2 states that "every person who shall monopolize, or attempt to monopolize, or combine or conspire with any other person or persons, to monopolize any part of the trade or commerce . . . shall be deemed guilty of a felony."

The Sherman Act targeted firms in several industries that had combined together during the 1870s and 1880s to form "trusts." In a trust, the firms were operated independently but gave voting control to a board of trustees. The board enforced collusive agreements for the firms to charge the same price and not to compete for each other's customers. The most notorious of the trusts was the Standard Oil Trust, organized by John D. Rockefeller. After the Sherman Act was passed, trusts disappeared, but the term **antitrust laws** has lived on to refer to the laws aimed at eliminating collusion and promoting competition among firms.

The Sherman Act prohibited trusts and collusive agreements, but it left several loopholes. For example, it was not clear whether it would be legal for two or more firms to merge to form a new, larger firm that would have substantial market power. A series of Supreme Court decisions interpreted the Sherman Act narrowly, and the result was a wave of mergers at the turn of the twentieth century. Included in these mergers was U.S. Steel Corporation, which was formed from dozens of smaller companies. U.S. Steel, organized by J. P. Morgan, was the first billion-dollar corporation, and it controlled two-thirds of steel production in the United States. The Sherman Act also left unclear whether any business practices short of outright collusion were illegal.

To address the loopholes in the Sherman Act, in 1914, Congress passed the Clayton Act and the Federal Trade Commission Act. Under the Clayton Act, a merger was illegal if its effect was "substantially to lessen competition, or to tend to create a monopoly." The Federal Trade Commission Act set up the Federal Trade Commission (FTC), which was given the power to police unfair business practices. The FTC has brought lawsuits against firms employing a variety of business practices, including deceptive advertising. In setting up the FTC, Congress divided the authority to police mergers. Currently, both the Antitrust Division of the U.S. Department of Justice and the FTC are responsible for merger policy. Table 15.1 lists the most important U.S. antitrust laws and the purpose of each.

## Mergers: The Trade-off between Market Power and Efficiency

The federal government regulates business mergers because it knows that if firms gain market power by merging, they may use that market power to raise prices and reduce output. As a result, the government is most concerned with **horizontal mergers**, or

**Collusion** An agreement among firms to charge the same price or otherwise not to compete.

**Antitrust laws** Laws aimed at eliminating collusion and promoting competition among firms.

**Horizontal merger** A merger between firms in the same industry.

| Law | Date Enacted | Purpose |
|---|---|---|
| Sherman Act | 1890 | Prohibited "restraint of trade," including price fixing and collusion. Also outlawed monopolization. |
| Clayton Act | 1914 | Prohibited firms from buying stock in competitors and from having directors serve on the boards of competing firms. |
| Federal Trade Commission Act | 1914 | Established the Federal Trade Commission (FTC) to help administer antitrust laws. |
| Robinson–Patman Act | 1936 | Prohibited firms from charging buyers different prices if the result would reduce competition. |
| Cellar–Kefauver Act | 1950 | Toughened restrictions on mergers by prohibiting any mergers that would reduce competition. |

**Table 15.1**

**Important U.S. Antitrust Laws**

**Vertical merger** A merger between firms at different stages of production of a good.

mergers between firms in the same industry. Horizontal mergers are more likely to increase market power than **vertical mergers**, which are mergers between firms at different stages of the production of a good. An example of a vertical merger would be a merger between a company making personal computers and a company making computer hard drives.

Two factors can complicate regulating horizontal mergers. First, the "market" that firms are in is not always clear. For example, if Hershey Foods wants to merge with Mars, Inc., maker of M&Ms, Snickers, and other candies, what is the relevant market? If the government looks just at the candy market, the newly merged company would have more than 70 percent of the market, a level at which the government would likely oppose the merger. What if the government looks at the broader market for snacks? In this market, Hershey and Mars compete with makers of potato chips, pretzels, and peanuts—and perhaps even producers of fresh fruit. Of course, if the government looked at the very broad market for food, then both Hershey and Mars have very small market shares, and there would be no reason to oppose their merger. In practice, the government defines the relevant market on the basis of whether there are close substitutes for the products being made by the merging firms. In this case, potato chips and the other snack foods mentioned are not close substitutes for candy. So, the government would consider the candy market to be the relevant market and would oppose the merger, on the grounds that the new firm would have too much market power.

The second factor that complicates merger policy is the possibility that the newly merged firm might be more efficient than the merging firms were individually. For example, one firm might have an excellent product but a poor distribution system for getting the product into the hands of consumers. A competing firm might have built a great distribution system but have an inferior product. Allowing these firms to merge might be good for both the firms and consumers. Or, two competing firms might each have an extensive system of warehouses that are only half full, but if the firms merged, they could consolidate their warehouses and significantly reduce their average costs.

Most of the mergers that come under scrutiny by the Department of Justice and the FTC are between large firms. For simplicity, though, let's consider a case in which all the firms in a perfectly competitive industry want to merge to form a monopoly. As we saw in Figure 15.5, as a result of this merger, prices will rise and output will fall, leading to a decline in consumer surplus and economic efficiency. But what if the larger, newly merged firm actually is more efficient than the smaller firms were? Figure 15.6 shows a possible result.

If costs aren't affected by the merger, we get the same result as in Figure 15.5: Price rises from $P_C$ to $P_M$, quantity falls from $Q_C$ to $Q_M$, consumer surplus is lower, and a loss of economic efficiency results. If the monopoly has lower costs than the competitive firms, it is possible for price to decline and quantity to increase. In Figure 15.6, note where $MR$ crosses $MC$ after the merger—this is the new profit-maximizing quantity,

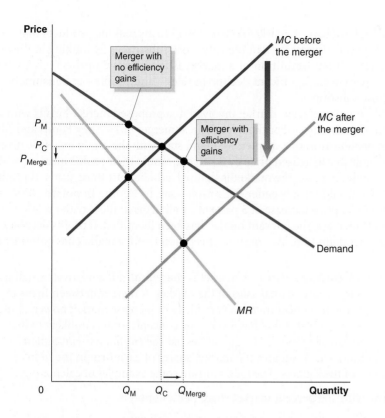

**Figure 15.6**

**A Merger That Makes Consumers Better Off**

This figure shows the result of all the firms in a perfectly competitive industry merging to form a monopoly. If costs are unaffected by the merger, the result is the same as in Figure 15.5 on page 501: Price rises from $P_C$ to $P_M$, quantity falls from $Q_C$ to $Q_M$, consumer surplus declines, and a loss of economic efficiency results. If, however, the monopoly has lower costs than the perfectly competitive firms, as shown by the marginal cost curve shifting to $MC$ after the merger, it is possible that the price will actually decline from $P_C$ to $P_{Merge}$ and that output will increase from $Q_C$ to $Q_{Merge}$ following the merger.

$Q_{Merge}$. The demand curve shows that the monopolist can sell this quantity at a price of $P_{Merge}$. Therefore, the price declines after the merger from $P_C$ to $P_{Merge}$, and quantity increases from $Q_C$ to $Q_{Merge}$. We have the following seemingly paradoxical result: *Although the newly merged firm has a great deal of market power, because it is more efficient, consumers are better off and economic efficiency is improved.* Of course, sometimes a merged firm will be more efficient and have lower costs, and other times it won't. Even if a merged firm is more efficient and has lower costs, that may not offset the increased market power of the firm enough to increase consumer surplus and economic efficiency.

As you might expect, whenever large firms propose a merger, they claim that the newly merged firm will be more efficient and have lower costs. They realize that without these claims, the Department of Justice and the FTC, along with the court system, are unlikely to approve the merger.

## The Department of Justice and FTC Merger Guidelines

For many years after the passage of the Sherman Act in 1890, lawyers from the Department of Justice enforced the antitrust laws. The lawyers rarely considered economic arguments, such as the possibility that consumers might be made better off by a merger if economic efficiency were significantly improved. This began to change in 1965, when Donald Turner became the first Ph.D. economist to head the Antitrust Division of the Department of Justice. Under Turner and his successors, economic analysis shaped antitrust policy. In 1973, the Economics Section of the Antitrust Division was established and staffed with economists who evaluate the economic consequences of proposed mergers.

Economists played a major role in the development of merger guidelines by the Department of Justice and the FTC in 1982. The guidelines made it easier for firms considering a merger to understand whether the government was likely to allow the merger or to oppose it. The guidelines were modified in 2010 and have three main parts:

1. Market definition
2. Measure of concentration
3. Merger standards

**Market Definition** A market consists of all firms making products that consumers view as close substitutes. We can identify close substitutes by looking at the effect of a price increase. If our definition of a market is too narrow, a price increase will cause firms to experience a significant decline in sales—and profits—as consumers switch to buying close substitutes.

Identifying the relevant market involved in a proposed merger begins with a narrow definition of the industry. For the hypothetical merger of Hershey Foods and Mars, Inc., discussed previously in this chapter, we might start with the candy industry. If all firms in the candy industry increased price by 5 percent, would their profits increase or decrease? If profits would increase, the market is defined as being just these firms. If profits would decrease, we would try a broader definition—say, by adding in potato chips and other snacks. Would a price increase of 5 percent by all firms in the broader market raise profits? If profits increase, the relevant market has been identified. If profits decrease, we consider a broader definition. We continue this process until a market has been identified.

**Measure of Concentration** A market is *concentrated* if a relatively small number of firms have a large share of total sales in the market. A merger between firms in a market that is already highly concentrated is very likely to increase market power. A merger between firms in an industry that has a very low concentration is unlikely to increase market power and can be ignored. The guidelines use the *Herfindahl-Hirschman Index (HHI)* of concentration, which squares the market shares of each firm in the industry and adds up the values of the squares. The following are some examples of calculating HHI:

- 1 firm, with 100 percent market share (a monopoly):

$$HHI = 100^2 = 10,000$$

- 2 firms, each with a 50 percent market share:

$$HHI = 50^2 + 50^2 = 5,000$$

- 4 firms, with market shares of 30 percent, 30 percent, 20 percent, and 20 percent:

$$HHI = 30^2 + 30^2 + 20^2 + 20^2 = 2,600$$

- 10 firms, each with market shares of 10 percent:

$$HHI = 10 \times (10^2) = 1,000$$

**Merger Standards** The Department of Justice and the FTC use the HHI calculation for a market to evaluate proposed horizontal mergers according to these standards:

- *Postmerger HHI below 1,500.* These markets are not concentrated, so mergers in them are not challenged.

- *Postmerger HHI between 1,500 and 2,500.* These markets are moderately concentrated. Mergers that raise the HHI by less than 100 probably will not be challenged. Mergers that raise the HHI by more than 100 may be challenged.

- *Postmerger HHI above 2,500.* These markets are highly concentrated. Mergers that increase the HHI by less than 100 points will not be challenged. Mergers that increase the HHI by 100 to 200 points may be challenged. Mergers that increase the HHI by more than 200 points will likely be challenged.

Increases in economic efficiency will be taken into account and can lead to approval of a merger that otherwise would be opposed, but the burden of showing that the efficiencies exist lies with the merging firms:

> The merging firms must substantiate efficiency claims so that the [Department of Justice and the FTC] can verify by reasonable means the likelihood and magnitude of each asserted efficiency. . . . Efficiency claims will not be considered if they are vague or speculative or otherwise cannot be verified by reasonable means.

# Making the Connection

## Should AT&T Have Been Allowed to Merge with T-Mobile?

In early 2011, AT&T agreed to buy T-Mobile from its parent firm Deutsche Telekom for $39 billion. AT&T is the second largest mobile wireless firm in the United States, and T-Mobile is the fourth largest. (In 2011, Verizon Wireless was the largest wireless firm, and Sprint Nextel was the third largest.) As we have seen, the two main ways that a merger between two large firms can increase the combined firm's profits are by (1) increasing market power so as to increase prices and (2) lowering costs through increased efficiency. The federal government may see the first motive as violating the antitrust laws, so firms typically emphasize the second motive. AT&T argued that the combined company, which would become the largest wireless firm in the United States, could operate at lower cost than could the companies operating separately. For instance, the two companies had 9,200 retail stores, but 41 percent of AT&T's stores had one or more T-Mobile stores within 1 mile. Closing hundreds of these stores would lower the combined company's costs. The combined company would also be able to reduce its technical and customer support staffs, among other savings. AT&T estimated the cost savings from the merger at $3 billion per year. In principle, these costs savings could lead to a situation like the one illustrated in Figure 15.6, where consumers benefit from a merger.

*The government didn't buy AT&T's argument that its purchase of T-Mobile would benefit consumers.*

AT&T needed to emphasize cost savings and efficiency gains because it was proposing a horizontal merger that would sharply increase concentration in the wireless industry. In fact, after studying the proposed merger for several months, the Antitrust Division of the Department of Justice filed a lawsuit to stop the merger. The government argued that the relevant market for judging the merger was the market for wireless services, because they argued that traditional landline telephones "are not regarded by consumers of mobile wireless telecommunications as reasonable substitutes." As a result, the government estimated that an increase in price by all mobile wireless companies would increase the companies' profits. In the national market, the merger would increase the HHI by nearly 700 points, from about 2,400 to about 3,100. Looking at just the market for wireless services purchased by businesses and the government, the HHI would increase from about 3,100 to about 3,400. In all of the 40 largest cities, the increase in HHI from the merger would be more than 200 points. These increases in HHI called the merger into question under the merger guidelines discussed earlier.

Despite these increases in HHI, the government might not have opposed the merger if it had accepted AT&T's argument that the merger would result in efficiencies that would lead to cost reductions. The government's merger guidelines state that the government will consider whether "efficiencies likely would be sufficient to reverse the merger's potential to harm customers in the relevant market . . . by preventing price increases in that market." However, the Antitrust Division's economists rejected AT&T's arguments that cost savings would offset the increased market power the newly merged firm would acquire. The government concluded, "Unless this acquisition is enjoined, customers of mobile wireless telecommunications services likely will face higher prices, less product variety and innovation, and poorer quality services due to reduced incentives to invest than would exist absent the merger."

The attempt by AT&T to merge with T-Mobile was shaping up as a classic antitrust case, with the firms involved arguing that the merger would increase economic efficiency and the government arguing that the reduction in price competition would more than offset the increase in efficiency.

Based on Thomas Catan and Spencer E. Ante, "U.S. Sues to Stop AT&T Deal," *Wall Street Journal*, September 1, 2011; Anton Troianovski, "T-Mobile Dealers Start to Hang Up," *Wall Street Journal*, June 23, 2011; Andrew Ross Sorkin, Michael J. De La Merced, and Jenna Wortham, "AT&T to Buy T-Mobile USA for $39 Billion," *New York Times*, March 20, 2011; and *United States v. AT&T Inc., T-Mobile USA, Inc., and Deutsche Telekom AG.*

**Your Turn:** Test your understanding by doing related related problem 5.15 on page 517 at the end of this chapter.

MyEconLab

**Regulating a Natural Monopoly**

A natural monopoly that is not subject to government regulation will charge a price equal to $P_M$ and produce $Q_M$. If government regulators want to achieve economic efficiency, they will set the regulated price equal to $P_E$, and the monopoly will produce $Q_E$. Unfortunately, $P_E$ is below average cost, and the monopoly will suffer a loss, shown by the shaded rectangle. Because the monopoly will not continue to produce in the long run if it suffers a loss, government regulators set a price equal to average cost, which is $P_R$ in the figure. The resulting production, $Q_R$, will be below the efficient level.

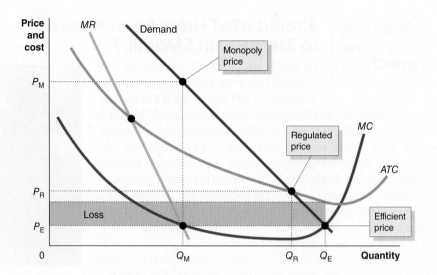

## Regulating Natural Monopolies

If a firm is a natural monopoly, competition from other firms will not play its usual role of forcing price down to the level where the company earns zero economic profit. As a result, local or state *regulatory commissions* usually set the prices for natural monopolies, such as firms selling natural gas or electricity. What price should these commissions set? Recall from Chapter 11 that economic efficiency requires the last unit of a good or service produced to provide an additional benefit to consumers equal to the additional cost of producing it. We can measure the additional benefit consumers receive from the last unit by the price, and we can measure the additional cost to the monopoly of producing the last unit by marginal cost. Therefore, to achieve economic efficiency, regulators should require that the monopoly charge a price equal to its marginal cost. There is, however, an important drawback to doing so, as illustrated in Figure 15.7, which shows the situation of a typical regulated natural monopoly.

Remember that with a natural monopoly, the average total cost curve is still falling when it crosses the demand curve. If unregulated, the monopoly will charge a price equal to $P_M$ and produce $Q_M$. To achieve economic efficiency, regulators should require the monopoly to charge a price equal to $P_E$. The monopoly will then produce $Q_E$. But here is the drawback: $P_E$ is less than average total cost, so the monopoly will be suffering a loss, shown by the area of the red-shaded rectangle. In the long run, the owners of the monopoly will not continue in business if they are experiencing losses. Realizing this, most regulators will set the regulated price, $P_R$, equal to the level of average total cost at which the demand curve intersects the *ATC* curve. At that price, the owners of the monopoly are able to break even on their investment by producing the quantity $Q_R$, although this quantity is below the efficient quantity, $Q_E$.

Continued from page 487

## Economics in Your Life

### Why Can't I Watch the NFL Network?

At the beginning of the chapter, we asked why some cable systems don't carry the NFL Network. You might think that the cable systems would want to televise one of the most popular sports in the nation. In most cities, a customer of a cable system can't switch to a competing cable system, so in many areas, the cable system may be the sole source of many programs. (Although some consumers have the option of switching to satellite television.) As a result, a cable system can increase its profits by, for example, not offering popular programming such as the NFL Network as part of its normal programming package, requiring instead that consumers upgrade to digital programming at a higher price.

# Conclusion

The more intense the level of competition among firms, the better a market works. In this chapter, we have seen that, compared with perfect competition, in a monopoly, the price of a good or a service is higher, output is lower, and consumer surplus and economic efficiency are reduced. Fortunately, true monopolies are rare. Even though most firms resemble monopolies in being able to charge a price above marginal cost, most markets have enough competition to keep the efficiency losses from market power low.

We've seen that barriers to entry are an important source of market power. Read *An Inside Look at Policy* on the next page for a discussion of the entry of Verizon into the market for cable TV in upstate New York to compete with Time Warner Cable.

# The End of the Cable TV Monopoly?

## TIMESUNION.COM

## Cable Fight Heats Up

Verizon is quickly making Schenectady County ground zero for the rollout of its FiOS TV service that competes with Time Warner Cable.

The village of Scotia was the first local municipality to strike a cable TV franchise deal with the New York City telecommunications giant.

And now Schenectady is poised to be the first major city in the region where FiOS TV will be available.

The Schenectady City Council will hold a public hearing on the plan Monday and could approve a franchise during its meeting that night. After approval of the franchise by the state Public Service Commission, Verizon would be able to start selling cable TV in the city, along with its FiOS Internet and phone products, which are currently available only in certain parts of the Capital Region.

**a** "Competition is good," said Chuck Steiner, president of The Chamber of Schenectady County. "The fact that they have chosen Schenectady County is very good for us as a community. It offers another option."

Time Warner has had a virtual monopoly on cable TV service and in most cases is the only company holding cable TV franchises in local municipalities.

**b** But several years ago Verizon began building its FiOS network to compete with local cable companies in the Northeast. It has slowly been negotiating franchises across the state, a process that is painstaking and also expensive because the agreements usually require Verizon to build out its system to the majority of citizens in a town or city within several years.

Verizon has also targeted Albany County—although not Albany city— and has gotten franchise agreements from the town of Bethlehem and the village of Colonie.

The towns of Guilderland and Colonie are next in line. The Guilderland town board will hold a public hearing Tuesday for the Verizon plan.

Guilderland Supervisor Ken Runion said the hearing was originally planned for earlier this month, but one of the recent snow storms prevented the necessary legal notice from being published on time.

Verizon spokesman John Bonomo said that discussions with the town of Colonie have progressed to the point that the town board is expected to discuss FiOS next month.

Bonomo has said that places like Bethlehem and Scotia that have already gotten PSC approval should see FiOS TV rolled out by the end of March. It's likely, though, that places like Guilderland and Schenectady won't get TV service until later in the spring, after the PSC approves their franchises as well.

**c** Verizon hasn't said how much FiOS TV will cost or how much its bundles of TV, Internet and phone will cost. However, Verizon is advertising its three-product bundle for under $85 a month on its website, which is less than Time Warner's current deal of $99 a month for new customers.

*Source:* "Cable fight heats up: Verizon pushes FiOS service in Schenectady to compete with Time Warner Cable," Times Union, February 24, 2011. Copyright © 2011 Times Union. Reprinted by permission.

# Key Points in the Article

Until 2011, Time Warner Cable had a virtual monopoly on cable TV services in upstate New York, and was the only company to hold cable TV franchises in most local communities in the region. Verizon has been constructing its FiOS fiber-optic network in the Northeast over the past several years while also negotiating franchise deals with local municipalities throughout New York State. Although the company is not yet publicly stating pricing for its services, Verizon's Web site lists a bundle price for TV, Internet, and home phone below what Time Warner charges.

## Analyzing the News

(a) The first major city in upstate New York scheduled to receive access to the Verizon TV service is Schenectady. This came as welcome news to Chuck Steiner, president of The Chamber of Schenectady County. Steiner acknowledged the benefit to the community of having an additional option beyond Time Warner for cable TV service. With approval of additional community franchises by the state Public Services Commission (PSC), Verizon expected to continue its expansion in the region throughout 2011.

(b) The process of entering a cable market is time-consuming and expensive. In addition to receiving franchise approval from individual communities and the PSC, the franchise agreements generally require Verizon to install fiber-optic connections to a majority of residents within each community it intends to serve. The necessary time and expense for a company to establish such services are significant barriers to entry and help explain why very few companies compete in the market for cable TV service.

(c) Verizon's Web site lists a monthly price for its three-product bundle of TV, Internet, and phone of $85, which is $14 less than Time Warner's new customer package of $99. As we learned in the chapter, barriers to entry enable a monopoly firm to retain the profits it earns, but when a competitor is able to enter the market, we would expect the profits of the original monopoly firm to decrease. The figure below illustrates what happens if entry results in the market becoming perfectly competitive. For simplicity, we assume that the marginal cost of providing cable services is constant, so the marginal cost curve is a horizontal line. Notice that with entry, output increases from $Q_M$ to $Q_C$, and price falls from $P_M$ to $P_C$. You can also see that consumer surplus

increases from areas $A + E$ to areas $A + E + B + C + D$, and the deadweight loss in the market (area $D$) is turned into consumer surplus. What were profits for the monopoly (areas $B + C$) are redistributed to consumers as consumer surplus. Economic profits fall to zero, and consumers benefit by paying a lower price. Unlike the example in the figure, the actual market for cable TV service in upstate New York does not become perfectly competitive with the entry of Verizon. However, consumers still benefit by receiving increased consumer surplus with the new, lower price option offered by Verizon and the probable matching of this lower price by Time Warner.

## Thinking Critically about Policy

1. Some cities require cable firms to pay a franchise fee in order to provide cable television services. What is the most a firm would be willing to pay as a franchise fee to be the sole provider of cable television in a market?

2. Would entry into the cable TV market in upstate New York ever be great enough to change the market to a perfectly competitive one (as we assume happens in the figure), with the price falling to $P_C$?

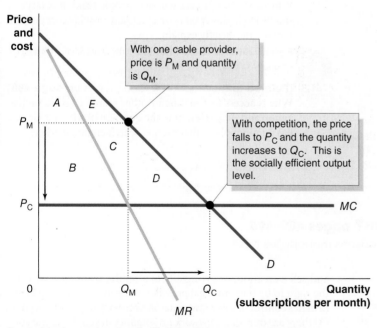

Competition lowers the price of cable TV and increases economic efficiency.

# Chapter Summary and Problems

## Key Terms

---

 **15.1** **Is Any Firm Ever Really a Monopoly?** pages 488–489

LEARNING OBJECTIVE: Define *monopoly*.

## Summary

A **monopoly** exists only in the rare situation in which a firm is producing a good or service for which there are no close substitutes. A narrow definition of monopoly that some economists use is that a firm has a monopoly if it can ignore the actions of all other firms. Many economists favor a broader definition of monopoly. Under the broader definition, a firm has a monopoly if no other firms are selling a substitute close enough that the firm's economic profits are competed away in the long run.

MyEconLab    Visit **www.myeconlab.com** to complete these exercises online and get instant feedback.

## Review Questions

**1.1** What is a monopoly? Can a firm be a monopoly if close substitutes for its product exist?

**1.2** If you own the only hardware store in a small town, do you have a monopoly?

**1.3** Is monopoly a good name for the game *Monopoly*? What aspects of the game involve monopoly? Explain briefly, using the definition of monopoly.

## Problems and Applications

**1.4** The great baseball player Ty Cobb was known for being very thrifty. Near the end of his life, he was interviewed by a reporter who was surprised to find that Cobb used candles, rather than electricity, to light his home. From Ty Cobb's point of view, was the local electric company a monopoly?

**1.5** **[Related to the** Chapter Opener **on page 487]** Some observers say that changes in the past few years have eroded the monopoly power of local cable TV companies, even if no other cable firms have entered their markets. What are these changes? Do these "monopoly" firms still have monopoly power?

**1.6** Are there any products for which there are no substitutes? Are these the only products for which it would be possible to have a monopoly? Briefly explain.

**1.7** **[Related to the** Making the Connection **on page 488]** A newspaper article has the headline "Google Says It's Actually Quite Small." According to the article:

> Google rejects the idea that it's in the search advertising business, an industry in which it holds more than a 70 percent share of revenue. Instead, the company says its competition is all advertising, a category broad enough to include newspaper, radio and highway billboards.

Why does Google care whether people think it is large or small? Do highway billboards actually provide competition for Google? Briefly explain.

From Jeff Horwitz, "Google Says It's Actually Quite Small," *Washington Post*, June 7, 2009.

**1.8** **[Related to the** Making the Connection **on page 488]** Why is access to YouTube by other search engines such as Yahoo and Bing relevant to the question of whether Google has a monopoly in the Internet search engine market?

---

 **15.2** **Where Do Monopolies Come From?** pages 489–495

LEARNING OBJECTIVE: Explain the four main reasons monopolies arise.

## Summary

To have a monopoly, barriers to entering the market must be so high that no other firms can enter. Barriers to entry may be high enough to keep out competing firms for four main reasons: (1) A government blocks the entry of more than one firm into a market by issuing a **patent**, which is the exclusive right to make a product for 20 years, or a **copyright**, which is the exclusive right to produce and sell a creation, or giving a firm a **public franchise**, which is the right to be the only legal provider of a good or service; (2) one firm has control of a key raw material necessary to produce a good; (3) there are important *network externalities* in supplying the good or service; or (4) economies of scale are so large that one firm has a *natural monopoly*. **Network externalities** refer to the situation where the usefulness of a product increases with the number of consumers who use it. A **natural monopoly** is a situation in which economies of scale are so large that one firm can supply the entire market at a lower average cost than can two or more firms.

## Review Questions

**2.1** What are the four most important ways a firm becomes a monopoly?

**2.2** If patents reduce competition, why does the federal government grant them?

**2.3** What is a public franchise? Are all public franchises natural monopolies?

**2.4** What is "natural" about a natural monopoly?

## Problems and Applications

**2.5** The U.S. Postal Service (USPS) is a monopoly because the federal government has blocked entry into the market for delivering first-class mail. Is the USPS also a natural monopoly? How can we tell? What would happen if the law preventing competition in this market were removed?

**2.6** Patents are granted for 20 years, but pharmaceutical companies can't use their patent-guaranteed monopoly powers for anywhere near this long because it takes several years to acquire FDA approval of drugs. Should the life of drug patents be extended to 20 years *after* FDA approval? What would be the costs and benefits of such an extension?

**2.7** Just as a new product or a new method of making a product receives patent protection from the government, books, articles, and essays receive copyright protection. Under U.S. law, authors have the exclusive right to their writings during their lifetimes—unless they sell this right, as most authors do to their publishers—and their heirs retain this exclusive right for 70 years after their death. The historian Thomas Macaulay once described the copyright law as "a

tax on readers to give a bounty to authors." In what sense does the existence of the copyright law impose a tax on readers? What "bounty" do copyright laws give authors? Discuss whether the government would be doing readers a favor by abolishing the copyright law.

Quote from Thomas Mallon, *Stolen Words: The Classic Book on Plagiarism*, [Boston: Houghton Mifflin Harcourt, 2001 (original ed. 1989)], p. 59.

**2.8** If firms incurred no cost in developing new technologies and new products, would there be any need for patents? Briefly explain.

**2.9** The German company Koenig & Bauer has 90 percent of the world market for presses that print currency. Discuss the factors that would make it difficult for new companies to enter this market.

**2.10** **[Related to the** Making the Connection **on page 490]** Would the Ecke family have been better off if it had patented its process for growing poinsettias? Briefly explain.

**2.11** **[Related to the** Making the Connection **on page 492]** Why was De Beers worried that people might resell their old diamonds? How did De Beers attempt to convince consumers that used diamonds were not good substitutes for new diamonds? How did De Beers's strategy affect the demand curve for new diamonds? How did De Beers's strategy affect its profits?

**2.12** **[Related to** Solved Problem 15.2 **on page 494]** Suppose that the quantity demanded per day for a product is 90 when the price is $35. The following table shows costs for a firm with a monopoly in this market:

| Quantity (per Day) | Total Cost |
| --- | --- |
| 30 | $1,200 |
| 40 | 1,400 |
| 50 | 2,250 |
| 60 | 3,000 |

Briefly explain whether this firm has a natural monopoly in this market.

---

<table><tr><td>**15.3**</td><td>**How Does a Monopoly Choose Price and Output?** pages 496–499<br>LEARNING OBJECTIVE: Explain how a monopoly chooses price and output.</td></tr></table>

## Summary

Monopolists face downward-sloping demand and marginal revenue curves and, like all other firms, maximize profit by producing where marginal revenue equals marginal cost. Unlike a perfect competitor, a monopolist that earns economic profits does not face the entry of new firms into the market. Therefore, a monopolist can earn economic profits even in the long run.

## Review Questions

**3.1** What is the relationship between a monopolist's demand curve and the market demand curve? What is the relationship between a monopolist's demand curve and its marginal revenue curve?

**3.2** In what sense is a monopolist a *price maker*?

**3.3** Draw a graph that shows a monopolist earning a profit. Be sure your graph includes the monopolist's demand, marginal revenue, average total cost, and marginal cost curves. Be sure to indicate the profit-maximizing level of output and price.

# Problems and Applications

**3.4** **[Related to** Solved Problem 15.3 **on page 498]** Ed Scahill has acquired a monopoly on the production of baseballs (don't ask how) and faces the demand and cost situation shown in the following table:

| Price | Quantity (per week) | Total Revenue | Marginal Revenue | Total Cost | Marginal Cost |
|-------|---------------------|---------------|------------------|------------|---------------|
| $20 | 15,000 | | | $330,000 | |
| 19 | 20,000 | | | 365,000 | |
| 18 | 25,000 | | | 405,000 | |
| 17 | 30,000 | | | 450,000 | |
| 16 | 35,000 | | | 500,000 | |
| 15 | 40,000 | | | 555,000 | |

a. Fill in the remaining values in the table.

b. If Scahill wants to maximize profits, what price should he charge, and how many baseballs should he sell? How much profit (or loss) will he make? Draw a graph to illustrate your answer. Your graph should be clearly labeled and should include: Scahill's demand, *ATC*, *AVC*, *AFC*, *MC*, and *MR* curves, the price he is charging, the quantity he is producing, and the area representing his profit (or loss).

c. Suppose the government imposes a tax of $50,000 per week on baseball production. Now what price should Scahill charge, how many baseballs should he sell, and what will his profit (or loss) be?

d. Suppose that the government raises the tax in part c. to $70,000. Now what price should Scahill charge, how many baseballs should he sell, and what will his profit (or loss) be? Will his decision on what price to charge and how much to produce be different in the short run than in the long run? Briefly explain.

**3.5** **[Related to** Solved Problem 15.3 **on page 498]** Use the information in Solved Problem 15.3 to answer the following questions.

a. What will Comcast do if the tax is $6.00 per month instead of $2.50? (*Hint:* Will its decision be different in the long run than in the short run?)

b. Suppose that the flat per-month tax is replaced with a tax on the firm of $0.50 per cable subscriber. Now how many subscriptions should Comcast sell if it wants to

maximize profit? What price should it charge? What is its profit? (Assume that Comcast will sell only the quantities listed in the table.)

**3.6** Before inexpensive pocket calculators were developed, many science and engineering students used slide rules to make numerical calculations. Slide rules are no longer produced, which means nothing prevents you from establishing a monopoly in the slide rule market. Draw a graph showing the situation your slide rule firm would be in. Be sure to include on your graph your demand, marginal revenue, average total cost, and marginal cost curves. Indicate the price you would charge and the quantity you would produce. Are you likely to make a profit or a loss? Show this area on your graph.

**3.7** Does a monopolist have a supply curve? Briefly explain. (*Hint:* Look again at the definition of a supply curve in Chapter 3 on page 78 and consider whether this applies to a monopolist.)

**3.8** **[Related to the** Don't Let This Happen to You **on page 499]** A student argues, "If a monopolist finds a way of producing a good at lower cost, he will not lower his price. Because he is a monopolist, he will keep the price and the quantity the same and just increase his profit." Do you agree? Use a graph to illustrate your answer.

**3.9** When home builders construct a new housing development, they usually sell to a single cable television company the rights to lay cable. As a result, anyone buying a home in that development is not able to choose between competing cable companies. Some cities have begun to ban such exclusive agreements. Williams Township, Pennsylvania, decided to allow any cable company to lay cable in the utility trenches of new housing developments. The head of the township board of supervisors argued, "What I would like to see and do is give the consumers a choice. If there's no choice, then the price [of cable] is at the whim of the provider." In a situation in which the consumers in a housing development have only one cable company available, is the price really at the whim of the company? Would a company in this situation be likely to charge, say, $500 per month for basic cable services? Briefly explain why or why not.

From Sam Kennedy, "Williams Township May Ban Exclusive Cable Provider Pacts," (*Allentown, Pennsylvania*) *Morning Call*, November 5, 2004.

**3.10** Will a monopoly that maximizes profit also be maximizing revenue? Will it be maximizing production? Briefly explain.

---

| **15.4** | **Does Monopoly Reduce Economic Efficiency?** pages 500–503 |
|----------|-----------------------------------------------------------|

LEARNING OBJECTIVE: Use a graph to illustrate how a monopoly affects economic efficiency.

## Summary

Compared with a perfectly competitive industry, a monopoly charges a higher price and produces less, which reduces consumer surplus and economic efficiency. Some loss of economic efficiency will occur whenever firms have **market power** and can charge a price greater than marginal cost. The total loss of economic efficiency in the U.S. economy due to market power is small, however,

because true monopolies are very rare. In most industries, competition will keep price much closer to marginal cost than would be the case in a monopoly.

MyEconLab Visit **www.myeconlab.com** to complete these exercises online and get instant feedback.

## Review Questions

**4.1** Suppose that a perfectly competitive industry becomes a monopoly. Describe the effects of this change on consumer surplus, producer surplus, and deadweight loss.

**4.2** Explain why market power leads to a deadweight loss. Is the total deadweight loss from market power for the economy large or small?

## Problems and Applications

**4.3** Review Figure 15.5 on page 501 on the inefficiency of monopoly. Will the deadweight loss due to monopoly be larger if the demand is elastic or if it is inelastic? Briefly explain.

**4.4** Economist Harvey Leibenstein argued that the loss of economic efficiency in industries that are not perfectly competitive has been understated. He argued that when competition is weak, firms are under less pressure to adopt the best techniques or to hold down their costs. He referred to this effect as "x-inefficiency." If x-inefficiency causes a firm's marginal costs to rise, show that the deadweight loss in Figure 15.5 understates the true deadweight loss caused by a monopoly.

**4.5** Most cities own the water system that provides water to homes and businesses. Some cities charge a flat monthly fee, while other cities charge by the gallon. Which method of pricing is more likely to result in economic efficiency in the water market? Be sure to refer to the definition of *economic efficiency* in your answer. Why do you think the same method of pricing isn't used by all cities?

**4.6** Review the concept of externalities on page 138 in Chapter 5. If a market is a monopoly, will a negative externality in production always lead to production beyond the level of economic efficiency? Use a graph to illustrate your answer.

---

**15.5** **Government Policy toward Monopoly, pages 503–509**
LEARNING OBJECTIVE: Discuss government policies toward monopoly.

## Summary

Because monopolies reduce consumer surplus and economic efficiency, most governments regulate monopolies. Firms that are not monopolies have an incentive to avoid competition by **colluding**, or agreeing to charge the same price or otherwise not to compete. In the United States, **antitrust laws** are aimed at deterring monopoly, eliminating collusion, and promoting competition among firms. The Antitrust Division of the U.S. Department of Justice and the Federal Trade Commission share responsibility for enforcing the antitrust laws, including regulating mergers between firms. A **horizontal merger** is a merger between firms in the same industry. A **vertical merger** is a merger between firms at different stages of production of a good. Local governments regulate the prices charged by natural monopolies.

MyEconLab    Visit **www.myeconlab.com** to complete these exercises online and get instant feedback.

## Review Questions

**5.1** What is the purpose of the antitrust laws? Who is in charge of enforcing these laws?

**5.2** What is the difference between a horizontal merger and a vertical merger? Which type of merger is more likely to increase the market power of a newly merged firm?

**5.3** Why would it be economically efficient to require a natural monopoly to charge a price equal to marginal cost? Why do most regulatory agencies require natural monopolies to charge a price equal to average cost instead?

## Problems and Applications

**5.4** Use the following graph for a monopoly to answer the questions:

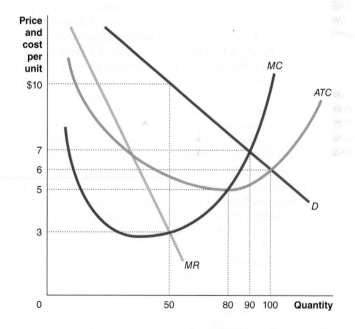

a. What quantity will the monopoly produce, and what price will the monopoly charge?

b. Suppose the monopoly is regulated. If the regulatory agency wants to achieve economic efficiency, what price should it require the monopoly to charge? How much output will the monopoly produce at this price? Will the monopoly make a profit if it charges this price? Briefly explain.

**5.5** Use the graph for a monopoly on the next page to answer the questions:

a. What quantity will the monopoly produce, and what price will the monopoly charge?

b. Suppose the government decides to regulate this monopoly and imposes a price ceiling of $18 (in other

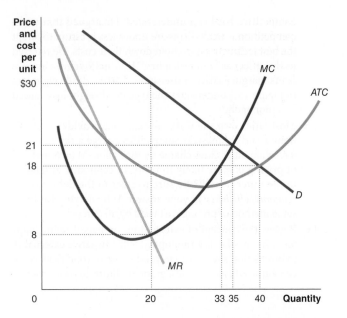

Petzinger, Jr., *Hard Landing: The Epic Contest for Power and Profits that Plunged the Airline Industry into Chaos*, (New York: Random House, 1995), pp. 149–150.

**5.9** Before they merged in 2008, Sirius Satellite Radio and XM Satellite Radio were the only two satellite radio firms. In announcing that it would not oppose the merger, the Justice Department said that "evidence developed in the investigation did not support defining a market limited to the two satellite radio firms." It believed that the two firms also competed with "other sources of audio entertainment, including traditional AM/FM radio, HD Radio, MP3 players (e.g., iPods), and audio offerings delivered through wireless telephones." Why would defining the size of the market in which the two firms competed be important to the Justice Department in deciding whether to oppose the merger?

Based on Department of Justice, "Statement of the Department of Justice's Antitrust Division on Its Decision to Close Its Investigation of XM Satellite Radio Holdings Inc.'s Merger with Sirius Satellite Radio Inc.," March 24, 2008.

**5.10** Look again at the section "The Department of Justice and FTC Merger Guidelines," which begins on page 505. Evaluate the following situations.

**a.** A market initially has 20 firms, each with a 5 percent market share. Of the firms, 4 propose to merge, leaving a total of 17 firms in the industry. Are the Department of Justice and the FTC likely to oppose the merger? Briefly explain.

**b.** A market initially has 5 firms, each with a 20 percent market share. Of the firms, 2 propose to merge, leaving a total of 4 firms in the industry. Are the Department of Justice and the Federal Trade Commission likely to oppose the merger? Briefly explain.

**5.11** In October 2008, Delta Air Lines completed its acquisition of Northwest Airlines. The newly merged company is the largest airline in the world. The following statement regarding the merger is from a Justice Department press release:

> After a thorough, six-month investigation, during which the [Antitrust] Division obtained extensive information from a wide range of market participants—including the companies, other airlines, corporate customers and travel agents—the Division has determined that the proposed merger between Delta and Northwest is likely to produce substantial and credible efficiencies that will benefit U.S. consumers and is not likely to substantially lessen competition.

What does the Justice Department mean by "substantial and credible efficiencies," and how might they benefit U.S. consumers? Why would a merger between two large airlines not be "likely to substantially lessen competition"?

Based on Andrew Ross Sorkin, "Regulators Approve Delta–Northwest Merger," *New York Times*, October 30, 2008; and Department of Justice, "Statement of the Department of Justice's Antitrust Division on Its Decision to Close Its Investigation of the Merger of Delta Air Lines Inc. and Northwest Airlines Corporation," October 29, 2008.

**5.12** The table on the next page shows the market shares during the last three months of 2010 for companies in the U.S.

words, the monopoly can charge less than $18 but can't charge more). Now what quantity will the monopoly produce, and what price will the monopoly charge? Will every consumer who is willing to pay this price be able to buy the product? Briefly explain.

**5.6** Consider the natural monopoly shown in Figure 15.7 on page 508. Assume that the government regulatory agency sets the regulated price, $P_R$, at the level of average total cost at which the demand curve intersects the *ATC* curve. If the firm knows that it will always be able to charge a price equal to its average total cost, does it have an incentive to reduce its average cost? Briefly explain.

**5.7** Draw a graph like Figure 15.6 on page 505 that shows a merger lowering costs. On your graph, show producer surplus and consumer surplus before a merger and consumer surplus and producer surplus after a merger.

**5.8** The following phone call took place in February 1982 between Robert Crandall, the chief executive officer of American Airlines, and Howard Putnam, the chief executive officer of Braniff Airways. Although Crandall didn't know it, Putnam was recording the call:

> **Crandall:** I think it's dumb . . . to sit here and pound the (obscenity) out of each other and neither one of us making a (obscenity) dime . . .
>
> **Putnam:** Do you have a suggestion for me?
>
> **Crandall:** Yes, I have a suggestion for you. Raise your . . . fares 20 percent. I'll raise mine the next morning.
>
> **Putnam:** Robert, we . . .
>
> **Crandall:** You'll make more money and I will, too.
>
> **Putnam:** We can't talk about pricing.
>
> **Crandall:** Oh (obscenity), Howard. We can talk about any . . . thing we want to talk about.

Who had a better understanding of antitrust law, Crandall or Putnam? Briefly explain.

Based on Mark Potts, "American Airlines Charged with Seeking a Monopoly," *Washington Post*, February 24, 1983; "Blunt Talk on the Phone," *New York Times*, February 24, 1983; and Thomas

personal computer (PC) market, which includes desk-based PCs, mobile PCs, such as mini-notebooks, but not media tablets, such as the iPad:

| Company | Market Share |
| --- | --- |
| Hewlett-Packard | 29% |
| Dell | 22 |
| Acer | 11 |
| Toshiba | 10 |
| Apple | 10 |
| Other | 18 |

Use the information in the section "The Department of Justice and FTC Merger Guidelines," which begins on page 505, to predict whether the Department of Justice and the FTC would be likely to oppose a merger between any of the five firms listed in the table. Assume that "Other" in the table consists of six firms, each of which has approximately a 3 percent share of the market.

Market share data from Gartner, Inc., www.gartner.com.

**5.13** The following table gives the market shares of the companies in the U.S. carbonated soft drink industry during 2008:

| Company | Market Share |
| --- | --- |
| Coca-Cola | 42% |
| PepsiCo | 30 |
| Dr Pepper Snapple | 16 |
| Other | 12 |

Use the information in the section "The Department of Justice and FTC Merger Guidelines," which begins on page 505, to predict whether the Department of Justice and the FTC would be likely to oppose a merger between any two of the three companies listed. Does your answer depend on how many companies are included in the "Other" category? Briefly explain.

Based on Andrew Ross Sorkin, "Dr. Pepper Snapple Bows to Lukewarm Reception," *New York Times*, May 8, 2008.

**5.14** According to a column in the *New York Times* by Austan Goolsbee of the University of Chicago, the French National Assembly approved a bill:

> . . . that would require Apple Computer to crack open the software codes of its iTunes music store and let the files work on players other than the iPod. . . . If the French gave away the codes, Apple would lose much of its rationale for improving iTunes.

**a.** Why would Apple no longer want to improve iTunes if its software codes were no longer secret?

**b.** Why would the French government believe it was a good idea to require Apple to make the codes public?

Based on Austan Goolsbee, "In iTunes War, France Has Met the Enemy. Perhaps It Is France," *New York Times*, April 27, 2006.

**5.15** **[Related to the** Making the Connection **on page 507]** The U.S. Department of Justice stated that it looked seriously at the benefits AT&T and T-Mobile described in their proposed merger. The Department of Justice concluded, however, that AT&T did not demonstrate that the deal "promised any efficiencies that would be sufficient to outweigh the transaction's substantial adverse impact on competition and consumers." What types of efficiencies could the proposed merger produce? What adverse effect could the proposed merger have on competition and consumers?

Based on Grant Gross, "Justice Department Wants AT&T, T-Mobile Merger Blocked," *PCWorld.com*, August 31, 2011.

# 16 Pricing Strategy

## Chapter Outline and Learning Objectives

# Getting into Walt Disney World: One Price Does Not Fit All

When you visit Walt Disney World in Florida, your age, home address, and occupation can determine how much you pay for admission. In 2011, the price for a one-day ticket for an adult was $90.53. The same ticket for a child, aged three to nine, was $84.14. Children under three were free. Adult Florida residents paid $81.47. Students at the University of Central Florida paid $57. Active members of the military paid $85. Why does Disney charge so many different prices for the same product?

In previous chapters, we assumed that firms charge all consumers the same price for a given product. In reality, many firms charge customers different prices, based on differences in their willingness to pay for the product. Firms often face complicated pricing problems. For example, the Walt Disney Company faces the problem of determining the profit-maximizing prices to charge different groups of consumers for admission to its Disneyland and Walt Disney World theme parks.

In the early 1950s, most amusement parks were collections of unrelated rides, such as roller coasters and Ferris wheels. Founder Walt Disney believed that a theme park, with attractions that emphasized storytelling over thrills, would be more appealing to families than were amusement parks. Disney hired an economist to evaluate the feasibility of such a park. Managers of existing parks gave this advice to the economist: "Tell your boss . . . to stick to what he knows and leave the amusement business to people who know it." Eventually, Disney convinced the ABC television network to provide funding in exchange for his providing them with a weekly television program.

When Disneyland opened in 1955, Disney decided to charge a low price—$1 for adults and $0.50 for children—for admission into the park and also to charge for tickets to the rides. This system of separate charges for admission and for the rides continued until the early 1980s. Today, Disney charges a high price for admission to Disneyland and Walt Disney World, but once a customer is in the park, the rides are free. In this chapter, we will study some common pricing strategies, and we will see how Disney and other firms use these strategies to increase their profits.

**AN INSIDE LOOK** on **page 538** discusses a two-part pricing strategy the University of Kansas has implemented for purchasing select season tickets to Jayhawks' football games.

Based on Disney World prices from mousesavers.com, September 1, 2011; Harrison Price, *Walt's Revolution! By the Numbers*, (Ripley Entertainment, Inc., 2004), p. 31; and Bruce Gordon and David Mumford, *Disneyland: The Nickel Tour*, (Santa Clarita, CA: Camphor Tree Publishers, 2000), pp. 174–175.

## Economics in Your Life

### Why So Many Prices to See a Movie?

Think about the movie theaters in your area. How much do you, as a student, pay to get into a theater? Would your parents pay the same amount? What about your grandparents? How about your little brother or sister? Is the price the same in the evening as in the afternoon? Why do you suppose movie theaters charge different prices to different groups of consumers?

If you buy popcorn at the movie theater, you pay the same price as everyone else. Why do you suppose people in certain age groups get a discount on movie admission but not on movie popcorn? As you read the chapter, see if you can answer these questions. You can check your answers against those we provide **on page 536** at the end of this chapter.

I n previous chapters, we saw that entrepreneurs continually seek out economic profit. Using pricing strategies is one way firms can attempt to increase their economic profit. One of these strategies, called *price discrimination*, involves firms setting different prices for the same good or service, as Disney does when setting admission prices at Walt Disney World. In Chapter 15, we analyzed the situation of a monopolist setting a single price for its product. In this chapter, we will see how a firm can increase its profits by charging a higher price to consumers who value the good more and a lower price to consumers who value the good less.

We will also analyze the widely used strategies of *odd pricing* and *cost-plus pricing*. Finally, we will analyze situations in which firms are able to charge consumers one price for the right to buy a good and a second price for each unit of the good purchased. Disney's old pricing scheme of charging for admission to Disney World and also charging for each ride is an example of a situation economists call a *two-part tariff*.

**16.1 LEARNING** OBJECTIVE

Define the law of one price and explain the role of arbitrage.

# Pricing Strategy, the Law of One Price, and Arbitrage

We saw in the chapter opener that sometimes firms can increase their profits by charging different prices for the same good. In fact, many firms rely on economic analysis to practice *price discrimination* by charging higher prices to some customers and lower prices to others. Some firms practice a sophisticated form of price discrimination in which they use technology to gather information on the preferences of consumers and their responsiveness to changes in prices. Managers use the information to rapidly adjust the prices of their goods and services. This practice of rapidly adjusting prices, called *yield management*, has been particularly important to airlines and hotels. There are limits, though, to the ability of firms to charge different prices for the same product. The key limit is the possibility in some circumstances that consumers who can buy a good at a low price will resell it to consumers who would otherwise have to buy at a high price.

## Arbitrage

According to the *law of one price*, identical products should sell for the same price everywhere. Let's explore why the law of one price usually holds true. Suppose that an Apple iPad sells for $499 in stores in Atlanta and for $429 in stores in San Francisco. Anyone who lives in San Francisco could buy iPads for $429 and resell them for $499 in Atlanta. They could sell them on eBay or Craigslist or ship them to someone they know in Atlanta who could sell them in local flea markets. Buying a product in one market at a low price and reselling it in another market at a high price is referred to as *arbitrage*. The profits received from engaging in arbitrage are referred to as *arbitrage profits*.

As the supply of iPads in Atlanta increases, the price of iPads in Atlanta will decline, and as the supply of iPads in San Francisco decreases, the price of iPads in San Francisco will rise. Eventually the arbitrage process will eliminate most, but not all, of the price difference. Some price difference will remain because sellers must pay to list iPads on eBay or to ship them to Atlanta. The costs of carrying out a transaction—by, for example, listing items on eBay and shipping them across the country—are called **transactions costs**. The law of one price holds exactly *only if transactions costs are zero*. As we will soon see, in cases in which it is impossible to resell a product, the law of one price will not hold, and firms will be able to practice price discrimination. Apart from this important qualification, we expect that arbitrage will result in a product selling for the same price everywhere.

**Transactions costs** The costs in time and other resources that parties incur in the process of agreeing to and carrying out an exchange of goods or services.

# Solved Problem 16.1

## Is Arbitrage Just a Rip-off?

People are often suspicious of arbitrage. Buying something at a low price and reselling it at a high price exploits the person buying at the high price. Or does it? Is this view correct?

If so, do the auctions on eBay serve any useful economic purpose?

## Solving the Problem

**Step 1:** **Review the chapter material.** This problem is about arbitrage, so you may want to review the section "Arbitrage" on page 520. If necessary, also review the discussion of the benefits from trade in Chapters 2 and 9.

**Step 2:** **Use the discussion of arbitrage and the discussion in earlier chapters of the benefits from trade to answer the questions.** Many of the goods on eBay have been bought at a low price and are being resold at a higher price. In fact, some people supplement their incomes by buying collectibles and other goods at garage sales and reselling them on eBay. Does eBay serve a useful economic purpose? Economists would say that it does. Consider the case of Lou, who buys collectible movie posters and resells them on eBay. Suppose Lou buys an *Avengers* poster at a garage sale for $30 and resells it on eBay for $60. Both the person who sold to Lou at the garage sale and the person who bought from him on eBay must have been made better off by the deals *or they would not have made them.* Lou has performed the useful service of locating the poster and making it available for sale on eBay. In carrying out this service, Lou has incurred costs, including the opportunity cost of his time spent searching garage sales, the opportunity cost of the funds he has tied up in posters he has purchased but not yet sold, and the cost of the fees eBay charges him. It is easy to sell goods on eBay, so over time, competition among Lou and other movie poster dealers should cause the difference between the prices of posters sold at garage sales and the prices on eBay to shrink until they are equal to the dealers' costs of reselling the posters.

**Your Turn:** For more practice, do related problems 1.5 and 1.6 on page 540 at the end of this chapter.

MyEconLab

# Why Don't All Firms Charge the Same Price?

The law of one price may appear to be violated even where transactions costs are zero and a product can be resold. For example, different Web sites may sell what seem to be identical products for different prices. We can resolve this apparent contradiction if we look more closely at what "product" an Internet Web site—or another business—actually offers for sale.

Suppose you want to buy a copy of John Grisham's best seller *The Litigators.* You use Google, mySimon.com, or some other search engine to compare the book's price at various Web sites. You get the results shown in Table 16.1.

Would you automatically buy the book from one of the last two sites listed rather than from Amazon.com or BarnesandNoble.com? We can think about why you might not. Consider what these sites offer for sale. Amazon.com is not just offering *The Litigators*; it is offering *The Litigators* delivered quickly to your home, well packaged so it's not

**Product: John Grisham's *The Litigators***

| Company | Price |
| --- | --- |
| Amazon.com | $15.23 |
| BarnesandNoble.com | 15.23 |
| WaitForeverForYourOrder.com | 14.50 |
| JustStartedinBusinessLastWednesday.com | 14.25 |

damaged in the mail, and charged to your credit card using a secure method that keeps your credit card number safe from computer hackers. As we discussed in Chapter 13, firms differentiate the products they sell in many ways. One way is by providing faster and more reliable delivery than competitors.

Amazon.com and BarnesandNoble.com have built reputations for fast and reliable service. New Internet booksellers who lack that reputation will have to differentiate their products on the basis of price, as the two fictitious firms listed in the table have done. So, the difference in the prices of products offered on Web sites does *not* violate the law of one price. A book Amazon.com offers for sale is not the same product as a book JustStartedinBusinessLastWednesday.com offers for sale.

**16.2 LEARNING** OBJECTIVE

Explain how a firm can increase its profits through price discrimination.

**Price discrimination** Charging different prices to different customers for the same product when the price differences are not due to differences in cost.

# Price Discrimination: Charging Different Prices for the Same Product

We saw at the beginning of this chapter that the Walt Disney Company charges different prices for the same product: admission to Disney World. Charging different prices to different customers for the same good or service when the price differences are not due to differences in cost is called **price discrimination**. But doesn't price discrimination contradict the law of one price? Why doesn't the possibility of arbitrage profits lead people to buy at the low price and resell at the high price?

## Don't Let This Happen to You

### Don't Confuse Price Discrimination with Other Types of Discrimination

Don't confuse price discrimination with discrimination based on race or gender. Discriminating on the basis of arbitrary characteristics, such as race or gender, is illegal under the civil rights laws. Price discrimination is legal because it involves charging people different prices on the basis of their willingness to pay rather than on the basis of arbitrary characteristics. There is a gray area, however, when companies charge different prices on the basis of gender. For example, insurance companies usually charge women lower prices than men for automobile insurance. The courts have ruled that this is not illegal discrimination under the civil rights laws because women, on average, have better driving records than men. Because the costs of insuring men are higher than the costs of insuring women, insurance companies are allowed to charge men higher prices. Notice that this is not actually price discrimination as we have defined it here. Price discrimination involves charging different prices for the same product *where the price differences are not due to differences in cost.*

MyEconLab

**Your Turn:** Test your understanding by doing related problem 2.10 on page 541 at the end of this chapter.

# The Requirements for Successful Price Discrimination

A successful strategy of price discrimination has three requirements:

1. A firm must possess market power.

2. Some consumers must have a greater willingness to pay for the product than other consumers, and the firm must be able to know what prices customers are willing to pay.

3. The firm must be able to divide up—or *segment*—the market for the product so that consumers who buy the product at a low price are not able to resell it at a high price. In other words, price discrimination will not work if arbitrage is possible.

A firm selling in a perfectly competitive market cannot practice price discrimination because it can only charge the market price. But because most firms do not sell in perfectly competitive markets, they have market power and can set the price of the good they sell. Many firms may also be able to determine that some customers have a greater willingness to pay for a product than others. However, the third requirement—that markets be segmented so that customers buying at a low price will not be able to resell the product—can be difficult to fulfill. For example, some people really love Big Macs and would be willing to pay $10 rather than do without one. Other people would not be willing to pay a penny more than $1 for a Big Mac. Even if McDonald's could identify differences in the willingness of its customers to pay for Big Macs, it would not be able to charge them different prices. Suppose McDonald's knows that Joe is willing to pay $10, whereas Jill will pay only $1. If McDonald's tries to charge Joe $10, he will just have Jill buy a Big Mac for him.

Only firms that can keep consumers from reselling a product are able to practice price discrimination. Because buyers cannot resell the product, the law of one price does not hold. For example, movie theaters know that many people are willing to pay more to see a movie in the evening than during the afternoon. As a result, theaters usually charge higher prices for tickets to evening showings than for tickets to afternoon showings. They keep these markets separate by making the tickets to afternoon showings a different color or by having the time printed on them and by having a ticket taker examine the tickets. That makes it difficult for someone to buy a lower-priced ticket in the afternoon and use the ticket to gain admission to an evening showing.

Figure 16.1 illustrates how the owners of movie theaters use price discrimination to increase their profits. The marginal cost to the movie theater owner from another person attending a showing is very small: a little more wear on a theater seat and a few more kernels of popcorn to be swept from the floor. In previous chapters, we assumed that marginal cost has a U shape. In Figure 16.1, we assume for simplicity that marginal cost is a constant $0.50, shown as a horizontal line. Panel (a) shows the demand for afternoon showings. In this segment of its market, the theater should maximize profit by selling the quantity of tickets for which marginal revenue equals marginal cost, or 450 tickets. We know from the demand curve that the theater can sell 450 tickets at a price of $7.25 per ticket. Panel (b) shows the demand for evening showings. Notice that charging $7.25 per ticket would *not* be profit maximizing in this market. At a price of $7.25, the theater sells 850 tickets, which is 225 more tickets than the profit-maximizing quantity of 625. By charging $7.25 for tickets to afternoon showings and $9.75 for tickets to evening showings, the theater has maximized profits.

Figure 16.1 also illustrates another important point about price discrimination: When firms can practice price discrimination, they will charge customers who are less sensitive to price—those whose demand for the product is *less elastic*—a higher price and charge customers who are more sensitive to price—those whose demand is *more elastic*—a lower price. In this case, the demand for tickets to evening showings is less elastic, so the price charged is higher, and the demand for tickets to afternoon showings is more elastic, so the price charged is lower.

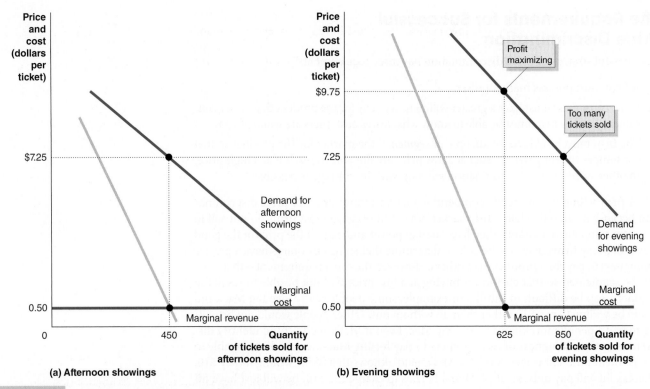

**(a) Afternoon showings**

**(b) Evening showings**

**Figure 16.1** **Price Discrimination by a Movie Theater**

Fewer people want to go to the movies in the afternoon than in the evening. In panel (a), the profit-maximizing price for a ticket to an afternoon showing is $7.25. Charging this same price for evening showings would not be profit maximizing, as panel (b) shows. At a price of $7.25, 850 tickets would be sold

to evening showings, which is more than the profit-maximizing number of 625 tickets. To maximize profits, the theater should charge $9.75 for tickets to evening showings.

# Solved Problem 16.2

## How Apple Uses Price Discrimination to Increase Profits

During the fall of 2011, Apple was selling MacBook Pro laptop computers with 13-inch screens on its Web site and in its retail stores for $1,499. But college students and faculty members could buy the same computer from Apple for $1,399. Why would Apple charge different prices for the same computer, depending on whether the buyer is an education customer? Draw two graphs to illustrate your answers: one for the general public and one for educational customers.

### Solving the Problem

**Step 1: Review the chapter material.** This problem is about using price discrimination to increase profits, so you may want to review the section "Price Discrimination: Charging Different Prices for the Same Product," which begins on page 522.

**Step 2: Explain why charging different prices to education customers and other customers will increase Apple's profits.** It makes sense for Apple to charge different prices if education customers have a different price elasticity of demand than do other customers. In that case, Apple will charge the market segment with the less elastic demand a higher price and the market segment with the more elastic demand a lower price. Because Apple is charging education customers the lower price, they must have a more elastic demand than do other customers.

**Step 3:** **Draw a graph to illustrate your answer.** Your graphs should look like the ones below, where we have chosen hypothetical quantities to illustrate the ideas. As in the case of movie theaters, you can assume for simplicity that the marginal cost is constant; in the graph we assume that the marginal cost is $400.

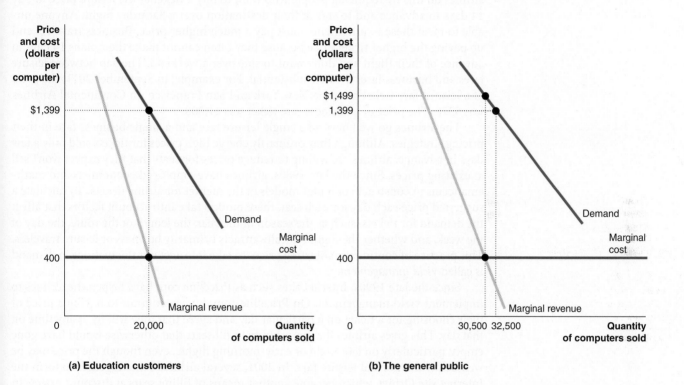

**(a) Education customers**          **(b) The general public**

Panel (a) shows that in the education customers segment of the market, marginal revenue equals marginal cost at 20,000 computers sold. Therefore, Apple should charge a price of $1,399 to maximize profits. But if Apple also charges $1,399 in the general public segment of the market, shown in panel (b), it will sell 32,500 computers, which is more than the profit-maximizing quantity. By charging $1,499 to the general public, Apple will sell 30,500 computers, the profit-maximizing quantity. We have shown that Apple maximizes its profits by charging education customers a lower price than it charges the general public. Notice that although the demand curve in panel (a) is more elastic, it is also steeper. This reminds us of the important point from Chapter 6 that elasticity is different from slope.

**Your Turn:** For more practice, do problems 2.11, 2.12, and 2.13 on pages 541–542 at the end of this chapter.          MyEconLab

# Airlines: The Kings of Price Discrimination

Airline seats are a perishable product. Once a plane has taken off from Chicago for Los Angeles, any seat that has not been sold on that particular flight will never be sold. In addition, the marginal cost of flying one additional passenger is low. This situation gives airlines a strong incentive to manage prices so that as many seats as possible are filled on each flight.

Airlines divide their customers into two main categories: business travelers and leisure travelers. Business travelers often have inflexible schedules, can't commit until the last minute to traveling on a particular day, and, most importantly, are not very sensitive to changes in price. The opposite is true for leisure travelers: They are flexible about when they travel, willing to buy their tickets well in advance, and sensitive to changes in price. Based on what we discussed earlier in this chapter, you can see that airlines will maximize profits by charging business travelers higher ticket prices than leisure travelers, but they need to determine who is a business traveler and who is a leisure traveler. Some airlines do this by requiring people who want to buy a ticket at the leisure price to buy 14 days in advance and to stay at their destination over a Saturday night. Anyone unable to meet these requirements must pay a much higher price. Business travelers end up paying the higher ticket price because they often cannot make their plans 14 days in advance of their flight and don't want to stay over a weekend. The gap between leisure fares and business fares is often substantial. For example, in September 2011, the price of a leisure-fare ticket between New York and San Francisco on Continental Airlines was $378. The price of a business-fare ticket was $1,008.

The airlines go well beyond a single leisure fare and a single business fare in their pricing strategies. Although they ordinarily charge high prices for tickets sold only a few days in advance, airlines are willing to reduce prices for seats that they expect won't sell at existing prices. Since the late 1980s, airlines have employed economists and mathematicians to construct computer models of the market for airline tickets. To calculate a suggested price each day for each seat, these models take into account factors that affect the demand for tickets, such as the season of the year, the length of the route, the day of the week, and whether the flight typically attracts primarily business or leisure travelers. This practice of continually adjusting prices to take into account fluctuations in demand is called *yield management*.

Since the late 1990s, Internet sites such as Priceline.com have helped the airlines to implement yield management. On Priceline.com, buyers commit to paying a price of their choosing for a ticket on a particular day and agree that they will fly at any time on that day. This gives airlines the opportunity to fill seats that otherwise would have gone empty, particularly on late-night or early-morning flights, even though the price may be well below the normal leisure fare. In 2001, several airlines came together to form the Internet site Orbitz, which became another means of filling seats at discount prices. In fact, in the past few years, the chance that you paid the same price for your airline ticket as the person sitting next to you has become quite small. Figure 16.2 shows an actual

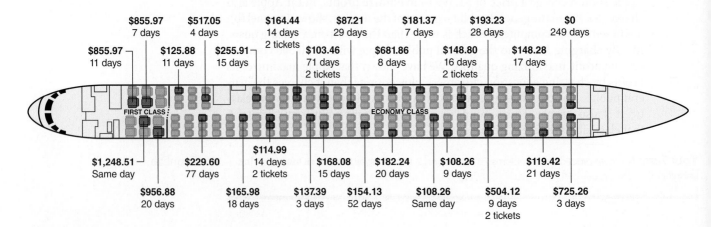

**Figure 16.2** **33 Customers and 27 Different Prices**

To fill as many seats on a flight as possible, airlines charge many different ticket prices. The 33 passengers on this United Air Lines flight from Chicago to Los Angeles paid 27 different prices for their tickets, including one passenger who used frequent flyer miles to obtain a free ticket. The first number in the figure is the price paid for the ticket; the second number is the number of days in advance that the ticket was purchased.

*Source:* "So, How Much Did You Pay for Your Ticket," by Matthew L. Wald. *The New York Times*, April 12, 1998. Copyright © 1998 by The New York Times Company.

United Air Lines flight from Chicago to Los Angeles. The 33 passengers on the flight paid 27 different prices for their tickets, including one passenger who used frequent flyer miles to obtain a free ticket.

| Making the Connection | ## How Colleges Use Yield Management |
|---|---|

Traditionally, colleges have based financial aid decisions only on the incomes of prospective students. In recent years, however, many colleges have started using yield management techniques, first developed for the airlines, to determine the amount of financial aid they offer different students. Colleges typically use a name such as "financial aid engineering" or "student enrollment management" rather than "yield management" to describe what they are doing. There is an important difference between the airlines and colleges: Colleges are interested not just in maximizing the revenue they receive from student tuition but also in increasing the academic quality of the students who enroll.

The "price" a college charges equals the full tuition minus any financial aid it provides students. When colleges use yield management techniques, they increase financial aid offers to students who are likely to be more price sensitive, and they reduce financial aid offers to students who are likely to be less price sensitive. As Stanford economist Caroline Hoxby puts it, "Universities are trying to find the people whose decisions will be changed by these [financial aid] grants." Some of the factors colleges use to judge how sensitive to price students are likely to be include whether they applied for early admission, whether they came for an on-campus interview, their intended major, their home state, and the level of their family's income. William F. Elliot, vice president for enrollment management at Carnegie Mellon University, advises, "If finances are a concern, you shouldn't be applying any place [for] early decision" because you are less likely to receive a large financial aid offer.

*Some colleges use yield management techniques to determine financial aid.*

Many students (and their parents) are critical of colleges that use yield management techniques in allocating financial aid. Some colleges, such as those in the Ivy League, have large enough endowments to meet all of their students' financial aid needs, so they don't practice yield management. Less well-endowed colleges defend the practice on the grounds that it allows them to recruit the best students at a lower cost in financial aid.

Based on Jacques Steinberg, "Early Signs That College Yields Did Not Change Dramatically," *New York Times*, May 8, 2009; Jane J. Kim and Anjali Athavaley, "Colleges Seek to Address Affordability," *Wall Street Journal*, May 3, 2007; and Albert B. Crenshaw, "Price Wars on Campus: Colleges Use Discounts to Draw Best Mix of Top Students, Paying Customers," *Washington Post*, October 15, 2002.

**Your Turn:** Test your understanding by doing related problem 2.14 on page 542 at the end of this chapter.

MyEconLab

## Perfect Price Discrimination

If a firm knew every consumer's willingness to pay—and could keep consumers who bought a product at a low price from reselling it—the firm could charge every consumer a different price. In this case of *perfect price discrimination*—also known as *first-degree price discrimination*—each consumer would have to pay a price equal to the consumer's willingness to pay and, therefore, would receive no consumer surplus. To see why, remember from Chapter 4 that consumer surplus is the difference between the highest price a consumer is willing to pay for a product and the price the consumer actually pays. But if the price the consumer pays is the maximum the consumer would be willing to pay, there is no consumer surplus.

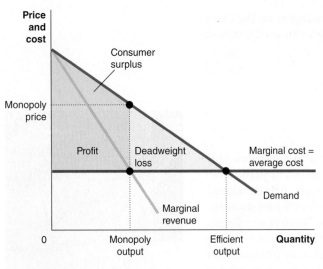

**(a) A monopolist who cannot practice price discrimination**

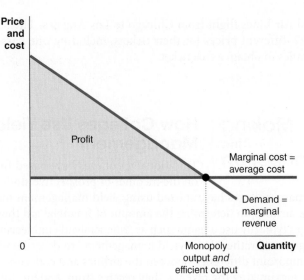

**(b) A monopolist practicing perfect price discrimination**

**Figure 16.3** **Perfect Price Discrimination**

Panel (a) shows the case of a monopolist who cannot practice price discrimination and, therefore, can charge only a single price for its product. The graph, like those in Chapter 15, shows that to maximize profits, the monopolist will produce the level of output where marginal revenue equals marginal cost. The resulting profit is shown by the area of the green rectangle. Given the monopoly price, the amount of consumer surplus in this market is shown by the area of the blue triangle. The economically efficient level of output occurs where price

equals marginal cost. Because the monopolist stops production at a level of output where price is above marginal cost, there is a deadweight loss equal to the area of the yellow triangle. In panel (b), the monopolist is able to practice perfect price discrimination by charging a different price to each consumer. The result is to convert both the consumer surplus *and* the deadweight loss from panel (a) into profit.

Figure 16.3 shows the effects of perfect price discrimination. To simplify the discussion, we assume that the firm is a monopoly and that it has constant marginal and average costs. Panel (a) should be familiar from Chapter 15. It shows the case of a monopolist who cannot practice price discrimination and, therefore, can charge only a single price for its product. The monopolist maximizes profits by producing the level of output where marginal revenue equals marginal cost. Recall that the economically efficient level of output occurs where price is equal to marginal cost, which is the level of output in a perfectly competitive market. Because the monopolist produces where price is greater than marginal cost, it causes a loss of economic efficiency equal to the area of the deadweight loss triangle in the figure.

Panel (b) shows the situation of a monopolist practicing perfect price discrimination. Because the firm can charge each consumer the maximum each consumer is willing to pay, its marginal revenue from selling one more unit is equal to the price of that unit. Therefore, the monopolist's marginal revenue curve becomes equal to its demand curve, and the firm will continue to produce up to the point where price is equal to marginal cost. It may seem like a paradox, but the ability to practice perfect price discrimination causes the monopolist to produce the efficient level of output. By doing so, the monopolist converts consumer surplus *and* what is deadweight loss in panel (a) into profits. In both panel (a) and panel (b), the profit shown is also producer surplus.

Even though the result in panel (b) is more economically efficient than the result in panel (a), consumers clearly are worse off because the amount of consumer surplus has been reduced to zero. We probably will never see a case of perfect price discrimination in the real world because firms typically do not know how much each consumer is willing to pay and therefore cannot charge each consumer a different price. Still, this extreme case helps us to see the two key results of price discrimination:

1. Profits increase.
2. Consumer surplus decreases.

Perfect price discrimination improves economic efficiency. Can we also say that this will be the case if price discrimination is less than perfect? Often, less-than-perfect price discrimination will improve economic efficiency. But under certain circumstances, it may actually reduce economic efficiency, so we can't draw a general conclusion.

## Price Discrimination across Time

Firms are sometimes able to engage in price discrimination over time. With this strategy, firms charge a higher price for a product when it is first introduced and a lower price later. Some consumers are *early adopters* who will pay a high price to be among the first to own certain new products. This pattern helps explain why DVD players, Blu-ray players, digital cameras, and flat-screen plasma televisions all sold for very high prices when they were first introduced. After the demand of the early adopters was satisfied, the companies reduced prices to attract more price-sensitive customers. For example, the price of DVD players dropped by 95 percent within five years of their introduction. Some of the price reductions over time for these products were also due to falling costs, as companies took advantage of economies of scale, but some represented price discrimination across time.

Book publishers routinely use price discrimination across time to increase profits. Hardcover editions of novels have much higher prices and are published months before paperback editions. For example, the hardcover edition of John Grisham's novel *The Litigators* was published in October 2011 at a price of $28.95. The paperback edition was published in June 2012 for $9.99. Although this difference in price might seem to reflect the higher costs of producing hardcover books, in fact, it does not. The marginal cost of printing another copy of the hardcover is about $1.50. The marginal cost of printing another copy of the paperback edition is only slightly less, about $1.25. So, the difference in price between the hardcover and paperback is driven primarily by differences in demand. John Grisham's most devoted fans want to read his next book at the earliest possible moment and are not very sensitive to price. Many casual readers are also interested in Grisham's books but will read something else if the price of Grisham's latest book is too high.

As Figure 16.4 shows, a publisher will maximize profits by segmenting the market—in this case across time—and by charging a higher price to the less elastic market segment and a lower price to the more elastic segment. (This example is similar to our earlier analysis of movie tickets in Figure 16.1 on page 524.) If the publisher had skipped the hardcover and issued only the paperback version at a price of $9.99 when the book was first published in October, its revenue would have dropped by the number of readers who bought the hardcover multiplied by the difference between the price of the hardcover and the price of the paperback, or $500,000 \times (\$28.95 - \$9.99) = \$9,480,000$.

## Can Price Discrimination Be Illegal?

In Chapter 15, we saw that Congress has passed *antitrust laws* to promote competition. Price discrimination may be illegal if its effect is to reduce competition in an industry. In 1936, Congress passed the Robinson–Patman Act, which outlawed price discrimination that reduced competition and which also contained language that could be interpreted as making illegal *all* price discrimination not based on differences in cost. In the 1960s, the Federal Trade Commission sued Borden, Inc., under this act because Borden was selling the same evaporated milk for two different prices. Cans with the Borden label were sold for a high price, and cans sold to supermarkets to be repackaged as the supermarkets' private brands were sold for a much lower price. The courts ultimately ruled that Borden had not violated the law because the price differences increased, rather than reduced, competition in the market

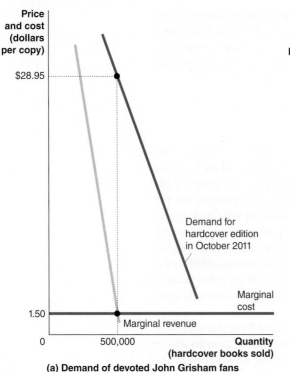

(a) Demand of devoted John Grisham fans

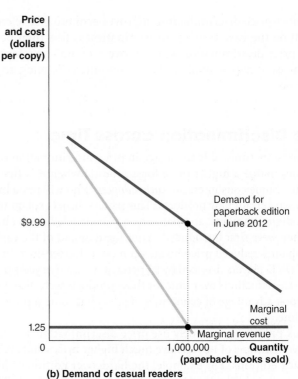

(b) Demand of casual readers

**Figure 16.4**   **Price Discrimination across Time**

Publishers issue most novels in hardcover at high prices to satisfy the demand of the novelists' most devoted fans. Later, publishers issue paperback editions at much lower prices to capture sales from casual readers. In panel (a), with a marginal cost of $1.50 per copy for a hardcover, the profit-maximizing level of output is 500,000 copies, which can be sold at a price of $28.95. In panel (b), the more elastic demand of casual readers and the slightly lower marginal cost result in a profit-maximizing output of 1,000,000 for the paperback edition, which can be sold at a price of $9.99.

for evaporated milk. In recent years, the courts have interpreted Robinson–Patman narrowly, allowing firms to use the types of price discrimination described in this chapter.

**Making the Connection** | **Price Discrimination with a Twist at Netflix**

Price discrimination usually refers to charging different prices to different consumers for the same good or service. But price discrimination can also involve charging the same price for goods or services of different quality. Netflix, an online DVD rental service, has apparently engaged in this second form of price discrimination. According to a newspaper story, "Netflix customers who pay the same price for the same service are often treated differently, depending on their rental patterns." Netflix subscribers pay a fixed monthly fee to rent a given number of DVDs. For instance, in 2011, Netflix was charging $23.98 per month to rent three DVDs at a time as well as receive unlimited streaming. (Many fewer movies are available for streaming than are available on DVD.) After a subscriber returns a DVD, Netflix mails that subscriber a new DVD. Subscribers under this plan can rent an unlimited number of DVDs per month, although they can have no more than three at any one time. Netflix has become very popular, with more than 24 million subscribers.

But does every Netflix subscriber receive service of the same quality? In particular, does every subscriber have an equal chance of receiving the latest movie released on DVD? Apparently not. Subscribers who rent the fewest movies per month

*Why does renting only a few movies get you better service with Netflix?*

have the best chance of receiving the latest releases and typically receive their DVDs faster. According to Netflix's DVD Terms and Conditions (the "fine print" that most subscribers don't read):

> In determining priority for shipping and inventory allocation, we may utilize many different factors.... For example, if all other factors are the same, we give priority to those members who receive the fewest DVDs through our service.... Also ... [the service you experience] may be different from the service we provide to other members on the same membership plan.

One Netflix subscriber was quoted in a newspaper article as saying, "Sometimes it would be two or three months before I got [a movie] once it came out on DVD. The longer I was a customer, the worse it got."

Why would Netflix provide better service to subscribers who rent only a few DVDs per month and poorer service to subscribers who rent many DVDs per month? Subscribers who rent many DVDs per month are likely to have less elastic demand—they really like watching movies—than subscribers who rent only a few DVDs per month. As we have seen in this chapter, firms can increase their profits by charging higher prices to consumers with less elastic demand and lower prices to consumers with more elastic demand. But this strategy works only if firms have a way of reliably separating consumers into groups on the basis of how elastic their demand is. When they first subscribe, Netflix has no way of separating its consumers on the basis of how elastic their demand is, so it has to charge the same price to everyone. But after a few months of observing a subscriber's pattern of rentals, Netflix has enough information to determine whether the subscriber's demand is more or less elastic. By reducing the level of service to subscribers with less elastic demand, Netflix is, in effect, raising the price these consumers pay relative to consumers who receive better service. In this way, Netflix engages in price discrimination and increases its profits over what they would be if every subscriber received the same service at the same price.

Based on Robin Raskin, "The Bottom of the Netflix Totem Pole," www.tech.yahoo.com, March 23, 2009; Alina Tugend, "Getting Movies from a Store or a Mailbox (or Just a Box)," *New York Times*, August 5, 2006; and "Netflix Critics Slam 'Throttling,'" *Associated Press*, February 10, 2006.

**Your Turn:** Test your understanding by doing related problem 2.17 on page 542 at the end of this chapter.

MyEconLab

# Other Pricing Strategies

**16.3 LEARNING** OBJECTIVE

Explain how some firms increase their profits through the use of odd pricing, cost-plus pricing, and two-part tariffs.

In addition to price discrimination, firms use many different pricing strategies, depending on the nature of their products, the level of competition in their markets, and the characteristics of their customers. In this section, we consider three important strategies: odd pricing, cost-plus pricing, and two-part tariffs.

## Odd Pricing: Why Is the Price $2.99 Instead of $3.00?

Many firms use what is called *odd pricing*—for example, charging $4.95 instead of $5.00, or $199 instead of $200. Surveys show that 80 percent to 90 percent of the products sold in supermarkets have prices ending in "9" or "5" rather than "0." Odd pricing has a long history. In the early nineteenth century, most goods in the United States were sold in general stores and did not have fixed prices. Instead, prices were often determined by haggling, much as prices of new cars are often determined today by haggling on dealers' lots. Later in the nineteenth century, when most products began to sell for a fixed price, odd pricing became popular.

Different explanations have been given for the origin of odd pricing. One explanation is that it began because goods imported from Great Britain had a reputation for high quality. When the prices of British goods in British currency—the pound—were translated into U.S. dollars, the result was an odd price. Because customers connected odd prices with high-quality goods, even sellers of domestic goods charged odd prices. Another explanation is that odd pricing began as an attempt to guard against employee theft. An odd price forced an employee to give the customer change, which reduced the likelihood that the employee would simply pocket the customer's money without recording the sale.

Whatever the origins of odd pricing, why do firms still use it today? The most obvious answer is that an odd price, say $9.99, seems somehow significantly—more than a penny—cheaper than $10.00. But do consumers really have this illusion? To find out, three market researchers conducted a study. We saw in Chapter 3 that demand curves can be estimated statistically. If consumers have the illusion that $9.99 is significantly cheaper than $10.00, they will demand a greater quantity of goods at $9.99—and other odd prices—than the estimated demand curve predicts. The researchers surveyed consumers about their willingness to purchase six different products—ranging from a block of cheese to an electric blender—at a series of prices. Ten of the prices were either odd cent prices—99 cents or 95 cents—or odd dollar prices—$95 or $99. Nine of these 10 odd prices resulted in an odd-price effect, with the quantity demanded being greater than predicted using the estimated demand curve. The study was not conclusive because it relied on surveys rather than on observing actual purchasing behavior and because it used only a small group of products, but the study does provide some evidence that using odd prices makes economic sense.

## Why Do Some Firms Use Cost-Plus Pricing?

Many firms use *cost-plus pricing*, which involves adding a percentage *markup* to average cost. With this pricing strategy, the firm first calculates average cost at a particular level of production, usually equal to the firm's expected sales. The firm then applies a percentage markup, say 30 percent, to the estimated average cost to arrive at the price. For example, if average cost is $100 and the percentage markup is 30 percent, the price will be $130. For a firm selling multiple products, the markup is intended to cover all costs, including those that the firm cannot assign to any particular product. Most firms have costs that are difficult to assign to one particular product. For example, the work performed by the employees in the accounting and finance departments at McDonald's applies to all of McDonald's products and can't be assigned directly to Big Macs or Happy Meals.

Making | Cost-Plus Pricing in the Publishing
the | Industry
Connection | Book publishing companies incur substantial costs for editing, designing, marketing, and warehousing books. These costs are difficult to assign directly to any particular book. Most publishers arrive at a price for a book by applying a markup to their production costs, which are usually divided into plant costs and manufacturing costs. Plant costs include typesetting the manuscript and preparing graphics or artwork for printing. Manufacturing costs include the costs of printing, paper, and binding the book.

Consider the following example for the hypothetical new book by Adam Smith, *How to Succeed at Economics without Really Trying*. We will assume that the book is

250 pages long, the publisher expects to sell 5,000 copies, and plant and manufacturing costs are as given in the following table:

| Plant Costs | | |
|---|---|---|
| | Typesetting | $3,500 |
| | Other plant costs | 2,000 |
| **Manufacturing Costs** | | |
| | Printing | $5,750 |
| | Paper | 6,250 |
| | Binding | 5,000 |
| **Total Production Cost** | | |
| | | $22,500 |

With total production cost of $22,500 and production of 5,000 books, the per-unit production cost is $22,500/5,000 = $4.50. Many publishers multiply the unit production cost number by 7 or 8 to arrive at the retail price they will charge customers in bookstores. In this case, multiplying by 7 results in a price of $31.50 for the book. The markup seems quite high, but publishers typically sell books to bookstores at a 40 percent discount. Although a customer in a bookstore will pay $31.50 for the book—or less, of course, if it is purchased from a bookseller that discounts the retail price—the publisher receives only $18.90. The difference between the $18.90 received from the bookstore and the $4.50 production cost equals the cost of editing, marketing, warehousing, paying a royalty to the author of the book, and all other costs, including the opportunity cost of the investment in the firm by its owners, plus any economic profit the owners receive.

Based on Beth Luey, *Handbook for Academic Authors*, Fifth Edition, (New York: Cambridge University Press, 2010).

**Your Turn:** Test your understanding by doing related problem 3.8 on page 543 at the end of this chapter.

MyEconLab

We have seen that firms maximize profit by producing the quantity where marginal revenue equals marginal cost and charging a price that will cause consumers to buy that quantity. The cost-plus approach doesn't appear to maximize profits unless the cost-plus price turns out to be the same as the price that will cause the quantity sold to be where marginal revenue is equal to marginal cost. Economists have two views of cost-plus pricing. One is that cost-plus pricing is simply a mistake that firms should avoid. The other view is that cost-plus pricing is a good way to come close to the profit-maximizing price when either marginal revenue or marginal cost is difficult to calculate.

Small firms often like cost-plus pricing because it is easy to use. Unfortunately, these firms can fall into the trap of mechanically applying a cost-plus pricing rule, which may result in charging prices that do not maximize profits. The most obvious problems with cost-plus pricing are that it ignores demand and focuses on average cost rather than marginal cost. If a firm's marginal cost is significantly different from its average cost at its current level of production, cost-plus pricing is unlikely to maximize profits.

Despite these problems, cost-plus pricing is used by some large firms that have the knowledge and resources to devise a better method of pricing if cost-plus pricing fails to maximize profits. Economists conclude that using cost-plus pricing may be the best way to determine the optimal price in two situations:

1. When marginal cost and average cost are roughly equal
2. When a firm has difficulty estimating its demand curve

In fact, most large firms that use cost-plus pricing do not just mechanically apply a markup to their estimate of average cost. Instead, they adjust the markup to reflect their best estimate of current demand. A large firm is likely to have a pricing policy committee that adjusts prices based on the current state of competition in the industry and the current state of the economy. If competition is strong in a weak economy, the pricing committee may decide to set price significantly below the cost-plus price.

In general, firms that take demand into account will charge lower markups on products that are more price elastic and higher markups on products that are less elastic. Supermarkets, where cost-plus pricing is widely used, have markups in the 5 percent to 10 percent range for products with more elastic demand, such as soft drinks and breakfast cereals, and markups in the 50 percent range for products with less elastic demand, such as fresh fruits and vegetables.

## Why Do Some Firms Use Two-Part Tariffs?

Some firms require consumers to pay an initial fee for the right to buy their product and an additional fee for each unit of the product purchased. For example, many golf and tennis clubs require members to buy an annual membership in addition to paying a fee each time they use the golf course or tennis court. Sam's Club requires consumers to pay a membership fee before shopping at its stores. Cellular phone companies charge a monthly fee and then have a per-minute charge after a certain number of minutes have been used. Economists refer to this situation as a **two-part tariff**.

**Two-part tariff** A situation in which consumers pay one price (or tariff) for the right to buy as much of a related good as they want at a second price.

The Walt Disney Company is in a position to use a two-part tariff by charging consumers for admission to Walt Disney World or Disneyland and also charging them to use the rides in the parks. As mentioned at the beginning of this chapter, at one time, the admission price to Disneyland was low, but people had to purchase tickets to go on the rides. Today, you must pay a high price for admission to Disneyland or Disney World, but the rides are free once you're in the park. Figure 16.5 helps us understand which of these pricing strategies is more profitable for Disney. The numbers in the figure are simplified to make the calculations easier.

Once visitors are inside the park, Disney is in the position of a monopolist: No other firm is operating rides in Disney World. So, we can draw panel (a) in Figure 16.5 to represent the market for rides at Disney World. This graph looks like the standard monopoly graph from Chapter 15. (Note that the marginal cost of another rider is quite low. We can assume that it is a constant $2 and equal to the average cost.) It seems obvious—but it will turn out to be wrong!—that Disney should determine the profit-maximizing quantity of ride tickets by setting marginal revenue equal to marginal cost. In this case, that would lead to 20,000 ride tickets sold per day at a price of $26 per ride. Disney's profit from selling *ride tickets* is shown by the area of the light-green rectangle, *B*. The area equals the difference between the $26 price and the average cost of $2, multiplied by the 20,000 tickets sold, or ($26 − $2) × 20,000 = $480,000. Disney also has a second source of profit from selling *admission tickets* to the park. Given the $26 price for ride tickets, what price would Disney be able to charge for admission tickets?

Let's assume the following for simplicity: The only reason people want admission to Disney World is to go on the rides, all consumers have the same individual demand curve for rides, and Disney knows what this demand curve is. This last assumption allows Disney to practice perfect price discrimination. More realistic assumptions would make the outcome of the analysis somewhat different but would not affect the main point of how Disney uses a two-part tariff to increase its profits. With these assumptions, we can use the concept of consumer surplus to calculate the maximum total amount consumers would be willing to pay for admission. Remember that consumer surplus is equal to the area below the demand curve and above the price line, shown by the dark-green triangle, *A*, in panel (a). The area represents the benefit to buyers from consuming the product. In this case, consumers would not be willing

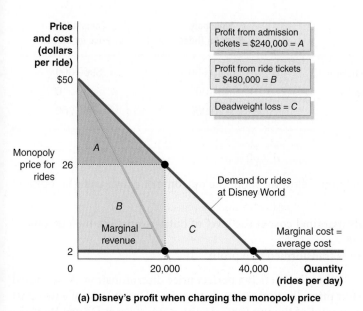

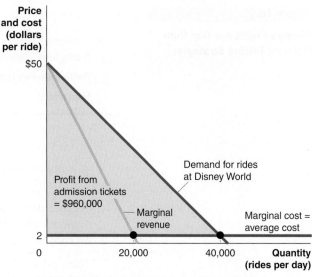

**Figure 16.5    A Two-Part Tariff at Disney World**

In panel (a), Disney charges the monopoly price of $26 per ride ticket and sells 20,000 ride tickets. Its profit from *ride tickets* is shown by the area of the light-green rectangle, *B*, $480,000. If Disney is in the position of knowing every consumer's willingness to pay, it can also charge a price for *admission tickets* that would result in the total amount paid for admission tickets being equal to total consumer surplus from the rides. Total consumer surplus from the rides

equals the area of the dark-green triangle, *A*, or $240,000. So, when charging the monopoly price, Disney's total profit equals $480,000 + $240,000 or $720,000. In panel (b), Disney charges the perfectly competitive price of $2, which results in a quantity of 40,000 ride tickets sold. At the lower ride ticket price, Disney can charge a higher price for admission tickets, which will increase its total profits from operating the park to the area of the light-green triangle, or $960,000.

to pay more for admission to the park than the consumer surplus they receive from the rides. In panel (a) of Figure 16.5, the total consumer surplus when Disney charges a price of $26 per ride is $240,000. (This number is easy to calculate if you remember that the formula for the area of a triangle is ½ × base × height, or ½ × 20,000 × $24.) Disney can set the price of admission tickets so that the *total* amount spent by buyers would be $240,000. In other words, Disney can set the price of admission to capture the entire consumer surplus from the rides. So, Disney's total profit from Disney World would be the $240,000 it receives from admission tickets plus the $480,000 in profit from the rides, or $720,000 per day.

Is this the most profit Disney can earn from selling admission tickets and ride tickets? The answer is "no." The key to understanding why is to notice that *the lower the price Disney charges for ride tickets, the higher the price it can charge for admission tickets.* Lower-priced ride tickets increase consumer surplus from the rides and, therefore, increase the willingness of buyers to pay a higher price for admission tickets. In panel (b) of Figure 16.5, we assume that Disney acts as it would in a perfectly competitive market and charges a price for ride tickets that is equal to marginal cost, or $2. Charging this price increases consumer surplus—*and* the maximum total amount that Disney can charge for admission tickets—from $240,000 to $960,000. (Once again, we use the formula for the area of a triangle to calculate the light-green area in panel (b): ½ × 40,000 × 48 = $960,000.) Disney's profits from the rides will decline to zero because it is now charging a price equal to average cost, *but its total profit from Disney World will rise from $720,000 per day to $960,000.* Table 16.2 summarizes this result.

What is the source of Disney's increased profit from charging a price equal to marginal cost? The answer is that Disney has converted what was deadweight loss when the monopoly price was charged—the area of triangle *C* in panel (a)—into consumer surplus. Disney then turns this consumer surplus into profit by increasing the price of admission tickets.

| | Monopoly Price for Rides | Competitive Price for Rides |
|---|---|---|
| **Table 16.2** | | |
| **Disney's Profits per Day from Different Pricing Strategies** | | |
| Profits from admission tickets | $240,000 | $960,000 |
| Profits from ride tickets | 480,000 | 0 |
| Total profit | 720,000 | 960,000 |

It is important to note the following about the outcome of a firm using an optimal two-part tariff:

1. Because price equals marginal cost at the level of output supplied, the outcome is economically efficient.
2. All consumer surplus is transformed into profit.

Notice that, in effect, Disney is practicing perfect price discrimination. As we noted in our discussion of perfect price discrimination on page 527, Disney's use of a two-part tariff has increased the amount of the product—in this case, rides at Disney World—consumers are able to purchase but has eliminated consumer surplus. Although it may seem paradoxical, consumer surplus was actually higher when consumers were being charged the monopoly price for the rides. The solution to the paradox is that although consumers pay a lower price for the rides when Disney employs a two-part tariff, the overall amount they pay to be at Disney World increases.

Disney actually does follow the profit-maximizing strategy of charging a high price for admission to the park and a very low price—zero—for the rides. It seems that Disney could increase its profits by raising the price for the rides from zero to the marginal cost of the rides. But the marginal cost is so low that it would not be worth the expense of printing ride tickets and hiring additional workers to sell the tickets and collect them at each ride. Finally, note that in practice Disney can't convert all consumer surplus into profit because (1) the demand curves of customers are not all the same, and (2) Disney does not know precisely what these demand curves are.

Continued from page 519

## Economics in Your Life

### Why So Many Prices to See a Movie?

At the beginning of the chapter, we asked you to think about what you pay for a movie ticket and what people in other age groups pay. A movie theater will try to charge different prices to different consumers, based on their willingness to pay. If you have two otherwise identical people, one a student and one not, you might assume that the student has less income, and thus a lower willingness to pay, than the non-student, and the movie theater would like to charge the student a lower price. The movie theater employee can ask to see a student ID to ensure that the theater is giving the discount to a student.

But why don't theaters practice price discrimination at the concession stand? It is likely that a student will also have a lower willingness to pay for popcorn, and the theater can check for a student ID at the time of purchase, but unlike with the entry ticket, the theater would have a hard time preventing the student from giving the popcorn to a non-student once inside the theater. Because it is easier to limit resale in movie admissions, we often see different prices for different groups. Because it is difficult to limit resale of popcorn and other movie concessions, all groups will typically pay the same price.

# Conclusion

Firms in perfectly competitive industries must sell their products at the market price. For firms in other industries—which means, of course, the vast majority of firms—pricing is an important part of the strategy used to maximize profits. We have seen in this chapter, for example, that if firms can successfully segment their customers into different groups on the basis of willingness to pay, they can increase their profits by charging different segments different prices.

Read *An Inside Look* on the next page for a discussion of a two-part pricing strategy the University of Kansas is considering to help pay for stadium renovations as well as other campus construction.

## ASSOCIATED PRESS

### Colleges add stadium seats with 'sports mortgages'

(a) Season ticket holders know the annual lament. The cost of prime seats keeps rising, even if the team is lousy.

Now, combine that frustration with cash-strapped college athletics departments, struggling to upgrade aging stadiums, and you've got the latest innovation in marketing for big-time athletics—the sports mortgage.

At Kansas, Jayhawk fans who sign up to pay as much as $105,000 over 10 years will earn the right to buy guaranteed top seats for football over the next three decades. In return, the seats themselves will stay locked in at 2010 prices.

California fans have even more latitude—30 years to pay for a half-century's worth of season football tickets. Like a home mortgage, the long-term deal requires the equivalent of annual interest payments.

(b) The new pricing plans are known as "equity seat rights," and are being pitched as a win-win for fans and teams. Die-hard fans can be certain of what they'll pay to see their favorite team well into the future—and can always sell tickets in the secondary market while taking a tax write-off for donating to a school. Teams can bank on extra revenue and avoid borrowing.

Stadium Capital Financing Group, the Chicago company behind the change, says it has the potential to transform how both college and pro teams court their most loyal fans. They're confident sports mortgages will overtake the personal seat license, which doesn't necessarily lock in ticket prices.

The only trick now is convincing fans it's a good deal.

"Even in difficult financial times, the price of the best seats in professional stadiums and university programs go up," said Lou Weisbach, Stadium Capital Financing's chief executive officer. "This is the ultimate solution for the shortfalls universities are facing in their athletics programs."

(c) At Kansas, mortgage sales are being targeted at the new 3,000-seat Gridiron Club, an addition to 90-year-old Memorial Stadium in Lawrence that will offer its members cushioned seats, catered food, private restrooms and preferred parking.

The school hopes the sales will not only cover the costs of $34 million in stadium renovations but eventually will raise a total of $200 million—without going into debt or relying on tax dollars.

That would pay for renovations to Allen Fieldhouse, home of the Kansas basketball team, and build a new "Olympic village" for the Jayhawk track and field, soccer and swim teams. Another $40 million would go toward academics.

Still, problems remain. The Gridiron Club's planned opening for the 2010 season has been delayed since the school has only been able to raise about $5 million of the needed $34 million, said Jim Marchiony, associate athletics director.

The football team's 2009 performance likely didn't help. After winning its first five games, the Jayhawks lost seven in a row. The season ended with the resignation of coach Mark Mangino amid allegations of mental and emotional abuse of players.

*Source:* Alan Scherzagier, "Colleges add stadium seats with 'sports mortgages'," *Associated Press,* March 30, 2010.

## Key Points in the Article

The University of Kansas is selling "sports mortgages" to those fans who want to purchase season tickets in its new 3,000-seat Gridiron Club. With a sports mortgage, those fans who want to purchase season tickets must also purchase the rights to these seats for as much as $105,000. The price of each game ticket is in addition to the one-time mortgage charge, but fans will be allowed to purchase these top seats for 30 years at 2010 prices. The University of Kansas is using this pricing plan as a way to pay for stadium renovations as well as other campus construction without having to go into debt or rely on state tax dollars for funding.

## Analyzing the News

**a** The sale of sports mortgages by the University of Kansas is an example of using a two-part tariff to sell season tickets to football games. A fan who wants to buy season tickets for seats in the new Gridiron Club must buy a mortgage as well as the tickets. The mortgages cost as much as $105,000 and can be paid over a 10-year period. The mortgage also guarantees the ticketholder the right to top seats at a fixed price for 30 years. The figure below shows how a sports team can use a two-part tariff to increase profit. Note that the figure uses simple, hypothetical numbers. The figure

assumes that the profit-maximizing monopoly price for a season ticket is $2,000. This assumes that tickets to individual games are sold for $250 each. (There are eight regular season home games.) Marginal cost is assumed to be zero in order to simplify the example. Therefore, without charging a mortgage fee, the total profit earned by the team would equal area $B$, or $110 million ($2,000 × 55,000). If the team knew the maximum amount each season ticket buyer was willing to pay, the team could charge a mortgage fee that would result in a total amount paid by all season ticket buyers equal to area $A$ – the total consumer surplus. The amount is equal to $82.5 million [½ × ($5,000 − $2,000) × 55,000]. The total profit earned by the university would increase to the area of $A$ plus the area of $B$, or $192.5 million.

**b** Pricing plans such as the sports mortgage are known as "equity seat rights" because they guarantee the seat holder top quality seats at locked-in prices for years into the future. Stadium Capital Financing Group is the company behind this pricing idea. This company believes that equity seat rights can benefit the fans by guaranteeing ticket prices and can benefit sports teams by giving them a new source of revenue. The equity seat rights pricing idea is the latest evolution of a two-part tariff known as the personal seat license, or PSL. With a personal seat license, those fans

who want to purchase season tickets must also purchase a license for each seat they want to use in the stadium, but ticket prices are not locked in at current levels. Several National Football League (NFL) teams have used, or are considering using, personal seat licenses to help finance new stadiums.

**c** At the University of Kansas, the revenue generated from the sale of equity seat rights is being used not only to finance $34 million in renovations to the football stadium, but may also be enough to cover additional renovations and new construction around the campus, therefore sparing the school from having to rely on tax revenues. Having season ticket holders pay for equity seat rights helps shift more of the burden of paying for new stadiums or renovations to those fans who use the stadium rather than the tax-paying general public, many of whom may never visit the facility.

## Thinking Critically

1. Many sports fans complain about the high prices professional sports teams charge to watch games played in new stadiums and arenas and argue that tickets are being increasingly sold to wealthy fans and corporations. Is it better for society for teams to charge high ticket prices or to lower prices so more fans can afford to watch their favorite teams play?

2. Suppose that after a new stadium is built for a National Football League (NFL) franchise, local government officials respond to complaints from fans by preventing the team from selling equity seat rights and by placing a ceiling on ticket prices. What effect would this policy have on the quantity demanded and the quantity supplied of tickets for this team? Would local citizens be better off as a result of the policy?

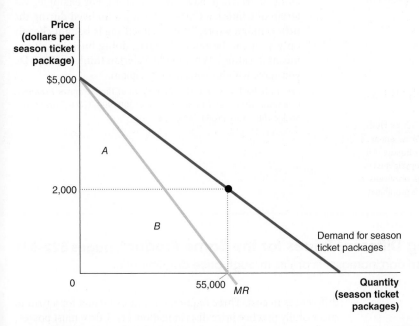

**A sports team can use a two-part tariff to increase profits.**

# Chapter Summary and Problems

## Key Terms

Price discrimination, p. 522      Transactions costs, p. 520      Two-part tariff, p. 534

 **16.1** **Pricing Strategy, the Law of One Price, and Arbitrage,** pages 520–522

LEARNING OBJECTIVE: Define the law of one price and explain the role of arbitrage.

## Summary

According to the *law of one price*, identical products should sell for the same price everywhere. If a product sells for different prices, it will be possible to make a profit through *arbitrage*: buying a product at a low price and reselling it at a high price. The law of one price will hold as long as arbitrage is possible. Arbitrage is sometimes blocked by high **transactions costs**, which are the costs in time and other resources incurred to carry out an exchange or because the product cannot be resold. Another apparent exception to the law of one price occurs when companies offset the higher price they charge for a product by providing superior or more reliable service to customers.

 MyEconLab    Visit **www.myeconlab.com** to complete these exercises online and get instant feedback.

## Review Questions

1.1 What is the law of one price? What is arbitrage?

1.2 Does a product always have to sell for the same price everywhere? Briefly explain.

## Problems and Applications

1.3 A newspaper article contains the following description of New York consumers avoiding the state's 8.375 percent sales tax by shopping in New Jersey:

> For years, shoppers from New York City have played a game of retail arbitrage, traveling to the many malls in northern New Jersey, a state where there is no tax on clothing and shoes.

Does this article use the word *arbitrage* correctly? Briefly explain.

Source: "Sales Tax Cut in City May Dim Allure of Stores Across Hudson," by Ken Belson and Nate Schweber. *The New York Times*, January 18, 2007. Copyright © 2007 by The New York Times Company. All rights reserved. Used by permission and protected by the copyright laws of the United States. The printing, copying, redistribution, or retransmission of the Material without express written permission is prohibited.

1.4 The following table contains the actual prices four Web sites charged for a Blu-ray of the movie *X-Men: First Class* in September 2011:

| | |
|---|---|
| Amazon | $24.99 |
| Wal-Mart | 24.96 |
| OrlandsBricks | 21.58 |
| ranch_records | 17.75 |

On Google's price comparison Web site, which allows customers to rate the seller, Amazon had 6,223 ratings, Wal-Mart had 835 ratings, ranch_records had 153 ratings, and OrlandsBricks had 0 ratings. Briefly explain whether the information in this table contradicts the law of one price.

1.5 **[Related to** Solved Problem 16.1 **on page 521]** Suppose California has many apple trees, and the price of apples there is low. Nevada has few apple trees, and the price of apples there is high. Abner buys low-priced California apples and ships them to Nevada, where he resells them at a high price. Is Abner exploiting Nevada consumers by doing this? Is Abner likely to earn economic profits in the long run? Briefly explain.

1.6 **[Related to** Solved Problem 16.1 **on page 521]** Suspicions of arbitrage have a long history. For example, Valerian of Cimiez, a Catholic bishop who lived during the fifth century, wrote, "When something is bought cheaply only so it can be retailed dearly, doing business always means cheating." What might Valerian think of eBay? Do you agree with his conclusion? Explain.

From Michael McCormick, *The Origins of the European Economy: Communications and Commerce*, A.D. 300–900, (New York: Cambridge University Press), 2001, p. 85.

**16.2** **Price Discrimination: Charging Different Prices for the Same Product,** pages 522–531

LEARNING OBJECTIVE: Explain how a firm can increase its profits through price discrimination.

## Summary

**Price discrimination** occurs if a firm charges different prices for the same product when the price differences are not due to differences in cost. Three requirements must be met for a firm to successfully practice price discrimination: (1) A firm must possess market power; (2) some consumers must have a greater willingness to pay for the product than other consumers, and firms must be able to know what customers are willing to pay; and (3) firms must be able to divide up—or segment—the market for the product so that consumers who buy the product at a low price cannot resell it a high price. In the case of *perfect price discrimination*, each consumer pays a price equal to the consumer's willingness to pay.

MyEconLab   Visit www.myeconlab.com to complete these exercises online and get instant feedback.

## Review Questions

**2.1** What is price discrimination? Under what circumstances can a firm successfully practice price discrimination?

**2.2** During a particular week, US Airways charged $498 for a round-trip ticket on a flight from New York to San Francisco, provided that the ticket was purchased at least 14 days in advance. The price of the same ticket purchased two days in advance was $833. Why does US Airways use this pricing strategy?

**2.3** What is yield management? Give an example of a firm using yield management to increase profits.

**2.4** What is perfect price discrimination? Is it likely to ever occur? Explain. Is perfect price discrimination economically efficient? Explain.

**2.5** Is it possible to practice price discrimination across time? Briefly explain.

## Problems and Applications

**2.6** According to an article in the *Wall Street Journal*:

> Airlines have increased restrictions on cheap fares by raising overnight requirements, upping what had commonly been only a one-night stay requirement to two and three nights. The overnights can be weeknights, so those tickets aren't as onerous as Saturday-night stay tickets. But the three-night requirement does limit the utility of discounted fares for road warriors.

What is a "road warrior"? Would a company put restrictions on a service that make the service less desirable to some of its customers?

From Scott McCartney, "Airlines Revive Minimum Stays on Cheap Fares," *Wall Street Journal*, August 19, 2008.

**2.7** An article on the AMC movie theater chain contained the following:

> In July, [AMC] announced plans to offer steeply discounted movie tickets to shows on Friday, Saturday and Sunday mornings. "Seventy-five percent of the revenue comes from the weekend," Mr. Brown [AMC's CEO] said. His recent initiatives are attempts to address the question: "Is there a way with price that you can create opportunity, a new market?"

Why would it be profitable for AMC to sell "steeply discounted" movie tickets for movies it shows on weekend mornings? Wouldn't the firm's revenues be higher if it charged the regular—higher—price for these showings? Briefly explain.

From Kate Kelly, "Box-Office Bounty Stirs Theater Deals," *Wall Street Journal*, August 10, 2006.

**2.8** Political columnist Michael Kinsley wrote, "The infuriating [airline] rules about Saturday night stayovers and so on are a crude alternative to administering truth serum and asking, 'So how much are you really willing to pay?'" Would a truth serum—or some other way of knowing how much people would be willing to pay for an airline ticket—really be all the airlines need to practice price discrimination? Briefly explain.

From Michael Kinsley, "Consuming Gets More Complicated," *Slate*, November 21, 2001.

**2.9** In 2011, the *New York Times* charged $828 to receive the newspaper delivered to your home every day for a year. Journalist Timothy Noah discovered, however, that when he called up the newspaper and threatened to end his subscription, he was offered a 50 percent discount. He became convinced that anyone who called up and threatened to end his or her subscription would be offered the same discount. Briefly explain whether the *New York Times* is practicing price discrimination.

Based on Timothy Noah, "Wise Up, Print Addicts!" www.slate.com, November 17, 2010.

**2.10** **[Related to the** Don't Let This Happen to You **on page 522]** A state law in California makes it illegal for businesses to charge men and women different prices for dry cleaning, laundry, tailoring, or hair grooming. The state legislator who introduced the law did so after a dry cleaner charged her more to have her shirts dry-cleaned than to have her husband's shirts dry-cleaned: "They charged me $1.50 for each of his, and he wears an extra large. They charged $3.50 for each of mine, and I wear a small." According to a newspaper article, "the dry cleaning proprietor told her that the price difference stemmed from the need for hand ironing her shirts because automatic presses are not made to handle small-sized women's garments." The law proved difficult to enforce, with many dry cleaners continuing to ignore it years after it was passed.

**a.** Was the dry cleaner practicing price discrimination, as defined in this chapter? Briefly explain.

**b.** Do you support laws like this one? Briefly explain.

Based on Veronique de Turenne, "Santa Monica Sues Nine Dry Cleaners under Gender Discrimination Law," *Los Angeles Times*, May 13, 2008; and Harry Brooks, "Law Mandates Equality in Dry Cleaning, Hair Styling," *North County (California) Times*, October 7, 2001.

**2.11** **[Related to** Solved Problem 16.2 **on page 524]** Use the graphs on the next page to answer the following questions.

**a.** If this firm wants to maximize profits, what price will it charge in Market 1, and what quantity will it sell?

**b.** If the firm wants to maximize profits, what price will it charge in Market 2, and what quantity will it sell?

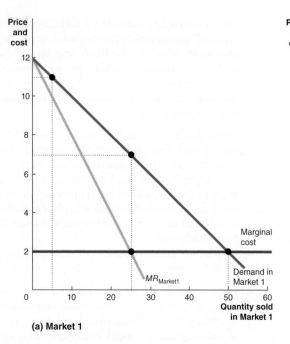

**(a) Market 1**

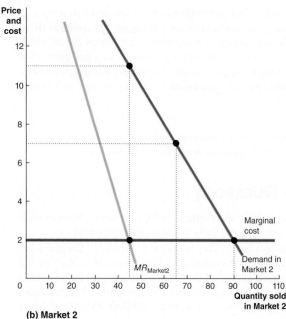

**(b) Market 2**

**2.12** **[Related to** Solved Problem 16.2 **on page 524]** In the fall of 2011, Apple was offering a $100 discount to students on MacBook Pro laptops but only $50 on MacBook Air laptops. The MacBook Air is a very thin, very light laptop that is particularly aimed at businesspeople who travel frequently. Why would Apple cut the price more for MacBook Pros than for MacBook Airs?

**2.13** **[Related to** Solved Problem 16.2 **on page 524]** In addition to discounting the price of computers purchased by students and faculty, Apple also sells certain computer models only to schools and universities. According to a discussion on the MacRumors blog:

> Apple has quietly launched a lower cost $999 iMac for educational institutions this morning. The new low-end model is labeled "Education only" and is not available for individuals. . . . Apple, in the past, has also offered special education only models for institutions. . . . has adjusted the hardware down in order to fit the sub-$1000 price point.

Is Apple engaging in price discrimination in following this policy? If so, why does it prepare special models for educational institutions rather than cutting the prices of existing models purchased by educational buyers? If this is not an example of price discrimination, why doesn't Apple offer these computers to the general public?

From "Apple Launches $999 iMac for Educational Institutions" by Arnold Kim. From www.macrumors.com, August 8, 2011. Reprinted with permission.

**2.14** **[Related to the** Making the Connection **on page 527]** Assume that the marginal cost of admitting one more student is constant for every university. Also assume that at every university, the demand for places in the freshman class is downward sloping. Now, suppose that the public becomes upset that universities charge different prices to different students. Responding to these concerns, the federal government requires universities to charge the same price to each student. In this situation, who will gain, and who will lose?

**2.15** **[Related to the** Chapter Opener **on page 519]** Why does Walt Disney World charge a lower admission price for children aged 3 to 9 than for adults? Why does Disney categorize a 10-year-old as an adult for this purpose? Why does it admit children under 3 for free? Why does it charge residents of Florida a lower price than it charges residents of other states?

**2.16** Briefly explain whether supermarket coupons are a form of price discrimination.

**2.17** **[Related to the** Making the Connection **on page 530]** Some Netflix subscriptions have a higher price and allow more—or unlimited—movies to be rented per month. Others have a lower price and allow fewer movies to be rented per month. Is Netflix practicing price discrimination by offering these different subscriptions? Briefly explain.

**2.18** Draw a graph that shows producer surplus, consumer surplus, and deadweight loss (if any) in a market where the seller practices perfect price discrimination. Profit-maximizing firms select an output at which marginal cost equals marginal revenue. Where is the marginal revenue curve in this graph?

---

| **16.3** | **Other Pricing Strategies,** pages 531–536 |
|---|---|

LEARNING OBJECTIVE: Explain how some firms increase their profits through the use of odd pricing, cost-plus pricing, and two-part tariffs.

## Summary

In addition to price discrimination, firms also use odd pricing, cost-plus pricing, and two-part tariffs as pricing strategies. Firms use *odd pricing*—for example, charging $1.99 rather than

$2.00—because consumers tend to buy more at odd prices than would be predicted from estimated demand curves. With *cost-plus pricing*, firms set the price for a product by adding a percentage markup to average cost. Using cost-plus pricing may be a good way to come close to the profit-maximizing price when marginal revenue or marginal cost is difficult to measure. Some firms can require consumers to pay an initial fee for the right to buy their product and an additional fee for each unit of the product purchased. Economists refer to this situation as a **two-part tariff**. Sam's Club, cell phone companies, and many golf and tennis clubs use two-part tariffs in pricing their products.

MyEconLab   Visit **www.myeconlab.com** to complete these exercises online and get instant feedback.

## Review Questions

**3.1**  What is odd pricing?

**3.2**  What is cost-plus pricing? Is using cost-plus pricing consistent with a firm maximizing profits? How does the elasticity of demand affect the percentage markup?

**3.3**  Give an example of a firm using a two-part tariff as part of its pricing strategy.

**3.4**  Why did the Walt Disney Company switch from charging for admission to Disneyland and charging for the rides to charging for admission and *not* charging for the rides?

## Problems and Applications

**3.5**  One leading explanation for odd pricing is that it allows firms to trick buyers into thinking they are paying less than they really are. If this is true, in what types of markets and among what groups of consumers would you be most likely to find odd pricing? Should the government ban this practice and force companies to round up their prices to the nearest dollar?

**3.6**  According to an article in the *Wall Street Journal*, McDonald's and Burger King have much larger markups on French fries and sodas than on hamburgers. Is it likely that the companies believe that the demand for French fries and sodas is more elastic or less elastic than the demand for hamburgers? Briefly explain.

Based on Diana Ransom, "Can They Really Make Money Off the Dollar Menu?" *Wall Street Journal*, May 21, 2009.

**3.7**  An article in the *Wall Street Journal* gave the following explanation of how products were traditionally priced at Parker-Hannifin Corporation:

> For as long as anyone at the 89-year-old company could recall, Parker used the same simple formula to determine prices of its 800,000 parts—from heat-resistant seals for jet engines to steel valves that hoist buckets on cherry pickers. Company managers would calculate how much it cost to make and deliver each product and add a flat percentage on top, usually aiming for about 35%. Many managers liked the method because it was straightforward.

Is it likely that this system of pricing maximized the firm's profits? Briefly explain.

From Timothy Aeppel, "Changing the Formula: Seeking Perfect Prices, CEO Tears Up the Rules," *Wall Street Journal*, March 27, 2007, p. A1.

**3.8**  [Related to the Making the Connection on page 532] Would you expect a publishing company to use a strict cost-plus pricing system for all its books? How might you find some indication about whether a publishing company actually was using cost-plus pricing for all its books?

**3.9**  Some professional sports teams charge fans a one-time lump sum for a personal seat license. The personal seat license allows a fan the right to buy season tickets each year. No one without a personal seat license can buy season tickets. After the original purchase from the team, the personal seat licenses usually can be bought and sold by fans—whoever owns the seat license in a given year can buy season tickets—but the team does not earn any additional revenue from this buying and selling. Suppose a new sports stadium has been built, and the team is trying to decide on the price to charge for season tickets.

    **a.**  Will the team make more profit from the combination of selling personal seat licenses and season tickets if it keeps the prices of the season tickets low or if it charges the monopoly price? Briefly explain.

    **b.**  After the first year, is the team's strategy for pricing season tickets likely to change?

    **c.**  Will it make a difference in the team's pricing strategy for season tickets if all the personal seat licenses are sold in the first year?

**3.10**  During the nineteenth century, the U.S. Congress encouraged railroad companies to build transcontinental railways across the Great Plains by giving them land grants. At that time, the federal government owned most of the land on the Great Plains. The land grants consisted of the land on which the railway was built and alternating sections of 1 square mile each on either side of the railway to a distance of 6 to 40 miles, depending on the location. The railroad companies were free to sell this land to farmers or anyone else who wanted to buy it. The process of selling the land took decades. Some economic historians have argued that the railroad companies charged lower prices to ship freight because they owned so much land along the tracks. Briefly explain the reasoning of these economic historians.

**3.11**  [Related to the Chapter Opener on page 519] If you visited Disneyland between 1955 and 1982, you could not go on most rides without buying a ticket for the ride—in addition to the ticket necessary to enter the park. Explain why this pricing strategy earned Disney lower profits than the current strategy of requiring visitors to purchase a ticket to enter the park but not requiring an additional ticket to be purchased for each ride.

**3.12**  Thomas Kinnaman, an economist at Bucknell University, has analyzed the pricing of garbage collection:

> Setting the appropriate fee for garbage collection can be tricky when there are both fixed and marginal costs of garbage collection. . . . A curbside price set equal to the average total cost of collection would have high garbage generators partially subsidizing the fixed costs of low garbage generators. For example, if the time that a truck idles outside a one-can household and a two-can household is the same, and the fees are set to cover the total cost of garbage collection, then the two-can household paying twice that of the one-can household has subsidized a portion of the collection costs of the one-can household.

Briefly explain how a city might solve this pricing problem by using a two-part tariff in setting the garbage collection fees it charges households.

"Examining the Justification for Residential Recycling," by Thomas C. Kinnaman from the *Journal of Economic Perspectives*, Vol. 20, No. 4, Fall 2006. Copyright © Thomas Kinnaman and the American Economic Association. Reprinted by permission.

## Chapter Outline and Learning Objectives

# Why Did the San Diego Padres Trade Their Best Player to the Boston Red Sox?

Few businesses generate as much passion as sports teams. Sports fans admire the skills of star athletes, but many question why they are paid high salaries "just for playing a game." Fans also can become frustrated when their teams lose the services of star players to wealthier teams that can afford to sign players to long-term contracts for large salaries. By the end of the 2010 season, Adrian Gonzalez had become one of the best players in Major League Baseball (MLB). Gonzalez was a three-time All-Star for the San Diego Padres and hit 161 home runs in five years, only 2 shy of the all-time record. At the end of the season, San Diego rewarded Gonzalez by exercising the team's option to pay him $6.2 million in 2011—and then traded him to the Boston Red Sox. Gonzalez would have become a free agent at the end of the 2011 season. The Padres had the second-lowest payroll of all MLB teams and could not afford to sign Gonzalez to a long-term contract. The Padres traded Gonzalez for three young—and inexpensive—players. Shortly after the 2011 season began, the Red Sox signed Gonzalez to a seven-year contract worth over $150 million. The Red Sox can afford to pay Gonzalez much more than the Padres could because of the higher revenues the team generates from ticket sales, cable television, and broadcast television and radio.

In Chapter 3, we developed a model for analyzing the demand and supply of goods and services. We will use some of the same concepts in this chapter to analyze the demand and supply of labor and other factors of production. But the markets for factors of production are not like markets for goods and services. The most obvious difference is that in factor markets, firms are demanders, and households are suppliers.

Another difference between the labor market and the markets for goods and services is that concepts of fairness arise more frequently in labor markets. When an athlete signs a contract for millions of dollars, people often wonder: "Why should someone playing a game get paid so much more than teachers, nurses, and other people doing more important jobs?" Because people typically earn most of their income from wages and salaries, they often view the labor market as the most important market in which they participate.

**AN INSIDE LOOK** on **page 572** applies the demand and supply model to the rapidly rising salaries of NCAA Division 1-A basketball coaches.

Based on Ian Browne, "Gonzalez, Red Sox Complete Seven-Year Deal," MLB.com, April 2011; and Jerry Crasnick, "Adrian Gonzalez to Red Sox," EPSN.com, December 5, 2010.

## Economics in Your Life

### How Can You Convince Your Boss to Give You a Raise?

Imagine that you have worked for a local sandwich shop for over a year and are preparing to ask for a raise. You might tell the manager that you are a good employee, with a good attitude and work ethic. You might also explain that you have learned more about your job and are now able to make sandwiches more quickly, track inventory more accurately, and work the cash register more effectively than when you were first hired. Will this be enough to convince your manager to give you a raise? How can you convince your manager that you are worth more money than you are currently being paid? As you read this chapter, see if you can answer these questions. You can check your answers against those we provide on **page 571** at the end of this chapter.

**Factors of production** Labor, capital, natural resources, and other inputs used to produce goods and services.

Firms use **factors of production**—such as labor, capital, and natural resources—to produce goods and services. For example, the Boston Red Sox use labor (baseball players), capital (Fenway Park), and natural resources (the land on which Fenway Park sits) to produce baseball games. In this chapter, we will explore how firms choose the profit-maximizing quantity of labor and other factors of production. The interaction between firms' demand for labor and households' supply of labor determines the equilibrium wage rate.

Because there are many different types of labor, there are many different labor markets. The equilibrium wage in the market for baseball players is much higher than the equilibrium wage in the market for college professors. We will explore why this is true. We will also explore how factors such as discrimination, unions, and compensation for dangerous or unpleasant jobs help explain differences among wages. We will then look at *personnel economics*, which is concerned with how firms can use economic analysis to design their employee compensation plans. Finally, we will analyze the markets for other factors of production.

---

**17.1 LEARNING OBJECTIVE**

Explain how firms choose the profit-maximizing quantity of labor to employ.

**Derived demand** The demand for a factor of production; it depends on the demand for the good the factor produces.

## The Demand for Labor

Up until now, we have concentrated on consumer demand for final goods and services. The demand for labor is different from the demand for final goods and services because it is a *derived demand*. A **derived demand** for a factor of production depends on the demand for the good the factor produces. You demand an Apple iPhone because of the utility you receive from making phone calls, texting, playing games, and listening to music. Apple's demand for the labor to make iPhones is derived from the underlying consumer demand for iPhones. As a result, we can say that Apple's demand for labor depends primarily on two factors:

1. The additional iPhones Apple can produce if it hires one more worker
2. The additional revenue Apple receives from selling the additional iPhones

(In fact, Apple's suppliers, rather than Apple itself, manufacture the iPhone. For simplicity, we are assuming here that Apple does the manufacturing.)

### The Marginal Revenue Product of Labor

**Marginal product of labor** The additional output a firm produces as a result of hiring one more worker.

Let's consider an example. To keep the main point clear, we'll assume that in the short run, Apple can increase production of iPhones only by increasing the quantity of labor it employs. The table in Figure 17.1 shows the relationship between the quantity of workers Apple hires, the quantity of iPhones it produces, the additional revenue from selling the additional iPhones, and the additional profit from hiring each additional worker.

For simplicity, we are keeping the scale of Apple's factory very small. We will also assume that Apple is a perfect competitor both in the market for selling cell phones and in the market for hiring labor. This means that Apple is a *price taker* in both markets. Although this is not realistic, the basic analysis would not change if we assumed that Apple can affect the price of cell phones and the wage paid to workers. Given these assumptions, suppose that Apple can sell as many iPhones as it wants at a price of $200 and can hire as many workers as it wants at a wage of $600 per week. Remember from Chapter 11 that the additional output a firm produces as a result of hiring one more worker is called the **marginal product of labor**. In the table in Figure 17.1, we calculate the marginal product of labor as the change in total output as each additional worker is hired. As we saw in Chapter 11, because of *the law of diminishing returns*, the marginal product of labor declines as a firm hires more workers.

When deciding how many workers to hire, a firm is not interested in how much *output* will increase as it hires another worker but in how much *revenue* will increase as it hires another worker. In other words, what matters is how much the firm's revenue will rise when it sells the additional output it can produce by hiring one more worker.

| Number of Workers | Output of iPhones per Week | Marginal Product of Labor (iPhones per week) | Product Price | Marginal Revenue Product of Labor (dollars per week) | Wage (dollars per week) | Additional Profit from Hiring One More Worker (dollars per week) |
|---|---|---|---|---|---|---|
| L | Q | MP | P | MRP = P x MP | W | MRP − W |
| 0 | 0 | — | $200 | — | $600 | — |
| 1 | 6 | 6 | 200 | $1,200 | 600 | $600 |
| 2 | 11 | 5 | 200 | 1,000 | 600 | 400 |
| 3 | 15 | 4 | 200 | 800 | 600 | 200 |
| 4 | 18 | 3 | 200 | 600 | 600 | 0 |
| 5 | 20 | 2 | 200 | 400 | 600 | −200 |
| 6 | 21 | 1 | 200 | 200 | 600 | −400 |

### Figure 17.1

**The Marginal Revenue Product of Labor and the Demand for Labor**

The marginal revenue product of labor equals the marginal product of labor multiplied by the price of the good. The marginal revenue product curve slopes downward because diminishing returns cause the marginal product of labor to decline as more workers are hired. A firm maximizes profits by hiring workers up to the point where the wage equals the marginal revenue product of labor. The marginal revenue product of labor curve is the firm's demand curve for labor because it tells the firm the profit-maximizing quantity of workers to hire at each wage. For example, using the demand curve shown in this figure, if the wage is $600, the firm will hire 4 workers.

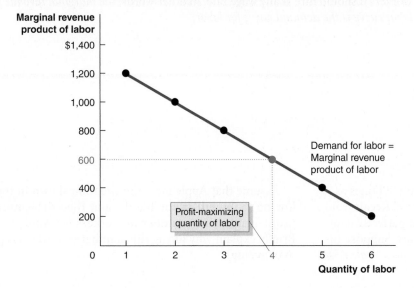

We can calculate this amount, which is called the **marginal revenue product of labor** (**MRP**), by multiplying the additional output produced by the product price. For example, consider what happens if Apple increases the number of workers hired from 2 to 3. The table in Figure 17.1 shows that hiring the third worker allows Apple to increase its weekly output of iPhones from 11 to 15, so the marginal product of labor is 4 iPhones. The price of the iPhones is $200, so the marginal revenue product of the third worker is 4 × $200 or $800. In other words, Apple adds $800 to its revenue as a result of hiring the third worker. In the graph, we plot the values of the marginal revenue product of labor at each quantity of labor.

To decide how many workers to hire, Apple must compare the additional revenue it earns from hiring another worker to the increase in its costs from paying that worker. The difference between the additional revenue and the additional cost is the additional profit (or loss) from hiring one more worker. This additional profit is shown in the last column of the table in Figure 17.1 and is calculated by subtracting the wage from the marginal revenue product of labor. As long as the marginal revenue product of labor is greater than the wage, Apple's profits are increasing, and it should continue to hire more workers. When the marginal revenue product of labor is less than the wage, Apple's profits are falling, and it should hire fewer workers. When the marginal revenue product of labor is equal to the wage, Apple has maximized its profits by hiring the optimal number of workers. The values in the table show that Apple should hire 4 workers. If Apple hires a fifth worker, the marginal revenue product of $400 will be less than the wage of $600, and its profits will fall by $200. Table 17.1 summarizes the relationship between the marginal revenue product of labor and the wage.

**Marginal revenue product of labor** (**MRP**) The change in a firm's revenue as a result of hiring one more worker.

| **Table 17.1** | When ... | the firm ... |
|---|---|---|
| **The Relationship between the Marginal Revenue Product of Labor and the Wage** | $MRP > W$, | should hire more workers to increase profits. |
| | $MRP < W$, | should hire fewer workers to increase profits. |
| | $MRP = W$, | is hiring the optimal number of workers and is maximizing profits. |

We can see from Figure 17.1 that if Apple has to pay a wage of $600 per week, it should hire 4 workers. If the wage were to rise to $1,000, then applying the rule that profits are maximized where the marginal revenue product of labor equals the wage, Apple should hire only 2 workers. Similarly, if the wage is only $400 per week, Apple should hire 5 workers. In fact, the marginal revenue product curve tells a firm how many workers it should hire at any wage rate. In other words, *the marginal revenue product of labor curve is the demand curve for labor.*

# Solved Problem 17.1

## Hiring Decisions by a Firm That Is a Price Maker

We have assumed that Apple can sell as many iPhones as it wants to sell, without having to cut the price. Recall from Chapter 12 that this is the case for firms in perfectly competitive markets. These firms are *price takers*. Suppose instead that a firm has market power and is a *price maker*, so that to increase sales, it must reduce the price.

Assume that Apple faces the situation shown in the following table. Fill in the blanks and then determine the profit-maximizing number of workers for Apple to hire. Briefly explain why hiring this number of workers is profit maximizing.

| (1) Quantity of Labor | (2) Output of iPhones per Week | (3) Marginal Product of Labor | (4) Product Price | (5) Total Revenue | (6) Marginal Revenue Product of Labor | (7) Wage | (8) Additional Profit from Hiring One Additional Worker |
|---|---|---|---|---|---|---|---|
| 0 | 0 | — | $200 | | — | $500 | — |
| 1 | 6 | 6 | 180 | | | 500 | |
| 2 | 11 | 5 | 160 | | | 500 | |
| 3 | 15 | 4 | 140 | | | 500 | |
| 4 | 18 | 3 | 120 | | | 500 | |
| 5 | 20 | 2 | 100 | | | 500 | |
| 6 | 21 | 1 | 80 | | | 500 | |

## Solving the Problem

**Step 1:** **Review the chapter material.** This problem is about determining the profit-maximizing quantity of labor for a firm to hire, so you may want to review the section "The Demand for Labor," which begins on page 546.

**Step 2:** **Fill in the blanks in the table.** As Apple hires more workers, it sells more iPhones and earns more revenue. You can calculate how revenue increases by multiplying the number of iPhones produced—shown in column (2)—by the price—shown in column (4). Then you can calculate the marginal revenue product of labor as the change in revenue as each additional worker is hired. (Notice that in this case, marginal revenue product is *not* calculated by multiplying the marginal product by the product price. Because Apple is a price maker, its marginal revenue from selling additional iPhones is less than the price of iPhones.) Finally, you can calculate the additional profit from hiring one more worker by subtracting the wage—shown in column (7)—from each worker's marginal revenue product.

| (1) Quantity of Labor | (2) Output of iPhones per Week | (3) Marginal Product of Labor | (4) Product Price | (5) Total Revenue | (6) Marginal Revenue Product of Labor | (7) Wage | (8) Additional Profit from Hiring One Additional Worker |
|---|---|---|---|---|---|---|---|
| 0 | 0 | — | $200 | $0 | — | $500 | — |
| 1 | 6 | 6 | 180 | 1,080 | $1,080 | 500 | $580 |
| 2 | 11 | 5 | 160 | 1,760 | 680 | 500 | 180 |
| 3 | 15 | 4 | 140 | 2,100 | 340 | 500 | −160 |
| 4 | 18 | 3 | 120 | 2,160 | 60 | 500 | −440 |
| 5 | 20 | 2 | 100 | 2,000 | −160 | 500 | −660 |
| 6 | 21 | 1 | 80 | 1,680 | −320 | 500 | −820 |

**Step 3:** **Use the information in the table to determine the profit-maximizing quantity of workers to hire.** To determine the profit-maximizing quantity of workers to hire, you need to compare the marginal revenue product of labor with the wage. Column (8) makes this comparison by subtracting the wage from the marginal revenue product. As long as the values in column (8) are positive, the firm should continue to hire workers. The marginal revenue product of the second worker is $680, and the wage is $500, so column (8) shows that hiring the second worker will add $180 to Apple's profits. The marginal revenue product of the third worker is $340, and the wage is $500, so hiring the third worker would reduce Apple's profits by $160. Therefore, Apple will maximize profits by hiring 2 workers.

**Your Turn:** For more practice, do problem 1.6 on page 574 at the end of this chapter.

MyEconLab

## The Market Demand Curve for Labor

We can determine the market demand curve for labor in the same way we determine a market demand curve for a good. We saw in Chapter 10 that the market demand curve for a good is determined by adding up the quantity of the good demanded by each consumer at each price. Similarly, the market demand curve for labor is determined by adding up the quantity of labor demanded by each firm at each wage, holding constant all other variables that might affect the willingness of firms to hire workers.

## Factors That Shift the Market Demand Curve for Labor

In constructing the demand curve for labor, we held constant all variables—except for the wage—that would affect the willingness of firms to demand labor. An increase or a decrease in the wage causes *an increase or a decrease in the quantity of labor demanded*, which we show by a movement along the demand curve. If any variable other than the wage changes, the result is *an increase or a decrease in the demand for labor*, which we show by a shift of the demand curve. The following are the five most important variables that cause the labor demand curve to shift:

**Human capital** The accumulated training and skills that workers possess.

1. ***Increases in human capital.*** **Human capital** represents the accumulated training and skills that workers possess. For example, a worker with a college education generally has more skills and is more productive than a worker who has only a high school diploma. If workers become more educated and are therefore able to produce more output per day, the demand for their services will increase, shifting the labor demand curve to the right.

2. ***Changes in technology.*** As new and better machinery and equipment are developed, workers become more productive. This effect causes the labor demand curve to shift to the right over time.

3. ***Changes in the price of the product.*** The marginal revenue product of labor depends on the price a firm receives for its output. A higher price increases the marginal revenue product and shifts the labor demand curve to the right. A lower price shifts the labor demand curve to the left.

4. ***Changes in the quantity of other inputs.*** Workers are able to produce more if they have more machinery and other inputs available to them. The marginal product of labor in the United States is higher than the marginal product of labor in most other countries in large part because U.S. firms provide workers with more machinery and equipment. Over time, workers in the United States have had increasing amounts of other inputs available to them, and that has increased their productivity and caused the demand for labor to shift to the right.

5. ***Changes in the number of firms in the market.*** If new firms enter the market, the demand for labor will shift to the right. If firms exit the market, the demand for labor will shift to the left. This effect is similar to the effect that increasing or decreasing the number of consumers in a market has on the demand for a good.

# The Supply of Labor

Having discussed the demand for labor, we can now consider the supply of labor. Of the many trade-offs each of us faces in life, one of the most important is how to divide up the 24 hours in a day between labor and leisure. Every hour spent posting to Facebook, walking on the beach, or in other forms of leisure is one hour less spent working. Because in devoting an hour to leisure we give up an hour's earnings from working, the *opportunity cost* of leisure is the wage. The higher the wage we could earn working, the higher the opportunity cost of leisure. Therefore, as the wage increases, we tend to take less leisure and work more. This relationship explains why the labor supply curve for most people is upward sloping, as Figure 17.2 shows.

**Figure 17.2**

**The Labor Supply Curve**

As the wage increases, the opportunity cost of leisure increases, causing individuals to supply a greater quantity of labor. Therefore, the labor supply curve is upward sloping.

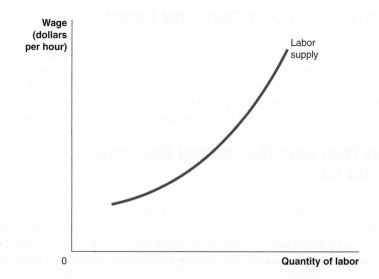

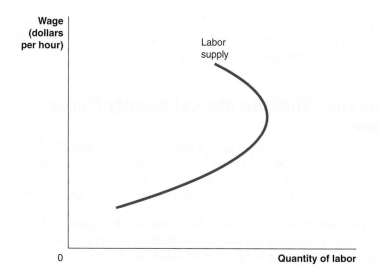

**Figure 17.3**

**A Backward-Bending Labor Supply Curve**

As the wage rises, a greater quantity of labor is usually supplied. As the wage climbs above a certain level, the individual is able to afford more leisure even though the opportunity cost of leisure is high. The result may be a smaller quantity of labor supplied.

Although we normally expect the labor supply curve for an individual to be upward sloping, it is possible that at very high wage levels, the labor supply curve of an individual might be *backward bending*, so that higher wages actually result in a *smaller* quantity of labor supplied, as shown in Figure 17.3. To understand why, recall the definitions of the *substitution effect* and the *income effect*, which we introduced in Chapter 3 and discussed more fully in Chapter 10. The substitution effect of a price change refers to the fact that an increase in price makes a good more expensive *relative* to other goods. In the case of a wage change, the substitution effect refers to the fact that an increase in the wage raises the opportunity cost of leisure and causes a worker to devote *more* time to working and less time to leisure.

The income effect of a price change refers to the change in the quantity demanded of a good that results from changes in consumer purchasing power as a result of a price change. An increase in the wage will clearly increase a consumer's purchasing power for any given number of hours worked. For a normal good, the income effect leads to a larger quantity demanded. Because leisure is a normal good, the income effect of a wage increase will cause a worker to devote *less* time to working and more time to leisure. So, the substitution effect of a wage increase causes a worker to supply a larger quantity of labor, but the income effect causes a worker to supply a smaller quantity of labor. Whether a worker supplies more or less labor following a wage increase depends on whether the substitution effect is larger than the income effect. Figure 17.3 shows the typical case of the substitution effect being larger than the income effect at low levels of wages—so the worker supplies a larger quantity of labor as the wage rises—and the income effect being larger than the substitution effect at high levels of wages—so the worker supplies a smaller quantity of labor as the wage rises. For example, suppose an attorney has become quite successful and can charge clients very high fees. Or suppose a rock band has become very popular and receives a large payment for every concert it performs. In these cases, there is a high opportunity cost for the lawyer to turn down another client to take a longer vacation or for the band to turn down another concert. But because their incomes are already very high, they may decide to give up additional income for more leisure. For the lawyer or the rock band, the income effect is larger than the substitution effect, and a higher wage causes them to supply *less* labor.

## The Market Supply Curve of Labor

We can determine the market supply curve of labor in the same way we determine a market supply curve of a good. We saw in Chapter 12 that the market supply curve of a good is determined by adding up the quantity of the good supplied by each firm at each price. Similarly, the market supply curve of labor is determined by adding up the quantity of labor supplied by each worker at each wage, holding constant all other variables that might affect the willingness of workers to supply labor.

## Factors That Shift the Market Supply Curve of Labor

In constructing the market supply curve of labor, we hold constant all other variables that would affect the willingness of workers to supply labor, except the wage. If any of these other variables change, the market supply curve will shift. The following are the three most important variables that cause the market supply curve of labor to shift:

1. *Increasing population.* As the population grows due to the number of births exceeding the number of deaths and due to immigration, the supply curve of labor shifts to the right. The effects of immigration on labor supply are largest in the markets for unskilled workers. In some large cities in the United States, for example, the majority of taxi drivers and workers in hotels and restaurants are immigrants. Some supporters of reducing immigration argue that wages in these jobs have been depressed by the increased supply of labor from immigrants.

2. *Changing demographics.* *Demographics* refers to the composition of the population. The more people who are between the ages of 16 and 65, the greater the quantity of labor supplied. During the 1970s and 1980s, the U.S. labor force grew particularly rapidly as members of the baby boom generation—born between 1946 and 1964—first began working. In contrast, a low birthrate in Japan has resulted in an aging population. The number of working-age people in Japan actually began to decline during the 1990s, causing the labor supply curve to shift to the left.

   A related demographic issue is the changing role of women in the labor force. In 1900, only 21 percent of women in the United States were in the labor force. By 1950, this figure had risen to 30 percent, and today it is 60 percent. This increase in the *labor force participation* of women has significantly increased the supply of labor in the United States.

3. *Changing alternatives.* The labor supply in any particular labor market depends, in part, on the opportunities available in other labor markets. For example, the problems in the financial services industry that began in 2007 reduced the opportunities for investment bankers, stockbrokers, and other financial workers. Many workers left this industry—causing the labor supply curve to shift to the left—and entered other markets, causing the labor supply curves to shift to the right in those markets. People who have lost jobs or who have low incomes are eligible for unemployment insurance and other payments from the government. The more generous these payments are, the less pressure unemployed workers have to quickly find another job. In many European countries, it is much easier than in the United States for unemployed workers to receive a greater replacement of their wage income from government payments. Many economists believe generous unemployment benefits help explain the higher unemployment rates experienced in some European countries.

**17.3 LEARNING** OBJECTIVE

Explain how equilibrium wages are determined in labor markets.

## Equilibrium in the Labor Market

In Figure 17.4, we bring together labor demand and labor supply to determine equilibrium in the labor market. We can use demand and supply to analyze changes in the equilibrium wage and the level of employment for the entire labor market, and we can also use it to analyze markets for different types of labor, such as baseball players or college professors.

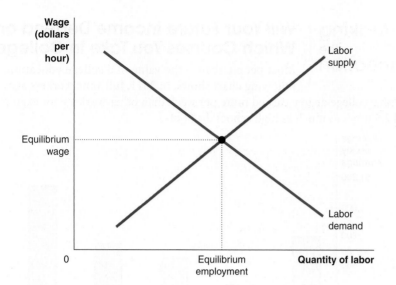

**Figure 17.4**

**Equilibrium in the Labor Market**

As in other markets, equilibrium in the labor market occurs where the demand curve for labor and the supply curve of labor intersect.

# The Effect on Equilibrium Wages of a Shift in Labor Demand

In many labor markets, increases over time in labor productivity will cause the demand for labor to increase. As Figure 17.5 shows, if labor supply is unchanged, an increase in labor demand will increase both the equilibrium wage and the number of workers employed.

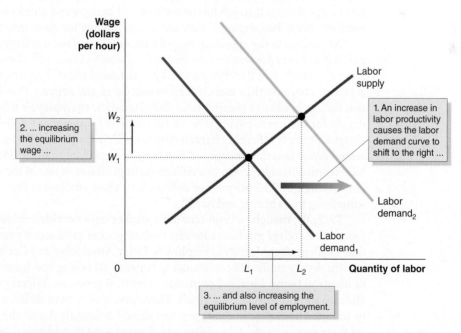

**Figure 17.5** The Effect of an Increase in Labor Demand

Increases in labor demand will cause the equilibrium wage and the equilibrium level of employment to rise:

1. If the productivity of workers rises, the marginal revenue product increases, causing the labor demand curve to shift to the right.

2. The equilibrium wage rises from $W_1$ to $W_2$.
3. The equilibrium level of employment rises from $L_1$ to $L_2$.

| Making the Connection | **Will Your Future Income Depend on Which Courses You Take in College?** |
|---|---|

Most people realize the value of a college education. As the following chart shows, in 2011, full-time workers ages 25 and over with a college degree earned more per week than other workers; for example, they earned 2.5 times as much as high school dropouts.

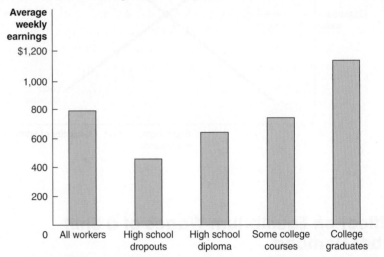

Data from U.S. Bureau of Labor Statistics, "Usual Weekly Earnings of Wage and Salary Workers," July 19, 2011.

Why do college graduates earn more than others? The obvious answer would seem to be that a college education provides skills that increase productivity. Some economists, though, advocate an alternative explanation, known as the *signaling hypothesis*, first proposed by Nobel Laureate A. Michael Spence of New York University. This hypothesis is based on the idea that job applicants will always have more information than will potential employers about how productive the applicants are likely to be. Although employers attempt through job interviews and background checks to distinguish "good workers" from "bad workers," they are always looking for more information.

According to the signaling hypothesis, employers see a college education as a signal that workers possess certain desirable characteristics: self-discipline, the ability to meet deadlines, and the ability to make a sustained effort. Employers value these characteristics because they usually lead to success in any activity. People generally believe that college graduates possess these characteristics, so employers often require a college degree for their best-paying jobs. In this view, the signal that a college education sends about a person's inherent characteristics—which the person presumably already possessed *before* entering college—is much more important than any skills the person may have learned in college. Or, as a college math professor of one of the authors put it (only half-jokingly): "The purpose of college is to show employers that you can succeed at something that's boring and hard."

Recently, though, several economic studies have provided evidence that the higher incomes of college graduates are due to their greater productivity rather than the signal that a college degree sends to employers. Orley Ashenfelter and Cecilia Rouse of Princeton University studied the relationship between schooling and income among 700 pairs of identical twins. Identical twins have identical genes, so differences in their inherent abilities should be relatively small. Therefore, if they have different numbers of years in school, differences in their earnings should be mainly due to the effect of schooling on their productivity. Ashenfelter and Rouse found that identical twins had returns of about 9 percent per additional year of schooling, enough to account for most of the gap in income between high school graduates and college graduates.

Daniel Hamermesh and Stephen G. Donald of the University of Texas studied the determinants of the earnings of college graduates 5 to 25 years after graduation. They collected extensive information on each person in their study, including the person's SAT scores, rank in high school graduating class, grades in every college course taken, and college major. Hamermesh and Donald discovered that, holding constant all other factors, business and engineering majors earned more than graduates with other majors. They also discovered that taking science and math courses has a large effect on future earnings: "A student who takes 15 credits of upper-division science and math courses and obtains a B average in them will earn about 10% more than an otherwise identical student in the same major . . . who takes no upper-division classes in these areas." This result held even after adjusting for a student's SAT score. The study by Hamermesh and Donald contradicts the signaling hypothesis because if that hypothesis is correct, the choice of courses taken in college should be of minor importance compared with the signal workers send to employers just by having completed college.

Based on Orley Ashenfelter and Cecilia Rouse, "Income, Schooling, and Ability: Evidence from a New Sample of Identical Twins," *Quarterly Journal of Economics*, Vol. 113, No. 1, February 1998, pp. 253–284; and Daniel S. Hamermesh and Stephen G. Donald, "The Effect of College Curriculum on Earnings: An Affinity Identifier for Non-Ignorable Non-Response Bias," *Journal of Econometrics*, Vol. 144, No. 2, June 2008, pp. 479–491.

**Your Turn:** Test your understanding by doing related problem 3.3 on page 576 at the end of this chapter.    MyEconLab

---

## The Effect on Equilibrium Wages of a Shift in Labor Supply

What is the effect on the equilibrium wage of an increase in labor supply due to population growth? As Figure 17.6 shows, if labor demand is unchanged, an increase in labor supply will decrease the equilibrium wage but increase the number of workers employed.

Whether the wage rises in a market depends on whether demand increases faster than supply. For example, as Facebook, Twitter, Zynga, and other social networking sites became increasingly popular, the demand for software engineers in California's Silicon Valley began to increase faster than the supply of new engineers graduating from college. By 2011, starting salaries for new graduates had increased from about $80,000 in 2009 to as much as $150,000. To keep their engineers from jumping to other employers, Google, Tagged, and other firms had to give their existing employees across-the-board raises. Start-up firms found that the salaries they needed to pay were raising their costs to levels that made it difficult to compete. If these escalating salaries lead more students to graduate with degrees in software engineering, the increased labor supply could eventually bring down salaries.

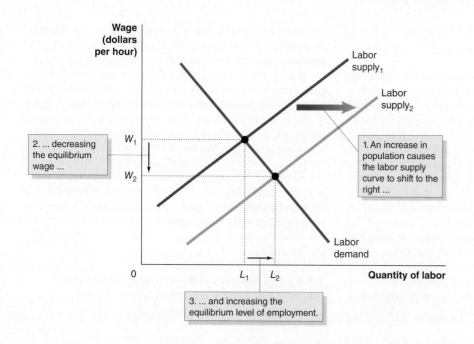

**Figure 17.6**

**The Effect of an Increase in Labor Supply**

Increases in labor supply will cause the equilibrium wage to fall but the equilibrium level of employment to rise:

1. As population increases, the labor supply curve shifts to the right.
2. The equilibrium wage falls from $W_1$ to $W_2$.
3. The equilibrium level of employment increases from $L_1$ to $L_2$.

**17.4 LEARNING** OBJECTIVE

Use demand and supply
analysis to explain how
compensating differentials,
discrimination, and labor
unions cause wages to differ.

# Explaining Differences in Wages

A key conclusion of our discussion of the labor market is that the equilibrium wage equals the marginal revenue product of labor. The more productive workers are and the higher the price for which workers' output can be sold, the higher the wages workers will receive. At the beginning of the chapter, we raised the question of why Major League Baseball players are paid so much more than most other workers. We are now ready to use demand and supply analysis to answer this question. Figure 17.7 shows the demand and supply curves for Major League Baseball players and the demand and supply curves for college professors.

Consider the marginal revenue product of baseball players, which is the additional revenue a team owner will receive from hiring one more player. Baseball players are hired to produce baseball games that are then sold to fans who pay admission to baseball stadiums and to radio and television stations that broadcast the games. Because a Major League Baseball team can sell each baseball game for a large amount, the marginal revenue product of baseball players is high. The supply of people with the ability to play Major League Baseball is also very limited. As a result, the average annual salary of the 750 Major League Baseball players was $3,305,000 in 2011.

The marginal revenue product of college professors is much lower than for baseball players. College professors are hired to produce college educations that are sold to students and their parents. Although one year's college tuition is quite high at many colleges, hiring one more professor allows a college to admit at most a few more students. So, the marginal revenue product of a college professor is much lower than the marginal revenue product of a baseball player. There are also many more people who possess the skills to be a college professor than possess the skills to be a Major League Baseball player. As a result, the average annual salary of the country's 1.5 million college professors was about $84,000 in 2011.

This still leaves unanswered the question raised at the beginning of this chapter: Why are the Boston Red Sox willing to pay Adrian Gonzalez more than the San Diego Padres, his previous team, were? Gonzlez's marginal product—which we can think of as the extra games a team will win by employing him—should be about the same in Boston as in San Diego. But his *marginal revenue product* will be higher in Boston. Because the

# Don't Let This Happen to You

### Remember That Prices and Wages Are Determined at the Margin

You have probably heard some variation of the following remark: "We could live without baseball, but we can't live without the garbage being hauled away. In a more rational world, garbage collectors would be paid more than baseball players." This remark seems logical: The total value to society of having the garbage hauled away certainly is greater than the total value of baseball games. But wages—like prices—do not depend on total value but on *marginal* value. The *additional* baseball games the Boston Red Sox expect to win by signing Adrian Gonzalez will result in millions of dollars in increased revenue. The supply of people with the ability to play Major League Baseball is very limited. The supply of people with the ability to be trash haulers is much greater. If a trash-hauling firm hires another worker, the *additional* trash-hauling services it can now offer will bring in a relatively small amount of

revenue. The *total* value of baseball games and the *total* value of trash hauling are not relevant in determining the relative salaries of baseball players and garbage collectors.

This point is related to the diamond and water paradox first noted by Adam Smith. On the one hand, water is very valuable—we literally couldn't live without it—but its price is very low. On the other hand, apart from a few industrial purposes, diamonds are used only for jewelry, yet their prices are quite high. We resolve the paradox by noting that the price of water is low because the supply is very large and the additional benefit consumers receive from the last gallon purchased is low. The price of diamonds is high because the supply is very small, and the additional benefit consumers receive from the last diamond purchased is high.

MyEconLab

**Your Turn:** Test your understanding by doing related problem 4.8 on page 576 at the end of this chapter.

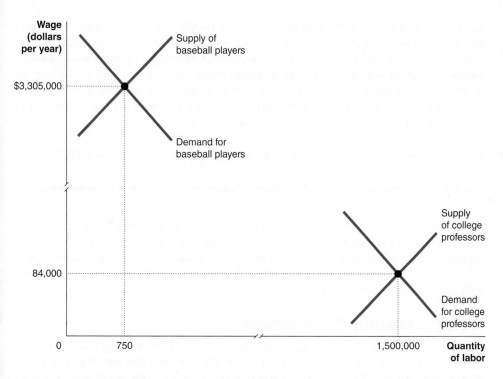

**Figure 17.7**

**Baseball Players Are Paid More Than College Professors**

The marginal revenue product of baseball players is very high, and the supply of people with the ability to play Major League Baseball is low. The result is that the 750 Major League Baseball players receive an average wage of $3,305,000. The marginal revenue product of college professors is much lower, and the supply of people with the ability to be college professors is much higher. The result is that the 1.5 million college professors in the United States receive an average wage of $84,000, far below the average wage of baseball players.

Red Sox have fans throughout the New England states, the number of their fans is much greater than the number of San Diego fans, so winning additional games will result in a greater increase in attendance at Boston Red Sox games than it would at San Diego Padres games. It will also result in a greater increase in viewers for Red Sox games on television. Therefore, the Red Sox are able to sell the extra wins that Gonzalez produces for much more than the Padres can. This difference explains why the Red Sox were willing to pay Gonzalez so much more than the Padres were willing to pay him.

## Making the Connection | Technology and the Earnings of "Superstars"

The gap between Adrian Gonzalez's salary and the salary of the lowest-paid baseball players is much greater than the gap between the salaries paid during the 1950s and 1960s to top players such as Mickey Mantle and Willie Mays and the salaries of the lowest-paid players. Similarly, the gap between the $15 million Angelina Jolie is paid to star in a movie and the salary paid to an actor in a minor role is much greater than the gap between the salaries paid during the 1930s and 1940s to stars such as Clark Gable and Cary Grant and the salaries paid to bit players. In fact, in most areas of sports and entertainment, the highest-paid performers—the "superstars"—now have much higher incomes relative to other members of their professions than was true a few decades ago.

The increase in the relative incomes of superstars is mainly due to technological advances. The spread of cable television has increased the number of potential viewers of Red Sox games, but many of those viewers will watch only if the Red Sox are winning. This increases the value to the Red Sox of winning games and, therefore, increases Gonzalez's marginal revenue product and the salary he can earn.

With Blu-ray discs, DVDs, Internet streaming video, and pay-per-view cable, the value to movie studios of producing a hit movie has risen greatly. Not surprisingly, movie studios have also increased their willingness to pay large salaries to stars such as Angelina Jolie and Will Smith because they think these superstars will significantly raise the chances that a film will be successful.

This process has been going on for a long time. For instance, before the invention of the motion picture, anyone who wanted to see a play had to attend the theater and

*Why does Angelina Jolie earn more today relative to the typical actor than stars did in the 1940s?*

see a live performance. Limits on the number of people who could see the best actors and actresses perform created an opportunity for many more people to succeed in the acting profession, and the gap between the salaries earned by the best actors and the salaries earned by average actors was relatively small. Today, when a hit movie starring Angelina Jolie is available on DVD or for downloading, millions of people will buy or rent it, and they will not be forced to spend money to see a lesser actress, as their great-great-grandparents might have been.

MyEconLab    **Your Turn:** Test your understanding by doing related problems 4.11 and 4.12 on page 577 at the end of this chapter.

---

Differences in marginal revenue products are the most important factor in explaining differences in wages, but they are not the whole story. To provide a more complete explanation for differences in wages, we must take into account three important aspects of labor markets: compensating differentials, discrimination, and labor unions. We begin with compensating differentials.

## Compensating Differentials

Suppose Paul runs a pizza parlor and acquires a reputation for being a bad boss who yells at his workers and is generally unpleasant. Two blocks away, Brendan also runs a pizza parlor, but Brendan is always very polite to his workers. We would expect in these circumstances that Paul will have to pay a higher wage than Brendan to attract and retain workers. Higher wages that compensate workers for unpleasant aspects of a job are called **compensating differentials**.

**Compensating differentials** Higher wages that compensate workers for unpleasant aspects of a job.

If working in a dynamite factory requires the same degree of training and education as working in a semiconductor factory but is much more dangerous, a larger number of workers will want to work making semiconductors than will want to work making dynamite. As a consequence, the wages of dynamite workers will be higher than the wages of semiconductor workers. We can think of the difference in wages as being the price of risk. As each worker decides on his or her willingness to assume risk and decides how much higher the wage must be to compensate for assuming more risk, wages will adjust so that dynamite factories will end up paying wages that are just high enough to compensate workers who choose to work there for the extra risk they assume. Only when workers in dynamite factories have been fully compensated with higher wages for the additional risk they assume will dynamite companies be able to attract enough workers.

One surprising implication of compensating differentials is that *laws protecting the health and safety of workers may not make workers better off.* To see this, suppose that dynamite factories pay wages of $25 per hour, and semiconductor factories pay wages of $20 per hour, with the $5 difference in wages being a compensating differential for the greater risk of working in a dynamite factory. Suppose that the government passes a law regulating the manufacture of dynamite in order to improve safety in dynamite factories. As a result of this law, dynamite factories are no longer any more dangerous than semiconductor factories. Once this happens, the wages in dynamite factories will decline to $20 per hour, the same as in semiconductor factories. Are workers in dynamite factories any better or worse off? Before the law was passed, their wages were $25 per hour, but $5 per hour was a compensating differential for the extra risk they were exposed to. Now their wages are only $20 per hour, but the extra risk has been eliminated. The conclusion seems to be that dynamite workers are no better off as a result of the safety legislation.

This conclusion is true, though, only if the compensating differential actually does compensate workers fully for the additional risk. Nobel Laureate George Akerlof of the University of California, Berkeley, and William Dickens of the Brookings Institution have argued that the psychological principle known as *cognitive dissonance* might cause workers to underestimate the true risk of their jobs. According to this principle, people prefer to think of themselves as intelligent and rational and tend to reject evidence that seems to contradict this image. Because working in a very hazardous job may seem irrational, workers in such jobs may refuse to believe that the jobs really are hazardous. Akerlof and Dickens present evidence that workers in chemical plants producing benzene and workers in nuclear power plants underestimate the hazards of their jobs. If this is true, the wages of these workers will not be high enough to compensate them fully for the risk they have assumed. So, in this situation, safety legislation may make workers better off.

<table>
<tr><td>## Making<br>the<br>Connection</td><td>## Are U.S. Firms Handicapped<br>by Paying for Their Employees'<br>Health Insurance?</td></tr>
</table>

When choosing among jobs, workers consider all aspects of each job. This includes how hazardous or otherwise unpleasant a job may be. It also includes the total compensation received from a job. To this point, we have assumed that compensation takes the form of wages. But many jobs also pay fringe benefits, such as employer contributions to retirement accounts or employer-provided health insurance.

So, it would be more accurate to describe the intersection of the labor demand and labor supply curves as determining the equilibrium compensation rather than the equilibrium wage. If the demand for, say, software engineers increases, the equilibrium compensation will increase. This increase in compensation could be partly an increase in wages and partly an increase in employer contributions to retirement accounts or to health insurance plans.

*Did paying for employees' health care contribute to Chrysler's bankruptcy in 2009?*

In many countries, the government either supplies health care directly by operating hospitals and employing doctors, or it pays for most health care expenses even if hospitals are not government owned and doctors are not government employees. By contrast, in the United States about two-thirds of the population is covered by private health insurance, most of which is provided by employers. As a result, at many firms in the United States, a significant portion of the compensation workers receive is in the form of employer payments for health insurance. Does paying for health insurance put U.S. firms at a disadvantage in competing with foreign firms that do not have this expense because their workers receive government-provided health care?

Some policymakers have argued that the bankruptcies of Chrysler and General Motors in 2009 were due, in part, to their making large payments for their workers' health insurance that their foreign competitors did not have to make. Some supporters of President Barack Obama's proposals to expand the government's role in providing health care have also argued that relieving U.S. firms from paying for health care would lower their costs relative to foreign competitors. But if labor markets determine equilibrium compensation, then a reduction in employer contributions for health insurance should lead to an offsetting increase in wages, leaving the total compensation paid by firms unaffected.

The Congressional Budget Office (CBO) undertakes studies of policy issues for Congress. In an overview of proposals for reforming health insurance in the United States, the CBO addressed this question:

> Some observers have asserted that domestic producers that provide health insurance to their workers face higher costs for compensation than competitors based in countries where insurance is not employment based and that fundamental changes to the health insurance system could reduce or eliminate that disadvantage. However, such a cost reduction is unlikely to occur. . . . The equilibrium level of overall compensation in the economy is determined by the supply of and the demand for labor. Fringe benefits (such as health insurance) are just part of that compensation. Consequently, the costs of fringe benefits are borne by workers largely in the form of lower cash wages than they would receive if no such benefits were provided by their employer. Replacing employment-based health care with a government-run system could reduce employers' payments for their workers'

insurance, but the amount that they would have to pay in overall compensation would remain essentially unchanged.

This is another case where basic demand and supply analysis provides important insights into a policy issue.

From Congress of the United States, Congressional Budget Office, *Key Issues in Analyzing Major Health Insurance Proposals*, December 2008, p. 167.

MyEconLab **Your Turn:** Test your understanding by doing related problem 4.17 on page 578 at the end of this chapter.

## Discrimination

**Economic discrimination** Paying a person a lower wage or excluding a person from an occupation on the basis of an irrelevant characteristic such as race or gender.

Table 17.2 shows that in the United States, white males on average earn more than other groups. One possible explanation for this is **economic discrimination**, which involves paying a person a lower wage or excluding a person from an occupation on the basis of an irrelevant characteristic such as race or gender.

If employers discriminated by hiring only white males for high-paying jobs or by paying white males higher wages than other groups working the same jobs, white males would have higher earnings, as Table 17.2 shows. However, excluding groups from certain jobs or paying one group more than another has been illegal in the United States since the passage of the Equal Pay Act of 1963 and the Civil Rights Act of 1964. Nevertheless, it is possible that employers are ignoring the law and practicing economic discrimination.

Most economists believe that only part of the gap between the wages of white males and the wages of other groups is due to discrimination. Instead, some of the gap is explained by three main factors:

1. Differences in education
2. Differences in experience
3. Differing preferences for jobs

**Differences in Education** Some of the difference between the incomes of white workers and the incomes of black workers can be explained by differences in education. Historically, African Americans have had less schooling than white people. Although the gap has closed significantly over the years, 90 percent of adult non-Hispanic white males in 2010 had graduated from high school, but only 82 percent of adult African-American males had. Thirty-one percent of white males had graduated from college, but only 16 percent of African-American males had. These statistics understate the true gap in education between black and white people because many black people receive a substandard education in inner-city schools. Not surprisingly, studies have shown that differing levels of education can account for a significant part of the gap between the

**Table 17.2**

**Why Do White Males Earn More Than Other Groups?**

| Group | Annual Earnings |
| --- | --- |
| White males | $51,699 |
| White females | 39,010 |
| Black males | 37,755 |
| Black females | 31,933 |
| Hispanic males | 31,554 |
| Hispanic females | 27,268 |

*Note:* The values are median annual earnings for persons who worked full time, year-round in 2009. Persons of Hispanic origin can be of any race.
Data from U.S. Bureau of the Census, Table PINC-10, "Current Population Survey," *Annual Social and Economic Supplement*, September 27, 2010.

earnings of white and black males. Some of the difference in educational levels between black and white people may itself reflect past and current discrimination by governments in failing to provide equal educational opportunities.

**Differences in Experience**  Women are much more likely than men to leave their jobs for a period of time after having a child. Women with several children will sometimes have several interruptions in their careers. Some women leave the workforce for several years until their children are of school age. As a result, on average, women with children have less workforce experience than do men of the same age. Because workers with greater experience are, on average, more productive, the difference in levels of experience helps to explain some of the difference in earnings between men and women. Providing some support for this explanation is the fact that, on average, married women earn about 25 percent less than married men, but women who have never been married—and whose careers are less likely to have been interrupted—earn only about 9 percent less than men who have never been married.

**Differing Preferences for Jobs**  Significant differences exist between the types of jobs held by women and men. Women represent 90 percent or more of the people employed in some relatively low-paying jobs, such as preschool teachers, dental assistants, and childcare workers, while men represent more than 90 percent of the people employed in some relatively high-paying jobs, such as airline pilots, engineering managers, and electricians. Although the overrepresentation of women in low-paying jobs and men in high-paying jobs may be due in part to discrimination, it is also likely to reflect differences in job preferences between men and women. For example, because many women interrupt their careers—at least briefly—when their children are born, they are more likely to take jobs where work experience is less important. Women may also be more likely to take jobs, such as teaching, that allow them to be home in the afternoons when their children return from school.

# Solved Problem 17.4

## Is Passing "Comparable Worth" Legislation a Good Way to Close the Gap between Men's and Women's Pay?

As we have seen, either because of discrimination or differing preferences, certain jobs are filled primarily by men, and other jobs are filled primarily by women. On average, the "men's jobs" have higher wages than the "women's jobs." Some observers have argued that many "men's jobs" are more highly paid than "women's jobs," despite the jobs being comparable in terms of the education and skills required and the working conditions involved. These observers have argued that the earnings gap between men and women could be closed at least partially if the government required employers to pay the same wages for jobs that have *comparable worth*. Many economists are skeptical of these proposals because they believe allowing markets to determine wages results in a more efficient outcome.

Suppose that electricians are currently being paid a market equilibrium wage of $800 per week, and dental assistants are being paid a market equilibrium wage of $500 per week. Comparable-worth legislation is passed, and a study finds that an electrician and a dental assistant have comparable jobs, so employers will now be required to pay workers in both jobs $650 per week. Analyze the effects of this requirement on the market for electricians and on the market for dental assistants. Be sure to use demand and supply graphs.

## Solving the Problem

**Step 1:**  **Review the chapter material.** This problem is about economic discrimination, so you may want to review the section "Discrimination," which begins on page 560.

**Step 2:** **Draw the graphs.** We saw in Chapter 4 that when the government sets the price in a market, the result is a surplus or a shortage, depending on whether the government-mandated price is above or below the competitive market equilibrium. A wage of $650 per week is below the market wage for electricians and above the market wage for dental assistants. Therefore, we expect the requirement to result in a shortage of electricians and a surplus of dental assistants.

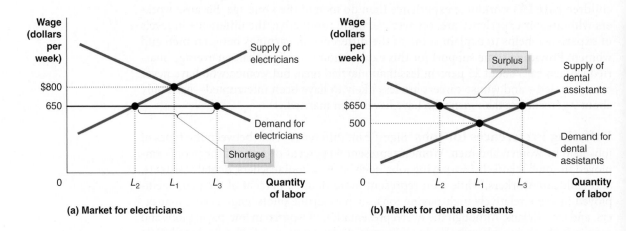

**(a) Market for electricians**

**(b) Market for dental assistants**

In panel (a), without comparable-worth legislation, the equilibrium wage for electricians is $800, and the equilibrium quantity of electricians hired is $L_1$. Setting the wage for electricians below equilibrium at $650 reduces the quantity of labor supplied in this occupation from $L_1$ to $L_2$ but increases the quantity of labor demanded by employers from $L_1$ to $L_3$. The result is a shortage of electricians equal to $L_3 - L_2$, as shown by the bracket in the graph.

In panel (b), without comparable-worth legislation, the equilibrium wage for dental assistants is $500, and the equilibrium quantity of dental assistants hired is $L_1$. Setting the wage for dental assistants above equilibrium at $650 increases the quantity of labor supplied in this occupation from $L_1$ to $L_3$ but reduces the quantity of labor demanded by employers from $L_1$ to $L_2$. The result is a surplus of dental assistants equal to $L_3 - L_2$, as shown by the bracket in the graph.

**Extra Credit:** Most economists are skeptical of government attempts to set wages and prices, as comparable-worth legislation would require. Supporters of comparable-worth legislation, by contrast, see differences between men's and women's wages as being mainly due to discrimination and are looking to government legislation as a solution.

MyEconLab    **Your Turn:** For more practice, do related problems 4.18 and 4.19 on page 578 at the end of this chapter.

---

### The Difficulty of Measuring Discrimination

When two people are paid different wages, discrimination may be the explanation. But differences in productivity or preferences may also be an explanation. Labor economists have attempted to measure what part of differences in wages between black workers and white workers and between men and women is due to discrimination and what part is due to other factors. Unfortunately, it is difficult to precisely measure differences in productivity or in worker preferences. As a result, we can't know exactly the extent of economic discrimination in the United States today.

| Making the Connection | **Does Greg Have an Easier Time Finding a Job Than Jamal?** |
|---|---|

One difficulty in accurately measuring economic discrimination is that two workers may not only differ in race and gender but also in characteristics that employers expect will affect the workers' productivity. If Worker A is hired instead of Worker B, is it because A is a white male, while B is a black female, or is it because of A's and B's other characteristics?

Marianne Bertrand of the University of Chicago and Sendhil Mullainathan of MIT found an ingenious way of getting around this difficulty. They responded to help wanted ads in newspapers by sending identical resumes, with the exception that half of the resumes were assigned an African-American–sounding name and half were assigned a white-sounding name. In other words, the characteristics of these fictitious people were the same, except for their names. In the absence of discrimination, resumes with African-American–sounding names, such as Jamal Jones, should have been as likely to get job interviews as the identical resumes with white-sounding names, such as Greg Baker. In fact, though, employers were 50 percent more likely to interview workers with white-sounding names than workers with African-American–sounding names. Bertrand and Mullainthan sent out more than 5,000 resumes to many different employers who were advertising for jobs in sales, administrative support, clerical services, and customer services. Their results were similar across these different types of jobs.

*Does having an African-American-sounding name make it more difficult to find a job?*

Some economists have questioned whether the study by Bertrand and Mullainathan, as well as other similar studies, actually do show that employers discriminate. They argue that employers may believe that the typical white job applicant and the typical black job applicant have different characteristics, apart from those included in the resumes, that may affect their productivity. If so, the employers may be responding to these differences in productivity rather than solely to the job applicant's race. Because Bertrand and Mullainthan based their artificial resumes on actual resumes, however, the artificial resumes probably include all the characteristics that actual job applicants think are relevant. Bertrand and Mullainathan believe that the results of their experiment show that "differential treatment by race . . . appears to still be prominent in the U.S. labor market."

Based on Marianne Bertrand and Sendhil Mullainathan, "Are Emily and Greg More Employable Than Lakisha and Jamal? A Field Experiment on Labor Market Discrimination," *American Economic Review*, Vol. 94, No. 4, September 2004, pp. 991–1013; and David Neumark, "Detecting Discrimination In Audit And Correspondence Studies," National Bureau of Economic Research, Working Paper 16448, October 2010.

**Your Turn:** Test your understanding by doing related problem 4.20 on page 578 at the end of this chapter.        MyEconLab

**Does It Pay to Discriminate?** Many economists believe that in the long run, markets can undermine economic discrimination. One reason is that *employers who discriminate pay an economic penalty*. To see why this is true, let's consider a simplified example. Suppose that men and women are equally qualified to be airline pilots and that, initially, airlines do not discriminate. In Figure 17.8, we divide the airlines into two groups: "A" airlines and "B" airlines. If neither group of airlines discriminates, we would expect them to pay an equal wage of $1,100 per week to both men and women pilots. Now suppose that "A" airlines decide to discriminate and to fire all their women pilots. This action will reduce the supply of pilots to these airlines and, as shown in panel (a), that will force up the wage from $1,100 to $1,300. At the same time, as women fired from the jobs with "A" airlines apply for jobs with "B" airlines, the supply of pilots to "B" airlines will increase, and the equilibrium wage will fall from $1,100 to $900. All the women pilots will end up being employed at the nondiscriminating airlines and will be paid a lower wage than the men who are employed by the discriminating airlines.

But this situation cannot persist for two reasons. First, male pilots employed by "B" airlines will also receive the lower wage. This lower wage gives them an incentive to quit their jobs at "B" airlines and apply at "A" airlines, which will shift the labor supply

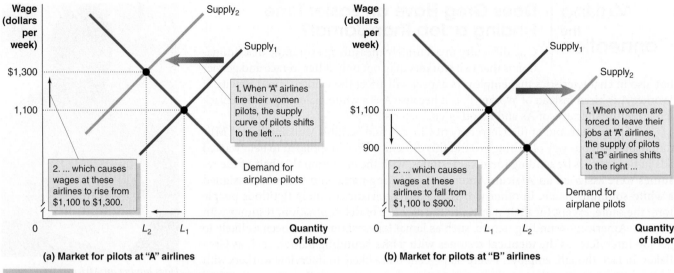

**Figure 17.8** Discrimination and Wages

In this hypothetical example, we assume that initially neither "A" airlines nor "B" airlines discriminate. As a result, men and women pilots receive the same wage of $1,100 per week at both groups of airlines. We then assume that "A" airlines discriminate by firing all their women pilots. Panel (a) shows that this reduces the supply of pilots to "A" airlines and raises the wage paid by these airlines from $1,100 to $1,300. Panel (b) shows that this increases the supply of pilots to "B" airlines and lowers the wage paid by these airlines from $1,100 to $900. All the women pilots will end up being employed at the nondiscriminating airlines and will be paid a lower wage than the men who are employed by the discriminating airlines.

curve for "B" airlines to the left and the labor supply curve for "A" airlines to the right. Second, "A" airlines are paying $1,300 per week to hire pilots who are no more productive than the pilots being paid $900 per week by "B" airlines. As a result, "B" airlines will have lower costs and will be able to charge lower prices. Eventually, "A" airlines will lose their customers to "B" airlines and will be driven out of business. The market will have imposed an economic penalty on the discriminating airlines. So, discrimination will not persist, and the wages of men and women pilots will become equal.

Can we conclude from this analysis that competition in markets will eliminate all economic discrimination? Unfortunately, this optimistic conclusion is not completely accurate. We know that until the Civil Rights Act of 1964 was passed, many firms in the United States refused to hire black workers. Even though this practice had persisted for decades, nondiscriminating competitors did not drive these firms out of business. Why not? There were three important factors:

1. *Worker discrimination.* In some cases, white workers refused to work alongside black workers. As a result, some industries—such as the important cotton textile industry in the South—were all white. Because of discrimination by white workers, an entrepreneur who wanted to use low-cost black labor might need to hire an all-black workforce. Some entrepreneurs tried this, but because black workers had been excluded from these industries, they often lacked the skills and experience to form an effective workforce.

2. *Customer discrimination.* Some white consumers were unwilling to buy from companies in certain industries if they employed black workers. This was not a significant barrier in manufacturing industries, where customers would not know the race of the workers producing the good. It was, however, a problem for firms in industries in which workers came into direct contact with the public.

3. *Negative feedback loops.* Our analysis in Figure 17.8 assumed that men and women pilots were equally qualified. However, if discrimination makes it difficult for a member of a group to find employment in a particular occupation, his or her incentive to be trained to enter that occupation is reduced. Consider the legal profession as an example. In 1952, future Supreme Court Justice Sandra Day O'Connor graduated third in her class at Stanford University Law School and was an editor of

the *Stanford Law Review*, but for some time she was unable to get a job as a lawyer because in those years, many law firms would not hire women. Facing such bleak job prospects, it's not surprising that relatively few women entered law school. As a result, a law firm that did not discriminate would have been unable to act like the nondiscriminating airlines in our example by hiring women lawyers at a lower salary and using this cost advantage to drive discriminating law firms out of business. In this situation, an unfortunate feedback loop was in place: Few women prepared to become lawyers because many law firms discriminated against women, and nondiscriminating law firms were unable to drive discriminating law firms out of business because there were too few women lawyers available.

Most economists agree that the market imposes an economic penalty on firms that discriminate, but because of the factors just discussed, it may take the market a very long time to eliminate discrimination entirely. The passage of the Civil Rights Act of 1964, which outlawed hiring discrimination on the basis of race and sex, greatly sped up the process of reducing economic discrimination in the United States.

## Labor Unions

Workers' wages can differ depending on whether the workers are members of labor unions. **Labor unions** are organizations of employees that have the legal right to bargain with employers about wages and working conditions. If a union is unable to reach an agreement with a company, it has the legal right to call a *strike*, which means its members refuse to work until a satisfactory agreement has been reached. As Figure 17.9 shows, a smaller fraction of the U.S. labor force is unionized than in most other high-income countries.

As Table 17.3 shows, in the United States, workers who are in unions receive higher wages than workers who are not in unions. Do union members earn more than nonunion members because they are in unions? The answer might seem to be "yes," but many union workers are in industries, such as automobile manufacturing, in which their marginal revenue products are high, so their wages would be high even if they were not unionized. Economists who have attempted to estimate statistically the effect of unionization on wages have concluded that being in a union increases a worker's wages about 10 percent, holding constant other factors, such as the industry the worker is in. A related question is whether unions raise the total amount of wages received by all workers, whether unionized or not. Because the share of national income received by workers has remained roughly constant over many years, most economists do not believe that unions have raised the total amount of wages received by workers.

> **Labor union** An organization of employees that has a legal right to bargain with employers about wages and working conditions.

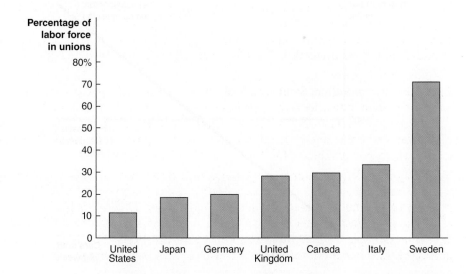

**Figure 17.9**

**The United States Is Less Unionized Than Most Other High-Income Countries**

The percentage of the labor force belonging to unions is lower in the United States than in most other high-income countries.
Data from Organization for Economic Cooperation and Development.

| Table 17.3 | | Average Weekly Earnings |
| --- | --- | --- |
| **Union Workers Earn More Than Nonunion Workers** | Union workers | $917 |
| | Nonunion workers | 717 |

*Note:* "Union workers" includes union members as well as workers who are represented by unions but who are not members of them.
Data from U.S. Bureau of Labor Statistics, *Union Members Summary*, January 21, 2011.

**17.5 LEARNING** OBJECTIVE

Discuss the role personnel economics can play in helping firms deal with human resources issues.

**Personnel economics** The application of economic analysis to human resources issues.

# Personnel Economics

Traditionally, labor economists have focused on issues such as the effects of labor unions on wages or the determinants of changes in average wages over time. They have spent less time analyzing *human resources issues*, which address how firms hire, train, and promote workers and set their wages and benefits. In recent years, some labor economists, including Edward Lazear of Stanford University and William Neilson of the University of Tennessee, have begun exploring the application of economic analysis to human resources issues. This new focus has become known as **personnel economics**.

Personnel economics analyzes the link between differences among jobs and differences in the way workers are paid. Jobs have different skill requirements, require more or less interaction with other workers, have to be performed in more or less unpleasant environments, and so on. Firms need to design compensation policies that take into account these differences. Personnel economics also analyzes policies related to other human resources issues, such as promotions, training, and pensions. In this brief overview, we look only at compensation policies.

## Should Workers' Pay Depend on How Much They Work or on How Much They Produce?

One issue personnel economics addresses is when workers should receive *straight-time pay*—a certain wage per hour or salary per week or month—and when they should receive *commission* or *piece-rate pay*—a wage based on how much output they produce.

Suppose, for example, that Anne owns a car dealership and is trying to decide whether to pay her salespeople a salary of $800 per week or a commission of $200 on each car they sell. Figure 17.10 compares the compensation a salesperson would receive under the two systems, according to the number of cars the salesperson sells.

### Figure 17.10

**Paying Car Salespeople by Salary or by Commission**

This figure compares the compensation a car salesperson receives if she is on a straight salary of $800 per week or if she receives a commission of $200 for each car she sells. With a straight salary, she receives $800 per week, no matter how many cars she sells. This outcome is shown by the horizontal line in the figure. If she receives a commission of $200 per car, her compensation will increase with every car she sells. This outcome is shown by the upward-sloping line. If she sells fewer than 4 cars per week, she would be better off with the $800 salary. If she sells more than 4 cars per week, she would be better off with the $200-per-car commission.

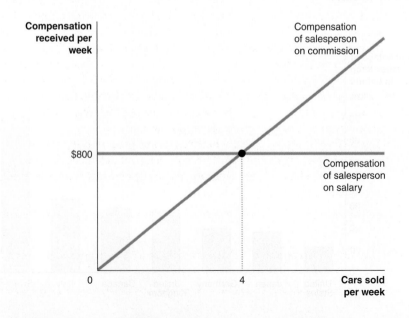

With a straight salary, the salesperson receives $800 per week, no matter how many cars she sells. This outcome is shown by the horizontal line in Figure 17.10. If she receives a commission of $200 per car, her compensation will increase with every car she sells. This outcome is shown by the upward-sloping line. A salesperson who sells fewer than 4 cars per week would earn more by receiving a straight salary of $800 per week. A salesperson who sells more than 4 cars per week would be better off receiving the $200-per-car commission. We can identify two advantages Anne would receive from paying her salespeople commissions rather than salaries: She would attract and retain the most productive employees, and she would provide an incentive to her employees to sell more cars.

Suppose that other car dealerships are all paying salaries of $800 per week. If Anne pays her employees on commission, any of her employees who are unable to sell at least 4 cars per week can improve their pay by going to work for one of her competitors. And any salespeople at Anne's competitors who can sell more than 4 cars per week can raise their pay by quitting and coming to work for Anne. Over time, Anne will find her least productive employees leaving, while she is able to hire new employees who are more productive.

Paying a commission also increases the incentive Anne's salespeople have to sell more cars. If Anne paid a salary, her employees would receive the same amount no matter how few cars they sold. An employee on salary might decide on a particularly hot or cold day that it was less trouble to stay inside the building than to go out on the car lot to greet potential customers. An employee on commission would know that the additional effort expended on selling more cars would be rewarded with additional compensation.

## Making the Connection | Raising Pay, Productivity, and Profits at Safelite AutoGlass

*A piece-rate system at Safelite AutoGlass led to increased worker wages and firm profits.*

Safelite Group, headquartered in Columbus, Ohio, is the parent company of Safelite AutoGlass, the nation's largest installer of auto glass, with 600 repair shops. In the mid-1990s, Safelite shifted from paying its glass installers hourly wages to paying them on the basis of how many windows they installed. Safelite already had in place a computer system that allowed it to easily track how many windows each worker installed per day. To make sure quality did not suffer, Safelite added a rule that if a workmanship-related defect occurred with an installed windshield, the worker would have to install a new windshield and would not be paid for the additional work.

Edward Lazear analyzed data provided by the firm and discovered that under the new piece-rate system, the number of windows installed per worker jumped 44 percent. Lazear estimated that half of this increase was due to increased productivity from workers who continued with the company and half was due to new hires being more productive than the workers they replaced who had left the company. Worker pay rose on average by about 9.9 percent. Ninety-two percent of workers experienced a pay increase, and one-quarter received an increase of at least 28 percent. Safelite's profits also increased as the cost to the company per window installed fell from $44.43 under the hourly wage system to $35.24 under the piece-rate system.

Sociologists sometimes question whether worker productivity can be increased through the use of monetary incentives. The experience of Safelite AutoGlass provides a clear example of workers reacting favorably to the opportunity to increase output in exchange for higher compensation.

Based on Edward P. Lazear, "Performance Pay and Productivity," *American Economic Review*, Vol. 90, No. 5, December 2000, pp. 1346–1361.

**Your Turn:** Test your understanding by doing related problem 5.8 on page 579 at the end of this chapter.   MyEconLab

## Other Considerations in Setting Compensation Systems

The discussion so far indicates that companies will find it more profitable to use a commission or piece-rate system of compensation rather than a salary system. In fact, many firms continue to pay their workers salaries, which means they are paying their workers on the basis of how long they work rather than on the basis of how much they produce. Firms may choose a salary system for several good reasons:

- *Difficulty measuring output.* Often it is difficult to attribute output to any particular worker. For example, projects carried out by an engineering firm may involve teams of workers whose individual contributions are difficult to distinguish. On assembly lines, such as those used in the automobile industry, the amount produced by each worker is determined by the speed of the line, which is set by managers rather than by workers. Managers at many firms perform such a wide variety of tasks that measuring their output would be costly, if it could be done at all.

- *Concerns about quality.* If workers are paid on the basis of the number of units produced, they may become less concerned about quality. An office assistant who is paid on the basis of the quantity of letters typed may become careless about how many typos the letters contain. In some cases, there are ways around this problem; for example, the assistant may be required to correct the mistakes on his or her own time, without pay.

- *Worker dislike of risk.* Piece-rate or commission systems of compensation increase the risk to workers because sometimes output declines for reasons not connected to the worker's effort. For example, if there is a very snowy winter, few customers may show up at Anne's auto dealership. Through no fault of their own, her salespeople may have great difficulty selling any cars. If they are paid a salary, their income will not be affected, but if they are on commission, their incomes may drop to low levels. The flip side of this is that by paying salaries, Anne assumes a greater risk. During a snowy winter, her payroll expenses will remain high even though her sales are low. With a commission system of compensation, her payroll expenses will decline along with her sales. But owners of firms are typically better able to bear risk than are workers. As a result, some firms may find that workers who would earn more under a commission system will prefer to receive a salary to reduce their risk. In these situations, paying a lower salary may reduce the firm's payroll expenses compared with what they would have been under a commission or piece-rate system.

Personnel economics is a relatively new field, but it holds great potential for helping firms deal more efficiently with human resources issues.

**17.6 LEARNING** OBJECTIVE

Show how equilibrium prices are determined in the markets for capital and natural resources.

# The Markets for Capital and Natural Resources

The approach we have used to analyze the market for labor can also be used to analyze the markets for other factors of production. We have seen that the demand for labor is determined by the marginal revenue product of labor because the value to a firm from hiring another worker equals the increase in the firm's revenue from selling the additional output it can produce by hiring the worker. The demand for capital and natural resources is determined in a similar way.

## The Market for Capital

Physical capital includes machines, equipment, and buildings. Firms sometimes buy capital, but we will focus on situations in which firms rent capital. A chocolate manufacturer renting a warehouse and an airline leasing a plane are examples of firms renting

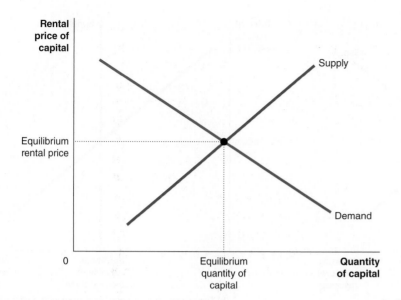

**Figure 17.11**

**Equilibrium in the Market for Capital**

The rental price of capital is determined by demand and supply in the market for capital. In equilibrium, the rental price of capital is equal to the marginal revenue product of capital.

capital. Like the demand for labor, the demand for capital is a derived demand. When a firm is considering increasing its capital by, for example, employing another machine, the value it receives equals the increase in the firm's revenue from selling the additional output it can produce by employing the machine. The *marginal revenue product of capital* is the change in the firm's revenue as a result of employing one more unit of capital, such as a machine. We have seen that the marginal revenue product of labor curve is the demand curve for labor. Similarly, the marginal revenue product of capital curve is the demand curve for capital.

Firms producing capital goods face increasing marginal costs, so the supply curve of capital goods is upward sloping, as are the supply curves for other goods and services. Figure 17.11 shows equilibrium in the market for capital. In equilibrium, suppliers of capital receive a rental price equal to the marginal revenue product of capital, just as suppliers of labor receive a wage equal to the marginal revenue product of labor.

## The Market for Natural Resources

The market for natural resources can be analyzed in the same way as the markets for labor and capital. When a firm is considering employing more natural resources, the value it receives equals the increase in the firm's revenue from selling the additional output it can produce by buying the natural resources. So, the demand for natural resources is also a derived demand. The *marginal revenue product of natural resources* is the change in a firm's revenue as a result of employing one more unit of natural resources, such as a barrel of oil. The marginal revenue product of natural resources curve is also the demand curve for natural resources.

Although the total quantity of most natural resources is ultimately fixed—as the humorist Will Rogers once remarked, "Buy land. They ain't making any more of it"—in many cases, the quantity supplied still responds to the price. For example, although the total quantity of oil deposits in the world is fixed, an increase in the price of oil will result in an increase in the quantity of oil supplied during a particular period. The result, as shown in panel (a) of Figure 17.12, is an upward-sloping supply curve. In some cases, however, the quantity of a natural resource that will be supplied is fixed and will not change as the price changes. The land available at a busy intersection is fixed, for example. In panel (b) of Figure 17.12, we illustrate this situation with a supply curve that is a vertical line, or perfectly inelastic. The price received by a factor of production that is in fixed supply is called an **economic rent** (or a **pure rent**) because, in this case, the price of the factor is determined only by demand. For example, if a new highway diverts much of the traffic from a previously busy intersection, the demand for the land will decline, and the price of the land will fall, but the quantity of the land will not change.

**Economic rent** (or **pure rent**) The price of a factor of production that is in fixed supply.

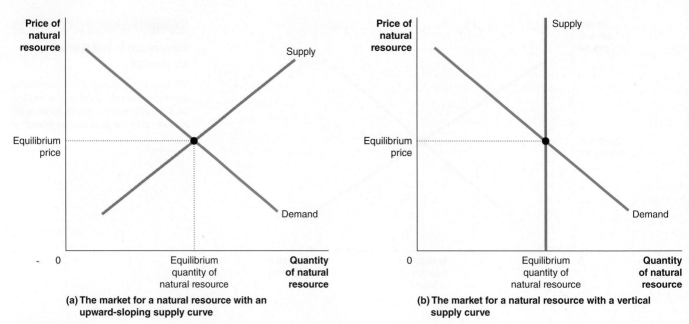

**Figure 17.12** **Equilibrium in the Market for Natural Resources**

In panel (a), the supply curve of a natural resource is upward sloping. The price of the natural resource is determined by the interaction of demand and supply. In panel (b), the supply curve of the natural resource is a vertical line, indicating that the quantity supplied does not respond to changes in price. In this case, the price of the natural resource is determined only by demand. The price of a factor of production with a vertical supply curve is called an *economic rent*, or a *pure rent*.

## Monopsony

**Monopsony** The sole buyer of a factor of production.

In Chapter 15, we analyzed the case of *monopoly*, where a firm is the sole *seller* of a good or service. What happens if a firm is the sole *buyer* of a factor of production? This case, which is known as **monopsony**, is comparatively rare. An example is a firm in an isolated town—perhaps a lumber mill in a small town in Washington or Oregon—that is the sole employer of labor in that location. In the nineteenth and early twentieth centuries, some coal mining firms were the sole employers in certain small towns in West Virginia, and some pineapple plantations were the sole employers on certain small islands in Hawaii. In these cases, not only would the firm own the mill, mine, or plantation, but it would also own the stores and other businesses in the town. Workers would have the choice of working for the sole employer in the town or moving to another town.

We know that a firm with a monopoly in an output market takes advantage of its market power to reduce the quantity supplied to force up the market price and increase its profits. A firm that has a monopsony in a factor market would employ a similar strategy: It would restrict the quantity of the factor demanded to force down the price of the factor and increase profits. A firm with a monopsony in a labor market will hire fewer workers and pay lower wages than would be the case in a competitive market. Because fewer workers are hired than would be hired in a competitive market, monopsony results in a deadweight loss. Monopoly and monopsony have similar effects on the economy: In both cases, a firm's market power results in a lower equilibrium quantity, a deadweight loss, and a reduction in economic efficiency compared with a competitive market.

In some cases, monopsony in labor markets is offset by worker membership in a labor union. A notable example of this is professional sports. For instance, Major League Baseball effectively has a monopsony on employing professional baseball players. (Although independent baseball leagues exist, none of the best players play for these teams, and the teams pay salaries that are a small fraction of those paid by Major League Baseball teams.) The monopsony power of the owners of Major League Baseball teams is offset by the power of the Major League Baseball Players Association, the union that represents baseball players. Bargaining between the representatives of Major League Baseball and the players' union has resulted in baseball players being paid something close to what they would be receiving in a competitive market.

# The Marginal Productivity Theory of Income Distribution

We have seen that in equilibrium, each factor of production receives a price equal to its marginal revenue product. We can use this fact to explain the distribution of income. Marginal revenue product represents the value of a factor's marginal contribution to producing goods and services. Therefore, individuals will receive income equal to the marginal contributions to production from the factors of production they own, including their labor. The more factors of production an individual owns and the more productive those factors are, the higher the individual's income will be. This approach to explaining the distribution of income is called the **marginal productivity theory of income distribution**. The theory was developed by John Bates Clark, who taught at Columbia University in the late nineteenth and early twentieth centuries.

**Marginal productivity theory of income distribution** The theory that the distribution of income is determined by the marginal productivity of the factors of production that individuals own.

Continued from page 545

## Economics in Your Life

### How Can You Convince Your Boss to Give You a Raise?

At the beginning of the chapter, we asked you to imagine that you work at a local sandwich shop and that you plan to ask your manager for a raise. One way to show the manager your worth is to demonstrate how many dollars your work earns for the sandwich shop: your marginal revenue product. You could certainly suggest that as you have become better at your job and have gained new skills, you have become a more productive employee; but, more importantly, you could say that your productivity results in increased revenue for the sandwich shop. By showing how your employment contributes to higher revenue and profit, you may be able to convince your manager to give you a raise.

# Conclusion

In this chapter, we used the demand and supply model from Chapter 3 to explain why wages differ among workers. The demand for workers depends on their productivity and on the price firms receive for the output the workers produce. The supply of workers to an occupation depends on the wages and working conditions offered by employers and on the skills required. The demand and supply for labor can also help us analyze such issues as economic discrimination and the effect of labor unions.

Read *An Inside Look* on the next page to see how demand and supply explain the rapidly rising salaries of NCAA Division 1-A basketball coaches.

# Basketball Coaches' Salaries: A March to Madness?

## STLTODAY.COM

## Salaries Escalate for College Basketball Coaches

(a) Before he was able to catapult Missouri to the Elite Eight in 2009, coach Mike Anderson's salary was respectable within the profession at $855,000. But that figure lacked the panache that announces a coach's arrival among the elite, at least financially speaking.

However, with salaries trending skyward, Anderson was able to join the growing $2 million club with astonishing swiftness.

A 58 percent raise from Mizzou put him at $1.35 million for two seasons. Then Arkansas upped the ante and lured him to Fayetteville with a 63 percent raise to $2.2 million annually.

In a job where $1 million was considered astronomical not long ago, Anderson is now helping to shatter the ceiling. Purdue's Matt Painter signed for $2.3 million last week, and Marquette's Buzz Williams received a contract reported by the Milwaukee Journal Sentinel at $2 million annually, more than double his previous pay.

Thus, 15 coaches have reached that milestone, with Missouri and possibly Oklahoma willing to offer similar money to their upcoming hires.

Although coaches are hired based on potential to produce a winner, it's ultimately about making money, according to Andrew Zimbalist, an economist and professor at Smith College in Massachusetts.

(b) "The general idea about how much a coach is worth is how much revenue did the program generate before and how much does it generate now," Zimbalist said. "What happens in college basketball and football is that since players don't get paid, the value they produce is attributed to the coach, and that's why they get paid so much."

In 2007, according to a USA Today study, one coach in the NCAA Tournament was making more than $2 million. Since that time, six coaches have surpassed $3 million, according to figures provided by St. Louis attorney Bob Lattinville of the law firm Stinson Morrison Hecker, which represents numerous college coaches....

(c) This week at his Final Four press conference, NCAA President Mark Emmert addressed the conundrum of rising salaries at a time when many colleges are having to make cuts.

He was asked specifically about Kentucky coach John Calipari's salary of $3.9 million at a time when staff and faculty can't get a raise.

"Kentucky and a number of other universities have decided that their coaches deserve to be well compensated, that that's a good investment for the institution," Emmert said. "And I'm not second-guessing them."

Lattinville argues that coaches are worth "every dime" because of the hours they work, the potential impact on their health and the public scrutiny they and their families must endure.

Illinois coach Bruce Weber received a raise from $1 million to $1.5 million two years ago during a budget crunch in the university system. However, the basketball program was hugely successful, ranking among the top 10 on the Forbes list from 2008 to 2010. In the 2009–10 season, Illinois basketball made a $9.4 million profit.

But Weber said he would like to think that coaches are paid for more than wins, losses and revenue capability.

"The immediate success is the W's and L's," he said. "The long-term success is the kids graduating, becoming good citizens and having good families. There are special cases where kids go to play pro basketball. And we put in an awful lot of time. If you have a whole day off every couple of weeks, you're fortunate."

Zimbalist is in favor of a salary cap but says it would require an antitrust exemption from Congress. He doesn't understand how some schools can offer salaries on par with NBA coaches while making a fraction of the revenue....

Lattinville said salaries will level off when universities and alumni become satisfied with teams being competitive and having a high caliber of student-athletes.

In other words, no time soon.

"People aren't satisfied with that, and there's enormous pressure on those guys to win," he said. "When a school terminates a coach, they complain they have to overpay. But we're all part of that problem."

Source: "Salaries Escalate for College Basketball Coaches" by Stu Durando from the *St. Louis Post-Dispatch*, April 3, 2011. Copyright © 2011 by St. Louis Post-Dispatch. Reprinted by permission.

## Key Points in the Article

As of April 2011, colleges and universities paid 15 NCAA Division 1-A basketball coaches salaries of $2 million or higher, with 6 of these coaches surpassing the $3 million salary mark. The high salaries have been questioned at a time when many schools are finding it necessary to cut expenses elsewhere. The schools justify the salaries because many basketball programs generate large revenues and profits, and the coaches are therefore viewed as good investments.

## Analyzing the News

Ⓐ Successful college basketball coaches such as Mike Anderson and John Calipari receive high salaries because their marginal products are high, and a fixed number of schools compete for the best coaches. In 2011, there were 345 NCAA Division 1-A men's basketball teams, so the labor supply curve in the figure below is vertical at a quantity of 345. The demand curve $D_1$ intersects the labor supply curve at $W_1$, the equilibrium wage or salary. The labor demand curve is the marginal revenue product of labor ($P \times MP_L$). The salaries are competitive and based on the ability of coaches to create winning programs and generate revenue.

Ⓑ Increases in the demand for coaches occur when there are increases in the revenue generated by the schools' basketball programs. A coach's value therefore depends not only on his win–loss record but also on the amount of revenue generated by the program. Schools often credit significant revenue increases following the hiring of a basketball coach to the hiring, and this analysis results in larger salaries. The figure below shows that as the demand for coaches increases to $D_2$, the equilibrium salary increases to $W_2$. Schools that bid up salaries know that higher salaries are needed to attract the best coaches, and winning programs result in greater revenue.

Ⓒ Not all 345 basketball programs can be successful at the same time. Athletic contests are zero-sum games with an equal number of wins and losses. Losing programs result in lower attendance and falling revenue, so schools have a financial interest in hiring coaches who can increase the schools' chances of winning. As long as basketball coaches are successful at increasing revenues for their schools, the demand for these coaches will continue to increase and, all else equal, the continued increase in demand will result in a continued increase in the equilibrium wage in the market for NCAA Division 1-A basketball coaches.

## Thinking Critically

1. Why do Division 1-A college basketball coaches earn higher salaries than most of their faculty colleagues?
2. Suppose that 100 non-Division 1-A colleges became Division 1-A colleges over a three-year period, raising the total number of Division 1-A college basketball programs to 445. How would this affect the (a) demand, (b) supply, and (c) equilibrium salary for basketball coaches?

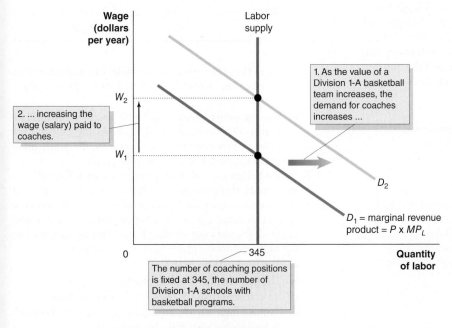

2. ... increasing the wage (salary) paid to coaches.

1. As the value of a Division 1-A basketball team increases, the demand for coaches increases ...

$D_2$

$D_1$ = marginal revenue product = $P \times MP_L$

The number of coaching positions is fixed at 345, the number of Division 1-A schools with basketball programs.

**The market for NCAA Division 1-A college basketball coaches.**

# Chapter Summary and Problems

## Key Terms

Compensating differentials, p. 558

Derived demand, p. 546

Economic discrimination, p. 560

Economic rent (or pure rent), p. 569

Factors of production, p. 546

Human capital, p. 550

Labor union, p. 565

Marginal product of labor, p. 546

Marginal productivity theory of income distribution, p. 571

Marginal revenue product of labor (*MRP*), p. 547

Monopsony, p. 570

Personnel economics, p. 566

---

### 17.1 The Demand for Labor, pages 546–550

LEARNING OBJECTIVE: Explain how firms choose the profit-maximizing quantity of labor to employ.

## Summary

The demand for labor is a **derived demand** because it depends on the demand consumers have for goods and services. The additional output produced by a firm as a result of hiring another worker is called the **marginal product of labor**. The amount by which a firm's revenue will increase as a result of hiring one more worker is called the **marginal revenue product of labor (*MRP*)**. A firm's marginal revenue product of labor curve is its demand curve for labor. Firms maximize profit by hiring workers up to the point where the wage is equal to the marginal revenue product of labor. The market demand curve for labor is determined by adding up the quantity of labor demanded by each firm at each wage, holding constant all other variables that might affect the willingness of firms to hire workers. The most important variables that shift the labor demand curve are changes in human capital, technology, the price of the product, the quantity of other inputs, and the number of firms in the market. **Human capital** is the accumulated training and skills that workers possess.

 **MyEconLab** Visit **www.myeconlab.com** to complete these exercises online and get instant feedback.

## Review Questions

1.1 In what sense is the demand for labor a derived demand?

1.2 What is the difference between the marginal product of labor and the marginal revenue product of labor?

1.3 Why is the demand curve for labor downward sloping?

1.4 What are the five most important variables that cause the market demand curve for labor to shift?

## Problems and Applications

1.5 Frank Gunter owns an apple orchard. He employs 87 apple pickers and pays them each $8 per hour to pick apples, which he sells for $1.60 per box. If Frank is maximizing profits, what is the marginal revenue product of the last worker he hired? What is that worker's marginal product?

1.6 **[Related to** Solved Problem 17.1 **on page 548]** Complete the following table for Terrell's Televisions:

| Number of Workers (L) | Output of Televisions per Week (Q) | Marginal Product of Labor (television sets per week) (MP) | Product Price (P) | Marginal Revenue Product of Labor (dollars per week) | Wage (dollars per week) (W) | Additional Profit from Hiring One More Worker (dollars per week) |
|---|---|---|---|---|---|---|
| 0 | 0 | — | $300 | — | $1,800 | — |
| 1 | 8 | — | 300 | — | 1,800 | — |
| 2 | 15 | — | 300 | — | 1,800 | — |
| 3 | 21 | — | 300 | — | 1,800 | — |
| 4 | 26 | — | 300 | — | 1,800 | — |
| 5 | 30 | — | 300 | — | 1,800 | — |
| 6 | 33 | — | 300 | — | 1,800 | — |

a. From the information in the table, can you determine whether this firm is a price taker or a price maker? Briefly explain.

b. Use the information in the table to draw a graph like Figure 17.1 on page 547 that shows the demand for labor by this firm. Be sure to indicate the profit-maximizing quantity of labor on your graph.

1.7 State whether each of the following events will result in a movement along the market demand curve for labor in electronics factories in China or whether it will cause the market demand curve for labor to shift. If the demand curve shifts, indicate whether it will shift to the left or to the right and draw a graph to illustrate the shift.

a. The wage rate declines.

b. The price of televisions declines.

c. Several firms exit the television market in Japan.

d. Chinese high schools introduce new vocational courses in assembling electronic products.

1.8 Baseball writer Rany Jazayerli assessed the Kansas City Royals outfielder Jose Guillen as follows: "Guillen has negative value the way his contract stands." How could a baseball player's contract cause him to have negative value to a baseball team?

Based on Rany Jazayerli, "Radical Situations Call for Radical Solutions," www.ranyontheroyals.com, June 6, 2009.

## 17.2 | The Supply of Labor, pages 550–552

LEARNING OBJECTIVE: Explain how people choose the quantity of labor to supply.

### Summary

As the wage increases, the opportunity cost of leisure increases, causing individuals to supply a greater quantity of labor. Normally, the labor supply curve is upward sloping, but it is possible that at very high wage levels, the supply curve might be backward bending. This outcome occurs when someone with a high income is willing to accept a somewhat lower income in exchange for more leisure. The market labor supply curve is determined by adding up the quantity of labor supplied by each worker at each wage, holding constant all other variables that might affect the willingness of workers to supply labor. The most important variables that shift the labor supply curve are increases in population, changing demographics, and changing alternatives.

 Visit www.myeconlab.com to complete these exercises online and get instant feedback.

### Review Questions

**2.1** How can we measure the opportunity cost of leisure? What are the substitution effect and the income effect resulting from a wage change? Why is the supply curve of labor usually upward sloping?

**2.2** What are the three most important variables that cause the market supply curve of labor to shift?

### Problems and Applications

**2.3** Daniel was earning $65 per hour and working 45 hours per week. Then Daniel's wage rose to $75 per hour, and as a result, he now works 40 hours per week. What can we conclude from this information about the income effect and the substitution effect of a wage change for Daniel?

**2.4** A columnist writing in the *Wall Street Journal* during the recession of 2007–2009 made the following observation about the "price of time":

> The recession is doing funny things with the price of time.

Technically it's risen in value. Although hardly anyone seems to have noticed, the government's latest figures show that hourly wages in real terms—which had pretty much stagnated for decades—have just jumped to their highest levels since the 1970s. You can thank cheaper prices in the stores, as well as higher pay.

What is the "price of time"? Is the columnist correct that when real hourly wages rise, the price of time increases? Briefly explain.

"Spend Some Time, Save Some Money," by Brett Arends from *Wall Street Journal*, May 19, 2009. Copyright © 2011 by Dow Jones & Company, Inc.. Reproduced with permission of Dow Jones & Company, Inc.

**2.5** Most labor economists believe that many adult males are on the vertical section of their labor supply curves. Use the concepts of income and substitution effects to explain under what circumstances an individual's labor supply curve would be vertical.

Based on Robert Whaples, "Is There Consensus among American Labor Economists? Survey Results on Forty Propositions," *Journal of Labor Research*, Vol. 17, No. 4, Fall 1996.

**2.6** Suppose that a large oil field is discovered in Michigan. By imposing a tax on the oil, the state government is able to eliminate the state income tax on wages. What is likely to be the effect on the labor supply curve in Michigan?

**2.7** The fraction of the U.S. population older than age 65 is increasing. What is the likely effect of the aging of the U.S. population on the supply curve for labor?

**2.8** State whether each of the following events will result in a movement along the market supply curve of agricultural labor in the United States or whether it will cause the market supply curve of agricultural labor to shift. If the supply curve shifts, indicate whether it will shift to the left or to the right and draw a graph to illustrate the shift.

a. The agricultural wage rate declines.

b. Wages outside agriculture increase.

c. The law is changed to allow for unlimited immigration into the United States.

## 17.3 | Equilibrium in the Labor Market, pages 552–555

LEARNING OBJECTIVE: Explain how equilibrium wages are determined in labor markets.

### Summary

The intersection between labor supply and labor demand determines the equilibrium wage and the equilibrium level of employment. If labor supply is unchanged, an increase in labor demand will increase both the equilibrium wage and the number of workers employed. If labor demand is unchanged, an increase in labor supply will lower the equilibrium wage and increase the number of workers employed.

MyEconLab Visit www.myeconlab.com to complete these exercises online and get instant feedback.

### Review Questions

**3.1** If the labor demand curve shifts to the left and the labor supply curve remains unchanged, what will happen to the equilibrium wage and the equilibrium level of employment? Illustrate your answer with a graph.

**3.2** If the labor supply curve shifts to the left and the labor demand curve remains unchanged, what will happen to the equilibrium wage and the equilibrium level of employment? Illustrate your answer with a graph.

# Problems and Applications

**3.3** **[Related to the** Making the Connection **on page 554]** Over time, the gap between the wages of workers with college degrees and the wages of workers without college degrees has been increasing. Shouldn't this gap have increased the incentive for workers to earn college degrees, thereby increasing the supply of college-educated workers and reducing the size of the gap?

**3.4** Reread the discussion on page 555 of changes in the salaries of software engineers. Use a graph to illustrate this situation. Make sure your graph has labor demand and supply curves for 2009 and 2011 and that the equilibrium point for each year is clearly indicated.

**3.5** Sean Astin, who played Sam in the *Lord of the Rings* movies, wrote the following about an earlier film he had appeared in: "Now I was in a movie I didn't respect, making obscene amounts of money (five times what a teacher makes, and teachers do infinitely more important work)." Are salaries determined by the importance of the work being done? If not, what are salaries determined by?

From Sean Astin, with Joe Layden, *There and Back Again: An Actor's Tale*, (New York: St. Martin's Press, 2004), p. 35.

**3.6** A newspaper article summarizes a study showing that "a standout kindergarten teacher is worth about $320,000 a year. That's the present value of the additional money that a full class of students can expect to earn over their careers. This estimate doesn't take into account social gains, like better health and less crime." Why are even standout kindergarten teachers paid salaries much lower than $320,000?

Based on David Leonhardt, "The Case for $320,000 Kindergarten Teachers," *New York Times*, July 27, 2010.

**3.7** In 541 A.D., an outbreak of bubonic plague hit the Byzantine Empire. Because the plague was spread by flea-infested rats that often lived on ships, ports were hit particularly hard. In some ports, more than 40 percent of the population died. The emperor, Justinian, was concerned that the wages of sailors were rising very rapidly as a result of the plague. In 544 A.D., he placed a ceiling on the wages of sailors. Use a demand and supply graph of the market for sailors to show the effect of the plague on the wages of sailors. Use the same graph to show the effect of Justinian's wage ceiling. Briefly explain what is happening in your graph.

Based on Michael McCormick, *The Origins of the European Economy*: Communications and Commerce, A.D., 300–900, (New York: Cambridge University Press, 2001), p. 109.

---

**17.4** **Explaining Differences in Wages,** pages 556–566

LEARNING OBJECTIVE: Use demand and supply analysis to explain how compensating differentials, discrimination, and labor unions cause wages to differ.

## Summary

The equilibrium wage is determined by the intersection of the labor demand curve and the labor supply curve. Some differences in wages are explained by **compensating differentials**, which are higher wages that compensate workers for unpleasant aspects of a job. Wages can also differ because of **economic discrimination**, which involves paying a person a lower wage or excluding a person from an occupation on the basis of irrelevant characteristics, such as race or gender. **Labor unions** are organizations of employees that have the legal right to bargain with employers about wages and working conditions. Being in a union increases a worker's wages about 10 percent, holding constant other factors, such as the industry in question.

 Visit **www.myeconlab.com** to complete these exercises online and get instant feedback.

## Review Questions

**4.1** What is a compensating differential? Give an example.

**4.2** Define *economic discrimination*. Is the fact that one group in the population has higher earnings than other groups evidence of economic discrimination? Briefly explain.

**4.3** In what sense do employers who discriminate pay an economic penalty? Is this penalty enough to eliminate discrimination? Briefly explain.

**4.4** Is the fraction of U.S. workers in labor unions larger or smaller than in other countries?

## Problems and Applications

**4.5** The journalist Michael Kinsley argued, "Free-market capitalism . . . works well for almost all by rewarding some people more than others." Discuss whether you agree.

From Michael Kinsley, "Curse You, Robert Caro!" *Slate*, November 21, 2002.

**4.6** Writing on the Baseball Prospectus Web site, Dan Fox argued, "What a player is really worth depends a great deal on the teams that are interested in signing him." Do you agree? Shouldn't a baseball player with a particular level of ability be worth the same to every team? Briefly explain.

From Dan Fox, "Schrodinger's Cat," www.baseballprospectus.com, May 17, 2007.

**4.7** **[Related to the** Chapter Opener **on page 545]** A student remarks, "I don't think the idea of marginal revenue product really helps explain differences in wages. After all, a ticket to a baseball game costs much less than college tuition, yet baseball players are paid much more than college professors." Do you agree with the student's reasoning?

**4.8** **[Related to the** Don't Let This Happen to You **on page 556]** Joe Morgan is a sportscaster and former baseball player. After he stated that he thought the salaries of Major League Baseball players were justified, a baseball fan wrote the following to Rob Neyer, a sports columnist:

Mr. Neyer,

What are your feelings about Joe Morgan's comment that players are justified in being paid what they're being paid? How is it ok for A-Rod [New York Yankees infielder Alex Rodriguez] to earn $115,000 per GAME while my boss works 80 hour weeks and earns $30,000 per year?

How would you answer this fan's questions?

From ESPN.com, August 30, 2002.

**4.9** Buster Olney, a columnist for ESPN.com, wondered why baseball teams pay the teams' managers and general managers less than they pay most baseball players:

> About two-thirds of the players on the [New York] Mets' roster will make more money than [manager Willie] Randolph; Willie will get somewhere in the neighborhood of half of an average major league salary for 2007. But Randolph's deal is right in line with what other managers are making, and right in the range of what the highest-paid general managers are making. . . . I have a hard time believing that Randolph or general manager Omar Minaya will have less impact on the Mets than left-handed reliever Scott Schoeneweis, who will get paid more than either the manager or GM.

Provide an economic explanation of why baseball managers and general managers are generally paid less than baseball players.

From "Managers Low on Pay Scale," by Buster Olney. ESPN.com, January 25, 2007.

**4.10** In early 2007, Nick Saban agreed to leave his job as head coach of the Miami Dolphins National Football League team to take a job as head football coach at the University of Alabama at a salary of $4 million per year for eight years. Ivan Maisel, a columnist for ESPN.com, wondered whether Saban was worth such a large salary: "Is Saban eight times better than the coach who outmaneuvered Bob Stoops of Oklahoma on Monday night? Boise State paid Chris Petersen $500,000 this season—and he still hasn't lost a game." Might Saban still be worth a salary of $4 million per year to Alabama even if he is not "eight times better" than a coach being paid $500,000 at another school? In your answer, be sure to refer to the difference between the marginal product of labor and the marginal revenue product of labor.

Based on Ivan Maisel, "Saban Will Find Crowded Pond in Tuscaloosa," ESPN.com, January 3, 2007.

**4.11** [Related to the Making the Connection on page 557] According to Alan Krueger, an economist at Princeton University, the share of concert ticket revenue received by the top 1 percent of all acts rose from 26 percent in 1982 to 56 percent in 2003. Does this information indicate that the top acts in 2003 must have been much better performers relative to other acts than was the case in 1982? If not, can you think of another explanation?

Based on Eduardo Porter, "More Than Ever, It Pays to Be the Top Executive," *New York Times*, May 25, 2007.

**4.12** [Related to the Making the Connection on page 557] Why are there superstar basketball players but no superstar plumbers?

**4.13** [Related to the Chapter Opener on page 545] Sam Goldwyn, a movie producer during Hollywood's Golden Age, once remarked about one of his stars: "We're overpaying him, but he's worth it."

**a.** In what sense did Goldwyn mean that he was overpaying this star?

**b.** If he was overpaying the star, why would the star have still been worth it?

**4.14** Prior to the early twentieth century, a worker who was injured on the job could collect damages only by suing his employer. To sue successfully, the worker—or his family, if the worker had been killed—had to show that the injury was due to the employer's negligence, that the worker did not know the job was hazardous, and that the worker's own negligence had not contributed to the accident. These lawsuits were difficult for workers to win, and even workers who had been seriously injured on the job often were unable to collect any damages from their employers. Beginning in 1910, most states passed workers' compensation laws that required employers to purchase insurance that would compensate workers for injuries suffered on the job. A study by Price Fishback and Shawn Kantor of the University of Arizona shows that after the passage of workers' compensation laws, wages received by workers in the coal and lumber industries fell. Briefly explain why passage of workers' compensation laws would lead to a fall in wages in some industries.

Based on Price V. Fishback and Shawn Everett Kantor, "Did Workers Pay for the Passage of Workers' Compensation Laws?" *Quarterly Journal of Economics*, Vol. 110, No. 3, August 1995, pp. 713–742.

**4.15** The following table is similar to Table 17.2 on page 560, except that it includes the earnings of Asian males and females. Does the fact that Asian males are the highest-earning group in the table affect the likelihood that economic discrimination is the best explanation for why earnings differ among the groups listed in the table? Briefly explain your argument.

| Group | Annual Earnings |
|---|---|
| Asian males | $52,154 |
| White males | 51,699 |
| Asian females | 43,601 |
| White females | 39,010 |
| Black males | 37,755 |
| Black females | 31,933 |
| Hispanic males | 31,544 |
| Hispanic females | 27,268 |

Data from U.S. Bureau of the Census, Current Population Survey, *Annual Social and Economic Supplement*, Table PINC-10, September 27, 2010.

**4.16** During the 1970s, many women changed their minds about whether they would leave the labor force after marrying and having children or whether they would be in the labor force most of their adult lives. In 1968, the National Longitudinal Survey asked a representative sample of women aged 14 to 24 whether they expected to be in the labor force at age 35. Twenty-nine percent of white women and 59 percent of black women responded that they expected to be in the labor force at that age. In fact, when these women were 35 years old, 60 percent of those who were married and 80 percent of those who were unmarried were in the labor force. In other words, many more women ended up being in the labor force than expected to be when they were of high school and college age. What effect did this fact have on the earnings of these women? Briefly explain.

Based on Claudia Goldin, *Understanding the Gender Gap: An Economic History of American Women*, (New York: Oxford University Press, 1990), p. 155.

**4.17** [**Related to the** Making the Connection **on page 559**] Some policymakers have proposed that all firms be required to make contributions to retirement plans for their employees. If such a proposal is enacted, what is likely to happen to the wages received by workers at firms that currently do not make contributions to their employees' retirement plans? Briefly explain your reasoning.

**4.18** [**Related to** Solved Problem 17.4 **on page 561**] Use the following graphs to answer the questions:

   **a.** What is the equilibrium quantity of trash collectors hired, and what is the equilibrium wage?

   **b.** What is the equilibrium quantity of receptionists hired, and what is the equilibrium wage?

   **c.** Briefly discuss why trash collectors might earn a higher weekly wage than receptionists.

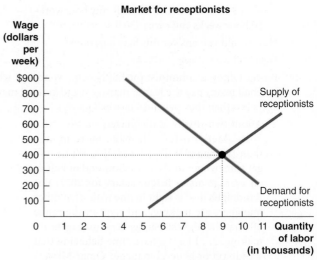

Market for receptionists

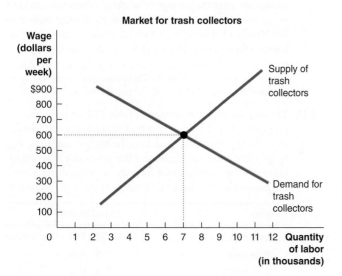

Market for trash collectors

   **d.** Suppose that comparable-worth legislation is passed, and the government requires that trash collectors and receptionists be paid the same wage, $500 per week. Now how many trash collectors will be hired and how many receptionists will be hired?

**4.19** [**Related to** Solved Problem 17.4 **on page 561**] In most universities, economics professors receive larger salaries than English professors. Suppose that the government requires that from now on, all universities must pay economics professors the same salaries as English professors. Use demand and supply graphs to analyze the effect of this requirement.

**4.20** [**Related to the** Making the Connection **on page 563**] Why might employers be more likely to interview a job applicant with a white-sounding name than an applicant with an African-American–sounding name? Leaving aside legal penalties, will employers who follow this practice incur an economic penalty? Briefly explain.

---

**17.5** **Personnel Economics, pages 566–568**

LEARNING OBJECTIVE: Discuss the role personnel economics can play in helping firms deal with human resources issues.

## Summary

**Personnel economics** is the application of economic analysis to human resources issues. One insight of personnel economics is that the productivity of workers can often be increased if firms move from straight-time pay to commission or piece-rate pay.

MyEconLab    Visit **www.myeconlab.com** to complete these exercises online and get instant feedback.

## Review Questions

**5.1** What is personnel economics?

**5.2** What are the two ways that the productivity of a firm's employees may increase when a firm moves from straight-time pay to commission or piece-rate pay?

**5.3** If piece-rate or commission systems of compensating workers have important advantages for firms, why don't more firms use them?

## Problems and Applications

**5.4** According to a study, the number of jobs in which firms used bonuses, commissions, or piece rates to tie workers' pay to their performance increased from an estimated 30 percent of all jobs in the 1970s to 40 percent in the 1990s. Why would systems that tie workers' pay to how much they produce have become increasingly popular with firms? The same study found that these pay systems were more common in higher-paid jobs than in lower-paid jobs. Briefly explain this result.

Based on Thomas Lemieux, W. Bentley MacLeod, and Daniel Parent, "Performance Pay and Wage Inequality," *Quarterly Journal of Economics*, Vol. 124, No. 1, February 2009, pp. 1–49.

**5.5** Many companies that pay workers an hourly wage require some minimum level of acceptable output. Suppose a company that has been using this system decides to switch to a piece-rate system under which workers are compensated on the basis of how much output they produce. Is it likely that workers under a piece-rate system will end up choosing to produce less than the minimum output required under the hourly wage system? Briefly explain.

**5.6** In most jobs, the harder you work, the more you earn. Some workers would rather work harder and earn more; others would rather work less hard, even though as a result they earn less. Suppose, though, that all workers at a company fall into the "work harder and earn more" group. Suppose also that the workers all have the same abilities. In these circumstances, would output per worker be the same under an hourly wage compensation system as under a piece-rate system? Briefly explain.

**5.7** For years, the Goodyear Tire & Rubber Company compensated its sales force by paying a salesperson a salary plus a bonus, based on the number of tires he or she sold. Eventually, Goodyear made two changes to this policy: (1) The basis for the bonus was changed from the *quantity* of tires sold to the *revenue* from the tires sold; and (2) salespeople were required to get approval from corporate headquarters in Akron, Ohio, before offering to sell tires to customers at reduced prices. Explain why these changes were likely to increase Goodyear's profits.

Based on Timothy Aeppel, "Amid Weak Inflation, Firms Turn Creative to Boost Prices," *Wall Street Journal*, September 18, 2002.

**5.8** **[Related to the** Making the Connection **on page 567]** What effect did the incentive pay system have on Safelite's marginal cost of installing replacement car windows? If all firms that replace car windows adopted an incentive pay system, what would happen to the price of replacing automobile glass? Who would ultimately benefit?

---

## 17.6 | The Markets for Capital and Natural Resources, pages 568–571

LEARNING OBJECTIVE: Show how equilibrium prices are determined in the markets for capital and natural resources.

## Summary

The approach used to analyze the market for labor can also be used to analyze the markets for other factors of production. In equilibrium, the price of capital is equal to the marginal revenue product of capital, and the price of natural resources is equal to the marginal revenue product of natural resources. The price received by a factor that is in fixed supply is called an **economic rent**, or a **pure rent**. A **monopsony** is the sole buyer of a factor of production. According to the **marginal productivity theory of income distribution**, the distribution of income is determined by the marginal productivity of the factors of production individuals own.

MyEconLab   Visit **www.myeconlab.com** to complete these exercises online and get instant feedback.

## Review Questions

**6.1** In equilibrium, what determines the price of capital? What determines the price of natural resources? What is the marginal productivity theory of income distribution?

**6.2** What is an economic rent? What is a monopsony?

## Problems and Applications

**6.3** Adam operates a pin factory. Suppose Adam faces the situation shown in the following table and the cost of renting a machine is $550 per week.

| Number of Machines | Output of Pins (boxes per week) | Marginal Product of Capital | Product Price (dollars per box) | Total Revenue | Marginal Revenue Product of Capital | Rental Cost per Machine | Additional Profit from Renting One Additional Machine |
|---|---|---|---|---|---|---|---|
| 0 | 0 | — | $100 | | — | $550 | |
| 1 | 12 | | 100 | | | 550 | |
| 2 | 21 | | 100 | | | 550 | |
| 3 | 28 | | 100 | | | 550 | |
| 4 | 34 | | 100 | | | 550 | |
| 5 | 39 | | 100 | | | 550 | |
| 6 | 43 | | 100 | | | 550 | |

a. Fill in the blanks in the table and determine the profit-maximizing number of machines for Adam to rent. Briefly explain why renting this number of machines is profit maximizing.

b. Draw Adam's demand curve for capital.

**6.4** Many people have predicted, using a model like the one in panel (b) of Figure 17.12 on page 570, that the price of natural resources should rise consistently over time in comparison with the prices of other goods because the demand curve for natural resources is continually shifting to the right, while the supply curve must be shifting to the left as natural resources are used up. However, the relative prices of most natural resources have not been increasing. Draw a graph that shows the demand and supply for natural resources that can explain why prices haven't risen even though demand has.

**6.5** In 1879, economist Henry George published *Progress and Poverty*, which became one of the best-selling books of the nineteenth century. In this book, George argued that all existing taxes should be replaced with a single tax on land. In Chapter 4, we discussed the concept of tax incidence, or the actual division of the burden of a tax between buyers and sellers in a market. If land is taxed, how will the burden of the tax be divided between the sellers of land and the buyers of land? Illustrate your answer with a graph of the market for land.

**6.6** The total amount of oil in the earth is not increasing. Does this mean that in the market for oil, the supply curve is perfectly inelastic? Briefly explain.

**6.7** In a competitive labor market, imposing a minimum wage should reduce the equilibrium level of employment. Will this also be true if the labor market is a monopsony? Briefly explain.

# Public Choice, Taxe and the Distributio of Income

## Chapter Outline and Learning Objectives

# Should the Government Use the Tax System to Reduce Inequality?

Taxes affect the incomes of households and the decisions made by businesses. For example, about 10 years ago, when the federal government cut the tax on dividends—payments corporations make to stockholders—many companies responded in a big way. Before the tax cut, Microsoft had never paid a dividend. After the tax cut, in a single year, Microsoft paid out more than $40 billion in dividends. Cutting the tax on dividends was intended to improve economic efficiency, but changing the tax code can serve other purposes as well.

The United States has the most unequal distribution of income of any high-income country, and income inequality in the United States has been increasing in recent years. As the 2012 presidential election campaign heated up, one of several issues separating President Barack Obama from Republican contender former Massachusetts Governor Mitt Romney was whether changes in the tax system should be used to reduce income inequality. President Obama argued that the tax cut on dividends, as well as other tax cuts enacted during the early 2000s, had increased the burden on individuals with low and moderate incomes, while the burden on the wealthy and on corporations had been reduced, increasing the level of income inequality. He proposed to use the tax code to help reduce this inequality. Romney argued that increasing income inequality had not been caused by changes in taxes and that increasing taxes on individuals with high incomes was likely to reduce economic efficiency while having little effect on inequality.

The questions raised by the debate over taxes during the 2012 election campaign were not new. Presidents John F. Kennedy and Ronald Reagan proposed significant cuts in income taxes that they claimed would enhance economic efficiency, while their opponents claimed that the tax cuts rewarded high-income taxpayers and increased income inequality. The design of the tax system and the criteria to use in evaluating it are important questions. Has the tax code improved economic efficiency? Has the government, through its tax and other policies, had much effect on the distribution of income? We explore these questions in this chapter.

**AN INSIDE LOOK AT POLICY** on **page 606** describes the arguments for and against using a tax on soda to reduce budget deficits.

Based on Jackie Calmes, "Obama Draws New Hard Line on Long-Term Debt Reduction," *New York Times*, September 19, 2011; and John D. McKinnon, "Millionaire's Tax to Be Tough Sell," *Wall Street Journal*, September 19, 2011.

## Economics in Your Life

### How Much Tax Should You Pay?

Government is ever present in your life. Just today, you likely drove on roads that the government paid to build and maintain. You may attend a public college or university, paid for, at least in part, by government. Where does a government get its money? By taxing citizens. Think of the different taxes you pay. Do you think you pay more than, less than, or just about your fair share in taxes? How do you determine what your fair share is? As you read this chapter, see if you can answer these questions. You can check your answers against those we provide on **page 605** at the end of this chapter.

**Public choice model** A model that applies economic analysis to government decision making.

W
e saw in Chapter 2 that the government plays a significant role in helping the market system work efficiently by providing secure rights to private property and an independent court system to enforce contracts. We saw in Chapter 5 that the government itself must sometimes supply goods— known as *public goods*—that private firms will not supply. But how do governments decide which policies to adopt? In recent years, economists led by Nobel Laureate James Buchanan and Gordon Tullock, formerly of the University of Virginia, have developed the **public choice model**, which applies economic analysis to government decision making. In this chapter, we will explore how public choice can help us understand how policymakers make decisions.

We will also discuss the principles that governments use to create tax policy. In particular, we will see how economists identify which taxes are most economically efficient. At the end of the chapter, we will discuss the extent to which government policy—including tax policy—affects the distribution of income.

**18.1 LEARNING** OBJECTIVE

Describe the public choice model and explain how it is used to analyze government decision making.

# Public Choice

In earlier chapters, we focused on explaining the actions of households and firms. We have assumed that households and firms act to make themselves as well off as possible. In particular, we have assumed that households choose the goods they buy to maximize their utility and that firms choose the quantities and prices of the goods they sell to maximize profits. Because government policy plays an important role in the economy, it is important also to consider how government policymakers—such as senators, governors, presidents, and state legislators—arrive at their decisions. One of the key insights from the public choice model is that policymakers are no different than consumers or managers of firms: Policymakers are likely to pursue their own self-interest, even if their self-interest conflicts with the public interest. In particular, we expect that public officials will take actions that are likely to result in their being reelected.

## How Do We Know the Public Interest? Models of Voting

It is possible to argue that elected officials simply represent the preferences of the voters who elect them. After all, it would seem logical that voters will not reelect a politician who fails to act in the public interest. A closer look at voting, however, makes it less clear that politicians are simply representing the views of the voters.

**The Voting Paradox** Many policy decisions involve multiple alternatives. Because the size of the federal budget is limited, policymakers face trade-offs. To take a simple example, suppose that there is $1 billion available in the budget, and Congress must choose whether to spend it on *only one* of three alternatives: (1) research on breast cancer, (2) subsidies for mass transit, or (3) increased border security. Assume that the votes of members of Congress will represent the preferences of their constituents. We might expect that Congress will vote for the alternative favored by a majority of the voters. In fact, though, there are circumstances in which majority voting will fail to result in a consistent decision. For example, suppose for simplicity that there are only three voters, and they have the preferences shown at the top of Table 18.1.

In the table, we show the three policy alternatives in the first column. The remaining columns show the voters' rankings of the alternatives. For example, Lena would prefer to see the money spent on cancer research. Her second choice is mass transit, and her third choice is border security. What happens if a series of votes are taken in which each pair of alternatives is considered in turn? The bottom of Table 18.1 shows the results of these votes. If the vote is between spending the money on cancer research and spending the money on mass transit, cancer research wins because Lena and David both prefer spending the money on cancer research to spending the money on mass transit. So, if the votes of members of Congress represent the preferences of voters, we have a

| Policy | Lena | David | Kathleen |
|---|---|---|---|
| Cancer research | 1st | 2nd | 3rd |
| Mass transit | 2nd | 3rd | 1st |
| Border security | 3rd | 1st | 2nd |

| Votes | Outcome |
|---|---|
| Cancer research versus mass transit | Cancer research wins |
| Mass transit versus border security | Mass transit wins |
| Border security versus cancer research | Border security wins |

**Table 18.1**

**The Voting Paradox**

clear verdict, and the money is spent on cancer research. Suppose, though, that the vote is between spending the money on mass transit and spending the money on border security. Then, because Lena and Kathleen prefer spending on mass transit to spending on border security, mass transit wins. Now, finally, suppose the vote is between spending on cancer research and spending on border security. Surprisingly, border security wins because that is what David and Kathleen prefer. The outcome of this vote is surprising because if voters prefer cancer research to mass transit and mass transit to border security, we would expect that consistency in decision making would ensure that they prefer cancer research to border security. But in this example, the collective preferences of the voters turn out not to be consistent. The failure of majority voting to always result in consistent choices is called the **voting paradox**.

This is an artificial example because we assumed that there were only three alternatives, there were only three voters, and a simple majority vote determined the outcomes. In fact, though, Nobel Laureate Kenneth Arrow of Stanford University has shown mathematically that the failure of majority votes to always represent voters' preferences is a very general result. The **Arrow impossibility theorem** states that no system of voting can be devised that will consistently represent the underlying preferences of voters. This theorem suggests that there is no way through democratic voting to ensure that the preferences of voters are translated into policy choices. In fact, the Arrow impossibility theorem suggests that voting might lead to shifts in policy that may not be efficient. For instance, which of the three alternatives for spending the $1 billion Congress will actually choose would depend on the order in which the alternatives happen to be voted on, which might change from one year to the next. So, with respect to economic issues, such as providing funding for public goods, we cannot count on the political process to necessarily result in an efficient outcome. In other words, the "voting market"—as represented by elections—may often do a less efficient job of representing consumer preferences than do markets for goods and services.

**The Median Voter Theorem** In practice, many political issues are decided by a majority vote. In those cases, what can we say about which voters' preferences the outcome is likely to represent? An important result known as the **median voter theorem** states that the outcome of a majority vote is likely to represent the preferences of the voter who is in the political middle. To take another simplified example, suppose there are five voters, and their preferences for spending on breast cancer research are shown in Figure 18.1. Their preferences range from Kathleen, who prefers to spend nothing on breast cancer research—preferring the funds to be spent on other programs or for federal spending to be reduced and taxes lowered—to Lena, who prefers to spend $6 billion.

In this case, David is the median voter because he is in the political middle; two voters would prefer to spend less than he does and two would prefer to spend more. To see why the median voter's preferences are likely to prevail, consider first a vote between David's preferred outcome of spending $2 billion and a proposal to spend $6 billion. Because only Lena favors $6 billion and the other voters all prefer spending less, the proposal to spend $2 billion would win four votes to one. Similarly, consider a vote between spending $2 billion and spending $1 billion. Three voters prefer spending more than $1 billion

**Voting paradox** The failure of majority voting to always result in consistent choices.

**Arrow impossibility theorem** A mathematical theorem that holds that no system of voting can be devised that will consistently represent the underlying preferences of voters.

**Median voter theorem** The proposition that the outcome of a majority vote is likely to represent the preferences of the voter who is in the political middle.

### Figure 18.1

**The Median Voter Theorem**

The median voter theorem states that the outcome of a majority vote is likely to represent the preferences of the voter who is in the political middle. In this case, David is in the political middle because two voters want to spend more on breast cancer research than he does and two voters want to spend less. In any vote between a proposal to spend $2 billion and a proposal to spend a different amount, a proposal to spend $2 billion will win.

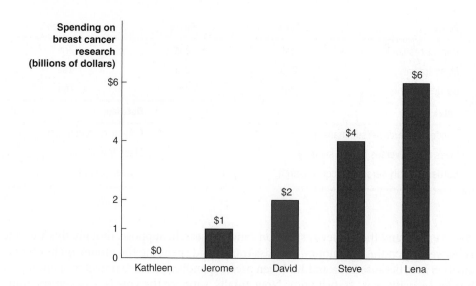

and only two prefer spending $1 billion or less, so the proposal to spend $2 billion will win three votes to two. Only the proposal to spend $2 billion will have the support of a majority when paired with proposals to spend a different amount. Notice also that the amount spent as a result of the voting is less than the amount that would result from taking the simple average of the voter's preferences, which would be $2.6 billion.

One implication of the median voter theorem is that the political process tends to serve individuals whose preferences are in the middle but not those individuals whose preferences are far away from the median. There is an important contrast between the political process, which results in collective actions in which everyone is obliged to participate, and the market process, in which individuals are free to participate or not. For instance, even though Kathleen would prefer not to spend government funds on breast cancer research, once a majority has voted to spend $2 billion, Kathleen is obliged to go along with the spending—and the taxes required to fund the spending. This is in contrast with the market for goods and services, where if, for instance, Kathleen disagrees with the majority of consumers who like iPods, she is under no obligation to buy one. Similarly, even though Lena and Steve might prefer to pay significantly higher taxes to fund additional spending on breast cancer research, they are obliged to go along with the lower level of spending the majority approved. If Lena would like to have her iPod gold plated, she can choose to do so, even if the vast majority of consumers would consider such spending a waste of money.

## Government Failure?

The voting models we have just looked at indicate that individuals are less likely to see their preferences represented in the outcomes of government policies than in the outcomes of markets. The public choice model goes beyond this observation to question whether the self-interest of policymakers is likely to cause them to take actions that are inconsistent with the preferences of voters, even where those preferences are clear. There are several aspects of how the political process works that might lead to this outcome.

**Rent seeking** Attempts by individuals and firms to use government action to make themselves better off at the expense of others.

**Rent Seeking** Economists usually focus on analyzing the actions of individuals and firms as they attempt to make themselves better off by interacting in markets. The public choice model shifts the focus to attempts by individuals and firms to engage in **rent seeking**, which is the use of government action to make themselves better off at the expense of others. One of the benefits of the market system is that it channels self-interested behavior in a way that benefits society as a whole. Although Apple developed the iPad to make profits, its actions increased the well-being of millions of consumers. When Samsung introduced the Galaxy Tab to compete with the iPad, it also was motivated by the desire for profit, but it further increased consumer well-being by expanding the choice of tablet computers available. Rent seeking, in contrast, can benefit a few individuals or firms at the expense of all other individuals and firms. For example, we saw in Chapter 9 that U.S. sugar firms have successfully convinced Congress to impose a quota on imports of sugar. The quota has benefited the owners of U.S. sugar firms and the people who work for them but has reduced consumer surplus, hurt U.S. candy companies and their workers, and reduced economic efficiency.

Because firms can benefit from government intervention in the economy, as the sugar companies have benefited from the sugar quota, they are willing to spend resources to attempt to secure these interventions. Members of Congress, state legislators, governors, and presidents need funds to finance their election campaigns. So, these policymakers may accept campaign contributions from rent-seeking firms and may be willing to introduce *special interest legislation* in their behalf.

**Logrolling and Rational Ignorance** Two other factors help explain why rent-seeking behavior can sometimes succeed. It may seem puzzling that the sugar quota has been enacted when  it helped very few workers and firms. Why would members of Congress vote for the sugar quota if they do not have sugar companies in their districts? One possibility is logrolling. *Logrolling* refers to the situation where a member of Congress votes to approve a bill in exchange for favorable votes from other members on other bills. For example, a member of Congress from Texas might vote for the sugar quota, even though none of the member's constituents will benefit from it. In exchange, members of Congress from districts where sugar producers are located will vote for legislation the member of Congress from Texas would like to see passed. This vote trading may result in a majority of Congress supporting legislation that benefits the economic interests of a few while harming the economic interests of a much larger group.

But if the majority of voters is harmed by rent-seeking legislation, how does it get passed, even given the effects of logrolling? In Chapter 9, we discussed one possible explanation with respect to the sugar quota. Although, collectively, consumer surplus declines by $6.08 billion per year because of the sugar quota, spread across a population of 310 million, the loss per person is only $20. Because the loss is so small, most people do not take it into account when deciding how to vote in elections, and many people are not even aware that the sugar quota exists. Other voters may be convinced to support restrictions on trade because the jobs saved by tariffs and quotas are visible and often highly publicized, while the jobs lost because of these restrictions and the reductions in consumer surplus are harder to detect. Because becoming informed on an issue may require time and effort and the economic payoff is often low, some economists argue that many voters are *rationally ignorant* of the effect of rent-seeking legislation. In this view, because voters frequently lack an economic incentive to become informed about pending legislation, the voters' preferences do not act as a constraint on legislators voting for rent-seeking legislation.

**Regulatory Capture** One way in which the government intervenes in the economy is by establishing a regulatory agency or commission that is given authority over a particular industry or type of product. For example, no firm is allowed to sell prescription drugs in the United States without first receiving authorization from the Food and Drug Administration (FDA). Ideally, regulatory agencies will make decisions in the public interest. The FDA should weigh the benefits to patients from quickly approving a new drug against the costs that the agency may overlook potentially dangerous side effects of the drug if approval is too rapid. However, because the firms being regulated are significantly affected by the regulatory agency's actions, the firms have an incentive to try to influence those actions. In extreme cases, this influence may lead the agency to make decisions that are in the best interests of the firms being regulated, even if these actions are not in the public interest. In that case, the agency has been subject to *regulatory capture* by the industry being regulated. Some economists point to the Interstate Commerce Commission (ICC) as an example of regulatory capture. Although Congress has since abolished the ICC, for decades it determined the prices that railroads and long-distance trucking firms could charge to haul freight. Congress originally established the ICC to safeguard the interests of consumers, but some economists have argued that for many years, the ICC operated to suppress competition, which was in the interests of the railroads and trucking firms rather than in the interests of consumers. Economists debate the extent to which regulatory capture explains the decisions of some government agencies.

In Chapter 5, we saw how the presence of externalities can lead to market failure, which is the situation where the market does not supply the economically efficient quantity of a good or service. Public choice analysis indicates that *government failure* can also occur. For the reasons we have discussed in this section, it is possible that government intervention in the economy may reduce economic efficiency rather than increase it. Economists disagree about the extent to which government failure results in serious economic inefficiency in the U.S. economy. Most economists, though, accept the basic argument of the public choice model that policymakers may have incentives to intervene in the economy in ways that do not promote efficiency and that proposals for such intervention should be evaluated with care.

### Is Government Regulation Necessary?

The public choice model raises important questions about the effect of government regulation on economic efficiency. But can we conclude that Congress should abolish agencies such as the Food and Drug Administration (FDA), the Environmental Protection Agency (EPA), and the Federal Trade Commission (FTC)? In fact, most economists agree that these agencies can serve useful purposes. For instance, in Chapter 5, we discussed how the EPA can help correct the effects of production externalities, such as pollution. Regulatory agencies can also improve economic efficiency in markets where consumers have difficulty obtaining the information they need to make informed purchases. For example, consumers have no easy way of detecting bacteria and other contaminants in food or determining whether prescription drugs are safe and effective. The FDA was established in the early twentieth century to monitor the nation's food supply following newspaper accounts of unsanitary practices in many meatpacking plants.

Although government regulation can clearly provide important benefits to consumers, we need to take into account the costs of regulations. Recent estimates indicate that the costs of federal regulations may be several thousand dollars per taxpayer. Economics can help policymakers devise regulations that provide benefits to consumers that exceed their costs.

**18.2 LEARNING** OBJECTIVE

Understand the tax system in the United States, including the principles that governments use to create tax policy.

## The Tax System

However the size of government and the types of activities it engages in are determined, government spending has to be financed. The government primarily relies on taxes to raise the revenue it needs. Some taxes, though, such as those on cigarettes or alcohol, are intended more to discourage what society views as undesirable behavior than to raise revenue. These are the most widely used taxes:

- *Individual income taxes.* The federal government, most state governments, and some local governments tax the wages, salaries, and other income of households and the profits of firms. The individual income tax is the largest source of revenue for the federal government. Because low-income people are exempted from paying federal individual income taxes, in recent years nearly half of all households have paid no federal income tax. In 2009, people who paid the individual income tax had an average income of $71,636 and paid federal individual income taxes of $8,307.

- *Social insurance taxes.* The federal government taxes wages and salaries to raise revenue for the Social Security and Medicare systems. *Social Security* makes payments to retired workers and to disabled individuals. *Medicare* helps pay the medical expenses of people over age 65. The Social Security and Medicare taxes are often referred to as "payroll taxes." As the U.S. population has aged, payroll taxes have increased. By 2011, 76 percent of taxpayers paid more in payroll taxes than in federal income taxes. The federal government and state governments also tax wages and salaries to raise revenue for the unemployment insurance system, which makes payments to workers who have lost their jobs.

- *Sales taxes.* Most state and local governments tax retail sales of most products. More than half the states exempt food from the sales tax, and a few states also exempt clothing.

- *Property taxes.* Most local governments tax homes, offices, factories, and the land they are built on. In the United States, the property tax is the largest source of funds for public schools.

- *Excise taxes.* The federal government and some state governments levy excise taxes on specific goods, such as gasoline, cigarettes, and beer.

## An Overview of the U.S. Tax System

Panels (a) and (b) of Figure 18.2 show the revenue sources of the federal, state, and local governments. Panel (a) shows that the federal government raises nearly 80 percent of its revenue from the social insurance taxes and from the individual income tax. Corporate income taxes and excise taxes account for much smaller fractions of federal revenues. In 2010, federal revenues of all types amounted to almost $2.4 trillion, or about $20,360 per household. Over the past 40 years, federal revenues as a share of gross domestic product (GDP; the value of all the goods and services produced in the U.S. economy) have typically remained in a fairly narrow range between 17 percent and 19 percent, with a low of 16 percent in 2009 and a high of 21 percent in 2000.

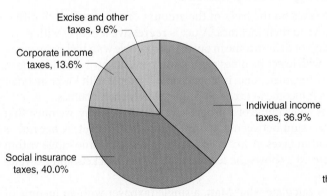

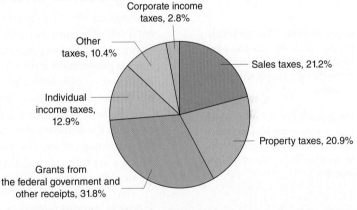

| Tax | Amount (billions) | Amount per Household | Percentage of Total Tax Receipts |
|---|---|---|---|
| Individual income taxes | $896 | $7,622 | 36.9% |
| Social insurance taxes | 971 | 8,256 | 40.0 |
| Corporate income taxes | 330 | 2803 | 13.6 |
| Excise and other taxes | 233 | 1,979 | 9.6 |
| Total | $2,430 | $20,660 | 100% |

| Tax | Amount (billions) | Amount per Household | Percentage of Total Tax Receipts |
|---|---|---|---|
| Sales taxes | $438 | $3,727 | 21.2% |
| Property taxes | 431 | 3,662 | 20.9 |
| Grants from the federal government and other receipts | 656 | 5,577 | 31.8 |
| Individual income taxes | 267 | 2,270 | 12.9 |
| Other taxes | 215 | 1,829 | 10.4 |
| Corporate income taxes | 58 | 492 | 2.8 |
| Total | $2,065 | $17,557 | 100% |

**(a) Sources of federal government revenue, 2010**

**(b) Sources of state and local government revenue, 2010**

**Figure 18.2**  **Federal, State, and Local Sources of Revenue, 2010**

Social insurance taxes are the most important source of revenue for the federal government, and individual income taxes are the second most important source. State and local governments receive the most revenue from sales taxes. State and local governments also receive large transfers from the federal government, in part to help pay for federally mandated programs. Many local governments depend on property taxes to raise most of their tax revenue.

Data from U.S. Department of Commerce, Bureau of Economic Analysis, "National Income and Product Accounts of the United States," Tables 3.2 and 3.3, August 26, 2011.

| Table 18.2 | Income | Tax Rate |
|---|---|---|
| **Federal Income Tax Brackets and Tax Rates for Single Taxpayers, 2011** | $0–$8,500 | 10% |
| | $8,501–$34,500 | 15 |
| | $34,501–$83,600 | 25 |
| | $83,601–$174,400 | 28 |
| | $174,401–$379,150 | 33 |
| | Over $379,150 | 35 |

Data from Internal Revenue Service.

Panel (b) shows that state and local governments rely on a different mix of revenue sources than does the federal government. In fact, in most years, the largest source of revenue for state and local governments is sales taxes. State and local governments also receive large grants from the federal government, which in 2010 were their largest source of revenue. These grants are intended in part to pay for programs that the federal government requires states and local governments to carry out. These programs, often called *federal mandates*, include the *Medicaid* program, which provides health care to poor people, and the Temporary Assistance for Needy Families (TANF) program, which provides financial assistance to poor families. During and after the 2007–2009 recession the federal government temporarily increased its grants to local governments. Local governments depend heavily on property taxes. Many local school districts, in particular, rely almost entirely on revenues from property taxes.

## Progressive and Regressive Taxes

**Regressive tax** A tax for which people with lower incomes pay a higher percentage of their income in tax than do people with higher incomes.

**Progressive tax** A tax for which people with lower incomes pay a lower percentage of their income in tax than do people with higher incomes.

Economists often categorize taxes on the basis of the amount of tax people with different levels of income pay relative to their incomes. A tax is **regressive** if people with lower incomes pay a higher percentage of their income in tax than do people with higher incomes. A tax is **progressive** if people with lower incomes pay a lower percentage of their income in tax than do people with higher incomes. A tax is *proportional* if people with lower incomes pay the same percentage of their income in tax as do people with higher incomes.

The federal income tax is an example of a progressive tax. To see why, we must first consider the important distinction between a tax rate and a tax bracket. A *tax rate* is the percentage of income paid in taxes. A *tax bracket* refers to the income range within which a tax rate applies. Table 18.2 shows the federal income tax brackets and tax rates for single taxpayers in 2011.

We can use Table 18.2 to calculate what Matt, a single taxpayer with an income of $100,000, pays in federal income tax. This example is somewhat simplified because we are ignoring the *exemptions* and *deductions* that taxpayers can use to reduce the amount of income subject to tax. For example, taxpayers are allowed to exclude from taxation a certain amount of income, called the *personal exemption*, that represents very basic living expenses. Ignoring Matt's exemptions and deductions, he will have to make the tax payment to the federal government shown in Table 18.3. Matt's first $8,500 of income is in the 10 percent bracket, so he pays $850 in taxes on that part of his income. His next $26,000 of income is in the 15 percent bracket, so he pays $3,900. His next $49,100 of income is in the 25 percent bracket, so he pays $12,275. His last $16,400 of income is in the 28 percent bracket, so he pays $4,592, which brings his total federal income tax bill to $21,617.

| Table 18.3 | On Matt's ... | Matt pays tax of ... |
|---|---|---|
| **Federal Income Tax Paid on Taxable Income of $100,000** | first $8,500 of income | $ 850 |
| | next $26,000 of income | 3,900 |
| | next $49,100 of income | 12,275 |
| | last $16,400 of income | 4,592 |
| | His total federal income tax payment is | $21,617 |

# Making the Connection

## Which Groups Pay the Most in Federal Taxes?

At the beginning of this chapter, we mentioned the ongoing debate over whether to increase taxes on people with high incomes. To evaluate this debate, it's useful to know how much each income group pays of the total taxes collected by the federal government. The following table shows projections for 2011 by the Tax Policy Center, with taxpayers divided into quintiles from the 20 percent with the lowest income to the 20 percent with the highest income. The last row also shows taxpayers whose incomes put them in the top 1 percent. Column (1) shows the percentage of total income earned by each income group. Column (2) shows the percentage of all federal taxes—including Social Security and Medicare payroll taxes—paid by each income group. Column (3) shows the average federal tax rate for each group, calculated by dividing total taxes paid by total income.

| Income Category | Percentage of Total Income Earned (1) | Percentage of Total Federal Taxes Paid (2) | All Federal Taxes Paid as a Fraction of Income (average federal tax rate) (3) |
|---|---|---|---|
| Lowest 20% | 3.7% | 0.2% | 0.8% |
| Second 20% | 8.5 | 2.7 | 5.8 |
| Third 20% | 13.5 | 9.3 | 12.5 |
| Fourth 20% | 19.5 | 18.1 | 16.6 |
| Highest 20% | 54.6 | 69.7 | 23.1 |
| **Total** | 100.0% | 100.0% | 18.1% |
| Highest 1% | 16.8 | 25.6 | 27.6 |

*Note:* Columns do not sum to precisely 100 percent due to rounding.
Source: "Income categories and Federal Taxes" from www.taxpolicy.org. Copyright © 2011 by The Urban Institute. Reprinted by permission.

The data in column (2) show that the 20 percent of taxpayers with the highest incomes pay 70 percent of federal taxes. This share is more than their share of total income earned, which is about 55 percent, as shown in column (1). Only taxpayers in the highest quintile pay a larger share of taxes than their share of income. Taxpayers whose incomes put them in the top 1 percent pay more than 25 percent of federal taxes. Many individuals in the lowest quintile of income, particularly those with children, receive tax credits from the federal government so that they in effect pay negative taxes. Column (3) indicates that average tax rates rise as income rises.

If we look at just the federal individual income tax considered separately from the payroll tax and other federal taxes, the results are similar. In 2011, taxpayers in the top 1 percent of the income distribution were projected to earn 17 percent of all income while paying 34 percent of all federal individual income taxes. The top 20 percent earned 55 percent of income while paying 85 percent of taxes. The bottom 40 percent of the income distribution earned 12 percent of income but actually paid *negative* 5 percent of federal individual income taxes when taking into account tax credits, such as the child tax credit.

We can conclude that the federal taxes are progressive. Whether the federal tax system should be made more or less progressive remains a source of political debate.

**Your Turn:** Test your understanding by doing related problem 2.9 on pages 609–610 at the end of this chapter.

MyEconLab

---

# Marginal and Average Income Tax Rates

The fraction of each additional dollar of income that must be paid in taxes is called the **marginal tax rate**. The **average tax rate** is the total tax paid divided by total income. When a tax is progressive, as is the federal income tax, the marginal and average tax rates

**Marginal tax rate** The fraction of each additional dollar of income that must be paid in taxes.

**Average tax rate** Total tax paid divided by total income.

differ. For example, in Table 18.3 on page 588, Matt had a marginal tax rate of 28 percent because that is the rate he paid on the last dollar of his income. But his average tax rate was:

$$\left(\frac{\$21,617}{\$100,000}\right) \times 100 = 21.6\%.$$

His average tax rate was lower than his marginal tax rate because the first $83,600 of his income was taxed at rates below his marginal rate of 28 percent.

When economists consider a change in tax policy, they generally focus on the marginal tax rate rather than the average tax rate because the marginal tax rate is a better indicator of how a change in a tax will affect people's willingness to work, save, and invest. For example, if Matt is considering working longer hours to raise his income, he will use his marginal tax rate to determine how much extra income he will earn after taxes. He will ignore his average tax rate because it does not represent the taxes he must pay on the *additional* income he earns. The higher the marginal tax rate, the lower the return he receives from working additional hours and the less likely he is to work those additional hours.

## The Corporate Income Tax

The federal government taxes the profits earned by corporations under the *corporate income tax*. Like the individual income tax, the corporate income tax is progressive, with the lowest tax rate being 15 percent and the highest being 35 percent. Unlike the individual income tax, however, where relatively few taxpayers are taxed at the highest rate, many corporations are in the 35 percent tax bracket.

Economists debate the costs and benefits of a separate tax on corporate profits. The corporate income tax ultimately must be paid by a corporation's owners—which are its shareholders—or by its employees, in the form of lower wages, or by its customers, in the form of higher prices. Some economists argue that if the purpose of the corporate income tax is to tax the owners of corporations, it would be better to do so directly by taxing the owners' incomes rather than by taxing the owners indirectly through the corporate income tax. Individual taxpayers already pay income taxes on the dividends and capital gains they receive from owning stock in corporations. In effect, the corporate income tax "double taxes" earnings on individual shareholders' investments in corporations. An alternative policy that avoids this double taxation would be for corporations to calculate their total profits each year and send a notice to each shareholder, indicating the shareholder's portion of the profits. The shareholder would then be required to include this amount as taxable income on his or her personal income tax. Under another alternative, the federal government could continue to tax corporate income through the corporate income tax but allow individual taxpayers to receive corporate dividends and capital gains tax-free. In 2003, Congress enacted a reduction on dividend and capital gains taxes to reduce double taxation.

## International Comparison of Corporate Income Taxes

In the past 10 years, several countries have cut corporate income taxes to increase investment spending and growth. Table 18.4 compares corporate income tax rates in several high-income countries. The tax rates given in the table include taxes at all levels of government. So, in the United States, for example, they include taxes imposed on corporate profits by state governments as well as by the federal government. The table shows that several countries, including Italy, Germany, and Ireland, significantly reduced corporate income tax rates between 2000 and 2010. Ireland, in particular, has been successful in using lower corporate income tax rates to attract foreign corporations to locate facilities there. Lower tax rates have led Microsoft, Intel, and Dell, among other U.S. firms, to base some of their operations in Ireland. The table also shows that corporate income tax rates are higher in the United States than in other high-income countries, except Japan.

| Country | Tax in 2000 | Tax in 2010 |
|---------|-------------|-------------|
| France | 37% | 33% |
| Germany | 52 | 29 |
| Ireland | 24 | 13 |
| Italy | 41 | 31 |
| Japan | 42 | 41 |
| Spain | 35 | 30 |
| Sweden | 28 | 26 |
| United Kingdom | 30 | 28 |
| United States | 40 | 40 |

**Table 18.4**

**Corporate Income Tax Rates around the World**

Data from KPMG, KPMG's Corporate and Indirect Tax Survey, 2010. pp. 65–69. (http://www.kpmg.com/Global/en/IssuesAndInsights/ArticlesPublications/Documents/Corp-and-Indirect-Tax-Oct12-2010.pdf).

# Evaluating Taxes

We have seen that to raise revenue, governments have available a variety of taxes. In selecting which taxes to use, governments take into account the following goals and principles:

- The goal of economic efficiency

- The ability-to-pay principle

- The horizontal-equity principle

- The benefits-received principle

- The goal of attaining social objectives

**The Goal of Economic Efficiency**   In Chapter 4, we analyzed the effect that taxes have on economic efficiency. We briefly review that discussion here. Whenever a government taxes an activity, it raises the cost of engaging in that activity, so less of that activity will occur. Figure 18.3 uses a demand and supply graph to illustrate this point for a sales tax. As we saw in Chapter 4, a sales tax increases the cost of supplying a good, which causes the supply curve to shift up by the amount of the tax. In the figure, the equilibrium price rises from $P_1$ to $P_2$, and the equilibrium quantity falls from $Q_1$ to $Q_2$. When a good is taxed, less of it is produced.

The government collects tax revenue equal to the tax per unit multiplied by the number of units sold. The green-shaded rectangle in Figure 18.3 represents the government's tax revenue. Although sellers appear to receive a higher price for the good—$P_2$—the price they receive after paying the tax falls to $P_3$. Because the price consumers pay has risen, consumer surplus has fallen. Because the price producers receive has also fallen,

**Figure 18.3**

**The Efficiency Loss from a Sales Tax**

This figure reviews the discussion from Chapter 4 on the efficiency loss from a tax. A sales tax increases the cost of supplying a good, which causes the supply curve to shift up, from $S_1$ to $S_2$. Without the tax, the equilibrium price of the good is $P_1$, and the equilibrium quantity is $Q_1$. After the tax is imposed, the equilibrium price rises to $P_2$, and the equilibrium quantity falls to $Q_2$. After paying the tax, producers receive $P_3$. The government receives tax revenue equal to the green-shaded rectangle. Some consumer surplus and some producer surplus become tax revenue for the government, and some become deadweight loss, shown by the yellow-shaded triangle. The deadweight loss is the *excess burden* of the tax.

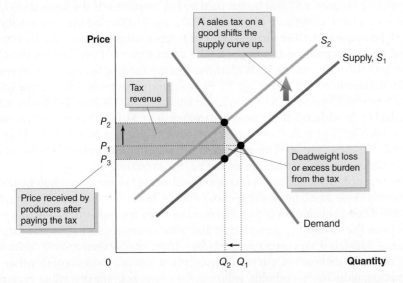

**Excess burden** A measure of the efficiency loss to the economy that results from a tax having reduced the quantity of a good produced; also known as the deadweight loss.

producer surplus has fallen. Some of the reduction in consumer surplus and producer surplus becomes tax revenue for the government. The rest of the reduction in consumer surplus and producer surplus is equal to the deadweight loss from the tax and is shown in the figure by the yellow-shaded triangle. The deadweight loss from a tax is known as the *excess burden* of the tax. The **excess burden** is a measure of the efficiency loss to the economy that results from the tax having reduced the quantity of the good produced. *A tax is efficient if it imposes a small excess burden relative to the tax revenue it raises.*

To improve the economic efficiency of a tax system, economists argue that the government should reduce its reliance on taxes that have a high deadweight loss relative to the revenue raised. The tax on interest earned from savings is an example of a tax with a high deadweight loss because savings often comes from income already taxed once. Therefore, taxing interest earned on savings from income that has already been taxed is essentially double taxation.

There are other examples of significant deadweight losses of taxation. High taxes on work can reduce the number of hours an individual works, as well as how hard the individual works or whether the individual starts a business. In each case, the reduction in the taxed activity—here, work—generates less government revenue, and individuals are worse off because the tax encourages them to change their behavior.

Taxation can have substantial effects on economic efficiency by altering incentives to work, save, or invest. A good illustration of this effect can be seen in the large differences between annual hours worked in Europe and in the United States. Europeans typically work fewer hours than do Americans. According to an analysis by Nobel Laureate Edward Prescott of Arizona State University, this difference was not always present. In the early 1970s, when European and U.S. tax rates on income were comparable, European and U.S. hours worked per employee were also comparable. Prescott finds that virtually all of the difference between labor supply in the United States and labor supply in France and Germany since that time is due to differences in their tax systems.

*Would a consumption tax be more efficient than an income tax?*

## Making the Connection | Should the United States Shift from an Income Tax to a Consumption Tax?

A key issue in recent debates over tax policy is whether the federal government should shift from relying on an income tax to relying on a *consumption tax*. Under the income tax, households pay taxes on all income earned. Under a consumption tax, households pay taxes only on the part of income they spend. Households pay taxes on saved income only if they spend the money at a later time.

To see how a shift from an income tax to a consumption tax can affect the economic incentives individuals face, consider the following example: Suppose a 20-year-old is deciding whether to save a $1,000 bonus paid by her employer. If she saves the $1,000 by putting it in a bank certificate of deposit (CD), the $1,000 *and* the interest she earns will both be taxed under the income tax, but neither will be taxed if the income tax is replaced by a consumption tax. Suppose she earns 6 percent per year on the CD and keeps it until she retires at age 70. With interest compounding tax free over 50 years, she will have accumulated $18,420 at age 70. Now suppose that under the income tax she is taxed at a rate of 33 percent. As a result, she will have only $670 of her bonus left after paying the tax. In addition, if she saves the money in a CD, her after-tax return each year is only 6 percent × (1 − 0.33) = 4 percent. Now saving her bonus in a CD at age 20 yields only $4,761 at age 70. This big difference in accumulation—$13,659—is the tax burden on saving, a burden that makes saving less attractive.

Many economists argue that a taxpayer's well-being is better measured by his or her consumption (how much he or she spends) than by his or her income (how much he or she earns). Taxing consumption may therefore be more appropriate than taxing income. Also, because the income tax taxes interest and other returns to saving, it taxes *future* consumption—which is what current saving is for—more heavily than *present* consumption. That is, under an income tax, current consumption is taxed more favorably than future consumption, reducing households' willingness to save, as in the preceding example.

Some economists oppose a shift from an income tax to a consumption tax because they believe a consumption tax will be more regressive than an income tax. These economists argue that people with very low incomes are able to save little or nothing and so would not be able to benefit from the increased incentives for saving that exist under a consumption tax.

Would a shift to a consumption tax be a radical change in the tax system? For many households, the answer is, perhaps surprisingly, "no." Most taxpayers can already put part of their savings into accounts where the funds deposited and the interest received are not taxed until the funds are withdrawn for retirement spending—for example, 401(k) plans and certain types of Individual Retirement Accounts (IRAs). In effect, individuals whose savings are mainly in these retirement accounts are already paying a consumption tax rather than an income tax. Reductions in tax rates on dividends and capital gains—which are both returns to savings—and other incentives to expand saving have further increased the role of consumption taxation.

**Your Turn:** Test your understanding by doing related problem 2.10 on page 610 at the end of this    MyEconLab
chapter.

---

The administrative burden of a tax represents another example of the deadweight loss of taxation. Individuals spend many hours during the year keeping records for income tax purposes, and they spend many more hours prior to April 15 preparing their tax returns. The opportunity cost of this time is billions of dollars each year and represents an administrative burden of the federal income tax. For corporations, complexity in tax planning arises in many areas. The federal government also has to devote resources to enforcing the tax laws. Although the government collects the revenue from taxation, the resources spent on administrative burdens benefit neither taxpayers nor the government.

Wouldn't tax simplification reduce the administrative burden and the deadweight loss of taxation? Yes. So why is the tax code complicated? In part, complexity arises because the political process has resulted in different types of income being taxed at different rates, requiring rules to limit taxpayers' ability to avoid taxes. In addition, interest groups seek benefits, while the majority of taxpayers, who do not benefit, find it difficult to organize a drive for a simpler tax system.

**The Ability-to-Pay Principle**  The *ability-to-pay principle* holds that when the government raises revenue through taxes, it is fair to expect a greater share of the tax burden to be borne by people who have a greater ability to pay. Usually this principle means raising more taxes from people with high incomes than from people with low incomes, which is sometimes referred to as *vertical equity*. The federal income tax is consistent with the ability-to-pay principle. The sales tax, in contrast, is not consistent with the ability-to-pay principle because low-income people tend to spend a larger fraction of their income than do high-income people. As a result, low-income people will pay a greater fraction of their income in sales taxes than will high-income people.

**The Horizontal-Equity Principle**  The *horizontal-equity principle* states that people in the same economic situation should be treated equally. Although this principle seems desirable, it is not easy to use in practice because it is sometimes difficult to determine whether two people are in the same economic situation. For example, two people with the same income are not necessarily in the same economic situation. Suppose one person does not work but receives an income of $50,000 per year entirely from interest received on bonds and another person receives an income of $50,000 per year from working at two jobs 16 hours a day. In this case, we could argue that the two people are in different economic situations and should not pay the same tax. Although policymakers and economists usually consider horizontal equity when evaluating proposals to change the tax system, it is not a principle they can follow easily.

**The Benefits-Received Principle**  According to the *benefits-received principle*, people who receive the benefits from a government program should pay the taxes that support the program. For example, if a city operates a marina used by private boat owners, the government can raise the revenue to operate the marina by levying a tax on the boat owners. Raising the revenue through a general income tax paid both by boat owners and non-boat owners would be inconsistent with the benefits-received principle. Because the government has many programs, however, it would be impractical to identify and tax the beneficiaries of every program.

**The Goal of Attaining Social Objectives** Taxes are sometimes used to attain social objectives. For example, the government might want to discourage smoking and drinking alcohol. Taxing cigarettes and alcoholic beverages is one way to help achieve this objective. Taxes intended to discourage certain activities are sometimes referred to as "sin taxes."

---

**18.3 LEARNING** OBJECTIVE

Understand the effect of price elasticity on tax incidence.

---

**Tax incidence** The actual division of the burden of a tax between buyers and sellers in a market.

---

# Tax Incidence Revisited: The Effect of Price Elasticity

In Chapter 4, we saw the difference between who is legally required to send a tax payment to the government and who actually bears the burden of a tax. Recall that the actual division of the burden of a tax between buyers and sellers in a market is known as **tax incidence**. We can go beyond the basic analysis of tax incidence by considering how the price elasticity of demand and price elasticity of supply affect how the burden of a tax is shared between consumers and firms.

In Chapter 4, we discussed whether consumers or firms bear the larger share of a 10-cents-per-gallon federal excise tax on gasoline. We saw that consumers paid the majority of the tax. We can expand on this conclusion by stating that consumers of gasoline pay a larger fraction of gasoline taxes than do sellers because the elasticity of demand for gasoline is smaller than the elasticity of supply. In fact, we can draw a general conclusion: *When the demand for a product is less elastic than the supply, consumers pay the majority of the tax on the product. When demand for a product is more elastic than the supply, firms pay the majority of the tax on the product.*

Figure 18.4 shows why this conclusion is correct. In Figure 18.4, $D_1$ is inelastic between points A and B, and $D_2$ is elastic between points A and C. With demand curve $D_1$, the 10-cents-per-gallon tax raises the market price of gasoline from \$4.00 (point A) to \$4.08 (point B) per gallon, so consumers pay 8 cents of the tax, and firms pay 2 cents. With $D_2$, the market price rises only to \$4.02 (point C) per gallon, and consumers pay only 2 cents of the tax. With demand curve $D_2$, sellers of gasoline receive only \$3.92 per gallon after paying the tax. So, the amount they receive per gallon after taxes falls from \$4.00 to \$3.92 per gallon, and they pay 8 cents of the tax.

---

# Don't Let This Happen to You

## Remember Not to Confuse Who Pays a Tax with Who Bears the Burden of the Tax

Consider the following statement: "Of course, I bear the burden of the sales tax on everything I buy. I can show you my sales receipts with the 6 percent sales tax clearly labeled. The seller doesn't bear that tax. I do."

The statement is incorrect. To understand why it is incorrect, think about what would happen to the price of a product if the sales tax on it were eliminated. Figure 18.4 shows that the price of the product would fall because the supply curve would shift down by the amount of the tax. The equilibrium price, however, would fall by less than the amount of the tax. (If you doubt that this is true, draw the graph to convince

yourself.) So, the gain from eliminating the tax would be received partly by consumers in the form of a lower price but also partly by sellers in the form of a new price that is higher than the amount they received from the old price minus the tax. Therefore, the burden from imposing a sales tax is borne partly by consumers and partly by sellers.

In determining the burden of a tax, what counts is not what is printed on the receipt for a product but what happens to the price of a product as a result of the tax.

MyEconLab

**Your Turn:** Test your understanding by doing related problem 3.9 on page 611 at the end of this chapter.

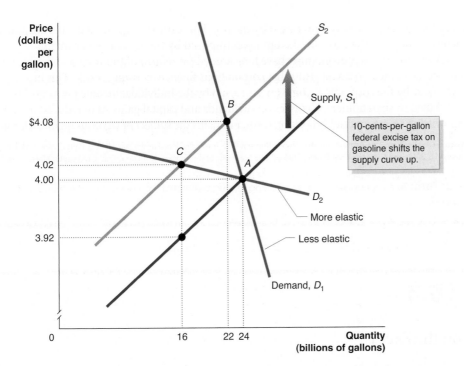

**Figure 18.4**

**The Effect of Elasticity on Tax Incidence**

When demand is more elastic than supply, consumers bear less of the burden of a tax. When supply is more elastic than demand, firms bear less of the burden of a tax. $D_1$ is inelastic between point $A$ and point $B$, and $D_2$ is elastic between point $A$ and point $C$. With demand curve $D_1$, a 10-cents-per-gallon tax raises the equilibrium price from \$4.00 (point $A$) to \$4.08 (point $B$), so consumers pay 8 cents of the tax, and firms pay 2 cents. With $D_2$, a 10-cents-per-gallon tax on gasoline raises the equilibrium price only from \$4.00 (point $A$) to \$4.02 (point $C$), so consumers pay 2 cents of the tax. Because in this case producers receive \$3.92 per gallon after paying the tax, their share of the tax is 8 cents per gallon.

## Making the Connection

## Do Corporations Really Bear the Burden of the Federal Corporate Income Tax?

During the 2012 presidential election campaign, hecklers at an Iowa appearance by former Massachusetts Governor Mitt Romney suggested that taxes on corporations be raised. Romney responded by saying, "Corporations are people, my friend." The hecklers responded, "No, they're not!" To which Romney responded, "Of course they are. Everything corporations earn ultimately goes to people. Where do you think it goes?" Romney was correct that corporations are legal persons in the eyes of the law. But what about the larger question: Who actually pays the corporate income tax? The incidence of the corporate income tax is one of the most controversial questions in the economics of tax policy. It is straightforward to determine the incidence of the gasoline tax using demand and supply analysis. Determining the incidence of the corporate income tax is more complicated because economists disagree about how corporations respond to the tax.

*Will this consumer be paying part of Apple's corporate income tax when she buys an iPad or an iPhone?*

A study by the Congressional Budget Office stated:

> A corporation may write its check to the Internal Revenue Service for payment of the corporate income tax, but the money must come from somewhere: from reduced returns to investors in the company, lower wages to its workers, or higher prices that consumers pay for the products the company produces.

Most economists agree that some of the burden of the corporate income tax is passed on to consumers in the form of higher prices. There is also some agreement that, because the corporate income tax reduces the rates of return received by investors, it results in less investment in corporations. This reduced investment means workers have less capital available to them. As we discussed in Chapter 17, when workers have less capital, their productivity and their wages both fall. In this way, some of the burden of the corporate income tax is shifted from corporations to workers in the form of lower wages. The deadweight loss or excess burden from the corporate income tax is substantial. A study by the Congressional Budget Office estimated that this excess burden could equal more than half of the revenues raised by the tax. This estimate would make the corporate income tax one of the most inefficient taxes imposed by the federal government.

As a consequence, economists have long argued for reform of the system of double taxing income earned on investments that corporations finance by issuing stock. This income is taxed once by the corporate income tax and again by the individual income tax as profits are distributed to shareholders. Tax rates on dividends and capital gains were reduced in 2003, but whether to reduce double taxation further remains the subject of vigorous political debate.

Based on Ashley Parker, "'Corporations Are People,' Romney Tells Iowa Hecklers Angry Over His Tax Policy," *New York Times*, August 11, 2011; and Congressional Budget Office, "The Incidence of the Corporate Income Tax," CBO paper, March 1996.

MyEconLab **Your Turn:** Test your understanding by doing related problem 3.7 on page 611 at the end of this chapter.

# Solved Problem 18.3

## The Effect of Price Elasticity on the Excess Burden of a Tax

Explain whether you agree or disagree with the following statement: "For a given supply curve, the excess burden of a tax will be greater when demand is less elastic than when it is more elastic." Illustrate your answer with a demand and supply graph.

## Solving the Problem

**Step 1:** **Review the chapter material.** This problem is about both excess burden and tax incidence, so you may want to review the section "Evaluating Taxes," which begins on page 591, and the section "Tax Incidence Revisited: The Effect of Price Elasticity," which begins on page 594.

**Step 2:** **Draw a graph to illustrate the relationship between tax incidence and excess burden.** Figure 18.4 on page 595 is a good example of the type of graph to draw. Be sure to indicate the areas representing excess burden.

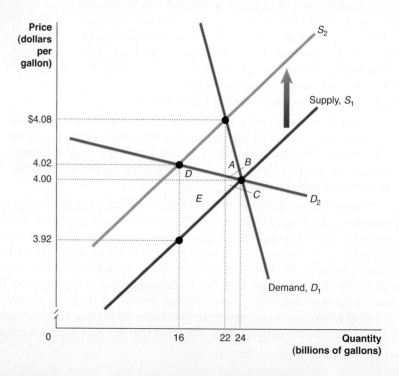

**Step 3:** **Use the graph to evaluate the statement.** As we have seen, for a given supply curve, when demand is more elastic, as with demand curve $D_2$, the fall in equilibrium quantity is greater than when demand is less elastic, as with demand curve $D_1$. The deadweight loss when demand is less elastic is shown by the area of the triangle made up of $A$, $B$, and $C$. The deadweight loss when demand is more elastic is shown by the area of the triangle made up of $B$, $C$, $D$, and $E$. The area of the deadweight loss is clearly larger when demand is more elastic than when it is less elastic. Recall that the excess burden of a tax is measured by the deadweight loss. Therefore, when demand is less elastic, the excess burden of a tax is *smaller* than when demand is more elastic. We can conclude that the statement is incorrect.

**Your Turn:** For more practice, do related problems 3.5 and 3.6 on pages 610–611 at the end of this chapter.

MyEconLab

# Income Distribution and Poverty

**18.4 LEARNING** OBJECTIVE

Discuss the distribution of income in the United States and understand the extent of income mobility.

In practice, in most economies, some individuals will have very high incomes, and some individuals will have very low incomes. But how unequal is the distribution of income in the United States today? How does this compare with the distribution of income in the United States in the past or with the distribution of income in other countries today? What determines the distribution of income? And, to return to an issue raised at the beginning of this chapter, how does the tax system affect the distribution of income? These are questions we will explore in the remainder of this chapter.

## Measuring the Income Distribution and Poverty

Tables 18.5 and 18.6 show that the distribution of income clearly is unequal. Table 18.5 shows that in 2010, while 13.7 percent of U.S. households had annual incomes less than $15,000, the top 21 percent of households had incomes greater than $100,000. Table 18.6 divides the population of the United States into five groups, from the 20 percent with the lowest incomes to the 20 percent with the highest incomes. The fraction of total income received by each of the five groups is shown for selected years. Table 18.6 reinforces the fact that income is unequally distributed in the United States. The first row shows that in 2011, the 20 percent of Americans with the lowest incomes received only 3.7 percent of all income, while the 20 percent with the highest incomes received 54.6 percent of all income.

Table 18.6 also shows that over time, there have been some changes in the distribution of income. There was a moderate decline in inequality between 1936 and 1980, followed by some increase in inequality during the years after 1980. We will discuss some reasons for the recent increase in income inequality later in this chapter.

| Annual Income | Percentage of All Households |
|---|---|
| $0–$14,999 | 13.7% |
| $15,000–$24,999 | 12.0 |
| $25,000–$34,999 | 10.9 |
| $35,000–$49,999 | 13.9 |
| $50,000–$74,999 | 17.7 |
| $75,000–$99,999 | 11.4 |
| $100,000 and over | 21.0 |

**Table 18.5**

**The Distribution of Household Income in the United States, 2010**

Data from Carmen DeNavas-Walt, Bernadette D. Proctor, and Jessica C. Smith, U.S. Census Bureau, Current Population Reports, P60–239, *Income, Poverty, and Health Insurance Coverage in the United States: 2009*, Washington, DC: U.S. Government Printing Office, September 2010, Table A-1.

| **Table 18.6** | Year | Lowest 20% | Second 20% | Third 20% | Fourth 20% | Highest 20% |
|---|---|---|---|---|---|---|
| **How Has the Distribution of Income Changed over Time?** | 2011 | 3.7% | 8.5% | 13.5% | 19.9% | 54.6% |
| | 1990 | 3.9 | 9.6 | 15.9 | 24.0 | 46.6 |
| | 1980 | 4.3 | 10.3 | 16.9 | 24.9 | 43.7 |
| | 1970 | 4.1 | 10.8 | 17.4 | 24.5 | 43.3 |
| | 1960 | 3.2 | 10.6 | 17.6 | 24.7 | 44.0 |
| | 1950 | 3.1 | 10.5 | 17.3 | 24.1 | 45.0 |
| | 1936 | 4.1 | 9.2 | 14.1 | 20.9 | 51.7 |

Data from Urban Institute and Brookings Institution, Tax Policy Center; U.S. Census Bureau, *Income in the United States, 2002*, P60–221, September 2003; and U.S. Census Bureau, *Historical Statistics of the United States, Colonial Times to 1970*, ( Washington, DC: U.S. Government Printing Office, 1975).

**Poverty line** A level of annual income equal to three times the amount of money necessary to purchase the minimum quantity of food required for adequate nutrition.

**Poverty rate** The percentage of the population that is poor according to the federal government's definition.

**The Poverty Rate in the United States** Much of the discussion of the distribution of income focuses on poverty. The federal government has a formal definition of poverty that was first developed in the early 1960s. According to this definition, a family is below the **poverty line** if its annual income is less than three times the amount of money necessary to purchase the minimum quantity of food required for adequate nutrition. In 2011, the poverty line was $22,350 for a family of four. Figure 18.5 shows the **poverty rate**, or the percentage of the U.S. population that was poor during each year between 1960 and 2010. Between 1960 and 1973, the poverty rate declined by half, falling from 22 percent of the population to 11 percent. In the past 40 years, however, the poverty rate has declined very little. In 2010 it was actually higher than it was in 1966.

Different groups in the population have substantially different poverty rates. Table 18.7 shows that while the overall poverty rate in 2010 was 15.1 percent, the rate among women who head a family with no husband present, among black people, and among Hispanic people was about twice as high. The poverty rates for white and Asian people as well as for married couples were below average.

## Explaining Income Inequality

The novelists Ernest Hemingway and F. Scott Fitzgerald supposedly once had a conversation about the rich. Fitzgerald said to Hemingway, "You know, the rich are different from you and me." To which Hemingway replied, "Yes. They have more money." Although witty, Hemingway's joke doesn't help answer the question of why the rich have more money. In Chapter 17, we provided one answer to the question when we discussed the *marginal productivity theory of income distribution*. We saw that in equilibrium, each factor of production receives a payment equal to its marginal revenue product. The

**Figure 18.5**

**Poverty in the United States, 1960–2010**

The poverty rate in the United States declined from 22 percent of the population in 1960 to 11 percent in 1973. Over the past 30 years, the poverty rate has fluctuated between 11 percent and 15 percent of the population.
Data from Carmen DeNavas-Walt, Bernadette D. Proctor, and Jessica C. Smith, U.S. Census Bureau, Current Population Reports, P60–239, *Income, Poverty, and Health Insurance Coverage in the United States: 2009*, (Washington, DC: U.S. Government Printing Office), September 2011.

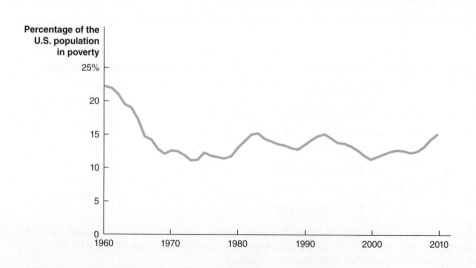

| | |
|---|---|
| All people | 15.1% |
| Female head of family, no husband present (all races) | 31.6 |
| Blacks | 27.4 |
| Hispanics | 26.6 |
| Asians | 12.1 |
| White, not Hispanic | 9.9 |
| Married couple | 6.2 |

**Table 18.7**

**Poverty Rates Vary across Groups, 2010**

*Note:* Hispanic people can be of any race.

Data from Carmen DeNavas-Walt, Bernadette D. Proctor, and Jessica C. Smith, U.S. Census Bureau, Current Population Reports, P60–238, *Income, Poverty, and Health Insurance Coverage in the United States: 2009*, (Washington, DC: U.S. Government Printing Office), September 2010, Table 4.

more factors of production an individual owns, and the more productive those factors are, the higher the individual's income will be.

For most people, of course, the most important factor of production they own is their labor. Therefore, the income they earn depends on how productive they are and on the prices of the goods and services their labor helps produce. Baseball player Adrian Gonzales will earn a salary of $21 million in 2012 because he is a very productive player, and his employer, the Boston Red Sox, can sell tickets and television rights to the baseball games Gonzalez plays in for a high price. Individuals who help to produce goods and services that can be sold for only a low price earn lower incomes.

Many people own other factors of production as well. For example, many people own capital by owning stock in corporations or by owning shares in mutual funds that buy the stock of corporations. Ownership of capital is not equally distributed, and income earned from capital is more unequally distributed than income earned from labor. Some people supply entrepreneurial skills by starting and managing businesses. Their income is increased by the profits from these businesses.

We saw in Table 18.6 that income inequality has increased during the past 25 years. Two factors that appear to have contributed to this increase are technological change and expanding international trade. Rapid technological change, particularly the development of information technology, has led to the substitution of computers and other machines for unskilled labor. This substitution has caused a decline in the wages of unskilled workers relative to other workers. Expanding international trade has put U.S. workers in competition with foreign workers to a greater extent than in the past. This competition has caused the wages of unskilled workers to be depressed relative to the wages of other workers. Some economists have also argued that the incomes of low-income workers have been depressed by competition with workers who have immigrated to the United States illegally.

Most economists believe that changes in tax laws have not played a major role in recent changes in income inequality. As Figure 18.6 shows, federal income tax rates have changed dramatically during the years covered in Table 18.6. For example, the top marginal income tax rate was 91 percent in the 1950s; it declined to 70 percent in the 1960s and to 28 percent in the 1980s. The rate then rose to 39.6 percent in the 1990s before declining to 35 percent in 2003. Because tax rates changed significantly but the distribution of income has changed relatively little, it is unlikely that changes in tax rates have had a large impact on the distribution of income.

Finally, like everything else in life, earning an income is subject to good and bad luck. A poor person who becomes a millionaire by winning the state lottery is an obvious example, as is a person whose earning power drastically declines as a result of a debilitating illness or accident. So, we can say that as a group, the people with high incomes are likely to have greater-than-average productivity and own greater-than-average amounts of capital. They are also likely to have experienced good luck. As a group, poor people are likely to have lower-than-average productivity and own lower-than-average amounts of capital. They are also likely to have been unlucky.

**Figure 18.6**

**The Top Marginal Income Tax Rate in the United States, 1950–2011**

The top marginal tax rate has varied dramatically since 1950, while the distribution of income has changed much less.
Data from the Urban Institute and the Brookings Institution, Tax Policy Center.

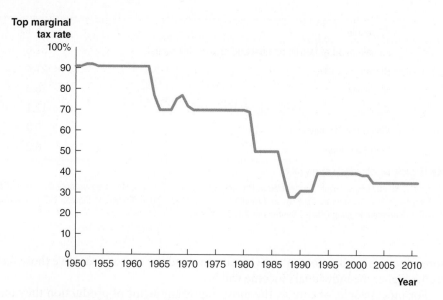

## Showing the Income Distribution with a Lorenz Curve

**Lorenz curve** A curve that shows the distribution of income by arraying incomes from lowest to highest on the horizontal axis and indicating the cumulative fraction of income earned by each fraction of households on the vertical axis.

Figure 18.7 presents the distribution of income using *Lorenz curves*. A **Lorenz curve** shows the distribution of income by arraying incomes from lowest to highest on the horizontal axis and indicating the cumulative fraction of income earned by each fraction of households on the vertical axis. If the distribution of income were perfectly equal, a Lorenz curve would be a straight line because the first 20 percent of households would earn 20 percent of total income, the first 40 percent of households would earn 40 percent of total income, and so on. Panel (a) of Figure 18.6 shows a Lorenz curve for the actual distribution of income in the United States in 1980 and another curve for the distribution of income in 2011, using the data from Table 18.6. We know that income

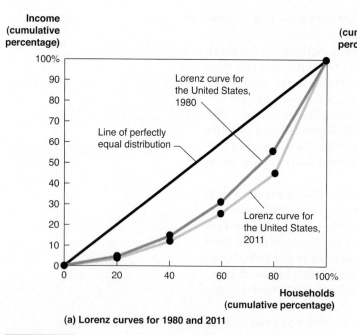

(a) Lorenz curves for 1980 and 2011

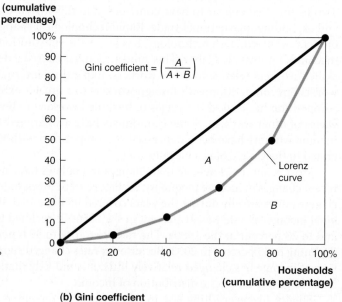

(b) Gini coefficient

**Figure 18.7** **The Lorenz Curve and Gini Coefficient**

In panel (a), the Lorenz curves show the distribution of income by arraying incomes from the lowest to the highest on the horizontal axis and indicating the cumulative fraction of income by each fraction of households on the vertical axis. The straight line represents perfect income equality. Because the Lorenz curve for 1980 is closer to the line of perfect equality than the Lorenz curve for 2011, we

know that income was more equally distributed in 1980 than in 2011. In panel (b), we show the Gini coefficient, which is equal to the area between the line of perfect income equality and the Lorenz curve—area *A*—divided by the whole area below the line of perfect equality—area *A* plus area *B*. The closer the Gini coefficient is to 1, the more unequal the income distribution.

was distributed more unequally in 2011 than in 1980 because the Lorenz curve for 2011 is farther away from the line of equal distribution than is the Lorenz curve for 1980.

Panel (b) illustrates how to calculate the *Gini coefficient*, which is one way of summarizing the information provided by a Lorenz curve. The Gini coefficient is equal to the area between the line of perfect income equality and the Lorenz curve—area *A* in panel (b)—divided by the whole area below the line of perfect equality—area *A* plus area *B* in panel (b). Or:

$$\text{Gini coefficient} = \left(\frac{A}{A + B}\right).$$

If the income distribution were completely *equal*, the Lorenz curve would be the same as the line of perfect income equality, area *A* would be zero, and the Gini coefficient would be zero. If the income distribution were completely *unequal*, area *B* would be zero, and the Gini coefficient would equal 1. Therefore, the greater the degree of income inequality, the greater the value of the Gini coefficient. In 1980, the Gini coefficient for the United States was 0.403. In 2011, it was 0.468, which tells us again that income inequality increased between 1980 and 2011.

## Problems in Measuring Poverty and the Distribution of Income

The measures of poverty and the distribution of income that we have discussed to this point may be misleading for two reasons. First, these measures are snapshots in time that do not take into account *income mobility*, which refers to changes in an individual's or a family's income over time. Second, they ignore the effects of government programs meant to reduce poverty.

**Income Mobility in the United States** We expect to see some income mobility. When you graduate from college, your income will rise as you assume a new job. A family may be below the poverty line one year because the main wage earner is unemployed but may rise well above the poverty line the next year, when that wage earner finds a job. A medical student may have a very low income for several years but a very high income after graduating and establishing a medical practice. It is also true that someone might have a high income one year—perhaps from making a very profitable investment in the stock market—and have a much lower income in future years.

Statistics on income mobility are more difficult to collect than statistics on income during a particular year because they involve following the same individuals over a number of years. A study by the U.S. Census Bureau tracked the incomes of the same households for each year from 2004 to 2007. Figure 18.8 shows the results of the study. Each column represents one quintile—or 20 percent—of households, arranged by their incomes in 2004. Reading up the column, we can see where the households that started in that quintile in 2004 ended up in 2007. For example, the bottom quintile (the first column) consists of households with incomes of less than $22,367 in 2004 (all values are measured in 2007 dollars to correct for the effects of inflation). About 69 percent of these households were still in the bottom quintile in 2007. Only a small number—1.6 percent—had moved all the way to the top quintile, but more than one-quarter had moved into either the second quintile or the middle quintile. At the other end of the income distribution, of those households in the top income quintile—with incomes of $92,886 or more—in 2004, only two-thirds were still in the top quintile in 2007. Given the relatively short time period involved, this study indicates that there is significant income mobility in the United States.

It should be noted that the U.S. economy experienced rapid growth between 2004 and 2007, which may have increased the degree of income mobility. However, an earlier study by Peter Gottschalk of Boston College and Sheldon Danziger of the University of Michigan also provides evidence of significant income mobility. In that study, only 47 percent of people who were in the lowest 20 percent of incomes in 1968 were still in the lowest bracket in 1991. More than 25 percent had incomes in 1991 that put them

### Income Mobility in the United States, 2004–2007

Each column represents one quintile—or 20 percent—of households, arranged by their incomes in 2004. Reading up the column, we can see where the households that started in that quintile in 2004 ended up in 2007. Only 69 percent of the households that were in the bottom quintile of income in 2004 were still in the bottom quintile in 2007. Only 68 percent of the households that were in the top quintile of income in 2004 were still in the top quintile in 2007.

*Note:* Incomes are in 2007 dollars to correct for the effects of inflation.

Based on U.S. Census Bureau, "Dynamics of Economic Well-Being: Movements in the U.S. Income Distribution, 2004–2007," *Current Population Reports,* P70–124, March 2011.

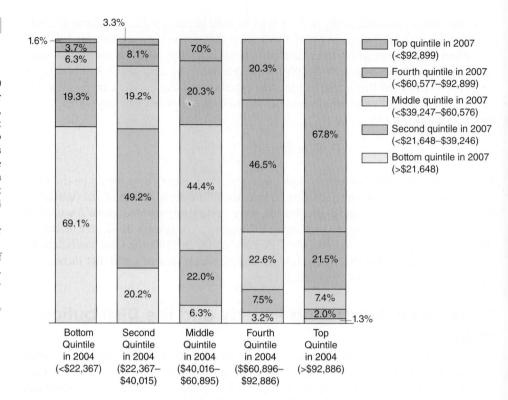

in the middle- or higher-income brackets. Of those people who were in the highest-income bracket in 1968, only 42 percent were still in the highest bracket in 1991. Almost 8 percent of this group had fallen to the lowest-income bracket.

Another study by the U.S. Census Bureau found that of people who were poor at some time during the years 2004 to 2006, about half were in poverty for four months or less. Of the people who were poor in January 2004, only about 23 percent remained in poverty every month through December 2006. Only 2.8 percent of the U.S. population was poor every month during those three years.

# Solved Problem 18.4

## Are Many Individuals Stuck in Poverty?

Evaluate the following statement:

Government statistics indicate that 14 percent of the population is below the poverty line. The fraction of the population in poverty has never dropped below 10 percent. Therefore, more than 10 percent of the population must cope with very low incomes year after year.

### Solving the Problem

**Step 1: Review the chapter material.** This problem is about income mobility, so you may want to review the section "Income Mobility in the United States," which begins on page 601.

**Step 2: Use the discussion in this chapter to evaluate the statement.** Although it is true that the poverty rate in the United States is never below 10 percent, it is not the same 10 percent of the population that is in poverty each year. This chapter discusses one U.S. Census Bureau study that showed that only about 69 percent of the people who were in the lowest 20 percent of the income distribution in 2004 were still in the lowest 20 percent in 2007. Another census study of the years from 2004 to 2006 showed that only 2.8 percent of the U.S. population was poor every month during those three years. Poverty remains a problem in the United States, but fortunately, the number of people who remain in poverty for many years is much smaller than the number who are in poverty during any one year.

Based on U.S. Census Bureau, "Dynamics of Economic Well-Being: Poverty 2004–2006," *Current Population Survey*, P70–123, March 2011; and U.S. Census Bureau, "Dynamics of Economic Well-Being: Movements in the U.S. Income Distribution, 2004–2007," *Current Population Reports*, P70–124, March 2011.

**Your Turn:** For more practice, do related problem 4.7 on page 611 at the end of this chapter.          MyEconLab

**The Effect of Taxes and Transfers**  A second reason the conventional statistics on poverty and income distribution may be misleading is that they omit the effects of government programs. Because of government programs, there is a difference between the income people earn and the income they actually have available to spend. The data in Tables 18.5 and 18.6 show the distribution of income before taxes are paid. We have seen that at the federal level, taxes are progressive, meaning that people with high incomes pay a larger share of their incomes in taxes than do people with low incomes. Therefore, income remaining after taxes is more equally distributed than is income before taxes. The tables also do not include income from *transfer payments* individuals receive from the government, such as Social Security payments to retired and disabled people. The Social Security system has been very effective in reducing the poverty rate among people older than 65. In 1960, 35 percent of people in the United States over age 65 had incomes below the poverty line. By 2010, only about 9 percent of people over 65 had incomes below the poverty line.

Individuals with low incomes also receive noncash benefits, such as food stamps, free school lunches, and rent subsidies. The government's Supplemental Nutrition Assistance Program, more commonly referred to as the *food stamp program*, has been a particularly important noncash benefit. Under this program, individuals with low incomes can buy, at a discount, coupons to purchase food in supermarkets. In 2011, more than 45 million people participated in this program, at a cost to the federal government of more than $70 billion. Because individuals with low incomes are more likely to receive transfer payments and other benefits from the government than are individuals with high incomes, the distribution of income is more equal if we take these benefits into account.

## Income Distribution and Poverty around the World

How does income inequality in the United States compare with income inequality in other countries? Table 18.8 compares the ratio of total income received by the 20 percent of the population with the lowest incomes and the 20 percent with the highest incomes in several countries. The countries are ranked from most unequal to least unequal. As the table shows, poor countries, such as Bolivia and Paraguay, typically have more unequal distributions of income than does the United States. The distribution of income in the United States is less equal than in some moderate-income countries, such as Chile and Argentina, but it is more equal than in other moderate-income countries, such as Thailand and Brazil. The United States has the most unequal distribution of income of any high-income country in the world. Of course, we must be careful with such comparisons because transfer payments are not counted in income. For example, the Social Security and Medicare systems in the United States are much more generous than the corresponding systems in Japan but less generous than those in France and Germany.

| Table 18.8 | | |
|---|---|---|
| **Income Inequality around the World** | Country | Ratio of Income Received by Highest 20% to Income Received by Lowest 20% |
| | Bolivia | 21.9 |
| | Brazil | 17.4 |
| | Thailand | 15.2 |
| | Paraguay | 15.0 |
| | United States | 14.8 |
| | Chile | 13.8 |
| | Argentina | 12.3 |
| | Canada | 9.1 |
| | Spain | 6.0 |
| | United Kingdom | 5.2 |
| | Italy | 5.2 |
| | Germany | 4.5 |
| | Ireland | 4.2 |
| | France | 4.4 |
| | Sweden | 3.7 |
| | Japan | 3.0 |

Data from the World Bank, Eurostat, and Statistics Canada.

Although poverty remains a problem in high-income countries, it is a much larger problem in poor countries. The level of poverty in much of sub-Saharan Africa, in particular, is a human catastrophe. In 2011, the poverty line in the United States for a family of four was an annual income of $22,350, but economists often use a much lower threshold income of $1 per day when calculating the rate of poverty in poor countries. As Table 18.9 shows, by this measure, according to estimates by Maxim Pinkovskiy of MIT and Xavier Sala-I-Martin of Columbia University, poverty declined from about 27 percent of the world population in 1970 to 5 percent in 2006, the most recent year for which statistics are available. The greatest reduction in poverty has taken place in Asia. In East Asia, which includes China, the poverty rate dropped spectacularly from about 60 percent in 1970 to less than 2 percent in 2006. In South Asia, which includes India, poverty rates dropped from 20 percent to less than 3 percent. Even in sub-Saharan Africa, poverty decreased from 40 percent in 1970 to 32 percent in 2006. Why has poverty fallen dramatically more in Asia than in Africa? The key explanation is that the countries of Asia have had higher rates of economic growth than have the countries of sub-Saharan Africa. Recent economic research demonstrates a positive relationship between economic growth and the incomes of lower-income people.

| Table 18.9 | | Percentage of the Population in Poverty | |
|---|---|---|---|
| **Poverty Has Declined Dramatically around the World Since 1970** | Region | 1970 | 2006 |
| | World | 26.8% | 5.4% |
| | East Asia | 58.8 | 1.7 |
| | South Asia | 20.1 | 2.6 |
| | Middle East and North Africa | 8.4 | 5.2 |
| | Latin America | 11.6 | 3.1 |
| | Sub-Saharan Africa | 39.9 | 31.8 |

Source: "Percentage of the Population in Poverty" by Xavier Sala-i-Martin and Maxim Pinkovskiy from "Parametric Estimations of the World Distribution of Income," National Bureau of Economic Research Working Paper 15433, October 2009. Copyright © 2009 by Xavier Sala-i-Martin and Maxim Pinkovskiy. Reprinted by permission.

Continued from page 581

## Economics in Your Life

### How Much Tax Should You Pay?

At the beginning of the chapter, we asked you to think about where government gets the money to provide goods and services and about whether you pay your fair share of taxes. After reading this chapter, you should see that you pay taxes in many different forms. When you work, you pay taxes on your income, both for individual income taxes and social insurance taxes. When you buy gasoline, you pay an excise tax, which, in part, pays for highways. When you buy goods at a local store, you pay state and local sales taxes, which the government uses to fund education and other services. Whether you are paying your fair share of taxes is a normative question. The U.S. tax system is progressive, so higher-income individuals pay more in taxes than do lower-income individuals. In fact, as we saw in the *Making the Connection* on page 589, people in the lowest 40 percent of the income distribution pay no federal income taxes at all. You may find that you will not pay much in federal income taxes in your first job after college. But as your income grows during your career, so will the percentage of your income you pay in taxes.

## Conclusion

The public choice model provides insights into how government decisions are made. The decisions of policymakers will not necessarily reflect the preferences of voters. Attempts by government to intervene in the economy may increase economic efficiency, as we saw in Chapter 5, but they may also lead to government failure and a reduction in economic efficiency.

A saying attributed to Benjamin Franklin states that "nothing in this world is certain but death and taxes." But which taxes? As we saw at the beginning of this chapter, politicians continue to debate whether the government should use the tax system and other programs to reduce the level of income inequality in the United States. The tax system represents a balance among the objectives of economic efficiency, ability to pay, paying for benefits received, and achieving social objectives. Those favoring government intervention to reduce inequality argue that it is unfair for some people to have much higher incomes than others. Others argue that income inequality largely reflects higher incomes resulting from greater skills and from entrepreneurial ability and that higher taxes reduce work, saving, and investment.

Many economists are skeptical of tax policy proposals intended to significantly reduce income inequality. They argue that a market system relies on individuals being willing to work hard and take risks, with the promise of high incomes if they are successful. Taking some of that income from them in the name of reducing income inequality reduces the incentives to work hard and take risks. As we saw in Chapter 1, policymakers are often faced with a trade-off between economic efficiency and equity. Ultimately, whether policies to reduce income inequality should be pursued is a normative question. Economics alone cannot decide the issue.

*An Inside Look at Policy* on the next page discusses how many states and cities are considering taxing soft drinks.

# Should a Tax on Soda Be Used to Reduce Budget Deficits?

## THE GAZETTE

## Taxing Soda Could Hit Lowest-Income Families Hardest, Study Says

As more budget-strapped states and cities consider taxing soda pop, the less educated and lower income households could be hit hardest, according to a new study published by the Federal Reserve Bank of Chicago.

Iowa taxes soda as general merchandise, and most other states tax such sweetened beverages as either food or general merchandise. Many states and a few cities are now also considering special taxes on soft drinks based on the premise that they contribute to growing national health epidemics of obesity and diabetes.

The Center for Science in the Public is supporting the drive to tax soda. It says several scientific studies have linked soft drinks to weight gain, and that frequent consumption is also linked to osteoporosis, tooth decay and erosion of tooth enamel. Weight gain is a risk factor for heart attacks, strokes, type two diabetes and cancer, the group says.

Legislation to expand soda taxation was filed in 17 states from 2009 through 2010 according to the Rudd Center for Food Policy and Obesity at Yale University. Only Colorado and Washington passed new legislation, but with many states facing budget shortfalls the soft drink taxes are expected to come up again in 2011. . . .

A study published in the March Chicago Fed Letter found that soda taxes will affect people differently depending on how much soda they purchase, where they buy it, the form of the soda tax, and whether they buy it with SNAP benefits, the federal program formerly known as food stamps.

The study found Americans living below poverty level obtain 9 percent of their daily calorie intake from "sugar sweetened beverages," compared to 5.6 percent for all Americans. Americans with less than a high school education obtained 7.4 percent of their calories from sugar sweetened beverages.

Sugar sweetened beverages were a significantly higher percentage of household food spending for less educated Americans than college graduates. College grads on average spend 1.9 percent of their food budget on soft drinks, versus 3.22 percent for Americans without a high school diploma.

The effect of soda taxes on consumption could depend heavily on the type of tax, the study found. Taxing soda based entirely on price could cause Americans to switch from cans to less expensive brands or larger containers such as two-liter bottles, the study found, because large containers typically cost less per ounce.

Taxing soda by the ounce could cause consumers to switch to beverages with a higher sugar content, the study found.

One way some tax proposals try to address the possible shifts in spending is by basing the tax solely on sugar content, according to the study, authored by Chicago Fed Senior Economist Leslie McGranahan and Northwestern University Associate Professor of Human Development Diane Whitmore Schanzenbach . . .

The Center for Science in the Public Interest says a federal excise tax of one cent per 12-ounce serving of soda would raise about $1.5 billion per year, while taxing it at 8 cents per 12-ounce serving would raise $11 billion. It proposes using the tax proceeds to fund education programs supporting healthier lifestyles. . . .

*Source:* "Taxing soda could hit lowest-income families hardest, study says," by David DeWitte in *The Gazette*, February 21, 2011. Copyright © 2011 Source Media Group News. Reprinted by permission.

| Education | Per Capita Spending on Soda | Average Daily Caloric Intake from Soda |
|---|---|---|
| Less than high school | $130.96 | 139 |
| High school grade | $141.79 | 159 |
| Some college | $147.02 | 131 |
| College graduate | $141.71 | 78 |

From Analysis of Bureau of Labor Statistics 2008 Consumer Expenditures Survey by Fed Senior Economist Leslie McGranahan and Northwestern University Associate Professor of Human Development Diane Whitmore Schanzenbach.

## Key Points in the Article

As budget shortfalls loom in many states and cities, a tax on soft drinks is being viewed as a way to not only raise revenue but also reduce consumption of a product that contributes to obesity, diabetes, and other health problems. A study published by the Federal Reserve Bank of Chicago indicates that a soda tax would affect demographic groups in different ways. For example, the percentage of food budgets spent on sugared beverages is lower for college graduates than for those without high school diplomas, and the caloric intake from soft drinks is highest for those living below the poverty level. So, the lowest-income families would feel the greatest impact from the implementation of a soda tax.

## Analyzing the News

In 2009, the U.S. Senate considered a proposal to place an excise tax on soda as a way to help pay for overhauling the nation's health care system. Although that proposal did not pass, several states are now considering a similar tax as a way to boost revenue during a time of budget shortfalls. Between 2009 and 2010, 17 states filed legislation to implement some form of a soda tax, with Colorado and

Washington passing versions of the tax. Proponents of the tax cite the health risks associated with sugared soft drinks and claim that the tax would reduce consumption and improve health.

A study conducted by Leslie McGranahan of the Federal Reserve Bank of Chicago and Diane Whitmore Schanzenbach of Northwestern University indicates that a soda tax will affect people in different ways, depending on the amount of soda purchased, where and how it is purchased, and the type of tax implemented. The study shows that the lowest-income families and people with less education consume the most soda and spend the highest fraction of their food budget on soda. As a consequence, these groups would feel the greatest impact of a soda tax. With a regressive tax, people with lower incomes pay a higher percentage of their income in tax than do people with higher incomes. Because people with less education tend to earn less than those with more education, the data indicate that a soda tax would be a regressive tax.

The Center for Science in the Public Interest claims that an 8-cent tax on a 12-ounce serving of soda would raise $11 billion per year. The figure below shows how an excise tax would affect the market

for soda. The original equilibrium is at point A. The tax would shift the supply curve for soda up, from $S_1$ to $S_2$. The equilibrium price would increase from $P_1$ to $P_2$, and the equilibrium quantity would decrease from $Q_1$ to $Q_2$. Point B is the new equilibrium point. The actual amount by which price and quantity would change depends on the price elasticity of the demand and supply of soda, as we saw in this chapter. The article does not report on the elasticity assumptions the Center for Science in the Public Interest made in computing its value of the revenue that would be raised by the tax. We do know, though, that the tax is expected to raise $11 billion per year. If the price of a 12-ounce soda is $1, then the quantity sold each year must be $137.5 billion (because $0.08 \times $137.5 billion = $11 billion). In the figure, the revenue from the tax equals the area of the green rectangle.

## Thinking Critically about Policy

1. The Federal Reserve Bank of Chicago study cited in the article indicates that a tax on soda could have the greatest effect on lower-income families. Some critics claim that the tax would not deter consumption. Draw a demand and supply graph that represents the market for soda, assuming that the tax would not deter consumption. How does this assumption affect the equilibrium price and quantity of soft drinks and the incidence of the tax?

2. Now assume that the demand for soda is perfectly elastic. Draw a demand and supply graph that represents this assumption. How does this assumption affect the equilibrium price and quantity of soft drinks and the incidence of the tax?

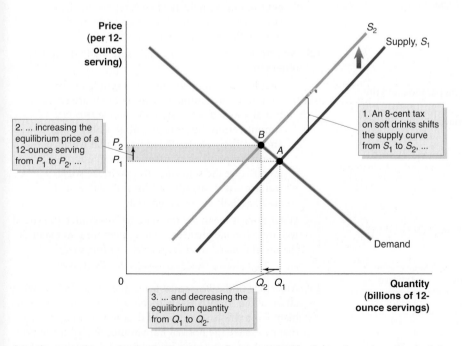

**2. ... increasing the equilibrium price of a 12-ounce serving from $P_1$ to $P_2$, ...**

**1. An 8-cent tax on soft drinks shifts the supply curve from $S_1$ to $S_2$, ...**

**3. ... and decreasing the equilibrium quantity from $Q_1$ to $Q_2$.**

A tax decreases the supply of soda. The amount of revenue raised by the tax depends on the elasticity of the demand and the elasticity of supply of the drinks.

# Chapter Summary and Problems

## Key Terms

Arrow impossibility theorem, p. 583

Average tax rate, p. 589

Excess burden, p. 592

Lorenz curve, p. 600

Marginal tax rate, p. 589

Median voter theorem, p. 583

Poverty line, p. 598

Poverty rate, p. 598

Progressive tax, p. 588

Public choice model, p. 582

Regressive tax, p. 588

Rent seeking, p. 584

Tax incidence, p. 594

Voting paradox, p. 583

**18.1** **Public Choice, pages 582–586**

LEARNING OBJECTIVE: Describe the public choice model and explain how it is used to analyze government decision making.

## Summary

The **public choice model** applies economic analysis to government decision making. The observation that majority voting may not always result in consistent choices is called the **voting paradox**. The **Arrow impossibility theorem** states that no system of voting can be devised that will consistently represent the underlying preferences of voters. The **median voter theorem** states that the outcome of a majority vote is likely to represent the preferences of the voter who is in the political middle. Individuals and firms sometimes engage in **rent seeking**, which is the use of government action to make themselves better off at the expense of others. Although government intervention can sometimes improve economic efficiency, public choice analysis indicates that *government failure* can also occur, reducing economic efficiency.

 MyEconLab   Visit **www.myeconlab.com** to complete these exercises online and get instant feedback.

## Review Questions

1.1  What is the public choice model?

1.2  What is the difference between the voting paradox and the Arrow impossibility theorem?

1.3  What is rent seeking, and how is it related to regulatory capture?

1.4  What is the relationship between market failure and government failure?

## Problems and Applications

1.5  Will the preferences shown in the following table lead to a voting paradox? Briefly explain.

| Policy | Lena | David | Kathleen |
|---|---|---|---|
| Cancer research | 1st | 2nd | 3rd |
| Mass transit | 2nd | 1st | 1st |
| Border security | 3rd | 3rd | 2nd |

1.6  Many political observers have noted that Republican presidential candidates tend to emphasize their conservative positions on policy issues while running for their party's nomination, and Democratic presidential candidates tend to emphasize their liberal positions on policy issues while running for their party's nomination. In the general election, though, Republican candidates tend to downplay their conservative positions and Democratic candidates tend to downplay their liberal positions. Can the median voter theorem help explain this pattern? Briefly explain.

1.7  Briefly explain whether you agree with the following argument:

> The median voter theorem will be an accurate predictor of the outcomes of elections when a majority of voters have preferences very similar to those of the median voter. When the majority of voters have preferences very different from those of the median voter, the median voter theorem will not lead to accurate predictions of the outcomes of elections.

1.8  An article in the *Economist* magazine made the following observation:

> People often complain that it is simplistic for economics to assume that individuals are rational and self-interested. Of course this is a simplification, but it is an enlightening one, and not flatly contradicted in the real world. The corresponding assumption about government—that the state aims to maximize social welfare—is contradicted by the real world about as flatly as you could wish.

What does it mean for the state to "maximize the social welfare"? If policymakers are not attempting to maximize the social welfare, what are they attempting to do?

From "The Grabbing Hand," *Economist*, February 11, 1999.

1.9  An article in the *Economist* magazine made the following observation: "In fact, as public choice theory shows, government has a whole set of special decision-making problems that can make the normal human mistakes of those decision-makers even worse." What "special decision-making problems" does government face according to public choice theory? Why might these problems make the mistakes of government decision makers worse?

From "Problem or Solution?" *Economist*, February 13, 2007.

1.10 Is the typical person likely to gather more information when buying a new car or when voting for a member of the House of Representatives? Briefly explain.

1.11 Nobel Laureate James Buchanan, who is one of the key figures in developing the public choice model, wrote: "The relevant difference between markets and politics does not lie in the kinds of values/interests that persons pursue, but in the conditions under which they pursue their various interests." Do you agree with this statement? Are there significant ways in which the business marketplace differs from the political marketplace?

From James M. Buchanan, "The Constitution of Economic Policy," *American Economic Review*, Vol. 77, No. 3, June 1987, p. 246.

---

## 18.2 The Tax System, pages 586–594

LEARNING OBJECTIVE: Understand the tax system in the United States, including the principles that governments use to create tax policy.

## Summary

Governments raise the funds they need through taxes. The most widely used taxes are income taxes, social insurance taxes, sales taxes, property taxes, and excise taxes. Governments take into account several important objectives when deciding which taxes to use: efficiency, ability to pay, horizontal equity, benefits received, and attaining social objectives. A **regressive tax** is a tax for which people with lower incomes pay a higher percentage of their incomes in tax than do people with higher incomes. A **progressive tax** is a tax for which people with lower incomes pay a lower percentage of their incomes in tax than do people with higher incomes. The **marginal tax rate** is the fraction of each additional dollar of income that must be paid in taxes. The **average tax rate** is the total tax paid divided by total income. When analyzing the impact of taxes on how much people are willing to work or save or invest, economists focus on the marginal tax rate rather than the average tax rate. The **excess burden** of a tax is the efficiency loss to the economy that results from a tax having reduced the quantity of a good produced.

 MyEconLab Visit **www.myeconlab.com** to complete these exercises online and get instant feedback.

## Review Questions

2.1 Which type of tax raises the most revenue for the federal government? Which type of tax raise the most revenue for state and local governments?

2.2 In September 2011, President Barack Obama proposed a new deficit reduction plan that included increasing tax rates on families earning $250,000 or more. If President Obama's proposals are enacted, is it likely that the U.S. tax system will become more progressive or less progressive? Be sure to provide a definition of *progressive tax* and *regressive tax* in your answer.

Based on Binyamin Appelbaum, "In Deficit Plan, Obama Drops Comprise for Confrontation," *New York Times*, September 19, 2011.

2.3 What is the difference between a marginal tax rate and an average tax rate? Which is more important in determining the effect of a change in taxes on economic behavior?

2.4 Briefly discuss each of the five goals and principles governments consider when deciding which taxes to use.

## Problems and Applications

2.5 Why does the federal government raise more tax revenue from taxes on individuals than from taxes on businesses?

2.6 On April 1, 2009, a 62-cent increase in the federal cigarette tax went into effect. The following data are from the Gallup-Healthways Well-Being Index for 2008:

| Percentage Who Smoke, by Annual Household Income | |
|---|---|
| **Income** | **Percentage Who Smoke** |
| Less than $12,000 | 34% |
| $12,000–$35,999 | 28 |
| $36,000–$59,999 | 22 |
| $60,000–$89,999 | 16 |
| $90,000+ | 13 |

Based on these data, would the federal cigarette tax be considered progressive or regressive? Be sure to define *progressive tax* and *regressive tax* in your answer.

Data from Lydia Saad, "Cigarette Tax Will Affect Low-Income Americans Most," *Gallup, Inc.*, April 1, 2009.

2.7 Many state governments have begun using lotteries to raise revenue. If we think of a lottery as a type of tax, is a lottery likely to be progressive or regressive? What data would you need to determine whether the burden of a lottery is progressive or regressive?

2.8 Use the information in Table 18.2 on page 588 to calculate the total federal income tax paid, the marginal tax rate, and the average tax rate for people with the following incomes. (For simplicity, assume that these people have no exemptions or deductions from their incomes.)

**a.** $25,000
**b.** $125,000
**c.** $300,000

2.9 **[Related to the** Making the Connection **on page 589]** President Barack Obama in his September 2011 deficit reduction plan proposed the so-called "'Buffett Rule,' named after billionaire Warren Buffett, who noted that he was paying a lower tax rate than his secretary. The "Buffett Rule" would set a new tax rate for those earning incomes of more than $1 million per year.

**a.** Looking at the table on page 589 for the percentage of federal taxes paid by the different income categories, is Mr. Buffett's situation of paying a lower tax rate than his secretary typical of the highest 1 percent of U.S. income earners?

**b.** According to an article in the *New York Times*, "[Buffett's] income comes mostly from his investments, which are taxed at the capital gains rate of 15 percent. His secretary is most likely paid a salary and bonus, which would be taxed as ordinary income, at a rate that goes as high as 35 percent." What are capital gains? Which goals and principles of evaluating taxes are relevant to considering whether the federal government should continue to tax capital gains at a lower rate than ordinary income? Briefly explain.

From Paul Sullivan, "'Buffett Rule' Is More Complicated Than Politics Suggest," *New York Times*, September 23, 2011.

**2.10** **[Related to the** Making the Connection **on page 592]** Currently, the Social Security and Medicare programs are

funded by payroll taxes rather than by the federal personal income tax. In 2011, the payroll tax for Social Security was 12.4 percent on wage, salary, and self-employment income up to $106,800. (Half of the tax is collected from employers and half from employees. In 2011, the employee portion was temporarily reduced from 6.2 percent to 4.2 percent.) Above that income level, the tax dropped to zero. The Medicare tax was 2.9 percent on all wage, salary, and self-employment income. Some economists and policymakers have proposed eliminating the payroll tax and shifting to funding Social Security and Medicare out of the federal personal income tax. Would this proposal make the federal income tax system as a whole more progressive or less progressive? Briefly explain.

**2.11** Almost all states levy sales taxes on retail products, but about half of them exempt purchases of food. In addition, virtually all services are exempt from state sales taxes. Evaluate these tax rate differences, using the goals and principles of taxation on pages 591–594.

**2.12** **[Related to the** Making the Connection **on page 592]** Suppose the government eliminates the income tax and replaces it with a consumption tax. Think about the effect of this on the market for automobiles. Can you necessarily tell what will happen to the price and quantity of automobiles? Briefly explain.

---

**18.3** **Tax Incidence Revisited: The Effect of Price Elasticity,** pages 594–597
LEARNING OBJECTIVE: Understand the effect of price elasticity on tax incidence.

## Summary

**Tax incidence** is the actual division of the burden of a tax. In most cases, buyers and sellers share the burden of a tax levied on a good or service. When the elasticity of demand for a product is smaller than the elasticity of supply, consumers pay the majority of the tax on the product. When the elasticity of demand for a product is larger than the elasticity of supply, sellers pay the majority of the tax on the product.

 Visit **www.myeconlab.com** to complete these exercises online and get instant feedback.

## Review Questions

**3.1** What is meant by *tax incidence*?
**3.2** Briefly discuss the effect of price elasticity of supply and demand on tax incidence.

## Problems and Applications

**3.3** According to the 2004 *Economic Report of the President*, "The actual incidence of a tax may have little to do with the legal specification of its incidence." Briefly explain what this statement means and discuss whether you agree or disagree with it.

**3.4** According to the 2004 *Economic Report of the President*, "Another crucial principle [of tax incidence] is that only people can pay taxes. Businesses and other artificial entities cannot pay taxes." Do you agree that businesses cannot

pay taxes? Don't businesses pay the federal corporate income tax? Briefly explain.

**3.5** **[Related to** Solved Problem 18.3 **on page 596]** Use the following graph of the market for cigarettes to answer the questions:

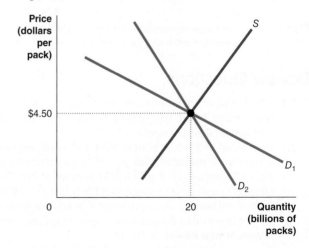

**a.** If the government imposes a 10-cents-per-pack tax on cigarettes, will the price consumers pay rise more if the demand curve is $D_1$ or if the demand curve is $D_2$? Briefly explain.

**b.** If the government imposes a 10-cents-per-pack tax on cigarettes, will the revenue to the government be greater if the demand curve is $D_1$ or if the demand curve is $D_2$? Briefly explain.

**c.** If the government imposes a 10-cents-per-pack tax on cigarettes, will the excess burden from the tax be greater if the demand curve is $D_1$ or if the demand curve is $D_2$? Briefly explain.

**3.6** **[Related to** Solved Problem 18.3 **on page 596]** Explain whether you agree with the following statement: "For a given demand curve, the excess burden of a tax will be greater when supply is less price elastic than when it is more elastic." Illustrate your answer with a demand and supply graph.

**3.7** **[Related to the** Making the Connection **on page 595]** Use a demand and supply model for the labor market to show the effect of the corporate income tax on workers. What factors would make the deadweight loss or excess burden from the tax larger or smaller?

**3.8** Governments often have multiple objectives in imposing a tax. In each part of this question, use a demand and supply graph to illustrate your answer.

**a.** If the government wants to minimize the excess burden from excise taxes, should these taxes be imposed on goods that are elastic or goods that are inelastic?

**b.** Suppose that rather than minimizing excess burden, the government is most interested in maximizing the revenue it receives from the tax. In this situation, should the government impose excise taxes on goods that are elastic or on goods that are inelastic?

**c.** Suppose that the government wants to discourage smoking and drinking alcohol. Will a tax be more effective in achieving this objective if the demand for these goods is elastic or if the demand is inelastic?

**3.9** **[Related to the** Don't Let This Happen to You **on page 594]** According to an article in the *New York Times*, during 2009 some New Yorkers were deciding to buy existing condominiums (condos) rather than newly constructed condos. One reason given was the following: "[Some buyers] seek to avoid the 1.825 percent transfer tax that buyers must pay on a brand-new condo. (In resales, the seller pays the tax.)" Analyze this reason for buying a resale rather than a new condo.

Based on Teri Karush Rogers, "Mint Condition, Low Miles," *New York Times*, May 29, 2009.

---

## **18.4** Income Distribution and Poverty, pages 597–605

**LEARNING OBJECTIVE:** Discuss the distribution of income in the United States and understand the extent of income mobility.

## Summary

No dramatic changes in the distribution of income have occurred over the past 70 years, although there was some decline in inequality between 1936 and 1980, and there has been some increase in inequality between 1980 and today. A **Lorenz curve** shows the distribution of income by arraying incomes from lowest to highest on the horizontal axis and indicating the cumulative fraction of income earned by each fraction of households on the vertical axis. About 12 percent of Americans are below the **poverty line**, which is defined as the annual income equal to three times the amount necessary to purchase the minimum quantity of food required for adequate nutrition. Over time, there has been significant income mobility in the United States. The United States has a more unequal distribution of income than do other high-income countries. The **poverty rate**—the percentage of the population that is poor—has been declining in most countries around the world, with the important exception of Africa. The *marginal productivity theory of income distribution* states that in equilibrium, each factor of production receives a payment equal to its marginal revenue product. The more factors of production an individual owns and the more productive those factors are, the higher the individual's income will be.

 MyEconLab    Visit **www.myeconlab.com** to complete these exercises online and get instant feedback.

## Review Questions

**4.1** Discuss the extent of income inequality in the United States. Has inequality in the distribution of income in the United States increased or decreased over time? Briefly explain.

**4.2** Define *poverty line* and *poverty rate*. How has the poverty rate changed in the United States since 1960?

**4.3** What is a Lorenz curve? What is a Gini coefficient? If a country had a Gini coefficient of 0.48 in 1960 and 0.44 in 2012, would income inequality in the country have increased or decreased?

**4.4** Describe the main factors economists believe cause inequality of income.

**4.5** Compare the distribution of income in the United States with the distribution of income in other high-income countries.

**4.6** Describe the trend in global poverty rates.

## Problems and Applications

**4.7** **[Related to** Solved Problem 18.4 **on page 602]** Evaluate the following statement: "Policies to redistribute income are desperately needed in the United States. Without such policies, the more than 15 percent of the population that is currently poor has no hope of ever climbing above the poverty line."

**4.8** **[Related to the** Chapter Opener **on page 581]** In his column on MSNBC.com, Robert J. Samuelson wrote, "As for what's caused greater inequality, we're also in the dark. The Reagan and Bush tax cuts are weak explanations, because gains have occurred in pretax incomes. . . . Up to a point, inequality is inevitable and desirable."

**a.** What are pretax incomes?

**b.** Evaluate Samuelson's argument that tax cuts are unlikely to have been the cause of greater income inequality in the United States.

**c.** Do you agree with Samuelson's argument that income inequality may be inevitable and desirable?

From Robert J. Samuelson, "The Rich and the Rest," MSNBC.com, April 18, 2007.

**4.9** Use the following Lorenz curve graph to answer the questions:

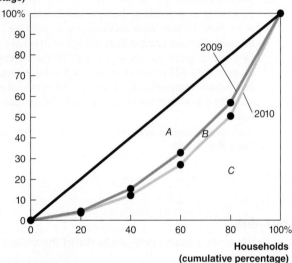

**a.** Did the distribution become more equal in 2010 than it was in 2009, or did it become less equal? Briefly explain.

**b.** If area $A$ = 2,150, area $B$ = 250, and area $C$ = 2,600, calculate the Gini coefficient for 2009 and the Gini coefficient for 2010.

**4.10** Draw a Lorenz curve showing the distribution of income for the five people in the following table.

| Name | Annual Earnings |
|------|-----------------|
| Lena | $70,000 |
| David | 60,000 |
| Steve | 50,000 |
| Jerome | 40,000 |
| Lori | 30,000 |

**4.11** Why do economists often use a lower poverty threshold for low-income countries than for high-income countries such as the United States? Is there a difference between *relative* poverty and *absolute* poverty? Briefly explain.

**4.12** Suppose that Congress and the president decide on a policy of bringing about a perfectly equal distribution of income. What factors might make this policy difficult to achieve? If it were possible to achieve the goal of this policy, would doing so be desirable?

**4.13** If everyone had the same income, would everyone have the same level of well-being?

**4.14** Suppose that a country has 20 million households. Ten million are poor households that each have labor market earnings of $20,000 per year, and 10 million are rich households that each have labor market earnings of $80,000 per year. If the government enacted a marginal tax of 10 percent on all labor market earnings above $20,000 and transferred this money to households earning $20,000 or less, would the incomes of the poor rise by $6,000 per year? Explain.

**4.15** A U.S. Census Bureau report showed that 46 percent of households living below the poverty line owned their own homes, 76 percent lived in dwellings with air-conditioning, about 75 percent owned cars, and 62 percent had cable or satellite TV reception. All these levels are considerably higher than they were for households below the poverty line a generation ago, but the official poverty rate is virtually unchanged over this period, as Figure 18.5 on page 598 shows. Going back to the official definition of *poverty*, how could ownership and purchases of these goods by the poor become more common while the poverty rate stayed the same?

**4.16** In a speech, Federal Reserve Chairman Ben Bernanke made the following observation: "Although we Americans strive to provide equality of economic opportunity, we do not guarantee equality of economic outcomes, nor should we." If the federal government wanted to, how could it "guarantee equality of economic outcomes"? If the government succeeded in making the distribution of income completely equal, what would be the benefits, and what would be the costs?

From "Remarks by Chairman Ben S. Bernanke before the Greater Omaha Chamber of Commerce, Omaha, Nebraska," February 6, 2007.

**4.17** In an article in the *Wall Street Journal*, Edward Lazear of Stanford University was quoted as saying: "There is some good news. . . . Most of the inequality reflects an increase in returns to 'investing in skills.'" Why would it be good news if it were true that most of the income inequality in the United States reflected an increase to returns in investing in skills?

From Greg Ip and John D. McKinnon, "Bush Reorients Rhetoric, Acknowledges Income Gap," *Wall Street Journal*, March 26, 2007, p. A2.

## Chapter Outline and Learning Objectives

# Ford Motor Company Feels the Effects of the Recession

In the more than 100 years that Ford Motor Company has been in business, its experiences have often mirrored those of the U.S. economy. So, it was no surprise that in the spring of 2009, with the U.S. economy suffering from its worst downturn since the 1930s, sales of Ford cars and trucks plummeted. In May 2009, Ford's sales were down 20 percent from a year earlier. Still, Ford was doing better than General Motors and Chrysler, Ford's two great American rivals, which had both declared bankruptcy. Those firms survived largely because the federal government invested more than $62 billion in them. While Ford suffered heavy losses, it did not require direct government aid.

By 2011, as the economy was slowly recovering from the downturn, Ford's sales were rising. Ford and the automobile industry as a whole were experiencing the effects of the *business cycle*, which refers to alternating periods of economic expansion and recession. Production and employment increase during expansions and fall during recessions.

Whether the general level of economic activity is increasing is important not just to firms such as Ford but also to workers wondering whether they will be able to keep their jobs and to college students wondering whether they will be able to find jobs when they graduate. One study found that during the slow recovery from the 2007–2009 recession, of those students who graduated from college in the spring of 2010, only 56 percent had found a job a year later. The average salary of those who did find a job was $27,000, down from an average of $30,000 for the classes of 2006 to 2008. What's more, students who graduate during recessions will continue to earn less for as long as 15 years after they graduate. The overall state of the economy is clearly important!

**AN INSIDE LOOK AT POLICY** on **page 634** discusses how uncertain economic conditions in 2011 and 2012 kept demand for automobiles below initial sales estimates.

Based on Sharon Terlep and Mike Ramsey, "August Auto Sales Perk Up," *The Wall Street Journal*, September 2, 2011; Catherine Rampell, "Many with New College Degrees Find the Job Market Humbling," *The New York Times*, May 18, 2011; and Lisa B. Kahn, "The Long-Term Labor Market Consequences of Graduating from College in a Bad Economy," *Labour Economics*, Vol. 17, No. 2, April 2010, pp. 303–316.

## Economics in Your Life

### What's the Best Country for You to Work In?

Suppose that an airline offers you a job after graduation in 2012. The firm has offices in Canada and China, and because you are fluent in English and Mandarin, you get to choose the country in which you will work and live. Gross domestic product (GDP) is a measure of an economy's total production of goods and services, so one factor in your decision is likely to be the growth rate of GDP in each country. Based on the International Monetary Fund's forecasts for 2012, GDP would increase by 2.6 percent in Canada but expand 9.5 percent in China. What effect do these two very different growth rates have on your decision to work and live in one country or the other? If China's much larger growth rate does not necessarily lead you to decide to work and live in China, why not? As you read this chapter, see if you can answer these questions. You can check your answers against those we provide on **page 633** at the end of this chapter.

**Microeconomics** The study of how households and firms make choices, how they interact in markets, and how the government attempts to influence their choices.

**Macroeconomics** The study of the economy as a whole, including topics such as inflation, unemployment, and economic growth.

**Business cycle** Alternating periods of economic expansion and economic recession.

**Expansion** The period of a business cycle during which total production and total employment are increasing.

**Recession** The period of a business cycle during which total production and total employment are decreasing.

**Economic growth** The ability of an economy to produce increasing quantities of goods and services.

**Inflation rate** The percentage increase in the price level from one year to the next.

As we saw in Chapter 1, we can divide economics into the subfields of microeconomics and macroeconomics. **Microeconomics** is the study of how households and firms make choices, how they interact in markets, and how the government attempts to influence their choices.

**Macroeconomics** is the study of the economy as a whole, including topics such as inflation, unemployment, and economic growth. In microeconomic analysis, economists generally study individual markets, such as the market for personal computers. In macroeconomic analysis, economists study factors that affect many markets at the same time. As we saw in the chapter opener, one important macroeconomic issue is the business cycle. The **business cycle** refers to the alternating periods of expansion and recession that the U.S. economy has experienced since at least the early nineteenth century. A business cycle **expansion** is a period during which total production and total employment are increasing. A business cycle **recession** is a period during which total production and total employment are decreasing. In the following chapters, we will discuss the factors that influence the business cycle and policies the government may use to reduce its effects.

Another important macroeconomic topic is **economic growth**, which refers to the ability of an economy to produce increasing quantities of goods and services. Economic growth is important because an economy that grows too slowly fails to raise living standards. In some countries in Africa, very little economic growth has occurred in the past 50 years, and many people remain in severe poverty. Macroeconomics analyzes both what determines a country's rate of economic growth and the reasons growth rates differ so greatly across countries.

Macroeconomics also analyzes what determines the total level of employment in an economy. As we will see, in the short run, the level of employment is significantly affected by the business cycle, but in the long run, the effects of the business cycle disappear, and other factors determine the level of employment. A related issue is why some economies are more successful than others at maintaining high levels of employment over time. Another important macroeconomic issue is what determines the **inflation rate**, or the percentage increase in the average level of prices from one year to the next. As with employment, inflation is affected both by the business cycle and by other long-run factors. Finally, macroeconomics is concerned with the linkages among economies: international trade and international finance.

Macroeconomic analysis provides information that consumers and firms need in order to understand current economic conditions and to help predict future conditions. A family may be reluctant to buy a house if employment in the economy is declining because some family members may be at risk of losing their jobs. Similarly, firms may be reluctant to invest in building new factories or to undertake major new expenditures on information technology if they expect that future sales may be weak. For example, in 2011, H. J. Heinz announced that it would close three of its factories in the United States. Heinz made that decision because macroeconomic forecasts indicated that consumer demand for its ketchup and other food products would increase only slowly. Macroeconomic analysis can also aid the federal government in designing policies that help the U.S. economy perform more efficiently.

In this chapter and Chapter 20, we begin our study of macroeconomics by considering how best to measure key macroeconomic variables. As we will see, there are important issues involved in measuring macroeconomic variables. We start by considering measures of total production and total income in an economy.

# Gross Domestic Product Measures Total Production

"Anemic GDP Figures Rattle Stocks"

"U.K. GDP Weak, but Could Have Been Worse"

"Concern Looms after Japan GDP Surprise"

"Malaysia's GDP Rises 4%"

"Indonesia's GDP Tops Forecast"

These headlines are from articles that appeared in the *Wall Street Journal* during 2011. Why is GDP so often the focus of news stories? In this section, we explore what GDP is and how it is measured. We also explore why knowledge of GDP is important to consumers, firms, and government policymakers.

## Measuring Total Production: Gross Domestic Product

Economists use **gross domestic product (GDP)** to measure total production. GDP is the market *value* of all *final* goods and services produced in a country during a period of time, typically one year. In the United States, the Bureau of Economic Analysis (BEA) in the Department of Commerce compiles the data needed to calculate GDP. The BEA issues reports on the GDP every three months. GDP is a central concept in macroeconomics, so we need to consider its definition carefully.

**Gross domestic product (GDP)** The market value of all final goods and services produced in a country during a period of time, typically one year.

### GDP Is Measured Using Market Values, Not Quantities

The word *value* is important in the definition of GDP. In microeconomics, we measure production in quantity terms: the number of cars Ford produces, the tons of wheat U.S. farmers grow, or the number of passengers American Airlines transports. When we measure total production in the economy, we can't just add together the quantities of every good and service because the result would be a meaningless jumble. Tons of wheat would be added to gallons of milk, numbers of passengers on flights, and so on. Instead, we measure production by taking the *value*, in dollar terms, of all the goods and services produced.

### GDP Includes Only the Market Value of Final Goods

In measuring GDP, we include only the value of *final goods and services*. A **final good or service** is one that is purchased by its final user and is not included in the production of any other good or service. Examples of final goods are a hamburger purchased by a consumer and a computer purchased by a business. Some goods and services, though, become part of other goods and services. For example, Ford does not produce tires for its cars and trucks; it buys them from tire companies, such as Goodyear and Michelin. The tires are an **intermediate good**, while a Ford truck is a final good. In calculating GDP, we include the value of the Ford truck but not the value of the tire. If we included the value of the tire, we would be *double counting*: The value of the tire would be counted once when the tire company sold it to Ford and a second time when Ford sold the truck, with the tire installed, to a consumer.

**Final good or service** A good or service purchased by a final user.

**Intermediate good or service** A good or service that is an input into another good or service, such as a tire on a truck.

### GDP Includes Only Current Production

GDP includes only production that takes place during the indicated time period. For example, GDP in 2012 includes only the goods and services produced during that year. In particular, GDP does *not* include the value of used goods. If you buy a DVD of *The Dark Knight Rises* from Amazon.com, the purchase is included in GDP. If six months later you resell the DVD on eBay, that transaction is not included in GDP.

# Solved Problem 19.1

## Calculating GDP

Suppose that a very simple economy produces only four goods and services: eye examinations, pizzas, textbooks, and paper. Assume that all the paper in this economy is used in the production of textbooks. Use the information in the following table to compute GDP for the year 2013:

| Production and Price Statistics for 2013 | | |
|---|---|---|
| (1) Product | (2) Quantity | (3) Price per Unit |
| Eye examinations | 100 | $50.00 |
| Pizzas | 80 | 10.00 |
| Textbooks | 20 | 100.00 |
| Paper | 2,000 | 0.10 |

## Solving the Problem

**Step 1:** **Review the chapter material.** This problem is about gross domestic product, so you may want to review the section "Measuring Total Production: Gross Domestic Product" on page 617.

**Step 2:** **Determine which goods and services listed in the table should be included in the calculation of GDP.** GDP is the value of all final goods and services. Therefore, we need to calculate the value of the final goods and services listed in the table. Eye examinations, pizzas, and textbooks are final goods. Paper would also be a final good if, for instance, a consumer bought it to use in a printer. However, here we are assuming that publishers purchase all the paper to use in manufacturing textbooks, so the paper is an intermediate good, and its value is not included in GDP.

**Step 3:** **Calculate the value of the three final goods and services listed in the table.** Value is equal to the quantity produced multiplied by the price per unit, so we multiply the numbers in column (1) by the numbers in column (2).

| Product | (1) Quantity | (2) Price per Unit | (3) Value |
|---|---|---|---|
| Eye examinations | 100 | $50 | $5,000 |
| Pizzas | 80 | 10 | 800 |
| Textbooks | 20 | 100 | 2,000 |

**Step 4:** **Add the value for each of the three final goods and services to find GDP.** GDP = Value of eye examinations produced + Value of pizzas produced + Value of textbooks produced = $5,000 + $800 + $2,000 = $7,800.

MyEconLab **Your Turn:** For more practice, do related problem 1.10 on page 637 at the end of this chapter.

## Production, Income, and the Circular-Flow Diagram

When we measure the value of total production in the economy by calculating GDP, we are simultaneously measuring the value of total income. To see why the value of total production is equal to the value of total income, consider what happens to the money you spend on a single product. Suppose you buy an Apple iPad for $499 at a Best Buy store. *All* of that $499 must end up as someone's income. Apple and Best Buy will receive some of the $499 as profits, workers at Apple will receive some as wages, the salesperson who sold you the iPad will receive some as salary, the firms that sell parts to Apple will receive some as profits, the workers for those firms will receive some as wages, and so on. Every penny must end up as someone's income. (Note, though, that any sales tax on the iPad will be collected by the store and sent to the government, without ending up as anyone's income.) Therefore, if we add up the value of every good and service sold in the economy, we must get a total that is exactly equal to the value of all the income in the economy.

The circular-flow diagram in Figure 19.1 was introduced in Chapter 2 to illustrate the interaction of firms and households in markets. We use it here to illustrate the flow of spending and money in the economy. Firms sell goods and services to three groups: domestic households, foreign firms and households, and the government. Expenditures by foreign firms and households (shown as "Rest of the World" in the diagram) on domestically produced goods and services are called *exports*. For example, American Airlines sells many tickets to passengers in Europe and Asia. As noted at the bottom of Figure 19.1, we can measure GDP by adding up the total expenditures of these groups on goods and services.

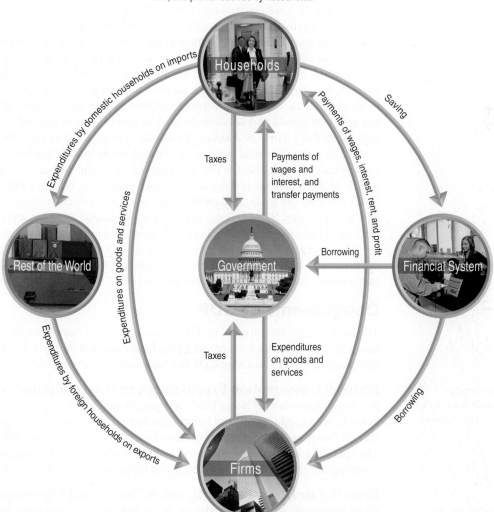

GDP can be measured by total wages, interest, rent, and profits received by households.

GDP can be measured by total expenditures on goods and services by households, firms, government, and the rest of the world.

**Figure 19.1**   The Circular Flow and the Measurement of GDP

The circular-flow diagram illustrates the flow of spending and money in the economy. Firms sell goods and services to three groups: domestic households, foreign firms and households, and the government. To produce goods and services, firms use factors of production: labor, capital, natural resources, and entrepreneurship. Households supply the factors of production to firms in exchange for income in the form of wages, interest, profit, and rent. Firms make payments of wages and interest to households in exchange for hiring workers and other factors of production. The sum of wages, interest, rent, and profit is total income in the economy. We can measure GDP as the total income received by households. The diagram also shows that households use their income to purchase goods and services, pay taxes, and save. Firms and the government borrow the funds that flow from households into the financial system. We can measure GDP either by calculating the total value of expenditures on final goods and services or by calculating the value of total income.

Firms use the *factors of production*—labor, capital, natural resources, and entrepreneurship—to produce goods and services. Households supply the factors of production to firms in exchange for income. We divide income into four categories: wages, interest, rent, and profit. Firms pay wages to households in exchange for labor services, interest for the use of capital, and rent for natural resources such as land. Profit is the income that remains after a firm has paid wages, interest, and rent. Profit is the return to entrepreneurs for organizing the other factors of production and for bearing the risk of producing and selling goods and services. As Figure 19.1 shows, federal, state, and local governments make payments of wages and interest to households in exchange for hiring workers and other factors of production. Governments also make *transfer payments* to households. **Transfer payments** include Social Security payments to retired and disabled people and unemployment insurance payments to unemployed workers. These payments are not included in GDP because they are not received in exchange for production of a new good or service. The sum of wages, interest, rent, and profit is total income in the economy. As noted at the top of Figure 19.1, we can measure GDP as the total income received by households.

> **Transfer payments** Payments by the government to households for which the government does not receive a new good or service in return.

The diagram also allows us to trace the ways that households use their income. Households spend some of their income on goods and services. Some of this spending is on domestically produced goods and services, and some is on foreign-produced goods and services. Spending on foreign-produced goods and services is known as *imports*. Households also use some of their income to pay taxes to the government. (Note that firms also pay taxes to the government.) Some of the income earned by households is not spent on goods and services or paid in taxes but is deposited in checking or savings accounts in banks or used to buy stocks or bonds. Banks and stock and bond markets make up the *financial system*. The flow of funds from households into the financial system makes it possible for the government and firms to borrow. As we will see, the health of the financial system is vital to an economy. Without the ability to borrow funds through the financial system, firms will have difficulty expanding and adopting new technologies. In fact, as we will discuss in Chapter 21, no country without a well-developed financial system has been able to sustain high levels of economic growth.

The circular-flow diagram shows that we can measure GDP either by calculating the total value of expenditures on final goods and services or by calculating the value of total income. We get the same dollar amount of GDP with both approaches.

## Components of GDP

The BEA divides its statistics on GDP into four major categories of expenditures: consumption, investment, government purchases, and net exports. Economists use these categories to understand why GDP fluctuates and to forecast future GDP.

**Personal Consumption Expenditures, or "Consumption"** Consumption expenditures are made by households and are divided into expenditures on *services*, such as medical care, education, and haircuts; expenditures on *nondurable goods*, such as food and clothing; and expenditures on *durable goods*, such as automobiles and furniture. The spending by households on new houses is not included in consumption. Instead, spending on new houses is included in the investment category, which we discuss next.

> **Consumption** Spending by households on goods and services, not including spending on new houses.

**Gross Private Domestic Investment, or "Investment"** Spending on *gross private domestic investment*, or simply **investment**, is divided into three categories. *Business fixed investment* is spending by firms on new factories, office buildings, and machinery used to produce other goods. *Residential investment* is spending by households and firms on new single-family and multi-unit houses. *Changes in business inventories* are also included in investment. Inventories are goods that have been produced but not yet sold. If Ford has $200 million worth of unsold cars at the beginning of the year and $350 million worth of unsold cars at the end of the year, then the firm has spent $150 million on inventory investment during the year.

> **Investment** Spending by firms on new factories, office buildings, machinery, and additions to inventories, plus spending by households and firms on new houses.

**Government Consumption and Gross Investment, or "Government Purchases"** **Government purchases** are spending by federal, state, and local governments on goods and services, such as teachers' salaries, highways, and aircraft carriers. Again, government spending on transfer payments is not included in government purchases because it does not result in the production of new goods and services.

> **Government purchases** Spending by federal, state, and local governments on goods and services.

## Don't Let This Happen to You

### Remember What Economists Mean by *Investment*

Notice that the definition of *investment* in this chapter is narrower than in everyday use. For example, people often say they are investing in the stock market or in rare coins. As we have seen, economists reserve the word *investment* for purchases of machinery, factories, and houses. Economists don't include purchases of stock or rare coins or deposits in savings accounts in the definition of investment because these activities don't result in the production of new goods. For example, a share of Microsoft stock

represents part ownership of that company. When you buy a share of Microsoft stock, nothing new is produced; there is just a transfer of that small piece of ownership of Microsoft. Similarly, buying a rare coin or putting $1,000 into a savings account does not result in an increase in production. GDP is not affected by any of these activities, so they are not included in the economic definition of investment.

### MyEconLab

**Your Turn:** Test your understanding by doing related problem 1.11 on page 637 at the end of this chapter.

**Net Exports of Goods and Services, or "Net Exports"** **Net exports** are equal to *exports* minus *imports*. Exports are goods and services produced in the United States and purchased by foreign firms, households, and governments. We add exports to our other categories of expenditures because otherwise we would not be including all spending on new goods and services produced in the United States. For example, if a farmer in South Dakota sells wheat to China, the value of the wheat is included in GDP because it represents production in the United States. Imports are goods and services produced in foreign countries and purchased by U.S. firms, households, and governments. We subtract imports from total expenditures because otherwise we would be including spending that does not result in production of new goods and services in the United States. For example, if U.S. consumers buy $1 billion worth of furniture manufactured in China, that spending is included in consumption expenditures. But the value of those imports is subtracted from GDP because the imports do not represent production in the United States.

**Net exports** Exports minus imports.

## An Equation for GDP and Some Actual Values

A simple equation sums up the components of GDP:

$$Y = C + I + G + NX.$$

The equation tells us that GDP (denoted as $Y$) equals consumption ($C$) plus investment ($I$) plus government purchases ($G$) plus net exports ($NX$). Figure 19.2 shows the values of the components of GDP for the year 2010. The graph in the figure highlights the fact that consumption is by far the largest component of GDP. The table provides a more detailed breakdown and shows several interesting points:

- Consumer spending on services is greater than the sum of spending on durable and nondurable goods. This greater spending on services reflects the continuing trend in the United States and other high-income countries away from the production of goods and toward the production of services. As the populations of these countries have become, on average, both older and wealthier, their demand for services such as medical care and financial advice has increased faster than their demand for goods.

- Business fixed investment is the largest component of investment. As we will see in later chapters, spending by firms on new factories, computers, and machinery can fluctuate. For example, a decline in business fixed investment played an important role in the 2007–2009 recession.

- Purchases made by state and local governments are greater than purchases made by the federal government. Because basic government activities, such as education and law enforcement, occur largely at the state and local levels, state and local government spending is greater than federal government spending.

| COMPONENTS OF GDP (billions of dollars) | | |
|---|---|---|
| **Consumption** | | $10,246 |
| Durable goods | $1,086 | |
| Nondurable goods | 2,302 | |
| Services | 6,859 | |
| **Investment** | | 1,795 |
| Business fixed investment | 1,390 | |
| Residential construction | 338 | |
| Change in business inventories | 67 | |
| **Government Purchases** | | 3,003 |
| Federal | 1,223 | |
| State and local | 1,780 | |
| **Net Exports** | | −517 |
| Exports | 1,840 | |
| Imports | 2,357 | |
| **Total GDP** | | $14,527 |

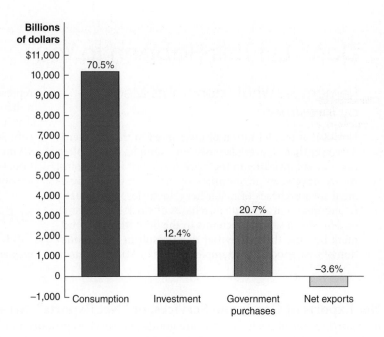

**Figure 19.2** **Components of GDP in 2010**

Consumption accounts for 70.5 percent of GDP, far more than any of the other components. In recent years, net exports typically have been negative, which reduces GDP. Note that the subtotals may not sum to the totals for each category because of rounding.
Data from U.S. Bureau of Economic Analysis.

- Imports are greater than exports, so net exports are negative. We will discuss in Chapter 29 why imports have typically been larger than exports for the U.S. economy.

## Making the Connection

### Will U.S. Consumers Be Spending Less?

We saw in Figure 19.2 that in 2010, consumption was 70.5 percent of GDP in the United States. As the figure below shows, consumption is a larger fraction of GDP in the United States than in most other high-income countries or in rapidly growing countries such as China and India.

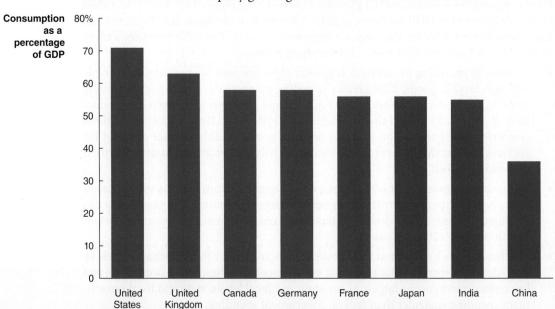

As shown in the following figure, over time, consumption in the United States has increased as a fraction of GDP. Through the mid-1980s, consumption was less than 65 percent of GDP. By the early 2000s, consumption had increased to 70 percent of GDP.

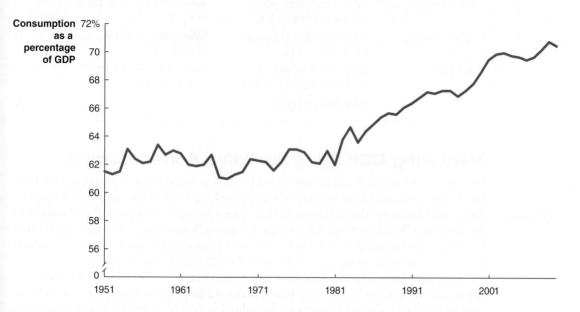

U.S. households financed this increased consumption partly by reducing saving and partly by increasing borrowing. While households were saving about 10 percent of their income in the mid-1980s, saving dropped to about 1 percent by 2005. Low saving rates were partly due to an increase in household wealth resulting from rising housing prices and rising stock prices. In many parts of the country, housing prices increased rapidly between 2001 and 2006. Stock prices, as measured by the Dow Jones Industrial Average and the S&P 500, reached record highs in October 2007. Some households felt less need to save out of their current incomes because their homes and their investments in the stock market were increasing in value.

During the early 2000s, many households borrowed against the increased value of their homes by taking out home equity loans, which many banks were increasingly willing to grant. Banks and other financial firms also loosened the requirements for issuing credit cards, so some households with flawed credit histories were able to borrow against their credit cards to finance their spending. The ratio of loans and other household debt to household income, which had been about 65 percent in the mid-1980s, rose to a record 133 percent in 2007 before declining to 102 percent in mid-2011.

Housing prices began to decline in 2006, and that decline accelerated with the start of the recession in December 2007. Stock prices also declined sharply. The combination of falling housing prices and falling stock prices wiped out trillions of dollars in household wealth. Banks and other financial institutions also tightened lending standards, making it more difficult for many households to borrow money. In the face of declining wealth and with reduced access to loans, household saving rates began to increase, rising above 6 percent by 2009.

As we will see in later chapters, increased household saving can be good news for the economy in the long run because it provides more funds that firms can borrow to finance investment, which can lead to more rapid rates of economic growth. But in the short run, in 2011, many firms—particularly firms such as Ford that sell consumer durables—worried that the slow recovery from the 2007–2009 recession was due in part to the determination of U.S. households to cut back on spending and increase saving.

Data from U.S. Bureau of Economic Analysis; Organization for Economic Cooperation and Development; and United Nations.

**Your Turn:** Test your understanding by doing related problem 1.12 on page 637 at the end of this chapter. MyEconLab

**Table 19.1**

**Calculating Value Added**

| Firm | Value of Product | Value Added | |
|---|---|---|---|
| Cotton farmer | Value of raw cotton = $1 | Value added by cotton farmer | = 1 |
| Textile mill | Value of raw cotton woven into cotton fabric = $3 | Value added by cotton textile mill = ($3 − $1) | = 2 |
| Shirt company | Value of cotton fabric made into a shirt = $15 | Value added by shirt manufacturer = ($15 − $3) | = 12 |
| L.L.Bean | Value of shirt for sale on L.L.Bean's Web site = $35 | Value added by L.L.Bean = ($35 − $15) | = 20 |
| | | **Total Value Added** | **= $35** |

## Measuring GDP Using the Value-Added Method

We have seen that GDP can be calculated by adding together all expenditures on final goods and services. An alternative way of calculating GDP is the *value-added method*. **Value added** refers to the additional market value a firm gives to a product and is equal to the difference between the price for which the firm sells a good and the price it paid other firms for intermediate goods. Table 19.1 gives a hypothetical example of the value added by each firm involved in the production of a shirt offered for sale on L.L.Bean's Web site.

**Value added** The market value a firm adds to a product.

Suppose a cotton farmer sells $1 of raw cotton to a textile mill. If, for simplicity, we ignore any inputs the farmer may have purchased from other firms—such as cotton-seed or fertilizer—then the farmer's value added is $1. The textile mill then weaves the raw cotton into cotton fabric, which it sells to a shirt company for $3. The textile mill's value added ($2) is the difference between the price it paid for the raw cotton ($1) and the price for which it can sell the cotton fabric ($3). Similarly, the shirt company's value added is the difference between the price it paid for the cotton fabric ($3) and the price it receives for the shirt from L.L.Bean ($15). L.L.Bean's value added is the difference be-tween the price it pays for the shirt ($15) and the price for which it can sell the shirt on its Web site ($35). Notice that *the price of the shirt on L.L.Bean's Web site is exactly equal to the sum of the value added by each firm involved in the production of the shirt*. We can calculate GDP by adding up the market value of every final good and service produced during a particular period. Or, we can arrive at the same value for GDP by adding up the value added of every firm involved in producing those final goods and services.

**19.2 LEARNING** OBJECTIVE

Discuss whether GDP is a good measure of well-being.

# Does GDP Measure What We Want It to Measure?

Economists use GDP to measure total production in the economy. For that purpose, we would like GDP to be as comprehensive as possible, not overlooking any significant pro-duction that takes place in the economy. Most economists believe that GDP does a good—but not flawless—job of measuring production. GDP is also sometimes used as a measure of well-being. Although it is generally true that the more goods and services people have, the better off they are, we will see that GDP provides only a rough measure of well-being.

## Shortcomings in GDP as a Measure of Total Production

When the BEA calculates GDP, it does not include two types of production: production in the home and production in the underground economy.

**Household Production** With few exceptions, the BEA does not attempt to estimate the value of goods and services that are not bought and sold in markets. If a carpenter makes and sells bookcases, the value of those bookcases will be counted in GDP. If the carpenter makes a bookcase for personal use, it will not be counted in GDP. *Household production* refers to goods and services people produce for themselves. The most important type of household production is the services a homemaker provides to the homemaker's family. If a person has been caring for children, cleaning the house, and preparing the family meals, the value of such services is not included in GDP. If the person then decides to work outside the home, enrolls the children in day care, hires a cleaning service, and begins buying the family's meals in restaurants, the value of GDP will rise by the amount paid for day care, cleaning services, and restaurant meals, even though production of these services has not actually increased.

**The Underground Economy**  Individuals and firms sometimes conceal the buying and selling of goods and services, in which case their production isn't counted in GDP. Individuals and firms conceal what they buy and sell for three basic reasons: They are dealing in illegal goods and services, such as drugs or prostitution; they want to avoid paying taxes on the income they earn; or they want to avoid government regulations. This concealed buying and selling is referred to as the **underground economy**. Estimates of the size of the underground economy in the United States vary widely, but it is probably at most 10 percent of measured GDP, or about $1.5 trillion. The underground economy in some low-income countries, such as Zimbabwe or Peru, may be more than half of measured GDP.

Is not counting household production or production in the underground economy a serious shortcoming of GDP? Most economists would answer "no" because the most important use of GDP is to measure changes in how the economy is performing over short periods of time, such as from one year to the next. For this purpose, omitting household production and production in the underground economy doesn't matter because there is not likely to be much change in household production or the size of the underground economy from one year to the next.

We also use GDP to measure how production of goods and services grows over fairly long periods of a decade or more. For this purpose, omitting household production and production in the underground economy may be more important. For example, beginning in the 1970s, the number of women working outside the home increased dramatically. Some of the goods and services—such as childcare and restaurant meals—produced in the following years were not true additions to total production; rather, they were replacing what had been household production.

> **Underground economy** Buying and selling of goods and services that is concealed from the government to avoid taxes or regulations or because the goods and services are illegal.

| Making the Connection | ## Why Do Many Developing Countries Have Such Large Underground Economies? |
|---|---|

Recent estimates put the size of the underground economy at 8 percent of measured GDP in the United States and 13 percent in Western Europe. The underground economy is much larger in many developing countries—perhaps 50 percent or more of measured GDP. In developing countries, the underground economy is often referred to as the *informal sector*, as opposed to the *formal sector*, in which output of goods and services is measured. Although it might not seem to matter whether production of goods and services is measured and included in GDP or unmeasured, a large informal sector can be a sign of government policies that are retarding economic growth.

Because firms in the informal sector are acting illegally, they tend to be smaller and have less capital than firms acting legally. The entrepreneurs who start firms in the informal sector may be afraid the government could someday close or confiscate their firms. Therefore, the entrepreneurs limit their investments in these firms. As a consequence, workers in these firms have less machinery and equipment to work with and so can produce fewer goods and services. Entrepreneurs in the informal sector also have to pay the costs of avoiding government authorities. For example, construction firms operating in the informal sector in Brazil have to employ lookouts who can warn workers to hide when government inspectors come around. In many countries, firms in the informal sector have to pay substantial bribes to government officials to remain in business. The informal sector is large

*In some developing countries, more than half the workers may be in the underground economy.*

in some developing economies because taxes are high and government regulations are extensive. For example, firms in Brazil pay 85 percent of all taxes collected, as compared with 41 percent in the United States. Not surprisingly, about half of all Brazilian workers are employed in the informal sector. In Zimbabwe and Peru, the fraction of workers in the informal sector may be as high as 60 or 70 percent. One estimate put the size of the informal sector in India at nearly 50 percent.

Many economists believe taxes in developing countries are so high because these countries are attempting to pay for government sectors that are as large relative to their economies as the government sectors of industrial economies. Including transfer payments, government spending in Brazil, for example, is 41 percent of measured GDP, compared to 36 percent in the United States. In the early twentieth century, when the United States was much poorer than it is today, government spending was only about 8 percent of GDP, so the tax burden on U.S. firms was much lower. In countries such as Brazil, bringing firms into the formal sector from the informal sector may require reductions in government spending and taxes. In most developing countries, however, voters are reluctant to see government services reduced.

Based on "Dynamic but Dirty," *Economist*, December 2, 2010; "Notes from the Underground," *Economist*, April 2, 2009; Mary Anastasia O'Grady, "Why Brazil's Underground Economy Grows and Grows," *Wall Street Journal*, September 10, 2004; and the International Monetary Fund.

MyEconLab **Your Turn:** Test your understanding by doing related problem 2.8 on page 638 at the end of this chapter.

## Shortcomings of GDP as a Measure of Well-Being

The main purpose of GDP is to measure a country's total production. GDP is also frequently used, though, as a measure of well-being. For example, newspaper and magazine articles often include tables that show the levels of GDP per person for different countries, which is usually referred to as *GDP per capita*. GDP per capita is calculated by dividing the value of GDP for a country by the country's population. These articles imply that people in the countries with higher levels of GDP per capita are better off. Although increases in GDP often do lead to increases in the well-being of the population, it is important to be aware that GDP is not a perfect measure of well-being for several reasons.

**The Value of Leisure Is Not Included in GDP** If an economic consultant decides to retire, GDP will decline even though the consultant may value increased leisure more than the income he or she was earning running a consulting firm. The consultant's well-being has increased, but GDP has decreased. In 1890, the typical American worked 60 hours per week. Today, the typical American works fewer than 40 hours per week. If Americans still worked 60-hour weeks, GDP would be much higher than it is, but the well-being of the typical person would be lower because less time would be available for leisure activities.

**GDP Is Not Adjusted for Pollution or Other Negative Effects of Production** When a dry cleaner cleans and presses clothes, the value of this service is included in GDP. If the chemicals the dry cleaner uses pollute the air or water, GDP is not adjusted to compensate for the costs of the pollution. Similarly, the value of cigarettes produced is included in GDP, with no adjustment made for the costs of the lung cancer that some smokers develop.

We should note, though, that increasing GDP often leads countries to devote more resources to pollution reduction. For example, in the United States between 1970 and 2011, as GDP was steadily increasing, emissions of the six main air pollutants declined by more than 50 percent. Developing countries often have higher levels of pollution than high-income countries because the lower GDPs of the developing countries make them more reluctant to spend resources on pollution reduction. Levels of pollution in China are much higher than in the United States, Japan, or the countries of Western

Europe. According to the World Health Organization, 7 of the 10 most polluted cities in the world are in China, but as Chinese GDP continues to rise, the country is likely to devote more resources to reducing pollution.

## GDP Is Not Adjusted for Changes in Crime and Other Social Problems

An increase in crime reduces well-being but may actually increase GDP if it leads to greater spending on police, security guards, and alarm systems. GDP is also not adjusted for changes in divorce rates, drug addiction, or other factors that may affect people's well-being.

## GDP Measures the Size of the Pie but Not How the Pie Is Divided Up   When a country's GDP increases, the country has more goods and services, but those goods and services may be very unequally distributed. Therefore, GDP may not provide good information about the goods and services consumed by the typical person.

To summarize, we can say that a person's well-being depends on many factors that are not considered in calculating GDP. Because GDP is designed to measure total production, it should not be surprising that it does an imperfect job of measuring well-being.

| | |
|---|---|
| **Making** <br> **the** <br> **Connection** | **Did World War II Bring Prosperity?** |

The Great Depression of the 1930s was the worst economic downturn in U.S. history. GDP declined by more than 25 percent between 1929 and 1933 and did not reach its 1929 level again until 1938. The unemployment rate remained at very high levels of 10 percent or more through 1940. Then, in 1941, the United States entered World War II. The graph below shows that GDP rose dramatically during the war years of 1941 to 1945. (The graph shows values for real GDP, which, as we will see in the next section, corrects measures of GDP for changes in the price level.) The unemployment rate also fell to very low levels—below 2 percent.

Traditionally, historians have argued that World War II brought prosperity back to the U.S. economy. But did it? Economist Robert Higgs argued that if we look at the well-being of the typical person, the World War II years were anything but prosperous. Higgs pointed out that increased production of tanks, ships, planes, and munitions accounted for most of the increase in GDP during those years. Between 1943 and 1945, more than 40 percent of the labor force was either in the military or producing war goods. As a result, between 1939 and 1944, production of clothing, radios, books, and other consumption goods per person increased only about 2 percent, leaving the quantity of consumption goods available to the typical person in 1944 still below what it had been in 1929. With the end of the war, true prosperity did return to the U.S. economy, and by 1946, production of consumption goods per person had risen by more than 25 percent from what it had been in 1929.

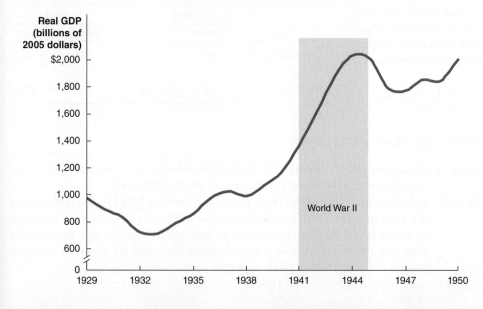

World War II was a period of extraordinary sacrifice and achievement by the "greatest generation." But statistics on GDP may give a misleading indication of whether it was also a period of prosperity.

Based on Robert Higgs, "Wartime Prosperity? A Reassessment of the U.S. Economy in the 1940s," *Journal of Economic History*, Vol. 52, No. 1, March 1992; Robert Higgs, "From Central Planning to the Market: The American Transition, 1945–1947," *Journal of Economic History*, Vol. 59, No. 3, September 1999; and data from the U.S. Bureau of Economic Analysis.

MyEconLab **Your Turn:** Test your understanding by doing related problem 2.10 on page 638 at the end of this chapter.

---

**19.3 LEARNING OBJECTIVE**

Discuss the difference between real GDP and nominal GDP.

# Real GDP versus Nominal GDP

Because GDP is measured in value terms, we have to be careful about interpreting changes over time. To see why, consider interpreting an increase in the total value of pickup truck production from $40 billion in 2012 to $44 billion in 2013. Can we be sure that because $44 billion is 10 percent greater than $40 billion, the number of trucks produced in 2013 was 10 percent greater than the number produced in 2012? We can draw this conclusion only if the average price of trucks did not change between 2012 and 2013. In fact, when GDP increases from one year to the next, the increase is due partly to increases in production of goods and services and partly to increases in prices. Because we are mainly interested in GDP as a measure of production, we need a way of separating the price changes from the quantity changes.

## Calculating Real GDP

**Nominal GDP** The value of final goods and services evaluated at current-year prices.

**Real GDP** The value of final goods and services evaluated at base-year prices.

The BEA separates price changes from quantity changes by calculating a measure of production called *real GDP*. **Nominal GDP** is calculated by summing the current values of final goods and services. **Real GDP** is calculated by designating a particular year as the *base year* and then using the prices of goods and services in the base year to calculate the value of goods and services in all other years. For instance, if the base year is 2005, real GDP for 2013 would be calculated by using prices of goods and services from 2005. By keeping prices constant, we know that changes in real GDP represent changes in the quantity of goods and services produced in the economy.

---

# Solved Problem 19.3

## Calculating Real GDP

Suppose that a very simple economy produces only the following three final goods and services: eye examinations, pizzas, and textbooks. Use the information in the table on the right to compute real GDP for the year 2013. Assume that the base year is 2005.

| Product | 2005 Quantity | 2005 Price | 2013 Quantity | 2013 Price |
|---|---|---|---|---|
| Eye examinations | 80 | $40 | 100 | $50 |
| Pizzas | 90 | 11 | 80 | 10 |
| Textbooks | 15 | 90 | 20 | 100 |

## Solving the Problem

**Step 1:** **Review the chapter material.** This problem is about calculating real GDP, so you may want to review the section above, "Calculating Real GDP."

**Step 2:** **Calculate the value of the three goods and services listed in the table, using the quantities for 2013 and the prices for 2005.** The definition on this page tells us that real GDP is the value of all final goods and services, evaluated at base-year prices. In this case, the base year is 2005, and we are given information on the price of each product in that year:

| Product | 2013 Quantity | 2005 Price | Value |
|---|---|---|---|
| Eye examinations | 100 | $40 | $4,000 |
| Pizzas | 80 | 11 | 880 |
| Textbooks | 20 | 90 | 1,800 |

**Step 3:  Add up the values for the three products to find real GDP.** Real GDP for 2013 equals the sum of:

Quantity of eye examination in 2013 $\times$ Price of eye examinations in 2005 = $4,000
Quantity of pizza produced in 2013 $\times$ Price of pizzas in 2005 = $880
Quantity of textbooks produced in 2013 $\times$ Price of textbooks in 2005 = $1,800
or, $6,680

**Extra Credit:** Notice that the quantities of each good produced in 2005 were irrelevant for calculating real GDP in 2013. Notice also that the value of $6,680 for real GDP in 2013 is lower than the value of $7,800 for nominal GDP in 2013 that we calculated in Solved Problem 19.1 on page 618.

**Your Turn:** For more practice, do related problem 3.4 on pages 638–639 at the end of this chapter.    MyEconLab

One drawback to calculating real GDP using base-year prices is that, over time, prices may change relative to each other. For example, the price of cell phones may fall relative to the price of milk. Because this change is not reflected in the fixed prices from the base year, the estimate of real GDP is somewhat distorted. The further away the current year is from the base year, the worse the problem becomes. To make the calculation of real GDP more accurate, in 1996, the BEA switched to using *chain-weighted prices*, and it now publishes statistics on real GDP in "chained (2005) dollars."

The details of calculating real GDP using chain-weighted prices are more complicated than we need to discuss here, but the basic idea is straightforward: Starting with the base year, the BEA takes an average of prices in that year and prices in the following year. It then uses this average to calculate real GDP in the year following the base year (currently the year 2005). For the next year—in other words, the year that is two years after the base year—the BEA calculates real GDP by taking an average of prices in that year and the previous year. In this way, prices in each year are "chained" to prices from the previous year, and the distortion from changes in relative prices is minimized.

Holding prices constant means that the *purchasing power* of a dollar remains the same from one year to the next. Ordinarily, the purchasing power of the dollar falls every year, as price increases reduce the amount of goods and services that a dollar can buy.

## Comparing Real GDP and Nominal GDP

Real GDP holds prices constant, which makes it a better measure than nominal GDP of changes in the production of goods and services from one year to the next. In fact, growth in the economy is almost always measured as growth in real GDP. If a headline in the *Wall Street Journal* states "U.S. Economy Grew 2.3% Last Year," the article will report that real GDP increased by 2.3 percent during the previous year.

We describe real GDP as being measured in "base-year dollars." For example, with a base year of 2005, nominal GDP in 2010 was $14,527 billion, and real GDP in 2010 was $13,088 billion in 2005 dollars. Because, on average, prices rise from one year to the next, real GDP is greater than nominal GDP in years before the base year and less than nominal GDP for years after the base year. In the base year, real GDP and nominal GDP are the same because both are calculated for the base year using the same prices and quantities. Figure 19.3 shows movements in nominal GDP and real GDP between 1990 and 2010. In the years before 2005, prices were, on average, lower than in 2005, so nominal GDP was lower than real GDP. In 2005, nominal and real GDP were equal. Since 2005, prices have been, on average, higher than in 2005, so nominal GDP is higher than real GDP.

## Figure 19.3

### Nominal GDP and Real GDP, 1990-2010

Currently, the base year for calculating GDP is 2005. In the years before 2005, prices were, on average, lower than in 2005, so nominal GDP was lower than real GDP. In 2005, nominal and real GDP were equal. Since 2005, prices have been, on average, higher than in 2005, so nominal GDP is higher than real GDP.

Data from U.S. Bureau of Economic Analysis.

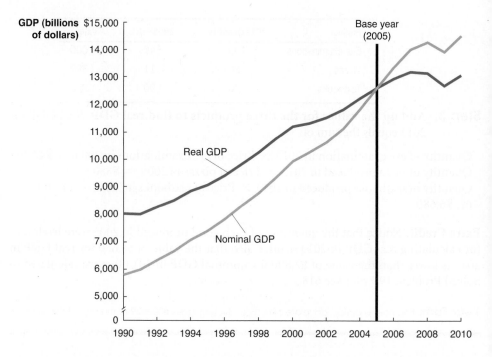

**Price level** A measure of the average prices of goods and services in the economy.

**GDP deflator** A measure of the price level, calculated by dividing nominal GDP by real GDP and multiplying by 100.

## The GDP Deflator

Economists and policymakers are interested not just in the level of total production, as measured by real GDP, but also in the *price level*. The **price level** measures the average prices of goods and services in the economy. One of the goals of economic policy is a stable price level. We can use values for nominal GDP and real GDP to compute a measure of the price level called the *GDP deflator*. We can calculate the **GDP deflator** by using this formula:

$$\text{GDP deflator} = \frac{\text{Nominal GDP}}{\text{Real GDP}} \times 100.$$

To see why the GDP deflator is a measure of the price level, think about what would happen if prices of goods and services rose while production remained the same. In that case, nominal GDP would increase, but real GDP would remain constant, so the GDP deflator would increase. In reality, both prices and production usually increase each year, but the more prices increase relative to the increase in production, the more nominal GDP increases relative to real GDP, and the higher the value for the GDP deflator. Increases in the GDP deflator allow economists and policymakers to track increases in the price level over time.

Remember that in the base year (currently 2005), nominal GDP is equal to real GDP, so the value of the GDP price deflator will always be 100 in the base year. The following table gives the values for nominal and real GDP for 2009 and 2010:

|  | 2009 | 2010 |
|---|---|---|
| **Nominal GDP** | $13,939 billion | $14,527 billion |
| **Real GDP** | $12,703 billion | $13,088 billion |

We can use the information from this table to calculate values for the GDP price deflator for 2009 and 2010:

| Formula | Applied to 2009 | Applied to 2010 |
|---|---|---|
| GDP deflator $= \dfrac{\text{Nominal GDP}}{\text{Real GDP}} \times 100$ | $\left(\dfrac{\$13,939 \text{ billion}}{\$12,703 \text{ billion}}\right) \times 100 = 110$ | $\left(\dfrac{\$14,527 \text{ billion}}{\$13,088 \text{ billion}}\right) \times 100 = 111$ |

From these values for the deflator, we can calculate that the price level increased by 0.9 percent between 2009 and 2010:

$$\left(\frac{111 - 110}{110}\right) \times 100 = 0.9\%.$$

In Chapter 20, we will see that economists and policymakers also rely on another measure of the price level, known as the consumer price index. In addition, we will discuss the strengths and weaknesses of different measures of the price level.

# Other Measures of Total Production and Total Income

**19.4 LEARNING** OBJECTIVE

Understand other measures of total production and total income.

*National income accounting* refers to the methods the BEA uses to track total production and total income in the economy. The statistical tables containing this information are called the *National Income and Product Accounts (NIPA)* tables. Every quarter, the BEA releases NIPA tables containing data on several measures of total production and total income. We have already discussed the most important measure of total production and total income: gross domestic product (GDP). In addition to computing GDP, the BEA computes the following four measures of production and income: gross national product, national income, personal income, and disposable personal income.

## Gross National Product (GNP)

We have seen that GDP is the value of final goods and services produced within the United States. *Gross national product (GNP)* is the value of final goods and services produced by residents of the United States, even if the production takes place *outside* the United States. U.S. firms have facilities in foreign countries, and foreign firms have facilities in the United States. Ford, for example, has assembly plants in the United Kingdom, and Toyota has assembly plants in the United States. GNP includes foreign production by U.S. firms but excludes U.S. production by foreign firms. For the United States, GNP is almost the same as GDP. For example, in 2010, GDP was $14,527 billion, and GNP was $14,716 billion, or only about 1 percent more than GDP.

For many years, GNP was the main measure of total production compiled by the federal government and used by economists and policymakers in the United States. However, in many countries other than the United States, a significant percentage of domestic production takes place in foreign-owned facilities. For those countries, GDP is much larger than GNP and is a more accurate measure of the level of production within the country's borders. As a result, many countries and international agencies had long preferred using GDP to using GNP. In 1991, the United States joined those countries in using GDP as its main measure of total production.

## National Income

In producing goods and services, some machinery, equipment, and buildings wear out and have to be replaced. The value of this worn-out machinery, equipment, and buildings is *depreciation*. In the NIPA tables, depreciation is referred to as the *consumption of fixed capital*. If we subtract this value from GDP, we are left with *national income*.

Previously in this chapter, we stressed that the value of total production is equal to the value of total income. This point is not strictly true if by "value of total production" we mean GDP and by "value of total income" we mean national income because national income will always be smaller than GDP by an amount equal to depreciation. In practice, though, the difference between the value of GDP and value of national income does not matter for most macroeconomic issues.

## Personal Income

Personal income is income received by households. To calculate personal income, we subtract the earnings that corporations retain rather than pay to shareholders in the form of dividends. We also add in the payments received by households from the government in the form of *transfer payments* or interest on government bonds.

## Disposable Personal Income

Disposable personal income is equal to personal income minus personal tax payments, such as the federal personal income tax. It is the best measure of the income households actually have available to spend.

Figure 19.4 shows the values of these measures of total production and total income for the year 2010 in a table and a graph.

## The Division of Income

Figure 19.1 on page 619 illustrates the important fact that we can measure GDP in terms of total expenditure or as the total income received by households. GDP calculated as the sum of income payments to households is sometimes referred to as *gross domestic income*. Figure 19.5 shows the division of total income among wages, interest, rent, profit, and certain non-income items. The non-income items are included in gross domestic income because sales taxes, depreciation, and a few other small items are included in the value of goods and services produced but are not directly received by households as income. *Wages* include all compensation received by employees, including fringe benefits such as health insurance. *Interest* is net interest received by households, or the difference between the interest received on savings accounts, government bonds, and other investments and the interest paid on car loans, home mortgages, and other debts. *Rent* is rent received by households. *Profits* include the profits of sole proprietorships, which are usually small businesses, and the profits of corporations. Figure 19.5 shows that the largest component of gross domestic income is wages, which are about three times as large as profits.

| Measure | Billions of dollars |
|---|---|
| GDP | $14,527 |
| GNP | 14,716 |
| National income | 12,840 |
| Personal income | 12,374 |
| Disposable personal income | 11,180 |

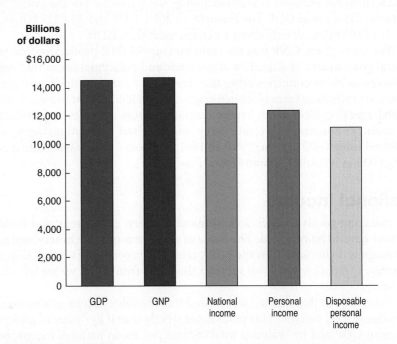

**Figure 19.4** **Measures of Total Production and Total Income, 2010**

The most important measure of total production and total income is gross domestic product (GDP). As we will see in later chapters, for some purposes, the other measures of total production and total income shown in the figure turn out to be more useful than GDP.
Data from U.S. Bureau of Economic Analysis.

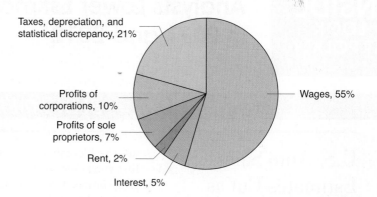

| | Billions of dollars |
|---|---|
| Wages | $7,981 |
| Interest | 748 |
| Rent | 350 |
| Profit | 2,455 |
|    Profits of sole proprietors | 1,036 |
|    Profits of corporations | 1,418 |
| Taxes, depreciation, and statistical discrepancy | 2,993 |

**Figure 19.5** **The Division of Income, 2010**

We can measure GDP in terms of total expenditure or as the total income received by households. The largest component of income received by households is wages, which are more than three times as large as the profits received by sole proprietors and the profits received by corporations combined.

Data from U.S. Bureau of Economic Analysis.

---

**Continued from page 615**

## Economics in Your Life

### What's the Best Country for You to Work In?

At the beginning of the chapter, we posed two questions: What effect should Canada's and China's two very different growth rates of GDP have on your decision to work and live in one country or the other? And if China's much higher growth rate does not necessarily lead you to decide to work and live in China, why not? This chapter has shown that although it is generally true that the more goods and services people have, the better off they are, GDP provides only a rough measure of well-being. GDP does not include the value of leisure; nor is it adjusted for pollution and other negative effects of production or crime and other social problems. So, in deciding where to live and work, you would need to balance China's much higher growth rate of GDP against these other considerations. You would also need to take into account that although China's *growth rate* is higher than Canada's, Canada's current *level* of real GDP is higher than China's.

---

# Conclusion

In this chapter, we have begun the study of macroeconomics by examining an important concept: how a nation's total production and income can be measured. Understanding GDP is important for understanding the business cycle and the process of long-run economic growth. In the next chapter, we discuss the issues involved in measuring two other key economic variables: the unemployment rate and the inflation rate.

Read *An Inside Look at Policy* on the next page for a discussion of how declining consumer confidence led analysts to lower their estimates of new automobile sales for 2011 and 2012.

# Analysts Lower Estimates for New Car Sales in 2011 and 2012

## BLOOMBERG

# U.S. Auto Sales Estimates Cut as Confidence Slows Rebound

Analysts are reducing estimates for U.S. automobile sales for 2011 and 2012, citing weak consumer confidence that has slowed the pace of recovery since May.

J.D. Power & Associates lowered its estimate for U.S. auto sales in 2011 by 300,000 light vehicles to 12.6 million, the Westlake Village, California-based researcher said today in a statement. J.D. Power reduced its estimate for next year by 600,000 cars and light trucks to 14.1 million.

The reduction by J.D. Power follows analysts at IHS Automotive in cutting expectations below the sales forecasts given by General Motors Co. (GM) and Ford Motor Co. (F), the largest U.S. automakers. JPMorgan Chase & Co., Goldman Sachs Group Inc. and RBC Capital Markets LLC also shaved estimates this month.

(a) "The thought of a second-half recovery is just not in the cards," Jeff Schuster, J.D. Power's executive director of global forecasting, said today in a phone interview. "It really comes down to consumer confidence and consumers just don't have any right now. There just really isn't a strong reason to go make that big-ticket purchase."

Consumer confidence in the U.S. economic outlook slumped in August to the lowest level since the recession, raising the risk that spending will dry up. The Bloomberg Consumer Comfort Index's monthly expectations gauge dropped to minus 34, the weakest since March 2009, from minus 22 in July.

Applications for unemployment benefits climbed last week to the highest level in a month, Labor Department figures showed today in Washington.

### Goldman Cuts

Goldman Sachs today lowered its 2012 U.S. auto sales estimate by 1 million light vehicles to 13.5 million. The New York–based investment bank sees 12.8 million deliveries this year. RBC Capital earlier this week lowered its estimates for 2011 by 200,000 units to 12.5 million and by 700,000 to 13.3 million for next year.

"Fragile U.S. consumer sentiment and recently tempered economic expectations" led to the reductions, Seth Weber, an RBC Capital analyst based in New York, said in an Aug. 16 research note. . . .

### GM, Ford Estimates

(b) GM and Dearborn, Michigan–based Ford forecast at least 13 million new-vehicle sales in 2011, including medium- and heavy- duty trucks. The U.S. averaged annual light-vehicle deliveries of 16.8 million vehicles from 2000 to 2007, according to Autodata Corp., a Woodcliff Lake, New Jersey–based research company.

"There's a lot of turmoil in the business and turmoil means uncertainty, so we're a little unsure of these numbers," Chief Executive Officer Dan Akerson of Detroit-based GM, told analysts Aug. 9. . . .

### No 'Snap Back'

(c) J.D. Power sees a 12.1 million seasonally adjusted annualized rate for August. Analysts and automakers had been predicting a "snap back" in demand once inventories recovered from the March earthquake and tsunami in Japan, which disrupted production and led to shortages of parts and finished vehicles.

"We're not seeing that snap back, and given all the variables out there it's a lower probability that we're going to see that happen this year," Schuster said today.

Sales ran at a seasonally adjusted annualized rate of 12.2 million through the first two weeks of August, Edmunds.com said in an e-mailed statement. The Santa Monica, California–based researcher still predicts 12.9 million deliveries this year and 13.9 million in 2012.

J.D. Power's estimate for full-year sales assumes that the industry will average a 12.8 million seasonally adjusted annualized rate in the last four months of the year, Schuster said. Lower gasoline prices and higher spending on sales incentives may help the sales pace accelerate to those levels late this year, he said.

If the pace of deliveries stays about flat, sales may finish the year at 12.4 million, according to J.D. Power's estimates.

"If August comes in at the level we're expecting, that gives us a really clear indication that we're running out" of time in 2011 "to get going again," Schuster said.

## Key Points in the Article

Citing declining consumer confidence in the economy, J.D. Power & Associates reduced its estimates for car and light truck sales in the United States by 300,000 vehicles for 2011 and by 600,000 for 2012. Other companies also announcing lower estimated sales include Goldman Sachs, RBC Capital, IHS Automotive, and JPMorgan Chase. Automakers and analysts had initially predicted an increase in new vehicle demand once inventories of new automobiles and auto parts stabilized following the March 2011 earthquake and tsunami in Japan, but uncertain economic conditions kept demand below the initial sales estimates.

## Analyzing the News

**a** Jeff Schuster of J.D. Power & Associates cited the lack of consumer confidence as a main reason for the decline in auto sales during the first half of 2011 and the lower estimates for the remainder of the year. In August, Bloomberg's consumer comfort index was the weakest it has been since March 2009, and consumer confidence in the economic outlook for the United States dropped to its lowest level since the recession. As you read in this chapter, automobiles are durable goods, and consumers are more likely to reduce purchases of durable goods when they are not confident about their jobs or their future

incomes. Automobiles have high prices, and as Schuster stated in the article, "There just really isn't a strong reason to go make that big-ticket purchase." Falling automobile sales reduce total consumption. Recall that consumption accounts for about 70 percent of GDP. The figure below shows that by June 2009, GDP had fallen for four consecutive quarters. Falling consumption contributed to the decline in GDP during that period. GDP began to rise again by September 2009, but the increases in GDP began to slow down in 2010, dropping to only 1 percent by June 2011. The significant slowdown in the growth of real GDP in 2011, as shown in the figure, reflects the lack of consumer confidence mentioned in the article and helps explain the lowered estimates for new car sales for the year.

**b** Following an increase in sales during 2010, both General Motors and Ford initially estimated that U.S. sales of new cars and trucks would increase to more than 13 million in 2011. Although the article does not mention any specific revised estimates from these companies, General Motors's CEO Dan Akerson was quoted on August 9 as saying, "There's a lot of turmoil in the business and turmoil means uncertainty, so we're a little unsure of these numbers." His statement seems to summarize the economic uncertainty discussed in the article.

**c** Initial estimates for new vehicle sales were lowered following the earthquake and tsunami that struck Japan in March

2011 and led to shortages of parts and new vehicles worldwide. Analysts and automakers had predicted that the market would "snap back" once these shortages had been eliminated, with demand for new vehicles increasing in the second half of the year. According to J.D. Power's Jeff Schuster, "We're not seeing that snap back, and given all the variables out there it's a lower probability that we're going to see that happen this year," again reflecting uncertainty and the lack of consumer confidence in the U.S. economy.

## Thinking Critically about Policy

1. The auto industry is cyclical: Auto sales rise during economic expansions and fall during economic recessions. Would you expect the same to be true of the markets for used vehicles and for vehicle repairs?

2. Ford and General Motors estimated that new vehicle sales in the United States would top 13 million in 2011. This sales number included medium- and heavy-duty trucks, which are more often purchased by businesses than households. Which component of GDP is affected by purchases of new vehicles by businesses? Which component of GDP is affected by purchases of new vehicles by households?

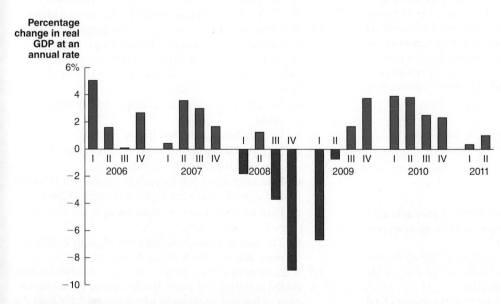

**Real GDP declined for four consecutive quarters in 2009.**

# Chapter Summary and Problems

## Key Terms

Business cycle, p. 616

Consumption, p. 620

Economic growth, p. 616

Expansion, p. 616

Final good or service, p. 617

GDP deflator, p. 630

Government purchases, p. 620

Gross domestic product (GDP), p. 617

Inflation rate, p. 616

Intermediate good or service, p. 617

Investment, p. 620

Macroeconomics, p. 616

Microeconomics, p. 616

Net exports, p. 621

Nominal GDP, p. 628

Price level, p. 630

Real GDP, p. 628

Recession, p. 616

Transfer payments, p. 620

Underground economy, p. 625

Value added, p. 624

### Gross Domestic Product Measures Total Production, pages 617–624

**LEARNING OBJECTIVE:** Explain how total production is measured.

## Summary

Economics is divided into the subfields of **microeconomics**—which studies how households and firms make choices—and **macroeconomics**—which studies the economy as a whole. An important macroeconomic issue is the **business cycle**, which refers to alternating periods of economic expansion and economic recession. An **expansion** is a period during which production and employment are increasing. A **recession** is a period during which production and employment are decreasing. Another important macroeconomic topic is **economic growth**, which refers to the ability of the economy to produce increasing quantities of goods and services. Macroeconomics also studies the **inflation rate**, or the percentage increase in the price level from one year to the next. Economists measure total production by **gross domestic product (GDP)**, which is the value of all *final goods and services* produced in an economy during a period of time. A **final good or service** is purchased by a final user. An **intermediate good or service** is an input into another good or service and is not included in GDP. When we measure the value of total production in the economy by calculating GDP, we are simultaneously measuring the value of total income. GDP is divided into four major categories of expenditures: consumption, investment, government purchases, and net exports. Government **transfer payments** are not included in GDP because they are payments to individuals for which the government does not receive a good or service in return. We can also calculate GDP by adding up the **value added** of every firm involved in producing final goods and services.

MyEconLab   Visit www.myeconlab.com to complete these exercises online and get instant feedback.

## Review Questions

1.1 Why in microeconomics do we measure production in terms of quantity, but in macroeconomics we measure production in terms of market value?

1.2 If the U.S. Bureau of Economic Analysis added up the values of every good and service sold during the year, would the total be larger or smaller than GDP?

1.3 In the circular flow of income, why must the value of total production in an economy equal the value of total income?

1.4 Describe the four major components of expenditures in GDP and write the equation used to represent the relationship between GDP and the four expenditure components.

1.5 What is the difference between the value of a firm's final product and the value added by the firm to the final product?

## Problems and Applications

1.6 A student remarks: "It doesn't make sense that intermediate goods are not counted in GDP. A computer chip is an intermediate good, and without it a PC won't work. So why don't we count the computer chip in GDP?" Provide an answer for the student's question.

1.7 Briefly explain whether each of the following transactions represents the purchase of a final good.

   a. The purchase of wheat from a wheat farmer by a bakery

   b. The purchase of an aircraft carrier by the federal government

   c. The purchase of French wine by a U.S. consumer

   d. The purchase of a new airliner by American Airlines

1.8 **[Related to the** Chapter Opener **on page 615]** Which component of GDP will be affected by each of the following transactions involving Ford Motor Company? If you believe that none of the components of GDP will be affected by the transactions, briefly explain why.

   a. You purchase a new Ford Escape Hybrid from a Ford dealer.

   b. You purchase a 2010 Ford Escape Hybrid from a friend.

   c. Ford purchases door handles for the Escape from an auto parts manufacturer in Indiana.

   d. Ford produces 1,000 Escapes in a factory in Missouri and ships them to a car dealer in Shanghai, China.

   e. Ford purchases new machine tools to use in its Missouri Escape factory.

   f. The state of Missouri builds a new highway to help improve access to the Ford Escape plant.

1.9 Is the value of a house built in 2000 and resold in 2013 included in the GDP of 2013? Briefly explain. Would the services of the real estate agent who helped sell (or buy) the house in 2013 be counted in GDP for 2013? Briefly explain.

**1.10** [Related to Solved Problem 19.1 **on page 618**] Suppose that a simple economy produces only four goods: textbooks, hamburgers, shirts, and cotton. Assume that all the cotton is used in the production of shirts. Use the information in the following table to calculate nominal GDP for 2013:

| Production and Price Statistics for 2013 | | |
|---|---|---|
| Product | Quantity | Price |
| Textbooks | 100 | $60.00 |
| Hamburgers | 100 | 2.00 |
| Shirts | 50 | 25.00 |
| Cotton | 80 | 0.60 |

**1.11** [Related to the Don't Let This Happen to You **on page 621**] Briefly explain whether you agree with the following statement: "In years when people buy many shares of stock, investment will be high and, therefore, so will GDP."

**1.12** [Related to the Making the Connection **on page 622**] An article on USAToday.com observed: "Consumer spending, once the driving force of the U.S. economy, is likely to remain stagnant for years as households struggle to cut debt and build up savings, economists say." Why does cutting debt and building up savings affect consumer spending? If consumer spending remains stagnant, what will be the likely effect on the economy?

Based on Karina Frayter, "Economists: Consumers Won't Save the Economy," USAToday.com, October 2, 2011.

**1.13** For the total value of expenditures on final goods and services to equal the total value of income generated from producing those final goods and services, all the money that a business receives from the sale of its product must be paid out as income to the owners of the factors of production. How can a business make a profit if it pays out as income all the money it receives?

**1.14** An artist buys scrap metal from a local steel mill as a raw material for her metal sculptures. Last year, she bought $5,000 worth of the scrap metal. During the year, she produced 10 metal sculptures that she sold for $800 each to a local art store. The local art store sold all of the sculptures to local art collectors, at an average price of $1,000 each. For the 10 metal sculptures, what was the total value added of the artist, and what was the total value added of the local art store?

---

**19.2** **Does GDP Measure What We Want It to Measure?** pages 624–628

LEARNING OBJECTIVE: Discuss whether GDP is a good measure of well-being.

## Summary

GDP does not include household production, which refers to goods and services people produce for themselves, nor does it include production in the **underground economy**, which consists of concealed buying and selling. The underground economy in some developing countries may be more than half of measured GDP. GDP is not a perfect measure of well-being because it does not include the value of leisure, it is not adjusted for pollution or other negative effects of production, and it is not adjusted for changes in crime and other social problems.

MyEconLab    Visit **www.myeconlab.com** to complete these exercises online and get instant feedback.

## Review Questions

**2.1** Why does the size of a country's GDP matter? How does it affect the quality of life of the country's people?

**2.2** What is the underground economy? Why do some countries have larger underground economies than do other countries?

**2.3** Why is GDP an imperfect measure of economic well-being? What types of production does GDP not measure? Even if GDP included these types of production, why would it still be an imperfect measure of economic well-being?

## Problems and Applications

**2.4** Which of the following are likely to increase measured GDP, and which are likely to reduce it?

a. The fraction of women working outside the home increases.

b. There is a sharp increase in the crime rate.

c. Higher tax rates cause some people to hide more of the income they earn.

**2.5** Michael Burda of Humboldt University in Germany and Daniel Hamermesh of the University of Texas examined how workers in the United States who lost their jobs between 2003 and 2006 spent their time. They discovered that during the period when they were unemployed, the decline in the number of hours of paid work done by these workers was almost the same as the increase in the number of hours these workers devoted to household production. Do Burda and Hamermesh's findings allow us to draw any conclusions about whether total production in the economy—whether that production is included in GDP or not—fell when these workers became unemployed? Does your answer depend on whether the household production they carried out while unemployed involved activities, such as child care, that the workers had been paying other people to perform before the workers lost their jobs? Briefly explain.

Based on Michael Burda and Daniel S. Hamermesh, "Unemployment, Market Work, and Household Production," *Economic Letters*, Vol. 107, May 2010, pp. 131–133.

**2.6** Does the fact that the typical American works less than 40 hours per week today and worked 60 hours per week in 1890 make the difference between the economic well-being of Americans today versus 1890 higher or lower than indicated by the difference in real GDP per capita today versus in 1890? Explain.

**2.7** Roger Ransom and Richard Sutch, economic historians at the University of California, Riverside, have estimated that African-American farmers in the U.S. South after the Civil War worked about 30 percent fewer hours per year than they had as slaves during the years before the Civil War. If after the Civil War, African-American farmers had continued to work these additional hours, their production and income would have been higher and so would have been U.S. GDP. Would the farmers' well-being also have been higher as a result of working these additional hours? Does your answer affect how we should interpret changes in U.S. GDP from before the Civil War to after the Civil War? Briefly explain.

Based on Roger L. Ransom and Richard Sutch, *One Kind of Freedom: The Economic Consequences of Emancipation*, Second Edition, (New York: Cambridge University Press), 2001.

**2.8** **[Related to the** Making the Connection **on page 625]** A report of the World Bank, an international organization devoted to increasing economic growth in developing countries, included the following statement: "Informal economic activities pose a particular measurement problem [in calculating GDP], especially in developing countries, where much economic activity may go unrecorded." What does the World Bank mean by "informal economic activities"? Why would these activities make it harder to measure GDP? Why might they make it harder to evaluate the standard of living in developing countries relative to the standard of living in the United States?

Based on The World Bank, *World Development Indicators*, (Washington, DC: The World Bank, 2003), p. 189.

**2.9** Each year, the United Nations publishes the Human Development Report, which provides information on the standard of living in nearly every country in the world. The report includes data on real GDP per person and also contains a broader measure of the standard of living called the Human Development Index (HDI). The HDI combines data on gross national income (GNI) per person with data on life expectancy at birth, average years of schooling, and expected years of schooling. (GNI is a measure of the total income per person in a country.) The following table shows values for GNI per person and the HDIs for several countries. Prepare one list that ranks countries from highest GNI per person to lowest and another list that ranks countries from highest HDI to lowest. Briefly discuss possible reasons for any differences in the rankings of countries in your two lists. (All values in the table are for the year 2010.)

| Country | Real GNI per Person | HDI |
|---|---|---|
| Australia | $38,692 | 0.937 |
| China | 7,258 | 0.663 |
| Greece | 27,580 | 0.855 |
| Iran | 11,764 | 0.702 |
| Norway | 58,810 | 0.938 |
| Singapore | 48,893 | 0.846 |
| South Korea | 29,518 | 0.877 |
| United Arab Emirates | 58,006 | 0.815 |
| United States | 47,094 | 0.902 |

Data from United Nations Development Programme, "The Human Development Index," (http://hdr.undp.org/en/statistics/hdi/).

**2.10** **[Related to the** Making the Connection **on page 627]** Think about the increases since 2001 in spending for the Department of Homeland Security and the wars in Afghanistan and Iraq. These increases represent government expenditures that have increased GDP. Briefly explain whether you think that these increases in GDP have made the typical person better off.

---

**19.3** **Real GDP versus Nominal GDP,** pages 628–631

LEARNING OBJECTIVE: Discuss the difference between real GDP and nominal GDP.

## Summary

**Nominal GDP** is the value of final goods and services evaluated at current-year prices. **Real GDP** is the value of final goods and services evaluated at *base-year* prices. By keeping prices constant, we know that changes in real GDP represent changes in the quantity of goods and services produced in the economy. When the **price level**, the average prices of goods and services in the economy, is increasing, real GDP is greater than nominal GDP in years before the base year and less than nominal GDP for years after the base year. The **GDP deflator** is a measure of the price level and is calculated by dividing nominal GDP by real GDP and multiplying by 100.

 MyEconLab    Visit **www.myeconlab.com** to complete these exercises online and get instant feedback.

## Review Questions

**3.1** Why does inflation make nominal GDP a poor measure of the increase in total production from one year to the next?

How does the U.S. Bureau of Economic Analysis deal with the problem inflation causes with nominal GDP?

**3.2** What is the GDP deflator, and how is it calculated?

**3.3** Assuming that inflation has occurred over time, what is the relationship between nominal GDP and real GDP in each of the following situations?
   **a.** In the years after the base year
   **b.** In the base year
   **c.** In the years before the base year

## Problems and Applications

**3.4** **[Related to** Solved Problem 19.3 **on page 628]** Suppose the information in the table on the next page is for a simple economy that produces only four goods and services: textbooks, hamburgers, shirts, and cotton. Assume that all the cotton is used in the production of shirts.

| Product | 2005 Quantity | 2005 Price | 2012 Quantity | 2012 Price | 2013 Quantity | 2013 Price |
|---------|----------|-------|----------|-------|----------|-------|
| Textbooks | 90 | $50.00 | 100 | $60.00 | 100 | $65.00 |
| Hamburgers | 75 | 2.00 | 100 | 2.00 | 120 | 2.25 |
| Shirts | 50 | 30.00 | 50 | 25.00 | 65 | 25.00 |
| Cotton | 100 | 0.80 | 800 | 0.60 | 120 | 0.70 |

a. Use the information in the table to calculate real GDP for 2012 and 2013, assuming that the base year is 2005.

b. What is the growth rate of real GDP during 2013?

**3.5** Briefly explain whether you agree or disagree with the following statements.

a. "If nominal GDP is less than real GDP, then the price level must have fallen during the year."

b. "Whenever real GDP declines, nominal GDP must also decline."

c. "If a recession is so severe that the price level declines, then we know that both real GDP and nominal GDP must decline."

d. "Nominal GDP declined between 2008 and 2009, therefore the GDP deflator must also have declined."

**3.6** The movie *Avatar* overtook *Titanic* as the highest-grossing movie of all time. An article on Forbes.com notes that "the average ticket price in 2008 (*Avatar* was released in 2009) was $7.18, up 56% from prices in 1997 when *Titanic* was in theaters." The article states that "A look at domestic grosses (box-office receipts) adjusted for inflation shows a more realistic view of *Avatar*'s performance."

a. Why would adjusting for inflation show a more realistic view of *Avatar*'s performance at the box office?

b. Which would be a more accurate measure of how well a movie has performed at the box office: The dollar value of tickets sold or the number of tickets sold? Why don't newspapers report the number of tickets sold rather than the dollar value of tickets sold? Would comparing the total number of tickets sold by all movies in 1939 with the total number of tickets sold by all movies in 2011 be a good way to measure how the relative importance of movies in the economy has changed over time? Briefly explain.

Based on Dorthy Pomerantz, "Is Avator Really King of the Box Office?" Forbes.com, January 27, 2010.

**3.7** Use the data in the following table to calculate the GDP deflator for each year (values are in billions of dollars):

| Year | Nominal GDP | Real GDP |
|------|-------------|----------|
| 2006 | $13,377 | $12,959 |
| 2007 | 14,029 | 13,206 |
| 2008 | 14,292 | 13,162 |
| 2009 | 13,939 | 12,703 |
| 2010 | 14,527 | 13,088 |

Which year from 2007 to 2010 saw the largest percentage increase in the price level, as measured by changes in the GDP deflator? Briefly explain.

## 19.4 | Other Measures of Total Production and Total Income, pages 631–633

LEARNING OBJECTIVE: Understand other measures of total production and total income.

## Summary

The most important measure of total production and total income is gross domestic product (GDP). As we will see in later chapters, for some purposes, the other measures of total production and total income shown in Figure 19.4 are actually more useful than GDP. These measures are gross national product (GNP), national income, personal income, and disposable personal income.

 Visit **www.myeconlab.com** to complete these exercises online and get instant feedback.

## Review Questions

**4.1** What is the difference between GDP and GNP? Briefly explain whether the difference is important for the United States.

**4.2** What are the differences between national income, personal income, and disposable personal income?

**4.3** What is gross domestic income? Which component of gross domestic income is the largest?

## Problems and Applications

**4.4** Suppose a country has many of its citizens temporarily working in other countries, and many of its firms have facilities in other countries. Furthermore, relatively few citizens of foreign countries are working in this country, and relatively few foreign firms have facilities in this country. In these circumstances, which would you expect to be larger for this country, GDP or GNP? Briefly explain.

**4.5** Suppose the amount the federal government collects in personal income taxes increases, while the level of GDP remains the same. What will happen to the values of national income, personal income, and disposable personal income?

**4.6** If you were attempting to forecast the level of consumption spending by households, which measure of total production or total income might be most helpful to you in making your forecast? Briefly explain.

**4.7** Briefly discuss the accuracy of the following statement: "Corporate profits are much too high: Most corporations make profits equal to 50 percent of the price of the products they sell."

# Unemployment and Inflation

## Chapter Outline and Learning Objectives

# Bank of America Announces Plans to Lay Off 30,000 Employees

When we study macroeconomics, we are looking at the big picture: total production, total employment, and the price level. Of course, the big picture is made up of millions of consumers, workers, and firms. Few industries have had as many problems in recent years as financial services, which includes businesses such as banks and brokerages. In September 2011, Bank of America, the second largest bank in the United States, announced that it would be laying off 30,000 of its 288,000 employees. To some extent, the layoffs reflected the problems banks had been having since the financial crisis that began in 2008 and the particular problems that Bank of America had experienced.

But the layoffs also were an indication of how slowly the U.S. economy was recovering from the economic recession of 2007–2009. Although the recession had ended in June 2009, unemployment remained high more than two years later. Economists at the White House and the Federal Reserve were forecasting that unemployment would not return to more normal levels for at least another two years. Some economists were even more pessimistic and had begun speaking of the "new normal," in which unemployment might be stuck at high levels for many years.

In this chapter, we will focus on measuring changes in unemployment as well as changes in the price level, or inflation. Because both unemployment and inflation are major macroeconomic problems, it is important to understand how they are measured. In later chapters, we will analyze why unemployment remained so high in the years following the end of the 2007–2009 recession. Read **AN INSIDE LOOK** on **page 668** for a discussion of how the U.S. Postal Service considered layoffs, office closings, and termination of Saturday deliveries to deal with declining revenues and mounting debts.

Based on Dan Fitzpatrick, "BofA Readies the Knife," *Wall Street Journal*, September 13, 2011; and Frank Bruni, "The Fall This Summer," *New York Times*, August 27, 2011.

## Economics in Your Life

### Should You Change Your Career Plans if You Graduate during a Recession?

Suppose that you are a sophomore majoring in either economics or finance. You plan to find a job in the banking industry after graduation. The economy is now in a deep recession, and the unemployment rate is the highest in your lifetime, at over 9 percent. Sizable layoffs have occurred in the banking industry. Should you change your major? Should you still consider a job in the banking industry? As you read this chapter, see if you can answer these questions. You can check your answers against those we provide on **page 667** at the end of this chapter.

U nemployment and inflation are the macroeconomic problems that are most often discussed in the media and during political campaigns. For many people, the state of the economy can be summarized in just two measures: the unemployment rate and the inflation rate. In the 1960s, Arthur Okun, who was chairman of the Council of Economic Advisers during President Lyndon Johnson's administration, coined the term *misery index*, which adds together the inflation rate and the unemployment rate to give a rough measure of the state of the economy. As we will see in later chapters, although unemployment and inflation are important problems in the short run, the long-run success of an economy is best judged by its ability to generate high levels of real GDP per person. We devote this chapter to discussing how the government measures the unemployment and inflation rates. In particular, we will look closely at the statistics on unemployment and inflation that the federal government issues each month.

**20.1 LEARNING** OBJECTIVE

Define the unemployment rate, the labor force participation rate, and the employment–population ratio and understand how they are computed.

# Measuring the Unemployment Rate, the Labor Force Participation Rate, and the Employment–Population Ratio

At 8:30 A.M. on a Friday early in each month, the U.S. Department of Labor reports its estimate of the previous month's unemployment rate. If the unemployment rate is higher or lower than expected, investors are likely to change their views on the health of the economy. The result is seen an hour later, when trading begins on the New York Stock Exchange. Good news about unemployment usually causes stock prices to rise, and bad news causes stock prices to fall. The unemployment rate can also have important political implications. In most presidential elections, the incumbent president is reelected if unemployment is falling early in the election year but is defeated if unemployment is rising. This relationship held true in 2004, when the unemployment rate was lower during the first six months of 2004 than it had been during the last six months of 2003, and incumbent George W. Bush was reelected.

The unemployment rate is a key macroeconomic statistic. But how does the Department of Labor prepare its estimates of the unemployment rate, and how accurate are these estimates? We will explore the answers to these questions in this section.

## The Household Survey

Each month, the U.S. Bureau of the Census conducts the *Current Population Survey* (often referred to as the *household survey*) to collect data needed to compute the unemployment rate. The bureau interviews adults in a sample of 60,000 households, chosen to represent the U.S. population, about the employment status of everyone in the household 16 years of age and older. The Department of Labor's Bureau of Labor Statistics (BLS) uses these data to calculate the monthly unemployment rate. People are considered *employed* if they worked during the week before the survey or if they were temporarily away from their jobs because they were ill, on vacation, on strike, or for other reasons. People are considered *unemployed* if they did not work in the previous week but were available for work and had actively looked for work at some time during the previous four weeks. The **labor force** is the sum of the *employed* and the *unemployed*. The **unemployment rate** is the percentage of the labor force that is unemployed.

**Labor force** The sum of employed and unemployed workers in the economy.

**Unemployment rate** The percentage of the labor force that is unemployed.

The BLS classifies people who do not have a job and who are not actively looking for a job as *not in the labor force*. People not in the labor force include retirees, homemakers, full-time students, and people on active military service, in prison, or in mental hospitals. Also not in the labor force are people who are available for work and who have actively looked for a job at some point during the previous 12 months but who have not looked during the previous four weeks. Some people have not actively looked for work during the previous four weeks for reasons such as transportation difficulties or

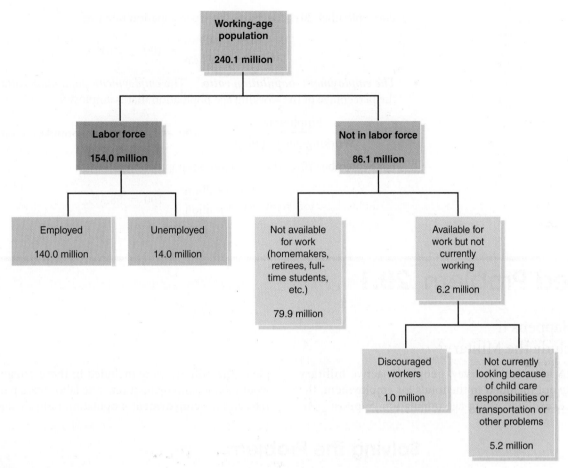

**Figure 20.1**   The Employment Status of the Civilian Working-Age Population, September 2011

In September 2011, the working-age population of the United States was 240.1 million. The working-age population is divided into those in the labor force (154.0 million) and those not in the labor force (86.1 million). The labor force is divided into the employed (140.0 million) and the unemployed (14.0 million). Those not in the labor force are divided into those not available for work (79.9 million) and those

available for work but not currently working (6.2 million). Finally, those available for work but not in the labor force are divided into discouraged workers (1.0 million) and those not currently looking for work for other reasons (5.2 million).
Data from U.S. Department of Labor, Bureau of Labor Statistics, *The Employment Situation—September 2011*, October 7, 2011.

childcare responsibilities. Other people who have not actively looked for work are called *discouraged workers*. **Discouraged workers** are available for work but have not looked for a job during the previous four weeks because they believe no jobs are available for them.

Figure 20.1 shows the employment status of the civilian working-age population in September 2011. We can use the information in the figure to calculate three important macroeconomic indicators:

**Discouraged workers** People who are available for work but have not looked for a job during the previous four weeks because they believe no jobs are available for them.

- *The unemployment rate.*   The unemployment rate measures the percentage of the labor force that is unemployed:

$$\frac{\text{Number of unemployed}}{\text{Labor force}} \times 100 = \text{Unemployment rate.}$$

Using the numbers from Figure 20.1, we can calculate the unemployment rate for September 2011:

$$\frac{14.0 \text{ million}}{154.0 \text{ million}} \times 100 = 9.1\%.$$

- *The labor force participation rate.*   The **labor force participation rate** measures the percentage of the working-age population that is in the labor force:

$$\frac{\text{Labor force}}{\text{Working-age-population}} \times 100 = \text{Labor force participation rate.}$$

**Labor force participation rate**
The percentage of the working-age population in the labor force.

For September 2011, the labor force participation rate was

$$\frac{154.0 \text{ million}}{240.1 \text{ million}} \times 100 = 64.1\%.$$

- **The employment–population ratio.** The *employment–population ratio* measures the percentage of the working age population that is employed:

$$\frac{\text{Employment}}{\text{Working-age population}} \times 100 = \text{Employment–population ratio.}$$

For September 2011, the employment–population ratio was

$$\frac{140.0 \text{ million}}{240.1 \text{ million}} \times 100 = 58.3\%.$$

# Solved Problem 20.1

## What Happens if You Include the Military?

In the BLS household survey, people on active military service are not included in the totals for employment, the labor force, or the working-age population. Suppose people in the military were included in these categories. How would the unemployment rate, the labor force participation rate, and the employment–population ratio change?

### Solving the Problem

**Step 1:** **Review the chapter material.** This problem is about calculating the unemployment rate and the labor force participation rate, so you may want to review the section "Measuring the Unemployment Rate, the Labor Force Participation Rate, and the Employment–Population Ratio," which begins on page 642.

**Step 2:** **Show that including the military decreases the measured unemployment rate.** The unemployment rate is calculated as

$$\frac{\text{Number of unemployed}}{\text{Labor force}} \times 100.$$

Including people in the military would increase the number of people counted as being in the labor force but would leave unchanged the number of people counted as unemployed. Therefore, the unemployment rate would decrease.

**Step 3:** **Show that including the military increases both the measured labor force participation rate and the measured employment–population ratio.** The labor force participation rate is calculated as

$$\frac{\text{Labor force}}{\text{Working-age population}} \times 100,$$

and the employment–population ratio is calculated as

$$\frac{\text{Employment}}{\text{Working-age population}} \times 100.$$

Including people in the military would increase the number of people in the labor force, the number of people employed, and the number of people in the working-age population all by the same amount. This change would increase the labor force participation rate and the employment–population ratio because adding the same number to both the numerator and the denominator of a fraction that is less than one increases the value of the fraction.

To see why this is true, consider the following simple example. Suppose that 100,000,000 people are in the working-age population and 50,000,000 are in the labor force, not counting people in the military. Suppose that 1,000,000 people are in the military. Then, the labor force participation rate excluding the military is

$$\frac{50,000,000}{100,000,000} \times 100 = 50\%,$$

and the labor force participation rate including the military is

$$\frac{51,000,000}{101,000,000} \times 100 = 50.5\%.$$

A similar calculation shows that including the military would increase the employment–population ratio.

**Your Turn:** For more practice, do related problem 1.9 on page 670 at the end of this chapter.    MyEconLab

## Problems with Measuring the Unemployment Rate

Although the BLS reports the unemployment rate measured to the tenth of a percentage point, it is not a perfect measure of the current state of joblessness in the economy. One problem that the BLS confronts is distinguishing between the unemployed and people who are not in the labor force. During an economic recession, for example, an increase in discouraged workers usually occurs, as people who have had trouble finding a job stop actively looking. Because these workers are not counted as unemployed, the unemployment rate as measured by the BLS may understate the true degree of joblessness in the economy. The BLS also counts people as being employed if they hold part-time jobs even though they would prefer to hold full-time jobs. In a recession, counting as "employed" a part-time worker who wants to work full time tends to understate the degree of joblessness in the economy and make the employment situation appear better than it is.

Not counting discouraged workers as unemployed and counting people as employed who are working part time, although they would prefer to be working full time, has a substantial effect on the measured unemployment rate. In Figure 20.2, the red line shows the official measure of the unemployment rate and the blue line shows what the unemployment rate would be if the BLS had counted as unemployed all people who were available for work but not actively looking for jobs and all people who were in part-time jobs but wanted full-time jobs. The difference between the two measures of the unemployment rate is substantial and was particularly large during the 2007–2009 recession and the slow recovery that followed the recession. For example, in September 2011, using the broader definition of unemployment would have increased the measured unemployment rate from 9.1 percent to 16.5 percent.

### Figure 20.2

**The Official Unemployment Rate and a Broad Measure of the Unemployment Rate, 1994–2011**

The red line shows the usual measure of the unemployment rate and the blue line shows what the unemployment rate would be if the BLS had counted as unemployed all people who were available for work but not actively looking for jobs and all people who were in part-time jobs but wanted full-time jobs. The difference between the measures was particularly large during the 2007–2009 recession and the weak recovery that followed. Shaded areas indicate months of recession. *Note:* The usual measure is BLS series U-3 and the broader measure is BLS series U-6. Data from U.S. Bureau of Labor Statistics.

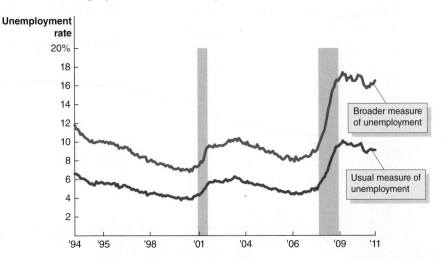

There are other measurement problems, however, that cause the measured unemployment rate to *overstate* the true extent of joblessness. These problems arise because the household survey does not verify the responses of people included in the survey. Some people who claim to be unemployed and actively looking for work may not be actively looking. A person might claim to be actively looking for a job to remain eligible for government payments to the unemployed. In this case, a person who is actually not in the labor force is counted as unemployed. Other people might be employed but engaged in illegal activity—such as drug dealing—or might want to conceal a legitimate job to avoid paying taxes. In these cases, individuals who are actually employed are counted as unemployed. These inaccurate responses to the survey bias the unemployment rate as measured by the BLS toward overstating the true extent of joblessness. We can conclude that, although the unemployment rate provides some useful information about the employment situation in the country, it is far from an exact measure of joblessness in the economy.

## Trends in Labor Force Participation

The labor force participation rate is important because it determines the amount of labor that will be available to the economy from a given population. The higher the labor force participation rate, the more labor that will be available and the higher a country's levels of GDP and GDP per person. Figure 20.3 highlights two important trends in the labor force participation rates of adults aged 16 and over in the United States since 1948: the rising labor force participation rate of adult women and the falling labor force participation rate of adult men.

The labor force participation rate of adult males has fallen from 87 percent in 1948 to 71 percent in 2010. Most of this decline is due to older men retiring earlier and younger men remaining in school longer. There has also been a decline in labor force participation among males who are not in school but who are too young to retire. Over the longer term, this decline appears to be partly due to Congress having made it easier for people to receive cash payments under the Social Security Disability Insurance program. In the shorter term, the decline is due to the severity of the 2007–2009 recession and the weakness of the recovery following the recession.

The decline in labor force participation among adult men has been more than offset by a sharp increase in the labor force participation rate for adult women, which rose from 33 percent in 1948 to 59 percent in 2010. As a result, the overall labor force participation rate rose from 59 percent in 1948 to 65 percent in 2010. The increase in the

### Figure 20.3

**Trends in the Labor Force: Participation Rates of Adult Men and Women since 1948**

The labor force participation rate of adult men has declined gradually since 1948, but the labor force participation rate of adult women has increased significantly, making the overall labor force participation rate higher today than it was in 1948.

Data from U.S. Bureau of Labor Statistics.

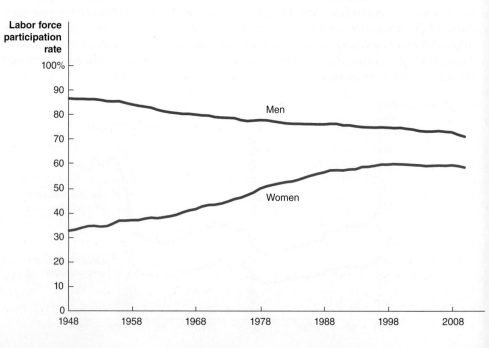

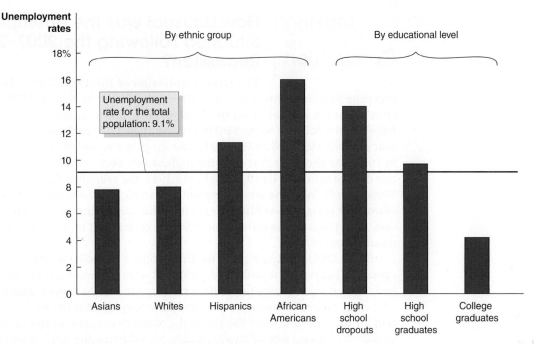

**Figure 20.4**    **Unemployment Rates in the United States, September 2011**

The unemployment rate of African Americans is the highest of the four ethnic groups shown, while the unemployment rate of Asians is the lowest. High school dropouts have an unemployment rate that is triple the unemployment rate for college graduates. *Notes:* The unemployment rates for ethnic groups apply to people 16 and older; the unemployment rates by educational attainment apply to people 25 and older. People identified as Hispanic may be of any race.

Data from U.S. Department of Labor, Bureau of Labor Statistics, *The Employment Situation—September 2011*, October 7, 2011.

labor force participation rate of women has several causes, including changing social attitudes due in part to the women's movement, federal legislation outlawing discrimination, increasing wages for women, and the typical family having fewer children.

## Unemployment Rates for Different Groups

Different groups in the population can have very different unemployment rates. Figure 20.4 shows unemployment rates in September 2011 for different ethnic groups and for groups with different levels of educational attainment. While the overall unemployment rate was 9.1 percent, Asians had an unemployment rate of 7.8 percent, and African Americans had an unemployment rate of 16.0 percent. The unemployment rate for people over age 25 without a high school degree was 14.0 percent, while the unemployment rate for college graduates was only 4.2 percent.

## How Long Are People Typically Unemployed?

The longer a person is unemployed, the greater the hardship. During the Great Depression of the 1930s, some people were unemployed for years at a time. In the modern U.S. economy, the typical unemployed person stays unemployed for a relatively brief period of time, although that time lengthens significantly during a severe recession. For example, in April 2007—which was during a period of economic expansion—82 percent of the people who were unemployed had been unemployed for less than six months. In September 2011, after the end of the 2007–2009 recession, but during a time when the economy was growing slowly, only 55 percent of the unemployed had been jobless for less than six months. The average period of unemployment was only 17 weeks in April 2007 but was 41 weeks in September 2011. The severity of unemployment during and after the 2007–2009 recession was a sharp break with the normal U.S. experience where the typical person who loses a job will find another one or be recalled to a previous job within a few months.

<table>
<tr><td>Making<br>the<br>Connection</td><td>

## How Unusual Was the Unemployment Situation Following the 2007–2009 Recession?

</td></tr>
</table>

The Great Depression of the 1930s left its mark on nearly everyone who lived through it. The Depression began in August 1929, became worse after the stock market crash of October 1929, and reached its low point in 1933, following the collapse of the banking system. Real GDP declined by more than 25 percent between 1929 and 1933—the largest drop ever recorded. The unemployment rate in 1933 was above 20 percent—the highest rate ever recorded. The unemployment rate did not return to its 1929 level until 1942, the year after the United States entered World War II. With the unemployment rate so high for so long, many people were out of work for years. As one historian put it, "What was distinctive about the Great Depression, in fact, was … the *extraordinary lengths of time* that most jobless men and women remained out of work."

By the 2000s, many people in the United States, including most economists and policymakers, believed that prolonged periods of unemployment such as the U.S. economy had suffered from during the 1930s were very unlikely to happen again. Although the 1981–1982 recession had been severe and the unemployment rate had risen above 10 percent for the first time since the 1930s, the recovery was strong, and many unemployed workers found new jobs relatively quickly. So, following the 2007–2009 recession, most economists and policymakers were unprepared for how slowly the unemployment rate declined and for how much the average period of unemployment rose. During the 1981–1982 recession, the unemployment rate peaked at 10.8 percent in December 1982, but 23 months later, in November 1984, it had already declined to 7.2 percent. In contrast, after the recession of 2007–2009, the unemployment rate peaked at 10.1 percent in October 2009, while 23 months later, it had declined by only 1 percentage point, to 9.1 percent. The figure below shows that the average period of unemployment was twice as high following the 2007–2009 recession as following any other recession since the end of World War II.

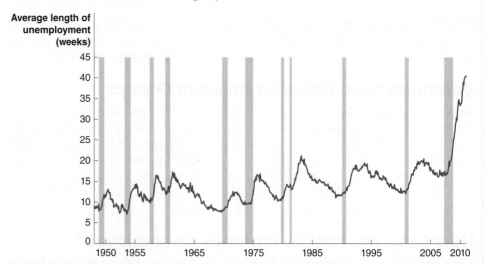

Unemployment was so persistent and widespread that a survey taken by the Pew Research Center in the spring of 2011 found that more than half of all households had experienced at least one member losing his or her job during the previous year. Another Pew survey taken in June 2011 found that more than half of people with jobs expected to receive a pay cut or to lose their job during the next year.

As we have seen, one drawback to the unemployment data is that workers who drop out of the labor market stop being counted as unemployed. As a result, some economists focus on the employment–population ratio because it measures the fraction of the population that has jobs. The figure on the next page shows the employment–population ratio for the period 1948 to 2011. The overall upward trend of the ratio reflects the increased labor force participation rate of women. In each recession, the employment–population ratio falls as some workers lose their jobs. The fall of the employment–population ratio was particularly dramatic during the recession of 2007–2009, and the ratio actually continued to decline during the two years following the end of the recession. The fall of the employment–population ratio may give an even better indication than does the unemployment rate of how weak the U.S. labor market was during and after the 2007–2009 recession.

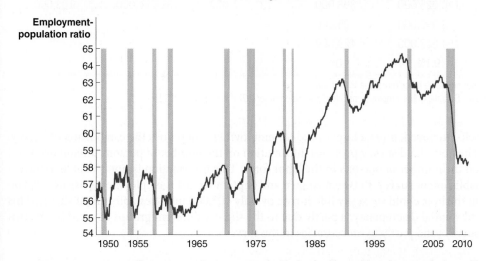

As we will see in later chapters, explaining the weakness of the U.S. labor market during and after the 2007–2009 recession had become a top priority of economists and policymakers.

Based on Alexander Keyssar, *Out of Work: The First Century of Unemployment in Massachusetts*, (New York: Cambridge University Press, 1986), p. 290; Federal Reserve Bank of St. Louis; U.S. Bureau of Labor Statistics; Pew Research Center, "The Recession, Economic Stress, and Optimism," May 4, 2011; and Pew Research Center, "Views of Personal Finances," June 23, 2011.

**Your Turn:** Test your understanding by doing related problem 1.11 on page 671 at the end of this chapter.    MyEconLab

---

# The Establishment Survey: Another Measure of Employment

In addition to the household survey, the BLS uses the *establishment survey*, sometimes called the *payroll survey*, to measure total employment in the economy. This monthly survey samples about 300,000 business establishments (such as factories, stores, and offices). A small company typically operates only one establishment, but a large company may operate many establishments. The establishment survey provides information on the total number of persons who are employed *and on a company payroll*. The establishment survey has four drawbacks. First, the survey does not provide information on the number of self-employed persons because they are not on a company payroll. Second, the survey may fail to count some persons employed at newly opened firms that are not included in the survey. Third, the survey provides no information on unemployment. Fourth, the initial employment values for the establishment survey can be significantly revised as data from additional establishments become available. Despite these drawbacks, the establishment survey has the advantage of being determined by actual payrolls rather than by unverified answers, as is the case with the household survey. In recent years, some economists have come to rely more on establishment survey data than on household survey data in analyzing current labor market conditions. Some financial analysts who forecast the future state of the economy to help forecast stock prices have also begun to rely more on establishment survey data than on household survey data.

Table 20.1 shows household survey and establishment survey data for the months of August and September 2011. Notice that the household survey, because it includes the

**Table 20.1** Household and Establishment Survey Data for August and September 2011

| | Household Survey | | | Establishment Survey | | |
|---|---|---|---|---|---|---|
| | August | September | Change | August | September | Change |
| Employed | 139,627,000 | 140,025,000 | 398,000 | 131,231,000 | 131,334,000 | 103,000 |
| Unemployed | 13,967,000 | 13,992,000 | 25,000 | | | |
| Labor force | 153,594,000 | 154,017,000 | 423,000 | | | |
| Unemployment rate | 9.1% | 9.1% | 0% | | | |

*Note:* The sum of employed and unemployed may not equal the labor force due to rounding.
Data from U.S. Department of Labor, Bureau of Labor Statistics, *The Employment Situation—September 2011*, October 7, 2011.

self-employed, gives a larger total for employment than does the establishment survey. The household survey provides information on the number of persons unemployed and on the number of persons in the labor force. This information is not available in the establishment survey. Between August and September 2011, employment rose by 398,000 in the household survey, while it rose by only 103,000 in the establishment survey. This substantial discrepancy is partly due to the slightly different groups covered by the two surveys and partly to inaccuracies in the surveys.

## Revisions in the Establishment Survey Employment Data: How Bad Was the 2007–2009 Recession?

Economists and policymakers rely on government economic data, such as the employment data from the establishment survey, to understand the current state of the economy. Given the size of the U.S. economy, though, government agencies, such as the Bureau of Economic Analysis, the Bureau of Labor Statistics, and the Census Bureau, need considerable time to gather complete and accurate data on GDP, employment, and other macroeconomic variables. To avoid long waits in supplying data to policymakers and the general public, government agencies typically issue preliminary estimates that they revise as additional information becomes available. As we noted earlier, the data from the BLS on employment as gathered in the establishment survey can be subject to particularly large revisions over time.

Figure 20.5 shows for each month from December 2007 to December 2010 the difference between the value for the change in employment as initially reported in the establishment survey and the revised value available in September 2011. The green bars show months for which the BLS revised its preliminary estimates to show that fewer jobs were lost (or more jobs were created) than originally reported, and the red bars show months for which the BLS revised its preliminary estimates to show that more jobs were lost (or fewer jobs were created). For example, the BLS initially reported that

### Figure 20.5

**Revisions to Employment Changes, as Reported in the Establishment Survey**

Over time, the BLS revises its preliminary estimates of changes in employment. During the 2007–2009 recession, many more jobs were lost than the preliminary estimates showed. The green bars show months for which the BLS revised its preliminary estimates to show fewer jobs lost (or more jobs created), and the red bars show months for which the BLS revised its preliminary estimates to show more jobs lost (or fewer jobs created).
Data from U.S. Bureau of Labor Statistics.

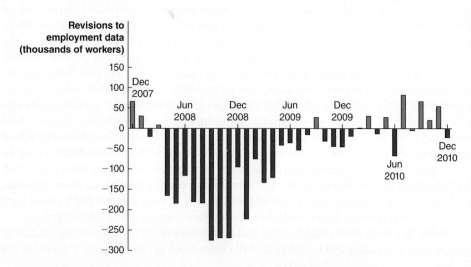

| | Number of Establishments | Number of Jobs |
|---|---|---|
| **Establishments Creating Jobs** | | |
| Existing establishments | 1,447,000 | 5,609,000 |
| New establishments | 382,000 | 1,345,000 |
| **Establishments Eliminating Jobs** | | |
| Existing establishments | 1,418,000 | 5,162,000 |
| Closing establishments | 352,000 | 1,229,000 |

**Table 20.2**

**Establishments Creating and Eliminating Jobs, September–December 2010**

Data from U.S. Bureau of Labor Statistics, *Business Employment Dynamics: Fourth Quarter 2010*, August 2, 2011.

employment declined by 159,000 jobs during September 2008. In fact, after additional data became available, the BLS revised its estimate to show that employment had declined by 434,000 jobs during the month—a difference of 275,000 more jobs lost. As the recession deepened between April 2008 and April 2009, the BLS's initial reports underestimated the number of jobs lost by 2.3 million. In other words, the recession of 2007–2009 turned out to be much more severe than economists and policymakers realized at the time.

## Job Creation and Job Destruction over Time

One important fact about employment is not very well known: The U.S. economy creates and destroys millions of jobs every year. In 2010, for example, about 26.6 million jobs were created, and about 25.4 million jobs were destroyed. This degree of job creation and destruction is not surprising in a vibrant market system where new firms are constantly being started, some existing firms are expanding, some existing firms are contracting, and some firms are going out of business. The creation and destruction of jobs results from changes in consumer tastes, technological progress, and the successes and failures of entrepreneurs in responding to the opportunities and challenges of shifting consumer tastes and technological change. The large volume of job creation and job destruction helps explain why during most years, the typical person who loses a job is unemployed for a relatively brief period of time.

*When the BLS announces each month the increases or decreases in the number of persons employed and unemployed, these are* net *figures.* That is, the change in the number of persons employed is equal to the total number of jobs created minus the number of jobs eliminated. Take, for example, the months from September to December 2010. During that period, 6,954,000 jobs were created, and 6,391,000 were eliminated, for a net increase of 563,000 jobs. Because the net change is so much smaller than the total job increases and decreases, the net change doesn't fully represent how dynamic the U.S. job market really is.

The data in Table 20.2 reinforce the idea of how large the volume of job creation and job elimination is over a period as brief as three months. The table shows the number of establishments (that is, offices, factories, or stores) creating and eliminating jobs during the period from September through December 2010. About 382,000 new establishments opened, creating 1.35 million new jobs, and 352,000 establishments closed, eliminating 1.23 million jobs.

## Types of Unemployment

Figure 20.6 illustrates that the unemployment rate follows the business cycle, rising during recessions and falling during expansions. Notice, though, that the unemployment rate never falls to zero. To understand why this is true, we need to discuss the three types of unemployment:

1. Frictional unemployment
2. Structural unemployment
3. Cyclical unemployment

**20.2 LEARNING** OBJECTIVE

Identify the three types of unemployment.

## Figure 20.6

### The Annual Unemployment Rate in the United States, 1950–2010

The unemployment rate rises during recessions and falls during expansions. Shaded areas indicate recessions.
Data from U.S. Bureau of Labor Statistics.

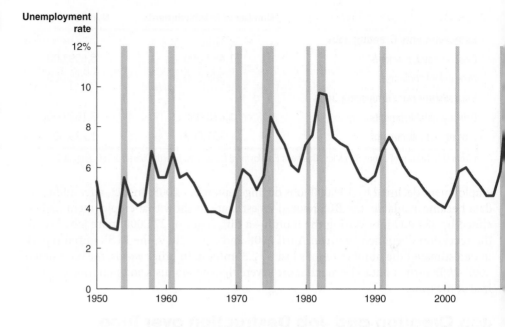

## Frictional Unemployment and Job Search

Workers have different skills, interests, and abilities, and jobs have different skill requirements, working conditions, and pay levels. As a result, a new worker entering the labor force or a worker who has lost a job probably will not find an acceptable job right away. Most workers spend at least some time engaging in *job search*, just as most firms spend time searching for a new person to fill a job opening. **Frictional unemployment** is short-term unemployment that arises from the process of matching workers with jobs. Some frictional unemployment is unavoidable. As we have seen, the U.S. economy creates and destroys millions of jobs each year. The process of job search takes time, so there will always be some workers who are frictionally unemployed because they are between jobs and in the process of searching for new ones.

**Frictional unemployment** Short-term unemployment that arises from the process of matching workers with jobs.

Some unemployment is due to seasonal factors, such as weather or fluctuations in demand for some products or services during different times of the year. For example, stores located in beach resort areas reduce their hiring during the winter, and ski resorts reduce their hiring during the summer. Department stores increase their hiring in November and December and reduce their hiring after New Year's Day. In agricultural areas, employment increases during harvest season and declines thereafter. Construction workers in many parts of the United States experience greater unemployment during the winter than during the summer. *Seasonal unemployment* refers to unemployment due to factors such as weather, variations in tourism, and other calendar-related events. Because seasonal unemployment can make the unemployment rate seem artificially high during some months and artificially low during other months, the BLS reports two unemployment rates each month—one that is *seasonally adjusted* and one that is not seasonally adjusted. The seasonally adjusted data eliminate the effects of seasonal unemployment. Economists and policymakers rely on the seasonally adjusted data as a more accurate measure of the current state of the labor market.

Would eliminating all frictional unemployment be good for the economy? No, because some frictional unemployment actually increases economic efficiency. Frictional unemployment occurs because workers and firms take the time necessary to ensure a good match between the attributes of workers and the characteristics of jobs. By devoting time to job search, workers end up with jobs they find satisfying and in which they can be productive. Of course, having more productive and better-satisfied workers is also in the best interest of firms.

# Structural Unemployment

By 2011, computer-generated three-dimensional animation, which was used in movies such as *Kung Fu Panda 2* and *Cars 2*, had become much more popular than traditional hand-drawn two-dimensional animation. Many people who were highly skilled in hand-drawn animation lost their jobs at Walt Disney Pictures, DreamWorks, and other movie studios. To become employed again, many of these people either became skilled in computer-generated animation or found new occupations. In the meantime, they were unemployed. Economists consider these animators *structurally unemployed*. **Structural unemployment** arises from a persistent mismatch between the job skills or attributes of workers and the requirements of jobs. While frictional unemployment is short term, structural unemployment can last for longer periods because workers need time to learn new skills. For example, employment by U.S. steel firms dropped by more than half between the early 1980s and the early 2000s as a result of competition from foreign producers and technological change that substituted machines for workers. Many steel-workers found new jobs in other industries only after lengthy periods of retraining.

Some workers lack even basic skills, such as literacy, or have addictions to alcohol or other drugs that make it difficult for them to perform adequately the duties of almost any job. These workers may remain structurally unemployed for years.

**Structural unemployment**
Unemployment that arises from a persistent mismatch between the skills and attributes of workers and the requirements of jobs.

# Cyclical Unemployment

When the economy moves into recession, many firms find their sales falling and cut back on production. As production falls, firms start laying off workers. Workers who lose their jobs because of a recession are experiencing **cyclical unemployment**. For example, Ford laid off workers during the recession of 2007–2009. As the economy slowly recovered from the recession, Ford began rehiring those workers. The Ford workers who had been laid off from their jobs during the recession and then rehired during the following expansion had experienced cyclical unemployment.

**Cyclical unemployment**
Unemployment caused by a business cycle recession.

# Full Employment

As the economy moves through the expansion phase of the business cycle, cyclical unemployment eventually drops to zero. The unemployment rate will not be zero, however, because of frictional and structural unemployment. As Figure 20.6 shows, the unemployment rate in the United States is rarely below 4 percent. When the only remaining unemployment is structural and frictional unemployment, the economy is said to be at *full employment*.

Economists consider frictional and structural unemployment as the normal underlying level of unemployment in the economy. The fluctuations around this normal level of unemployment that we see in Figure 20.6 are mainly due to the changes in the level of cyclical unemployment. This normal level of unemployment, which is the sum of frictional and structural unemployment, is called the **natural rate of unemployment**. Economists disagree on the exact value of the natural rate of unemployment, and there is good reason to believe it varies over time. Currently, most economists estimate the natural rate to be between 5 percent and 6 percent. The natural rate of unemployment is also sometimes called the *full-employment rate of unemployment*.

**Natural rate of unemployment**
The normal rate of unemployment, consisting of frictional unemployment plus structural unemployment.

## Making the Connection | How Should We Categorize Unemployment at Bank of America?

We saw at the beginning of the chapter that in the fall of 2011, Bank of America, the second largest bank in the United States, announced that it would be laying off 30,000 of its 288,000 employees. Was the unemployment caused by the layoffs at Bank of America frictional unemployment, structural unemployment, or cyclical unemployment? In answering this question, we should acknowledge that categorizing unemployment as frictional, structural, or cyclical is useful in understanding the sources of unemployment, but it can be difficult to apply

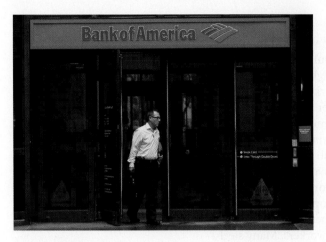

*The people who lost their jobs at Bank of America fit into more than one category of unemployment.*

these categories in a particular case. The BLS, for instance, provides estimates of total unemployment but does not classify it as frictional, structural, or cyclical.

Despite these difficulties, we can roughly categorize the unemployment caused by Bank of America's announcement. We begin by considering the three basic reasons the layoffs occurred: the long-term decline in the commercial banking sector; the recession of 2007–2009 that temporarily reduced the demand for mortgages and other loans; and the particular problems that Bank of America was experiencing in 2011. Each reason corresponds to a category of unemployment. During the housing boom of the mid-2000s, the financial sector of the economy, including banks, expanded rapidly. The financial sector began to contract during the recession of 2007–2009 as the need for mortgages and other loans began to decline. Employment in the financial sector was still declining in the fall of 2011. Although some of this decline was related to the severity of the recession and the slowness of the recovery, many economists believed that employment in the financial sector was unlikely to return to the levels seen at the height of the housing boom in 2005 and 2006. Therefore, some of the employees laid off by Bank of America were unlikely to find new jobs without leaving the financial sector, so they had become structurally unemployed. Some of the decline in demand for loans and other banking and financial services was due to the effects of the 2007–2009 recession rather than to long-term problems in the financial sector. So, some of the workers Bank of America laid off were cyclically unemployed and could expect to find other jobs with financial firms after the economic recovery strengthened.

Finally, Bank of America was suffering from some problems that were not shared by all other banks. In 2008, after the recession had already begun, Bank of America purchased Countrywide Financial for over $4 billion. Countrywide had been the leading mortgage lender in the United States. Unfortunately, many of its loans had been made to borrowers with poor credit who defaulted on their loans once housing prices began to decline. Managers at Bank of America had underestimated the problems at Countrywide, which continued to suffer losses into 2011. In addition, some of Countrywide's lending practices were disputed in lawsuits that might cost Bank of America billions of dollars to settle. Bank of America would have laid off fewer workers if it had not been suffering from these problems. As a result, it was likely that some of these workers would be able to find jobs at competing banks after relatively brief job searches. These workers were frictionally unemployed.

Based on Dan Fitzpatrick, "BofA Readies the Knife," *Wall Street Journal*, September 13, 2011; "Bank Withdrawals," *Economist*, August 9, 2011; and Nelson D. Schwartz, "Bank of America Confirms Plan to Cut 30,000 Positions," *New York Times*, September 12, 2011.

MyEconLab  **Your Turn:** Test your understanding by doing related problem 2.6 on page 671 at the end of this chapter.

---

**20.3 LEARNING** OBJECTIVE

Explain what factors determine the unemployment rate.

# Explaining Unemployment

We have seen that some unemployment is a result of the business cycle. In later chapters, we will explore the causes of the business cycle, which will help us understand the causes of cyclical unemployment. In this section, we will look at the factors that determine the levels of frictional and structural unemployment.

## Government Policies and the Unemployment Rate

Workers search for jobs by sending out resumes, registering with Internet job sites such as Monster.com, and getting job referrals from friends and relatives. Firms fill job openings by advertising in newspapers, listing openings online, participating in job fairs, and recruiting on college campuses. Government policy can aid these private efforts. Governments can help reduce the level of frictional unemployment by pursuing policies that help speed up the process of matching unemployed workers with unfilled jobs. Governments can help reduce structural unemployment by implementing policies that aid worker retraining. For example, the federal government's Trade Adjustment Assistance program offers training to workers whose firms laid them off as a result of competition from foreign firms.

Some government policies, however, can add to the level of frictional and structural unemployment. These government policies increase the unemployment rate either by increasing the time workers devote to searching for jobs, by providing disincentives for firms to hire workers, or by keeping wages above their market level.

**Unemployment Insurance and Other Payments to the Unemployed** Suppose you have been in the labor force for a few years but have just lost your job. You could probably find a low-wage job immediately if you needed to—perhaps at Wal-Mart or McDonald's. But you might decide to search for a better, higher-paying job by sending out resumes and responding to want ads and Internet job postings. Remember that the *opportunity cost* of any activity is the highest-valued alternative that you must give up to engage in that activity. In this case, the opportunity cost of continuing to search for a job is the salary you are giving up at the job you could have taken. The longer you search, the greater your chances of finding a better, higher-paying job, but the longer you search, the more salary you have given up by not working, so the greater the opportunity cost.

In the United States and most other industrial countries, the unemployed are eligible for *unemployment insurance payments* from the government. In the United States, these payments vary by state but are generally equal to about half the average wage. The unemployed spend more time searching for jobs because they receive these payments. This additional time spent searching raises the unemployment rate. Does this mean that the unemployment insurance program is a bad idea? Most economists would say no. Before Congress established the unemployment insurance program at the end of the 1930s, unemployed workers suffered very large declines in their incomes, which led them to greatly reduce their spending. This reduced spending contributed to the severity of recessions. Unemployment insurance helps the unemployed maintain their income and spending, which lessens the personal hardship of being unemployed and also helps reduce the severity of recessions.

In the United States, unemployed workers are generally eligible to receive unemployment insurance payments equal to about half their previous wage for only six months, although this period is typically extended during recessions, as happened during and after the recession of 2007–2009. After that, the opportunity cost of continuing to search for a job rises. In many other high-income countries, such as Canada and most of the countries of Western Europe, workers are eligible to receive unemployment payments for a year or more, and the payments may equal 70 percent to 80 percent of their previous wage. In addition, many of these countries have generous *social insurance programs* that allow unemployed adults to receive some government payments even after their eligibility for unemployment insurance has ended. In the United States, very few government programs make payments to healthy adults, with the exception of the Temporary Assistance for Needy Families program, which allows single parents to receive payments for up to five years. Although there are many reasons unemployment rates may differ across countries, most economists believe that because the opportunity cost of job search is lower in Canada and countries of Western Europe, unemployed workers in those countries search longer for jobs and, therefore, the unemployment rates in those countries tend to be higher than in the United States. During the 2007–2009 recession, however, unemployment rates were lower in Canada and Germany than in the United States.

**Minimum Wage Laws** In 1938, the federal government enacted a national minimum wage law. At first, the lowest legal wage firms could pay workers was $0.25 per hour. Over the years, Congress has gradually raised the minimum wage; in 2011, it was $7.25 per hour. Some states and cities also have minimum wage laws. For example, in 2011, the minimum wage in California was $8.00 per hour, and the minimum wage in

San Francisco was $9.92 per hour. If the minimum wage is set above the market wage determined by the demand and supply of labor, the quantity of labor supplied will be greater than the quantity of labor demanded. Some workers will be unemployed who would have been employed if there were no minimum wage. As a result, the unemployment rate will be higher than it would be without a minimum wage. Economists agree that the current minimum wage is above the market wage for some workers, but they disagree on the amount of unemployment that has resulted. Because teenagers generally have relatively few job-related skills, they are the group most likely to receive the minimum wage. Studies estimate that a 10 percent increase in the minimum wage reduces teenage employment by about 2 percent. Because teenagers and others receiving the minimum wage are a relatively small part of the labor force, most economists believe that, at its present level, the effect of the minimum wage on the unemployment rate in the United States is fairly small.

## Labor Unions

*Labor unions* are organizations of workers that bargain with employers for higher wages and better working conditions for their members. In unionized industries, the wage is usually above what otherwise would be the market wage. This above-market wage results in employers in unionized industries hiring fewer workers, but does it also significantly increase the overall unemployment rate in the economy? Most economists would say the answer is "no" because only about 9 percent of workers outside the government sector are unionized. Although unions remain strong in a few industries, such as airlines, automobiles, steel, and telecommunications, most industries in the United States are not unionized. The result is that most workers who can't find jobs in unionized industries because the wage is above its market level can find jobs in other industries.

## Efficiency Wages

**Efficiency wage** A higher-than-market wage that a firm pays to increase worker productivity.

Many firms pay higher-than-market wages not because the government requires them to or because they are unionized but because they believe doing so will increase their profits. This may seem like a paradox: Wages are the largest cost for many employers, so paying higher wages seems like a good way for firms to lower profits rather than to increase them. The key to understanding the paradox is that the level of wages can affect the level of worker productivity. Many studies have shown that workers are motivated by higher wages to work harder. An **efficiency wage** is a higher-than-market wage that a firm pays to motivate workers to be more productive. Can't firms ensure that workers work hard by supervising them? In some cases, they can. For example, a telemarketing firm can monitor workers electronically to ensure that they make the required number of phone calls per hour. In many business situations, however, it is much more difficult to monitor workers. Many firms must rely on workers being motivated enough to work hard. By paying a wage above the market wage, a firm raises the costs to workers of losing their jobs because many alternative jobs will pay only the market wage. The increase in productivity that results from paying the high wage can more than offset the extra cost of the wage, thereby lowering the firm's costs of production.

Because the efficiency wage is above the market wage, it results in the quantity of labor supplied being greater than the quantity of labor demanded, just as do minimum wage laws and unions. So, efficiency wages are another reason economies experience some unemployment even when cyclical unemployment is zero.

**20.4 LEARNING** OBJECTIVE

Define price level and inflation rate and understand how they are computed.

# Measuring Inflation

One of the facts of economic life is that the prices of most goods and services rise over time. As a result, the cost of living continually rises. In 1914, Henry Ford began paying his workers a wage of $5 per day, which was more than twice as much as other automobile manufacturers were paying. Ford's $5-a-day wage provided his workers with a middle-class income because prices were so low. In 1914, Ford's Model T, the best-selling car in the country, sold for less than $600, the price of a man's suit was $15, the price of a ticket to a movie theater was $0.15, and the price of a box of Kellogg's Corn Flakes was $0.08. In 2011, with the cost of living being much higher than it was in 1914, the minimum wage law required firms to pay a wage of at least $7.25 per *hour*, more than Ford's highly paid workers earned in a day.

Knowing how the government compiles the employment and unemployment statistics is important in interpreting them. The same is true of the government's statistics on the cost of living. As we saw in Chapter 19, the **price level** measures the average prices of goods and services in the economy. The **inflation rate** is the percentage increase in the price level from one year to the next. In Chapter 19, we introduced the *GDP deflator* as a measure of the price level. The GDP deflator is the broadest measure we have of the price level because it includes the price of every final good and service. But for some purposes it is too broad. For example, if we want to know how inflation affects the typical household, the GDP price deflator may be misleading because it includes the prices of products such as large electric generators and machine tools that are included in the investment component of GDP but are not purchased by the typical household. In this chapter, we will focus on measuring the inflation rate by changes in the *consumer price index* because changes in this index come closest to measuring changes in the cost of living as experienced by the typical household. We will also briefly discuss a third measure of inflation: the *producer price index*.

**Price level** A measure of the average prices of goods and services in the economy.

**Inflation rate** The percentage increase in the price level from one year to the next.

## The Consumer Price Index

To obtain prices of a representative group of goods and services, the BLS surveys 30,000 households nationwide on their spending habits. It uses the results of this survey to construct a *market basket* of 211 types of goods and services purchased by the typical urban family of four. Figure 20.7 shows the goods and services in the market basket, grouped into eight broad categories. Almost three-quarters of the market basket falls into the categories of housing, transportation, and food. Each month, hundreds of BLS employees visit 23,000 stores in 87 cities and record prices of the goods and services in the market basket. Each price in the consumer price index is given a weight equal to the fraction of the typical family's budget spent on that good or service. The **consumer price index (CPI)** is an average of the prices of the goods and services purchased by the typical urban family of four. One year is chosen as the base year, and the value of the CPI is set equal to 100 for that year. In any year other than the base year, the CPI is equal to the ratio of the dollar amount necessary to buy the market basket of goods in that year divided by the dollar amount necessary to buy the market basket of goods in

**Consumer price index (CPI)** An average of the prices of the goods and services purchased by the typical urban family of four.

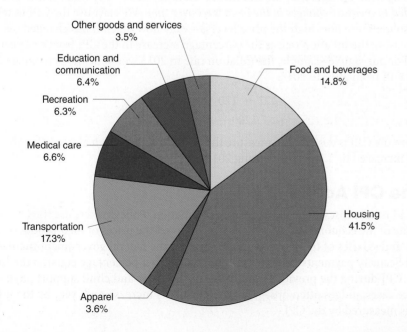

Other goods and services
3.5%

Education and communication
6.4%

Recreation
6.3%

Medical care
6.6%

Transportation
17.3%

Apparel
3.6%

Food and beverages
14.8%

Housing
41.5%

**Figure 20.7**

**The CPI Market Basket, December 2010**

The Bureau of Labor Statistics surveys 30,000 households on their spending habits. The results are used to construct a *market basket* of goods and services purchased by the typical urban family of four. The chart shows these goods and services, grouped into eight broad categories. The percentages represent the expenditure shares of the categories within the market basket. The categories of housing, transportation, and food make up about three-quarters of the market basket. Data from U.S. Bureau of Labor Statistics.

the base year, multiplied by 100. Because the CPI measures the cost to the typical family to buy a representative basket of goods and services, it is sometimes referred to as the *cost-of-living index.*

A simple example can clarify how the CPI is constructed. For purposes of this example, we assume that the market basket has only three products: eye examinations, pizzas, and books:

| Product | Base Year (1999) Quantity | Price | Expenditures | 2012 Price | 2012 Expenditures (on base-year quantities) | 2013 Price | 2013 Expenditures (on base-year quantities) |
|---|---|---|---|---|---|---|---|
| Eye examinations | 1 | $50.00 | $50.00 | $100.00 | $100.00 | $85.00 | $85.00 |
| Pizzas | 20 | 10.00 | 200.00 | 15.00 | 300.00 | 14.00 | 280.00 |
| Books | 20 | 25.00 | 500.00 | 25.00 | 500.00 | 27.50 | 550.00 |
| TOTAL | | | $750.00 | | $900.00 | | $915.00 |

Suppose that during the base year, 1999, a survey determines that each month, the typical family purchases 1 eye examination, 20 pizzas, and 20 books. At 1999 prices, the typical family must spend $750.00 to purchase this market basket of goods and services. The CPI for every year after the base year is determined by dividing the amount necessary to purchase the market basket in that year by the amount required in the base year, then multiplying by 100. Notice that the quantities of the products purchased in 2012 and 2013 are irrelevant in calculating the CPI because *we are assuming that households buy the same market basket of products each month.* Using the numbers in the table, we can calculate the CPI for 2012 and 2013:

| Formula | Applied to 2012 | Applied to 2013 |
|---|---|---|
| $CPI = \dfrac{\text{Expenditures in the current year}}{\text{Expenditures in the base year}} \times 100$ | $\left(\dfrac{\$900}{\$750}\right) \times 100 = 120$ | $\left(\dfrac{\$915}{\$750}\right) \times 100 = 122$ |

How do we interpret values such as 120 and 122? First, recognize that they are *index numbers*, which means they are not measured in dollars or any other units. *The CPI is intended to measure changes in the price level over time.* We can't use the CPI to tell us in an absolute sense how high the price level is—only how much it has changed over time. We measure the inflation rate as the percentage increase in the CPI from one year to the next. For our simple example, the inflation rate in 2013 would be the percentage change in the CPI from 2012 to 2013:

$$\left(\frac{122-120}{120}\right) \times 100 = 1.7\%.$$

Because the CPI is designed to measure the cost of living, we can also say that the cost of living increased by 1.7 percent during 2013.

## Is the CPI Accurate?

The CPI is the most widely used measure of inflation. Policymakers use the CPI to track the state of the economy. Businesses use it to help set the prices of their products and the wages and salaries of their employees. Each year, the federal government increases the Social Security payments made to retired workers by a percentage equal to the increase in the CPI during the previous year. In setting alimony and child support payments in divorce cases, judges often order that the payments increase each year by the inflation rate, as measured by the CPI.

# Don't Let This Happen to You

## Don't Miscalculate the Inflation Rate

Suppose you are given the data in the following table and are asked to calculate the inflation rate for 2010:

| Year | CPI |
|------|-----|
| 2009 | 216 |
| 2010 | 219 |

It is tempting to avoid any calculations and simply to report that the inflation rate in 2010 was 119 percent because 219 is a 119 percent increase from 100. But 119 percent would be the wrong answer. A value for the CPI of 219 in

2010 tells us that the price level in 2010 was 119 percent higher than in the base year, but the inflation rate is the percentage increase in the price level from the previous year, *not* the percentage increase from the base year. The correct calculation of the inflation rate for 2010 is:

$$\left( \frac{219 - 216}{216} \right) \times 100 = 1.4\%.$$

MyEconLab

**Your Turn:** Test your understanding by doing related problem 4.5 on page 672 at the end of this chapter.

It is important that the CPI be as accurate as possible, but there are four biases that cause changes in the CPI to overstate the true inflation rate:

- *Substitution bias.* In constructing the CPI, the BLS assumes that each month, consumers purchase the same amount of each product in the market basket. In fact, consumers are likely to buy fewer of those products that increase most in price and more of those products that increase least in price (or fall the most in price). For instance, if apple prices rise rapidly during the month while orange prices fall, consumers will reduce their apple purchases and increase their orange purchases. Therefore, the prices of the market basket consumers actually buy will rise less than the prices of the market basket the BLS uses to compute the CPI.

- *Increase in quality bias.* Over time, most products included in the CPI improve in quality: Automobiles become more durable and side air bags become standard equipment, computers become faster and have more memory, dishwashers use less water while getting dishes cleaner, and so on. Increases in the prices of these products partly reflect their improved quality and partly are pure inflation. The BLS attempts to make adjustments so that only the pure inflation part of price increases is included in the CPI. These adjustments are difficult to make, however, so the recorded price increases overstate the pure inflation in some products.

- *New product bias.* For many years, the BLS updated the market basket of goods used in computing the CPI only every 10 years. So, new products introduced between updates were not included in the market basket. For example, the 1987 update took place before cell phones were introduced. Although millions of American households used cell phones by the mid-1990s, they were not included in the CPI until the 1997 update. The prices of many products, such as cell phones, Blu-ray players, and LED televisions, decrease in the years immediately after they are introduced. If the market basket is not updated frequently, these price decreases are not included in the CPI.

- *Outlet bias.* During the mid-1990s, many consumers began to increase their purchases from discount stores such as Sam's Club and Costco. By the late 1990s, the Internet began to account for a significant fraction of sales of some products. Because the BLS continued to collect price statistics from traditional full-price retail stores, the CPI did not reflect the prices some consumers actually paid.

Most economists believe these biases cause changes in the CPI to overstate the true inflation rate by 0.5 percentage point to 1 percentage point. That is, if the CPI indicates that the inflation rate was 3 percent, it is probably between 2 percent and 2.5 percent. The BLS continues to take steps to reduce the size of the bias. For example, the BLS has reduced the size of the substitution and new product biases by updating the market basket every 2 years rather than every 10 years. The BLS has reduced the size of the outlet bias by conducting a point-of-purchase survey to track where consumers actually make their purchases. Finally, the BLS has used statistical methods to reduce the size of the quality bias. Prior to these changes, the size of the total bias in the CPI was probably greater than 1 percent.

## The Producer Price Index

**Producer price index (PPI)** An average of the prices received by producers of goods and services at all stages of the production process.

In addition to the GDP deflator and the CPI, the government also computes the **producer price index (PPI)**. Like the CPI, the PPI tracks the prices of a market basket of goods. But, whereas the CPI tracks the prices of goods and services purchased by the typical household, the PPI tracks the prices firms receive for goods and services at all stages of production. The PPI includes the prices of intermediate goods, such as flour, cotton, yarn, steel, and lumber; and raw materials, such as raw cotton, coal, and crude petroleum. If the prices of these goods rise, the cost to firms of producing final goods and services will rise, which may lead firms to increase the prices of goods and services purchased by consumers. Changes in the PPI therefore can give an early warning of future movements in the CPI.

**20.5 LEARNING** OBJECTIVE

Use price indexes to adjust for the effects of inflation.

# Using Price Indexes to Adjust for the Effects of Inflation

You are likely to receive a much higher salary after graduation than your parents did 25 or more years ago, but prices 25 years ago were, on average, much lower than prices today. Put another way, the purchasing power of a dollar was much higher 25 years ago because the prices of most goods and services were much lower. Price indexes such as the CPI give us a way of adjusting for the effects of inflation so that we can compare dollar values from different years. For example, suppose your mother received a salary of $20,000 in 1984. By using the CPI, we can calculate what $20,000 in 1984 was equivalent to in 2010. The consumer price index is 104 for 1984 and 219 for 2010. Because 219/104 = 2.1, we know that, on average, prices were about 2.1 times as high in 2010 as in 1984. We can use this result to inflate a salary of $20,000 received in 1984 to its value in terms of 2010 purchasing power:

$$\text{Value in 2010 dollars} = \text{Value in 1984 dollars} \times \left( \frac{\text{CPI in 2010}}{\text{CPI in 1984}} \right)$$
$$= \$20,000 \times \left( \frac{219}{104} \right) = \$42,115.$$

Our calculation shows that if you were paid a salary of $42,115 in 2010, you would be able to purchase roughly the same amount of goods and services that your mother could have purchased with a salary of $20,000 in 1984. Economic variables that are calculated in current-year prices are referred to as *nominal variables*. The calculation we have just made uses a price index to adjust a nominal variable—your mother's salary—for the effects of inflation.

For some purposes, we are interested in tracking changes in an economic variable over time rather than in seeing what its value would be in today's dollars. In that case, to correct for the effects of inflation, we can divide the nominal variable by a price index and multiply by 100 to obtain a *real variable*. The real variable will be measured in dollars of the base year for the price index. Currently, the base year for the CPI is the average of prices in the years 1982 to 1984.

# Solved Problem 20.5

## Calculating Real Average Hourly Earnings

In addition to data on employment, the BLS establishment survey gathers data on average hourly earnings of production workers. Production workers are all workers, except for managers and professionals. Average hourly earnings are the wages or salaries earned by these workers per hour. Economists closely follow average hourly earnings because they are a broad measure of the typical worker's income. Use the information in the following table to calculate real average hourly earnings for each year. What was the percentage change in real average hourly earnings between 2009 and 2010?

| Year | Nominal Average Hourly Earnings | CPI (1982–1984 = 100) |
|------|------|------|
| 2008 | $21.62 | 216.2 |
| 2009 | 22.21 | 215.9 |
| 2010 | 22.59 | 218.6 |

## Solving the Problem

**Step 1:** **Review the chapter material.** This problem is about using price indexes to correct for inflation, so you may want to review the section "Using Price Indexes to Adjust for the Effects of Inflation" on page 660.

**Step 2:** **Calculate real average hourly earnings for each year.** To calculate real average hourly earnings for each year, divide nominal average hourly earnings by the CPI and multiply by 100. For example, real average hourly earnings for 2008 are equal to

$$\left(\frac{\$21.62}{216.2}\right) \times 100 = \$10.00.$$

These are the results for all three years:

| Year | Nominal Average Hourly Earnings | CPI (1982–1984 = 100) | Real Average Hourly Earnings (1982–1984 dollars) |
|------|------|------|------|
| 2008 | $21.62 | 216.2 | $10.00 |
| 2009 | 22.21 | 215.9 | 10.29 |
| 2010 | 22.59 | 218.6 | 10.33 |

**Step 3:** **Calculate the percentage change in real average earnings from 2009 to 2010.** This percentage change is equal to

$$\left(\frac{\$10.33 - \$10.29}{\$10.29}\right) \times 100 = 0.4\%.$$

We can conclude that real average hourly earnings increased slightly between 2009 and 2010.

**Extra Credit:** The values we computed for real average hourly earnings are in 1982–1984 dollars. Because this period is more than 25 years ago, the values are somewhat difficult to interpret. We can convert the earnings to 2010 dollars by using the method we used earlier to calculate your mother's salary. But notice that, for purposes of calculating the *change* in the value of real average hourly earnings over time, the base year of the price index doesn't matter. The change from 2009 to 2010 would have still been 0.4 percent, no matter what the base year of the price index was. If you don't see that this is true, test it by using the mother's salary method to calculate real average hourly earnings for 2009 and 2010 in 2010 dollars. Then calculate the percentage change. Unless you make an arithmetic error, you should find that the answer is still 0.4 percent.

MyEconLab **Your Turn:** For more practice, do related problems 5.3, 5.4, 5.5, and 5.6 on pages 673–674 at the end of this chapter.

---

**20.6 LEARNING** OBJECTIVE

Distinguish between the nominal interest rate and the real interest rate.

**Nominal interest rate** The stated interest rate on a loan.

**Real interest rate** The nominal interest rate minus the inflation rate.

# Real versus Nominal Interest Rates

The difference between nominal and real values is important when money is being borrowed and lent. As we saw in Chapter 8, the *interest rate* is the cost of borrowing funds, expressed as a percentage of the amount borrowed. If you lend someone $1,000 for one year and charge an interest rate of 6 percent, the borrower will pay back $1,060, or 6 percent more than the amount you lent. But is $1,060 received one year from now really 6 percent more than $1,000 today? If prices rise during the year, you will not be able to buy as much with $1,060 one year from now as you could with that amount today. Your true return from lending the $1,000 is equal to the percentage change in your purchasing power after taking into account the effects of inflation.

The stated interest rate on a loan is the **nominal interest rate**. The **real interest rate** corrects the nominal interest rate for the effect of inflation on purchasing power. As a simple example, suppose that the only good you purchase is DVDs, and at the beginning of the year, the price of DVDs is $10.00. With $1,000, you can purchase 100 DVDs. If you lend the $1,000 out for one year at an interest rate of 6 percent, you will receive $1,060 at the end of the year. Suppose the inflation rate during the year is 2 percent, so that the price of DVDs has risen to $10.20 by the end of the year. How has your purchasing power increased as a result of making the loan? At the beginning of the year, your $1,000 could purchase 100 DVDs. At the end of the year, your $1,060 can purchase $1,060/$10.20 = 103.92 DVDs. In other words, you can purchase almost 4 percent more DVDs. So, in this case, the real interest rate you received from lending was a little less than 4 percent (actually, 3.92 percent). For low rates of inflation, a convenient approximation for the real interest rate is

$$\text{Real interest rate} = \text{Nominal interest rate} - \text{Inflation rate}.$$

In our example, we can calculate the real interest rate by using this formula as 6 percent − 2 percent = 4 percent, which is close to the actual value of 3.92 percent. If the inflation rate during the year was 4 percent, the real interest rate would be only 2 percent. Holding the nominal interest rate constant, the higher the inflation rate, the lower the real interest rate. Notice that if the inflation rate turns out to be higher than expected, borrowers pay and lenders receive a lower real interest rate than either of them expected. For example, if both you and the person to whom you lent the $1,000 expected the inflation rate to be 2 percent, you both expected the real interest rate on the loan to be 4 percent. If inflation actually turns out to be 4 percent, the real interest rate on the loan will be 2 percent: That's bad news for you but good news for your borrower.

For the economy as a whole, we can measure the nominal interest rate as the interest rate on three-month U.S. Treasury bills. U.S. Treasury bills are short-term loans investors make to the federal government. We can use inflation as measured by changes in the CPI to calculate the real interest rate on Treasury bills. Figure 20.8 shows the nominal and real interest rates for the years 1970 through 2010. Notice that when the inflation rate is low, as it has been during most years since the early 1990s, the gap between the nominal and real interest rates is small. When the inflation rate is high, as it was during the mid- to late 1970s, the gap between the nominal and real interest rates becomes large. In fact, a particular nominal interest rate can be associated in different periods with very different real interest rates. For example, during late 1975, the nominal interest rate was about 5.5 percent, but because the inflation rate was 7 percent,

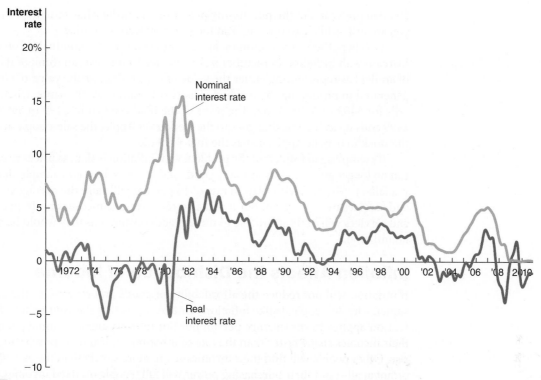

**Figure 20.8**    **Nominal and Real Interest Rates, 1970–2010**

The real interest rate is equal to the nominal interest rate minus the inflation rate. The real interest rate provides a better measure of the true cost of borrowing and the true return on lending than does the nominal interest rate. The nominal interest rate in the figure is the interest rate on three-month U.S. Treasury bills.

The inflation rate is measured by the percentage change in the CPI from the same quarter during the previous year.
Data from Federal Reserve Bank of St. Louis.

the real interest rate was −1.5 percent. In early 1987, the nominal interest rate was also 5.5 percent, but because the inflation rate was only 2 percent, the real interest rate was 3.5 percent.

This example shows that it is impossible to know whether a particular nominal interest rate is "high" or "low." It all depends on the inflation rate. *The real interest rate provides a better measure of the true cost of borrowing and the true return from lending than does the nominal interest rate.* When firms are deciding whether to borrow the funds to buy an investment good, such as a new factory, they will look at the real interest rate because the real interest rate measures the true cost to the firm of borrowing.

Is it possible for the nominal interest rate to be less than the real interest rate? Yes, but only when the inflation rate is negative. A negative inflation rate is referred to as **deflation** and occurs on the rare occasions when the price level falls. During the years shown in Figure 20.8, the inflation rate as measured by changes in the CPI was only negative during the first nine months of 2009.

**Deflation** A decline in the price level.

# Does Inflation Impose Costs on the Economy?

**20.7 LEARNING** OBJECTIVE

Discuss the problems that inflation causes.

Imagine waking up tomorrow morning and finding that every price in the economy has doubled. The prices of food, gasoline, DVDs, computers, houses, and haircuts have all doubled. But suppose that all wages and salaries have also doubled. Will this doubling of prices and wages matter? Think about walking into Best Buy, expecting to find an iPad selling for $499. Instead, you find it selling for $998. Will you turn around and walk out? Probably not, because your salary has also increased overnight from $45,000 per year to

$90,000 per year. So, the purchasing power of your salary has remained the same, and you are just as likely to buy the iPad today as you were yesterday.

This hypothetical situation makes an important point: Nominal incomes generally increase with inflation. Remember from Chapter 19 that we can think of the $499 price of an iPad as representing either the value of the product or the value of all the income generated in producing the product. The two amounts are the same, whether the iPad sells for $499 or $998. When the price of the iPad rises from $499 to $998, that extra $499 ends up as income that goes to the workers at Apple, the salespeople at Best Buy, or the stockholders of Apple, just as the first $499 did.

It's tempting to think that the problem with inflation is that, as prices rise, consumers can no longer afford to buy as many goods and services, but our example shows that this is a fallacy. An expected inflation rate of 10 percent will raise the average price of goods and services by 10 percent, but it will also raise average incomes by 10 percent. Goods and services will be as affordable to the average consumer as they would be if there were no inflation.

## Inflation Affects the Distribution of Income

If inflation will not reduce the affordability of goods and services to the average consumer, why do people dislike inflation? One reason is that the argument in the previous section applies to the *average* person but not to every person. Some people will find their incomes rising faster than the rate of inflation, and so their purchasing power will rise. Other people will find their incomes rising more slowly than the rate of inflation—or not at all—and their purchasing power will fall. People on fixed incomes are particularly likely to be hurt by inflation. If a retired worker receives a pension fixed at $3,000 per month, over time, inflation will reduce the purchasing power of that payment. In that way, inflation can change the distribution of income in a manner that strikes many people as being unfair.

The extent to which inflation redistributes income depends in part on whether the inflation is *anticipated*—in which case consumers, workers, and firms can see it coming and can prepare for it—or *unanticipated*—in which case they do not see it coming and do not prepare for it.

## The Problem with Anticipated Inflation

Like many of life's problems, inflation is easier to manage if you see it coming. Suppose that everyone knows that the inflation rate for the next 10 years will be 10 percent per year. Workers know that unless their wages go up by at least 10 percent per year, the real purchasing power of their wages will fall. Businesses will be willing to increase workers' wages enough to compensate for inflation because they know that the prices of the products they sell will increase. Lenders will realize that the loans they make will be paid back with dollars that are losing 10 percent of their value each year, so they will charge a higher interest rate to compensate. Borrowers will be willing to pay these higher interest rates because they also know they are paying back these loans with dollars that are losing value. So far, there don't seem to be costs to anticipated inflation.

Even when inflation is perfectly anticipated, however, some individuals will experience a cost. Inevitably, there will be a redistribution of income, as some people's incomes fall behind even an anticipated level of inflation. In addition, firms and consumers have to hold some paper money to facilitate their buying and selling. Anyone holding paper money will find its purchasing power decreasing each year by the rate of inflation. To avoid this cost, workers and firms will try to hold as little paper money as possible, but they will have to hold some. In addition, firms that print catalogs listing the prices of their products will have to reprint them more frequently. Supermarkets and other stores that mark prices on packages or on store shelves will have to devote more time and labor to changing the marked prices. The costs to firms of changing prices are called **menu costs**. At moderate levels of anticipated inflation, menu costs are relatively small, but at very high levels of inflation, such as those experienced in

**Menu costs** The costs to firms of changing prices.

some developing countries, menu costs and the costs due to paper money losing value can become substantial. Finally, even anticipated inflation acts to raise the taxes paid by investors and raises the cost of capital for business investment. These effects arise because investors are taxed on the nominal payments they receive rather than on the real payments.

## The Problem with Unanticipated Inflation

In any high-income economy—such as the United States—households, workers, and firms routinely enter into contracts that commit them to make or receive certain payments for years in the future. For example, when firms sign wage contracts, they commit to paying a specified wage for the duration of the contract. When people buy homes, they usually borrow most of the amount they need from a bank. These loans, called *mortgage loans*, commit a borrower to make a fixed monthly payment for the length of the loan. Most mortgage loans are for long periods, often as long as 30 years.

To make these long-term commitments, households, workers, and firms must forecast the rate of inflation. If a firm believes the inflation rate over the next three years will be 6 percent per year, signing a three-year contract with a union that calls for wage increases of 8 percent per year may seem reasonable because the firm may be able to raise its prices by at least the rate of inflation each year. If the firm believes that the inflation rate will be only 2 percent over the next three years, paying wage increases of 8 percent may significantly reduce its profits or even force it out of business.

When people borrow money or banks lend money, they must forecast the inflation rate so they can calculate the real rate of interest on a loan. In 1980, banks were charging interest rates of 18 percent or more on mortgage loans. This rate seems very high compared to the less than 5 percent charged on such loans in 2011, but the inflation rate in 1980 was more than 13 percent and was expected to remain high. In fact, the inflation rate declined unexpectedly during the early 1980s. By 1983, the inflation rate was only about 3 percent. People who borrowed money for 30 years at the high interest rates of 1980 soon found that the real interest rate on their loans was much higher than they expected.

When the actual inflation rate turns out to be very different from the expected inflation rate, some people gain, and other people lose. This outcome seems unfair to most people because they are either winning or losing only because something unanticipated has happened. This apparently unfair redistribution is a key reason people dislike unanticipated inflation.

| Making | What's So Bad about Falling Prices? |
|---|---|
| the Connection | |

We have just discussed how inflation being higher than expected can cause problems for consumers, workers, and firms. But what if an economy begins to experience falling prices—*deflation*, rather than inflation? A falling price level might seem like good news for the economy. After all, falling prices should encourage consumers to increase their spending as goods and services become less expensive. In fact, though, deflation tends to have the opposite effect on consumers. Episodes of deflation are relatively rare, but we can draw some lessons from two important deflationary episodes: the United States during the 1930s and Japan during the 1990s. In both cases, many consumers reduced their spending in the face of falling prices, apparently because they were waiting for prices to go even lower. Waiting for falling prices to go even lower was also a problem for the U.S. housing market in the late 2000s. A large run-up in housing prices took place from 2002 to 2006. When prices began to decline, many potential buyers postponed purchases in the expectation that prices would continue to fall.

The figure on the next page shows annual changes in the consumer price index in the United States during the years between 1925 and 1940. The beginning of the Great Depression in 1929 caused the country to experience severe deflation.

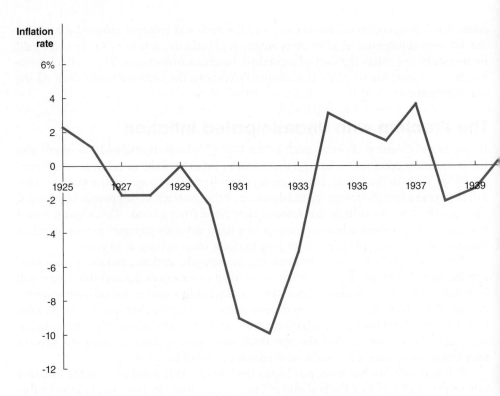

The deflation of the 1930s hurt the U.S. economy not just because it may have led some consumers to postpone purchases but also because it increased the burden on borrowers. For example, suppose that in 1929 you had borrowed money for five years at a nominal interest rate of 5 percent. What real interest rate would you have paid during those years? We have seen that to calculate the real interest rate, we need to subtract the inflation rate from the nominal interest rate. With deflation, the change in the price level is negative, so to calculate the real interest rate, we are in effect *adding* the change in the price level to the nominal interest rate. The following table uses the actual deflation rate in each year to calculate the resulting real interest rates on your loan:

|                                      | 1929 | 1930 | 1931 | 1932 | 1933 |
|--------------------------------------|------|------|------|------|------|
| Nominal interest rate                | 5%   | 5%   | 5%   | 5%   | 5%   |
| Change in the consumer price index   | 0    | −2.3 | −9.0 | −9.9 | −5.1 |
| Real interest rate                   | 5    | 7.30 | 14.00| 14.90| 10.10|

The bottom row of the table shows that although the nominal interest rate on your loan is only 5 percent, in three of the five years the real interest rate you pay is greater than 10 percent. In fact, high real interest rates inflicted serious losses on both household and business borrowers during the early 1930s and contributed to the severity of the Great Depression.

During the 2001 and 2007–2009 recessions, some policymakers and economists feared that the U.S. economy would experience deflation. Fortunately, significant deflation did not occur. If it had, those recessions would likely have been more severe than they were.

MyEconLab **Your Turn:** Test your understanding by doing related problem 7.9 on page 675 at the end of this chapter.

Continued from page 641

## Economics in Your Life

At the beginning of this chapter, we asked whether layoffs in the banking industry should cause you to change your major and give up your plans to pursue a career in banking. We have learned in this chapter that unemployment rates are higher and layoffs are more common in a recession than in an economic expansion. Because you are a sophomore, you will graduate a few years later, when the recession will likely have ended and the unemployment rate will have declined. You might also want to investigate whether the layoffs in the banking industry represent a permanent contraction in the size of the industry or whether they reflect a temporary decline due to the recession. If the reduction of banking jobs is more likely to be permanent, then you might consider a career in another industry. If the layoffs appear to be related to the current recession, then you probably do not need to change your career plans.

## Conclusion

Inflation and unemployment are key macroeconomic problems. Presidential elections are often won and lost on the basis of which candidate is able to convince the public that he or she can best deal with these problems. Many economists, however, would argue that, in the long run, maintaining high rates of growth of real GDP per person is the most important macroeconomic concern. Only when real GDP per person is increasing will a country's standard of living increase. We turn in the next chapter to discussing the important issue of economic growth.

Read *An Inside Look* on the next page for a discussion of cost-cutting proposals by officials at the U.S. Postal Service for dealing with a loss of $8 billion in 2010.

## ASSOCIATED PRESS

## Postal Service Considers Cutting 120,000 Jobs

The financially strapped U.S. Postal Service is considering cutting as many as 120,000 jobs.

Facing a second year of losses totaling $8 billion or more, the agency also wants to pull its workers out of the retirement and health benefits plans covering federal workers and set up its own benefit systems.

Congressional approval would be needed for either step, and both could be expected to face severe opposition from postal unions which have contracts that ban layoffs.

**a** The post office has cut 110,000 jobs over the last four years and is currently engaged in eliminating 7,500 administrative staff.

But the loss of mail to the Internet and the decline in advertising caused by the recession have rocked the agency.

Postal officials have said they will be unable to make a $5.5 billion payment to cover future employee health care costs due Sept. 30. It is the only federal agency required to make such a payment but, because of the complex way government finances are counted, eliminating it would make the federal budget deficit appear $5.5 billion larger.

If Congress doesn't act and current losses continue, the post office will be unable to make that payment at the end of September because it will have reached its borrowing limit and simply won't have the cash to do so, the agency said earlier.

In that event, Postmaster General Patrick Donahoe said, "Our intent is to continue to deliver the mail, pay our employees and pay our suppliers."

**b** Postal officials have sought congressional assistance repeatedly over the last few years, including requests to be allowed to end Saturday mail delivery, and several bills have been proposed, but none has been acted on.

In addition the post office recently said it is considering closing 3,653 post offices, stations and other facilities, about one-10th of its offices around the country, in an effort to save money. Offices under consideration for closing are largely rural with little traffic.

And in June the post office suspended contributions to its employees' pension fund, which it said was overfunded.

**c** In its 2010 annual report the post office reported a loss of more than $8 billion on revenues of $67 billion and expenses of $75 billion.

And even while total mail volume fell from 202 billion items to 170 billion from 2008 to 2010 the number of places the agency has to deliver mail increased by 1.7 million as Americans built new homes, offices and businesses.

The latest cutback plans were first reported by *The Washington Post*, which said a notice to employees informing them of its proposals stated: "Financial crisis calls for significant actions; we will be insolvent next month due to significant declines in mail volume and retiree health benefit prefunding costs imposed by Congress."

## Key Points in the Article

In 2011, the U.S. Postal Service considered layoffs as a way to deal with a second consecutive year of heavy losses. Officials with the cash-strapped Postal Service stated that it would not be able to make a $5.5 billion payment to its health care plan without cutting its losses. In addition to layoffs, the agency has proposed cutting costs by restructuring its employee retirement and health care plans, eliminating Saturday delivery, and shutting down approximately one-tenth of its offices. Postal officials need congressional approval to move forward with any of these actions, and significant opposition was expected from postal unions and some members of Congress.

## Analyzing the News

**a** The recession and a changing economy help explain the growing losses at the U.S. Postal Service. Many companies are sending fewer advertisements and catalogs to potential customers as a result of the recession. This reduction in through-the-mail advertising has had a direct effect on postal revenues. In addition to the decline in advertisements, the Postal Service has seen a continued decline in the use of first-class mail, with a growing number of customers using the Internet to send and pay bills and as a means of communication.

The postal system is just one area of the economy that is facing declining revenues and mounting debts. The economic recession that began in 2007 and its lingering effects have led to higher unemployment. The figure below shows the unemployment rates in different sectors of the economy during August 2011. The overall unemployment rate was 9.1 percent, much higher than the 4.6 percent in August 2007. The construction sector and the hospitality and leisure sector suffered the most in the economic downturn, with the unemployment rate in each above 10 percent. The health care and education, mining, financial, and government workers sectors were least affected; their unemployment rates were below 6.5 percent.

**b** Layoffs are not the only cost-cutting measure the Postal Service is considering. Over the past several years, postal officials have proposed ending Saturday delivery service and have recently suggested closing more than 3,600 post offices and other facilities. The Postal Service is a semi-independent federal agency, and its operating expenses are primarily paid for by those who use the service. However, the Postal Service must receive congressional approval to undertake actions such as employee layoffs, delivery schedule changes, and office closings. The need for congressional approval makes it much more difficult and time-consuming for the Postal

Service to proceed with cost-cutting measures than if the service were a private firm.

**c** The U.S. Postal Service reported a loss of $8 billion in 2010 and expected to lose that much or more in 2011. The recent losses resulted primarily from a drop in the volume of mail being sent, with 32 billion fewer items being mailed in 2010 than in 2008. In addition to this drop in volume, the postal system added an additional 1.7 million new addresses for mail delivery during this time, adding to its costs at a time of declining revenue.

## Thinking Critically

1. The article indicates that much of the Postal Service's financial difficulties have arisen due to a decline in advertising and to a loss of mail to the Internet. Assuming that the Postal Service does eliminate 120,000 jobs, would it be best to think of these laid-off workers as being frictionally, structurally, or cyclically unemployed? Briefly explain.

2. The figure indicates that the unemployment rate in the construction sector in August 2011 was 13.5 percent, which was almost 50 percent greater than the overall unemployment rate. Beginning in 2006, housing construction entered a period of decline that some economists believed might last for several years. If housing construction had entered a long-lived period of decline, how should we characterize the unemployment in construction: frictional, structural, cyclical, or some combination of these types?

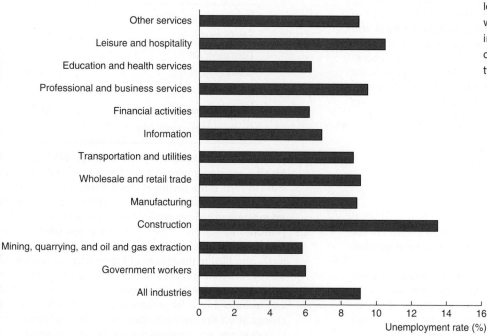

Unemployment rates vary widely across different sectors of the economy.

# Chapter Summary and Problems

## Key Terms

Consumer price index (CPI), p. 657

Cyclical unemployment, p. 653

Deflation, p. 663

Discouraged workers, p. 643

Efficiency wage, p. 656

Frictional unemployment, p. 652

Inflation rate, p. 657

Labor force, p. 642

Labor force participation rate, p. 643

Menu costs, p. 664

Natural rate of unemployment, p. 653

Nominal interest rate, p. 662

Price level, p. 657

Producer price index (PPI), p. 660

Real interest rate, p. 662

Structural unemployment, p. 653

Unemployment rate, p. 642

 **20.1** **Measuring the Unemployment Rate, the Labor Force Participation Rate, and the Employment–Population Ratio, pages 642–651**

LEARNING OBJECTIVE: Define the unemployment rate, the labor force participation rate, and the employment–population ratio and understand how they are computed.

## Summary

The U.S. Bureau of Labor Statistics uses the results of the monthly household survey to calculate the *unemployment rate,* the *labor force participation rate,* and the *employment–population ratio.* The **labor force** is the total number of people who have jobs plus the number of people who do not have jobs but are actively looking for them. The **unemployment rate** is the percentage of the labor force that is unemployed. **Discouraged workers** are people who are available for work but who are not actively looking for a job because they believe no jobs are available for them. Discouraged workers are not counted as unemployed. The **labor force participation rate** is the percentage of the working-age population in the labor force. Since 1950, the labor force participation rate of women has been rising, while the labor force participation rate of men has been falling. The employment–population ratio measures the percentage of the working-age population that is employed. Asians, whites, and college graduates have below-average unemployment rates. African Americans, Hispanics, and high school dropouts have above-average unemployment rates. Except during severe recessions, the typical unemployed person finds a new job or returns to his or her previous job within a few months. Each year, millions of jobs are created in the United States, and millions of jobs are destroyed.

MyEconLab    Visit www.myeconlab.com to complete these exercises online and get instant feedback.

## Review Questions

**1.1** How is the unemployment rate measured? What are the three conditions someone needs to meet to be counted as unemployed?

**1.2** What are the problems in measuring the unemployment rate? In what ways does the official BLS measure of the unemployment rate understate the true degree of unemployment? In what ways does the official BLS measure overstate the true degree of unemployment?

**1.3** Which groups tend to have above-average unemployment rates, and which groups tend to have below-average unemployment rates?

**1.4** What does the labor force participation rate measure? Since 1950, how have the labor force participation rates of men and women changed?

**1.5** What does the employment-population ratio measure? How does an unemployed person dropping out of the labor force affect the unemployment rate? How does it affect the employment-population ratio?

**1.6** What is the difference between the household survey and the establishment survey? Which survey do many economists prefer for measuring changes in employment? Why?

## Problems and Applications

**1.7** Fill in the missing values in the following table of data collected in the household survey for September 2011:

| | |
|---|---|
| Working-age population | |
| Employment | 140,025,000 |
| Unemployment | |
| Unemployment rate | 9.1% |
| Labor force | |
| Labor force participation rate | 64.2% |
| Employment-population ratio | |

**1.8** [Related to the Chapter Opener **on page 641**] The Ford Motor Company employed many fewer people in 2011 than it did in 1980. Is this decline in employment frictional, structural, cyclical, or some combination of these factors? What information would you need to arrive at a definite answer?

**1.9** [Related to Solved Problem 20.1 **on page 644**] Homemakers are not included in the employment or labor force totals compiled in the Bureau of Labor Statistics household survey. They are included in the working-age population totals. Suppose that homemakers were counted as employed and included in the labor force statistics. How would that change affect the unemployment rate, the labor force participation rate, and the employment–population ratio?

**1.10** Look again at Table 20.1 on page 650. Between August and September 2011, the household survey shows that the total number of people employed increased by 398,000. Yet the unemployment rate remained the same. Shouldn't the unemployment rate fall when the number of people employed increases? Briefly explain.

**1.11** **[Related to the** Making the Connection **on page 648]** An article published in the *New York Times* in July 2011 argued that: "For the second straight year, the recovery in the job market has essentially stalled. This chart, showing the share of adults with jobs, offers the best summary you'll find." The "share of adults with jobs" is known more formally as the employment-population ratio. Why might the employment-population ratio provide the "best summary" of the state of the job market rather than the unemployment rate?

Based on David Leonhardt, "Overly Optimistic, Once Again," *New York Times*, July 8, 2011.

**1.12** Is it possible for the total number of people who are unemployed to increase while the unemployment rate decreases? Briefly explain.

**1.13** In a speech delivered in the summer of 2011, President Barack Obama observed, "Even though the economy is growing, even though it's created more than two million jobs over the past 15 months, we still face some tough times." Is it likely that the U.S. economy created only about two million jobs during this time period? If not, what was President Obama referring to?

Based on Catherine Rampell, "Hiring in U.S. Slowed in May With 54,000 Jobs Added," *New York Times*, June 3, 2011.

---

## 20.2 | Types of Unemployment, pages 651–654

LEARNING OBJECTIVE: Identify the three types of unemployment.

## Summary

There are three types of unemployment: frictional, structural, and cyclical. **Frictional unemployment** is short-term unemployment that arises from the process of matching workers with jobs. One type of frictional unemployment is *seasonal unemployment*, which refers to unemployment due to factors such as weather, variations in tourism, and other calendar-related events. **Structural unemployment** arises from a persistent mismatch between the job skills or attributes of workers and the requirements of jobs. **Cyclical unemployment** is caused by a business cycle recession. The **natural rate of unemployment** is the normal rate of unemployment, consisting of structural unemployment and frictional unemployment. The natural rate of unemployment is also sometimes called the *full-employment rate of unemployment*.

 MyEconLab   Visit www.myeconlab.com to complete these exercises online and get instant feedback.

## Review Questions

**2.1** What are the three types of unemployment?

**2.2** What is the relationship between frictional unemployment and job search?

**2.3** What is the natural rate of unemployment? What is the relationship between the natural rate of unemployment and full employment? Would it be better for economists

to define full employment as being an unemployment rate equal to zero?

## Problems and Applications

**2.4** Macroeconomic conditions affect the decisions firms and families make. Why, for example, might a student graduating from college enter the job market during an economic expansion but apply for graduate school during a recession?

**2.5** A politician makes the following argument: "The economy would operate more efficiently if frictional unemployment were eliminated. Therefore, a goal of government policy should be to reduce the frictional rate of unemployment to the lowest possible level." Briefly explain whether you agree with this argument.

**2.6** **[Related to the** Making the Connection **on page 653]** What advice for finding a job would you give someone who is frictionally unemployed? What advice would you give someone who is structurally unemployed? What advice would you give someone who is cyclically unemployed?

**2.7** Recall from Chapter 3 the definitions of *normal goods* and *inferior goods*. During an economic expansion, would you rather be working in an industry that produces a normal good or in an industry that produces an inferior good? Why? During a recession, would you rather be working in an industry that produces a normal good or an inferior good? Why?

---

## 20.3 | Explaining Unemployment, pages 654–656

LEARNING OBJECTIVE: Explain what factors determine the unemployment rate.

## Summary

Government policies can reduce the level of frictional and structural unemployment by aiding the search for jobs and the retraining of workers. Some government policies, however, can add to the

level of frictional and structural unemployment. Unemployment insurance payments can raise the unemployment rate by extending the time that unemployed workers search for jobs. Government policies have caused the unemployment rates in most other high-income countries typically to be higher than in the United

States. Wages above market levels can also increase unemployment. Wages may be above market levels because of the minimum wage, labor unions, and *efficiency wages*. An **efficiency wage** is a higher-than-market wage that a firm pays to increase worker productivity.

 Visit **www.myeconlab.com** to complete these exercises online and get instant feedback.

## Review Questions

**3.1** What effect does the payment of government unemployment insurance have on the unemployment rate? On the severity of recessions?

**3.2** Discuss the effect of each of the following on the unemployment rate.
   **a.** The federal minimum wage law
   **b.** Labor unions
   **c.** Efficiency wages

**3.3** Why has the unemployment rate in the United States typically been lower than the unemployment rates in Canada and countries in Western Europe?

## Problems and Applications

**3.4** In 2007, Ségolène Royal, who was running unsuccessfully for president of France, proposed that workers who lost their jobs would receive unemployment payments equal to 90 percent of their previous wages during their first year of unemployment. If this proposal were enacted, what would likely be the effect on the unemployment rate in France? Briefly explain.

Based on Alessandra Galloni and David Gauthier-Villars, "France's Royal Introduces Platform Ahead of Election," *Wall Street Journal*, February 12, 2007.

**3.5** If Congress eliminated the unemployment insurance system, what would be the effect on the level of frictional unemployment? What would be the effect on the level of real GDP? Would well-being in the economy be increased? Briefly explain.

**3.6** Discuss the likely effect of each of the following on the unemployment rate:
   **a.** The length of time workers are eligible to receive unemployment insurance payments doubles.
   **b.** The minimum wage is abolished.
   **c.** Most U.S. workers join labor unions.
   **d.** More companies make information on job openings easily available on Internet job sites.

**3.7** Why do you think the minimum wage was set at only $0.25 per hour in 1938? Wouldn't this wage have been well below the equilibrium wage?

**3.8** An economic consultant studies the labor policies of a firm where it is difficult to monitor workers and prepares a report in which she recommends that the firm raise employee wages. At a meeting of the firm's managers to discuss the report, one manager makes the following argument: "I think the wages we are paying are fine. As long as enough people are willing to work here at the wages we are currently paying, why should we raise them?" What argument can the economic consultant make to justify her advice that the firm should increase its wages?

**3.9** Costco typically pays its workers higher wages than does Wal-Mart. One analyst argues that Costco pays higher wages "because it requires higher-skilled workers to sell higher-cost products to more affluent customers." If this analyst is correct, can we conclude that Costco is paying efficiency wages and Wal-Mart is not? Briefly explain.

Based on Loti Montgomery, "Maverick Costco CEO Joins Push to Raise Minimum Wage," *Washington Post*, January 30, 2007.

---

**20.4** **Measuring Inflation, pages 656–660**

LEARNING OBJECTIVE: Define price level and inflation rate and understand how they are computed.

## Summary

The **price level** measures the average prices of goods and services. The **inflation rate** is equal to the percentage change in the price level from one year to the next. The federal government compiles statistics on three different measures of the price level: the consumer price index (CPI), the GDP price deflator, and the producer price index (PPI). The **consumer price index (CPI)** is an average of the prices of goods and services purchased by the typical urban family of four. Changes in the CPI are the best measure of changes in the cost of living as experienced by the typical household. Biases in the construction of the CPI cause changes in it to overstate the true inflation rate by 0.5 percentage point to 1 percentage point. The **producer price index (PPI)** is an average of prices received by producers of goods and services at all stages of production.

MyEconLab Visit **www.myeconlab.com** to complete these exercises online and get instant feedback.

## Review Questions

**4.1** Briefly describe the three major measures of the price level.

**4.2** Which price index does the government use to measure changes in the cost of living?

**4.3** What potential biases exist in calculating the consumer price index? What steps has the Bureau of Labor Statistics taken to reduce the size of the biases?

**4.4** What is the difference between the consumer price index and the producer price index?

## Problems and Applications

**4.5** **[Related to the** Don't Let This Happen to You **on page 659]** Briefly explain whether you agree or disagree with the following statement: "I don't believe the government price statistics. The CPI for 2010 was 218, but I know that the inflation rate couldn't have been as high as 118 percent in 2010."

**4.6** In calculating the consumer price index for the year, why does the BLS use the quantities in the market basket, rather than the quantities purchased during the current year?

**4.7** In October 2011, Apple introduced the iPhone 4S, which had new features, including an improved camera and voice control, but sold at the same price as the previous iPhone model. How was the consumer price index affected by the introduction of the iPhone 4S?

Based on Ian Sherr and Greg Bensinger, "New Apple iPhone Snared Big Sales on First Weekend," *Wall Street Journal*, October 18, 2011.

**4.8** Consider a simple economy that produces only three products: haircuts, hamburgers, and DVDs. Use the information in the following table to calculate the inflation rate for 2012, as measured by the consumer price index.

| Product | Base Year (1999) Quantity | Base Year (1999) Price | 2011 Price | 2012 Price |
|---------|------|------|------|------|
| Haircuts | 2 | $10.00 | $11.00 | $16.20 |
| Hamburgers | 10 | 2.00 | 2.45 | 2.40 |
| DVDs | 6 | 15.00 | 15.00 | 14.00 |

**4.9** The Standard & Poor's/Case-Shiller Home Price Index is one of the leading indicators of housing price trends in the United States. The base year for the index is January 2000. The following table lists index numbers for July 2010 and July 2011 for five cities:

| City | July 2010 | July 2011 |
|------|-----------|-----------|
| New York | 173.8 | 167.2 |
| Miami | 147.5 | 140.7 |
| Phoenix | 109.51 | 99.8 |
| Dallas | 117.8 | 114.0 |
| San Diego | 162.6 | 152.9 |

**a.** Calculate the percentage change in housing prices from July 2010 to July 2011 for each of these five cities. In which city did housing prices change the most? The least?

**b.** Can you determine on the basis of these numbers which city had the most expensive homes in July 2011? Briefly explain.

Data from "S&P/Case-Shiller Home Price Indices," *Standard & Poor's Financial Services, LLC*, September 2011.

---

**20.5** | # Using Price Indexes to Adjust for the Effects of Inflation, pages 660–662
LEARNING OBJECTIVE: Use price indexes to adjust for the effects of inflation.

## Summary

Price indexes are designed to measure changes in the price level over time, not the absolute level of prices. To correct for the effects of inflation, we can divide a *nominal variable* by a price index and multiply by 100 to obtain a *real variable*. The real variable will be measured in dollars of the base year for the price index.

 Visit **www.myeconlab.com** to complete these exercises online and get instant feedback.

## Review Questions

**5.1** What is the difference between a nominal variable and a real variable?

**5.2** Briefly explain how you can use data on nominal wages for 2004 to 2011 and data on the consumer price index for the same years to calculate the real wage for these years.

## Problems and Applications

**5.3** **[Related to** Solved Problem 20.5 **on page 661]** In 1924, the famous novelist F. Scott Fitzgerald wrote an article for the *Saturday Evening Post* titled "How to Live on $36,000 a Year," in which he wondered how he and his wife had managed to spend all of that very high income without saving any of it. The CPI in 1924 was 17, and the CPI in 2010 was 218. What income would you have needed in 2010 to have had the same purchasing power that Fitzgerald's $36,000 had in 1924? Be sure to show your calculation.

From F. Scott Fitzgerald, "How to Live on $36,000 a Year," *Saturday Evening Post*, April 5, 1924.

**5.4** **[Related to** Solved Problem 20.5 **on page 661]** Use the information in the following table to determine the percentage changes in the U.S. and French *real* minimum wages between 1957 and 2010. Does it matter for your answer that you have not been told the base year for the U.S. CPI or the French CPI? Was the percentage increase in the price level greater in the United States or in France during these years?

| | United States | | France | |
|------|------|------|------|------|
| Year | Minimum Wage (dollars per hour) | CPI | Minimum Wage (euros per hour) | CPI |
| 1957 | $1.00 | 27 | €0.19 | 10 |
| 2010 | 7.25 | 215 | 8.86 | 128 |

Based on John M. Abowd, Francis Kramarz, Thomas Lemieux, and David N. Margolis, "Minimum Wages and Youth Employment in France and the United States," in D. Blanchflower and R. Freeman, eds., *Youth Employment and Joblessness in Advanced Countries*, (Chicago: University of Chicago Press, 1999), pp. 427–472 (the value for the minimum wage is given in francs; it was converted to euros at a conversion rate of 1 euro = 6.55957 francs); Insee online data bank, www.insee.fr; U.S. Department of Labor; and U.S. Bureau of Labor Statistics.

**5.5** **[Related to** Solved Problem 20.5 **on page 661]** The Great Depression was the worst economic disaster in U.S. history in terms of declines in real GDP and increases in the unemployment rate. Use the data in the table on the next page to calculate the percentage decline in real GDP between 1929 and 1933:

| Year | Nominal GDP (billions of dollars) | GDP Price Deflator 2005 = 100 |
|------|-----------------------------------|-------------------------------|
| 1929 | $103.6 | 10.6 |
| 1933 | 56.4 | 7.9 |

**5.6** **[Related to** Solved Problem 20.5 **on page 661]** The following table shows the top 10 films of all time through October 2011, measured by box office receipts in the United States, as well as several other notable films farther down the list.

The CPI in 2010 was 218. Use this information and the data in the table to calculate the box office receipts for each film in 2010 dollars. Assume that each film generated all of its box office receipts during the year it was released. Use your results to prepare a new list of the top 10 films, based on their earnings in 2010 dollars. (Some of the films, such as the first *Star Wars* film, *Gone with the Wind*, and *Snow White and the Seven Dwarfs*, were re-released several times, so their receipts were actually earned during several different years, but we will ignore that complication.)

Data from The Internet Movie database, www.imdb.com.

| Rank | Film | Total Box Office Receipts | Year Released | CPI |
|------|------|---------------------------|---------------|-----|
| 1 | Avatar | $760,505,847 | 2009 | 215 |
| 2 | Titanic | $600,779,824 | 1997 | 161 |
| 3 | The Dark Knight | 533,316,061 | 2008 | 215 |
| 4 | Star Wars | 460,935,655 | 1977 | 61 |
| 5 | Shrek 2 | 436,471,036 | 2004 | 189 |
| 6 | E.T.: The Extra-Terrestrial | 434,949,459 | 1982 | 97 |
| 7 | Star Wars: Episode I—The Phantom Menace | 431,065,444 | 1999 | 167 |
| 8 | Pirates of the Caribbean: Dead Man's Chest | 423,032,628 | 2006 | 202 |
| 9 | Toy Story 3 | 414,984,497 | 2010 | 218 |
| 10 | Spider-Man | 403,706,375 | 2002 | 180 |
| 56 | Jaws | 260,000,000 | 1975 | 54 |
| 115 | Gone with the Wind | 198,655,278 | 1939 | 14 |
| 130 | Snow White and the Seven Dwarfs | 184,925,485 | 1937 | 14 |
| 187 | The Sound of Music | 163,214,286 | 1965 | 32 |
| 212 | One Hundred and One Dalmatians | 153,000,000 | 1961 | 30 |

---

## 20.6 Real versus Nominal Interest Rates, pages 662–663

LEARNING OBJECTIVE: Distinguish between the nominal interest rate and the real interest rate.

## Summary

The stated interest rate on a loan is the **nominal interest rate**. The **real interest rate** is the nominal interest rate minus the inflation rate. Because it is corrected for the effects of inflation, the real interest rate provides a better measure of the true cost of borrowing and the true return from lending than does the nominal interest rate. The nominal interest rate is always greater than the real interest rate unless the economy experiences *deflation*. **Deflation** is a decline in the price level.

MyEconLab Visit www.myeconlab.com to complete these exercises online and get instant feedback.

## Review Questions

**6.1** What is the difference between the nominal interest rate and the real interest rate?

**6.2** If inflation is expected to increase, what will happen to the nominal interest rate? Briefly explain.

**6.3** The chapter explains that it is impossible to know whether a particular nominal interest rate is "high" or "low." Briefly explain why.

**6.4** If the economy is experiencing deflation, will the nominal interest rate be higher or lower than the real interest rate?

## Problems and Applications

**6.5** The following appeared in a newspaper article: "Inflation in the Lehigh Valley during the first quarter of [the year] was less than half the national rate. . . . So, unlike much of the nation, the fear here is deflation—when prices sink so low the CPI drops below zero." Do you agree with the reporter's definition of *deflation*? Briefly explain.

From Dan Shope, "Valley's Inflation Rate Slides," *Morning Call* (Allentown, PA), July 9, 1996.

**6.6** Suppose you were borrowing money to buy a car. Which of these situations would you prefer: The interest rate on your car loan is 20 percent and the inflation rate is 19 percent or the interest rate on your car loan is 5 percent and the inflation rate is 2 percent? Briefly explain.

**6.7** Describing the situation in England in 1920, the historian Robert Skidelsky wrote the following: "Who would not borrow at 4 percent a year, with prices going up 4 percent a *month*?" What was the real interest rate paid by borrowers in this situation? (*Hint:* What is the annual inflation rate, if the monthly inflation rate is 4 percent?)

Based on Robert Skidelsky, John Maynard Keynes: Volume 2, The Economist as Saviour 1920–1937, (New York: The Penguin Press), 1992, p. 39.

**6.8** Suppose that the only good you purchase is hamburgers and that at the beginning of the year, the price of a hamburger is $2.00. Suppose you lend $1,000 for one year at an interest rate of 5 percent. At the end of the year, a hamburger costs $2.08. What is the real rate of interest you earned on your loan?

**6.9** During the 1990s, Japan experienced periods of deflation and low nominal interest rates that approached zero percent. Why would lenders of funds agree to a nominal interest rate of almost zero percent? (Hint: Were real interest rates in Japan also low during this period?)

---

## 20.7 Does Inflation Impose Costs on the Economy? pages 663–666

**LEARNING OBJECTIVE: Discuss the problems that inflation causes.**

## Summary

Inflation does not reduce the affordability of goods and services to the average consumer, but it does impose costs on the economy. When inflation is anticipated, its main costs are that paper money loses some of its value and firms incur *menu costs*. **Menu costs** include the costs of changing prices on products and printing new catalogs. When inflation is unanticipated, the actual inflation rate can turn out to be different from the expected inflation rate. As a result, income is redistributed as some people gain and some people lose.

 Visit **www.myeconlab.com** to complete these exercises online and get instant feedback.

## Review Questions

**7.1** Why do nominal incomes generally increase with inflation? If nominal incomes increase with inflation, does inflation reduce the purchasing power of the average consumer? Briefly explain.

**7.2** How can inflation affect the distribution of income?

**7.3** Which is a greater problem: anticipated inflation or unanticipated inflation? Briefly explain.

**7.4** What problems does deflation cause?

## Problems and Applications

**7.5** What are menu costs? What effect has the Internet had on the size of menu costs?

**7.6** Suppose that the inflation rate turns out to be much higher than most people expected. In that case, would you rather have been a borrower or a lender? Briefly explain.

**7.7** Suppose James and Frank both retire this year. For income from retirement, James will rely on a pension from his company that pays him a fixed $2,500 per month for as long as he lives. James hasn't saved anything for retirement. Frank has no pension but has saved a considerable amount, which he has invested in certificates of deposit (CDs) at his bank. Currently, Frank's CDs pay him interest of $2,300 per month.

  **a.** Ten years from now, is James or Frank likely to have a higher real income? In your answer, be sure to define *real income*.

  **b.** Now suppose that instead of being a constant amount, James's pension increases each year by the same percentage as the CPI. For example, if the CPI increases by 5 percent in the first year after James retires, then his pension in the second year equals $2,500 + ($2,500 × 0.05) = $2,625. In this case, 10 years from now, is James or Frank likely to have a higher real income?

**7.8** Suppose that News Corporation, the owner of the *Wall Street Journal*, and the investors buying the firm's bonds both expect a 2 percent inflation rate for the year. Given this expectation, suppose the nominal interest rate on the bonds is 6 percent and the real interest rate is 4 percent. Suppose that a year after the investors purchase the bonds, the inflation rate turns out to be 6 percent, rather than the 2 percent that had been expected. Who gains and who loses from the unexpectedly high inflation rate?

**7.9** **[Related to the** Making the Connection **on page 665]** During the late nineteenth century in the United States, many farmers borrowed heavily to buy land. During most of the period between 1870 and the mid-1890s, the United States experienced mild deflation: The price level declined each year. Many farmers engaged in political protests during these years, and deflation was often a subject of their protests. Explain why farmers would have felt burdened by deflation.

CHAPTER

# 21

# Economic Growth, the Financial System, and Business Cycle

## Chapter Outline and Learning Objectives

# Growth and the Business Cycle at Boeing

In December 1903, at Kitty Hawk, North Carolina, the Wright Flyer became the first human-piloted, machine-powered, heavier-than-air craft to fly—for all of 12 seconds and a distance of 120 feet. Roughly a century later, on November 10, 2005, the Boeing 777-200LR became the first commercial aircraft to fly nonstop more than halfway around the world—for 22 hours and 42 minutes, across 13,422 miles. This tremendous advance in aviation technology has been matched by technological progress in many other areas of the economy. In this chapter, we begin to explore how technological change has affected the standard of living in the United States and elsewhere around the world.

William Boeing established the Boeing Company in 1916. Today, Boeing is one of the world's largest manufacturers of commercial jetliners, military aircraft, satellites, missiles, and defense systems. The company employs more than 165,000 people in 70 countries. Boeing's experiences have often mirrored two key macroeconomic facts: In the long run, the U.S. economy has experienced economic growth, and in the short run, the economy has experienced a series of business cycles. Boeing has also experienced growth over the long run, while being affected by the business cycle.

In 2007, Boeing received a record 1,413 orders for new commercial jets, as the United States and much of the rest of the world was experiencing a period of strong economic growth. As the U.S. and world economies entered a recession in 2008, Boeing's orders fell to 662, and then plummeted to 142 in 2009. As the economy improved in 2010, Boeing's orders rebounded to 530. In 2011, Randy Tinseth, vice president for marketing at Boeing Commercial Airplanes, predicted that, despite the recent short-run swings in orders, long-run prospects for the airline industry were good: "Not only is there strong demand for air travel and new airplanes today, but the fundamental drivers of air travel—including economic growth, world trade and liberalization—all point to a healthy long-term demand."

In this chapter, we provide an overview of long-run growth and the business cycle and discuss their importance for firms, for consumers, and for the economy as a whole.

Read **AN INSIDE LOOK** on **page 704** for a discussion of how the International Air Transport Association uses projected global GDP numbers to forecast lower profits in the airline industry during 2012.

Based on David Pearson, "Boeing Sees Rising Aircraft Demand," *Wall Street Journal*, June 16, 2011; Julie Johnson, "Boeing Aircraft Orders Rebound in 2010," *Chicago Tribune*, January 6, 2011; and James Wallace, "Boeing 777 Stretches Its Wings, Record," *Seattle Post Intelligencer*, November 11, 2005.

## Economics in Your Life

### Do You Help the Economy More if You Spend or if You Save?

Suppose that you have received an income tax refund check from the U.S. government. You are not sure what to do with the money, so you ask your two roommates for advice. One roommate tells you that if you want to help the economy, you should save all the money because a country's economic growth depends on the amount of saving by households. The other roommate disagrees and advises you to spend all the money because consumer spending is a major component of gross domestic product (GDP), and your spending would help increase production and create more jobs. Which of your two roommates is right? As you read this chapter, see if you can answer this question. You can check your answer against the one we provide on **page 702** at the end of this chapter.

A successful economy is capable of increasing production of goods and services faster than the growth in population. Attaining this level of growth is the only way that the standard of living of the average person in a country can increase. Unfortunately, many economies around the world are not growing at all or are growing very slowly. Most people in those countries live on about the same levels of income as their ancestors did decades, or even centuries, ago. In the United States and other developed countries, however, incomes and living standards are much higher today than they were 50 years ago. An important macroeconomic topic is why some countries grow much faster than others.

As we will see, one determinant of economic growth is the ability of firms to expand their operations, buy additional equipment, train workers, and adopt new technologies. To carry out these activities, firms must acquire funds from households, either directly through financial markets—such as the stock and bond markets—or indirectly through financial intermediaries—such as banks. Financial markets and financial intermediaries together comprise the *financial system*. In this chapter, we present an overview of the financial system and see how funds flow from households to firms through the *market for loanable funds*.

Since at least the early nineteenth century, the U.S. economy has experienced periods of expanding production and employment followed by periods of recession during which production and employment decline. As we noted in Chapter 19, these alternating periods of expansion and recession are called the **business cycle**. The business cycle is not uniform: Each period of expansion is not the same length, nor is each period of recession, but every period of expansion in U.S. history has been followed by a period of recession, and every period of recession has been followed by a period of expansion.

In this chapter, we begin to explore two key aspects of macroeconomics: the long-run growth that has steadily raised living standards in the United States and the short-run fluctuations of the business cycle.

**Business cycle** Alternating periods of economic expansion and economic recession.

**21.1 LEARNING** OBJECTIVE

Discuss the importance of long-run economic growth.

## Long-Run Economic Growth

Most people in the United States, Western Europe, Japan, and other high-income countries expect that over time, their standard of living will improve. They expect that year after year, firms will introduce new and improved products, new prescription drugs and better surgical techniques will overcome more diseases, and their ability to afford these goods and services will increase. For most people, these are reasonable expectations.

In 1900, the United States was already enjoying the highest standard of living in the world. Yet in that year, only 3 percent of U.S. homes had electricity, only 15 percent had indoor flush toilets, and only 25 percent had running water. The lack of running water meant that before people could cook or bathe, they had to pump water from wells and haul it to their homes in buckets—on average about 10,000 gallons per year per family. Not surprisingly, water consumption averaged only about 5 gallons per person per day, compared with about 150 gallons today. The result was that people washed themselves and their clothing only infrequently. A majority of families living in cities had to use outdoor toilets, which they shared with other families. Diseases such as smallpox, typhus, dysentery, and cholera were still common. In 1900, 5,000 of the 45,000 children born in Chicago died before their first birthday. Life expectancy at birth was about 47 years, compared with 78 years in 2011. Few families had electric lights, relying instead on the limited illumination provided by burning candles or burning kerosene or coal oil in lamps. Many homes were heated in the winter by burning coal, which contributed to

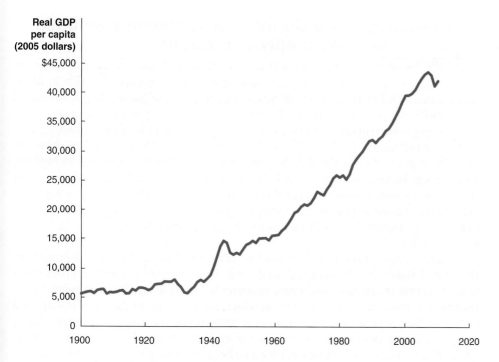

**Figure 21.1**

**The Growth in Real GDP per Capita, 1900–2010**

Measured in 2005 dollars, real GDP per capita in the United States grew from about $5,600 in 1900 to about $42,200 in 2010. The average American in the year 2010 could buy nearly eight times as many goods and services as the average American in the year 1900.

Data from Louis D. Johnston and Samuel H. Williamson, "What Was the U.S. GDP Then?" MeasuringWorth, 2011; and U.S. Bureau of Economic Analysis.

the severe pollution that fouled the air of most large cities. There were no modern appliances, and most women worked inside the home at least 80 hours per week. The typical American homemaker in 1900 baked a half-ton of bread per year.

The process of **long-run economic growth** brought the typical American from the standard of living of 1900 to the standard of living of today. The best measure of the standard of living is real GDP per person, which is usually referred to as *real GDP per capita*. So, we measure long-run economic growth by increases in real GDP per capita over long periods of time, generally decades or more. We use real GDP rather than nominal GDP to adjust for changes in the price level over time. Figure 21.1 shows the growth in real GDP per capita in the United States from 1900 to 2010. The figure shows that although real GDP per capita fluctuates because of the short-run effects of the business cycle, over the long run, the trend is strongly upward. It is the upward trend in real GDP per capita that we focus on when discussing long-run economic growth.

The values in Figure 21.1 are measured in prices of the year 2005, so they represent constant amounts of purchasing power. In 1900, real GDP per capita was about $5,600. Over a century later, in 2010, it had risen to about $42,200, which means that the average American in 2010 could purchase nearly eight times as many goods and services as the average American in 1900. Large as it is, this increase in real GDP per capita actually understates the true increase in the standard of living of Americans in 2010 compared with 1900. Many of today's goods and services were not available in 1900. For example, if you lived in 1900 and became ill with a serious infection, you would have been unable to purchase antibiotics to treat your illness—no matter how high your income. You might have died from an illness for which even a very poor person in today's society could receive effective medical treatment. Of course, the quantity of goods and services that a person can buy is not a perfect measure of how happy or contented that person may be. The level of education, life expectancy, crime, spiritual well-being, pollution, and many other factors ignored in calculating GDP contribute to a person's happiness. Nevertheless, economists rely heavily on comparisons of real GDP per capita because it is the best means of comparing the performance of one economy over time or the performance of different economies at any particular time.

**Long-run economic growth** The process by which rising productivity increases the average standard of living.

Making the Connection | **The Connection between Economic Prosperity and Health**

We can see the direct effect of economic growth on living standards by looking at improvements in health in high-income countries over the past 100 years. The research of Robert Fogel, winner of the Nobel Prize in Economics, highlights the close connection between economic growth, improvements in technology, and improvements in human physiology. One important measure of health is life expectancy at birth. As the graph below shows, in 1900, life expectancy was less than 50 years in the United States, the United Kingdom, and France. Today, life expectancy is about 80 years. Although life expectancies in the lowest-income countries remain very short, some countries that have begun to experience economic growth have seen dramatic increases in life expectancies. For example, life expectancy in India has more than doubled from 27 years in 1900 to 67 years today.

Many economists believe there is a link between health and economic growth. In the United States and Western Europe during the nineteenth century, improvements in agricultural technology and rising incomes led to dramatic improvements in the nutrition of the average person. The development of the germ theory of disease and technological progress in the purification of water in the late nineteenth century led to sharp declines in sickness due to waterborne diseases. As people became taller, stronger, and less susceptible to disease, they also became more productive. Today, economists studying economic development have put increasing emphasis on the need for low-income countries to reduce disease and increase nutrition if they are to experience economic growth.

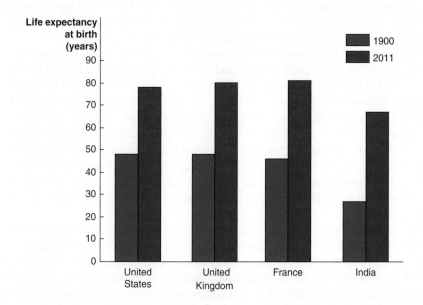

Many researchers believe that the state of human physiology will continue to improve as technology advances. In high-income countries, life expectancy at birth is expected to rise from about 80 years today to about 90 years by the middle of the twenty-first century. Technological advances will continue to reduce the average number of hours worked per day and the number of years the average person spends in the paid workforce. Individuals spend about 10 hours per day sleeping, eating, and bathing. Their remaining "discretionary hours" are divided between paid work and leisure. The graph on the next page is based on estimates by Robert Fogel that contrast how individuals in the United States will divide their time in 2040 compared with 1880 and 1995. Not only will technology and economic growth allow people in the near future to live longer lives, but a much smaller fraction of those lives will need to be spent at paid work.

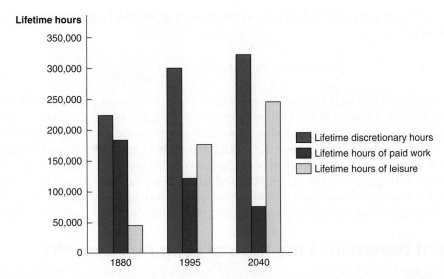

Based on Robert William Fogel, *The Escape from Hunger and Premature Death, 1700–2100*, (New York: Cambridge University Press, 2004); and U.S. Central Intelligence Agency, *The 2011 World Factbook*, online version.

**Your Turn:** Test your understanding by doing related problem 1.8 on page 706 at the end of this chapter.

MyEconLab

## Calculating Growth Rates and the Rule of 70

The growth rate of real GDP or real GDP per capita during a particular year is equal to the percentage change from the previous year. For example, measured in prices of the year 2005, real GDP equaled $12,703 billion in 2009 and rose to $13,088 billion in 2010. We calculate the growth of real GDP in 2010 as:

$$\left(\frac{\$13{,}088 \text{ billion} - \$12{,}703 \text{ billion}}{\$12{,}703 \text{ billion}}\right) \times 100 = 3.0\%.$$

For longer periods of time, we can use the *average annual growth rate*. For example, real GDP in the United States was $2,004 billion in 1950 and $13,088 billion in 2010. To find the average annual growth rate during this 60-year period, we compute the annual growth rate that would result in $2,004 billion increasing to $13,088 billion over 60 years. In this case, the growth rate is 3.2 percent. That is, if $2,004 billion grows at an average rate of 3.2 percent per year, after 60 years, it will have grown to $13,088 billion.

For shorter periods of time, we get approximately the same answer by averaging the growth rate for each year. For example, real GDP in the United States *fell* by 0.3 percent in 2008, *fell* by 3.5 percent in 2009, and grew by 3.0 percent in 2010. So, the average annual growth rate of real GDP for the period 2008–2010 was −0.3 percent, which is the average of the three annual growth rates:

$$\frac{-0.3\% + (-3.5\%) + 3.0\%}{3} = -0.3\%$$

Note that during this period, the "growth" rate was actually negative because real GDP declined during the recession years of 2008 and 2009. Finally, when discussing long-run economic growth, we usually shorten "average annual growth rate" to "growth rate."

We can judge how rapidly an economic variable is growing by calculating the number of years it would take to double. For example, if real GDP per capita in a country doubles, say, every 20 years, most people in the country will experience significant increases in their standard of living over the course of their lives. If real GDP per capita doubles only every 100 years, increases in the standard of living will occur too slowly to notice. One easy way to calculate approximately how many years it will take real GDP per capita to double is to use the *rule of 70*. The formula for the rule of 70 is as follows:

$$\text{Number of years to double} = \frac{70}{\text{Growth rate}}.$$

For example, if real GDP per capita is growing at a rate of 5 percent per year, it will double in $70/5 = 14$ years. If real GDP per capita is growing at a rate of 2 percent per year, it will take $70/2 = 35$ years to double. These examples illustrate an important point that we will discuss further in Chapter 22: Small differences in growth rates can have large effects on how rapidly the standard of living in a country increases. Finally, notice that the rule of 70 applies not just to growth in real GDP per capita but to growth in any variable. For example, if you invest $1,000 in the stock market, and your investment grows at an average annual rate of 7 percent, your investment will double to $2,000 in 10 years.

## What Determines the Rate of Long-Run Growth?

**Labor productivity** The quantity of goods and services that can be produced by one worker or by one hour of work.

In Chapter 22, we will explore the sources of economic growth in more detail and discuss why growth in the United States and other high-income countries has been so much faster than growth in low-income countries. For now, we will focus on the basic point that *increases in real GDP per capita depend on increases in labor productivity*. **Labor productivity** is the quantity of goods and services that can be produced by one worker or by one hour of work. In analyzing long-run growth, economists usually measure labor productivity as output per hour of work to avoid the effects of fluctuations in the length of the workday and in the fraction of the population employed. If the quantity of goods and services consumed by the average person is to increase, the quantity of goods and services produced per hour of work must also increase. Why in 2010 was the average American able to consume almost eight times as many goods and services as the average American in 1900? Because the average American worker in 2010 was eight times as productive as the average American worker in 1900.

If increases in labor productivity are the key to long-run economic growth, what causes labor productivity to increase? Economists believe two key factors determine labor productivity: the quantity of capital per hour worked and the level of technology. Therefore, economic growth occurs if the quantity of capital per hour worked increases and if technological change occurs.

**Increases in Capital per Hour Worked** Workers today in high-income countries such as the United States have more physical capital available than workers in low-income countries or workers in the high-income countries of 100 years ago. Recall that **capital** refers to manufactured goods that are used to produce other goods and services. Examples of capital are computers, factory buildings, machine tools, warehouses, and trucks. The total amount of physical capital available in a country is known as the country's *capital stock*.

**Capital** Manufactured goods that are used to produce other goods and services.

As the capital stock per hour worked increases, worker productivity increases. A secretary who uses a personal computer can produce more documents per day than a secretary who uses only a typewriter. A worker who uses a backhoe can excavate more earth than a worker who uses only a shovel.

*Human capital* refers to the accumulated knowledge and skills workers acquire from education and training or from their life experiences. For example, workers with a college education generally have more skills and are more productive than workers who have only a high school degree. Increases in human capital are particularly important in stimulating economic growth.

**Technological Change** Economic growth depends more on *technological change* than on increases in capital per hour worked. *Technology* refers to the processes a firm uses to turn inputs into outputs of goods and services. Technological change is an increase in the quantity of output firms can produce, using a given quantity of inputs. Technological change can come from many sources. For example, a firm's managers may rearrange a factory floor or the layout of a retail store to increase production and sales. Most technological change, however, is embodied in new machinery, equipment, or software.

A very important point is that just accumulating more inputs—such as labor, capital, and natural resources—will not ensure that an economy experiences economic growth unless technological change also occurs. For example, the Soviet Union failed to maintain a high rate of economic growth, even though it continued to increase the quantity of capital available per hour worked, because it experienced relatively little technological change.

In implementing technological change, *entrepreneurs* are of crucial importance. Recall from Chapter 2 that an entrepreneur is someone who operates a business, bringing together the factors of production—labor, capital, and natural resources—to produce goods and services. In a market economy, entrepreneurs make the crucial decisions about whether to introduce new technology to produce better or lower-cost products. Entrepreneurs also decide whether to allocate a firm's resources to research and development that can result in new technologies. One of the difficulties centrally planned economies have in sustaining economic growth is that managers employed by the government are usually much slower to develop and adopt new technologies than entrepreneurs in a market system.

# Solved Problem 21.1

## The Role of Technological Change in Growth

Between 1960 and 1995, real GDP per capita in Singapore grew at an average annual rate of 6.2 percent. This very rapid growth rate results in the level of real GDP per capita doubling about every 11.3 years. In 1995, Alwyn Young of the London School of Economics published an article in which he argued that Singapore's growth depended more on increases in capital per hour worked, increases in the labor force participation rate, and the transfer of workers from agricultural to nonagricultural jobs than on technological change. If Young's analysis was correct, predict what was likely to happen to Singapore's growth rate in the years after 1995.

## Solving the Problem

**Step 1: Review the chapter material.** This problem is about what determines the rate of long-run growth, so you may want to review the section "What Determines the Rate of Long-Run Growth?" which begins on page 682.

**Step 2: Predict what happened to the growth rate in Singapore after 1995.** As countries begin to develop, they often experience an increase in the labor force participation rate, as workers who are not part of the paid labor force respond to rising wage rates. Many workers also leave the agricultural sector—where output per hour worked is often low—for the nonagricultural sector. These changes increase real GDP per capita, but they are "one-shot" changes that eventually come to an end, as the labor force participation rate and the fraction of the labor force outside agriculture both approach the levels found in high-income countries. Similarly, as we already noted, increases in capital per hour worked cannot sustain high rates of economic growth unless they are accompanied by technological change.

We can conclude that Singapore was unlikely to sustain its high growth rates in the years after 1995. In fact, from 1996 to 2010, the growth of real GDP per capita slowed to an average rate of 3.2 percent per year. Although this growth rate is comparable to rates experienced in high-income countries, such as the United States, it leads to a doubling of real GDP per capita only every 21.9 years rather than every 11.3 years.

Based on Alwyn Young, "The Tyranny of Numbers: Confronting the Statistical Realities of the East Asian Growth Experience," *Quarterly Journal of Economics*, Vol. 110, No. 3, August 1995, pp. 641–680; and International Monetary Fund, *World Economic Outlook Database*, September 2011.

**Your Turn:** For more practice, do related problem 1.12 on page 707 at the end of this chapter.      MyEconLab

Finally, an additional requirement for economic growth is that the government must provide secure rights to private property. As we saw in Chapter 2, a market system cannot function unless rights to private property are secure. In addition, the government can help the market work and aid economic growth by establishing an independent court system that enforces contracts between private individuals. Many economists would also say that the government has a role in facilitating the development of an efficient financial system, as well as systems of education, transportation, and communication. Economist Richard Sylla of New York University has argued that every country that has experienced economic growth first experienced a "financial revolution." For example, before the United States was able to experience significant economic growth in the early nineteenth century, the country's banking and monetary systems were reformed under the guidance of Alexander Hamilton, who was appointed the country's first secretary of the Treasury in 1789. Without supportive government policies, long-run economic growth is unlikely to occur.

| Making the Connection | ## What Explains Rapid Economic Growth in Botswana? |
|---|---|

Economic growth in much of sub-Saharan Africa has been very slow. As desperately poor as most of these countries were in 1960, some are even poorer today. The growth rate in one country in this region stands out, however, as being exceptionally rapid. The graph below shows the average annual growth rate in real GDP per capita between 1960 and 2009 for Botswana and the six most populous sub-Saharan countries. Botswana's average annual growth rate over this 49-year period was three times as great as that of Tanzania and South Africa, which were the second and third-fastest-growing countries in the group. Botswana may seem an unlikely country to experience rapid growth because it has been hard hit by the HIV epidemic. Despite the disruptive effects of the epidemic, growth in real per capita GDP continued to be rapid, with the International Monetary Fund projecting increases in real GDP per capita of 5.9 percent in 2010 and 5.0 percent in 2011.

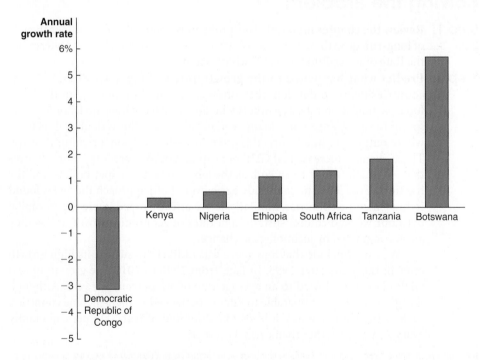

*Note:* Data for Democratic Republic of Congo are for 1970–2004.

Source: Authors' calculations from data in Alan Heston, Robert Summers, and Bettina Aten, *Penn World Table*, Version 7.0, Center for International Comparisons of Production, Income and Prices at the University of Pennsylvania, June 3, 2011.

What explains Botswana's rapid growth rate? Several factors have been important. Botswana avoided the civil wars that plagued other African countries during these years. The country also benefited from earnings from diamond exports. But many economists believe the pro-growth policies of Botswana's government are the most important reason for the country's success. Economists Shantayanan Devarajan of the World Bank, William Easterly of New York University, and Howard Pack of the University of Pennsylvania summarized these policies as follows:

> The government [of Botswana] made it clear it would protect private property rights. It was a "government of cattlemen" who were attuned to commercial interests. . . . The relative political stability and relatively low corruption also made Botswana a favorable location for investment. Botswana's relatively high level of press freedom and democracy (continuing a pre-colonial tradition that held chiefs responsible to tribal members) held the government responsible for any economic policy mistakes.

These policies—protecting private property, avoiding political instability and corruption, and allowing press freedom and democracy—may seem a straightforward recipe for providing an environment in which economic growth can occur. As we will see in Chapter 22, however, in practice, these are policies many countries have difficulty implementing successfully.

Based on International Monetary Fund, *World Economic Outlook Database*, September 2011; and Shantayanan Devarajan, William Easterly, and Howard Pack, "Low Investment Is Not the Constraint on African Development," *Economic Development and Cultural Change*, Vol. 51, No. 3, April 2003, pp. 547–571.

**Your Turn:** Test your understanding by doing related problem 1.14 on page 707 at the end of this chapter.    MyEconLab

# Potential GDP

Because economists take a long-run perspective in discussing economic growth, the concept of *potential GDP* is useful. **Potential GDP** is the level of real GDP attained when all firms are producing at capacity. The capacity of a firm is *not* the maximum output the firm is capable of producing. A Boeing assembly plant could operate 24 hours per day for 52 weeks per year and would be at its maximum production level. The plant's capacity, however, is measured by its production when operating on normal hours, using a normal workforce. If all firms in the economy were operating at capacity, the level of total production of final goods and services would equal potential GDP. Potential GDP increases over time as the labor force grows, new factories and office buildings are built, new machinery and equipment are installed, and technological change takes place.

Growth in potential GDP in the United States is estimated to be about 3.3 percent per year. In other words, each year, the capacity of the economy to produce final goods and services expands by 3.3 percent. The *actual* level of real GDP may increase by more or less than 3.3 percent as the economy moves through the business cycle. Figure 21.2 shows movements in actual and potential GDP for the years since 1989. The smooth red line represents potential GDP, and the blue line represents actual real GDP. Notice that in each of the three recessions since 1989, actual real GDP has fallen below potential GDP. During the 2007–2009 recession, the gap between actual real GDP and potential GDP was particularly large, which is an indication of how severe the recession was.

**Potential GDP** The level of real GDP attained when all firms are producing at capacity.

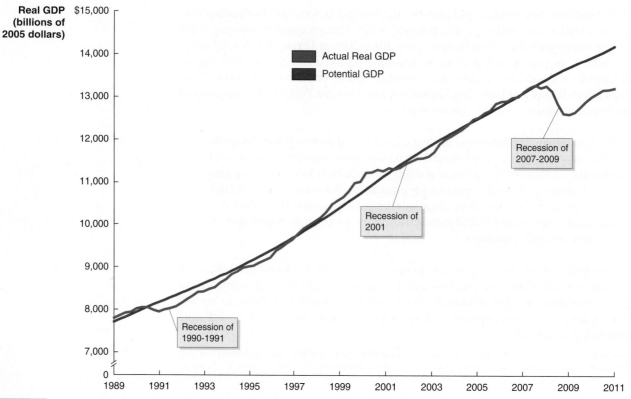

**Figure 21.2** **Actual and Potential GDP**

Potential GDP increases every year as the labor force and the capital stock grow and technological change occurs. The smooth red line represents potential GDP, and the blue line represents actual real GDP. During the three recessions since 1989, actual real GDP has been less than potential GDP.
Data from Federal Reserve Bank of St. Louis.

**21.2 LEARNING** OBJECTIVE

Discuss the role of the financial system in facilitating long-run economic growth.

# Saving, Investment, and the Financial System

The process of economic growth depends on the ability of firms to expand their operations, buy additional equipment, train workers, and adopt new technologies. Firms can finance some of these activities from *retained earnings*, which are profits that are reinvested in the firm rather than paid to the firm's owners. For many firms, retained earnings are not sufficient to finance the rapid expansion required in economies experiencing high rates of economic growth. Firms can acquire funds from households, either directly through financial markets—such as the stock and bond markets—or indirectly through financial intermediaries—such as banks. Financial markets and financial intermediaries together comprise the **financial system**. Without a well-functioning financial system, economic growth is impossible because firms will be unable to expand and adopt new technologies. As we noted earlier, no country without a well-developed financial system has been able to sustain high levels of economic growth.

**Financial system** The system of financial markets and financial intermediaries through which firms acquire funds from households.

## An Overview of the Financial System

The financial system channels funds from savers to borrowers and channels returns on the borrowed funds back to savers. Recall from Chapter 8 that in **financial markets**, such as the stock market or the bond market, firms raise funds by selling financial securities directly to savers. A *financial security* is a document—sometimes in electronic form—that states the terms under which funds pass from the buyer of the security— who is providing funds—to the seller. *Stocks* are financial securities that represent partial

**Financial markets** Markets where financial securities, such as stocks and bonds, are bought and sold.

ownership of a firm. If you buy one share of stock in General Electric, you become one of millions of owners of that firm. *Bonds* are financial securities that represent promises to repay a fixed amount of funds. When General Electric sells a bond, the firm promises to pay the purchaser of the bond an interest payment each year for the term of the bond, as well as a final payment of the amount of the loan.

**Financial intermediaries**, such as banks, mutual funds, pension funds, and insurance companies, act as go-betweens for borrowers and lenders. In effect, financial intermediaries borrow funds from savers and lend them to borrowers. When you deposit funds in your checking account, you are lending your funds to the bank. The bank may lend your funds (together with the funds of other savers) to an entrepreneur who wants to start a business. Suppose Lena wants to open a laundry. Rather than you lending money directly to Lena's Laundry, the bank acts as a go-between for you and Lena. Intermediaries pool the funds of many small savers to lend to many individual borrowers. The intermediaries pay interest to savers in exchange for the use of savers' funds and earn a profit by lending money to borrowers and charging borrowers a higher rate of interest on the loans. For example, a bank might pay you as a depositor a 3 percent rate of interest, while it lends the money to Lena's Laundry at a 6 percent rate of interest.

Banks, mutual funds, pension funds, and insurance companies also make investments in stocks and bonds on behalf of savers. For example, *mutual funds* sell shares to savers and then use the funds to buy a portfolio of stocks, bonds, mortgages, and other financial securities. Large mutual fund companies, such as Fidelity, Vanguard, and Dreyfus, offer many stock and bond funds. Some funds hold a wide range of stocks or bonds; others specialize in securities issued by a particular industry or sector, such as technology; and others invest as index funds in fixed market baskets of securities, such as shares of the Standard & Poor's 500 firms. Over the past 30 years, the role of mutual funds in the financial system has increased dramatically. Today, competition among hundreds of mutual fund firms gives investors thousands of funds from which to choose.

In addition to matching households that have excess funds with firms that want to borrow funds, the financial system provides three key services for savers and borrowers: risk sharing, liquidity, and information. *Risk* is the chance that the value of a financial security will change relative to what you expect. For example, you may buy a share of stock in Google at a price of $450, only to have the price fall to $100. Most individual savers are not gamblers and seek a steady return on their savings rather than erratic swings between high and low earnings. The financial system provides risk sharing by allowing savers to spread their money among many financial investments. For example, you can divide your money among a bank certificate of deposit, individual bonds, and a mutual fund.

*Liquidity* is the ease with which a financial security can be exchanged for money. The financial system provides the service of liquidity by providing savers with markets in which they can sell their holdings of financial securities. For example, savers can easily sell their holdings of the stocks and bonds issued by large corporations on the major stock and bond markets.

A third service that the financial system provides savers is the collection and communication of *information*, or facts about borrowers and expectations about returns on financial securities. For example, Lena's Laundry may want to borrow $10,000 from you. Finding out what Lena intends to do with the funds and how likely she is to pay you back may be costly and time-consuming. By depositing $10,000 in the bank, you are, in effect, allowing the bank to gather this information for you. Because banks specialize in gathering information on borrowers, they are able to do it faster and at a lower cost than can individual savers. The financial system plays an important role in communicating information. If you read a news story announcing that an automobile firm has invented a car with an engine that runs on water, how would you determine the effect of that discovery on the firm's profits? Financial markets do the job for you by incorporating information into the prices of stocks, bonds, and other financial securities. In this example, the expectation of higher future profits would boost the prices of the automobile firm's stock and bonds.

**Financial intermediaries** Firms, such as banks, mutual funds, pension funds, and insurance companies, that borrow funds from savers and lend them to borrowers.

## The Macroeconomics of Saving and Investment

As we have seen, the funds available to firms through the financial system come from saving. When firms use funds to purchase machinery, factories, and office buildings, they are engaging in investment. In this section, we explore the macroeconomics of saving and investment. A key point we will develop is that *the total value of saving in the economy must equal the total value of investment*. We saw in Chapter 19 that *national income accounting* refers to the methods the Bureau of Economic Analysis uses to keep track of total production and total income in the economy. We can use some relationships from national income accounting to understand why total saving must equal total investment.

We begin with the relationship between GDP ($Y$) and its components, consumption ($C$), investment ($I$), government purchases ($G$), and net exports ($NX$):

$$Y = C + I + G + NX.$$

Remember that GDP is a measure of both total production in the economy and total income.

In an *open economy*, there is interaction with other economies in terms of both trading of goods and services and borrowing and lending. All economies today are open economies, although they vary significantly in the extent of their openness. In a *closed economy*, there is no trading or borrowing and lending with other economies. For simplicity, we will develop the relationship between saving and investment for a closed economy. This allows us to focus on the most important points in a simpler framework. We will consider the case of an open economy in Chapter 29.

In a closed economy, net exports are zero, so we can rewrite the relationship between GDP and its components as

$$Y = C + I + G.$$

If we rearrange this relationship, we have an expression for investment in terms of the other variables:

$$I = Y - C - G.$$

This expression tells us that in a closed economy, investment spending is equal to total income minus consumption spending and minus government purchases.

We can also derive an expression for total saving. *Private saving* is equal to what households retain of their income after purchasing goods and services ($C$) and paying taxes ($T$). Households receive income for supplying the factors of production to firms. This portion of household income is equal to $Y$. Households also receive income from government in the form of *transfer payments* ($TR$). Recall that transfer payments include Social Security payments and unemployment insurance payments. We can write an expression for private saving ($S_{\text{Private}}$):

$$S_{\text{Private}} = Y + TR - C - T.$$

The government also engages in saving. *Public saving* ($S_{\text{Public}}$) equals the amount of tax revenue the government retains after paying for government purchases and making transfer payments to households:

$$S_{\text{Public}} = T - G - TR.$$

So, total saving in the economy ($S$) is equal to the sum of private saving and public saving:

$$S = S_{\text{Private}} + S_{\text{Public}},$$

or:

$$S = (Y + TR - C - T) + (T - G - TR),$$

or:

$$S = Y - C - G.$$

The right side of this expression is identical to the expression we derived earlier for investment spending. So, we can conclude that total saving must equal total investment:

$$S = I.$$

When the government spends the same amount that it collects in taxes, there is a *balanced budget*. When the government spends more than it collects in taxes, there is a *budget deficit*. In the case of a deficit, $T$ is less than $G+TR$, which means that public saving is negative. Negative saving is also known as *dissaving*. How can public saving be negative? When the federal government runs a budget deficit, the U.S. Department of the Treasury sells Treasury bonds to borrow the money necessary to fund the gap between taxes and spending. In this case, rather than adding to the total amount of saving available to be borrowed for investment spending, the government is subtracting from it. (Notice that if households borrow more than they save, the total amount of saving will also fall.) With less saving, investment must also be lower. We can conclude that, holding constant all other factors, there is a lower level of investment spending in the economy when there is a budget deficit than when there is a balanced budget.

When the government spends less than it collects in taxes, there is a *budget surplus*. A budget surplus increases public saving and the total level of saving in the economy. A higher level of saving results in a higher level of investment spending. Therefore, holding constant all other factors, there is a higher level of investment spending in the economy when there is a budget surplus than when there is a balanced budget.

The U.S. federal government has experienced dramatic swings in the state of its budget over the past 20 years. In 1992, the federal budget deficit was $297.4 billion. The federal budget had a surplus of $189.5 billion in 2000, but a dramatic decline in taxes and increase in government spending resulting from the recession of 2007–2009 led to record deficits of $1.4 trillion in 2009 and $1.5 trillion in 2010.

## The Market for Loanable Funds

We have seen that the value of total saving must equal the value of total investment, but we have not yet discussed how this equality is actually brought about in the financial system. We can think of the financial system as being composed of many markets through which funds flow from lenders to borrowers: the market for certificates of deposit at banks, the market for stocks, the market for bonds, the market for mutual fund shares, and so on. For simplicity, we can combine these markets into a single market for *loanable funds*. In the model of the **market for loanable funds**, the interaction of borrowers and lenders determines the market interest rate and the quantity of loanable funds exchanged. As we will discuss in Chapter 29, firms can also borrow from savers in other countries. For the remainder of this chapter, we will assume that there are no interactions between households and firms in the United States and those in other countries.

**Market for loanable funds** The interaction of borrowers and lenders that determines the market interest rate and the quantity of loanable funds exchanged.

**Demand and Supply in the Loanable Funds Market** The demand for loanable funds is determined by the willingness of firms to borrow money to engage in new investment projects, such as building new factories or carrying out research and development of new products. In determining whether to borrow funds, firms compare the return they expect to make on an investment with the interest rate they must pay to borrow the necessary funds. For example, if Home Depot is considering opening several new stores and expects to earn a return of 15 percent on its investment, the investment will be profitable if Home Depot can borrow the funds at an interest rate of 10 percent but will not be profitable if the interest rate is 20 percent. In Figure 21.3, the demand for loanable funds is downward sloping because the lower the interest rate, the more investment projects firms can profitably undertake, and the greater the quantity of loanable funds they will demand.

The supply of loanable funds is determined by the willingness of households to save and by the extent of government saving or dissaving. When households save, they reduce the amount of goods and services they can consume and enjoy today. The willingness

## Figure 21.3

### The Market for Loanable Funds

The demand for loanable funds is determined by the willingness of firms to borrow money to engage in new investment projects. The supply of loanable funds is determined by the willingness of households to save and by the extent of government saving or dissaving. Equilibrium in the market for loanable funds determines the real interest rate and the quantity of loanable funds exchanged.

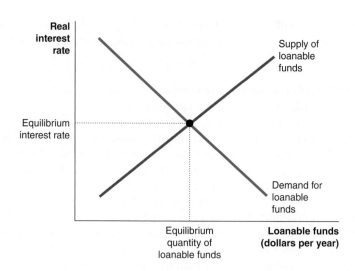

of households to save rather than consume their incomes today will be determined in part by the interest rate they receive when they lend their savings. The higher the interest rate, the greater the reward for saving and the larger the amount of funds households will save. Therefore, the supply curve for loanable funds in Figure 21.3 is upward sloping because the higher the interest rate, the greater the quantity of saving supplied.

In Chapter 20, we discussed the distinction between the *nominal interest rate* and the *real interest rate*. The nominal interest rate is the stated interest rate on a loan. The real interest rate corrects the nominal interest rate for the effect of inflation and is equal to the nominal interest rate minus the inflation rate. Because both borrowers and lenders are interested in the real interest rate they will receive or pay, equilibrium in the market for loanable funds determines the real interest rate rather than the nominal interest rate.

*Who was better for economic growth: Scrooge the saver or Scrooge the spender?*

**Making the Connection** | **Ebenezer Scrooge: Accidental Promoter of Economic Growth?**

Ebenezer Scrooge's name has become synonymous with miserliness. Before his reform at the end of Charles Dickens's *A Christmas Carol*, Scrooge is extraordinarily reluctant to spend money. Although he earns a substantial income, he lives in a cold, dark house that he refuses to heat or light adequately, and he eats a meager diet of gruel because he refuses to buy more expensive food. Throughout most of the book, Dickens portrays Scrooge's behavior in an unfavorable way. Only at the end of the book, when the reformed Scrooge begins to spend lavishly on himself and others, does Dickens praise his behavior.

As economist Steven Landsburg of the University of Rochester points out, however, economically speaking, it may be the pre-reform Scrooge who is more worthy of praise:

> In this whole world, there is nobody more generous than the miser—the man who could deplete the world's resources but chooses not to. The only difference between miserliness and philanthropy is that the philanthropist serves a favored few while the miser spreads his largess far and wide.

We can extend Landsburg's discussion to consider whether the actions of the pre-reform Scrooge or the actions of the post-reform Scrooge are more helpful to economic growth. Pre-reform Scrooge spends very little, investing most of his income in the financial markets. These funds became available for firms to borrow to build new factories and to carry out research and development. Post-reform Scrooge spends much more—and saves much less. Funds that he had previously saved are now spent on food for Bob Cratchit's family and on "making merry" at Christmas. In other words, the actions of post-reform Scrooge contribute to more consumption goods being produced and fewer investment goods. We can conclude that Scrooge's reform caused economic growth to slow down—if only by a little. The larger point is, of course, that savers provide the funds that are indispensable for the investment spending that economic growth requires, and the only way to save is to not consume.

From "What I Like About Scrooge," *Slate*, December 9, 2004.

**Your Turn:** Test your understanding by doing related problem 2.16 on page 708 at the end of this chapter.   MyEconLab

## Explaining Movements in Saving, Investment, and Interest Rates

Equilibrium in the market for loanable funds determines the quantity of loanable funds that will flow from lenders to borrowers each period. It also determines the real interest rate that lenders will receive and that borrowers must pay. We draw the demand curve for loanable funds by holding constant all factors, other than the interest rate, that affect the willingness of borrowers to demand funds. We draw the supply curve by holding constant all factors, other than the interest rate, that affect the willingness of lenders to supply funds. A shift in either the demand curve or the supply curve will change the equilibrium interest rate and the equilibrium quantity of loanable funds.

If, for example, the profitability of new investment increases due to technological change, firms will increase their demand for loanable funds. Figure 21.4 shows the effect of an increase in demand in the market for loanable funds. As in the markets for goods and services we studied in Chapter 3, an increase in demand in the market for loanable funds shifts the demand curve to the right. In the new equilibrium, the interest rate increases from $i_1$ to $i_2$, and the equilibrium quantity of loanable funds increases from $L_1$ to $L_2$. Notice that an increase in the quantity of loanable funds means that both the quantity of saving by households and the quantity of investment by firms have increased.

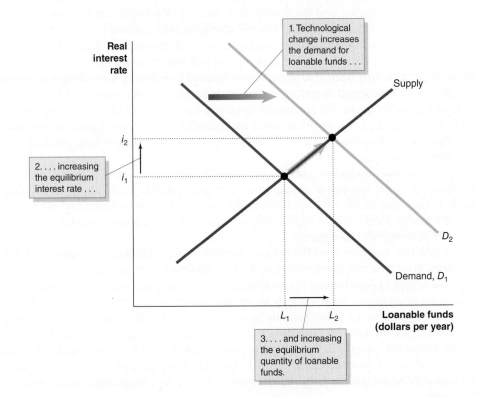

**Figure 21.4**

**An Increase in the Demand for Loanable Funds**

An increase in the demand for loanable funds increases the equilibrium interest rate from $i_1$ to $i_2$, and it increases the equilibrium quantity of loanable funds from $L_1$ to $L_2$. As a result, saving and investment both increase.

**Figure 21.5**

**The Effect of a Budget Deficit on the Market for Loanable Funds**

When the government begins running a budget deficit, the supply of loanable funds shifts to the left. The equilibrium interest rate increases from $i_1$ to $i_2$, and the equilibrium quantity of loanable funds falls from $L_1$ to $L_2$. As a result, saving and investment both decline.

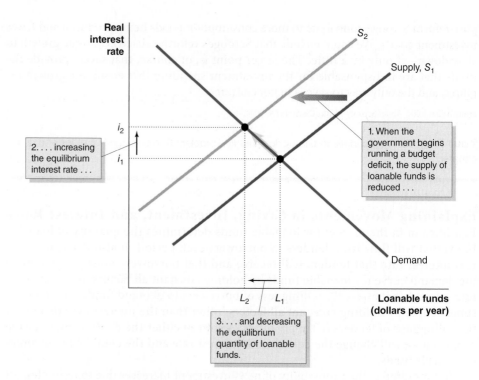

2. . . . increasing the equilibrium interest rate . . .

1. When the government begins running a budget deficit, the supply of loanable funds is reduced . . .

3. . . . and decreasing the equilibrium quantity of loanable funds.

**Crowding out** A decline in private expenditures as a result of an increase in government purchases.

Increasing investment increases the capital stock and the quantity of capital per hour worked, helping to increase economic growth.

We can also use the market for loanable funds to examine the effect of a government budget deficit. Putting aside the effects of foreign saving—which we will consider in Chapter 29—recall that if the government begins running a budget deficit, it reduces the total amount of saving in the economy. Suppose the government increases spending, which results in a budget deficit. We illustrate the effects of the budget deficit in Figure 21.5 by shifting the supply of loanable funds to the left. In the new equilibrium, the interest rate is higher, and the equilibrium quantity of loanable funds is lower. Running a deficit has reduced the level of total saving in the economy and, by increasing the interest rate, has also reduced the level of investment spending by firms. By borrowing to finance its budget deficit, the government will have *crowded out* some firms that would otherwise have been able to borrow to finance investment. **Crowding out** refers to a decline in investment spending as a result of an increase in government purchases. In Figure 21.5, the decline in investment spending due to crowding out is shown by the movement from $L_1$ to $L_2$ on the demand for loanable funds curve. Lower investment spending means that the capital stock and the quantity of capital per hour worked will not increase as much.

A government budget surplus has the opposite effect of a deficit: A budget surplus increases the total amount of saving in the economy, shifting the supply of loanable funds to the right. In the new equilibrium, the interest rate will be lower, and the quantity of loanable funds will be higher. We can conclude that a budget surplus increases the level of saving and investment.

In practice, however, the effect of government budget deficits and surpluses on the equilibrium interest rate is relatively small. (This finding reflects in part the importance of global saving in determining the interest rate.) For example, a recent study found that increasing government borrowing by an amount equal to 1 percent of GDP would increase the equilibrium real interest rate by only about 0.003 percentage point. However, this small effect on interest rates does not imply that we can ignore the effect of deficits on economic growth. Paying off government debt in the future may require higher taxes, which can depress economic growth. In 2011, many economists and policymakers were concerned that the large deficits projected for future years might be an obstacle to growth.

# Solved Problem 21.2

## How Would a Consumption Tax Affect Saving, Investment, the Interest Rate, and Economic Growth?

Some economists and policymakers have suggested that the federal government shift from relying on an income tax to relying on a *consumption tax*. Under the income tax, households pay taxes on all income earned. Under a consumption tax, households pay taxes only on the income they spend.

Households would pay taxes on saved income only if they spent the money at a later time. Use the market for loanable funds model to analyze the effect on saving, investment, the interest rate, and economic growth of switching from an income tax to a consumption tax.

## Solving the Problem

**Step 1:** **Review the chapter material.** This problem is about applying the market for loanable funds model, so you may want to review the section "Explaining Movements in Saving, Investment, and Interest Rates," which begins on page 691.

**Step 2:** **Explain the effect of switching from an income tax to a consumption tax.** Households are interested in the return they receive from saving after they have paid their taxes. For example, consider someone who puts his savings in a certificate of deposit at an interest rate of 4 percent and whose tax rate is 25 percent. Under an income tax, this person's after-tax return to saving is 3 percent $[4 - (4 \times 0.25)]$. Under a consumption tax, income that is saved is not taxed, so the return rises to 4 percent. We can conclude that moving from an income tax to a consumption tax would increase the return to saving, causing the supply of loanable funds to increase.

**Step 3:** **Draw a graph of the market for loanable funds to illustrate your answer.** The supply curve for loanable funds will shift to the right as the after-tax return to saving increases under the consumption tax. The equilibrium interest rate will fall, and the levels of saving and investment will both increase. Because investment increases, the capital stock and the quantity of capital per hour worked will grow, and the rate of economic growth should increase. Note that the size of the fall in the interest rate and size of the increase in loanable funds shown in the graph are larger than the effects that most economists expect would actually result from the replacement of the income tax with a consumption tax.

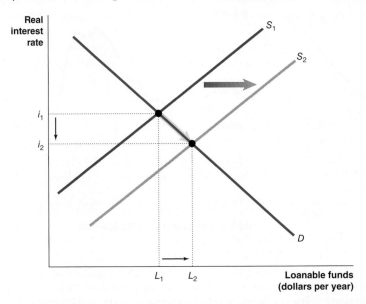

**Your Turn:** For more practice, do related problem 2.15 on page 708 at the end of this chapter.    MyEconLab

**21.3 LEARNING** OBJECTIVE

Explain what happens during
the business cycle.

# The Business Cycle

Figure 21.1 on page 679 illustrates the tremendous increase during the past 110 years in the standard of living of the average American. But close inspection of the figure reveals that real GDP per capita did not increase every year during this time. For example, during the first half of the 1930s, real GDP per capita *fell* for several years in a row. What accounts for these fluctuations in the long-run upward trend?

## Some Basic Business Cycle Definitions

The fluctuations in real GDP *per capita* shown in Figure 21.1 reflect the underlying fluctuations in real GDP. Since at least the early nineteenth century, the U.S. economy has experienced business cycles that consist of alternating periods of expanding and contracting economic activity. Because real GDP is our best measure of economic activity, the business cycle is usually illustrated using movements in real GDP.

During the *expansion phase* of the business cycle, production, employment, and income are increasing. The period of expansion ends with a *business cycle peak*. Following the business cycle peak, production, employment, and income decline as the economy enters the *recession phase* of the cycle. The recession comes to an end with a *business cycle trough*, after which another period of expansion begins. Figure 21.6 illustrates the phases of the business cycle. Panel (a) shows an idealized business cycle, with real GDP increasing smoothly in an expansion to a business cycle peak and then decreasing smoothly in a recession to a business cycle trough, which is followed by another expansion. Panel (b) shows the somewhat messier reality of an actual business cycle by plotting fluctuations in real GDP during the period from 2005 to 2011. The figure shows that the expansion that began in 2001 continued until a business cycle peak was reached in December 2007. The following recession was the longest and the most severe since the Great Depression of the 1930s. The severity of the recession led some economists to refer to it as the "Great Recession." A business cycle trough was reached in June 2009, when the next expansion began. Although real GDP grew following the business cycle trough, the growth was slower than is typical at the beginning of a business cycle expansion.

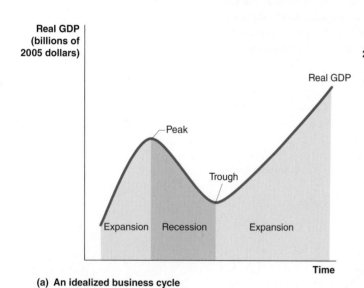

**(a) An idealized business cycle**

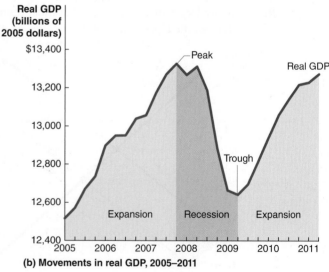

**(b) Movements in real GDP, 2005–2011**

**Figure 21.6**   **The Business Cycle**

Panel (a) shows an idealized business cycle, with real GDP increasing smoothly in an expansion to a business cycle peak and then decreasing smoothly in a recession to a business cycle trough, which is followed by another expansion. The periods of expansion are shown in green, and the period of recession is shown

in red. Panel (b) shows the actual movements in real GDP for 2005 to 2011. The recession that began following the business cycle peak in December 2007 was the longest and the most severe since the Great Depression of the 1930s.

| Peak | Trough | Length of Recession |
|------|--------|---------------------|
| July 1953 | May 1954 | 10 months |
| August 1957 | April 1958 | 8 months |
| April 1960 | February 1961 | 10 months |
| December 1969 | November 1970 | 11 months |
| November 1973 | March 1975 | 16 months |
| January 1980 | July 1980 | 6 months |
| July 1981 | November 1982 | 16 months |
| July 1990 | March 1991 | 8 months |
| March 2001 | November 2001 | 8 months |
| December 2007 | June 2009 | 18 months |

**Table 21.1**

**The U.S. Business Cycle**

Data from National Bureau of Economic Research.

## How Do We Know When the Economy Is in a Recession?

The federal government produces many statistics that make it possible to monitor the economy. But the federal government does not officially decide when a recession begins or when it ends. Instead, most economists accept the decisions of the Business Cycle Dating Committee of the National Bureau of Economic Research (NBER), a private research group located in Cambridge, Massachusetts. Although writers for newspapers and magazines often define a recession as two consecutive quarters of declining real GDP, the NBER has a broader definition: "A recession is a significant decline in activity spread across the economy, lasting more than a few months, visible in industrial production, employment, real income, and wholesale–retail trade."

The NBER is fairly slow in announcing business cycle dates because it takes time to gather and analyze economic statistics. Typically, the NBER will announce that the economy is in a recession only well after the recession has begun. For instance, the NBER did not announce that a recession had begun in December 2007 until 11 months later, at the end of November 2008. Table 21.1 lists the business cycle peaks and troughs identified by the NBER for the years since 1950. The length of each recession is the number of months from each peak to the following trough.

**Making the Connection** | ### Can a Recession Be a Good Time for a Business to Expand?

During a recession, business managers have to quickly make many decisions, such as whether to reduce production, cut prices, close stores or other facilities, or lay off workers. In addition to making decisions aimed at dealing with the immediate effects of the recession, managers also have to consider how to prepare for the expansion that will follow the recession. Managers know that every recession, even one as severe as the recession of 2007–2009, will be followed by an expansion during which demand for their products is likely to increase. But it can be difficult to commit resources to future expansion when current conditions are bleak and when the end of the recession is difficult to predict.

The payoff, though, to preparing for future growth can be very large. For example, at the end of World War II in 1945, many economists and business managers expected that the U.S. economy would enter a severe recession. Sears and Montgomery Ward were the two largest department store chains in the country. Sears CEO Robert Wood, expecting continuing prosperity, moved to open new stores across the country, while Sewell Avery, CEO of Montgomery Ward, expecting falling incomes and rising unemployment, refused to authorize any new stores and closed a number of existing ones. As a result, when strong economic growth occurred during the late 1940s, Sears rapidly gained market share at Montgomery Ward's expense.

*Businesses such as Intel viewed the recession of 2007–2009 as an opportunity to expand operations.*

Following the September 11, 2001, terrorist attacks, the managers of many hotels expected a prolonged period of reduced travel. They responded by laying off workers and postponing or canceling new construction. Isadore Sharp, the chairman and CEO of Four Seasons Hotels, decided that although the recession would severely hurt the hotel industry, the effects would be short-lived. He decided to push ahead with construction of 18 hotels and begin construction of 10 more. By his own account, "We maintained or enhanced our market share in most regions, contrary to the predictions of various industry experts." In a letter to his shareholders in March 2002, he wrote: "We are well positioned for the economic recovery expected later this year."

During the severe recession of 2007–2009, managers had similar decisions to make. Based in Greensboro, North Carolina, VF Corporation is the largest apparel maker in the world. While many firms, such as J.Crew, Anne Klein, and Liz Claiborne, were closing stores or postponing opening new ones, VF CEO Eric Wiseman pushed ahead, opening 89 stores in 2008 and 70 in 2009. One retail analyst was quoted as saying: "Unfortunately, many companies pull in the reins in a downturn, but these are often the best opportunities to grow." Similarly, Intel, the computer chip manufacturer, decided in early 2009 to proceed with a $7 billion expansion of its factories in the United States, while many rival firms were reducing their spending on new factories as computer sales declined. Intel's CEO Paul Otellini was quoted as saying, "I thought it was important for a company like Intel to stand up and say we have confidence." Heavy equipment manufacturer Caterpillar, Inc., announced that it would build several new facilities and expand some existing ones in order "to meet the expected increase in customer demand."

Through 2011, the recovery from the 2007–2009 recession was much slower than the typical recovery, which led some economists and analysts to wonder whether continued slow growth might make the decision by some businesses to expand less profitable than expected. So, how the decisions by VF, Intel, and Caterpillar will turn out remains to be seen, but, over the long run, for many firms, betting on the future of the U.S. economy has paid off.

Based on Robert Sobel, *When Giants Stumble*, (Paramus, NJ: Prentice Hall, 1999); Isadore Sharp, *Four Seasons: The Story of a Business Philosophy*, (New York: Portfolio, 2009); Bob Tita, "Caterpillar to Expand Kansas Plant," *Wall Street Journal*, August 18, 2011; Rachel Dodes, "VF Dresses Up Its Operations, Bucking Recession," *Wall Street Journal*, March 31, 2009; and Don Clark, "Intel to Invest $7 Billion in U.S. Plants," *Wall Street Journal*, February 10, 2009.

MyEconLab    **Your Turn:** Test your understanding by doing related problem 3.7 on page 709 at the end of this chapter.

## What Happens during the Business Cycle?

Each business cycle is different. The lengths of the expansion and recession phases and which sectors of the economy are most affected are rarely the same in any two cycles. But most business cycles share certain characteristics, which we will discuss in this section. As the economy nears the end of an expansion, interest rates are usually rising, and the wages of workers are usually rising faster than prices. As a result of rising interest rates and rising wages, the profits of firms will be falling. Typically, toward the end of an expansion, both households and firms will have substantially increased their debts. These debts are the result of the borrowing that firms and households undertake to help finance their spending during the expansion.

A recession will often begin with a decline in spending by firms on capital goods, such as machinery, equipment, new factories, and new office buildings, or by households on new houses and consumer durables, such as furniture and automobiles. As spending declines, firms selling capital goods and consumer durables will find their sales declining. As sales decline, firms cut back on production and begin to lay off workers. Rising unemployment and falling profits reduce income, which leads to further declines in spending.

As the recession continues, economic conditions gradually begin to improve. The declines in spending eventually come to an end; households and firms begin to reduce their debt, thereby increasing their ability to spend; and interest rates decline, making it more likely that households and firms will borrow to finance new spending. Firms begin to increase their spending on capital goods as they anticipate the need for additional production during the next expansion. Increased spending by households on consumer durables and by businesses on capital goods will finally bring the recession to an end and begin the next expansion.

**The Effect of the Business Cycle on Boeing** *Durables* are goods that are expected to last for three or more years. Consumer durables include furniture, appliances, and automobiles, and producer durables include machine tools, electric generators, and commercial airplanes. *Nondurables* are goods that are expected to last for fewer than three years. Consumer nondurables include goods such as food and clothing. Durables are affected more by the business cycle than are nondurables. During a recession, workers reduce spending if they lose their jobs, fear losing their jobs, or suffer wage cuts. Because people can often continue using their existing furniture, appliances, or automobiles, they are more likely to postpone spending on durables than spending on nondurables. Similarly, when firms experience declining sales and profits during a recession, they often cut back on purchases of producer durables.

We mentioned in our discussion of Boeing at the beginning of this chapter that the firm's sales are significantly affected by the business cycle. Panel (a) of Figure 21.7 shows movements in real GDP for each quarter from the beginning of 1990 through the end of 2010. We can see both the upward trend in real GDP over time and the effects of the recessions of 1990–1991, 2001, and 2007–2009. Panel (b) shows movements in the total

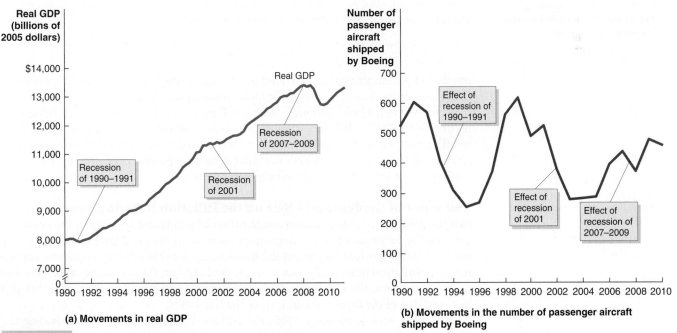

**(a) Movements in real GDP**

**(b) Movements in the number of passenger aircraft shipped by Boeing**

**Figure 21.7** **The Effect of the Business Cycle on Boeing**

Panel (a) shows movements in real GDP for each quarter from the beginning of 1990 through the end of 2010. Panel (b) shows movements in the number of passenger aircraft shipped by Boeing for the same years. In panel (b), the effects of the recessions on Boeing are typically more dramatic than the effects on

the economy as a whole, although Boeing suffered a relatively mild decline in deliveries during the 2007–2009 recession.

Data from U.S. Bureau of Economic Analysis; and Boeing.

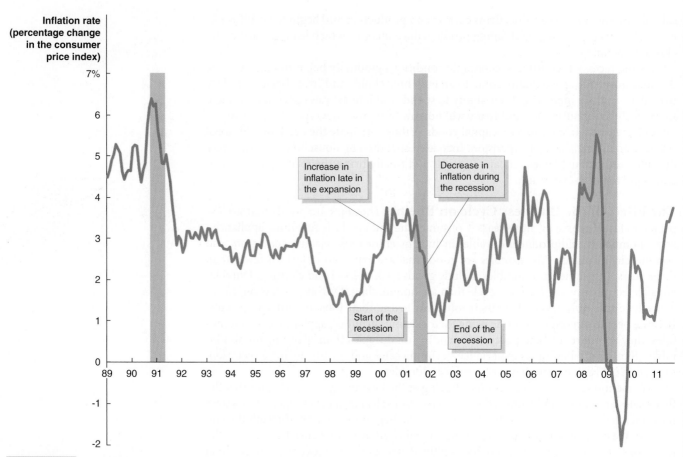

**Figure 21.8** **The Effect of Recessions on the Inflation Rate**

Toward the end of a typical expansion, the inflation rate begins to rise. Recessions, marked by the shaded vertical bars, cause the inflation rate to fall. By the end of a recession, the inflation rate is significantly below what it had been at the beginning of the recession.

*Note:* The points on the figure represent the annual inflation rate measured by the percentage change in the consumer price index from the same month during the previous year. Data from U.S. Bureau of Labor Statistics.

number of passenger aircraft delivered by Boeing during the same years. The effects of the recessions on Boeing are typically more dramatic and long-lived than the effects on the economy as a whole, although Boeing suffered a relatively mild decline in deliveries during the 2007–2009 recession as increased demand from foreign airlines helped to offset declines in demand from U.S. airlines. In each of the recessions shown, U.S. airlines suffered declines in ticket sales and cut back on purchases of aircraft. As a result, Boeing suffered declines in sales during each recession.

**The Effect of the Business Cycle on the Inflation Rate** In Chapter 20, we saw that the *price level* measures the average prices of goods and services in the economy and that the *inflation rate* is the percentage increase in the price level from one year to the next. An important fact about the business cycle is that during economic expansions, the inflation rate usually increases, particularly near the end of the expansion, and during recessions, the inflation rate usually decreases. Figure 21.8 illustrates that this has been true of the three recessions since the late 1980s.

In every recession since 1950, the inflation rate has been lower during the 12 months after the recession ends than it was during the 12 months before the recession began. The average decline in the inflation rate has been about 2.5 percentage points. This result is not surprising. During a business cycle expansion, spending by businesses and households is strong, and producers of goods and services find it easier to raise prices. As spending declines during a recession, firms have a more difficult

# Don't Let This Happen to You

## Don't Confuse the Price Level and the Inflation Rate

Do you agree with the following statement: "The consumer price index is a widely used measure of the inflation rate"? This statement may sound plausible, but it is incorrect. As we saw in Chapter 20, the consumer price index is a measure of the *price level*, not of the inflation rate. We can measure the inflation rate as the *percentage change* in the consumer price index from one year to the next. In macroeconomics, it is important not to confuse the level of a variable with the change in the variable. To give another example, real GDP does not measure economic growth. Economic growth is measured by the percentage change in real GDP from one year to the next.

### MyEconLab

**Your Turn:** Test your understanding by doing related problem 3.6 on page 709 at the end of this chapter.

time selling their goods and services and are likely to increase prices less than they otherwise might have.

**The Effect of the Business Cycle on the Unemployment Rate**   Recessions cause the inflation rate to fall, but they cause the unemployment rate to increase. As firms see their sales decline, they begin to reduce production and lay off workers. Figure 21.9

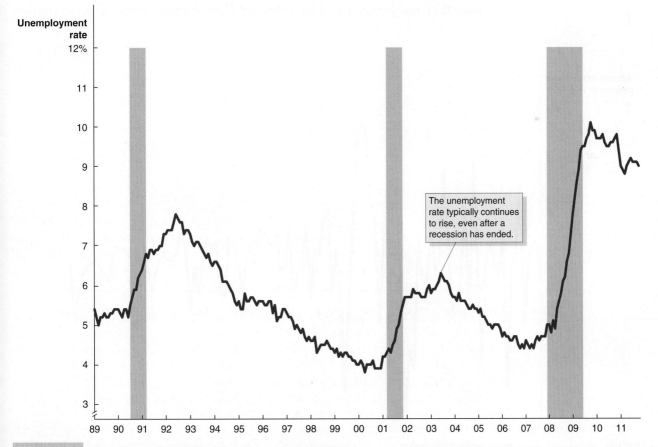

The unemployment rate typically continues to rise, even after a recession has ended.

**Figure 21.9   How Recessions Affect the Unemployment Rate**

Unemployment rises during recessions and falls during expansions. The reluctance of firms to hire new employees during the early stages of a recovery means that the unemployment rate usually continues to rise even after the recession has ended.

Data from U.S. Bureau of Labor Statistics.

shows that this has been true of the three recessions since the late 1980s. Notice in the figure that the unemployment rate continued to rise even after the recessions of 1990–1991, 2001, and 2007–2009 had ended. This pattern, which is typical, is due to two factors. First, even though employment begins to increase as the recession ends, it may be increasing more slowly than the growth in the labor force resulting from population growth. If employment grows slowly enough relative to the growth in the labor force, it is possible for the unemployment rate to increase. Second, some firms continue to operate well below their capacity even after a recession has ended and production has begun to increase. As a result, at first, firms may not hire back all the workers they have laid off and may even continue for a while to lay off more workers.

During the recessions since 1950, the unemployment rate has risen on average by about 1.2 percentage points during the 12 months after a recession has begun. So, on average, more than 1 million more workers have been unemployed during the 12 months after a recession has begun than during the previous 12 months.

**Is the "Great Moderation" Over?** Figure 21.10, which shows the year-to-year percentage changes in real GDP since 1900, illustrates a striking change in fluctuations in real GDP beginning around 1950. Before 1950, real GDP went through much greater year-to-year fluctuations than it has since that time. Fluctuations since the mid-1980s have been particularly mild. By the early twenty-first century, some economists had begun referring to the absence of severe recessions in the United States as the "Great Moderation." However, economists began questioning this view with the recession that began in December 2007. This recession was the longest and most severe since the Great Depression of the 1930s and was referred to as the Great Contraction.

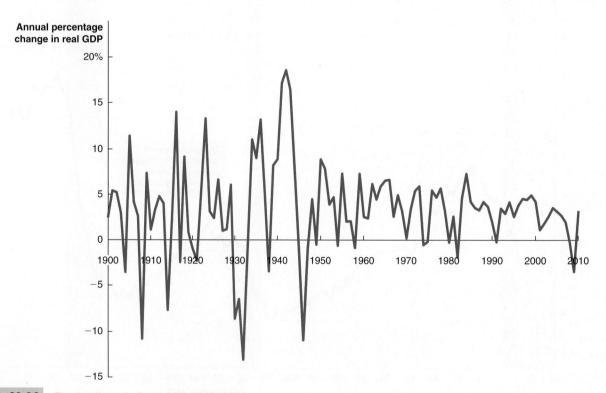

**Figure 21.10** Fluctuations in Real GDP, 1900–2010

Fluctuations in real GDP were greater before 1950 than they have been since 1950.

Data from Louis D. Johnston and Samuel H. Williamson, "What Was the U.S. GDP Then?" Measuring Worth, 2011; and U.S. Bureau of Economic Analysis.

| Period | Average Length of Expansions | Average Length of Recessions |
|---|---|---|
| 1870–1900 | 26 months | 26 months |
| 1900–1950 | 25 months | 19 months |
| 1950–2009 | 61 months | 11 months |

**Table 21.2**

**Until 2007, the Business Cycle Had Become Milder**

*Note:* The World War I and World War II periods have been omitted from the computations in the table. The expansion that began in June 2009 is not included.
Data from National Bureau of Economic Research.

The percentage decline in real GDP during 2009 was the largest since 1932. Economists and policymakers were unsure whether the Great Moderation would return with the end of the Great Contraction.

The unusual severity of the 2007–2009 recession can be seen by comparing its length to the lengths of other recent recessions. Table 21.2 shows that in the late nineteenth century, the average length of recessions was the same as the average length of expansions. During the first half of the twentieth century, the average length of expansions decreased slightly, and the average length of recessions decreased significantly. As a result, expansions were about six months longer than recessions during these years. The most striking change came after 1950, when the length of expansions greatly increased and the length of recessions decreased. After 1950, expansions were more than five times as long as recessions. In other words, in the late nineteenth century, the U.S. economy spent as much time in recession as it did in expansion. After 1950, the U.S. economy experienced long expansions interrupted by relatively short recessions.

The recession of 2007–2009 is an exception to this experience of relatively short, mild recessions. The recession lasted 18 months, the longest of the post-1950 period. Does the length and depth of the 2007–2009 recession indicate that the United States is returning to an era of severe fluctuations in real GDP? A full answer to this question will not be possible for at least several years. But in the next section, we provide some perspective on the question by considering why the period from 1950 to 2007 was one of relative macroeconomic stability.

## Will the U.S. Economy Return to Stability?

Shorter recessions, longer expansions, and less severe fluctuations in real GDP have resulted in a significant improvement in the economic well-being of Americans. Economists have offered several explanations for why the U.S. economy experienced a period of relative stability from 1950 to 2007:

- *The increasing importance of services and the declining importance of goods.* As services such as medical care or investment advice have become a much larger fraction of GDP, there has been a corresponding relative decline in the production of goods. For example, at one time, manufacturing production accounted for about 40 percent of GDP, but in 2010, it accounted for less than 12 percent. Manufacturing production, particularly production of durable goods such as automobiles, fluctuates more than the production of services. Because durable goods are usually more expensive than services, during a recession households will cut back more on purchases of durables than they will on purchases of services.

- *The establishment of unemployment insurance and other government transfer programs that provide funds to the unemployed.* Before the 1930s, programs such as unemployment insurance, which provides government payments to workers who lose their jobs, and Social Security, which provides government payments to retired and disabled workers, did not exist. These and other government programs make it possible for workers who lose their jobs during recessions to have higher incomes and, therefore, to spend more than they would otherwise. This additional spending may have helped to shorten recessions.

- *Active federal government policies to stabilize the economy.* Before the Great Depression of the 1930s, the federal government did not attempt to end recessions or prolong expansions. Because the Great Depression was so severe, with the unemployment rate rising to more than 20 percent of the labor force and real GDP declining by almost 30 percent, public opinion began favoring government attempts to stabilize the economy. In the years since World War II, the federal government has actively tried to use macroeconomic policy measures to end recessions and prolong expansions. Many economists believe that these government policies have played a key role in stabilizing the economy. Other economists, however, argue that active government policy has had little effect. The debate over the role of macroeconomic policy became particularly intense during and after the 2007–2009 recession. We will consider the debate over macroeconomic policy further in Chapters 26 and 27, when we discuss the federal government's *monetary* and *fiscal policies.*

- *The increased stability of the financial system.* The severity of the Great Depression of the 1930s was caused in part by instability in the financial system. More than 5,000 banks failed between 1929 and 1933, reducing the savings of many households and making it difficult for households and firms to obtain the credit needed to maintain their spending. In addition, a decline of more than 80 percent in stock prices greatly reduced the wealth of many households and made it difficult for firms to raise funds by selling stock. In Chapters 25 and 26, we will discuss some of the institutional changes that resulted in increased stability in the financial system during the years after the Great Depression. Most economists believe that the return of financial instability during the 2007–2009 recession is a key reason the recession was so severe. If the United States is to return to macroeconomic stability, stability will first have to return to the financial system.

Continued from page 677

## Economics in Your Life

### Do You Help the Economy More if You Spend or if You Save?

At the beginning of the chapter, we posed a question: Which of your two roommates is right: The one who argues that you would help the economy more by saving your tax refund check, or the one who argues that you should spend it? In this chapter, we have seen that consumption spending promotes the production of more consumption goods and services—such as jeans and haircuts—and fewer investment goods and services—such as physical capital and worker education. Saving—and, therefore, not consuming—is necessary to fund investment expenditure. So, saving your refund check will help the economy over the long run. But if the economy is in a recession, spending your refund check will spur more production of consumption goods. In a sense, then, both of your roommates are correct: Spending your check will help stimulate the economy during a recession, while saving it will help the economy grow over the long run.

# Conclusion

The U.S. economy remains a remarkable engine for improving the well-being of Americans. The standard of living of Americans today is much higher than it was 100 years ago. But households and firms are still subject to the ups and downs of the business cycle. In the following chapters, we will continue our analysis of this basic fact of macroeconomics: Ever-increasing long-run prosperity is achieved in the context of short-run instability.

Read *An Inside Look* on the next page for a discussion of how the airline industry revises profit estimates based on global GDP projections.

# Airlines Face the Business Cycle

## RTTNEWS

## IATA Lifts 2011 Airline Profit Forecast; Expects Fall in 2012

The International Air Transport Association or IATA on Tuesday lifted its airline industry profit forecast for fiscal 2011, citing better than expected passenger demand in most regions, even though cargo markets were weak. Meanwhile, it expects lower profit for the year 2012, with a very tough environment going ahead.

**(a)** For the year 2011, IATA currently expects industry profit to be $6.9 billion, compared to a previous projection of $4 billion. Meanwhile, the agency emphasized that profitability, with a net margin rate of 1.2 percent, is still exceptionally weak, despite the improvements, considering the industry's total revenues of $594 billion.

In an early June announcement, IATA, which represents around 230 airlines in over 115 countries, had slashed its profit outlook for the year from an earlier projection of $8.6 billion, citing high oil prices, natural disasters in Japan, and the political unrest in the Middle East and North Africa. The latest forecast is significantly lower than the $18 billion net profit recorded in 2010.

**(b)** For the year 2011, passenger numbers are expected to grow 5.9 percent, compared to a previous forecast of 4.4 percent growth, reflecting stronger than anticipated demand, despite the gloomy economic outlook. Total passenger numbers would now be 2.833 billion, up from the previous forecast of 2.793 billion.

Tighter supply and demand conditions in passenger markets over the first half is expected to offset the impact of a weaker second half.

Meanwhile, IATA slashed its forecast for air freight's full-year volume growth to 1.4 percent from 5.5 percent. Airlines are expected to carry 46.4 million tonnes of cargo in 2011, down from the previous forecast of 48.2 million. The agency does not expect a revival in air freight before 2012.

For the year, passenger revenues are now projected to be $464 billion, $7 billion higher than the June forecast, while freight revenue projections fell by $5 billion to $67 billion reflecting weaker freight markets.

IATA said its forecast is built around global projected GDP growth of 2.5 percent in 2011 falling to 2.4 percent in 2012.

IATA also lifted profit forecast for all regions, despite the ongoing impacts of the Japanese earthquake and tsunami in Asia and potential demand shocks associated with political instability in Middle East.

Meanwhile, IATA expects African carriers to break even, compared to previous loss forecast.

**(c)** Tony Tyler, IATA's Director General and CEO, stated that the airlines are competing in a very tough environment and that 2012 will be even more difficult.

For 2012, IATA projects profits to fall to $4.9 billion on revenues of $632 billion for a net margin of just 0.8 percent. Passenger markets are expected to grow 4.6 percent, and cargo markets by 4.2 percent.

IATA said the fourth quarter of 2011 and the first half of 2012 may well see the weakest point for air transport markets, with debt-burdened Western economies set for an extended period of weak economic activity.

Tyler stated, "Relatively stronger economic growth and some rebound in cargo will help Asia Pacific airlines to maintain their 2012 profits close to 2011 levels at $2.3 billion. The rest of the industry will see declining profitability. And the worst hit is expected to be Europe where the economic crisis means the industry is only expected to return a combined profit of $300 million. A long slow struggle lies ahead."

*Source:* "IATA Lifts 2011 Airline Profit Forecast; Expects Fall In 2012," *RTTNews*, September 20, 2011. Copyright © 2011 by RTT News. Reprinted by permission.

## Key Points in the Article

An airline industry trade association, the International Air Transport Association (IATA), revised its profit forecast for the industry for 2011 to $6.9 billion in September, up from $4 billion in June. Profit forecasts were increased for all regions of the globe. The higher profits, which are still less than the $18 billion profit recorded in 2010, would mainly be the result of increased demand for passenger travel, with passenger numbers projected to increase by 5.9 percent for the year. Freight volume, however, is expected to grow only 1.4 percent for the year, down from the earlier estimate of 5.5 percent. For 2012, IATA projects industry profits to decline to $4.9 billion, despite expected growth in passengers and freight of 4.6 percent and 4.2 percent, respectively. IATA's revised profit forecasts are based on projected global GDP growth of 2.5 percent in 2011 and 2.4 percent in 2012.

## Analyzing the News

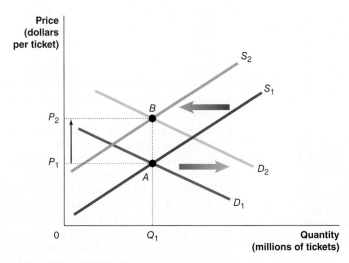 In 2010, the airline industry rebounded from the effects of the global economic recession, recording net profits of $18 billion.

However, the rebound was short-lived. An airline industry trade association, IATA, has twice lowered its forecast of profit for the industry for 2011. IATA reduced its original estimate of $8.6 billion to $4 billion in June and then increased that estimate to $6.9 billion in September. These 2011 profit estimates are considerably less than the $18 billion profit the industry earned in 2010. As IATA noted, the profit margin of 1.2 percent is very weak for an industry with total revenue of $594 billion.

(b) Despite the expected decline in profits from 2010 and a cautious economic outlook, passenger numbers are expected to increase in 2011 by 5.8 percent from the previous year, to a total of 2.833 billion. During the recession of 2007–2009, airlines decreased ticket prices and cut back on flights in response to decreasing demand. While the number of flights has remained lower than prior to the recession, ticket prices began to rise in 2010 as passenger demand increased. As we saw in Chapter 3, an increase in market demand causes an increase in the equilibrium market price and an increase in the equilibrium quantity, while a decrease in market supply causes an increase in the equilibrium price and a decrease in the equilibrium quantity. The demand curve shifts to the right from $D_1$ to $D_2$, showing the increase in market demand for air travel, and the supply curve shifts to the left from $S_1$ to $S_2$, showing the decrease in market supply of air travel as airlines cut back on the number of flights they offered. Both the increase in demand and the decrease in supply cause the equilibrium price to increase. The increase in demand causes the equilibrium quantity to increase and the decrease in supply causes the equilibrium quantity to decrease. In the graph, the equilibrium quantity is shown to have remained constant at $Q_1$, because of shifts of equal magnitude of supply and demand.

(c) The IATA industry outlook for 2012 is not encouraging. Airline profits are projected to fall to $4.9 billion, with the profit margin decreasing to 0.8 percent. At the same time, revenues are projected to increase to $632 billion, with passenger travel up 4.6 percent and freight up 4.2 percent. The airline industry is expected to suffer a decline in profits despite an increase in passengers and freight and a rise in total revenue.

## Thinking Critically

1. Suppose the U.S. government regulated U.S. airline ticket prices. How might such a policy affect the profitability of U.S. airlines during a weak economy?
2. Suppose the U.S. government decides to provide U.S. airlines with low-interest loans, regardless of their creditworthiness, in an attempt to help the airlines increase their profits. Would such a policy be likely to succeed? Briefly explain.

For air travel, higher demand and lower supply cause higher ticket prices.

# Chapter Summary and Problems

## Key Terms

Business cycle, p. 678

Capital, p. 682

Crowding out, p. 692

Financial intermediaries, p. 687

Financial markets, p. 686

Financial system, p. 686

Labor productivity, p. 682

Long-run economic growth, p. 679

Market for loanable funds, p. 689

Potential GDP, p. 685

 **21.1** **Long-Run Economic Growth,** pages 678–686

LEARNING OBJECTIVE: Discuss the importance of long-run economic growth.

## Summary

The U.S. economy has experienced both *long-run economic growth* and the *business cycle*. The **business cycle** refers to alternating periods of economic expansion and economic recession. **Long-run economic growth** is the process by which rising productivity increases the standard of living of the typical person. Because of economic growth, the typical American today can buy almost eight times as much as the typical American of 1900. Long-run growth is measured by increases in real GDP per capita. Increases in real GDP per capita depend on increases in labor productivity. **Labor productivity** is the quantity of goods and services that can be produced by one worker or by one hour of work. Economists believe two key factors determine labor productivity: the quantity of capital per hour worked and the level of technology. **Capital** refers to manufactured goods that are used to produce other goods and services. *Human capital* is the accumulated knowledge and skills workers acquire from education, training, or their life experiences. Economic growth occurs if the quantity of capital per hour worked increases and if technological change occurs. Economists often discuss economic growth in terms of growth in **potential GDP**, which is the level of GDP attained when all firms are producing at capacity.

MyEconLab   Visit www.myeconlab.com to complete these exercises online and get instant feedback.

## Review Questions

**1.1** By how much did real GDP per capita increase in the United States between 1900 and 2010? Discuss whether the increase in real GDP per capita is likely to be greater or smaller than the true increase in living standards.

**1.2** What is the rule of 70? If real GDP per capita grows at a rate of 7 percent per year, how many years will it take to double?

**1.3** What is the most important factor in explaining increases in real GDP per capita in the long run?

**1.4** What two key factors cause labor productivity to increase over time?

**1.5** What is potential real GDP? Does potential real GDP remain constant over time?

## Problems and Applications

**1.6** Briefly discuss whether you would rather live in the United States of 1900 with an income of $1,000,000 per year or the United States of 2012 with an income of $50,000 per year. Assume that the incomes for both years are measured in 2012 dollars.

**1.7** A question from Chapter 19 asked about the relationship between real GDP and the standard of living in a country. Based on what you read about economic growth in this chapter, elaborate on the importance of growth in GDP, particularly real GDP per capita, to the quality of life of a country's citizens.

**1.8** **[Related to the** Making the Connection **on page 680]** Think about the relationship between economic prosperity and life expectancy. What implications does this relationship have for the size of the health care sector of the economy? In particular, is this sector likely to expand or contract in coming years?

**1.9** Use the table to answer the following questions.

| Year | Real GDP (billions of 2005 dollars) |
|------|-------------------------------------|
| 1990 | $8,034 |
| 1991 | 8,015 |
| 1992 | 8,287 |
| 1993 | 8,523 |
| 1994 | 8,871 |

**a.** Calculate the growth rate of real GDP for each year from 1991 to 1994.

**b.** Calculate the average annual growth rate of real GDP for the period from 1991 to 1994.

**1.10** Real GDP per capita in the United States, as mentioned in the chapter, grew from about $5,600 in 1900 to about $42,200 in 2010, which represents an annual growth rate of 1.8 percent. If the United States continues to grow at this rate, how many years will it take for real GDP per capita to double? If government economic policies meant to stimulate economic growth result in the annual growth rate increasing to 2.0 percent, how many years will it take for real GDP per capita to double?

**1.11** A study conducted by the Moscow-based management consulting firm Strategy Partners found that average labor productivity in Russia is only 17 percent of labor productivity in the United States. What factors would cause U.S. labor productivity to be nearly six times higher than Russian labor productivity?

Based on Jason Bush, "Why Is Russia's Productivity So Low?" *BusinessWeek*, May 8, 2009.

**1.12** **[Related to** Solved Problem 21.1 **on page 683]** An article in the *Economist* magazine compares Panama to Singapore. It quotes Panama's president as saying: "We copy a lot from Singapore and we need to copy more." The article observes that: "Panama is not even one-fifth as rich as its Asian model on a per-person basis. But Singapore would envy its growth: from 2005 to 2010 its economy expanded by more than 8% a year, the fastest rate in the Americas." Judging from the experience of Singapore, if Panama is to maintain these high growth rates, what needs to be true about the sources of Panama's growth?

Based on "A Singapore for Central America?" *Economist*, July 14, 2011.

**1.13** A newspaper article on labor productivity in the United States observes that, " . . . the best measure of productivity is probably output per hour, not output per person." Briefly explain whether you agree.

From David Leonhardt, "Even More Productive than Americans," *New York Times*, January 26, 2011.

**1.14** **[Related to the** Making the Connection **on page 684]** If the keys to Botswana's rapid economic growth seem obvious, why have other countries in the region had so much difficulty following them?

---

**21.2** **Saving, Investment, and the Financial System, pages 686–693**

LEARNING OBJECTIVE: Discuss the role of the financial system in facilitating long-run economic growth.

## Summary

Financial markets and financial intermediaries together comprise the **financial system**. A well-functioning financial system is an important determinant of economic growth. Firms acquire funds from households, either directly through financial markets—such as the stock and bond markets—or indirectly through financial intermediaries—such as banks. The funds available to firms come from *saving*. There are two categories of saving in the economy: *private saving* by households and *public saving* by the government. The value of total saving in the economy is always equal to the value of total investment spending. In the model of the **market for loanable funds**, the interaction of borrowers and lenders determines the market interest rate and the quantity of loanable funds exchanged.

 **MyEconLab** Visit **www.myeconlab.com** to complete these exercises online and get instant feedback.

## Review Questions

**2.1** Why is the financial system of a country important for long-run economic growth? Why is it essential for economic growth that firms have access to adequate sources of funds?

**2.2** How does the financial system—either financial markets or financial intermediaries—provide risk sharing, liquidity, and information for savers and borrowers?

**2.3** Briefly explain why the total value of saving in the economy must equal the total value of investment.

**2.4** What are loanable funds? Why do businesses demand loanable funds? Why do households supply loanable funds?

## Problems and Applications

**2.5** Suppose you can receive an interest rate of 3 percent on a certificate of deposit at a bank that is charging borrowers 7 percent on new car loans. Why might you be unwilling to loan money directly to someone who wants to borrow from you to buy a new car, even if that person offers to pay you an interest rate higher than 3 percent?

**2.6** An International Monetary Fund Factsheet makes the following observation regarding stable financial systems: "A sound financial system is . . . essential for supporting economic growth." Do you agree with this observation? Briefly explain.

Based on "Financial System Soundness," *International Monetary Fund Factsheet*, April 2009.

**2.7** Consider the following data for a closed economy:

$Y = \$11$ trillion

$C = \$8$ trillion

$I = \$2$ trillion

$TR = \$1$ trillion

$T = \$3$ trillion

Use these data to calculate the following:

a. Private saving
b. Public saving
c. Government purchases
d. The government budget deficit or budget surplus

**2.8** Consider the following data for a closed economy:

$Y = \$12$ trillion

$C = \$8$ trillion

$G = \$2$ trillion

$S_{Public} = -\$0.5$ trillion

$T = \$2$ trillion

Use these data to calculate the following:

a. Private saving
b. Investment spending
c. Transfer payments
d. The government budget deficit or budget surplus

**2.9** In problem 2.8, suppose that government purchases increase from $2 trillion to $2.5 trillion. If the values for $Y$ and $C$ are unchanged, what must happen to the values of $S$ and $I$? Briefly explain.

**2.10** Use the graph on the next page to answer the following questions:

a. Does the shift from $S_1$ to $S_2$ represent an increase or a decrease in the supply of loanable funds?
b. With the shift in supply, what happens to the equilibrium quantity of loanable funds?

c. With the change in the equilibrium quantity of loan-able funds, what happens to the quantity of saving? What happens to the quantity of investment?

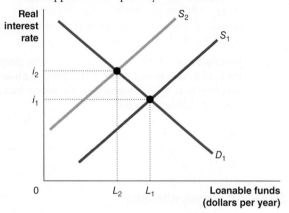

2.11 Use this graph to answer the following questions:

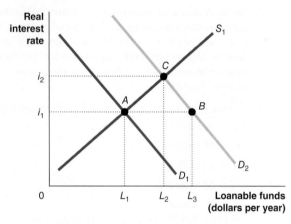

a. With the shift in the demand for loanable funds, what happens to the equilibrium real interest rate and the equilibrium quantity of loanable funds?

b. How can the equilibrium quantity of loanable funds increase when the real interest rate increases? Doesn't the quantity of loanable funds demanded decrease when the interest rate increases?

c. How much would the quantity of loanable funds demanded have increased if the interest rate had remained at $i_1$?

d. How much does the quantity of loanable funds supplied increase with the increase in the interest rate from $i_1$ to $i_2$?

2.12 Suppose that the economy is currently in a recession and that economic forecasts indicate that the economy will soon enter an expansion. What is the likely effect of the expansion on the expected profitability of new investment in plant and equipment? In the market for loanable funds, graph and explain the effect of the forecast of an economic expansion, assuming that borrowers and lenders believe the forecast is accurate. What happens to the equilibrium real interest rate and the quantity of loanable funds? What happens to the quantity of saving and investment?

2.13 Firms care about their after-tax rate of return on investment projects. In the market for loanable funds, graph and explain the effect of an increase in taxes on business profits. (For simplicity, assume no change in the federal budget deficit or budget surplus.) What happens to the equilibrium real interest rate and the quantity of loanable funds? What will be the effect on the quantity of investment by firms and the economy's capital stock in the future?

2.14 The federal government in the United States has been running very large budget deficits.

a. Use a market for loanable funds graph to illustrate the effect of the federal budget deficits. What happens to the equilibrium real interest rate and the quantity of loanable funds? What happens to the quantity of saving and investment?

b. Now suppose that households believe that deficits will be financed by higher taxes in the near future, and households increase their saving in anticipation of paying those higher taxes. Briefly explain how your analysis in part a will be affected.

2.15 **[Related to** Solved Problem 21.2 **on page 693]** Savers are taxed on the nominal interest payments they receive rather than the real interest payments. Suppose the government shifted from taxing nominal interest payments to taxing only real interest payments. (That is, savers could subtract the inflation rate from the nominal interest rate they received and only pay taxes on the resulting real interest rate.) Use a market for loanable funds graph to analyze the effects of this change in tax policy. What happens to the equilibrium real interest rate and the equilibrium quantity of loanable funds? What happens to the quantity of saving and investment?

2.16 **[Related to the** Making the Connection **on page 690]** The *Making the Connection* claims that Ebenezer Scrooge promoted economic growth more when he was a miser and saved most of his income than when he reformed and began spending freely. Suppose, though, that most of his spending after he reformed involved buying food for the Cratchits and other poor families. Many economists believe that there is a close connection between how much very poor people eat and how much they are able to work and how productive they are while working. Does this fact affect the conclusion about whether the pre-reform or post-reform Scrooge had a more positive impact on economic growth? Briefly explain.

---

**21.3** ## The Business Cycle, pages 694–702

LEARNING OBJECTIVE: Explain what happens during the business cycle.

## Summary

During the expansion phase of the business cycle, production, employment, and income are increasing. The period of expansion ends with a business cycle peak. Following the business cycle peak, production, employment, and income decline during the recession phase of the cycle. The recession comes to an end with a business cycle trough, after which another period of expansion begins. The inflation rate usually rises near the end of a business cycle expansion and then falls during a recession. The unemployment rate declines during the later part of an expansion and increases during a recession. The unemployment rate often continues to increase even after an expansion has begun. Economists have not found a method to predict when recessions will begin and end. Recessions are difficult to predict because they are due to more than one cause. Until the severe recession of 2007–2009, recessions had been milder and the economy had been more stable in the period since 1950.

MyEconLab    Visit **www.myeconlab.com** to complete these exercises online and get instant feedback.

## Review Questions

**3.1** What are the names of the following events that occur during a business cycle?
   a. The high point of economic activity
   b. The low point of economic activity
   c. The period between the high point of economic activity and the following low point
   d. The period between the low point of economic activity and the following high point

**3.2** Briefly describe the effect of the business cycle on the inflation rate and the unemployment rate. Why might the unemployment rate continue to rise during the early stages of a recovery?

**3.3** Briefly compare the severity of recessions before and after 1950. What explanations have economists offered for the period of relative macroeconomic stability from 1950 to 2007?

## Problems and Applications

**3.4** **[Related to the** Chapter Opener **on page 677]** Briefly explain whether production of each of the following goods is likely to fluctuate more or less than real GDP does during the business cycle:

   a. Ford F-150 trucks
   b. McDonald's Big Macs
   c. Kenmore refrigerators
   d. Huggies diapers
   e. Boeing passenger aircraft

**3.5** The National Bureau of Economic Research, a private group, is responsible for declaring when recessions begin and end. Can you think of reasons the Bureau of Economic Analysis, part of the federal government, might not want to take on this responsibility?

**3.6** **[Related to the** Don't Let This Happen to You **on page 699]** "Real GDP in 2010 was $13.1 trillion. This value is a large number. Therefore, economic growth must have been high during 2010." Briefly explain whether you agree with this statement.

**3.7** **[Related to the** Making the Connection **on page 695]** As we have seen, some firms prosper by expanding during recessions. What risks do firms take when they pursue this strategy? Are there circumstances in particular industries under which a more cautious approach might be advisable? Briefly explain.

**3.8** Imagine that you own a business and that during the next recession, you lay off 10 percent of your workforce. When economic activity picks up and your sales begin to increase, why might you not immediately start rehiring workers?

**3.9** An article in the *Economist* magazine refers to "The Great Delusion of a Great Moderation. . . ." What is the Great Moderation? By 2011, why might some people have considered the Great Moderation to have been a delusion?

Based on "Lending a Hand," *Economist*, September 10, 2011.

# Long-Run Economic Growth: Sources and Policies

# Google's Dilemma in China

Google was founded in 1998 by Larry Page and Sergey Brin. By 2011, Google employed more than 28,000 people and had annual revenues exceeding $29 billion. But Google encountered problems when expanding into China in 2006. The Chinese government insisted on regulating how people in that country access the Internet. In setting up Google.cn, Google had to agree to block searches of sensitive topics, such as the 1989 pro-democracy demonstrations in Tiananmen Square.

In late 2009, hackers stole some of Google's most important intellectual property by breaking into its computer system. Company executives suspected that Chinese government officials were involved in the theft. In January 2010, Google decided it would no longer cooperate with the Chinese government to censor Internet searchers and moved its Chinese search service from the mainland to Hong Kong.

Google's problems highlight one of the paradoxes of China in recent years: very rapid economic growth occurring in the context of government regulations that can stifle that growth. From the time the Communist Party seized control of China in 1949 until the late 1970s, the government controlled production, and the country experienced very little economic growth. China moved away from a *centrally planned economy* in 1978, and real GDP per capita grew at a rate of 6.5 percent per year between 1979 and 1995; it grew at the white-hot rate of more than 9 percent per year between 1996 and 2010. These rapid growth rates have transformed the Chinese economy: Real GDP per capita today is 10 times higher than it was 50 years ago.

But, as the experience of Google has shown, China is not a democracy, and the Chinese government has failed to fully establish the rule of law, particularly with respect to the consistent enforcement of property rights. This is a problem for the long-term prospects of the Chinese economy because without the rule of law, entrepreneurs cannot fulfill their role in the market system of bringing together the factors of production—labor, capital, and natural resources—to produce goods and services.

Read **AN INSIDE LOOK** on **page 740** for a discussion of China's long-term plan to decrease its reliance on investment spending as a means of achieving sustainable economic growth.

Based on Steven Levy, "Inside Google's China Misfortune," *Fortune*, April 15, 2011; and Kathrin Hille, "China Renews Google's Website License," *Financial Times*, September 7, 2011.

## Economics in Your Life

### Would You Be Better Off without China?

Suppose that you could choose to live and work in a world with the Chinese economy growing very rapidly or in a world with the Chinese economy as it was before 1978—very poor and growing slowly. Which world would you choose to live in? How does the current high-growth, high-export Chinese economy affect you as a consumer? How does it affect you as someone about to start a career? As you read the chapter, see if you can answer these questions. You can check your answers against those we provide on **page 738** at the end of this chapter.

E
conomic growth is not inevitable. For most of human history, no sustained increases in output per capita occurred, and, in the words of the philosopher Thomas Hobbes, the lives of most people were "poor, nasty, brutish, and short." Sustained economic growth first began with the Industrial Revolution in England in the late eighteenth century. From there, economic growth spread to the United States, Canada, and the countries of Western Europe. Following World War II, rapid economic growth also began in Japan and, eventually, in several other Asian countries, but the economies of many other countries stagnated, leaving their people mired in poverty.

Real GDP per capita is the best measure of a country's standard of living because it represents the ability of the average person to buy goods and services. Economic growth occurs when real GDP per capita increases. Why have countries such as the United States and the United Kingdom, which had high standards of living at the beginning of the twentieth century, continued to grow rapidly? Why have countries such as Argentina, which at one time had relatively high standards of living, failed to keep pace? Why was the Soviet Union unable to sustain the rapid growth rates of its early years? Why are some countries that were very poor at the beginning of the twentieth century still very poor today? And why have some countries, such as South Korea and Japan, that once were very poor now become much richer? What explains China's very rapid recent growth rates? In this chapter, we will develop a *model of economic growth* that helps us answer these important questions.

**22.1 LEARNING** OBJECTIVE

Define economic growth, calculate economic growth rates, and describe global trends in economic growth.

# Economic Growth over Time and around the World

You live in a world that is very different from the world when your grandparents were young. You can listen to music on an iPod that fits in your pocket; your grandparents played vinyl records on large stereo systems. You can pick up a cell phone or send a text message to someone in another city, state, or country; your grandparents mailed letters that took days or weeks to arrive. More importantly, you have access to health care and medicines that have prolonged life and improved its quality. In many poorer countries, however, people endure grinding poverty and have only the bare necessities of life, just as their great-grandparents did.

The difference between you and people in poor countries is that you live in a country that has experienced substantial economic growth. With economic growth, an economy produces both increasing quantities of goods and services and better goods and services. It is only through economic growth that living standards can increase, but through most of human history, no economic growth took place. Even today, billions of people are living in countries where economic growth is extremely slow.

## Economic Growth from 1,000,000 B.C. to the Present

In 1,000,000 B.C., our ancestors survived by hunting animals and gathering edible plants. Farming was many years in the future, and production was limited to food, clothing, shelter, and simple tools. Bradford DeLong, an economist at the University of California, Berkeley, estimates that in those primitive circumstances, GDP per capita was about $140 per year in 2010 dollars, which was the minimum amount necessary to sustain life. DeLong estimates that real GDP per capita worldwide was still $140 in the year 1300 A.D. In other words, no sustained economic growth occurred between 1,000,000 B.C. and 1300 A.D. A peasant toiling on a farm in France in the year 1300 was no better off than his ancestors thousands of years before. In fact, for most of human existence, the typical person had only the bare minimum of food, clothing, and shelter necessary to sustain life. Few people survived beyond age 40, and most people suffered from debilitating illnesses.

Significant economic growth did not begin until the **Industrial Revolution**, which started in England around the year 1750. The production of cotton cloth in

**Industrial Revolution** The application of mechanical power to the production of goods, beginning in England around 1750.

factories using machinery powered by steam engines marked the beginning of the Industrial Revolution. Before that time, production of goods had relied almost exclusively on human or animal power. The use of mechanical power spread to the production of many other goods, greatly increasing the quantity of goods each worker could produce. First England and then other countries, such as the United States, France, and Germany, experienced *long-run economic growth*, with sustained increases in real GDP per capita that eventually raised living standards in those countries to the high levels of today.

| Making the Connection | ## Why Did the Industrial Revolution Begin in England? |
| --- | --- |

The Industrial Revolution was a key turning point in human history. Before the Industrial Revolution, economic growth was slow and halting. After the Industrial Revolution, economic growth became rapid and sustained in a number of countries. Although historians and economists agree on the importance of the Industrial Revolution, they have not reached a consensus on why it happened in the time and place that it did. Why the eighteenth century and not the sixteenth century or the twenty-first century? Why England and not China or India or Africa or Japan?

*The British government's guarantee of property rights set the stage for the Industrial Revolution.*

There is always a temptation to read history backward. We know when and where the Industrial Revolution occurred; therefore, it had to happen where it did and when it did. But what was so special about England in the eighteenth century? Nobel Laureate Douglass North, of Washington University in St. Louis, has argued that institutions in England differed significantly from those in other countries in ways that greatly aided economic growth. North believes that the Glorious Revolution of 1688 was a key turning point. After that date, the British Parliament, rather than the king, controlled the government. The British court system also became independent of the king. As a result, the British government was credible when it committed to upholding private property rights, protecting wealth, and eliminating arbitrary increases in taxes. These institutional changes gave entrepreneurs the incentive to make the investments necessary to use the important technological developments of the second half of the eighteenth century—particularly the spinning jenny and the water frame, which were used in the production of cotton textiles, and the steam engine, which was used in mining and in the manufacture of textiles and other products. Without the institutional changes, entrepreneurs would have been reluctant to risk their property or their wealth by starting new businesses.

Although not all economists agree with North's specific argument about the origins of the Industrial Revolution, we will see that most economists accept the idea that economic growth is not likely to occur unless a country's government provides the type of institutional framework North describes.

Based on Douglass C. North, *Understanding the Process of Economic Change*, (Princeton, NJ: Princeton University Press, 2005); and Douglass C. North and Barry R. Weingast, "Constitutions and Commitment: The Evolution of Institutions Governing Public Choice in Seventeenth-Century England," *Journal of Economic History*, Vol. 49, No. 4, December 1989.

**Your Turn:** Test your understanding by doing related problem 1.3 on page 742 at the end of this chapter.    MyEconLab

---

Figure 22.1 shows how growth rates of real GDP per capita for the entire world have changed over long periods. Prior to 1300 A.D., there were no sustained increases in real GDP per capita. Over the next 500 years, to 1800, there was very slow growth. Significant growth began in the nineteenth century, as a result of the Industrial Revolution. A further acceleration in growth occurred during the twentieth century, as the average growth rate increased from 1.3 percent per year to 2.3 percent per year.

**Average Annual Growth Rates for the World Economy**

World economic growth was essentially zero in the years before 1300, and it was very slow—an average of only 0.2 percent per year—before 1800. The Industrial Revolution made possible the sustained increases in real GDP per capita that have allowed some countries to attain high standards of living. Data from J. Bradford DeLong, "Estimating World GDP, One Million B.C.–Present," working paper, University of California, Berkeley.

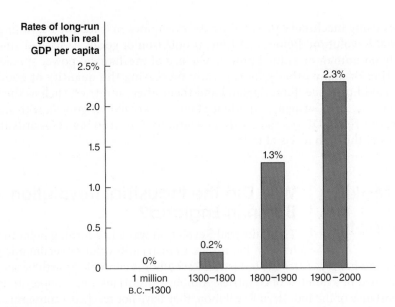

## Small Differences in Growth Rates Are Important

The difference between 1.3 percent and 2.3 percent may seem trivial, but over long periods, small differences in growth rates can have a large effect. For example, suppose you have $100 in a savings account earning an interest rate of 1.3 percent, which means you will receive an interest payment of $1.30 this year. If the interest rate on the account is 2.3 percent, you will earn $2.30. The difference of an extra $1.00 interest payment seems insignificant. But if you leave the interest as well as the original $100 in your account for another year, the difference becomes greater because now the higher interest rate is applied to a larger amount—$102.30—and the lower interest rate is applied to a smaller amount—$101.30. This process, known as *compounding*, magnifies even small differences in interest rates over long periods of time. Over a period of 50 years, your $100 would grow to $312 at an interest rate of 2.3 percent but to only $191 at an interest rate of 1.3 percent.

The principle of compounding applies to economic growth rates as well as to interest rates. For example, in 1950, real GDP per capita in Argentina was $5,474 (measured in 2005 dollars), which was larger than Italy's real GDP per capita of $5,361. Over the next 60 years, the economic growth rate in Italy averaged 2.8 percent per year, while in Argentina, the growth rate was only 1.4 percent per year. Although this difference in growth rates of only 1.4 percentage points may seem small, in 2010, real GDP per capita in Italy had risen to $27,930, while real GDP per capita in Argentina was only $12,931. In other words, because of a relatively small difference in the growth rates of the two economies, the standard of living of the typical person in Italy went from being below that of the typical person in Argentina to being much higher. The important point to keep in mind is this: *In the long run, small differences in economic growth rates result in big differences in living standards.*

## Why Do Growth Rates Matter?

Why should anyone care about growth rates? Growth rates matter because an economy that grows too slowly fails to raise living standards. In some countries in Africa and Asia, very little economic growth has occurred in the past 50 years, so many people remain in severe poverty. In high-income countries, only 4 out of every 1,000 babies die before they are they one year old. In the poorest countries, more than 100 out of every 1,000 babies die before they are one year old, and millions of children die annually from diseases that could be avoided by having access to clean water or that could be cured by using medicines that cost only a few dollars.

Although their problems are less dramatic, countries that experience slow growth have also missed opportunities to improve the lives of their citizens. For example, the failure of Argentina to grow as rapidly as the other countries that had similar levels of GDP per capita in 1950 has left many of its people in poverty. Life expectancy in Argentina is lower than in the United States and other high-income countries, and nearly twice as many babies in Argentina die before age one.

# Don't Let This Happen to You

## Don't Confuse the Average Annual Percentage Change with the Total Percentage Change

When economists talk about growth rates over a period of more than one year, the numbers are always *average annual percentage changes* and *not* total percentage changes. For example, in the United States, real GDP per capita was $13,213 in 1950 and $42,205 in 2010. The percentage change in real GDP per capita between these two years is

$$\left(\frac{\$42,205 - \$13,213}{\$13,213}\right) \times 100 = 219\%.$$

However, this is *not* the growth rate between the two years. The growth rate between these two years is the rate at which $13,213 in 1950 would have to grow on average *each year* to end up as $42,205 in 2010, which is 2.0 percent.

MyEconLab

**Your Turn:** Test your understanding by doing related problem 1.6 on page 743 at the end of this chapter.

## "The Rich Get Richer and . . ."

We can divide the world's economies into two groups: the *high-income countries*, sometimes also referred to as the *industrial countries*, and the poorer countries, or *developing countries*. The high-income countries include the countries of Western Europe, Australia, Canada, Japan, New Zealand, and the United States. The developing countries include most of the countries of Africa, Asia, and Latin America. In the 1980s and 1990s, a small group of countries, mostly East Asian countries such as Singapore, South Korea, and Taiwan, experienced high rates of growth and are sometimes referred to as the *newly industrializing countries*. Figure 22.2 shows the

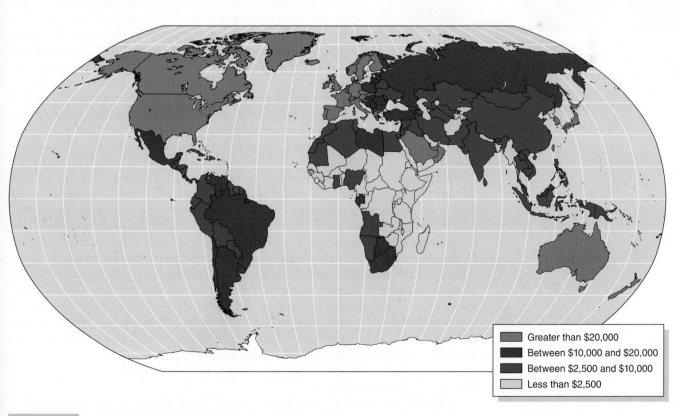

Greater than $20,000
Between $10,000 and $20,000
Between $2,500 and $10,000
Less than $2,500

**Figure 22.2** **GDP per Capita, 2010**

GDP per capita is measured in U.S. dollars, corrected for differences across countries in the cost of living.

levels of GDP per capita around the world in 2010. GDP is measured in U.S. dollars, corrected for differences across countries in the cost of living. In 2010, GDP per capita ranged from a high of $82,600 in Luxembourg to a low of $300 in the African countries of Burundi and the Democratic Republic of the Congo. To understand why the gap between rich and poor countries exists, we need to look at what causes economies to grow.

## Making the Connection

# Is Income All That Matters?

The more income you have, the more goods and services you can buy. When people are surviving on very low incomes of $2 per day or less, their ability to buy even minimal amounts of food, clothing, and housing is limited. So, most economists argue that unless the incomes of the very poor increase significantly, they will be unable to attain a higher standard of living. In some countries—primarily those colored yellow in Figure 22.2—the growth in average income has been very slow, or even negative, over a period of decades. Many economists and policymakers have concluded that the standard of living in these countries has been largely unchanged for many years.

Recently, however, some economists have argued that if we look beyond income to other measures of the standard of living, we can see that even the poorest countries have made significant progress in recent decades. For example, Charles Kenny, an economist with the World Bank, argues that "those countries with the lowest quality of life are making the fastest progress in improving it—across a range of measures including health, education, and civil and political liberties." For example, between 1960 and 2010, deaths among children declined, often by more than 50 percent, in nearly all countries, including most of those with the lowest incomes. Even in sub-Saharan Africa, where growth in incomes has been very slow, the percentage of children dying before age five has decreased by more than 30 percent over the past 50 years. Similarly, the percentage of people able to read and write has more than doubled in sub-Saharan Africa since 1970. Many more people now live in democracies where basic civil rights are respected than at any other time in world history. Although some countries, such as Somalia, the Democratic Republic of the Congo, and Afghanistan, have suffered from civil wars, political instability has also decreased in many countries in recent years, which has reduced the likelihood of dying from violence.

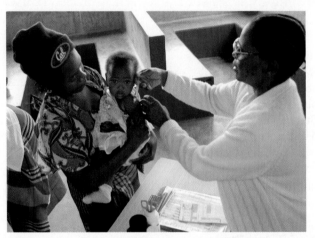

*In sub-Saharan Africa and other parts of the world, increases in technology and knowledge are leading to improvements in health care and the standard of living.*

What explains these improvements in health, education, democracy, and political stability? William Easterly, an economist at New York University, has found that although at any given time, countries that have a higher income also have a higher standard of living, over time increases in income *within a particular country* typically have very little effect on the country's standard of living in terms of health, education, individual rights, political stability, and similar factors. Kenny's argument and Easterly's finding are connected: Some increases in living standards do not require significant increases in income. The key factors in raising living standards in low-income countries have been increases in technology and knowledge—such as the development of inexpensive vaccines that reduce epidemics or the use of mosquito-resistant netting that reduces prevalence of malaria—that are inexpensive enough to be widely available. Changes in attitudes, such as placing a greater value on education, particularly for girls, or increasing support for political freedoms, have also played a role in improving conditions in low-income countries.

There are limits, of course, to how much living standards can increase if incomes stagnate. Ultimately, much higher rates of economic growth will be necessary for low-income countries to significantly close the gap in living standards with high-income countries.

Based on Charles Kenny, *Getting Better*, (New York: Basic Books, 2011); Ursula Casabonne and Charles Kenny, "The Best Things in Life Are (Nearly) Free: Technology, Knowledge, and Global Health," *World Development*, forthcoming; and William Easterly, "Life during Growth," *Journal of Economic Growth*, Vol. 4, No. 3, September 1999, pp. 239–276.

**Your Turn:** Test your understanding by doing related problems 1.7 and 1.8 on page 743 at the end of this chapter.

MyEconLab

# What Determines How Fast Economies Grow?

**22.2 LEARNING** OBJECTIVE

Use the economic growth model to explain why growth rates differ across countries.

To explain changes in economic growth rates over time within countries and differences in growth rates among countries, we need to develop an *economic growth model*. An **economic growth model** explains growth rates in real GDP per capita over the long run. As we noted in Chapter 21, the average person can buy more goods and services only if the average worker produces more goods and services. Recall that **labor productivity** is the quantity of goods and services that can be produced by one worker or by one hour of work. Because of the importance of labor productivity in explaining economic growth, the economic growth model focuses on the causes of long-run increases in labor productivity.

How can a country's workers become more productive? Economists believe two key factors determine labor productivity: the quantity of capital per hour worked and the level of technology. Therefore, the economic growth model focuses on technological change and changes over time in the quantity of capital available to workers in explaining changes in real GDP per capita. Recall that **technological change** is a change in the quantity of output firms can produce using a given quantity of inputs.

There are three main sources of technological change:

- *Better machinery and equipment.* Beginning with the steam engine during the Industrial Revolution, the invention of new machinery has been an important source of rising labor productivity. Today, continuing improvements in computers, factory machine tools, electric generators, and many other machines contribute to increases in labor productivity.

- *Increases in human capital.* Capital refers to *physical capital*, including computers, factory buildings, machine tools, warehouses, and trucks. The more physical capital workers have available, the more output they can produce. **Human capital** is the accumulated knowledge and skills that workers acquire from education and training or from their life experiences. As workers increase their human capital through education or on-the-job training, their productivity also increases. The more educated workers are, the greater is their human capital.

- *Better means of organizing and managing production.* Labor productivity increases if managers can do a better job of organizing production. For example, the *just-in-time system*, first developed by Toyota Motor Corporation, involves assembling goods from parts that arrive at the factory at exactly the time they are needed. With this system, Toyota needs fewer workers to store and keep track of parts in the factory, so the quantity of goods produced per hour worked increases.

Note that technological change is *not* the same thing as more physical capital. New capital can embody technological change, as when a faster computer chip is embodied in a new computer. But simply adding more capital that is the same as existing capital is not technological change. To summarize, we can say that a country's standard of living will be higher the more capital workers have available on their jobs, the better the capital, the more human capital workers have, and the better the job business managers do in organizing production.

**Economic growth model** A model that explains growth rates in real GDP per capita over the long run.

**Labor productivity** The quantity of goods and services that can be produced by one worker or by one hour of work.

**Technological change** A change in the quantity of output a firm can produce using a given quantity of inputs.

**Human capital** The accumulated knowledge and skills that workers acquire from education and training or from their life experiences.

# The Per-Worker Production Function

The economic growth model explains increases in real GDP per capita over time as resulting from increases in just two factors: the quantity of physical capital available to workers and technological change. Often when analyzing economic growth, we look at increases in real GDP *per hour worked* and increases in capital *per hour worked*. We use measures of GDP per hour and capital per hour rather than per person so we can analyze changes in the underlying ability of an economy to produce more goods with a given amount of labor without having to worry about changes in the fraction of the population working or in the length of the workday. We can illustrate the economic growth model using the **per-worker production function**, which is the relationship between real GDP per hour worked and capital per hour worked, *holding the level of technology constant*. Figure 22.3 shows the per-worker production function as a graph. In the figure, we measure capital per hour worked along the horizontal axis and real GDP per hour worked along the vertical axis. Letting *K* stand for capital, *L* stand for labor, and *Y* stand for real GDP, real GDP per hour worked is *Y/L*, and capital per hour worked is *K/L*. The curve represents the production function. Notice that we do not explicitly show technological change in the figure. We assume that as we move along the production function, the level of technology remains constant. As we will see, we can illustrate technological change using this graph by *shifting up* the curve representing the production function.

The figure shows that increases in the quantity of capital per hour worked result in movements up the per-worker production function, increasing the quantity of output each worker produces. When *holding technology constant*, however, equal increases in the amount of capital per hour worked lead to *diminishing* increases in output per hour worked. For example, increasing capital per hour worked from $20,000 to $30,000 increases real GDP per hour worked from $200 to $350, an increase of $150. Another $10,000 increase in capital per hour worked, from $30,000 to $40,000, increases real GDP per hour worked from $350 to $475, an increase of only $125. Each additional $10,000 increase in capital per hour worked results in progressively smaller increases in real GDP per hour worked. In fact, at very high levels of capital per hour worked, further increases in capital per hour worked will not result in any increase in real GDP per hour worked. This effect results from the *law of diminishing returns*, which states that as we add more of one input—in this case, capital—to a fixed quantity of another input—in this case, labor—output increases by smaller additional amounts.

Why are there diminishing returns to capital? Consider a simple example in which you own a copy store. At first you have 10 employees but only 1 copy machine, so each of your workers is able to produce relatively few copies per day. When you buy a second copy

**Per-worker production function**
The relationship between real GDP per hour worked and capital per hour worked, holding the level of technology constant.

---

**Figure 22.3**

**The Per-Worker Production Function**

The per-worker production function shows the relationship between capital per hour worked and real GDP per hour worked, holding technology constant. Increases in capital per hour worked increase output per hour worked but at a diminishing rate. For example, an increase in capital per hour worked from $20,000 to $30,000 increases real GDP per hour worked from $200 to $350. An increase in capital per hour worked from $30,000 to $40,000 increases real GDP per hour worked only from $350 to $475. Each additional $10,000 increase in capital per hour worked results in a progressively smaller increase in output per hour worked.

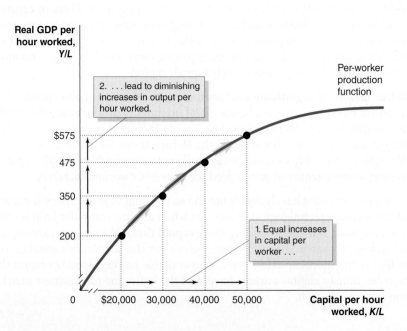

machine, your employees will be able to produce more copies. Adding additional copy machines will continue to increase your output—but by increasingly smaller amounts. For example, adding a twentieth copy machine to the 19 you already have will not increase the copies each worker is able to make by nearly as much as adding a second copy machine did. Eventually, adding additional copying machines will not increase your output at all.

## Which Is More Important for Economic Growth: More Capital or Technological Change?

Technological change helps economies avoid diminishing returns to capital. Let's consider two simple examples of the effects of technological change. First, suppose you have 10 copy machines in your copy store. Each copy machine can produce 10 copies per minute. You don't believe that adding an eleventh machine identical to the 10 you already have will significantly increase the number of copies your employees can produce in a day. Then you find out that a new copy machine has become available that produces 20 copies per minute. If you replace your existing machines with the new machines, the productivity of your workers will increase. The replacement of existing capital with more productive capital is an example of technological change.

Or suppose you realize that the layout of your store could be improved. Maybe the paper for the machines is on shelves at the back of the store, which requires your workers to spend time walking back and forth whenever the machines run out of paper. By placing the paper closer to the copy machines, you can improve the productivity of your workers. Reorganizing how production takes place so as to increase output is also an example of technological change.

## Technological Change: The Key to Sustaining Economic Growth

Figure 22.4 shows the effect of technological change on the per-worker production function. Technological change shifts up the per-worker production function and allows an economy to produce more real GDP per hour worked with the same quantity of capital per hour worked. For example, if the current level of technology puts the economy on production function$_1$, then when capital per hour worked is $50,000, real GDP per hour worked is $575. Technological change that shifts the economy to production function$_2$

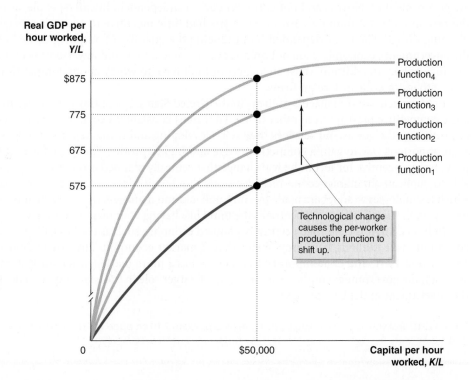

### Figure 22.4

**Technological Change Increases Output per Hour Worked**

Technological change shifts up the production function and allows more output per hour worked with the same amount of capital per hour worked. For example, along Production function$_1$ with $50,000 in capital per hour worked, the economy can produce $575 in real GDP per hour worked. However, an increase in technology that shifts the economy to Production function$_2$ makes it possible to produce $675 in real GDP per hour worked with the same level of capital per hour worked.

makes it possible to produce $675 in goods and services per hour worked with the same level of capital per hour worked. Further increases in technology that shift the economy to higher production functions result in further increases in real GDP per hour worked. Because of diminishing returns to capital, continuing increases in real GDP per hour worked can be sustained only if there is technological change. Remember that a country will experience increases in its standard of living only if it experiences increases in real GDP per hour worked. Therefore, we can draw the following important conclusion: *In the long run, a country will experience an increasing standard of living only if it experiences continuing technological change.*

*The fall of the Berlin Wall in 1989 symbolized the failure of Communism.*

Making the Connection | **What Explains the Economic Failure of the Soviet Union?**

The economic growth model can help explain one of the most striking events of the twentieth century: the economic collapse of the Soviet Union. The Soviet Union was formed from the old Russian Empire following the Communist revolution of 1917. Under Communism, the Soviet Union was a centrally planned economy where the government owned nearly every business and made all production and pricing decisions. In 1960, Nikita Khrushchev, the leader of the Soviet Union, addressed the United Nations in New York City. He declared to the United States and the other democracies, "We will bury you. Your grandchildren will live under Communism."

Many people at the time took Khrushchev's boast seriously. Capital per hour worked grew rapidly in the Soviet Union from 1950 through the 1980s. At first, these increases in capital per hour worked also produced rapid increases in real GDP per hour worked. Rapid increases in real GDP per hour worked during the 1950s caused some economists in the United States to predict incorrectly that the Soviet Union would someday surpass the United States economically. In fact, diminishing returns to capital meant that the additional factories the Soviet Union was building resulted in smaller and smaller increases in real GDP per hour worked.

The Soviet Union did experience some technological change—but at a rate much slower than in the United States and other high-income countries. Why did the Soviet Union fail the crucial requirement for growth: implementing new technologies? The key reason is that in a centrally planned economy, the people managing most businesses are government employees and not entrepreneurs or independent businesspeople, as is the case in market economies. Soviet managers had little incentive to adopt new ways of doing things. Their pay depended on producing the quantity of output specified in the government's economic plan, not on discovering new, better, and lower-cost ways to produce goods. In addition, these managers did not have to worry about competition from either domestic or foreign firms.

Entrepreneurs and managers of firms in the United States, by contrast, are under intense competitive pressure from other firms. They must constantly search for better ways of producing the goods and services they sell. Developing and using new technologies is an important way to gain a competitive edge and higher profits. The drive for profit provides an incentive for technological change that centrally planned economies are unable to duplicate. In market economies, decisions about which investments to make and which technologies to adopt are made by entrepreneurs and managers who have their own money on the line. Nothing concentrates the mind like having your own funds at risk.

In hindsight, it is clear that a centrally planned economy, such as the Soviet Union's, could not, over the long run, grow faster than a market economy. The Soviet Union collapsed in 1991, and contemporary Russia now has a more market-oriented system, although the government continues to play a much larger role in the economy than does the government in the United States.

MyEconLab **Your Turn:** Test your understanding by doing related problem 2.10 on page 744 at the end of this chapter.

# Solved Problem 22.2

## Using the Economic Growth Model to Analyze the Failure of the Soviet Economy

Use the economic growth model and the information in the *Making the Connection* on page 720 to analyze the economic problems the Soviet Union encountered.

### Solving the Problem

**Step 1: Review the chapter material.** This problem is about using the economic growth model to explain the failure of the Soviet economy, so you may want to review the *Making the Connection* on page 720.

**Step 2: Draw a graph like Figure 22.3 on page 718 to illustrate the economic problems of the Soviet Union.** For simplicity, assume that the Soviet Union experienced no technological change.

The Soviet Union experienced rapid increases in capital per hour worked from 1950 through the 1980s, but its failure to implement new technology meant that output per hour worked grew at a slower and slower rate.

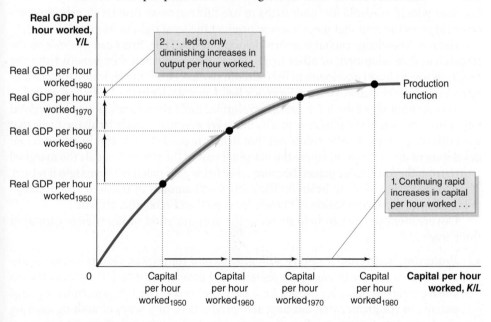

**Extra Credit:** The Soviet Union hoped to raise the standard of living of its citizens above that enjoyed in the United States and other high-income countries. Its strategy was to make continuous increases in the quantity of capital available to its workers. The economic growth model helps us understand the flaws in this policy for achieving economic growth.

**Your Turn:** For more practice, do related problems 2.7 and 2.8 on page 744 at the end of this chapter.     MyEconLab

## New Growth Theory

The economic growth model we have been using was first developed in the 1950s by Nobel Laureate Robert Solow of MIT. According to this model, productivity growth is the key factor in explaining long-run growth in real GDP per capita. In recent years, some economists have become dissatisfied with this model because it does not

**New growth theory** A model of long-run economic growth that emphasizes that technological change is influenced by economic incentives and so is determined by the working of the market system.

explain the factors that determine productivity growth. What has become known as the **new growth theory** was developed by Paul Romer, an economist at Stanford University, to provide a better explanation of the sources of productivity change. Romer argues that the rate of technological change is influenced by how individuals and firms respond to economic incentives. Earlier accounts of economic growth did not explain technological change or attributed it to factors such as chance scientific discoveries.

Romer argues that the accumulation of *knowledge capital* is a key determinant of economic growth. Firms add to an economy's stock of knowledge capital when they engage in research and development or otherwise contribute to technological change. We have seen that accumulation of physical capital is subject to diminishing returns: Increases in capital per hour worked lead to increases in real GDP per hour worked but at a decreasing rate. Romer argues that the same is true of knowledge capital *at the firm level*. As firms add to their stock of knowledge capital, they increase their output but at a decreasing rate. At the level of the entire economy rather than just individual firms, however, Romer argues that knowledge capital is subject to *increasing returns*. Increasing returns can exist because knowledge, once discovered, becomes available to everyone. The use of physical capital, such as a computer or machine tool, is *rival* because if one firm uses it, other firms cannot, and it is *excludable* because the firm that owns the capital can keep other firms from using it. The use of knowledge capital, such as the chemical formula for a drug that cures cancer, is nonrival, however, because one firm's using that knowledge does not prevent another firm from using it. Knowledge capital is also nonexcludable because once something like a chemical formula becomes known, it becomes widely available for other firms to use (unless, as we discuss shortly, the government gives the firm that invents a new product the legal right to its exclusive use).

Because knowledge capital is nonrival and nonexcludable, firms can *free ride* on the research and development of other firms. Firms free ride when they benefit from the results of research and development they did not pay for. For example, transistor technology was first developed at Western Electric's Bell Laboratories in the 1950s and served as the basic technology of the information revolution. Bell Laboratories, however, received only a tiny fraction of the immense profits that were eventually made by all the firms that used this technology. Romer points out that firms are unlikely to invest in research and development up to the point where the marginal cost of the research equals the marginal return from the knowledge gained because *other* firms gain much of the marginal return. Therefore, there is likely to be an inefficiently small amount of research and development, slowing the accumulation of knowledge capital and economic growth.

Government policy can help increase the accumulation of knowledge capital in three ways:

**Patent** The exclusive right to produce a product for a period of 20 years from the date the patent is applied for.

- *Protecting intellectual property with patents and copyrights.* Governments can increase the incentive to engage in research and development by giving firms the exclusive rights to their discoveries for a period of years. The U.S. government grants patents to companies that develop new products or new ways of making existing products. A **patent** gives a firm the exclusive legal right to a new product for a period of 20 years from the date a patent on the product is applied for. For example, a pharmaceutical firm that develops a drug that cures cancer can secure a patent on the drug, keeping other firms from manufacturing the drug without permission. The profits earned during the period the patent is in force provide firms with an incentive for undertaking the research and development. The patent system has drawbacks, however. In filing for a patent, a firm must disclose information about the product or process. This information enters the public record and may help competing firms develop products or processes that are similar but that do not infringe on the patent. To avoid this problem, a firm may try to keep the results of its research a *trade secret*, without patenting it. (A famous example of a trade secret is the formula for Coca-Cola.) Tension also arises between the government's objectives of providing patent protection that gives firms the incentive to engage in research and development and making sure that the knowledge gained through the research is widely available, which increases the positive effect of the knowledge on the economy. Economists debate the features of an ideal patent system.

Just as a new product or a new method of making a product receives patent protection, books, films, and other artistic works receive *copyright* protection. Under U.S. law, the creator of a book, a film, or other artistic work has the exclusive right to use the creation during the creator's lifetime. The creator's heirs retain this exclusive right for 70 years after the creator's death.

- *Subsidizing research and development.* The government can use subsidies to increase the quantity of research and development that takes place. In the United States, the federal government conducts some research directly. For example, the National Institutes of Health conducts medical research. The government also subsidizes research by providing grants to researchers in universities through the National Science Foundation and other agencies. Finally, the government provides tax benefits to firms that invest in research and development.

- *Subsidizing education.* People with technical training carry out research and development. If firms are unable to capture all the profits from research and development, they will pay lower wages and salaries to technical workers. These lower wages and salaries reduce the incentive to workers to receive this training. If the government subsidizes education, it can increase the number of workers who have technical training. In the United States, the government subsidizes education by directly providing free education from grades kindergarten through 12 and by providing support for public colleges and universities. The government also provides student loans at reduced interest rates.

These government policies can bring the accumulation of knowledge capital closer to the optimal level.

## Joseph Schumpeter and Creative Destruction

The new growth theory has revived interest in the ideas of Joseph Schumpeter. Born in Austria in 1883, Schumpeter served briefly as that country's finance minister. In 1932, he became an economics professor at Harvard. Schumpeter developed a model of growth that emphasized his view that new products unleash a "gale of creative destruction" that drives older products—and, often, the firms that produced them—out of the market. According to Schumpeter, the key to rising living standards is not small changes to existing products but, rather, new products that meet consumer wants in qualitatively better ways. For example, in the early twentieth century, the automobile displaced the horse-drawn carriage by meeting consumer demand for personal transportation in a way that was qualitatively better. In the early twenty-first century, the DVD and the DVD player displaced the VHS tape and the VCR by better meeting consumer demand for watching films at home. Downloading or streaming movies from the Internet may be in the process of displacing the DVD just as the DVD displaced the VHS tape.

To Schumpeter, the entrepreneur is central to economic growth: "The function of entrepreneurs is to reform or revolutionize the pattern of production by exploiting an invention or, more generally, an untried technological possibility for producing new commodities or producing an old one in a new way."

The profits an entrepreneur hopes to earn provide the incentive for bringing together the factors of production—labor, capital, and natural resources—to start new firms and introduce new goods and services. Successful entrepreneurs can use their profits to finance the development of new products and are better able to attract funds from investors.

## Economic Growth in the United States

**22.3 LEARNING** OBJECTIVE

Discuss fluctuations in productivity growth in the United States.

The economic growth model can help us understand the record of growth in the United States. Figure 22.5 shows average annual growth rates in real GDP per hour worked since 1800. As the United States experienced the Industrial Revolution during the nineteenth century, U.S. firms increased the quantities of capital per hour worked. New technologies

## Figure 22.5

### Average Annual Growth Rates in Real GDP per Hour Worked in the United States

The growth rate in the United States increased from 1800 through the mid-1970s. Then, for more than 20 years, growth slowed before increasing again in the mid-1990s. Note: The values for 1800–1900 are real GDP per worker. The values for 1900–2010 are real GDP per hour worked and are the authors' calculations, based on the methods used in Neville Francis and Valerie A. Ramey, "The Source of Historical Economic Fluctuations: An Analysis Using Long-Run Restrictions," in Jeffrey Frankel, Richard Clarida, and Francesco Giavazzi, eds., *International Seminar in Macroeconomics*, (Chicago: University of Chicago Press, 2005); the authors thank Neville Francis for kindly providing data through 2004.

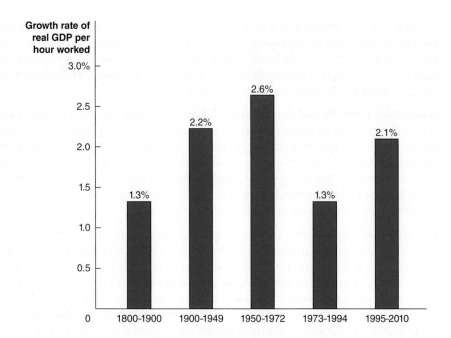

such as the steam engine, the railroad, and the telegraph also became available. Together, these factors resulted in an average annual growth rate of real GDP per worker of 1.3 percent from 1800 to 1900. Real GDP per capita grew at the slower rate of 1.1 percent during this period. At this growth rate, real GDP *per capita* would double about every 63 years, which means that living standards were growing steadily but relatively slowly.

By the twentieth century, technological change had been institutionalized. Many large corporations began to set up research and development facilities to improve the quality of their products and the efficiency with which they produced them. Universities also began to conduct research that had business applications. After World War II, many corporations began to provide significant funds to universities to help pay for research. In 1950, the federal government created the National Science Foundation, whose main goal is to support university researchers. The accelerating rate of technological change led to more rapid growth rates.

## Economic Growth in the United States since 1950

Continuing technological change allowed the U.S. economy to avoid the diminishing returns to capital that stifled growth in the Soviet economy. In fact, until the 1970s, the growth rate of the U.S. economy accelerated over time. As Figure 22.5 shows, growth in the first half of the twentieth century was faster than growth during the nineteenth century, and growth in the immediate post–World War II period from 1950 to 1972 was faster yet. Then the unexpected happened: For more than 20 years, from 1973 to 1994, the growth rate of real GDP per hour worked slowed. The growth rate during these years was more than 1 percentage point per year lower than during the 1950–1972 period. Beginning in the mid-1990s, the growth rate picked up again, although it remained below the levels of the immediate post–World War II period.

## What Caused the Productivity Slowdown of 1973–1994?

Several explanations have been offered for the productivity slowdown of the mid-1970s to mid-1990s, but none is completely satisfying. Some economists argue that productivity really didn't slow down; it only *appears* to have slowed down because of problems in measuring productivity accurately. After 1970, services—such as haircuts and financial advice—became a larger fraction of GDP, and goods—such as automobiles and hamburgers—became a smaller fraction. It is more difficult to measure increases in the output of services than to measure increases in the output of goods. For example, before banks began using automated teller machines (ATMs) in the 1980s, you could withdraw money only by going to a bank before closing time—which was usually 3:00 P.M. Once ATMs became available, you could withdraw money at any time of the day or night at a variety of locations. This increased convenience from ATMs does not show up in GDP. If it did, measured output per hour worked would have grown more rapidly.

There may also be a measurement problem in accounting for improvements in the environment and in health and safety. During these years, new laws required firms to spend billions of dollars reducing pollution, improving workplace safety, and redesigning products to improve their safety. This spending did not result in additional output that would be included in GDP—although it may have increased overall well-being. If these increases in well-being had been included in GDP, measured output per hour worked would have grown more rapidly.

In the early 1980s, many economists thought the rapid oil price increases that occurred between 1974 and 1979 explained the productivity slowdown, but the productivity slowdown continued after U.S. firms had fully adjusted to high oil prices. In fact, it continued into the late 1980s and early 1990s, when oil prices declined.

Some economists argue that deterioration in the U.S. educational system may have contributed to the slowdown in growth from the mid-1970s to mid-1990s. Scores on some standardized tests began to decline in the 1970s, which may indicate that workers entering the labor force were less well educated and less productive than in earlier decades. Another possibility is that the skills required to perform many jobs increased during the 1970s and 1980s, while the preparation that workers had received in school did not keep pace.

The United States was not alone in experiencing the slowdown in productivity. All the high-income countries experienced a growth slowdown between the mid-1970s and the mid-1990s. Because all the high-income economies began producing more services and fewer goods and enacted stricter environmental regulations at about the same time, explanations of the productivity slowdown that emphasize measurement problems become more plausible. In the end, though, economists are still debating why the productivity slowdown took place.

## Can the United States Maintain High Rates of Productivity Growth?

As Figure 22.5 shows, productivity growth, as measured by increases in real GDP per hour worked, increased between 1995 and 2010 compared to the previous 20-year period. Some economists argue that the development of a "new economy" based on information technology caused the higher productivity growth that began in the mid-1990s. The spread of ever-faster and increasingly less expensive computers has made communication and data processing easier and faster than ever before. Today, a single desktop computer has more computing power than all the mainframe computers NASA used to control the *Apollo* spacecrafts that landed on the moon in the late 1960s and early 1970s.

Faster data processing has had a major effect on nearly every firm. Business record keeping, once done laboriously by hand, is now done more quickly and accurately by computer. The increase in Internet use during the 1990s brought changes to the ways firms sell to consumers and to each other. Cell phones, laptop computers, and wireless Internet access allow people to work away from the office, both at home and while traveling. These developments have significantly increased labor productivity.

Many economists are optimistic that the increases in productivity that began in the mid-1990s will continue. The use of computers, as well as information and communications technology in general, increases as prices continue to fall. By 2011, well-equipped desktop computers could be purchased for less than $300. Further innovations in information and communications technology may continue to contribute to strong productivity growth. Some economists are skeptical, however, about the ability of the economy to continue to sustain high rates of productivity growth. These economists argue that in the 1990s, innovations in information and communications technology—such as the development of the World Wide Web, Windows 95, and computerized inventory control systems—raised labor productivity by having a substantial effect on how businesses operated. By the early 2000s, these economists argue, innovations in information and communications technology were having a greater effect on consumer products, such as cell phones, than on labor productivity. If the increases in output per hour worked that began in the mid-1990s do continue, this trend will be good news for increases in living standards in the United States.

# Why Isn't the Whole World Rich?

The economic growth model tells us that economies grow when the quantity of capital per hour worked increases and when technological change takes place. This model seems to provide a good blueprint for developing countries to become rich: (1) Increase the quantity of capital per hour worked and (2) use the best available technology. There are economic incentives for both of these things to happen in poor countries. The profitability of using additional capital or better technology is generally greater in a developing country than in a high-income country. For example, replacing an existing computer with a new, faster computer will generally have a relatively small payoff for a firm in the United States. In contrast, installing a new computer in a Zambian firm where records have been kept by hand is likely to have an enormous payoff.

This observation leads to an important conclusion: *The economic growth model predicts that poor countries will grow faster than rich countries.* If this prediction is correct, we should observe poor countries catching up to rich countries in levels of GDP per capita (or income per capita). Has this **catch-up**—or *convergence*—actually occurred? Here we come to a paradox: If we look only at the countries that currently have high incomes, we see that the lower-income countries have been catching up to the higher-income countries, but the developing countries as a group have not been catching up to the high-income countries as a group.

**Catch-up** The prediction that the level of GDP per capita (or income per capita) in poor countries will grow faster than in rich countries.

## Catch-up: Sometimes but Not Always

We can construct a graph that makes it easier to see whether catch-up is happening. In Figure 22.6, the horizontal axis shows the initial level of real GDP per capita, and the vertical axis shows the rate at which real GDP per capita is growing. We can then plot points on the graph for rich and poor countries. Each point represents the combination

### Figure 22.6

**The Catch-up Predicted by the Economic Growth Model**

According to the economic growth model, countries that start with lower levels of real GDP per capita should grow faster (points near the top of the line) than countries that start with higher levels of real GDP per capita (points near the bottom of the line).

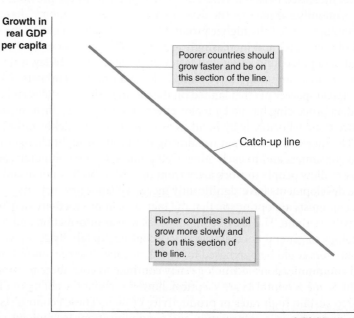

of a country's initial level of real GDP per capita and its growth rate over the following years. Low-income countries should be in the upper-left part of the graph because they would have low initial levels of real GDP per capita but fast growth rates. High-income countries should be in the lower-right part of the graph because they would have high initial levels of real GDP per capita but slow growth rates.

### Catch-up among the High-Income Countries

If we look at only the countries that currently have high incomes, we can see the catch-up predicted by the economic growth model. Figure 22.7 shows that the high-income countries that had the lowest incomes in 1960, such as Taiwan, Korea, and Singapore, grew the fastest between 1960 and 2009. Countries that had the highest incomes in 1960, such as Switzerland and the United States, grew the slowest.

### Are the Developing Countries Catching Up to the High-Income Countries?

If we expand our analysis to include every country for which statistics are available, it becomes more difficult to find the catch-up predicted by the economic growth model. Figure 22.8 does not show a consistent relationship between the level of real GDP in 1960 and growth from 1960 to 2009. Some countries that had low levels of real GDP per capita in 1960, such as Niger, Madagascar, and the Democratic Republic of the Congo, actually experienced *negative* economic growth: They had *lower* levels of real GDP per capita in 2009 than in 1960. Other countries that started with low levels of real GDP per capita, such as Malaysia and South Korea, grew rapidly. Some middle-income countries in 1960, such as Venezuela, hardly grew between 1960 and 2009, while others, such as Israel, experienced significant growth.

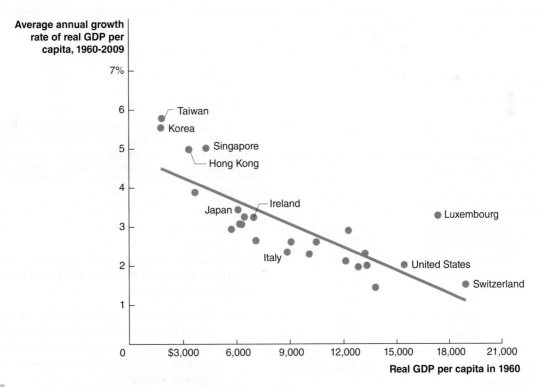

**Figure 22.7**    There Has Been Catch-up among High-Income Countries

If we look only at countries that currently have high incomes, we see that countries such as Taiwan, Korea, and Singapore that had the lowest incomes in 1960 grew the fastest between 1960 and 2009. Countries such as Switzerland and the United States that had the highest incomes in 1960 grew the slowest.

*Note:* Data are real GDP per capita in 2005 dollars. Each point in the figure represents one high-income country.

Authors' calculations from data in Alan Heston, Robert Summers, and Bettina Aten, *Penn World Table Version 7.0*, Center for International Comparisons of Production, Income and Prices at the University of Pennsylvania, June 3, 2011.

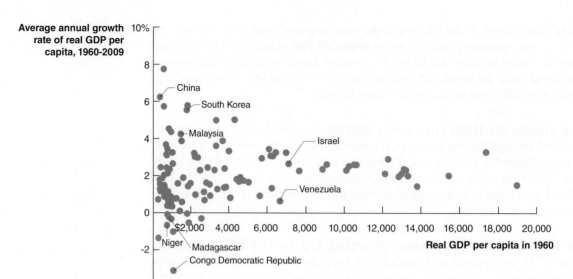

**Figure 22.8** **Most of the World Hasn't Been Catching Up**

If we look at all countries for which statistics are available, we do not see the catch-up predicted by the economic growth model. Some countries that had low levels of real GDP per capita in 1960, such as Niger, Madagascar, and the Democratic Republic of the Congo, actually experienced *negative* economic growth. Other countries that started with low levels of real GDP per capita, such as Malaysia and South Korea, grew rapidly. Some middle-income countries in 1960, such as Venezuela, hardly grew between 1960 and 2009, while others, such as Israel, experienced significant growth.

*Note:* Data are real GDP per capita in 2005 dollars. Each point in the figure represents one country.

Authors' calculations from data in Alan Heston, Robert Summers, and Bettina Aten, *Penn World Table Version 7.0*, Center for International Comparisons of Production, Income and Prices at the University of Pennsylvania, June 3, 2011.

# Solved Problem 22.4

## The Economic Growth Model's Prediction of Catch-up

The economic growth model makes predictions about the relationship between an economy's initial level of real GDP per capita relative to other economies and how fast the economy will grow in the future.

**a.** Consider the statistics in the following table:

| Country | Real GDP per Capita in 1960 (2005 dollars) | Annual Growth in Real GDP per Capita, 1960–2009 |
|---|---|---|
| Taiwan | $1,826 | 5.78% |
| Panama | 2,171 | 3.21 |
| Brazil | 2,877 | 2.43 |
| Algeria | 4,077 | 0.81 |
| Venezuela | 6,662 | 0.64 |

Are these statistics consistent with the economic growth model? Briefly explain.

**b.** Now consider the statistics in the following table:

| Country | Real GDP per Capita in 1960 (2005 dollars) | Annual Growth in Real GDP per Capita, 1960–2009 |
|---|---|---|
| Japan | $6,094 | 3.44% |
| Belgium | 10,241 | 2.52 |
| United Kingdom | 12,842 | 1.97 |
| New Zealand | 13,803 | 1.44 |

Are these statistics consistent with the economic growth model? Briefly explain.

**c.** Construct a new table that lists all nine countries, from lowest real GDP per capita in 1960 to highest, along with their growth rates. Are the statistics in your new table consistent with the economic growth model?

## Solving the Problem

**Step 1: Review the chapter material.** This problem is about catch-up in the economic growth model, so you may want to review the section "Why Isn't the Whole World Rich?" which begins on page 726.

Step 2:  **Explain whether the statistics in the table in part a are consistent with the economic growth model.** These statistics are consistent with the economic growth model. The countries with the lowest levels of real GDP per capita in 1960 had the fastest growth rates between 1960 and 2009, and the countries with the highest levels of real GDP per capita had the slowest growth rates.

Step 3:  **Explain whether the statistics in the table in part b are consistent with the economic growth model.** These statistics are also consistent with the economic growth model. Once again, the countries with the lowest levels of real GDP per capita in 1960 had the fastest growth rates between 1960 and 2009, and the countries with the highest levels of real GDP per capita had the slowest growth rates.

Step 4:  **Construct a table that includes all nine countries from the tables in parts a and b and discuss the results.**

| Country | Real GDP per Capita in 1960 (2005 dollars) | Annual Growth in Real GDP per Capita, 1960–2009 |
|---|---|---|
| Taiwan | $1,826 | 5.78% |
| Panama | 2,171 | 3.21 |
| Brazil | 2,877 | 2.43 |
| Algeria | 4,077 | 0.81 |
| Japan | 6,094 | 3.44 |
| Venezuela | 6,662 | 0.64 |
| Belgium | 10,241 | 2.52 |
| United Kingdom | 12,842 | 1.97 |
| New Zealand | 13,803 | 1.44 |

The statistics in the new table are not consistent with the predictions of the economic growth model. For example, New Zealand and the United Kingdom had higher levels of real GDP per capita in 1960 than did Algeria and Venezuela. The economic growth model predicts that New Zealand and the United Kingdom should, therefore, have grown more slowly than Algeria and Venezuela. The data in the table show, however, that New Zealand and the United Kingdom grew faster. Similarly, Belgium grew faster than Brazil, even though its real GDP per capita was already much higher than Brazil's in 1960.

**Extra Credit:** The statistics in these tables confirm what we saw in Figures 22.7 and 22.8 on pages 727–728: There has been catch-up among the high-income countries, but there has not been catch-up if we include in the analysis all the countries of the world.

**Your Turn:** For more practice, do problems 4.5 and 4.6 on page 746 at the end of this chapter.    MyEconLab

# Why Haven't Most Western European Countries, Canada, and Japan Caught Up to the United States?

Figure 22.7 indicates that there has been catch-up among the high-income countries over the past 50 years. If we look at the catch-up of other high-income countries to the United States, we discover a surprising fact: Over the past 20 years, other high-income countries have actually fallen further behind the United States rather than catching up to it. Figure 22.9 shows real GDP per capita in Canada, Japan, and the five largest economies in Western Europe relative to real GDP per capita in the United States. The blue bars show real GDP per capita in 1990 relative to the United States, and the red bars show real GDP per capita in 2010 relative to the United States. In each case, relative levels of real GDP per capita were lower in 2010 than they were in 1990. Each of these countries experienced significant catch-up to the United States between 1960 and 1990, but they have experienced no catch-up since 1990.

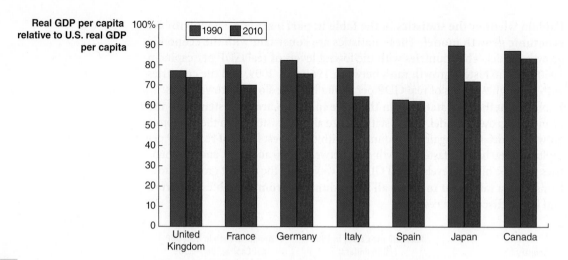

**Figure 22.9** **Other High-Income Countries Have Stopped Catching Up to the United States**

The blue bars show real GDP per capita in 1990 relative to the United States, and the red bars show real GDP per capita in 2010 relative to the United States. In each case, relative levels of real GDP per capita are lower in 2010 than they were in 1990, which means that these countries have ceased catching up to the United States.

Data from Alan Heston, Robert Summers, and Bettina Aten, *Penn World Table Version 7.0*, Center for International Comparisons of Production, Income and Prices at the University of Pennsylvania, June 3, 2011; and U.S. Central Intelligence Agency, *The World Factbook*, online version, www.cia.gov/library/publications/the-world-factbook.

Why have other high-income countries had trouble completely closing the gap in real GDP per capita with the United States? Many economists believe there are two main explanations: the greater flexibility of U.S. labor markets and the greater efficiency of the U.S. financial system. U.S. labor markets are more flexible than labor markets in other countries for several reasons. In many European countries, government regulations make it difficult for firms to fire workers and thereby make firms reluctant to hire workers in the first place. As a result, many younger workers have difficulty finding jobs, and once a job is found, a worker tends to remain in it even if his or her skills and preferences are not a good match for the characteristics of the job. In the United States, by contrast, government regulations are less restrictive, workers have an easier time finding jobs, and workers change jobs fairly frequently. This high rate of job mobility ensures a better match between workers' skills and preferences and the characteristics of jobs, which increases labor productivity. Many European countries also have restrictive work rules that limit the flexibility of firms to implement new technologies. These rules restrict the tasks firms can ask workers to perform and the number of hours they work. So, the rules reduce the ability of firms to use new technologies that may require workers to learn new skills, perform new tasks, or work during the night or early mornings.

Workers in the United States tend to enter the labor force earlier, retire later, and experience fewer long spells of unemployment than do workers in Europe. As we noted in Chapter 20, unemployed workers in the United States typically receive smaller government payments for a shorter period of time than do unemployed workers in Canada and most of the countries of Western Europe. Because the opportunity cost of being unemployed is lower in those countries, the unemployment rate tends to be higher, and the fraction of the labor force that is unemployed for more than one year also tends to be higher. Studies have shown that workers who are employed for longer periods tend to have greater skills, greater productivity, and higher wages. Many economists believe that the design of the U.S. unemployment insurance program has contributed to the greater flexibility of U.S. labor markets and to higher rates of growth in labor productivity and real GDP per capita.

As we have seen, technological change is essential for rapid productivity growth. To obtain the funds needed to implement new technologies, firms turn to the financial system. It is important that funds for investment be not only available but also allocated efficiently. We saw in Chapter 8 that large corporations can raise funds by selling stocks and bonds in financial markets. U.S. corporations benefit from the efficiency of U.S. financial markets. The level of legal protection of investors is relatively high in

U.S. financial markets, which encourages both U.S. and foreign investors to buy stocks and bonds issued by U.S. firms. The volume of trading in U.S. financial markets also ensures that investors will be able to quickly sell the stocks and bonds they buy. This *liquidity* serves to attract investors to U.S. markets.

Smaller firms that are unable to issue stocks and bonds often obtain funding from banks. Entrepreneurs founding new firms—"start-ups"—particularly firms that are based on new technologies, generally find that investors are unwilling to buy their stocks and bonds because the firms lack records of profitability. Banks are also reluctant to lend to new firms founded to introduce new and unfamiliar technologies. However, some technology start-ups obtain funds from *venture capital firms*. Venture capital firms raise funds from institutional investors, such as pension funds, and from wealthy individuals. The owners of venture capital firms closely examine the business plans of start-up firms, looking for those that appear most likely to succeed. In exchange for providing funding, a venture capital firm often becomes part owner of the start-up and may even play a role in managing the firm. A successful venture capital firm is able to attract investors who would not otherwise be willing to provide funds to start-ups because the investors would lack enough information on the start-up. A number of well-known U.S. high-technology firms, such as Google, relied on venture capitals firms to fund their early expansion. The ability of venture capital firms to finance technology-driven start-up firms may be giving the United States an advantage in bringing new products and new processes to market.

The U.S. financial system suffered severe problems between 2007 and 2009. But, over the long run, it has succeeded in efficiently allocating investment funds.

## Why Don't More Low-Income Countries Experience Rapid Growth?

The economic growth model predicts that the countries that were very poor in 1960 should have grown rapidly over the next 50 years. As we have just seen, a few did, but most did not. Why are many low-income countries growing so slowly? There is no single answer, but most economists point to four key factors:

- Failure to enforce the rule of law

- Wars and revolutions

- Poor public education and health

- Low rates of saving and investment

**Failure to Enforce the Rule of Law**  In the years since 1960, increasing numbers of developing countries, including China, have abandoned centrally planned economies in favor of more market-oriented economies. For entrepreneurs in a market economy to succeed, however, the government must guarantee private **property rights** and enforce contracts. Unless entrepreneurs feel secure in their property, they will not risk starting a business. It is also difficult for businesses to operate successfully in a market economy unless they can use an independent court system to enforce contracts. The **rule of law** refers to the ability of a government to enforce the laws of the country, particularly with respect to protecting private property and enforcing contracts. The failure of many developing countries to guarantee private property rights and to enforce contracts has hindered their economic growth.

Consider, for example, the production of shoes in a developing country. Suppose the owner of a shoe factory signs a contract with a leather tannery to deliver a specific quantity of leather on a particular date for a particular price. On the basis of this contract, the owner of the shoe factory signs a contract to deliver a specific quantity of shoes to a shoe wholesaler. This contract specifies the quantity of shoes to be delivered, the quality of the shoes, the delivery date, and the price. The owner of the leather tannery uses the contract with the shoe factory to enter into a contract with cattle ranchers

**Property rights**  The rights individuals or firms have to the exclusive use of their property, including the right to buy or sell it.

**Rule of law**  The ability of a government to enforce the laws of the country, particularly with respect to protecting private property and enforcing contracts.

for the delivery of hides. The shoe wholesaler enters into contracts to deliver shoes to retail stores, where they are sold to consumers. For the flow of goods from cattle ranchers to shoe customers to operate efficiently, each business must carry out the terms of the contract it has signed. In developed countries, such as the United States, businesses know that if they fail to carry out a contract, they may be sued in court and forced to compensate the other party for any economic damages.

Many developing countries do not have functioning, independent court systems. Even if a court system does exist, a case may not be heard for many years. In some countries, bribery of judges and political favoritism in court rulings are common. If firms cannot enforce contracts through the court system, they will insist on carrying out only face-to-face cash transactions. For example, the shoe manufacturer will wait until the leather producer brings the hides to the factory and will then buy them for cash. The wholesaler will wait until the shoes have been produced before making plans for sales to retail stores. Production still takes place, but it is carried out more slowly and inefficiently. With slow and inefficient production, firms have difficulty finding investors willing to provide them with the funds they need to expand.

| Making the Connection | # What Do Parking Tickets in New York City Tell Us about Poverty in the Developing World? |

In many developing countries, government officials insist on receiving bribes to process most transactions. For example, someone may need to pay an official before being allowed to open a shoe store or to purchase farm land. This corruption represents a breakdown in the rule of law. Generally, the more corrupt a country's government, the lower the country's growth rate. Economists at the World Bank have developed an index that ranks the countries of the world from most corrupt to least corrupt. The figure below compares GDP per capita in the 20 most corrupt and the 20 least corrupt countries. GDP per capita is more than 10 times higher in the least corrupt countries than in the most corrupt countries.

But does corruption cause countries to be poor, or does a country's being poor lead to its being corrupt? Some economists have made the controversial argument that corruption may be the result of culture. If a culture of corruption exists in a country, then the country may have great difficulty establishing an honest government that is willing to enforce the rule of law. Economists Raymond Fisman of the Columbia Business School and Edward Miguel of the University of California, Berkeley, came up with an ingenious method of testing whether a culture of corruption exists in some countries. Every country in the world sends delegates to the United Nations in New York City. Under international law, these delegates cannot be prosecuted for violating U.S. laws, including parking regulations. So, a delegate to the United Nations can double park or park next to a fire hydrant and ignore any parking ticket he or she would receive.

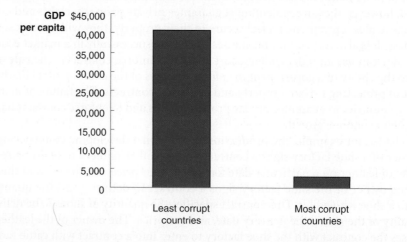

Fisman and Miguel argue that if a culture of corruption exists in some countries, the delegates from these countries will be more likely to ignore parking tickets than will the delegates from countries without a culture of corruption. Fisman and Miguel gathered statistics on the number of parking violations per delegate and compared the statistics to the World Bank's index of corruption. They found that as the level of corruption in a country increases, so does the number of parking violations by the country's United Nations delegates. For example, the figure below shows that the 15 percent of countries that are most corrupt had more than 10 times as many parking violations as the 15 percent of countries that are least corrupt.

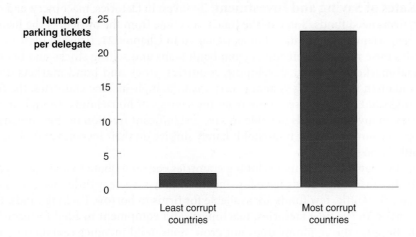

Of course, ignoring parking regulations is a relatively minor form of corruption. But if Fisman and Miguel are correct, and a culture of corruption has taken hold in some developing countries, then it may be a difficult task to reform their governments enough to establish the rule of law.

Based on Raymond Fisman and Edward Miguel, *Economic Gangsters*, (Princeton, NJ: Princeton University Press, 2008), Chapter 4; Daniel Kaufmann, Aart Kraay, and Massimo Mastruzzi, *Governance Matters V: Aggregate Governance Indicators, 1996–2007*, World Bank working paper; and International Monetary Fund, *World Economic Outlook Database*, April 2009.

**Your Turn:** Test your understanding by doing related problem 4.8 on page 746 at the end of this chapter.    MyEconLab

---

**Wars and Revolutions** Many of the countries that were very poor in 1960 have experienced extended periods of war or violent changes of government during the years since. These wars have made it impossible for countries such as Afghanistan, Angola, Ethiopia, the Central African Republic, and the Congo to accumulate capital or adopt new technologies. In fact, conducting any kind of business has been very difficult. The positive effect on growth of ending war was shown in Mozambique, which suffered through almost two decades of civil war and declining real GDP per capita. With the end of civil war, Mozambique experienced a strong annual growth rate of 3.7 percent in real GDP per capita from 1990 to 2009.

**Poor Public Education and Health** We have seen that human capital is one of the determinants of labor productivity. Many low-income countries have weak public school systems, so many workers are unable to read and write. Few workers acquire the skills necessary to use the latest technology.

Many low-income countries suffer from diseases that are either nonexistent or treated readily in high-income countries. For example, few people in developed countries suffer from malaria, but more than 1 million Africans die from it each year.

Treatments for AIDS have greatly reduced deaths from this disease in the United States and Europe. But millions of people in low-income countries continue to die from AIDS. These countries often lack the resources, and their governments are often too ineffective, to provide even routine medical care, such as childhood vaccinations.

People who are sick work less and are less productive when they do work. Poor nutrition or exposure to certain diseases in childhood can leave people permanently weakened and can affect their intelligence as adults. Poor health has a significant negative effect on the human capital of workers in developing countries.

**Low Rates of Saving and Investment** To invest in factories, machinery, and computers, firms need funds. Some of the funds can come from the owners of the firm and from their friends and families, but as we noted in Chapter 21, firms in high-income countries raise most of their funds from bank loans and selling stocks and bonds in financial markets. In most developing countries, stock and bond markets do not exist, and often the banking system is very weak. In high-income countries, the funds that banks lend to businesses come from the savings of households. In high-income countries, many households are able to save a significant fraction of their income. In developing countries, many households barely survive on their incomes and, therefore, have little or no savings.

The low savings rates in developing countries can contribute to a vicious cycle of poverty. Because households have low incomes, they save very little. Because households save very little, few funds are available for firms to borrow. Lacking funds, firms do not invest in the new factories, machinery, and equipment needed for economic growth. Because the economy does not grow, household incomes remain low, as do their savings, and so on.

## The Benefits of Globalization

One way for a developing country to break out of the vicious cycle of low saving and investment and low growth is through foreign investment. **Foreign direct investment (FDI)** occurs when corporations build or purchase facilities in foreign countries. **Foreign portfolio investment** occurs when an individual or a firm buys stocks or bonds issued in another country. Foreign direct investment and foreign portfolio investment can give a low-income country access to funds and technology that otherwise would not be available. Until recently, many developing countries were reluctant to take advantage of this opportunity.

From the 1940s through the 1970s, many developing countries closed themselves off from the global economy. They did this for several reasons. During the 1930s and early 1940s, the global trading and financial system collapsed as a result of the Great Depression and World War II. Developing countries that relied on exporting to the high-income countries were hurt economically. Also, many countries in Africa and Asia achieved independence from the colonial powers of Europe during the 1950s and 1960s and were afraid of being dominated by them economically. As a result, many developing countries imposed high tariffs on foreign imports and strongly discouraged or even prohibited foreign investment. This made it difficult to break out of the vicious cycle of poverty.

The policies of high tariff barriers and avoiding foreign investment failed to produce much growth, so by the 1980s, many developing countries began to change policies. The result was **globalization**, which refers to the process of countries becoming more open to foreign trade and investment.

If we measure globalization by the fraction of a country's GDP accounted for by exports, we see that globalization and growth are strongly positively associated. Figure 22.10 shows that developing countries that were more globalized grew faster during the 1990s than developing countries that were less globalized. Globalization has benefited developing countries by making it easier for them to get investment funds and technology.

**Foreign direct investment (FDI)** The purchase or building by a corporation of a facility in a foreign country.

**Foreign portfolio investment** The purchase by an individual or a firm of stocks or bonds issued in another country.

**Globalization** The process of countries becoming more open to foreign trade and investment.

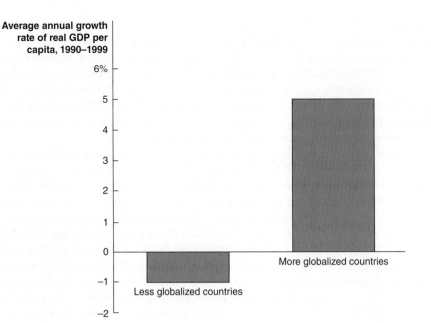

Average annual growth rate of real GDP per capita, 1990–1999

**Figure 22.10**

**Globalization and Growth**

Developing countries that were more open to foreign trade and investment grew much faster during the 1990s than developing countries that were less open.
Data from David Dollar, "Globalization, Inequality, and Poverty since 1980," *World Bank Research Observer*, Vol. 20, No. 2, Fall 2005, pp. 145–175.

# Growth Policies

**22.5 LEARNING** OBJECTIVE

Discuss government policies that foster economic growth.

What can governments do to promote long-run economic growth? We have seen that even small differences in growth rates compounded over the years can lead to major differences in standards of living. Therefore, there is potentially a very high payoff to government policies that increase growth rates. We have already discussed some of these policies in this chapter. In this section, we explore additional policies.

## Enhancing Property Rights and the Rule of Law

A market system cannot work well unless property rights are enforced. Entrepreneurs are unlikely to risk their own funds, and investors are unlikely to lend their funds to entrepreneurs, unless property is safe from being arbitrarily seized. We have seen that in many developing countries, the rule of law and property rights are undermined by government *corruption*. In some developing countries, it is impossible for an entrepreneur to obtain a permit to start a business without paying bribes, often to several different government officials. Is it possible for a country to reform a corrupt government bureaucracy?

Although today the United States ranks among the least corrupt countries, recent research by economists Edward Glaeser and Claudia Goldin of Harvard University has shown that in the late nineteenth and early twentieth centuries, corruption was a significant problem in the United States. The fact that political reform movements and crusading newspapers helped to reduce corruption in the United States to relatively low levels by the 1920s provides some hope for reform movements that aim to reduce corruption in developing countries today.

Property rights are unlikely to be secure in countries that are afflicted by wars and civil strife. For a number of countries, increased political stability is a necessary prerequisite to economic growth.

## Making the Connection

### Will China's Standard of Living Ever Exceed That of the United States?

In 2010, GDP per capita in the United States was more than six times higher than GDP per capita in China. However, the growth rate of real GDP per capita in the United States has averaged only 1.9 percent per year since 1980, compared to China's average rate of 8.9 percent per year over the same time period. If these growth rates were to continue, then China's standard of living would exceed the U.S. standard of living in the year 2038. However, for China to maintain its high rates of growth in real GDP per capita, it would have to maintain high rates of productivity growth, which is unlikely for several reasons. First, the United States invests more in activities, such as research and development, that result in new technologies and increases in productivity. Second, much of China's growth is likely due to the transition from a centrally planned economy to a market economy, so China's growth rate is likely to decrease as the transition is completed.

Another looming problem is demographic. Because of China's low birthrate, the country will soon experience a decline in its labor force. Over the next two decades, the population of men and women between 15 and 29 years will fall by roughly 100 million, or about 30 percent. China will also experience a large increase in older workers, a group that will likely be less educated and less healthy than younger workers. Given current trends, the U.S. Census Bureau projects fewer people under age 50 in China in 2030 than today, including fewer people in their twenties and early thirties and many more people in their sixties and older. China still has potential sources for enhancing productivity, including the migration of rural workers to more productive urban jobs and wider application of technical know-how. These factors can fuel future growth, but at some point, China's demographic problems could slow growth.

*Some economists argue that China may have overinvested in physical capital, such as bullet trains.*

Perhaps most troubling for China is the fact that, as we saw in the chapter opener, the country remains autocratic, with the Communist Party refusing to allow meaningful elections and continuing to limit freedom of expression. Secure property rights and the rule of law have never been fully established in China. Some observers believe that the lack of political freedom in China may ultimately lead to civil unrest, which could slow growth rates. Whether or not civil unrest eventually develops, the lack of democracy in China may already be resulting in problems that could slow growth in the near future. Nouriel Roubini, an economist at New York University, argues that China's Communist Party may be repeating some of the mistakes committed by the Soviet Communist Party decades ago. He argues that by employing policies that have resulted in investment being 50 percent of GDP, the government may have boosted short-term growth at the expense of the health of the economy in the long term. He notes that:

> China is rife with overinvestment in physical capital, infrastructure, and property. To a visitor, this is evident in sleek but empty airports and bullet trains . . . highways to nowhere, thousands of colossal new central and provincial government buildings, ghost towns, and brand-new aluminum smelters kept closed to prevent global prices from plunging.

China has been engaged in an economic experiment: Can a country maintain high rates of economic growth in the long run while denying its citizens basic political rights?

Based on Nicholas Eberstadt, "The Demographic Future," *Foreign Affairs*, Vol. 89, No. 6, November/December 2010, pp. 54–64; and Nouriel Roubini, "Beijing's Empty Bullet Trains," *Slate*, April 14, 2011.

MyEconLab **Your Turn:** Test your understanding by doing related problem 5.4 on page 747 at the end of this chapter.

## Improving Health and Education

Recently, many economists have become convinced that poor health is a major impediment to growth in some countries. As we saw in Chapter 21, the research of Nobel Laureate Robert Fogel emphasizes the important interaction between health and economic growth. As people's health improves and they become stronger and less susceptible to disease, they also become more productive. Recent initiatives in developing countries to increase vaccinations against infectious diseases, to improve access to treated water, and to improve sanitation have begun to reduce rates of illness and death.

We discussed earlier in this chapter Paul Romer's argument that there are increasing returns to knowledge capital. Nobel Laureate Robert Lucas of the University of Chicago similarly argues that there are increasing returns to *human* capital. Lucas argues that productivity increases as the total stock of human capital increases but that these productivity increases are not completely captured by individuals as they decide how much education to purchase. Therefore, the market may produce an inefficiently low level of education and training unless education is supported by the government. Some researchers have been unable to find evidence of increasing returns to human capital, but many economists believe that government subsidies for education have played an important role in promoting economic growth.

The rising incomes that result from economic growth can help developing countries deal with the brain drain. The *brain drain* refers to highly educated and successful individuals leaving developing countries for high-income countries. This migration occurs when successful individuals believe that economic opportunities are very limited in the domestic economy. Rapid economic growth in India and China in recent years has resulted in more entrepreneurs, engineers, and scientists deciding to remain in those countries rather than leave for the United States or other high-income countries.

## Policies That Promote Technological Change

One of the lessons from the economic growth model is that technological change is more important than increases in capital in explaining long-run growth. Government policies that facilitate access to technology are crucial for low-income countries. The easiest way for developing countries to gain access to technology is through foreign direct investment, where foreign firms are allowed to build new facilities or to buy domestic firms. Recent economic growth in India has been greatly aided by the Indian government's relaxation of regulations on foreign investment. Relaxing these regulations made it possible for India to gain access to the technology of Dell, Microsoft, and other multinational corporations.

In high-income countries, government policies can aid the growth of technology by subsidizing research and development. As we noted previously, in the United States, the federal government conducts some research and development on its own and also provides grants to researchers in universities. Tax breaks to firms undertaking research and development also facilitate technological change.

## Policies That Promote Saving and Investment

We noted in Chapter 21 that firms turn to the loanable funds market to finance expansion and research and development. Policies that increase the incentives to save and invest will increase the equilibrium level of loanable funds and may increase the level of real GDP per capita. As we also discussed in Chapter 21, tax incentives can lead to increased savings. In the United States, many workers are able to save for retirement by placing funds in 401(k) or 403(b) plans or in Individual Retirement Accounts (IRAs). Income placed in these accounts is not taxed until it is withdrawn during retirement. Because the funds are allowed to accumulate tax free, the return is increased, which raises the incentive to save.

Governments also increase incentives for firms to engage in investment in physical capital by using *investment tax credits*. Investment tax credits allow firms to deduct from their taxes some fraction of the funds they have spent on investment. Reductions in the taxes firms pay on their profits also increase the after-tax return on investments.

## Is Economic Growth Good or Bad?

Although we didn't state so explicitly, in this chapter we have assumed that economic growth is desirable and that governments should undertake policies that will increase growth rates. It seems undeniable that increasing the growth rates of very low-income countries would help relieve the daily suffering that many people in those countries endure. But some people are unconvinced that, at least in the high-income countries, further economic growth is desirable.

The arguments against further economic growth tend to be motivated either by concern about the effects of growth on the environment or by concern about the effects of the globalization process that has accompanied economic growth in recent years. In 1973, the Club of Rome published a controversial book titled *The Limits to Growth*, which predicted that economic growth would likely grind to a halt in the United States and other high-income countries because of increasing pollution and the depletion of natural resources, such as oil. Although these dire predictions have not yet come to pass, many people remain concerned that economic growth may be contributing to global warming, deforestation, and other environmental problems.

In Chapter 9, we discussed the opposition to globalization. We noted that some people believe that globalization has undermined the distinctive cultures of many countries, as imports of food, clothing, movies, and other goods have displaced domestically produced goods. We have seen that allowing foreign direct investment is an important way in which low-income countries can gain access to the latest technology. Some people, however, see multinational firms that locate in low-income countries as unethical because they claim the firms are paying very low wages and are failing to follow the same safety and environmental regulations they are required to follow in high-income countries.

As with many other normative questions, economic analysis can contribute to the ongoing political debate over the consequences of economic growth, but it cannot settle the issue.

Continued from page 711

## Economics in Your Life

### Would You Be Better Off without China?

At the beginning of the chapter, we asked you to imagine that you could choose to live and work in a world with the Chinese economy growing very rapidly or in a world with the Chinese economy as it was before 1978—very poor and growing slowly. Which world would you choose to live in? How does the current high-growth, high-export Chinese economy affect you as a consumer? How does it affect you as someone about to start a career?

It's impossible to walk into stores in the United States without seeing products imported from China. Many of these products were at one time made in the United States. Imports from China replace domestically produced goods when the imports are either less expensive or of higher quality than the domestic goods they replace. Therefore, the rapid economic growth that has enabled Chinese firms to be competitive with firms in the United States has benefited you as a consumer: You have lower-priced goods and better goods available for purchase than you would if China had remained very poor. As you begin your career, there are some U.S. industries that, because of competition from Chinese firms, will have fewer jobs to offer. But, as we saw when discussing international trade in Chapter 9, expanding trade changes the types of products each country makes, and, therefore, the types of jobs available, but it does not affect the total number of jobs. So, the economic rise of China will affect the mix of jobs available to you in the United States but will not make finding a job any more difficult.

# Conclusion

For much of human history, most people have had to struggle to survive. Even today, two-thirds of the world's population lives in extreme poverty. The differences in living standards among countries today are a result of many decades of sharply different rates of economic growth. According to the economic growth model, increases in the quantity of capital per hour worked and increases in technology determine how rapidly increases will occur in real GDP per hour worked and a country's standard of living. The keys to higher living standards seem straightforward: Establish the rule of law, provide basic education and health care for the population, increase the amount of capital per hour worked, adopt the best technology, and participate in the global economy. However, for many countries, these policies have proved very difficult to implement.

Having discussed what determines the growth rate of economies, we will turn in the following chapters to the question of why economies experience short-run fluctuations in output, employment, and inflation. First, read *An Inside Look at Policy* on the next page for a discussion of the Chinese government's attempts to become less dependent on investment spending for economic growth.

# Despite a Plan for Change, Investment Still Spurs China's Growth

## REUTERS

## Analysis: China Unlikely to Cool Investment as Its Growth Engine

China's long-term plan to cut reliance on investment as a growth engine is clashing with its short-term need for protection against a worsening global outlook.

Beijing has made it clear that consumption, not investment, must eventually do more of the work to drive the world's No. 2 economy.

But with debt troubles in the United States and Europe casting doubt on worldwide demand, it's likely China will keep investing by the billions for now, even if that takes Beijing further from its ultimate goal.

**(a)** Chinese consumers are a long way from becoming big spenders, so massive investment is still the fastest and easiest way for China to prop up its economy if push comes to shove. . . .

Without doubt, having heavy investment carries a price. Analysts say it generates waste and excess capacity, fuels inflation and produces diminishing economic returns. State investment is like an unsustainable life-support system that China needs to wean itself off.

In 2009—the last year for which figures are available—investment made up 65 percent of China's gross domestic product, a far higher share than in other major or Asian economies. Household consumption, however, accounted for just 35 percent, compared with 70 percent in the United States.

### (b) Unstable, Unbalanced, Uncoordinated

In the words of China Premier Wen Jiabao, the Chinese growth model is on all counts unstable, unbalanced, uncoordinated and ultimately unsustainable.

Some of the more bearish economists argue that wasteful investment is inflating a property price bubble and saddling banks with bad loans, sowing the seeds of a future crisis.

An example of healthier investment, economists say, would be companies stepping up capital expenditures on improving China's manufacturing technologies. . . .

### Rebalancing, Some Day

On the surface, China seems serious about following through on promises to invest less to rebalance its economy, and it has good reasons to be wary of repeating its 2008 spending spree.

Some of the 4 trillion yuan ($626 billion) stimulus package announced in 2008 was squandered on ill-advised projects and economists now worry that a sizable fraction of loans to local governments won't be repaid.

Banks may be wary of extending more large loans, making it difficult for local governments to invest their way to growth in the future. . . .

### Homes Priced Out of Reach

Soaring property prices have put homes out of reach for many ordinary Chinese, and that has become a source of public ire. Keenly aware of that, Beijing wants to build more public homes to keep them affordable.

And with the real estate market accounting for a quarter of total investment in the first half of this year, China could get decent bang for its buck if it ramps up spending in the sector. . . .

To be sure, Beijing says it wants to cure China of its penchant for investment-driven growth. Under its broad five-year economic plan starting from 2011, it envisions a fairer Chinese economy where consumption climbs on rising incomes. . . .

### (c) Few Big Spenders

Many analysts have said that Chinese consumers cannot pull their weight as big spenders because the bulk of national income goes to the state instead of workers. A flimsy social safety net encourages high saving rates.

For younger workers, consumption tends to be higher, but between expensive housing and strong cultural pressure to support aging parents and grandparents, they too face limits on how much they can spend.

In a paper published last month, the International Monetary Fund outlined key reforms China should implement to empower its consumers.

It called for a liberalization of financial markets; a reduction in personal income taxes; better healthcare services, increasing the cost of land, energy and pollution; raising dividend payouts from state firms, and improving labor mobility.

However, it would be years before these reforms take effect. . . .

## Key Points in the Article

The Chinese economy has been growing at a rapid pace over the past decade, due in large part to high levels of investment. However, the Chinese government has stated that its recent growth will be unsustainable without a shift away from investment spending. The government has established a five-year economic plan that calls for greater reliance on consumption as a means to sustain economic growth. Many analysts believe that achieving this goal will not happen anytime soon because (1) a majority of national income goes to the government instead of workers, and (2) other reforms are needed before Chinese consumers have the willingness and the financial ability to significantly increase consumption.

## Analyzing the News

**a** As you read in the chapter, the quantity of capital available to workers is a source of long-run economic growth. From 1996 to 2010, China experienced an annual growth rate of real GDP per capita of more than 9 percent. Much of this growth came from investment in capital goods. In 2009, investment spending accounted for 65 percent of Chinese GDP, a far higher percentage than in other major economies, and consumption was only 35 percent. In contrast, consumption spending is 70 percent of GDP in the United States. Relying on investment as a means of economic growth is not a long-run solution, though, as eventually an economy encounters diminishing returns to capital. Because of diminishing returns to capital, further increases in the quantity of capital would result in even smaller increases in real GDP per worker. The production function in the figure below illustrates this point: An increase in capital per hour worked from $(K/L)_{2010}$ to $(K/L)_{2011}$ leads to an increase in output per hour worked from $(Y/L)_{2010}$ to $(Y/L)_{2011}$. This increase in output per hour is much smaller than the increase resulting from the same size increase in capital per hour worked from $(K/L)_{2001}$ to $(K/L)_{2002}$, when the level of capital per hour worked was much smaller.

**b** Chinese Premier Wen Jiabao understands that the country's current economic growth model is unsustainable in the long run, yet China has continued on the path of high rates of investment. A main reason for this strategy has been a decrease in worldwide demand caused by the global economic downturn. While this investment strategy is not sustainable in the long run, some economists have suggested that increasing government expenditures on research and development in an effort to improve China's manufacturing technologies would be a good option for the Chinese economy.

**c** A primary reason that China has yet to succeed in increasing consumption is because Chinese consumers have low incomes and high savings rates. A large portion of Chinese national income currently goes to the government rather than to workers, although China has announced its desire to increase income levels to encourage more consumption. Increasing consumption may take time, though, as the following reforms may be needed to encourage consumers to increase spending: reduced personal income taxes, liberalized financial markets, and improved labor mobility.

## Thinking Critically About Policy

1. What policies can the Chinese government pursue to raise the country's long-run economic growth without further increases in investment spending? How would these policies affect China's per-worker production function?

2. According to the article, consumption in China has not grown significantly because a "flimsy social safety net encourages high saving rates." Explain what the article means by "flimsy social safety net." Why would a flimsy social safety net lead to high saving rates and low rates of consumption? Briefly explain.

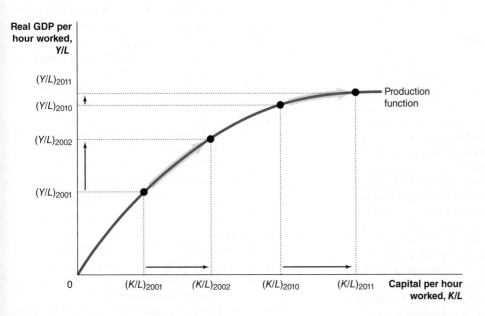

Continuous increases in capital per hour worked lead to smaller and smaller increases in output per hour worked.

# Chapter Summary and Problems

## Key Terms

Catch-up, p. 726

Economic growth model, p. 717

Foreign direct investment (FDI), p. 734

Foreign portfolio investment, p. 734

Globalization, p. 734

Human capital, p. 717

Industrial Revolution, p. 712

Labor productivity, p. 717

New growth theory, p. 722

Patent, p. 722

Per-worker production function, p. 718

Property rights, p. 731

Rule of law, p. 731

Technological change, p. 717

---

**22.1**  **Economic Growth over Time and around the World, pages 712–717**

LEARNING OBJECTIVE: Define economic growth, calculate economic growth rates, and describe global trends in economic growth.

## Summary

Until around 1300 A.D., most people survived with barely enough food. Living standards began to rise significantly only after the **Industrial Revolution** began in England in the 1700s, with the application of mechanical power to the production of goods. The best measure of a country's standard of living is its level of real GDP per capita. Economic growth occurs when real GDP per capita increases, thereby increasing the country's standard of living.

MyEconLab    Visit **www.myeconlab.com** to complete these exercises online and get instant feedback.

## Review Questions

1.1  Why does a country's rate of economic growth matter?

1.2  Explain the difference between the total percentage increase in real GDP between 1999 and 2009 and the average annual growth rate in real GDP between the same years.

## Problems and Applications

1.3  **[Related to the** Making the Connection **on page 713]** Economists Carol Shiue and Wolfgang Keller of the University of Texas at Austin published a study of "market efficiency" in the eighteenth century in England, other European countries, and China. If the markets in a country are efficient, a product should have the same price wherever in the country it is sold, allowing for the effect of transportation costs. If prices are not the same in two areas within a country, it is possible to make profits by buying the product where its price is low and reselling it where its price is high. This trading will drive prices to equality. Trade is most likely to occur, however, if entrepreneurs feel confident that their gains will not be seized by the government and that contracts to buy and sell can be enforced in the courts. Therefore, in the eighteenth century, the more efficient a country's markets, the more its institutions favored long-run growth. Shiue and Keller found that in 1770, the efficiency of markets in England was significantly greater than the efficiency of markets elsewhere in Europe and in China. How does this finding relate to

Douglas North's argument concerning why the Industrial Revolution occurred in England?

Based on Carol H. Shiue and Wolfgang Keller, "Markets in China and Europe on the Eve of the Industrial Revolution," *American Economic Review*, Vol. 97, No. 4, September 2007, pp. 1189–1216.

1.4  Use the data on real GDP in this table to answer the following questions.

| Country | 2007 | 2008 | 2009 | 2010 |
|---|---|---|---|---|
| Brazil | 1,295.7 | 1,362.6 | 1,353.8 | 1,455.2 |
| Mexico | 8,806.7 | 8,911.4 | 8,362.4 | 8,815.3 |
| Thailand | 4,259.5 | 4,368.4 | 4,265.1 | 4,597.0 |

*Note:* All values are in billions of units of domestic currency at constant prices.

Data from International Monetary Fund.

a.  Which country experienced the highest rate of economic growth during 2008 (that is, for which country did real GDP increase the most from 2007 to 2008)?

b.  Which country experienced the worst economic recession during 2009? Briefly explain.

c.  Which country experienced the highest average annual growth rate between 2008 and 2010?

d.  Does it matter for your answer that each country's real GDP is measured in a different currency? Briefly explain.

1.5  Andover Bank and Lowell Bank each sell one-year certificates of deposit (CDs). The interest rates on these CDs are given in the following table for a three-year period:

| Bank | 2011 | 2012 | 2013 |
|---|---|---|---|
| Andover Bank | 5% | 5% | 5% |
| Lowell Bank | 2 | 6 | 7 |

Suppose you deposit $1,000 in a CD in each bank at the beginning of 2011. At the end of 2011, you take your $1,000 and any interest earned and invest it in a CD for the following year. You do this again at the end of 2012. At the end of 2013, will you have earned more on your Andover Bank CDs or on your Lowell Bank CDs? Briefly explain.

**1.6** **[Related to the** Don't Let This Happen to You **on page 715]** Use the data for the United States in this table to answer the following questions:

| Year | Real GDP per Capita (2005 prices) |
|------|-----------------------------------|
| 2006 | $ 43,332 |
| 2007 | 43,726 |
| 2008 | 43,178 |
| 2009 | 41,313 |
| 2010 | 42,205 |

a. What was the percentage change in real GDP per capita between 2006 and 2010?

b. What was the average annual growth rate in real GDP per capita between 2006 and 2010? (*Hint:* Remember from Chapter 21 that the average annual growth rate for relatively short periods can be approximated by averaging the growth rates for each year during the period.)

**1.7** **[Related to the** Making the Connection **on page 716]** In his book *The White Man's Burden*, William Easterly reports that

> A vaccination campaign in southern Africa virtually eliminated measles as a killer of children. Routine childhood immunization combined with measles vaccination in seven southern Africa nations starting in 1996 virtually eliminated measles in those countries by 2000. A national campaign in Egypt to make parents aware of the use of oral rehydration therapy from 1982 to 1989 cut childhood

deaths from diarrhea by 82 percent over that period.

a. Is it likely that real GDP per capita increased significantly in southern Africa and Egypt as a result of the near elimination of measles and the large decrease in childhood deaths from diarrhea? If these events did not increase real GDP per capita, is it still possible that they increased the standard of living in southern Africa and Egypt? Briefly explain.

b. Which seems more achievable for a developing country: the elimination of measles and childhood deaths from diarrhea or sustained increases in real GDP per capita? Briefly explain.

From William Easterly, *The White Man's Burden: Why the West's Efforts to Aid the Rest Have Done So Much Ill and So Little Good*, (New York: The Penguin Press, 2006), p. 241.

**1.8** **[Related to the** Making the Connection **on page 716]** Economist Charles Kenny of the World Bank has argued that:

> The process technologies—institutions like laws and inventory management systems—that appear central to raising incomes per capita flow less like water and more like bricks. But ideas and inventions—the importance of ABCs and vaccines for DPT—really might flow more easily across borders and over distances.

If Kenny is correct, what are the implications of these facts for the ability of low-income countries to rapidly increase their rates of growth of real GDP per capita in the decades ahead? What are the implications for the ability of these countries to increase their standards of living? Briefly explain.

From Charles Kenny, *Getting Better*, (New York: Basic Books, 2011), p. 117.

---

**22.2** **What Determines How Fast Economies Grow?** pages 717–723

LEARNING OBJECTIVE: Use the economic growth model to explain why growth rates differ across countries.

## Summary

An **economic growth model** explains changes in real GDP per capita in the long run. **Labor productivity** is the quantity of goods and services that can be produced by one worker or by one hour of work. Economic growth depends on increases in labor productivity. Labor productivity will increase if there is an increase in the amount of *capital* available to each worker or if there is an improvement in *technology*. **Technological change** is a change in the ability of a firm to produce a given level of output with a given quantity of inputs. There are three main sources of technological change: better machinery and equipment, increases in human capital, and better means of organizing and managing production. **Human capital** is the accumulated knowledge and skills that workers acquire from education and training or from their life experiences. We can say that an economy will have a higher standard of living the more capital it has per hour worked, the more human capital its workers have, the better its capital, and the better the job its business managers do in organizing production.

The **per-worker production function** shows the relationship between capital per hour worked and output per hour worked,

holding technology constant. *Diminishing returns to capital* means that increases in the quantity of capital per hour worked will result in diminishing increases in output per hour worked. Technological change shifts up the per-worker production function, resulting in more output per hour worked at every level of capital per hour worked. The economic growth model stresses the importance of changes in capital per hour worked and technological change in explaining growth in output per hour worked. **New growth theory** is a model of long-run economic growth that emphasizes that technological change is influenced by how individuals and firms respond to economic incentives.

One way governments can promote technological change is by granting **patents**, which are exclusive rights to a product for a period of 20 years from the date the patent is applied for. To Joseph Schumpeter, the entrepreneur is central to the "creative destruction" by which the standard of living increases as qualitatively better products replace existing products.

 MyEconLab  Visit **www.myeconlab.com** to complete these exercises online and get instant feedback.

# Review Questions

**2.1** Using the per-worker production function graph from Figures 22.3 and 22.4 on pages 718–719, show the effect on real GDP per hour worked of an increase in capital per hour worked, holding technology constant. Now, again using the per-worker production function graph, show the effect on real GDP per hour worked of an increase in technology, holding constant the quantity of capital per hour worked.

**2.2** What are the consequences for growth of diminishing returns to capital? How are some economies able to maintain high growth rates despite diminishing returns to capital?

**2.3** Why are firms likely to underinvest in research and development, which slows the accumulation of knowledge capital, slowing economic growth? Briefly discuss three ways in which government policy can increase the accumulation of knowledge capital.

**2.4** What is the *new growth theory*? How does the new growth theory differ from the growth theory developed by Robert Solow?

# Problems and Applications

**2.5** According to a study by an economist at the Federal Reserve Bank of Minneapolis, during the mid-1980s, managers at iron mines in Canada and the United States increased output per hour worked by 100 percent through changes in work rules that increased workers' effort per hour worked and increased the efficiency of workers' effort. Briefly explain whether this increase in output per hour worked is an example of an improvement in technology.

Based on James A. Schmitz, Jr., "What Determines Labor Productivity? Lessons from the Dramatic Recovery of the U.S. and Canadian Iron-Ore Industries Following Their Early 1980s Crisis," Federal Reserve Bank of Minneapolis Research Department Staff Report 286, February 2005.

**2.6** Which of the following will result in a movement along China's per-worker production function, and which will result in a shift of China's per-worker production function? Briefly explain.

**a.** Capital per hour worked increases from 5 million yuan per hour worked to 6 million yuan per hour worked.

**b.** The Chinese government doubles its spending on support for university research.

**c.** A reform of the Chinese school system results in more highly trained Chinese workers.

**2.7** **[Related to** Solved Problem 22.2 **on page 721]** Use the graph at the top of the next column. to answer the following questions.

**a.** True or false: The movement from point *A* to point *B* shows the effects of technological change.

**b.** True or false: The economy can move from point *B* to point *C* only if there are no diminishing returns to capital.

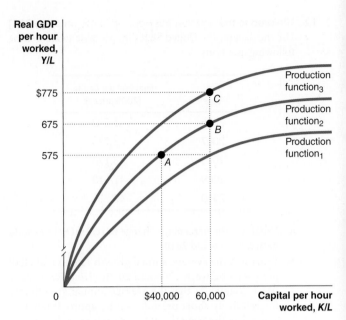

**c.** True or false: To move from point *A* to point *C*, the economy must increase the amount of capital per hour worked and experience technological change.

**2.8** **[Related to** Solved Problem 22.2 **on page 721]** Shortly before the fall of the Soviet Union, the economist Gur Ofer of Hebrew University of Jerusalem, wrote this: "The most outstanding characteristic of Soviet growth strategy is its consistent policy of very high rates of investment, leading to a rapid growth rate of [the] capital stock." Explain why this turned out to be a very poor growth strategy.

From Gur Ofer, "Soviet Economic Growth, 1928–1985," *Journal of Economic Literature*, Vol. 25, No. 4, December 1987, p. 1,784.

**2.9** Why is the role of the entrepreneur much more important in the new growth theory than in the traditional economic growth model?

**2.10** **[Related to the** Making the Connection **on page 720]** The *Making the Connection* argues that a key difference between market economies and centrally planned economies, like that of the former Soviet Union, is as follows:

> In market economies, decisions about which investments to make and which technologies to adopt are made by entrepreneurs and managers with their own money on the line. In the Soviet system, these decisions were usually made by salaried bureaucrats trying to fulfill a plan formulated in Moscow.

But in large corporations, investment decisions are often made by salaried managers who do not have their own money on the line. These managers are spending the money of the firm's shareholders rather than their own money. Why, then, do the investment decisions of salaried managers in the United States tend to be better for the long-term growth of the economy than were the decisions of salaried bureaucrats in the Soviet Union?

**22.3** **Economic Growth in the United States,** pages 723–726

LEARNING OBJECTIVE: Discuss fluctuations in productivity growth in the United States.

## Summary

Productivity in the United States grew rapidly from the end of World War II until the mid-1970s. Growth then slowed down for 20 years before increasing again after 1995. Economists continue to debate the reasons for the growth slowdown of the mid-1970s to mid-1990s. Leading explanations for the productivity slowdown are measurement problems, high oil prices, and a decline in labor quality. Because Western Europe and Japan experienced a productivity slowdown at the same time as the United States, explanations that focus on factors affecting only the United States are unlikely to be correct. Some economists argue that the development of a "new economy" based on information technology caused the higher productivity growth that began in the mid-1990s. Economists debate whether the higher productivity growth that began in the mid-1990s will continue.

 MyEconLab    Visit **www.myeconlab.com** to complete these exercises online and get instant feedback.

## Review Questions

3.1 Describe the record of productivity growth in the United States from 1800 to the present. What explains the slowdown in productivity growth from the mid-1970s to the mid-1990s? Why did productivity growth increase beginning in 1995?

3.2 Why do some economists believe that the higher productivity growth rates that began in the mid-1990s can be sustained?

## Problems and Applications

3.3 Figure 22.5 on page 724 shows growth rates in real GDP per hour worked in the United States for various periods from 1900 onward. How might the growth rates in the figure be different if they were calculated for real GDP *per capita* instead of per hour worked? (*Hint:* How do you think the number of hours worked per person has changed in the United States since 1900?)

3.4 An article in the *Wall Street Journal* observes: "For 2008, productivity grew an astounding 2.8% from 2007 even as the economy suffered through its worst recession in decades." How is it possible for labor productivity—output per hour worked—to increase if output—real GDP—is falling?

From Brian Blackstone, "Productivity Proves Resilient," *Wall Street Journal*, April 29, 2009.

3.5 Economist Robert Gordon of Northwestern University has argued that:

> My interpretation of the [information] revolution is that it is increasingly burdened by diminishing returns. The push to ever smaller devices runs up against the fixed size of the human finger that must enter information on the device. Most of the innovations since 2000 have been directed to consumer enjoyment rather than business productivity, including video games, DVD players, and iPods. iPhones are nice, but the ability to reschedule business meetings and look up corporate documents while on the road already existed by 2003.

If Gordon's observations about the information revolution are correct, what are the implications for future labor productivity growth rates in the United States?

From Robert J. Gordon, "Revisiting U.S. Productivity Growth over the Past Century with a View of the Future," National Bureau of Economic Research Working Paper 15834, March 2010.

---

**22.4** **Why Isn't the Whole World Rich?** pages 726–735

LEARNING OBJECTIVE: Explain economic catch-up and discuss why many poor countries have not experienced rapid economic growth.

## Summary

The economic growth model predicts that poor countries will grow faster than rich countries, resulting in **catch-up**. In recent decades, some poor countries have grown faster than rich countries, but many have not. Some poor countries do not experience rapid growth for four main reasons: wars and revolutions, poor public education and health, failure to enforce the rule of law, and low rates of saving and investment. The **rule of law** refers to the ability of a government to enforce the laws of the country, particularly with respect to protecting private property and enforcing contracts. **Globalization** has aided countries that have opened their economies to foreign trade and investment. **Foreign direct investment (FDI)** is the purchase or building by a corporation of a facility in a foreign country. **Foreign portfolio investment** is the purchase by an individual or firm of stocks or bonds issued in another country.

MyEconLab    Visit **www.myeconlab.com** to complete these exercises online and get instant feedback.

## Review Questions

4.1 Why does the economic growth model predict that poor countries should catch up to rich countries in income per capita? Have poor countries been catching up to rich countries?

**4.2** In what ways does the United States have greater flexibility in its labor markets and greater efficiency in its financial system than other higher income countries such as those in Europe? How might this greater flexibility in labor markets and greater efficiency in financial markets lead to higher growth rates in real GDP per capita?

**4.3** What are the main reasons many poor countries have experienced slow growth?

**4.4** What does *globalization* mean? How have developing countries benefited from globalization?

## Problems and Applications

**4.5** [Related to Solved Problem 22.4 **on page 728**] Briefly explain whether the statistics in the following table are consistent with the economic growth model's predictions of catch-up.

| Country | Real GDP per Capita in 1960 | Growth in Real GDP per Capita, 1960–2009 |
|---|---|---|
| China | $363 | 6.23% |
| Uganda | 655 | 1.16 |
| Madagascar | 1,268 | –0.23 |
| Ireland | 6,971 | 3.25 |
| United States | 15,438 | 2.02 |

Authors' calculations from data in Alan Heston, Robert Summers, and Bettina Aten, *Penn World Table Version 7.0*, Center for International Comparisons of Production, Income and Prices at the University of Pennsylvania, June 3, 2011.

**4.6** [Related to Solved Problem 22.4 **on page 728**] In the following figure, each dot represents a country, with its initial real GDP per capita and its growth rate of real GDP per capita.

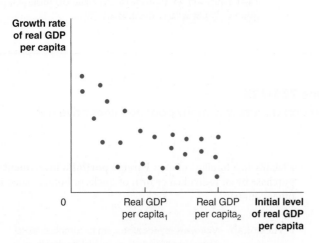

**a.** For the range of initial GDP per capita from 0 to Real GDP per capita$_2$, does the figure support the economic growth model's prediction of catch-up? Briefly explain.

**b.** For the range of initial GDP per capita from 0 to Real GDP per capita$_1$, does the figure support the catch-up prediction? Briefly explain.

**c.** For the range from initial Real GDP per capita$_1$ to Real GDP per capita$_2$, does the figure support the catch-up prediction? Briefly explain.

**4.7** An opinion column in the *Economist* argued, "Globalisation, far from being the greatest cause of poverty, is its only feasible cure." What does globalization have to do with reducing poverty?

From Clive Crook, "Globalisation and Its Critics," *Economist*, September 27, 2001.

**4.8** [Related to the Making the Connection **on page 732**] The relationship that Raymond Fisman and Edward Miguel found between the extent of corruption in a country and the number of parking violations committed by the country's United Nations delegates in New York isn't perfect. For example, "Ecuador and Colombia both have perfectly clean parking slates, despite the experts' view of them as fairly corrupt places." Does this observation invalidate Fisman and Miguel's conclusions about whether the parking violations data provide evidence in favor of there being a culture of corruption in some countries? Briefly explain.

Based on Raymond Fisman and Edward Miguel, *Economic Gangsters*, (Princeton, NJ: Princeton University Press, 2009), p. 89.

**4.9** In a speech in 2009, President Barack Obama made the following observations: "I know that for many, the face of globalization is contradictory. . . . Trade can bring new wealth and opportunities, but also huge disruptions and change in communities." How does trade bring "new wealth and opportunities"? How does trade bring "huge disruptions and change"?

From "Obama's Speech in Cairo," *Wall Street Journal*, June 4, 2009.

**4.10** A columnist in the *New York Times* observes that, "many analysts agree that economic reform, of which integration into the global economy was a key element, has lifted millions of people out of poverty in India. What does "integration into the global economy" mean? How might integration into the global economy reduce poverty in India?

From Vivek Dehejia, "Has Globalization Helped India's Poor?" *New York Times*, October 7, 2011.

**4.11** The Roman Empire lasted from 27 B.C. to 476 A.D. The empire was wealthy enough to build such monuments as the Roman Coliseum. Roman engineering skill was at a level high enough that aqueducts built during the empire to carry water long distances remained in use for hundreds of years. Yet the empire's growth rate of real GDP per capita was very low, perhaps zero. Why didn't the Roman Empire experience sustained economic growth? What would the world be like today if it had? (*Note:* There are no definite answers to this question; it is intended to get you to think about the preconditions for economic growth.)

**22.5** | **Growth Policies, pages 735-738**

LEARNING OBJECTIVE: Discuss government policies that foster economic growth.

## Summary

Governments can attempt to increase economic growth through policies that enhance property rights and the rule of law, improve health and education, subsidize research and development, and provide incentives for savings and investment. Whether continued economic growth is desirable is a normative question that cannot be settled by economic analysis.

MyEconLab   Visit www.myeconlab.com to complete these exercises online and get instant feedback.

## Review Questions

**5.1** Briefly describe three government policies that can increase economic growth.

**5.2** Can economics arrive at the conclusion that economic growth will always improve economic well-being? Briefly explain.

## Problems and Applications

**5.3** **[Related to the** Chapter Opener **on page 711]** In discussing the future of China, the *Economist* magazine observed:

> And there are ... clear limits to the march of freedom in China; although personal and economic freedoms have multiplied, political freedoms have been disappointingly constrained since Hu Jintao became president in 2003.

Briefly discuss whether the limits on political freedom in China are likely to eventually become an obstacle to its continued rapid economic growth.

From "China's Dash for Freedom," *Economist*, July 31, 2008.

**5.4** **[Related to the** Making the Connection **on page 735]** In China, why may a lower birthrate lead to slower growth in real GDP per capita? Why might high levels of spending on investment in China lead to high rates of growth in the short run, but not in the long run?

**5.5** Is it likely to be easier for the typical developing country to improve the state of public health or to improve the average level of education? Briefly explain.

**5.6** Briefly explain which of the following policies are likely to increase the rate of economic growth in the United States.

  **a.** Congress passes an investment tax credit, which reduces a firm's taxes if it installs new machinery and equipment.

  **b.** Congress passes a law that allows taxpayers to reduce their income taxes by the amount of state sales taxes they pay.

  **c.** Congress provides more funds for low-interest loans to college students.

**5.7** Economist George Ayittey, in an interview on PBS about economic development in Africa, stated that of the 54 African countries, only 8 had a free press. For Africa's economic development, Ayittey argued strongly for the establishment of a free press. Why would a free press be vital for the enhancement of property rights and the rule of law? How could a free press help reduce corruption?

From George Ayittey, *Border Jumpers*, Anchor Interview Transcript, WideAngle, PBS.org, July 24, 2005.

**5.8** More people in high-income countries than in low-income countries tend to believe that rapid rates of economic growth are not desirable. Recall the concept of a "normal good" from Chapter 3. Does this concept provide insight into why some people in high-income countries might be more concerned with certain consequences of rapid economic growth than are people in low-income countries?

# Aggregate Expenditure and Output in the Short Run

## Chapter Outline and Learning Objectives

# Fluctuating Demand Helps—
# and Hurts—Intel and Other Firms

Intel is the world's largest semiconductor manufacturer and a major supplier of the microprocessors and memory chips found in most personal computers. Robert Noyce and Gordon Moore founded the firm in 1968. The performance of computers has improved very rapidly over the past 40 years, making possible the information revolution, in which Intel has been a key participant. By 2010, Intel had more than 82,000 employees and annual revenues of over $43 billion. Because of its dependence on computer sales, Intel is vulnerable to the swings of the business cycle. During the 2001 recession, for example, Intel's revenue fell 21 percent, and the firm laid off 5,000 workers. Intel was also hurt by the 2007–2009 recession. During the last quarter of 2008, its revenues fell 90 percent, and it laid off 6,000 workers.

But Intel bounced back in 2010, as the U.S. economy recovered from the recession. Real GDP grew by 3.0 percent in 2010. Increased demand for computers and other technology-based products, especially in China and other emerging markets, increased the demand for the parts Intel sells to computer manufacturers. Intel's revenue continued to grow through the first half of 2011, although analysts cautioned that a slowdown in real GDP growth—only 0.4 percent in the first quarter of 2011 and 1.3 percent in the second quarter—could eventually reduce Intel's sales.

Other firms also suffered from the slow economic growth in 2011. Cisco Systems, a manufacturer of computer networking equipment, announced that it would lay off 6,500 employees. Lockheed Martin, supplier of weapons to the Department of Defense, also announced plans to lay off 6,500 employees. Layoffs were not limited to technology firms. Cracker Barrel Old Country Store joined the list of firms cutting workers. Steven Ricchiuto, chief economist at Mizuho Securities, explained, "They're looking to reduce staff [and this] means they don't see a pickup in demand going forward."

These firms were cutting production and employment as a result of the sluggish growth of total spending, or *aggregate expenditure*. In this chapter, we will explore how changes in aggregate expenditure affect the level of total production in the economy.

**AN INSIDE LOOK** on **page 782** discusses the expected rebound in sales in the restaurant industry following the recession of 2007–2009.

Based on Conor Dougherty, "Layoffs Deepen Gloom," *The Wall Street Journal*, July 21, 2011; and Kathryn Glass, "Intel's Quarterly Results Beat Expectations, *FOXBusiness.com*," July 20, 2011.

## Economics in Your Life

### When Consumer Confidence Falls, Is Your Job at Risk?

Suppose that while attending college, you work part time, assembling desktop computers for a large computer company. One morning, you read in the local newspaper that consumer confidence in the economy has fallen and, consequently, many households expect their future income to be dramatically less than their current income. Should you be concerned about losing your job? What factors should you consider in deciding how likely your company is to lay you off? As you read the chapter, see if you can answer these questions. You can check your answers against those we provide on **page 781** at the end of this chapter.

**Aggregate expenditure (*AE*)** Total spending in the economy: the sum of consumption, planned investment, government purchases, and net exports.

I n Chapter 22, we analyzed the determinants of long-run growth in the economy. In the short run, as we saw in Chapter 21, the economy experiences a business cycle around the long-run upward trend in real GDP. In this chapter, we begin exploring the causes of the business cycle by examining the effect of changes in total spending on real GDP.

During some years, total spending in the economy, or **aggregate expenditure (*AE*)**, and total production of goods and services increase by the same amount. If this happens, most firms will sell about what they expected to sell, and they probably will not increase or decrease production or the number of workers they hire. During other years, total spending in the economy increases more than the production of goods and services. In those years, firms will increase production and hire more workers. But at other times, such as during 2008 and early 2009, total spending does not increase as much as total production. As a result, firms cut back on production and lay off workers, and the economy moves into a recession. In this chapter, we will explore why changes in total spending play such an important role in the economy.

Understand how macroeconomic equilibrium is determined in the aggregate expenditure model.

**Aggregate expenditure model** A macroeconomic model that focuses on the short-run relationship between total spending and real GDP, assuming that the price level is constant.

# The Aggregate Expenditure Model

The business cycle involves the interaction of many economic variables. A simple model called the *aggregate expenditure model* can help us begin to understand the relationships among some of these variables. Recall from Chapter 19 that GDP is the value of all the final goods and services produced in an economy during a particular year. Real GDP corrects nominal GDP for the effects of inflation. The **aggregate expenditure model** focuses on the short-run relationship between total spending and real GDP. An important assumption of the model is that the price level is constant. In Chapter 24, we will develop a more complete model of the business cycle that relaxes the assumption of constant prices.

The key idea of the aggregate expenditure model is that *in any particular year, the level of GDP is determined mainly by the level of aggregate expenditure.* To understand the relationship between aggregate expenditure and real GDP, we need to look more closely at the components of aggregate expenditure.

## Aggregate Expenditure

Economists first began to study the relationship between changes in aggregate expenditure and changes in GDP during the Great Depression of the 1930s. The United States, the United Kingdom, and other industrial countries suffered declines in real GDP of 20 percent or more during the early 1930s. In 1936, the English economist John Maynard Keynes published a book, *The General Theory of Employment, Interest, and Money*, that systematically analyzed the relationship between changes in aggregate expenditure and changes in GDP. Keynes identified four components of aggregate expenditure that together equal GDP (these are the same four components we discussed in Chapter 19):

- *Consumption (C).* This is spending by households on goods and services, such as automobiles and haircuts.

- *Planned investment (I).* This is planned spending by firms on capital goods, such as factories, office buildings, and machine tools, and by households on new homes.

- *Government purchases (G).* This is spending by local, state, and federal governments on goods and services, such as aircraft carriers, bridges, and the salaries of FBI agents.

- *Net exports (NX).* This is spending by foreign firms and households on goods and services produced in the United States minus spending by U.S. firms and households on goods and services produced in other countries.

So, we can write

> Aggregate expenditure = Consumption + Planned investment
> + Government purchases + Net exports,

or

$$AE = C + I + G + NX.$$

Governments around the world gather statistics on aggregate expenditure on the basis of these four components. And economists and business analysts usually explain changes in GDP in terms of changes in these four components of spending.

## The Difference between Planned Investment and Actual Investment

Before considering further the relationship between aggregate expenditure and GDP, we need to consider an important distinction: Notice that *planned* investment spending, rather than actual investment spending, is a component of aggregate expenditure. You might wonder how the amount that businesses plan to spend on investment can be different from the amount they actually spend. We can begin resolving this puzzle by remembering that goods that have been produced but have not yet been sold are referred to as **inventories**. Changes in inventories are included as part of investment spending, along with spending on machinery, equipment, office buildings, and factories. We assume that the amount businesses plan to spend on machinery and office buildings is equal to the amount they actually spend, but the amount businesses plan to spend on inventories may be different from the amount they actually spend.

**Inventories** Goods that have been produced but not yet sold.

For example, Doubleday Publishing may print 1.5 million copies of the latest John Grisham novel, expecting to sell them all. If Doubleday does sell all 1.5 million, its inventories will be unchanged, but if it sells only 1.2 million, it will have an unplanned increase in inventories. In other words, changes in inventories depend on sales of goods, which firms cannot always forecast with perfect accuracy.

For the economy as a whole, we can say that actual investment spending will be greater than planned investment spending when there is an unplanned increase in inventories. Actual investment spending will be less than planned investment spending when there is an unplanned decrease in inventories. *Therefore, actual investment will equal planned investment only when there is no unplanned change in inventories.* In this chapter, we will use *I* to represent planned investment. We will also assume that the government data on investment spending compiled by the U.S. Bureau of Economic Analysis represents planned investment spending. This is a simplification, however, because the government collects data on actual investment spending, which equals planned investment spending only when unplanned changes in inventories are zero.

## Macroeconomic Equilibrium

Macroeconomic equilibrium is similar to microeconomic equilibrium. In microeconomics, equilibrium in the apple market occurs at the point at which the quantity of apples demanded equals the quantity of apples supplied. When we have equilibrium in the apple market, the quantity of apples produced and sold will not change unless the demand for apples or the supply of apples changes. For the economy as a whole, macroeconomic equilibrium occurs where total spending, or aggregate expenditure, equals total production, or GDP:

> Aggregate expenditure = GDP.

As we saw in Chapter 22, over the long run, real GDP in the United States grows, and the standard of living rises. In this chapter, we are interested in understanding why GDP fluctuates in the short run. To simplify the analysis of macroeconomic equilibrium, we assume that the economy is not growing. In the next chapter, we discuss the more realistic case of macroeconomic equilibrium in a growing economy. If we assume that the economy is not growing, then equilibrium GDP will not change unless aggregate expenditure changes.

## Adjustments to Macroeconomic Equilibrium

The apple market isn't always in equilibrium because sometimes the quantity of apples demanded is greater than the quantity supplied, and sometimes the quantity supplied is greater than the quantity demanded. The same outcome holds for the economy as a whole. Sometimes the economy is in macroeconomic equilibrium, and sometimes it isn't. When aggregate expenditure is greater than GDP, the total amount of spending in the economy is greater than the total amount of production. With spending being greater than production, many businesses will sell more goods and services than they had expected to sell. For example, the manager of a Home Depot store might like to keep 50 refrigerators in stock to give customers the opportunity to see a variety of different sizes and models. If sales are unexpectedly high, the store may end up with only 20 refrigerators. In that case, the store will have an unplanned decrease in inventories: Its inventory of refrigerators will decline by 30.

How will the store manager react when more refrigerators are sold than expected? The manager is likely to order more refrigerators. If other stores selling refrigerators are experiencing similar sales increases and are also increasing their orders, then General Electric, Whirlpool, and other refrigerator manufacturers will significantly increase their production. These manufacturers may also increase the number of workers they hire. If the increase in sales is affecting not just refrigerators but also other appliances, automobiles, furniture, computers, and other goods and services, then GDP and total employment will begin to increase. In summary, *when aggregate expenditure is greater than GDP, inventories will decline, and GDP and total employment will increase.*

Now suppose that aggregate expenditure is less than GDP. With spending being less than production, many businesses will sell fewer goods and services than they had expected to sell, so their inventories will increase. For example, the manager of the Home Depot store who wants 50 refrigerators in stock may find that because of slow sales, the store has 75 refrigerators, so the store manager will cut back on orders for new refrigerators. If other stores also cut back on their orders, General Electric and Whirlpool will reduce production and lay off workers.

If the decrease in sales is affecting not just refrigerators but also many other goods and services, GDP and total employment will begin to decrease. These events happened at many firms during 2008. In summary, *when aggregate expenditure is less than GDP, inventories will increase, and GDP and total employment will decrease.*

Only when aggregate expenditure equals GDP will firms sell what they expected to sell. In that case, their inventories will be unchanged, and they will not have an incentive to increase or decrease production. The economy will be in macroeconomic equilibrium. Table 23.1 summarizes the relationship between aggregate expenditure and GDP.

**Table 23.1**

**The Relationship between Aggregate Expenditure and GDP**

| If... | then... | and... |
|---|---|---|
| aggregate expenditure is *equal* to GDP | inventories are *unchanged* | the economy is in *macroeconomic equilibrium.* |
| aggregate expenditure is *less* than GDP | inventories *rise* | GDP and employment *decrease.* |
| aggregate expenditure is *greater* than GDP | inventories *fall* | GDP and employment *increase.* |

Increases and decreases in aggregate expenditure cause the year-to-year changes we see in GDP. Economists devote considerable time and energy to forecasting what will happen to each component of aggregate expenditure. If economists forecast that aggregate expenditure will decline in the future, that is equivalent to forecasting that GDP will decline and that the economy will enter a recession. Individuals and firms closely watch these forecasts because changes in GDP can have dramatic consequences. When GDP is increasing, so are wages, profits, and job opportunities. Declining GDP can be bad news for workers, firms, and job seekers.

When economists forecast that aggregate expenditure is likely to decline and that the economy is headed for a recession, the federal government may implement *macroeconomic policies* in an attempt to head off the decrease in expenditure and keep the economy from falling into recession. We discuss these macroeconomic policies in Chapters 26 and 27.

# Determining the Level of Aggregate Expenditure in the Economy

**23.2 LEARNING** OBJECTIVE

Discuss the determinants of the four components of aggregate expenditure and define marginal propensity to consume and marginal propensity to save.

To better understand how macroeconomic equilibrium is determined in the aggregate expenditure model, we look more closely at the components of aggregate expenditure. Table 23.2 lists the four components of aggregate expenditure for the year 2010. Each component is measured in *real* terms, meaning that it is corrected for inflation by being measured in billions of 2005 dollars. Consumption is clearly the largest component of aggregate expenditure. Investment and government purchases are of roughly similar size. Net exports were negative because in 2010, as in most years since the early 1970s, the United States imported more goods and services than it exported. Next, we consider the variables that determine each of the four components of aggregate expenditure.

## Consumption

Figure 23.1 shows movements in real consumption from 1979 through the second quarter of 2011. Notice that consumption follows a smooth, upward trend. Only during periods of recession does the growth in consumption decline.

The following are the five most important variables that determine the level of consumption:

• Current disposable income

• Household wealth

• Expected future income

• The price level

• The interest rate

We now discuss how changes in each of these variables affect consumption.

| Expenditure Category | Real Expenditure (billions of 2005 dollars) |
|---|---|
| Consumption | $9,221 |
| Planned investment | 1,715 |
| Government purchases | 2,557 |
| Net exports | −422 |

**Table 23.2**

**Components of Real Aggregate Expenditure, 2010**

Data from U.S. Bureau of Economic Analysis.

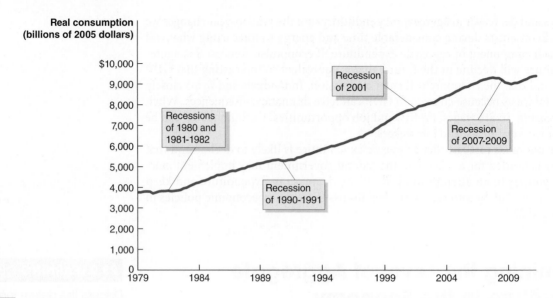

**Figure 23.1** Real Consumption

Consumption follows a smooth, upward trend, interrupted only infrequently by brief recessions.

*Note:* The values are quarterly data seasonally adjusted at an annual rate.
Data from U.S. Bureau of Economic Analysis.

**Current Disposable Income** The most important determinant of consumption is the current disposable income of households. Recall from Chapter 19 that disposable income is the income remaining to households after they have paid the personal income tax and received government *transfer payments*, such as Social Security payments. For most households, the higher their disposable income, the more they spend, and the lower their income, the less they spend. Macroeconomic consumption is the total of all the consumption of U.S. households. So, we would expect consumption to increase when the current disposable income of households increases and to decrease when the current disposable income of households decreases. As we discussed in Chapter 19, total income in the United States expands during most years. Only during recessions, which happen infrequently, does total income decline. The main reason for the general upward trend in consumption shown in Figure 23.1 is that disposable income has followed a similar upward trend.

**Household Wealth** Consumption depends in part on the wealth of households. A household's *wealth* is the value of its *assets* minus the value of its *liabilities*. Recall from Chapter 8 that an asset is anything of value owned by a person or a firm, and a liability is anything owed by a person or a firm. A household's assets include its home, stock and bond holdings, and bank accounts. A household's liabilities include any loans that it owes. A household with $10 million in wealth is likely to spend more than a household with $10,000 in wealth, even if both households have the same disposable income. Therefore, when the wealth of households increases, consumption should increase, and when the wealth of households decreases, consumption should decrease. Shares of stock are an important category of household wealth. When stock prices increase, household wealth will increase, and so should consumption. For example, a family whose stock holdings increase in value from $50,000 to $100,000 may be willing to spend a larger fraction of its income because it is less concerned with adding to its savings. A decline in stock prices should lead to a decline in consumption. Economists who have studied the determinants of consumption have concluded that permanent increases in wealth have a larger impact than temporary increases. A recent estimate of the effect of changes in wealth on consumption spending indicates that, for every permanent $1 increase in household wealth, consumption spending will increase by between 4 and 5 cents per year.

| Making the Connection | ## Do Changes in Housing Wealth Affect Consumption Spending? |
|---|---|

From 2000 to 2006, housing prices increased sharply in many parts of the United States. The figure below shows the S&P/Case-Shiller index of housing prices, which represents changes in the prices of single-family homes. As measured by this index, housing prices increased nearly 90 percent between the beginning of 2000 and the beginning of 2006. Housing prices then declined over 30 percent between the beginning of 2006 and the beginning of 2009. *Housing wealth* equals the market value of houses minus the value of loans people have taken out to pay for the houses. For example, someone who owns a house with a market price of $200,000 and who has a mortgage of $150,000 would have housing wealth of $50,000. Between 2000 and 2005, total housing wealth increased by about $5.5 trillion before falling by $7.0 trillion through mid-2011.

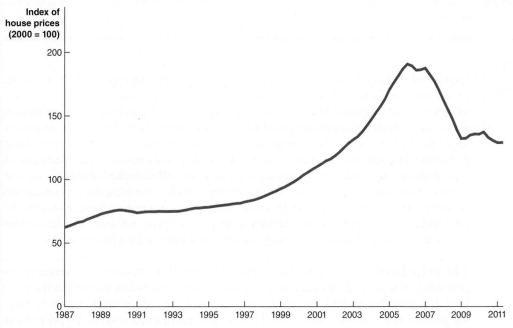

Data from S&P/Case-Shiller, standardandpoors.com.

Did these big swings in housing wealth affect consumption spending? Economists are divided in their opinions. Charles Calomiris of Columbia University, Stanley Longhofer of the Barton School of Business, and William Miles of Wichita State University argue that changes in housing wealth have little or no effect on consumption. They argue that consumers do not consider houses to be assets similar to their holdings of stocks and bonds because they own houses primarily so they can consume the housing services a home provides. Only consumers who intend to sell their current house and buy a smaller one—for example, "empty nesters" whose children have left home—will benefit from an increase in housing prices. But taking the population as a whole, the number of empty nesters may be smaller than the number of first-time home buyers plus the number of homeowners who want to buy larger houses. These two groups are hurt by rising home prices. Although it appears that consumption increases when housing prices increase, in fact, increases in income are responsible for both the increases in housing prices and the increases in consumption; increases in housing prices have no independent effect on consumption. (This is an example of the omitted variable problem discussed on page 32 of the appendix to Chapter 1.)

Atif Mian and Amir Sufi, both of the University of Chicago, strongly disagree with Calomiris, Longhofer, and Miles. Mian and Sufi tracked a sample of 70,000 consumers from 1998 to 2008 and found that consumers living in cities that experienced dramatic increases in housing prices borrowed heavily as their housing wealth increased. Consumers used these borrowed funds to increase their spending on goods and services.

Mian and Sufi believe that the sharp decline in consumption spending in 2008—the largest since 1980—occurred because falling housing prices resulted in lower housing wealth and lower consumer borrowing to finance spending.

The debate over the effect of changes in housing wealth on consumption spending illustrates an important fact about macroeconomics: Many macroeconomic variables, such as GDP, housing prices, consumption spending, and investment spending, rise and fall at about the same time during the business cycle. Because many macroeconomic variables move together, economists sometimes have difficulty determining whether movements in one variable are causing movements in another variable.

Based on Atif R. Mian and Amir Sufi, "House Prices, Home Equity–Based Borrowing, and the U.S. Household Leverage Crisis," *American Economic Review*, Vol. 101, No. 5, August 2011, pp. 2132–2156; Atif Mian and Amir Sufi, "Housing Bubble Fueled Consumer Spending," *Wall Street Journal*, June 25, 2009; Charles W. Calomiris, Stanley D. Longhofer, and William Miles, "The (Mythical?) Housing Wealth Effect," National Bureau of Economic Research Working Paper 15075, June 2009; and Charles W. Calomiris, Stanley D. Longhofer, and William Miles, "The (Mythical?) Housing Wealth Effect," *Wall Street Journal*, June 22, 2009.

MyEconLab **Your Turn:** Test your understanding by doing related problem 2.11 on page 785 at the end of this chapter.

**Expected Future Income**  Consumption depends in part on expected future income. Most people prefer to keep their consumption fairly stable from year to year, even if their income fluctuates significantly. Some salespeople, for example, earn most of their income from commissions (fixed percentages of the price) on the products they sell. A salesperson might have a high income in some years and a much lower income in other years. Most people in this situation keep their consumption steady and do not increase it during good years and then drastically cut it back during slower years. If we looked only at the current income of someone in this situation, we might have difficulty estimating the person's current consumption. Instead, we need to take into account the person's expected future income. We can conclude that current income explains current consumption well *but only when current income is not unusually high or unusually low compared with expected future income.*

**The Price Level**  Recall from Chapter 20 that the *price level* measures the average prices of goods and services in the economy. Consumption is affected by changes in the price level. It is tempting to think that an increase in prices will reduce consumption by making goods and services less affordable. In fact, the effect of an increase in the price of *one* product on the quantity demanded of that product is different from the effect of an increase in the price level on *total* spending by households on goods and services. Changes in the price level affect consumption mainly through their effect on household wealth. An increase in the price level will result in a decrease in the *real* value of household wealth. For example, if you have $2,000 in a checking account, the higher the price level, the fewer goods and services you can buy with your money. If the price level falls, the real value of your $2,000 increases. Therefore, as the price level rises, the real value of your wealth declines, and so will your consumption, at least a little. Conversely, if the price level falls—which happens very rarely in the United States—your consumption will increase.

**The Interest Rate**  Finally, consumption depends on the interest rate. When the interest rate is high, the reward for saving is increased, and households are likely to save more and spend less. In Chapter 20, we discussed the distinction between the *nominal interest rate* and the *real interest rate*. The nominal interest rate is the stated interest rate on a loan or a financial investment such as a bond. The real interest rate corrects the nominal interest rate for the effect of inflation and is equal to the nominal interest rate minus the inflation rate. Because households are concerned with the payments they will make or receive after the effects of inflation are taken into account, consumption spending depends on the real interest rate.

We saw in Chapter 19 that consumption spending is divided into three categories: spending on *services*, such as medical care, education, and haircuts; spending on *nondurable goods*, such as food and clothing; and spending on *durable goods*, such as automobiles and furniture. Spending on durable goods is most likely to be affected by changes in the interest rate because a high real interest rate increases the cost of spending financed by borrowing. The monthly payment on a four-year car loan will be higher if the real interest rate on the loan is 4 percent than if the real interest rate is 2 percent.

**The Consumption Function**  Panel (a) in Figure 23.2 illustrates the relationship between consumption and disposable income during the years 1960 to 2010. In panel (b), we draw a straight line through the points representing consumption and disposable income. The fact that most of the points lie almost on the line shows the close relationship between consumption and disposable income. Because changes in consumption depend on changes in disposable income, we can say that *consumption is a function of disposable income*. The relationship between consumption spending and disposable income illustrated in panel (b) of Figure 23.2 is called the **consumption function**.

The slope of the consumption function, which is equal to the change in consumption divided by the change in disposable income, is referred to as the **marginal propensity to consume (MPC)**. Using the Greek letter delta, $\Delta$, to represent "change in," $C$ to represent consumption spending, and $YD$ to represent disposable income, we can write the expression for the $MPC$ as follows:

$$MPC = \frac{\text{Change in consumption}}{\text{Change in disposable income}} = \frac{\Delta C}{\Delta YD}.$$

For example, between 2006 and 2007, consumption spending increased by $208 billion, while disposable income increased by $228 billion. The marginal propensity to consume was, therefore:

$$\frac{\Delta C}{\Delta YD} = \frac{\$208 \text{ billion}}{\$228 \text{ billion}} = 0.91.$$

The value for the $MPC$ tells us that households in 2007 spent 91 percent of the increase in their household income.

> **Consumption function**  The relationship between consumption spending and disposable income.
>
> **Marginal propensity to consume (MPC)**  The slope of the consumption function: The amount by which consumption spending changes when disposable income changes.

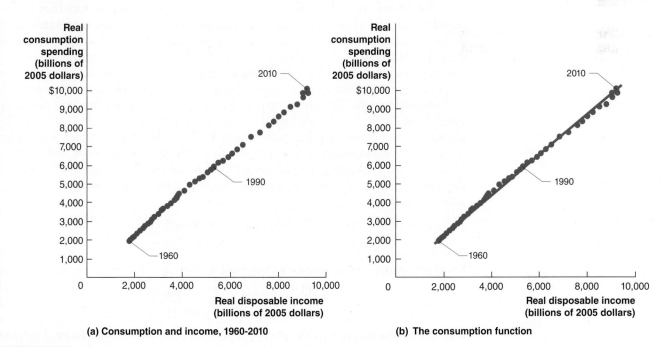

**(a) Consumption and income, 1960-2010**          **(b) The consumption function**

**Figure 23.2**  **The Relationship between Consumption and Income, 1960–2010**

Panel (a) shows the relationship between consumption and income. The points represent combinations of real consumption spending and real disposable income for the years 1960 to 2010. In panel (b), we draw a straight line through the points from panel (a). The line, which represents the relationship between consumption and disposable income, is called the *consumption function*. The slope of the consumption function is the marginal propensity to consume.

Data from U.S. Bureau of Economic Analysis.

We can also use the *MPC* to determine how much consumption will change as income changes. To see this relationship, we rewrite the expression for the *MPC*:

$$\text{Change in consumption} = \text{Change in disposable income} \times MPC.$$

For example, with an *MPC* of 0.91, a $10 billion increase in disposable income will increase consumption by $10 billion $\times$ 0.91, or $9.1 billion.

## The Relationship between Consumption and National Income

We have seen that consumption spending by households depends on disposable income. We now shift our focus slightly to the similar relationship that exists between consumption spending and GDP. We make this shift because we are interested in using the aggregate expenditure model to explain changes in real GDP rather than changes in disposable income. The first step in examining the relationship between consumption and GDP is to recall from Chapter 19 that the differences between GDP and national income are small and can be ignored without affecting our analysis. In fact, in this and the following chapters, we will use the terms *GDP* and *national income* interchangeably. Also recall that disposable income is equal to national income plus government transfer payments minus taxes. Taxes minus government transfer payments are referred to as *net taxes*. So, we can write the following:

$$\text{Disposable income} = \text{National income} - \text{Net taxes}.$$

We can rearrange the equation like this:

$$\text{National income} = \text{GDP} = \text{Disposable income} + \text{Net taxes}.$$

The table in Figure 23.3 shows hypothetical values for national income (or GDP), net taxes, disposable income, and consumption spending. Notice that national income and disposable income differ by a constant amount, which is equal to net taxes of $1,000 billion. In reality, net taxes are not a constant amount because they are affected by changes in income. As income rises, net taxes rise because some taxes, such as the personal income tax, increase and some government transfer payments, such as government payments to unemployed workers, fall. Nothing important is affected in our analysis, however, by our simplifying assumption that net taxes are constant. The graph in Figure 23.3 shows a line representing the relationship between consumption and national income. The line is very similar to the consumption function shown in panel (b) of Figure 23.2. We defined the marginal propensity to consume (*MPC*) as the change in consumption divided by the change in disposable income, which is the slope of the consumption function. In fact, notice that if we calculate the slope of the line in Figure 23.3 between points *A* and *B*, we get a result that will not change whether we use the values for national income or the values for disposable income. Using the values for national income:

$$\frac{\Delta C}{\Delta Y} = \frac{\$5,250\text{ billion} - \$3,750\text{ billion}}{\$7,000\text{ billion} - \$5,000\text{ billion}} = 0.75.$$

Using the corresponding values for disposable income from the table:

$$\frac{\Delta C}{\Delta YD} = \frac{\$5,250\text{ billion} - \$3,750\text{ billion}}{\$6,000\text{ billion} - \$4,000\text{ billion}} = 0.75.$$

It should not be surprising that we get the same result in either case. National income and disposable income differ by a constant amount, so changes in the two numbers always give us the same value, as shown in the last two columns of the table in Figure 23.3. Therefore, we can graph the consumption function using national income rather than using disposable income. We can also calculate the *MPC* using either the change in national income or the change in disposable income and always get the same value.

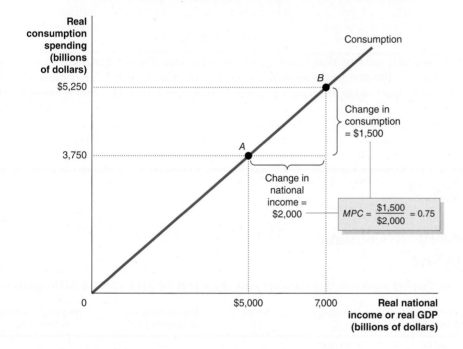

| National Income or GDP (billions of dollars) | Net Taxes (billions of dollars) | Disposable Income (billions of dollars) | Consumption (billions of dollars) | Change in National Income (billions of dollars) | Change in Disposable Income (billions of dollars) |
|---|---|---|---|---|---|
| $1,000 | $1,000 | $0 | $750 | — | — |
| 3,000 | 1,000 | 2,000 | 2,250 | $2,000 | $2,000 |
| 5,000 | 1,000 | 4,000 | 3,750 | 2,000 | 2,000 |
| 7,000 | 1,000 | 6,000 | 5,250 | 2,000 | 2,000 |
| 9,000 | 1,000 | 8,000 | 6,750 | 2,000 | 2,000 |
| 11,000 | 1,000 | 10,000 | 8,250 | 2,000 | 2,000 |
| 13,000 | 1,000 | 12,000 | 9,750 | 2,000 | 2,000 |

### Figure 23.3

**The Relationship between Consumption and National Income**

Because national income differs from disposable income only by net taxes—which, for simplicity, we assume are constant—we can graph the consumption function using national income rather than disposable income. We can also calculate the MPC, which is the slope of the consumption function, using either the change in national income or the change in disposable income and always get the same value. The slope of the consumption function between point A and point B is equal to the change in consumption—$1,500 billion—divided by the change in national income—$2,000 billion—or 0.75.

## Income, Consumption, and Saving

To complete our discussion of consumption, we can look briefly at the relationships among income, consumption, and saving. Households either spend their income, save it, or use it to pay taxes. For the economy as a whole, we can write the following:

$$\text{National income} = \text{Consumption} + \text{Saving} + \text{Taxes}.$$

When national income increases, there must be some combination of an increase in consumption, an increase in saving, and an increase in taxes:

$$\text{Change in national income} = \text{Change in consumption} + \text{Change in saving} + \text{Change in taxes}.$$

Using symbols, where $Y$ represents national income (and GDP), $C$ represents consumption, $S$ represents saving, and $T$ represents taxes, we can write the following:

$$Y = C + S + T$$

and

$$\Delta Y = \Delta C + \Delta S + \Delta T.$$

To simplify, we can assume that taxes are always a constant amount, in which case $\Delta T = 0$ so the following is also true:

$$\Delta Y = \Delta C + \Delta S.$$

**Marginal propensity to save (*MPS*)**
The amount by which saving changes when disposable income changes.

We have already seen that the marginal propensity to consume equals the change in consumption divided by the change in income. We can define the **marginal propensity to save (*MPS*)** as the amount by which saving increases when disposable income increases. We can measure the *MPS* as the change in saving divided by the change in disposable income. In calculating the *MPS*, as in calculating the *MPC*, we can safely ignore the difference between national income and disposable income.

If we divide the last equation on the previous page by the change in income, $\Delta Y$, we get an equation that shows the relationship between the marginal propensity to consume and the marginal propensity to save:

$$\frac{\Delta Y}{\Delta Y} = \frac{\Delta C}{\Delta Y} + \frac{\Delta S}{\Delta Y}$$

or

$$1 = MPC + MPS.$$

This equation tells us that when taxes are constant, the marginal propensity to consume plus the marginal propensity to save must always equal 1. They must add up to 1 because part of any increase in income is consumed, and whatever remains must be saved.

# Solved Problem **23.2**

## Calculating the Marginal Propensity to Consume and the Marginal Propensity to Save

Fill in the blanks in the following table. For simplicity, assume that taxes are zero. Show that the *MPC* plus the *MPS* equals 1.

| National Income and Real GDP (*Y*) | Consumption (*C*) | Saving (*S*) | Marginal Propensity to Consume (*MPC*) | Marginal Propensity to Save (*MPS*) |
|---|---|---|---|---|
| $9,000 | $8,000 | | — | — |
| 10,000 | 8,600 | | | |
| 11,000 | 9,200 | | | |
| 12,000 | 9,800 | | | |
| 13,000 | 10,400 | | | |

## Solving the Problem

**Step 1:** **Review the chapter material.** This problem is about the relationship among income, consumption, and saving, so you may want to review the section "Income, Consumption, and Saving," which begins on page 759.

**Step 2:** **Fill in the table.** We know that $Y = C + S + T$. With taxes equal to zero, this equation becomes $Y = C + S$. We can use this equation to fill in the "Saving" column. We can use the equations for the *MPC* and the *MPS* to fill in the other two columns:

$$MPC = \frac{\Delta C}{\Delta Y}$$

$$MPS = \frac{\Delta S}{\Delta Y}$$

For example, to calculate the value of the *MPC* in the second row, we have:

$$MPC = \frac{\Delta C}{\Delta Y} = \frac{\$8,600 - \$8,000}{\$10,000 - \$9,000} = \frac{\$600}{\$1,000} = 0.6.$$

To calculate the value of the *MPS* in the second row, we have:

$$MPS = \frac{\Delta S}{\Delta Y} = \frac{\$1,400 - \$1,000}{\$10,000 - \$9,000} = \frac{\$400}{\$1,000} = 0.4.$$

| National Income and Real GDP (Y) | Consumption (C) | Saving (S) | Marginal Propensity to Consume (MPC) | Marginal Propensity to Save (MPS) |
|---|---|---|---|---|
| $9,000 | $8,000 | $1,000 | — | — |
| 10,000 | 8,600 | 1,400 | 0.6 | 0.4 |
| 11,000 | 9,200 | 1,800 | 0.6 | 0.4 |
| 12,000 | 9,800 | 2,200 | 0.6 | 0.4 |
| 13,000 | 10,400 | 2,600 | 0.6 | 0.4 |

**Step 3:** **Show that the *MPC* plus the *MPS* equals 1.** At every level of national income, the *MPC* is 0.6 and the *MPS* is 0.4. Therefore, the *MPC* plus the *MPS* is always equal to 1.

**Your Turn:** For more practice, do related problem 2.13 on page 785 at the end of this chapter.    MyEconLab

# Planned Investment

Figure 23.4 shows movements in real investment spending from 1979 through the second quarter of 2011. Notice that, unlike consumption, investment does not follow a smooth, upward trend. Investment declined significantly during the recessions of 1980, 1981–1982, 1990–1991, 2001, and 2007–2009.

The four most important variables that determine the level of investment are:

- Expectations of future profitability

- Interest rate

- Taxes

- Cash flow

**Expectations of Future Profitability** Investment goods, such as factories, office buildings, and machinery and equipment, are long lived. A firm is unlikely to build a new factory unless it is optimistic that the demand for its product will remain strong for at least several years. When the economy moves into a recession, many firms postpone

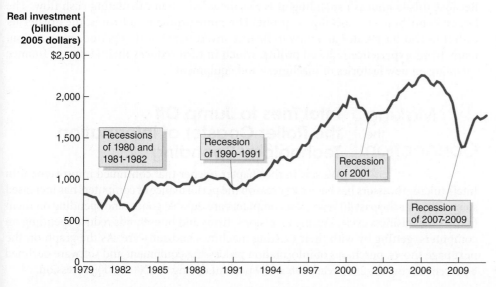

**Figure 23.4**

**Real Investment**

Investment is subject to larger changes than is consumption. Investment declined significantly during the recessions of 1980, 1981–1982, 1990–1991, 2001, and 2007–2009.

*Note:* The values are quarterly data, seasonally adjusted at an annual rate.

Data from U.S. Bureau of Economic Analysis.

buying investment goods even if the demand for their own product is strong because they are afraid that the recession may become worse. During an expansion, some firms may become optimistic and begin to increase spending on investment goods even before the demand for their own product has increased. The key point is this: *The optimism or pessimism of firms is an important determinant of investment spending.*

Residential construction is included in investment spending. Since 1990, residential construction has averaged about 30 percent of total investment spending. But the swings in residential construction have been quite substantial, ranging from 36 percent of investment spending at the height of the housing boom in 2005, down to 18 percent in 2011. The sharp decline in spending on residential construction beginning in 2006 helped to bring on the 2007–2009 recession and contributed to the recession's severity.

**Interest Rate** Some business investment is financed by borrowing, which takes the form of issuing corporate bonds or receiving loans from banks. Households also borrow to finance most of their spending on new homes. The higher the interest rate, the more expensive it is for firms and households to borrow. Because households and firms are interested in the cost of borrowing after taking into account the effects of inflation, investment spending depends on the real interest rate. Therefore, holding the other factors that affect investment spending constant, there is an inverse relationship between the real interest rate and investment spending: *A higher real interest rate results in less investment spending, and a lower real interest rate results in more investment spending.* As we will discuss further in Chapter 26, the ability of households to borrow money at very low real interest rates helps explain the rapid increase in spending on residential construction from 2002 to 2006.

**Taxes** Taxes affect the level of investment spending. Firms focus on the profits that remain after they have paid taxes. The federal government imposes a *corporate income tax* on the profits corporations earn, including profits from the new buildings, equipment, and other investment goods they purchase. A reduction in the corporate income tax increases the after-tax profitability of investment spending. An increase in the corporate income tax decreases the after-tax profitability of investment spending. *Investment tax incentives* also increase investment spending. An investment tax incentive provides firms with a tax reduction when they spend on new investment goods.

**Cash flow** The difference between the cash revenues received by a firm and the cash spending by the firm.

**Cash Flow** Most firms do not borrow to finance spending on new factories, machinery, and equipment. Instead, they use their own funds. **Cash flow** is the difference between the cash revenues received by a firm and the cash spending by the firm. Neither noncash receipts nor noncash spending is included in cash flow. For example, tax laws allow firms to count depreciation to replace worn out or obsolete machinery and equipment as a cost, even if new machinery and equipment have not actually been purchased. Because this is noncash spending, it is not included when calculating cash flow. The largest contributor to cash flow is profit. The more profitable a firm is, the greater its cash flow and the greater its ability to finance investment. During periods of recession, many firms experience reduced profits, which in turn reduces their ability to finance spending on new factories or machinery and equipment.

| Making the Connection | Intel Tries to Jump Off the Roller Coaster of Information Technology Spending |

We saw in the chapter opener that continued improvement in Intel's microprocessors has been a key reason the performance of computers has increased so rapidly over the past 40 years. But computers are durable goods, and spending on them follows the business cycle. During recessions, firms and households reduce spending on computers, getting by with their existing machines and software. As the graph on the next page shows, purchases of information processing equipment and software declined 8 percent during the 2001 recession and 9 percent during the 2007–2009 recession.

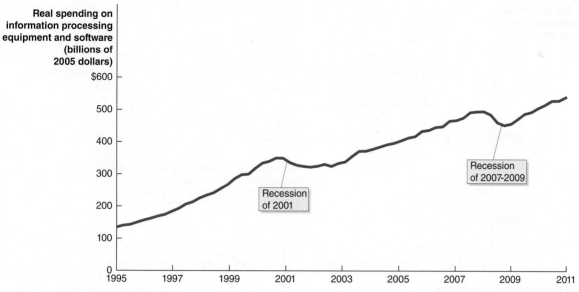

Data from U.S. Bureau of Economic Analysis.

We saw in Chapter 21 that Intel CEO Paul Otellini remained optimistic about the future demand for computers and pressed ahead in 2009 with a $7 billion expansion of Intel factories in the United States. But Otellini was also concerned that its dependence on sales of microprocessors to Apple, Dell, and other computer firms made it vulnerable to sharp declines in sales during recessions. To help deal with this vulnerability, Intel began to develop memory chips that could be used in portable consumer electronic devices, such as Apple's iPod, and in cell phones. Intel made progress toward this goal when it came to an agreement with Nokia, which manufactures about 40 percent of cell phones sold worldwide, to collaborate on the development of new portable devices.

The cell phone market was particularly attractive to Intel because more than 1 billion cell phones are sold each year, as opposed to several hundred million computers. Sales of cell phones also declined much less during the recession of 2007–2009 than did sales of personal computers. Otellini believed Intel's experience with computer chips would allow the company to expand into making chips for other devices because, he argued, "All consumer electronics—and I mean all—are aimed at bringing the Internet into devices." By 2011, the new factories the firm started building in 2009 had begun to develop results, including production of the Atom chip that it adapted for use in cell phones. But Intel faced stiff competition from existing chip suppliers, such as Qualcomm, Texas Instruments, and NVIDIA, and whether it would succeed in becoming less dependent on sales of personal computers remained to be seen.

Based on Tiernan Ray, "ARM Elbows Out Intel in the Post-PC World," *Barron's*, September 17, 2011; Ashlee Vance, "Intel's Bet on Innovation Pays Off in Faster Chips," *New York Times*, January 14, 2010; Don Clark, "Intel Makes Another Run at Phones with Nokia," *Wall Street Journal*, June 24, 2009; and Michael V. Copeland, "Intel's Secret Plan," cnnmoney.com, May 13, 2009.

**Your Turn:** Test your understanding by doing related problem 2.14 on page 785 at the end of this chapter.     MyEconLab

## Government Purchases

Total government purchases include all spending by federal, local, and state governments for goods and services. Recall from Chapter 19 that government purchases do not include transfer payments, such as Social Security payments by the federal government or pension payments by local governments to retired police officers and firefighters because the government does not receive a good or service in return.

Figure 23.5 shows levels of real government purchases from 1979 through the second quarter of 2011. Government purchases grew steadily for most of this period, with

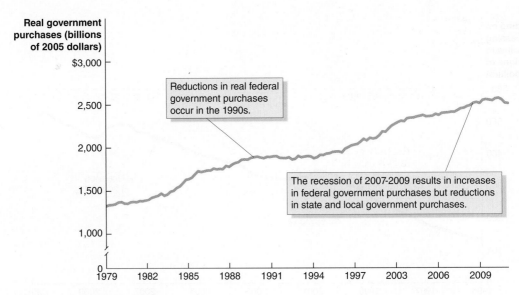

**Figure 23.5** **Real Government Purchases**

Government purchases grew steadily for most of the 1979–2011 period, with the exception of the early 1990s, when concern about the federal budget deficit caused real government purchases to fall for three years, beginning in 1992.

*Note:* The values are quarterly data, seasonally adjusted at an annual rate. Data from U.S. Bureau of Economic Analysis.

the exception of the early 1990s, when Congress and Presidents George H. W. Bush and Bill Clinton enacted a series of spending reductions after they became concerned that spending by the federal government was growing much faster than tax receipts. As a result, real government purchases declined for three years, beginning in 1992. Contributing to the slow growth of government purchases during the 1990s was the end of the Cold War between the United States and the Soviet Union in 1989. Real federal government spending on national defense declined by 24 percent from 1990 to 1998, before rising by 60 percent between 1998 and 2011, in response to the war on terrorism and the wars in Iraq and Afghanistan. As we will discuss further in Chapter 27, total federal government purchases increased sharply beginning in 2009, as President Barack Obama and Congress attempted to offset declining consumption and investment spending during the recession. Increased federal government purchases were partially offset, however, by lower state and local government purchases.

## Net Exports

Net exports equal exports minus imports. We can calculate net exports by taking the value of spending by foreign firms and households on goods and services produced in the United States and *subtracting* the value of spending by U.S. firms and households on goods and services produced in other countries. Figure 23.6 illustrates movements in real net exports from 1979 through the second quarter of 2011. During nearly all these years, the United States imported more goods and services than it exported, so net exports were negative. Net exports usually increase when the U.S. economy is in recession—although this happened to only a minor extent during the 2001 recession—and fall when the U.S. economy is expanding. We will explore the behavior of net exports further in Chapter 29.

The following are the three most important variables that determine the level of net exports:

• The price level in the United States relative to the price levels in other countries

• The growth rate of GDP in the United States relative to the growth rates of GDP in other countries

• The exchange rate between the dollar and other currencies

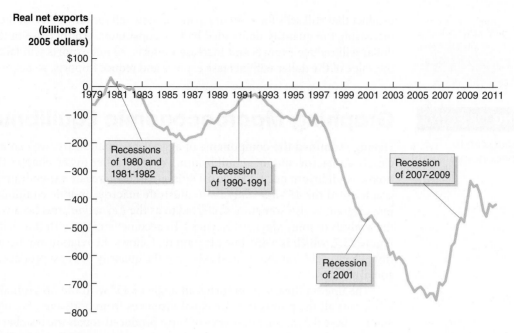

**Figure 23.6    Real Net Exports**

Net exports were negative in most years between 1979 and 2011. Net exports have usually increased when the U.S. economy is in recession and decreased when the U.S. economy is expanding, although they fell during most of the 2001 recession.

*Note:* The values are quarterly data, seasonally adjusted at an annual rate. Data from U.S. Bureau of Economic Analysis.

**The Price Level in the United States Relative to the Price Levels in Other Countries**  If inflation in the United States is lower than inflation in other countries, prices of U.S. products increase more slowly than the prices of products of other countries. This slower increase in the U.S. price level increases the demand for U.S. products relative to the demand for foreign products. So, U.S. exports increase and U.S. imports decrease, which increases net exports. The reverse happens during periods when the inflation rate in the United States is higher than the inflation rates in other countries: U.S. exports decrease and U.S. imports increase, which decreases net exports.

**The Growth Rate of GDP in the United States Relative to the Growth Rates of GDP in Other Countries**  As GDP increases in the United States, the incomes of households rise, leading them to increase their purchases of goods and services. Some of the additional goods and services purchased with rising incomes are produced in the United States, but some are imported. When incomes rise faster in the United States than in other countries, U.S. consumers' purchases of foreign goods and services increase faster than foreign consumers' purchases of U.S. goods and services. As a result, net exports fall. When incomes in the United States rise more slowly than incomes in other countries, net exports rise.

**The Exchange Rate between the Dollar and Other Currencies**  As the value of the U.S. dollar rises, the foreign currency price of U.S. products sold in other countries rises, and the dollar price of foreign products sold in the United States falls. For example, suppose that the exchange rate between the Japanese yen and the U.S. dollar is 100 Japanese yen for one U.S. dollar, or ¥100 = $1. At this exchange rate, someone in the United States could buy ¥100 for $1, or someone in Japan could buy $1 for ¥100. Leaving aside transportation costs, at this exchange rate, a U.S. product that sells for $1 in the United States will sell for ¥100 in Japan, and a Japanese product that sells for ¥100 in Japan will sell for $1 in the United States. If the exchange rate changes to ¥150 = $1, then the value of the dollar will have risen because it takes more yen to buy $1. At the new exchange rate, the U.S. product that still sells for $1 in the United States will now sell for ¥150 in Japan, reducing the quantity demanded by Japanese consumers. The Japanese product that still sells for ¥100 in Japan will now sell for only $0.67 in the United States, increasing the quantity demanded by U.S. consumers. An increase in the value of the dollar will reduce exports and increase imports, so net exports will fall. A decrease in the value of the dollar will increase exports and reduce imports, so net exports will rise.

**23.3 LEARNING** OBJECTIVE

Use a 45°-line diagram to illustrate macroeconomic equilibrium.

# Graphing Macroeconomic Equilibrium

Having examined the components of aggregate expenditure, we can now look more closely at macroeconomic equilibrium. We saw earlier in the chapter that macroeconomic equilibrium occurs when GDP is equal to aggregate expenditure. We can use a graph called the *45°-line diagram* to illustrate macroeconomic equilibrium. (The 45°-line diagram is also sometimes referred to as the *Keynesian cross* because it is based on the analysis of John Maynard Keynes.) To become familiar with this diagram, consider Figure 23.7, which is a 45°-line diagram that shows the relationship between the quantity of Pepsi sold (on the vertical axis) and the quantity of Pepsi produced (on the horizontal axis).

The line on the diagram forms an angle of 45° with the horizontal axis. The line represents all the points that are equal distances from both axes. So, points such as *A* and *B*, where the number of bottles of Pepsi produced equals the number of bottles sold, are on the 45° line. Points such as *C*, where the quantity sold is greater than the quantity produced, lie above the line. Points such as *D*, where the quantity sold is less than the quantity produced, lie below the line.

Figure 23.8 is similar to Figure 23.7 except that it measures real national income, or real GDP (*Y*), on the horizontal axis and planned real aggregate expenditure (*AE*) on the vertical axis. Because macroeconomic equilibrium occurs where planned aggregate expenditure equals GDP, *we know that all points of macroeconomic equilibrium must lie along the 45° line.* For all points above the 45° line, planned aggregate expenditure will be greater than GDP. For all points below the 45° line, planned aggregate expenditure will be less than GDP.

The 45° line shows many potential points of macroeconomic equilibrium. During any particular year, only one of these points will represent the actual level of equilibrium

**Figure 23.7**

**An Example of a 45°-Line Diagram**

The 45° line shows all the points that are equal distances from both axes. Points such as *A* and *B*, at which the quantity produced equals the quantity sold, are on the 45° line. Points such as *C*, at which the quantity sold is greater than the quantity produced, lie above the line. Points such as *D*, at which the quantity sold is less than the quantity produced, lie below the line.

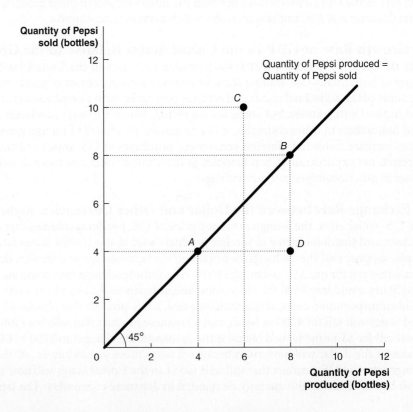

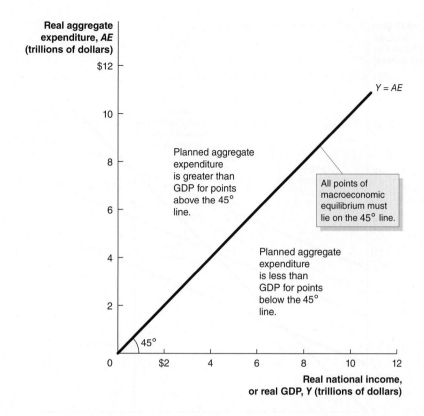

**Figure 23.8**

**The Relationship between Planned Aggregate Expenditure and GDP on a 45°-Line Diagram**

Every point of macroeconomic equilibrium is on the 45° line, where planned aggregate expenditure equals GDP. At points above the line, planned aggregate expenditure is greater than GDP. At points below the line, planned aggregate expenditure is less than GDP.

real GDP, given the actual level of planned real expenditure. To determine this point, we need to draw a line on the graph to show the *aggregate expenditure function*. The aggregate expenditure function shows us the amount of planned aggregate expenditure that will occur at every level of national income, or GDP.

Changes in GDP have a much greater effect on consumption than on planned investment, government purchases, or net exports. We assume for simplicity that the variables that determine planned investment, government purchases, and net exports all remain constant, as do the variables other than GDP that affect consumption. For example, we assume that a firm's level of planned investment at the beginning of the year will not change during the year, even if the level of GDP changes.

Figure 23.9 shows the aggregate expenditure function on the 45°-line diagram. The lowest upward-sloping line, $C$, represents the consumption function, as shown in Figure 23.2, panel (b), on page 757. The quantities of planned investment, government purchases, and net exports are constant because we assumed that the variables they depend on are constant. So, the level of planned aggregate expenditure at any level of GDP is the amount of consumption spending at that level of GDP plus the sum of the constant amounts of planned investment, government purchases, and net exports. In Figure 23.9, we add each component of spending successively to the consumption function line to arrive at the line representing planned aggregate expenditure ($AE$). The $C + I$ line is higher than the $C$ line by the constant amount of planned investment; the $C + I + G$ line is higher than the $C + I$ line by the constant amount of government purchases; and the $C + I + G + NX$ line is higher than the $C + I + G$ line by the constant amount of $NX$. (In many years, however, $NX$ is negative, which would cause the $C + I + G + NX$ line to be *below* the $C + I + G$ line.) The $C + I + G + NX$ line shows all four components of expenditure and is the aggregate expenditure ($AE$) function. At the point where the $AE$ line crosses the 45° line, planned aggregate expenditure is equal to GDP, and the economy is in macroeconomic equilibrium.

Figure 23.10 makes the relationship between planned aggregate expenditure and GDP clearer by showing only the 45° line and the $AE$ line. The figure shows that the $AE$ line intersects the 45° line at a level of real GDP of $10 trillion. Therefore, $10 trillion represents the equilibrium level of real GDP. To see why this is true, consider the situation if real GDP were only $8 trillion. By moving vertically from $8 trillion on the

## Figure 23.9

### Macroeconomic Equilibrium on the 45°-Line Diagram

Macroeconomic equilibrium occurs where the aggregate expenditure (AE) line crosses the 45° line. The lowest upward-sloping line, C, represents the consumption function. The quantities of planned investment, government purchases, and net exports are constant because we assumed that the variables they depend on are constant. So, the total of planned aggregate expenditure at any level of GDP is the amount of consumption at that level of GDP plus the sum of the constant amounts of planned investment, government purchases, and net exports. We successively add each component of spending to the consumption function line to arrive at the line representing aggregate expenditure.

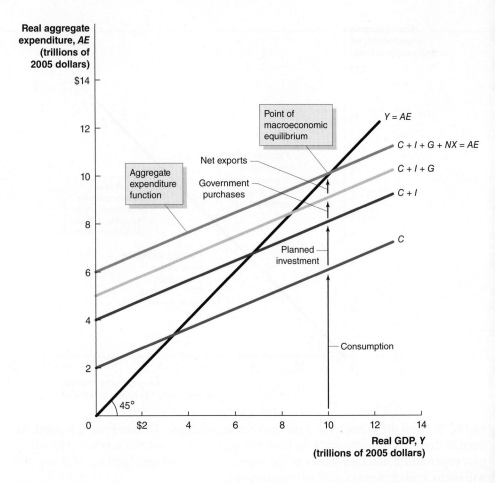

horizontal axis up to the AE line, we see that planned aggregate expenditure will be greater than $8 trillion at this level of real GDP. Whenever total spending is greater than total production, firms' inventories will fall. The fall in inventories is equal to the vertical distance between the AE line, which shows the level of total spending, and the 45° line, which shows the $8 trillion of total production. Unplanned declines in inventories lead firms to increase their production. As real GDP increases from $8 trillion, so will total income and, therefore, consumption. The economy will move up the AE line as consumption increases. The gap between total spending and total production will fall, but as long as the AE line is above the 45° line, inventories will continue to decline, and firms will continue to expand production. When real GDP rises to $10 trillion, inventories stop falling, and the economy will be in macroeconomic equilibrium.

As Figure 23.10 shows, if GDP is initially $12 trillion, planned aggregate expenditure will be less than GDP, and firms will experience an unplanned increase in inventories. Rising inventories lead firms to decrease production. As GDP falls from $12 trillion, consumption will also fall, which causes the economy to move down the AE line. The gap between planned aggregate expenditure and GDP will fall, but as long as the AE line is below the 45° line, inventories will continue to rise, and firms will continue to cut production. When GDP falls to $10 trillion, inventories will stop rising, and the economy will be in macroeconomic equilibrium.

## Showing a Recession on the 45°-Line Diagram

Notice that *macroeconomic equilibrium can occur at any point on the 45° line*. Ideally, we would like equilibrium to occur at *potential GDP*. At potential GDP, firms will be operating at their normal level of capacity, and the economy will be at the *natural rate of unemployment*. As we saw in Chapter 20, at the natural rate of unemployment, the economy will be at *full employment*: Everyone in the labor force who wants a job will have one, except the structurally and frictionally unemployed. However, for equilibrium

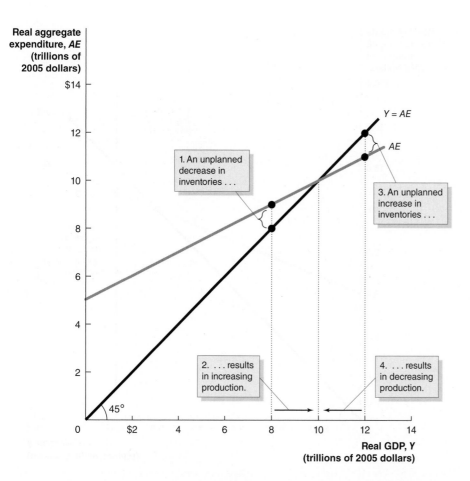

**Figure 23.10**

**Macroeconomic Equilibrium**

Macroeconomic equilibrium occurs where the *AE* line crosses the 45° line. In this case, that occurs at GDP of $10 trillion. If GDP is less than $10 trillion, the corresponding point on the *AE* line is above the 45° line, planned aggregate expenditure is greater than total production, firms will experience an unplanned decrease in inventories, and GDP will increase. If GDP is greater than $10 trillion, the corresponding point on the *AE* line is below the 45° line, planned aggregate expenditure is less than total production, firms will experience an unplanned increase in inventories, and GDP will decrease.

to occur at the level of potential GDP, planned aggregate expenditure must be high enough. As Figure 23.11 shows, if there is insufficient total spending, equilibrium will occur at a lower level of real GDP. Many firms will be operating below their normal capacity, and the unemployment rate will be above the natural rate of unemployment.

Suppose that the level of potential GDP is $10 trillion. As Figure 23.11 shows, when GDP is $10 trillion, planned aggregate expenditure is below $10 trillion, perhaps because business firms have become pessimistic about their future profitability and have reduced their investment spending. The shortfall in planned aggregate expenditure that leads to the recession can be measured as the vertical distance between the *AE* line and the 45° line at the level of potential GDP. The shortfall in planned aggregate expenditure is exactly equal to the unplanned increase in inventories that would occur if the economy were initially at a level of GDP of $10 trillion. The unplanned increase in inventories measures the amount by which current planned aggregate expenditure is too low for the current level of production to be the equilibrium level. Or, put another way, if any of the four components of aggregate expenditure increased by this amount, the *AE* line would shift upward and intersect the 45° line at GDP of $10 trillion, and the economy would be in macroeconomic equilibrium at full employment.

Figure 23.11 shows that macroeconomic equilibrium will occur when real GDP is $9.8 trillion. Because this is 2 percent below the potential level of real GDP of $10 trillion, many firms will be operating below their normal capacity, and the unemployment rate will be well above the natural rate of unemployment. The economy will remain at this level of real GDP until there is an increase in one or more of the components of aggregate expenditure.

# The Important Role of Inventories

Whenever planned aggregate expenditure is less than real GDP, some firms will experience unplanned increases in inventories. If firms do not cut back their production promptly when spending declines, they will accumulate inventories. If firms accumulate

## Figure 23.11

### Showing a Recession on the 45°-Line Diagram

When the aggregate expenditure line inter-sects the 45° line at a level of GDP below potential GDP, the economy is in recession. The figure shows that potential GDP is $10 trillion, but because planned aggregate expenditure is too low, the equilibrium level of GDP is only $9.8 trillion, where the $AE$ line intersects the 45° line. As a result, some firms will be operating below their normal capacity, and unemployment will be above the natural rate of unemployment. We can measure the shortfall in planned aggregate expenditure as the vertical distance between the $AE$ line and the 45° line at the level of potential GDP.

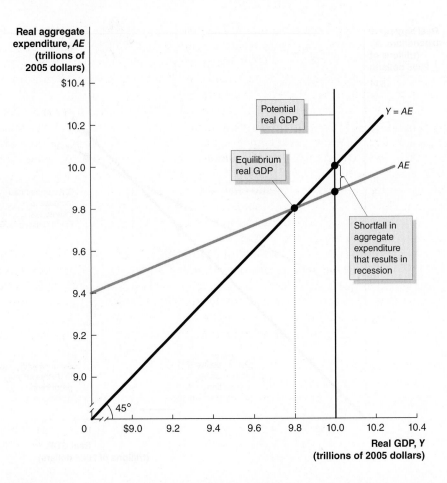

excess inventories, then even if spending quickly returns to its normal levels, firms will have to sell their excess inventories before they can return to producing at normal levels. For example, almost half of the sharp 6.7 percent annual rate of decline in real GDP during the first quarter of 2009 resulted from firms cutting production as they sold off unintended accumulations of inventories.

## A Numerical Example of Macroeconomic Equilibrium

In forecasting real GDP, economists rely on quantitative models of the economy. We can increase our understanding of the causes of changes in real GDP by considering a simple numerical example of macroeconomic equilibrium. Although simplified, this example captures some of the key features contained in the quantitative models that economic forecasters use. Table 23.3 shows several hypothetical combinations of real

### Table 23.3 Macroeconomic Equilibrium

| Real GDP (Y) | Consumption (C) | Planned Investment (I) | Government Purchases (G) | Net Exports (NX) | Planned Aggregate Expenditure (AE) | Unplanned Change in Inventories | Real GDP Will... |
|---|---|---|---|---|---|---|---|
| $8,000 | $6,200 | $1,500 | $1,500 | −$500 | $8,700 | −$700 | increase |
| 9,000 | 6,850 | 1,500 | 1,500 | −500 | 9,350 | −350 | increase |
| 10,000 | 7,500 | 1,500 | 1,500 | −500 | 10,000 | 0 | be in equilibrium |
| 11,000 | 8,150 | 1,500 | 1,500 | −500 | 10,650 | +350 | decrease |
| 12,000 | 8,800 | 1,500 | 1,500 | −500 | 11,300 | +700 | decrease |

*Note:* The values are in billions of 2005 dollars.

GDP and planned aggregate expenditure. The first column lists real GDP. The next four columns list levels of the four components of planned aggregate expenditure that occur at the corresponding level of real GDP. We assume that planned investment, government purchases, and net exports do not change as GDP changes. Because consumption depends on GDP, it increases as GDP increases.

In the first row, GDP of $8,000 billion (or $8 trillion) results in consumption of $6,200 billion. Adding consumption, planned investment, government purchases, and net exports across the row gives planned aggregate expenditure of $8,700 billion, which is shown in the sixth column. Because planned aggregate expenditure is greater than GDP, inventories will fall by $700 billion. This unplanned decline in inventories will lead firms to increase production, and GDP will increase. GDP will continue to increase until it reaches $10,000 billion. At that level of GDP, planned aggregate expenditure is also $10,000 billion, unplanned changes in inventories are zero, and the economy is in macroeconomic equilibrium.

In the last row of Table 23.3, GDP of $12,000 billion results in consumption of $8,800 billion and planned aggregate expenditure of $11,300 billion. Because planned aggregate expenditure is less than GDP, inventories will increase by $700 billion. This unplanned increase in inventories will lead firms to decrease production, and GDP will decrease. GDP will continue to decrease until it reaches $10,000 billion, unplanned changes in inventories are zero, and the economy is in macroeconomic equilibrium.

Only when real GDP equals $10,000 billion will the economy be in macroeconomic equilibrium. At other levels of real GDP, planned aggregate expenditure will be higher or lower than GDP, and the economy will be expanding or contracting.

# Don't Let This Happen to You

## Don't Confuse Aggregate Expenditure with Consumption Spending

Macroeconomic equilibrium occurs where planned aggregate expenditure equals GDP. But, remember that planned aggregate expenditure equals the sum of consumption spending, planned investment spending, government purchases, and net exports, *not* consumption spending by itself. If GDP were equal to consumption, the economy would not be in equilibrium. Planned investment plus government purchases plus net exports will always be a positive number. Therefore, if consumption were equal to GDP, aggregate expenditure would have to be greater than GDP. In that case, inventories would be decreasing, and GDP would be *increasing*; GDP would not be in equilibrium.

Test your understanding of macroeconomic equilibrium with this problem:

*Question:* Do you agree with the following argument?

The chapter says macroeconomic equilibrium occurs where planned aggregate expenditure equals GDP. GDP is equal to national income. So, at equilibrium, planned aggregate expenditure must equal national income. But, we know that consumers do not spend all of their income: They save at least some and use some to pay taxes. Therefore, aggregate expenditure will never equal national income, and the basic macroeconomic story is incorrect.

*Answer:* As discussed in Chapter 19, national income equals GDP (disregarding depreciation, as we have throughout this chapter). So, it is correct to say that in macroeconomic equilibrium, planned aggregate expenditure must equal national income. But the last sentence of the argument is incorrect because it assumes that aggregate expenditure is the same as consumption spending. Because of saving and taxes, consumption spending is always much less than national income, but in equilibrium, the sum of consumption spending, planned investment spending, government purchases, and net exports does, in fact, equal GDP and national income. So, the argument is incorrect because it confuses consumption spending with aggregate expenditure.

MyEconLab

**Your Turn:** Test your understanding by doing related problem 3.11 on page 786 at the end of this chapter.

# Solved Problem 23.3

## Determining Macroeconomic Equilibrium

Fill in the blanks in the following table and determine the equilibrium level of real GDP.

| Real GDP (Y) | Consumption (C) | Planned Investment (I) | Government Purchases (G) | Net Exports (NX) | Planned Aggregate Expenditure (AE) | Unplanned Change in Inventories |
|---|---|---|---|---|---|---|
| $8,000 | $6,200 | $1,675 | $1,675 | −$500 | | |
| 9,000 | 6,850 | 1,675 | 1,675 | −500 | | |
| 10,000 | 7,500 | 1,675 | 1,675 | −500 | | |
| 11,000 | 8,150 | 1,675 | 1,675 | −500 | | |
| 12,000 | 8,800 | 1,675 | 1,675 | −500 | | |

*Note: The values are in billions of 2005 dollars.*

## Solving the Problem

**Step 1:** **Review the chapter material.** This problem is about determining macroeconomic equilibrium, so you may want to review the section "A Numerical Example of Macroeconomic Equilibrium," which begins on page 770.

**Step 2:** **Fill in the missing values in the table.** We can calculate the missing values in the last two columns by using two equations:

$$\text{Planned aggregate expenditure } (AE) = \text{Consumption } (C)$$
$$+ \text{ Planned investment } (I) + \text{ Government purchases } (G)$$
$$+ \text{ Net exports } (NX)$$

and

$$\text{Unplanned change in inventories} = \text{Real GDP } (Y)$$
$$- \text{Planned aggregate expenditure } (AE).$$

For example, to fill in the first row, we have $AE = \$6,200$ billion + $\$1,675$ billion + $\$1,675$ billion + $(-\$500$ billion$) = \$9,050$ billion; and unplanned change in inventories = $\$8,000$ billion − $\$9,050$ billion = $-\$1,050$ billion.

| Real GDP (Y) | Consumption (C) | Planned Investment (I) | Government Purchases (G) | Net Exports (NX) | Planned Aggregate Expenditure (AE) | Unplanned Change in Inventories |
|---|---|---|---|---|---|---|
| $8,000 | $6,200 | $1,675 | $1,675 | −$500 | $9,050 | −$1,050 |
| 9,000 | 6,850 | 1,675 | 1,675 | −500 | 9,700 | −700 |
| 10,000 | 7,500 | 1,675 | 1,675 | −500 | 10,350 | −350 |
| 11,000 | 8,150 | 1,675 | 1,675 | −500 | 11,000 | 0 |
| 12,000 | 8,800 | 1,675 | 1,675 | −500 | 11,650 | 350 |

**Step 3:** **Determine the equilibrium level of real GDP.** Once you fill in the table, you should see that equilibrium real GDP must be $11,000 billion because only at that level is real GDP equal to planned aggregate expenditure.

MyEconLab **Your Turn:** For more practice, do related problem 3.12 on page 787 at the end of this chapter.

# The Multiplier Effect

To this point, we have seen that aggregate expenditure determines real GDP in the short run and we have seen how the economy adjusts if it is not in equilibrium. We have also seen that whenever aggregate expenditure changes, there will be a new level of equilibrium real GDP. In this section, we will look more closely at the effects of a change in aggregate expenditure on equilibrium real GDP. We begin the discussion with Figure 23.12, which illustrates the effects of an increase in planned investment spending. We assume that the economy starts in equilibrium at point $A$, at which real GDP is $9.6 trillion. Firms then become more optimistic about their future profitability and increase spending on factories, machinery, and equipment by $100 billion. This increase in investment spending shifts the $AE$ line up by $100 billion, from the dark tan line ($AE_1$) to the light tan line ($AE_2$). The new equilibrium occurs at point $B$, at which real GDP is $10.0 trillion, which equals potential real GDP.

Notice that the initial $100 billion increase in planned investment spending results in a $400 billion increase in equilibrium real GDP. The increase in planned investment spending has had a *multiplied effect* on equilibrium real GDP. It is not only investment spending that will have this multiplied effect; any increase in *autonomous expenditure* will shift up the aggregate expenditure function and lead to a multiplied increase in equilibrium GDP. **Autonomous expenditure** does not depend on the level of GDP. In the aggregate expenditure model we have been using, planned investment spending, government spending, and net exports are all autonomous expenditures. Consumption actually has both an autonomous component, which does not depend on the level of GDP, and a nonautonomous—or *induced*—component that does depend on the level of GDP. For example, if households decide to spend more of their incomes—and save less—at every level of income, there will be an autonomous increase in consumption spending, and the aggregate expenditure function will shift up. If, however, real GDP increases and households increase their consumption spending, as indicated by the consumption function, the economy will move up along the aggregate expenditure function, and the increase in consumption spending will be nonautonomous.

The ratio of the increase in equilibrium real GDP to the increase in autonomous expenditure is called the **multiplier**. The series of induced increases in consumption spending that results from an initial increase in autonomous expenditure is called the **multiplier effect**. The multiplier effect occurs because an initial increase in autonomous expenditure sets off a series of increases in real GDP.

**23.4 LEARNING** OBJECTIVE

Describe the multiplier effect and use the multiplier formula to calculate changes in equilibrium GDP.

**Autonomous expenditure** An expenditure that does not depend on the level of GDP.

**Multiplier** The increase in equilibrium real GDP divided by the increase in autonomous expenditure.

**Multiplier effect** The process by which an increase in autonomous expenditure leads to a larger increase in real GDP.

### Figure 23.12

#### The Multiplier Effect

The economy begins at point $A$, at which equilibrium real GDP is $9.6 trillion. A $100 billion increase in planned investment shifts up aggregate expenditure from $AE_1$ to $AE_2$. The new equilibrium is at point $B$, where real GDP is $10.0 trillion, which is potential real GDP. Because of the multiplier effect, a $100 billion increase in investment results in a $400 billion increase in equilibrium real GDP.

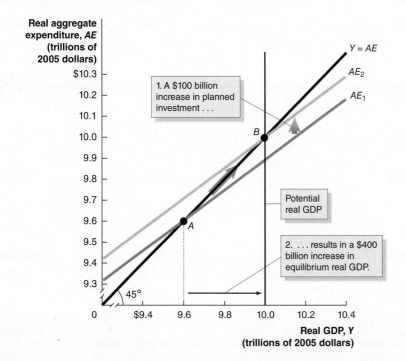

We can look more closely at the multiplier effect shown in Figure 23.12. Suppose the whole $100 billion increase in investment spending shown in the figure consists of firms building additional factories and office buildings. Initially, this additional spending will cause the construction of factories and office buildings to increase by $100 billion, so GDP will also increase by $100 billion. Remember that increases in production result in equal increases in national income. So, this increase in real GDP of $100 billion is also an increase in national income of $100 billion. In this example, the income is received as wages and salaries by the employees of the construction firms, as profits by the owners of the firms, and so on. After receiving this additional income, these workers, managers, and owners will increase their consumption of cars, appliances, furniture, and many other products. If the marginal propensity to consume (*MPC*) is 0.75, we know the increase in consumption spending will be $75 billion. This additional $75 billion in spending will cause the firms making the cars, appliances, and other products to increase production by $75 billion, so GDP will rise by $75 billion. This increase in GDP means national income has also increased by another $75 billion. This increased income will be received by the owners and employees of the firms producing the cars, appliances, and other products. These workers, managers, and owners in turn will increase their consumption spending, and the process of increasing production, income, and consumption will continue.

Eventually, the total increase in consumption will be $300 billion (we will soon show how we know this is true). This $300 billion increase in consumption combined with the initial $100 billion increase in investment spending will result in a total change in equilibrium GDP of $400 billion. Table 23.4 summarizes how changes in GDP and spending caused by the initial $100 billion increase in investment will result in equilibrium GDP rising by $400 billion. We can think of the multiplier effect occurring in rounds of spending. In round 1, there is an increase of $100 billion in autonomous

**Table 23.4**

**The Multiplier Effect in Action**

| | Additional Autonomous Expenditure (investment) | Additional Induced Expenditure (consumption) | Total Additional Expenditure = Total Additional GDP |
|---|---|---|---|
| Round 1 | $100 billion | $0 | $100 billion |
| Round 2 | 0 | 75 billion | 175 billion |
| Round 3 | 0 | 56 billion | 231 billion |
| Round 4 | 0 | 42 billion | 273 billion |
| Round 5 | 0 | 32 billion | 305 billion |
| . | . | . | . |
| . | . | . | . |
| Round 10 | 0 | 8 billion | 377 billion |
| . | . | . | . |
| . | . | . | . |
| Round 15 | 0 | 2 billion | 395 billion |
| . | . | . | . |
| . | . | . | . |
| Round 19 | 0 | 1 billion | 398 billion |
| . | . | . | . |
| . | . | . | . |
| Round $n$ | 0 | 0 | 400 billion |

expenditure—the $100 billion in planned investment spending in our example—which causes GDP to rise by $100 billion. In round 2, induced expenditure rises by $75 billion (which equals the $100 billion increase in real GDP in round 1 multiplied by the *MPC*). The $75 billion in induced expenditure in round 2 causes a $75 billion increase in real GDP, which leads to a $56 billion increase in induced expenditure in round 3, and so on. The final column sums up the total increases in expenditure, which equal the total increase in GDP. In each round, the additional induced expenditure becomes smaller because the *MPC* is less than 1. By round 10, additional induced expenditure is only $8 billion, and the total increase in GDP from the beginning of the process is $377 billion. By round 19, the process is almost complete: Additional induced expenditure is only about $1 billion, and the total increase in GDP is $398 billion. Eventually, the process will be finished, although we cannot say precisely how many spending rounds it will take, so we simply label the last round *n* rather than give it a specific number.

We can calculate the value of the multiplier in our example by dividing the increase in equilibrium real GDP by the increase in autonomous expenditure:

$$\frac{\Delta Y}{\Delta I} = \frac{\text{Change in real GDP}}{\text{Change in investment spending}} = \frac{\$400 \text{ billion}}{\$100 \text{ billion}} = 4.$$

With a multiplier of 4, each increase in autonomous expenditure of $1 will result in an increase in equilibrium GDP of $4.

| Making the Connection | ## The Multiplier in Reverse: The Great Depression of the 1930s |

An increase in autonomous expenditure causes an increase in equilibrium real GDP, but the reverse is also true: A decrease in autonomous expenditure causes a decrease in real GDP. Many Americans became aware of this fact in the 1930s, when reductions in autonomous expenditure were magnified by the multiplier into the largest decline in real GDP in U.S. history.

In August 1929, the economy reached a business cycle peak, and a downturn in production began. In October, the stock market crashed, destroying billions of dollars of wealth and increasing pessimism among households and firms. Both consumption spending and planned investment spending declined. The passage by the U.S. Congress of the Smoot–Hawley Tariff Act in June 1930 helped set off a trade war that reduced net exports. A series of banking crises that began in fall 1930 limited the ability of households and firms to finance consumption and investment. As aggregate expenditure declined, many firms experienced declining sales and began to lay off workers. Falling levels of production and income induced further declines in consumption spending, which led to further cutbacks in production and employment, leading to further declines in income, and so on, in a downward spiral. The following table shows the severity of the economic downturn by contrasting the business cycle peak of 1929 with the business cycle trough of 1933:

*The multiplier effect contributed to the very high levels of unemployment during the Great Depression.*

| Year | Consumption | Investment | Net Exports | Real GDP | Unemployment Rate |
|------|-------------|------------|-------------|----------|-------------------|
| 1929 | $737 billion | $102 billion | −$11 billion | $977 billion | 3.2% |
| 1933 | $601 billion | $19 billion | −$12 billion | $716 billion | 24.9% |

*Note:* The values are in 2005 dollars.
Data from U.S. Bureau of Economic Analysis; and U.S. Bureau of Labor Statistics.

We can use a 45°-line diagram to illustrate the multiplier effect working in reverse during these years. The economy was at potential real GDP in 1929, before the declines in aggregate expenditure began. Declining consumption, planned investment, and net exports shifted the aggregate expenditure function down from $AE_{1929}$ to $AE_{1933}$, reducing equilibrium real GDP from $977 billion in 1929 to $716 billion in 1933. The depth and length of this economic downturn led to its being labeled the Great Depression.

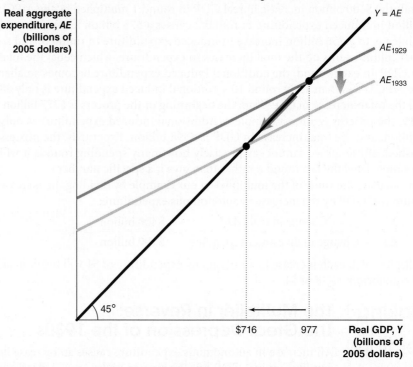

The severity of the Great Depression forced thousands of firms to declare bankruptcy. Even firms that survived experienced sharp declines in sales. By 1933, production at U.S. Steel had declined 90 percent, and production at General Motors had declined more than 75 percent. High rates of unemployment forced many families into poverty and a daily struggle for survival. Recovery from the business cycle trough in 1933 was slow. Real GDP did not regain its 1929 level until 1936, and a growing labor force meant that the unemployment rate did not fall below 10 percent until the United States entered World War II in 1941.

MyEconLab **Your Turn:** Test your understanding by doing related problem 4.4 on page 787 at the end of this chapter.

## A Formula for the Multiplier

Table 23.4 shows that during the multiplier process, each round of increases in consumption is smaller than in the previous round, so eventually, the increases will come to an end, and we will have a new macroeconomic equilibrium. But how do we know that when we add all the increases in GDP, the total will be $400 billion? We can show that this is true by first writing out the total change in equilibrium GDP:

The total change in equilibrium real GDP equals the initial increase in planned investment spending = $100 billion

*Plus* the first induced increase in consumption = $MPC \times \$100$ billion

*Plus* the second induced increase in consumption = $MPC \times (MPC \times \$100$ billion) $= MPC^2 \times \$100$ billion

*Plus* the third induced increase in consumption = $MPC \times (MPC^2 \times \$100$ billion) $= MPC^3 \times \$100$ billion

*Plus* the fourth induced increase in consumption = $MPC \times (MPC^3 \times \$100$ billion) $= MPC^4 \times \$100$ billion

And so on . . .

Or:

$$\text{Total change in GDP} = \$100\,\text{billion} + MPC \times \$100\,\text{billion} + MPC^2$$
$$\times \$100\,\text{billion} + MPC^3 \times \$100\,\text{billion} + MPC^4 \times \$100\,\text{billion} + \ldots)$$

where the ellipsis (...) indicates that the expression contains an infinite number of similar terms.

If we factor out the $100 billion from each expression, we have:

$$\text{Total change in GDP} = \$100\,\text{billion} \times (1 + MPC + MPC^2 + MPC^3$$
$$+ MPC^4 + \ldots)$$

Mathematicians have shown that an expression like the one in the parentheses sums to

$$\frac{1}{1 - MPC}.$$

In this case, the $MPC$ is equal to 0.75. So, we can now calculate that the change in equilibrium GDP $= 1\,\text{billion} \times [1/(1- 0.75)] = 100\,\text{billion} \times 4 = 400\,\text{billion}$. We have also derived a general formula for the multiplier:

$$\text{Multiplier} = \frac{\text{Change in equilibrium real GDP}}{\text{Change in autonomous expenditure}} = \frac{1}{1 - MPC}.$$

In this case, the multiplier is $1/(1 - 0.75)$, or 4, which means that for each additional $1 of autonomous spending, equilibrium GDP will increase by $4. A $100 billion increase in planned investment spending results in a $400 billion increase in equilibrium GDP. Notice that the value of the multiplier depends on the value of the $MPC$. In particular, the larger the value of the $MPC$, the larger the value of the multiplier. For example, if the $MPC$ were 0.9 instead of 0.75, the value of the multiplier would increase from 4 to $1/(1 - 0.9) = 10$.

## Summarizing the Multiplier Effect

You should note four key points about the multiplier effect:

1. The multiplier effect occurs both when autonomous expenditure increases and when it decreases. For example, with an $MPC$ of 0.75, a *decrease* in planned investment of $100 billion will lead to a *decrease* in equilibrium income of $400 billion.
2. The multiplier effect makes the economy more sensitive to changes in autonomous expenditure than it would otherwise be. Between the fourth quarter of 2005 and the first quarter of 2009, spending on residential construction declined more than 50 percent. This decline in spending set off a series of declines in production, income, and spending, so that firms such as automobile dealerships and clothing stores, which are far removed from the housing industry, also experienced sales declines. Because of the multiplier effect, a decline in spending and production in one sector of the economy can lead to declines in spending and production in many other sectors of the economy.
3. The larger the $MPC$, the larger the value of the multiplier. With an $MPC$ of 0.75, the multiplier is 4, but with an $MPC$ of 0.50, the multiplier is only 2. This direct relationship between the value of the $MPC$ and the value of the multiplier holds true because the larger the $MPC$, the more additional consumption takes place after each rise in income during the multiplier process.
4. The formula for the multiplier, $1/(1 - MPC)$, is oversimplified because it ignores some real-world complications, such as the effect that increases in GDP have on imports, inflation, interest rates, and individual income taxes. These effects combine to cause the simple formula to overstate the true value of the multiplier. Beginning in Chapter 24, we will start to take into account these real-world complications.

# Solved Problem 23.4

## Using the Multiplier Formula

Use the information in the table to answer the following questions:

| Real GDP (Y) | Consumption (C) | Planned Investment (I) | Government Purchases (G) | Net Exports (NX) |
|---|---|---|---|---|
| $8,000 | $6,900 | $1,000 | $1,000 | −$500 |
| 9,000 | 7,700 | 1,000 | 1,000 | −500 |
| 10,000 | 8,500 | 1,000 | 1,000 | −500 |
| 11,000 | 9,300 | 1,000 | 1,000 | −500 |
| 12,000 | 10,100 | 1,000 | 1,000 | −500 |

*Note:* The values are in billions of 2005 dollars.

a. What is the equilibrium level of real GDP?

b. What is the *MPC*?

c. Suppose government purchases increase by $200 billion. What will be the new equilibrium level of real GDP? Use the multiplier formula to determine your answer.

## Solving the Problem

**Step 1: Review the chapter material.** This problem is about the multiplier process, so you may want to review the section "The Multiplier Effect," which begins on page 773.

**Step 2: Determine equilibrium real GDP.** Just as in Solved Problem 23.2 on page 760, we can find macroeconomic equilibrium by calculating the level of planned aggregate expenditure for each level of real GDP.

| Real GDP (Y) | Consumption (C) | Planned Investment (I) | Government Purchases (G) | Net Exports (NX) | Planned Aggregate Expenditure (AE) |
|---|---|---|---|---|---|
| $8,000 | $6,900 | $1,000 | $1,000 | −$500 | $8,400 |
| 9,000 | 7,700 | 1,000 | 1,000 | −500 | 9,200 |
| 10,000 | 8,500 | 1,000 | 1,000 | −500 | 10,000 |
| 11,000 | 9,300 | 1,000 | 1,000 | −500 | 10,800 |
| 12,000 | 10,100 | 1,000 | 1,000 | −500 | 11,600 |

We can see that macroeconomic equilibrium will occur when real GDP equals $10,000 billion.

**Step 3: Calculate the *MPC*.**

$$MC = \frac{\Delta C}{\Delta Y}.$$

In this case:

$$MPC = \frac{\$800 \text{ billion}}{\$1,000 \text{ billion}} = 0.8.$$

**Step 4: Use the multiplier formula to calculate the new equilibrium level of real GDP.** We could find the new level of equilibrium real GDP by constructing a new table with government purchases increased from $1,000 to $1,200. But the multiplier allows us to calculate the answer directly. In this case:

$$\text{Multiplier} = \frac{1}{1 - MPC} = \frac{1}{1 - 0.8} = 5.$$

So:

Change in equilibrium real GDP = Change in autonomous expenditure × 5.

Or:

Change in equilibrium real GDP $= \$200$ billion $\times 5 = \$1,000$ billion.

Therefore:

New level of equilibrium GDP $= \$10,000$ billion $+ \$1,000$ billion
$= \$11,000$ billion.

**Your Turn:** For more practice, do related problem 4.5 on page 787 at the end of this chapter.    MyEconLab

## The Paradox of Thrift

We saw in Chapters 21 and 22 that an increase in savings can increase the rate of economic growth in the long run by providing funds for investment. But in the short run, if households save more of their income and spend less of it, aggregate expenditure and real GDP will decline. In discussing the aggregate expenditure model, John Maynard Keynes argued that if many households decide at the same time to increase their saving and reduce their spending, they may make themselves worse off by causing aggregate expenditure to fall, thereby pushing the economy into a recession. The lower incomes in the recession might mean that total saving does not increase, despite the attempts by many individuals to increase their own saving. Keynes referred to this outcome as the *paradox of thrift* because what appears to be something favorable to the long-run performance of the economy might be counterproductive in the short run.

As we mentioned in Chapter 19, households had been saving very little of their income in the mid-2000s but increased their saving markedly in late 2008 and 2009. The personal saving rate is saving by households as a percentage of disposable personal income. By mid-2009, the personal saving rate had increased to 6 percent. Some economists argued that this increase in saving contributed to the recession by reducing consumption spending. Other economists were more skeptical of the reasoning behind the paradox of thrift. As we saw in Chapter 21, an increase in saving, by increasing the supply of loanable funds, should lower the real interest rate and increase the level of investment spending. This increase in investment spending might offset some or all of the decline in consumption spending attributable to increased saving. Economists continue to debate the short-run effects of an increase in saving.

## The Aggregate Demand Curve

When demand for a product increases, firms usually respond by increasing production, but they are also likely to increase prices. Similarly, when demand falls, production falls, but often, prices also fall. We would expect, then, that an increase or a decrease in aggregate expenditure would affect not just real GDP but also the *price level*. Will a change in the price level, in turn, affect the components of aggregate expenditure? In fact, as we will see, increases in the price level cause aggregate expenditure to fall, and decreases in the price level cause aggregate expenditure to rise. There are three main reasons for this inverse relationship between changes in the price level and changes in aggregate expenditure. We discussed the first two reasons earlier in this chapter, when considering the factors that determine consumption and net exports:

- A rising price level decreases consumption by decreasing the real value of household wealth; a falling price level has the reverse effect.

- If the price level in the United States rises relative to the price levels in other countries, U.S. exports will become relatively more expensive, and foreign imports will become relatively less expensive, causing net exports to fall. A falling price level in the United States has the reverse effect.

- When prices rise, firms and households need more money to finance buying and selling. If the central bank (the Federal Reserve in the United States) does not

**23.5 LEARNING** OBJECTIVE

Understand the relationship between the aggregate demand curve and aggregate expenditure.

increase the money supply, the result will be an increase in the interest rate. In Chapter 25, we will analyze in more detail why this happens. As we discussed earlier in this chapter, at a higher interest rate, investment spending falls as firms borrow less money to build new factories or to install new machinery and equipment and households borrow less money to buy new houses. A falling price level has the reverse effect: Other things being equal, interest rates will fall, and investment spending will rise.

We can now incorporate the effect of a change in the price level into the basic aggregate expenditure model, in which equilibrium real GDP is determined by the intersection of the aggregate expenditure ($AE$) line and the 45° line. Remember that we measure the price level as an index number with a value of 100 in the base year. If the price level rises from, say, 100 to 103, consumption, planned investment, and net exports will all fall, causing the $AE$ line to shift down on the 45°-line diagram. The $AE$ line shifts down because with higher prices, less spending will occur in the economy at every level of GDP. Panel (a) of Figure 23.13 shows that the downward shift of the $AE$ line results in a lower level of equilibrium real GDP.

If the price level falls from, say, 100 to 97, then investment, consumption, and net exports will all rise. As panel (b) of Figure 23.13 shows, the $AE$ line will shift up, which will cause equilibrium real GDP to increase.

Figure 23.14 summarizes the effect of changes in the price level on real GDP. The table shows the combinations of price level and real GDP from Figure 23.13. The graph plots the numbers from the table. In the graph, the price level is measured on the vertical axis, and real GDP is measured on the horizontal axis. The relationship shown in Figure 23.14 between the price level and the level of planned aggregate expenditure is known as the **aggregate demand ($AD$) curve**.

**Aggregate demand ($AD$) curve** A curve that shows the relationship between the price level and the level of planned aggregate expenditure in the economy, holding constant all other factors that affect aggregate expenditure.

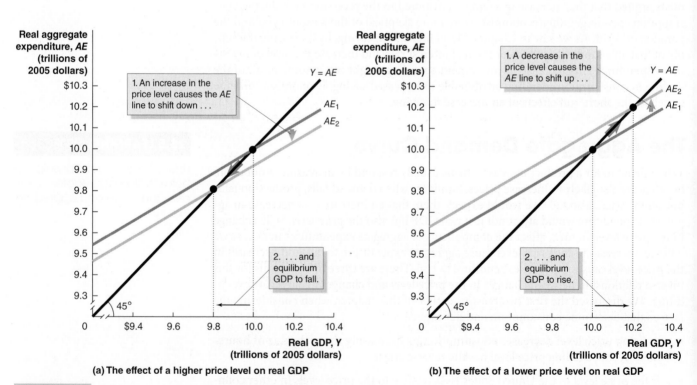

**(a) The effect of a higher price level on real GDP**

**(b) The effect of a lower price level on real GDP**

**Figure 23.13** **The Effect of a Change in the Price Level on Real GDP**

In panel (a), an increase in the price level results in declining consumption, planned investment, and net exports and causes the aggregate expenditure line to shift down from $AE_1$ to $AE_2$. As a result, equilibrium real GDP declines from $10.0 trillion to $9.8 trillion. In panel (b), a decrease in the price level results in

rising consumption, planned investment, and net exports and causes the aggregate expenditure line to shift up from $AE_1$ to $AE_2$. As a result, equilibrium real GDP increases from $10.0 trillion to $10.2 trillion.

| Price level | Equilibrium real GDP |
|---|---|
| 97 | $10.2 trillion |
| 100 | 10.0 trillion |
| 103 | 9.8 trillion |

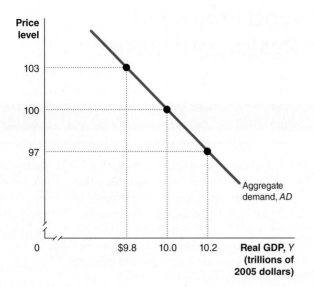

**Figure 23.14**

**The Aggregate Demand Curve**

The aggregate demand (*AD*) curve shows the relationship between the price level and the level of planned aggregate expenditure in the economy. When the price level is 97, real GDP is $10.2 trillion. An increase in the price level to 100 causes consumption, investment, and net exports to fall, which reduces real GDP to $10.0 trillion.

Continued from page 749

## Economics in Your Life

### When Consumer Confidence Falls, Is Your Job at Risk?

At the beginning of this chapter, we asked you to suppose that you work part time assembling desktop computers for a large computer company. You have learned that consumer confidence in the economy has fallen and that many households expect their future income to be dramatically less than their current income. Should you be concerned about losing your job? We have seen in this chapter that if consumers expect their future incomes to decline, they will cut their consumption spending, and consumption spending is more than two-thirds of aggregate expenditure. So, if the decline in consumer confidence is correctly forecasting a decline in consumption spending, then aggregate expenditures and GDP will also likely decline. If the economy moves into a recession, spending on computers by households and firms is likely to fall, which could reduce your firm's sales and possibly cost you a job. Before you panic, though, keep in mind that surveys of consumer confidence do not have a good track record in predicting recessions, so you may not have to move back in with your parents after all.

## Conclusion

In this chapter, we examined a key macroeconomic idea: In the short run, the level of GDP is determined mainly by the level of aggregate expenditure. When economists forecast changes in GDP, they do so by forecasting changes in the four components of aggregate expenditure. We constructed an aggregate demand curve by taking into account how changes in the price level affect aggregate expenditure.

But our story is incomplete. In Chapter 24, we will analyze the *aggregate supply curve*. Then, we will use the aggregate demand curve and the aggregate supply curve to show how equilibrium real GDP and the equilibrium price level are simultaneously determined.

We also need to discuss the roles that the financial system and government policy play in determining real GDP and the price level in the short run. We will cover these important topics in the next three chapters. Before moving on, read *An Inside Look* on the next page, for a discussion of how a rebound in sales in the restaurant industry affects aggregate expenditure in the economy.

# Turnaround Projected for the Restaurant Industry

## Restaurant Industry Sales Turn Positive in 2011 after Three Tough Years

Restaurant industry sales are expected to reach a record $604 billion and post positive growth in 2011 after a three-year period of negative real sales growth, according to National Restaurant Association research released today. The Association's 2011 *Restaurant Industry Forecast* projects an industry sales increase of 3.6 percent over 2010 sales, which equals 1.1 percent in real (inflation-adjusted) terms.

**ⓐ** The nation's 960,000 restaurants will continue to be strong contributors to the recovery of the nation's economy, with industry sales representing 4 percent of the U.S. gross domestic product and employees comprising nearly 10 percent of the U.S. workforce. Its total economic impact exceeds $1.7 trillion, as every dollar spent in restaurants generates $2.05 spent in the overall economy. Restaurants are the nation's second-largest private sector employer with 12.8 million employees.

"As the national economy is slowly improving, the restaurant industry is climbing out of its most challenging period in decades to post positive real sales growth in 2011," said Hudson Riehle, senior vice president of the Research and Knowledge Group for the National Restaurant Association. "As in 2010, restaurant industry job growth is expected to outpace the national economy this year, emphasizing the importance of the industry to the nation's economy."

"The U.S. restaurant industry is an economic juggernaut whose annual sales are larger than 90 percent of the world's economies—if it were a country, it would rank as the 18th largest economy in the world. While pockets of challenges remain, we are looking forward to a brighter future in 2011," he added.

### Industry Segment Growth

**ⓑ** Continuing the trend from last year, the quick-service restaurant segment is expected to post slightly stronger sales growth than the full-service segment. Quick-service restaurants are projected to post sales of $167.7 billion this year, a gain of 3.3 percent over 2010. Sales at full-service restaurants are projected to reach $194.6 billion in 2011, an increase of 3.1 percent in current dollars over 2010. . . .

### State and Regional Sales Growth

Among the 50 states, North Carolina is expected to post the strongest sales growth in 2011 at 4.2 percent (industry sales are projected at $14.1 billion), followed by Idaho ($1.8 billion) and Virginia ($12.8 billion) at 4.0 percent. Forecast to post growth at 3.9 percent: Colorado ($8.6 billion), Florida ($30.1 billion), Maryland ($9.4 billion) and Texas ($36.7 billion).

Of the nine U.S. Census regions, the South Atlantic is expected to post the strongest restaurant sales growth at 3.9 percent, totaling $93.9 billion among its eight states (Delaware, Florida, Georgia, Maryland, North Carolina, South Carolina, Virginia and West Virginia) and the District of Columbia.

### Workforce Outlook

**ⓒ** The restaurant industry posted modest job growth last year, and that growth is expected to accelerate in 2011. This year, the industry will add jobs at a rate of 2.4 percent, compared with the 1.8 percent expected for the national economy. In the next decade, the industry will add 1.3 million positions.

In the states, the restaurant industries in Texas and Florida will show the strongest job growth over the next 10 years at roughly 17 percent, followed by Arizona and Alabama at roughly 16 percent.

### Consumer and Menu Trends

According to the National Restaurant Association's 2011 *Restaurant Industry Forecast*, consumers today spend 49 percent of their food budget in the restaurant community, compared with only 25 percent in 1955. The economic downturn has created a substantial pent-up demand for restaurant services—more than two out of five consumers say they are not dining out or using takeout as often as they would like—which positions the restaurant industry for growth in 2011. . . .

## Key Points in the Article

The National Restaurant Association expected industry sales to reach $604 billion in 2011, up 3.6 percent from 2010. Both the quick-service and full-service segments of the market were expected to grow. The strongest growth was expected in the South Atlantic region, with an annual increase in sales of 3.9 percent and total sales exceeding $93 billion. Employment for the industry was also expected to increase by 2.4 percent in 2011, higher than the 1.8 percent expected growth in employment for the economy as a whole. Over the next decade, the restaurant industry is expected to add 1.3 million jobs, with Texas and Florida leading the way.

## Analyzing the News

(a) The National Restaurant Association's 2011 industry forecast projects growth in an industry that has been on the decline for the previous three years. For 2011, sales at the 960,000 restaurants in the United States are expected to account for 4 percent of U.S. GDP, and the 12.8 million employees at these restaurants will account for almost 10 percent of the nation's labor force. The association states that the industry has an economic effect of more than $1.7 trillion, with every dollar spent in restaurants generating an estimated total of $2.05 in spending in the economy.

(b) Sales in both the quick-service and full-service segments of the restaurant industry were expected to grow in 2011. Quick-service restaurant sales, a segment comprising primarily of fast-food outlets, are expected to be $167.7 billion, a 3.3 percent increase for the year. Full-service sales, or sales at restaurants that offer table service, are projected at $194.6 billion, representing an increase of 3.1 percent. Consumer purchases of restaurant meals would be counted as part of consumption spending. The figure below illustrates the effect of an increase in real aggregate expenditure on real GDP. The economy begins at equilibrium at point $A$, and real GDP is $Y_1$. As a result of an increase in consumption spending, aggregate expenditure shifts up from $AE_1$ to $AE_2$, and the new equilibrium moves from point $A$ to point $B$. In this case, real GDP increases from $Y_1$ to $Y_2$.

(c) The expected increase in sales in the restaurant industry is expected to result in an increase in industry employment during 2011. Following job losses in 2008 and 2009, the industry did experience slight job growth in 2010, and employment growth is expected to be 2.4 percent in 2011. This growth rate outpaces the expected job growth rate for the national economy by 33 percent. The restaurant industry employs nearly 10 percent of the nation's workforce, so an increase in job growth in this industry can be quite significant for the economy. As employment increases, the level of aggregate expenditure should also increase because the increase in employment will result in additional consumer spending in the economy. In the figure below, an increase in aggregate expenditure from $AE_1$ to $AE_2$, first causes the amount of planned aggregate expenditure to be greater than real GDP at point $A$. Firms then respond to the increase in sales by increasing production and employment until the economy reaches equilibrium at point $B$ and real GDP eventually increases from $Y_1$ to $Y_2$.

## Thinking Critically

1. The article states that $1 spent in restaurants results in $2.05 spent in the entire economy. Suppose the U.S. government issues to each citizen $500 in vouchers that can only be spent in restaurants. How would this program affect aggregate expenditure and equilibrium real GDP?

2. Suppose that in an effort to aid the economy, the federal government enacts a law that prohibits any imported food products to be used in restaurants. How would this law affect aggregate expenditure and equilibrium real GDP in the United States? Does your answer depend on how the governments of other countries react to the law? Briefly explain.

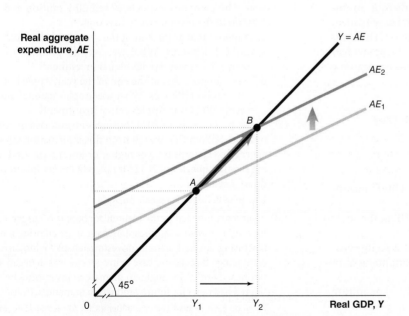

An increase in aggregate expenditure results in an increase in real GDP.

# Chapter Summary and Problems

## Key Terms

Aggregate demand (*AD*) curve, p. 780

Aggregate expenditure (*AE*), p. 750

Aggregate expenditure model, p. 750

Autonomous expenditure, p. 773

Cash flow, p. 762

Consumption function, p. 757

Inventories, p. 751

Marginal propensity to consume (*MPC*), p. 757

Marginal propensity to save (*MPS*), p. 760

Multiplier, p. 773

Multiplier effect, p. 773

---

**23.1** **The Aggregate Expenditure Model, pages 750–753**

LEARNING OBJECTIVE: Understand how macroeconomic equilibrium is determined in the aggregate expenditure model.

### Summary

**Aggregate expenditure** (*AE*) is the total amount of spending in the economy. The **aggregate expenditure model** focuses on the relationship between total spending and real GDP in the short run, assuming that the price level is constant. In any particular year, the level of GDP is determined by the level of total spending, or aggregate expenditure, in the economy. The four components of aggregate expenditure are consumption (*C*), planned investment (*I*), government purchases (*G*), and net exports (*NX*). When aggregate expenditure is greater than GDP, there is an unplanned decrease in **inventories**, which are goods that have been produced but not yet sold, and GDP and total employment will increase. When aggregate expenditure is less than GDP, there is an unplanned increase in inventories, and GDP and total employment will decline. When aggregate expenditure is equal to GDP, firms will sell what they expected to sell, production and employment will be unchanged, and the economy will be in macroeconomic equilibrium.

 Visit **www.myeconlab.com** to complete these exercises online and get instant feedback.

### Review Questions

**1.1** What is the key idea in the aggregate expenditure macroeconomic model?

**1.2** What is the main reason for changes in GDP in the short run?

**1.3** What are inventories? What usually happens to inventories at the beginning of a recession? At the beginning of an expansion?

**1.4** Which of the following does the aggregate expenditure model seek to explain: long-run economic growth, the business cycle, inflation, and cyclical unemployment?

### Problems and Applications

**1.5** Into which category of aggregate expenditure would each of the following transactions fall?
   a. The Jones family buys a new car.
   b. The San Diego Unified School District buys 12 new school buses.
   c. The Jones family buys a newly constructed house from the Garcia Construction Co.
   d. A consumer in Japan orders a computer online from Dell.
   e. Prudential insurance company purchases 250 new computers from Dell.

**1.6** Suppose Apple plans to produce 20.2 million iPhones this year. The company expects to sell 20.1 million and add 100,000 to the inventories in its stores.
   a. Suppose that at the end of the year, Apple has sold 19.9 million iPhones. What was Apple's planned investment? What was Apple's actual investment?
   b. Now suppose that at the end of the year, Apple has sold 20.3 million iPhones. What was Apple's planned investment? What was Apple's actual investment?

**1.7** In the first quarter of 2011, business inventories increased by $49.1 billion. Can we tell from this information whether aggregate expenditure was higher or lower than GDP during the first quarter of 2011? If not, what other information do we need?

Data from Bureau of Economic Analysis.

**1.8** A survey conducted by the Institute for Supply Management in June 2011 showed a significant increase in inventories in manufacturing. An analyst for the investment bank Goldman Sachs commented that the increase in inventories was "a negative for future activity." Why might an increase in inventories be considered bad news for future production in manufacturing?

Based on Kelly Evans, "Factories Offer a Clue to Second-Half Hopes," *Wall Street Journal*, July 15, 2011.

---

**23.2** **Determining the Level of Aggregate Expenditure in the Economy, pages 753–766**

LEARNING OBJECTIVE: Discuss the determinants of the four components of aggregate expenditure and define marginal propensity to consume and marginal propensity to save.

### Summary

The five determinants of consumption are current disposable income, household wealth, expected future income, the price level, and the interest rate. The **consumption function** is the relationship between consumption and disposable income. The **marginal propensity to consume** (*MPC*) is the change in consumption divided by the change in disposable income. The **marginal**

**propensity to save** (*MPS*) is the change in saving divided by the change in disposable income. The determinants of planned investment are expectations of future profitability, real interest rate, taxes, and **cash flow**, which is the difference between the cash revenues received by a firm and the cash spending by the firm. Government purchases include spending by the federal government and by local and state governments for goods and services. Government purchases do not include *transfer payments*, such as Social Security payments by the federal government or pension payments by local governments to retired police officers and firefighters. The three determinants of net exports are changes in the price level in the United States relative to changes in the price levels in other countries, the growth rate of GDP in the United States relative to the growth rates of GDP in other countries, and the exchange rate between the dollar and other currencies.

MyEconLab    Visit www.myeconlab.com to complete these exercises online and get instant feedback.

## Review Questions

**2.1** In the aggregate expenditure model, why is it important to know the factors that determine consumption spending, investment spending, government purchases, and net exports?

**2.2** Give an example of each of the four categories of aggregate expenditure.

**2.3** What are the five main determinants of consumption spending? Which of these is the most important? How would a rise in stock prices or housing prices affect consumption spending?

**2.4** Compare what happened to real investment between 1979 and the second quarter of 2011 with what happened to real consumption during that period.

**2.5** What are the four main determinants of investment? How would a change in interest rates affect investment?

**2.6** What are the three main determinants of net exports? How would an increase in the growth rate of GDP in the BRIC nations (Brazil, Russia, India, and China) affect U.S. net exports?

## Problems and Applications

**2.7** [**Related to the** Chapter Opener **on page 749**] Suppose a major U.S. furniture manufacturer is forecasting demand for its products during the next year. How will the forecast be affected by each of the following?
   a. A survey shows a sharp rise in consumer confidence that income growth will be increasing
   b. Real interest rates are expected to increase
   c. The exchange rate value of the U.S. dollar is expected to increase
   d. Planned investment spending in the economy is expected to decrease

**2.8** Draw the consumption function and label each axis. Show the effect of an increase in income on consumption spending. Does the change in income cause a movement along the consumption function or a shift of the consumption function? How would an increase in expected future income or an increase in household wealth affect the consumption function? Would these increases cause a movement along the consumption function or a shift of the consumption function?

**2.9** Many people have difficulty borrowing as much money as they want to, even if they are confident that their incomes in the future will be high enough to easily pay back the borrowed funds. For example, many students in medical school will earn high incomes after they graduate and become physicians. If they could, they would probably borrow now in order to live more comfortably while in medical school and pay the loans back out of their higher future income. Unfortunately, banks are usually reluctant to make loans to people who currently have low incomes, even if there is a good chance that their incomes will be much higher in the future. If people could always borrow as much as they want to, would you expect consumption to become more or less sensitive to current income? Briefly explain.

**2.10** An economics student raises the following objection: "The textbook said that a higher interest rate lowers investment, but this doesn't make sense. I know that if I can get a higher interest rate, I am certainly going to invest more in my savings account." Do you agree with this reasoning?

**2.11** [**Related to the** Making the Connection **on page 755**] Writing about the state of the British economy, an article in the *Economist* argued: "Spending will be hit . . . by weak stock-markets and shrinking housing wealth." Would Calomiris, Longhofer, and Miles agree with this argument? Would Mian and Sufi? Briefly explain.

Based on "Combating the Recession," *Economist*, January 8, 2009.

**2.12** Unemployed workers receive unemployment insurance payments from the government. Does the existence of unemployment insurance make it likely that consumption will fluctuate more or fluctuate less over the business cycle than it would in the absence of unemployment insurance? Briefly explain.

**2.13** [**Related to** Solved Problem 23.2 **on page 760**] Fill in the blanks in the following table. Assume for simplicity that taxes are zero. Also assume that the values represent billions of 2005 dollars.

| National Income and Real GDP (Y) | Consumption (C) | Saving (S) | Marginal Propensity to Consume (MPC) | Marginal Propensity to Save (MPS) |
|---|---|---|---|---|
| $9,000 | $8,000 | | — | — |
| 10,000 | 8,750 | | | |
| 11,000 | 9,500 | | | |
| 12,000 | 10,250 | | | |
| 13,000 | 11,000 | | | |

**2.14** [**Related to the** Making the Connection **on page 762**] We saw that Intel hopes to increase sales of microprocessors used in cell phones and other small consumer electronics products. During a recession, why would spending on these products be more stable than spending on computers?

## 23.3 Graphing Macroeconomic Equilibrium, pages 766–772

LEARNING OBJECTIVE: Use a 45°-line diagram to illustrate macroeconomic equilibrium.

## Summary

The 45°-line diagram shows all the points where aggregate expenditure equals real GDP. On the 45°-line diagram, macroeconomic equilibrium occurs where the line representing the aggregate expenditure function crosses the 45° line. The economy is in recession when the aggregate expenditure line intersects the 45° line at a level of GDP that is below potential GDP. Numerically, macroeconomic equilibrium occurs when:

Consumption + Planned investment +
Government purchases + Net exports = GDP.

MyEconLab Visit www.myeconlab.com to complete these exercises online and get instant feedback.

## Review Questions

3.1 What is the meaning of the 45° line in the 45°-line diagram?

3.2 Use a 45°-line diagram to illustrate macroeconomic equilibrium. Make sure your diagram shows the aggregate expenditure function and the level of equilibrium real GDP and that your axes are properly labeled.

3.3 What does the slope of the aggregate expenditure line equal? How is the slope of the aggregate expenditure line related to the slope of the consumption function?

3.4 What is the macroeconomic consequence if firms accumulate large amounts of unplanned inventory at the beginning of a recession?

3.5 What is the difference between aggregate expenditure and consumption spending?

## Problems and Applications

3.6 At point A in the following graph, is planned aggregate expenditure greater than, equal to, or less than GDP? What about at point B? At point C? For points A and C, indicate the vertical distance that measures the unintended change in inventories.

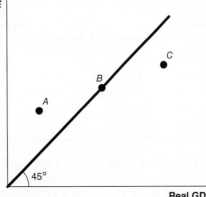

3.7 Suppose we drop the assumption that net exports do not depend on real GDP. Draw a graph with the value of net exports on the vertical axis and the value of real GDP on

the horizontal axis. Now, add a line representing the relationship between net exports and real GDP. Does your net exports line have a positive or negative slope? Briefly explain.

3.8 A Federal Reserve Board publication makes the following observation: "The impact of inventory increases on the business cycle depends upon whether [the increases] are planned or unplanned." Do you agree? Briefly explain.

3.9 Jack Lavery, former chief economist at Merrill Lynch, made the following observation about the U.S. economy in April 2009: "I expect inventory drawdown to be even more pronounced in the second quarter, which will contribute to the fourth successive quarterly decline in real GDP." What does Lavery mean by "inventory drawdown"? What component of aggregate expenditure would be affected by an inventory drawdown? Why would this contribute to GDP decline?

Based on Jack Lavery, "Real GDP Declines Far More Than Predicted," minyanville.com, April 29, 2009.

3.10 Consider the following table, which shows the change in inventories for each quarter from 2007:I to 2011:II measured in billions of 2005 dollars. Provide a macroeconomic explanation for this pattern. (Hint: When did the recession during this period begin and end?)

| Year | Quarter | Change in Inventories |
|------|---------|----------------------|
| 2007 | I | $17.3 |
|  | II | 44.9 |
|  | III | 36.1 |
|  | IV | 12.6 |
| 2008 | I | −12.5 |
|  | II | −14.2 |
|  | III | −38.1 |
|  | IV | −80.3 |
| 2009 | I | −161.6 |
|  | II | −183.0 |
|  | III | −178.7 |
|  | IV | −56.5 |
| 2010 | I | 39.9 |
|  | II | 64.6 |
|  | III | 92.3 |
|  | IV | 38.3 |
| 2011 | I | 49.1 |
|  | II | 39.1 |

3.11 [**Related to the** Don't Let This Happen to You **on page 771**] Briefly explain whether you agree with the following argument: "The equilibrium level of GDP is determined by the level of aggregate expenditure. Therefore, GDP will decline only if households decide to spend less on goods and services."

**3.12** **[Related to** Solved Problem 23.3 **on page 772]** Fill in the missing values in the following table. Assume that the value of the *MPC* does not change as real GDP changes. Also assume that the values represent billions of 2005 dollars.

| Real GDP (Y) | Consumption (C) | Planned Investment (I) | Government Purchases (G) | Net Exports (NX) | Planned Aggregate Expenditure (AE) | Unplanned Change in Inventories |
|---|---|---|---|---|---|---|
| $9,000 | $7,600 | $1,200 | $1,200 | −$400 | | |
| 10,000 | 8,400 | 1,200 | 1,200 | −400 | | |
| 11,000 | | 1,200 | 1,200 | −400 | | |
| 12,000 | | 1,200 | 1,200 | −400 | | |
| 13,000 | | 1,200 | 1,200 | −400 | | |

a. What is the value of the *MPC*?

b. What is the value of equilibrium real GDP?

---

**23.4** **The Multiplier Effect, pages 773–779**

LEARNING OBJECTIVE: Describe the multiplier effect and use the multiplier formula to calculate changes in equilibrium GDP.

## Summary

**Autonomous expenditure** is expenditure that does not depend on the level of GDP. An autonomous change is a change in expenditure not caused by a change in income. An *induced change* is a change in aggregate expenditure caused by a change in income. An autonomous change in expenditure will cause rounds of induced changes in expenditure. Therefore, an autonomous change in expenditure will have a *multiplier effect* on equilibrium GDP. The **multiplier effect** is the process by which an increase in autonomous expenditure leads to a larger increase in real GDP. The **multiplier** is the ratio of the change in equilibrium GDP to the change in autonomous expenditure. The formula for the multiplier is

$$\frac{1}{1-MPC}.$$

Because of the paradox of thrift, an attempt by many individuals to increase their saving may lead to a reduction in aggregate expenditure and a recession.

 MyEconLab Visit **www.myeconlab.com** to complete these exercises online and get instant feedback.

## Review Questions

**4.1** What is the multiplier effect? Use a 45°-line diagram to illustrate the multiplier effect of a decrease in government purchases.

**4.2** What is the formula for the multiplier? Explain why this formula is considered to be too simple.

## Problems and Applications

**4.3** In Figure 23.12 on page 773, the economy is initially in equilibrium at point *A*. Aggregate expenditure and real

GDP both equal $9.6 trillion. The increase in investment of $100 billion increases aggregate expenditure to $9.7 trillion. If real GDP increases to $9.7 trillion, will the economy be in equilibrium? Briefly explain. What happens to aggregate expenditure when real GDP increases to $9.7 trillion?

**4.4** **[Related to the** Making the Connection **on page 775]** If the multiplier had a value of 4 in 1929, how large must the change in autonomous expenditure have been to cause the decline in real GDP between 1929 and 1933 shown in the table on page 775? If the multiplier had a value of 2, how large must the change in autonomous expenditure have been?

**4.5** **[Related to** Solved Problem 23.4 **on page 778]** Use the information in the following table to answer the following questions. Assume that the values represent billions of 2005 dollars.

| Real GDP (Y) | Consumption (C) | Planned Investment (I) | Government Purchases (G) | Net Exports (NX) |
|---|---|---|---|---|
| $8,000 | $7,300 | $1,000 | $1,000 | −$500 |
| 9,000 | 7,900 | 1,000 | 1,000 | −500 |
| 10,000 | 8,500 | 1,000 | 1,000 | −500 |
| 11,000 | 9,100 | 1,000 | 1,000 | −500 |
| 12,000 | 9,700 | 1,000 | 1,000 | −500 |

a. What is the equilibrium level of real GDP?

b. What is the *MPC*?

c. Suppose net exports increase by $400 billion. What will be the new equilibrium level of real GDP? Use the multiplier formula to determine your answer.

**4.6** If the marginal propensity to consume is 0.75, by how much will an increase in planned investment spending of $400 billion shift up the aggregate expenditure line? By how much will it increase equilibrium real GDP?

**4.7** Explain whether each of the following would cause the value of the multiplier to be larger or smaller.
   a. An increase in real GDP increases imports.
   b. An increase in real GDP increases interest rates.
   c. An increase in in real GDP increases the marginal propensity to consume.
   d. An increase in real GDP causes the average tax rate paid by households to decrease.
   e. An increase in real GDP increases the price level.

**4.8** Explain whether you agree with the following statement:

> Some economists claim that the recession of 2007–2009 was caused by a decline in spending on residential construction. This can't be true. If there had just been a decline in spending on residential construction, the only firms hurt would have been home builders and firms selling lumber and other goods used in building houses. In fact, many firms experienced falling sales during that recession, including automobile, appliance, and furniture firms.

**4.9** Suppose booming economies in the BRIC nations (Brazil, Russia, India, and China) causes net exports to rise by $75 billion in the United States. If the *MPC* is 0.8, what will be the change in equilibrium GDP?

**4.10** Would a larger multiplier lead to longer and more severe recessions or shorter and less severe recessions? Briefly explain.

**4.11** Use the following graph to answer the questions.

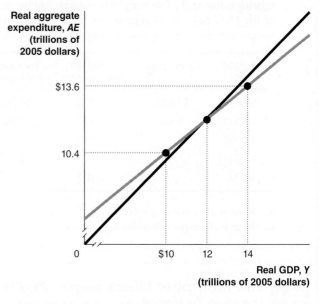

a. What is the value of equilibrium real GDP?
b. What is the value of the *MPC*?
c. What is the value of the multiplier?
d. What is the value of unplanned changes in inventories when real GDP has each of the following values?
   • $10 trillion
   • $12 trillion
   • $14 trillion

---

**23.5** **The Aggregate Demand Curve,** pages 779–781

LEARNING OBJECTIVE: Understand the relationship between the aggregate demand curve and aggregate expenditure.

## Summary

Increases in the price level cause a reduction in consumption, investment, and net exports. This causes the aggregate expenditure function to shift down on the 45°-line diagram, leading to a lower equilibrium real GDP. A decrease in the price level leads to a higher equilibrium real GDP. The **aggregate demand curve** shows the relationship between the price level and the level of aggregate expenditure, holding constant all factors other than the price level that affect aggregate expenditure.

MyEconLab    Visit **www.myeconlab.com** to complete these exercises online and get instant feedback.

## Review Questions

**5.1** Briefly explain the difference between aggregate expenditure and aggregate demand.

**5.2** Briefly explain which components of aggregate expenditure are affected by a change in the price level.

**5.3** Does a change in the price level cause a movement along the aggregate expenditure line or a shift of the aggregate expenditure line? Does a change in the price level cause a movement along the aggregate demand curve or a shift of the aggregate demand curve?

## Problems and Applications

**5.4** Briefly explain why the aggregate expenditure line is upward sloping, while the aggregate demand curve is downward sloping.

**5.5** Briefly explain whether you agree with the following statement: "The reason the aggregate demand curve slopes downward is that when the price level is higher, people cannot afford to buy as many goods and services."

**5.6** Suppose that exports become more sensitive to changes in the price level in the United States. That is, when the price level in the United States rises, exports decline by more than they previously did. Will this change make the aggregate demand curve steeper or less steep? Briefly explain.

# Appendix

## The Algebra of Macroeconomic Equilibrium

**LEARNING** OBJECTIVE

Apply the algebra of macroeconomic equilibrium.

In this chapter, we relied primarily on graphs and tables to illustrate the aggregate expenditure model of short-run real GDP. Graphs help us understand economic change *qualitatively*. When we write an economic model using equations, we make it easier to make *quantitative estimates*. When economists forecast future movements in GDP, they often rely on *econometric models*. An econometric model is an economic model written in the form of equations, where each equation has been statistically estimated, using methods similar to the methods used in estimating demand curves that we briefly described in Chapter 3. We can use equations to represent the aggregate expenditure model described in this chapter.

The following equations are based on the example shown in Table 23.3 on page 770. *Y* stands for real GDP, and the numbers (with the exception of the *MPC*) represent billions of dollars.

1. $C = 1,000 + 0.65\,Y$     Consumption function

2. $I = 1,500$     Planned investment function

3. $G = 1,500$     Government spending function

4. $NX = -500$     Net export function

5. $Y = C + I + G + NX$     Equilibrium condition

The first equation is the consumption function. The *MPC* is 0.65, and 1,000 is autonomous consumption, which is the level of consumption that does not depend on income. If we think of the consumption function as a line on the 45°-line diagram, 1,000 would be the intercept, and 0.65 would be the slope. The "functions" for the other three components of planned aggregate expenditure are very simple because we have assumed that these components are not affected by GDP and, therefore, are constant. Economists who use this type of model to forecast GDP would, of course, use more realistic investment, government, and net export functions. The *parameters* of the functions—such as the value of autonomous consumption and the value of the *MPC* in the consumption function—would be estimated statistically, using data on the values of each variable over a period of years.

In this model, GDP is in equilibrium when it equals planned aggregate expenditure. Equation 5—the equilibrium condition—shows us how to calculate equilibrium in the model: We need to substitute equations 1 through 4 into equation 5. Doing so gives us the following:

$$Y = 1,000 + 0.65Y + 1,500 + 1,500 - 500.$$

We need to solve this expression for *Y* to find equilibrium GDP. The first step is to subtract 0.65*Y* from both sides of the equation:

$$Y - 0.65Y = 1,000 + 1,500 + 1,500 - 500.$$

Then, we solve for *Y*:

$$0.35Y = 3,500.$$

Or:

$$Y = \frac{3,500}{0.35} = 10,000.$$

To make this result more general, we can replace particular values with general values represented by letters:

1. $C = \bar{C} + MPC(Y)$      Consumption function
2. $I = \bar{I}$      Planned investment function
3. $G = \bar{G}$      Government spending function
4. $NX = \overline{NX}$      Net export function
5. $Y = C + I + G + NX$      Equilibrium condition

The letters with bars over them represent fixed, or autonomous, values. So, for example, $\bar{C}$ represents autonomous consumption, which had a value of 1,000 in our original example. Now, solving for equilibrium, we get

$$Y = \bar{C} + MPC(Y) + \bar{I} + \bar{G} + \overline{NX},$$

or

$$Y - MPC(Y) = \bar{C} + \bar{I} + \bar{G} + \overline{NX},$$

or

$$Y(1 - MPC) = \bar{C} + \bar{I} + \bar{G} + \overline{NX},$$

or

$$Y = \frac{\bar{C} + \bar{I} + \bar{G} + \overline{NX}}{1 - MPC}.$$

Remember that $1/(1 - MPC)$ is the multiplier, and all four variables in the numerator of the equation represent autonomous expenditure. Therefore, an alternative expression for equilibrium GDP is:

Equilibrium GDP = Autonomous expenditure × Multiplier.

---

**23A** **The Algebra of Macroeconomic Equilibrium, pages 789–790**
LEARNING OBJECTIVE: Apply the algebra of macroeconomic equilibrium.

 Visit **www.myeconlab.com** to complete these exercises online and get instant feedback.

## Review Questions

**23A.1** Write a general expression for the aggregate expenditure function. If you think of the aggregate expenditure function as a line on the 45°-line diagram, what would be the intercept and what would be the slope, using the general values represented by letters?

**23A.2** Find equilibrium GDP using the following macroeconomic model (where the numbers, with the exception of the *MPC*, represent billions of dollars).

1. $C = 1,500 + 0.75\ Y$      Consumption function
2. $I = 1,250$      Planned investment function

3. $G = 1,250$      Government spending function
4. $NX = 2500$      Net export function
5. $Y = C + I + G + NX$      Equilibrium condition

**23A.3** For the macroeconomic model in problem 23A.2, write the aggregate expenditure function. For GDP of $16,000, what is the value of aggregate expenditure, and what is the value of the unintended change in inventories? For GDP of $12,000, what is the value of aggregate expenditure, and what is the value of the unintended change in inventories?

**23A.4** Suppose that autonomous consumption is 500, government purchases are 1,000, planned investment spending is 1,250, net exports are −250, and the *MPC* is 0.8. What is equilibrium GDP?

# Aggregate Demand and Aggregate Supply Analysis

## Chapter Outline and Learning Objectives

# The Fortunes of FedEx Follow the Business Cycle

FedEx plays a large role in moving packages around the United States and around the world. The value of packages handled by FedEx is about 4 percent of U.S. GDP and 1.5 percent of global GDP. Some Wall Street analysts use a "FedEx indicator" to guage the state of the economy because there is usually a close relationship between fluctuations in FedEx's business and fluctuations in GDP.

Fred Smith came up with the idea for the company in 1965, in an undergraduate term paper. He proposed an entirely new system of delivering packages: One firm would control shipping freight, from pickup to delivery. The firm would operate its own planes on a "hub-and-spoke" system: Packages would be collected and flown to a central hub, where they would be sorted and then flown to their destination for final delivery by truck.

Despite FedEx's tremendous success over the past 40 years, the business cycle has always affected the company's business. For example, as the U.S. entered a recession in December 2007, businesses and individuals cut back on shipping packages. In the first quarter of 2008, FedEx reported its first loss, after 11 straight years of profits. As the 2007–2009 recession dragged on, FedEx announced in March 2009 that it was laying off 1,000 employees and was imposing a 5 to 20 percent pay cut on its remaining employees. By September 2009, economic conditions had begun to improve, and FedEx announced that its profits for the three months ending on August 31 were 35 percent higher than its executives had expected. But as U.S. GDP growth slowed in 2011, so did FedEx's fortunes. Weak consumer demand and half-empty cargo planes led FedEx to announce in September that it was lowering its forecast for end-of-the-year profits. Fred Smith explained: "We expect sluggish economic growth will continue.... The consumer just doesn't have an appetite" for increased spending.

To understand how the business cycle affects FedEx and other firms, we need to explore the effects that recessions and expansions have on production, employment, and prices.

**AN INSIDE LOOK** on **page 818** discusses why a slowdown in cargo shipments signals problems in the wider economy.

Based on Lynn Adler, "FedEx Pares 2012 Outlook, Shares Hit 2-Year Low," *Reuters*, September 22, 2011; Hal Weiztman, "FedEx to Cut Costs by $1 Bn," *Financial Times*, March 19, 2009; "FedEx Confirms 1,000 Layoffs, 500 in Memphis," *Memphis Business Journal*, April 3, 2009; Bob Sechler, "FedEx Boosts Outlook," *Wall Street Journal*, September 11, 2009; and David Gaffen, "The FedEx Indicator," *Wall Street Journal*, February 20, 2007.

## Economics in Your Life

### Is an Employer Likely to Cut Your Pay during a Recession?

Suppose that you have worked as a barista for a local coffeehouse for two years. From on-the-job training and experience, you have honed your coffee-making skills and mastered the perfect latte. Then the economy moves into a recession, and sales at the coffeehouse decline. Is the owner of the coffeehouse likely to cut the prices of lattes and other drinks? Suppose the owner asks to meet with you to discuss your wages for next year. Is the owner likely to cut your pay? As you read the chapter, see if you can answer these questions. You can check your answers against those we provide on **page 817** at the end of this chapter.

W e saw in Chapter 21 that the U.S. economy has experienced a long-run upward trend in real GDP. This upward trend has resulted in the standard of living in the United States being much higher today than it was 50 years ago. In the short run, however, real GDP fluctuates around this long-run upward trend because of the business cycle. Fluctuations in GDP lead to fluctuations in employment. These fluctuations in real GDP and employment are the most visible and dramatic part of the business cycle. During recessions, we are more likely to see factories close, small businesses declare bankruptcy, and workers lose their jobs. During expansions, we are more likely to see new businesses open and new jobs created. In addition to these changes in output and employment, the business cycle causes changes in wages and prices. Some firms react to a decline in sales by cutting back on production, but they may also cut the prices they charge and the wages they pay. Other firms respond to a recession by raising prices and workers' wages by less than they otherwise would have.

In this chapter, we expand our story of the business cycle by developing the aggregate demand and aggregate supply model. This model will help us analyze the effects of recessions and expansions on production, employment, and prices.

**24.1 LEARNING** OBJECTIVE

Identify the determinants of aggregate demand and distinguish between a movement along the aggregate demand curve and a shift of the curve.

**Aggregate demand and aggregate supply model** A model that explains short-run fluctuations in real GDP and the price level.

**Aggregate demand (AD) curve** A curve that shows the relationship between the price level and the quantity of real GDP demanded by households, firms, and the government.

**Short-run aggregate supply (SRAS) curve** A curve that shows the relationship in the short run between the price level and the quantity of real GDP supplied by firms.

# Aggregate Demand

To understand what happens during the business cycle, we need an explanation of why real GDP, the unemployment rate, and the inflation rate fluctuate. We have already seen that fluctuations in the unemployment rate are caused mainly by fluctuations in real GDP. In this chapter, we use the **aggregate demand and aggregate supply model** to explain short-run fluctuations in real GDP and the price level. As Figure 24.1 shows, real GDP and the price level in this model are determined in the short run by the intersection of the *aggregate demand curve* and the *aggregate supply curve*. Fluctuations in real GDP and the price level are caused by shifts in the aggregate demand curve or in the aggregate supply curve.

The **aggregate demand (AD) curve** shows the relationship between the price level and the quantity of real GDP demanded by households, firms, and the government. The **short-run aggregate supply (SRAS) curve** shows the relationship in the short run between the price level and the quantity of real GDP supplied by firms. The aggregate demand and short-run aggregate supply curves in Figure 24.1 look similar to the individual market demand and supply curves we studied in Chapter 3. However, because these curves apply to the whole economy, rather than to just a single market, the aggregate demand and aggregate supply model is very different from the model of demand and supply in individual markets. Because we are dealing with the economy as a whole, we need

### Figure 24.1

### Aggregate Demand and Aggregate Supply

In the short run, real GDP and the price level are determined by the intersection of the aggregate demand curve and the short-run aggregate supply curve. In the figure, real GDP is measured on the horizontal axis, and the price level is measured on the vertical axis by the GDP deflator. In this example, the equilibrium real GDP is $14.0 trillion, and the equilibrium price level is 100.

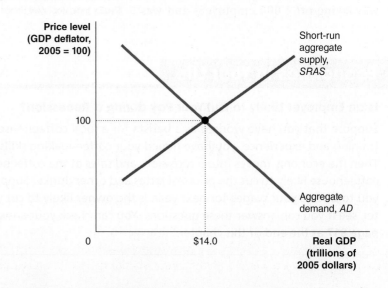

*macroeconomic* explanations of why the aggregate demand curve is downward sloping, why the short-run aggregate supply curve is upward sloping, and why the curves shift. We begin by explaining why the aggregate demand curve is downward sloping.

# Why Is the Aggregate Demand Curve Downward Sloping?

We saw in Chapter 19 that GDP has four components: consumption ($C$), investment ($I$), government purchases ($G$), and net exports ($NX$). If we let $Y$ stand for GDP, we have the following relationship:

$$Y = C + I + G + NX.$$

The aggregate demand curve is downward sloping because a fall in the price level increases the quantity of real GDP demanded. To understand why this is true, we need to look at how changes in the price level affect each component of aggregate demand. We begin with the assumption that government purchases are determined by the policy decisions of lawmakers and are not affected by changes in the price level. We can then consider the effect of changes in the price level on the three other components: consumption, investment, and net exports.

## The Wealth Effect: How a Change in the Price Level Affects Consumption

Current income is the most important variable determining the consumption of households. As income rises, consumption will rise, and as income falls, consumption will fall. But consumption also depends on household wealth. A household's wealth is the difference between the value of its assets and the value of its debts. Consider two households, both with incomes of $80,000 per year. The first household has wealth of $5 million, and the second household has wealth of $50,000. The first household is likely to spend more of its income than the second household. So, as total household wealth rises, consumption will rise. Some household wealth is held in cash or other *nominal assets* that lose value as the price level rises and gain value as the price level falls. For instance, if you have $10,000 in cash, a 10 percent increase in the price level will reduce the purchasing power of that cash by 10 percent. When the price level rises, the *real value* of household wealth declines, and so will consumption, thereby reducing the demand for goods and services. When the price level falls, the real value of household wealth rises, and so will consumption and the demand for goods and services. This effect of the price level on consumption is called the *wealth effect*, and it is one reason the aggregate demand curve is downward sloping.

## The Interest-Rate Effect: How a Change in the Price Level Affects Investment

When prices rise, households and firms need more money to finance buying and selling. Therefore, when the price level rises, households and firms will try to increase the amount of money they hold by withdrawing funds from banks, borrowing from banks, or selling financial assets, such as bonds. These actions tend to drive up the interest rate charged on bank loans and the interest rate on bonds. (In Chapter 26, we analyze in more detail the relationship between money and interest rates.) A higher interest rate raises the cost of borrowing for firms and households. As a result, firms will borrow less to build new factories or to install new machinery and equipment, and households will borrow less to buy new houses. To a smaller extent, consumption will also fall as households borrow less to finance spending on automobiles, furniture, and other durable goods. So, because a higher price level increases the interest rate and reduces investment spending, it also reduces the quantity of goods and services demanded. A lower price level will decrease the interest rate and increase investment spending, thereby increasing the quantity of goods and services demanded. This effect of the price level on investment is known as the *interest-rate effect*, and it is a second reason the aggregate demand curve is downward sloping.

## The International-Trade Effect: How a Change in the Price Level Affects Net Exports

*Net exports* equal spending by foreign households and firms on goods and services produced in the United States minus spending by U.S. households and firms on goods and services produced in other countries. If the price level in the United States rises relative to the price levels in other countries, U.S. exports will become relatively more expensive, and foreign imports will become relatively less expensive. Some consumers in foreign countries will shift from buying U.S. products to buying domestic products, and some U.S. consumers will also shift from buying U.S. products to buying imported products. U.S. exports will fall, and U.S. imports will rise, causing net exports to fall, thereby reducing the quantity of goods and services demanded. A lower price level in the United States relative to other countries has the reverse effect, causing net exports to rise, increasing the quantity of goods and services demanded. This effect of the price level on net exports is known as the *international-trade effect*, and it is a third reason the aggregate demand curve is downward sloping.

## Shifts of the Aggregate Demand Curve versus Movements along It

An important point to remember is that the aggregate demand curve tells us the relationship between the price level and the quantity of real GDP demanded, *holding everything else constant*. If the price level changes but other variables that affect the willingness of households, firms, and the government to spend are unchanged, the economy will move up or down a stationary aggregate demand curve. If any variable other than the price level changes, the aggregate demand curve will shift. For example, if government purchases increase and the price level remains unchanged, the aggregate demand curve will shift to the right at every price level. Or, if firms become pessimistic about the future profitability of investment and cut back spending on factories and machinery, the aggregate demand curve will shift to the left.

## The Variables That Shift the Aggregate Demand Curve

The variables that cause the aggregate demand curve to shift fall into three categories:

- Changes in government policies
- Changes in the expectations of households and firms
- Changes in foreign variables

**Monetary policy** The actions the Federal Reserve takes to manage the money supply and interest rates to pursue macroeconomic policy objectives.

**Changes in Government Policies** As we will discuss further in Chapters 26 and 27, the federal government uses monetary policy and fiscal policy to shift the aggregate demand curve. **Monetary policy** involves actions the Federal Reserve—the nation's central bank—takes to manage the money supply and interest rates and to ensure the flow of funds from lenders to borrowers. The Federal Reserve takes these actions to attain macroeconomic policy objectives, such as high employment, price stability, and high rates of economic growth. For example, by lowering interest rates, the Federal Reserve can lower the cost to firms and households of borrowing. Lowering borrowing costs increases consumption and investment spending, which shifts the aggregate demand curve to the right. Higher interest rates shift the aggregate demand curve to the left. **Fiscal policy** involves changes in federal taxes and purchases that are intended to achieve macroeconomic policy objectives. Because government purchases are one component of aggregate demand, an increase in government purchases shifts the aggregate demand curve to the right, and a decrease in government purchases shifts the aggregate demand curve to the left. An increase in personal income taxes reduces the amount of spendable income available to households. Higher personal income taxes reduce consumption spending and shift the aggregate demand curve to the left. Lower personal income taxes shift the aggregate demand curve to the right. Increases in business taxes reduce the profitability of investment spending and shift the aggregate demand curve to the left. Decreases in business taxes shift the aggregate demand curve to the right.

**Fiscal policy** Changes in federal taxes and purchases that are intended to achieve macroeconomic policy objectives.

**Changes in the Expectations of Households and Firms** If households become more optimistic about their future incomes, they are likely to increase their current

# Don't Let This Happen to You

## Understand Why the Aggregate Demand Curve Is Downward Sloping

The aggregate demand curve and the demand curve for a single product are both downward sloping—but for different reasons. When we draw a demand curve for a single product, such as apples, we know that it will slope downward because as the price of apples rises, apples become more expensive relative to other products—such as oranges—and consumers will buy fewer apples and more of the other products. In other words, consumers substitute other products for apples. When the overall price level rises, the prices of all domestically produced goods and services are rising, so consumers have no other domestic products to which they can switch. The aggregate demand curve slopes downward for the reasons given on pages 795–796: A lower price level raises the real value of household wealth (which increases consumption), lowers interest rates (which increases investment and consumption), and makes U.S. exports less expensive and foreign imports more expensive (which increases net exports).

MyEconLab

**Your Turn:** Test your understanding by doing related problem 1.6 on page 820 at the end of this chapter.

consumption. This increased consumption will shift the aggregate demand curve to the right. If households become more pessimistic about their future incomes, the aggregate demand curve will shift to the left. Similarly, if firms become more optimistic about the future profitability of investment spending, the aggregate demand curve will shift to the right. If firms become more pessimistic, the aggregate demand curve will shift to the left.

**Changes in Foreign Variables** If firms and households in other countries buy fewer U.S. goods or if firms and households in the United States buy more foreign goods, net exports will fall, and the aggregate demand curve will shift to the left. As we saw in Chapter 19, when real GDP increases, so does the income available for consumers to spend. If real GDP in the United States increases faster than real GDP in other countries, U.S. imports will increase faster than U.S. exports, and net exports will fall. Net exports will also fall if the *exchange rate* between the dollar and foreign currencies rises because the price in foreign currency of U.S. products sold in other countries will rise, and the dollar price of foreign products sold in the United States will fall. For example, if the current exchange rate between the dollar and the euro is $1 = €1 then a $500 iPad exported from the United States to France will cost €500 in France, and a €50 bottle of French wine will cost $50 in the United States. But if the exchange rate rises to $1 = €1.50, the iPad's price will rise to €750 in France, causing its sales to decline, and the price of the French wine will fall to $33.33 per bottle in the United States, causing its sales to increase. U.S. exports will fall, U.S. imports will rise, and the aggregate demand curve will shift to the left.

An increase in net exports at every price level will shift the aggregate demand curve to the right. Net exports will increase if real GDP grows more slowly in the United States than in other countries or if the value of the dollar falls against other currencies. A change in net exports that results from a change in the price level in the United States will result in a movement along the aggregate demand curve, *not* a shift of the aggregate demand curve.

# Solved Problem 24.1

## Movements along the Aggregate Demand Curve versus Shifts of the Aggregate Demand Curve

Suppose the current price level is 110, and the current level of real GDP is $14.2 trillion. Illustrate each of the following situations on a graph.

a. The price level rises to 115, while all other variables remain constant.

b. Firms become pessimistic and reduce their investment. Assume that the price level remains constant.

## Solving the Problem

**Step 1:** **Review the chapter material.** This problem is about understanding the difference between movements along an aggregate demand curve and shifts of an aggregate demand curve, so you may want to review the section "Shifts of the Aggregate Demand Curve versus Movements along It," on page 796.

**Step 2:** **To answer part a. draw a graph that shows a movement along the aggregate demand curve.** Because there will be a movement along the aggregate demand curve but no shift of the aggregate demand curve, your graph should look like this:

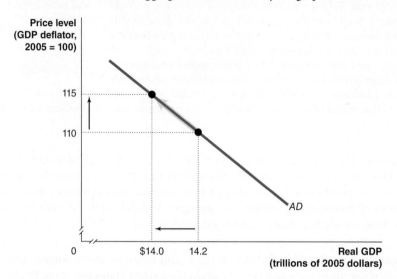

We don't have enough information to be certain what the new level of real GDP demanded will be. We only know that it will be less than the initial level of $14.2 trillion; the graph shows the value as $14.0 trillion.

**Step 3:** **To answer part b. draw a graph that shows a shift of the aggregate demand curve.** We know that the aggregate demand curve will shift to the left, but we don't have enough information to know how far to the left it will shift. Let's assume that the shift is $300 billion (or $0.3 trillion). In that case, your graph should look like this:

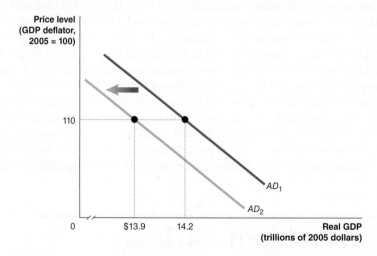

The graph shows a parallel shift in the aggregate demand curve so that at every price level, the quantity of real GDP demanded declines by $300 billion. For example, at a price level of 110, the quantity of real GDP demanded declines from $14.2 trillion to $13.9 trillion.

MyEconLab    **Your Turn:** For more practice, do related problem 1.7 on page 821 at the end of this chapter.

Table 24.1 summarizes the most important variables that cause the aggregate demand curve to shift. The table shows the shift in the aggregate demand curve that results from an increase in each of the variables. A *decrease* in these variables would cause the aggregate demand curve to shift in the opposite direction.

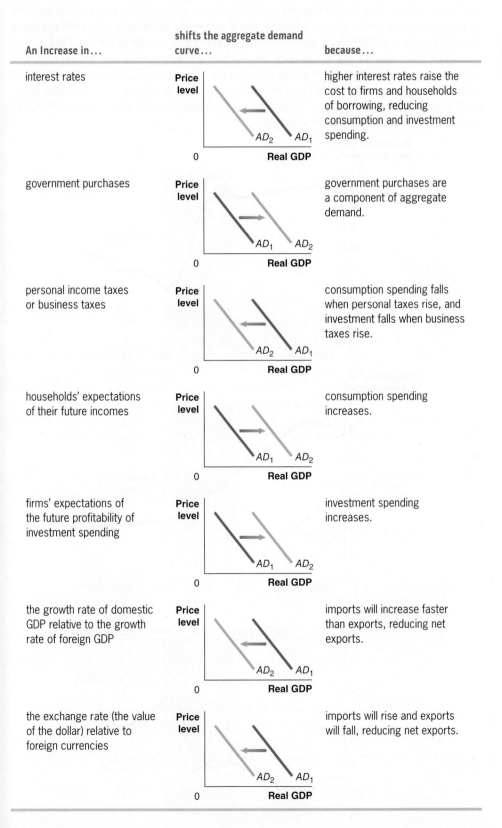

| An Increase in... | shifts the aggregate demand curve... | because... |
|---|---|---|
| interest rates | | higher interest rates raise the cost to firms and households of borrowing, reducing consumption and investment spending. |
| government purchases | | government purchases are a component of aggregate demand. |
| personal income taxes or business taxes | | consumption spending falls when personal taxes rise, and investment falls when business taxes rise. |
| households' expectations of their future incomes | | consumption spending increases. |
| firms' expectations of the future profitability of investment spending | | investment spending increases. |
| the growth rate of domestic GDP relative to the growth rate of foreign GDP | | imports will increase faster than exports, reducing net exports. |
| the exchange rate (the value of the dollar) relative to foreign currencies | | imports will rise and exports will fall, reducing net exports. |

**Table 24.1**

**Variables That Shift the Aggregate Demand Curve**

<table>
<tr><td>Making<br>the<br>Connection</td><td>**Which Components of Aggregate<br>Demand Changed the Most during<br>the 2007–2009 Recession?**</td></tr>
</table>

The recession of 2007–2009 was the longest and most severe since the Great Depression of the 1930s. We can gain some insight into the reasons for the length and severity of the 2007–2009 recession by looking at changes over time in the components of aggregate demand. In the graphs below, we show changes in three components of aggregate demand that showed the largest movements between the first quarter of 2005 and the second quarter of 2011: consumption, spending on residential construction, and net exports. The red bars represent the 2007–2009 recession. We know that potential GDP, or the level of GDP when all firms are producing at capacity, grows over time. So, economists are often interested in measuring changes in the components of aggregate demand *relative to potential GDP*, which is what we have done in these graphs.

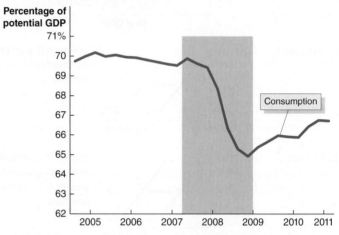

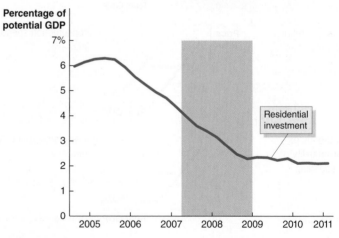

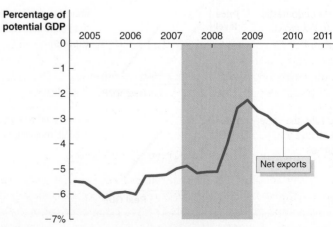

The figure allows us to note a number of facts about the 2007–2009 recession:

- In the two years before the beginning of the recession, spending on residential construction had already declined significantly relative to potential GDP.

- For more than two years following the end of the recession, spending on residential construction did not increase relative to potential GDP.

- Consumption, which usually remains relatively stable during a recession, declined significantly relative to potential GDP during the recession and remained low for more than two years after the recession had ended.

- Net exports increased just before, during, and after the recession. (Because net exports were negative throughout this period, it increased by becoming a smaller negative number.)

Although not shown in the graphs, business fixed investment and changes in business inventories—the nonresidential construction components of investment spending—actually rose relative to potential GDP during the recession. Government purchases remained fairly stable relative to potential GDP throughout the recession, before declining in late 2010 and the first half of 2011. Federal government purchases surged during the recession, but state and local governments reduced their spending as falling household incomes and falling business profits reduced state and local tax revenues.

We can briefly account for these facts. The housing sector underwent a boom from 2002 to 2005, with rapid increases in both housing prices and spending on new housing. The housing boom, though, turned into a housing bust beginning in 2006, which explains the sharp decline in spending on residential construction. The continued low levels of spending on residential construction helps explain why the recession was the longest since the Great Depression and why the economic expansion that began in June 2009 was relatively weak. As one newspaper article noted in late 2011: "Americans aren't spending because their home values are declining and employment prospects are dimming, and housing and employment is struggling because Americans won't spend."

High levels of unemployment reduced household incomes and led to declines in consumption spending. In addition, many households increased their saving and paid off debts, further reducing consumption spending. The continuing low levels of consumption spending also contributed to the severity of the recession and the weakness of the following expansion. Finally, efforts by the Federal Reserve to reduce interest rates helped to lower the value of the U.S. dollar, thereby reducing the prices of U.S. exports and increasing the prices of foreign imports. The result was an increase in net exports. (We will discuss further the effect of Federal Reserve policy on net exports in Chapters 26 and 29.)

Based on U.S. Bureau of Economic Analysis; Congressional Budget Office; and S. Mitra Kalita, "Housing's Job Engine Falters," *Wall Street Journal*, October 5, 2011.

**Your Turn:** Test your understanding by doing related problem 1.8 on page 821 at the end of this chapter.

MyEconLab

# Aggregate Supply

**24.2 LEARNING** OBJECTIVE

Identify the determinants of aggregate supply and distinguish between a movement along the short-run aggregate supply curve and a shift of the curve.

The aggregate demand curve is one component of the aggregate demand and aggregate supply model. Now we turn to aggregate supply, which shows the effect of changes in the price level on the quantity of goods and services that firms are willing and able to supply. Because the effect of changes in the price level on aggregate supply is very different in the short run from what it is in the long run, we use two aggregate supply curves: one for the short run and one for the long run. We start by considering the *long-run aggregate supply curve*.

## The Long-Run Aggregate Supply Curve

In Chapter 22, we saw that in the long run, the level of real GDP is determined by the number of workers, the *capital stock*—including factories, office buildings, and machinery and equipment—and the available technology. Because changes in the price level

### Figure 24.2

#### The Long-Run Aggregate Supply Curve

Changes in the price level do not affect the level of aggregate supply in the long run. Therefore, the long-run aggregate supply (*LRAS*) curve is a vertical line at the potential level of real GDP. For instance, the price level was 113 in 2011, and potential real GDP was $14.3 trillion. If the price level had been 123, or if it had been 103, long-run aggregate supply would still have been a constant $14.3 trillion. Each year, the long-run aggregate supply curve shifts to the right, as the number of workers in the economy increases, more machinery and equipment are accumulated, and technological change occurs.

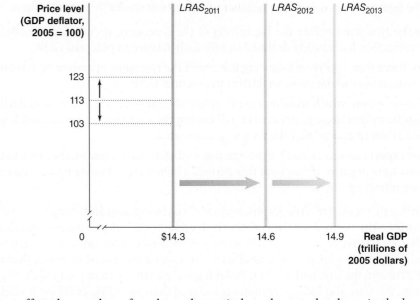

**Long-run aggregate supply (*LRAS*) curve** A curve that shows the relationship in the long run between the price level and the quantity of real GDP supplied.

do not affect the number of workers, the capital stock, or technology, *in the long run, changes in the price level do not affect the level of real GDP.* Remember that the level of real GDP in the long run is called *potential GDP,* or *full-employment GDP.* At potential GDP, firms will operate at their normal level of capacity, and everyone who wants a job will have one, except the structurally and frictionally unemployed. There is no reason for this normal level of capacity to change just because the price level has changed. The **long-run aggregate supply (*LRAS*) curve** shows the relationship in the long run between the price level and the quantity of real GDP supplied. As Figure 24.2 shows, in 2011, the price level was 113, and potential real GDP was $14.3 trillion. If the price level had been 123, or if it had been 103, long-run aggregate supply would still have been a constant $14.3 trillion. Therefore, the *LRAS* curve is a vertical line.

Figure 24.2 also shows that the long-run aggregate supply curve shifts to the right each year. This shift occurs because potential real GDP increases each year, as the number of workers in the economy increases, the economy accumulates more machinery and equipment, and technological change occurs. Figure 24.2 shows potential real GDP increasing from $14.3 trillion in 2011 to $14.6 trillion in 2012 and to $14.9 trillion in 2013.

## The Short-Run Aggregate Supply Curve

While the *LRAS* curve is vertical, the *SRAS* curve is upward sloping. The *SRAS* curve is upward sloping because, over the short run, as the price level increases, the quantity of goods and services firms are willing to supply will increase. The main reason firms behave this way is that, *as prices of final goods and services rise, prices of inputs—such as the wages of workers or the price of natural resources—rise more slowly.* Profits rise when the prices of the goods and services firms sell rise more rapidly than the prices they pay for inputs. Therefore, a higher price level leads to higher profits and increases the willingness of firms to supply more goods and services. A secondary reason the *SRAS* curve slopes upward is that, as the price level rises or falls, some firms are slow to adjust their prices. A firm that is slow to raise its prices when the price level is increasing may find its sales increasing and, therefore, will increase production. A firm that is slow to reduce its prices when the price level is decreasing may find its sales falling and, therefore, will decrease production.

Why do some firms adjust prices more slowly than others, and why might the wages of workers and the prices of other inputs change more slowly than the prices of final goods and services? Most economists believe the explanation is that *some firms and workers fail to accurately predict changes in the price level.* If firms and workers could predict the future price level exactly, the short-run aggregate supply curve would be the same as the long-run aggregate supply curve.

But how does the failure of workers and firms to predict the price level accurately result in an upward-sloping *SRAS* curve? Economists are not in complete agreement on this point, but we can briefly discuss the three most common explanations:

1. Contracts make some wages and prices "sticky."
2. Firms are often slow to adjust wages.
3. Menu costs make some prices sticky.

**Contracts Make Some Wages and Prices "Sticky"** Prices or wages are said to be "sticky" when they do not respond quickly to changes in demand or supply. Contracts can make wages or prices sticky. For example, suppose United Parcel Service (UPS) negotiates a three-year contract with the Independent Pilots Association, the union for the pilots who fly the company's cargo planes, during a time when the economy is in recession and the volume of packages being shipped is falling. Suppose that after the union signs the contract, the economy begins to expand rapidly, and the volume of packages shipped increases, so that UPS can raise the rates it charges. UPS will find that shipping more packages will be profitable because the prices it charges are rising, while the wages it pays its pilots are fixed by contract. Or a steel mill might have signed a multiyear contract to buy coal, which is used in making steel, at a time when the demand for steel was stagnant. If steel demand and steel prices begin to rise rapidly, producing additional steel will be profitable because coal prices will remain fixed by contract. In both of these cases, rising prices lead to higher output. If these examples are representative of enough firms in the economy, a rising price level should lead to a greater quantity of goods and services supplied. In other words, the short-run aggregate supply curve will be upward sloping.

Notice, though, that if the pilots at UPS or the managers of the coal companies had accurately predicted what would happen to prices, this prediction would have been reflected in the contracts, and UPS and the steel mill would not have earned greater profits when prices rose. In that case, rising prices would not have led to higher output.

**Firms Are Often Slow to Adjust Wages** We just noted that the wages of many union workers remain fixed by contract for several years. Many nonunion workers also have their wages or salaries adjusted only once a year. For instance, suppose you accept a job at a management consulting firm in June, at a salary of $45,000 per year. The firm probably will not adjust your salary until the following June, even if the prices it can charge for its services later in the year are higher or lower than the firm had expected them to be when they hired you. If firms are slow to adjust wages, a rise in the price level will increase the profitability of hiring more workers and producing more output. A fall in the price level will decrease the profitability of hiring more workers and producing more output. Once again, we have an explanation for why the short-run aggregate supply curve slopes upward.

It is worth noting that firms are often slower to *cut* wages than to increase them. Cutting wages can have a negative effect on the morale and productivity of workers and can also cause some of a firm's best workers to quit and look for jobs elsewhere.

**Menu Costs Make Some Prices Sticky** Firms base their prices today partly on what they expect future prices to be. For instance, before it prints menus, a restaurant has to decide the prices it will charge for meals. Many firms print catalogs that list the prices of their products. If demand for their products is higher or lower than the firms had expected, they may want to charge prices that are different from the ones printed in their menus or catalogs. Changing prices would be costly, however, because it would involve printing new menus or catalogs. The costs to firms of changing prices are called **menu costs**. To see why menu costs can lead to an upward-sloping short-run aggregate supply curve, consider the effect of an unexpected increase in the price level. In this case, firms will want to increase the prices they charge. Some firms, however, may not be willing to increase prices because of menu costs. Because of their relatively low prices, these firms will find their sales increasing, which will cause them to increase output. Once again, we have an explanation for a higher price level leading to a larger quantity of goods and services supplied.

**Menu costs** The costs to firms of changing prices.

## Shifts of the Short-Run Aggregate Supply Curve versus Movements along It

It is important to remember the difference between a shift in a curve and a movement along a curve. The short-run aggregate supply curve tells us the short-run relationship between the price level and the quantity of goods and services firms are willing to supply, *holding constant all other variables that affect the willingness of firms to supply goods and services*. If the price level changes but other variables are unchanged, the economy will move up or down a stationary aggregate supply curve. If any variable other than the price level changes, the aggregate supply curve will shift.

## Variables That Shift the Short-Run Aggregate Supply Curve

We now briefly discuss the five most important variables that cause the short-run aggregate supply curve to shift.

**Increases in the Labor Force and in the Capital Stock** A firm will supply more output at every price if it has more workers and more physical capital. The same is true of the economy as a whole. So, as the labor force and the capital stock grow, firms will supply more output at every price level, and the short-run aggregate supply curve will shift to the right. In Japan, the population is aging, and the labor force is decreasing. Holding other variables constant, this decrease in the labor force causes the short-run aggregate supply curve in Japan to shift to the left.

**Technological Change** As positive technological change takes place, the productivity of workers and machinery increases, which means firms can produce more goods and services with the same amount of labor and machinery. This increase in productivity reduces the firms' costs of production and, therefore, allows them to produce more output at every price level. As a result, the short-run aggregate supply curve shifts to the right.

**Expected Changes in the Future Price Level** If workers and firms believe that the price level is going to increase by 3 percent during the next year, they will try to adjust their wages and prices accordingly. For instance, if a labor union believes there will be 3 percent inflation next year, it knows that wages must rise 3 percent to preserve the purchasing power of those wages. Similar adjustments by other workers and firms will result in costs increasing throughout the economy by 3 percent. The result, shown in Figure 24.3, is that the short-run aggregate supply curve will shift to the left, so that any

### Figure 24.3

**How Expectations of the Future Price Level Affect the Short-Run Aggregate Supply Curve**

The *SRAS* curve shifts to reflect worker and firm expectations of future prices.

1. If workers and firms expect that the price level will rise by 3 percent, from 100 to 103, they will adjust their wages and prices by that amount.

2. Holding constant all other variables that affect aggregate supply, the short-run aggregate supply curve will shift to the left.

If workers and firms expect that the price level will be lower in the future, the short-run aggregate supply curve will shift to the right.

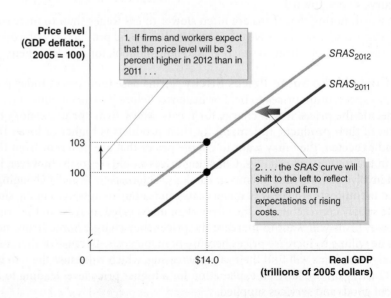

level of real GDP is now associated with a price level that is 3 percent higher. In general, *if workers and firms expect the price level to increase by a certain percentage, the SRAS curve will shift by an equivalent amount*, holding constant all other variables that affect the *SRAS* curve.

### Adjustments of Workers and Firms to Errors in Past Expectations about the Price Level

Workers and firms sometimes make incorrect predictions about the price level. As time passes, they will attempt to compensate for these errors. Suppose, for example, that the Independent Pilots Association signs a contract with UPS that provides for only small wage increases because the company and the union both expect only small increases in the price level. If increases in the price level turn out to be unexpectedly large, the union will take this into account when negotiating the next contract. The higher wages UPS pilots receive under the new contract will increase UPS's costs and result in UPS needing to receive higher prices to produce the same level of output. If workers and firms across the economy are adjusting to the price level being higher than expected, the *SRAS* curve will shift to the left. If they are adjusting to the price level being lower than expected, the *SRAS* curve will shift to the right.

### Unexpected Changes in the Price of an Important Natural Resource

An unexpected event that causes the short-run aggregate supply curve to shift is known as a **supply shock**. Supply shocks are often caused by unexpected increases or decreases in the prices of important natural resources that can cause firms' costs to be different from what they had expected. Oil prices can be particularly volatile. Some firms use oil in the production process. Other firms use products, such as plastics, that are made from oil. If oil prices rise unexpectedly, the costs of production will rise for these firms. Some utilities also burn oil to generate electricity, so electricity prices will rise. Rising oil prices lead to rising gasoline prices, which raise transportation costs for many firms. Because firms face rising costs, they will supply the same level of output only if they receive higher prices, and the short-run aggregate supply curve will shift to the left.

**Supply shock** An unexpected event that causes the short-run aggregate supply curve to shift.

Because the U.S. economy has experienced at least some inflation every year since the 1930s, workers and firms always expect next year's price level to be higher than this year's price level. Holding everything else constant, expectations of a higher price level will cause the *SRAS* curve to shift to the left. But everything else is not constant because every year, the U.S. labor force and the U.S. capital stock expand, and changes in technology occur, which cause the *SRAS* curve to shift to the right. Whether in any particular year the *SRAS* curve shifts to the left or to the right depends on how large an impact these variables have during that year.

Table 24.2 summarizes the most important variables that cause the *SRAS* curve to shift. The table shows the shift in the *SRAS* curve that results from an *increase* in each of the variables. A *decrease* in these variables would cause the *SRAS* curve to shift in the opposite direction.

## Macroeconomic Equilibrium in the Long Run and the Short Run

**24.3 LEARNING** OBJECTIVE

Use the aggregate demand and aggregate supply model to illustrate the difference between short-run and long-run macroeconomic equilibrium.

Now that we have discussed the components of the aggregate demand and aggregate supply model, we can use it to analyze changes in real GDP and the price level. In Figure 24.4, we bring the aggregate demand curve, the short-run aggregate supply curve, and the long-run aggregate supply curve together in one graph, to show the *long-run macroeconomic equilibrium* for the economy. In the figure, equilibrium occurs at real GDP of $14.0 trillion and a price level of 100. Notice that in long-run equilibrium, the short-run aggregate supply curve and the aggregate demand curve intersect at a point on the long-run aggregate supply curve. Because equilibrium occurs at a point along the long-run aggregate supply curve, we know the economy is at potential real GDP: Firms will be

| Table 24.2 | An increase in . . . | shifts the short-run aggregate supply curve . . . | because . . . |
|---|---|---|---|
| **Variables That Shift the Short-Run Aggregate Supply Curve** | the labor force or the capital stock | 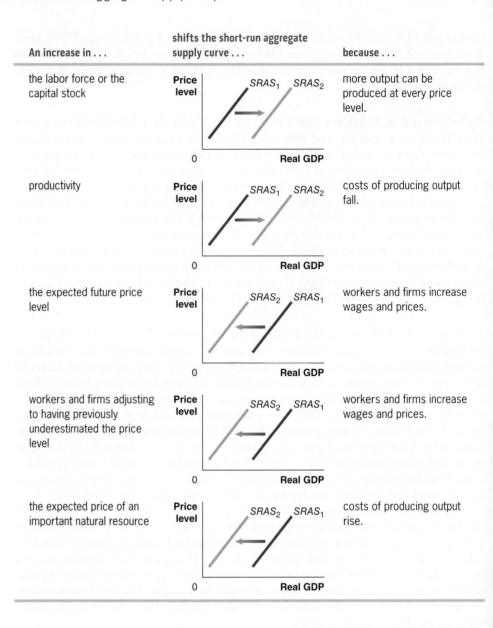 | more output can be produced at every price level. |
| | productivity | | costs of producing output fall. |
| | the expected future price level | | workers and firms increase wages and prices. |
| | workers and firms adjusting to having previously underestimated the price level | | workers and firms increase wages and prices. |
| | the expected price of an important natural resource | | costs of producing output rise. |

---

| Figure 24.4 | |
|---|---|

### Long-Run Macroeconomic Equilibrium

In long-run macroeconomic equilibrium, the *AD* and *SRAS* curves intersect at a point on the *LRAS* curve. In this case, equilibrium occurs at real GDP of $14.0 trillion and a price level of 100.

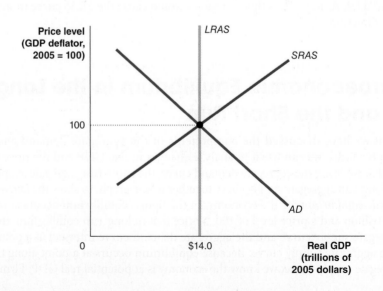

operating at their normal level of capacity, and everyone who wants a job will have one, except the structurally and frictionally unemployed. We know, however, that the economy is often not in long-run macroeconomic equilibrium. In the following section, we discuss the economic forces that can push the economy away from long-run equilibrium.

## Recessions, Expansions, and Supply Shocks

Because the full analysis of the aggregate demand and aggregate supply model can be complicated, we begin with a simplified case, using two assumptions:

1. The economy has not been experiencing any inflation. The price level is currently 100, and workers and firms expect it to remain at 100 in the future.
2. The economy is not experiencing any long-run growth. Potential real GDP is $14.0 trillion and will remain at that level in the future.

These assumptions are simplifications because in reality, the U.S. economy has experienced at least some inflation every year since the 1930s, and the potential real GDP also increases every year. However, the assumptions allow us to understand more easily the key ideas of the aggregate demand and aggregate supply model. In this section, we examine the short-run and long-run effects of recessions, expansions, and supply shocks.

### *Recession*

### The Short-Run Effect of a Decline in Aggregate Demand
Suppose that rising interest rates cause firms to reduce spending on factories and equipment and cause households to reduce spending on new homes. The decline in investment that results will shift the aggregate demand curve to the left, from $AD_1$ to $AD_2$, as shown in Figure 24.5. The economy moves from point $A$ to a new *short-run macroeconomic equilibrium*, where the $AD_2$ curve intersects the $SRAS_1$ curve at point $B$. In the new short-run equilibrium, real GDP has declined from $14.0 trillion to $13.8 trillion and is below its potential level. This lower level of GDP will result in declining profitability for many firms and layoffs for some workers: the economy will be in recession.

### Adjustment Back to Potential GDP in the Long Run
We know that a recession will eventually end because there are forces at work that push the economy back to potential GDP in the long run. Figure 24.5 shows how the economy moves from recession back to potential GDP. The shift from $AD_1$ to $AD_2$ initially leads to a short-run equilibrium, with the price level having fallen from 100 to 98 (point $B$). Workers and firms will

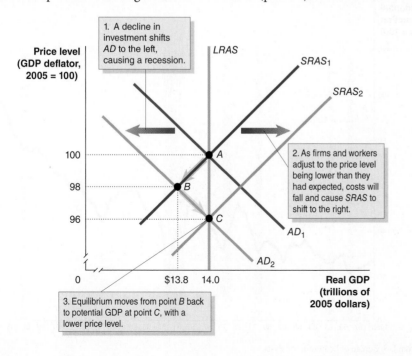

**Figure 24.5**

**The Short-Run and Long-Run Effects of a Decrease in Aggregate Demand**

In the short run, a decrease in aggregate demand causes a recession. In the long run, it causes only a decrease in the price level. ·

begin to adjust to the price level being lower than they had expected it to be. Workers will be willing to accept lower wages—because each dollar of wages is able to buy more goods and services—and firms will be willing to accept lower prices. In addition, the unemployment resulting from the recession will make workers more willing to accept lower wages, and the decline in demand will make firms more willing to accept lower prices. As a result, the *SRAS* curve will shift to the right, from $SRAS_1$ to $SRAS_2$. At this point, the economy will be back in long-run equilibrium (point *C*). The shift from $SRAS_1$ to $SRAS_2$ will not happen instantly. It may take the economy several years to return to potential GDP. The important conclusion is that a decline in aggregate demand causes a recession in the short run, but in the long run it causes only a decline in the price level.

Economists refer to the process of adjustment back to potential GDP just described as an *automatic mechanism* because it occurs without any actions by the government. An alternative to waiting for the automatic mechanism to end a recession is for the government to use monetary and fiscal policy to shift the *AD* curve to the right and restore potential GDP more quickly. We will discuss monetary and fiscal policy in Chapters 26 and 27. Economists debate whether it is better to wait for the automatic mechanism to end recessions or whether it is better to use monetary and fiscal policy.

## Making the Connection | Does It Matter What Causes a Decline in Aggregate Demand?

We have seen that GDP has four components and that a decrease in any of the four components can cause the aggregate demand curve to shift to the left, bringing on a recession. In practice, though, most recessions in the United States since World War II have begun with a decline in residential construction. Edward Leamer of the University of California, Los Angeles has gone so far as to argue that "housing *is* the business cycle," meaning that declines in residential construction are the most important reason for the declines in aggregate demand that lead to recessions. The shaded periods in the graph below represent recessions. The graph shows that spending on residential construction has declined prior to every recession since 1955.

The figure shows again a fact that we noted earlier in the chapter: The decline in residential construction during the 2007–2009

*The collapse in spending on housing added to the severity of the 2007–2009 recession.*

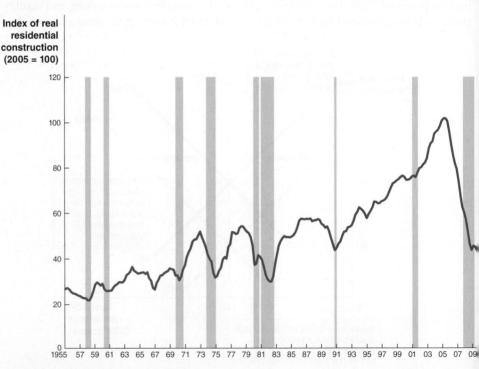

Index of real residential construction (2005 = 100)

Data from U.S. Bureau of Economic Analysis.

recession was particularly severe. Spending on residential construction declined by almost 60 percent from the fourth quarter of 2005 to the second quarter of 2010. Largely because of these problems in the housing sector, the decline in real GDP during the recession of 2007–2009 was larger than during any other recession since the Great Depression of the 1930s.

What causes declines in spending on residential construction, and why was the decline that preceded the 2007–2009 recession so severe? As we discussed in Chapter 21, late in a business cycle expansion, the inflation rate and interest rates start to increase. As we will discuss in Chapter 26, higher interest rates often result from monetary policy actions as the Federal Reserve tries to slow down the economy and reduce the rate of inflation. Higher interest rates reduce consumer demand for new houses by increasing the cost of loans.

But the collapse in residential construction prior to and during the recession of 2007–2009 was due more to the deflating of the "housing bubble" of 2002–2005 and to the financial crisis that began in 2007 than to higher interest rates. We will discuss both the housing bubble and the financial crisis later in this chapter. At this point, we can note that research by Carmen M. Reinhart of the University of Maryland and Kenneth S. Rogoff of Harvard University shows that declines in aggregate demand that result from financial crises tend to be larger and more long lasting than declines due to other factors. So, the experience of 2007–2009 indicates that, in fact, the source of the decline in aggregate demand can be important in determining the severity of a recession.

Based on Edward E. Leamer, "Housing Is the Business Cycle," in *Housing, Housing Finance, and Monetay Policy*, Federal Reserve Bank of Kansas City, August 2007; and Carmen M. Reinhart and Kenneth S. Rogoff, "The Aftermath of Financial Crises," *American Economic Review*, Vol. 99, No. 2, May 2009, pp. 466–472.

**Your Turn:** Test your understanding by doing related problem 3.6 on page 822 at the end of this chapter.

MyEconLab

*Expansion*

### The Short-Run Effect of an Increase in Aggregate Demand

Suppose that instead of becoming pessimistic, many firms become optimistic about the future profitability of new investment, as happened during the information technology and telecommunications booms of the late 1990s. The resulting increase in investment will shift the *AD* curve to the right, as shown in Figure 24.6. Equilibrium moves from point *A* to point *B*. Real GDP rises from $14.0 trillion to $14.3 trillion, and the price level rises from 100 to 103. The economy will be above potential real GDP: Firms are operating

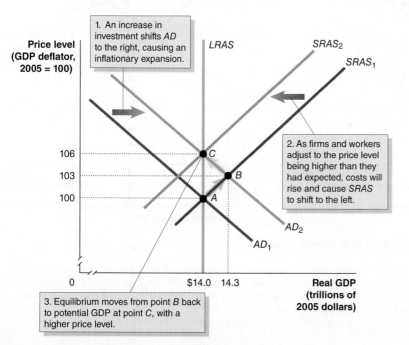

1. An increase in investment shifts *AD* to the right, causing an inflationary expansion.

2. As firms and workers adjust to the price level being higher than they had expected, costs will rise and cause *SRAS* to shift to the left.

3. Equilibrium moves from point *B* back to potential GDP at point *C*, with a higher price level.

**Figure 24.6**

**The Short-Run and Long-Run Effects of an Increase in Aggregate Demand**

In the short run, an increase in aggregate demand causes an increase in real GDP. In the long run, it causes only an increase in the price level.

beyond their normal level of capacity, and some workers who would ordinarily be structurally or frictionally unemployed or who would not be in the labor force are employed.

**Adjustment Back to Potential GDP in the Long Run** Just as an automatic mechanism brings the economy back to potential GDP from a recession, an automatic mechanism brings the economy back from a short-run equilibrium beyond potential GDP. Figure 24.6 illustrates this mechanism. The shift from $AD_1$ to $AD_2$ initially leads to a short-run equilibrium, with the price level rising from 100 to 103 (point $B$). Workers and firms will begin to adjust to the price level being higher than they had expected. Workers will push for higher wages—because each dollar of wages is able to buy fewer goods and services—and firms will charge higher prices. In addition, the low levels of unemployment resulting from the expansion will make it easier for workers to negotiate for higher wages, and the increase in demand will make it easier for firms to receive higher prices. As a result, the *SRAS* curve will shift to the left, from $SRAS_1$ to $SRAS_2$. At this point, the economy will be back in long-run equilibrium. Once again, the shift from $SRAS_1$ to $SRAS_2$ will not happen instantly. The process of returning to potential GDP may stretch out for more than a year.

*Supply Shock*

**The Short-Run Effect of a Supply Shock** Suppose oil prices increase substantially. This supply shock will increase many firms' costs and cause the *SRAS* curve to shift to the left, as shown in panel (a) of Figure 24.7. Notice that the price level is higher in the new short-run equilibrium (102 rather than 100), but real GDP is lower ($13.7 trillion rather than $14 trillion). This unpleasant combination of inflation and recession is called **stagflation**.

**Stagflation** A combination of inflation and recession, usually resulting from a supply shock.

**Adjustment Back to Potential GDP in the Long Run** The recession caused by a supply shock increases unemployment and reduces output. This eventually results in workers being willing to accept lower wages and firms being willing to accept lower

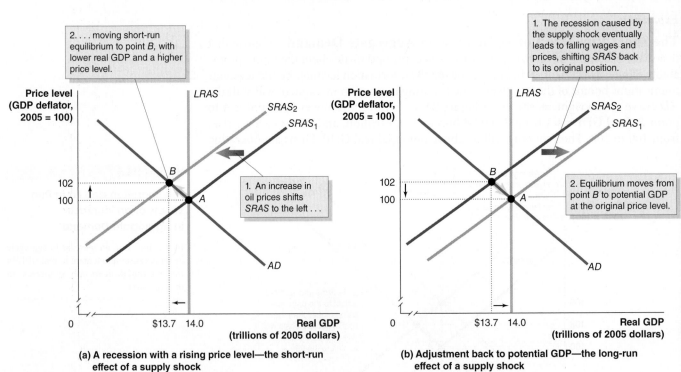

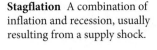

**(a) A recession with a rising price level—the short-run effect of a supply shock**

**(b) Adjustment back to potential GDP—the long-run effect of a supply shock**

**Figure 24.7** The Short-Run and Long-Run Effects of a Supply Shock

Panel (a) shows that a supply shock, such as a large increase in oil prices, will cause a recession and a higher price level in the short run. The recession caused by the supply shock increases unemployment and reduces output. In panel (b), rising unemployment and falling output result in workers being willing to accept lower wages and firms being willing to accept lower prices. The short-run aggregate supply curve shifts from $SRAS_2$ to $SRAS_1$. Equilibrium moves from point $B$ back to potential GDP and the original price level at point $A$.

prices. In panel (b) of Figure 24.7, the short-run aggregate supply curve shifts from $SRAS_2$ to $SRAS_1$, moving the economy from point $B$ back to point $A$. The economy is back to potential GDP at the original price level. It may take several years for this process to be completed. An alternative would be to use monetary and fiscal policy to shift the aggregate demand to the right. Using policy in this way would bring the economy back to potential GDP more quickly but would result in a permanently higher price level.

| Making the Connection | How Long Does It Take to Return to Potential GDP? Economic Forecasts Following the Recession of 2007-2009 |
|---|---|

Making accurate macroeconomic forecasts is difficult. As we have seen, many factors can cause aggregate demand or aggregate supply to shift. Because it is challenging to predict how much aggregate demand and aggregate supply will shift, economists often have difficulty predicting the beginning and end of a recession. The Federal Reserve, foreign central banks, other government agencies, large banks, forecasting firms, and academic economists use a variety of forecasting models to predict changes in GDP. Most forecasting models consist of equations that represent the macroeconomic relationships—such as the relationship between disposable income and consumption spending—that underlie the aggregate demand and aggregate supply model. After economists have statistically estimated the equations using economic data, they can use the models to forecast values for GDP and the price level.

*Alan Krueger, the chair of the Council of Economic Advisers in the Obama administration, provided an estimate of how long the economy would take to return to potential GDP.*

Most economists agree that an automatic mechanism brings the economy back to potential GDP in the long run. But how long is the long run? When the recession of 2007–2009 ended in June 2009, the economy was far from potential GDP. Even two years later, in mid-2011, real GDP remained more than 7 percent below potential GDP. How long would it take for the economy to finally return to potential GDP? The figure below shows the Congressional Budget Office's estimates of potential GDP along with three forecasts of real GDP made in 2011 by the following:

- Economists on the president's staff at the White House
- Officials at the Federal Reserve
- Economists at the Congressional Budget Office (CBO)

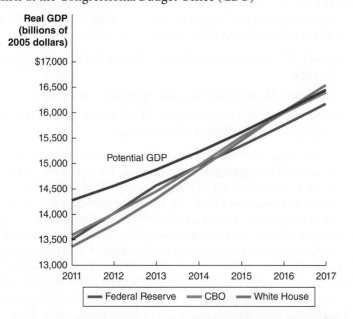

The forecasts of the White House and the CBO agreed that real GDP would not return to potential GDP until 2016. The projections of the Federal Reserve were even more pessimistic, with real GDP remaining below potential GDP in 2017. These forecasts indicate how severe the 2007–2009 recession was in that real GDP was not expected to return to potential GDP until nearly seven years after the end of the recession. Prior to the

2007–2009 recession, the recession of 1981–1982 had been the most severe since the Great Depression. Yet it took less than three years after the end of that recession for real GDP to return to potential GDP.

These macroeconomic forecasts played an important role in the policy debates of 2011 and 2012. As we will discuss in Chapters 26 and 27, economists and policymakers disagreed about why the U.S. economy would take so long to return to potential GDP and about what measures the federal government might take to shorten the time.

Note: The Federal Reserve's forecast uses averages of the forecasts of the individual members of the Federal Open Market Committee.

Based on Board of Governors of the Federal Reserve System, "Economic Projections of Federal Reserve Board Members and Federal Reserve Bank Presidents, April 2011," April 27, 2011; Congressional Budget Office, "Data Underlying Selected Economic Figures, Real Gross Domestic Product, 1980–2021," January 27, 2011; and Office of Management and Budget, "Budget of the U.S. Government, Fiscal Year 2012, Mid-Session Review," September 1, 2011.

MyEconLab | **Your Turn:** Test your understanding by doing related problem 3.9 on page 823 at the end of this chapter.

**24.4 LEARNING** OBJECTIVE

Use the dynamic aggregate demand and aggregate supply model to analyze macroeconomic conditions.

# A Dynamic Aggregate Demand and Aggregate Supply Model*

The basic aggregate demand and aggregate supply model used so far in this chapter provides important insights into how short-run macroeconomic equilibrium is determined. Unfortunately, the model also provides some misleading results. For instance, it incorrectly predicts that a recession caused by the aggregate demand curve shifting to the left will cause the price level to fall, which has not happened for an entire year since the 1930s. The difficulty with the basic model arises from the following two assumptions we made: (1) The economy does not experience continuing inflation, and (2) the economy does not experience long-run growth. We can develop a more useful aggregate demand and aggregate supply model by dropping these assumptions. The result will be a model that takes into account that the economy is not *static*, with an unchanging level of potential real GDP and no continuing inflation, but *dynamic*, with potential real GDP that grows over time and inflation that continues every year. We can create a *dynamic aggregate demand and aggregate supply model* by making changes to the basic model that incorporate the following important macroeconomic facts:

- Potential real GDP increases continually, shifting the long-run aggregate supply curve to the right.
- During most years, the aggregate demand curve shifts to the right.
- Except during periods when workers and firms expect high rates of inflation, the short-run aggregate supply curve shifts to the right.

Figure 24.8 illustrates how incorporating these macroeconomic facts changes the basic aggregate demand and aggregate supply model. We start with $SRAS_1$ and $AD_1$ intersecting at point $A$, at a price level of 100 and real GDP of \$14.0 trillion. Because this intersection occurs at a point on $LRAS_1$, we know the economy is in long-run equilibrium. The long-run aggregate supply curve shifts to the right, from $LRAS_1$ to $LRAS_2$. This shift occurs because during the year, potential real GDP increases as the U.S. labor force and the U.S. capital stock increase and technological progress occurs. The short-run aggregate supply curve shifts from $SRAS_1$ to $SRAS_2$. This shift occurs because the same variables that cause the long-run aggregate supply curve to shift to the right will also increase the quantity of goods and services that firms are willing to supply in the short run. Finally, the aggregate demand curve shifts to the right, from $AD_1$ to $AD_2$. The aggregate demand curve shifts for several reasons: As the population grows and incomes rise, consumption will increase over time. As the economy grows, firms will expand capacity, and new firms will be formed, increasing investment. An expanding

*This section may be omitted without loss of continuity.

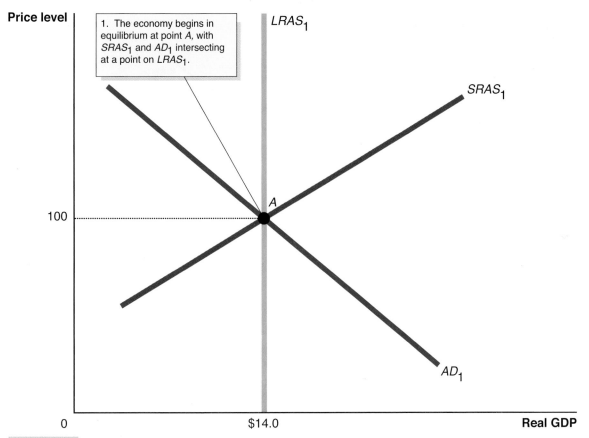

Figure 24.8    **A Dynamic Aggregate Demand and Aggregate Supply Model**

We start with the basic aggregate demand and aggregate supply model.

population and an expanding economy require increased government services, such as more police officers and teachers, so government purchases will increase.

The new equilibrium in Figure 24.8 occurs at point $B$, where $AD_2$ intersects $SRAS_2$ on $LRAS_2$. In the new equilibrium, the price level remains at 100, while real GDP increases to $14.3 trillion. Notice that there has been no inflation because the price level is unchanged, at 100. There has been no inflation because aggregate demand and aggregate supply shifted to the right by exactly as much as long-run aggregate supply. We would not expect this to be the typical situation for two reasons. First, the $SRAS$ curve is also affected by workers' and firms' expectations of future changes in the price level and by supply shocks. These variables can partially or completely offset the normal tendency of the $SRAS$ curve to shift to the right over the course of a year. Second, we know that consumers, firms, and the government may cut back on expenditures. This reduced spending will result in the aggregate demand curve shifting to the right less than it normally would or, possibly, shifting to the left. In fact, as we will see shortly, *changes in the price level and in real GDP in the short run are determined by shifts in the* SRAS *and* AD *curves.*

## What Is the Usual Cause of Inflation?

The dynamic aggregate demand and aggregate supply model provides a more accurate explanation than the basic model of the source of most inflation. If total spending in the economy grows faster than total production, prices rise. Figure 24.9 illustrates this point by showing that if the $AD$ curve shifts to the right by more than the $LRAS$ curve, inflation results because equilibrium occurs at a higher price level, point $B$. In the new equilibrium, the $SRAS$ curve has shifted to the right by less than the $LRAS$ curve because the anticipated increase in prices offsets some of the technological change and increases in the labor force and capital stock that occur during the year. Although inflation generally

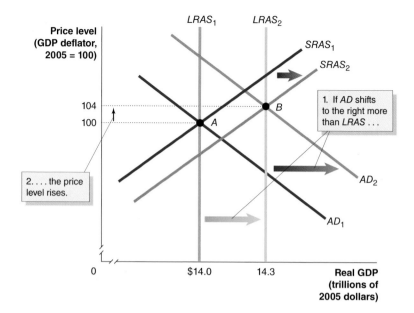

**Using Dynamic Aggregate Demand and Aggregate Supply to Understand Inflation**

The most common cause of inflation is total spending increasing faster than total production.

1. The economy begins at point *A*, with real GDP of $14.0 trillion and a price level of 100. An increase in full-employment real GDP from $14.0 trillion to $14.3 trillion causes long-run aggregate supply to shift from $LRAS_1$ to $LRAS_2$. Aggregate demand shifts from $AD_1$ to $AD_2$.

2. Because *AD* shifts to the right by more than the *LRAS* curve, the price level in the new equilibrium rises from 100 to 104.

results from total spending growing faster than total production, a shift to the left of the short-run aggregate supply curve can also cause an increase in the price level, as we saw earlier, in the discussion of supply shocks.

As we saw in Figure 24.8, if aggregate demand increases by the same amount as short-run and long-run aggregate supply, the price level will not change. In this case, the economy experiences economic growth without inflation.

## The Recession of 2007–2009

We can use the dynamic aggregate demand and aggregate supply model to analyze the recession of 2007–2009. The recession began in December 2007, with the end of the economic expansion that had begun in November 2001. Several factors combined to bring on the recession:

- **The end of the housing bubble.** The figure in the *Making the Connection* on page 808 shows that spending on residential construction increased rapidly from 2002 to 2005, before declining more than 60 percent between the end of 2005 and the beginning of 2010. The increase in spending on housing was partly the result of actions the Federal Reserve had taken to lower interest rates during and after the recession of 2001. As interest rates on mortgage loans declined, more consumers began to buy new homes. But by 2005, it was clear that a speculative bubble was partly responsible for the rapidly rising prices of both newly built and existing homes. A bubble occurs when people become less concerned with the underlying value of an asset—either a physical asset, such as a house, or a financial asset, such as a stock—and focus instead on expectations of the price of the asset increasing. In some areas of the country, such as California, Arizona, and Florida, many homes were purchased by investors who intended to resell them for higher prices than they paid for them and did not intend to live in them. Some popular television programs explored ways that people could "flip" houses by buying and quickly reselling them. Speculative bubbles eventually end, and the housing bubble started to deflate in 2006. Both new home sales and housing prices began to decline. The growth of aggregate demand slowed as spending on residential construction—a component of investment spending—fell. We will discuss the housing bubble further in Chapter 26.

- **The financial crisis.** Problems in the housing market were bad news for workers and firms involved with residential construction. In addition, falling housing prices led to an increased number of borrowers defaulting on their mortgage loans. These defaults caused banks and some other financial institutions to suffer heavy losses. Beginning in the spring of 2008, the U.S. Department of the Treasury and the Federal Reserve intervened to save several large financial institutions from bankruptcy. We will look at the details of the financial crisis in Chapters 25 and 26. For now we can note that the financial crisis led to a "credit crunch" that made it difficult for many households and firms to obtain the loans they needed to finance their spending. This drying up of credit contributed to declines in consumption spending and investment spending.

- ***The rapid increase in oil prices during 2008.*** Oil prices, which had been as low as $34 per barrel in 2004, had risen to $140 per barrel by mid-2008. The increase in the price of oil appeared to be caused by increased demand in rapidly growing economies, particularly India and China, and by the difficulty in developing new supplies of oil in the short run. With the deepening of the recession, worldwide demand for oil declined, and oil prices fell to about $40 per barrel in early 2009. As we have seen in this chapter, rising oil prices can result in a *supply shock* that causes the short-run aggregate supply curve to shift to the left. Although rising oil prices contributed to the severity of the recession, they had less impact than some economists had predicted. The U.S. economy appears to have become less vulnerable to increases in oil prices. Increases in the price of oil during the 1970s and early 1980s led many firms to switch to less-oil-dependent production processes. For example, FedEx and other firms used more fuel-efficient jets and trucks. As a result, the U.S. economy was consuming almost 60 percent less oil per dollar of GDP than it had in the mid-1970s. During 2008, oil price increases did not shift the short-run aggregate supply curve as far to the left as similar increases had 30 years earlier.

Figure 24.10 illustrates the beginning of the recession by showing the economy's short-run macroeconomic equilibrium in 2007 and 2008. In the figure, short-run equilibrium for 2007 occurs where $AD_{2007}$ intersects $SRAS_{2007}$ at real GDP of $13.21 trillion and a price level of 106.2. Real GDP in 2007 was slightly above potential real GDP of $13.20 trillion, shown by $LRAS_{2007}$. During 2008, aggregate demand shifted to the right, from $AD_{2007}$ to $AD_{2008}$. Aggregate demand increased by less than potential GDP because of the negative effects of the bursting of the housing bubble and the financial crisis on consumption spending and investment spending. The supply shock from higher oil prices caused short-run aggregate supply to shift to the left, from $SRAS_{2007}$ to $SRAS_{2008}$. Short-run equilibrium for 2008 occurred at real GDP of $13.16 trillion and a price level of 108.6. A large gap opened between short-run equilibrium real GDP and potential GDP. Not surprisingly, unemployment rose from 4.6 percent in 2007 to 5.8 percent in 2008. The price level increased only from 106.2 to 108.6, so the inflation rate was a low 2.3 percent.

The recession persisted into 2009, as potential real GDP increased to $13.78 trillion, while real GDP fell to $12.70 trillion. This increased gap between real GDP and potential GDP caused the unemployment rate to soar to 9.3 percent—the highest unemployment

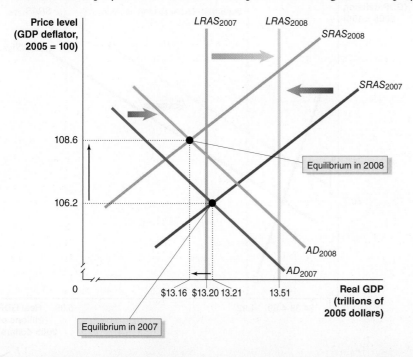

### Figure 24.10

### The Beginning of the Recession of 2007–2009

Between 2007 and 2008, the *AD* curve shifted to the right, but not by nearly enough to offset the shift to the right of the *LRAS* curve, which represented the increase in potential real GDP from $13.20 trillion to $13.51 trillion. Because of a sharp increase in oil prices, short-run aggregate supply shifted to the left, from $SRAS_{2007}$ to $SRAS_{2008}$. Real GDP decreased from $13.21 trillion in 2007 to $13.16 trillion in 2008, which was far below the potential real GDP, shown by $LRAS_{2008}$. As a result, the unemployment rate rose from 4.6 percent in 2007 to 5.8 percent in 2008. Because the increase in aggregate demand was small, the price level increased only from 106.2 in 2007 to 108.6 in 2008, so the inflation rate for 2008 was only 2.3 percent.

rate since the recession of 1981–1982 and the second highest since the Great Depression of the 1930s. Although the recession ended in June 2009, real GDP grew only slowly during 2010 and 2011, leaving the unemployment rate above 9 percent.

The severity of the recession of 2007–2009 resulted in some of the most dramatic changes in government economic policy since the Great Depression. We will explore these new policies in Chapters 26 and 27.

# Solved Problem 24.4

## Showing the Oil Shock of 1974–1975 on a Dynamic Aggregate Demand and Aggregate Supply Graph

The 1974–1975 recession clearly illustrates how a supply shock affects the economy. Following the Arab–Israeli War of 1973, the Organization of the Petroleum Exporting Countries (OPEC) increased the price of a barrel of oil from less than $3 to more than $10. Use this information and the statistics in the following table to draw a dynamic aggregate demand and aggregate supply graph showing macroeconomic equilibrium for 1974 and 1975. Assume that the aggregate demand curve did not shift between 1974 and 1975. Provide a brief explanation of your graph.

|  | Actual Real GDP | Potential Real GDP | Price Level |
|---|---|---|---|
| 1974 | $4.89 trillion | $4.92 trillion | 30.7 |
| 1975 | $4.88 trillion | $5.09 trillion | 33.6 |

Data from U.S. Bureau of Economic Analysis; and Congressional Budget Office.

## Solving the Problem

**Step 1:** **Review the chapter material.** This problem is about using the dynamic aggregate demand and aggregate supply model, so you may want to review the section "A Dynamic Aggregate Demand and Aggregate Supply Model," which begins on page 812.

**Step 2:** **Use the information in the table to draw the graph.** You need to draw five curves: *SRAS* and *LRAS* for both 1974 and 1975 and *AD*, which is the same for both years. You know that the two *LRAS* curves will be vertical lines at the values given for potential GDP in the table. Because of the large supply shock, you know that the *SRAS* curve shifted to the left. You are instructed to assume that the *AD* curve did not shift. Your graph should look like this:

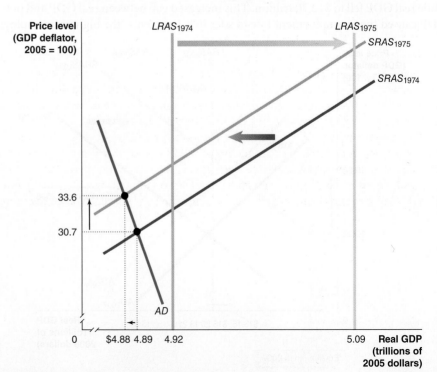

**Step 3:** **Explain your graph.** $LRAS_{1974}$ and $LRAS_{1975}$ are at the levels of potential real GDP for each year. Macroeconomic equilibrium for 1974 occurs where the $AD$ curve intersects the $SRAS_{1974}$ curve, with real GDP of $4.89 trillion and a price level of 30.7. Macroeconomic equilibrium for 1975 occurs where the $AD$ curve intersects the $SRAS_{1975}$ curve, with real GDP of $4.88 trillion and a price level of 33.6.

**Extra Credit:** As a result of the supply shock, the economy moved from an equilibrium output just below potential GDP in 1974 (the recession actually began right at the end of 1973) to an equilibrium well below potential GDP in 1975. With real GDP in 1975 about 4.1 percent below its potential level, the unemployment rate soared from 5.6 percent in 1974 to 8.5 percent in 1975.

**Your Turn:** For more practice, do related problems 4.5 and 4.6 on pages 823–824 at the end of this chapter.

MyEconLab

---

**Continued from page 793**

## Economics in Your Life

### Is an Employer Likely to Cut Your Pay during a Recession?

At the beginning of this chapter, we asked you to consider whether during a recession your employer is likely to reduce your pay and cut the prices of the products he or she sells. In this chapter, we saw that even during a recession, the price level rarely falls. In fact, in the United States, the GDP deflator has not fallen for an entire year since the 1930s. Although some firms reduced prices during the recession of 2007–2009, most firms did not. So, the owner of the coffeehouse where you work will probably not cut the price of lattes unless sales have declined drastically. We also saw that most firms are more reluctant to cut wages than to increase them because wage cuts can have a negative effect on worker morale and productivity. Because the recession of 2007–2009 was particularly severe, some firms did cut wages. But given that you are a highly skilled barista, your employer is unlikely to cut your wages for fear that you might quit and work for a competitor.

---

# Conclusion

Chapter 3 demonstrated the power of the microeconomic model of demand and supply in explaining how the prices and quantities of individual products are determined. This chapter showed that we need a different model to explain the behavior of the whole economy. We saw that the macroeconomic model of aggregate demand and aggregate supply explains fluctuations in real GDP and the price level.

Fluctuations in real GDP, employment, and the price level have led the federal government to implement macroeconomic policies. We will explore these policies in Chapters 26 and 27, but first, in Chapter 25, we consider the role money plays in the economy.

Read *An Inside Look* on the next page for a discussion of how a decline in air cargo shipments caused the airline industry to be concerned about the health of the economy.

# Smaller Freight Volumes Signal Continued Economic Troubles

## BLOOMBERG

## Air Cargo Down as Comerica Mulls Recession Risk: Freight Markets

(a) Sagging cargo shipments in the belly of passenger jets at carriers such as United Continental Holdings Inc. (UAL) and Delta Air Lines Inc. (DAL) are stoking concern that the U.S. economy risks a double-dip recession.

United's cargo traffic plunged 17 percent in August for the fourth straight drop that exceeded 10 percent, while Delta's cargo was little changed for three months in a row and American Airlines extended a streak of decreases that began in May.

"We have a lot of consumer nervousness over the economy," Delta Chief Cargo Officer Neel Shah said in a telephone interview. "One day people feel good, and the next day they feel bad, and it's that volatility that's the problem."

(b) Cargo is a bellwether for the carriers' main business of flying people, said Hunter Keay, a Wolfe Trahan & Co. analyst. While cargo is less than 4 percent of sales at the biggest U.S. airlines, their monthly reports offer more-timely soundings on the $60 billion global airfreight market than quarterly results from FedEx Corp. (FDX) and United Parcel Service Inc. (UPS).

Frequent flights and broad networks help airlines win business for everything from U.S. mail to electronics, along with niche shipments such as sushi-grade seafood, baby chicks for poultry farms and caskets containing human remains.

"The decline in air cargo is yet another indicator among so many that suggests the economy continues to be weak and may be inching closer to recession," said Robert Dye, Comerica Inc. (CMA)'s chief economist. . . .

The slide in air-carrier cargo correlates with "consumer confidence falling off a cliff" in August, Dye said in an interview from Dallas. The Bloomberg Consumer Comfort Index slid to minus 49.3 in the week ended Sept. 4, 2011's second-worst reading, and stayed at that level last week.

Dye rates the risk of a recession at 45 percent. Mark Vitner, senior economist at Wells Fargo Securities LLC in Charlotte, North Carolina, put the chances at one in three. The cargo drop "flies in the face" of assertions that shipping disruptions from Japan's earthquake had been resolved, he said.

"I don't think it's unreasonable to look at these cargo numbers and grow a little suspicious on what it means for passenger trends," Keay, who is based in New York, said in an interview.

Analysts and investors have been watching for signs of a return to recession because unemployment has hovered at about 9 percent or more for two years, damping consumer confidence and spending. . . .

The airline-cargo slowdown began in May, following Japan's March 11 earthquake and tsunami. Carriers also cited tougher comparisons with a year earlier when many businesses replenished inventory as the economy improved.

At Atlanta-based Delta, cargo traffic had been growing by 15 percent in March and April before cooling to a 2.1 percent pace for May. Traffic has been little changed since then. Exports are down from China and Japan, and domestic U.S. loads are shrinking, Shah said. . . .

(c) "Historically, cargo has been a pretty good leading indicator for business and premium traffic by about three to six months," Michael Linenberg, a Deutsche Bank AG analyst in New York, said in a note last month. "Business and premium traffic tends to lead leisure travel by a similar time frame."

Even as industry executives such as Delta President Ed Bastian said this week at a conference hosted by Linenberg that travel demand was firm, some also signaled their concern with steps to shrink passenger capacity.

Delta said it would trim 2012 flying by 2 percent to 3 percent, while American said it would pare available seats next quarter by 0.5 percent and said its plans for next year are under review. United and Delta previously scaled back on seating for the end of this year.

"Cargo is usually the canary in the mine shaft," Delta's Shah said. "I don't know if we're going to face that sort of situation this time. Passenger demand is holding up quite well, yet everyone is being very cautious with costs and capacity."

*Source:* "Air Cargo Down as Comerica Mulls Recession Risk: Freight Markets," by Mary Jane Credeur from *Bloomberg*, September 15, 2011. Copyright © 2011 by Bloomberg. Reprinted by permission of the YGS Group.

## Key Points in the Article

Although cargo shipments account for only a small percentage of total business for the major airlines, they have historically been good indicators of future passenger travel. A decline in shipments has some industry analysts concerned that passenger air travel may also experience declines in the next 6 to 12 months. Airlines have reacted with planned cuts in passenger service. The air cargo slowdown began in May 2011, occurring alongside a drop in consumer confidence tied to an unemployment rate that continued to exceed 9 percent. Some analysts view the decline in cargo shipments and the airlines' actions to scale back passenger service as an indication that an already-sluggish economy may be slipping even further.

## Analyzing the News

ⓐ Three major U.S. airlines indicated in August 2011 that air cargo shipments remained sluggish or had declined since May. While shipments with Delta Air Lines were little changed, those at American Airlines and United Air Lines fell for the fourth consecutive month, with the percentage of United's shipments falling by double digits each month.

ⓑ Air cargo shipments are viewed as an indicator of the future volume of passenger travel and also the state of the economy in general. Cargo accounts for less than 4 percent of sales at the nation's largest airlines, but trends in the cargo segment often precede similar trends in the passenger segment. With their extensive networks and large number of daily flights, airlines have attracted a vast array of cargo customers, so the decline in cargo reflects the lower volume of shipments occurring in a number of industries across the country. According to Robert Dye, the chief economist at Comerica, this "is yet another indicator among so many that suggests the economy continues to be weak and may be inching closer to recession." We can use the aggregate demand and aggregate supply model to analyze what happened to the U.S. economy during the 2007–2009 recession. The figure below shows that the economy during the fourth quarter of 2007 was in long-run equilibrium. Real GDP in 2005 dollars was $13.4 trillion, and the price level was 107.4. Declines in consumption and investment spending caused the aggregate demand curve to shift to the left, from $AD_{Q4,2007}$ to $AD_{Q1,2009}$. Meanwhile, aggregate supply also decreased, partly as a result of lower capital investment and increases in oil and commodity prices in 2008. The short-run aggregate supply curve shifts to the left, from $SRAS_{Q4,2007}$ to $SRAS_{Q1,2009}$, but the decline in aggregate supply is greater than the decline in aggregate demand. As a result, short-run real GDP fell to $12.7 trillion in the first quarter of 2009, and the price level rose to 108.6. Since the end of the recession, the economy has improved slightly, but real GDP had grown to only $13.3 trillion by the second quarter of 2011, still less than it was at the beginning of the recession, and the price level had increased to 116.0.

ⓒ Because the trends in cargo shipments often indicate future trends in passenger air travel, airlines initiated plans to reduce passenger capacity for late 2011 and 2012. This is yet another indication of a fear that the economy may be slowing down and could be moving toward another recession.

## Thinking Critically

1. Between the fourth quarter of 2007 and the first quarter of 2009, the U.S. unemployment rate rose from 4.8 percent to 8.5 percent. In the aggregate demand and aggregate supply graph shown, where would the long-run aggregate supply curve have been in 2009? Briefly explain.

2. For the second quarter of 2011, real GDP in 2005 dollars was $13.3 trillion and the price level was 116.0. Use an aggregate demand and aggregate supply graph to illustrate the changes from the first quarter of 2009 to the second quarter of 2011 and explain what happened to aggregate demand and aggregate supply to result in these changes.

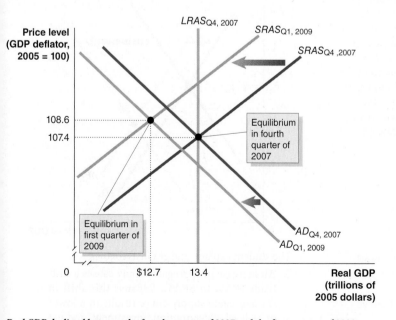

Real GDP declined between the fourth quarter of 2007 and the first quarter of 2009.

# Chapter Summary and Problems

## Key Terms

Aggregate demand and aggregate supply model, p. 794

Aggregate demand (*AD*) curve, p. 794

Fiscal policy, p. 796

Long-run aggregate supply (*LRAS*) curve, p. 802

Menu costs, p. 803

Monetary policy, p. 796

Short-run aggregate supply (*SRAS*) curve, p. 794

Stagflation, p. 810

Supply shock, p. 805

 **Aggregate Demand, pages 794–801**

LEARNING OBJECTIVE: Identify the determinants of aggregate demand and distinguish between a movement along the aggregate demand curve and a shift of the curve.

## Summary

The **aggregate demand and aggregate supply model** enables us to explain short-run fluctuations in real GDP and price level. The **aggregate demand curve** shows the relationship between the price level and the level of planned aggregate expenditures by households, firms, and the government. The **short-run aggregate supply curve** shows the relationship in the short run between the price level and the quantity of real GDP supplied by firms. The **long-run aggregate supply curve** shows the relationship in the long run between the price level and the quantity of real GDP supplied. The four components of aggregate demand are consumption (*C*), investment (*I*), government purchases (*G*), and net exports (*NX*). The aggregate demand curve is downward sloping because a decline in the price level causes consumption, investment, and net exports to increase. If the price level changes but all else remains constant, the economy will move up or down a stationary aggregate demand curve. If any variable other than the price level changes, the aggregate demand curve will shift. The variables that cause the aggregate demand curve to shift are divided into three categories: changes in government policies, changes in the expectations of households and firms, and changes in foreign variables. For example, **monetary policy** involves the actions the Federal Reserve takes to manage the money supply and interest rates to pursue macroeconomic policy objectives. When the Federal Reserve takes actions to change interest rates, consumption and investment spending will change, shifting the aggregate demand curve. **Fiscal policy** involves changes in federal taxes and purchases that are intended to achieve macroeconomic policy objectives. Changes in federal taxes and purchases shift the aggregate demand curve.

MyEconLab   Visit www.myeconlab.com to complete these exercises online and get instant feedback.

## Review Questions

1.1 What relationship is shown by the aggregate demand curve? What relationship is shown by the aggregate supply curve?

1.2 Explain the three reasons the aggregate demand curve slopes downward.

1.3 What are the differences between the *AD* curve and the demand curve for an individual product, such as apples?

1.4 What variables cause the *AD* curve to shift? For each variable, identify whether an increase in that variable will cause the *AD* curve to shift to the right or to the left.

## Problems and Applications

1.5 Explain how each of the following events would affect the aggregate demand curve.
   a. An increase in the price level
   b. An increase in government purchases
   c. Higher state income taxes
   d. Higher interest rates
   e. Faster income growth in other countries

1.6 [Related to the Don't Let This Happen to You on page 797] A student was asked to draw an aggregate demand and aggregate supply graph to illustrate the effect of an increase in aggregate supply. The student drew the following graph:

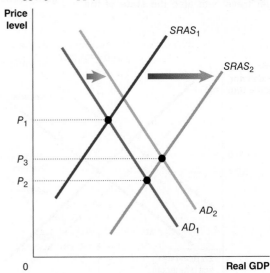

The student explains the graph as follows:

An increase in aggregate supply causes a shift from *SRAS₁* to *SRAS₂*. Because this shift in the aggregate supply curve results in a lower price level, consumption, investment, and net exports will increase. This change causes the aggregate demand curve to shift to the right, from $AD_1$ to $AD_2$. We know that real GDP will increase, but we can't be sure whether the price level will rise or fall because that depends on whether the aggregate supply curve or the aggregate demand curve has shifted farther to the right. I assume that aggregate supply shifts out farther than aggregate demand, so I show the final price level, $P_3$, as being lower than the initial price level, $P_1$.

Explain whether you agree with the student's analysis. Be careful to explain exactly what—if anything—you find wrong with this analysis.

**1.7** **[Related to** Solved Problem 24.1 **on page 797]** Explain whether each of the following will cause a shift of the $AD$ curve or a movement along the $AD$ curve.
a. Firms become more optimistic and increase their spending on machinery and equipment.
b. The federal government increases taxes in an attempt to reduce a budget deficit.
c. The U.S. economy experiences 4 percent inflation.

**1.8** **[Related to the** Making the Connection **on page 800]** If real GDP in the United States declined by more during the 2007–2009 recession than did real GDP in Canada, China, and other trading partners of the United States, would the effect be to increase or decrease U.S. net exports? Briefly explain.

---

## **24.2** Aggregate Supply, pages 801–805

LEARNING OBJECTIVE: Identify the determinants of aggregate supply and distinguish between a movement along the short-run aggregate supply curve and a shift of the curve.

### Summary

The **long-run aggregate supply curve** is a vertical line because in the long run, real GDP is always at its potential level and is unaffected by the price level. The short-run aggregate supply curve slopes upward because workers and firms fail to predict accurately the future price level. The three main explanations of why this failure results in an upward-sloping aggregate supply curve are that (1) contracts make wages and prices "sticky;" (2) businesses often adjust wages slowly; and (3) menu costs make some prices sticky. **Menu costs** are the costs to firms of changing prices on menus or in catalogs. If the price level changes but all else remains constant, the economy will move up or down a stationary aggregate supply curve. If any variable other than the price level changes, the aggregate supply curve will shift. The aggregate supply curve shifts as a result of increases in the labor force and capital stock, technological change, expected increases or decreases in the future price level, adjustments of workers and firms to errors in past expectations about the price level, and unexpected increases or decreases in the price of an important raw material. A **supply shock** is an unexpected event that causes the short-run aggregate supply curve to shift.

 Visit **www.myeconlab.com** to complete these exercises online and get instant feedback.

### Review Questions

**2.1** Explain why the long-run aggregate supply curve is vertical.
**2.2** What variables cause the long-run aggregate supply curve to shift? For each variable, identify whether an increase in that variable will cause the long-run aggregate supply curve to shift to the right or to the left.
**2.3** Why does the short-run aggregate supply curve slope upward?
**2.4** What variables cause the short-run aggregate supply curve to shift? For each variable, identify whether an increase in that variable will cause the short-run aggregate supply curve to shift to the right or to the left.

### Problems and Applications

**2.5** Explain how each of the following events would affect the long-run aggregate supply curve.
a. A higher price level
b. An increase in the labor force
c. An increase in the quantity of capital goods
d. Technological change

**2.6** An article in the *Economist* magazine noted that "the economy's potential to supply goods and services [is] determined by such things as the labour force and capital stock, as well as inflation expectations." Do you agree with this list of the determinants of potential GDP? Briefly explain.

Based on "Money's Muddled Message," *Economist*, May 19, 2009.

**2.7** Explain how each of the following events would affect the short-run aggregate supply curve.
a. An increase in the price level
b. An increase in what the price level is expected to be in the future
c. A price level that is currently higher than expected
d. An unexpected increase in the price of an important raw material
e. An increase in the labor force participation rate

**2.8** Suppose that workers and firms could always predict next year's price level with perfect accuracy. Briefly explain whether in these circumstances the *SRAS* curve would still slope upward.

**2.9** Workers and firms often enter into contracts that fix prices or wages, sometimes for years at a time. If the price level turns out to be higher or lower than was expected when the contract was signed, one party to the contract will lose out. Briefly explain why, despite knowing this, workers and firms still sign long-term contracts.

**2.10** What are menu costs? How has the widespread use of computers and the Internet affected menu costs? If menu costs were eliminated, would the short-run aggregate supply curve be a vertical line? Briefly explain.

# Macroeconomic Equilibrium in the Long Run and the Short Run, pages 805–812

**LEARNING OBJECTIVE:** Use the aggregate demand and aggregate supply model to illustrate the difference between short-run and long-run macroeconomic equilibrium.

## Summary

In long-run macroeconomic equilibrium, the aggregate demand and short-run aggregate supply curves intersect at a point *on* the long-run aggregate supply curve. In short-run macroeconomic equilibrium, the aggregate demand and short-run aggregate supply curves often intersect at a point *off* the long-run aggregate supply curve. An automatic mechanism drives the economy to long-run equilibrium. If short-run equilibrium occurs at a point below potential real GDP, wages and prices will fall, and the short-run aggregate supply curve will shift to the right until potential GDP is restored. If short-run equilibrium occurs at a point beyond potential real GDP, wages and prices will rise, and the short-run aggregate supply curve will shift to the left until potential GDP is restored. Real GDP can be temporarily above or below its potential level, either because of shifts in the aggregate demand curve or because supply shocks lead to shifts in the aggregate supply curve. **Stagflation** is a combination of inflation and recession, usually resulting from a supply shock.

MyEconLab   Visit www.myeconlab.com to complete these exercises online and get instant feedback.

## Review Questions

3.1 What is the relationship among the *AD*, *SRAS*, and *LRAS* curves when the economy is in long-run macroeconomic equilibrium?

3.2 Why might a supply shock lead to stagflation?

3.3 Why are the long-run effects of an increase in aggregate demand on price and output different from the short-run effects?

## Problems and Applications

3.4 Draw a basic aggregate demand and aggregate supply graph (with *LRAS* constant) that shows the economy in long-run equilibrium.

a. Assume that there is a large increase in demand for U.S. exports. Show the resulting short-run equilibrium on your graph. In this short-run equilibrium, is the unemployment rate likely to be higher or lower than it was before the increase in exports? Briefly explain. Explain how the economy adjusts back to long-run equilibrium. When the economy has adjusted back to long-run equilibrium, how have the values of each of the following changed relative to what they were before the increase in exports:
   i   Real GDP
   ii  The price level
   iii The unemployment rate

b. Assume that there is an unexpected increase in the price of oil. Show the resulting short-run equilibrium on your graph. Explain how the economy adjusts back to long-run equilibrium. In this short-run equilibrium, is the unemployment rate likely to be higher or lower than it was before the increase in exports? Briefly explain. When the economy has adjusted back to long-run equilibrium, how have the values of each of the following changed relative to what they were before the unexpected increase in the price of oil:
   i   Real GDP
   ii  The price level
   iii The unemployment rate

3.5 List four variables that would cause a decrease in real GDP (if large enough, a recession). Indicate whether changes in each variable increase or decrease aggregate demand or short-run aggregate supply. Next, state four variables that would cause an increase in the price level (short-run inflation). Indicate whether changes in the variable increase or decrease aggregate demand or short-run aggregate supply.

3.6 **[Related to the** Making the Connection **on page 808]** Edward Leamer of the University of California, Los Angeles, has argued that "housing *is* the business cycle." Why would spending on housing be likely to fluctuate more than spending by households on consumer durables, such as automobiles or furniture, or spending by firms on plant and equipment?

Based on Edward E. Leamer, "Housing Is the Business Cycle," *Housing, Housing Finance, and Monetary Policy*, Federal Reserve Bank of Kansas City, August 2007.

3.7 Consider the data in the following table for the years 1969 and 1970 (where the values for real GDP and potential GDP are in 2005 dollars):

| Year | Actual Real GDP | Potential GDP | Unemployment Rate |
|------|-----------------|---------------|-------------------|
| 1969 | $4.26 trillion  | $4.19 trillion | 3.5% |
| 1970 | $4.27 trillion  | $4.34 trillion | 4.9% |

Data from U.S. Bureau of Labor Statistics; and U.S. Bureau of Economic Analysis.

a. In 1969, actual real GDP was greater than potential real GDP. Explain how this is possible.

b. Even though real GDP in 1970 was slightly greater than real GDP in 1969, the unemployment rate increased substantially from 1969 to 1970. Why did this increase in unemployment occur?

c. Was the inflation rate in 1970 likely to have been higher or lower than the inflation rate in 1969? Does your answer depend on whether the recession that began in December 1969 was caused by a change in a component of aggregate demand or by a supply shock?

3.8 Use the graph on the next page to answer the following questions:

a. Which of the points *A*, *B*, *C*, or *D* can represent a long-run equilibrium?

b. Suppose that initially the economy is at point *A*. If aggregate demand increases from $AD_1$ to $AD_2$, which point represents the economy's short-run equilibrium? Which point represents the eventual long-run equilibrium? Briefly explain how the economy adjusts from the short-run equilibrium to the long-run equilibrium.

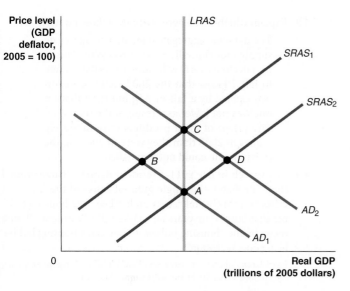

Price level (GDP deflator, 2005 = 100)

Real GDP (trillions of 2005 dollars)

**3.9 [Related to the** Making the Connection **on page 811]**
In early 2009, Christina Romer, who was then chair of the Council of Economic Advisers, and Jared Bernstein, who was then an economic adviser to Vice President Joseph Biden,

forecast how long they expected it would take for real GDP to return to potential GDP, assuming that Congress passed fiscal policy legislation proposed by President Obama:

> It should be understood that all of the estimates presented in this memo are subject to significant margins of error. There is the obvious uncertainty that comes from modeling a hypothetical package rather than the final legislation passed by the Congress. But, there is the more fundamental uncertainty that comes with any estimate of the effects of a program. Our estimates of economic relationships . . . are derived from historical experience and so will not apply exactly in any given episode. Furthermore, the uncertainty is surely higher than normal now because the current recession is unusual both in its fundamental causes and its severity.

Why would the causes of a recession and its severity affect the accuracy of forecasts of when the economy would return to potential GDP?

From Christina Romer and Jared Bernstein, *The Job Impact of the American Recovery and Reinvestment Plan*, January 9, 2009, p. 2.

---

**24.4** **A Dynamic Aggregate Demand and Aggregate Supply Model,** pages 812–817
LEARNING OBJECTIVE: Use the dynamic aggregate demand and aggregate supply model to analyze macroeconomic conditions.

## Summary

To make the aggregate demand and aggregate supply model more realistic, we need to make it *dynamic* by incorporating three facts that were left out of the basic model: (1) Potential real GDP increases continually, shifting the long-run aggregate supply curve to the right; (2) during most years, aggregate demand shifts to the right; and (3) except during periods when workers and firms expect high rates of inflation, the aggregate supply curve shifts to the right. The dynamic aggregate demand and aggregate supply model allows us to analyze macroeconomic conditions, including the beginning of the 2007–2009 recession.

 Visit **www.myeconlab.com** to complete these exercises online and get instant feedback.

## Review Questions

4.1 What are the key differences between the basic aggregate demand and aggregate supply model and the dynamic aggregate demand and aggregate supply model?

4.2 In the dynamic aggregate demand and aggregate supply model, what is the result of aggregate demand increasing more quickly than potential real GDP? What is the result of aggregate demand increasing more slowly than potential real GDP?

4.3 Briefly discuss the factors that brought on the recession of 2007–2009.

## Problems and Applications

4.4 Draw a dynamic aggregate demand and aggregate supply graph showing the economy moving from potential GDP in 2013 to potential GDP in 2014 , with no inflation. Your graph should contain the *AD*, *SRAS*, and *LRAS* curves for both 2013 and 2014 and should indicate the short-run macroeconomic equilibrium for each year and the directions in which the curves have shifted. Identify what must happen to have growth during 2014 without inflation.

4.5 **[Related to** Solved Problem 24.4 **on page 816]** Consider the information in the following table for the first two years of the Great Depression (where the values for real GDP and potential GDP are in 2005 dollars):

| Year | Actual Real GDP | Potential GDP | Price Level |
|------|-----------------|---------------|-------------|
| 1929 | $977.0 billion | $977.7 billion | 10.6 |
| 1930 | $892.8 billion | $1,011.4 billion | 10.2 |

Data from U.S. Bureau of Labor Statistics; and U.S. Bureau of Economic Analysis.

a. The table shows that something happened during 1929–1930 that has not happened during the recessions of the past 50 years. What is it?

b. Draw a dynamic aggregate demand and aggregate supply graph to illustrate what happened during these years. Your graph should contain the *AD*, *SRAS*, and *LRAS* curves for both 1929 and 1930 and should indicate the short-run macroeconomic equilibrium for each year and the directions in which the curves shifted.

**4.6** **[Related to** Solved Problem 24.4 **on page 816]** Look at the table in Solved Problem 24.4. The price level for 1974 is given as 30.7, and the price level for 1975 is given as 33.6. The values for the price level are well below 100. Does this indicate that inflation must have been low during these years? Briefly explain.

**4.7** In the graph below, suppose that the economy moves from point *A* in year 1 to point *B* in year 2. Using the graph, briefly explain your answer to each of the questions.
   **a.** What is the growth rate in potential real GDP from year 1 to year 2?
   **b.** Is the unemployment rate in year 2 higher or lower than in year 1?
   **c.** What is the inflation rate in year 2?
   **d.** What is the growth rate of real GDP in year 2?

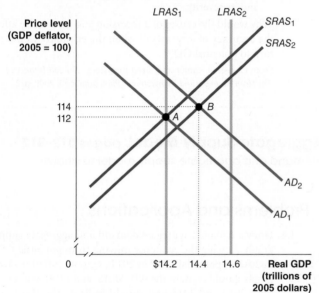

**4.8** Explain whether you agree with the following statement:
   The dynamic aggregate demand and aggregate supply model predicts that a recession caused by a decline in *AD* will cause the inflation rate to fall. I know that the 2007–2009 recession was caused by a fall in *AD*, but the inflation rate was not lower as a result of the recession. The prices of most products were definitely higher in 2008 than they were in 2007, so the inflation rate could not have fallen.

**4.9** In a speech in late 2011, President Barack Obama argued that: "Probably the single greatest cause of the financial crisis and this brutal recession has been the housing bubble that burst four years ago." What did President Obama mean by the "housing bubble"? How can a housing bubble bring on a recession?
   From Laura Meckler, "Obama Says Plan Will Cut Mortgage Payments for Millions," *Wall Street Journal*, October 24, 2011.

**4.10** **[Related to the** Chapter Opener **on page 793]** An article in the *Wall Street Journal* in late 2011 notes that "FedEx Corp.'s forecast for record holiday shipping this year shows that U.S. customers are buying more things online. But retailers still anticipate a soft holiday season, with the growth in shipping volume largely expected to come from shoppers scouring the Web for cheap deals." What are the implications of this information for the usefulness of the "FedEx indicator" discussed in the chapter opener?
   Based on Bob Sechler and Jennifer Levitz, "More Boxes for FedEx," *Wall Street Journal*, October 25, 2011.

# Appendix

## Macroeconomic Schools of Thought

**LEARNING** OBJECTIVE

Understand macroeconomic schools of thought.

Macroeconomics became a separate field of economics in 1936, with the publication of John Maynard Keynes's book *The General Theory of Employment, Interest, and Money*. Keynes, an economist at the University of Cambridge in England, was attempting to explain the devastating Great Depression of the 1930s. As we discussed in Chapter 23, real GDP in the United States declined more than 25 percent between 1929 and 1933 and did not return to its potential level until the United States entered World War II in 1941. The unemployment rate soared to 25 percent by 1933 and did not return to its 1929 level until 1942. Keynes developed a version of the aggregate demand and aggregate supply model to explain these facts. The widespread acceptance during the 1930s and 1940s of Keynes's model became known as the **Keynesian revolution**.

In fact, using the aggregate demand and aggregate supply model remains the most widely accepted approach to analyzing macroeconomic issues. Because the model has been modified significantly from Keynes's day, many economists who use the model today refer to themselves as *new Keynesians*. The new Keynesians emphasize the importance of the stickiness of wages and prices in explaining fluctuations in real GDP. A significant number of economists, however, dispute whether using the aggregate demand and aggregate supply model, as we have discussed it in this chapter, is the best way to analyze macroeconomic issues. These alternative *schools of thought* use models that differ significantly from the standard aggregate demand and aggregate supply model. We can briefly consider each of the three major alternative models:

1. The monetarist model
2. The new classical model
3. The real business cycle model

**Keynesian revolution** The name given to the widespread acceptance during the 1930s and 1940s of John Maynard Keynes's macroeconomic model.

## The Monetarist Model

The monetarist model—also known as the neo-Quantity Theory of Money model—was developed beginning in the 1940s by Milton Friedman, an economist at the University of Chicago who was awarded the Nobel Prize in Economics in 1976. Friedman argued that the Keynesian approach overstates the amount of macroeconomic instability in the economy. In particular, he argued that the economy will ordinarily be at potential real GDP. In the book *A Monetary History of the United States: 1867–1960*, written with Anna Jacobson Schwartz, Friedman argued that most fluctuations in real output were caused by fluctuations in the money supply rather than by fluctuations in consumption spending or investment spending. Friedman and Schwartz argued that the severity of the Great Depression was caused by the Federal Reserve's allowing the quantity of money in the economy to fall by more than 25 percent between 1929 and 1933.

In the United States, the Federal Reserve is responsible for managing the quantity of money. As we will discuss further in Chapter 26, the Federal Reserve has typically focused more on controlling interest rates than on controlling the money supply. Friedman has argued that the Federal Reserve should change its practices and adopt a **monetary growth rule**, which is a plan for increasing the quantity of money at a fixed rate. Friedman believed that adopting a monetary growth rule would reduce fluctuations in real GDP, employment, and inflation.

Friedman's ideas, which are referred to as **monetarism**, attracted significant support during the 1970s and early 1980s, when the economy experienced high rates of unemployment and inflation. The support for monetarism declined during the late 1980s and 1990s, when the unemployment and inflation rates were relatively low. In Chapter 25, we will discuss the *quantity theory of money*, which underlies the monetarist model.

**Monetary growth rule** A plan for increasing the quantity of money at a fixed rate that does not respond to changes in economic conditions.

**Monetarism** The macroeconomic theories of Milton Friedman and his followers, particularly the idea that the quantity of money should be increased at a constant rate.

# The New Classical Model

The new classical model was developed in the mid-1970s by a group of economists including Nobel Laureate Robert Lucas of the University of Chicago, Nobel Laureate Thomas Sargent of New York University, and Robert Barro of Harvard University. Some of the views held by the new classical macroeconomists are similar to those held by economists before the Great Depression. Keynes referred to the economists before the Great Depression as "classical economists." Like the classical economists, the new classical macroeconomists believe that the economy normally will be at potential real GDP. They also believe that wages and prices adjust quickly to changes in demand and supply. Put another way, they believe the stickiness in wages and prices emphasized by the new Keynesians is unimportant.

**New classical macroeconomics** The macroeconomic theories of Robert Lucas and others, particularly the idea that workers and firms have rational expectations.

Lucas argues that workers and firms have *rational expectations*, meaning that they form their expectations of the future values of economic variables, such as the inflation rate, by making use of all available information, including information on variables—such as changes in the quantity of money—that might affect aggregate demand. If the actual inflation rate is lower than the expected inflation rate, the actual real wage will be higher than the expected real wage. These higher real wages will lead to a recession because they will cause firms to hire fewer workers and cut back on production. As workers and firms adjust their expectations to the lower inflation rate, the real wage will decline, and employment and production will expand, bringing the economy out of recession. The ideas of Lucas and his followers are referred to as the **new classical macroeconomics**. Supporters of the new classical model agree with supporters of the monetarist model that the Federal Reserve should adopt a monetary growth rule. They argue that a monetary growth rule will make it easier for workers and firms to accurately forecast the price level, thereby reducing fluctuations in real GDP.

# The Real Business Cycle Model

Beginning in the 1980s, some economists, including Nobel Laureates Finn Kydland of Carnegie Mellon University and Edward Prescott of Arizona State University, began to argue that Lucas was correct in assuming that workers and firms formed their expectations rationally and that wages and prices adjust quickly to supply and demand but was wrong about the source of fluctuations in real GDP. They argue that fluctuations in real GDP are caused by temporary shocks to productivity. These shocks can be negative, such as a decline in the availability of oil or other raw materials, or positive, such as technological change that makes it possible to produce more output with the same quantity of inputs.

**Real business cycle model** A macroeconomic model that focuses on real, rather than monetary, causes of the business cycle.

According to this school of thought, shifts in the aggregate demand curve have no impact on real GDP because the short-run aggregate supply curve is vertical. Other schools of thought believe that the short-run aggregate supply curve is upward sloping and that only the *long-run* aggregate supply curve is vertical. Fluctuations in real GDP occur when a negative productivity shock causes the short-run aggregate supply curve to shift to the left—reducing real GDP—or a positive productivity shock causes the short-run aggregate supply curve to shift to the right—increasing real GDP. Because this model focuses on "real" factors—productivity shocks—rather than changes in the quantity of money to explain fluctuations in real GDP, it is known as the **real business cycle model**.

| Making the Connection | **Karl Marx: Capitalism's Severest Critic** |
| --- | --- |

The schools of macroeconomic thought we have discussed in this appendix are considered part of mainstream economic theory because of their acceptance of the market system as the best means of raising living standards in the long run. One quite influential critic of mainstream economic theory was Karl Marx. Marx was born in Trier, Germany, in 1818. After graduating from the University of Berlin in 1841, he began a career as a political journalist and agitator. His political activities caused him to be expelled first from Germany and then from France and Belgium. In 1849, he moved to London, where he spent the remainder of his life.

In 1867, Marx published the first volume of his greatest work, *Das Kapital*. Marx read closely the most prominent mainstream economists, including Adam Smith, David Ricardo, and John Stuart Mill. But Marx believed that he understood how market systems would evolve in the long run much better than those earlier authors. Marx argued that the market system would eventually be replaced by a Communist economy, in which the workers would control production. He believed in the *labor theory of value*, which attributed all of the value of a good or service to the labor embodied in it. According to Marx, the owners of businesses—capitalists—did not earn profits by contributing anything of value to the production of goods or services. Instead, capitalists earned profits because their "monopoly of the means of production"—their ownership of factories and machinery—allowed them to exploit workers by paying them wages that were much lower than the value of workers' contribution to production.

Marx argued that the wages of workers would be driven to levels that allowed only bare survival. He also argued that small firms would eventually be driven out of business by larger firms, forcing owners of small firms into the working class. Control of production would ultimately be concentrated in the hands of a few firms, which would have difficulty selling the goods they produced to the impoverished masses. A final economic crisis would lead the working classes to rise up, seize control of the economy, and establish Communism. Marx died in 1883, without having provided a detailed explanation of how the Communist economy would operate.

*Karl Marx predicted that a final economic crisis would lead to the collapse of the market system.*

Marx had relatively little influence on mainstream thinking in the United States, but several political parties in Europe were guided by his ideas. In 1917, the Bolshevik party seized control of Russia and established the Soviet Union, the first Communist state. Although the Soviet Union was a vicious dictatorship under Vladimir Lenin and his successor, Joseph Stalin, its prestige rose when it avoided the macroeconomic difficulties that plagued the market economies during the 1930s. By the late 1940s, Communist parties had also come to power in China and the countries of Eastern Europe. Poor economic performance contributed to the eventual collapse of the Soviet Union and its replacement by a market system, although one in which government intervention is still widespread. The Communist Party remains in power in China, but the economy is evolving toward a market system. Today, only North Korea and Cuba have economies that claim to be based on the ideas of Karl Marx.

## Key Terms

Keynesian revolution, p. 825

Monetarism, p. 825

Monetary growth rule, p. 825

New classical macroeconomics, p. 826

Real business cycle model, p. 826

# Money, Banks, and the Federal Reserve System

## Chapter Outline and Learning Objectives

# Coca-Cola Dries Up as Money Floods Zimbabwe

People in Africa buy 36 billion bottles of Coca-Cola a year. In 2008, Zimbabwe, a country in southern Africa, ran out of locally produced Coke for the first time in at least 40 years. Because they could not obtain U.S. dollars, local Coke bottlers were not able to import from the United States the concentrated syrup used to make the soft drink. A meager amount of Coke was imported from South Africa, but a single bottle sold for around 15 billion Zimbabwean dollars! Zimbabwe was suffering the effects of an inflation rate so high that it is called a *hyperinflation*. Zimbabwe's hyperinflation was of epic proportions, perhaps the worst in world history. When it was first introduced in 1980, 1 Zimbabwean dollar was worth 1.47 U.S. dollars. By the end of 2008, the exchange rate was 1 U.S. dollar to 2 *billion* Zimbabwean dollars, and prices for some large transactions in Zimbabwe were calculated in quadrillions (15 zeros) and quintillions (18 zeros).

In addition to the Coke shortage, Zimbabweans were suffering shortages of fuel, food, and other basic goods. As the value of the Zimbabwean currency fell against other currencies, it was difficult for local businesses such as the Coke bottlers to find anyone willing to exchange U.S. dollars for Zimbabwean dollars. What made Zimbabwe's currency almost worthless? The government of Zimbabwe had decided to pay for all of its expenses by printing more and more money. The faster the government printed money, the faster prices rose. Eventually, both foreigners and local residents refused to accept the Zimbabwean dollar in exchange for goods and services, and the country's economy plunged into a devastating recession, with real GDP falling more than 12 percent during 2008. In early 2009, the government issued 100 trillion dollar bills, not enough for a bus ticket in Harare, Zimbabwe's capital city. Eventually, in 2009, a new Zimbabwean government took the drastic step of abandoning its own currency and making the U.S. dollar the country's official currency.

**AN INSIDE LOOK AT POLICY** on **page 856** discusses how banks in 2011 increased their loans to both consumers and businesses and how that affected the recovery from the recession of 2007–2009.

Based on Angus Shaw, "Coca Cola Dries Up in Zimbabwe," newzimbabwe.com, December 1, 2008; Patrick McGroarty and Farai Mutsaka, "How to Turn 100 Trillion Dollars into Five and Feel Good About It," *Wall Street Journal*, May 11, 2011; Marcus Walker and Andrew Higgins, "Zimbabwe Can't Paper Over Its Million-Percent Inflation Anymore," *Wall Street Journal*, July 2, 2008; and "Wait and See," *Economist*, February 5, 2009.

## Economics in Your Life

### What if Money Became Increasingly Valuable?

Most people are used to the fact that as prices rise each year, the purchasing power of money falls. You will be able to buy fewer goods and services with $1,000 one year from now than you can buy today, and you will be able to buy even fewer goods and services the year after that. In fact, with an inflation rate of just 3 percent, in 25 years, $1,000 will buy only what $475 can buy today. Suppose, though, that you could live in an economy where the purchasing power of money rose each year? What would be the advantages and disadvantages of living in such an economy? As you read the chapter, see if you can answer these questions. You can check your answers against those we provide on **page 854** at the end of this chapter.

I n this chapter, we will explore the role of money in the economy. We will see how the banking system creates money and what policy tools the Federal Reserve uses to manage the quantity of money. We will also look at the crisis in the banking system during the past few years. At the end of the chapter, we will explore the link between changes in the quantity of money and changes in the price level. What you learn in this chapter will serve as an important foundation for understanding monetary policy and fiscal policy, which we study in the next three chapters.

**25.1 LEARNING OBJECTIVE**

Define money and discuss the four functions of money.

**Money** Assets that people are generally willing to accept in exchange for goods and services or for payment of debts.

**Asset** Anything of value owned by a person or a firm.

**Commodity money** A good used as money that also has value independent of its use as money.

# What Is Money, and Why Do We Need It?

Could an economy function without money? We know the answer to this question is "yes" because there are many historical examples of economies in which people traded goods for other goods rather than using money. For example, a farmer on the American frontier during colonial times might have traded a cow for a plow. Most economies, though, use money. What is money? The economic definition of **money** is any asset that people are generally willing to accept in exchange for goods and services or for payment of debts. Recall from Chapter 8 that an **asset** is anything of value owned by a person or a firm. There are many possible kinds of money: In West Africa, at one time, cowrie shells served as money. During World War II, prisoners of war used cigarettes as money.

## Barter and the Invention of Money

To understand the importance of money, let's consider further the situation in economies that do not use money. These economies, where goods and services are traded directly for other goods and services, are called *barter economies*. Barter economies have a major shortcoming. To illustrate this shortcoming, consider a farmer on the American frontier in colonial days. Suppose the farmer needed another cow and proposed trading a spare plow to a neighbor for one of the neighbor's cows. If the neighbor did not want the plow, the trade would not happen. For a barter trade to take place between two people, each person must want what the other one has. Economists refer to this requirement as a *double coincidence of wants*. The farmer who wants the cow might eventually be able to obtain one if he first trades with some other neighbor for something the neighbor with the cow wants. However, it may take several trades before the farmer is ultimately able to trade for what the neighbor with the cow wants. Locating several trading partners and making several intermediate trades can take considerable time and energy.

The problems with barter give societies an incentive to identify a product that most people will accept in exchange for what they have to trade. For example, in colonial times, animal skins were very useful in making clothing. The first governor of Tennessee actually received a salary of 1,000 deerskins per year, and the secretary of the Treasury received 450 otter skins per year. A good used as money that also has value independent of its use as money is called a **commodity money**. Historically, once a good became widely accepted as money, people who did not have an immediate use for it would be willing to accept it. A colonial farmer—or the governor of Tennessee—might not want a deerskin, but as long as he knew he could use the deerskin to buy other goods and services, he would be willing to accept it in exchange for what he had to sell.

Trading goods and services is much easier when money becomes available. People only need to sell what they have for money and then use the money to buy what they want. If the colonial family could find someone to buy their plow, they could use the money to buy the cow they wanted. The family with the cow would accept the money because they knew they could use it to buy what they wanted. When money is available, families are less likely to produce everything or nearly everything they need themselves and more likely to specialize.

Most people in modern economies are highly specialized. They do only one thing—work as a nurse, an accountant, or an engineer—and use the money they earn to buy everything else they need. As we discussed in Chapter 2, people become much more productive by specializing because they can pursue their *comparative advantage*. The high income levels in modern economies are based on the specialization that money makes possible. We can now answer the question, "Why do we need money?" *By making exchange easier, money allows people to specialize and become more productive.*

## The Functions of Money

Anything used as money—whether a deerskin, a cowrie seashell, cigarettes, or a dollar bill—should fulfill the following four functions:

- Medium of exchange
- Unit of account
- Store of value
- Standard of deferred payment

**Medium of Exchange**  Money serves as a medium of exchange when sellers are willing to accept it in exchange for goods or services. When the local supermarket accepts your $5 bill in exchange for bread and milk, the $5 bill is serving as a medium of exchange. With a medium of exchange, people can sell goods and services for money and use the money to buy what they want. An economy is more efficient when a single good is recognized as a medium of exchange.

**Unit of Account**  In a barter system, each good has many prices. A cow may be worth two plows, 20 bushels of wheat, or six axes. Once a single good is used as money, each good has a single price rather than many prices. This function of money gives buyers and sellers a *unit of account*, a way of measuring value in the economy in terms of money. Because the U.S. economy uses dollars as money, each good has a price in terms of dollars.

**Store of Value**  Money allows value to be stored easily: If you do not use all your dollars to buy goods and services today, you can hold the rest to use in the future. Money is not the only store of value, however. Any asset—shares of Coca-Cola stock, Treasury bonds, real estate, or Renoir paintings, for example—represents a store of value. Financial assets, such as stocks and bonds, offer an important benefit relative to holding money because they pay a higher rate of interest or may increase in value in the future. Other assets also have advantages relative to money because they provide services. A house, for example, offers you a place to sleep.

Why, then, do people hold any money? The answer has to do with *liquidity*, or the ease with which an asset can be converted into the medium of exchange. Because money is the medium of exchange, it is the most liquid asset. If you want to buy something and you need to sell an asset to do so, you are likely to incur a cost. For example, if you want to buy a car and need to sell bonds or stocks in order to do so, you will need to pay a commission to your broker. To avoid such costs, people are willing to hold some of their wealth in the form of money, even though other assets offer a greater return as a store of value.

**Standard of Deferred Payment**  Money is useful because it can serve as a standard of deferred payment in borrowing and lending. Money can facilitate exchange at a *given point in time* by providing a medium of exchange and unit of account. Money can facilitate exchange *over time* by providing a store of value and a standard of deferred payment. For example, a computer manufacturer may buy hard drives from another firm in exchange for the promise of making payment in 60 days.

How important is it that money be a reliable store of value and standard of deferred payment? People care about how much food, clothing, and other goods and services their dollars will buy. The value of money depends on its purchasing power, which refers to its ability to buy goods and services. Inflation causes a decline in purchasing power because with rising prices, a given amount of money can purchase fewer goods and services. When inflation reaches the levels seen in Zimbabwe, money is no longer a reliable store of value or standard of deferred payment.

## What Can Serve as Money?

Having a medium of exchange helps to make transactions easier, allowing the economy to work more efficiently. The next logical question is this: What can serve as money? That is, which assets should be used as the medium of exchange? We saw earlier that an asset must, at a minimum, be generally accepted as payment to serve as money. In practical terms, however, it must be even more.

Five criteria make a good suitable for use as a medium of exchange:

1. The good must be *acceptable* to (that is, usable by) most people.
2. It should be of *standardized quality* so that any two units are identical.
3. It should be *durable* so that value is not lost by spoilage.
4. It should be *valuable* relative to its weight so that amounts large enough to be useful in trade can be easily transported.
5. The medium of exchange should be *divisible* because different goods are valued differently.

Dollar bills meet all these criteria. What determines the acceptability of dollar bills as a medium of exchange? Basically, it is through self-fulfilling expectations: You value something as money only if you believe that others will accept it from you as payment. A society's willingness to use paper dollars as money makes dollars an acceptable medium of exchange.

**Commodity Money** Commodity money has value independent of its use as money. Gold, for example, was a common form of money in the nineteenth century because it was a medium of exchange, a unit of account, a store of value, and a standard of deferred payment. But commodity money has a significant problem: Its value depends on its purity. Therefore, someone who wanted to cheat could mix impure metals with a precious metal. Another problem with using gold as money was that the money supply was difficult to control because it depended partly on unpredictable discoveries of new gold fields.

**Fiat Money** It can be inefficient for an economy to rely on only gold or other precious metals for its money supply. What if you had to transport bars of gold to settle your transactions? Not only would doing so be difficult and costly, but you would run the risk of being robbed. To get around this problem, private institutions or governments began to store gold and issue paper certificates that could be redeemed for gold. In modern economies, paper currency is generally issued by a *central bank*, which is an agency of the government that regulates the money supply. The **Federal Reserve** is the central bank of the United States. Today, no government in the world issues paper currency that can be redeemed for gold. Paper currency has no value unless it is used as money, and it is therefore not a commodity money. Instead, paper currency is a **fiat money**, which has no value except as money. If paper currency has no value except as money, why do consumers and firms use it?

If you look at the top of a U.S. dollar bill, you will see that it is actually a *Federal Reserve Note*, issued by the Federal Reserve. Because U.S. dollars are fiat money, the Federal Reserve is not required to give you gold or silver for your dollar bills. Federal Reserve currency is *legal tender* in the United States, which means the federal government requires that it be accepted in payment of debts and requires that cash or checks denominated in dollars be used in payment of taxes. Despite being legal tender, dollar bills would not be a good medium of exchange and could not serve as money if they weren't widely accepted by people. The key to this acceptance is that *households and firms have confidence that if they accept paper dollars in exchange for goods and services, the dollars will not lose much value during the time they hold them*. Without this confidence, dollar bills would not serve as a medium of exchange.

**Federal Reserve** The central bank of the United States.

**Fiat money** Money, such as paper currency, that is authorized by a central bank or governmental body and that does not have to be exchanged by the central bank for gold or some other commodity money.

| Making the Connection | **Apple Didn't Want My Cash!** |

If Federal Reserve Notes are legal tender, doesn't that mean that everyone in the United States, including every business, has to accept paper money? The answer to this question is "no," as a woman in California found out when she went to an Apple store in Palo Alto and tried to buy an iPad using $600 in currency. At that point, the iPad had just been released, and Apple did not want to sell large numbers to people who were buying them to resell on eBay, Craigslist, or elsewhere. So, a customer wanting to buy an iPad had to pay either with a credit card or a debit card, which would make it easier for Apple to keep track of anyone attempting to buy more than the limit of two per customer.

*The law doesn't require Apple to accept paper money from these customers.*

Because Federal Reserve Notes are legal tender, creditors must accept them in payment of debts, and the government will accept them in payment of taxes. However, as this incident makes clear, firms do not have to accept cash as payment for goods and services. As the U.S. Treasury Department explains on its Web site:

> There is . . . no Federal statute mandating that a private business, a person or an organization must accept currency or coins as payment for goods and/or services. . . . For example, a bus line may prohibit payment of fares in pennies or dollar bills. In addition, movie theaters, convenience stores and gas stations may refuse to accept large denomination currency (usually notes above $20) as a matter of policy.

The woman who tried to buy an iPad for cash was disabled and on a limited income, so the incident led to bad publicity for Apple. As a result, Apple decided to lift its ban on paying for iPads with cash, provided that the customer was willing to set up an Apple account at the time of purchase. In addition, Apple presented a free iPad to the customer who was originally turned down when she tried to pay with cash.

Based on Michael Winter, "Apple Ends No-Cash Policy and California Woman Gets Free iPad," www.usatoday.com, May 20, 2010; and U.S. Treasury, "FAQs: Currency," http://www.treasury.gov/resource-center/faqs/Currency/Pages/edu_faq_currency_index2.aspx.

**Your Turn:** Test your understanding by doing related problem 1.9 on page 859 at the end of this chapter.

MyEconLab

# How Is Money Measured in the United States Today?

**25.2 LEARNING** OBJECTIVE

Discuss the definitions of the money supply used in the United States today.

A narrow definition of money would include only those assets that obviously function as a medium of exchange: currency, checking account deposits, and traveler's checks. These assets can easily be used to buy goods and services and thus act as a medium of exchange. This strict interpretation is too narrow, however, as a measure of the money supply in the real world. Many other assets can fill the role of a medium of exchange, although they are not as liquid as checking account deposits or cash. For example, you can convert your savings account at a bank to cash.

In the United States, the Federal Reserve has conducted several studies of the appropriate definition of *money*. The job of defining the money supply has become more difficult during the past two decades, as innovation in financial markets and institutions has created new substitutes for traditional checking accounts. Outside the United States, other central banks use similar measures. Next, we will look more closely at the Fed's definitions of the money supply.

# M1: The Narrowest Definition of the Money Supply

Figure 25.1 illustrates the definitions of the money supply. The narrowest definition is called **M1**. It includes:

**M1** The narrowest definition of the money supply: The sum of currency in circulation, checking account deposits in banks, and holdings of traveler's checks.

1. *Currency*, which is all the paper money and coins that are in circulation, where "in circulation" means not held by banks or the government
2. The value of all checking account deposits at banks
3. The value of traveler's checks (Because this last category is so small—about $4.4 billion in August 2011—relative to the other two categories, we will ignore it in our discussion of the money supply.)

Although currency has a larger value than checking account deposits, checking account deposits are used much more often than currency to make payments. More than 80 percent of all expenditures on goods and services are made with checks rather than with currency. In fact, the total amount of currency in circulation—$977 billion in August 2011—is a misleading number. This amount is more than $2,800 per person—adult or child—in the United States. If this sounds like an unrealistically large amount of currency to be held per person, it is. Economists estimate that more than 60 percent of U.S. currency is actually outside the borders of the United States.

Who holds these dollars outside the United States? Foreign banks and foreign governments hold some dollars, but most are held by households and firms in countries where there is not much confidence in the local currency. When inflation rates are very high, many households and firms do not want to hold their domestic currency because it is losing its value too rapidly. The value of the U.S. dollar will be much more stable than their domestic currency. If enough people are willing to accept dollars as well as—or instead of—domestic currency, dollars become a second currency for the country. As we saw in the chapter opener, when inflation soared in Zimbabwe, the government was led to adopt the U.S. dollar as the country's official currency.

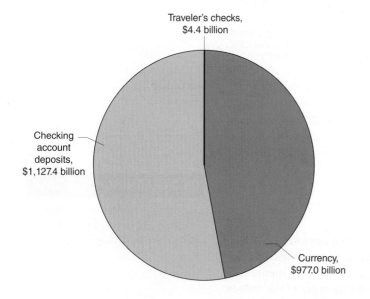

**(a)  M1 = $2,108.8 billion**

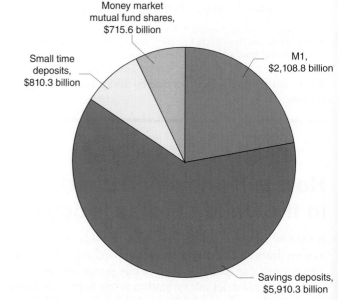

**(b)  M2 = $9,544.9 billion**

**Figure 25.1**    Measuring the Money Supply, August 2011

The Federal Reserve uses two different measures of the money supply: M1 and M2. M2 includes all the assets in M1, as well as the additional assets shown in panel (b).

Data from Board of Governors of the Federal Reserve System, "Federal Reserve Statistical Release, H6," September 29, 2011.

# Making the Connection

## Do We Still Need the Penny?

We have seen that fiat money has no value except as money. Governments actually make a profit from issuing fiat money because fiat money is usually produced using paper or low-value metals that cost far less than the face value of the money.

For example, it costs only about 4 cents for the federal Bureau of Engraving and Printing to manufacture a $20 bill. The government's profit from issuing fiat money—which is equal to the difference between the face value of the money and its production cost—is called *seigniorage*.

With small-denomination coins—like pennies or nickels—there is a possibility that the coins will cost more to produce than their face value. This was true in the early 1980s, when the rising price of copper meant the federal government was spending more than 1 cent to produce a penny. That led the government to switch from making pennies from copper to making them from zinc. Unfortunately, by 2007, the rising price of zinc meant that once again, the penny cost more than 1 cent to produce. Although the price of zinc later declined, many economists began to ask whether the penny should simply be abolished. Not only does it sometimes cost more to produce than it is worth, but inflation has eroded its purchasing power to such an extent that some people just find the penny to be a nuisance. Many people will not bother to pick up a penny from the sidewalk. In fact, several other countries, including Great Britain, Australia, and the European countries that use the euro, have eliminated their lowest-denomination coins; Canada is also considering doing so.

*Unfortunately, these cost the government more than a penny to produce.*

Some economists, though, have argued that eliminating the penny would subject consumers to a "rounding tax." For example, a good that had been priced at $2.99 will cost $3.00 if the penny is eliminated. Some estimates have put the cost to consumers of the rounding tax as high as $600 million. But Robert Whaples, an economist at Wake Forest University, after analyzing almost 200,000 transactions from a convenience store chain, concludes that "the 'rounding tax' is a myth. In reality, the number of times consumers' bills would be rounded upward is almost exactly equal to the number of times they would be rounded downward."

François Velde, an economist at the Federal Reserve Bank of Chicago, has come up with perhaps the most ingenious solution to the problem of the penny: The federal government would simply declare that Lincoln pennies are now worth 5 cents. There would then be two 5-cent coins in circulation—the current Jefferson nickels and the current Lincoln pennies—and no 1-cent coins. In the future, only the Lincoln coins—now worth 5 cents—would be minted. This would solve the problem of consumers and retail stores having to deal with pennies, it would make the face value of the Lincoln 5-cent coin greater than its cost of production, and it would also deal with the problem that the current Jefferson nickel frequently costs more than 5 cents to produce. But will Lincoln pennies actually be accepted as being worth 5 cents simply because the government says so? The answer is "yes" because as long as the government is willing to exchange 20 Lincoln coins for a paper dollar, everyone else will be willing to do so as well. Of course, if this plan were adopted, anyone with a hoard of pennies would find that their money would be worth five times as much overnight!

Whether or not pennies get turned into nickels, it seems very likely that one way or another, the penny will eventually disappear from the U.S. money supply.

Based on Robert Whaples, "Why Keeping the Penny No Longer Makes Sense," *USA Today*, July 12, 2006; Austan Goolsbee, "Now That a Penny Isn't Worth Much, It's Time to Make It Worth 5 Cents," *New York Times*, February 1, 2007; François Velde, "What's a Penny (or a Nickel) Really Worth?" Federal Reserve Bank of Chicago, Chicago Fed Letter, No. 235a, February 2007; and Nicholas Kohler, "A Penny Dropped," macleans.ca, January 14, 2011.

**Your Turn:** Test your understanding by doing related problems 2.10 and 2.11 on page 859 at the end of this chapter.

MyEconLab

## M2: A Broader Definition of Money

Before 1980, U.S. law prohibited banks from paying interest on checking account deposits. Households and firms held checking account deposits primarily to buy goods and services. M1 was, therefore, very close to the function of money as a medium of exchange. Almost all currency, checking account deposits, and traveler's checks were held with the intention of buying and selling, not with the intention of storing value. In 1980, the law was changed to allow banks to pay interest on certain types of checking accounts. This change reduced the difference between checking accounts and savings accounts, although people are still not allowed to write checks against their savings account balances.

After 1980, economists began to pay closer attention to a broader definition of the money supply, **M2**. As panel (b) of Figure 25.1 shows, M2 includes everything that is in M1, plus savings account deposits, small-denomination time deposits—such as certificates of deposit (CDs)—balances in money market deposit accounts in banks, and noninstitutional money market fund shares. Small-denomination time deposits are similar to savings accounts, but the deposits are for a fixed period of time—usually from six months to several years—and withdrawals before that time are subject to a penalty. Mutual fund companies sell shares to investors and use the funds raised to buy financial assets such as stocks and bonds. Some of these mutual funds, such as Vanguard's Treasury Money Market Fund or Fidelity's Cash Reserves Fund, are called *money market mutual funds* because they invest in very short-term bonds, such as U.S. Treasury bills. The balances in these funds are included in M2. Each week, the Federal Reserve publishes statistics on M1 and M2. In the discussion that follows, we will use the M1 definition of the money supply because it corresponds most closely to money as a medium of exchange.

There are two key points to keep in mind about the money supply:

1. The money supply consists of *both* currency and checking account deposits.
2. Because balances in checking account deposits are included in the money supply, banks play an important role in the way the money supply increases and decreases. We will discuss this second point further in the next section.

**M2** A broader definition of the money supply: It includes M1 plus savings account balances, small-denomination time deposits, balances in money market deposit accounts in banks, and noninstitutional money market fund shares.

# Don't Let This Happen to You

### Don't Confuse Money with Income or Wealth

According to *Forbes* magazine, Bill Gates's wealth of $56 billion makes him the second-richest person in the world. He also has a very large income, but how much money does he have? Your *wealth* is equal to the value of your assets minus the value of any debts you have. Your *income* is equal to your earnings during the year. Bill Gates's earnings as chairman of Microsoft and from his investments are very large. But his *money* is just equal to what he has in currency and in checking accounts. Only a small proportion of Gates's $56 billion in wealth is likely to be in currency or checking accounts. Most of his wealth is invested in stocks and bonds and other financial assets that are not included in the definition of money.

In everyday conversation, we often describe someone who is wealthy or who has a high income as "having a lot of money." But when economists use the word *money*, they are usually referring to currency plus checking account deposits. It is important to keep straight the differences between wealth, income, and money.

Just as money and income are not the same for a person, they are not the same for the whole economy. National income in the United States was equal to $12.8 trillion in 2010. The money supply in 2010 was $1.8 trillion (using the M1 measure). There is no reason national income in a country should be equal to the country's money supply, nor will an increase in a country's money supply necessarily increase the country's national income.

Based on "The World's Billionaires," *Forbes*, March 19, 2011.

MyEconLab

**Your Turn:** Test your understanding by doing related problems 2.7 and 2.8 on page 859 at the end of this chapter.

# Solved Problem 25.2

## The Definitions of M1 and M2

Suppose you decide to withdraw $2,000 from your checking account and use the money to buy a bank certificate of deposit (CD). Briefly explain how this will affect M1 and M2.

### Solving the Problem

**Step 1:** **Review the chapter material.** This problem is about the definitions of the money supply, so you may want to review the section "How Is Money Measured in the United States Today?" which begins on page 833.

**Step 2:** **Use the definitions of M1 and M2 to answer the problem.** Funds in checking accounts are included in both M1 and M2. Funds in CDs are included only in M2. It is tempting to answer this problem by saying that shifting $2,000 from a checking account to a CD reduces M1 by $2,000 and increases M2 by $2,000, but the $2,000 in your checking account was already counted in M2. So, the correct answer is that your action reduces M1 by $2,000 but leaves M2 unchanged.

**Your Turn:** For more practice, do related problems 2.5 and 2.6 on page 859 at the end of this chapter. MyEconLab

## What about Credit Cards and Debit Cards?

Many people buy goods and services with credit cards, yet credit cards are not included in definitions of the money supply. The reason is that when you buy something with a credit card, you are in effect taking out a loan from the bank that issued the credit card. Only when you pay your credit card bill at the end of the month—often with a check or an electronic transfer from your checking account—is the transaction complete. In contrast, with a debit card, the funds to make the purchase are taken directly from your checking account. In either case, the cards themselves do not represent money.

# How Do Banks Create Money?

We have seen that the most important component of the money supply is checking accounts in banks. To understand the role money plays in the economy, we need to look more closely at how banks operate. Banks are profit-making private businesses, just like bookstores and supermarkets. Some banks are quite small, with just a few branches, and they do business in a limited area. Others are among the largest corporations in the United States, with hundreds of branches spread across many states. The key role that banks play in the economy is to accept deposits and make loans. By doing this, they create checking account deposits.

## Bank Balance Sheets

To understand how banks create money, we need to briefly examine a typical bank balance sheet. Recall from Chapter 8 that on a balance sheet, a firm's assets are listed on the left, and its liabilities and stockholders' equity are listed on the right. Assets are the value of anything owned by the firm, liabilities are the value of anything the firm owes, and stockholders' equity is the difference between the total value of assets and the total value of liabilities. Stockholders' equity represents the value of the firm if it had to be closed, all its assets were sold, and all its liabilities were paid off. A corporation's stockholders' equity is also referred to as its *net worth*.

Figure 25.2 shows the actual balance sheet of a large bank. The key assets on a bank's balance sheet are its *reserves*, loans, and holdings of securities, such as U.S. Treasury bills.

**25.3 LEARNING** OBJECTIVE

Explain how banks create money.

| Assets (in millions) | | Liabilities and Stockholders' Equity (in millions) | |
|---|---|---|---|
| Reserves | $108,427 | Deposits | $1,010,430 |
| Loans | 898,555 | Short-term borrowing | 394,572 |
| Securities | 896,097 | Long-term debt | 359,180 |
| Buildings and equipment | 14,306 | Other liabilities | 272,479 |
| Other assets | 347,524 | Total liabilities | $2,036,661 |
| | | | |
| | | Stockholders' equity | 228,248 |
| Total assets | $2,264,909 | Total liabilities and stockholders' equity | $2,264,909 |

**Reserves** Deposits that a bank keeps as cash in its vault or on deposit with the Federal Reserve.

**Required reserves** Reserves that a bank is legally required to hold, based on its checking account deposits.

**Required reserve ratio** The minimum fraction of deposits banks are required by law to keep as reserves.

**Excess reserves** Reserves that banks hold over and above the legal requirement.

**Reserves** are deposits that a bank has retained rather than loaned out or invested. Banks keep reserves either physically within the bank, as *vault cash,* or on deposit with the Federal Reserve. Banks are required by law to keep as reserves 10 percent of their checking account deposits above a threshold level, which in 2011 was $58.8 million. These reserves are called **required reserves**. The minimum fraction of deposits that banks are required to keep as reserves is called the **required reserve ratio**. We can abbreviate the required reserve ratio as $RR$. Any reserves that banks hold over and above the legal requirement are called **excess reserves**. The balance sheet in Figure 25.2 shows that loans are this bank's largest asset, which is true of most banks.

Banks make *consumer loans* to households and *commercial loans* to businesses. A loan is an asset to a bank because it represents a promise by the person taking out the loan to make certain specified payments to the bank. A bank's reserves and its holdings of securities are also assets because they are things of value owned by the bank.

As with most banks, this bank's largest liability is its deposits. Deposits include checking accounts, savings accounts, and certificates of deposit. Deposits are liabilities to banks because they are owed to the households or firms that have deposited the funds. If you deposit $100 in your checking account, the bank owes you the $100, and you can ask for it back at any time. So, your checking account is an asset to you, and it is a liability to the bank.

## Using T-Accounts to Show How a Bank Can Create Money

It is easier to show how banks create money by using a T-account than by using a balance sheet. A T-account is a stripped-down version of a balance sheet that shows only how a transaction *changes* a bank's balance sheet. For example, suppose you deposit $1,000 in currency into an account at Bank of America. This transaction raises the total deposits at Bank of America by $1,000 and also raises its reserves by $1,000. We show this on the following T-account:

| Assets | | Liabilities | |
|---|---|---|---|
| Reserves | +$1,000 | Deposits | +$1,000 |

> Your deposit of $1,000 into your checking account increases Bank of America's assets and liabilities by the same amount.

Remember that because the total value of all the entries on the right side of a balance sheet must always be equal to the total value of all the entries on the left side of a balance sheet, any transaction that increases (or decreases) one side of the balance sheet must also increase (or decrease) the other side of the balance sheet. In this case, the T-account shows that we increased both sides of the balance sheet by $1,000.

Initially, this transaction does not increase the money supply. The currency component of the money supply declines by $1,000 because the $1,000 you deposited is no longer in circulation and, therefore, is not counted in the money supply. But the decrease in currency is offset by a $1,000 increase in the checking account deposit component of the money supply.

This initial change is not the end of the story, however. Banks are required to keep 10 percent of deposits as reserves. Because the Federal Reserve pays banks only a low rate of interest on their reserves, banks have an incentive to loan out or buy securities with the other 90 percent. In this case, Bank of America can keep $100 as required reserves and loan out the other $900, which represents excess reserves. Suppose Bank of America loans out the $900 to someone to buy a very inexpensive used car. Bank of America could give the $900 to the borrower in currency, but usually banks make loans by increasing the borrower's checking account. We can show this with another T-account:

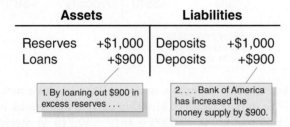

| Assets | | Liabilities | |
|---|---|---|---|
| Reserves | +$1,000 | Deposits | +$1,000 |
| Loans | +$900 | Deposits | +$900 |

1. By loaning out $900 in excess reserves . . .

2. . . . Bank of America has increased the money supply by $900.

A key point to recognize is that *by making this $900 loan, Bank of America has increased the money supply by $900*. The initial $1,000 in currency you deposited into your checking account has been turned into $1,900 in checking account deposits—a net increase in the money supply of $900.

But the story does not end here. The person who took out the $900 loan did so to buy a used car. To keep things simple, let's suppose he buys the car for exactly $900 and pays by writing a check on his account at Bank of America. The seller of the used car will now deposit the check in her bank. That bank may also be a branch of Bank of America, but in most cities, there are many banks, so let's assume that the seller of the car has her account at a branch of PNC Bank. Once she deposits the check, PNC Bank will send it to Bank of America to *clear* the check and collect the $900. We show the result in the following T-accounts:

### Bank of America

| Assets | | Liabilities | |
|---|---|---|---|
| Reserves | +$100 | Deposits | +$1,000 |
| Loans | +$900 | | |

1. When the $900 check that was deposited in a PNC account arrives to be cleared, the increase in Bank of America's reserves (shown in the previous T-account) falls by $900, to $100 . . .

2. . . . and the increase in Bank of America's deposits falls by $900, to $1,000.

### PNC Bank

| Assets | | Liabilities | |
|---|---|---|---|
| Reserves | +$900 | Deposits | +$900 |

After the check drawn on the account at Bank of America clears, PNC's reserves and deposits both increase by $900.

After the car buyer's check clears, Bank of America has lost $900 in deposits—the amount loaned to the car buyer—and $900 in reserves—the amount it had to pay PNC when PNC sent Bank of America the car buyer's check. PNC has an increase in checking account deposits of $900—the deposit of the car seller—and an increase in reserves of $900—the amount it received from Bank of America.

PNC has 100 percent reserves against this new $900 deposit, when it needs only 10 percent reserves. The bank has an incentive to keep $90 as reserves and to loan out the other $810, which are excess reserves. If PNC does this, we can show the change in its balance sheet by using another T-account:

**PNC Bank**

| **Assets** | | **Liabilities** | |
|---|---|---|---|
| Reserves | +$900 | Deposits | +$900 |
| Loans | +$810 | Deposits | +$810 |

By making an $810 loan, PNC has increased both its loans and its deposits by $810.

In loaning out the $810 in excess reserves, PNC creates a new checking account deposit of $810. The initial deposit of $1,000 in currency into Bank of America has now resulted in the creation of $1,000 + $900 + $810 = $2,710 in checking account deposits. The money supply has increased by $2,710 − $1,000 = $1,710.

The process is still not finished. The person who borrows the $810 will spend it by writing a check against his account. Whoever receives the $810 will deposit it in her bank, which could be a Bank of America branch or a PNC branch or a branch of some other bank. That new bank—if it's not PNC—will send the check to PNC and will receive $810 in new reserves. That new bank will have an incentive to loan out 90 percent of these reserves—keeping 10 percent to meet the legal requirement—and the process will go on. At each stage, the additional loans being made and the additional deposits being created are shrinking by 10 percent, as each bank has to withhold that amount as required reserves. We can use a table to show the total increase in checking account deposits set off by your initial deposit of $1,000. The dots in the table represent additional rounds in the money creation process:

| Bank | Increase in Checking Account Deposits | |
|---|---|---|
| Bank of America | $1,000 | |
| PNC | + 900 | ( = 0.9 × $1,000) |
| Third Bank | + 810 | ( = 0.9 × $900) |
| Fourth Bank | + 729 | ( = 0.9 × $810) |
| • | + • | |
| • | + • | |
| • | + • | |
| Total change in checking account deposits | = $10,000 | |

## The Simple Deposit Multiplier

Your initial deposit of $1,000 increased the reserves of the banking system by $1,000 and led to a total increase in checking account deposits of $10,000. The ratio of the amount of deposits created by banks to the amount of new reserves is called the **simple deposit multiplier**. In this case, the simple deposit multiplier is equal to $10,000/$1,000 = 10. Why 10? How do we know that your initial $1,000 deposit ultimately leads to a total increase in deposits of $10,000?

There are two ways to answer this question. First, each bank in the process is keeping reserves equal to 10 percent of its deposits. For the banking system as a whole, the total increase in reserves is $1,000—the amount of your original currency deposit. Therefore, the system as a whole will end up with $10,000 in deposits because $1,000 is 10 percent of $10,000.

**Simple deposit multiplier** The ratio of the amount of deposits created by banks to the amount of new reserves.

A second way to answer the question is by deriving an expression for the simple deposit multiplier. The total increase in deposits equals:

$$\$1,000 + [0.9 \times \$1,000] + [(0.9 \times 0.9) \times \$1,000] + [(0.9 \times 0.9 \times 0.9) \times \$1,000] + \ldots$$

or

$$\$1,000 + [0.9 \times \$1,000] + [0.9^2 \times \$1,000] + [0.9^3 \times \$1,000] + \ldots$$

or

$$\$1,000 + (1 + 0.9 + 0.9^2 + 0.9^3 + \ldots).$$

The rules of algebra tell us that an expression like the one in the parentheses sums to:

$$\frac{1}{1 - 0.9}.$$

Simplifying further, we have

$$\frac{1}{0.10} = 10.$$

So

$$\text{Total increase in deposit} = \$1,000 \times 10 = \$10,000.$$

Note that 10 is equal to 1 divided by the required reserve ratio, *RR*, which in this case is 10 percent, or 0.10. This gives us another way of expressing the simple deposit multiplier:

$$\text{Simple deposit multiplier} = \frac{1}{RR}.$$

This formula makes it clear that the higher the required reserve ratio, the smaller the simple deposit multiplier. With a required reserve ratio of 10 percent, the simple deposit multiplier is 10. If the required reserve ratio were 20 percent, the simple deposit multiplier would fall to 1/0.20, or 5. We can use this formula to calculate the total increase in checking account deposits from an increase in bank reserves due to, for instance, currency being deposited in a bank:

$$\text{Change in checking account deposits} = \text{Change in bank reserves} \times \frac{1}{RR}.$$

For example, if \$100,000 in currency is deposited in a bank and the required reserve ratio is 10 percent, then

$$\text{Change in checking account deposits} = \$100,000 \times \frac{1}{0.10}$$

$$= \$100,000 \times 10 = \$1,000,000.$$

# Don't Let This Happen to You

## Don't Confuse Assets and Liabilities

Consider the following reasoning: "How can checking account deposits be a liability to a bank? After all, they are something of value that is in the bank. Therefore, checking account deposits should be counted as a bank *asset* rather than as a bank liability."

This statement is incorrect. The balance in a checking account represents something the bank *owes* to the owner of the account. Therefore, it is a liability to the bank, although it is an asset to the owner of the account. Similarly, your car loan is a liability to you—because it is a debt you owe to the bank—but it is an asset to the bank.

MyEconLab

**Your Turn:** Test your understanding by doing related problem 3.12 on page 860 at the end of this chapter.

# Solved Problem 25.3

## Showing How Banks Create Money

Suppose you deposit $5,000 in currency into your checking account at a branch of PNC Bank, which we will assume has no excess reserves at the time you make your deposit. Also assume that the required reserve ratio is 0.10.

   **a.** Use a T-account to show the initial effect of this transaction on PNC's balance sheet.

   **b.** Suppose that PNC makes the maximum loan it can from the funds you deposited. Use a T-account to show the initial effect on PNC's balance sheet from granting the loan. Also include in this T-account the transaction from question a.

   **c.** Now suppose that whoever took out the loan in question b. writes a check for this amount and

that the person receiving the check deposits it in Bank of America. Show the effect of these transactions on the balance sheets of PNC Bank and Bank of America *after the check has cleared*. On the T-account for PNC Bank, include the transactions from questions a. and b.

   **d.** What is the maximum increase in checking account deposits that can result from your $5,000 deposit? What is the maximum increase in the money supply that can result from your deposit? Explain.

## Solving the Problem

**Step 1:** **Review the chapter material.** This problem is about how banks create checking account deposits, so you may want to review the section "Using T-Accounts to Show How a Bank Can Create Money," which begins on page 838.

**Step 2:** **Answer part a. by using a T-account to show the effect of the deposit.** Keeping in mind that T-accounts show only the changes in a balance sheet that result from the relevant transaction and that assets are on the left side of the account and liabilities are on the right side, we have:

**PNC Bank**

| Assets | | Liabilities | |
|---|---|---|---|
| Reserves | +$5,000 | Deposits | +$5,000 |

Because the bank now has your $5,000 in currency in its vault, its reserves (and, therefore, its assets) have risen by $5,000. But this transaction also increases your checking account balance by $5,000. Because the bank owes you this money, the bank's liabilities have also risen by $5,000.

**Step 3:** **Answer part b. by using a T-account to show the effect of the loan.** The problem tells you to assume that PNC Bank currently has no excess reserves and that the required reserve ratio is 10 percent. This requirement means that if the bank's checking account deposits go up by $5,000, the bank must keep $500 as reserves and can loan out the remaining $4,500. Remembering that new loans usually take the form of setting up, or increasing, a checking account for the borrower, we have:

**PNC Bank**

| Assets | | Liabilities | |
|---|---|---|---|
| Reserves | +$5,000 | Deposits | +$5,000 |
| Loans | +$4,500 | Deposits | +$4,500 |

The first line of the T-account shows the transaction from question a. The second line shows that PNC has loaned out $4,500 by increasing the checking account of the borrower by $4,500. The loan is an asset to PNC because it represents a promise by the borrower to make certain payments spelled out in the loan agreement.

**Step 4:** **Answer part c. by using T-accounts for PNC and Bank of America to show the effect of the check clearing.** We now show the effect of the borrower having spent the $4,500 he received as a loan from PNC. The person who received the $4,500 check deposits it in her account at Bank of America. We need two T-accounts to show this activity:

**PNC Bank**

| Assets | | Liabilities | |
|---|---|---|---|
| Reserves | +$500 | Deposits | +$5,000 |
| Loans | +$4,500 | | |

**Bank of America**

| Assets | | Liabilities | |
|---|---|---|---|
| Reserves | +$4,500 | Deposits | +$4,500 |

Look first at the T-account for PNC. Once Bank of America sends the check written by the borrower to PNC, PNC loses $4,500 in reserves, and Bank of America gains $4,500 in reserves. The $4,500 is also deducted from the account of the borrower. PNC is now satisfied with the result. It received a $5,000 deposit in currency from you. When that money was sitting in the bank vault, it wasn't earning any interest for PNC. Now $4,500 of the $5,000 has been loaned out and is earning interest. These interest payments allow PNC to cover its costs and earn a profit, which it has to do to remain in business.

Bank of America now has an increase in deposits of $4,500, resulting from the check being deposited, and an increase in reserves of $4,500. Bank of America is in the same situation as PNC was in question a: It has excess reserves as a result of this transaction and a strong incentive to lend them out.

**Step 5:** **Answer part d. by using the simple deposit multiplier formula to calculate the maximum increase in checking account deposits and the maximum increase in the money supply.** The simple deposit multiplier expression is (remember that $RR$ is the required reserve ratio)

$$\text{Change in checking account deposits} = \text{Change in bank reserves} \times \frac{1}{RR}.$$

In this case, bank reserves rose by $5,000 as a result of your initial deposit, and the required reserve ratio is 0.10, so:

$$\text{Change in checking account deposits} = \$5,000 \times \frac{1}{0.10}$$

$$= \$5,000 \times 10 = \$50,000.$$

Because checking account deposits are part of the money supply, it is tempting to say that the money supply has also increased by $50,000. Remember, though, that your $5,000 in currency was counted as part of the money supply while you had it, but it is not included when it is sitting in a bank vault. Therefore:

$$\text{Increase in checking account deposits} - \text{Decline in currency in circulation} = \text{Change in the money supply}$$

or

$$\$50,000 - \$5,000 = \$45,000.$$

MyEconLab **Your Turn:** For more practice, do related problem 3.10 on page 860 at the end of the chapter.

## The Simple Deposit Multiplier versus the Real-World Deposit Multiplier

The story we have told about the way an increase in reserves in the banking system leads to the creation of new deposits and, therefore, an increase in the money supply has been simplified in two ways. First, we assumed that banks do not keep any excess reserves. That is, we assumed that when you deposited $1,000 in currency into your checking account at Bank of America, it loaned out $900, keeping only the $100 in required reserves. In fact, banks often keep some excess reserves to guard against the possibility that many depositors may simultaneously make withdrawals from their accounts. During the financial crisis that began in 2007, banks kept substantial excess reserves. The more excess reserves banks keep, the smaller the deposit multiplier. Imagine an extreme case in which Bank of America keeps your entire $1,000 as reserves. If Bank of America does not loan out any of your deposit, the process described earlier—loans leading to the creation of new deposits, leading to the making of additional loans, and so on—will not take place. The $1,000 increase in reserves will lead to a total increase of $1,000 in deposits, and the deposit multiplier will be only 1, not 10.

Second, we assumed that the whole amount of every check is deposited in a bank; no one takes any of it out as currency. In reality, households and firms keep roughly constant the amount of currency they hold relative to the value of their checking account balances. So, we would expect to see people increasing the amount of currency they hold as the balances in their checking accounts rise. Once again, think of the extreme case. Suppose that when Bank of America makes the initial $900 loan to the borrower who wants to buy a used car, the seller of the car cashes the check instead of depositing it. In that case, PNC does not receive any new reserves and does not make any new loans. Once again, the $1,000 increase in your checking account at Bank of America is the only increase in deposits, and the deposit multiplier is 1.

The effect of these two factors is to reduce the real-world deposit multiplier to about 2.5 during normal times. This means that a $1 increase in the reserves of the banking system results in about a $2.50 increase in deposits. During the financial crisis of 2007–2009, the surge in bank holdings of excess reserves reduced the multiplier to about 1.

Although the story of the deposit multiplier can be complicated, the key point to bear in mind is that the most important part of the money supply is the checking account balance component. When banks make loans, they increase checking account balances, and the money supply expands. Banks make new loans whenever they gain reserves. The whole process can also work in reverse: If banks lose reserves, they reduce their outstanding loans and deposits, and the money supply contracts.

We can summarize these important conclusions:

1. When banks gain reserves, they make new loans, and the money supply expands.
2. When banks lose reserves, they reduce their loans, and the money supply contracts.

# The Federal Reserve System

Many people are surprised to learn that banks do not keep locked away in their vaults all the funds that are deposited in checking accounts. The United States, like nearly all other countries, has a **fractional reserve banking system**, which means that banks keep less than 100 percent of deposits as reserves. When people deposit money in a bank, the bank loans most of the money to someone else. What happens, though, if depositors want their money back? This would seem to be a problem because banks have loaned out most of the money and can't easily get it back.

In practice, though, withdrawals are usually not a problem for banks. On a typical day, about as much money is deposited as is withdrawn. If a small amount more is withdrawn than deposited, banks can cover the difference from their excess reserves or by borrowing from other banks. Sometimes depositors lose confidence in a bank when they question the value of the bank's underlying assets, particularly its loans. Often, the reason for a loss of confidence is bad news, whether true or false. When many depositors simultaneously decide to withdraw their money from a bank, there is a **bank run**. If many banks experience runs at the same time, the result is a **bank panic**. It is possible for one bank to handle a run by borrowing from other banks, but if many banks simultaneously experience runs, the banking system may be in trouble.

A *central bank*, like the Federal Reserve in the United States, can help stop a bank panic by acting as a *lender of last resort*. In acting as a lender of last resort, a central bank makes loans to banks that cannot borrow funds elsewhere. The banks can use these loans to pay off depositors. When the panic ends and the depositors put their money back in their accounts, the banks can repay the loans to the central bank.

## The Establishment of the Federal Reserve System

Bank panics lead to severe disruptions in business activity because households and firms have trouble gaining access to their accounts and may be unable to borrow money. Not surprisingly, in the United States, each bank panic in the late nineteenth and early twentieth centuries was accompanied by a recession. With the intention of putting an end to bank panics, in 1913, Congress passed the Federal Reserve Act, setting up the Federal Reserve System—often referred to as "the Fed." The system began operation in 1914, with the authority to make loans to banks. The loans the Fed makes to banks are called **discount loans**, and the interest rate it charges on the loans is called the **discount rate**. When a bank receives a loan from the Fed, its reserves increase by the amount of the loan.

The Fed's first test as a lender of last resort came in the early years of the Great Depression of the 1930s, when many banks were hit by bank runs as depositors pulled funds out of checking and savings accounts. Although the Fed had been established to act as a lender of last resort, Fed officials declined to make loans to many banks because the officials were worried that banks experiencing runs had made bad loans and other investments. The Fed believed that making loans to banks that were in financial trouble because of bad investments might reduce the incentive bank managers had to be careful in their investment decisions. Partly due to the Fed's unwillingness to act as a lender of last resort, more than 5,000 banks failed during the early 1930s. Today, many economists are critical of the Fed's decisions in the early 1930s because they believe these decisions increased the severity of the Great Depression. In 1934, Congress established the Federal Deposit Insurance Corporation (FDIC) to insure deposits in most banks up to a limit, which is currently $250,000 per deposit. Deposit insurance has greatly reduced bank runs because it has reassured all but the largest depositors that their deposits are safe, even if their bank goes out of business. During the financial crisis of 2007–2009, some banks experienced runs when depositors with funds exceeding the deposit insurance limit feared that they would suffer losses if their banks failed.

To aid the Fed in carrying out its responsibilities, in 1913 Congress divided the country into 12 Federal Reserve districts, as shown in Figure 25.3. Each district has its

**25.4 LEARNING** OBJECTIVE

Discuss the three policy tools the Federal Reserve uses to manage the money supply.

**Fractional reserve banking system** A banking system in which banks keep less than 100 percent of deposits as reserves.

**Bank run** A situation in which many depositors simultaneously decide to withdraw money from a bank.

**Bank panic** A situation in which many banks experience runs at the same time.

**Discount loans** Loans the Federal Reserve makes to banks.

**Discount rate** The interest rate the Federal Reserve charges on discount loans.

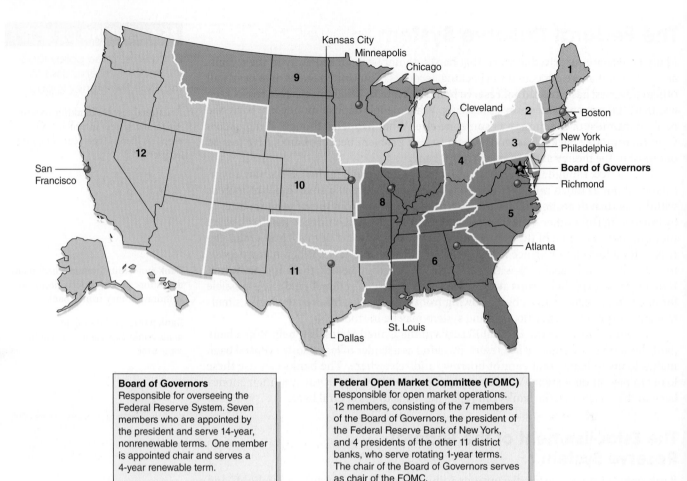

**Board of Governors**
Responsible for overseeing the
Federal Reserve System. Seven
members who are appointed by
the president and serve 14-year,
nonrenewable terms. One member
is appointed chair and serves a
4-year renewable term.

**Federal Open Market Committee (FOMC)**
Responsible for open market operations.
12 members, consisting of the 7 members
of the Board of Governors, the president of
the Federal Reserve Bank of New York,
and 4 presidents of the other 11 district
banks, who serve rotating 1-year terms.
The chair of the Board of Governors serves
as chair of the FOMC.

**Figure 25.3** **The Federal Reserve System**

The United States is divided into 12 Federal Reserve districts, each of which has a Federal Reserve bank. The real power within the Federal Reserve System, however, lies in Washington, DC, with the Board of Governors, which consists of 7 members appointed by the president. Monetary policy is carried out by the 14-member Federal Open Market Committee.

Data from Board of Governors of the Federal Reserve System.

own Federal Reserve bank, which provides services to banks in that district. The real power of the Fed, however, lies in Washington, DC, with the Board of Governors. The seven members of the Board of Governors are appointed by the president of the United States to 14-year, nonrenewable terms. One member of the Board of Governors is chosen to be chair and serves a 4-year, renewable term. In 2012, the chair of the Board of Governors was Ben Bernanke. In addition to acting as a lender of last resort to banks, the Fed acts as a bankers' bank, providing services such as check clearing to banks, and also has the responsibility of managing the nation's money supply.

## How the Federal Reserve Manages the Money Supply

Although Congress established the Fed primarily to stop bank panics by acting as a lender of last resort, today the Fed is also responsible for managing the money supply. As we will discuss in more detail in Chapter 26, managing the money supply is part of **monetary policy**, which the Fed undertakes to pursue macroeconomic objectives. To manage the money supply, the Fed uses three *monetary policy tools*:

**Monetary policy** The actions the Federal Reserve takes to manage the money supply and interest rates to pursue macroeconomic policy objectives.

1. Open market operations
2. Discount policy
3. Reserve requirements

Remember that the most important component of the money supply is checking account deposits. Not surprisingly, all three of the Fed's policy tools are aimed at affecting the reserves of banks as a means of changing the volume of checking account deposits.

**Open Market Operations** Eight times per year, the **Federal Open Market Committee (FOMC)** meets in Washington, DC, to discuss monetary policy. The committee has 12 voting members: the 7 members of the Federal Reserve's Board of Governors, the president of the Federal Reserve Bank of New York, and 4 presidents from the other 11 Federal Reserve banks. These 4 presidents serve one-year rotating terms on the FOMC. The chair of the Board of Governors also serves as the chair of the FOMC.

**Federal Open Market Committee (FOMC)** The Federal Reserve committee responsible for open market operations and managing the money supply in the United States.

The U.S. Treasury borrows money by selling bills, notes, and bonds. Remember that the *maturity* of a financial asset is the period of time until the purchaser receives payment of the face value or principal. Usually, bonds have face values of $1,000. Treasury bills have maturities of 1 year or less, Treasury notes have maturities of 2 years to 10 years, and Treasury bonds have maturities of 30 years. To increase the money supply, the FOMC directs the *trading desk*, located at the Federal Reserve Bank of New York, to *buy* U.S. Treasury securities—most frequently bills, but sometimes notes or bonds—from the public. When the sellers of the Treasury securities deposit the funds in their banks, the reserves of banks rise. This increase in reserves starts the process of increasing loans and checking account deposits that increases the money supply. To decrease the money supply, the FOMC directs the trading desk to *sell* Treasury securities. When the buyers of the Treasury securities pay for them with checks, the reserves of their banks fall. This decrease in reserves starts a contraction of loans and checking account deposits that reduces the money supply. The buying and selling of Treasury securities is called **open market operations**.

There are three reasons the Fed conducts monetary policy principally through open market operations. First, because the Fed initiates open market operations, it completely controls their volume. Second, the Fed can make both large and small open market operations. Third, the Fed can implement its open market operations quickly, with no administrative delay or required changes in regulations. Many other central banks, including the European Central Bank and the Bank of Japan, also use open market operations to conduct monetary policy.

**Open market operations** The buying and selling of Treasury securities by the Federal Reserve in order to control the money supply.

The Federal Reserve is responsible for putting the paper currency of the United States into circulation. Recall that if you look at the top of a dollar bill, you see the words "Federal Reserve Note." When the Fed takes actions to increase the money supply, commentators sometimes say that it is "printing more money." The main way the Fed increases the money supply, however, is not by printing more currency but by buying Treasury securities. Similarly, to reduce the money supply, the Fed does not set fire to stacks of paper currency. Instead, it sells Treasury securities. We will spend more time discussing how and why the Fed manages the money supply in Chapter 26, when we discuss monetary policy.

**Discount Policy** As we have seen, when a bank borrows money from the Fed by taking out a discount loan, the interest rate the bank pays is known as the discount rate. By lowering the discount rate, the Fed can encourage banks to take additional loans and thereby increase their reserves. With more reserves, banks will make more loans to households and firms, which will increase checking account deposits and the money supply. Raising the discount rate will have the reverse effect.

**Reserve Requirements** When the Fed reduces the required reserve ratio, it converts required reserves into excess reserves. For example, suppose a bank has $100 million in checking account deposits, and the required reserve ratio is 10 percent. The bank will be required to hold $10 million as reserves. If the Fed reduces the required reserve ratio to 8 percent, the bank will need to hold only $8 million as reserves. The Fed can thereby convert $2 million worth of reserves from required reserves to excess reserves. This $2 million is then available for the bank to lend out. If the Fed *raises* the required reserve ratio from 10 percent to 12 percent, it will have the reverse effect.

The Fed changes reserve requirements much more rarely than it conducts open market operations or changes the discount rate. Because changes in reserve requirements require significant alterations in banks' holdings of loans and securities, frequent changes would be disruptive. Also, because the Fed pays banks only a low interest rate on reserves, the use of reserve requirements to manage the money supply effectively places a tax on banks' deposit-taking and lending activities, which can be costly for the economy.

## The "Shadow Banking System" and the Financial Crisis of 2007–2009

The banks we have been discussing in this chapter are *commercial banks*, whose most important economic role is to accept funds from depositors and lend those funds to borrowers. In Chapter 8, we noted that large firms can sell stocks and bonds on financial markets but that investors are typically unwilling to buy stocks and bonds from small and medium-sized firms because they lack sufficient information on the financial health of smaller firms. So, smaller firms—and households—have traditionally relied on bank loans for their credit needs. In the past 20 years, however, two important developments have occurred in the financial system: (1) Banks have begun to resell many of their loans rather than keep them until they are paid off, and (2) financial firms other than commercial banks have become sources of credit to businesses.

**Securitization Comes to Banking** Traditionally, when a bank made a *residential mortgage loan* to a household to buy a home or made a commercial loan to a business, the bank would keep the loan and collect the payments until the loan was paid off. A financial asset—such as a loan or a stock or a bond—is considered a **security** if it can be bought and sold in a *financial market* as, for instance, shares of stock issued by the Coca-Cola Company can be bought and sold on the New York Stock Exchange. When a financial asset is first sold, the sale takes place in the *primary market*. Subsequent sales take place in the *secondary market*. Prior to 1970, most loans were not securities because they could not be resold—there was no secondary market for them. First, residential mortgages and then other loans, including car loans and commercial loans, began to be *securitized*. The process of **securitization** involves creating a secondary market in which loans that have been bundled together can be bought and sold in financial markets, just as corporate or government bonds are. Figure 25.4 outlines the securitization process.

**Security** A financial asset—such as a stock or a bond—that can be bought and sold in a financial market.

**Securitization** The process of transforming loans or other financial assets into securities.

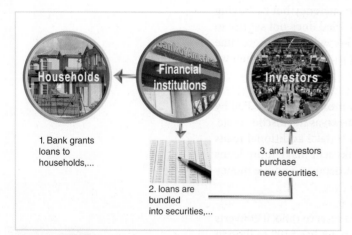

(a) Securitizing a loan

1. Bank grants loans to households,...

2. loans are bundled into securities,...

3. and investors purchase new securities.

(b) The flow of payments on a securitized loan

1. Banks collect loan payments from households,...

2. collect a fee for processing the payments ...

3. and send the payments to investors.

**Figure 25.4** **The Process of Securitization**

Panel (a) shows how in the securitization process banks grant loans to households and bundle the loans into securities that are then sold to investors. Panel (b) shows that banks collect payments on the original loans and, after taking a fee, send the payments to the investors who bought the securities.

We will discuss the process of securitization further in Chapter 26, when we discuss monetary policy.

**The Shadow Banking System** In addition to the changes resulting from securitization, the financial system was transformed in the 1990s and 2000s by the increasing importance of nonbank financial firms. Investment banks, such as Goldman Sachs and Morgan Stanley, differ from commercial banks in that they do not accept deposits, and they rarely lend directly to households. Instead, investment banks traditionally concentrated on providing advice to firms issuing stocks and bonds or considering mergers with other firms. In the late 1990s, investment banks expanded their buying of mortgages, bundling large numbers of them together as bonds known as *mortgage-backed securities*, and reselling them to investors. Mortgage-backed securities proved very popular with investors because they often paid higher interest rates than other securities with comparable default risk.

*Money market mutual funds* have also increased their importance in the financial system over time. These funds sell shares to investors and use the money to buy short-term securities such as Treasury bills and commercial paper issued by corporations. Commercial paper represents short-term borrowing corporations use to fund their day-to-day operations. Many corporations that previously met such needs by borrowing from banks began instead to sell commercial paper to money market mutual funds.

*Hedge funds* raise money from wealthy investors and use sophisticated investment strategies that often involve significant risk. By 2005, hedge funds had become an important source of demand for securitized loans and an important source of loans to other financial firms.

In 2008, Timothy Geithner, who became Treasury secretary in the Obama administration, referred to investment banks, money market mutual funds, hedge funds, and other financial firms engaged in similar activities as the "shadow banking system." By raising money from individual investors and providing it directly or indirectly to firms and households, these firms were carrying out a function that at one time was almost exclusively the domain of commercial banks.

**The Financial Crisis of 2007–2009** The firms in the shadow banking system differed from commercial banks in two important ways: First, the government agencies—including the Federal Reserve—that regulated the commercial banking system did not regulate these firms. Second, these firms were more highly *leveraged*—that is, they relied more heavily on borrowed money to finance their operations—than were commercial banks. If a firm uses a small amount of its own money and a lot of borrowed money to make an investment, both the firm's potential profits and its potential losses are increased. For example, suppose a firm invests $100 of its own money. If the investment earns a return of $3, the firm has earned 3 percent ($3/$100) on its funds. But if the firm's investment consists of $10 of its own money and $90 it has borrowed, a return of $3 becomes a return of 30 percent ($3/$10) on the firm's $10 investment. If the investment loses $2, however, the firm's return is −20 percent (−$2/$10). Leveraged investments have a potential for both large gains and large losses.

As mentioned earlier, commercial banks have rarely experienced runs since Congress established federal deposit insurance in the 1930s. However, beginning in 2007, firms in the shadow banking system were quite vulnerable to runs. As we will discuss further in Chapter 26, the underlying cause of the financial crisis of 2007–2009 was problems in the U.S. housing market. As housing prices began to fall, a significant number of borrowers began to default on their mortgages, which caused mortgage-backed securities to lose value. Financial firms, including both commercial banks and many firms in the shadow banking system, that had invested in these securities suffered heavy losses. The more leveraged the firm, the larger the losses. Although deposit insurance helped commercial banks avoid runs, investment banks and other financial firms that had borrowed short term and invested the funds long term were in trouble. As lenders refused to renew their short-term loans, many of these firms had to sell their holdings of securities in an attempt to raise cash. But as the prices of these securities continued to fall, the losses to these firms increased.

In the spring of 2008, the investment bank Bear Stearns was saved from bankruptcy only when the Federal Reserve arranged for it to be acquired by JPMorgan Chase. In the fall of 2008, the Federal Reserve and the U.S. Treasury decided not to take action to save the investment bank Lehman Brothers, which failed. The failure of Lehman Brothers reverberated throughout the financial system, setting off a panic. The process of securitization—apart from government-guaranteed residential mortgages—ground to a halt. The well-publicized difficulties of a money market mutual fund that had suffered losses on loans to Lehman Brothers led to a wave of withdrawals from these funds. In turn, the funds were no longer able to fulfill their role as buyers of corporate commercial paper. As banks and other financial firms sold assets and cut back on lending to shore up their financial positions, the flow of funds from savers to borrowers was disrupted. The resulting credit crunch significantly worsened the recession that had begun in December 2007.

**The Fed's Response** The Fed, in combination with the U.S. Treasury, took vigorous action to deal with the financial panic. We will discuss the Fed's actions further in Chapter 27, but for now, we can mention several particularly important policy actions. First, in the fall of 2008, under the Troubled Asset Relief Program (TARP), the Fed and Treasury began attempting to stabilize the commercial banking system by providing funds to banks in exchange for stock. Taking partial ownership of private commercial banks was an unprecedented move by the federal government. The Fed also modified its discount policy by setting up several new "lending facilities." These lending facilities made it possible for the Fed to grant discount loans to financial firms—such as investment banks—that had not previously been eligible. In addition, the Fed addressed problems in the commercial paper market by directly buying commercial paper for the first time since the 1930s.

Although the recession continued into 2009, the extraordinary actions of the Treasury and Fed appeared to have stabilized the financial system. Still, even by late 2011, the flow of funds from savers to borrowers had not yet returned to normal levels, and economists and policymakers were debating the wisdom of some of the Fed's actions. We will return to the Fed's response to the recession of 2007–2009 in Chapter 27.

**25.5 LEARNING** OBJECTIVE

Explain the quantity theory of money and use it to explain how high rates of inflation occur.

# The Quantity Theory of Money

People have been aware of the connection between increases in the money supply and inflation for centuries. In the sixteenth century, the Spanish conquered Mexico and Peru and shipped large quantities of gold and silver from those countries back to Spain. The gold and silver were minted into coins and spent across Europe to further the political ambitions of the Spanish kings. Prices in Europe rose steadily during these years, and many observers discussed the relationship between this inflation and the flow of gold and silver into Europe from the Americas.

## Connecting Money and Prices: The Quantity Equation

In the early twentieth century, Irving Fisher, an economist at Yale, formalized the connection between money and prices by using the *quantity equation*:

$$M \times V = P \times Y.$$

The quantity equation states that the money supply ($M$) multiplied by the *velocity of money* ($V$) equals the price level ($P$) multiplied by real output ($Y$). Fisher defined the

**velocity of money**, often referred to simply as "velocity," as the average number of times each dollar of the money supply is used to purchase goods and services included in GDP. Rewriting the original equation by dividing both sides by $M$, we have the equation for velocity:

$$V = \frac{P \times Y}{M}.$$

**Velocity of money** The average number of times each dollar in the money supply is used to purchase goods and services included in GDP.

If we use M1 to measure the money supply, the GDP price deflator to measure the price level, and real GDP to measure real output, the value for velocity for 2010 was

$$V = \frac{1.11 \times \$13,088 \text{ billion}}{\$1,832 \text{ billion}} = 7.9.$$

This result tells us that, on average during 2010, each dollar of M1 was spent about eight times on goods or services included in GDP.

Because velocity is defined to be equal to $(P \times Y)/M$, we know that the quantity equation must always hold true: The left side *must* be equal to the right side. A theory is a statement about the world that might possibly be false. Therefore, the quantity equation is not a theory. Irving Fisher turned the quantity equation into the **quantity theory of money** by asserting that velocity was constant. He argued that the average number of times a dollar is spent depends on how often people get paid, how often they do their grocery shopping, how often businesses mail bills, and other factors that do not change very often. Because this assertion may be true or false, the quantity theory of money is, in fact, a theory.

**Quantity theory of money** A theory about the connection between money and prices that assumes that the velocity of money is constant.

## The Quantity Theory Explanation of Inflation

The quantity equation gives us a way of showing the relationship between changes in the money supply and changes in the price level, or inflation. To see this relationship more clearly, we can use a handy mathematical rule that states that an equation where variables are multiplied together is equal to an equation where the *growth rates* of these variables are *added* together. So, we can transform the quantity equation from

$$M \times V = P \times Y$$

to

Growth rate of the money supply + Growth rate of velocity =
Growth rate of the price level (or inflation rate) + Growth rate of real output.

This way of writing the quantity equation is more useful for investigating the effect of changes in the money supply on the inflation rate. Remember that the growth rate for any variable is the percentage change in the variable from one year to the next. The growth rate of the price level is the inflation rate, so we can rewrite the quantity equation to help understand the factors that determine inflation:

Inflation rate = Growth rate of the money supply +
Growth rate of velocity − Growth rate of real output.

If Irving Fisher was correct that velocity is constant, then the growth rate of velocity will be zero. That is, if velocity is, say, always eight, then its percentage change from one year to the next will always be zero. This assumption allows us to rewrite the equation one last time:

Inflation rate = Growth rate of the money supply − Growth rate of real output.

This equation leads to the following predictions:

1. If the money supply grows at a faster rate than real GDP, there will be inflation.
2. If the money supply grows at a slower rate than real GDP, there will be deflation. (Recall that *deflation* is a decline in the price level.)
3. If the money supply grows at the same rate as real GDP, the price level will be stable, and there will be neither inflation nor deflation.

It turns out that Irving Fisher was wrong in asserting that the velocity of money is constant. From year to year, there can be significant fluctuations in velocity. As a result, the predictions of the quantity theory of money do not hold every year, but most economists agree that the quantity theory provides useful insight into the long-run relationship between the money supply and inflation: *In the long run, inflation results from the money supply growing at a faster rate than real GDP.*

## How Accurate Are Estimates of Inflation Based on the Quantity Theory?

Note that the accuracy of the quantity theory depends on whether the key assumption that velocity is constant is correct. If velocity is not constant, then there may not be a tight link between increases in the money supply and increases in the price level. For example, an increase in the quantity of money might be offset by a decline in velocity, leaving the price level unaffected. Because velocity can move erratically in the short run, we would not expect the quantity equation to provide good forecasts of inflation in the short run. Over the long run, however, there is a strong link between changes in the money supply and inflation. Panel (a) of Figure 25.5 shows the relationship between the growth of the M2 measure of the money supply and the inflation rate by decade in the United States. (We use M2 here because data on M2 are available for a longer period of time than for M1.) Because of variations in the rate of growth of real GDP and in velocity, there is not an exact relationship between the growth rate of M2 and the inflation rate. But there is a clear pattern that decades with higher growth rates in the money supply were also decades with higher inflation rates. In other words, most of the variation in inflation rates across decades can be explained by variation in the rates of growth of the money supply.

Panel (b) provides further evidence consistent with the quantity theory by looking at rates of growth of the money supply and rates of inflation across countries for the decade from 1999 to 2008. Although there is not an exact relationship between rates

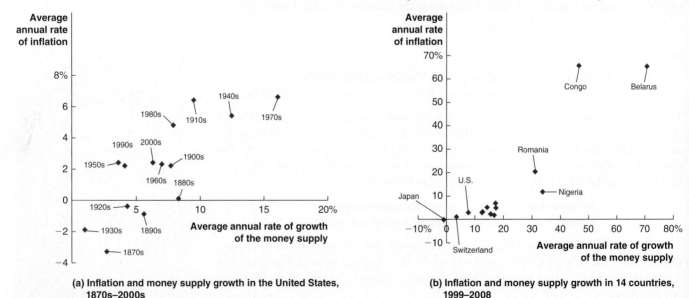

**(a) Inflation and money supply growth in the United States, 1870s–2000s**

**(b) Inflation and money supply growth in 14 countries, 1999–2008**

**Figure 25.5** **The Relationship between Money Growth and Inflation over Time and around the World**

Panel (a) shows that, by and large, in the United States, the rate of inflation has been highest during the decades in which the money supply has increased most rapidly, and the rate of inflation has been lowest during the decades in which the money supply has increased least rapidly. Panel (b) shows that for the decade from 1999 to 2008, there is not an exact relationship between money supply growth and inflation, but in countries such as the United States, Japan, and Switzerland, both the growth rate of the money supply and the rate of inflation

were low, while countries such as Belarus, the Congo, and Romania had both high rates of growth of the money supply and high rates of inflation.

Data from: Panel (a): for 1870s to 1960s, Milton Friedman and Anna J. Schwartz, *Monetary Trends in the United States and United Kingdom: Their Relation to Income, Prices, and Interest Rates, 1867–1975*, (Chicago: University of Chicago Press, 1982), Table 4.8; and for the 1970s to 2000s: Federal Reserve Board of Governors and U.S. Bureau of Economic Analysis; Panel (b): World Bank.

# Conclusion

Money plays a key role in the functioning of an economy by facilitating trade in goods and services and by making specialization possible. Without specialization, no advanced economy can prosper. Households and firms, banks, and the central bank (the Federal Reserve in the United States) are participants in the process of creating the money supply. In Chapter 26, we will explore how the Federal Reserve uses monetary policy to promote its economic objectives.

*An Inside Look at Policy* on the next page discusses how an increase in bank lending to consumers and businesses is a positive signal for the economy.

# Increased Lending Boosts Money Supply Growth

## FISCAL TIMES

## Bank Lending Signals a Strengthening Economy

The financial crisis of 2008 rocked the foundation of the U.S. banking sector. The shock left banks short of capital and hesitant to lend, even as the recession cut deeply into loan demand. The Federal Reserve has pumped in an ocean of lendable funds, trying to prime the process of bringing banks and borrowers together. But many still wonder when, if ever, bank lending will return to normal.

We're not there yet, but recent signs have been encouraging. Despite the sluggish economy, loan growth is finally beginning to pick up in key areas, reflecting both greater willingness to lend and increased desire to borrow. Loan volume of U.S. commercial banks rose at a one percent annual rate in June as expansion in business loans and non-mortgage consumer lending more than offset the ongoing contraction in real estate financing. It was the third consecutive monthly increase after steady declines for more than two years. . . .

(a) Lending to businesses is leading the credit upswing. The volume of commercial and industrial (C&I) loans in the second quarter rose at a 9.6 percent annual rate, the largest increase in 2½ years. Banks have progressively eased lending standards for C&I loans to large and medium-sized companies for the past six quarters. Small companies have seen easier terms and conditions in each of the past four quarters. Economists expect to see signs that this loosening in standards is continuing when the Fed issues it third-quarter report from bank senior loan officers in mid-August.

More credit is starting to flow to small businesses, as well. That's important, because small firms account for about half of U.S. job creation, and depend greatly on banks for credit, unlike large corporations that have the option to raise funds in the capital markets by issuing bonds. In the second quarter, the balance of banks reporting stronger vs. weaker demand for commercial and industrial (C&I) loans by small businesses was positive for the first time in five years, according to the latest Fed survey. Another positive sign is the gradual rise in C&I loans made by small banks, whose customers tend to be small local companies. Small-bank C&I loan volume has been rising gradually in 2011 after hitting bottom late last year.

Despite increased attention by policymakers over the past year to the dearth of small business lending, the problem has been not so much banks' unwillingness to lend but simply a lack of loan demand, reflecting weak sales. Although the percentage of small companies saying credit is harder to get is still somewhat higher than before the recession, it has fallen steadily over the past two years, from a peak of 16 percent, to 9 percent in June, according to the National Federation of Independent Business.

(b) Banks are also warming to consumer loans. Despite sluggish job markets, households have made great progress in getting their financial obligations under control, allowing qualified borrowers to take on more debt. So far this year, monthly financial obligations of households have fallen to only 16.4 percent of household income, the lowest since 1994. In the second quarter, the percentage of banks reporting increased demand for auto loans was the highest since 2003.

Banks began easing lending standards for auto loans, credit cards, and other borrowing this time last year. In the 2011 second quarter the percentage of loan officers saying they were more willing to make consumer loans rose to the highest level in 17 years. . . .

(c) The ebb and flow of bank lending during recessions and recoveries exerts a powerful force on any business cycle. Aside from this cycle's problems in mortgage lending, banks are finally beginning to behave as they usually do in a recovery. Barring some new shock, especially from the debt troubles in Washington or Europe, evidence that loan growth is beginning to expand in response to easier lending standards and stronger loan demand is a key sign that the recovery has staying power.

Source: "Bank Lending Signals a Strengthening Economy" by James C. Cooper, from *Fiscal Times* website, August 1st, 2011. Copyright © 2011 by The Fiscal Times. Reprinted with permission.

## Key Points in the Article

The financial crisis of 2007–2009 resulted in decreases in both the supply of funds available to lend and in the demand for those funds. Despite the Federal Reserve's infusion of large amounts of funds into the economy, bank lending continued to decline for more than two years. In April 2011, loan volumes finally began to increase. The largest increase occurred in business lending, with the volume of commercial and industrial (C&I) loans rising at an annual rate of 9.6 percent for the second quarter of 2011, which was the largest increase in over two years. The increase in small business lending was particularly encouraging, with banks in the second quarter reporting increased demand for small business loans for the first time in five years. The market for consumer loans was improving as well. As consumer debt as a percentage of income fell to its lowest level since 1994, banks became more willing to make consumer loans. The expansion of loan growth was a positive sign for the economy during what had been a sluggish recovery from the recession.

## Analyzing the News

ⓐ As we saw in Chapter 9, banks help channel funds from savers to borrowers by making loans to individuals and

businesses. Rising defaults on home loans after the housing bubble burst led to the collapse of a number of financial intermediaries in 2008, and loan volume declined for more than two years. Growth in the market for loans reemerged in the second quarter of 2011, with business loans leading the upswing. Commercial and industrial loans rose at an annual rate of 9.6 percent as banks continued to loosen lending requirements for small, medium, and large companies. As Figure 1 below shows, the percentage change in commercial and industrial bank loans turned positive toward the end of 2010, and it accelerated for much of the second quarter of 2011.

ⓑ Loans to consumers began to increase in mid-2011. Following the collapse of financial markets in 2008, banks were much less willing to make consumer loans, increasing their lending standards as households' financial obligations grew. The decrease in the supply of funds available to households was met with a decrease in the demand for these funds as households worked to reduce their debts. As household debts became more manageable, banks became increasingly willing to make consumer loans, as shown in Figure 2 below.

ⓒ As you read in this chapter, banks create money by loaning out excess reserves. Because of the money multiplier process, a given amount of new reserves

results in a multiple increase in bank deposits. In an attempt to bring lenders and borrowers together following the financial crisis of 2008, the Federal Reserve made a large amount of new funds available to financial markets. These extra funds had the potential to affect the economy as banks, responding to an increase in demand, finally began to see an increase in loans in 2011. The increases in excess reserves, bank deposits, and loan volume are indications that the economy was in the expansion phase of the business cycle and were positive signs for continued economic recovery.

## Thinking Critically About Policy

1. During the financial crisis of 2007–2009, the Fed attempted to stimulate the economy by taking actions to increase the money supply. How effective would these actions be if banks remained reluctant to make consumer loans while households remained reluctant to obtain loans? Briefly explain.

2. The quantity theory of money predicts that a large increase in the money supply will result in inflation. Why, then, even though the money supply increased rapidly was inflation relatively low during the recession of 2007–2009 and its immediate aftermath?

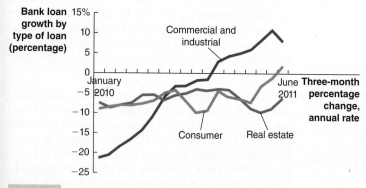

**Figure 1**

Loans to businesses and consumers are growing, but real estate loans keep falling.

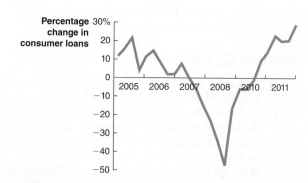

**Figure 2**

More banks say they are willing to make consumer loans.

# Chapter Summary and Problems

## Key Terms

Asset, p. 830

Bank panic, p. 845

Bank run, p. 845

Commodity money, p. 830

Discount loans, p. 845

Discount rate, p. 845

Excess reserves, p. 838

Federal Open Market Committee (FOMC), p. 847

Federal Reserve, p. 832

Fiat money, p. 832

Fractional reserve banking system, p. 845

M1, p. 834

M2, p. 836

Monetary policy, p. 846

Money, p. 830

Open market operations, p. 847

Quantity theory of money, p. 851

Required reserve ratio, p. 838

Required reserves, p. 838

Reserves, p. 838

Securitization, p. 848

Security, p. 848

Simple deposit multiplier, p. 840

Velocity of money, p. 851

---

**25.1** **What Is Money, and Why Do We Need It? pages 830–833**
LEARNING OBJECTIVE: Define money and discuss the four functions of money.

## Summary

A *barter economy* is an economy that does not use money and in which people trade goods and services directly for other goods and services. Barter trade occurs only if there is a *double coincidence of wants*, where both parties to the trade want what the other one has. Because barter is inefficient, there is strong incentive to use **money**, which is any **asset** that people are generally willing to accept in exchange for goods or services or in payment of debts. An *asset* is anything of value owned by a person or a firm. A **commodity money** is a good used as money that also has value independent of its use as money. Money has four functions: It is a medium of exchange, a unit of account, a store of value, and a standard of deferred payment. The *gold standard* was a monetary system under which the government produced gold coins and paper currency that were convertible into gold. The gold standard collapsed in the early 1930s. Today, no government in the world issues paper currency that can be redeemed for gold. Instead, paper currency is **fiat money**, which has no value except as money.

MyEconLab   Visit www.myeconlab.com to complete these exercises online and get instant feedback.

## Review Questions

**1.1** A baseball fan with an Albert Pujols baseball card wants to trade it for a Derek Jeter baseball card, but everyone the fan knows who has a Jeter card doesn't want a Pujols card. What do economists call the problem this fan is having?

**1.2** What is the difference between commodity money and fiat money?

**1.3** What are the four functions of money? Can something be considered money if it does not fulfill all four functions?

**1.4** Why do businesses accept paper currency when they know that, unlike a gold coin, the paper the currency is printed on is worth very little?

## Problems and Applications

**1.5** The English economist William Stanley Jevons described a world tour during the 1880s by a French singer, Mademoiselle Zélie. One stop on the tour was a theater in the Society Islands, part of French Polynesia in the South Pacific. She performed for her usual fee, which was one-third of the receipts. This turned out to be three pigs, 23 turkeys, 44 chickens, 5,000 coconuts, and "considerable quantities of bananas, lemons, and oranges." She estimated that all of this would have had a value in France of 4,000 francs. According to Jevons, "as Mademoiselle could not consume any considerable portion of the receipts herself, it became necessary in the meantime to feed the pigs and poultry with the fruit." Do the goods Mademoiselle Zélie received as payment fulfill the four functions of money described in the chapter? Briefly explain.

Based on W. Stanley Jevons, *Money and the Mechanism of Exchange*, (New York: D. Appleton and Company, 1889), pp. 1–2.

**1.6** **[Related to the** Chapter Opener **on page 829]** An article in the New York Times provides the following description of a hospital in Zimbabwe: "People lined up on the veranda of the American mission hospital here from miles around to barter for doctor visits and medicines, clutching scrawny chickens, squirming goats and buckets of maize." Why wouldn't the people buying medical services at this hospital use money to pay for the medical services they are buying?

From Celia W. Dugger, "Zimbabwe Health Care, Paid With Peanuts," *New York Times*, December 18, 2011.

**1.7** In the late 1940s, the Communists under Mao Zedong were defeating the government of China in a civil war. The paper currency issued by the Chinese government was losing much of its value, and most businesses refused to accept it. At the same time, there was a paper shortage in Japan. During these years, Japan was still under military occupation by the United States, following its defeat in World War II. Some of the U.S. troops in Japan realized that they could use dollars to buy up vast amounts of paper currency in China, ship it to Japan to be recycled into paper, and make a substantial profit. Under these circumstances, was the Chinese paper currency a commodity money or a fiat money? Briefly explain.

**1.8** According to Peter Heather, a historian at the University of Oxford, during the Roman Empire, the German tribes

east of the Rhine River produced no coins of their own but used Roman coins instead:

> Although no coinage was produced in Germania, Roman coins were in plentiful circulation and could easily have provided a medium of exchange (already in the first century, Tacitus tells us, Germani of the Rhine region were using good-quality Roman silver coins for this purpose).

a. What is a medium of exchange?

b. What does the author mean when he writes that Roman coins could have provided the German tribes with a medium of exchange?

c. Why would any member of a German tribe have been willing to accept a Roman coin from another member of the tribe in exchange for goods or services when the tribes were not part of the Roman Empire and were not governed by Roman law?

Based on Peter Heather, *The Fall of the Roman Empire: A New History of Rome and the Barbarians*, (New York: Oxford University Press, 2006), p. 89.

1.9 **[Related to the** Making the Connection **on page 833]** Suppose that Congress changes the law to require all firms to accept paper currency in exchange for whatever they are selling. Briefly discuss who would gain and who would lose from this legislation.

---

## 25.2   How Is Money Measured in the United States Today? pages 833–837

LEARNING OBJECTIVE: Discuss the definitions of the money supply used in the United States today.

## Summary

The narrowest definition of the money supply in the United States today is **M1**, which includes currency, checking account balances, and traveler's checks. A broader definition of the money supply is **M2**, which includes everything that is in M1, plus savings accounts, small-denomination time deposits (such as certificates of deposit [CDs]), money market deposit accounts in banks, and noninstitutional money market fund shares.

 MyEconLab   Visit www.myeconlab.com to complete these exercises online and get instant feedback.

## Review Questions

2.1 What is the main difference between the M1 and M2 definitions of the money supply?

2.2 Why does the Federal Reserve use two definitions of the money supply rather than one?

2.3 Distinguish among money, income, and wealth. Which one of the three does the central bank of a country control?

## Problems and Applications

2.4 Briefly explain whether each of the following is counted in M1.
 a. The coins in your pocket
 b. The funds in your checking account
 c. The funds in your savings account
 d. The traveler's checks that you have left over from a trip
 e. Your Citibank Platinum MasterCard

2.5 **[Related to** Solved Problem 25.2 **on page 837]** Suppose you have $2,000 in currency in a shoebox in your closet. One day, you decide to deposit the money in a checking account. Briefly explain how this will affect M1 and M2.

2.6 **[Related to** Solved Problem 25.2 **on page 837]** Suppose you decide to withdraw $100 in currency from your checking account. What is the effect on M1? Ignore any actions the bank may take as a result of your having withdrawn the $100.

2.7 **[Related to the** Don't Let This Happen to You **on page 836]** Briefly explain whether you agree with the following

statement: "I recently read that more than half of the money issued by the government is actually held by people in foreign countries. If that's true, then the United States is less than half as wealthy as government statistics indicate."

2.8 **[Related to the** Don't Let This Happen to You **on page 836]** A newspaper article contains the statement: "Income is only one way of measuring wealth." Do you agree that income is a way of measuring wealth?

From Sam Roberts, "As the Data Show, There's a Reason the Wall Street Protesters Chose New York," *New York Times*, October 25, 2011.

2.9 The paper currency of the United States is technically called "Federal Reserve Notes." The following excerpt is from the Federal Reserve Act: "Federal Reserve Notes . . . shall be redeemed in lawful money on demand at the Treasury Department of the United States, in the city of Washington, District of Columbia, or at any Federal Reserve bank." If you took a $20 bill to the Treasury Department or a Federal Reserve bank, with what type of "lawful money" is the government likely to redeem it?

2.10 **[Related to the** Making the Connection **on page 835]** In the nineteenth century, the Canadian government had difficulty getting banks and the public to accept the penny, which had been introduced a few years before. As a result, the government offered pennies for sale at a 20 percent discount. One account of this episode describes what the Canadian government did as "negative seigniorage." What is seigniorage? Why might the Canadian government's selling pennies at a 20 percent discount be considered "negative seigniorage"?

Based on Nicholas Kohler, "A Penny Dropped," macleans.ca, January 14, 2011.

2.11 **[Related to the** Making the Connection **on p 835]** There are currently about 1.4 billion pennies in circulation. Suppose the proposal of economist François Velde to make the current penny worth 5 cents were adopted. What would be the effect on the value of M1? Is this change likely to have much impact on the economy? (*Hint*: According to the information given in this chapter, what is the current value of M1?)

Based on Austan Goolsbee, "Now That a Penny Isn't Worth Much, It's Time to Make It Worth 5 Cents," *New York Times*, February 1, 2007.

**25.3** **How Do Banks Create Money?** pages 837–844

LEARNING OBJECTIVE: Explain how banks create money.

## Summary

On a bank's balance sheet, *reserves* and loans are assets, and deposits are liabilities. **Reserves** are deposits that the bank has retained rather than loaned out or invested. **Required reserves** are reserves that banks are legally required to hold. The fraction of deposits that banks are required to keep as reserves is called the **required reserve ratio**. Any reserves banks hold over and above the legal requirement are called **excess reserves**. When a bank accepts a deposit, it keeps only a fraction of the funds as reserves and loans out the remainder. In making a loan, a bank increases the checking account balance of the borrower. When the borrower uses a check to buy something with the funds the bank has loaned, the seller deposits the check in his bank. The seller's bank keeps part of the deposit as reserves and loans out the remainder. This process continues until no banks have excess reserves. In this way, the process of banks making new loans increases the volume of checking account balances and the money supply. This money creation process can be illustrated with T-accounts, which are stripped-down versions of balance sheets that show only how a transaction changes a bank's balance sheet. The **simple deposit multiplier** is the ratio of the amount of deposits created by banks to the amount of new reserves. An expression for the simple deposit multiplier is $1/RR$.

MyEconLab Visit **www.myeconlab.com** to complete these exercises online and get instant feedback.

## Review Questions

**3.1** What are the largest asset and the largest liability of a typical bank?

**3.2** Suppose you decide to withdraw $100 in cash from your checking account. Draw a T-account showing the effect of this transaction on your bank's balance sheet.

**3.3** What does it mean to say that banks "create money"?

**3.4** Give the formula for the simple deposit multiplier. If the required reserve ratio is 20 percent, what is the maximum increase in checking account deposits that will result from an increase in bank reserves of $20,000?

**3.5** What causes the real-world money multiplier to be smaller than the simple deposit multiplier?

## Problems and Applications

**3.6** An article on The Motley Fool Web site states:

> Deposits are the lifeblood of banks. Bank of America for example, had nearly $1 trillion in deposits at the end of March, representing nearly half of its total liabilities. Citigroup and Wells Fargo held around $800 billion each in deposits at the end of the first quarter.

Briefly explain the statement "deposits are the life-blood of banks."

"Should Your Bank Deposits Be at Risk?" by Matt Koppenheffer from www.fool.com, May 21, 2009. Copyright © 2009 by The Motley Fool. Reprinted by permission.

**3.7** The following is from an article on community banks: "Their commercial-lending businesses, funded by their stable deposit bases, make them steady earners." What is commercial lending? In what sense are loans "funded" by deposits?

From Karen Richardson, "Clean Books Bolster Traditional Lenders," *Wall Street Journal*, April 30, 2007.

**3.8** "Most of the money supply of the United States is created by banks making loans." Briefly explain whether you agree with this statement.

**3.9** Would a series of bank runs in a country decrease the total quantity of M1? Wouldn't a bank run simply move funds in a checking account to currency in circulation? How could that movement of funds decrease the quantity of money?

**3.10** **[Related to** Solved Problem 25.3 **on page 842]** Suppose you deposit $2,000 in currency into your checking account at a branch of Bank of America, which we will assume has no excess reserves at the time you make your deposit. Also assume that the required reserve ratio is 0.20, or 20 percent.

a. Use a T-account to show the initial impact of this transaction on Bank of America's balance sheet.

b. Suppose that Bank of America makes the maximum loan it can from the funds you deposited. Using a T-account, show the initial impact of granting the loan on Bank of America's balance sheet. Also include on this T-account the transaction from part a.

c. Now suppose that whoever took out the loan in part b writes a check for this amount and that the person receiving the check deposits it in a branch of Citibank. Show the effect of these transactions on the balance sheets of Bank of America and Citibank *after the check has been cleared*. (On the T-account for Bank of America, include the transactions from parts a and b.)

d. What is the maximum increase in checking account deposits that can result from your $2,000 deposit? What is the maximum increase in the money supply? Explain.

**3.11** Consider the following simplified balance sheet for a bank:

| Assets | | Liabilities | |
|---|---|---|---|
| Reserves | $10,000 | Deposits | $70,000 |
| Loans | $66,000 | Stockholders' equity | $6,000 |

a. If the required reserve ratio is 0.10, or 10 percent, how much in excess reserves does the bank hold?

b. What is the maximum amount by which the bank can expand its loans?

c. If the bank makes the loans in part b, show the *immediate* impact on the bank's balance sheet.

**3.12** **[Related to the** Don't Let This Happen to You **on page 841]** Briefly explain whether you agree with the following statement: "Assets are things of value that people own. Liabilities are debts. Therefore, a bank will always consider a checking account deposit to be an asset and a car loan to be a liability."

**25.4** The Federal Reserve System, pages 845–850

LEARNING OBJECTIVE: Discuss the three policy tools the Federal Reserve uses to manage the money supply.

## Summary

The United States has a **fractional reserve banking system** in which banks keep less than 100 percent of deposits as reserves. In a **bank run**, many depositors decide simultaneously to withdraw money from a bank. In a **bank panic**, many banks experience runs at the same time. The **Federal Reserve System** ("the Fed") is the central bank of the United States. It was originally established in 1913 to stop bank panics. The recession of 2007–2009 put renewed emphasis on the Fed's goal of financial market stability. **Monetary policy** refers to the actions the Federal Reserve takes to manage the money supply and interest rates to pursue macroeconomic policy objectives. The Fed's three monetary policy tools are open market operations, discount policy, and reserve requirements. **Open market operations** are the buying and selling of Treasury securities by the Federal Reserve. The loans the Fed makes to banks are called **discount loans**, and the interest rate the Fed charges on discount loans is the **discount rate**. The **Federal Open Market Committee (FOMC)** meets in Washington, DC, eight times per year to discuss monetary policy. In the past 20 years, a "shadow banking system" has developed. During the financial crisis of 2007–2009, the existence of the shadow banking system complicated the Fed's policy response. A **security** is a financial asset—such as a stock or a bond—that can be bought and sold in a financial market. The process of **securitization** involves creating a secondary market in which loans that have been bundled together can be bought and sold in financial markets just as corporate or government bonds are.

MyEconLab    Visit **www.myeconlab.com** to complete these exercises online and get instant feedback.

## Review Questions

4.1 Why did Congress decide to set up the Federal Reserve System in 1913?

4.2 What policy tools does the Fed use to control the money supply? Which tool is the most important?

4.3 Why does an open market purchase of Treasury securities by the Federal Reserve increase bank reserves? Why does an open market sale of Treasury securities by the Federal Reserve decrease bank reserves?

4.4 What is the "shadow banking system"? Why were the financial firms of the shadow banking system more vulnerable than commercial banks to bank runs?

## Problems and Applications

4.5 The text explains that the United States has a "fractional reserve banking system." Why do most depositors seem to be unworried that banks loan out most of the deposits they receive?

4.6 Suppose that you are a bank manager, and the Federal Reserve raises the required reserve ratio from 10 percent to 12 percent. What actions would you need to take? How would your actions and those of other bank managers end up affecting the money supply?

4.7 Suppose that the Federal Reserve makes a $10 million discount loan to First National Bank (FNB) by increasing FNB's account at the Fed.

   a. Use a T-account to show the impact of this transaction on FNB's balance sheet. Remember that the funds a bank has on deposit at the Fed count as part of its reserves.

   b. Assume that before receiving the discount loan, FNB has no excess reserves. What is the maximum amount of this $10 million that FNB can lend out?

   c. What is the maximum total increase in the money supply that can result from the Fed's discount loan? Assume that the required reserve ratio is 10 percent.

4.8 In a speech delivered in June 2008, Timothy Geithner, then president of the Federal Reserve Bank of New York and later U.S. Treasury secretary, said:

> The structure of the financial system changed fundamentally during the boom. . . . [The] non-bank financial system grew to be very large. . . . [The] institutions in this parallel financial system [are] vulnerable to a classic type of run, but without the protections such as deposit insurance that the banking system has in place to reduce such risks.

   a. What did Geithner mean by the "non-bank financial system"?

   b. What is a "classic type of run," and why were institutions in the nonbank financial system vulnerable to it?

   c. Why would deposit insurance provide the banking system with protection against runs?

From Timothy F. Geithner, "Reducing Systemic Risk in a Dynamic Financial System," remarks at the Economics Club of New York, June 9, 2008.

4.9 When the Federal Reserve steps in as the lender of last resort to prevent a bank panic, does this constitute a "bail out of the banks"? Briefly explain.

**25.5** **The Quantity Theory of Money,** pages 850–855

LEARNING OBJECTIVE: Explain the quantity theory of money and use it to explain how high rates of inflation occur.

## Summary

The *quantity equation*, which relates the money supply to the price level, is $M \times V = P \times Y$ where $M$ is the money supply, $V$ is the *velocity of money*, $P$ is the price level, and $Y$ is real output. The **velocity of money** is the average number of times each dollar in the money supply is spent during the year. Economist Irving Fisher developed the **quantity theory of money**, which assumes that the velocity of money is constant. If the quantity theory of money is correct, the inflation rate should equal the rate of growth of the money supply minus the rate of growth of real output. Although the quantity theory of money is not literally correct because the velocity of money is not constant, it is true that in the long run, inflation results from the money supply growing faster than real GDP. When governments attempt to raise revenue by selling large quantities of bonds to the central bank, the money supply will increase rapidly, resulting in a high rate of inflation.

 **MyEconLab** Visit **www.myeconlab.com** to complete these exercises online and get instant feedback.

## Review Questions

**5.1** What is the quantity theory of money? What explanation does the quantity theory provide for inflation?

**5.2** Is the quantity theory of money better able to explain the inflation rate in the long run or in the short run? Briefly explain.

**5.3** What is hyperinflation? Why do governments sometimes allow it to occur?

## Problems and Applications

**5.4** If the money supply is growing at a rate of 6 percent per year, real GDP is growing at a rate of 3 percent per year, and velocity is constant, what will the inflation rate be? If velocity is increasing 1 percent per year instead of remaining constant, what will the inflation rate be?

**5.5** Suppose that during one period, the velocity of money is constant and during another period, it undergoes large fluctuations. During which period will the quantity theory of money be more useful in explaining changes in the inflation rate? Briefly explain.

**5.6** In an article titled "We Should Celebrate Price Deflation" in the *American Free Press*, Professor Peter Spencer of York University in England is quoted as saying: "This printing of money 'will keep the [deflation] wolf from the door.'" In the same article, Ambrose Evans-Pritchard, a writer for the London-based newspaper *The Telegraph*, is quoted as saying: "Deflation has . . . insidious traits. It causes shoppers to hold back. Once this psychology gains a grip, it can gradually set off a self-feeding spiral that is hard to stop."

  **a.** What is price deflation?

  **b.** What does Professor Spencer mean by the statement, "This printing of money 'will keep the [deflation] wolf from the door'"?

  **c.** Why would deflation cause "shoppers to hold back," and what does Evans-Pritchard mean when he says, "Once this psychology gains a grip, it can gradually set off a self-feeding spiral that is hard to stop"?

  Based on Doug French, "We Should Celebrate Price Deflation," *American Free Press*, November 17, 2008.

**5.7** During the Civil War, the Confederate States of America printed lots of its own currency—Confederate dollars—to fund the war. By the end of the war, the Confederate government had printed nearly 1.5 billion paper dollars. How would such a large quantity of Confederate dollars have affected the value of the Confederate currency? With the war drawing to an end, would Southerners have been as willing to use and accept Confederate dollars? How else could they have made exchanges?

  Based on Federal Reserve Bank of Richmond, "Textual Transcript of Confederate Currency."

**5.8** [**Related to the** Chapter Opener **on page 829**] In April 2009, the African nation of Zimbabwe suspended the use of its own currency, the Zimbabwean dollar. According to an article from the Voice of America, "Hyperinflation in 2007 and 2008 made Zimbabwe's currency virtually worthless despite the introduction of bigger and bigger notes, including a 10 trillion dollar bill." Zimbabwe's Economic Planning Minister, Elton Mangoma, was quoted as saying the Zimbabwean dollar "will be out for at least a year," and in January 2009, the government of Zimbabwe made the U.S. dollar the country's official currency. Why would hyperinflation make a currency "virtually worthless"? How might using the U.S. dollar as its currency help to stabilize Zimbabwe's economy?

  From Voice of America News, "Zimbabwe Suspends Use of Own Currency," voanews.com, April 12, 2009.

**5.9** [**Related to the** Chapter Opener **on page 829**] A *New York Times* article on Zimbabwe describes conditions in summer 2008 as follows: "Official inflation soared to 2.2 million percent in Zimbabwe—by far the highest in the world . . . [and] unemployment has reached 80 percent." Is there a connection between the very high inflation rate and the very high rate of unemployment? Briefly explain.

  From "Inflation Soars to 2 Million Percent in Zimbabwe," *New York Times*, July 17, 2008.

**5.10** [**Related to the** Making the Connection **on page 853**] During the German hyperinflation of the 1920s, many households and firms in Germany were hurt economically. Do you think any groups in Germany benefited from the hyperinflation? Briefly explain.

## Chapter Outline and Learning Objectives

# Monetary Policy, Toll Brothers, and the Housing Market

If you lose your job or are afraid that you might, you are not likely to buy a new house. It's not surprising, then, that residential construction tends to fall during a recession. In addition, recessions often begin after the Federal Reserve increases interest rates to slow the growth in aggregate demand in order to reduce the inflation rate. Higher interest rates increase the cost of buying houses, further reducing demand for them. Not surprisingly, firms that build homes usually don't do well during recessions. For example, during the recessions of 1974–1975 and 1981–1982, residential construction declined by more than 30 percent.

The recession of 2001 was different, however. In early 2001, the members of the Federal Reserve's Federal Open Market Committee (FOMC) concluded that a recession was about to begin and took action to drive down interest rates. This action succeeded in heading off what some economists had predicted would be a prolonged and severe recession. In fact, the Fed's strategy resulted in spending on residential construction actually rising by 5 percent during the 2001 recession.

Toll Brothers is a homebuilder headquartered in Huntingdon Valley, Pennsylvania.

Toll Brothers' profit actually increased during 2001. However, the recession of 2007–2009 was a different story. Toll Brothers suffered a record loss of more than $750 million— and it wasn't alone. Nearly all homebuilders suffered severe declines in sales, and many went bankrupt. The key problem was that by 2005, the housing market boom had turned into a "bubble." In a bubble, prices soar to levels that are not sustainable. When the housing bubble finally burst in 2006, sales of new homes and prices of existing homes began a sharp decline. By 2007, the economy had entered a recession. This time, unfortunately, the Fed found that cutting interest rates was not enough to revive the housing market or the general economy. Beginning in 2008, the Fed was forced to turn to new policies to try to pull the economy out of recession.

In this chapter, we will study how monetary policy affects economic activity. Read **AN INSIDE LOOK AT POLICY** on **page 896** for a discussion of "Operation Twist," the Federal Reserve's attempt to boost the economy in late 2011.

Based on Toll Brothers, *Annual Report*, 2010.

## Economics in Your Life

### Should You Buy a House during a Recession?

If you are like most college students, buying a house is one of the farthest things from your mind. But suppose you think forward a few years to when you might be married and maybe even (gasp!) have children. Leaving behind years of renting apartments, you are considering buying a house. But, suppose that according to an article in the *Wall Street Journal*, a majority of economists are predicting that a recession is likely to begin soon. What should you do? Would this be a good time or a bad time to buy a house? As you read the chapter, see if you can answer these questions. You can check your answers against those we provide on **page 895** at the end of this chapter.

I n Chapter 25, we saw that banks play an important role in providing credit to households and firms, and in creating the money supply. We also saw that Congress established the Federal Reserve to stabilize the financial system and that the Fed is responsible for managing the money supply. In this chapter, we will discuss the Fed's four main policy goals: (1) price stability, (2) high employment, (3) stability of financial markets and institutions, and (4) economic growth. We will explore how the Federal Reserve decides which *monetary policy* actions to take to achieve its goals.

**26.1 LEARNING** OBJECTIVE

Define monetary policy and describe the Federal Reserve's monetary policy goals.

**Monetary policy** The actions the Federal Reserve takes to manage the money supply and interest rates to pursue macroeconomic policy goals.

# What Is Monetary Policy?

In 1913, Congress passed the Federal Reserve Act, creating the Federal Reserve System ("the Fed"). The main responsibility of the Fed was to make discount loans to banks to prevent the bank panics we discussed in Chapter 25. As a result of the Great Depression of the 1930s, Congress amended the Federal Reserve Act to give the Federal Reserve's Board of Governors broader responsibility to act "so as to promote effectively the goals of maximum employment, stable prices, and moderate long-term interest rates."

Since World War II, the Federal Reserve has carried out an active *monetary policy*. **Monetary policy** refers to the actions the Fed takes to manage the money supply and interest rates to pursue its macroeconomic policy goals.

## The Goals of Monetary Policy

The Fed has four main *monetary policy goals* that are intended to promote a well-functioning economy:

1. Price stability
2. High employment
3. Stability of financial markets and institutions
4. Economic growth

We briefly consider each of these goals.

**Price Stability** As we have seen in previous chapters, rising prices erode the value of money as a medium of exchange and a store of value. Especially after inflation rose dramatically and unexpectedly during the 1970s, policymakers in most industrial countries have had price stability as a policy goal. Figure 26.1 shows that from the early 1950s until 1968, the inflation rate remained below 4 percent per year. Inflation was above

**Figure 26.1**

**The Inflation Rate, January 1952–August 2011**

For most of the 1950s and 1960s, the inflation rate in the United States was 4 percent or less. During the 1970s, the inflation rate increased, peaking during 1979–1981, when it averaged more than 10 percent. After 1992, the inflation rate was usually less than 4 percent, until increases in oil prices pushed it above 5 percent during summer 2008. The effects of the recession caused several months of deflation—a falling price level—during early 2009.
*Note:* The inflation rate is measured as the percentage change in the consumer price index (CPI) from the same month in the previous year.

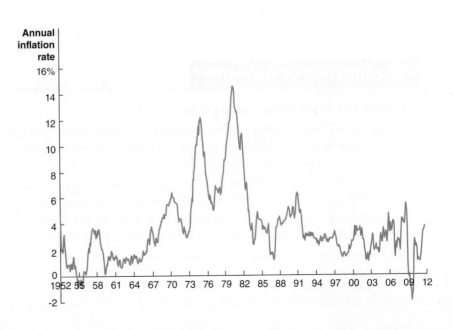

4 percent for most of the 1970s. In early 1979, the inflation rate increased to more than 10 percent, where it remained until late 1981, when it began to rapidly fall back to the 4 percent range. After 1992, the inflation rate was usually below 4 percent, until rapid increases in gasoline prices helped push it above 5 percent in summer 2008. The effects of the recession caused several months of deflation—a falling price level—during early 2009.

The inflation rates during the years 1979–1981 were the highest the United States has ever experienced during peacetime. When Paul Volcker became chairman of the Federal Reserve's Board of Governors in August 1979, he made fighting inflation his top policy goal. Alan Greenspan, who succeeded Volcker in August 1987, and Ben Bernanke, who succeeded Greenspan in January 2006, continued to focus on inflation. Volcker, Greenspan, and Bernanke argued that if inflation is low over the long run, the Fed will have the flexibility it needs to lessen the impact of recessions. Although the severity of the 2007–2009 recession led the Fed to adopt extraordinary policy measures that we will discuss later in this chapter, price stability remains a key policy goal of the Fed.

**High Employment**   In addition to price stability, high employment, or a low rate of unemployment, is an important monetary policy goal. Unemployed workers and underused factories and office buildings reduce GDP below its potential level. Unemployment causes financial distress and decreases the self-esteem of workers who lack jobs. The goal of high employment extends beyond the Fed to other branches of the federal government. At the end of World War II, Congress passed the Employment Act of 1946, which stated that it was the "responsibility of the Federal Government ... to foster and promote ... conditions under which there will be afforded useful employment, for those able, willing, and seeking to work, and to promote maximum employment, production, and purchasing power." Because price stability and high employment are explicitly mentioned in the Employment Act, it is sometimes said that the Fed has a *dual mandate* to attain these two goals.

**Stability of Financial Markets and Institutions**   Resources are lost when financial markets and institutions are not efficient in matching savers and borrowers. Firms with the potential to produce goods and services that consumers value cannot obtain the financing they need to design, develop, and market those products. Savers waste resources looking for satisfactory investments. The Fed promotes the stability of financial markets and institutions so that an efficient flow of funds from savers to borrowers will occur. As we saw in Chapter 25, the financial crisis of 2007–2009 brought the issue of stability in financial markets to the forefront.

The financial crisis of 2007–2009 was similar to the banking crises that led Congress to create the Federal Reserve System in 1913. A key difference is that while earlier banking crises affected commercial banks, the events of 2007–2009 also affected investment banks. Investment banks can be subject to *liquidity problems* because they often borrow short term—sometimes as short as overnight—and invest the funds in longer-term investments. Commercial banks borrow from households and firms in the form of checking and savings deposits, while investment banks borrow primarily from other financial firms, such as other investment banks, mutual funds, or hedge funds, which are similar to mutual funds but typically engage in more complex—and risky—investment strategies. Just as commercial banks can experience crises if depositors begin to withdraw funds, investment banks can experience crises if other financial firms stop offering them short-term loans. In 2008, the Fed decided to ease the liquidity problems facing investment banks by temporarily allowing them to receive discount loans, which had previously been available only to commercial banks. Later in this chapter, we will discuss in more detail the new policies the Fed enacted to help deal with the financial crisis.

**Economic Growth**   We discussed in Chapters 21 and 22 the importance of economic growth to raising living standards. Policymakers aim to encourage *stable* economic growth because it allows households and firms to plan accurately and encourages the long-run investment that is needed to sustain growth. Policy can spur economic growth

by providing incentives for saving to ensure a large pool of investment funds, as well as by providing direct incentives for business investment. Congress and the president, however, may be better able to increase saving and investment than is the Fed. For example, Congress and the president can change the tax laws to increase the return to saving and investing. In fact, some economists question whether the Fed can play a role in promoting economic growth beyond attempting to meet its goals of price stability, high employment, and financial stability.

In the next section, we will look at how the Fed attempts to attain its monetary policy goals. Although the Fed has multiple monetary policy goals, during most periods, its most important goals have been price stability and high employment. But the turmoil in financial markets that began in 2007 led the Fed to put new emphasis on the goal of financial market stability.

**26.2 LEARNING** OBJECTIVE

Describe the Federal Reserve's monetary policy targets and explain how expansionary and contractionary monetary policies affect the interest rate.

# The Money Market and the Fed's Choice of Monetary Policy Targets

The Fed aims to use its policy tools to achieve its monetary policy goals. Recall from Chapter 25 that the Fed's policy tools are open market operations, discount policy, and reserve requirements. At times, the Fed encounters conflicts between its policy goals. For example, as we will discuss later in this chapter, the Fed can raise interest rates to reduce the inflation rate. But, as we saw in Chapter 24, higher interest rates typically reduce household and firm spending, which may result in slower growth and higher unemployment. So, a policy that is intended to achieve one monetary policy goal, such as reducing inflation, may have an adverse effect on another policy goal, such as high employment.

## Monetary Policy Targets

The Fed tries to keep both the unemployment and inflation rates low, but it can't affect either of these economic variables directly. The Fed cannot tell firms how many people to employ or what prices to charge for their products. Instead, the Fed uses variables, called *monetary policy targets*, that it can affect directly and that, in turn, affect variables, such as real GDP, employment, and the price level, that are closely related to the Fed's policy goals. The two main monetary policy targets are the money supply and the interest rate. As we will see, the Fed typically uses the interest rate as its policy target.

It's important to bear in mind that while the Fed has typically used the money supply and the interest rate as its targets, these targets were not central to the Fed's policy decisions during the recession of 2007–2009. As we will discuss later in this chapter, because U.S. financial markets suffered a degree of disruption not seen since the Great Depression of the 1930s, the Fed was forced to develop new policy tools. However, it is still important to have a good grasp of how the Fed carries out policy during normal times.

## The Demand for Money

The Fed's two monetary policy targets are related in an important way. To see this relationship, we first need to examine the demand and supply for money. Figure 26.2 shows the demand curve for money. The interest rate is on the vertical axis, and the quantity of money is on the horizontal axis. Here we are using the M1 definition of money, which equals currency in circulation plus checking account deposits. Notice that the demand curve for money is downward sloping.

To understand why the demand curve for money is downward sloping, consider that households and firms have a choice between holding money and holding other financial assets, such as U.S. Treasury bills. Money has one particularly desirable characteristic: You can use it to buy goods, services, or financial assets. Money also has one undesirable characteristic: It earns either no interest or a very low rate of interest. The currency in your wallet earns no interest, and the money in your checking account earns

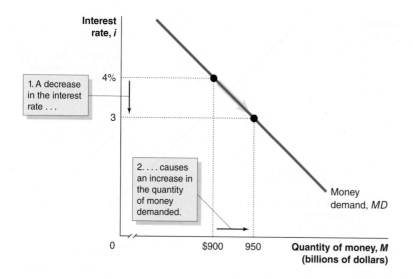

**1. A decrease in the interest rate . . .**

**2. . . . causes an increase in the quantity of money demanded.**

**Figure 26.2**

**The Demand for Money**

The money demand curve slopes downward because lower interest rates cause households and firms to switch from financial assets such as U.S. Treasury bills to money. All other things being equal, a fall in the interest rate from 4 percent to 3 percent will increase the quantity of money demanded from $900 billion to $950 billion. An increase in the interest rate will decrease the quantity of money demanded.

either no interest or very little interest. Alternatives to money, such as U.S. Treasury bills, pay interest but have to be sold if you want to use the funds to buy something. When interest rates rise on financial assets such as U.S. Treasury bills, the amount of interest that households and firms lose by holding money increases. When interest rates fall, the amount of interest households and firms lose by holding money decreases. Remember that *opportunity cost* is what you have to forgo to engage in an activity. The interest rate is the opportunity cost of holding money.

We now have an explanation of why the demand curve for money slopes downward: When interest rates on Treasury bills and other financial assets are low, the opportunity cost of holding money is low, so the quantity of money demanded by households and firms will be high; when interest rates are high, the opportunity cost of holding money will be high, so the quantity of money demanded will be low. In Figure 26.2, a decrease in interest rates from 4 percent to 3 percent causes the quantity of money demanded by households and firms to rise from $900 billion to $950 billion.

## Shifts in the Money Demand Curve

We saw in Chapter 3 that the demand curve for a good is drawn holding constant all variables, other than the price, that affect the willingness of consumers to buy the good. Changes in variables other than the price cause the demand curve to shift. Similarly, the demand curve for money is drawn holding constant all variables, other than the interest rate, that affect the willingness of households and firms to hold money. Changes in variables other than the interest rate cause the demand curve to shift. The two most important variables that cause the money demand curve to shift are real GDP and the price level.

An increase in real GDP means that the amount of buying and selling of goods and services will increase. This additional buying and selling increases the demand for money as a medium of exchange, so the quantity of money households and firms want to hold increases at each interest rate, shifting the money demand curve to the right. A decrease in real GDP decreases the quantity of money demanded at each interest rate, shifting the money demand curve to the left. A higher price level increases the quantity of money required for a given amount of buying and selling. Eighty years ago, for example, when the price level was much lower and someone could purchase a new car for $500 and a salary of $30 per week put you in the middle class, the quantity of money demanded by households and firms was much lower than today, even adjusting for the effect of the lower real GDP and smaller population of those years. An increase in the price level increases the quantity of money demanded at each interest rate, shifting the money demand curve to the right. A decrease in the price level decreases the quantity of money demanded at each interest rate, shifting the money demand curve to the left. Figure 26.3 illustrates shifts in the money demand curve.

**Shifts in the Money Demand Curve**

Changes in real GDP or the price level cause the money demand curve to shift. An increase in real GDP or an increase in the price level will cause the money demand curve to shift from $MD_1$ to $MD_2$. A decrease in real GDP or a decrease in the price level will cause the money demand curve to shift from $MD_1$ to $MD_3$.

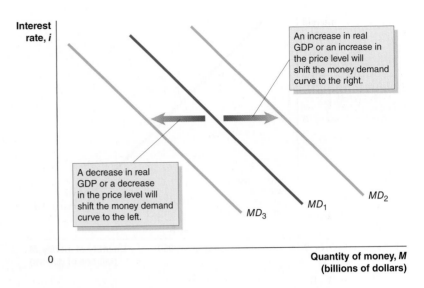

## How the Fed Manages the Money Supply: A Quick Review

Having discussed money demand, we now turn to money supply. In Chapter 25, we saw how the Federal Reserve manages the money supply. Eight times per year, the Federal Open Market Committee (FOMC) meets in Washington, DC. If the FOMC decides to increase the money supply, it orders the trading desk at the Federal Reserve Bank of New York to purchase U.S. Treasury securities. The sellers of these Treasury securities deposit the funds they receive from the Fed in banks, which increases the banks' reserves. Typically, the banks loan out most of these reserves, which creates new checking account deposits and expands the money supply. If the FOMC decides to decrease the money supply, it orders the trading desk to sell Treasury securities, which decreases banks' reserves and contracts the money supply.

## Equilibrium in the Money Market

In Figure 26.4, we include both the money demand and money supply curves. We can use this figure to see how the Fed affects both the money supply and the interest rate. For simplicity, we assume that the Federal Reserve is able to completely control the money supply. Therefore, the money supply curve is a vertical line, and changes

**The Effect on the Interest Rate When the Fed Increases the Money Supply**

When the Fed increases the money supply, households and firms will initially hold more money than they want, relative to other financial assets. Households and firms use the money they don't want to hold to buy Treasury bills and make deposits in interest-paying bank accounts. This increase in demand allows banks and sellers of Treasury bills and similar securities to offer lower interest rates. Eventually, interest rates will fall enough that households and firms will be willing to hold the additional money the Fed has created. In the figure, an increase in the money supply from $900 billion to $950 billion causes the money supply curve to shift to the right, from $MS_1$ to $MS_2$, and causes the equilibrium interest rate to fall from 4 percent to 3 percent.

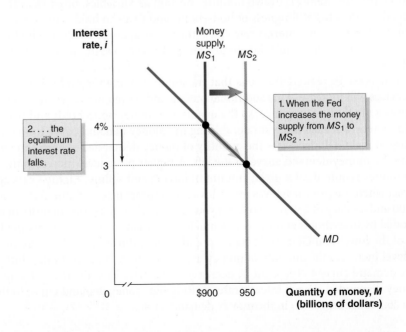

in the interest rate have no effect on the quantity of money supplied. Just as with other markets, equilibrium in the *money market* occurs where the money demand curve crosses the money supply curve. If the Fed increases the money supply, the money supply curve will shift to the right, and the equilibrium interest rate will fall. In Figure 26.4, when the Fed increases the money supply from $900 billion to $950 billion, the money supply curve shifts from $MS_1$ to $MS_2$, and the equilibrium interest rate falls from 4 percent to 3 percent.

In the money market, the adjustment from one equilibrium to another equilibrium is a little different from the adjustment in the market for a good. In Figure 26.4, the money market is initially in equilibrium, with an interest rate of 4 percent and a money supply of $900 billion. When the Fed increases the money supply by $50 billion, households and firms have more money than they want to hold at an interest rate of 4 percent. What do households and firms do with the extra $50 billion? They are most likely to use the money to buy short-term financial assets, such as Treasury bills, or to deposit the money in interest-paying bank accounts, such as certificates of deposit. This increase in demand for interest-paying bank accounts and short-term financial assets allows banks to offer lower interest rates on certificates of deposit, and it allows sellers of Treasury bills and similar assets to also offer lower interest rates. As the interest rates on certificates of deposit, Treasury bills, and other short-term assets fall, the opportunity cost of holding money also falls. Households and firms move down the money demand curve. Eventually the interest rate will have fallen enough that households and firms are willing to hold the additional $50 billion worth of money the Fed has created, and the money market will be back in equilibrium. To summarize: *When the Fed increases the money supply, the short-term interest rate must fall until it reaches a level at which households and firms are willing to hold the additional money.*

Figure 26.5 shows what happens when the Fed decreases the money supply. The money market is initially in equilibrium, at an interest rate of 4 percent and a money supply of $900 billion. If the Fed decreases the money supply to $850 billion, households and firms will be holding less money than they would like, relative to other financial assets, at an interest rate of 4 percent. To increase their money holdings, they will sell Treasury bills and other short-term financial assets and withdraw funds from certificates of deposit and other interest-paying bank accounts. Banks will have to offer higher interest rates in order to retain depositors, and sellers of Treasury bills and similar securities will have to offer higher interest rates in order to find buyers. Rising short-term interest rates increase the opportunity cost of holding money, causing households and firms to move up the money demand curve. Equilibrium is finally restored at an interest rate of 5 percent.

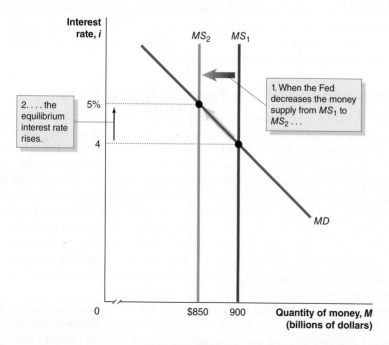

**Figure 26.5**

**The Effect on Interest Rates When the Fed Decreases the Money Supply**

When the Fed decreases the money supply, households and firms will initially hold less money than they want, relative to other financial assets. Households and firms will sell Treasury bills and other financial assets and withdraw money from interest-paying bank accounts. These actions will increase interest rates. Eventually, interest rates will rise to the point at which households and firms will be willing to hold the smaller amount of money that results from the Fed's actions. In the figure, a reduction in the money supply from $900 billion to $850 billion causes the money supply curve to shift to the left, from $MS_1$ to $MS_2$, and causes the equilibrium interest rate to rise from 4 percent to 5 percent.

## A Tale of Two Interest Rates

In Chapter 21, we discussed the loanable funds model of the interest rate. In that model, the equilibrium interest rate is determined by the demand and supply for loanable funds. Why do we need two models of the interest rate? The answer is that the loanable funds model is concerned with the *long-term real rate of interest*, and the money market model is concerned with the *short-term nominal rate of interest*. The long-term real rate of interest is the interest rate that is most relevant when savers consider purchasing a long-term financial investment such as a corporate bond. It is also the rate of interest that is most relevant to firms that are borrowing to finance long-term investment projects such as new factories or office buildings, or to households that are taking out mortgage loans to buy new homes.

When conducting monetary policy, however, the short-term nominal interest rate is the most relevant interest rate because it is the interest rate most affected by increases and decreases in the money supply. Often—but not always—there is a close connection between movements in the short-term nominal interest rate and movements in the long-term real interest rate. So, when the Fed takes actions to increase the short-term nominal interest rate, usually the long-term real interest rate also increases. In other words, as we will discuss in the next section, when the interest rate on Treasury bills rises, the real interest rate on mortgage loans usually also rises, although sometimes only after a delay.

## Choosing a Monetary Policy Target

As we have seen, the Fed uses monetary policy targets to affect economic variables such as real GDP or the price level, that are closely related to the Fed's policy goals. The Fed can use either the money supply or the interest rate as its monetary policy target. As Figure 26.5 shows, the Fed is capable of affecting both. The Fed has generally focused more on the interest rate than on the money supply. Since 1980, deregulation and financial innovations, including paying interest on checking accounts and the introduction of money market mutual funds, have made M1 less relevant as a measure of the medium of exchange. For a time, these developments led the Fed to rely on M2, a broader measure of the money supply that had a more stable historical relationship to economic growth. Even this relationship broke down in the early 1990s. In July 1993, then Fed Chairman Alan Greenspan informed the U.S. Congress that the Fed would cease using M1 or M2 targets to guide the conduct of monetary policy. The Fed has correspondingly increased its reliance on interest rate targets.

There are many different interest rates in the economy. For purposes of monetary policy, the Fed has targeted the interest rate known as the *federal funds rate*. In the next section, we discuss the federal funds rate before examining how targeting the interest rate can help the Fed achieve its monetary policy goals.

## The Importance of the Federal Funds Rate

Recall from Chapter 25 that every bank must keep 10 percent of its checking account deposits above a certain threshold amount as reserves, either as currency held in the bank or as deposits with the Fed. The Fed pays banks a low interest rate on their reserve deposits, so banks normally have an incentive to invest reserves above the 10 percent minimum. As the financial crisis that began in 2007 deepened during 2008, bank reserves soared as banks attempted to meet an increase in deposit withdrawals and as they became reluctant to lend to any borrowers except those with the most flawless credit histories. These conditions were very unusual, however. In normal times, banks keep few excess reserves, and when they need additional reserves, they borrow in the *federal funds market* from banks that have reserves available. The **federal funds rate** is the interest rate banks charge each other on loans in the federal funds market. The loans in that market are usually very short term, often just overnight.

Despite the name, the Fed does not legally set the federal funds rate. Instead, the rate is determined by the supply of reserves relative to the demand for them. Because the Fed can increase and decrease the supply of bank reserves through open

**Federal funds rate** The interest rate banks charge each other for overnight loans.

of growth of the money supply and rates of inflation across countries, panel (b) shows that countries where the money supply grew rapidly tended to have high inflation rates, while countries where the money supply grew more slowly tended to have much lower inflation rates. Not included in panel (b) are data for the African country of Zimbabwe, which we mentioned at the beginning of the chapter. Over this decade, the money supply in Zimbabwe grew by more than 7,500 percent per year. The result was an accelerating rate of inflation that eventually reached 15 billion percent during 2008. Zimbabwe was suffering from hyperinflation—that is, a rate of inflation that exceeds 100 percent per year.

## High Rates of Inflation

Why do governments allow high rates of inflation? The quantity theory can help us to understand the reasons for high rates of inflation, such as that experienced by Zimbabwe. Very high rates of inflation—in excess of 100 percent per year—are known as *hyperinflation*. Hyperinflation is caused by central banks increasing the money supply at a rate far in excess of the growth rate of real GDP. A high rate of inflation causes money to lose its value so rapidly that households and firms avoid holding it. If, as happened in Zimbabwe, the inflation becomes severe enough, people stop using paper currency, so it no longer serves the important functions of money discussed earlier in this chapter. Economies suffering from high inflation usually also suffer from very slow growth, if not severe recession.

Given the dire consequences that follow from high inflation, why do governments cause it by expanding the money supply so rapidly? The main reason is that governments often want to spend more than they are able to raise through taxes. Developed countries, such as the United States, can usually bridge gaps between spending and taxes by borrowing through selling bonds to the public. Developing countries, such as Zimbabwe, often have difficulty selling bonds because investors are skeptical of their ability to pay back the money. If they are unable to sell bonds to the public, governments in developing countries will force their central banks to purchase them. As we discussed previously, when a central bank buys bonds, the money supply will increase.

| Making the Connection | The German Hyperinflation of the Early 1920s |
|---|---|

When Germany lost World War I, a revolution broke out that overthrew Kaiser Wilhelm II and installed a new government known as the Weimar Republic. In the peace treaty of 1919, the Allies—the United States, Great Britain, France, and Italy—imposed payments called *reparations* on the new German government. The reparations were meant as compensation to the Allies for the damage Germany had caused during the war. It was very difficult for the German government to use tax revenue to cover both its normal spending and the reparations.

The German government decided to pay for the difference between its spending and its tax revenues by selling bonds to the central bank, the Reichsbank. After a few years, the German government fell far behind in its reparations payments. In January 1923, the French government sent troops into the German industrial area known as the Ruhr to try to collect the payments directly. German workers in the Ruhr went on strike, and the German government decided to support them by paying their salaries. Raising the funds to do so was financed by an inflationary monetary policy: The German government sold bonds to the Reichsbank, thereby increasing the money supply.

*During the hyperinflation of the 1920s, people in Germany used paper currency to light their stoves.*

The inflationary increase in the money supply was very large: The total number of marks—the German currency—in circulation rose from 115 million in January 1922 to 1.3 billion in January 1923 and then to 497 billion *billion*, or 497,000,000,000,000,000,000, in December 1923. Just as the quantity theory predicts, the result was a staggeringly high rate of inflation. The German price index that stood at 100 in 1914 and 1,440 in January 1922 had risen to 126,160,000,000,000 in December 1923. The German mark became worthless. The German government ended the hyperinflation by (1) negotiating a new agreement with the Allies that reduced its reparations payments, (2) reducing other government expenditures and raising taxes to balance its budget, and (3) replacing the existing mark with a new mark. Each new mark was worth 1 trillion old marks. The German central bank was also limited to issuing a total of 3.2 billion new marks.

These steps were enough to bring the hyperinflation to an end—but not before the savings of anyone holding the old marks had been wiped out. Most middle-income Germans were extremely resentful of this outcome. Many historians believe that the hyperinflation greatly reduced the allegiance of many Germans to the Weimar Republic and may have helped pave the way for Adolph Hitler and the Nazis to seize power 10 years later.

Based on Thomas Sargent, "The End of Four Big Hyperinflations," *Rational Expectations and Inflation*, (New York: Harper & Row, 1986).

MyEconLab **Your Turn:** Test your understanding by doing related problem 5.10 on page 862 at the end of this chapter.

Continued from page 829

## Economics in Your Life

### What if Money Became Increasingly Valuable?

At the beginning of the chapter, we asked you to consider whether you would like to live in an economy in which the purchasing power of money rises every year. The first thing to consider when thinking about the advantages and disadvantages of this situation is that the only way for the purchasing power of money to increase is for the price level to fall; in other words, *deflation* must occur. Because the price level in the United States hasn't fallen for an entire year since the 1930s, most people alive today have experienced only rising price levels—and declining purchasing power of money. Would replacing rising prices with falling prices necessarily be a good thing? It might be tempting to say "yes," because if you have a job, your salary will buy more goods and services each year. But, in fact, just as a rising price level results in most wages and salaries rising each year, a falling price level is likely to mean falling wages and salaries each year. So, it is likely that, on average, people would not see the purchasing power of their incomes increase, even if the purchasing power of any currency they hold would increase. There can also be a significant downside to deflation, particularly if the transition from inflation to deflation happens suddenly. In Chapter 20, we defined the real interest rate as being equal to the nominal interest rate minus the inflation rate. If an economy experiences deflation, then the real interest rate will be greater than the nominal interest rate. A rising real interest rate can be bad news for anyone who has borrowed, including homeowners who may have substantial mortgage loans. So, you are probably better off living in an economy experiencing mild inflation than one experiencing deflation.

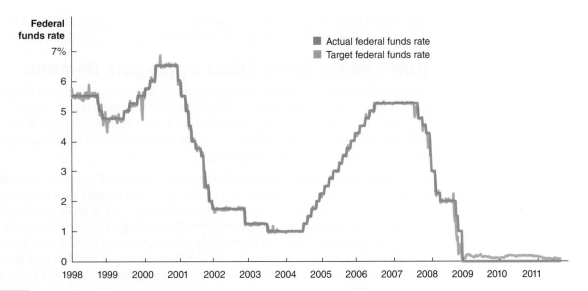

**Figure 26.6    Federal Funds Rate Targeting, January 1998–September 2011**

The Fed does not set the federal funds rate, but its ability to increase or decrease bank reserves quickly through open market operations keeps the actual federal funds rate close to the Fed's target rate. The orange line is the Fed's target for the federal funds rate, and the jagged green line represents the actual value for the federal funds rate on a weekly basis.

Note: The federal funds target for the period after December 2008 was 0 to 0.25 percent.
Data from Board of Governers of the Federal Reserve System.

market operations, it can set a *target* for the federal funds rate and usually come very close to hitting it. The FOMC announces a target for the federal funds rate after each meeting. In Figure 26.6, the orange line shows the Fed's targets for the federal funds rate since 1998. The jagged green line represents the actual federal funds rate on a weekly basis. The figure shows the rapid declines in the target for the federal funds rate beginning in September 2007, as the Fed responded to the start of the financial crisis. In December 2008, the Fed announced a range of 0 to 0.25 percent as its target. The actual federal funds rate fluctuated between 0.06 and 0.23 percent. These very low federal funds rates reflect the severity of the financial crisis.

The federal funds rate is not directly relevant for households and firms. Only banks can borrow or lend in the federal funds market. However, changes in the federal funds rate usually result in changes in interest rates on other short-term financial assets, such as Treasury bills, and changes in interest rates on long-term financial assets, such as corporate bonds and mortgages. A change in the federal funds rate has a greater effect on short-term interest rates than on long-term interest rates, and its effect on long-term interest rates may occur only after a lag in time. Although a majority of economists support the Fed's choice of the interest rate as its monetary policy target, some economists believe the Fed should concentrate on the money supply instead. We will discuss the views of these economists later in this chapter.

# Monetary Policy and Economic Activity

Remember that the Fed uses the federal funds rate as a monetary policy target because it has good control of the federal funds rate through open market operations and because it believes that changes in the federal funds rate will ultimately affect economic variables that are related to its monetary policy goals. It is important to consider again the distinction between the nominal interest rate and the real interest rate. Recall that we calculate the real interest rate by subtracting the inflation rate from the nominal interest rate. Ultimately, the ability of the Fed to use monetary policy to affect economic variables such as real GDP depends on its ability to affect real interest rates, such as the real interest rates on mortgages and corporate bonds. Because the federal funds rate is a short-term nominal interest rate, the Fed sometimes has difficulty affecting long-term

**26.3 LEARNING** OBJECTIVE

Use aggregate demand and aggregate supply graphs to show the effects of monetary policy on real GDP and the price level.

real interest rates. Nevertheless, for purposes of the following discussion, we will assume that the Fed is able to use open market operations to affect long-term real interest rates.

## How Interest Rates Affect Aggregate Demand

Changes in interest rates affect *aggregate demand*, which is the total level of spending in the economy. Recall from Chapter 24 that aggregate demand has four components: consumption, investment, government purchases, and net exports. Changes in interest rates will not affect government purchases, but they will affect the other three components of aggregate demand in the following ways:

- *Consumption.* Many households finance purchases of consumer durables, such as automobiles and furniture, by borrowing. Lower interest rates lead to increased spending on durables because they lower the total cost of these goods to consumers by lowering the interest payments on loans. Higher interest rates raise the cost of consumer durables, and households will buy fewer of them. Lower interest rates also reduce the return to saving, leading households to save less and spend more. Higher interest rates increase the return to saving, leading households to save more and spend less.

- *Investment.* Firms finance most of their spending on machinery, equipment, and factories out of their profits or by borrowing. Firms borrow either from the financial markets by issuing corporate bonds or from banks. Higher interest rates on corporate bonds or on bank loans make it more expensive for firms to borrow, so they will undertake fewer investment projects. Lower interest rates make it less expensive for firms to borrow, so they will undertake more investment projects. Lower interest rates can also increase investment through their effect on stock prices. As interest rates decline, stocks become a more attractive investment relative to bonds. The increase in demand for stocks raises their price. An increase in stock prices sends a signal to firms that the future profitability of investment projects has increased. By issuing additional shares of stocks, firms can acquire the funds they need to buy new factories and equipment, thereby increasing investment.

  Finally, spending by households on new homes is also part of investment. When interest rates on mortgage loans rise, the cost of buying new homes rises, and fewer new homes will be purchased. When interest rates on mortgage loans fall, more new homes will be purchased.

- *Net exports.* Recall that net exports are equal to spending by foreign households and firms on goods and services produced in the United States minus spending by U.S. households and firms on goods and services produced in other countries. The value of net exports depends partly on the exchange rate between the dollar and foreign currencies. When the value of the dollar rises, households and firms in other countries will pay more for goods and services produced in the United States, but U.S. households and firms will pay less for goods and services produced in other countries. As a result, the United States will export less and import more, so net exports fall. When the value of the dollar falls, net exports will rise. If interest rates in the United States rise relative to interest rates in other countries, investing in U.S. financial assets will become more desirable, causing foreign investors to increase their demand for dollars, which will increase the value of the dollar. As the value of the dollar increases, net exports will fall. If interest rates in the United States decline relative to interest rates in other countries, the value of the dollar will fall, and net exports will rise.

## The Effects of Monetary Policy on Real GDP and the Price Level

In Chapter 24, we developed the *aggregate demand and aggregate supply model* to explain fluctuations in real GDP and the price level. In the basic version of the model, we assume that there is no economic growth, so the long-run aggregate supply curve

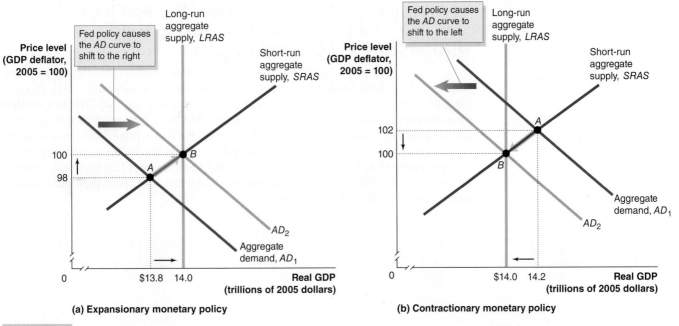

**(a) Expansionary monetary policy**

**(b) Contractionary monetary policy**

**Figure 26.7**     **Monetary Policy**

In panel (a), the economy begins in a recession at point A, with real GDP of $13.8 trillion and a price level of 98. An expansionary monetary policy causes aggregate demand to shift to the right, from $AD_1$ to $AD_2$, increasing real GDP from $13.8 trillion to $14.0 trillion and the price level from 98 to 100 (point B). With real GDP back at its potential level, the Fed can meet its goal of high employment.

In panel (b), the economy begins at point A, with real GDP at $14.2 trillion and the price level at 102. Because real GDP is greater than potential GDP, the economy experiences rising wages and prices. A contractionary monetary policy causes aggregate demand to shift to the left, from $AD_1$ to $AD_2$, decreasing real GDP from $14.2 trillion to $14.0 trillion and the price level from 102 to 100 (point B). With real GDP back at its potential level, the Fed can meet its goal of price stability.

does not shift. In panel (a) of Figure 26.7, we assume that the economy is in short-run equilibrium at point A, where the aggregate demand $(AD_1)$ curve intersects the short-run aggregate supply (SRAS) curve. Real GDP is below potential real GDP, as shown by the LRAS curve, so the economy is in a recession, with some firms operating below normal capacity and some workers having been laid off. To reach its goal of high employment, the Fed needs to carry out an **expansionary monetary policy** by increasing the money supply and decreasing interest rates. Lower interest rates cause an increase in consumption, investment, and net exports, which shifts the aggregate demand curve to the right, from $AD_1$ to $AD_2$. Real GDP increases from $13.8 trillion to potential GDP of $14.0 trillion, and the price level rises from 98 to 100 (point B). The policy successfully returns real GDP to its potential level. Rising production leads to increasing employment, allowing the Fed to achieve its goal of high employment.

In panel (b) of Figure 26.7, the economy is in short-run equilibrium at point A, with real GDP of $14.2 trillion, which is above potential real GDP of $14.0 trillion. With some firms producing beyond their normal capacity and the unemployment rate very low, wages and prices are increasing. To reach its goal of price stability, the Fed needs to carry out a **contractionary monetary policy** by decreasing the money supply and increasing interest rates. Higher interest rates cause a decrease in consumption, investment, and net exports, which shifts the aggregate demand curve from $AD_1$ to $AD_2$. Real GDP decreases from $14.2 trillion to $14.0 trillion, and the price level falls from 102 to 100 (point B). Why would the Fed want to intentionally cause real GDP to decline? Because in the long run, real GDP cannot continue to remain above potential GDP. Attempting to keep real GDP above potential GDP would result in rising inflation. As aggregate demand declines and real GDP returns to its potential level, upward pressure on wages and prices will be reduced, allowing the Fed to achieve its goal of price stability.

We can conclude that the Fed can use monetary policy to affect the price level and, in the short run, the level of real GDP, allowing it to attain its policy goals of high employment and price stability.

**Expansionary monetary policy** The Federal Reserve's decreasing interest rates to increase real GDP.

**Contractionary monetary policy** The Federal Reserve's increasing interest rates to reduce inflation.

**Making**
**the**
**Connection**

## Too Low for Zero: The Fed Tries "Quantitative Easing" and "Operation Twist"

Figure 26.6 shows that in December 2008, the Fed pushed the target for the federal funds rate to nearly zero and kept it there through 2011. Because the 2007–2009 recession was so severe, even this very low rate did little to stimulate the economy. To lower the federal funds rate, the Fed buys Treasury bills through open market purchases, which increases bank reserves. Banks then lend out these reserves. As the figure below shows, however, in late 2008, many banks began piling up excess reserves rather than lending the funds out. Total bank reserves had been less than $50 billion in August 2008, but with the deepening of the financial crisis, they had soared to more than $900 billion by May 2009.

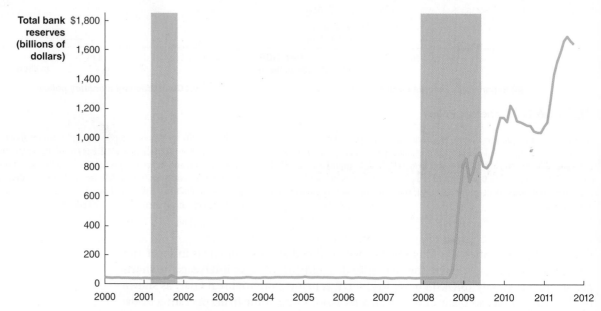

Data from The Federal Reserve Bank of St. Louis.

The increase in bank reserves was partly due to the Fed's decision in October 2008 to start paying interest of 0.25 percent on bank reserves held as deposits at the Fed. Primarily, though, the increase in reserves occurred because banks were reluctant to make loans at low interest rates to households and firms whose financial positions had been damaged by the recession. Some economists believed the Fed was facing a situation known as a *liquidity trap*, in which short-term interest rates are pushed to zero, leaving the central bank unable to lower them further. Some economists believe that liquidity traps occurred in the United States during the 1930s and in Japan during the 1990s.

Not being able to push the target for the federal funds rate below zero was a problem for the Fed. Glenn Rudebusch, an economist at the Federal Reserve Bank of San Francisco, calculated that given how high the unemployment rate was, the appropriate target for the federal funds rate was –5 percent. Because the federal funds rate cannot be negative, the Fed turned to other policies. In particular, the Fed decided to embark on a policy of *quantitative easing*, which involves buying securities beyond the short-term Treasury securities that are usually involved in open market operations. The Fed began purchasing 10-year Treasury notes to keep their interest rates from rising. Interest rates on home mortgage loans typically move closely with interest rates on 10-year Treasury notes. The Fed also purchased certain *mortgage-backed securities*. The Fed's objective was to keep interest rates on mortgages low and to keep funds flowing into the mortgage market in order to help stimulate demand for housing.

The Fed's first round of quantitative easing began in November 2008 and ended in June 2010. With the economy recovering only slowly, in November 2010, the Fed announced a second round of quantitative easing (dubbed QE2). With QE2, the Fed bought an additional $600 billion in long-term Treasury securities through June 2011. In September 2011, with the economic recovery remaining weak, the Fed announced a new program under which it would purchase $400 billion in long-term Treasury securities while selling an equal amount of shorter-term Treasury securities. This program, which some people in financial markets called "Operation Twist," had the same objective as quantitative easing: to reduce interest rates on long-term Treasury securities in order to increase aggregate demand.

Later in this chapter, we will consider other new programs the Fed put in place to deal with the recession of 2007–2009 and the slow recovery that followed, as its traditional focus on lowering the federal funds rate to stimulate the economy proved ineffective.

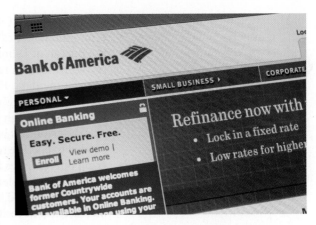

*The Fed pushed interest rates to very low levels during 2008 and 2009.*

Based on Glenn Rudebusch, "The Fed's Monetary Policy Response to the Current Crisis," FRBSF Economic Letter, May 22, 2009.

**Your Turn:** Test your understanding by doing related problems 3.11 and 3.12 on page 900 at the end of this chapter.

MyEconLab

# Can the Fed Eliminate Recessions?

Panel (a) of Figure 26.7 on page 875 shows an expansionary monetary policy that performs perfectly by shifting the *AD* curve to bring the economy back to potential GDP. In fact, however, this ideal is very difficult for the Fed to achieve, as the length and severity of the 2007–2009 recession indicates. In practice, the best the Fed can do is keep recessions shorter and milder than they would otherwise be.

If the Fed is to be successful in offsetting the effects of the business cycle, it needs to quickly recognize the need for a change in monetary policy. If the Fed is late in recognizing that a recession has begun or that the inflation rate is increasing, it may not be able to implement a new policy soon enough to do much good. In fact, implementing a policy too late may actually destabilize the economy. To see how this can happen, consider Figure 26.8. The straight line represents the long-run growth trend in real GDP in the United States. On average, real GDP grows about 3.3 percent per year. The actual path of real GDP differs from the underlying trend because of the business cycle, which is shown by the red curved line. As we saw in Chapter 21, the actual business cycle is more irregular than the stylized cycle shown here.

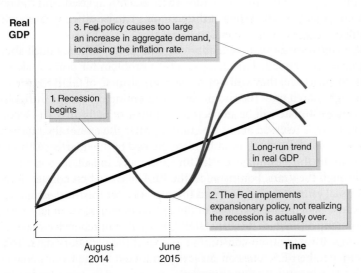

**Figure 26.8**

**The Effect of a Poorly Timed Monetary Policy on the Economy**

The upward-sloping straight line represents the long-run growth trend in real GDP. The curved red line represents the path real GDP takes because of the business cycle. If the Fed is too late in implementing a change in monetary policy, real GDP will follow the curved blue line. The Fed's expansionary monetary policy results in too great an increase in aggregate demand during the next expansion, which causes an increase in the inflation rate.

Suppose that a recession begins in August 2014. Because it takes months for economic statistics to be gathered by the Commerce Department, the Census Bureau, the Bureau of Labor Statistics, and the Fed itself, there is a *lag*, or delay, before the Fed recognizes that a recession has begun. Then it takes time for the Fed's economists to analyze the data. Finally, in June 2015, the FOMC concludes that the economy is in recession and begins an expansionary monetary policy. As it turns out, June 2015 is actually the trough of the recession, meaning that the recession has already ended, and an expansion has begun. In these circumstances, the Fed's expansionary policy is not needed to end the recession. The increase in aggregate demand caused by the Fed's lowering interest rates is likely to push the economy beyond potential real GDP and cause a significant acceleration in inflation. Real GDP ends up following the path indicated by the blue curved line. The Fed has inadvertently engaged in a *procyclical policy*, which increases the severity of the business cycle, as opposed to a *countercyclical policy*, which is meant to reduce the severity of the business cycle, and which is what the Fed intends to use. As we saw in Chapter 21, the typical recession since 1950 has lasted less than one year, which increases the likelihood that the Fed may accidentally engage in a procyclical policy. Making this mistake is, of course, less likely in a long and severe recession such as the recession of 2007–2009.

It is not unusual for employment or manufacturing production to decline for a month or two in the middle of an expansion. Distinguishing these minor ups and downs from the beginning of a recession is difficult. The National Bureau of Economic Research (NBER) announces dates for the beginning and end of recessions that most economists generally accept. An indication of how difficult it is to determine when recessions begin and end is that the NBER generally makes its announcements only after a considerable delay. The NBER did not announce that a recession had begun in March 2001 until November 2001, which is the same month it later determined that the recession had ended. The NBER did not announce that a recession had begun in December 2007 until December 2008. Failing to react until well after a recession has begun (or ended) can be a serious problem for the Fed. In the case of the 2007–2009 recession, however, the Fed did promptly cut the federal funds rate in September 2007, in response to the beginning of the financial crisis, even though the recession did not actually begin until two months later.

| Making the Connection | ### Trying to Hit a Moving Target: Making Policy with "Real-Time Data" |
|---|---|

The Fed relies on macroeconomic data to formulate monetary policy. One key piece of economic data is GDP, which is calculated quarterly by the Bureau of Economic Analysis (BEA). Unfortunately for Fed policymakers, the GDP data the BEA provides are frequently revised, and the revisions can be large enough that the actual state of the economy can be different from what it at first appeared to be.

The BEA's *advance estimate* of a quarter's GDP is not released until about a month after the quarter has ended. This delay can be a problem for policymakers because it means that, for instance, they will not receive an estimate of GDP for the period from January through March until the end of April. Presenting even more difficulty is the fact that the advance estimate will be subject to a number of revisions. The second estimate of a quarter's GDP is released about two months after the end of the quarter. The third estimate is released about three months after the end of the quarter. Although the BEA used to refer to the third estimate as the "final estimate," in fact, it continues to revise its estimates through the years. For instance, the BEA releases first annual, second annual, and third annual estimates one, two, and three years after the third estimate. Nor is that the end, because benchmark revisions of the estimates will occur in later years.

Why so many estimates? Because GDP is such a comprehensive measure of output in the economy, it is very time-consuming to collect the necessary data. To provide the advance estimate, the BEA relies on surveys conducted by the Commerce Department of retail sales and manufacturing shipments, as well as data from trade organizations, estimates of government spending, and so on. As time passes, these organizations gather additional data, and the BEA is able to refine its estimates.

Do these revisions to the GDP estimates matter? Sometimes they do, as the following example indicates. At the beginning of 2001, there were some indications that the U.S. economy might be headed for recession. The dot-com stock market bubble had burst the previous spring, wiping out trillions of dollars in stockholder wealth. Overbuilding of fiber-optic cable networks and other information technology also weighed on the economy. The advance estimate of the first quarter's GDP, though, showed a reasonably healthy increase in real GDP of 2.0% at an annual rate. It seemed as if there was nothing for government policymakers to be worried about. But, as the graph below shows, that estimate of 2.0% was revised a number of times over the years, mostly downward. Currently, BEA data indicate that real GDP actually declined by 1.3% at an annual rate during the first quarter of 2001. This swing of more than 3 percentage points is a large difference—a difference that changes the picture of what happened during the first quarter of 2001 from one of an economy experiencing moderate growth to one of an economy suffering a significant decline. The National Bureau of Economic Research dates the recession of 2001 as having begun in March, but some economists believe it actually began at the end of 2000. The current BEA estimates of GDP provide some support for this view.

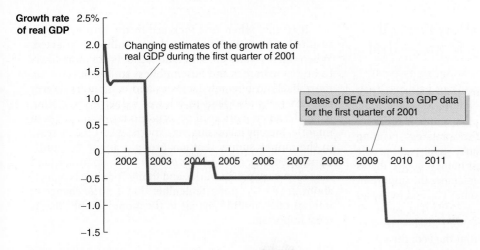

This example shows that in addition to the other problems the Federal Reserve encounters in successfully conducting monetary policy, it must make decisions using data that may be subject to substantial revisions.

Based on Federal Reserve Bank of Philadelphia, "Historical Data Files for the Real-Time Data Set," August 24, 2010; and Bruce T. Grimm and Teresa Weadock, "Gross Domestic Product: Revisions and Source Data," *Survey of Current Business*, Vol. 86, No. 2, February 2006, pp. 11–15.

**Your Turn:** Test your understanding by doing related problems 3.13 and 3.14 on pages 900 and 901 at the end of this chapter.                    MyEconLab

---

# A Summary of How Monetary Policy Works

Table 26.1 compares the steps involved in expansionary and contractionary monetary policies. We need to note an important qualification to this summary. At every point, we should add the phrase "relative to what would have happened without the policy." Table 26.1 isolates the impact of monetary policy, *holding constant all other factors affecting the variables involved.* In other words, we are invoking the *ceteris paribus* condition, discussed in Chapter 3. This point is important because, for example, a contractionary monetary policy does not cause the price level to fall; rather, a contractionary monetary policy causes the price level *to rise by less than it would have risen without the policy.* One final note on terminology: An expansionary monetary policy is sometimes referred to as a *loose* policy, or an *easy* policy. A contractionary monetary policy is sometimes referred to as a *tight* policy.

**Table 26.1** **Expansionary and Contractionary Monetary Policies**

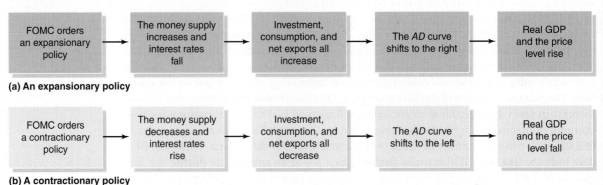

**(a) An expansionary policy**

FOMC orders an expansionary policy → The money supply increases and interest rates fall → Investment, consumption, and net exports all increase → The *AD* curve shifts to the right → Real GDP and the price level rise

**(b) A contractionary policy**

FOMC orders a contractionary policy → The money supply decreases and interest rates rise → Investment, consumption, and net exports all decrease → The *AD* curve shifts to the left → Real GDP and the price level fall

# Don't Let This Happen to You

## Remember That with Monetary Policy, It's the Interest Rates—Not the Money—That Counts

It is tempting to think of monetary policy working like this: If the Fed wants more spending in the economy, it increases the money supply, and people spend more because they now have more money. If the Fed wants less spending in the economy, it decreases the money supply, and people spend less because they now have less money. In fact, that is *not* how monetary policy works. Remember the important difference between money and income: The Fed increases the money supply by buying Treasury bills. The sellers of the Treasury bills have just exchanged one asset—Treasury bills—for another asset—a check from the Fed; the sellers have *not* increased their income. Even though the money supply is now larger, no one's income has increased, so no one's spending should be affected.

It is only when this increase in the money supply results in lower interest rates that spending is affected. When interest rates are lower, households are more likely to buy new homes and automobiles, and businesses are more likely to buy new factories and computers. Lower interest rates also lead to a lower value of the dollar, which lowers the prices of exports and raises the prices of imports, thereby increasing net exports. It isn't the increase in the money supply that has brought about this additional spending; *it's the lower interest rates.* To understand how monetary policy works, and to interpret news reports about the Fed's actions, remember that it is the change in interest rates, not the change in the money supply, that is most important.

MyEconLab

**Your Turn:** Test your understanding by doing related problem 3.15 on page 901 at the end of this chapter.

---

**26.4 LEARNING** OBJECTIVE

Use the dynamic aggregate demand and aggregate supply model to analyze monetary policy.

# Monetary Policy in the Dynamic Aggregate Demand and Aggregate Supply Model\*

The overview of monetary policy we just finished contains a key idea: The Fed can use monetary policy to affect aggregate demand, thereby changing the price level and the level of real GDP. The discussion of monetary policy illustrated by Figure 26.7 on page 875 is simplified, however, because it ignores two important facts about the economy: (1) The economy experiences continuing inflation, with the price level rising every year, and (2) the economy experiences long-run growth, with the *LRAS* curve shifting to the right every year. In Chapter 24, we developed a *dynamic aggregate demand and aggregate supply model* that takes into account these two facts. In this section, we use the dynamic model to gain a more complete understanding of monetary policy. Let's briefly review the dynamic model. Recall from Chapter 24 that over time, the U.S. labor force and U.S. capital stock will increase. Technological change will also occur. The result will be an increase in potential real GDP, which we show by the long-run aggregate supply

\* This section may be omitted without loss of continuity.

curve shifting to the right. These factors will also result in firms supplying more goods and services at any given price level in the short run, which we show by the short-run aggregate supply curve shifting to the right. During most years, the aggregate demand curve will also shift to the right, indicating that aggregate expenditure will be higher at every price level. There are several reasons aggregate expenditure usually increases: As population grows and incomes rise, consumption will increase over time. Also, as the economy grows, firms expand capacity, and new firms are established, increasing investment spending. Finally, an expanding population and an expanding economy require increased government services, such as more police officers and teachers, so government purchases will expand.

## The Effects of Monetary Policy on Real GDP and the Price Level: A More Complete Account

During certain periods, $AD$ does not increase enough during the year to keep the economy at potential GDP. This slow growth in aggregate demand may be due to households and firms becoming pessimistic about the future state of the economy, leading them to cut back their spending on consumer durables, houses, and factories. As we have seen, the collapse of the housing bubble and the resulting financial crisis had a negative effect on aggregate demand during the 2007–2009 recession. Other possibilities exist as well: The federal government might decide to balance the budget by cutting back its purchases, or recessions in other countries might cause a decline in U.S. exports. In the hypothetical situation shown in Figure 26.9, in the first year, the economy is in equilibrium, at potential real GDP of $14.0 trillion and a price level of 100 (point A). In the second year, $LRAS$ increases to $14.4 trillion, but $AD$ increases only to $AD_{2(\text{without policy})}$, which is not enough to keep the economy in macroeconomic equilibrium at potential GDP. If the Fed does not intervene, the short-run equilibrium will occur at $14.3 trillion (point B). The $100 billion gap between this level of real GDP and potential real GDP at $LRAS_2$ means that some firms are operating at less than their normal capacity. Incomes and profits will fall, firms will begin to lay off workers, and the unemployment rate will rise.

Economists at the Federal Reserve closely monitor the economy and continually update forecasts of future levels of real GDP and prices. When these economists anticipate that aggregate demand is not growing fast enough to allow the economy to remain at full employment, they present their findings to the FOMC, which decides

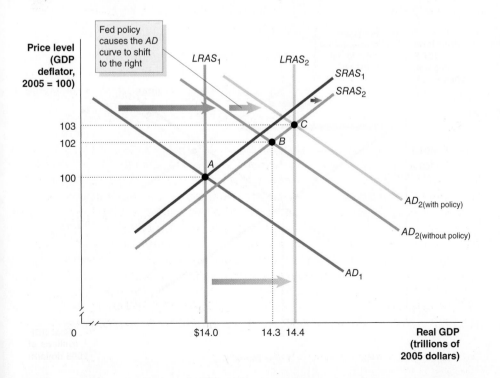

### Figure 26.9

### An Expansionary Monetary Policy

The economy begins in equilibrium at point A, with real GDP of $14.0 trillion and a price level of 100. Without monetary policy, aggregate demand will shift from $AD_1$ to $AD_{2(\text{without policy})}$, which is not enough to keep the economy at full employment because long-run aggregate supply has shifted from $LRAS_1$ to $LRAS_2$. The economy will be in short-run equilibrium at point B, with real GDP of $14.3 trillion and a price level of 102. By lowering interest rates, the Fed increases investment, consumption, and net exports sufficiently to shift aggregate demand to $AD_{2(\text{with policy})}$. The economy will be in equilibrium at point C, with real GDP of $14.4 trillion, which is its full employment level, and a price level of 103. The price level is higher than it would have been if the Fed had not acted to increase spending in the economy.

whether circumstances require a change in monetary policy. For example, suppose that the FOMC meets and considers a forecast from the staff indicating that during the following year, a gap of $100 billion will open between equilibrium real GDP and potential real GDP. In other words, the macroeconomic equilibrium illustrated by point *B* in Figure 26.9 will occur. The FOMC may then decide to carry out an expansionary monetary policy to lower interest rates to stimulate aggregate demand. The figure shows the results of a successful attempt to do this: *AD* has shifted to the right, and equilibrium occurs at potential GDP (point *C*). The Fed will have successfully headed off the falling incomes and rising unemployment that otherwise would have occurred. Bear in mind that we are illustrating a perfectly executed monetary policy that keeps the economy at potential GDP, which is difficult to achieve in practice for reasons already discussed.

Notice in Figure 26.9 that the expansionary monetary policy caused the inflation rate to be higher than it would have been. Without the expansionary policy, the price level would have risen from 100 to 102, so the inflation rate for the year would have been 2 percent. By shifting the aggregate demand curve, the expansionary policy caused the price level to increase from 102 to 103, raising the inflation rate from 2 percent to 3 percent.

## Using Monetary Policy to Fight Inflation

In addition to using an expansionary monetary policy to reduce the severity of recessions, the Fed can also use a contractionary monetary policy to keep aggregate demand from expanding so rapidly that the inflation rate begins to increase. Figure 26.10 shows the situation during 2005 and 2006, when the Fed faced this possibility. During 2005, the economy was at equilibrium at potential GDP, but Fed Chair Alan Greenspan and other members of the FOMC were concerned that the continuing boom in the housing market might lead aggregate demand to increase so rapidly that the inflation rate would begin to accelerate. The Fed had been gradually increasing the target for the federal funds rate since mid-2004.

When Ben Bernanke assumed office as Fed chair in early 2006, he advocated continued increases in the target for the federal funds rate to slow the growth in aggregate demand. By June 2006, the target for the federal funds rate had been raised

### Figure 26.10

#### A Contractionary Monetary Policy in 2006

The economy began 2005 in equilibrium at point *A*, with real GDP equal to potential GDP of $12.6 trillion and a price level of 100.0. From 2005 to 2006, potential GDP increased from $12.6 trillion to $12.9 trillion, as long-run aggregate supply increased from $LRAS_{2005}$ to $LRAS_{2006}$. The Fed raised interest rates because it believed the housing boom was causing aggregate demand to increase too rapidly. Without the increase in interest rates, aggregate demand would have shifted from $AD_{2005}$ to $AD_{2006(without\ policy)}$, and the new short-run equilibrium would have occurred at point *B*. Real GDP would have been $13.2 trillion—$300 billion greater than potential GDP—and the price level would have been 104.5. The increase in interest rates resulted in aggregate demand increasing only to $AD_{2006(with\ policy)}$. Equilibrium occurred at point *C*, with real GDP of $13.0 trillion being only $100 billion greater than potential GDP and the price level rising only to 103.2.

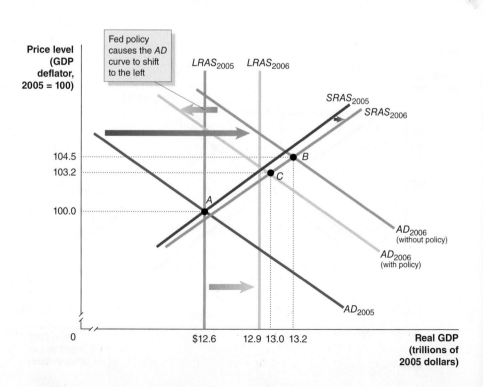

to 5.25 percent, from the low rate of 1 percent that had prevailed from June 2003 to May 2004. The FOMC issues a statement after each meeting that summarizes the committee's views on the current state of the economy and gives some indication of how monetary policy might change in the near future. After its meeting on June 29, 2006, the FOMC included the following remarks in its statement:

> The Federal Open Market Committee decided today to raise its target for the federal funds rate ... to 5-1/4 percent. Recent indicators suggest that economic growth is moderating from its quite strong pace earlier this year, partly reflecting a gradual cooling of the housing market and the lagged effects of increases in ... interest rates.... Although the moderation in the growth of aggregate demand should help to limit inflation pressures over time, the Committee judges that some inflation risks remain.

The committee kept the target for the federal funds rate constant at 5.25 percent until September 2007, when concern about difficulties in financial markets led it to cut the target to 4.75 percent. Although it is impossible to know exactly what would have happened during 2006 without the Fed's policy change, Figure 26.10 presents a plausible scenario. The figure shows that without the Fed's actions to increase interest rates, aggregate demand would have shifted farther to the right, and equilibrium would have occurred at a level of real GDP that was beyond the potential level. The price level would have risen from 100.0 in 2005 to 104.5 in 2006, meaning that the inflation rate would have been 4.5 percent. Because the Fed kept aggregate demand from increasing as much as it otherwise would have, equilibrium occurred at potential real GDP, and the price level in 2006 rose to only 103.2, keeping the inflation rate at 3.2 percent.

# Solved Problem 26.4

## The Effects of Monetary Policy

The hypothetical information in the following table shows what the values for real GDP and the price level will be in 2015 if the Fed does *not* use monetary policy:

| Year | Potential GDP | Real GDP | Price Level |
|------|---------------|----------|-------------|
| 2014 | $15.2 trillion | $15.2 trillion | 114 |
| 2015 | 15.6 trillion | 15.4 trillion | 116 |

a. If the Fed wants to keep real GDP at its potential level in 2015, should it use an expansionary policy or a contractionary policy? Should the trading desk buy Treasury bills or sell them?

b. Suppose the Fed's policy is successful in keeping real GDP at its potential level in 2015. State whether each of the following will be higher or lower than if the Fed had taken no action:
   i Real GDP
   ii Potential real GDP
   iii The inflation rate
   iv The unemployment rate

c. Draw an aggregate demand and aggregate supply graph to illustrate your answer. Be sure that your graph contains *LRAS* curves for 2014 and 2015; *SRAS* curves for 2014 and 2015; *AD* curve for 2014 and 2015, with and without monetary policy action; and equilibrium real GDP and the price level in 2015, with and without policy.

## Solving the Problem

**Step 1:** **Review the chapter material**. This problem is about the effects of monetary policy on real GDP and the price level, so you may want to review the section "The Effects of Monetary Policy on Real GDP and the Price Level: A More Complete Account," which begins on page 881.

**Step 2:** **Answer the questions in part a. by explaining how the Fed can keep real GDP at its potential level.** The information in the table tells us that without monetary policy, the economy will be below potential real GDP in 2015. To keep real GDP at its potential level, the Fed must undertake an expansionary policy. To carry out an expansionary policy, the trading desk needs to buy Treasury bills. Buying Treasury bills will increase reserves in the banking system. Banks will increase their loans, which will increase the money supply and lower the interest rate.

**Step 3:** **Answer part b. by explaining the effect of the Fed's policy.** If the Fed's policy is successful, real GDP in 2015 will increase from $15.4 trillion, as given in the table, to its potential level of $15.6 trillion. Potential real GDP is not affected by monetary policy, so its value will not change. Because the level of real GDP will be higher, the unemployment rate will be lower than it would have been without policy. The expansionary monetary policy shifts the *AD* curve to the right, so short-run equilibrium will move up the short-run aggregate supply (*SRAS*) curve, and the price level will be higher.

**Step 4:** **Answer part c. by drawing the graph.** Your graph should look similar to Figure 26.9.

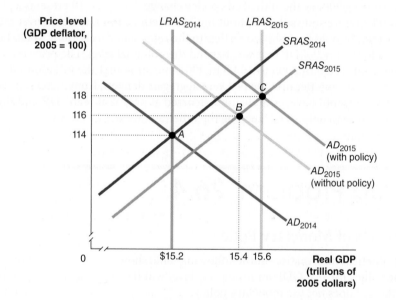

The economy starts in equilibrium in 2014 at point *A*, with the *AD* and *SRAS* curves intersecting along the *LRAS* curve. Real GDP is at its potential level of $15.2 trillion, and the price level is 114. Without monetary policy, the *AD* curve shifts to $AD_{2015(\text{without policy})}$, and the economy is in short-run equilibrium at point *B*. Because potential real GDP has increased from $15.2 trillion to $15.6 trillion, short-run equilibrium real GDP of $15.4 trillion is below the potential level. The price level has increased from 114 to 116. With policy, the *AD* curve shifts to $AD_{2015(\text{with policy})}$, and the economy is in equilibrium at point *C*. Real GDP is at its potential level of $15.6 trillion. We don't have enough information to be sure of the new equilibrium price level. We do know that it will be higher than 116. The graph shows the price level rising to 118. Therefore, without the Fed's expansionary policy, the inflation rate in 2015 would have been about 1.8 percent. With policy, it will be about 3.5 percent.

**Extra Credit:** Bear in mind that in reality, the Fed is unable to use monetary policy to keep real GDP exactly at its potential level, as this problem suggests.

MyEconLab **Your Turn:** For more practice, do related problems 4.4 and 4.5 on pages 901–902 at the end of this chapter.

# A Closer Look at the Fed's Setting of Monetary Policy Targets

We have seen that in carrying out monetary policy, the Fed changes its target for the federal funds rate, depending on the state of the economy. During times when the economy is not experiencing a financial crisis, is using the federal funds rate as a target the best way to conduct monetary policy? If the Fed targets the federal funds rate, how should it decide what the target level should be? In this section, we consider some important issues concerning the Fed's targeting policy.

## Should the Fed Target the Money Supply?

Some economists have argued that rather than use an interest rate as its monetary policy target, the Fed should use the money supply. Many of the economists who make this argument belong to a school of thought known as *monetarism*. The leader of the monetarist school was Nobel Laureate Milton Friedman, who was skeptical that the Fed would be able to correctly time changes in monetary policy.

Friedman and his followers favored replacing *monetary policy* with a *monetary growth rule*. Ordinarily, we expect monetary policy to respond to changing economic conditions: When the economy is in recession, the Fed reduces interest rates, and when inflation is increasing, the Fed raises interest rates. A monetary growth rule, in contrast, is a plan for increasing the money supply at a constant rate that does not change in response to economic conditions. Friedman and his followers proposed a monetary growth rule of increasing the money supply every year at a rate equal to the long-run growth rate of real GDP, which is about 3.3 percent. If the Fed adopted this monetary growth rule, it would stick to it through changing economic conditions.

But what happens under a monetary growth rule if the economy moves into recession? Shouldn't the Fed abandon the rule to drive down interest rates? Friedman argued that the Fed should stick to the rule even during recessions because, he believed, active monetary policy destabilizes the economy, increasing the number of recessions and their severity. By keeping the money supply growing at a constant rate, Friedman argued, the Fed would greatly increase economic stability.

Although during the 1970s some economists and politicians pressured the Federal Reserve to adopt a monetary growth rule, most of that pressure has disappeared in recent years. A key reason is that the fairly close relationship between movements in the money supply and movements in real GDP and the price level that existed before 1980 has become much weaker. Since 1980, the growth rate of M1 has been unstable. In some years, M1 has grown more than 10 percent, while in other years, it has actually fallen. Yet despite these wide fluctuations in the growth of M1, growth in real GDP has been fairly stable, and inflation has remained low during most years.

## Why Doesn't the Fed Target Both the Money Supply and the Interest Rate?

Most economists believe that an interest rate is the best monetary policy target, but, as we have just seen, other economists believe the Fed should target the money supply. Why doesn't the Fed satisfy both groups by targeting both the money supply and an interest rate? The simple answer to this question is that the Fed can't target both at the same time. To see why, look at Figure 26.11, which shows the money market.

Remember that the Fed controls the money supply, but it does not control money demand. Money demand is determined by decisions of households and firms as they weigh the trade-off between the convenience of money and its low interest rate compared with other financial assets. Suppose the Fed is targeting the interest rate and decides, given conditions in the economy, that the interest rate should be 5 percent.

## Figure 26.11

**The Fed Can't Target Both the Money Supply and the Interest Rate**

The Fed is forced to choose between using either an interest rate or the money supply as its monetary policy target. In this figure, the Fed can set a target of $900 billion for the money supply or a target of 5 percent for the interest rate, but the Fed can't hit both targets because it can achieve only combinations of the interest rate and the money supply that represent equilibrium in the money market.

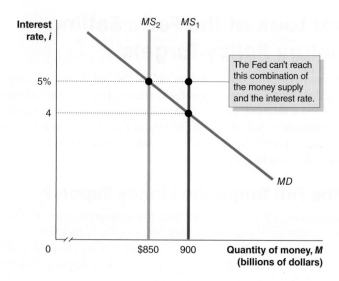

Or, suppose the Fed is targeting the money supply and decides that the money supply should be $900 billion. Figure 26.11 shows that the Fed can bring about an interest rate of 5 percent or a money supply of $900 billion, but it can't bring about both. The point representing an interest rate of 5 percent and a money supply of $900 billion is not on the money demand curve, so it can't represent an equilibrium in the money market. Only combinations of the interest rate and the money supply that represent equilibrium in the money market are possible.

The Fed has to choose between targeting an interest rate and targeting the money supply. For most of the period since World War II, the Fed has chosen an interest rate target.

## The Taylor Rule

**Taylor rule** A rule developed by John Taylor that links the Fed's target for the federal funds rate to economic variables.

How does the Fed choose a target for the federal funds rate? The discussions at the meetings of the FOMC can be complex, and they take into account many economic variables. John Taylor of Stanford University has analyzed the factors involved in Fed decision making and developed the **Taylor rule** to explain federal funds rate targeting. The Taylor rule begins with an estimate of the value of the equilibrium real federal funds rate, which is the federal funds rate—adjusted for inflation—that would be consistent with real GDP being equal to potential real GDP in the long run. According to the Taylor rule, the Fed should set the target for the federal funds rate so that it is equal to the sum of the inflation rate, the equilibrium real federal funds rate, and two additional terms. The first of these additional terms is the *inflation gap*—the difference between current inflation and a target rate; the second is the *output gap*—the percentage difference between real GDP and potential real GDP. The inflation gap and output gap are each given "weights" that reflect their influence on the federal funds target rate. With weights of 1/2 for both gaps, we have the following Taylor rule:

Federal funds target rate = Current inflation rate + Real equilibrium federal funds rate + ((1/2) × Inflation gap) + ((1/2) × Output gap).

The Taylor rule includes expressions for the inflation gap and the output gap because the Fed is concerned about both inflation and fluctuations in real GDP. Taylor demonstrated that if the equilibrium real federal funds rate is 2 percent and the target rate of inflation is 2 percent, the preceding expression does a good job of explaining changes in the Fed's target for the federal funds rate during most years. Consider an example in which the current inflation rate is 1 percent, and real GDP is 1 percent below potential real GDP. In that case, the inflation gap is 1 percent −2 percent = −1 percent and the output gap is also −1 percent. Inserting these values in the Taylor rule, we can calculate the predicted value for the federal funds target rate:

$$\text{Federal funds target rate} = 1\% + 2\% + ((1/2) \times -1\%) + ((1/2) \times -1\%) = 2\%.$$

The Taylor rule accurately predicted changes in the federal funds target during the period of Alan Greenspan's leadership of the Federal Reserve. For the period of the late 1970s and early 1980s, when Paul Volcker was chairman of the Federal Reserve, the Taylor rule predicts a federal funds rate target *lower* than the actual target the Fed used. This indicates that Chairman Volcker kept the federal funds rate at an unusually high level to bring down the very high inflation rates plaguing the economy in the late 1970s and early 1980s. In contrast, using data from the chairmanship of Arthur Burns from 1970 to 1978, the Taylor rule predicts a federal funds rate target *higher* than the actual target. This indicates that Chairman Burns kept the federal funds rate at an unusually low level during these years, which helps to explain why the inflation rate grew worse. During the mid-2000s the actual federal funds rate was also lower than the predicted federal funds rate. Some economists, including Taylor, argue that these low targets for the federal funds rate contributed to the excessive increase in spending on housing that we will discuss in the next section.

Although the Taylor rule does not account for changes in the target inflation rate or the equilibrium interest rate, many economists view the rule as a convenient tool for analyzing the federal funds target.

## Should the Fed Target Inflation?

Over the past decade, many economists and central bankers, including the current Fed chair, Ben Bernanke, have proposed using *inflation targeting* as a framework for conducting monetary policy. With **inflation targeting**, the central bank commits to achieving a publicly announced inflation target of, for example, 2 percent. Inflation targeting does not impose an inflexible rule on the central bank. The central bank would still be free, for example, to take action in case of a severe recession. Nevertheless, monetary policy goals and operations would focus on inflation and inflation forecasts. Inflation targeting has been adopted by the central banks of New Zealand (1989), Canada (1991), the United Kingdom (1992), Finland (1993), Sweden (1993), and Spain (1994), and by the European Central Bank. Inflation targeting has also been used in some newly industrializing countries, such as Chile, South Korea, Mexico, and South Africa, as well as in some transition economies in Eastern Europe, such as the Czech Republic, Hungary, and Poland. Experience with inflation targeting has varied, but typically the move to inflation targeting has been accompanied by lower inflation (sometimes at the cost of temporarily higher unemployment).

**Inflation targeting** Conducting monetary policy so as to commit the central bank to achieving a publicly announced level of inflation.

Should the Fed adopt an inflation target? Arguments in favor of inflation targeting focus on four points. First, as we have already discussed, in the long run, real GDP returns to its potential level, and potential real GDP is not affected by monetary policy. Therefore, in the long run, the Fed can affect inflation but not real GDP. Having an explicit inflation target would draw the public's attention to this fact. Second, by announcing an inflation target, the Fed would make it easier for households and firms to form accurate expectations of future inflation, improving their planning and the efficiency of the economy. Third, an announced inflation target would help institutionalize good U.S. monetary policy. An inflation target would reduce the chances of abrupt changes in policy occurring as members join and leave the FOMC. Finally, an inflation target would promote accountability for the Fed by providing a yardstick against which Congress and the public could measure the Fed's performance.

Inflation targeting also has opponents, who typically raise three points. First, having a numeric target for inflation reduces the flexibility of monetary policy to address other policy goals. Second, inflation targeting assumes that the Fed can accurately forecast future inflation rates, which is not always the case. Finally, holding the Fed accountable only for an inflation goal may make it less likely that the Fed will achieve other important policy goals.

Although Ben Bernanke becoming chair of the Fed in January 2006 appeared to increase the chances that the Fed would adopt a policy of inflation targeting, the necessity of dealing with the recession of 2007–2009 at least temporarily pushed the issue off the Fed's agenda.

*The Fed excludes food and energy prices from its main measure of inflation.*

## Making the Connection | How Does the Fed Measure Inflation?

To attain its goal of price stability, the Fed has to consider carefully the best way to measure the inflation rate. As we saw in Chapter 20, the consumer price index (CPI) is the most widely used measure of inflation. But we also saw that the CPI suffers from biases that cause it to overstate the true underlying rate of inflation. An alternative measure of changes in consumer prices can be constructed from the data gathered to calculate GDP. We saw in Chapter 19 that the GDP deflator is a broad measure of the price level that includes the price of every good or service that is in GDP. Changes in the GDP deflator are not a good measure of inflation experienced by the typical consumer, worker, or firm, however, because the deflator includes prices of goods, such as industrial equipment, that are not widely purchased. The *personal consumption expenditures price index (PCE)* is a measure of the price level that is similar to the GDP deflator, except it includes only the prices of goods from the consumption category of GDP.

In 2000, the Fed announced that it would rely more on the PCE than on the CPI in tracking inflation. The Fed noted three advantages that the PCE has over the CPI:

1. The PCE is a so-called chain-type price index, as opposed to the market-basket approach used in constructing the CPI. As we saw in Chapter 20, because consumers shift the mix of products they buy each year, the market-basket approach causes the CPI to overstate actual inflation. A chain-type price index allows the mix of products to change each year.

2. The PCE includes the prices of more goods and services than the CPI, so it is a broader measure of inflation.

3. Past values of the PCE can be recalculated as better ways of computing price indexes are developed and as new data become available. This allows the Fed to better track historical trends in the inflation rate.

In 2004, the Fed announced that it would begin to rely on a subcategory of the PCE: the so-called core PCE, which excludes food and energy prices. Prices of food and energy tend to fluctuate up and down for reasons that may not be related to the causes of general inflation and that cannot easily be controlled by monetary policy. Oil prices, in particular, have moved dramatically up and down in recent years. Therefore, a price index that includes food and energy prices may not give a clear view of underlying trends in inflation. The following graph shows movements in the CPI, the PCE, and the core PCE from January 1999 through September 2011. Although the three measures of inflation move roughly together, the core PCE has been more stable than the others. Note in particular that in early 2009, when the CPI and the PCE were indicating that the economy was experiencing deflation, the core PCE was still showing moderate inflation rates of about 1.5 percent.

If you want to know what the Fed thinks the current inflation rate is, the best idea is to look at data on the core PCE. These data are published monthly by the Bureau of Economic Analysis.

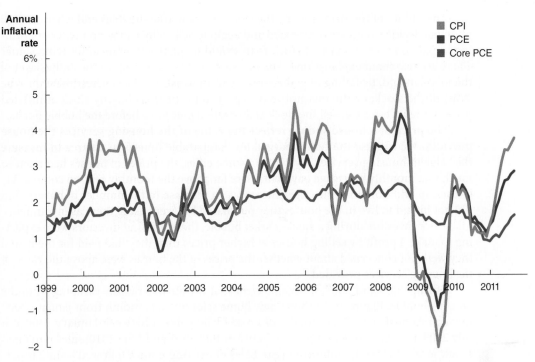

Data from U.S. Bureau of Economic Analysis; and U.S. Bureau of Labor Statistics.

**Your Turn:** Test your understanding by doing related problem 5.8 on page 902 at the end of this chapter.

MyEconLab

# Fed Policies during the 2007–2009 Recession

**26.6 LEARNING** OBJECTIVE

Discuss the policies the Federal Reserve used during the 2007–2009 recession.

As we have seen, the Fed's traditional response to a recession is to lower the target for the federal funds rate. The severity of the recession of 2007–2009, particularly the problems in financial markets during those years, complicated the Fed's job. By December 2008, the Fed had effectively lowered the target for the federal funds rate to zero, but the zero interest rate alone did not achieve the Fed's desired expansionary effect on the economy. In this section, we will discuss some of the additional policy measures the Fed took during the 2007–2009 recession. Some of these measures were used for the first time in the Fed's history.

## The Inflation and Deflation of the Housing Market Bubble

To understand the 2007–2009 recession and the difficulties in financial markets that occurred during it, we need to start by considering the housing market. As we mentioned in the chapter opener, the Fed lowered the target for the federal funds rate during the 2001 recession to stimulate demand for housing. The policy was successful, and most builders, such as Toll Brothers, experienced several years of high demand. By 2005, however, many economists argued that a "bubble" had formed in the housing market. As we discussed in Chapter 8, the price of any asset reflects the returns the owner of the asset expects to receive. For example, the price of a share of stock reflects the profitability of the firm issuing the stock because the owner of a share of stock has a claim on the firm's profits and assets. Many economists believe, however, that sometimes a *stock market bubble* can form when the prices of stocks rise above levels that can be justified by the profitability of the firms issuing the stock. Stock market bubbles end when enough investors decide stocks are overvalued and begin to sell. Why would an investor be willing to pay more for a share of stock than would be justified by its underlying value? There are two main explanations: The investor may be caught up in the enthusiasm of the moment and, by failing to gather sufficient information, may overestimate the true value of the stock; or the investor may expect to profit from buying stock at inflated prices if the investor can sell the stock at an even higher price before the bubble bursts.

The price of a house should reflect the value of the housing services the house provides. We can use the rents charged for comparable houses in an area to measure the value of housing services. By 2005, in some cities, the prices of houses had risen so much that monthly mortgage payments were far above the monthly rent on comparable houses. In addition, in some cities, there was an increase in the number of buyers who did not intend to live in the houses they purchased but were using them as investments. Like stock investors during a stock market bubble, these housing investors were expecting to make a profit by selling houses at higher prices than they had paid for them, and they were not concerned about whether the prices of the houses were above the value of the housing services provided.

During 2006 and 2007, it became clear that the air was rapidly escaping from the housing bubble. Figure 26.12 shows new home sales for each month from January 2000 through August 2011. New home sales rose by 60 percent between January 2000 and July 2005 and then fell by 80 percent between July 2005 and May 2010; sales remained at low levels during the following year. Sales of existing homes followed a similar pattern. Prices of new and existing homes in most markets also began to decline beginning in 2006, and the inventory of unsold homes offered for sale soared. Some homebuyers began having trouble making their loan payments. When lenders foreclosed on some of these loans, the lenders sold the homes, causing housing prices to decline further. *Subprime loans* are loans granted to borrowers with flawed credit histories. Some mortgage lenders that had concentrated on making subprime loans suffered heavy losses and

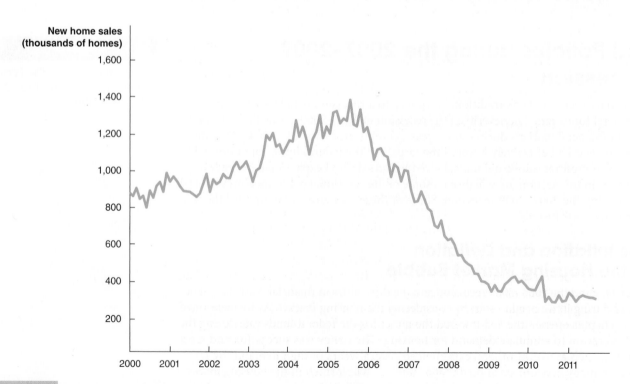

**Figure 26.12** **The Housing Bubble**

Sales of new homes in the United States went on a roller-coaster ride, rising by 60 percent between January 2000 and July 2005, before falling by 80 percent between July 2005 and May 2010.

*Note:* The data are seasonally adjusted at an annual rate.
Data from U.S. Bureau of the Census.

went out of business, and most banks and other lenders tightened the requirements for borrowers. This *credit crunch* made it more difficult for potential homebuyers to obtain mortgages, further depressing the market.

The decline in the housing market affected other markets as well. For example, with home prices falling, consumption spending on furniture, appliances, and home improvements declined as many households found it more difficult to borrow against the value of their homes.

Was the housing bubble the result of overly optimistic expectations by homebuyers and builders who believed that new residential construction and housing prices would continue to rise at rapid rates indefinitely? While overly optimistic expectations may have played some role in the housing bubble, many economists believe that changes in the market for mortgages may have played a bigger role.

## The Changing Mortgage Market

Until the 1970s, the commercial banks and savings and loans that granted mortgages kept the loans until the borrowers paid them off. As we saw in Chapter 25, a financial asset such as a mortgage is a security only if it can be resold in a secondary market. Many members of Congress believed that home ownership could be increased by creating a secondary market in mortgages. If banks and savings and loans could resell mortgages, then, in effect, individual investors would be able to provide funds for mortgages. The process would work like this: If a bank or savings and loan granted a mortgage and then resold the mortgage to an investor, the bank could use the funds received from the investor to grant another mortgage. In this way, banks and savings and loans could grant more mortgage loans because they would no longer depend only on deposits for the funds needed to make the loans. One barrier to creating a secondary market in mortgages was that most investors were unwilling to buy mortgages because they were afraid of losing money if the borrower stopped making payments, or *defaulted*, on the loan.

To reassure investors, Congress used two *government-sponsored enterprises (GSEs)*: the Federal National Mortgage Association ("Fannie Mae") and the Federal Home Loan Mortgage Corporation ("Freddie Mac"). These two institutions stand between investors and banks that grant mortgages. Fannie Mae and Freddie Mac sell bonds to investors and use the funds to purchase mortgages from banks. By the 1990s, a large secondary market existed in mortgages, with funds flowing from investors through Fannie Mae and Freddie Mac to banks and, ultimately, to individuals and families borrowing money to buy houses.

## The Role of Investment Banks

By the 2000s, further changes had taken place in the mortgage market. First, investment banks became significant participants in the secondary market for mortgages. As we have seen, investment banks, such as Goldman Sachs and Morgan Stanley, differ from commercial banks in that they do not take in deposits and rarely lend directly to households. Instead, investment banks concentrate on providing advice to firms issuing stocks and bonds or considering mergers with other firms. Investment banks began buying mortgages, bundling large numbers of them together as bonds known as *mortgage-backed securities*, and reselling them to investors. Mortgage-backed securities proved very popular with investors because they often paid higher interest rates than other securities with comparable default risk.

Second, by the height of the housing bubble in 2005 and early 2006, lenders had greatly loosened the standards for obtaining a mortgage loan. Traditionally, only borrowers with good credit histories and who were willing to make a down payment equal to at least 20 percent of the value of the house they were buying would be able to receive a mortgage. By 2005, however, lenders were issuing many mortgages to subprime borrowers with flawed credit histories. In addition, "Alt-A" borrowers who stated—but did not document—their incomes and borrowers who made very small down payments found it easier to take out loans. Lenders also created new types of *adjustable-rate mortgages* that allowed borrowers to pay a very low interest rate for the first few years of the mortgage and then pay a higher rate in later years. The chance that the borrowers using these nontraditional mortgages would default was higher than for borrowers using traditional mortgages. Why would borrowers take out mortgages if they doubted that they could make the payments, and why would lenders grant these mortgages? The answer seems to be that both borrowers and lenders were anticipating that housing prices would continue to rise, which would reduce the chance that borrowers would default on the mortgages and would also make it easier for borrowers to convert to more traditional mortgages in the future.

Unfortunately, the decline in housing prices led to rising defaults among subprime and Alt-A borrowers, borrowers with adjustable-rate mortgages, and borrowers who had made only small down payments. When borrowers began defaulting on mortgages, the value of many mortgage-backed securities declined sharply. Investors feared that if they purchased these securities, they would not receive the promised payments because the payments on the securities depended on borrowers making their mortgage payments, which an increasing number were failing to do. Many commercial and investment banks owned these mortgage-backed securities, so the decline in the value of the securities caused these banks to suffer heavy losses. By mid-2007, the decline in the value of mortgage-backed securities and the large losses suffered by commercial and investment banks began to cause turmoil in the financial system. Many investors refused to buy mortgage-backed securities, and some investors would buy only bonds issued by the U.S. Treasury.

## Making the Connection | The Wonderful World of Leverage

Traditionally, most people taking out a mortgage make a down payment equal to 20 percent of the price of the house and borrow the remaining 80 percent. During the housing boom, however, many people purchased houses with down payments of 5 percent or less. In this sense, borrowers were highly *leveraged*, which means that their investment in their house was made mostly with borrowed money.

To see how leverage works in the housing market, consider the following example: Suppose you buy a $200,000 house on January 1, 2014. On January 1, 2015, the price of the house—if you decide to sell it—has risen to $220,000. What return have you earned on your investment in the house? The answer depends on how much you invested when you bought the house. For example, if you paid $200,000 in cash for the house, your return on that $200,000 investment is the $20,000 increase in the price of the house divided by your $200,000 investment, or 10 percent. Suppose that rather than paying cash, you made a down payment of 20 percent, or $40,000, and borrowed the rest by taking out a mortgage loan of $160,000. Now the return on your investment in the house is the $20,000 increase in the price of the house divided by your $40,000 investment, or 50 percent. If the down payment is less than 20 percent, your return on investment will be higher. The second column in the table below shows how the return on your investment increases as your down payment decreases:

*Making a very small down payment on a home mortgage leaves a buyer vulnerable to falling house prices.*

|  | Return on your investment from . . . | |
| --- | --- | --- |
| Down Payment | A 10 Percent Increase in the Price of Your House | A 10 Percent Decrease in the Price of Your House |
| 100% | 10% | −10% |
| 20 | 50 | −50 |
| 10 | 100 | −100 |
| 5 | 200 | −200 |

An investment financed at least partly by borrowing is called a *leveraged investment*. As this example shows, the larger the fraction of an investment financed by borrowing, the greater the degree of leverage in the investment, and the greater the potential return. But as the third column in the table shows, the reverse is also true: The greater the leverage, the greater the potential loss. To see why, consider once again that you buy a house for $200,000, except that in this case, after one year the price of the house falls to $180,000. If you paid $200,000 in cash for the house—so your leverage was zero—the $20,000 decline in the price of the house represents a loss of 10 percent of your investment. But if you made a down payment of only $10,000 and borrowed the remaining $190,000, then the $20,000 decline in the price of the house represents a loss of 200 percent of your investment. In fact, the house is now worth $10,000 less than the amount of your mortgage loan. The *equity* in your house is the difference between the market price of the house and the amount you owe on a loan. If the amount you owe is greater than the price of the house, you have *negative equity*. A home owner who has negative equity is also said to be "upside down" on his or her mortgage.

When the housing bubble burst and housing prices started to fall, many people found that they had negative equity. In that situation, some people defaulted on their loans, sometimes by simply moving out and abandoning their homes. Leverage had contributed to the housing boom and bust and the severity of the 2007–2009 recession.

**Your Turn:** Test your understanding by doing related problem 6.8 on page 903 at the end of this chapter.

MyEconLab

# The Fed and the Treasury Department Respond

Because the problems in financial markets resulting from the bursting of the housing bubble were so profound, the Fed entered into an unusual partnership with the U.S. Treasury Department to develop suitable policies. Fed Chairman Ben Bernanke and U.S. Treasury Secretaries Henry Paulson (in the Bush administration) and Timothy Geithner (in the Obama administration) responded to the crisis by intervening in financial markets in unprecedented ways.

**Initial Fed and Treasury Actions** The financial crisis significantly worsened following the bankruptcy of the investment bank Lehman Brothers on September 15, 2008. So it is useful to look at the actions taken by the Fed and Treasury before and after that date. First, although the Fed traditionally made loans only to commercial banks, in March 2008, it announced it would temporarily make discount loans to *primary dealers*—firms that participate in regular open market transactions with the Fed. This change was intended to provide short-term funds to these dealers, some of which are investment banks. Second, also in March, the Fed announced that it would loan up to $200 billion of Treasury securities in exchange for mortgage-backed securities. This temporary program made it possible for primary dealers that owned mortgage-backed securities that were difficult or impossible to sell, to have access to Treasury securities that they could use as collateral for short-term loans. Third, once again in March, the Fed and the Treasury helped JPMorgan Chase acquire the investment bank Bear Stearns, which was on the edge of failing. The Fed agreed that if JPMorgan Chase would acquire Bear Stearns, the Fed would guarantee any losses JPMorgan Chase suffered on Bear Stearns's holdings of mortgage-backed securities, up to a limit of $29 billion. The Fed and Treasury were convinced that the failure of Bear Stearns had the potential of causing a financial panic, as many investors and financial firms would have stopped making short-term loans to other investment banks. Finally, in early September, the Treasury moved to have the federal government take control of Fannie Mae and Freddie Mac. Although Fannie Mae and Freddie Mac had been sponsored by the federal government, they were actually private businesses whose stock was bought and sold on the New York Stock Exchange. Under the Treasury's plan, Fannie Mae and Freddie Mac were each provided with up to $100 billion in exchange for 80 percent ownership of the firms. The firms were placed under the supervision of the Federal Housing Finance Agency. The Treasury believed that the bankruptcy of Fannie Mae and Freddie Mac would have caused a collapse in confidence in mortgage-backed securities, further devastating this already weak housing market.

**Responses to the Failure of Lehman Brothers** Some economists and policy-makers criticized the decision by the Fed and the Treasury to help arrange the sale of Bear Stearns to JPMorgan Chase. Their main concern was with what is known as the *moral hazard problem*, which is the possibility that managers of financial firms such as Bear Stearns might make riskier investments if they believe that the federal government will save them from bankruptcy. The Treasury and Fed acted to save Bear Stearns because they believed that the failure of a large financial firm could have wider economic repercussions. As we discussed in Chapter 25, when a financial firm sells off its holdings of bonds and other assets, it causes their prices to fall, which in turn can undermine the financial position of other firms that also own these assets. In September 2008, when the investment bank Lehman Brothers was near bankruptcy, the Fed and the Treasury had to weigh the moral hazard problem against the possibility that the failure of Lehman Brothers would lead to further declines in asset prices and endanger the financial positions of other firms.

The Fed and the Treasury decided to allow Lehman Brothers to go bankrupt, which it did on September 15. The adverse reaction in financial markets was stronger than the Fed and Treasury had expected, which led them to reverse course two days later, when the Fed agreed to provide an $85 billion loan to the American International Group (AIG)—the largest insurance company in the United States—in exchange for an 80 percent ownership stake, effectively giving the federal government control of the company. One important result of the failure of Lehman Brothers was the heavy losses suffered by Reserve Primary Fund, a money market mutual fund that had invested in loans to Lehman Brothers. The problems at Reserve led many investors to withdraw their funds from it and other money market funds. These withdrawals reduced the ability of the money market funds to purchase commercial paper from corporations. Because in recent years corporations had become dependent on selling commercial paper to finance their operations, the Treasury and the Fed moved to stabilize this market and ensure that the flow of funds from investors to corporations continued. The Treasury announced a plan to provide insurance for deposits in money market mutual funds, similar to the existing insurance on bank deposits. The Fed announced that for a limited time it would lend directly to corporations by purchasing three-month commercial paper issued by non-financial corporations.

Finally, in October 2008, Congress passed the *Troubled Asset Relief Program (TARP)*, under which the Treasury attempted to stabilize the commercial banking system by providing funds to banks in exchange for stock. Taking partial ownership positions in private commercial banks was an unprecedented action for the federal government.

Clearly, the recession of 2007–2009 and the accompanying financial crisis had led the Fed and the Treasury to implement new approaches to policy. Many of these new approaches were controversial because they involved partial government ownership of financial firms, implicit guarantees to large financial firms that they would not be allowed to go bankrupt, and unprecedented intervention in financial markets. Although the approaches were new, they were intended to achieve the traditional macroeconomic policy goals of high employment, price stability, and stability of financial markets. What remains to be seen is whether these new approaches represent a permanent increase in federal government involvement in U.S. financial markets or whether the end of the recession will see policy return to more traditional approaches.

Continued from page 865

## Economics in Your Life

### Should You Buy a House during a Recession?

At the beginning of this chapter, we asked whether buying a house during a recession is a good idea. Clearly, there are many considerations to keep in mind when buying a house, which is the largest purchase you are likely to make in your lifetime. Included among these considerations are the price of the house relative to other comparable houses in the neighborhood, whether house prices in the neighborhood have been rising or falling, and the location of the house relative to stores, work, and good schools. Also important is the interest rate you will have to pay on the mortgage loan you would need in order to buy the house. As we have seen in this chapter, during a recession the Fed often takes actions to lower interest rates. So, mortgage rates are typically lower during a recession than at other times. You may want to take advantage of low interest rates to buy a house during a recession. But, recessions are also times of rising unemployment, and you would not want to make a commitment to borrow a lot of money for 15 or more years if you were in significant danger of losing your job. We can conclude, then, that if your job seems secure, buying a house during a recession may be a good idea.

# Conclusion

Monetary policy is one way governments pursue goals for inflation, employment, and financial stability. Many journalists and politicians refer to the chairman of the Federal Reserve as second only to the president of the United States in his ability to affect the U.S. economy. Congress and the president, however, also use their power over spending and taxes to try to stabilize the economy. In Chapter 27, we discuss how *fiscal policy*—changes in government spending and taxes—affect the economy.

Read *An Inside Look at Policy* on the next page for a discussion of the Federal Reserve's new policies designed to reenergize the sluggish U.S. housing market.

## ATLANTIC

# Will the Fed's New Policies Revitalize the Housing Market?

Congress is gridlocked, consumers are pessimistic, and firms are barely hiring. To speed this recovery up—or to prevent a double dip—it might be up to the Federal Reserve. Last week it announced its latest attempt to revitalize the economy. Its chief target appears to be the still anemic housing market. Will the new policies work?

### The Fed's Plan

**(a)** The central bank will take two different actions meant to jumpstart the economy. First, there's "Operation Twist." The Fed will attempt to push down long-term interest rates by purchasing $400 billion in Treasury securities with six to 30 year terms. The program will last for nine months—through June 2012.

But here's the clever part: the Fed will sell shorter-dated Treasuries in exchange for bank reserves. This will prevent the Fed from having to expand its balance sheet to purchase longer-term Treasury securities. The relative increase in short term rates should be small, since short-term Treasuries are in high demand. . . .

The Fed announced another policy change as well. It has been reinvesting its maturing principal in additional Treasury securities. The central bank will refine that approach by investing maturing principal from its agency bonds and mortgage-backed securities in additional agency mortgage-backed securities. In this way, it will keep the size of its mortgage securities exposure level. But more importantly, this action will also increase the demand for mortgage-backed securities, which should push down mortgage interest rates.

### The Medicine the Housing Market Needs?

In fact, the major target for all of the Fed's new action appears to be the U.S. housing market. Both Operation Twist and the new MBS reinvestment policy should help to push down mortgage interest rates. And they're low already: this week Freddie Mac reports the average 30-year mortgage interest rate at just 4.09%. Through the Fed's new policy, rates should easily dip below 4%.

Operation Twist could also help the reinvestment policy to have a more dramatic effect: as mortgage interest rates begin to decline, we should see mortgage refinancing soar. That means more maturing principal, which will provide even more capital for the Fed to reinvest in MBS to push down mortgage interest rates even further. . . .

### But Will It Boost the Economy?

**(b)** If mortgage interest rates decline significantly, then we'll almost certainly see more refinancing occur. That will provide a little bit of stimulus. Some Americans will lower their monthly mortgage payment. The impact that this has on the economy depends on how much these payments are lowered and how many people take advantage of the opportunity. That additional money they'll have can then be spent to stimulate the economy.

**(c)** What's less clear, however, is whether or not the very low mortgage interest rates will lead to more home sales. Over the past year, even though interest rates were extremely low, they weren't enough to push more buyers into the market. Will even lower rates do the trick?

If home sales do increase, then prices may begin to stabilize—at least for a time. If the market isn't near the bottom, then once interest rates begin rising again, sales could decline and prices could begin to drop again. This is what we saw when the home buyer credit created a temporary burst of demand.

What we probably won't see is a significant increase in construction. The market still has plenty of existing inventory to work through before more homes are needed. So unless home demand truly explodes, we shouldn't expect a tidal wave of construction jobs.

As always, the effectiveness of the Fed's policy relies on the willingness of consumers, banks, and businesses to play along. First, Americans will need to seek refinancing and home purchases. Then, the banks must be willing to provide the credit for those new loans. If that encourages more spending due to consumers having more money in their pockets, then firms could begin hiring more aggressively. That's the plan—we'll see if it works.

*Source:* Daniel Indiviglio, "Will the Fed's New Policies Revitalize the Housing Market?" *The Atlantic*, September 24, 2011. Reprinted by permission of The Atlantic Monthly Group. All rights reserved.

## Key Points in the Article

In late 2011, the Federal Reserve announced two new policies to stimulate the economy. One policy, referred to as "Operation Twist," has the Fed purchasing longer-term Treasury securities in an attempt to lower long-term interest rates. With the second policy, the Fed will invest maturing principal from its mortgage-backed securities and agency bonds in additional mortgage-backed securities, a move the Fed hopes will lower interest rates on mortgages. The primary focus of both policies is aiding the still-sluggish U.S. housing market. A decline in mortgage rates should encourage refinancing, leading to lower monthly mortgage payments and, therefore, more income to spend on other goods and services. Lower mortgage rates might also boost home sales, and this increase in demand may help stabilize housing prices. Whether these new Fed policies will be effective in boosting the economy by stimulating the housing market depends both on the willingness of banks to provide new mortgage loans and on the willingness of consumers to take advantage of the lower mortgage rates to either refinance existing loans or to purchase new homes.

## Analyzing the News

(a) In December 2008, the Fed pushed the target for the federal funds rate to nearly zero, where it remained through 2011. Due to the severity of the 2007–2009 recession, this very low rate still did little to stimulate the economy. Because the federal funds rate cannot go below zero, the Fed embarked on a policy of quantitative easing: purchasing longer-term securities such as 10-year Treasury notes and certain mortgage-backed securities in an effort to keep mortgage rates low and help increase the demand for housing. With the economy remaining weak and the housing market still lethargic, the Fed announced its intention of implementing two new policies to attempt to boost the economy by increasing the demand for housing. With Operation Twist, the Fed will attempt to lower long-term interest rates by selling shorter-term Treasury securities and using the proceeds to buy Treasury securities with 6- to 30-year terms. The Fed will also invest the maturing principal from its mortgage-backed securities in additional mortgage-backed securities, which should reduce mortgage interest rates by increasing the demand for these securities.

(b) The Fed hopes that a significant decrease in mortgage rates will encourage current homeowners to refinance their mortgages to lower their monthly payments. Lower mortgage payments will provide these homeowners with additional funds that can be spent on more goods and services, helping to stimulate the economy.

(c) The figure below shows the average annual interest rates for federal funds, 30-year mortgages, and 10- and 30-year Treasury securities from 2001 through September 2011. By attempting to decrease the rates on these longer-term Treasury securities, the Fed hopes to reduce mortgage rates and increase home sales. An increase in home sales should help to stabilize home prices and boost the economy.

## Thinking Critically About Policy

1. More than 80 percent of mortgages in the United States involve fixed interest rates rather than adjustable interest rates. How would the effect of monetary policy on aggregate demand change if there were more adjustable-rate mortgages than fixed-rate mortgages?

2. According to the figure, the federal funds rate began to increase dramatically in 2004, reaching a level closest to the 30-year fixed mortgage rate in 2007 before rapidly falling from 2007 to 2009. Explain how this rate change corresponds to the bursting of the U.S. housing bubble in 2005 and what the change in the federal funds rate indicates about the monetary policy employed by the Fed beginning in 2004.

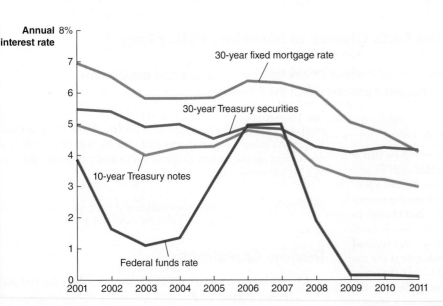

The average annual rates for federal funds, 30-year mortgages, and 10- and 30-year Treasury securities from 2001 through September 2011.

# Chapter Summary and Problems

## Key Terms

Contractionary monetary policy, p. 875

Expansionary monetary policy, p. 875

Federal funds rate, p. 872

Inflation targeting, p. 887

Monetary policy, p. 866

Taylor rule, p. 886

 **26.1** **What Is Monetary Policy?** pages 866–868
LEARNING OBJECTIVE: Define monetary policy and describe the Federal Reserve's monetary policy goals.

### Summary

**Monetary policy** is the actions the Fed takes to manage the money supply and interest rates to pursue its macroeconomic policy goals. The Fed has four *monetary policy goals* that are intended to promote a well-functioning economy: price stability, high employment, stability of financial markets and institutions, and economic growth.

MyEconLab   Visit www.myeconlab.com to complete these exercises online and get instant feedback.

### Review Questions

1.1 When Congress established the Federal Reserve in 1913, what was its main responsibility? When did Congress broaden the Fed's responsibilities?
1.2 What are the Fed's four monetary policy goals?
1.3 Why is the Fed sometimes said to have a "dual mandate"?
1.4 How can investment banks be subject to liquidity problems?

### Problems and Applications

1.5 What is a bank panic? What role did bank panics play in the decision by Congress to establish the Federal Reserve?
1.6 Why is price stability one of the Fed's monetary policy goals? What problems can high inflation rates cause for the economy?
1.7 A former Federal Reserve official argued that at the Fed, "the objectives of price stability and low long-term interest rates are essentially the same objective." Briefly explain his reasoning.
From William Poole, "Understanding the Fed," Federal Reserve Bank of St. Louis Review, Vol. 89, No. 1, January/February 2007, p. 4.

1.8 Stock prices rose rapidly in 2005, as did housing prices in many parts of the country. By 2008, both stock prices and housing prices were declining sharply. Some economists have argued that rapid increases and decreases in the prices of assets such as shares of stock or houses can damage the economy. Currently, stabilizing asset prices is not one of the Federal Reserve's policy goals. In what ways would a goal of stabilizing asset prices be different from the four goals listed on page 866? Do you believe that stabilizing asset prices should be added to the list of the Fed's policy goals? Briefly explain.

 **26.2** **The Money Market and the Fed's Choice of Monetary Policy Targets,** pages 868–873
LEARNING OBJECTIVE: Describe the Federal Reserve's monetary policy targets and explain how expansionary and contractionary monetary policies affect the interest rate.

### Summary

The Fed's *monetary policy targets* are economic variables that it can affect directly and that in turn affect variables such as real GDP and the price level that are closely related to the Fed's policy goals. The two main monetary policy targets are the money supply and the interest rate. The Fed has most often chosen to use the interest rate as its monetary policy target. The Federal Open Market Committee announces a target for the **federal funds rate** after each meeting. The federal funds rate is the interest rate banks charge each other for overnight loans. To lower the interest rate, the Fed increases the money supply. To raise the interest rate, the Fed decreases the money supply. In a graphical analysis of the money market, when the money supply curve shifts to the right, the result is a movement down the money

demand curve and a new equilibrium at a lower interest rate. When the money supply curve shifts to the left, the result is a movement up the money demand curve and a new equilibrium at a higher interest rate.

MyEconLab   Visit www.myeconlab.com to complete these exercises online and get instant feedback.

### Review Questions

2.1 What is a monetary policy target? Why does the Fed use policy targets?
2.2 What do economists mean by the demand for money? What is the advantage of holding money? What is the disadvantage?

**2.3** Draw a demand and supply graph showing equilibrium in the money market. Suppose the Fed wants to lower the equilibrium interest rate. Show on the graph how the Fed would accomplish this objective.

**2.4** What is the federal funds rate? What role does it play in monetary policy?

## Problems and Applications

**2.5** In the graph of the money market below, what could cause the money supply curve to shift from $MS_1$ to $MS_2$? What could cause the money demand curve to shift from $MD_1$ to $MD_2$?

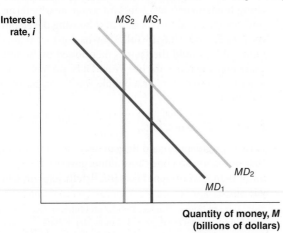

**2.6** The following is from a December 2008 article in the *Wall Street Journal*:

> The Federal Reserve cut its target interest rate Tuesday to historic lows between zero and a quarter percentage point. . . . After two days of discussion among Fed officials, the central bank said it would use every weapon from its arsenal to lift the U.S. from

recession. . . . Another Fed lending rate, the discount rate, will go to half a percentage point, a level last seen in the 1940s.

a. What is the name of the "target interest rate" mentioned in this article?

b. Briefly explain who borrows money and who lends money at this "target interest rate."

c. What is the discount rate, and how is it different from the "target interest rate" mentioned in the article?

From "Fed Cuts Rates Near Zero to Battle Slump," *Wall Street Journal*, December 17, 2008.

**2.7** If the Federal Reserve purchases $100 million worth of U.S. Treasury bills from the public, predict what will happen to the money supply. Explain your reasoning.

**2.8** In response to problems in financial markets and a slowing economy, the Federal Open Market Committee (FOMC) began lowering its target for the federal funds rate from 5.25 percent in September 2007. Over the next year, the FOMC cut its federal funds rate target in a series of steps. Writing in the *New York Times*, economist Steven Levitt observed, "The Fed has been pouring more money into the banking system by cutting the target federal funds rate to 0 to 0.25 percent in December 2008." What is the relationship between the federal funds rate falling and the money supply increasing? How does lowering the target for the federal funds rate "pour money" into the banking system?

From Steven D. Levitt, "The Financial Meltdown Now and Then," *New York Times*, May 12, 2009.

**2.9** In a column in the *Wall Street Journal*, two economists at the Council on Foreign Relations argue: "Simply put, the Fed must choose between managing the level of reserves and managing rates. It cannot do both." Do you agree? Briefly explain.

From Benn Steil and Paul Swartz, "Bye-Bye to the Fed-Funds Rate," *Wall Street Journal*, August 19, 2010.

---

**26.3** **Monetary Policy and Economic Activity,** pages 873–880

LEARNING OBJECTIVE: Use aggregate demand and aggregate supply graphs to show the effects of monetary policy on real GDP and the price level.

## Summary

An **expansionary monetary policy** lowers interest rates to increase consumption, investment, and net exports. This increased spending causes the aggregate demand (*AD*) curve to shift out more than it otherwise would, raising the level of real GDP and the price level. An expansionary monetary policy can help the Fed achieve its goal of high employment. A **contractionary monetary policy** raises interest rates to decrease consumption, investment, and net exports. This decreased spending causes the aggregate demand curve to shift out less than it otherwise would, reducing both the level of real GDP and the inflation rate below what they would be in the absence of policy. A contractionary monetary policy can help the Fed achieve its goal of price stability.

 Visit **www.myeconlab.com** to complete these exercises online and get instant feedback.

## Review Questions

**3.1** How does an increase in interest rates affect aggregate demand? Briefly discuss how each component of aggregate demand is affected.

**3.2** If the Fed believes the economy is about to fall into recession, what actions should it take? If the Fed believes the inflation rate is about to increase, what actions should it take?

**3.3** What were "quantitative easing" and "Operation Twist" and what was the Fed's objective in using them?

## Problems and Applications

**3.4** **[Related to the** Chapter Opener **on page 865]** An article in the *New York Times* in March 2002 reported that the housing market had been surprisingly strong during the previous year. According to the article, "In trying to explain the resilience of the housing market in the face of rising unemployment, shrinking stock portfolios and a soft economy, economists start with the Federal Reserve." Why start with the Federal Reserve in trying to explain the strength of the housing market during the 2001 recession?

From Daniel Altman, "Economy's Rock: Homes, Homes, Homes," *New York Times*, March 30, 2002.

**3.5** In explaining why monetary policy did not pull Japan out of a recession in the early 2000s, an official at the Bank of Japan was quoted as saying that despite "major increases in the money supply," the money "stay[ed] in banks." Explain what the official meant by saying that the money stayed in banks. Why would that be a problem? Where does the money go if an expansionary monetary policy is successful?

Based on James Brooke, "Critics Say Koizumi's Economic Medicine Is a Weak Tea," *New York Times*, February 27, 2002.

**3.6** According to an article in the *Wall Street Journal*:

> In February… [Japan's] gauge of core consumer prices slipped 0.1% from a year earlier…. The Bank of Japan said last year it would regard prices as stable if they rose from zero to 2% a year…. The Bank of Japan's target for short-term interest rates is just 0.5%…. "It will be very difficult for the BOJ [Bank of Japan] to raise interest rates when prices are below the range it defines as stable," says Teizo Taya, special counselor for the Daiwa Institute of Research and a former BOJ policy board member.

    **a.** What is the term for a falling price level?

    **b.** Why would the Bank of Japan, the Japanese central bank, be reluctant to raise its target for short-term interest rates if the price level is falling?

    **c.** Why would a country's central bank consider a falling price level to be undesirable?

"Japan's Consumer Prices May Threaten Economy," by Yuka Hayashi from *Wall Street Journal*, April 25, 2007. Copyright © 2011 by Dow Jones & Company, Inc. Reproduced with permission of Dow Jones & Company, Inc.

**3.7** An article by three economists at the Federal Reserve Bank of Richmond notes that by the fall of 2011, many unemployed people in the United States had been out of work for more than six months. The economists argue that: "After a long period of unemployment, affected workers may become effectively unemployable." They conclude that: "Policy options [such as providing additional training] that increase the ability of unemployed workers to find work … may be more effective at reducing unemployment than additional monetary stimulus."

    **a.** What is a policy of monetary stimulus?

    **b.** If many unemployed people have been out of work for a long time, why might policies that increase their ability to find jobs be more effective in reducing unemployment than a policy of monetary stimulus?

From Andreas Hornstein, Thomas A. Lubik, and Jessie Romero, "Potential Causes and Implications of the Rise in Long-Term Unemployment," Federal Reserve Bank of Richmond, Economic Brief, September 2011.

**3.8** William McChesney Martin, who was Federal Reserve chairman from 1951 to 1970, was once quoted as saying, "The role of the Federal Reserve is to remove the punchbowl just as the party gets going." What did he mean?

**3.9** **[Related to the** Chapter Opener **on page 865]** At the beginning of 2005, Robert Toll, CEO of Toll Brothers, argued that the United States was not experiencing a housing bubble. Instead, he argued that higher house prices reflected restrictions imposed by local governments on building new houses. He argued that the restrictions resulted from "NIMBY"—"Not in My Back Yard"—politics. Many existing homeowners are reluctant to see nearby farms and undeveloped land turned into new housing developments. As a result, according to Toll, "Towns don't want anything built." Why would the factors mentioned by Robert Toll cause housing prices to rise? Would it be possible to decide whether these factors or a bubble was the cause of rising housing prices?

From Shawn Tully, "Toll Brothers: The New King of the Real Estate Boom," *Fortune*, April 5, 2005.

**3.10** Former president Ronald Reagan once stated that inflation "has one cause and one cause alone: government spending more than government takes in." Briefly explain whether you agree.

From Edward Nelson, "Budget Deficits and Interest Rates," *Monetary Trends*, Federal Reserve Bank of St. Louis, March 2004.

**3.11** **[Related to the** Making the Connection **on page 876]** John Maynard Keynes is said to have remarked that using an expansionary monetary policy to pull an economy out of a deep recession can be like "pushing on a string." Briefly explain what Keynes is likely to have meant.

**3.12** **[Related to the** Making the Connection **on page 876]** Martin Feldstein, an economist at Harvard University, has argued that QE2 led consumers to decrease saving and increase spending: "A likely reason for the fall in the saving rate and the resulting rise in consumer spending was the sharp increase in the stock market, which rose by 15% between August [2010] and the end of the year. That, of course, is what the Fed had been hoping for."

    **a.** Why might QE2, which resulted in a decline in interest rates on long-term Treasury securities, have resulted in an increase in stock prices?

    **b.** Why was the Fed hoping for consumers to increase their spending in late 2010?

From Martin Feldstein, "Quantitative Easing and America's Economic Rebound," www.project-syndicate.org, February 24, 2011.

**3.13** **[Related to the** Making the Connection **on page 878]** The following is from a Federal Reserve publication:

> In practice, monetary policymakers do not have up-to-the-minute, reliable information about the state of the economy and prices. Information is limited because of lags in the publication of data. Also, policymakers have less-than-perfect understanding of the way the economy works, including the knowledge of when and to what extent policy actions will affect aggregate demand. The operation of the economy changes over time, and with it the response of

the economy to policy measures. These limitations add to uncertainties in the policy process and make determining the appropriate setting of monetary policy... more difficult.

If the Fed itself admits that there are many obstacles in the way of effective monetary policy, why does the Fed still engage in active monetary policy rather than use a monetary growth rule, as suggested by Milton Friedman and his followers?

From Board of Governors of the Federal Reserve System, *The Federal Reserve System: Purposes and Functions*, Washington, DC, 1994.

**3.14** **[Related to the** Making the Connection **on page 878]** If policymakers at the Fed are aware that GDP data are sometimes subject to large revisions, how might this affect their views about how best to conduct policy?

**3.15** **[Related to the** Don't Let This Happen to You **on page 880]** Briefly explain whether you agree with the following statement: "The Fed has an easy job. Say it wants to increase real GDP by $200 billion. All it has to do is increase the money supply by that amount."

---

<table>
<tr><td>**26.4**</td><td>**Monetary Policy in the Dynamic Aggregate Demand and Aggregate Supply Model, pages 880–884**<br>LEARNING OBJECTIVE: Use the dynamic aggregate demand and aggregate supply model to analyze monetary policy.</td></tr>
</table>

## Summary

We can use the *dynamic aggregate demand and aggregate supply model* introduced in Chapter 24 to look more closely at expansionary and contractionary monetary policies. The dynamic aggregate demand and aggregate supply model takes into account that (1) the economy experiences continuing inflation, with the price level rising every year, and (2) the economy experiences long-run growth, with the *LRAS* curve shifting to the right every year. In the dynamic model, an expansionary monetary policy tries to ensure that the aggregate demand curve will shift far enough to the right to bring about macroeconomic equilibrium with real GDP equal to potential GDP. A contractionary monetary policy attempts to offset movements in aggregate demand that would cause macroeconomic equilibrium to occur at a level of real GDP that is greater than potential real GDP.

 Visit www.myeconlab.com to complete these exercises online and get instant feedback.

## Review Questions

4.1 What are the key differences between how we illustrate an expansionary monetary policy in the basic aggregate demand and aggregate supply model and in the dynamic aggregate demand and aggregate supply model?

4.2 What are the key differences between how we illustrate a contractionary monetary policy in the basic aggregate demand and aggregate supply model and in the dynamic aggregate demand and aggregate supply model?

## Problems and Applications

4.3 Explain whether you agree with this argument:

> If the Fed actually ever carried out a contractionary monetary policy, the price level would fall. Because the price level has not fallen in the United States over an entire year since the 1930s, we can conclude that the Fed has not carried out a contractionary policy since the 1930s.

**4.4** **[Related to** Solved Problem 26.4 **on page 883]** Use this graph to answer the following questions.

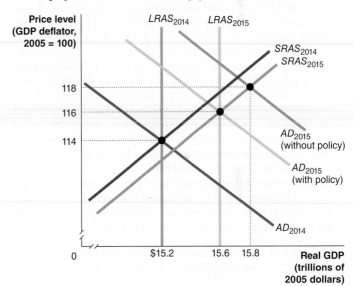

a. If the Fed does not take any policy action, what will be the level of real GDP and the price level in 2015?

b. If the Fed wants to keep real GDP at its potential level in 2015, should it use an expansionary policy or a contractionary policy? Should the trading desk be buying Treasury bills or selling them?

c. If the Fed takes no policy action, what will be the inflation rate in 2015? If the Fed uses monetary policy to keep real GDP at its full-employment level, what will be the inflation rate in 2015?

**4.5** **[Related to** Solved Problem 26.4 **on page 883]** The hypothetical information in the following table shows what the situation will be in 2015 if the Fed does *not* use monetary policy.

| Year | Potential GDP | Real GDP | Price Level |
|------|--------------|----------|-------------|
| 2014 | $15.2 trillion | $15.2 trillion | 110.0 |
| 2015 | 15.6 trillion | 15.8 trillion | 115.5 |

a. If the Fed wants to keep real GDP at its potential level in 2015, should it use an expansionary policy or a contractionary policy? Should the trading desk be buying T-bills or selling them?

b. If the Fed's policy is successful in keeping real GDP at its potential level in 2015, state whether each of the following will be higher, lower, or the same as it would have been if the Fed had taken no action:

  i. Real GDP

  ii. Potential real GDP

  iii. The inflation rate

  iv. The unemployment rate

c. Draw an aggregate demand and aggregate supply graph to illustrate the effects of the Fed's policy. Be sure that your graph contains *LRAS* curves for 2014 and 2015; *SRAS* curves for 2014 and 2015; *AD* curves for 2014 and 2015, with and without monetary policy action; and equilibrium real GDP and the price level in 2015, with and without policy.

---

**26.5** | **A Closer Look at the Fed's Setting of Monetary Policy Targets,** pages 885–889

LEARNING OBJECTIVE: Discuss the Fed's setting of monetary policy targets.

## Summary

Some economists have argued that the Fed should use the money supply, rather than an interest rate, as its monetary policy target. Milton Friedman and other monetarists argued that the Fed should adopt a monetary growth rule of increasing the money supply every year at a fixed rate. Support for this proposal declined after 1980 because the relationship between movements in the money supply and movements in real GDP and the price level weakened. John Taylor analyzed the factors involved in Fed decision making and developed the **Taylor rule** for federal funds targeting. The Taylor rule links the Fed's target for the federal funds rate to economic variables. Over the past decade, many economists and central bankers have expressed significant interest in using **inflation targeting**, under which monetary policy is conducted to commit the central bank to achieving a publicly announced inflation target. A number of foreign central banks have adopted inflation targeting, but the Fed has not. The Fed's performance in the 1980s, 1990s, and early 2000s generally received high marks from economists, even without formal inflation targeting.

 **MyEconLab** Visit **www.myeconlab.com** to complete these exercises online and get instant feedback.

## Review Questions

5.1 What is a monetary rule, as opposed to a monetary policy? What monetary rule would Milton Friedman have liked the Fed to follow? Why has support for a monetary rule of the kind advocated by Friedman declined since 1980?

5.2 For more than 20 years, the Fed has used the federal funds rate as its monetary policy target. Why doesn't the Fed target the money supply at the same time?

5.3 What is the Taylor rule? What is its purpose?

## Problems and Applications

5.4 Suppose that the equilibrium real federal funds rate is 2 percent and the target rate of inflation is 2 percent. Use the following information and the Taylor rule to calculate the federal funds rate target:

  Current inflation rate = 4 percent
  Potential real GDP = $14.0 trillion
  Real GDP = $14.14 trillion

5.5 According to an article in the *Economist*:

> Calculations by David Mackie, of J.P. Morgan, show that virtually throughout the past six years, interest rates in the euro area have been lower than a Taylor rule would have prescribed, refuting the popular wisdom that the [European Central Bank] cares less about growth than does the Fed.

Why would keeping interest rates "lower than a Taylor rule would have prescribed" be an indication that the European Central Bank cared more about growth than popular wisdom held?

From "The European Central Bank: Haughty Indifference, or Masterly Inactivity?" *Economist*, July 14, 2005.

5.6 Glenn Rudebusch, an economist at the Federal Reserve Bank of San Francisco, argues that if the Fed had followed the Taylor rule during the recession of 2007–2009, then by the end of 2009 the target for the federal funds rate would have been −5 percent. Provide values for the Taylor rule equation given on page 886 that would result in a negative target for the federal funds rate. Is it possible for the federal funds rate to be negative?

Based on Glenn Rudebusch, "The Fed's Monetary Policy Response to the Current Crisis," *FRBSF Economic Letter*, May 22, 2009.

5.7 While serving as the president of the Federal Reserve Bank of St. Louis, William Poole stated, "Although my own preference is for zero inflation properly managed, I believe that a central bank consensus on some other numerical goal of reasonably low inflation is more important than the exact number." Briefly explain why the economy might gain the benefits of an explicit inflation target even if the target chosen is not a zero rate of inflation.

From William Poole, "Understanding the Fed," *Federal Reserve Bank of St. Louis Review*, Vol. 89, No. 1, January/February 2007, p. 4.

5.8 **[Related to the** Making the Connection **on page 888]** If the core PCE is a better measure of the inflation rate than is the CPI, why is the CPI more widely used? In particular, can you think of reasons the federal government uses the CPI when deciding how much to increase Social Security payments to retired workers to keep the purchasing power of the payments from declining?

**26.6** **Fed Policies during the 2007–2009 Recession**, pages 889–894

LEARNING OBJECTIVE: Discuss the policies the Federal Reserve used during the 2007–2009 recession.

## Summary

A housing bubble that began to deflate in 2006 led to the recession of 2007–2009 and an accompanying financial crisis. In response, the Federal Reserve instituted a variety of policy actions. In a series of steps, it cut the target for the federal funds rate from 5.25 percent in September 2007 to effectively zero in December 2008. The decline in the housing market caused wider problems in the financial system, as defaults on home mortgages rose and the value of mortgage-backed securities declined. The Fed and the U.S. Treasury Department implemented a series of new policies to provide liquidity and restore confidence. The Fed expanded the types of firms eligible for discount loans and began lending directly to corporations by purchasing commercial paper. Under the *Troubled Asset Relief Program*, the Treasury provided financial support to banks and other financial firms in exchange for part ownership. The Treasury also moved to have the federal government take control of Fannie Mae and Freddie Mac, government-sponsored firms that play a central role in the mortgage market. The failure of the investment bank Lehman Brothers in September 2008 led to a deepening of the financial crisis and provided the motivation for some of the new policies. Ultimately, the new policies stabilized the financial system, but their long-term effects remain the subject of debate.

MyEconLab   Visit **www.myeconlab.com** to complete these exercises online and get instant feedback.

## Review Questions

**6.1** What is a mortgage? What were the important developments in the mortgage market during the years after 1970?

**6.2** Beginning in 2008, the Federal Reserve and the U.S. Treasury Department responded to the financial crisis by intervening in financial markets in unprecedented ways. Briefly summarize the actions of the Fed and Treasury.

## Problems and Applications

**6.3** Some economists argue that one cause of the financial problems resulting from the housing crisis was the fact that lenders who grant mortgages no longer typically hold the mortgages until they are paid off. Instead, lenders usually resell their mortgages in secondary markets. How might a lender intending to resell a mortgage act differently than a lender intending to hold a mortgage?

**6.4** An article in a Federal Reserve publication observes that "20 or 30 years ago, local financial institutions were the only option for some borrowers. Today, borrowers have access to national (and even international) sources of mortgage finance." What caused this change in the sources of mortgage finance? What would be the likely consequence of this change for the interest rates borrowers have to pay on mortgages? Briefly explain.

From Daniel J. McDonald and Daniel L. Thornton, "A Primer on the Mortgage Market and Mortgage Finance," *Federal Reserve Bank of St. Louis Review*, January/February 2008.

**6.5** Charles Calomiris, an economist at Columbia University, was quoted as saying the following of the initiatives of the Treasury and Fed during the financial crisis of 2007–2009: "It has been a really head-spinning range of unprecedented and bold actions. . . . That is exactly as it should be. But I'm not saying that it's without some cost and without some risk." What was unprecedented about the Treasury and Fed's actions? What risks did these actions involve?

From Steven R. Weisman, "With Bold Steps, Fed Chief Quiets Some Criticism," *New York Times*, May 28, 2008.

**6.6** Recall that "securitization" is the process of turning a loan, such as a mortgage, into a bond that can be bought and sold in secondary markets. An article in the *Economist* notes:

> That securitization caused more subprime mortgages to be written is not in doubt. By offering access to a much deeper pool of capital, securitization helped to bring down the cost of mortgages and made home-ownership more affordable for borrowers with poor credit histories.

What is a "subprime mortgage"? What is a "deeper pool of capital"? Why would securitization give mortgage borrowers access to a deeper pool of capital? Would a subprime borrower be likely to pay a higher or a lower interest rate than a borrower with a better credit history? Under what circumstances might a lender prefer to loan money to a borrower with a poor credit history rather than to a borrower with a good credit history? Briefly explain.

From "Ruptured Credit," *Economist*, May 15, 2008.

**6.7** In the fall of 2011, investors began to fear that some European governments, particularly Greece and Italy, might default on the bonds they had issued, making the prices of the bonds fall sharply. Many European banks owned these bonds, and some investors worried that these banks might also be in financial trouble. An article in the *Economist* magazine referred to the "prospect of another Lehman moment." The article noted that, "Governments are once again having to step in to support their banks." What did the article mean by another "Lehman moment"? Why might European governments have felt the need to support their banks in order to avoid another Lehman moment?

From "Here We Go Again," *Economist*, October 8, 2011.

**6.8** **[Related to the** Making the Connection **on page 892]** Suppose you buy a house for $150,000. One year later, the market price of the house has risen to $165,000. What is the return on your investment in the house if you made a down payment of 20 percent and took out a mortgage loan for the other 80 percent? What if you made a down payment of 5 percent and borrowed the other 95 percent? Be sure to show your calculations in your answer.

## Chapter Outline and Learning Objectives

# Does Government Spending Create Jobs?

Tutor-Saliba was founded in Southern California in 1949 and is today one of the largest heavy construction firms in the United States. In the fall of 2011, workers employed by Tutor-Saliba were hard at work on the Caldecott Tunnel in Northern California. The project would expand the tunnel through the Berkeley Hills from six lanes to eight in order to ease congestion between the cities of Orinda and Oakland. Part of the funding for the project came from the American Recovery and Reinvestment Act (ARRA, often referred to as the "stimulus bill"), which President Barack Obama and Congress had enacted in early 2009, in an attempt to increase aggregate demand during the recession of 2007–2009. Without this funding, the state of California would not have gone ahead with the project. The ARRA is an example of *discretionary fiscal policy* aimed at increasing real GDP and employment. To carry out the Caldecott Tunnel project, Tutor-Saliba hired an additional 106 workers. A spokesperson for the state agency in charge of the project argued that the increased employment effects from the project were even larger: "There is a ripple effect. There's truckers and equipment builders, and the deli in Orinda has never been as busy before."

The project to expand the Caldecott Tunnel is an example of increased government spending leading to increased employment. Or is it? A majority of economists agree that increased government spending leads to increased employment. But some economists argue that government spending shifts employment from one group of workers to another but doesn't increase *total* employment. Casey Mulligan, an economist at the University of Chicago, compares the effect of increases in government spending on projects like the Caldecott Tunnel to the effect of the New York Yankees building a new Yankee Stadium on the north side of East 161st Street in New York, across the street from the old Yankee Stadium on the south side of East 161st Street: "Not surprisingly, . . . spending by consumers, news organizations and entertainment businesses, among others, on the north side of East 161st Street was a lot more than it had been in years past. . . . [But] much of what happened north of East 161st Street was just a displacement of activity from the south side, rather than a creation of new activity."

The debate over the effects of government spending were particularly important during 2011 because the economy was recovering slowly from the 2007–2009 recession, with the unemployment rate remaining above 9 percent. In this chapter, we will examine discretionary fiscal policy and the debate over its effects. **AN INSIDE LOOK AT POLICY** on **page 936** discusses whether government-sponsored infrastructure spending is an effective means to create jobs in a slow-growing U.S. economy.

Based on Zusha Elinson, "Caldecott Tunnel Edges Forward, Tribute to Stimulus Bill," *New York Times*, September 10, 2011; and Casey B. Mulligan, "Local and National Stimulus," *New York Times*, August 24, 2011.

## Economics in Your Life

### What Would You Do with $500?

Suppose that the federal government announces that it will immediately mail you, and everyone else in the economy, a $500 tax rebate. In addition, you expect that in future years, your taxes will also be $500 less than they would otherwise have been. How will you respond to this increase in your disposable income? What effect will this tax rebate likely have on equilibrium real GDP in the short run? As you read the chapter, see if you can answer these questions. You can check your answers against those we provide on **page 935** at the end of this chapter.

I n Chapter 26, we discussed how the Federal Reserve uses monetary policy to pursue macroeconomic policy goals, including price stability and high employment. In this chapter, we will explore how the government uses *fiscal policy*, which involves changes in taxes and government purchases, to achieve similar policy goals. As we have seen, in the short run, the price level and the levels of real GDP and total employment in the economy depend on aggregate demand and short-run aggregate supply. The government can affect the levels of both aggregate demand and aggregate supply through fiscal policy. We will explore how Congress and the president decide which fiscal policy actions to take to achieve their goals. We will also discuss the debates among economists and policymakers over the effectiveness of fiscal policy.

Define fiscal policy.

**Fiscal policy** Changes in federal taxes and purchases that are intended to achieve macroeconomic policy objectives.

# What Is Fiscal Policy?

Since the end of World War II, the federal government has been committed under the Employment Act of 1946 to intervening in the economy "to promote maximum employment, production, and purchasing power." As we saw in Chapter 26, the Federal Reserve closely monitors the economy, and the Federal Open Market Committee meets eight times per year to decide whether to change monetary policy. Less frequently, Congress and the president also make changes in taxes and government purchases to achieve macroeconomic policy objectives, such as high employment, price stability, and high rates of economic growth. Changes in federal taxes and spending that are intended to achieve macroeconomic policy objectives are called **fiscal policy**.

## What Fiscal Policy Is and What It Isn't

In the United States, federal, state, and local governments all have responsibility for taxing and spending. Economists typically use the term *fiscal policy* to refer only to the actions of the federal government. State and local governments sometimes change their taxing and spending policies to aid their local economies, but these are not fiscal policy actions because they are not intended to affect the national economy. The federal government makes many decisions about taxes and spending, but not all of these decisions are fiscal policy actions because they are not intended to achieve macroeconomic policy goals. For example, a decision to cut the taxes of people who buy hybrid cars is an environmental policy action, not a fiscal policy action. Similarly, the spending increases to fund the war on terrorism and the wars in Iraq and Afghanistan were part of defense and homeland security policy, not fiscal policy.

## Automatic Stabilizers versus Discretionary Fiscal Policy

**Automatic stabilizers** Government spending and taxes that automatically increase or decrease along with the business cycle.

There is an important distinction between *automatic stabilizers* and *discretionary fiscal policy*. Some types of government spending and taxes, which automatically increase and decrease along with the business cycle, are referred to as **automatic stabilizers**. The word *automatic* in this case refers to the fact that changes in these types of spending and taxes happen without actions by the government. For example, when the economy is expanding and employment is increasing, government spending on unemployment insurance payments to workers who have lost their jobs will automatically decrease. During a recession, as employment declines, this type of spending will automatically increase. Similarly, when the economy is expanding and incomes are rising, the amount the government collects in taxes will increase as people pay additional taxes on their higher incomes. When the economy is in recession, the amount the government collects in taxes will fall.

With discretionary fiscal policy, the government takes actions to change spending or taxes. The tax cuts Congress passed in 2008, 2009, and 2010 are examples of discretionary fiscal policy actions.

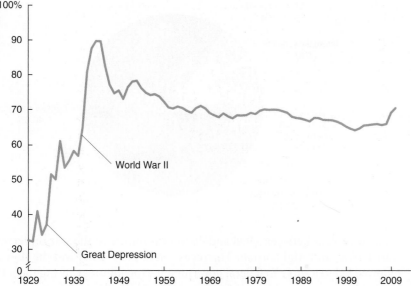

Federal Expenditures as a percentage of total government expenditures

World War II

Great Depression

**Figure 27.1**

**The Federal Government's Share of Total Government Expenditures, 1929–2010**

Until the Great Depression of the 1930s, the majority of government spending in the United States occurred at the state and local levels. Since World War II, the federal government's share of total government expenditures has been between two-thirds and three-quarters.
Data from U.S. Bureau of Economic Analysis.

## An Overview of Government Spending and Taxes

To provide a context for understanding fiscal policy, it is important to understand the big picture of government taxing and spending. Before the Great Depression of the 1930s, the majority of government spending took place at the state and local levels. As Figure 27.1 shows, the size of the federal government expanded significantly during the crisis of the Great Depression. Since World War II, the federal government's share of total government expenditures has been between two-thirds and three-quarters.

Economists often measure government spending relative to the size of the economy by calculating government spending as a percentage of GDP. Remember that there is a difference between federal government *purchases* and federal government *expenditures*. When the federal government purchases an aircraft carrier or the services of an FBI agent, it receives a good or service in return. Federal government expenditures include purchases plus all other federal government spending. As Figure 27.2 shows, federal government *purchases* as a percentage of GDP have actually been falling since the end of the Korean War in the early 1950s. Total federal *expenditures* as a percentage of GDP rose from 1950 to the early 1990s and then fell from 1992 to 2001, before rising again. The decline in expenditures between 1992 and 2001 was partly the result of the end of the Cold War between the Soviet Union and the United States, which allowed for a substantial reduction in defense spending. Real federal government spending on national defense declined by almost 25 percent between 1990 and 1998, before rising by more

Spending as a percentage of GDP

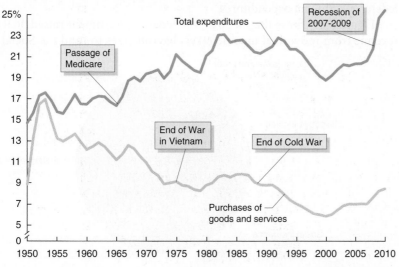

Total expenditures

Recession of 2007-2009

Passage of Medicare

End of War in Vietnam

End of Cold War

Purchases of goods and services

**Figure 27.2**

**Federal Purchases and Federal Expenditures as a Percentage of GDP, 1950–2010**

As a fraction of GDP, the federal government's *purchases* of goods and services have been declining since the Korean War in the early 1950s. Total *expenditures* by the federal government—including transfer payments—as a fraction of GDP slowly rose from 1950 through the early 1990s and fell from 1992 to 2001, before rising again. The recession of 2007–2009 and the slow recovery that followed led to a surge in federal government expenditures causing them to rise to their highest level as a percentage of GDP since World War II.
Data from U.S. Bureau of Economic Analysis.

**Federal Government Expenditures, 2010**

Federal government *purchases* can be divided into defense spending—which makes up 22.1 percent of the federal budget—and spending on everything else the federal government does—from paying the salaries of FBI agents, to operating the national parks, to supporting scientific research—which makes up 9.4 percent of the budget. In addition to purchases, there are three other categories of federal government *expenditures*: interest on the national debt, grants to state and local governments, and transfer payments. Transfer payments rose from about 25 percent of federal government expenditures in the 1960s to nearly 46.6 percent in 2010.
Data from U.S. Bureau of Economic Analysis.

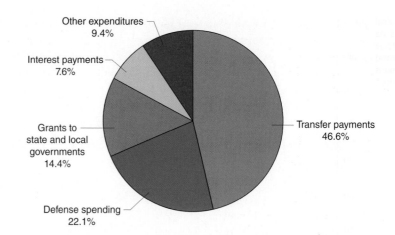

than 60 percent between 1998 and 2010 in response to the war on terrorism and the wars in Iraq and Afghanistan. The recession of 2007–2009 and the slow recovery that followed led to a surge in federal government expenditures causing them to rise to their highest level as a percentage of GDP since World War II.

In addition to purchases, there are three other categories of federal government expenditures: *interest on the national debt, grants to state and local governments*, and *transfer payments*. Interest on the national debt represents payments to holders of the bonds the federal government has issued to borrow money. Grants to state and local governments are payments made by the federal government to support government activity at the state and local levels. For example, to help reduce crime, Congress implemented a program of grants to local governments to hire more police officers. The largest and fastest-growing category of federal expenditures is transfer payments. Some of these programs, such as Social Security and unemployment insurance, began in the 1930s. Others, such as Medicare, which finances health care for the elderly, or the food stamps and Temporary Assistance for Needy Families programs, which are intended to aid the poor, began in the 1960s or later.

Figure 27.3 shows that in 2010, transfer payments were 46.6 percent of federal government expenditures. In the 1960s, transfer payments were only about 25 percent of federal government expenditures. As the U.S. population ages and medical costs continue to increase, federal government spending on the Social Security and Medicare programs will continue to increase, causing transfer payments to consume an increasing share of federal expenditures. Figure 27.3 shows that spending on most of the federal government's day-to-day activities—including running federal agencies such as the Environmental Protection Agency, the Federal Bureau of Investigation, the National Park Service, and the Immigration and Naturalization Service—makes up only 9.4 percent of federal government expenditures.

Figure 27.4 shows that in 2010, the federal government raised 36.9 percent of its revenue from individual income taxes. Payroll taxes to fund the Social Security and

**Federal Government Revenue, 2010**

In 2010, individual income taxes raised 36.9 percent of the federal government's revenues. Corporate income taxes raised 13.6 percent of revenue. Payroll taxes to fund the Social Security and Medicare programs rose from less than 10 percent of federal government revenues in 1950 to 40.0 percent in 2010. The remaining 9.6 percent of revenues were raised from excise taxes, tariffs on imports, and other sources.
Data from U.S. Bureau of Economic Analysis.

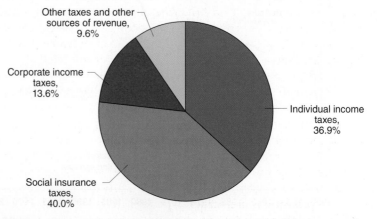

Medicare programs raised 40 percent of federal revenues. The tax on corporate profits raised 13.6 percent of federal revenues. The remaining 9.6 percent of federal revenues were raised from excise taxes on certain products, such as cigarettes and gasoline, from tariffs on goods imported from other countries, and from other sources, such as payments by companies that cut timber on federal lands.

| Making<br>the<br>Connection | ## Is Spending on Social Security and Medicare a Fiscal Time Bomb? |
|---|---|

Social Security, established in 1935 to provide payments to retired workers, began as a "pay-as-you-go" system, meaning that payments to current retirees were paid from taxes collected from current workers. In the early years of the program, many workers were paying into the system, and there were relatively few retirees. For example, in 1940, more than 35 million workers were paying into the system, and only 222,000 people were receiving benefits—a ratio of more than 150 workers to each beneficiary. In those early years, most retirees received far more in benefits than they had paid in taxes. For example, the first beneficiary was a legal secretary named Ida May Fuller. She worked for three years while the program was in place and paid total taxes of only $24.75. During her retirement, she collected $22,888.92 in benefits.

*Will the federal government be able to keep the promises made by the Social Security and Medicare programs?*

The Social Security and Medicare programs have been very successful in reducing poverty among elderly Americans, but in recent years, the ability of the federal government to finance current promises has been called into doubt. After World War II, the United States experienced a "baby boom," as birthrates rose and remained high through the early 1960s. Falling birthrates after 1965 have meant long-run problems for the Social Security system, as the number of workers per retiree has continually declined. Currently, there are only about three workers per retiree, and that ratio is expected to decline to two workers per retiree by 2035. Congress has attempted to deal with this problem by raising the age to receive full benefits from 65 to 67 and by increasing payroll taxes. In 1940, the combined payroll tax paid by workers and firms was 2 percent; in 2011, it was 15.3 percent (although a tax cut temporarily reduced it to 13.3 percent for that year).

Under the Medicare program, which was established in 1965, the federal government provides health care coverage to people age 65 and over. The long-term financial situation for Medicare is an even greater cause for concern than is Social Security. As Americans live longer and as new—and expensive—medical procedures are developed, the projected expenditures under the Medicare program will eventually far outstrip projected tax revenues. The federal government also faces increasing expenditures under the Medicaid program, which is administered by state governments and provides health care coverage to low-income people. In 2010, federal spending on Social Security, Medicare, and Medicaid equaled 10.4 percent of GDP. Spending on these three programs was less than 3 percent of GDP in 1962. The Congressional Budget Office (CBO) indicates that spending on these three programs will rise to 15.2 percent of GDP in 2030, 18.9 percent by 2050, and 25.8 percent by 2085. The graph on the next page illustrates these forecasts. Over the past 40 years, the federal government has spent an average of about 18.5 percent of GDP on *all programs* combined—from buying aircraft carriers to paying the salaries of FBI agents. So, if current trends continue, the federal government will eventually be spending, as a fraction of GDP, more on these three programs than it currently does on all programs combined. Over the coming decades, the gap between the benefits projected to be paid under the Social Security and Medicare programs and projected tax revenues is a staggering $72 *trillion*, or nearly five times the value of GDP in 2011. If current projections are accurate, policymakers are faced with the choice of significantly restraining spending on these programs, greatly increasing taxes on households and firms, or implementing some combination of spending restraints and tax increases. The alternatives will all clearly involve considerable pain. A report from the Congressional Budget Office concluded, "Even if taxation reached levels that were unprecedented in the United States, current spending policies could become financially unsustainable."

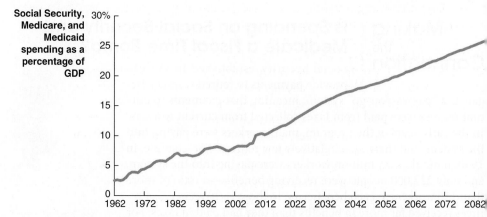

*Note:* The graph gives the Congressional Budget Office's "alternative fiscal scenario" of future spending.

A lively political debate has taken place over the future of the Social Security and Medicare programs. Some policymakers have proposed increasing taxes to fund future benefit payments. The tax increases needed, however, could be as much as 50 percent higher than current rates, and tax increases of that magnitude could discourage work effort, entrepreneurship, and investment, thereby slowing economic growth. There have also been proposals to slow the rate of growth of future benefits, while guaranteeing benefits to current recipients. While this strategy would avoid the need to raise taxes significantly, it would also require younger workers to save more for their retirement. Some economists and policymakers have argued for slower benefit growth for higher-income workers while leaving future benefits unchanged for lower-income workers. Whatever changes are ultimately made in the Medicare and Social Security programs, this policy debate is one of the most important for young people.

Based on Congressional Budget Office, The Long-Term Budget Outlook, June 2011; Congressional Budget Office, *Baseline Projections of Mandatory Outlays*, January 2009; 112th Congress, 1st Session, "The 2011 Annual Report of the Board of Trustees of the Federal Old-Age and Survivors Insurance and Disability Insurance Trust Funds," House Document 112–23, May 13, 2011; and the Social Security Administration Web site (www.ssa.gov).

MyEconLab   **Your Turn:** Test your understanding by doing related problems 1.6 and 1.7 on page 938 at the end of this chapter.

---

**27.2 LEARNING** OBJECTIVE

Explain how fiscal policy affects aggregate demand and how the government can use fiscal policy to stabilize the economy.

# The Effects of Fiscal Policy on Real GDP and the Price Level

The federal government uses macroeconomic policies to offset the effects of the business cycle on the economy. We saw in Chapter 26 that the Federal Reserve carries out monetary policy through changes in the money supply and interest rates. Congress and the president carry out fiscal policy through changes in government purchases and taxes. Because changes in government purchases and taxes lead to changes in aggregate demand, they can affect the level of real GDP, employment, and the price level. When the economy is in a recession, *increases* in government purchases or *decreases* in taxes will increase aggregate demand. As we saw in Chapter 24, the inflation rate may increase when real GDP is beyond potential GDP. Decreasing government purchases or raising taxes can slow the growth of aggregate demand and reduce the inflation rate.

# Expansionary and Contractionary Fiscal Policy

*Expansionary fiscal policy* involves increasing government purchases or decreasing taxes. An increase in government purchases will increase aggregate demand directly because government purchases are a component of aggregate demand. A cut in taxes has an indirect effect on aggregate demand. Remember from Chapter 19 that the income households have available to spend after they have paid their taxes is called *disposable income.* Cutting the individual income tax will increase household disposable income and consumption spending. Cutting taxes on business income can increase aggregate demand by increasing business investment.

Figure 27.5 shows the results of an expansionary fiscal policy, using the basic version of the aggregate demand and aggregate supply model. In this model, there is no economic growth, so the long-run aggregate supply (*LRAS*) curve does not shift. Notice that this figure is very similar to Figure 26.7 on page 875, which shows the effects of an expansionary monetary policy. The goal of both expansionary monetary policy and expansionary fiscal policy is to increase aggregate demand relative to what it would have been without the policy.

In panel (a) of Figure 27.5, we assume that the economy is in short-run equilibrium at point *A*, where the aggregate demand (*AD₁*) curve intersects the short-run aggregate supply (*SRAS*) curve. Real GDP is below potential real GDP, so the economy is in recession, with some firms operating below normal capacity and some workers having been laid off. To bring real GDP back to potential GDP, Congress and the president increase government purchases or cut taxes, which will shift the aggregate demand curve to the right, from *AD₁* to *AD₂*. Real GDP increases from \$14.2 trillion to potential GDP of \$14.4 trillion, and the price level rises from 98 to 100 (point *B*). The policy has successfully returned real GDP to its potential level. Rising production will lead to increasing employment, reducing the unemployment rate.

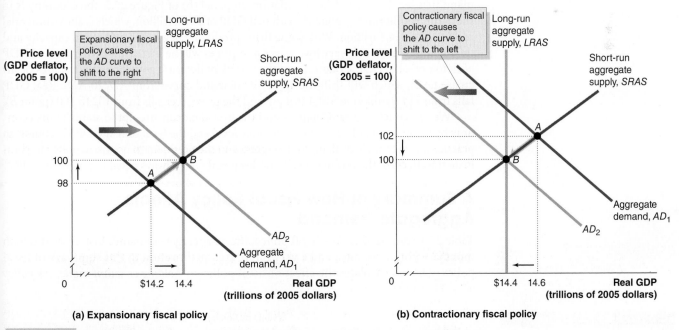

(a) Expansionary fiscal policy

(b) Contractionary fiscal policy

## Figure 27.5 Fiscal Policy

In panel (a), the economy begins in recession at point *A*, with real GDP of \$14.2 trillion and a price level of 98. An expansionary fiscal policy will cause aggregate demand to shift to the right, from *AD₁* to *AD₂*, increasing real GDP from \$14.2 trillion to \$14.4 trillion and the price level from 98 to 100 (point *B*). In panel (b), the economy begins at point *A*, with real GDP at \$14.6 trillion

and the price level at 102. Because real GDP is greater than potential GDP, the economy will experience rising wages and prices. A contractionary fiscal policy will cause aggregate demand to shift to the left, from *AD₁* to *AD₂*, decreasing real GDP from \$14.6 trillion to \$14.4 trillion and the price level from 102 to 100 (point *B*).

# Don't Let This Happen to You

## Don't Confuse Fiscal Policy and Monetary Policy

If you keep in mind the definitions of *money*, *income*, and *spending*, the difference between monetary policy and fiscal policy will be clearer. Students often make these two related mistakes: (1) They think of monetary policy as the Fed fighting recessions by increasing the money supply so people will have more money to spend; and (2) they think of fiscal policy as Congress and the president fighting recessions by spending more money. In this view, the only difference between fiscal policy and monetary policy is the source of the money.

To understand what's wrong with the descriptions of fiscal policy and monetary policy just given, first remember that the problem during a recession is not that there is too little *money*—currency plus checking account deposits—but too little *spending*. There may be too little spending for a number of reasons. For example, households may cut back on their spending on cars and houses because they are pessimistic about the future. Firms may cut back their spending because they have lowered their estimates of the future profitability of new machinery and factories.

Or the major trading partners of the United States—such as Japan and Canada—may be suffering from recessions, which cause households and firms in those countries to cut back their spending on U.S. products.

The purpose of expansionary monetary policy is to lower interest rates, which in turn increases aggregate demand. When interest rates fall, households and firms are willing to borrow more to buy cars, houses, and factories. The purpose of expansionary fiscal policy is to increase aggregate demand either by having the government directly increase its own purchases or by cutting taxes to increase household disposable income and, therefore, consumption spending.

Just as increasing or decreasing the money supply does not have a direct effect on government spending or taxes, increasing or decreasing government spending or taxes does not have a direct effect on the money supply. Fiscal policy and monetary policy have the same goals, but they have different effects on the economy.

MyEconLab

**Your Turn:** Test your understanding by doing related problem 2.6 on page 939 at the end of this chapter.

*Contractionary fiscal policy* involves decreasing government purchases or increasing taxes. Policymakers use contractionary fiscal policy to reduce increases in aggregate demand that seem likely to lead to inflation. In panel (b) of Figure 27.5, the economy is in short-run equilibrium at point *A*, with real GDP of $14.6 trillion, which is above potential real GDP of $14.4 trillion. With some firms producing beyond their normal capacity and the unemployment rate very low, wages and prices will be increasing. To bring real GDP back to potential GDP, Congress and the president decrease government purchases or increase taxes, which will shift the aggregate demand curve from $AD_1$ to $AD_2$. Real GDP falls from $14.6 trillion to $14.4 trillion, and the price level falls from 102 to 100 (point *B*).

We can conclude that Congress and the president can attempt to stabilize the economy by using fiscal policy to affect the price level and the level of real GDP. Of course, in practice it is extremely difficult for Congress and the president to use fiscal policy to eliminate the effects of the business cycle and keep real GDP always equal to potential GDP.

## A Summary of How Fiscal Policy Affects Aggregate Demand

Table 27.1 summarizes how fiscal policy affects aggregate demand. Just as we did with monetary policy, we must add a very important qualification to this summary of fiscal policy: The table isolates the effect of fiscal policy *by holding constant monetary policy*

**Table 27.1**

**Countercyclical Fiscal Policy**

| Problem | Type of Policy | Actions by Congress and the President | Result |
|---|---|---|---|
| Recession | Expansionary | Increase government spending or cut taxes | Real GDP and the price level rise. |
| Rising inflation | Contractionary | Decrease government spending or raise taxes | Real GDP and the price level fall. |

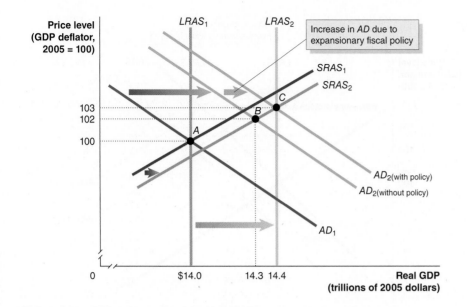

**Figure 27.6**

**An Expansionary Fiscal Policy in the Dynamic Model**

The economy begins in equilibrium at point $A$, at potential real GDP of \$14.0 trillion and a price level of 100. Without an expansionary policy, aggregate demand will shift from $AD_1$ to $AD_{2(\text{without policy})}$, which is not enough to keep the economy at potential GDP because long-run aggregate supply has shifted from $LRAS_1$ to $LRAS_2$. The economy will be in short-run equilibrium at point $B$, with real GDP of \$14.3 trillion and a price level of 102. Increasing government purchases or cutting taxes will shift aggregate demand to $AD_{2(\text{with policy})}$. The economy will be in equilibrium at point $C$, with real GDP of \$14.4 trillion, which is its potential level, and a price level of 103. The price level is higher than it would have been without an expansionary fiscal policy.

*and all other factors affecting the variables involved.* In other words, we are again invoking the *ceteris paribus* condition we discussed in Chapter 3. This point is important because, for example, a contractionary fiscal policy does not cause the price level to fall. A contractionary fiscal policy causes the price level *to rise by less than it would have without the policy.*

# Fiscal Policy in the Dynamic Aggregate Demand and Aggregate Supply Model*

**27.3 LEARNING OBJECTIVE**

Use the dynamic aggregate demand and aggregate supply model to analyze fiscal policy.

The overview of fiscal policy we just finished contains a key idea: Congress and the president can use fiscal policy to affect aggregate demand, thereby changing the price level and the level of real GDP. The discussion of expansionary and contractionary fiscal policy illustrated by Figure 27.5 on page 911 is simplified, however, because it ignores two important facts about the economy: (1) The economy experiences continuing inflation, with the price level rising every year, and (2) the economy experiences long-run growth, with the *LRAS* curve shifting to the right every year. In Chapter 24, we developed a *dynamic aggregate demand and aggregate supply model* that took these two facts into account. In this section, we use the dynamic model to gain a more complete understanding of fiscal policy.

To briefly review the dynamic model, recall that over time, potential real GDP increases, which we show by the long-run aggregate supply curve shifting to the right. The factors that cause the *LRAS* curve to shift also cause firms to supply more goods and services at any given price level in the short run, which we show by the short-run aggregate supply curve shifting to the right. Finally, during most years, the aggregate demand curve also shifts to the right, indicating that aggregate expenditure is higher at every price level.

Figure 27.6 shows the results of an expansionary fiscal policy using the dynamic aggregate demand and aggregate supply model. Notice that this figure is very similar to Figure 26.9 on page 881, which showed the effects of an expansionary monetary policy. The goal of both expansionary monetary policy and expansionary fiscal policy is to increase aggregate demand relative to what it would have been without the policy.

In the hypothetical situation shown in Figure 27.6, the economy begins in equilibrium at potential real GDP of \$14.0 trillion and a price level of 100 (point $A$). In the second year, *LRAS* increases to \$14.4 trillion, but *AD* increases only to $AD_{2(\text{without policy})}$,

*This section may be omitted without loss of continuity.

## Figure 27.7

### A Contractionary Fiscal Policy in the Dynamic Model

The economy begins in equilibrium at point *A*, with real GDP of $14.0 trillion and a price level of 100. Without a contractionary policy, aggregate demand will shift from $AD_1$ to $AD_{2(\text{without policy})}$, which results in a short-run equilibrium beyond potential GDP at point *B*, with real GDP of $14.5 trillion and a price level of 105. Decreasing government purchases or increasing taxes can shift aggregate demand to $AD_{2(\text{with policy})}$. The economy will be in equilibrium at point *C*, with real GDP of $14.4 trillion, which is its potential level, and a price level of 103. The inflation rate will be 3 percent, as opposed to the 5 percent it would have been without the contractionary fiscal policy.

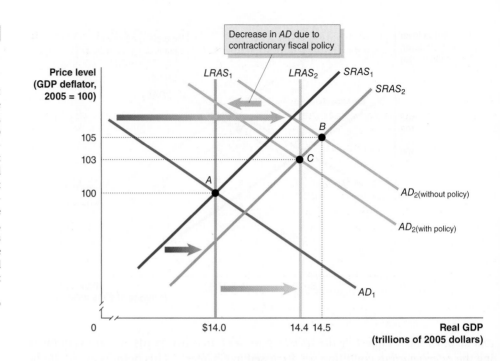

which is not enough to keep the economy in macroeconomic equilibrium at potential GDP. Let's assume that the Fed does not react to the situation with an expansionary monetary policy. In that case, without an expansionary fiscal policy of spending increases or tax reductions, the short-run equilibrium will occur at $14.3 trillion (point *B*). The $100 billion gap between this level of real GDP and the potential level means that some firms are operating at less than their full capacity. Incomes and profits will be falling, firms will begin to lay off workers, and the unemployment rate will rise.

Increasing government purchases or cutting taxes can shift aggregate demand to $AD_{2(\text{with policy})}$. The economy will be in equilibrium at point *C*, with real GDP of $14.4 trillion, which is its potential level, and a price level of 103. The price level is higher than it would have been without an expansionary fiscal policy.

*Contractionary fiscal policy* involves decreasing government purchases or increasing taxes. Policymakers use contractionary fiscal policy to reduce increases in aggregate demand that seem likely to lead to inflation. In Figure 27.7, the economy again begins at potential real GDP of $14.0 trillion and a price level of 100 (point *A*). Once again, *LRAS* increases to $14.4 trillion in the second year. In this scenario, the shift in aggregate demand to $AD_{2(\text{without policy})}$ results in a short-run macroeconomic equilibrium beyond potential GDP (point *B*). If we assume that the Fed does not respond to the situation with a contractionary monetary policy, the economy will experience a rising inflation rate. Decreasing government purchases or increasing taxes can keep real GDP from moving beyond its potential level. The result, shown in Figure 27.7, is that in the new equilibrium at point *C*, the inflation rate is 3 percent rather than 5 percent.

**27.4 LEARNING** OBJECTIVE

Explain how the government purchases and tax multipliers work.

# The Government Purchases and Tax Multipliers

We saw in the chapter opener that in 2009, Congress and the president authorized spending to widen the Caldecott Tunnel in Northern California, in an attempt to increase aggregate demand during the recession of 2007–2009. Suppose that Congress and the president decide to spend $100 billion on expanding the Caldecott Tunnel and similar projects. (The total increase in federal spending under the ARRA was actually about $500 billion, including the $180 million spent to widen the Caldecott Tunnel.) How much will equilibrium real GDP increase as a result of this increase in government purchases? We might expect that the answer is greater than $100 billion because the initial increase in aggregate demand should lead to additional increases in income and spending. For example, to expand the Caldecott Tunnel, the California state government hired Tutor-Saliba, a private construction firm. Tutor-Saliba and the subcontractors it used hired workers to carry out the project. The firms that carried out the many other projects authorized under the ARRA also hired new workers. Newly hired workers are likely to increase their spending on cars, furniture, appliances, and other products. Sellers of these products will increase their production and hire more workers, and so on. At each step, real GDP and income will rise, thereby increasing consumption spending and aggregate demand. These additional waves of hiring are what the spokesperson for the state agency in charge of the Caldecott Tunnel project referred to in the chapter opener as a "ripple effect" from the project.

Economists refer to the initial increase in government purchases as *autonomous* because it is a result of a decision by the government and is not directly caused by changes in the level of real GDP. The increases in consumption spending that result from the initial autonomous increase in government purchases are *induced* because they are caused by the initial increase in autonomous spending. Economists refer to the series of induced increases in consumption spending that result from an initial increase in autonomous expenditures as the **multiplier effect**.

Figure 27.8 illustrates how an increase in government purchases affects the aggregate demand curve. The initial increase in government purchases causes the aggregate demand curve to shift to the right because total spending in the economy is now higher at every price level. The shift to the right from $AD_1$ to the dashed $AD$ curve represents the effect of the initial increase of $100 billion in government purchases. Because this initial increase in government purchases raises incomes and leads to further increases in consumption spending, the aggregate demand curve will ultimately shift from $AD_1$ all the way to $AD_2$.

To better understand the multiplier effect, let's start with a simplified analysis in which we assume that the price level is constant. In other words, initially we will ignore the effect of an upward-sloping *SRAS*. Figure 27.9 shows how spending and real GDP increase over a number of periods, beginning with the initial increase in government purchases in the first period. The initial spending in the first period raises real GDP and total income in the economy by $100 billion. How much additional consumption spending will result from $100 billion in additional income? We know that in addition to increasing their consumption spending on domestically produced goods, households will save some of the increase in income, use some to pay income taxes, and use some to purchase imported goods, which will have no direct effect on spending and production in the U.S. economy. In Figure 27.9, we assume that in the second period, households increase their consumption spending by

**Multiplier effect** The series of induced increases in consumption spending that results from an initial increase in autonomous expenditures.

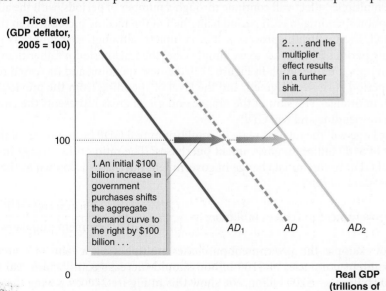

**Figure 27.8**

**The Multiplier Effect and Aggregate Demand**

An initial increase in government purchases of $100 billion causes the aggregate demand curve to shift to the right, from $AD_1$ to the dashed $AD$ curve, and represents the effect of the initial increase of $100 billion in government purchases. Because this initial increase raises incomes and leads to further increases in consumption spending, the aggregate demand curve will ultimately shift further to the right, to $AD_2$.

| Period | Additional Spending This Period | Cumulative Increase in Spending and Real GDP |
|--------|--------------------------------|---------------------------------------------|
| 1 | $100 billion in government purchases | $100 billion |
| 2 | $50 billion in consumption spending | $150 billion |
| 3 | $25 billion in consumption spending | $175 billion |
| 4 | $12.5 billion in consumption spending | $187.5 billion |
| 5 | $6.25 billion in consumption spending | $193.75 billion |
| 6 | $3.125 billion in consumption spending | $196.875 billion |
| . | . | . |
| . | . | . |
| $n$ | 0 | $200 billion |

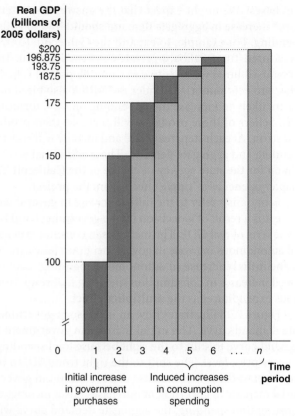

**Figure 27.9** **The Multiplier Effect of an Increase in Government Purchases**

Following an initial increase in government purchases, spending and real GDP increase over a number of periods due to the multiplier effect. The new spending and increased real GDP in each period is shown in green, and the level of spending from the previous period is shown in orange. The sum of the orange and green areas represents the cumulative increase in spending and real GDP. In total, equilibrium real GDP will increase by $200 billion as a result of an initial increase of $100 billion in government purchases.

one-half of the increase in income from the first period—or by $50 billion. This spending in the second period will, in turn, increase real GDP and income by an additional $50 billion. In the third period, consumption spending will increase by $25 billion, or one-half of the $50 billion increase in income from the second period.

The multiplier effect will continue through a number of periods, with the additional consumption spending in each period being half of the income increase from the previous period. Eventually, the process will be complete, although we cannot say precisely how many periods it will take, so we simply label the final period $n$ rather than give it a specific number. In the graph in Figure 27.9, the new spending and increased real GDP in each period is shown in green, and the level of spending from the previous period is shown in orange. The sum of the orange and green areas represents the cumulative increase in spending and real GDP.

How large will the total increase in equilibrium real GDP be as a result of the initial increase of $100 billion in government purchases? The ratio of the change in equilibrium real GDP to the initial change in government purchases is known as the *government purchases multiplier*:

$$\text{Government purchases multiplier} = \frac{\text{Change in equilibrium real GDP}}{\text{Change in government purchases}}.$$

If, for example, the government purchases multiplier has a value of 2, an increase in government purchases of $100 billion should increase equilibrium real GDP by $2 \times \$100 \text{ billion} = \$200 \text{ billion}$. We show this in Figure 27.9 by having the cumulative increase in real GDP equal $200 billion.

Tax cuts also have a multiplier effect. Cutting taxes increases the disposable income of households. When household disposable income rises, so will consumption spending. These increases in consumption spending will set off further increases in real GDP and income, just as increases in government purchases do. Suppose we consider a change in taxes of a specific amount—say, a tax cut of $100 billion—with the tax *rate* remaining unchanged. The expression for this tax multiplier is

$$\text{Tax multiplier} = \frac{\text{Change in equilibrium real GDP}}{\text{Change in taxes}}.$$

The tax multiplier is a negative number because changes in taxes and changes in real GDP move in opposite directions: An increase in taxes reduces disposable income, consumption, and real GDP, and a decrease in taxes raises disposable income, consumption, and real GDP. For example, if the tax multiplier is −1.6, a $100 billion *cut* in taxes will increase real GDP by −1.6 × −$100 billion = $160 billion. We would expect the tax multiplier to be smaller in absolute value than the government purchases multiplier. To see why, think about the difference between a $100 billion increase in government purchases and a $100 billion decrease in taxes. The whole of the $100 billion in government purchases results in an increase in aggregate demand. But households will save rather than spend some portion of a $100 billion decrease in taxes, and they will spend some portion on imported goods. The fraction of the tax cut that households save or spend on imports will not increase aggregate demand. Therefore, the first period of the multiplier process will see a smaller increase in aggregate demand than occurs when there is an increase in government purchases, and the total increase in equilibrium real GDP will be smaller.

## The Effect of Changes in Tax Rates

A change in tax *rates* has a more complicated effect on equilibrium real GDP than does a tax cut of a fixed amount. To begin with, the value of the tax rate affects the size of the multiplier effect. The higher the tax rate, the smaller the multiplier effect. To see why, think about the size of the additional spending increases that take place in each period following an increase in government purchases. The higher the tax rate, the smaller the amount of any increase in income that households have available to spend, which reduces the size of the multiplier effect. So, a cut in tax rates affects equilibrium real GDP through two channels: (1) A cut in tax rates increases the disposable income of households, which leads them to increase their consumption spending, and (2) a cut in tax rates increases the size of the multiplier effect.

## Taking into Account the Effects of Aggregate Supply

To this point, as we discussed the multiplier effect, we assumed that the price level was constant. We know, though, that because the *SRAS* curve is upward sloping, when the *AD* curve shifts to the right, the price level will rise. As a result of the rise in the price level, equilibrium real GDP will not increase by the full amount that the multiplier effect indicates. Figure 27.10 illustrates how an upward-sloping *SRAS* curve affects the size of the multiplier. To keep the graph relatively simple, we assume that the *SRAS* and *LRAS* curves do not shift. The economy starts at point *A*, with real GDP below its potential level. An increase in government purchases shifts the aggregate demand curve from $AD_1$ to the dashed *AD* curve. Just as in Figure 27.8, the multiplier effect causes a further shift in aggregate demand to $AD_2$. If the price level remained constant, real GDP would increase from $13.0 trillion at point *A* to $14.2 trillion at point *B*. However, because the *SRAS* curve is upward sloping, the price level rises from 100 to 103, reducing the total quantity of goods and services demanded in the economy. The new equilibrium occurs at point *C*, with real GDP having risen to $14.0 trillion, or by $200 billion less than if the price level had remained unchanged. We can conclude that the actual change in real GDP resulting from an increase in government purchases or a cut in taxes will be less than indicated by the simple multiplier effect with a constant price level.

**Figure 27.10**

**The Multiplier Effect and Aggregate Supply**

The economy is initially at point *A*. An increase in government purchases causes the aggregate demand curve to shift to the right, from $AD_1$ to the dashed *AD* curve. The multiplier effect results in the aggregate demand curve shifting further to the right, to $AD_2$ (point *B*). Because of the upward-sloping supply curve, the shift in aggregate demand results in a higher price level. In the new equilibrium at point *C*, both real GDP and the price level have increased. The increase in real GDP is less than indicated by the multiplier effect with a constant price level.

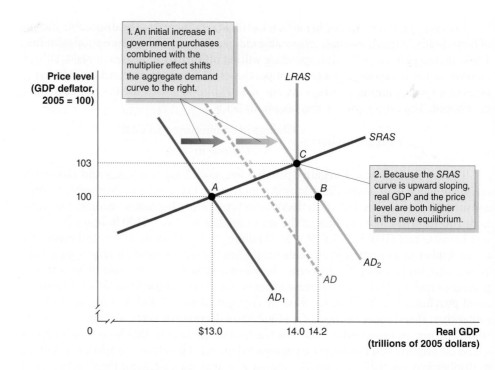

1. An initial increase in government purchases combined with the multiplier effect shifts the aggregate demand curve to the right.

2. Because the *SRAS* curve is upward sloping, real GDP and the price level are both higher in the new equilibrium.

## The Multipliers Work in Both Directions

Increases in government purchases and cuts in taxes have a positive multiplier effect on equilibrium real GDP. Decreases in government purchases and increases in taxes also have a multiplier effect on equilibrium real GDP, but in this case, the effect is negative. For example, an increase in taxes will reduce household disposable income and consumption spending. As households buy fewer cars, furniture, refrigerators, and other products, the firms that sell these products will cut back on production and begin laying off workers. Falling incomes will lead to further reductions in consumption spending. A reduction in government spending on defense would set off a similar process of decreases in real GDP and income. The cutback would be felt first by defense contractors selling directly to the government, and then it would spread to other firms.

We look more closely at the government purchases multiplier and the tax multiplier in the appendix to this chapter.

# Solved Problem 27.4

## Fiscal Policy Multipliers

Briefly explain whether you agree with the following statement: "Real GDP is currently $14.2 trillion, and potential real GDP is $14.4 trillion. If Congress and the president would increase government purchases by $200 billion or cut taxes by $200 billion, the economy could be brought to equilibrium at potential GDP."

### Solving the Problem

**Step 1:** **Review the chapter material.** This problem is about the multiplier process, so you may want to review the section "The Government Purchases and Tax Multipliers," which begins on page 914.

**Step 2:** **Explain how the necessary increase in purchases or cut in taxes is less than $200 billion because of the multiplier effect.** The statement is incorrect because it does not consider the multiplier effect. Because of the multiplier effect, an increase in government purchases or a decrease in taxes of less than $200 billion is necessary to increase equilibrium real GDP by $200 billion. For instance, assume that the government purchases multiplier is 2 and the tax multiplier is −1.6. We can then calculate the necessary increase in government purchases as follows:

$$\text{Government purchases multiplier} = \frac{\text{Change in equilibrium real GDP}}{\text{Change in government purchases}}$$

$$2 = \frac{\$200 \text{ billion}}{\text{Change in government purchases}}$$

$$\text{Change in government purchases} = \frac{\$200 \text{ billion}}{2} = \$100 \text{ billion.}$$

And the necessary change in taxes:

$$\text{Tax multiplier} = \frac{\text{Change in equilibrium real GDP}}{\text{Change in taxes}}$$

$$-1.6 = \frac{\$200 \text{ billion}}{\text{Change in taxes}}$$

$$\text{Change in taxes} = \frac{\$200 \text{ billion}}{-1.6} = -\$125 \text{ billion.}$$

**Your Turn:** For more practice, do related problem 4.6 on page 940 at the end of this chapter.    MyEconLab

# The Limits of Using Fiscal Policy to Stabilize the Economy

**27.5 LEARNING** OBJECTIVE

Discuss the difficulties that can arise in implementing fiscal policy.

Poorly timed fiscal policy, like poorly timed monetary policy, can do more harm than good. As we discussed in Chapter 26, it takes time for policymakers to collect statistics and identify changes in the economy. If the government decides to increase spending or cut taxes to fight a recession that is about to end, the effect may be to increase the inflation rate. Similarly, cutting spending or raising taxes to slow down an economy that has actually already moved into recession can increase the length and depth of the recession.

Getting the timing right can be more difficult with fiscal policy than with monetary policy for two main reasons. Control over monetary policy is concentrated in the hands of the Federal Open Market Committee, which can change monetary policy at any of its meetings. By contrast, the president and a majority of the 535 members of Congress have to agree on changes in fiscal policy. The delays caused by the legislative process can be very long. For example, in 1962, President John F. Kennedy concluded that the U.S. economy was operating below potential GDP and proposed a tax cut to stimulate aggregate demand. Congress eventually agreed to the tax cut—but not until 1964. The events of 2001 and 2009 show, though, that it is sometimes possible to authorize changes in fiscal policy relatively quickly. When George W. Bush came into office in January 2001, the economy was on the verge of recession, and he immediately proposed a tax cut. Congress passed the tax cut, and the president signed it into law in early June 2001. Similarly, Barack Obama proposed a stimulus package as soon as he came into office in January 2009, and Congress had passed the proposal by February.

Even after a change in fiscal policy has been approved, it takes time to implement the policy. Suppose Congress and the president agree to increase aggregate demand by spending $30 billion more on constructing subway systems in several cities. It will probably take at least several months to prepare detailed plans for the construction. Local governments will then ask for bids from private construction companies. Once the winning bidders have been selected, they will usually need several months to begin the project. Only then will significant amounts of spending actually take place. This delay may push the spending beyond the end of the recession that the spending was intended to fight. Delays of this type are less of a concern during long and severe recessions, such as that of 2007–2009.

## Does Government Spending Reduce Private Spending?

In addition to the timing problem, using increases in government purchases to increase aggregate demand presents another potential problem. We have been assuming that when the federal government increases its purchases by $30 billion, the multiplier effect will cause the increase in aggregate demand to be greater than $30 billion. However, the size of the multiplier effect may be limited if the increase in government purchases causes one of the nongovernment, or private, components of aggregate expenditures—consumption, investment, or net exports—to fall. A decline in private expenditures as a result of an increase in government purchases is called **crowding out**.

**Crowding out** A decline in private expenditures as a result of an increase in government purchases.

## Crowding Out in the Short Run

Consider the case of a temporary increase in government purchases. Suppose the federal government decides to fight a recession by spending $30 billion more this year on subway construction. When the $30 billion has been spent, the program will end, and government spending will drop back to its previous level. As the spending takes place, income and real GDP will increase. These increases in income and real GDP will cause households and firms to increase their demand for currency and checking account balances to accommodate the increased buying and selling. Figure 27.11 shows the result, using the money market graph introduced in Chapter 26.

At higher levels of real GDP and income, households and firms demand more money at every interest rate. When the demand for money increases, the equilibrium interest rate will rise. Higher interest rates will result in a decline in each component of private expenditures. Consumption spending and investment spending will decline because households will borrow less to buy houses, cars, furniture, and appliances, and firms will borrow less to buy factories, computers, and machine tools. Net exports will

### Figure 27.11

**An Expansionary Fiscal Policy Increases Interest Rates**

If the federal government increases spending, the demand for money will increase from Money demand₁ to Money demand₂ as real GDP and income rise. With the supply of money constant, at $950 billion, the result is an increase in the equilibrium interest rate from 3 percent to 5 percent, which crowds out some consumption, investment, and net exports.

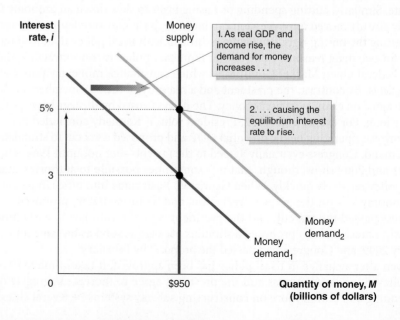

also decline because higher interest rates in the United States will attract foreign investors. German, Japanese, and Canadian investors will want to exchange the currencies of their countries for U.S. dollars to invest in U.S. Treasury bills and other U.S. financial assets. This increased demand for U.S. dollars will cause an increase in the exchange rate between the dollar and other currencies. When the dollar increases in value, the prices of U.S. products in foreign countries rise—causing a reduction in U.S. exports—and the prices of foreign products in the United States fall—causing an increase in U.S. imports. Falling exports and rising imports mean that net exports are falling.

The greater the sensitivity of consumption, investment, and net exports to changes in interest rates, the more crowding out will occur. In a deep recession, many firms may be so pessimistic about the future and have so much excess capacity that investment spending will fall to very low levels and will be unlikely to fall much further, even if interest rates rise. In this case, crowding out is unlikely to be a problem. If the economy is close to potential GDP, however, and firms are optimistic about the future, an increase in interest rates may result in a significant decline in investment spending.

Figure 27.12 shows that crowding out may reduce the effectiveness of an expansionary fiscal policy. The economy begins in short-run equilibrium at point $A$, with real GDP at $14.2 trillion. Real GDP is below potential GDP, so the economy is in recession. Suppose that Congress and the president decide to increase government purchases to bring the economy back to potential GDP. In the absence of crowding out, the increase in government purchases will shift aggregate demand to $AD_{2(\text{no crowding out})}$ and bring the economy to equilibrium at real GDP of $14.4 trillion, which is the potential level of GDP (point $B$). But the higher interest rate resulting from the increased government purchases will reduce consumption, investment, and net exports, causing aggregate demand to shift back to $AD_{2(\text{crowding out})}$. The result is a new short-run equilibrium at point $C$, with real GDP of $14.3 trillion, which is $100 billion short of potential GDP.

## Crowding Out in the Long Run

Most economists agree that in the short run, an increase in government spending results in partial, but not complete, crowding out. What is the long-run effect of a *permanent* increase in government spending? In this case, most economists agree that the result is complete crowding out. In the long run, the decline in investment, consumption, and net exports exactly offsets the increase in government purchases, and aggregate demand remains unchanged. To understand crowding out in the long run, recall from Chapter 24 that *in the long run, the economy returns to potential GDP*. Suppose that the economy is currently at potential GDP and that government purchases are 35 percent of GDP. In

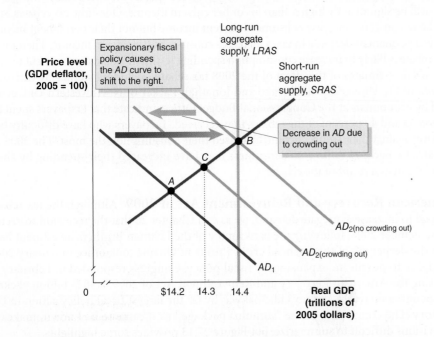

### Figure 27.12

### The Effect of Crowding Out in the Short Run

The economy begins in a recession, with real GDP of $14.2 trillion (point $A$). In the absence of crowding out, an increase in government purchases will shift aggregate demand to $AD_{2(\text{no crowding out})}$ and bring the economy to equilibrium at potential real GDP of $14.4 trillion (point $B$). But the higher interest rate resulting from the increased government purchases will reduce consumption, investment, and net exports, causing aggregate demand to shift to $AD_{2(\text{crowding out})}$. The result is a new short-run equilibrium at point $C$, with real GDP of $14.3 trillion, which is $100 billion short of potential real GDP.

that case, private expenditures—the sum of consumption, investment, and net exports—will make up the other 65 percent of GDP. If government purchases are increased permanently to 37 percent of GDP, in the long run, private expenditures must fall to 63 percent of GDP. There has been complete crowding out: Private expenditures have fallen by the same amount that government purchases have increased. If government spending is taking a larger share of GDP, then private spending must take a smaller share.

An expansionary fiscal policy does not have to cause complete crowding out in the short run. If the economy is below potential real GDP, it is possible for both government purchases and private expenditures to increase. But in the long run, any permanent increase in government purchases must come at the expense of private expenditures. Keep in mind, however, that it may take several—possibly many—years to arrive at this long-run outcome.

## Fiscal Policy in Action: Did the Stimulus Package of 2009 Work?

As we have seen, Congress and the president can increase government purchases and cut taxes to increase aggregate demand either to avoid a recession or to shorten the length or severity of a recession that is already under way. The recession of 2007–2009 occurred during the end of the presidency of George W. Bush and the beginning of the presidency of Barack Obama. Both presidents used fiscal policy to fight the recession.

In early 2008, economists advising President Bush believed that the housing crisis, the resulting credit crunch, and rising oil prices were pushing the economy into a recession. (As we now know, a recession had actually already begun in December 2007.) These economists proposed cutting taxes to increase household disposable income, which would increase consumption spending and aggregate demand. Congress enacted a tax cut that took the form of *rebates* of taxes already paid. Rebate checks totaling $95 billion were sent to taxpayers between April and July 2008.

How effective were the rebates in increasing consumption spending? While economists are still studying the issue, economic analysis can give us some insight. Many economists believe that consumers base their spending on their *permanent income* rather than just on their *current income*. A consumer's permanent income reflects the consumer's expected future income. By basing spending on permanent income, a consumer can smooth out consumption over a period of years. For example, a medical student may have very low current income but a high expected future income. The student may borrow against this high expected future income rather than having to consume at a very low level in the present. Some people, however, have difficulty borrowing against their future income because banks or other lenders may not be convinced that a borrower's future income really will be significantly higher than his or her current income. One-time tax rebates, such as the one in 2008, increase consumers' current income but not their permanent income. Only a permanent decrease in taxes increases consumers' permanent income. Therefore, a tax rebate is likely to increase consumption spending less than would a permanent tax cut.

Some estimates of the effect of the 2008 tax rebate, including studies by Christian Broda of the University of Chicago and Jonathan Parker of Northwestern University, and by economists at the Congressional Budget Office, indicate that taxpayers spent between 33 and 40 percent of the rebates they received. Taxpayers who have difficulty borrowing against their future income increased their consumption the most. The 2008 tax rebates totaled $95 billion, so consumers may have increased their spending by about $35 billion as a result of the rebate.

**American Recovery and Reinvestment Act of 2009** Although the tax rebates helped to increase aggregate demand, we saw in Chapter 26 that the recession worsened in September 2008, following the bankruptcy of the Lehman Brothers investment bank and the deepening of the financial crisis. President Obama took office in January 2009, pledging to pursue an expansionary fiscal policy. Congress responded in February by passing the American Recovery and Reinvestment Act of 2009, a $825 billion package of spending increases and tax cuts that was by far the largest fiscal policy action in U.S. history. The complexity of the "stimulus package," as it came to be known, makes its provisions difficult to summarize, but Figure 27.13 provides some highlights.

policy had failed during the New Deal was raised again. Economic historians have argued, however, that despite the increases in government spending, Congress and the president had not, in fact, implemented an expansionary fiscal policy during the 1930s. In separate studies, economists E. Cary Brown of MIT and Larry Peppers of Washington and Lee University argued that there was a cyclically adjusted budget deficit during only one year of the 1930s, and that one deficit was small. The following table provides data supporting their arguments. (All variables in the table are nominal rather than real.) The second column shows federal government expenditures increasing from 1933 to 1936, falling in 1937, and then increasing in 1938 and 1939. The third column shows a similar pattern, with the federal budget being in deficit each year after 1933 except for 1937. The fourth column, however, shows that in each year after 1933, the federal government ran a cyclically adjusted budget *surplus*. Because the level of income was so low and the unemployment rate was so high during these years, tax collections were far below what they would have been if the economy had been at potential GDP. As the fifth column shows, in 1933 and again in 1937 to 1939, the cyclically adjusted surpluses were large relative to GDP.

| Year | Federal Government Expenditures (billions of dollars) | Actual Federal Budget Deficit or Surplus (billions of dollars) | Cyclically Adjusted Budget Deficit or Surplus (billions of dollars) | Cyclically Adjusted Budget Deficit or Surplus as a Percentage of GDP |
|------|------|------|------|------|
| 1929 | $2.6 | $1.0 | $1.24 | 1.20% |
| 1930 | 2.7 | 0.2 | 0.81 | 0.89 |
| 1931 | 4.0 | −2.1 | −0.41 | −0.54 |
| 1932 | 3.0 | −1.3 | 0.50 | 0.85 |
| 1933 | 3.4 | −0.9 | 1.06 | 1.88 |
| 1934 | 5.5 | −2.2 | 0.09 | 0.14 |
| 1935 | 5.6 | −1.9 | 0.54 | 0.74 |
| 1936 | 7.8 | −3.2 | 0.47 | 0.56 |
| 1937 | 6.4 | 0.2 | 2.55 | 2.77 |
| 1938 | 7.3 | −1.3 | 2.47 | 2.87 |
| 1939 | 8.4 | −2.1 | 2.00 | 2.17 |

Although President Roosevelt proposed many new government spending programs, he had also promised during the 1932 presidential election campaign to balance the federal budget. He achieved a balanced budget only in 1937, but his reluctance to allow the actual budget deficit to grow too large helps explain why the cyclically adjusted budget remained in surplus. Many economists today would agree with E. Cary Brown's conclusion: "Fiscal policy, then, seems to have been an unsuccessful recovery device in the 'thirties—not because it did not work, but because it was not tried."

Based on E. Cary Brown, "Fiscal Policy in the 'Thirties: A Reappraisal," *American Economic Review*, Vol. 46, No. 5, December 1956, pp. 857–879; Larry Peppers, "Full Employment Surplus Analysis and Structural Changes," *Explorations in Economic History*, Vol. 10, Winter 1973, pp. 197–210; and U.S. Bureau of Economic Analysis.

**Your Turn:** Test your understanding by doing related problem 6.8 on page 942 at the end of this chapter.    MyEconLab

# Solved Problem 27.6

## The Effect of Economic Fluctuations on the Budget Deficit

The federal government's budget deficit was $207.8 billion in 1983 and $185.4 billion in 1984. A student comments, "The government must have acted during 1984 to raise taxes or cut spending or both." Do you agree? Briefly explain.

## Solving the Problem

**Step 1:** **Review the chapter material.** This problem is about the federal budget as an automatic stabilizer, so you may want to review the section "How the Federal Budget Can Serve as an Automatic Stabilizer," which begins on page 927.

**Step 2:** **Explain how changes in the budget deficit can occur without Congress and the president acting.** If Congress and the president take action to raise taxes or cut spending, the federal budget deficit will decline. But the deficit will also decline automatically when GDP increases, even if the government takes no action. When GDP increases, rising household incomes and firm profits result in higher tax revenues. Increasing GDP also usually means falling unemployment, which reduces government spending on unemployment insurance and other transfer payments. So, you should disagree with the comment. A falling deficit does not mean that the government *must* have acted to raise taxes or cut spending.

**Extra Credit:** Although you don't have to know it to answer the question, GDP did increase from $3.5 trillion in 1983 to $3.9 trillion in 1984.

MyEconLab **Your Turn:** For more practice, do related problem 6.6 on page 942 at the end of this chapter.

## Should the Federal Budget Always Be Balanced?

Although many economists believe that it is a good idea for the federal government to have a balanced budget when the economy is at potential GDP, few economists believe that the federal government should attempt to balance its budget every year. To see why economists take this view, consider what the government would have to do to keep the budget balanced during a recession, when the federal budget automatically moves into deficit. To bring the budget back into balance, the government would have to raise taxes or cut spending, but these actions would reduce aggregate demand, thereby making the recession worse. Similarly, when GDP increases above its potential level, the budget automatically moves into surplus. To eliminate this surplus, the government would have to cut taxes or increase government spending. But these actions would increase aggregate demand, thereby pushing GDP further beyond potential GDP and increasing the risk of higher inflation. To balance the budget every year, the government might have to take actions that would destabilize the economy.

Some economists argue that the federal government should normally run a deficit, even at potential GDP. When the federal budget is in deficit, the U.S. Treasury sells bonds to investors to raise the funds necessary to pay the government's bills. Borrowing to pay the bills is a bad policy for a household, a firm, or the government when the bills are for current expenses, but it is not a bad policy if the bills are for long-lived capital goods. For instance, most families pay for a new home by taking out a 15- to 30-year mortgage. Because houses last many years, it makes sense to pay for a house out of the income the family makes over a long period of time rather than out of the income received in the year the house is bought. Businesses often borrow the funds to buy machinery, equipment, and factories by selling 30-year corporate bonds. Because these capital goods generate profits for the businesses over many years, it makes sense to pay for them over a period of years as well. By similar reasoning, when the federal government contributes to the building of a new highway, bridge, or subway, it may want to borrow funds by selling Treasury bonds. The alternative is to pay for these long-lived capital goods out of the tax revenues received in the year the goods were purchased. But that means that the taxpayers in that year have to bear the whole burden of paying for the projects, even though taxpayers for many years in the future will be enjoying the benefits.

# The Federal Government Debt

Every time the federal government runs a budget deficit, the Treasury must borrow funds from investors by selling Treasury securities. For simplicity, we will refer to all Treasury securities as "bonds." When the federal government runs a budget surplus, the Treasury pays off some existing bonds. Figure 27.14 on page 927 shows that there are many more years of federal budget deficits than years of federal budget surpluses. As a result, the total number of Treasury bonds outstanding has grown over the years. The total value of U.S. Treasury bonds outstanding is referred to as the *federal government debt* or, sometimes, as the *national debt*. Each year the federal budget is in deficit, the federal government debt grows. Each year the federal budget is in surplus, the debt shrinks.

Figure 27.15 shows federal government debt as a percentage of GDP in the years since 1901. The ratio of debt to GDP increased during World Wars I and II and the Great Depression, reflecting the large government budget deficits of those years. After the end of World War II, GDP grew faster than the debt until the early 1980s, which caused the ratio of debt to GDP to fall. The large budget deficits of the 1980s and early 1990s sent the debt-to-GDP ratio climbing. The budget surpluses of 1998 to 2001 caused the debt-to-GDP ratio to fall, but it rose again with the return of deficits beginning in 2002. The large deficits beginning in 2008 caused the ratio to spike up to its highest level since 1947.

## Is Government Debt a Problem?

Debt can be a problem for a government for the same reasons that debt can be a problem for a household or a business. If a family has difficulty making the monthly mortgage payment, it will have to cut back spending on other goods and services. If the family is unable to make the payments, it will have to *default* on the loan and will probably lose its house. The federal government is not in danger of defaulting on its debt. Ultimately, the government can raise the funds it needs through taxes to make the interest payments on the debt. If the debt becomes very large relative to the economy, however, the government may have to raise taxes to high levels or cut back on other types of spending to make the interest payments on the debt. Interest payments are currently about 10 percent of total federal expenditures. At this level, tax increases or significant cutbacks in other types of federal spending are not required.

In the long run, a debt that increases in size relative to GDP, as was happening after 2008, can pose a problem. As we discussed previously, crowding out of investment spending may occur if an increasing debt drives up interest rates. Lower investment spending means a lower capital stock in the long run and a reduced capacity of the economy to produce goods and services. This effect is somewhat offset if some of the government debt was incurred to finance improvements in *infrastructure*, such as

## Figure 27.15

### The Federal Government Debt, 1901–2011

The federal government debt increases whenever the federal government runs a budget deficit. The large deficits incurred during World Wars I and II, the Great Depression, and the 1980s and early 1990s increased the ratio of debt to GDP. The large deficits of 2009 to 2011 caused the ratio to spike up to its highest level since 1947.

Data from U.S. Bureau of the Census, *Historical Statistics of the United States, Colonial Times to 1970*, Washington, DC: U.S. Government Printing Office, 1975; Budget of the United States Government, Fiscal Year 2003, Historical Printing Office, 2002; Federal Reserve Bank of St. Louis, *National Economic Trends*, October 2011; and Congressional Budget Office.

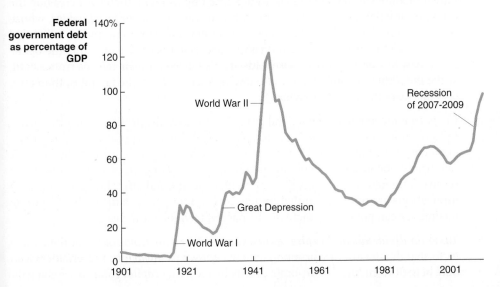

bridges, highways, and ports; to finance education; or to finance research and development. Improvements in infrastructure, a better-educated labor force, and additional research and development can add to the productive capacity of the economy.

# The Effects of Fiscal Policy in the Long Run

Some fiscal policy actions are intended to meet the short-run goal of stabilizing the economy. Other fiscal policy actions are intended to have long-run effects by expanding the productive capacity of the economy and increasing the rate of economic growth. Because these policy actions primarily affect aggregate supply rather than aggregate demand, they are sometimes referred to as *supply-side economics*. Most fiscal policy actions that attempt to increase aggregate supply do so by changing taxes to increase the incentives to work, save, invest, and start a business.

## The Long-Run Effects of Tax Policy

**Tax wedge** The difference between the pretax and posttax return to an economic activity.

The difference between the pretax and posttax return to an economic activity is known as the **tax wedge**. The tax wedge applies to the *marginal tax rate*, which is the fraction of each additional dollar of income that must be paid in taxes. For example, the U.S. federal income tax has several tax brackets, which are the income ranges within which a tax rate applies. In 2011, for a single taxpayer, the tax rate was 10 percent on the first $8,500 earned during a year. The tax rate rose for higher income brackets, until it reached 35 percent on income earned above $379,150. Suppose you are paid a wage of $20 per hour. If your marginal income tax rate is 25 percent, then your after-tax wage is $15, and the tax wedge is $5. When discussing the model of demand and supply in Chapter 3, we saw that increasing the price of a good or service increases the quantity supplied. So, we would expect that reducing the tax wedge by cutting the marginal tax rate on income would result in a larger quantity of labor supplied because the after-tax wage would be higher. Similarly, we saw in Chapter 21 that a reduction in the income tax would increase the after-tax return to saving, causing an increase in the supply of loanable funds, a lower equilibrium interest rate, and an increase in investment spending. In general, economists believe that the smaller the tax wedge for any economic activity—such as working, saving, investing, or starting a business—the more of that economic activity that will occur. When workers, savers, investors, or entrepreneurs change their behavior as a result of a tax change, economists say that there has been a *behavioral response* to the tax change.

We can look briefly at the effects on aggregate supply of cutting each of the following taxes:

- *Individual income tax.* As we have seen, reducing the marginal tax rates on individual income will reduce the tax wedge faced by workers, thereby increasing the quantity of labor supplied. Many small businesses are *sole proprietorships*, whose profits are taxed at the individual income tax rates. Therefore, cutting the individual income tax rates also raises the return to entrepreneurship, encouraging the opening of new businesses. Most households are also taxed on their returns from saving at the individual income tax rates. Reducing marginal income tax rates, therefore, also increases the return to saving.

- *Corporate income tax.* The federal government taxes the profits earned by corporations under the corporate income tax. In 2011, most corporations faced a marginal corporate tax rate of 35 percent. Cutting the marginal corporate income tax rate would encourage investment spending by increasing the return corporations receive from new investments in equipment, factories, and office buildings. Because innovations are often embodied in new investment goods, cutting the corporate income tax can potentially increase the pace of technological change.

- *Taxes on dividends and capital gains.* Corporations distribute some of their profits to shareholders in the form of payments known as *dividends*. Shareholders also may benefit from higher corporate profits by receiving *capital gains*. A capital gain is the increase in the price of an asset, such as a share of stock. Rising profits usually result in rising stock prices and capital gains to shareholders. Individuals pay taxes on both dividends and capital gains (although the tax on capital gains can be postponed if the stock is not sold). As a result, the same earnings are, in effect, taxed twice: once when a corporation pays the corporate income tax on its profits and a second time when the profits are received by individual investors in the form of dividends or capital gains. Economists debate the costs and benefits of a separate tax on corporate profits. With the corporate income tax remaining in place, one way to reduce the "double taxation" problem is to reduce the taxes on dividends and capital gains. These taxes were, in fact, reduced in 2003, and in 2011, the marginal tax rates on dividends and capital gains were still well below the top marginal tax rate on individual income. Lowering the tax rates on dividends and capital gains increases the supply of loanable funds from households to firms, increasing saving and investment and lowering the equilibrium real interest rate.

## Tax Simplification

In addition to the potential gains from cutting individual taxes, there are also gains from tax simplification. The complexity of the tax code has created a whole industry of tax preparation services, such as H&R Block. At almost 3,000 pages long, the tax code is extremely complex. The Internal Revenue Service estimates that taxpayers spend more than 6.4 billion hours each year filling out their tax forms, or about 45 hours per tax return. Households and firms have to deal with more than 480 tax forms to file their federal taxes. It is not surprising that there are more H&R Block offices around the country than Starbucks coffeehouses.

If the tax code were greatly simplified, the economic resources currently used by the tax preparation industry would be available to produce other goods and services. In addition to wasting resources, the complexity of the tax code may also distort the decisions made by households and firms. For example, the tax rate on dividends has clearly affected whether corporations pay dividends. When Congress passed a reduction in the tax on dividends in 2003, many firms—including Microsoft—began paying dividends for the first time. A simplified tax code would increase economic efficiency by reducing the number of decisions households and firms make solely to reduce their tax payments.

## The Economic Effect of Tax Reform

We can analyze the economic effects of tax reduction and simplification by using the aggregate demand and aggregate supply model. Figure 27.16 shows that without tax changes, the long-run aggregate supply curve will shift from $LRAS_1$ to $LRAS_2$. This shift represents the increases in the labor force and the capital stock and the technological change that would occur even without tax reduction and simplification. To focus on the effect of tax changes on aggregate supply, we will ignore any shifts in the short-run aggregate supply curve, and we will assume that the aggregate demand curve remains unchanged, at $AD_1$. In this case, equilibrium moves from point $A$ to point $B$, with real GDP increasing from $Y_1$ to $Y_2$ and the price level decreasing from $P_1$ to $P_2$.

If tax reduction and simplification are effective, the economy will experience increases in labor supply, saving, investment, and the formation of new firms. Economic efficiency will also be improved. Together these factors will result in an increase in the quantity of real GDP supplied at every price level. We show the effects of the tax changes in Figure 27.16 by a shift in the long-run aggregate supply curve to $LRAS_3$. With aggregate demand remaining unchanged, the equilibrium in the economy moves from point $A$ to point $C$ (rather than to point $B$, which is the equilibrium without tax changes), with real GDP increasing from $Y_1$ to $Y_3$ and the price level decreasing from $P_1$ to $P_3$. Notice that compared with the equilibrium without tax changes (point $B$), the equilibrium with tax changes (point $C$) occurs at a lower price level and a higher level of real GDP. We can conclude that the tax changes have benefited the economy by increasing output and employment while at the same time reducing the price level.

**Figure 27.16**

**The Supply-Side Effects of a Tax Change**

The economy's initial equilibrium is at point *A*. With no tax change, the long-run aggregate supply curve shifts to the right, from $LRAS_1$ to $LRAS_2$. Equilibrium moves to point *B*, with the price level falling from $P_1$ to $P_2$ and real GDP increasing from $Y_1$ to $Y_2$. With tax reductions and simplifications, the long-run aggregate supply curve shifts further to the right, to $LRAS_3$, and equilibrium moves to point *C*, with the price level falling to $P_3$ and real GDP increasing to $Y_3$.

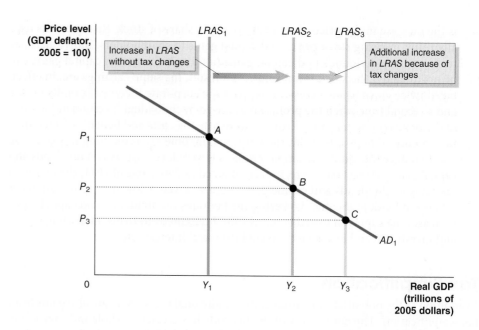

Clearly, our analysis is unrealistic because we have ignored the changes in aggregate demand and short-run aggregate supply that will occur. How would a more realistic analysis differ from the simplified one in Figure 27.16? The change in real GDP would be the same because in the long run, real GDP is equal to its potential level, which is represented by the long-run aggregate supply curve. The results for the price level would be different, however, because we would expect both aggregate demand and short-run aggregate supply to shift to the right. The likeliest case is that the price level would end up higher in the new equilibrium than in the original equilibrium. However, because the position of the long-run aggregate supply curve is further to the right as a result of the tax changes, the increase in the price level will be smaller; that is, the price level at point *C* is likely to be lower than $P_2$, even if it is higher than $P_3$, although—as we will discuss in the next section—not all economists would agree. We can conclude that a successful policy of tax reductions and simplifications will benefit the economy by increasing output and employment and, at the same time, may result in smaller increases in the price level.

## How Large Are Supply-Side Effects?

Most economists would agree that there are supply-side effects to reducing taxes: Decreasing marginal income tax rates will increase the quantity of labor supplied, cutting the corporate income tax will increase investment spending, and so on. The magnitude of the effects is the subject of considerable debate, however. For example, some economists argue that the increase in the quantity of labor supplied following a tax cut will be limited because many people work a number of hours set by their employers and lack the opportunity to work additional hours. Similarly, some economists believe that tax changes have only a small effect on saving and investment. In this view, saving and investment are affected much more by changes in income or changes in expectations of the future profitability of new investment due to technological change or improving macroeconomic conditions than they are by tax changes.

Economists who are skeptical of the magnitude of supply-side effects believe that tax cuts have their greatest effect on aggregate demand rather than on aggregate supply. In their view, focusing on the effect of tax cuts on aggregate demand, while ignoring any effect on aggregate supply, yields accurate forecasts of future movements in real GDP and the price level, which indicates that the supply-side effects must be small. If tax changes have only small effects on aggregate supply, it is unlikely that they will reduce the size of price increases to the extent shown in the analysis in Figure 27.16.

Ultimately, the debate over the size of the supply-side effects of tax policy can be resolved only through careful study of the effects of differences in tax rates on labor supply and on saving and investment decisions. Some recent studies have arrived at conflicting conclusions, however. For example, a study by Nobel Laureate Edward Prescott of Arizona State University concludes that the differences between the United States and Europe with respect to the average number of hours worked per week and the average number of weeks worked per year are due to differences in taxes. The lower marginal tax rates in the United States compared with Europe increase the return to working for U.S. workers and result in a larger quantity of labor supplied. But another study by Alberto Alesina and Edward Glaeser of Harvard University and Bruce Sacerdote of Dartmouth College argues that the more restrictive labor market regulations in Europe explain the shorter work weeks and longer vacations of European workers and that differences in taxes have only a small effect.

As in other areas of economics, differences among economists in their estimates of the supply-side effects of tax changes may narrow over time as they conduct more studies.

Continued from page 905

## Economics in Your Life

### What Would You Do with $500?

At the beginning of the chapter, we asked how you would respond to a $500 tax rebate and what effect this tax rebate would likely have on equilibrium real GDP in the short run. This chapter has shown that tax cuts increase disposable income and that when there is a permanent increase in disposable income, consumption spending increases. So, you will likely respond to a permanent $500 increase in your disposable income by increasing your spending. How much your spending increases depends in part on your overall financial situation. As mentioned in the chapter, people who are able to borrow usually try to smooth out their spending over time and don't increase spending much in response to a one-time increase in their income. But if you are a student struggling to get by on a low income and you are unable to borrow against the higher income you expect to earn in the future, you may well spend most of the rebate. This chapter has also shown that tax cuts have a multiplier effect on the economy. That is, an increase in consumption spending sets off further increases in real GDP and income. So, if the economy is not already at potential GDP, this tax rebate will likely increase equilibrium real GDP in the short run.

## Conclusion

In this chapter, we have seen how the federal government uses changes in government purchases and taxes to achieve its economic policy goals. We have seen that economists debate the effectiveness of discretionary fiscal policy actions intended to stabilize the economy. Congress and the president share responsibility for economic policy with the Federal Reserve. In Chapter 28, we will discuss further some of the challenges that the Federal Reserve encounters as it carries out monetary policy. In Chapters 29 and 30, we will look more closely at the international economy, including how monetary and fiscal policy are affected by the linkages between economies.

Read *An Inside Look at Policy* on the next page for a discussion of the arguments for and against using infrastructure spending to increase employment.

# Obama Proposes Additional Spending to Stimulate the Economy

## U.S. NEWS & WORLD REPORT

## Are Infrastructure Projects the Answer to America's Jobs Problem?

Infrastructure spending is expected to be one of the chief components of the jobs plan that President Obama will unveil in September. The idea of spending on public works projects like road-building as economic stimulus has been a mainstay of jobs proposals from both congressional Democrats and the White House in recent years. But opponents question its efficiency at creating jobs—and its cost.

**(a)** According to data from Moody's Analytics, which performs economic analysis and forecasting, infrastructure spending is more effective, dollar for dollar, than many forms of tax cuts at boosting jobs growth. But after passing legislation, going through the appropriations process, identifying projects, planning, and hiring workers, the time it takes the federal government bureaucracy to get that money out the door can mean delayed or even diminished economic impact. Add to that a particularly slow-moving Congress with a propensity for partisan divides that slow or halt much legislation—and the current climate of budget-cutting—and a potentially promising policy move could be greatly undercut or never enacted.

Many Republican lawmakers have in the past decried spending on infrastructure. When President Obama introduced the idea of a national infrastructure bank in September 2010, Representative Eric Cantor called it "yet another government stimulus effort" and House Speaker John Boehner called it "more of the same failed 'stimulus' spending," alluding to the 2009 American Recovery and Reinvestment Act that the president introduced to counteract the Great Recession. That $787-billion stimulus package created far fewer jobs than the White House had initially predicted, a point that stimulus critics often make. But not all Republicans are opposed to infrastructure spending; Texas Senator Kay Bailey Hutchison, for example, co-sponsored a bill with Massachusetts Democrat John Kerry in March, proposing an infrastructure bank.

**(b)** The theory behind infrastructure spending is the multiplier effect: the idea that every dollar in government expenditures can increase GDP by more than one dollar by starting economic chain reactions: the government pays firms for goods and services and those firms then pay employees who then spend their paychecks.

Moody's Analytics estimates that the multiplier effect for increases in government spending is generally larger than the multiplier for tax cuts. Any additional dollar spent on permanent tax cuts adds to GDP by significantly less than a dollar. Making the Bush tax cuts permanent, for example, would add to GDP by $0.29 for every dollar of revenue reduction, according to calculations from Moody's. Infrastructure spending would add by $1.59 for every dollar spent, while extending unemployment insurance and temporarily increasing food stamps would add even more.

**(c)** The mitigating factor, then, is the speed (or lack thereof) with which infrastructure spending works. In past recessions, infrastructure projects have taken so long to get off the ground that their effects were only felt after recovery had begun, says Alan Viard, resident scholar at the American Enterprise Institute, a conservative think tank. "Dollar for dollar, [tax cuts and direct government payments] may not stimulate the economy as much as infrastructure spending, but they can be timed effectively. . . . If we expect [economic weakness] to last long enough for new infrastructure spending to come online, we've really got pretty serious problems. . . ."

It is difficult to dispute that tax cuts and direct government payments could provide rapid stimulus, but like any policy, those also have their downsides. "It's true that if you want an instant stimulus, you'd send people checks. . . . And a certain amount of that would be lost. Some would go to savings and paying back debt, and a fair amount would go to buying things that are not made in the U.S.," says Ross Eisenbrey, vice president of the liberal Economic Policy Institute. . . .

*Source:* "Are Infrastructure Projects the Answer to America's Jobs Problem? Disappointing stimulus package gives ammunition to the policy's opponents," by Danielle Kurtzleban from *U.S. News & World Report,* August 22, 2011. Copyright © 2011 by Wright's Media. Reprinted by permission.

## Key Points in the Article

Proponents of spending on infrastructure as a means of stimulating the economy argue that for each dollar spent, infrastructure spending is more effective than tax cuts at creating jobs. They also estimate that the multiplier effect for increases in government spending is larger than the multiplier effect for tax cuts. Those opposed to using infrastructure spending as a way to increase employment argue that the 2009 American Recovery and Reinvestment Act created considerably fewer jobs than had been predicted. An important factor in determining job creation through infrastructure spending is the time needed for the spending to occur and to have its full effect on the economy. Although infrastructure spending may stimulate the economy more than tax cuts, it may also take a long time for Congress to approve spending programs and for the programs actually to take effect.

## Analyzing the News

ⓐ As you read in this chapter, expansionary fiscal policy involves increasing government purchases or decreasing taxes to increase aggregate demand. The Obama administration introduced the American Recovery and Reinvestment Act in 2009, a stimulus package designed to combat the recession that began in December 2007. A portion of this stimulus package was designated for infrastructure spending, and the administration believed that it would have a greater economic effect than the less-than-successful tax rebate program implemented by the Bush administration in 2008. According to Moody's Analytics, an economic analysis and forecasting company, each dollar of infrastructure spending has a greater effect on job growth than does each dollar in tax cuts, but infrastructure spending is subject to potentially significant time delays because Congress needs to approve the spending, infrastructure projects need to be identified and planned, and workers need to be hired. The amount of time it takes to actually implement these projects can delay or even weaken their economic effect.

ⓑ An increase in infrastructure spending is subject to the multiplier effect, where every dollar spent will increase GDP by more than one dollar. The figure below shows aggregate demand increasing from $AD_1$ to $AD$ when infrastructure spending is first increased. The amount of the increase is equal to the initial increase in government spending. Due to the multiplier effect, aggregate demand continues to increase, from $AD$ to $AD_2$. The increase in spending therefore results in a larger increase in real GDP. Moody's Analytics estimates that the multiplier for infrastructure spending is 1.59, so for every $1 increase in spending, real GDP will increase by $1.59.

ⓒ The length of time it takes for infrastructure spending to affect the economy can make a large difference in the overall effectiveness of the spending. If the spending only starts after a relatively long period of time, the economy may have already begun to recover by the time the additional spending can have an effect. In this case, the expansionary fiscal policy could expand aggregate demand by too great an amount, leading to an eventual increase in inflation.

## Thinking Critically About Policy

1. President Obama's economic team calculated the effects of its economic stimulus package using estimates of the government spending multiplier. Some economists, though, argue that administration economists have overestimated the sizes of the government purchases and tax multipliers. Other economists have argued that the sizes of these multipliers were underestimated. Why do economists have difficulty in reaching agreement on the sizes of these multipliers?

2. The Obama administration's stimulus spending resulted in a large increase in the federal budget deficit. Administration economists, however, were relatively unconcerned that crowding out would reduce the effect of the stimulus spending on real GDP. Briefly explain what crowding out is and why the administration was relatively unconcerned about it as it implemented the stimulus package.

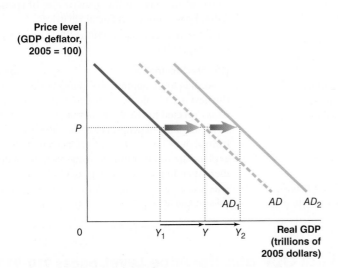

**The effect on aggregate demand of infrastructure spending.**

# Chapter Summary and Problems

## Key Terms

Automatic stabilizers, p. 906

Budget deficit, p. 927

Budget surplus, p. 927

Crowding out, p. 920

Cyclically adjusted budget deficit or surplus, p. 928

Fiscal policy, p. 906

Multiplier effect, p. 915

Tax wedge, p. 932

---

**27.1** **What Is Fiscal Policy?** pages 906–910

LEARNING OBJECTIVE: Define fiscal policy.

## Summary

**Fiscal policy** involves changes in federal taxes and purchases that are intended to achieve macroeconomic policy objectives. **Automatic stabilizers** are government spending and taxes that automatically increase or decrease along with the business cycle. Since World War II, the federal government's share of total government expenditures has been between two-thirds and three-quarters. Federal government *expenditures* as a percentage of GDP rose from 1950 to the early 1990s and fell between 1992 and 2001, before rising again. Federal government *purchases* have declined as a percentage of GDP since the end of the Korean War in the early 1950s. The largest component of federal expenditures is transfer payments. The largest sources of federal government revenue are individual income taxes, followed by social insurance taxes, which are used to fund the Social Security and Medicare systems.

 MyEconLab  Visit **www.myeconlab.com** to complete these exercises online and get instant feedback.

## Review Questions

1.1 What is fiscal policy? Who is responsible for fiscal policy?

1.2 What is the difference between fiscal policy and monetary policy?

1.3 What is the difference between federal purchases and federal expenditures? Are federal purchases higher today as a percentage of GDP than they were in 1960? Are federal expenditures as a percentage of GDP higher?

## Problems and Applications

1.4 In 2009, Congress and the president enacted "cash for clunkers" legislation that paid people buying new cars up to $4,500 if they traded in an older, low-gas-mileage car. Was this piece of legislation an example of fiscal policy? Does it depend on what goals Congress and the president had in mind when they enacted the legislation?

Based on Justin Lahart, "Trade-in Program Tunes Up Economic Engine," *Wall Street Journal*, August 4, 2009.

1.5 Based on the discussion in this chapter, which source of government revenue shown in Figure 27.4 on page 908 do you think is likely to increase the most in the future? Briefly explain.

1.6 **[Related to the** Making the Connection **on page 909]** According to a Congressional Budget Office report:

> By the end of this decade, an increasing number of baby boomers will have reached retirement age.... CBO therefore estimates that, unless changes are made to Social Security, spending for the program will rise from 4.8 percent of GDP today to 6.1 percent by 2035.

Who are the baby boomers? Why should their retirement cause an increase in the growth rate of spending by the federal government on Social Security?

From Congressional Budget Office, *CBO's 2011 Long-Term Budget Outlook*, June 2011, p. 53.

1.7 **[Related to the** Making the Connection **on page 909]** According to a Congressional Budget Office report, "During the next decade alone, the number of people over the age of 65 is expected to rise by more than a third. Over the longer term, the share of people age 65 or older is projected to grow from about 13 percent now to 20 percent in 2035...." Briefly explain the implications of these facts for federal government spending as a percentage of GDP in 2035.

From Congressional Budget Office, *CBO's 2011 Long-Term Budget Outlook*, June 2011, p. 7.

---

**27.2** **The Effects of Fiscal Policy on Real GDP and the Price Level,** pages 910–913

LEARNING OBJECTIVE: Explain how fiscal policy affects aggregate demand and how the government can use fiscal policy to stabilize the economy.

## Summary

To fight recessions, Congress and the president can increase government purchases or cut taxes. This expansionary policy causes the aggregate demand curve to shift out more than it otherwise would, raising the level of real GDP and the price level. To fight rising inflation, Congress and the president can decrease government purchases or raise taxes. This contractionary policy causes the aggregate demand curve to shift out less than it otherwise would, reducing the increase in real GDP and the price level.

MyEconLab  Visit **www.myeconlab.com** to complete these exercises online and get instant feedback.

## Review Questions

**2.1** What is an expansionary fiscal policy? What is a contractionary fiscal policy?

**2.2** If Congress and the president decide that an expansionary fiscal policy is necessary, what changes should they make in government spending or taxes? What changes should they make if they decide that a contractionary fiscal policy is necessary?

## Problems and Applications

**2.3** Briefly explain whether you agree with the following statements: "An expansionary fiscal policy involves an increase in government purchases or an increase in taxes. A contractionary fiscal policy involves a decrease in government purchases or a decrease in taxes."

**2.4** Identify each of the following as (i) part of an expansionary fiscal policy, (ii) part of a contractionary fiscal policy, or (iii) not part of fiscal policy.
   **a.** The corporate income tax rate is increased.
   **b.** Defense spending is increased.
   **c.** The Federal Reserve lowers the target for the federal funds rate.
   **d.** Families are allowed to deduct all their expenses for day care from their federal income taxes.
   **e.** The individual income tax rate is decreased.
   **f.** The state of New Jersey builds a new highway in an attempt to expand employment in the state.

**2.5** Use an aggregate demand and aggregate supply graph to illustrate the situation where the economy begins in equilibrium at potential GDP and then the demand for housing sharply declines. What actions can Congress and the president take to move the economy back to potential GDP? Show the results of these actions on your graph.

**2.6** **[Related to the** Don't Let This Happen to You **on page 912]** Is it possible for Congress and the president to carry out an expansionary fiscal policy if the money supply does not increase? Briefly explain.

**2.7** A political commentator argues: "Congress and the president are more likely to enact an expansionary fiscal policy than a contractionary fiscal policy because expansionary policies are popular and contractionary policies are unpopular." Briefly explain whether you agree.

---

**27.3** **Fiscal Policy in the Dynamic Aggregate Demand and Aggregate Supply Model,** pages 913–914

LEARNING OBJECTIVE: Use the dynamic aggregate demand and aggregate supply model to analyze fiscal policy.

## Summary

We can use the *dynamic aggregate demand and aggregate supply model* introduced in Chapter 24 to look more closely at expansionary and contractionary fiscal policies. The dynamic aggregate demand and aggregate supply model takes into account that (1) the economy experiences continuing inflation, with the price level rising every year, and (2) the economy experiences long-run growth, with the *LRAS* curve shifting to the right every year. In the dynamic model, an expansionary fiscal policy tries to ensure that the aggregate demand curve will shift far enough to the right to bring about macroeconomic equilibrium, with real GDP equal to potential GDP. A contractionary fiscal policy attempts to offset movements in aggregate demand that would cause macroeconomic equilibrium to occur at a level of real GDP that is greater than potential real GDP.

 Visit www.myeconlab.com to complete these exercises online and get instant feedback.

## Review Questions

**3.1** What are the key differences between how we illustrate an expansionary fiscal policy in the basic aggregate demand and aggregate supply model and in the dynamic aggregate demand and aggregate supply model?

**3.2** What are the key differences between how we illustrate a contractionary fiscal policy in the basic aggregate demand and aggregate supply model and in the dynamic aggregate demand and aggregate supply model?

## Problems and Applications

**3.3** Use the graph to answer the following questions.

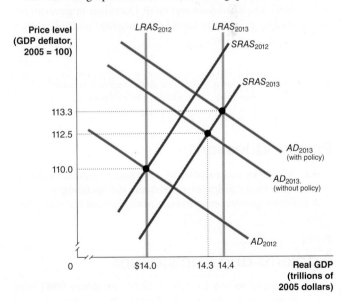

**a.** If the government takes no policy actions, what will be the values of real GDP and the price level in 2013?

**b.** What actions can the government take to bring real GDP to its potential level in 2013?

**c.** If the government takes no policy actions, what will be the inflation rate in 2013? If the government uses fiscal policy to keep real GDP at its potential level, what will be the inflation rate in 2013?

3.4 The hypothetical information in the following table shows what the situation will be in 2015 if the Fed does *not* use fiscal policy:

| Year | Potential GDP | Real GDP | Price Level |
|------|--------------|----------|-------------|
| 2014 | $15.0 trillion | $15.0 trillion | 110.0 |
| 2015 | $15.4 trillion | $15.0 trillion | 111.5 |

a. If Congress and the president want to keep real GDP at its potential level in 2015, should it use an expansionary policy or a contractionary policy? In your answer, be sure to explain whether Congress and the president should be increasing or decreasing government purchases and taxes.

b. If Congress and the president are successful in keeping real GDP at its potential level in 2015, state whether each of the following will be higher, lower, or the same as it would have been if they had taken no action:
i   Real GDP
ii  Potential real GDP
iii The inflation rate
iv  The unemployment rate

c. Draw an aggregate demand and aggregate supply graph to illustrate your answer. Be sure that your graph contains *LRAS* curves for 2014 and 2015; *SRAS* curves for 2014 and 2015; *AD* curves for 2014 and 2015, with and without fiscal policy action; and equilibrium real GDP and the price level in 2015, with and without fiscal policy.

3.5 Use a dynamic aggregate demand and aggregate supply graph to illustrate the change in macroeconomic equilibrium from 2015 to 2016, assuming that the economy experiences deflation during 2016. In order for deflation to take place in 2016, does the economy also have to be experiencing a recession?

---

<table><tr><td>27.4</td><td></td></tr></table> **The Government Purchases and Tax Multipliers, pages 914–919**

LEARNING OBJECTIVE: Explain how the government purchases and tax multipliers work.

## Summary

Because of the **multiplier effect**, an increase in government purchases or a cut in taxes will have a multiplied effect on equilibrium real GDP. The *government purchases multiplier* is equal to the change in equilibrium real GDP divided by the change in government purchases. The *tax multiplier* is equal to the change in equilibrium real GDP divided by the change in taxes. Increases in government purchases and cuts in taxes have a positive multiplier effect on equilibrium real GDP. Decreases in government purchases and increases in taxes have a negative multiplier effect on equilibrium real GDP.

 Visit **www.myeconlab.com** to complete these exercises online and get instant feedback.

## Review Questions

4.1 Why does a $1 increase in government purchases lead to more than a $1 increase in income and spending?

4.2 Define *government purchases multiplier* and *tax multiplier*.

## Problems and Applications

4.3 **[Related to the** Chapter Opener **on page 905]** Why would the Caldecott tunnel in Northern California and similar construction projects elsewhere in the country be expected to help the economy in the short run? A spokesperson for the California state agency in charge of the project mentioned that the Caldecott tunnel project would have a "ripple effect" on employment. What does the spokesperson mean by a ripple effect?

4.4 In *The General Theory of Employment, Interest, and Money,* John Maynard Keynes wrote:

> If the Treasury were to fill old bottles with banknotes, bury them at suitable depths in disused coal mines which are then filled up to the surface with town rubbish, and leave it to private enterprise . . . to dig the notes up again . . . there need be no more unemployment and, with the help of the repercussions, the real income of the community . . . would probably become a good deal greater than it is.

Which important macroeconomic effect is Keynes discussing here? What does he mean by "repercussions"? Why does he appear unconcerned about whether government spending is wasteful?

4.5 Suppose that real GDP is currently $13.1 trillion, potential real GDP is $13.5 trillion, the government purchases multiplier is 2, and the tax multiplier is –1.6.
a. Holding other factors constant, by how much will government purchases need to be increased to bring the economy to equilibrium at potential GDP?
b. Holding other factors constant, by how much will taxes have to be cut to bring the economy to equilibrium at potential GDP?
c. Construct an example of a *combination* of increased government spending and tax cuts that will bring the economy to equilibrium at potential GDP.

4.6 **[Related to** Solved Problem 27.4 **on page 918]** Briefly explain whether you agree with the following statement:

> Real GDP is currently $14.7 trillion, and potential real GDP is $14.4 trillion. If Congress and the president would decrease government purchases by $300 billion or increase taxes by $300 billion, the economy could be brought to equilibrium at potential GDP.

**4.7** A Federal Reserve publication discusses an estimate of the tax multiplier that gives it a value of 1.2 after one year and 2.8 after two years. Briefly explain why the tax multiplier might have a larger value after two years than after one year.

From Sylvain Leduc, "Fighting Downturns with Fiscal Policy," Federal Reserve Bank of San Francisco Economic Letter, June 19, 2009.

**4.8** If the short-run aggregate supply (*SRAS*) curve were a horizontal line at the current price level, what would be the effect on the size of the government purchases and tax multipliers?

---

 **The Limits of Using Fiscal Policy to Stabilize the Economy,** pages 919–926

LEARNING OBJECTIVE: Discuss the difficulties that can arise in implementing fiscal policy.

## Summary

Poorly timed fiscal policy can do more harm than good. Getting the timing right with fiscal policy can be difficult because obtaining approval from Congress for a new fiscal policy can be a very long process and because it can take months for an increase in authorized spending to actually take place. Because an increase in government purchases may lead to a higher interest rate, it may result in a decline in consumption, investment, and net exports. A decline in private expenditures as a result of an increase in government purchases is called **crowding out**. Crowding out may cause an expansionary fiscal policy to fail to meet its goal of keeping the economy at potential GDP.

MyEconLab  Visit www.myeconlab.com to complete these exercises online and get instant feedback.

## Review Questions

**5.1** Which can be changed more quickly: monetary policy or fiscal policy? Briefly explain.

**5.2** What is meant by crowding out? Explain the difference between crowding out in the short run and in the long run.

## Problems and Applications

**5.3** Some economists argue that because increases in government spending crowd out private spending, increased government spending will reduce the long-run growth rate of real GDP.

a. Is this most likely to happen if the private spending being crowded out is consumption spending, investment spending, or net exports? Briefly explain.

b. In terms of its effect on the long-run growth rate of real GDP, would it matter if the additional government

spending involves (i) increased spending on highways and bridges or (ii) increased spending on national parks? Briefly explain.

**5.4** In 2011, an article in the *Economist* argued that "heavy public debt risks more than just crowding out private investment. It can, in the extreme, bring on insolvency." What does the article mean by "heavy public debts"? How might heavy public debts lead to insolvency?

From "Running Out of Road," *Economist*, June 16, 2011.

**5.5** We saw that in calculating the stimulus package's effect on real GDP, economists in the Obama administration estimated that the government purchases multiplier has a value of 1.57. John F. Cogan, Tobias Cwik, John B. Taylor, and Volker Wieland argue that the value is only 0.61.

a. Briefly explain how the government purchases multiplier can have a value less than 1.

b. Why does an estimate of the size of the multiplier matter in evaluating the effects of an expansionary fiscal policy?

Based on John Cogan, Tobias Cwik, John Taylor, and Volker Wieland, "New Keynesian Versus Old Keynesian Government Spending Multipliers," *Journal of Economic Dynamics and Control*, Control, Vol. 34, No. 3, March 2010, pp. 281–295.

**5.6** **[Related to the** Making the Connection **on page 924]** Why would recessions accompanied by a financial crisis be more severe than recessions that do not involve bank crises? Were the large budget deficits of $1.4 trillion in fiscal year 2009 and $1.3 trillion in fiscal year 2010 primarily the result of the stimulus package of 2009? Briefly explain.

**5.7** Suppose that at the same time Congress and the president pursue an expansionary fiscal policy, the Federal Reserve pursues an expansionary monetary policy. How might an expansionary monetary policy affect the extent of crowding out in the short run?

---

 **Deficits, Surpluses, and Federal Government Debt,** pages 927–932

LEARNING OBJECTIVE: Define federal budget deficit and federal government debt and explain how the federal budget can serve as an automatic stabilizer.

## Summary

A **budget deficit** occurs when the federal government's expenditures are greater than its tax revenues. A **budget surplus** occurs when the federal government's expenditures are less than its tax revenues. A budget deficit automatically increases during recessions

and decreases during expansions. The automatic movements in the federal budget help to stabilize the economy by cushioning the fall in spending during recessions and restraining the increase in spending during expansions. The **cyclically adjusted budget deficit or surplus** measures what the deficit or surplus would be if the economy were at potential GDP. The federal government debt is the value of outstanding bonds issued by the U.S. Treasury. The national debt is a problem if interest payments on it require taxes to be raised substantially or require other federal expenditures to be cut.

MyEconLab Visit www.myeconlab.com to complete these exercises online and get instant feedback.

## Review Questions

**6.1** In what ways does the federal budget serve as an automatic stabilizer for the economy?

**6.2** What is the cyclically adjusted budget deficit or surplus? Suppose that the economy is currently at potential GDP, and the federal budget is balanced. If the economy moves into recession, what will happen to the federal budget?

**6.3** Why do few economists argue that it would be a good idea to balance the federal budget every year?

**6.4** What is the difference between the federal budget deficit and federal government debt?

## Problems and Applications

**6.5** In a column in the *Financial Times*, the prime minister and the finance minister of the Netherlands argue that the European Union, an organization of 27 countries in Europe, should appoint "a commissioner for budgetary discipline." They believe that "The new commissioner should be given clear powers to set requirements for the budgetary policy of countries that run excessive deficits." What is an "excessive" budget deficit? Does judging whether a deficit is excessive depend in part on whether the country is in a recession? How can budgetary policies be used to reduce a budget deficit?

From Mark Rutte and Jan Kees de Jager, "Expulsion from the Euro-zone Has to Be the Final Penalty," *Financial Times*, September 7, 2011.

**6.6** [Related to Solved Problem 27.6 **on page 929**] The federal government's budget surplus was $189.4 billion in 2000 and $41.8 billion in 2001. What does this information tell us about fiscal policy actions that Congress and the president took during those years?

**6.7** The federal government calculates its budget on a fiscal year that begins each year on October 1 and ends the following September 30. At the beginning of the 2005 fiscal year, the Congressional Budget Office (CBO) forecast that the federal budget deficit would be $368 billion. The actual budget deficit for fiscal 2005 was only $319 billion. Federal expenditures were $37 billion less than the CBO had forecast, and federal revenue was $12 billion more than the CBO had forecast.

**a.** Is it likely that the economy grew faster or more slowly during fiscal 2005 than the CBO had expected? Explain your reasoning.

**b.** Suppose that Congress and the president were committed to balancing the budget each year. Does what happened during 2005 provide any insight into difficulties they might run into in trying to balance the budget every year?

**6.8** [Related to the Making the Connection **on page 928**] The following is from a message by President Hoover to Congress, dated May 5, 1932:

> I need not recount that the revenues of the Government as estimated for the next fiscal year show a decrease of about $1,700,000,000 below the fiscal year 1929, and inexorably require a broader basis of taxation and a drastic reduction of expenditures in order to balance the Budget. Nothing is more necessary at this time than balancing the Budget.

Do you think President Hoover was correct in saying that, in 1932, nothing was more necessary than balancing the federal government's budget? Explain.

**6.9** According to an article in the *Wall Street Journal*, "Federal Reserve Chairman Ben Bernanke warned Congress and the White House that the U.S. economy will suffer if they don't move soon to rein in the federal budget deficit." How might the economy suffer from large federal deficits? How can Congress and the president "rein in" the federal budget deficit?

From Jon Hilsenrath and Brian Blackstone, "Bernanke Urges Deficit Reduction, Sees Growth This Year," *Wall Street Journal*, June 4, 2009.

**6.10** An editorial in the *Wall Street Journal* declares, "We don't put much stock in future budget forecasts because they depend on so many variables." What variables would a forecast of future federal budget deficits depend on? What is it about these variables that makes future budget deficits difficult to predict?

From "Fiscal Revelation," *Wall Street Journal*, February 6, 2007.

**6.11** An article in the *Economist* described the situation in Japan in mid-2009: "Nor is there much sign that Japan's gaping budget deficits have crowded out private investment. [Interest rates] on long-term Japanese bonds . . . are still only 1.45%, even as gross public debt is heading for 200% of GDP." Why would "gaping budget deficits" be expected to lead to crowding out? Why does the fact that interest rates in Japan have not risen indicate that crowding out may not yet be a problem?

From "Damage Assessment," *Economist*, May 14, 2009.

**6.12** A political columnist wrote the following:

> Today . . . the main purpose [of government's issuing bonds] is to let craven politicians launch projects they know the public, at the moment, would rather not fully finance. The tab for these projects will not come due, probably, until after the politicians have long since departed for greener (excuse the expression) pastures.

Do you agree with this commentator's explanation for why some government spending is financed through tax receipts and other government spending is financed through borrowing, by issuing bonds? Briefly explain.

"The Bond Issue Won't Be Repaid by Park Tolls," by Paul Carpenter from the *Morning Call*, May 26, 2002. Copyright © 2002 by the Morning Call. Reprinted by permission. All rights reserved.

## **27.7** The Effects of Fiscal Policy in the Long Run, pages 932–935

LEARNING OBJECTIVE: Discuss the effects of fiscal policy in the long run.

## Summary

Some fiscal policy actions are intended to have long-run effects by expanding the productive capacity of the economy and increasing the rate of economic growth. Because these policy actions primarily affect aggregate supply rather than aggregate demand, they are sometimes referred to as *supply-side economics*. The difference between the pretax and posttax return to an economic activity is known as the **tax wedge**. Economists believe that the smaller the tax wedge for any economic activity—such as working, saving, investing, or starting a business—the more of that economic activity will occur. Economists debate the size of the supply-side effects of tax changes.

MyEconLab    Visit www.myeconlab.com to complete these exercises online and get instant feedback.

## Review Questions

**7.1** What is meant by "supply-side economics"?

**7.2** What is the "tax wedge"?

## Problems and Applications

**7.3** It seems that both households and businesses would benefit if the federal income tax were simpler and tax forms were easier to fill out. Why then have the tax laws become increasingly complicated?

**7.4** Some economists and policymakers have argued in favor of a "flat tax." A flat tax would replace the current individual income tax system, with its many tax brackets, exemptions, and deductions, with a new system containing a single tax rate and few, or perhaps no, deductions and exemptions. Suppose a political candidate hired you to develop two arguments in favor of a flat tax. What two arguments would you advance? Alternatively, if you were hired to develop two arguments against a flat tax, what two arguments would you advance?

**7.5** Suppose that an increase in marginal tax rates on individual income affects both aggregate demand and aggregate supply. Briefly describe the effect of the tax increase on equilibrium real GDP and the equilibrium price level. Will the changes in equilibrium real GDP and the price level be larger or smaller than they would be if the tax increase affected only aggregate demand? Briefly explain.

**7.6** Writing in the *Wall Street Journal*, Martin Feldstein, an economist at Harvard University, argues that "behavioral responses" of taxpayers to the cuts in marginal tax rates enacted in 1986 resulted in "an enormous rise in the taxes paid, particularly by those who experienced the greatest reductions in marginal tax rates." How is it possible for cuts in marginal tax rates to result in an increase in total taxes collected? What does Feldstein mean by a "behavioral response" to tax cuts?

Based on Martin Feldstein, "The Tax Reform Evidence from 1986," *Wall Street Journal*, October 24, 2011.

# Appendix

**LEARNING** OBJECTIVE

Apply the multiplier formula.

## A Closer Look at the Multiplier

In this chapter, we saw that changes in government purchases and changes in taxes have a multiplied effect on equilibrium real GDP. In this appendix, we will build a simple economic model of the multiplier effect. When economists forecast the effect of a change in spending or taxes, they often rely on *econometric models*. As we saw in the appendix to Chapter 23, an econometric model is an economic model written in the form of equations, where each equation has been statistically estimated, using methods similar to those used in estimating demand curves, as briefly described in Chapter 3. In this appendix, we will start with a model similar to the one we used in the appendix to Chapter 23.

## An Expression for Equilibrium Real GDP

We can write a set of equations that includes the key macroeconomic relationships we have studied in this and previous chapters. It is important to note that in this model, we will be assuming that the price level is constant. We know that this is unrealistic because an upward-sloping *SRAS* curve means that when the aggregate demand curve shifts, the price level will change. Nevertheless, our model will be approximately correct when changes in the price level are small. It also serves as an introduction to more complicated models that take into account changes in the price level. For simplicity, we also start out by assuming that taxes, $T$, do not depend on the level of real GDP, $Y$. We also assume that there are no government transfer payments to households. Finally, we assume that we have a closed economy, with no imports or exports. The numbers (with the exception of the *MPC*) represent billions of dollars:

| | |
|---|---|
| (1) $C = 1,000 + 0.75(Y - T)$ | Consumption function |
| (2) $I = 1,500$ | Planned investment function |
| (3) $G = 1,500$ | Government purchases function |
| (4) $T = 1,000$ | Tax function |
| (5) $Y = C + I + G$ | Equilibrium condition |

The first equation is the consumption function. The marginal propensity to consume, or *MPC*, is 0.75, and 1,000 is the level of autonomous consumption, which is the level of consumption that does not depend on income. We assume that consumption depends on disposable income, which is $Y - T$. The functions for planned investment spending, government spending, and taxes are very simple because we have assumed that these variables are not affected by GDP and, therefore, are constant. Economists who use this type of model to forecast GDP would, of course, use more realistic planned investment, government purchases, and tax functions.

Equation (5)—the equilibrium condition—states that equilibrium GDP equals the sum of consumption spending, planned investment spending, and government purchases. To calculate a value for equilibrium real GDP, we need to substitute equations (1) through (4) into equation (5). This substitution gives us the following:

$$Y = 1,000 + 0.75(Y - 1,000) + 1,500 + 1,500$$
$$= 1,000 + 0.75Y - 750 + 1,500 + 1,500.$$

We need to solve this equation for $Y$ to find equilibrium GDP. The first step is to subtract $0.75Y$ from both sides of the equation:

$$Y - 0.75Y = 1,000 - 750 + 1,500 + 1,500.$$

Then, we solve for $Y$:

$$0.25Y = 3,250$$

or

$$Y = \frac{3,250}{0.25} = 13,000.$$

To make this result more general, we can replace particular values with general values represented by letters:

| | |
|---|---|
| $C = \overline{C} + MPC(Y - T)$ | Consumption function |
| $I = \overline{I}$ | Planned investment function |
| $G = \overline{G}$ | Government purchases function |
| $T = \overline{T}$ | Tax function |
| $Y = C + I + G$ | Equilibrium condition |

The letters with bars above them represent fixed, or *autonomous*, values that do not depend on the values of other variables. So, $\overline{C}$ represents autonomous consumption, which had a value of 1,000 in our original example. Now, solving for equilibrium, we get:

$$Y = \overline{C} + MPC(Y - \overline{T}) + \overline{I} + \overline{G}$$

or

$$Y - MPC(Y) = \overline{C} - (MPC \times \overline{T}) + \overline{I} + \overline{G}$$

or

$$Y(1 - MPC) = \overline{C} - (MPC \times \overline{T}) + \overline{I} + \overline{G}$$

or

$$Y = \frac{\overline{C} - (MPC \times \overline{T}) + \overline{I} + \overline{G}}{1 - MPC}.$$

# A Formula for the Government Purchases Multiplier

To find a formula for the government purchases multiplier, we need to rewrite the last equation for changes in each variable rather than levels. Letting $\Delta$ stand for the change in a variable, we have

$$\Delta Y = \frac{\Delta \overline{C} - (MPC \times \Delta \overline{T}) + \Delta \overline{I} + \Delta \overline{G}}{1 - MPC}.$$

If we hold constant changes in autonomous consumption spending, planned investment spending, and taxes, we can find a formula for the government purchases multiplier, which is the ratio of the change in equilibrium real GDP to the change in government purchases:

$$\Delta Y = \frac{\Delta G}{1 - MPC}$$

or

$$\text{Government purchases multiplier} = \frac{\Delta Y}{\Delta G} = \frac{1}{1 - MPC}.$$

For an $MPC$ of 0.75, the government purchases multiplier will be

$$\frac{1}{1 - 0.75} = 4.$$

...chases multiplier of 4 means that an increase in government spend-
...will increase equilibrium real GDP by 4 × $10 billion = $40 billion.

## ...ula for the Tax Multiplier

...find a formula for the tax multiplier. We start again with this equation:

$$\Delta Y = \frac{\Delta \overline{C} - (MPC \times \Delta \overline{T}) + \Delta \overline{I} + \Delta \overline{G}}{1 - MPC}.$$

...we hold constant the values of autonomous consumption spending, planned in-
...ment spending, and government purchases, but we allow the value of taxes to
...nge:

$$\Delta Y = \frac{- MPC \times \Delta T}{1 - MPC}.$$

Or:

$$\text{The tax multiplier} = \frac{\Delta Y}{\Delta T} = \frac{-MPC}{1 - MPC}.$$

For an *MPC* of 0.75, the tax multiplier will be:

$$\frac{-0.75}{1 - 0.75} = -3.$$

The tax multiplier is a negative number because an increase in taxes causes a decrease
in equilibrium real GDP, and a decrease in taxes causes an increase in equilibrium real
GDP. A tax multiplier of −3 means that a decrease in taxes of $10 billion will increase
equilibrium real GDP by −3 × −$10 billion = $30 billion. In this chapter, we discussed the economic reasons for the tax multiplier being smaller than the government
spending multiplier.

## The "Balanced Budget" Multiplier

What will be the effect of equal increases (or decreases) in government purchases and
taxes on equilibrium real GDP? At first, it might appear that the tax increase would exactly
offset the government purchases increase, leaving real GDP unchanged. But we have just
seen that the government purchases multiplier is larger (in absolute value) than the tax
multiplier. We can use our formulas for the government purchases multiplier and the tax
multiplier to calculate the net effect of increasing government purchases by $10 billion at
the same time that taxes are increased by $10 billion:

$$\text{Increase in real GDP from the increase in government purchases} = \$10 \text{ billion} \times \frac{1}{1 - MPC}$$

$$\text{Decrease in real GDP from the increase in taxes} = \$10 \text{ billion} \times \frac{-MPC}{1 - MPC}$$

So, the combined effect equals

$$\$10 \text{ billion} \times \left[ \left( \frac{1}{1 - MPC} \right) + \left( \frac{- MPC}{1 - MPC} \right) \right]$$

or

$$\$10 \text{ billion} \times \left( \frac{1 - MPC}{1 - MPC} \right) = \$10 \text{ billion}.$$

The balanced budget multiplier is, therefore, equal to $(1 - MPC)/(1 - MPC)$, or 1. Equal dollar increases and decreases in government purchases and in taxes lead to the same dollar increase in real GDP in the short run.

# The Effects of Changes in Tax Rates on the Multiplier

We now consider the effect of a change in the tax *rate*, as opposed to a change in a fixed amount of taxes. Changing the tax rate actually changes the value of the multiplier. To see this, suppose that the tax rate is 20 percent, or 0.2. In that case, an increase in household income of $10 billion will increase *disposable income* by only $8 billion [or 10 billion $\times (1 - 0.2)$]. In general, an increase in income can be multiplied by $(1 - t)$ to find the increase in disposable income, where $t$ is the tax rate. So, we can rewrite the consumption function as:

$$C = \overline{C} + MPC(1 - t)Y.$$

We can use this expression for the consumption function to find an expression for the government purchases multiplier, using the same method we used previously:

$$\text{Government purchases multiplier} = \frac{\Delta Y}{\Delta G} = \frac{1}{1 - MPC(1 - t)}.$$

We can see the effect of changing the tax rate on the size of the multiplier by trying some values. First, assume that $MPC = 0.75$ and $t = 0.2$. Then:

$$\text{Government purchases multiplier} = \frac{\Delta Y}{\Delta G} = \frac{1}{1 - 0.75(1 - 0.2)} = \frac{1}{1 - 0.6} = 2.5.$$

This value is smaller than the multiplier of 4 that we calculated by assuming that there was only a fixed amount of taxes (which is the same as assuming that the marginal tax *rate* was zero). This multiplier is smaller because spending in each period is now reduced by the amount of taxes households must pay on any additional income they earn. We can calculate the multiplier for an $MPC$ of 0.75 and a lower tax rate of 0.1:

$$\text{Government purchases multiplier} = \frac{\Delta Y}{\Delta G} = \frac{1}{1 - 0.75(1 - 0.1)} = \frac{1}{1 - 0.675} = 3.1.$$

Cutting the tax rate from 20 percent to 10 percent increased the value of the multiplier from 2.5 to 3.1.

# The Multiplier in an Open Economy

Up to now, we have assumed that the economy is closed, with no imports or exports. We can consider the case of an open economy by including net exports in our analysis. Recall that net exports equal exports minus imports. Exports are determined primarily by factors—such as the exchange value of the dollar and the levels of real GDP in other countries—that we do not include in our model. So, we will assume that exports are fixed, or autonomous:

$$\text{Exports} = \overline{\text{Exports}}$$

Imports will increase as real GDP increases because households will spend some portion of an increase in income on imports. We can define the *marginal propensity to import (MPI)* as the fraction of an increase in income that is spent on imports. So, our expression for imports is

$$\text{Imports} = MPI \times Y.$$

We can substitute our expressions for exports and imports into the expression we derived earlier for equilibrium real GDP:

$$Y = \overline{C} + MPC(1 - t)Y + \overline{I} + \overline{G} + [\overline{Exports} - (MPI \times Y)],$$

where the expression $[\overline{Exports} - (MPI \times Y)]$ represents net exports. We can now find an expression for the government purchases multiplier by using the same method we used previously:

$$\text{Government purchases multiplier} = \frac{\Delta Y}{\Delta G} = \frac{1}{1 - [MPC(1 - t) - MPI]}.$$

We can see the effect of changing the value of the marginal propensity to import on the size of the multiplier by trying some values of key variables. First, assume that $MPC = 0.75$, $t = 0.2$, and $MPI = 0.1$. Then:

$$\text{Government purchases multiplier} = \frac{\Delta Y}{\Delta G} = \frac{1}{1 - (0.75(1 - 0.2) - 0.1)} = \frac{1}{1 - 0.5} =$$

This value is smaller than the multiplier of 2.5 that we calculated by assuming that there were no exports or imports (which is the same as assuming that the marginal propensity to import was zero). This multiplier is smaller because spending in each period is now reduced by the amount of imports households buy with any additional income they earn. We can calculate the multiplier with $MPC = 0.75$, $t = 0.2$, and a higher $MPI$ of 0.2:

$$\text{Government purchases multiplier} = \frac{\Delta Y}{\Delta G} = \frac{1}{1 - (0.75(1 - 0.2) - 0.2)} = \frac{1}{1 - 0.4} =$$

Increasing the marginal propensity to import from 0.1 to 0.2 decreases the value of the multiplier from 2 to 1.7. We can conclude that countries with a higher marginal propensity to import will have smaller multipliers than countries with a lower marginal propensity to import.

Bear in mind that the multiplier is a short-run effect which assumes that the economy is below the level of potential real GDP. In the long run, the economy is at potential real GDP, so an increase in government purchases causes a decline in the nongovernment components of real GDP but leaves the level of real GDP unchanged.

The analysis in this appendix is simplified compared to what would be carried out by an economist forecasting the effects of changes in government purchases or changes in taxes on equilibrium real GDP in the short run. In particular, our assumption that the price level is constant is unrealistic. However, looking more closely at the determinants of the multiplier has helped us see more clearly some important macroeconomic relationships.

---

**27A** | **A Closer Look at the Multiplier,** pages 944–948
LEARNING OBJECTIVE: Apply the multiplier formula.

## Problem and Applications

**27A.1** Assuming a fixed amount of taxes and a closed economy, calculate the value of the government purchases multiplier, the tax multiplier, and the balanced budget multiplier if the marginal propensity to consume equals 0.6.

**27A.2** Calculate the value of the government purchases multiplier if the marginal propensity to consume equals 0.8, the tax rate equals 0.25, and the marginal propensity to import equals 0.2.

**27A.3** Use a graph to show the change in the aggregate demand curve resulting from an increase in government purchases if the government purchases multiplier equals 2. Now, on the same graph, show the change in the aggregate demand curve resulting from an increase in government purchases if the government purchases multiplier equals 4.

**27A.4** Using your understanding of multipliers, explain why an increase in the tax rate would decrease the size of the government purchases multiplier. Similarly, explain why a decrease in the marginal propensity to import would increase the size of the government purchases multiplier.

# Inflation, Unemployment, and Federal Reserve Policy

## Chapter Outline and Learning Objectives

# Why Does CarMax Worry about Monetary Policy?

The Federal Reserve is continually balancing the risks of inflation against the risks of unemployment. A contractionary monetary policy that would help rein in inflation risks pushing the economy into recession. An expansionary policy that can reduce the effects of recession risks increasing inflation. Consider the following example of the Fed's balancing act: In an attempt to cool the inflationary effect of a booming housing market, the Fed raised the target for the federal funds rate to 5.25 percent in June 2006 and kept it there until September 2007. At that point, a rapidly declining housing market led the Fed to begin cutting the federal funds rate, although well into 2008, the Fed remained worried that rising oil and commodity prices could increase the inflation rate.

Behind the roller-coaster ride of GDP, unemployment, and inflation are individual firms and workers. In 1991, former executives from Circuit City, the now-defunct consumer electronics store, started CarMax, using a new business model. They believed customers would buy from dealers who offered a large selection of cars with non-negotiable prices. Salespeople would earn flat commissions so there would be no incentive to coax customers to buy the most expensive models. Today, CarMax has more than 100 "superstore" locations.

Monetary policy affects the performance of both new and used car companies.

When the Federal Reserve raised interest rates in 2006 and kept them high through mid-2007, it meant higher costs for consumers who borrow money to buy cars.

By late 2008, the Fed had slashed the federal funds rate to near-zero levels. Although car dealers were hit hard by the recession, CarMax's sales began to recover in 2009. Many consumers who balked at buying new cars viewed used cars as an affordable alternative, and low-interest loans reduced the monthly payments they would make. Though interest rates remained low and incomes had risen in 2010 and 2011, CarMax sales began to slip. Unemployment remained high, and consumer confidence was low. As CEO Thomas Folliard noted: "When you look at the product that we sell, it almost always requires a loan, and somebody has . . . to be confident in signing up for [a loan, which can be] six and seven years long now on cars."

In this chapter, we will further explore the Fed's attempts to balance its goals of price stability and high employment. **AN INSIDE LOOK AT POLICY** on **page 974** discusses how the Fed attempts to reduce unemployment without causing a significant increase in inflation.

Based on Caitlin Nish, "Economy Crimps CarMax Sales," *Wall Street Journal*, September 22, 2011; and Michael Myser, "The Wal-Mart of Used Cars," *Business 2.0*, October 2, 2006.

## Economics in Your Life

### Is It Wise to Delay a Job Search?

Your friend was recently laid off from her entry-level job as a computer analyst. You call to console her, but she does not seem very upset. "Our state offers workers up to 99 weeks of unemployment compensation. I have almost two years before I have to find a new job. With my education and job experience, I should be able to find a new job by then without much trouble." Your friend did well in school, but you are not sure that waiting almost two years to find a new job is a good idea. What advice would you give someone who has decided to wait nearly two years to look for a new job? As you read this chapter, see if you can answer this question. You can check your answer against the one we provide on **page 973** at the end of this chapter.

An important consideration for the Federal Reserve as it carries out monetary policy is that in the short run, there can be a trade-off between unemployment and inflation: Lower unemployment rates can result in higher inflation rates. In the long run, however, this trade-off disappears, and the unemployment rate is independent of the inflation rate. In this chapter, we will explore the relationship between inflation and unemployment in both the short run and the long run, and we will discuss what this relationship means for monetary policy. We will also provide an overview of how monetary policy has evolved over the years and conclude with a discussion of the debate over Fed policy during the 2007–2009 recession.

**28.1 LEARNING** OBJECTIVE

Describe the Phillips curve and the nature of the short-run trade-off between unemployment and inflation.

# The Discovery of the Short-Run Trade-off between Unemployment and Inflation

Ordinarily, unemployment and inflation are the two great macroeconomic problems the Fed must deal with in the short run. As we saw in Chapter 24, when aggregate demand increases, unemployment usually falls, and inflation rises. When aggregate demand decreases, unemployment usually rises and inflation falls. As a result, there is a *short-run trade-off* between unemployment and inflation: Higher unemployment is usually accompanied by lower inflation, and lower unemployment is usually accompanied by higher inflation. As we will see later in this chapter, this trade-off exists in the short run—a period that may be as long as several years—but disappears in the long run.

Although today the short-run trade-off between unemployment and inflation plays a role in the Fed's monetary policy decisions, this trade-off was not widely recognized until the late 1950s. In 1957, New Zealand economist A. W. Phillips plotted data on the unemployment rate and the inflation rate in Great Britain and drew a curve showing their average relationship. Since that time, a graph showing the short-run relationship between the unemployment rate and the inflation rate has been called a **Phillips curve**. (Phillips actually measured inflation by the percentage change in wages rather than by the percentage change in prices. Because wages and prices usually move together, this difference is not important to our discussion.) Figure 28.1 shows a graph similar to the one Phillips prepared. Each point on the Phillips curve represents a possible combination of the unemployment rate and the inflation rate that might be observed in a given year. Point *A* represents a year in which the inflation rate is 4 percent and the unemployment rate is 5 percent, and point *B* represents a year in which the inflation rate

**Phillips curve** A curve showing the short-run relationship between the unemployment rate and the inflation rate.

### Figure 28.1

**The Phillips Curve**

A. W. Phillips was the first economist to show that there is usually an inverse relationship between unemployment and inflation. Here we can see this relationship at work: In the year represented by point *A*, the inflation rate is 4 percent and the unemployment rate is 5 percent. In the year represented by point *B*, the inflation rate is 2 percent and the unemployment rate is 6 percent.

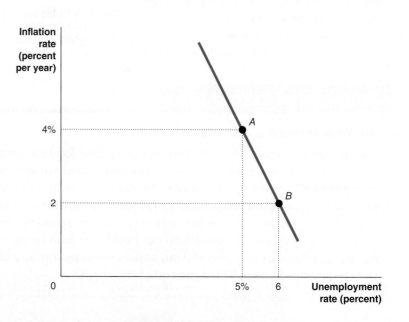

is 2 percent and the unemployment rate is 6 percent. Phillips documented that there is usually an *inverse relationship* between unemployment and inflation. During years when the unemployment rate is low, the inflation rate tends to be high, and during years when the unemployment rate is high, the inflation rate tends to be low.

## Explaining the Phillips Curve with Aggregate Demand and Aggregate Supply Curves

The inverse relationship between unemployment and inflation that Phillips discovered is consistent with the aggregate demand and aggregate supply analysis we developed in Chapter 24. Figure 28.2 shows why this inverse relationship exists.

Panel (a) shows the aggregate demand and aggregate supply model from Chapter 24, and panel (b) shows the Phillips curve. For simplicity, in panel (a), we are using the basic aggregate demand and aggregate supply model, and we are assuming that the long-run aggregate supply curve and the short-run aggregate supply curve do not shift. To take a hypothetical example, assume that the economy in 2013 is at point *A*, with real GDP of $14.0 trillion and a price level of 100. If there is weak growth in aggregate demand, in 2014, the economy moves to point *B*, with real GDP of $14.3 trillion and a price level of 102. The inflation rate is 2 percent and the unemployment rate is 6 percent, which corresponds to point *B* on the Phillips curve in panel (b). If there is strong growth in aggregate demand, in 2014, the economy moves to point *C*, with real GDP of $14.6 trillion and a price level of 104. Strong aggregate demand growth results in a higher inflation rate of 4 percent but a lower unemployment rate of 5 percent. This combination of higher inflation and lower unemployment is shown as point *C* on the Phillips curve in panel (b).

To summarize, the aggregate demand and aggregate supply model indicates that slow growth in aggregate demand leads to both higher unemployment and lower inflation. This relationship explains why there is a short-run trade-off between unemployment and inflation, as shown by the downward-sloping Phillips curve. The *AD–AS*

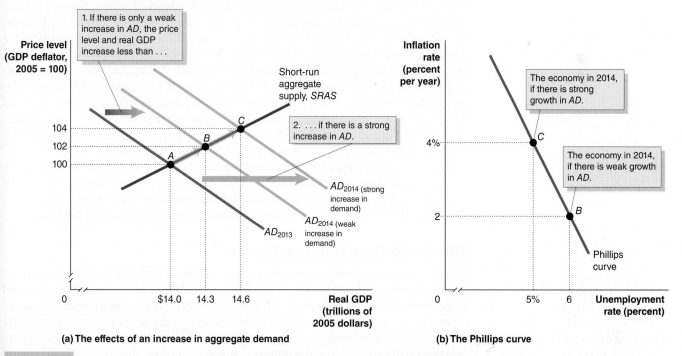

**Figure 28.2    Using Aggregate Demand and Aggregate Supply to Explain the Phillips Curve**

In panel (a), the economy in 2013 is at point *A*, with real GDP of $14.0 trillion and a price level of 100. If there is weak growth in aggregate demand, in 2014, the economy moves to point *B*, with real GDP of $14.3 trillion and a price level of 102. The inflation rate is 2 percent and the unemployment rate is 6 percent, which corresponds to point *B* on the Phillips curve in panel (b). If there is strong growth in aggregate demand, in 2014, the economy moves to point *C*, with real GDP of $14.6 trillion and a price level of 104. Strong aggregate demand growth results in a higher inflation rate of 4 percent but a lower unemployment rate of 5 percent. This combination of higher inflation and lower unemployment is shown as point *C* on the Phillips curve in panel (b).

model and the Phillips curve are different ways of illustrating the same macroeconomic events. The Phillips curve has an advantage over the aggregate demand and aggregate supply model, however, when we want to analyze explicitly *changes* in the inflation and unemployment rates.

## Is the Phillips Curve a Policy Menu?

During the 1960s, some economists argued that the Phillips curve represented a *structural relationship* in the economy. A **structural relationship** depends on the basic behavior of consumers and firms and remains unchanged over long periods. Structural relationships are useful in formulating economic policy because policymakers can anticipate that these relationships are constant—that is, the relationships will not change as a result of changes in policy.

If the Phillips curve were a structural relationship, it would present policymakers with a reliable menu of combinations of unemployment and inflation. Potentially, policymakers could use expansionary monetary and fiscal policies to choose a point on the curve that had lower unemployment and higher inflation. They could also use contractionary monetary and fiscal policies to choose a point that had lower inflation and higher unemployment. Because many economists and policymakers in the 1960s viewed the Phillips curve as a structural relationship, they believed it represented a *permanent trade-off between unemployment and inflation*. As long as policymakers were willing to accept a permanently higher inflation rate, they would be able to keep the unemployment rate permanently lower. Similarly, a permanently lower inflation rate could be attained at the cost of a permanently higher unemployment rate. As we discuss in the next section, however, economists came to realize that the Phillips curve did *not*, in fact, represent a permanent trade-off between unemployment and inflation.

## Is the Short-Run Phillips Curve Stable?

During the 1960s, the basic Phillips curve relationship seemed to hold because a stable trade-off appeared to exist between unemployment and inflation. In the early 1960s, the inflation rate was low, and the unemployment rate was high. In the late 1960s, the unemployment rate had declined, and the inflation rate had increased. Then in 1968, in his presidential address to the American Economic Association, Milton Friedman of the University of Chicago argued that the Phillips curve did *not* represent a *permanent* trade-off between unemployment and inflation. At almost the same time, Edmund Phelps of Columbia University published an academic paper making a similar argument. Friedman and Phelps noted that economists had come to agree that the long-run aggregate supply curve was vertical (a point we discussed in Chapter 24). If this observation were true, the Phillips curve could not be downward sloping in the long run. A critical inconsistency exists between a vertical long-run aggregate supply curve and a long-run Phillips curve that is downward sloping. Friedman and Phelps argued, in essence, that there is no trade-off between unemployment and inflation in the long run.

## The Long-Run Phillips Curve

To understand the argument that there is no permanent trade-off between unemployment and inflation, first recall that the level of real GDP in the long run is also referred to as *potential GDP*. At potential GDP, firms will operate at their normal level of capacity, and everyone who wants a job will have one, except the structurally and frictionally unemployed. Friedman defined the **natural rate of unemployment** as the unemployment rate that exists when the economy is at potential GDP. The actual unemployment rate will fluctuate in the short run but will always come back to the natural rate in the long run. In the same way, the actual level of real GDP will fluctuate in the short run but will always come back to its potential level in the long run.

In the long run, a higher or lower price level has no effect on real GDP because real GDP is always at its potential level in the long run. In the same way, in the long run, a higher or lower inflation rate will have no effect on the unemployment rate because the

**Structural relationship** A relationship that depends on the basic behavior of consumers and firms and that remains unchanged over long periods.

**Natural rate of unemployment** The unemployment rate that exists when the economy is at potential GDP.

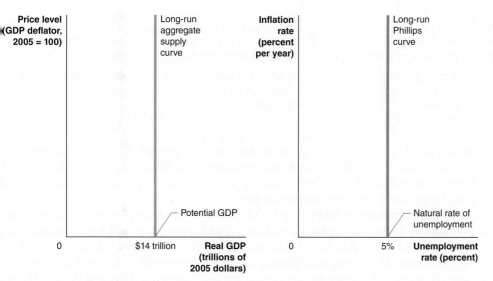

**Figure 28.3**

**A Vertical Long-Run Aggregate Supply Curve Means a Vertical Long-Run Phillips Curve**

Milton Friedman and Edmund Phelps argued that there is no trade-off between unemployment and inflation in the long run. If real GDP automatically returns to its potential level in the long run, the unemployment rate must return to the natural rate of unemployment in the long run. In this figure, we assume that potential GDP is $14 trillion and the natural rate of unemployment is 5 percent.

unemployment rate is always equal to the natural rate in the long run. Figure 28.3 illustrates Friedman's conclusion that the long-run aggregate supply curve is a vertical line at the potential real GDP, and *the long-run Phillips curve is a vertical line at the natural rate of unemployment.*

## The Role of Expectations of Future Inflation

If the long-run Phillips curve is a vertical line, *no trade-off exists between unemployment and inflation in the long run.* This conclusion seemed to contradict the experience of the 1950s and 1960s, which showed a stable trade-off between unemployment and inflation. Friedman argued that the statistics from those years actually showed only a short-run trade-off between inflation and unemployment.

The short-run trade-off existed—but only because workers and firms sometimes expected the inflation rate to be either higher or lower than it turned out to be. Differences between the expected inflation rate and the actual inflation rate could lead the unemployment rate to rise above or dip below the natural rate. To see why, consider a simple case of Ford negotiating a wage contract with the United Auto Workers (UAW) union. Remember that both Ford and the UAW are interested in the real wage, which is the nominal wage corrected for inflation. Suppose, for example, that Ford and the UAW agree on a wage of $31.50 per hour to be paid during 2015. Both Ford and the UAW expect that the price level will increase from 100 in 2014 to 105 in 2015, so the inflation rate will be 5 percent. We can calculate the real wage Ford expects to pay and the UAW expects to receive as follows:

$$\text{Real wage} = \frac{\text{Nominal wage}}{\text{Price level}} \times 100 = \frac{\$31.50}{105} \times 100 = \$30.$$

But suppose that the actual inflation rate turns out to be higher or lower than the expected inflation rate of 5 percent. Table 28.1 shows the effect on the actual real wage. If the price level rises only to 102 during 2015, the inflation rate will be 2 percent, and the actual real wage will be $30.88, which is higher than Ford and the UAW had expected. With a higher real wage, Ford will hire fewer workers than it had planned to at

| Nominal Wage | Expected Real Wage | | Actual Real Wage | |
|---|---|---|---|---|
| | Expected $P_{2015} = 105$ | Actual $P_{2015} = 102$ | Actual $P_{2015} = 108$ | |
| | Expected inflation = 5% | Actual inflation = 2% | Actual inflation = 8% | |
| $31.50 | $\dfrac{\$31.50}{105} \times 100 = \$30$ | $\dfrac{\$31.50}{102} \times 100 = \$30.88$ | $\dfrac{\$31.50}{108} \times 100 = \$29.17$ | |

**Table 28.1**

**The Effect of Unexpected Price Level Changes on the Real Wage**

| Table 28.2 | If . . . | then . . . | and . . . |
|---|---|---|---|
| **The Basis for the Short-Run Phillips Curve** | actual inflation is greater than expected inflation, | the actual real wage is less than the expected real wage, | the unemployment rate falls. |
| | actual inflation is less than expected inflation, | the actual real wage is greater than the expected real wage, | the unemployment rate rises. |

the expected real wage of $30. If the inflation rate is 8 percent, the actual real wage will be $29.17, and Ford will hire more workers than it had planned to hire. If Ford and the UAW expected a higher or lower inflation rate than actually occurred, other firms and workers probably made the same assumption.

If actual inflation is higher than expected inflation, actual real wages in the economy will be lower than expected real wages, and many firms will hire more workers than they had planned to hire. Therefore, the unemployment rate will fall. If actual inflation is lower than expected inflation, actual real wages will be higher than expected, many firms will hire fewer workers than they had planned to hire, and the unemployment rate will rise. Table 28.2 summarizes this argument.

Friedman and Phelps concluded that *an increase in the inflation rate increases employment (and decreases unemployment) only if the increase in the inflation rate is unexpected.* Friedman argued that in 1968, the unemployment rate was 3.6 percent rather than 5 percent only because the inflation rate of 4 percent was above the 1 percent to 2 percent inflation that workers and firms had expected: "There is always a temporary trade-off between inflation and unemployment; there is no permanent trade-off. The temporary trade-off comes not from inflation per se, but from unanticipated inflation."

## Making the Connection | Do Workers Understand Inflation?

A higher inflation rate can lead to lower unemployment if *both* workers and firms mistakenly expect the inflation rate to be lower than it turns out to be. But this same result might be due to firms forecasting inflation more accurately than workers do or to firms understanding better the effects of inflation. Some large firms employ economists to help them gather and analyze information that is useful in forecasting inflation. Many firms also have human resources or employee compensation departments that gather data on wages paid at competing firms and analyze trends in compensation. Workers generally rely on much less systematic information about wages and prices. Workers also often fail to realize a fact we discussed in Chapter 20: *Expected inflation increases the value of total production and the value of total income by the same amount.* Therefore, although not all wages will rise as prices rise, inflation will increase the average wage in the economy at the same time that it increases the average price.

*Will wage increases keep up with inflation?*

Robert Shiller, an economist at Yale University, conducted a survey on inflation and discovered that, although most economists believe an increase in inflation will lead quickly to an increase in wages, a majority of the general public thinks otherwise. As part of the survey, Shiller asked how "the effect of general inflation on wages or salary relates to your own experience and your own job." The most popular response was: "The price increase will create extra profits for my employer, who can now sell output for more; there will be no effect on my pay. My employer will see no reason to raise my pay."

Shiller also asked the following question:

Imagine that next year the inflation rate unexpectedly doubles. How long would it probably take, in these times, before your income is increased enough so that you can afford the same things as you do today? In other words, how long will it be before a full inflation correction in your income has taken place?

Eighty-one percent of the public answered either that it would take several years for the purchasing power of their income to be restored or that it would never be restored.

If workers fail to understand that rising inflation leads over time to comparable increases in wages, then when inflation increases, in the short run, firms can increase wages by less than inflation without needing to worry about workers quitting or their morale falling. Once again, we have a higher inflation rate, leading in the short run to lower real wages and lower unemployment. In other words, we have an explanation for a downward-sloping short-run Phillips curve.

Based on Robert J. Shiller, "Why Do People Dislike Inflation?" in *Reducing Inflation: Motivation and Strategy* by Christina D. Romer and David H. Romer, eds., (Chicago: University of Chicago Press, 1997).

**Your Turn:** Test your understanding by doing related problems 1.12 and 1.13 on page 977 at the end of this chapter.

MyEconLab

---

# The Short-Run and Long-Run Phillips Curves

If there is both a short-run Phillips curve and a long-run Phillips curve, how are the two curves related? We can begin answering this question with the help of Figure 28.4, which represents macroeconomic conditions in the United States during the 1960s. In the late 1960s, workers and firms were still expecting the inflation rate to be about 1.5 percent, as it had been from 1960 to 1965. Expansionary monetary and fiscal policies, however, had moved the short-run equilibrium up the short-run Phillips curve to an inflation rate of 4.5 percent and an unemployment rate of 3.5 percent. This very low unemployment rate was possible only because the real wage rate was unexpectedly low.

Once workers and firms began to expect that the inflation rate would continue to be about 4.5 percent, they changed their behavior. Firms knew that only nominal wage increases of more than 4.5 percent would increase real wages. Workers realized that unless they received a nominal wage increase of at least 4.5 percent, their real wage would be falling. Higher expected inflation rates had an effect throughout the economy. For example, as we saw in Chapter 25, when banks make loans, they are interested in the *real interest rate* on the loan. The real interest rate is the nominal interest rate minus the expected inflation rate. If banks need to receive a real interest rate of 3 percent on home mortgage loans and expect the inflation rate to be 1.5 percent, they will charge a nominal interest rate of 4.5 percent. If banks revise their expectations of the inflation rate to 4.5 percent, they will increase the nominal interest rate they charge on mortgage loans to 7.5 percent.

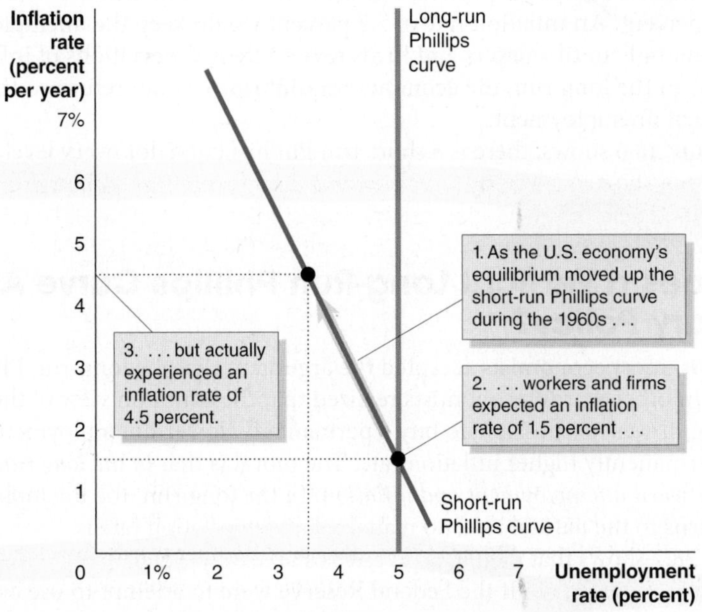

**28.2 LEARNING OBJECTIVE**

Explain the relationship between the short-run and long-run Phillips curves.

**Figure 28.4**

**The Short-Run Phillips Curve of the 1960s and the Long-Run Phillips Curve**

In the late 1960s, U.S. workers and firms were expecting the 1.5 percent inflation rates of the recent past to continue. However, expansionary monetary and fiscal policies moved the short-run equilibrium up the short-run Phillips curve to an inflation rate of 4.5 percent and an unemployment rate of 3.5 percent.

**Figure 28.5**

**Expectations and the Short-Run Phillips Curve**

By the end of the 1960s, workers and firms had revised their expectations of inflation from 1.5 percent to 4.5 percent. As a result, the short-run Phillips curve shifted up, which made the short-run trade-off between unemployment and inflation worse.

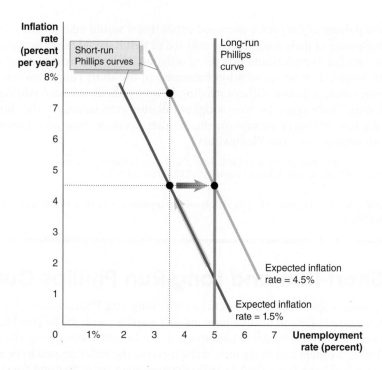

## Shifts in the Short-Run Phillips Curve

The new, higher expected inflation rate can become *embedded* in the economy, meaning that workers, firms, consumers, and the government all take the inflation rate into account when making decisions. The short-run trade-off between unemployment and inflation now takes place from this higher, less favorable level, as shown in Figure 28.5.

As long as workers and firms expected the inflation rate to be 1.5 percent, the short-run trade-off between unemployment and inflation was the more favorable one shown by the lower Phillips curve. Along this Phillips curve, an inflation rate of 4.5 percent was enough to drive down the unemployment rate to 3.5 percent. Once workers and firms adjusted their expectations to an inflation rate of 4.5 percent, the short-run trade-off deteriorated to the one shown by the higher Phillips curve. At this higher expected inflation rate, the real wage rose, causing some workers to lose their jobs, and the economy's equilibrium returned to the natural rate of unemployment of 5 percent—but now with an inflation rate of 4.5 percent rather than 1.5 percent. On the higher short-run Phillips curve, an inflation rate of 7.5 percent would be necessary to reduce the unemployment rate to 3.5 percent. An inflation rate of 7.5 percent would keep the unemployment rate at 3.5 percent only until workers and firms revised their expectations of inflation up to 7.5 percent. In the long run, the economy's equilibrium would return to the 5 percent natural rate of unemployment.

As Figure 28.6 shows, there is a short-run Phillips curve for every level of expected inflation. Each short-run Phillips curve intersects the long-run Phillips curve at the expected inflation rate.

## How Does a Vertical Long-Run Phillips Curve Affect Monetary Policy?

By the 1970s, most economists accepted the argument that the long-run Phillips curve is vertical. In other words, economists realized that the common view of the 1960s had been wrong: It was *not* possible to buy a permanently lower unemployment rate at the cost of a permanently higher inflation rate. The moral is that *in the long run, there is no trade-off between unemployment and inflation*. In the long run, the unemployment rate always returns to the natural rate, no matter what the inflation rate is.

Figure 28.7 shows that the inflation rate is stable only when the unemployment rate is equal to the natural rate. If the Federal Reserve were to attempt to use expansionary

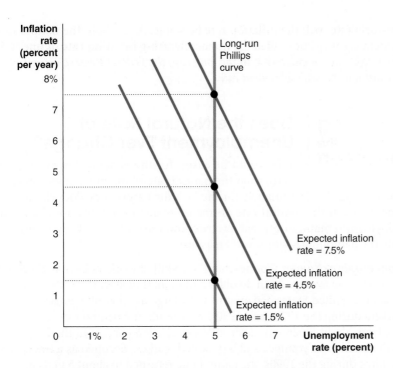

**Figure 28.6**

**A Short-Run Phillips Curve for Every Expected Inflation Rate**

There is a different short-run Phillips curve for every expected inflation rate. Each short-run Phillips curve intersects the long-run Phillips curve at the expected inflation rate.

monetary policy to push the economy to a point such as *A*, where the unemployment rate is below the natural rate, the result would be increasing inflation as the economy moved up the short-run Phillips curve. If the economy remained below the natural rate long enough, the short-run Phillips curve would shift up as workers and firms adjusted to the new, higher inflation rate. During the 1960s and 1970s, the short-run Phillips curve did shift up, presenting the economy with a more unfavorable short-run trade-off between unemployment and inflation.

If the Federal Reserve used contractionary policy to push the economy to a point such as *B*, where the unemployment rate is above the natural rate, the inflation rate would decrease. If the economy remained above the natural rate long enough, the short-run Phillips curve would shift down as workers and firms adjusted to the new, lower inflation rate. Only at a point such as *C*, where the unemployment rate is equal

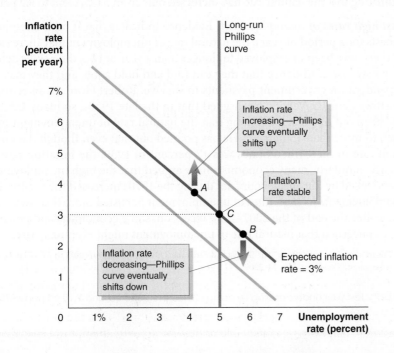

**Figure 28.7**

**The Inflation Rate and the Natural Rate of Unemployment in the Long Run**

The inflation rate is stable only if the unemployment rate equals the natural rate of unemployment (point *C*). If the unemployment rate is below the natural rate (point *A*), the inflation rate increases, and, eventually, the short-run Phillips curve shifts up. If the unemployment rate is above the natural rate (point *B*), the inflation rate decreases, and, eventually, the short-run Phillips curve shifts down.

**Nonaccelerating inflation rate of unemployment (NAIRU)** The unemployment rate at which the inflation rate has no tendency to increase or decrease.

to the natural rate, will the inflation rate be stable. As a result, the natural rate of unemployment is sometimes called the **nonaccelerating inflation rate of unemployment (NAIRU)**. We can conclude that *in the long run, the Federal Reserve can affect the inflation rate but not the unemployment rate.*

*An increase in the number of younger and less skilled workers in an economy can make the natural rate of unemployment increase.*

## Making the Connection | Does the Natural Rate of Unemployment Ever Change?

Life would be easier for the Federal Reserve if it knew exactly what the natural rate of unemployment was and if that rate never changed. Unfortunately for the Fed, the natural rate does change over time. Remember that at the natural rate of unemployment, only frictional and structural unemployment remain. Frictional or structural unemployment can change—thereby changing the natural rate—for several reasons:

- *Demographic changes.* Younger and less skilled workers have higher unemployment rates, on average, than do older and more skilled workers. Because of the baby boom, the United States had an unusually large number of younger and less skilled workers during the 1970s and 1980s. As a result, the natural rate of unemployment rose from about 5 percent in the 1960s to about 6 percent in the 1970s and 1980s. As the number of younger and less skilled workers declined as a fraction of the labor force during the 1990s, the natural rate returned to about 5 percent.

- *Labor market institutions.* As we discussed in Chapter 20, labor market institutions such as the unemployment insurance system, unions, and legal barriers to firing workers can increase the economy's unemployment rate. Because many European countries have generous unemployment insurance systems, strong unions, and restrictive policies on firing workers, the natural rate of unemployment in most European countries has been well above the rate in the United States. In 2011, some economists believed that many workers in the United States had become less mobile because of the bursting of the housing bubble. These economists argued that because workers either were unable to sell their homes or were unwilling to do so because they did not want to sell for a low price, they were less likely to move from a geographic area of high unemployment to one of lower unemployment. Economists at JPMorgan Chase estimated that this lack of mobility might have increased the natural rate of unemployment to about 6 percent. Economists at the Congressional Budget Office disagreed, estimating that the natural rate had increased only from 5.0 percent to 5.2 percent.

- *Past high rates of unemployment.* Evidence indicates that if high unemployment persists for a period of years, the natural rate of unemployment may increase. When workers have been unemployed for longer than a year or two, their skills deteriorate, they may lose confidence that they can find and hold a job, and they may become dependent on government payments to survive. Robert Gordon, an economist at Northwestern University, has argued that in the late 1930s, so many U.S. workers had been out of work for so long that the natural rate of unemployment may have risen to more than 15 percent. He has pointed out that even though the unemployment rate in the United States was 17 percent in 1939, the inflation rate did not change. Similarly, many economists have argued that the high unemployment rates experienced by European countries during the 1970s increased their natural rates of unemployment. As high rates of unemployment persisted more than two and a half years after the end of the 2007–2009 recession, some economists and policymakers were concerned that natural rate of unemployment might eventually rise.

Based on Congressional Budget Office: "The Budget and Economic Outlook: Fiscal Years 2011 to 2021," January 2011; and "Damage Assessment," *Economist*, May 14, 2009.

MyEconLab **Your Turn:** Test your understanding by doing related problems 2.9 and 2.10 on page 978 at the end of this chapter.

# Solved Problem 28.2

## Changing Views of the Phillips Curve

Writing in a Federal Reserve publication, Bennett McCallum, an economist at Carnegie Mellon University, argues that during the 1970s, the Fed was "acting under the influence of 1960s academic ideas that posited the existence of a long-run and exploitable Phillips-type tradeoff between inflation and unemployment rates." What does McCallum mean by a "long-run and exploitable Phillips-type tradeoff"? How would the Fed have attempted to exploit this long-run trade-off? What would be the consequences for the inflation rate?

## Solving the Problem

**Step 1:** **Review the chapter material.** This problem is about the relationship between the short-run and long-run Phillips curves, so you may want to review the section "The Short-Run and Long-Run Phillips Curves," which begins on page 957.

**Step 2:** **Explain what a "long-run exploitable Phillips-type tradeoff" means.** A "long-run exploitable Phillips-type tradeoff" means a Phillips curve that in the long run is downward sloping rather than vertical. An "exploitable" trade-off is one that the Fed could take advantage of to *permanently* reduce unemployment, at the expense of higher inflation, or to permanently reduce inflation, at the expense of higher unemployment.

**Step 3:** **Explain how the inflation rate will accelerate if the Fed tries to exploit a long-run trade-off between unemployment and inflation.** As we have seen, during the 1960s, the Fed conducted expansionary monetary policies to move up what it thought was a stationary short-run Phillips curve. By the late 1960s, these policies resulted in very low unemployment rates. In the long run, there is no stable trade-off between unemployment and inflation. Attempting to permanently keep the unemployment rate at very low levels leads to a rising inflation rate, which is what happened in the late 1960s and early 1970s.

Based on Bennett T. McCallum, "Recent Developments in Monetary Policy Analysis: The Roles of Theory and Evidence," Federal Reserve Bank of Richmond, *Economic Quarterly*, Winter 2002, p. 73.

**Your Turn:** For more practice, do related problem 2.6 on page 978 at the end of this chapter.

MyEconLab

# Expectations of the Inflation Rate and Monetary Policy

**28.3 LEARNING** OBJECTIVE

Discuss how expectations of the inflation rate affect monetary policy.

How long can the economy remain at a point that is on the short-run Phillips curve but not on the long-run Phillips curve? It depends on how quickly workers and firms adjust their expectations of future inflation to changes in current inflation. The experience in the United States over the past 60 years indicates that how workers and firms adjust their expectations of inflation depends on how high the inflation rate is. There are three possibilities:

- *Low inflation.* When the inflation rate is low, as it was during most of the 1950s, the early 1960s, the 1990s, and the 2000s, workers and firms tend to ignore it. For example, if the inflation rate is low, a restaurant may not want to pay for printing new menus that would show slightly higher prices.

- *Moderate but stable inflation.* For the four-year period from 1968 to 1971, the inflation rate in the United States stayed in the narrow range between 4 percent and

5 percent. This rate was high enough that workers and firms could not ignore it without seeing their real wages and profits decline. It was also likely that the next year's inflation rate would be very close to the current year's inflation rate. In fact, workers and firms during the 1960s acted as if they expected changes in the inflation rate during one year to continue into the following year. People are said to have *adaptive expectations* of inflation if they assume that future rates of inflation will follow the pattern of rates of inflation in the recent past.

- *High and unstable inflation.* Inflation rates above 5 percent during peacetime have been rare in U.S. history, but the inflation rate was above 5 percent every year from 1973 through 1982. Not only was the inflation rate high during these years, it was also unstable—rising from 6 percent in 1973 to 11 percent in 1974, before falling below 6 percent in 1976 and rising again to 13.5 percent in 1980. In the mid-1970s, Nobel Laureates Robert Lucas of the University of Chicago and Thomas Sargent of New York University argued that the gains to accurately forecasting inflation had dramatically increased. Workers and firms that failed to correctly anticipate the fluctuations in inflation during these years could experience substantial declines in real wages and profits. Therefore, Lucas and Sargent argued, people should use all available information when forming their expectations of future inflation. Expectations formed by using all available information about an economic variable are called **rational expectations**.

**Rational expectations** Expectations formed by using all available information about an economic variable.

## The Effect of Rational Expectations on Monetary Policy

Lucas and Sargent pointed out an important consequence of rational expectations: An expansionary monetary policy would not work. In other words, there might not be a trade-off between unemployment and inflation, even in the short run. By the mid-1970s, most economists had accepted the idea that an expansionary monetary policy could cause the actual inflation rate to be higher than the expected inflation rate. This gap between actual and expected inflation would cause the actual real wage to fall below the expected real wage, and the unemployment rate would be pushed below the natural rate. The economy's short-run equilibrium would move up the short-run Phillips curve.

Lucas and Sargent argued that this explanation of the Phillips curve assumed that workers and firms either ignored inflation or used adaptive expectations in making their forecasts of inflation. If workers and firms have rational expectations, they will use all available information, *including knowledge of the effects of Federal Reserve policy*. If workers and firms know that an expansionary monetary policy will raise the inflation rate, they should use this information in their forecasts of inflation. If they do, an expansionary monetary policy will not cause the actual inflation rate to be above the expected inflation rate. Instead, the actual inflation rate will equal the expected inflation rate, the actual real wage will equal the expected real wage, and the unemployment rate will not fall below the natural rate.

Figure 28.8 illustrates this argument. Suppose the economy begins at point *A*, where the short-run Phillips curve intersects the long-run Phillips curve. The actual and expected inflation rates are both equal to 1.5 percent, and the unemployment rate equals the natural rate of 5 percent. Then suppose the Fed engages in an expansionary monetary policy. If workers ignore inflation or if they form their expectations adaptively, the expansionary monetary policy will cause the actual inflation rate to be higher than the expected inflation rate, and the short-run equilibrium will move from point *A* on the short-run Phillips curve to point *B*. The inflation rate will rise to 4.5 percent, and the unemployment rate will fall to 3.5 percent. The decline in unemployment will be only temporary, however. Eventually, workers and firms will adjust to the fact that the actual inflation rate is 4.5 percent, not the 1.5 percent they had expected. The short-run Phillips curve will shift up, and the unemployment rate will return to 5 percent at point *C*.

Lucas and Sargent argued that if workers and firms have rational expectations, they will realize that the Fed's expansionary policy will result in an inflation rate of

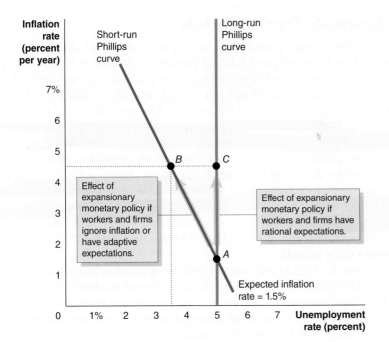

**Figure 28.8**

**Rational Expectations
and the Phillips Curve**

If workers and firms ignore inflation, or
if they have adaptive expectations, an expansionary monetary policy will cause the
short-run equilibrium to move from point *A*
on the short-run Phillips curve to point *B*;
inflation will rise, and unemployment will
fall. If workers and firms have rational expectations, an expansionary monetary
policy will cause the short-run equilibrium
to move up the long-run Phillips curve from
point *A* to point *C*. Inflation will still rise, but
there will be no change in unemployment.

4.5 percent. Therefore, as soon as the Fed announces its new policy, workers and firms
should adjust their expectations of inflation from 1.5 percent to 4.5 percent. There will
be no temporary decrease in the real wage, leading to a temporary increase in employment and real GDP. Instead, the short-run equilibrium will move immediately from
point *A* to point *C* on the long-run Phillips curve. The unemployment rate will never
drop below 5 percent, and the *short-run* Phillips curve will be vertical.

## Is the Short-Run Phillips Curve Really Vertical?

The claim by Lucas and Sargent that the short-run Phillips curve is vertical and that
an expansionary monetary policy cannot reduce the unemployment rate below the
natural rate surprised many economists. An obvious objection to the argument of
Lucas and Sargent was that the record of the 1950s and 1960s seemed to show that
there was a short-run trade-off between unemployment and inflation and that, therefore, the short-run Phillips curve was downward sloping and not vertical. Lucas and
Sargent argued that the apparent short-run trade-off was actually the result of *unexpected* changes in monetary policy. During those years, the Fed did not announce
changes in policy, so workers, firms, and financial markets had to *guess* when the Fed
had begun using a new policy. In that case, an expansionary monetary policy might
cause the unemployment rate to fall because workers and firms would be taken by
surprise, and their expectations of inflation would be too low. Lucas and Sargent
argued that a policy that was announced ahead of time would not cause a change in
unemployment.

Many economists have remained skeptical of the argument that the short-run
Phillips curve is vertical. The two main objections raised are that (1) workers and firms
actually may not have rational expectations, and (2) the rapid adjustment of wages and
prices needed for the short-run Phillips curve to be vertical will not actually take place.
Many economists doubt that people are able to use information on the Fed's monetary
policy to make reliable forecasts of the inflation rate. If workers and firms do not know
what effect an expansionary monetary policy will have on the inflation rate, the actual
real wage may still end up being lower than the expected real wage. Also, firms may
have contracts with their workers and suppliers that keep wages and prices from adjusting quickly. If wages and prices adjust slowly, then even if workers and firms have
rational expectations, an expansionary monetary policy may still be able to reduce the
unemployment rate in the short run.

## Real Business Cycle Models

During the 1980s, some economists, including Nobel Laureates Finn Kydland of Carnegie Mellon University and Edward Prescott of Arizona State University, argued that Robert Lucas was correct in assuming that workers and firms formed their expectations rationally and that wages and prices adjust quickly but that Lucas was wrong in assuming that fluctuations in real GDP are caused by unexpected changes in the money supply. Instead, Kydland and Prescott argued that fluctuations in "real" factors, particularly *technology shocks*, explain deviations of real GDP from its potential level. Technology shocks are changes to the economy that make it possible to produce either more output—a positive shock—or less output—a negative shock—with the same number of workers, machines, and other inputs. Real GDP will be above its previous potential level following a positive technology shock and below its previous potential level following a negative technology shock. Because these models focus on real factors—rather than on changes in the money supply—to explain fluctuations in real GDP, they are known as **real business cycle models**.

**Real business cycle models** Models that focus on real rather than monetary explanations of fluctuations in real GDP.

The approach of Lucas and Sargent and the real business cycle models are sometimes grouped together under the label *the new classical macroeconomics* because these approaches share the assumptions that people have rational expectations and that wages and prices adjust rapidly. Some of the assumptions of the new classical macroeconomics are similar to those held by economists before the Great Depression of the 1930s. John Maynard Keynes, in his 1936 book *The General Theory of Employment, Interest, and Money*, referred to these earlier economists as "classical economists." Like the classical economists, the new classical macroeconomists believe that the economy will normally be at its potential level.

Economists who find the assumptions of rational expectations and rapid adjustment of wages and prices appealing are likely to accept the real business cycle model approach. Other economists are skeptical of these models because the models explain recessions as being caused by negative technology shocks. Negative technology shocks are uncommon and, apart from the oil price increases of the 1970s, real business cycle theorists have had difficulty identifying shocks that would have been large enough to cause recessions. Some economists have begun to develop real business cycle models that allow for the possibility that changes in the money supply may affect the level of real GDP. If real business cycle models continue to develop along these lines, they may eventually converge with the approaches the Fed uses.

**28.4 LEARNING** OBJECTIVE

Use a Phillips curve graph to show how the Federal Reserve can permanently lower the inflation rate.

# Federal Reserve Policy from the 1970s to the Present

We have already seen that the high inflation rates of the late 1960s and early 1970s were due in part to the Federal Reserve's attempts to keep the unemployment rate below the natural rate. By the mid-1970s, the Fed also had to deal with the inflationary impact of the Organization of the Petroleum Exporting Countries (OPEC) oil price increases. By the late 1970s, as the Fed attempted to deal with the problem of high and worsening inflation rates, it received conflicting policy advice. Many economists argued that the inflation rate could be reduced only at the cost of a temporary increase in the unemployment rate. Followers of the Lucas–Sargent rational expectations approach, however, argued that a painless reduction in the inflation rate was possible. Before analyzing the actual policies used by the Fed, we can look at why the oil price increases of the mid-1970s made the inflation rate worse.

## The Effect of a Supply Shock on the Phillips Curve

As we saw in Chapter 24, the increases in oil prices in 1974 resulting from actions by OPEC caused the short-run aggregate supply curve to shift to the left. This shift is shown in panel (a) of Figure 28.9. (For simplicity, in this panel, we use the basic

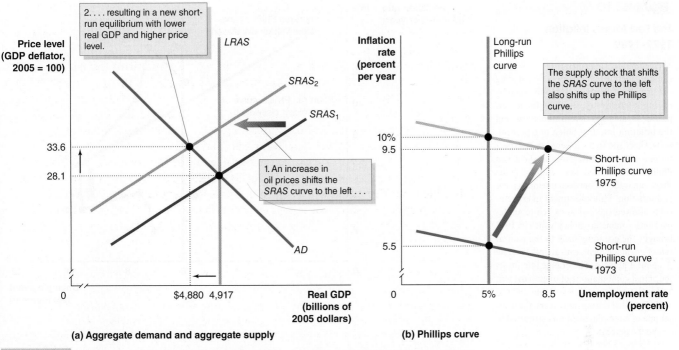

**Figure 28.9**    A Supply Shock Shifts the *SRAS* Curve and the Short-Run Phillips Curve

When OPEC increased the price of a barrel of oil from less than $3 to more than $10, in panel (a), the *SRAS* curve shifted to the left. Between 1973 and 1975, real GDP declined from $4,917 billion to $4,880 billion, and the price level rose from 28.1 to 33.6. Panel (b) shows that the supply shock shifted up the Phillips curve.

In 1973, the U.S. economy had an inflation rate of about 5.5 percent and an unemployment rate of about 5 percent. By 1975, the inflation rate had risen to about 9.5 percent and the unemployment rate to about 8.5 percent.

rather than dynamic *AD–AS* model.) The result was a higher price level and a lower level of real GDP. On a Phillips curve graph—panel (b) of Figure 28.9—we can shift the short-run Phillips curve up to show that the inflation rate and unemployment rate both increased.

As the Phillips curve shifted up, the economy moved from an unemployment rate of about 5 percent and an inflation rate of about 5.5 percent in 1973 to an unemployment rate of 8.5 percent and an inflation rate of about 9.5 percent in 1975. This combination of rising unemployment and rising inflation placed the Federal Reserve in a difficult position. If the Fed used an expansionary monetary policy to fight the high unemployment rate, the *AD* curve would shift to the right, and the economy's equilibrium would move up the short-run Phillips curve. Real GDP would increase, and the unemployment rate would fall—but at the cost of higher inflation. If the Fed used a contractionary monetary policy to fight the high inflation rate, the *AD* curve would shift to the left, and the economy's equilibrium would move down the short-run Phillips curve. As a result, real GDP would fall, and the inflation rate would be reduced—but at the cost of higher unemployment. In the end, the Fed chose to fight high unemployment with an expansionary monetary policy, even though that decision worsened the inflation rate.

## Paul Volcker and Disinflation

By the late 1970s, the Federal Reserve had gone through a two-decade period of continually increasing the rate of growth of the money supply. In August 1979, President Jimmy Carter appointed Paul Volcker as chairman of the Board of Governors of the Federal Reserve System. Along with most other economists, Volcker was convinced that high inflation rates were damaging the economy. To reduce inflation, Volcker began reducing the annual growth rate of the money supply. This contractionary monetary policy raised interest rates, causing a decline in aggregate demand. Figure 28.10 uses the

**Figure 28.10**

## The Fed Tames Inflation, 1979–1989

The Fed, under Chairman Paul Volcker, began fighting inflation in 1979 by reducing the growth of the money supply, thereby raising interest rates. By 1982, the unemployment rate had risen to 10 percent, and the inflation rate had fallen to 6 percent. As workers and firms lowered their expectations of future inflation, the short-run Phillips curve shifted down, improving the short-run trade-off between unemployment and inflation. This adjustment in expectations allowed the Fed to switch to an expansionary monetary policy, which by 1987 brought the economy back to the natural rate of unemployment, with an inflation rate of about 4 percent. The orange line shows the actual combinations of unemployment and inflation for each year from 1979 to 1989. Note that during these years, the natural rate of unemployment was estimated to be about 6 percent.

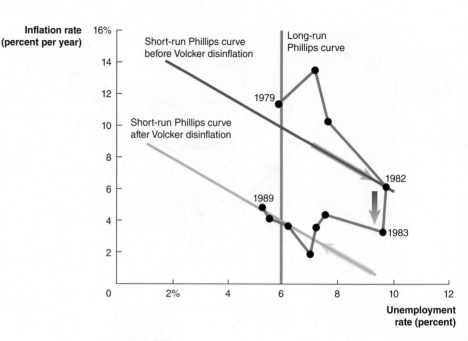

**Disinflation** A significant reduction in the inflation rate.

Phillips curve model to analyze the movements in unemployment and inflation from 1979 to 1989.

The Fed's contractionary monetary policy shifted the economy's short-run equilibrium down the short-run Phillips curve, lowering the inflation rate from 11 percent in 1979 to 6 percent in 1982—but at a cost of raising the unemployment rate from 6 percent to 10 percent. As workers and firms lowered their expectations of future inflation, the short-run Phillips curve shifted down, improving the short-run trade-off between unemployment and inflation. This adjustment in expectations allowed the Fed to switch to an expansionary monetary policy. By 1987, the economy was back to the natural rate of unemployment, which during these years was about 6 percent. The orange line in Figure 28.10 shows the actual combinations of unemployment and inflation for each year from 1979 to 1989.

Under Volcker's leadership, the Fed had reduced the inflation rate from more than 10 percent to less than 5 percent. The inflation rate has generally remained below 5 percent ever since. A significant reduction in the inflation rate is called **disinflation**. In fact, this episode is often referred to as the "Volcker disinflation." The disinflation had come at a very high price, however. From September 1982 through June 1983, the unemployment rate was above 10 percent, the first time this had happened since the end of the Great Depression of the 1930s.

Some economists argue that the Volcker disinflation provided evidence against the view that workers and firms have rational expectations. Volcker's announcement in October 1979 that he planned to use a contractionary monetary policy to bring down the inflation rate was widely publicized. If workers and firms had rational expectations, we might have expected them to have quickly reduced their expectations of future inflation. The economy should have moved smoothly down the long-run Phillips curve. As we have seen, however, the economy moved down the existing short-run Phillips curve, and only after several years of high unemployment did the Phillips curve shift down. Apparently, workers and firms had adaptive expectations—only changing their expectations of future inflation after the current inflation rate had fallen.

Robert Lucas and Thomas Sargent argue, however, that a less painful disinflation would have occurred if workers and firms had *believed* Volcker's announcement that he was fighting inflation. The problem was that previous Fed chairmen had made similar promises throughout the 1970s, but inflation had continued to get worse. By 1979, the

# Don't Let This Happen to You

## Don't Confuse Disinflation with Deflation

Disinflation refers to a decline in the *inflation rate*. *Deflation* refers to a decline in the *price level*. Paul Volcker and the Federal Reserve brought about a substantial disinflation in the United States during the years between 1979 and 1983. The inflation rate fell from over 11 percent in 1979 to below 5 percent in 1984. Yet even in 1984, there was no deflation: The price level was still rising—but at a slower rate.

The last period of significant deflation in the United States was in the early 1930s, during the Great Depression. The following table shows the consumer price index for each of those years.

Because the price level fell each year from 1929 to 1933, there was deflation.

| Year | Consumer Price Index | Deflation Rate |
|------|---------------------|----------------|
| 1929 | 17.1 | — |
| 1930 | 16.7 | −2.3% |
| 1931 | 15.2 | −9.0 |
| 1932 | 13.7 | −9.9 |
| 1933 | 13.0 | −5.1 |

MyEconLab

**Your Turn:** Test your understanding by doing related problem 4.5 on page 980 at the end of this chapter.

credibility of the Fed was at a low point. Some support for Lucas's and Sargent's argument comes from surveys of business economists at the time, which showed that they also reduced their forecasts of future inflation only slowly, even though they were well aware of Volcker's announcement of a new policy.

# Solved Problem 28.4

## Using Monetary Policy to Lower the Inflation Rate

Consider the following hypothetical situation: The economy is currently at the natural rate of unemployment of 5 percent. The actual inflation rate is 6 percent, and, because it has remained at 6 percent for several years, this is also the rate that workers and firms expect to see in the future. The

Federal Reserve decides to reduce the inflation rate permanently to 2 percent. How can the Fed use monetary policy to achieve this objective? Be sure to use a Phillips curve graph in your answer.

## Solving the Problem

**Step 1: Review the chapter material.** This problem is about using a Phillips curve graph to show how the Fed can fight inflation, so you may want to review the section "Paul Volcker and Disinflation," which begins on page 965.

**Step 2: Explain how the Fed can use monetary policy to reduce the inflation rate.** To reduce the inflation rate significantly, the Fed will have to raise the target for the federal funds rate. Higher interest rates will reduce aggregate demand, raise unemployment, and move the economy's equilibrium down the short-run Phillips curve.

**Step 3: Illustrate your argument with a Phillips curve graph.** How much the unemployment rate would have to rise to drive down the inflation rate from 6 percent to 2 percent depends on the steepness of the short-run Phillips curve.

Here we have assumed that the unemployment rate would have to rise from 5 percent to 7 percent.

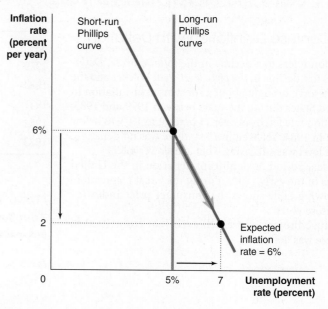

**Step 4:** **Show on your graph the reduction in the inflation rate from 6 percent to 2 percent.** For the decline in the inflation rate to be permanent, the expected inflation rate has to decline from 6 percent to 2 percent. We can show this decline on our graph:

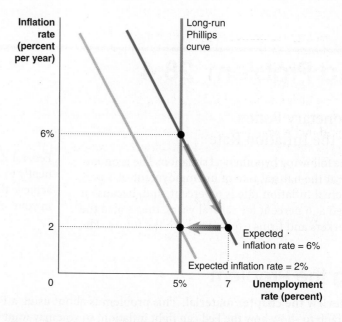

Once the short-run Phillips curve has shifted down, the Fed can use an expansionary monetary policy to push the economy back to the natural rate of unemployment. This policy is similar to the one carried out by the Fed after Paul Volcker became chairman in 1979. The downside to these policies of disinflation is that they lead to significant increases in unemployment.

**Extra Credit:** A follower of the new classical macroeconomics approach would have a more optimistic view of the consequences of using monetary policy to lower the inflation rate from 6 percent to 2 percent. According to this approach, the Fed's policy announcement should cause people to immediately revise downward their expectations of future inflation from 6 percent to 2 percent. The economy's short-run equilibrium would move directly down the long-run Phillips curve from an inflation rate of 6 percent to an inflation rate of 2 percent, while keeping the unemployment rate constant at 5 percent. For the reasons discussed in this chapter, many economists are skeptical that disinflation can be brought about so painlessly.

**Your Turn:** For more practice, do related problems 4.7 and 4.8 on page 980 at the end of this chapter.

MyEconLab

## Alan Greenspan, Ben Bernanke, and the Crisis in Monetary Policy

President Ronald Reagan appointed Alan Greenspan to succeed Paul Volcker as Fed chairman in 1987. Greenspan served a term of more than 18 years. When he stepped down in January 2006, President George W. Bush appointed Ben Bernanke to take his place. Like Volcker, Greenspan and Bernanke were determined to keep the inflation rate low. Table 28.3 shows that the average annual inflation rate was lower during Greenspan's term and Bernanke's term through late 2011 than it had been during the terms of their three most immediate predecessors. Under Greenspan's leadership of the Fed, inflation was reduced nearly to the low levels experienced during the term of Chairman William McChesney Martin in the 1950s and 1960s. Greenspan's term was marked by only two short and mild recessions, in 1990–1991 and 2001. When Greenspan left office in 2006, he was widely applauded by economists, policymakers, and the media.

But with the severity of the 2007–2009 recession, some critics questioned whether decisions made by the Fed under Greenspan's leadership might have played a role in bringing on the crisis. We will discuss those arguments after briefly reviewing two other developments in monetary policy during the past 20 years:

- *Deemphasizing the money supply.* Greenspan's term was notable for the Fed's continued movement away from using the money supply as a monetary policy target. We saw in Chapter 25 that during the 1980s and 1990s, the close relationship between growth in the money supply and inflation broke down. Before 1987, the Fed would announce annual targets for how much M1 and M2 would increase during the year. In February 1987, near the end of Paul Volcker's term, the Fed announced that it would no longer set targets for M1. In July 1993, Alan Greenspan announced that the Fed also would no longer set targets for M2. Instead, the Federal Open Market Committee (FOMC) has relied on setting targets for the federal funds rate to meet its goals of price stability and high employment.

- *The importance of Fed credibility.* The Fed learned an important lesson during the 1970s: Workers, firms, and investors in stock and bond markets have to view Fed announcements as credible if monetary policy is to be effective. As inflation

**Table 28.3**

**The Record of Fed Chairmen and Inflation**

| Federal Reserve Chairman | Term | Average Annual Inflation Rate During Term |
|---|---|---|
| William McChesney Martin | April 1951–January 1970 | 2.2% |
| Arthur Burns | February 1970–January 1978 | 6.5 |
| G. William Miller | March 1978–August 1979 | 9.1 |
| Paul Volcker | August 1979–August 1987 | 6.2 |
| Alan Greenspan | August 1987–January 2006 | 3.1 |
| Ben Bernanke | January 2006– | 2.4 |

*Note:* Data for Bernanke are through October 2011.
Data from U.S. Bureau of Labor Statistics; and Federal Reserve Board of Governors.

worsened throughout the late 1960s and the 1970s, the Fed announced repeatedly that it would take actions to reduce inflation. In fact, policies were either not implemented or were ineffective, and inflation rose. These repeated failures to follow through on announced policies had greatly reduced the Fed's credibility by the time Paul Volcker took office in August 1979. The contractionary monetary policy that the Fed announced in October 1979 had less effect on the expectations of workers, firms, and investors than it would have had if the Fed's credibility had been greater. It took a severe recession to convince people that this time, the inflation rate really was coming down. Only then were workers willing to accept lower nominal wage increases, banks willing to accept lower interest rates on mortgage loans, and investors willing to accept lower interest rates on bonds.

Over the past two decades, the Fed has taken steps to enhance its credibility. Most importantly, whenever a change in Fed policy has been announced, the change has actually taken place. In addition, Greenspan revised the previous Fed policy of keeping secret the target for the federal funds rate. Since February 1994, any change in the target rate has been announced at the conclusion of the FOMC meeting at which the change is made. In addition, the minutes of the FOMC meetings are now made public after a brief delay. In February 2000, the Fed helped make its intentions for future policy clearer by announcing at the end of each FOMC meeting whether it considered the economy in the future to be at greater risk of higher inflation or of recession. In 2011, Ben Bernanke held a press conference following an FOMC meeting, which was the first time a Fed chair had done so.

**The Decision to Intervene in the Failure of Long-Term Capital Management** Greenspan's ability to help guide the economy through a long period of economic stability and his moves to enhance Fed credibility were widely applauded. However, two actions by the Fed during Greenspan's term have been identified as possibly contributing to the financial crisis that increased the length and severity of the 2007–2009 recession. One was the decision during 1998 to help save the hedge fund Long-Term Capital Management (LTCM). Hedge funds raise money, typically from wealthy investors, and use sophisticated investment strategies that often involve significant risk. Hedge funds generally rely heavily on borrowing in order to leverage their investments, thereby increasing potential returns. LTCM included as partners Robert Merton and Myron Scholes, who had both been awarded the Nobel Prize in Economics.

In the spring of 1998, LTCM suffered heavy losses on several of its investments, partly because the Russian government announced it would no longer make payments on some of its bonds, causing their value to plummet. Other financial firms that had loaned money to LTCM feared that the hedge fund would go bankrupt and began to push for repayment of their loans. We saw in Chapter 25 that a run on a financial firm can cause widespread problems in the financial system. If LTCM had been forced to quickly sell all of its investments, the prices of the securities it owned would have declined, causing problems for other financial firms that held the same securities. The Fed was concerned that a sudden failure of LTCM might lead to failures of other financial firms. With the support of Alan Greenspan, William McDonough, president of the Federal Reserve Bank of New York, held a meeting between the management of LTCM and the other financial firms to which LTCM owed money. The other firms were persuaded to give LTCM enough time to slowly sell off—or "unwind"—its investments to keep the prices of those investments from falling too rapidly and to avoid a financial panic.

The Fed's actions succeeded in avoiding wider damage from LTCM's failure, but some critics argued that the Fed's intervention had negative consequences in the long run because it allowed the owners of LTCM and the firms that had loaned LTCM money to avoid the full consequences of LTCM's failed investments. These critics argued that the Fed's intervention set the stage for other firms—particularly highly leveraged investment banks and hedge funds—to take on excessive risk, with the expectation that the Fed would intervene on their behalf should they suffer heavy losses on the investments.

Although some critics see the Fed's actions in the case of LTCM as encouraging the excessive risk taking that helped result in the financial crisis of 2007–2009, other observers doubt that the behavior of managers of financial firms were much affected by the Fed's actions.

### The Decision to Keep the Target for the Federal Funds Rate at 1 Percent from June 2003 to June 2004

In response to the popping of the dot-com stock bubble in the spring of 2000, the beginning of a recession in March 2001, and the terrorist attacks of September 11, 2001, the Fed successively lowered the target for the federal funds rate. The target rate was cut in a series of steps from 6.5 percent in May 2000 to 1 percent in June 2003. The target remained at 1 percent until it was raised to 1.25 percent in June 2004. The Fed's decision to continue cutting the target for the federal funds rate for more than 18 months after the end of the recession in November 2001 and to keep the rate at 1 percent for another year has been criticized. At the time, the FOMC argued that although the recession of 2001 was mild, the very low inflation rates of late 2001 and 2002 raised the possibility that the U.S. economy could slip into a period of deflation. As we discussed in Chapter 26, deflation can damage the economy by raising real interest rates and by causing consumers to postpone purchases, based on the expectation that future prices will be lower than current prices.

Critics argued, though, that by keeping interest rates low for an extended period, the Fed helped to fuel the housing bubble that eventually deflated beginning in 2006, with disastrous results for the economy. We have seen that the origins of the housing bubble are complex and that contributing factors included the increase in securitization of mortgages, the willingness of banks and other lenders to give loans to subprime and Alt-A borrowers, and the widespread use of adjustable-rate mortgages that allowed borrowers to qualify for larger loans than would have been possible using conventional mortgages. Economists will continue to debate whether the Fed's policy of keeping the target for the federal funds rate very low for an extended period caused the housing bubble.

## Has the Fed Lost Its Independence?

The financial crisis of 2007–2009 led the Fed to move well beyond the federal funds rate as the focus of monetary policy. With the target federal funds rate having been driven to zero without much expansionary effect on the economy, some observers began to speak of a "crisis in monetary policy." We reviewed the Fed's new policy initiatives in Chapters 25 and 26. Like other policies that represent a sharp break with the past, the Fed's actions had both supporters and critics. At this point, we can review the debate over whether the Fed's policy actions reduced its independence. The Fed worked closely with the Treasury Department in arranging to inject funds into the commercial banking system by taking partial ownership of some banks and in several other policy actions. Typically, the chairman of the Fed has formulated policy independently of the secretary of the Treasury, who is a political appointee and can be replaced at any time by the president of the United States. Close collaboration between the Fed and the Treasury, were it to continue, raises the question of whether the Fed will be able to pursue policies independent from those of the administration in power. In addition, by 2011, the Fed's extensive interventions in the financial system had led members of Congress to scrutinize—and in many cases, criticize—Fed policy to an unusual degree. Some observers worried that this intense congressional oversight might limit the Fed's freedom of action in the future.

The main reason to keep the Fed—or any country's central bank—independent of the rest of the government is to avoid inflation. Whenever a government is spending more than it is collecting in taxes, it must borrow the difference by selling bonds. The governments of many developing countries have difficulty finding anyone other than their central bank to buy their bonds. The more bonds the central bank buys, the faster the money supply grows, and the higher the inflation rate will be. Even in developed countries, governments that control their central banks may be tempted to sell bonds to the central bank rather than to the public.

### The More Independent the Central Bank, the Lower the Inflation Rate

For 16 high-income countries, the greater the degree of central bank independence from the rest of the government, the lower the inflation rate. Central bank independence is measured by an index ranging from 1 (minimum independence) to 4 (maximum independence). During these years, Germany had a high index of independence of 4 and a low average inflation rate of just over 3 percent. New Zealand had a low index of independence of 1 and a high average inflation rate of over 7 percent.

"Central Bank Independence and Macroeconomic Performance: Some Comparative Evidence" by Alberto Alesina and Lawrence H. Summer from the *Journal of Money, Credit and Banking*, Vol. 25, No. 2, May 1993. Copyright © 1993 by the Ohio State University. Reprinted by permission.

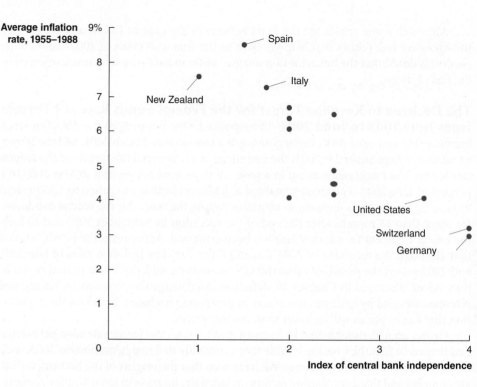

Another fear is that if the government controls the central bank, it may use that control to further its political interests. It is difficult in any democratic country for a government to be reelected at a time of high unemployment. If the government controls the central bank, it may be tempted just before an election to increase the money supply and drive down interest rates to increase production and employment. In the United States, for example, a president who had direct control over the Fed might be tempted to increase the money supply just before running for reelection, even if doing so led in the long run to higher inflation and accompanying economic costs.

We might expect that the more independent a country's central bank is, the lower the inflation rate in the country and the less independent a country's central bank, the higher the inflation rate. In a classic study, Alberto Alesina and Lawrence Summers, who were both at the time economists at Harvard University, tested this idea by comparing the degree of central bank independence and the inflation rate for 16 high-income countries during the years 1955–1988. Figure 28.11 shows the results.

Countries with highly independent central banks, such as the United States, Switzerland, and Germany, had lower inflation rates than countries whose central banks had little independence, such as New Zealand, Italy, and Spain. In the past few years, New Zealand and Canada have granted their banks more independence, at least partly to better fight inflation.

Whether the changes in the Fed's policies and procedures during and after the 2007–2009 recession will have lasting effects on its independence remains to be seen.

Continued from page 951

## Economics in Your Life

### Is It Wise to Delay a Job Search?

At the beginning of the chapter, we posed this question: What advice would you give someone who has decided to wait nearly two years to look for a new job? As we discussed in the chapter, evidence shows that many of those who are unemployed for longer than a year or two find it more difficult to find new employment than if they searched for a new job soon after they were laid off. The longer workers are unemployed, especially in a high-technology field, the more their skills deteriorate. By delaying her job search, your friend risks being unemployed for longer than two years. Eventually, she may have to be retrained or take additional courses in a different field in order to find a job. Tell your friend to start her job search right away!

# Conclusion

The workings of the contemporary economy are complex. The attempts by the Federal Reserve to keep the U.S. economy near the natural rate of unemployment with a low rate of inflation have not always been successful. Economists continue to debate the best way for the Fed to proceed.

*An Inside Look at Policy* on the next page discusses the challenges the Federal Reserve faces in trying to reduce unemployment without increasing inflation.

# Can the Fed Balance the Trade-off between Unemployment and Inflation?

## NEWSWEEK

### Ben Bernanke's Bet on Jobs and Inflation

Federal Reserve Chairman Ben Bernanke glided smoothly through his first regular news conference the other day—an event both remarkable and unremarkable. It was remarkable for symbolizing the Fed's ongoing transformation from a citadel of secrecy into an agency that tries to explain itself to the public. "The original attitude . . . was that it was no one's business what they did—and if you wanted to figure it out, do so yourself," says economist Allan Meltzer, author of a history of the Fed. Until now, there had been no news conferences, a legacy of the tight-lipped past.

**(a)** What was unremarkable is that reporters' questions focused on an old issue: How much can the Fed reduce unemployment without stoking inflation? Bernanke's bet is: a lot. He's embraced super-easy credit to cut the appalling 8.8 percent jobless rate; that's 13.5 million people, nearly half out of work for six months or more. Since late 2008, the Fed has held short-term interest rates near zero. To cut long-term rates, the Fed is buying gobs of Treasury bonds and mortgage securities: $1.725 trillion from late 2008 to March 2010; an additional $600 billion from last November through June. These purchases are known as QE1 and QE2, for "quantitative easing."

But there's a growing debate about whether all the pump-priming is helping recovery or simply fostering inflation. The economy's fate may hang on who's right. Studies by Fed economists are, not surprisingly, supportive. One estimated that QE1 and QE2 lowered long-term interest rates by about 0.5 percentage points and saved nearly 3 million jobs; the jobless rate otherwise could have approached 11 percent. Many private economists are less impressed; they suspect the benefits of QE1 faded with QE2. . . .

**(b)** Meanwhile, inflation creeps up. Over the past year, the consumer price index rose 2.7 percent; six months earlier, the year-over-year gain was only 1.2 percent. Bernanke blames higher oil and food prices, reflecting temporary factors (the war in Libya, poor harvests) that may be reversed. The danger of an inflationary wage-price spiral, goes this argument, is negligible because unemployment is high and pay is stagnant.

Maybe. But inflation's dynamics might be changing. Here's why. The recession caused enormous factory and business closures; now, there's less capacity to meet rising demand. Companies have more power to raise prices; a depreciating dollar compounds the effect by making imports more expensive. . . .

The problem might become more widespread. The Fed regularly measures manufacturers' production capacity. From 2007 to 2010, it fell 5.4 percent. That's the largest drop since

the statistics began being kept in 1948; the only other annual decline occurred in 2003 and was a scant 0.25 percent.

**(c)** The Fed is attacked from both the left (for doing too little to create jobs) and the right (for doing too much and tempting inflation), notes former Fed vice chairman Donald Kohn. Bernanke aims for a middle course. One argument for a less secretive Fed is this: Investors, managers and workers who better understand the Fed's goals won't futilely try to defy them. The Fed's very commitment to low inflation will restrain wages and prices. Up to a point, this may be true. But public relations alone won't control behavior. Actions outrank intentions.

The lesson of the 1970s' great inflation (13 percent in 1980) is that once prices begin to rise consistently, they feed on themselves. The fallout is disastrous. People and companies can't plan for the future; recessions become more frequent. Unexpectedly high inflation would probably doom today's cheap credit policy. The Fed would have to raise rates. Criticism from both left and right would intensify. So, much is riding on Bernanke's bet: If he loses, we all lose.

## Key Points in the Article

In an effort to reduce the unemployment rate and increase real GDP, the Fed held its target for the federal funds rate close to zero for three years beginning in late 2008. The Fed also successfully lowered long-term interest rates with its quantitative easing programs. While Fed economists argue that the Fed's policies helped save nearly 3 million jobs, some economists are concerned that these policies did more to increase inflation than to assist the recovery. From mid-2010 to mid-2011, the consumer price index rose 2.7 percent, with the largest increase coming in the last six months. Some observers criticized Fed Chairman Ben Bernanke for not doing enough to lower unemployment, while others criticized him for doing too much and fanning the flames of inflation. Bernanke argues, however, that the Fed's recent policy actions will help reduce the unemployment rate without causing a significant increase in the inflation rate.

## Analyzing the News

**ⓐ** Fed Chairman Ben Bernanke argues that Fed policies that have reduced both short-term and long-term interest rates will be successful in lowering the high unemployment rate while keeping inflation in check. But some economists are convinced that monetary policy actions are doing less to improve the job situation and more to generate inflation. As you read in this chapter, A. W. Phillips discovered an inverse short-run relationship between the unemployment rate and the inflation rate. The figure below shows the short-run Phillips curve relationship from July 2008 through July 2011. For the months from July 2008 to July 2009, the Phillips curve relationship appears to fit the data well, as the unemployment rate rose from 5.8 percent to 9.5 percent while the inflation rate, measured by the percent change of the consumer price index, fell from 5.6 percent to −2.10 percent.

**ⓑ** The figure below also shows that from July 2009 to July 2011, the short-run

Phillips curve relationship is less clear, as the unemployment rate remained between 9 and 10 percent, while the inflation rate rose from −2.10 percent to 3.63 percent. The article states that the dynamics of inflation may be changing and prices may rise due to reduced capacity coupled with increasing demand. As you learned in this chapter, if a higher inflation rate becomes expected in the economy, the short-run Phillips curve will shift up, and the short-run trade-off between unemployment and inflation will take place at a higher inflation rate. In the figure, the data from July 2010 to July 2011 could be indicating that workers and firms are expecting the inflation rate to increase.

**ⓒ** Some critics argue that the Fed has not done enough to create jobs and others claim that the Fed's actions will generate inflation. However, Bernanke is sticking with the policy decisions he believes will boost employment while keeping inflation under control. By announcing these policies and moving forward with them, the Fed maintains its credibility and therefore has a better chance of meeting its goals.

## Thinking Critically about Policy

1. Suppose that the unemployment rate in mid-2011 was the same as it actually was, but the inflation rate during those months averaged 10 percent rather than the rate shown in the figure. What effect might the higher inflation rates have had on the Fed's monetary policy?

2. Suppose the unemployment rate is currently equal to the nonaccelerating inflation rate of unemployment (NAIRU) of 5 percent, and the inflation rate is 0 percent. If the Fed wants to raise the inflation rate permanently to 2 percent, what should it do? Explain your answer using a Phillips curve graph.

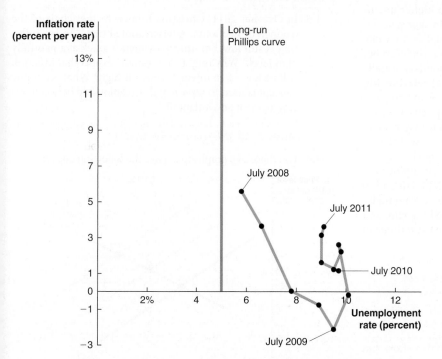

The short-run Phillips curve can be seen in the data for the period from July 2008 to July 2011.

# Chapter Summary and Problems

## Key Terms

Disinflation, p. 966

Natural rate of unemployment, p. 954

Nonaccelerating inflation rate of unemployment (NAIRU), p. 960

Phillips curve, p. 952

Rational expectations, p. 962

Real business cycle models, p. 964

Structural relationship, p. 954

---

**28.1** **The Discovery of the Short-Run Trade-off between Unemployment and Inflation,** pages 952–957

LEARNING OBJECTIVE: Describe the Phillips curve and the nature of the short-run trade-off between unemployment and inflation.

## Summary

The **Phillips curve** illustrates the short-run trade-off between the unemployment rate and the inflation rate. The inverse relationship between unemployment and inflation shown by the Phillips curve is consistent with the aggregate demand and aggregate supply analysis developed in Chapter 24. The aggregate demand and aggregate supply (AD–AS) model indicates that slow growth in aggregate demand leads to both higher unemployment and lower inflation, and rapid growth in aggregate demand leads to both lower unemployment and higher inflation. This relationship explains why there is a short-run trade-off between unemployment and inflation. Many economists initially believed that the Phillips curve was a **structural relationship** that depended on the basic behavior of consumers and firms and that remained unchanged over time. If the Phillips curve were a stable relationship, it would present policymakers with a menu of combinations of unemployment and inflation from which they could choose. Nobel Laureate Milton Friedman argued that there is a **natural rate of unemployment**, which is the unemployment rate that exists when the economy is at potential GDP and to which the economy always returns. As a result, there is no trade-off between unemployment and inflation in the long run, and the long-run Phillips curve is a vertical line at the natural rate of unemployment.

MyEconLab Visit **www.myeconlab.com** to complete these exercises online and get instant feedback.

## Review Questions

1.1 What is the Phillips curve? Draw a graph of a short-run Phillips curve.

1.2 What actions should the Fed take if it wants to move from a point on the short-run Phillips curve representing high unemployment and low inflation to a point representing lower unemployment and higher inflation?

1.3 Why did economists during the early 1960s think of the Phillips curve as a "policy menu"? Were they correct to think of it in this way? Briefly explain.

1.4 Why did Milton Friedman argue that the Phillips curve did not represent a permanent trade-off between unemployment and inflation? In your answer, be sure to explain what Friedman meant by the "natural rate of unemployment."

## Problems and Applications

1.5 In October 2011, Christina Romer, former chair of the Council of Economic Advisers, noted that, "Today, inflation is still low, but unemployment is stuck at a painfully high level." Why might we normally expect that inflation will be low when unemployment is high? What economic concept is used to represent this relationship between unemployment and inflation?

From Christina D. Romer, "Dear Ben: It's Time for Your Volcker Moment," *New York Times*, October 29, 2011.

1.6 Use these two graphs to answer the following questions:

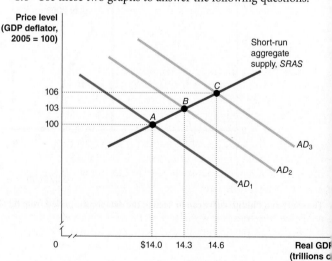

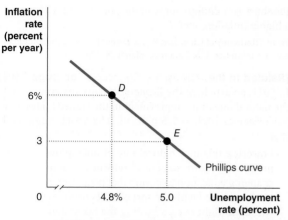

a. Briefly explain which point on the Phillips curve graph represents the same economic situation as point *B* on the aggregate demand and aggregate supply graph.

b. Briefly explain which point on the Phillips curve graph represents the same economic situation as point *C* on the aggregate demand and aggregate supply graph.

1.7 Given that the Phillips curve is derived from the aggregate demand and aggregate supply model, why do we use the Phillips curve analysis? What benefits does the Phillips curve analysis offer compared to the aggregate demand and aggregate supply model?

1.8 Briefly explain whether you agree with the following statement: "Any economic relationship that changes as economic policy changes is not a structural relationship."

1.9 In macroeconomics courses in the 1960s and early 1970s, some economists argued that one of the U.S. political parties was willing to have higher unemployment in order to achieve lower inflation and that the other major political party was willing to have higher inflation in order to achieve lower unemployment. Why might such views of the trade-off between inflation and unemployment have existed in the 1960s? Why are such views rare today?

1.10 General Juan Perón, the former dictator of Argentina, once said of the labor market in his country, "Prices have gone up the elevator, and wages have had to use the stairs." In this situation, what was happening to real wages in Argentina? Was unemployment likely to have been relatively high or relatively low?

From Robert J. Shiller, "Why Do People Dislike Inflation?" in Christina D. Romer and David H. Romer, eds., *Reducing Inflation: Motivation and Strategy*, (Chicago: University of Chicago Press, 1997).

1.11 This chapter argues that if the price level increases over time, the average wage should increase by the same amount. Why is this true?

1.12 **[Related to the** Making the Connection **on page 956]** Robert Shiller asked a sample of the general public and a sample of economists the following question: "Do you agree that preventing high inflation is an important national priority, as important as preventing drug abuse or preventing deterioration in the quality of our schools?" Fifty-two percent of the general public, but only 18 percent of economists, fully agreed. Why does the general public believe inflation is a bigger problem than economists do?

1.13 **[Related to the** Making the Connection **on page 956]** When Shiller asked a sample of the general public what they thought caused inflation, the most frequent answer he received was "greed." Do you agree that greed causes inflation? Briefly explain.

1.14 **[Related to the** Chapter Opener **on page 951]** Why might a firm such as CarMax, which we discussed in the chapter opener, pay more attention than firms in, say, the restaurant or clothing industries, to the Federal Reserve raising or lowering interest rates? In other words, why are movements in interest rates particularly important to CarMax?

---

| 28.2 | **The Short-Run and Long-Run Phillips Curves,** pages 957–961 |

LEARNING OBJECTIVE: Explain the relationship between the short-run and long-run Phillips curves.

## Summary

There is a short-run trade-off between unemployment and inflation only if the actual inflation rate differs from the inflation rate that workers and firms had expected. There is a different short-run Phillips curve for every expected inflation rate. Each short-run Phillips curve intersects the long-run Phillips curve at the expected inflation rate. With a vertical long-run Phillips curve, it is not possible to buy a permanently lower unemployment rate at the cost of a permanently higher inflation rate. If the Federal Reserve attempts to keep the economy below the natural rate of unemployment, the inflation rate will increase. Eventually, the expected inflation rate will also increase, which causes the short-run Phillips curve to shift up and pushes the economy back to the natural rate of unemployment. The reverse happens if the Fed attempts to keep the economy above the natural rate of unemployment. In the long run, the Federal Reserve can affect the inflation rate but not the unemployment rate.

## Review Questions

2.1 Suppose that the expected inflation rate increases from 4 percent to 6 percent. What will happen to the short-run Phillips curve?

2.2 What is the relationship between the short-run Phillips curve and the long-run Phillips curve?

2.3 Why is it inconsistent to believe that the long-run aggregate supply curve is vertical and the long-run Phillips curve is downward sloping?

## Problems and Applications

2.4 Use the following information to draw a graph showing the short-run and long-run Phillips curves:

  Natural rate of unemployment = 5 percent
  Current rate of unemployment = 4 percent
  Expected inflation rate = 4 percent
  Current inflation rate = 6 percent

Be sure your graph shows the point where the short-run and long-run Phillips curves intersect.

**2.5** In 1968, Herbert Stein, who would later serve on President Nixon's Council of Economic Advisers, wrote, "Some who would opt for avoiding inflation would say that in the long run such a policy would cost little, if any, additional unemployment." Was Stein correct? Did most economists in 1968 agree with him? Briefly explain.

From Herbert Stein, *The Fiscal Revolution in America*, (Chicago: University of Chicago Press, 1969), p. 382.

**2.6** **[Related to** Solved Problem 28.2 **on page 961]** In a speech in September 1975, then Fed Chairman Arthur Burns said the following:

> There is no longer a meaningful trade-off between unemployment and inflation. In the current environment, a rapidly rising level of consumer prices will not lead to the creation of new jobs. . . . Highly expansionary monetary and fiscal policies might, for a short time, provide some additional thrust to economic activity. But inflation would inevitably accelerate—a development that would create even more difficult economic problems than we have encountered over the past year.

How do Burns's views in this speech compare with the views at the Fed in the late 1960s? Why do you think he specifically says that "in the current environment" there is no trade-off between unemployment and inflation?

From Arthur F. Burns, "The Real Issues of Inflation and Unemployment," in Federal Reserve Bank of New York, *Federal Reserve Readings on Inflation*, February 1979.

**2.7** In testifying before Congress, former Federal Reserve Chairman Alan Greenspan remarked, "The challenge of monetary policy is to interpret data on the economy and financial markets with an eye to anticipating future inflationary forces and to countering them by taking action in advance." Why should the Fed take action in anticipation of inflation becoming worse? Why not just wait until the increase in the inflation rate has occurred?

From Nicoletta Batini and Andrew G. Haldane, "Forward-Looking Rules for Monetary Policy," in John B. Taylor, ed., *Monetary Policy Rules*, (Chicago: University of Chicago Press, 1999), p. 157.

**2.8** In Congressional testimony, Federal Reserve Chairman Ben Bernanke said:

> Another significant factor influencing medium-term trends in inflation is the public's expectations of inflation. These expectations have an important bearing on whether transitory influences on prices, such as changes in energy costs, become embedded in wage and price decisions and so leave a lasting imprint on the rate of inflation.

What did Bernanke mean when he said that the public's expectations of inflation could "become embedded in wage and price decisions"? What would be the effect on the short-run Phillips curve of the public coming to expect a higher inflation rate?

From "Testimony of Chairman Ben S. Bernanke before the Joint Economic Committee, U.S. Congress," March 28, 2007.

**2.9** **[Related to the** Making the Connection **on page 960]** In 2011, an article in the *Economist* magazine argued that the natural rate of unemployment in the United States may have risen as high as 7.5 percent. The article suggested that:

> Lowering this new natural rate of unemployment will require structural reforms, such as changing education to ensure that people enter work equipped with the sort of skills firms are willing to fight over, adjusting the tax system and modernising the welfare safety net, and more broadly creating a climate conducive to entrepreneurship and innovation.

Why should policymakers be concerned with lowering the natural rate of unemployment? How would the "structural reforms" listed in the article contribute to lowering the natural rate of unemployment? Would the Fed be able to implement any of these reforms? Briefly explain.

From "The Great Mismatch," *Economist*, September 10, 2011.

**2.10** **[Related to the** Making the Connection **on page 960]** An article in a publication of the Federal Reserve Bank of San Francisco described the natural rate of unemployment in 2011:

> Recent labor market developments, including mismatches in the skills of workers and jobs, extended unemployment benefits, and very high rates of long-term joblessness, may be impeding the return to "normal" unemployment rates of around 5%. An examination of alternative measures of labor market conditions suggests that the "normal" unemployment rate may have risen as much as 1.7 percentage points to about 6.7%, although much of this increase is likely to prove temporary.

**a.** Explain why each of the factors mentioned—mismatches in the skills of workers and jobs, extended unemployment benefits, and very high rates of long-term joblessness—might increase the natural rate of unemployment.

**b.** Draw short-run and long-run Phillips curves that illustrate the effects of the natural rate of unemployment increasing from 5.0 percent to 6.7 percent. Briefly explain your graph.

**c.** The article states that, "Even with such an increase (in the natural rate of unemployment), sizable labor market slack is expected to persist for years." What is "labor market slack"? Show on your short-run Phillips curve in part b. the situation where the economy is experiencing labor market slack.

From Justin Weidner and John C. Williams, "What Is the New Normal Unemployment Rate?" *FRBSF Economic Letter*, February 14, 2011.

## **28.3** Expectations of the Inflation Rate and Monetary Policy, pages 961–964

LEARNING OBJECTIVE: Discuss how expectations of the inflation rate affect monetary policy.

## Summary

When the inflation rate is moderate and stable, workers and firms tend to have *adaptive expectations*. That is, they form their expectations under the assumption that future inflation rates will follow the pattern of inflation rates in the recent past. During the high and unstable inflation rates of the mid- to late 1970s, Robert Lucas and Thomas Sargent argued that workers and firms would have *rational expectations*. **Rational expectations** are formed by using all the available information about an economic variable, including the effect of the policy being used by the Federal Reserve. Lucas and Sargent argued that if people have rational expectations, expansionary monetary policy will not work. If workers and firms know that an expansionary monetary policy is going to raise the inflation rate, the actual inflation rate will be the same as the expected inflation rate. Therefore, the unemployment rate won't fall. Many economists remain skeptical of Lucas and Sargent's argument in its strictest form. **Real business cycle models** focus on "real" factors—technology shocks—rather than changes in the money supply to explain fluctuations in real GDP.

MyEconLab    Visit www.myeconlab.com to complete these exercises online and get instant feedback.

## Review Questions

**3.1** Why do workers, firms, banks, and investors in financial markets care about the future rate of inflation? How do they form their expectations of future inflation? Do current conditions in the economy have any bearing on how they form their expectations?

**3.2** What does it mean to say that workers and firms have rational expectations?

**3.3** Why did Robert Lucas and Thomas Sargent argue that the Phillips curve might be vertical in the short run? What difference would it make for monetary policy if they were right?

## Problems and Applications

**3.4** During a time when the inflation rate is increasing each year for a number of years, are adaptive expectations or rational expectations likely to give the more accurate forecasts? Briefly explain.

**3.5** An article in the *Economist* magazine contains the following: "Robert Lucas . . . showed how incorporating

expectations into macroeconomic models muddled the framework economists prior to the 'rational expectations revolution' thought they saw so clearly." What economic framework did economists change as the result of Lucas's arguments? Do all economists agree with Lucas's main conclusions about the effectiveness of monetary policy? Briefly explain.

From "How to Know What Causes What," *Economist*, October 10, 2011.

**3.6** Would a monetary policy intended to bring about disinflation cause a greater increase in unemployment if workers and firms have adaptive expectations or if they have rational expectations? Briefly explain.

**3.7** If both the short-run and long-run Phillips curves are vertical, what will be the effect on the inflation rate and the unemployment rate of an expansionary monetary policy? Use a Phillips curve graph to illustrate your answer.

**3.8** An article in the *Wall Street Journal* contains the following about the views of William Poole, who was then the president of the Federal Reserve Bank of St. Louis:

> Mr. Poole said both inflation expectations and the output gap—the spare room the economy has between what it's producing and what it could potentially produce—go into the inflation process. But "inflation expectations . . . trump the gap. If inflation expectations were to rise, that development by itself would tend to drag the inflation rate up . . . and it might take a very long time before the (output gap) would be able to offset what's going on with inflation expectations."

**a.** Use the short-run and long-run Phillips curves to explain what Poole meant in saying that both inflation expectations and the output gap affect the current inflation rate.

**b.** In terms of Phillips curve analysis, what are the implications of Poole's claim that "it might take a very long time before the (output gap) would be able to offset what's going on with inflation expectations"?

**c.** Why might inflation expectations be slow to respond to the output gap?

"Fed Policy Maker Warns of Rising Inflation," by Greg Ip from *Wall Street Journal*, June 6, 2006. Copyright © 2011 by Dow Jones & Company, Inc. Reproduced with permission of Dow Jones & Company, Inc.

## **28.4** Federal Reserve Policy from the 1970s to the Present, pages 964–972

LEARNING OBJECTIVE: Use a Phillips curve graph to show how the Federal Reserve can permanently lower the inflation rate.

## Summary

Inflation worsened through the 1970s. Paul Volcker became Fed chairman in 1979, and, under his leadership, the Fed used contractionary monetary policy to reduce inflation. A significant reduction in the inflation rate is called **disinflation**. This contractionary

monetary policy pushed the economy down the short-run Phillips curve. As workers and firms lowered their expectations of future inflation, the short-run Phillips curve shifted down, improving the short-run trade-off between unemployment and inflation. This change in expectations allowed the Fed to switch to an expansionary monetary policy to bring the economy back to the natural rate of unemployment. During Alan Greenspan's term as Fed chairman, inflation remained low, and the credibility of the Fed increased. In recent years, some economists have argued that monetary policy decisions during Greenspan's term may have contributed to the problems the financial system experienced during the 2007–2009 recession. Some economists and policymakers fear that actions taken by the Fed during the 2007–2009 recession may have reduced its independence.

MyEconLab    Visit **www.myeconlab.com** to complete these exercises online and get instant feedback.

## Review Questions

**4.1** What was the "Volcker disinflation"? What happened to the unemployment rate during the period of the Volcker disinflation?

**4.2** Why is the credibility of the Fed's policy announcements particularly important?

**4.3** Why do most economists believe that it is important for a country's central bank to be independent of the rest of the country's central government?

## Problems and Applications

**4.4** According to an article in *BusinessWeek*, many workers who retired in the year 2000 expected to live off the interest they would receive from bank certificates of deposit or money market mutual funds. "Then came disinflation—and a steep fall in interest rates." What is disinflation, and why should it lead to a fall in interest rates?

From Peter Coy, "The Surprise Threat to Nest Eggs," *BusinessWeek*, July 28, 2003.

**4.5** [Related to the Don't Let This Happen to You **on page 967**] Look again at the table on prices during the early 1930s on page 967. Was there disinflation during 1933? Briefly explain.

**4.6** Suppose the current inflation rate and the expected inflation rate are both 4 percent. The current unemployment rate and the natural rate of unemployment are both 5 percent. Use a Phillips curve graph to show the effect on the economy of a severe supply shock. If the Federal Reserve keeps monetary policy unchanged, what will happen eventually to the unemployment rate? Show this on your Phillips curve graph.

**4.7** [Related to Solved Problem 28.4 **on page 967**] Suppose the inflation rate has been 15 percent for the past four years. The unemployment rate is currently at the natural rate of unemployment of 5 percent. The Federal Reserve decides that it wants to permanently reduce the inflation rate to 5 percent. How can the Fed use monetary policy to achieve this objective? Be sure to use a Phillips curve graph in your answer.

**4.8** [Related to Solved Problem 28.4 **on page 967**] In 1995, some economists argued that the natural rate of

unemployment was 6 percent. Then Fed Chairman Alan Greenspan was convinced that the natural rate was actually about 5 percent. If Greenspan had accepted the view that the natural rate was 6 percent, how might monetary policy have been different during the late 1990s?

**4.9** During the recession of 2007–2009, some economists were concerned that the U.S. economy might begin experiencing deflation. An article in the Federal Reserve Bank of San Francisco's *Economic Letter* stated: "A popular version of the well-known Phillips curve model of inflation predicts that we are on the cusp of a deflationary spiral in which prices will fall at ever increasing rates over the next several years."

  **a.** How might a deflationary spiral occur in the Phillips curve model?

  **b.** Why do you think that a deflationary spiral did not actually occur during or after the recession of 2007–2009?

From John C. Williams, "The Risk of Deflation," *FRBSF Economic Letter*, March 27, 2009.

**4.10** According to an article in the *Wall Street Journal*, "J.P. Morgan Chase economist Michael Feroli finds that in the past two decades it has taken a far larger drop in the jobless rate to boost inflation by one percentage point than it did in the previous 25 years." If this economist is correct, has the short-run Phillips curve become steeper during the past 25 years or less steep? If true, would this fact have any implications for monetary policy? Briefly explain.

From Greg Ip, "Fed Sees Inflation Rise as Fleeting," *Wall Street Journal*, August 4, 2006.

**4.11** Robert Lucas has been quoted as saying: "In practice, it is much more painful to put a modern economy through a deflation than the monetary theory we have would lead us to expect. I take this to mean that we have 'price stickiness.'" What does Lucas mean by "the monetary theory we have"? What events may have led Lucas to conclude that it is more painful to reduce the inflation rate than theory would predict? Why does he conclude that the U.S. economy apparently has "price stickiness"?

From Paul A. Samuelson and William A. Barnett, eds., *Inside Economist's Mind: Conversations with Eminent Economists*, (Malden, MA: Blackwell Publishing, 2007).

**4.12** During the 2012 presidential election campaign, Texas Governor Rick Perry criticized the actions of Fed Chair Ben Bernanke. Perry argued that, "Printing more money to play politics at this particular time in American history is almost . . . treasonous in my opinion." An article in the *Wall Street Journal* commented that despite Perry's remarks, ". . . Bernanke is willing to embrace the political independence embedded in his role to do what Fed officials think the economy needs." How is "political independence" embedded in the role of Fed chair? Why did Congress initially decide to make the Fed independent of the rest of the federal government?

From Sudeep Reddy, "Rick Perry's Attack on Bernanke Highlights Political Risks Facing the Fed," *Wall Street Journal*, August 16, 2011.

# Macroeconomics in an Open Econo

## Chapter Outline and Learning Objectives

# A Strong Dollar Hurts McDonald's Profits

The McDonald's Big Mac is one of the most widely available products in the world. McDonald's has 32,000 outlets in 118 countries, serving 60 million customers per day. The company's stock was one of only two in the Dow Jones Industrial Average to post a gain in 2008, which was a bad year for most U.S. firms. During the recession of 2007–2009, McDonald's prospered as many consumers switched to eating out at fast-food restaurants rather than at restaurants that provide table service. The success of McDonald's continued into 2010, with the company's stock price increasing 22.5 percent, more than double the 11 percent gain in the Dow Jones Industrial Average.

With expansion in the U.S. market limited, McDonald's has grown in recent years mostly by expanding in foreign markets. About 34 percent of its sales come from the United States; 40 percent from Europe; 20 percent from the Middle East, Asia, and Africa; and about 6 percent from Canada and Latin America. Because McDonald's has restaurants in so many different countries, it receives revenue in many different currencies. As a result, the company's revenue and profits are affected by fluctuations in the value of the dollar in exchange for other currencies. In some years, converting revenue from foreign currencies yields more dollars than in other years. For example, in August 2011, global revenues for McDonald's increased by 11.3 percent from the previous year when measured in local currency—pounds in Great Britain, euros in France, yen in Japan. But when measured in terms of dollars, the company's revenues rose by only 5.4 percent. Why the discrepancy? The value of the dollar had increased relative to most other currencies. So, converting pounds, euros, and yen into dollars yielded fewer dollars for McDonald's.

What explains fluctuations in the exchange rate between the dollar and other currencies? In this chapter and the next, we will look more closely at how exchange rates are determined and at other important issues involving the international financial system. Read **AN INSIDE LOOK** on **page 1004** for a discussion of the effects of a decrease in the value of the U.S. dollar relative to other currencies.

Based on Dimitra Defotis, "McDonald's Shares Hit New High; Sales Strong in EU," *Barron's*, July 22, 2011; and McDonald's, "Financial Press Release," September 9, 2011.

## Economics in Your Life

### The South Korean Central Bank and Your Car Loan

Suppose that you are shopping for a new car, which you plan to finance with a loan from a local bank. One morning, as you head out the door to visit another automobile dealership, you hear the following newsflash on the radio: "The Bank of Korea, South Korea's central bank, announces it will sell its large holdings of U.S. Treasury bonds." What effect will the Bank of Korea's decision to sell its U.S. Treasury bonds likely have on the interest rate you pay on your car loan? As you read this chapter, see if you can answer this question. You can check your answer against the one we provide on **page 1003** at the end of this chapter.

I n Chapter 8, we looked at the basics of international trade. In this chapter, we look more closely at the linkages among countries at the macroeconomic level. Countries are linked by trade in goods and services and by flows of financial investment. We will see how policymakers in all countries take these linkages into account when conducting monetary policy and fiscal policy.

**Open economy** An economy that has interactions in trade or finance with other countries.

**Closed economy** An economy that has no interactions in trade or finance with other countries.

**Balance of payments** The record of a country's trade with other countries in goods, services, and assets.

**Current account** The part of the balance of payments that records a country's net exports, net income on investments, and net transfers.

**Balance of trade** The difference between the value of the goods a country exports and the value of the goods a country imports.

# The Balance of Payments: Linking the United States to the International Economy

Today, consumers, firms, and investors routinely interact with consumers, firms, and investors in other economies. A consumer in France may use computer software produced in the United States, watch a television made in South Korea, and wear a sweater made in Italy. A firm in the United States may sell its products in dozens of countries around the world. An investor in London may sell a U.S. Treasury bill to an investor in Mexico City. Nearly all economies are **open economies** and have extensive interactions in trade or finance with other countries. Open economies interact by trading goods and services and by making investments in each other's economies. A **closed economy** has no interactions in trade or finance with other countries. No economy today is completely closed, although a few countries, such as North Korea, have very limited economic interactions with other countries.

A good way to understand the interactions between one economy and other economies is through the **balance of payments**, which is a record of a country's trade with other countries in goods, services, and assets. Just as the U.S. Bureau of Economic Analysis is responsible for collecting data on the GDP, it is also responsible for collecting data on the balance of payments. Table 29.1 shows the balance of payments for the United States in 2010. Notice that the table contains three "accounts": the *current account*, the *financial account*, and the *capital account*.

## The Current Account

The **current account** records *current*, or short-term, flows of funds into and out of a country. The current account for the United States includes exports and imports of goods and services (recall from Chapter 19 that the difference between exports and imports of goods and services is called *net exports*); income received by U.S. residents from investments in other countries; income paid on investments in the United States owned by residents of other countries (the difference between investment income received and investment income paid is called *net income on investments*); and the difference between transfers made to residents of other countries and transfers received by U.S. residents from other countries (called *net transfers*). If you make a donation to a charity caring for orphans in Afghanistan, it would be included in net transfers. Any payments received by U.S. residents are positive numbers in the current account, and any payments made by U.S. residents are negative numbers in the current account.

**The Balance of Trade** Part of the current account is the **balance of trade**, which is the difference between the value of the goods a country exports and the value of the goods a country imports. The balance of trade is the largest item in the current account and is often a topic that politicians and the media discuss. If a country exports more goods than it imports, it has a *trade surplus*. If a country exports less than it imports, it has a *trade deficit*. In 2010, the United States had a trade deficit of $646 billion. In the same year, Japan had a trade surplus of $76 billion, and China had a trade surplus of $183 billion. Figure 29.1 shows imports and exports of goods between the United States and its trading partners and between Japan and its trading partners. The data show that the United States ran a trade deficit in 2010 with all its major trading partners and with every region of the world except for Latin America. Japan ran trade deficits with China,

| CURRENT ACCOUNT | | |
| --- | --- | --- |
| Exports of goods | $1,289 | |
| Imports of goods | −1,935 | |
| Balance of trade | | −646 |
| Exports of services | 549 | |
| Imports of services | −403 | |
| Balance of services | | 146 |
| Income received on investments | 663 | |
| Income payments on investments | −498 | |
| Net income on investments | | 165 |
| Net transfers | | −136 |
| Balance on current account | | −471 |
| **FINANCIAL ACCOUNT** | | |
| Increase in foreign holdings of assets in the United States | 1,259 | |
| Increase in U.S. holdings of assets in foreign countries | −1,005 | |
| Balance on financial account | | 254 |
| **BALANCE ON CAPITAL ACCOUNT** | | 0 |
| Statistical discrepancy | | 217 |
| Balance of payments | | 0 |

**Table 29.1**

**The Balance of Payments, 2010 (billions of dollars)**

The sum of the balance of trade and the balance of services equals net exports.

Data from U.S. Bureau of Economic Analysis, "U.S. International Transactions: Second Quarter 2011," September 15, 2011.

the Middle East, and Africa, and it ran trade surpluses with other regions. (Note that exports from the United States to Japan in panel (a) of Figure 29.1 should equal imports by Japan from the United States in panel (b). These two numbers are different because international trade statistics are not measured exactly.)

### Net Exports Equals the Sum of the Balance of Trade and the Balance of Services

In previous chapters, we saw that *net exports* is a component of aggregate expenditures. Net exports is not explicitly shown in Table 29.1, but we can calculate it by adding together the balance of trade and the balance of services. The *balance of services* is the difference between the value of the services a country exports and the value of the services a country imports. Notice that, technically, net exports is *not* equal to the current account balance because this account also includes net income on investments and net transfers. But these other two items are relatively small, so, as we will see later in this chapter, it is often a convenient simplification to think of net exports as being equal to the current account balance.

## The Financial Account

The **financial account** records purchases of assets a country has made abroad and foreign purchases of assets in the country. The financial account records long-term flows of funds into and out of a country. There is a *capital outflow* from the United States when an investor in the United States buys a bond issued by a foreign company or government or when a U.S. firm builds a factory in another country. There is a *capital inflow* into the United States when a foreign investor buys a bond issued by a U.S. firm or by the government or when a foreign firm builds a factory in the United States. Notice that we

**Financial account** The part of the balance of payments that records purchases of assets a country has made abroad and foreign purchases of assets in the country.

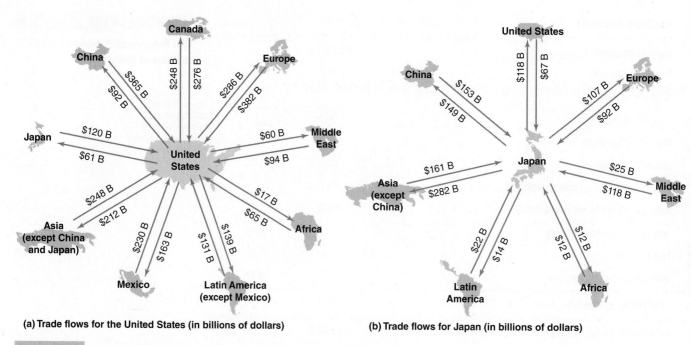

**(a) Trade flows for the United States (in billions of dollars)**

**(b) Trade flows for Japan (in billions of dollars)**

**Figure 29.1** Trade Flows for the United States and Japan, 2010

Panel (a) shows that in 2010, the United States ran a trade deficit with all its major trading partners and with every region of the world except for Latin America. Panel (b) shows that Japan ran trade deficits with China, Latin America, and the Middle East, and it ran trade surpluses with the United States, Europe, and Asia. In each panel, the green arrows represent exports from the United States or Japan, and the red arrows represent imports.

*Note:* Japanese data are converted from yen to dollars at the average 2010 exchange rate of 87.8 yen per dollar.

Data from U.S. Bureau of Economic Analysis, "U.S. International Transactions: Second Quarter 2011," September 15, 2011.

are using the word *capital* here to apply not just to physical assets, such as factories, but also to financial assets, such as shares of stock. When firms build or buy facilities in foreign countries, they are engaging in *foreign direct investment*. When investors buy stock or bonds issued in another country, they are engaging in *foreign portfolio investment*.

Another way of thinking of the balance on the financial account is as a measure of *net capital flows*, or the difference between capital inflows and capital outflows. (Here we are omitting a few transactions included in the capital account, as discussed in the next section.) A concept closely related to net capital flows is **net foreign investment**, which is equal to capital outflows minus capital inflows. Net capital flows and net foreign investment are always equal but have opposite signs: When net capital flows are positive, net foreign investment is negative, and when net capital flows are negative, net foreign investment is positive. Net foreign investment is also equal to net foreign direct investment plus net foreign portfolio investment. Later in this chapter, we will use the relationship between the balance on the financial account and net foreign investment to understand an important aspect of the international economic system.

**Net foreign investment** The difference between capital outflows from a country and capital inflows, also equal to net foreign direct investment plus net foreign portfolio investment.

## The Capital Account

A third, less important, part of the balance of payments is called the *capital account*. The **capital account** records relatively minor transactions, such as migrants' transfers—which consist of goods and financial assets people take with them when they leave or enter a country—and sales and purchases of nonproduced, nonfinancial assets. A nonproduced, nonfinancial asset is a copyright, patent, trademark, or right to natural resources. The definitions of the financial account and the capital account are often misunderstood because the capital account prior to 1999 recorded all the transactions included now in both the financial account and the capital account. In other words, capital account transactions went from being a very important part of the balance of

**Capital account** The part of the balance of payments that records relatively minor transactions, such as migrants' transfers and sales and purchases of nonproduced, nonfinancial assets.

payments to being a relatively unimportant part. Because the balance on what is now called the capital account is so small—only $152 million in 2010—for simplicity we will ignore it in the remainder of this chapter.

## Why Is the Balance of Payments Always Zero?

The sum of the current account balance, the financial account balance, and the capital account balance equals the balance of payments. Table 29.1 shows that the balance of payments for the United States in 2010 was zero. It's not just by chance that this balance was zero; *the balance of payments is always zero*. Notice that the current account balance in 2010 was –$471 billion. The balance on the financial account (which has the opposite sign to the balance on the current account) was $254 billion. To make the balance on the current account equal the balance on the financial account, the balance of payments includes an entry called the *statistical discrepancy*. (Remember that we are ignoring the balance on the capital account. If we included it, we would say that the statistical discrepancy takes on a value equal to the difference between the current account balance and the sum of the balance on the financial account and the balance on the capital account.)

Why does the U.S. Department of Commerce include the statistical discrepancy entry to force the balance of payments to equal zero? If the sum of the current account balance and the financial account balance does not equal zero, some imports or exports of goods and services or some capital inflows or capital outflows were not measured accurately.

To better understand why the balance of payments must equal zero every year, consider the following: In 2010, the United States spent $471 billion more on goods, services, and other items in the current account than it received. What happened to that $471 billion? We know that every dollar of that $471 billion was used by foreign individuals or firms to invest in the United States or was added to foreign holdings of dollars. We know this because logically there is nowhere else for the dollars to go: If the dollars weren't spent on U.S. goods and services—and we know they weren't because in that case they would have shown up in the current account—they must have been spent on investments in the United States or not spent at all. Dollars that aren't spent are added to foreign holdings of dollars. Changes in foreign holdings of dollars are known

## Don't Let This Happen to You

### Don't Confuse the Balance of Trade, the Current Account Balance, and the Balance of Payments

The terminology of international economics can be tricky. Remember that the *balance of trade* includes only trade in goods; it does not include services. This observation is important because the United States, for example, usually imports more *goods* than it exports, but it usually exports more *services* than it imports. As a result, the U.S. trade deficit is almost always larger than the current account deficit. The *current account balance* includes the balance of trade, the balance of services, net investment income, and net transfers. Net investment income and net transfers are much smaller than the balance of trade and the balance of services.

Even though the *balance of payments* is equal to the sum of the current account balance and the financial account balance—and must equal zero—you may sometimes see references to a balance of payments "surplus" or "deficit." These references have two explanations. The first is that the person making the reference has confused the balance of payments with either the balance of trade or the current account balance. This is a very common mistake. The second explanation is that the person is not including official reserve transactions in the financial account. If we separate changes in U.S. holdings of foreign currencies and changes in foreign holdings of U.S. dollars from other financial account entries, the current account balance and the financial account balance do not have to sum to zero, and there can be a balance of payments surplus or deficit. This may sound complicated—and it is! But don't worry. How official reserve transactions are accounted for is not crucial to understanding the basic ideas behind the balance of payments.

MyEconLab

**Your Turn:** Test your understanding by doing related problem 1.6 on page 1006 at the end of this chapter.

as *official reserve transactions*. Foreign investment in the United States and additions to foreign holdings of dollars both show up as positive entries in the U.S. financial account. Therefore, a current account deficit must be exactly offset by a financial account surplus, leaving the balance of payments equal to zero. Similarly, a country that runs a current account surplus, such as China or Japan, must run a financial account deficit of exactly the same size. If a country's current account surplus is not exactly equal to its financial account deficit, or if a country's current account deficit is not exactly equal to its financial account surplus, some transactions must not have been accounted for. The statistical discrepancy is included in the balance of payments to compensate for these uncounted transactions.

# Solved Problem 29.1

## Understanding the Arithmetic of Open Economies

Test your understanding of the relationship between the current account and the financial account by evaluating the following assertion by a political commentator:

The industrial countries are committing economic suicide. Every year, they invest more and more in developing countries. Every year, more U.S., Japanese, and European manufacturing firms move their factories to developing countries. With extensive new factories and low wages, developing countries now export far more to the industrial countries than they import.

## Solving the Problem

**Step 1:** **Review the chapter material.** This problem is about the relationship between the current account and the financial account, so you may want to review the section "Why Is the Balance of Payments Always Zero?" which begins on page 987.

**Step 2:** **Explain the errors in the commentator's argument.** The argument sounds plausible. It would be easy to find statements similar to this one in recent books and articles by well-known political commentators. But the argument contains an important error: The commentator has failed to understand the relationship between the current account and the financial account. The commentator asserts that developing countries are receiving large capital inflows from industrial countries. In other words, developing countries are running financial account surpluses. The commentator also asserts that developing countries are exporting more than they are importing. In other words, they are running current account surpluses. As we have seen in this section, it is impossible to run a current account surplus *and* a financial account surplus simultaneously. A country that runs a current account surplus *must* run a financial account deficit and vice versa.

**Extra Credit:** Most emerging economies that have received large inflows of foreign investment during the past two decades, such as South Korea, Thailand, and Malaysia, have run current account deficits: They import more goods and services than they export. Emerging economies, such as Singapore, that run current account surpluses also run financial account deficits: They invest more abroad than other countries invest in them.

The point here is not obvious; if the point was obvious, it wouldn't confuse so many intelligent politicians, journalists, and political commentators. Unless you understand the relationship between the current account and the financial account, you won't be able to understand a key aspect of the international economy.

MyEconLab **Your Turn:** For more practice, do related problems 1.7, 1.8, and 1.9 on page 1006 at the end of this chapter.

# The Foreign Exchange Market and Exchange Rates

**29.2 LEARNING** OBJECTIVE

Explain how exchange rates are determined and how changes in exchange rates affect the prices of imports and exports.

A firm that operates entirely within the United States will price its products in dollars and will use dollars to pay its suppliers' bills, wages and salaries to its workers, interest to its bondholders, and dividends to its shareholders. A multinational corporation such as McDonald's, in contrast, may sell its products in many different countries and receive payments in many different currencies. Its suppliers and workers may also be spread around the world and may have to be paid in local currencies. Corporations may also use the international financial system to borrow in a foreign currency. For example, during a period of rapid expansion in East Asian countries such as Thailand and South Korea during the late 1990s, many large firms received dollar loans from foreign banks. When firms make extensive use of foreign currencies, they must deal with fluctuations in the exchange rate.

The **nominal exchange rate** is the value of one country's currency in terms of another country's currency. Economists also calculate the *real exchange rate*, which corrects the nominal exchange rate for changes in prices of goods and services. We discuss the real exchange rate later in this chapter. The nominal exchange rate determines how many units of a foreign currency you can purchase with $1. For example, the exchange rate between the U.S. dollar and the Japanese yen can be expressed as ¥100 = $1. (This exchange rate can also be expressed as how many U.S. dollars are required to buy 1 Japanese yen: $0.01 = ¥1.) The market for foreign exchange is very active. Every day, the equivalent of more than $3 trillion worth of currency is traded in the foreign exchange market. The exchange rates that result from this trading are reported on a number of online sites devoted to economic news and in the business or financial sections of most newspapers.

**Nominal exchange rate** The value of one country's currency in terms of another country's currency.

Banks and other financial institutions around the world employ currency traders, who are linked together by computer. Rather than exchange large amounts of paper currency, they buy and sell deposits in banks. A bank buying or selling dollars will actually be buying or selling dollar bank deposits. Dollar bank deposits exist not just in banks in the United States but also in banks around the world. Suppose that the Crédit Agricole bank in France wants to sell U.S. dollars and buy Japanese yen. The bank may exchange U.S. dollar deposits that it owns for Japanese yen deposits owned by the Deutsche Bank in Germany. Businesses and individuals usually obtain foreign currency from banks in their own country.

## Making the Connection | Exchange Rate Listings

Many online sites, such as wsj.com, Bloomberg.com, or finance.yahoo.com, as well as the financial pages of most newspapers list the exchange rates between the dollar and other important currencies. The exchange rates in the following table are for October 13, 2011. The euro is the common currency used by 17 European countries, including France, Germany, and Italy.

| | Exchange Rate between the Dollar and the Indicated Currency | |
|---|---|---|
| Currency | Units of Foreign Currency per U.S. Dollar | U.S. Dollars per Unit of Foreign Currency |
| Canadian dollar | 1.023 | 0.978 |
| Japanese yen | 76.870 | 0.013 |
| Mexican peso | 13.449 | 0.074 |
| British pound | 0.635 | 1.574 |
| Euro | 0.727 | 1.375 |

*You can find information on exchange rates on many online sites that report economic news and in the financial pages of most newspapers.*

Notice that the expression for the exchange rate stated as units of foreign currency per U.S. dollar is the *reciprocal* of the exchange rate stated as U.S. dollars per unit of foreign currency. So, the exchange rate between the U.S. dollar and the British pound can be stated as either 0.635 British pounds per U.S. dollar or 1/0.635 = 1.574 U.S. dollars per British pound.

Banks are the most active participants in the market for foreign exchange. Typically, banks buy currency for slightly less than the amount for which they sell it. This spread between the buying and selling prices allows banks to cover their expenses from currency trading and to make a profit. Therefore, when most businesses and individuals buy foreign currency from a bank, they receive fewer units of foreign currency per dollar than would be indicated by the exchange rate shown on online business sites or printed in the newspaper.

Based on *Wall Street Journal*, October 13, 2011.

MyEconLab **Your Turn:** Test your understanding by doing related problem 2.6 on page 1007 at the end of this chapter.

The market exchange rate is determined by the interaction of demand and supply, just as other prices are. Let's consider the demand for U.S. dollars in exchange for Japanese yen. There are three sources of foreign currency demand for the U.S. dollar:

1. Foreign firms and households that want to buy goods and services produced in the United States.

2. Foreign firms and households that want to invest in the United States either through foreign direct investment—buying or building factories or other facilities in the United States—or through foreign portfolio investment—buying stocks and bonds issued in the United States.

3. Currency traders who believe that the value of the dollar in the future will be greater than its value today.

## Equilibrium in the Market for Foreign Exchange

Figure 29.2 shows the demand and supply of U.S. dollars for Japanese yen. Notice that as we move up the vertical axis in Figure 29.2, the value of the dollar increases relative to the value of the yen. When the exchange rate is ¥150 = $1, the dollar is worth 1.5 times as much relative to the yen as when the exchange rate is ¥100 = $1. Consider, first, the demand curve for dollars in exchange for yen. The demand curve has the normal downward slope. When the value of the dollar is high, the quantity of dollars demanded will be low. A Japanese investor will be more likely to buy a $1,000 bond issued by the U.S. Treasury when the exchange rate is ¥100 = $1 and the investor pays only ¥100,000

### Figure 29.2

**Equilibrium in the Foreign Exchange Market**

When the exchange rate is ¥150 to the dollar, it is above its equilibrium level, and there will be a surplus of dollars. When the exchange rate is ¥100 to the dollar, it is below its equilibrium level, and there will be a shortage of dollars. At an exchange rate of ¥120 to the dollar, the foreign exchange market is in equilibrium.

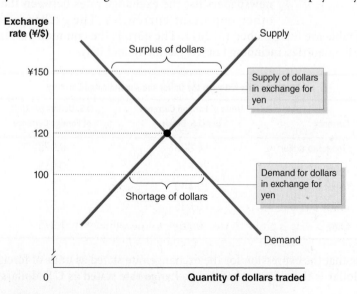

to buy $1,000 than when the exchange rate is ¥150 = $1 and the investor must pay ¥150,000. Similarly, a Japanese firm is more likely to buy $150 million worth of microchips from Intel Corporation when the exchange rate is ¥100 = $1 and the microchips can be purchased for ¥15 billion than when the exchange rate is ¥150 = $1 and the microchips cost ¥22.5 billion.

Consider, now, the supply curve of dollars in exchange for yen. The supply curve has the normal upward slope. When the value of the dollar is high, the quantity of dollars supplied in exchange for yen will be high. A U.S. investor will be more likely to buy a ¥200,000 bond issued by the Japanese government when the exchange rate is ¥200 = $1 and he needs to pay only $1,000 to buy ¥200,000 than when the exchange rate is ¥100 = $1 and he must pay $2,000. The owner of a U.S. electronics store is more likely to buy ¥20 million worth of television sets from the Sony Corporation when the exchange rate is ¥200 = $1 and she only needs to pay $100,000 to purchase the televisions than when the exchange rate is ¥100 = $1 and she must pay $200,000.

As in any other market, equilibrium occurs in the foreign exchange market where the quantity supplied equals the quantity demanded. In Figure 29.2, ¥120 = $1 is the equilibrium exchange rate. At exchange rates above ¥120 = $1, there will be a surplus of dollars and downward pressure on the exchange rate. The surplus and the downward pressure will not be eliminated until the exchange rate falls to ¥120 = $1. If the exchange rate is below ¥120 = $1, there will be a shortage of dollars and upward pressure on the exchange rate. The shortage and the upward pressure will not be eliminated until the exchange rate rises to ¥120 = $1. Surpluses and shortages in the foreign exchange market are eliminated very quickly because the volume of trading in major currencies such as the dollar and the yen is very large, and currency traders are linked together by computer.

**Currency appreciation** occurs when the market value of a country's currency increases relative to the value of another country's currency. **Currency depreciation** occurs when the market value of a country's currency decreases relative to the value of another country's currency.

**Currency appreciation** An increase in the market value of one currency relative to another currency.

**Currency depreciation** A decrease in the market value of one currency relative to another currency.

## How Do Shifts in Demand and Supply Affect the Exchange Rate?

Shifts in the demand and supply curves cause the equilibrium exchange rate to change. Three main factors cause the demand and supply curves in the foreign exchange market to shift:

1. Changes in the demand for U.S.-produced goods and services and changes in the demand for foreign-produced goods and services

2. Changes in the desire to invest in the United States and changes in the desire to invest in foreign countries

3. Changes in the expectations of currency traders about the likely future value of the dollar and the likely future value of foreign currencies

### Shifts in the Demand for Foreign Exchange
Consider how the three factors listed above will affect the demand for U.S. dollars in exchange for Japanese yen. During an economic expansion in Japan, the incomes of Japanese households will rise, and the demand by Japanese consumers and firms for U.S. goods will increase. At any given exchange rate, the demand for U.S. dollars will increase, and the demand curve will shift to the right. Similarly, if interest rates in the United States rise, the desirability of investing in U.S. financial assets will increase, and the demand curve for dollars will also shift to the right. **Speculators** are currency traders who buy and sell foreign exchange in an attempt to profit from changes in exchange rates. If a speculator becomes convinced that the value of the dollar is going to rise relative to the value of the yen, the speculator will sell yen and buy dollars. If the current exchange rate is ¥120 = $1, and the speculator is convinced that it will soon rise to ¥140 = $1, the speculator could sell ¥600,000,000 and receive $5,000,000 (= ¥600,000,000/¥120) in return. If the speculator is correct

**Speculators** Currency traders who buy and sell foreign exchange in an attempt to profit from changes in exchange rates.

and the value of the dollar rises against the yen to ¥140 = $1, the speculator will be able to exchange $5,000,000 for ¥700,000,000 (=$5,000,000 × ¥140), for a profit of ¥100,000,000.

To summarize, the demand curve for dollars shifts to the right when incomes in Japan rise, when interest rates in the United States rise, or when speculators decide that the value of the dollar will rise relative to the value of the yen.

During a recession in Japan, Japanese incomes will fall, reducing the demand for U.S.-produced goods and services and shifting the demand curve for dollars to the left. Similarly, if interest rates in the United States fall, the desirability of investing in U.S. financial assets will decrease, and the demand curve for dollars will shift to the left. Finally, if speculators become convinced that the future value of the dollar will be lower than its current value, the demand for dollars will fall, and the demand curve will shift to the left.

**Shifts in the Supply of Foreign Exchange** The factors that affect the supply curve for dollars are similar to those that affect the demand curve for dollars. An economic expansion in the United States increases the incomes of Americans and increases their demand for goods and services, including goods and services made in Japan. As U.S. consumers and firms increase their spending on Japanese products, they must supply dollars in exchange for yen, which causes the supply curve for dollars to shift to the right. Similarly, an increase in interest rates in Japan will make financial investments in Japan more attractive to U.S. investors. These higher Japanese interest rates will cause the supply of dollars to shift to the right, as U.S. investors exchange dollars for yen. Finally, if speculators become convinced that the future value of the yen will be higher relative to the dollar than it is today, the supply curve of dollars will shift to the right as traders attempt to exchange dollars for yen.

A recession in the United States will decrease the demand for Japanese products and cause the supply curve for dollars to shift to the left. Similarly, a decrease in interest rates in Japan will make financial investments in Japan less attractive and cause the supply curve of dollars to shift to the left. If traders become convinced that the future value of the yen will be lower relative to the dollar, the supply curve will also shift to the left.

**Adjustment to a New Equilibrium** The factors that affect the demand and supply for currencies are constantly changing. Whether the exchange rate increases or decreases depends on the direction and size of the shifts in the demand curve and supply curve. For example, as Figure 29.3 shows, if the demand curve for dollars in exchange for Japanese yen shifts to the right by more than the supply curve shifts, the equilibrium exchange rate will increase.

**Figure 29.3**

**Shifts in the Demand and Supply Curve Resulting in a Higher Exchange Rate**

Holding other factors constant, an increase in the supply of dollars will decrease the equilibrium exchange rate. An increase in the demand for dollars will increase the equilibrium exchange rate. In the case shown in this figure, the demand curve and the supply curve have both shifted to the right. Because the demand curve has shifted to the right by more than the supply curve, the equilibrium exchange rate has increased from ¥120 to $1 at point A to ¥130 to $1 at point B.

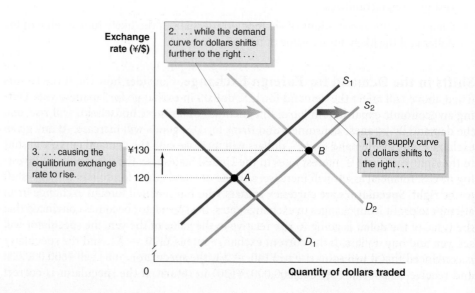

## Making the Connection

## What Explains the Fall and Rise and Fall of the Dollar?

An American vacationing in Paris during the spring of 2002 could have bought a meal for €50 and paid the equivalent of $44 for it. In the summer of 2008, that same €50 meal would have cost the equivalent of $79. A few months later, in early 2009, it would have cost only $64. In the fall of 2011, it would have cost $69. Clearly, during these years, the value of the dollar in exchange for the euro was going through substantial fluctuations. And it wasn't just against the euro that the dollar was losing value, then regaining some of it, and then losing it again. The graph below shows fluctuations for the period from 1990 to late 2011 in an index of the value of the dollar against an average of other major currencies, such as the euro, the British pound, the Canadian dollar, and the Japanese yen. The shaded areas indicate recessions.

The graph indicates that although the dollar gained value against other currencies for a brief period during late 2008 and early 2009, and again during mid-2010, overall it has lost value since 2002. What explains the decline in the value of the dollar? We have just seen that an increase in the demand by foreign investors for U.S. financial assets can increase the value of the dollar, and a decrease in the demand for U.S. financial assets can decrease the value of the dollar. The increase in the value of the dollar in the late 1990s, as shown in the graph, was driven by strong demand from foreign investors for U.S. stocks and bonds, particularly U.S. Treasury securities. This increase in demand was not primarily due to higher U.S. interest rates but to problems in the international financial system that we will discuss in Chapter 30. Many investors saw U.S. financial assets as a safe haven in times of financial problems because the investors believed the U.S. Treasury was unlikely to default on its bonds.

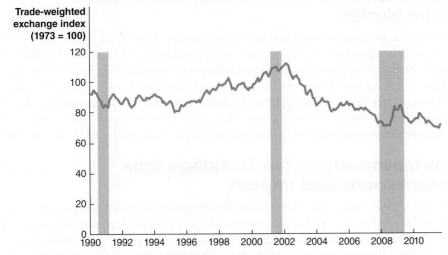

Data from Federal Reserve Bank of St. Louis.

Conditions began to change in 2002, however, for a couple of reasons. First, as we saw in Chapter 26, the Fed began aggressively cutting the target for the federal funds rate to deal with the recession of 2001 and the initially slow recovery that followed. By May 2003, the target for the federal funds rate was at a historically low level of 1 percent. Low U.S. interest rates mean that investors are likely to buy foreign assets rather than U.S. assets, which depresses the demand for dollars and lowers the exchange value of the dollar. Although the Fed did begin raising the target for the federal funds rate in 2004, it resumed cutting the target in the fall of 2007. Low U.S. interest rates have played a role in the declining value of the dollar. Second, many investors and some central banks became convinced that the value of the dollar was too high in 2002 and that it was likely to decline in the future. As we will see later in this chapter, the United States has run large current account deficits since the early 2000s. Many investors believed that the substantial increase in the supply of dollars in exchange for foreign currencies that resulted from these current account deficits would ultimately result in a significant decline in the value of the dollar. Once investors become convinced that the value of a country's currency will decline, they become reluctant to hold that country's financial assets. A decreased willingness by foreign investors to buy U.S. financial assets decreases the demand for dollars and lowers the exchange value of the dollar.

What explains the increase in the value of the dollar in late 2008 and early 2009 and again in mid-2010? The increase was largely the result of the deepening of the financial crisis in the fall of 2008. Just as during the financial crisis of the late 1990s, many investors saw U.S. Treasury securities as a safe haven and demanded dollars in order to invest in them. By the summer of 2009, the easing in the financial crisis resulted in the dollar resuming its decline. Worries that some European governments—particularly Greece—might default on their government bonds caused a temporary increase in the value of the dollar during mid-2010. A smaller increase in the value of the dollar during 2011 caused the problems for McDonald's mentioned in the chapter opener.

The fall in the value of the dollar over the long run has been bad news for U.S. tourists traveling abroad and for anyone in the United States buying foreign goods and services. It has been good news, however, for U.S. firms exporting goods and services to other countries.

**MyEconLab** **Your Turn:** Test your understanding by doing related problems 2.14 and 2.15 on page 1008 at the end of this chapter.

## Some Exchange Rates Are Not Determined by the Market

To this point, we have assumed that exchange rates are determined in the market. This assumption is a good one for many currencies, including the U.S. dollar, the euro, the Japanese yen, and the British pound. Some currencies, however, have *fixed exchange rates* that do not change over long periods. For example, for more than 10 years, the value of the Chinese yuan was fixed against the U.S. dollar at a rate of 8.28 yuan to the dollar. As we will discuss in more detail in Chapter 30, a country's central bank has to intervene in the foreign exchange market to buy and sell its currency to keep the exchange rate fixed.

## How Movements in the Exchange Rate Affect Exports and Imports

When the market value of the dollar increases, the foreign currency price of U.S. exports rises, and the dollar price of foreign imports falls. For example, suppose that initially the market exchange rate between the U.S. dollar and the euro is $1 = €1. In that case, an Apple iPhone that has a price of $200 in the United States will have a price of €200 in France. A bottle of French wine that has a price of €50 in France will have a price of $50 in the United States. Now suppose the market exchange rate between the U.S. dollar and the euro changes to $1.20 = €1. Because it now takes more dollars to buy a euro, the dollar has *depreciated* against the euro, and the euro has *appreciated* against the dollar. The depreciation of the dollar has decreased the euro price of the iPhone from €200 to $200/(1.20 \text{ dollars}/\text{euro}) = €167$. The dollar price of the French wine has risen from $50 to €50 × 1.20 \text{ dollars}/\text{euro} = $60$. As a result, we would expect more iPhones to be sold in France and less French wine to be sold in the United States.

To generalize, we can conclude that a depreciation in the domestic currency will increase exports and decrease imports, thereby increasing net exports. As we saw in previous chapters, net exports is a component of aggregate demand. If real GDP is currently below potential GDP, then, holding all other factors constant, a depreciation in the domestic currency should increase net exports, aggregate demand, and real GDP. An appreciation in the domestic currency should have the opposite effect: Exports should fall, and imports should rise, which will reduce net exports, aggregate demand, and real GDP.

## Don't Let This Happen to You

### Don't Confuse What Happens When a Currency Appreciates with What Happens When It Depreciates

One of the most confusing aspects of exchange rates is that they can be expressed in two ways. We can express the exchange rate between the dollar and the yen either as how many yen can be purchased with $1 or as how many dollars can be purchased with ¥1. That is, we can express the exchange rate as ¥100 = $1 or as $0.01 = ¥1. When a currency appreciates, it increases in value relative to another currency. When it depreciates, it decreases in value relative to another currency.

If the exchange rate changes from ¥100 = $1 to ¥120 = $1, the dollar has appreciated and the yen has depreciated because it now takes more yen to buy $1. If the exchange rate changes from $0.01 = ¥1 to $0.015 = ¥1,

however, the dollar has depreciated and the yen has appreciated because it now takes more dollars to buy ¥1. This situation can appear somewhat confusing because the exchange rate seems to have "increased" in both cases. To determine which currency has appreciated and which has depreciated, it is important to remember that an appreciation of the domestic currency means that it now takes *more* units of the foreign currency to buy one unit of the domestic currency. A depreciation of the domestic currency means it takes *fewer* units of the foreign currency to buy one unit of the domestic currency. This observation holds no matter which way we express the exchange rate.

MyEconLab

**Your Turn:** Test your understanding by doing related problem 2.5 on page 1007 at the end of the chapter.

---

# Solved Problem **29.2**

## The Effect of Changing Exchange Rates on the Prices of Imports and Exports

In June 2011, the average price of goods imported into the United States from Canada fell 2.1 percent. Is it likely that the value of the U.S. dollar appreciated or depreciated versus the Canadian dollar during this period? Is it likely that the average price in Canadian dollars of goods exported from the United States to Canada during June 2011 rose or fell?

## Solving the Problem

**Step 1:** **Review the chapter material.** This problem is about changes in the value of a currency, so you may want to review the section "How Movements in the Exchange Rate Affect Exports and Imports" on page 994.

**Step 2:** **Explain whether the value of the U.S. dollar appreciated or depreciated against the Canadian dollar.** We know that if the U.S. dollar appreciates against the Canadian dollar, it will take more Canadian dollars to purchase 1 U.S. dollar, and, equivalently, fewer U.S. dollars will be required to purchase 1 Canadian dollar. A Canadian consumer or business will need to pay more Canadian dollars to buy products imported from the United States: A good or service that had been selling for 100 Canadian dollars will now sell for more than 100 Canadian dollars. A U.S. consumer or business will have to pay fewer U.S. dollars to buy products imported from Canada: A good or service that had been selling for 100 U.S. dollars will now sell for fewer than 100 U.S. dollars. We can conclude that if the price of goods imported into the United States from Canada fell, the value of the U.S. dollar must have appreciated versus the Canadian dollar.

**Step 3:** **Explain what happened to the average price in Canadian dollars of goods exported from the United States to Canada.** If the U.S. dollar appreciated relative to the Canadian dollar, the average price in Canadian dollars of goods exported from the United States to Canada will have risen.

**Your Turn:** For more practice, do related problem 2.10 on page 1008 at the end of this chapter.　　MyEconLab

## The Real Exchange Rate

**Real exchange rate** The price of domestic goods in terms of foreign goods.

We have seen that an important factor in determining the level of a country's exports to and imports from another country is the relative prices of each country's goods. The relative prices of two countries' goods are determined by two factors: the relative price levels in the two countries and the nominal exchange rate between the two countries' currencies. Economists combine these two factors in the **real exchange rate**, which is the price of domestic goods in terms of foreign goods. Recall that the price level is a measure of the average prices of goods and services in an economy. We can calculate the real exchange rate between two currencies as

$$\text{Real exchange rate} = \text{Nominal exchange rate} \times \left( \frac{\text{Domestic price level}}{\text{Foreign price level}} \right).$$

Notice that changes in the real exchange rate reflect both changes in the nominal exchange rate and changes in the relative price levels. For example, suppose that the exchange rate between the U.S. dollar and the British pound is $1 = £1, the price level in the United States is 100, and the price level in the United Kingdom is also 100. Then the real exchange rate between the dollar and the pound is

$$\text{Real exchange rate} = 1 \text{ pound/dollar} \times \left( \frac{100}{100} \right) = 1.00.$$

Now suppose that the nominal exchange rate increases to 1.1 pounds per dollar, while the price level in the United States rises to 105 and the price level in the United Kingdom remains 100. In this case, the real exchange rate will be

$$\text{Real exchange rate} = 1.1 \text{ pound/dollar} \times \left( \frac{105}{100} \right) = 1.15.$$

The increase in the real exchange rate from 1.00 to 1.15 tells us that the prices of U.S. goods and services are now 15 percent higher than they were relative to British goods and services.

Real exchange rates are reported as index numbers, with one year chosen as the base year. As with the consumer price index, the main value of the real exchange rate is in tracking changes over time—in this case, changes in the relative prices of domestic goods in terms of foreign goods.

**29.3 LEARNING** OBJECTIVE

Explain the saving and investment equation.

# The International Sector and National Saving and Investment

Having studied what determines the exchange rate, we are now ready to explore further the linkages between the U.S. economy and foreign economies. As we saw in Figure 9.1 on page 275, until 1970, U.S. imports and exports were usually 4 percent to 5 percent of GDP. Imports and exports are now two to three times as large a fraction of U.S. GDP. Imports have also consistently been larger than exports, meaning that net exports have been negative.

## Net Exports Equal Net Foreign Investment

If your spending is greater than your income, what can you do? You can sell some assets—maybe those 20 shares of stock in the Walt Disney Company your grandparents gave you—or you can borrow money. A firm can be in the same situation: If a firm's costs are greater than its revenues, it has to make up the difference by selling assets or by borrowing. A country is in the same situation when it imports more than it exports: The country must finance the difference by selling assets—such as land, office buildings, or factories—or by borrowing.

In other words, for any country, a current account deficit must be exactly offset by a financial account surplus. When a country sells more assets to foreigners than it buys from foreigners, or when it borrows more from foreigners than it lends to foreigners— as it must if it is running a current account deficit—the country experiences a net capital inflow and a financial account surplus. Remember that net exports is roughly equal to the current account balance. Remember also that the financial account balance is roughly equal to net capital flows, which are in turn equal to net foreign investment but with the opposite sign. To review these two points, look again at Table 29.1 on page 985, which shows that the current account balance is determined mainly by the balance of trade and the balance of services, and the financial account is equal to net capital flows. Also, remember the definition of net foreign investment.

When imports are greater than exports, net exports are negative, and there will be a net capital inflow as people in the United States sell assets and borrow to pay for the surplus of imports over exports. Therefore, net capital flows will be equal to net exports (but with the opposite sign), and net foreign investment will also be equal to net exports (and with the same sign). Because net exports are usually negative for the United States, in most years, the United States must be a net borrower from abroad, and U.S. net foreign investment will be negative.

We can summarize this discussion with the following equations:

$$\text{Current account balance} + \text{Financial account balance} = 0$$

or

$$\text{Current account balance} = -\text{Financial account balance}$$

or

$$\text{Net exports} = \text{Net foreign investment.}$$

This equation tells us, once again, that countries such as the United States that import more than they export must borrow more from abroad than they lend abroad: If net exports are negative, net foreign investment will also be negative by the same amount. Countries such as Japan and China that export more than they import must lend abroad more than they borrow from abroad: If net exports are positive, net foreign investment will also be positive by the same amount.

## Domestic Saving, Domestic Investment, and Net Foreign Investment

As we saw in Chapter 21, the total saving in any economy is equal to saving by the private sector plus saving by the government sector, which we called *public saving*. When the government runs a budget surplus by spending less than it receives in taxes, it is saving. When the government runs a budget deficit, public saving is negative. Negative saving is also known as *dissaving*. We can write the following expression for the level of saving in the economy:

$$\text{National saving} = \text{Private saving} + \text{Public saving}$$

or

$$S = S_{\text{private}} + S_{\text{public}}.$$

Private saving is equal to what households have left of their income after spending on consumption goods and paying taxes (for simplicity, we assume that transfer payments are zero):

$$\text{Private saving} = \text{National income} - \text{Consumption} - \text{Taxes}$$

or

$$S_{\text{private}} = Y - C - T.$$

Public saving is equal to the difference between government spending and taxes:

$$\text{Government saving} = \text{Taxes} - \text{Government spending}$$

or

$$S_{\text{public}} = T - G.$$

Finally, remember the basic macroeconomic equation for GDP or national income:

$$Y = C + I + G + NX.$$

We can use this last equation, our definitions of private and public saving, and the fact that net exports equal net foreign investment to arrive at an important relationship, known as the **saving and investment equation**:

**Saving and investment equation** An equation that shows that national saving is equal to domestic investment plus net foreign investment.

National saving = Domestic investment + Net foreign investment

or

$$S = I + NFI.$$

This equation is an *identity* because it must always be true, given the definitions we have used.

The saving and investment equation tells us that a country's saving will be invested either domestically or overseas. If you save $1,000 and use the funds to buy a bond issued by General Motors, GM may use the $1,000 to renovate a factory in the United States (*I*) or to build a factory in China (*NFI*) as a joint venture with a Chinese firm.

# Solved Problem 29.3

## Arriving at the Saving and Investment Equation

Use the definitions of private and public saving, the equation for GDP or national income, and the fact that net exports must equal net foreign investment to arrive at the saving and investment equation.

### Solving the Problem

**Step 1:** **Review the chapter material.** This problem is about the saving and investment equation, so you may want to review the section "Domestic Saving, Domestic Investment, and Net Foreign Investment," which begins on page 997.

**Step 2:** **Derive an expression for national saving (*S*) in terms of national income (*Y*), consumption (*C*), and government purchases (*G*).** We can bring together the four equations we need to use:

1. $S_{\text{private}} = Y - C - T$
2. $S_{\text{public}} = T - G$
3. $Y = C + I + G + NX$
4. $NX = NFI$

Because national saving (*S*) appears in the saving and investment equation, we need to find an equation for it in terms of the other variables. Adding equation 1 plus equation 2 yields national saving:

$$S = S_{\text{private}} + S_{\text{public}} = (Y - C - T) + (T - G) = Y - C - G.$$

**Step 3:** **Use the result from Step 2 to derive an expression for national saving in terms of investment (*I*) and net exports (*NX*).** Because GDP (*Y*) does not appear in the saving and investment equation, we need to substitute the expression for it given in equation (3):

$$S = (C + I + G + NX) - C - G$$

and simplify:

$$S = I + NX.$$

**Step 4: Use the results of Steps 2 and 3 to derive the saving and investment equation.** Finally, substitute net foreign investment for net exports:

$$S = I + NFI.$$

**Your Turn:** For more practice, do related problem 3.8 on page 1009 at the end of this chapter.    MyEconLab

---

A country such as the United States that has negative net foreign investment must be saving less than it is investing domestically. To see this, rewrite the saving and investment equation by moving domestic investment to the left side:

$$S - I = NFI.$$

If net foreign investment is negative—as it is for the United States nearly every year—domestic investment ($I$) must be greater than national saving ($S$).

The level of saving in Japan has been well above domestic investment. The result has been high levels of Japanese net foreign investment. For example, Japanese automobile companies Toyota, Honda, and Nissan have all constructed factories in the United States. Sony purchased the Columbia Pictures film studio. Japan has made many similar investments in countries around the world, which has sometimes caused resentment in those countries. There were some protests in the United States in the 1980s, for example, when Japanese investors purchased the Pebble Beach golf course in California and the Rockefeller Center complex in New York City.

Japan needs a high level of net exports to help offset a low level of domestic investment. When exports of a product begin to decline and imports begin to increase, governments are often tempted to impose tariffs or quotas to reduce imports. (See Chapter 9 to review tariffs and quotas and their negative effects on the economy.) In fact, many Japanese firms have been urging the Japanese government to impose trade restrictions on imports from China.

# The Effect of a Government Budget Deficit on Investment

**29.4 LEARNING** OBJECTIVE

Explain the effect of a government budget deficit on investment in an open economy.

The link we have just developed among saving, investment, and net foreign investment can help us understand some of the effects of changes in a government's budget deficit. When the government runs a budget deficit, national saving will decline unless private saving increases by the amount of the budget deficit, which is unlikely. As the saving and investment equation ($S = I + NFI$) shows, the result of a decline in national saving must be a decline in either domestic investment or net foreign investment. Why, though, does an increase in the government budget deficit cause a fall in domestic investment or net foreign investment?

To understand the answer to this question, remember that if the federal government runs a budget deficit, the U.S. Treasury must raise an amount equal to the deficit by selling bonds. To attract investors, the Treasury may have to raise the interest rates on its bonds. As interest rates on Treasury bonds rise, other interest rates, including those on corporate bonds and bank loans, will also rise. Higher interest rates will discourage some firms from borrowing funds to build new factories or to buy new equipment or computers. Higher interest rates on financial assets in the United States will attract foreign investors. Investors in Canada, Japan, or China will have to buy U.S. dollars to be able to purchase bonds in the United States. This greater demand for dollars will increase their value relative to foreign currencies. As the value of the dollar rises, exports from the United States will fall, and imports to the United States will rise. Net exports and, therefore, net foreign investment will fall.

**Figure 29.4**

**The Twin Deficits, 1978–2010**

During the early 1980s, large federal budget deficits occurred at the same time as large current account deficits, but twin deficits did not occur in most other periods during these years.

Data from U.S. Bureau of Economic Analysis.

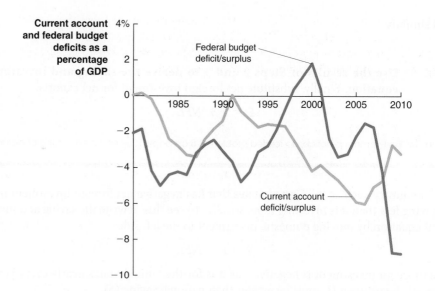

When a government budget deficit leads to a decline in net exports, the result is sometimes referred to as the *twin deficits*, which refers to the possibility that a government budget deficit will also lead to a current account deficit. The twin deficits idea first became widely discussed in the United States during the early 1980s, when the federal government ran a large budget deficit that resulted in high interest rates, a high exchange value of the dollar, and a large current account deficit.

Figure 29.4 shows that in the early 1980s, the United States had large federal budget deficits and large current account deficits. The figure also shows, however, that the twin deficits idea does not match the experience of the United States after 1990. The large federal budget deficits of the early 1990s occurred at a time of relatively small current account deficits, and the budget surpluses of the late 1990s occurred at a time of then-record current account deficits. Both the current account deficit and the federal budget deficit increased in the early 2000s, but the federal budget deficit declined in the mid-2000s much more than did the current account deficit. Beginning in 2008, the federal budget deficit soared, more than doubling as a percentage of GDP, while the current account deficit declined.

The experience of other countries also shows only mixed support for the twin deficits idea. Germany ran large budget deficits and large current account deficits during the early 1990s, but both Canada and Italy ran large budget deficits during the 1980s without running current account deficits. The saving and investment equation shows that an increase in the government budget deficit will not lead to an increase in the current account deficit, provided that either private saving increases or domestic investment declines. According to the twin deficits idea, when the federal government ran budget surpluses in the late 1990s, the current account should also have been in surplus, or at least the current account deficit should have been small. In fact, the increase in national saving due to the budget surpluses was more than offset by a sharp decline in private saving, and the United States ran very large current account deficits.

**Making the Connection**

## Why Is the United States Called the "World's Largest Debtor"?

The following graph shows the current account balance as a percentage of GDP for the United States for the period 1950–2010. The United States has had a current account deficit every year since 1982, with the exception of 1991. Between 1950 and 1975, the United States ran a current account deficit in only five years. Many economists believe that the current account deficits of the 1980s were closely related to the federal budget deficits of those years. High interest rates attracted foreign investors to U.S. bonds, which raised the exchange rate between the dollar and foreign currencies. The high exchange rate reduced U.S. exports and increased imports, leading to current account deficits.

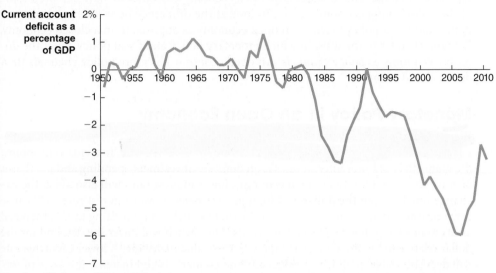

Data from U.S. Bureau of Economic Analysis.

As the federal budget deficit narrowed in the mid-1990s and disappeared in the late 1990s, the foreign exchange value of the dollar remained high—and large current account deficits continued—because foreign investors persisted in investing in the United States, despite low interest rates. In the late 1990s, a number of countries around the world, such as South Korea, Indonesia, Brazil, and Russia, suffered severe economic problems. In a process known as a *flight to quality*, many investors sold their investments in those countries and bought investments in the United States. In addition, the strong performance of the U.S. stock market through the spring of 2000 attracted many investors. Finally, the sharp decline in private saving in the United States that began during the late 1990s also contributed to the U.S. current account deficit. The fall in the value of the dollar after 2008 helped reduce the size of the current account deficit, although the deficit still remained substantial.

Do persistent current account deficits represent a problem for the United States? Current account deficits result in U.S. net foreign investment being negative. Each year, foreign investors accumulate many more U.S. assets than U.S. investors accumulate foreign assets. At the end of 2010, foreign investors owned about $2.5 trillion more of U.S. assets—such as stocks, bonds, and factories—than U.S. investors owned of foreign assets, which is why the United States is sometimes called "the world's largest debtor." But the continued willingness of foreign investors to buy U.S. stocks and bonds and foreign companies to build factories in the United States can be seen as a vote of confidence in the strength of the U.S. economy and the buying power of U.S. consumers. When private saving rates declined in the United States to historically low levels in the mid-2000s, only the continued flow of funds from foreign investors made it possible for the United States to maintain the high levels of domestic investment required for economic growth. Beginning in 2009, private saving rates increased, but public saving turned sharply negative as the federal budget deficit soared. Domestic investment in the United States remains reliant on funds from foreign investment.

**Your Turn:** Test your understanding by doing related problem 4.7 on page 1010 at the end of this chapter. MyEconLab

**29.5 LEARNING** OBJECTIVE

Compare the effectiveness of monetary policy and fiscal policy in an open economy and in a closed economy.

# Monetary Policy and Fiscal Policy in an Open Economy

When we discussed monetary policy and fiscal policy in Chapters 26 and 27, we did not emphasize that the United States is an open economy. Now that we have explored some of the links among economies, we can look at the difference between how monetary policy and fiscal policy work in an open economy as opposed to in a closed economy. Economists refer to the ways in which monetary policy and fiscal policy affect the domestic economy as *policy channels*. An open economy has more policy channels than does a closed economy.

## Monetary Policy in an Open Economy

When the Federal Reserve engages in an expansionary monetary policy, it buys Treasury securities to lower interest rates and stimulate aggregate demand. In a closed economy, the main effect of lower interest rates is on domestic investment spending and purchases of consumer durables. In an open economy, lower interest rates will also affect the exchange rate between the dollar and foreign currencies. Lower interest rates will cause some investors in the United States and abroad to switch from investing in U.S. financial assets to investing in foreign financial assets. This switch will lower the demand for the dollar relative to foreign currencies and cause its value to decline. A lower exchange rate will decrease the price of U.S. products in foreign markets and increase the price of foreign products in the United States. As a result, net exports will increase. This additional policy channel will increase the ability of an expansionary monetary policy to affect aggregate demand.

When the Fed wants to reduce aggregate demand to reduce inflation, it engages in a contractionary monetary policy. The Fed sells Treasury securities to increase interest rates and reduce aggregate demand. In a closed economy, the main effect is once again on domestic investment spending and purchases of consumer durables. In an open economy, higher interest rates will lead to a higher foreign exchange value of the dollar. The prices of U.S. products in foreign markets will increase, and the prices of foreign products in the United States will fall. As a result, net exports will fall. The contractionary policy will have a larger effect on aggregate demand, and therefore it will be more effective in slowing down the growth in economic activity. To summarize: *Monetary policy has a greater effect on aggregate demand in an open economy than in a closed economy.*

## Fiscal Policy in an Open Economy

To engage in an expansionary fiscal policy, the federal government increases its purchases or cuts taxes. Increases in government purchases directly increase aggregate demand. Tax cuts increase aggregate demand by increasing household disposable income and business income, which results in increased consumption spending and investment spending. An expansionary fiscal policy may result in higher interest rates. In a closed economy, the main effect of higher interest rates is to reduce domestic investment spending and purchases of consumer durables. In an open economy, higher interest rates will also lead to an increase in the foreign exchange value of the dollar and a decrease in net exports. Therefore, in an open economy, an expansionary fiscal policy may be less effective because the *crowding out effect* may be larger. In a closed economy, only consumption and investment are crowded out by an expansionary fiscal policy. In an open economy, net exports may also be crowded out.

The government can fight inflation by using a contractionary fiscal policy to slow the growth of aggregate demand. A contractionary fiscal policy cuts government purchases or raises taxes to reduce household disposable income and consumption spending. It also reduces the federal budget deficit (or increases the budget surplus), which may lower interest rates. Lower interest rates will increase domestic investment and purchases of consumer durables, thereby offsetting some of the reduction in government spending and increases in taxes. In an open economy, lower interest rates will also reduce the foreign exchange value of the dollar and increase net exports. Therefore, in an open economy, a contractionary fiscal policy will have a smaller effect on aggregate demand and therefore will be less effective in slowing down an economy. In summary: *Fiscal policy has a smaller effect on aggregate demand in an open economy than in a closed economy.*

Continued from page 983

## Economics in Your Life

### The South Korean Central Bank and Your Car Loan

At the beginning of the chapter, we posed this question: What effect will the Bank of Korea's decision to sell its U.S. Treasury bonds likely have on the interest rate that you pay on your car loan? To sell its holdings of Treasury bonds, South Korea's central bank may have to offer them at a lower price. When the prices of bonds fall, the interest rates on them rise. As the interest rates on U.S. Treasury bonds increase, the interest rates on corporate bonds and bank loans, including car loans, may also increase. So, the decision of the Bank of Korea has the potential to increase the interest rate you pay on your car loan. In practice, the interest rate on your car loan is likely to be affected only if the Bank of Korea sells a very large number of bonds and if investors consider it likely that other foreign central banks may soon do the same thing. The basic point is important, however: Economies are interdependent, and interest rates in the United States are not determined entirely by the actions of people in the United States.

# Conclusion

At one time, U.S. policymakers—and economics textbooks—ignored the linkages between the United States and other economies. In the modern world, these linkages have become increasingly important, and economists and policymakers must take them into account when analyzing the economy. In Chapter 30, we will discuss further how the international financial system operates.

Read *An Inside Look* on the next page for a discussion of the falling value of the U.S. dollar against major foreign currencies through the first half of 2011.

# Struggling Economy Contributes to a Weak Dollar

## U.S. NEWS & WORLD REPORT

## What a Weak Dollar Means for Consumers

The value of U.S. currency might seem trivial in the face of soaring gas prices and high unemployment, but the ripple effects of a chronically weak greenback impacts consumers both here and abroad. The U.S. Dollar Index, which tracks a basket of foreign currencies, has fallen almost 5 percent year-to-date. Despite a recent rebound, just last month it tumbled to levels not seen since the worst days of the financial crisis in 2008.

But how did the dollar drop to this point, and more importantly, how much should you worry?

The answer is complicated, but it has much to do with fundamental supply-and-demand dynamics, says Adolfo Laurenti, deputy chief economist at Chicago-based financial services firm Mesirow Financial. Stronger economies tend to attract investors, putting pressure on the supply of that country's currency and driving up its value. "The stronger the country's economy, the more people want to go and invest in that country and the stronger the currency is expected to be," Laurenti says. On the flip side, investors tend to avoid struggling economies, which lessens demand for investment in the country and weakens its currency.

**(a)** The Federal Reserve's bond buying programs have also had a hand in pushing the dollar lower by driving interest rates to all-time lows. While meant to reduce the cost of borrowing to spur economic growth, low interest rates have stunted yields on financial products such as bonds, reducing demand for investments denominated in dollars and weakening the currency.

"What we're seeing now is that other economies, as they come out of recession faster than we are and [are] experiencing more robust growth than we are, their central banks are starting to tighten and raise interest rates making those countries look more attractive," says J. Bradford Jensen, associate professor of international business and economics at the McDonough School of Business at Georgetown University. "They might sell U.S. dollar-denominated assets to purchase assets in other currencies, which puts downward pressure on the dollar."

**(b)** The specter of inflation also remains on investors' minds. "The Fed's bond buying created very low interest rates and created fear for many investors that future inflation will go up," Laurenti says. "Higher inflation expectations and lower yields on financial assets tend to bring weaker currency, and that's exactly what we are seeing for the dollar."

**(c)** But investors aren't the only ones who have to worry about the impact of inflation. Consumers, too, are bound to see the cost of goods inching up if the dollar remains weak. Although weaker currency helps exporters by making U.S.-produced goods more attractive in the global market, it also makes imports more expensive. U.S. companies can only absorb those higher costs for so long before they start passing hikes on to consumers.

"If you buy goods from abroad and their price continues to escalate, sooner or later, those rising costs will need to be offset in the United States by passing higher costs to the consumer," Laurenti says. "That would, in turn, generate higher inflation." Higher inflation erodes the purchasing power of consumers, which could put strain on the U.S. consumer spending-driven economy.

A weak dollar is a double-edged sword, says Axel Merk, founder of Merk Investments and author of *Sustainable Wealth*. U.S. exporters might see a bump in quarterly earnings as a result of a weaker dollar, but the benefits will be short-lived, he says. The fundamental issue, Merk says, is that advanced economies rarely compete on the prices of goods, because they can't. "When you think of low-end consumer goods that compete on price, you think of Vietnam," he says. "We have no chance to compete with Vietnam. We have to compete in high tech. We have to compete on value added."

# Key Points in the Article

Through 2011, the Federal Reserve had kept interest rates at historically low levels in an effort to stimulate growth. As a result, the value of the dollar had declined relative to foreign currencies. At the same time, the central banks of some countries that were experiencing faster recoveries from the recession had begun to tighten their monetary policies by raising interest rates. Higher interest rates made those economies more attractive to investors and strengthened their currencies relative to the dollar. If the dollar remains weak, consumers will likely feel the effect in the form of rising prices for imported products. These rising prices will increase the U.S. inflation rate, reducing the purchasing power of consumers.

## Analyzing the News

(a) In an effort to boost economic growth in the United States, the Federal Reserve has purchased very large quantities of Treasury bonds, which has helped to push U.S. interest rates to record low levels. The low interest rates have lowered the demand for dollar-denominated investments. A decrease in the demand for U.S. financial assets by foreign investors decreases the demand for U.S. dollars, which in turn decreases the dollar's value against foreign currencies. Figure 1 below shows movements in the value of the dollar since 2002. The index used to measure the value of the dollar is an average of the exchange rates between the dollar and the currencies of major trading partners of the United States. Beginning in 2002, the dollar has declined gradually over time, rising in 2008 and 2009, and then declining again through the middle of 2011.

(b) As you read in this chapter, lower interest rates result in a decline in the demand for financial assets by foreign investors. Figure 2 shows the exchange rate between the dollar and the euro. A decrease in the demand for U.S. assets by foreign investors causes a decrease in the demand for dollars in exchange for euros, so that the demand curve for the dollar shifts from $D_1$ to $D_2$. As a result, the exchange rate falls from €0.80 per $1 to €0.75 per $1. The low interest rates resulting from the Fed's bond-buying programs also have some investors concerned about the possibility that the U.S. inflation rate will increase in the future. Expectations of higher inflation combined with lower yields on financial securities have the potential to weaken the value of a currency relative to other currencies. Adolfo Laurenti of the financial services company Mesirow Financial believes this is what has happened to the U.S. dollar.

(c) Concerns about rising inflation can affect consumers as well as investors. A weak dollar makes imports more expensive in the United States. If the dollar remains weak, U.S. companies that sell imported products and those that use imports in the manufacture of products will likely need to pass these higher costs along to U.S. consumers by raising prices. The result would be higher inflation and reduced consumer purchasing power.

## Thinking Critically

1. How would a decrease in the value of the U.S. dollar relative to other currencies affect future U.S. trade deficits?
2. Suppose the value of the U.S. dollar increased. Which sectors of the U.S. economy would benefit from such an adjustment? Briefly explain.

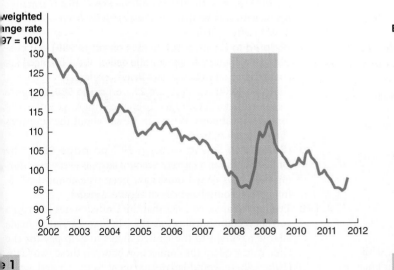

**Figure 1**

k U.S. economy led to a decline of the U.S. dollar. The shaded area indicates a recession.
Trade weighted exchange index, St. Louis Federal Reserve; and Board of Governors of the Federal System.

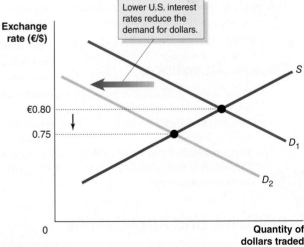

**Figure 2**

Lower interest rates reduce the value of the dollar against the euro.

# Chapter Summary and Problems

## Key Terms

Balance of payments, p. 984

Balance of trade, p. 984

Capital account, p. 986

Closed economy, p. 984

Currency appreciation, p. 991

Currency depreciation, p. 991

Current account, p. 984

Financial account, p. 985

Net foreign investment, p. 986

Nominal exchange rate, p. 989

Open economy, p. 984

Real exchange rate, p. 996

Saving and investment equation, p. 998

Speculators, p. 991

---

**29.1** **The Balance of Payments: Linking the United States to the International Economy,** pages 984–988

LEARNING OBJECTIVE: Explain how the balance of payments is calculated.

## Summary

Nearly all economies are **open economies** that trade with and invest in other economies. A **closed economy** has no transactions in trade or finance with other economies. The **balance of payments** is the record of a country's trade with other countries in goods, services, and assets. The **current account** records a country's net exports, net investment income, and net transfers. The **financial account** shows investments a country has made abroad and foreign investments received by the country. The **balance of trade** is the difference between the value of the goods a country exports and the value of the goods a country imports. **Net foreign investment** is the difference between capital outflows from a country and capital inflows. The **capital account** is a part of the balance of payments that records relatively minor transactions. Apart from measurement errors, the sum of the current account and the financial account must equal zero. Therefore, the balance of payments must also equal zero.

 Visit **www.myeconlab.com** to complete these exercises online and get instant feedback.

## Review Questions

**1.1** What is the relationship among the current account, the financial account, and the balance of payments?

**1.2** What is the difference between net exports and the current account balance?

**1.3** Explain whether you agree with the following statement: "The United States has run a balance of payments deficit every year since 1982."

## Problems and Applications

**1.4** In 2010, France had a current account deficit of €41.0 billion (approximately $54.4 billion). Did France experience a net capital outflow or a net capital inflow during 2010? Briefly explain.

**1.5** Use the information in the following table to prepare a balance of payments account, like the one shown in Table 29.1 on page 985. Assume that the balance on the capital account is zero.

| | |
|---|---:|
| Increase in foreign holdings of assets in the United States | $1,181 |
| Exports of goods | 856 |
| Imports of services | −256 |
| Statistical discrepancy | ? |
| Net transfers | −60 |
| Exports of services | 325 |
| Income received on investments | 392 |
| Imports of goods | −1,108 |
| Increase in U.S. holdings of assets in foreign countries | −1,040 |
| Income payments on investments | −315 |

**1.6** [**Related to the** Don't Let This Happen to You **on page 987**] In 2010, Germany had a trade surplus of $204 billion and a current account balance of $188 billion. Explain how Germany's current account surplus could be smaller than its trade surplus. In 2010, would we expect that Germany's balance on financial account would have been −$188 billion? Briefly explain.

**1.7** [**Related to** Solved Problem 29.1 **on page 988**] Is it possible for a country to run a trade deficit and a financial account deficit simultaneously? Briefly explain.

**1.8** [**Related to** Solved Problem 29.1 **on page 988**] Suppose we know that a country has been receiving large inflows of foreign investment. What can we say about the country's current account balance?

**1.9** [**Related to** Solved Problem 29.1 **on page 988**] The United States ran a current account surplus every year during the 1960s. What must have been true about the U.S. financial account balance during those years?

**1.10** The only year since 1982 that the United States has run a current account surplus was 1991. In that year, Japan made a large payment to the United States to help pay for the Gulf War. Explain the connection between these two facts. (*Hint:* Where would Japan's payment to the United States appear in the balance of payments?)

**1.11** According to this chapter, the U.S. trade deficit is almost always larger than the U.S. current account deficit. Why is this true?

**1.12** An article in the *New York Times* observes that, "China is quickly shifting from being a country known for exports to one capable of making huge investments in global financial markets, analysts say." Is there a connection between China's exports and its financial investments in other countries? Your answer should mention China's current account and its financial account.

From David Barboza, "China's Growing Overseas Portfolio," *New York Times*, May 9, 2011.

---

## 29.2  The Foreign Exchange Market and Exchange Rates, pages 989–996

LEARNING OBJECTIVE: Explain how exchange rates are determined and how changes in exchange rates affect the prices of imports and exports.

## Summary

The **nominal exchange rate** is the value of one country's currency in terms of another country's currency. The exchange rate is determined in the foreign exchange market by the demand and supply of a country's currency. Changes in the exchange rate are caused by shifts in demand or supply. The three main sets of factors that cause the supply and demand curves in the foreign exchange market to shift are changes in the demand for U.S.-produced goods and services and changes in the demand for foreign-produced goods and services; changes in the desire to invest in the United States and changes in the desire to invest in foreign countries; and changes in the expectations of currency traders—particularly **speculators**—concerning the likely future values of the dollar and the likely future values of foreign currencies. **Currency appreciation** occurs when a currency's market value increases relative to another currency. **Currency depreciation** occurs when a currency's market value decreases relative to another currency. The **real exchange rate** is the price of domestic goods in terms of foreign goods. The real exchange rate is calculated by multiplying the nominal exchange rate by the ratio of the domestic price level to the foreign price level.

 MyEconLab    Visit **www.myeconlab.com** to complete these exercises online and get instant feedback.

## Review Questions

**2.1**  If the exchange rate between the Japanese yen and the U.S. dollar expressed in terms of yen per dollar is ¥75 = $1, what is the exchange rate when expressed in terms of dollars per yen?

**2.2**  Suppose that the current exchange rate between the dollar and the euro is €0.7 = $1. If the exchange rate changes to €0.8 = $1, has the euro appreciated or depreciated against the dollar?

**2.3**  Why do foreign households and foreign firms demand U.S. dollars in exchange for foreign currency? Why do U.S. households and U.S. firms supply U.S. dollars in exchange for foreign currency?

**2.4**  What are the three main sets of factors that cause the supply and demand curves in the foreign exchange market to shift?

## Problems and Applications

**2.5**  [Related to the Don't Let This Happen to You **on page 995**] If we know the exchange rate between Country A's currency and Country B's currency and we know the exchange rate between Country B's currency and Country C's currency, then we can compute the exchange rate between Country A's currency and Country C's currency.

**a.**  Suppose the exchange rate between the Japanese yen and the U.S. dollar is currently ¥75 = $1 and the exchange rate between the British pound and the U.S. dollar is £0.62 = $1. What is the exchange rate between the yen and the pound?

**b.**  Suppose the exchange rate between the yen and dollar changes to ¥85 = $1 and the exchange rate between the pound and dollar changes to £0.55 = $1. Has the dollar appreciated or depreciated against the yen? Has the dollar appreciated or depreciated against the pound? Has the yen appreciated or depreciated against the pound?

**2.6**  [Related to the Making the Connection **on page 989**] In January 1, 2002, there were 15 member countries in the European Union. Twelve of those countries eliminated their own individual currencies and began using a new common currency, the euro. For a three-year period from January 1, 1999, through December 31, 2001, these 12 countries priced goods and services in terms of both their own currencies and the euro. During that period, the value of their currencies was fixed against each other and against the euro. So during that time, the dollar had an exchange rate against each of these currencies and against the euro. The information in the following table shows the fixed exchange rates of four European currencies against the euro and their exchange rates against the U.S. dollar on March 2, 2001. Use the information below to calculate the exchange rate between the dollar and the euro (in euros per dollar) on March 2, 2001.

| Currency | Units per Euro (fixed) | Units per U.S. Dollar (as of March 2, 2001) |
|---|---|---|
| German mark | 1.9558 | 2.0938 |
| French franc | 6.5596 | 7.0223 |
| Italian lira | 1,936.2700 | 2,072.8700 |
| Portuguese escudo | 200.4820 | 214.6300 |

**2.7**  Graph the demand and supply of U.S. dollars for euros and label each axis. Show graphically and explain the effect of an increase in interest rates in Europe by the European Central Bank (ECB) on the demand and supply of dollars and the resulting change in the exchange rate of euros for U.S. dollars.

**2.8**  Graph the demand and supply of U.S. dollars for euros and label each axis. Suppose that higher federal budget deficits result in higher U.S. interest rates. Use your graph to show the effect higher U.S. interest rates on the demand and supply of dollars and the resulting change in the exchange rate of euros for U.S. dollars. Why might the change in the exchange rate lead to a current account deficit?

2.9 Use the graph to answer the following questions.

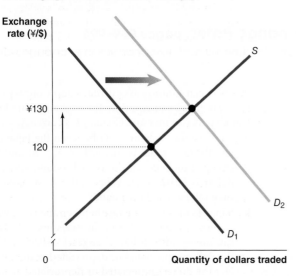

a. Briefly explain whether the dollar appreciated or depreciated against the yen.

b. Which of the following events could have caused the shift in demand shown in the graph?
   i. Interest rates in the United States have declined.
   ii. Income rises in Japan.
   iii. Speculators begin to believe the value of the dollar will be higher in the future.

2.10 **[Related to** Solved Problem 29.2 **on page 995]** When a country's currency appreciates, is this generally good news or bad news for the country's consumers? Is it generally good news or bad news for the country's businesses? Explain your reasoning.

2.11 An article about U.S. wheat exports is titled "Wheat Gains as Export Demand May Rise on Dollar Drop…"
   a. What does the title mean by a "dollar drop"?
   b. Why would the dollar's drop increase the demand for U.S. wheat exports?

   From Whitney McFerron, "Wheat Gains as Export Demand May Rise on Dollar Drop, EU Rain," www.businessweek.com, October 27, 2011.

2.12 **[Related to the** Chapter Opener **on page 983]** An article describing global sales for McDonald's contains the following information: "However, global sales in dollar terms declined 4.6 per cent for the month, but would have increased 3.2 per cent in constant currencies."
   a. What does the article mean by "constant currencies"?
   b. If global sales for McDonald's declined in dollar terms but would have risen in constant currencies, what must have happened during this period to the value of the dollar in exchange for other currencies? Briefly explain.

   From Jonathan Birchall, "Strong Sales to Hit McDonald's Profits," *Financial Times,* July 27, 2011.

2.13 The following is from an article from Reuters:

   The dollar rallied broadly for its best day in more than a month on Thursday and the euro tumbled to an eight-month low as mounting concerns about the global economy drove investors to seek safety and liquidity.

   What assets were investors purchasing to seek safety and liquidity, and why did the purchases lead to a dollar rally?

   From Gertrude Chavez-Dreyfuss, "Dollar Gains as Global Gloom Spurs Flight to Safety," Reuters.com, September 23, 2011.

2.14 **[Related to the** Making the Connection **on page 993]** The humorist Dave Barry once wrote the following: "In economic news, the Federal Reserve Board, responding to recession fears and the continued weakening of the dollar, votes unanimously to be paid in euros." Granted that Barry was joking, what advantages would there be to U.S. citizens being paid in euros at a time when the dollar was "weakening"? Why did the dollar lose value against most other currencies beginning in 2002?

   From Dave Barry, *Dave Barry's History of the Millenium (So Far),* (New York: Berkeley Books, 2008), pp. 230–231.

2.15 **[Related to the** Making the Connection **on page 993]** The following is from an article in the *Wall Street Journal:*

   [Peter] Schiff's Darien, Conn., broker-dealer firm, Euro Pacific Capital Inc., advised its clients to bet that the dollar would weaken significantly and that foreign stocks would outpace their U.S. peers. Instead, the dollar advanced against most currencies, magnifying the losses from foreign stocks Mr. Schiff steered his investors into.

   What does it mean to say that "the dollar advanced against most currencies"? Why would this advance magnify the losses to U.S. investors from investing in foreign stocks?

   From Scott Patterson, Joanna Slater, and Craig Karmin, "Right Forecast by Schiff, Wrong Plan?" *Wall Street Journal,* January 30, 2009.

---

**29.3** **The International Sector and National Saving and Investment,** pages 996–999

LEARNING OBJECTIVE: Explain the saving and investment equation.

## Summary

A current account deficit must be exactly offset by a financial account surplus. The financial account is equal to net capital flows, which is equal to net foreign investment but with the opposite sign. Because the current account balance is roughly equal to net exports, we can conclude that net exports will equal net foreign investment. National saving is equal to private saving plus government saving. Private saving is equal to national income minus consumption and minus taxes. Government saving is the difference between taxes and government spending. As we saw in previous chapters, GDP (or national income) is equal to the sum of investment, consumption, government spending, and net exports. We can use this fact, our definitions of private and government saving, and the fact that net exports equal net foreign investment to arrive at an important relationship known as the **saving and investment equation**: $S = I + NFI$.

## Review Questions

3.1 Explain the relationship between net exports and net foreign investment.

3.2 What is the saving and investment equation? If national saving declines, what will happen to domestic investment and net foreign investment?

3.3 If a country saves more than it invests domestically, what must be true of its net foreign investment?

## Problems and Applications

3.4 Writing in the *Wall Street Journal*, David Wessel makes the following observation:

> Trend one: The U.S. has been buying more than $1 billion a day more from the rest of the world than it has been selling.... Trend two: Foreigners have been investing more than $1 billion a day of their savings in U.S. stocks, bonds, office towers, factories, and companies.

Is it coincidence that both of Wessel's "trends" involve $1 billion per day? Briefly explain.

"Pain from the Dollar's Decline Will Mostly Be Felt Overseas," by David Wessel from *Wall Street Journal*, June 13, 2002. Copyright © 2011 by Dow Jones & Company, Inc. Reproduced with permission of Dow Jones & Company, Inc.

3.5 In 2010, domestic investment in Japan was 20.6 percent of GDP, and Japanese net foreign investment was 1.3 percent of GDP. What percentage of GDP was Japanese national saving?

3.6 In 2010, France's net foreign investment was negative. Which was larger in France in 2010: national saving or domestic investment? Briefly explain.

3.7 Briefly explain whether you agree with the following statement: "Because in 2010 national saving was a smaller percentage of GDP in the United States than in the United Kingdom, domestic investment must also have been a smaller percentage of GDP in the United States than in the United Kingdom."

3.8 **[Related to** Solved Problem 29.3 **on page 998]** Look again at Solved Problem 29.3, in which we derived the saving and investment equation $S = I + NX$. In deriving this equation, we assumed that national income was equal to $Y$. But $Y$ only includes income *earned* by households. In the modern U.S. economy, households receive substantial transfer payments—such as Social Security payments and unemployment insurance payments—from the government. Suppose that we define national income as being equal to $Y + TR$, where $TR$ equals government transfer payments, and we also define government spending as being equal to $G + TR$. Show that after making these adjustments, we end up with the same saving and investment equation.

3.9 Use the saving and investment equation to explain why the United States experienced large current account deficits in the late 1990s.

3.10 Former congressman and presidential candidate Richard Gephardt once proposed that tariffs be imposed on imports from countries with which the United States has a trade deficit. If this proposal were enacted and if it were to succeed in reducing the U.S. current account deficit to zero, what would be the likely effect on domestic investment spending within the United States? Assume that no other federal government economic policy is changed. (*Hint*: Use the saving and investment equation to answer this question.)

3.11 According to a May 2009 article from *Reuters*:

> Net capital inflows into the United States were $23.2 billion in March, reversing a revised net outflow of $91.1 billion in the previous month.... It shows that money was returning into U.S. dollars.... The dollar extended gains against the euro, which last traded down 0.5 percent at $1.3572.

From the U.S. point of view, do the changes mentioned in the first sentence represent an increase or a decrease in net foreign investment? Why would this change in net foreign investment show that "money was returning into U.S. dollars" and cause the exchange value of the dollar to rise?

"U.S. Net Capital Inflows for March at $23.2 Billion," by Wanfeng Zhou from *Reuters*, May 15, 2009. All rights reserved. Republication or redistribution of Thomson Reuters content, including by framing or similar means, is expressly prohibited without the prior written consent of Thomson Reuters. Thomson Reuters and its logo are registered trademarks of the Thomson Reuters group of companies around the world. Copyright © 2011 by Thomson Reuters. Thomson Reuters journalists are subject to an Editorial Handbook which requires fair presentation and disclosure of relevant interests.

---

## 29.4 | The Effect of a Government Budget Deficit on Investment, pages 999–1001

LEARNING OBJECTIVE: Explain the effect of a government budget deficit on investment in an open economy.

## Summary

When the government runs a budget deficit, national saving will decline unless private saving increases by the full amount of the budget deficit, which is unlikely. As the saving and investment equation $(S = I + NFI)$ shows, the result of a decline in national saving must be a decline in either domestic investment or net foreign investment.

## Review Questions

4.1 What happens to national saving when the government runs a budget surplus? What is the twin deficits idea?

Did it hold for the United States in the 1990s? Briefly explain.

4.2 Why were the early and mid-1980s particularly difficult times for U.S. exporters?

4.3 Why is the United States sometimes called the "World's largest debtor"?

## Problems and Applications

4.4 Tim Condon, an economist at the European bank ING, was quoted in the *Wall Street Journal* in 2011 as predicting that "China's current account or saving-investment surplus [will be in] the 1–2% of GDP range…" Is he correct in referring to China's current account as being the same as its saving-investment surplus? Briefly explain. If the Chinese government runs a large budget deficit, what will be the likely effect on its current account?

From Josh Chin, "Economists React: Chinese Imports Way Up in August," *Wall Street Journal*, September 12, 2011.

4.5 According to an article in the *Wall Street Journal*:

Economists at China International Capital Corp., or CICC, say the companies that will suffer most from a stronger yuan are textile and apparel makers and office equipment producers…. That could also mean a sting for clothing retailers such as Wal-Mart Stores Inc. that buy a lot from China….

a. Does a "stronger yuan" mean that the yuan will exchange for more or fewer dollars?

b. How can both Chinese companies, such as apparel makers, and foreign companies, such as Wal-Mart and Carrefour, be hurt by a stronger yuan?

c. What effect will a stronger yuan be likely to have on the Chinese current account? What effect is it likely to have on the U.S. current account?

From Jason Dean, Norihiko Shirouzu, Clare Ansberry and Kersten Zhang, "Yuan Impact: General Manufacturing," *Wall Street Journal*, June 21, 2010.

4.6 The text states, "The budget surpluses of the late 1990s occurred at a time of then-record current account deficits." Holding everything else constant, what would the likely impact have been on domestic investment in the United States if the current account had been balanced instead of being in deficit?

4.7 **[Related to the** Making the Connection **on page 1000]** Why might "the continued willingness of foreign investors to buy U.S. stocks and bonds and foreign companies to build factories in the United States" result in the United States running a current account deficit?

---

**29.5** **Monetary Policy and Fiscal Policy in an Open Economy,** pages 1002–1003

LEARNING OBJECTIVE: Compare the effectiveness of monetary policy and fiscal policy in an open economy and in a closed economy.

## Summary

When the Federal Reserve engages in an expansionary monetary policy, it buys government bonds to lower interest rates and increase aggregate demand. In a closed economy, the main effect of lower interest rates is on domestic investment spending and purchases of consumer durables. In an open economy, lower interest rates will also cause an increase in net exports. When the Fed wants to slow the rate of economic growth to reduce inflation, it engages in a contractionary monetary policy. With a contractionary policy, the Fed sells government bonds to increase interest rates and reduce aggregate demand. In a closed economy, the main effect is once again on domestic investment and purchases of consumer durables. In an open economy, higher interest rates will also reduce net exports. We can conclude that monetary policy has a greater impact on aggregate demand in an open economy than in a closed economy. To engage in an expansionary fiscal policy, the government increases government spending or cuts taxes. An expansionary fiscal policy can lead to higher interest rates. In a closed economy, the main effect of higher interest rates is on domestic investment spending and spending on consumer durables. In an open economy, higher interest rates will also reduce net exports. A contractionary fiscal policy will reduce the budget deficit and may lower interest rates. In a closed economy, lower interest rates increase domestic investment and spending on consumer durables.

In an open economy, lower interest rates also increase net exports. We can conclude that fiscal policy has a smaller impact on aggregate demand in an open economy than in a closed economy.

 MyEconLab    Visit **www.myeconlab.com** to complete these exercises online and get instant feedback.

## Review Questions

5.1 What is meant by a "policy channel"?

5.2 Why does monetary policy have a greater effect on aggregate demand in an open economy than in a closed economy?

5.3 Why does fiscal policy have a smaller effect on aggregate demand in an open economy than in a closed economy?

## Problems and Applications

5.4 An article in the *Economist* magazine describes Ireland as "an extraordinarily open economy." Is fiscal policy in Ireland likely to be more or less effective than it would be in a less open economy? Briefly explain.

From "Celtic Cross," *Economist*, May 26, 2011.

**5.5** Suppose that Federal Reserve policy leads to higher interest rates in the United States.

    **a.** How will this policy affect real GDP in the short run if the United States is a closed economy?

    **b.** How will this policy affect real GDP in the short run if the United States is an open economy?

    **c.** How will your answer to part b. change if interest rates also rise in the countries that are the major trading partners of the United States?

**5.6** An economist remarks, "In the 1960s, fiscal policy would have been a better way to stabilize the economy, but now I believe that monetary policy is better." What has changed about the U.S. economy that might have led the economist to this conclusion?

**5.7** Suppose the federal government increases spending without also increasing taxes. In the short run, how will this action affect real GDP and the price level in a closed economy? How will the effects of this action differ in an open economy?

## Chapter Outline and Learning Objectives

# Don't Let This Happen to You

## Remember That Modern Currencies Are Fiat Money

Although the United States has not been on the gold standard since 1933, many people still believe that somehow gold continues to "back" U.S. currency. The U.S. Department of the Treasury still owns billions of dollars worth of gold bars, most of which are stored at the Fort Knox Bullion Depository in Kentucky. (Even more gold is stored in a basement of the Federal Reserve Bank of New York, which holds about one-quarter of the world's gold supply—almost 10 percent of all the gold ever mined. This gold, however, is entirely owned by foreign governments and international agencies.) The gold in Fort Knox no longer has any connection to the amount of paper money issued by the Federal Reserve. As we saw in Chapter 25, U.S. currency—like the currencies of other countries—is *fiat money*, which means it has no value except as money. The link between gold and money that existed for centuries has been broken in modern economies.

MyEconLab

**Your Turn:** Test your understanding by doing related problem 1.3 on page 1032 at the end of this chapter.

# The Current Exchange Rate System

**30.2 LEARNING** OBJECTIVE

Discuss the three key features of the current exchange rate system.

**Euro** The common currency of many European countries.

The current exchange rate system has three important aspects:

1. The United States allows the dollar to float against other major currencies.
2. Seventeen countries in Europe have adopted a single currency, the **euro**.
3. Some developing countries have attempted to keep their currencies' exchange rates fixed against the dollar or another major currency.

We begin our discussion of the current exchange rate system by looking at the changing value of the dollar over time. In discussing the value of the dollar, we can look further at what determines exchange rates in the short run and in the long run.

## The Floating Dollar

Since 1973, the value of the U.S. dollar has fluctuated widely against other major currencies. Panel (a) of Figure 30.1 shows the exchange rate between the U.S. dollar and the Canadian dollar between January 1973 and October 2011, and panel (b) shows the

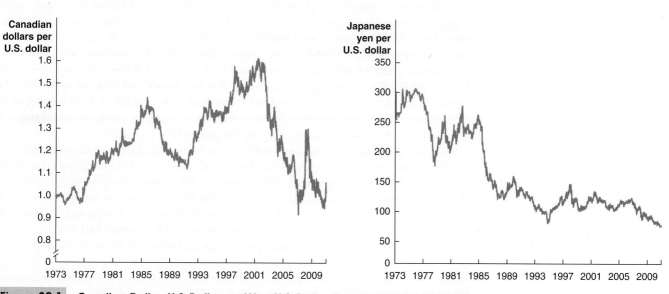

**Figure 30.1** Candian Dollar-U.S. Dollar and Yen-U.S. Dollar Exchange Rates, 1973-2011

Panel (a) shows that from the end of the Bretton Woods system in 1973 through October 2011, the U.S. dollar gained slightly in value against the Canadian dollar. Panel (b) shows that during the same period, the U.S. dollar lost value against the Japanese yen.
Data from Federal Reserve Board of Governors.

exchange rate between the U.S. dollar and the Japanese yen for the same period. Remember that the dollar increases in value when it takes more units of foreign currency to buy $1, and it falls in value when it takes fewer units of foreign currency to buy $1. From January 1973 to October 2011, the U.S. dollar lost more than 74 percent in value against the yen, while it gained about 2 percent in value against the Canadian dollar.

*In 2011, many individual Canadians purchased second homes in Arizona, thanks to the favorable exchange rate.*

## Making the Connection

## The Canadian Province of . . . Arizona?

In 2011, there seemed to be a lot of Canadians buying houses in Phoenix and other cities in Arizona. For many years, some Canadians have found buying a second home in Arizona or Florida a good way to avoid the harsh Canadian winters. As Figure 30.1 shows, the value of the U.S. dollar has been declining relative to the Canadian dollar for most of the period since 2000. Although the value of the U.S. dollar soared by more than 30 percent relative to the Canadian dollar during the height of the financial crisis in 2008, it continued to decline during most of the period after the crisis had ended. The falling value of the U.S. dollar was a great help to Canadian buyers of U.S. homes.

In late 2001, it took 1.60 Canadian dollars to purchase 1 U.S. dollar. So, a Canadian purchasing a house in Phoenix priced at $125,000 would have had to pay $200,000 in Canadian dollars. In the summer of 2011, it took only 0.95 Canadian dollars to purchase 1 U.S. dollar. The stronger Canadian dollar meant that a Canadian could now purchase a house in Phoenix priced at $125,000 for only $118,750 in Canadian dollars. In other words, the decline in the value of the U.S. dollar resulted in a more than 40 percent reduction in the price of the house in Canadian dollars. As one Canadian who was buying a vacation home in Desert Ridge, Arizona, put it: "It's purchasing power, plain and simple. In the days when our dollar was 60 or 65 [U.S.] cents, I wouldn't even be talking to you. The strong Canadian dollar has created a lot of opportunities for Canadians." In addition to the decline in the value of the U.S. dollar, many Canadians found Arizona to be an ideal place to buy a second home because overbuilding in the state during the housing bubble had resulted in many property owners being willing to accept sharply lower prices (in U.S. dollars). Little wonder that by 2011, restaurants and bars in Arizona began staging Canada Day celebrations to attract the growing Canadian population.

In addition to individual Canadians looking to buy second homes in Arizona, some Canadian investors bought multiple properties, hoping to resell them for a profit in the future after local housing prices had risen and after the value of the U.S. dollar had increased relative to the Canadian dollar. Some Canadian manufacturers have also shifted operations to the United States. For example, E.H. Price, a firm that produces ventilation systems for commercial buildings and is headquartered in Winnipeg, Canada, doubled the size of its operations in the United States, where nearly half of its sales were. The rising value of the Canadian dollar would have priced its products out of the U.S. market if it had continued manufacturing the products in Canada.

Of course, further fluctuations in the value of the U.S. dollar could pose problems for Canadians buying and investing in the United States. For example, if the value of the U.S. dollar were to continue to decline, then Canadians who bought second homes in the United States or Canadian investors buying multiple U.S. homes would take a loss in terms of Canadian dollars should they decide to sell. An increase in the value of the U.S. dollar would be good news for Canadian owners of U.S. houses but bad news for Canadian manufacturers if they intended to export goods to Canada from their U.S. plants.

Based on Chana R. Schoenberger, "Canadians Warm to Phoenix," *Wall Street Journal*, October 8, 2011; Julie Schmit, "Foreign Buyers Lifting U.S. Home Sales," *USA Today*, July 14, 2011; and Barrie McKenna, "For Canadian Manufacturers, Foreign Assets Tantalizingly Cheap," *(Toronto) Globe and Mail*, June 12, 2011.

MyEconLab **Your Turn:** Test your understanding by doing related problem 2.6 on page 1033 at the end of this chapter.

# What Determines Exchange Rates in the Long Run?

Over the past 40 years, why has the value of the U.S. dollar fallen against the Japanese yen but risen slightly against the Canadian dollar? In the short run, the two most important causes of exchange rate movements are changes in interest rates—which cause investors to change their views of which countries' financial investments will yield the highest returns—and changes in investors' expectations about the future values of currencies. Over the long run, other factors are also important in explaining movements in exchange rates.

**The Theory of Purchasing Power Parity**  It seems reasonable that, in the long run, exchange rates should be at a level that makes it possible to buy the same amount of goods and services with the equivalent amount of any country's currency. In other words, the purchasing power of every country's currency should be the same. The idea that in the long run, exchange rates move to equalize the purchasing powers of different currencies is referred to as the theory of **purchasing power parity**.

**Purchasing power parity**  The theory that in the long run, exchange rates move to equalize the purchasing powers of different currencies.

To make the theory of purchasing power parity clearer, consider a simple example. Suppose that a Hershey candy bar has a price of $1 in the United States and £1 in the United Kingdom and that the exchange rate is £1 = $1. In that case, at least with respect to candy bars, the dollar and the pound have equivalent purchasing power. If the price of a Hershey bar increases to £2 in the United Kingdom but stays at $1 in the United States, the exchange rate will have to change to £2 per $1 in order for the pound to maintain its relative purchasing power. As long as exchange rates adjust to reflect purchasing power, it will be possible to buy a Hershey bar for $1 in the United States or to exchange $1 for £2 and buy the candy bar in the United Kingdom.

If exchange rates are not at the values indicated by purchasing power parity, it appears that there are opportunities to make profits. For example, suppose a Hershey candy bar sells for £2 in the United Kingdom and $1 in the United States, and the exchange rate between the dollar and the pound is £1 = $1. In this case, it would be possible to exchange £1 million for $1 million and use the dollars to buy 1 million Hershey bars in the United States. The Hershey bars could then be shipped to the United Kingdom, where they could be sold for £2 million. The result of these transactions would be a profit of £1 million (minus any shipping costs). In fact, if the dollar–pound exchange rate does not reflect the purchasing power for many products—not just Hershey bars—this process could be repeated until extremely large profits were made. In practice, though, as people attempted to make these profits by exchanging pounds for dollars, they would bid up the value of the dollar until it reached the purchasing power exchange rate of £2 = $1. Once the exchange rate reflected the purchasing power of the two currencies, there would be no further opportunities for profit. This mechanism appears to guarantee that exchange rates will be at the levels determined by purchasing power parity.

Three real-world complications, though, keep purchasing power parity from being a complete explanation of exchange rates, even in the long run:

1. ***Not all products can be traded internationally.*** Where goods are traded internationally, profits can be made whenever exchange rates do not reflect their purchasing power parity values. However, more than half of all goods and services produced in the United States and most other countries are not traded internationally. When goods are not traded internationally, their prices will not be the same in every country. For instance, suppose that the exchange rate is £1 for $1, but the price for having a cavity filled by a dentist is twice as high in the United States as it is in the United Kingdom. In this case, there is no way to buy up the low-priced British service and resell it in the United States. Because many goods and services are not traded internationally, exchange rates will not reflect exactly the relative purchasing powers of currencies.

2. ***Products and consumer preferences are different across countries.*** We expect the same product to sell for the same price around the world, but if a product is similar but not identical to another product, their prices might be different. For example, a 3-ounce Hershey candy bar may sell for a different price in the United States than

does a 3-ounce Cadbury candy bar in the United Kingdom. Prices of the same product may also differ across countries if consumer preferences differ. If consumers in the United Kingdom like candy bars more than do consumers in the United States, a Hershey candy bar may sell for more in the United Kingdom than in the United States.

3. *Countries impose barriers to trade.* Most countries, including the United States, impose *tariffs* and *quotas* on imported goods. A **tariff** is a tax imposed by a government on imports. A **quota** is a government-imposed limit on the quantity of a good that can be imported. For example, the United States has a quota on imports of sugar. As a result, the price of sugar in the United States is much higher than the price of sugar in other countries. Because of the quota, there is no legal way to buy up the cheap foreign sugar and resell it in the United States.

**Tariff** A tax imposed by a government on imports.

**Quota** A numerical limit that a government imposes on the quantity of a good that can be imported into the country.

### Making the Connection | The Big Mac Theory of Exchange Rates

In a lighthearted attempt to test the accuracy of the theory of purchasing power parity, the *Economist* magazine regularly compares the prices of Big Macs in different countries. If purchasing power parity holds, you should be able to take the dollars required to buy a Big Mac in the United States and exchange them for the amount of foreign currency needed to buy a Big Mac in any other country. The following table is for July 2011, when Big Macs were selling for an average price of $4.07 in the United States. The "implied exchange rate" shows what the xchange rate would be if purchasing power parity held for Big Macs. For example, a Big Mac sold for 20.0 pesos in Argentina and $4.07 in the United States, so for purchasing power parity to hold, the exchange rate should have been 20.0 pesos/$4.07, or 4.91 pesos = $1. The actual exchange rate in July 2011 was 4.13 pesos = $1. So, on Big Mac purchasing power parity grounds, the Argentine peso was *overvalued* against the dollar by 19 percent $(((4.91 - 4.13)/4.13) \times 100 = 19 \text{ percent})$. That is, if Big Mac purchasing power parity held, it would have taken 19 percent more Argentine pesos to buy a dollar than it actually did.

*Is the price of a Big Mac in Buenos Aires the same as the price of a Big Mac in New York?*

Could you take advantage of this difference between the purchasing power parity exchange rate and the actual exchange rate to become fabulously wealthy by buying up low-priced Big Macs in New York and reselling them at a higher price in Buenos Aires? Unfortunately, the low-priced U.S. Big Macs would be a soggy mess by the time you got them to Buenos Aires. The fact that Big Mac prices are not the same around the world illustrates one reason purchasing power parity does not hold exactly: Many goods are not traded internationally.

| Country | Big Mac Price | Implied Exchange Rate | Actual Exchange Rate |
|---------|---------------|-----------------------|----------------------|
| Mexico | 32.0 pesos | 7.86 pesos per dollar | 11.70 pesos per dollar |
| Japan | 320 yen | 78.62 yen per dollar | 78.40 yen per dollar |
| United Kingdom | 2.39 pounds | 0.59 pound per dollar | 0.61 pound per dollar |
| Switzerland | 6.50 Swiss francs | 1.60 Swiss francs per dollar | 0.81 Swiss francs per dollar |
| Indonesia | 22,534 rupiahs | 5,537 rupiahs per dollar | 8,523 rupiahs per dollar |
| Canada | 4.73 Canadian dollars | 1.16 Canadian dollars per U.S. dollar | 0.95 Canadian dollars per U.S. dollar |
| China | 14.7 yuan | 3.61 yuan per dollar | 6.45 yuan per dollar |

Data from "Currency Comparisons, to Go," *Economist*, July 28, 2011.

MyEconLab  **Your Turn:** Test your understanding by doing related problem 2.11 on page 1033 at the end of this chapter.

# Solved Problem 30.2

## Calculating Purchasing Power Parity Exchange Rates Using Big Macs

Fill in the missing values in the following table. Remember that the implied exchange rate shows what the exchange rate would be if purchasing power parity held for Big Macs. Assume that the Big Mac is selling for $4.07 in the United States. Explain whether the U.S. dollar is overvalued or undervalued relative to each currency and predict what will happen in the future to each exchange rate. Finally, calculate the implied exchange rate between the Polish zloty and the Brazilian real (plural: reais) and explain which currency is undervalued in terms of Big Mac purchasing power parity.

| Country | Big Mac Price | Implied Exchange Rate | Actual Exchange Rate |
|---|---|---|---|
| Brazil | 9.50 reais | | 1.54 reais per dollar |
| Poland | 8.63 zlotys | | 2.80 zlotys per dollar |
| South Korea | 3,700 won | | 1,056 won per dollar |
| Malaysia | 7.20 ringgits | | 2.97 ringgits per dollar |

## Solving the Problem

**Step 1:** **Review the chapter material.** This problem is about the theory of purchasing power parity, as illustrated by prices of Big Macs, so you may want to review the sections "The Theory of Purchasing Power Parity," which begins on page 1017, and the Making the Connection "The Big Mac Theory of Exchange Rates" on page 1018.

**Step 2:** **Fill in the table.** To calculate the purchasing power parity exchange rate, divide the foreign currency price of a Big Mac by the U.S. price. For example, the implied exchange rate between the Brazilian real and the U.S. dollar is 9.50 reais/$4.07, or 2.33 reais per dollar.

| Country | Big Mac Price | Implied Exchange Rate | Actual Exchange Rate |
|---|---|---|---|
| Brazil | 9.50 reais | 2.33 reais per dollar | 1.54 reais per dollar |
| Poland | 8.63 zlotys | 2.12 zlotys per dollar | 2.80 zlotys per dollar |
| South Korea | 3,700 won | 909 won per dollar | 1,056 won per dollar |
| Malaysia | 7.20 ringgits | 1.77 ringgits per dollar | 2.97 ringgits per dollar |

**Step 3:** **Explain whether the U.S. dollar is overvalued or undervalued against the other currencies.** The dollar is overvalued if the actual exchange rate is greater than the implied exchange rate, and it is undervalued if the actual exchange rate is less than the implied exchange rate. In this case, the dollar is overvalued against the zloty, the won, and the ringgit, but it is undervalued against the real. So, we would predict that in the future the value of the dollar should rise against the real but fall against the zloty, the won, and the ringgit.

**Step 4:** **Calculate the implied exchange rate between the zloty and the real.** The implied exchange rate between the zloty and the real is 8.63 zlotys/9.50 reais, or 0.91 zlotys per real. We can calculate the actual exchange rate by taking the ratio of zlotys per dollar to reais per dollar: 2.80 zlotys/1.54 reais, or 1.82 zlotys per real. Therefore, the zloty is undervalued relative to the real because our Big Mac purchasing power parity calculation tells us that it should take fewer zlotys to buy a real than it actually does.

Data from "Currency Comparisons, to Go," *Economist*, July 28, 2011.

**Your Turn:** For more practice, do related problem 2.12 on page 1033 at the end of this chapter.   MyEconLab

**The Four Determinants of Exchange Rates in the Long Run** We can take into account the shortcomings of the theory of purchasing power parity to develop a more complete explanation of how exchange rates are determined in the long run. There are four main determinants of exchange rates in the long run:

1. *Relative price levels.* The purchasing power parity theory is correct in arguing that in the long run, the most important determinant of exchange rates between two countries' currencies is their relative price levels. If prices of goods and services rise faster in Canada than in the United States, the value of the Canadian dollar has to decline to maintain demand for Canadian products. Over the past 30 years, prices in Canada have risen slightly faster than average prices in the United States, while prices in Japan have risen more slowly. The relationship among inflation rates helps explain why the U.S. dollar has increased slightly in value against the Canadian dollar while losing value against the Japanese yen.

2. *Relative rates of productivity growth.* When the productivity of a firm increases, the firm is able to produce more goods and services using fewer workers, machines, or other inputs. The firm's costs of production fall, and usually so do the prices of its products. If the average productivity of Japanese firms increases faster than the average productivity of U.S. firms, Japanese products will have relatively lower prices than U.S. products, which increases the quantity demanded of Japanese products relative to U.S. products. As a result, the value of the yen should rise against the dollar. For most of the period from the early 1970s to the early 1990s, Japanese productivity increased faster than U.S. productivity, which contributed to the fall in the value of the dollar versus the yen. However, between 1992 and 2011, U.S. productivity increased faster than Japanese productivity.

3. *Preferences for domestic and foreign goods.* If consumers in Canada increase their preferences for U.S. products, the demand for U.S. dollars will increase relative to the demand for Canadian dollars, and the U.S. dollar will increase in value relative to the Canadian dollar. During the 1970s and 1980s, many U.S. consumers increased their preferences for Japanese products, particularly automobiles and consumer electronics. This greater preference for Japanese products helped to increase the value of the yen relative to the dollar.

4. *Tariffs and quotas.* The U.S. sugar quota forces firms such as Hershey Foods Corporation to buy expensive U.S. sugar rather than less expensive foreign sugar. The quota increases the demand for dollars relative to the currencies of foreign sugar producers and, therefore, leads to a higher exchange rate. Changes in tariffs and quotas have not been a significant factor in explaining trends in the U.S. dollar–Canadian dollar or U.S. dollar–yen exchange rates.

Because these four factors change over time, the value of one country's currency can increase or decrease by substantial amounts in the long run. These changes in exchange rates can create problems for firms. A decline in the value of a country's currency lowers the foreign currency prices of the country's exports and increases the prices of imports. An increase in the value of a country's currency has the reverse effect. Firms can be both helped and hurt by exchange rate fluctuations.

## The Euro

A second key aspect of the current exchange rate system is that most Western European countries have adopted a single currency. After World War II, many of the countries of Western Europe wanted to more closely integrate their economies. In 1957, Belgium, France, West Germany, Italy, Luxembourg, and the Netherlands signed the Treaty of Rome, which established the European Economic Community, often referred to as the European Common Market. Tariffs and quotas on products being shipped within the European Common Market were greatly reduced. Over the years, Britain, Sweden, Denmark, Finland, Austria, Greece, Ireland, Spain, and Portugal joined the European Economic Community, which was renamed the European Union (EU) in 1991. By 2011, 27 countries were members of the EU.

**Figure 30.2**

**Countries Adopting the Euro**

The 17 member countries of the European Union that have adopted the euro as their common currency as of 2011 are shaded with red hash marks. The members of the EU that have not adopted the euro are colored tan. Countries in white are not members of the EU.

EU members decided to move to a common currency beginning in 1999. Three of the 15 countries that were then members of the EU—the United Kingdom, Denmark, and Sweden—decided to retain their domestic currencies. The move to a common currency took place in several stages. On January 1, 1999, the exchange rates of the 12 participating countries (risen to 17 in 2011) were permanently fixed against each other and against the common currency, the *euro*. At first the euro was a pure *unit of account*. No euro currency was actually in circulation, although firms began quoting prices in both the domestic currency and euros. On January 1, 2002, euro coins and paper currency were introduced, and on June 1, 2002, the old domestic currencies were withdrawn from circulation. Figure 30.2 shows the countries in the EU that had adopted the euro as of 2011. These countries are sometimes referred to as the "euro zone."

A new European Central Bank (ECB) was also established. Although the central banks of the member countries continue to exist, the ECB has assumed responsibility for monetary policy and for issuing currency. The ECB is run by a governing council that consists of a six-member executive board—appointed by the participating governments—and the governors of the central banks of the 17 member countries that have adopted the euro. The ECB represents a unique experiment in allowing a multinational organization to control the domestic monetary policies of independent countries.

## Making the Connection | Can the Euro Survive?

The euro was first introduced as a currency at the beginning of 2002. The period from then until the beginning of the global economic downturn at the end of 2007 was one of relative economic stability in most of Europe. With low interest rates, low inflation rates, and expanding employment and production, the advantages of the euro seemed obvious. The countries using the euro no longer had to deal with problems caused by fluctuating exchange rates. Having a common currency also makes it easier for consumers and firms to buy and sell across borders. It is no longer

*German Chancellor Angela Merkel, then Greek Prime Minister George Papandreou, left, and French President Nicolas Sarkozy debated how to handle Greece's financial rescue.*

necessary for someone in France to exchange francs for marks in order to do business in Germany. Having a single currency reduces costs and increases competition. Some of the lower-income European countries seemed to particularly prosper under the euro. The Spanish economy grew at a rate of 3.9 percent between 1999 and 2007. The unemployment rate in Spain had been nearly 20 percent in the mid-1990s, but it had dropped to 7.9 percent in 2007. Ireland and Greece also experienced rapid growth during these years.

But by 2008, with the global recession gathering force, some economists and policymakers were starting to question whether the euro was making the economic crisis worse. The countries using the euro are not able to pursue independent monetary policies, which are instead determined by the ECB from its headquarters in Frankfurt, Germany. Countries that were particularly hard hit by the recession—for example, Spain, where the unemployment rate had more than doubled to 18 percent by 2009 and was nearly 21 percent in 2011—were unable to pursue a more expansionary policy than the ECB was willing to implement for the euro zone as a whole. Similarly, countries could not attempt to revive their exports by allowing their exchange rates to depreciate because (1) most of their exports were to other euro zone countries, and (2) the value of the euro was determined by factors affecting the euro zone as a whole.

Problems in the euro zone were made worse by a *sovereign debt* crisis that developed in 2010. Sovereign debt refers to bonds issued by a government. The recession of 2007–2009 caused large increases in government spending and reductions in tax revenues in a number of European countries, particularly Greece, Ireland, Spain, Portugal, and Italy. The resulting government budget deficits were paid for by issuing government bonds. By the spring of 2010, many investors had come to doubt the ability of Greece, in particular, to make the interest payments on the bonds. If Greece defaulted and stopped making interest payments on its bonds, investors would be likely to stop buying bonds issued by several other European governments, and the continuation of the euro would be called into question. The ECB helped Greece avoid a default by directly buying its bonds. The bank extended similar help to Spain, Ireland, and Italy. The International Monetary Fund and the European Union put together aid packages meant to keep Greece and other countries from defaulting. In exchange for the aid, these countries were required to cut government spending and raise taxes even though doing so resulted in significant protests from unions, students, and other groups. In late 2011, it was not yet clear whether the actions the European Union had taken would be sufficient to keep Greece and possibly other countries from defaulting on their bonds.

During the years of the gold standard, countries couldn't run expansionary monetary policies and were unable to have their exchange rates depreciate. During the Great Depression of the 1930s, these drawbacks to remaining on the gold standard led one country after another to abandon it, and by the mid-1930s, the gold standard had collapsed. In 2011, some economists and policymakers were predicting a similar abandonment of the euro. There were significant reasons, though, that no government had yet been willing to consider reverting from the euro to its own currency. Because many euro zone countries export a significant fraction of GDP to other euro zone countries, exchange rate stability has been important to their economic stability, making these countries reluctant to abandon the euro. In addition, some of the European countries hit hardest by the recession, particularly Spain and Ireland, were suffering from the bursting of housing bubbles. More expansionary monetary policies or depreciating exchange rates were unlikely to result in economic recovery until the effects of the collapse in residential construction had run its course. So, it was unclear that the constraints imposed by the euro were holding back recovery in Europe. Finally, because so many contracts and agreements among households, firms, and governments in Europe were written in euros, abandoning the euro was likely to be disruptive to the financial system and to trade.

The ultimate fate of the euro will help to answer the question of whether independent countries with diverse economies can successfully maintain a joint monetary policy and a single currency.

Based on Jack Ewing, Stephen Castle, and Liz Alderman, "Debt Plan Is Delayed in Europe," *New York Times*, October 20, 2011; Terence Roth, "Setting Up the Greek Default," *Wall Street Journal*, October 11, 2011; and "Solving the Euro-Zone Crisis," *Economist*, October 6, 2011.

**Your Turn:** Test your understanding by doing related problem 2.15 on page 1034 at the end of this chapter.

MyEconLab

# Pegging against the Dollar

A final key aspect of the current exchange rate system is that some developing countries have attempted to keep their exchange rates fixed against the dollar or another major currency. Having a fixed exchange rate can provide important advantages for a country that has extensive trade with another country. When the exchange rate is fixed, business planning becomes much easier. For instance, if the South Korean won increases in value relative to the dollar, Hyundai, the Korean car manufacturer, may have to raise the dollar price of cars it exports to the United States, thereby reducing sales. If the exchange rate between the Korean won and the dollar is fixed, Hyundai's planning is much easier.

In the 1980s and 1990s, an additional reason developed for having fixed exchange rates. During those decades, the flow of foreign investment funds to developing countries, particularly those in East Asia, increased substantially. It became possible for firms in countries such as Korea, Thailand, Malaysia, and Indonesia to borrow dollars directly from foreign investors or indirectly from foreign banks. For example, a Thai firm might borrow U.S. dollars from a Japanese bank. If the Thai firm wants to build a new factory in Thailand with the borrowed dollars, it has to exchange the dollars for the equivalent amount of Thai currency, the baht. When the factory opens and production begins, the Thai firm will be earning the additional baht it needs to exchange for dollars to make the interest payments on the loan. A problem arises if the value of the baht falls against the dollar. Suppose that the exchange rate is 25 baht per dollar when the firm takes out the loan. A Thai firm making an interest payment of $100,000 per month on a dollar loan could buy the necessary dollars for 2.5 million baht. But if the value of the baht declines to 50 baht to the dollar, it would take 5 million baht to buy the dollars necessary to make the interest payment. These increased payments might be a crushing burden for the Thai firm. The government of Thailand would have a strong incentive to avoid this problem by keeping the exchange rate between the baht and the dollar fixed.

Finally, in the 1980s and 1990s, some countries feared the inflationary consequences of a floating exchange rate. When the value of a currency falls, the prices of imports rise. If imports are a significant fraction of the goods consumers buy, a fall in the value of the currency may significantly increase the inflation rate. During the 1990s, an important part of Brazil's and Argentina's anti-inflation policies was a fixed exchange rate against the dollar. (As we will see, though, there are difficulties with following a fixed exchange rate policy, and, ultimately, both Brazil and Argentina abandoned fixed exchange rates.)

### The East Asian Exchange Rate Crisis of the Late 1990s
When a country keeps its currency's exchange rate fixed against another country's currency, it is **pegging** its currency. It is not necessary for both countries involved in a peg to agree to it. When a developing country has pegged the value of its currency against the dollar, the responsibility for maintaining the peg has been entirely with the developing country.

Countries attempting to maintain a peg can run into problems, however. We saw in Chapter 4 that when the government fixes the price of a good or service, the result can be persistent surpluses or shortages. Figure 30.3 shows the exchange rate between the dollar and the Thai baht. The figure is drawn from the Thai point of view, so we measure the exchange rate on the vertical axis as dollars per baht. The figure represents the situation in the 1990s, when the government of Thailand pegged the exchange rate

**Pegging** The decision by a country to keep the exchange rate fixed between its currency and another country's currency.

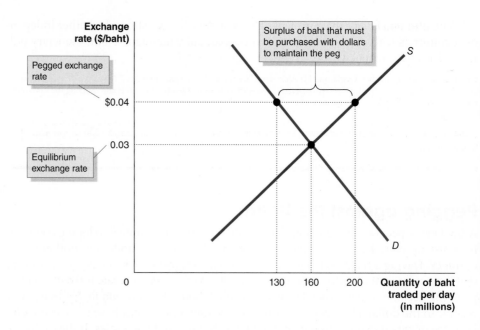

between the dollar and the baht above the equilibrium exchange rate, as determined by demand and supply. A currency pegged at a value above the market equilibrium exchange rate is said to be *overvalued*. A currency pegged at a value below the market equilibrium exchange rate is said to be *undervalued*.

Pegging made it easier for Thai firms to export products to the United States and protected Thai firms that had taken out dollar loans. The pegged exchange rate was 25.19 baht to the dollar, or about $0.04 to the baht. By 1997, this exchange rate was well above the market equilibrium exchange rate of 35 baht to the dollar, or about $0.03 to the baht. The result was a surplus of baht on the foreign exchange market. To keep the exchange rate at the pegged level, the Thai central bank, the Bank of Thailand, had to buy these baht with dollars. In doing so, the Bank of Thailand gradually used up its holdings of dollars, or its *dollar reserves*. To continue supporting the pegged exchange rate, the Bank of Thailand borrowed additional dollar reserves from the International Monetary Fund (IMF). The Bank of Thailand also raised interest rates to attract more foreign investors to investments in Thailand, thereby increasing the demand for the baht. The Bank of Thailand took these actions even though allowing the value of the baht to decline against the dollar would have helped Thai firms exporting to the United States by reducing the dollar prices of their goods. The Thai government was afraid of the negative consequences of abandoning the peg even though the peg had led to the baht being overvalued.

Although higher domestic interest rates helped attract foreign investors, they made it more difficult for Thai firms and households to borrow the funds they needed to finance their spending. As a consequence, domestic investment and consumption declined, pushing the Thai economy into recession. International investors realized that there were limits to how high the Bank of Thailand would be willing to push interest rates and how many dollar loans the IMF would be willing to extend to Thailand. These investors began to speculate against the baht by exchanging baht for dollars at the official, pegged exchange rate. If, as they expected, Thailand was forced to abandon the peg, they would be able to buy back the baht at a much lower exchange rate, making a substantial profit. Because these actions by investors make it more difficult to maintain a fixed exchange rate, they are referred to as *destabilizing speculation*. Figure 30.4 shows the results of this destabilizing speculation. The decreased demand for baht shifted the demand curve for baht from $D_1$ to $D_2$, increasing the quantity of baht the Bank of Thailand needed to buy in exchange for dollars.

Foreign investors also began to sell off their investments in Thailand and exchange the baht they received for dollars. This *capital flight* forced the Bank of Thailand to run through its dollar reserves. Dollar loans from the IMF temporarily allowed Thailand to defend the pegged exchange rate. Finally, on July 2, 1997, Thailand abandoned its

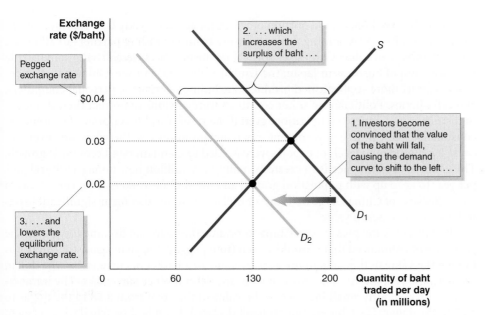

**Exchange rate ($/baht)**

Pegged exchange rate

2. . . . which increases the surplus of baht . . .

1. Investors become convinced that the value of the baht will fall, causing the demand curve to shift to the left . . .

3. . . . and lowers the equilibrium exchange rate.

**Figure 30.4**

**Destabilizing Speculation against the Thai Baht**

In 1997, the pegged exchange rate of $0.04 = 1 baht was above the equilibrium exchange rate of $0.03 = 1 baht. As investors became convinced that Thailand would have to abandon its pegged exchange rate against the dollar and allow the value of the baht to fall, they decreased their demand for baht, causing the demand curve to shift from $D_1$ to $D_2$. The new equilibrium exchange rate became $0.02 = 1 baht. To defend the pegged exchange rate, the Bank of Thailand had to increase the quantity of baht it purchased in exchange for dollars from 70 million per day to 140 million. The *destablizing speculation* by investors caused Thailand to abandon its pegged exchange rate in July 1997.

pegged exchange rate against the dollar and allowed the baht to float. Thai firms that had borrowed dollars were now faced with interest payments that were much higher than they had planned. Many firms were forced into bankruptcy, and the Thai economy plunged into a deep recession.

Many currency traders became convinced that other East Asian countries, such as South Korea, Indonesia, and Malaysia, would have to follow Thailand and abandon their pegged exchange rates. The result was a wave of speculative selling of these countries' currencies. These waves of selling—sometimes referred to as *speculative attacks*—were difficult for countries to fight off. Even if a country's currency was not initially overvalued at the pegged exchange rate, the speculative attacks would cause a large reduction in the demand for the country's currency. The demand curve for the currency would shift to the left, which would force the country's central bank to quickly run through its dollar reserves. Within a few months, South Korea, Indonesia, the Philippines, and Malaysia abandoned their pegged currencies. All these countries also plunged into recession.

**The Decline in Pegging** Following the disastrous events experienced by the East Asian countries, the number of countries with pegged exchange rates declined sharply. Most countries that continue to use pegged exchange rates are small and trade primarily with a single, much larger, country. So, for instance, several Caribbean countries continue to peg against the dollar, and several former French colonies in Africa that formerly pegged against the French franc now peg against the euro. Overall, the trend has been toward replacing pegged exchange rates with managed floating exchange rates.

**The Chinese Experience with Pegging** As we discussed in Chapter 22, in 1978, China began to move away from central planning and toward a market system. The result was a sharp acceleration in economic growth. Real GDP per capita grew at a rate of 6.5 percent per year between 1979 and 1995 and at the very rapid rate of more than 9 percent per year between 1996 and 2010. An important part of Chinese economic policy was the decision in 1994 to peg the value of the Chinese currency, the yuan, to the dollar at a fixed rate of 8.28 yuan to the dollar. Pegging against the dollar ensured that Chinese exporters would face stable dollar prices for the goods they sold in the United States. By the early 2000s, many economists argued that the yuan was undervalued against the dollar, possibly significantly so. Many U.S. firms claimed that the undervaluation of the yuan gave Chinese firms an unfair advantage in competing with U.S. firms.

To support the undervalued exchange rate, the Chinese central bank had to buy large amounts of dollars with yuan. By 2005, the Chinese government had accumulated more than $700 billion, a good portion of which it had used to buy U.S. Treasury bonds. In addition, China was coming under pressure from its trading partners to allow the yuan to increase in value. Chinese exports of textile products were driving some textile producers out of business in Japan, the United States, and Europe. China had also begun to export more sophisticated products, including televisions, personal computers, and cell phones. Politicians in other countries were anxious to protect their domestic industries from Chinese competition, even if the result was higher prices for domestic consumers. The Chinese government was reluctant to revalue the yuan, however, because it believed high levels of exports were needed to maintain rapid economic growth. The Chinese economy needs to create as many as 20 million new nonagricultural jobs per year to keep up with population growth and the shift of workers from rural areas to cities. Because of China's large holdings of dollars, it would also incur significant losses if the yuan increases in value.

By July 2005, the pressure on China to revalue the yuan had become too great. The government announced that it would switch from pegging the yuan against the dollar to linking the value of the yuan to the average value of a basket of currencies—the dollar, the Japanese yen, the euro, the Korean won, and several other currencies. The immediate effect was a fairly small increase in the value of the yuan from 8.28 to the dollar to 8.11 to the dollar. The Chinese central bank declared that it had switched from a peg to a managed floating exchange rate. Some economists and policymakers were skeptical, however, that much had actually changed because the initial increase in the value of the yuan had been small and because the Chinese central bank did not explain the details of how the yuan would be linked to the basket of other currencies. By late 2011, the value of the yuan had slowly increased to 6.38 to the dollar. Despite this increase, some economists and policymakers still believed that the yuan was overvalued and urged the Chinese government to allow its currency to become more responsive to changes in demand and supply in the foreign exchange markets.

## Making the Connection | Crisis and Recovery in South Korea

Korea spent the first part of the twentieth century as a colony of Japan. In 1945, at the end of World War II, Korea was divided into Communist North Korea and democratic South Korea. North Korea's invasion of South Korea in June 1950 set off the Korean War, which devastated South Korea, before ending in 1953. Despite these difficult beginnings, by the 1960s, the South Korean economy was growing rapidly. As one of the *newly industrializing countries*, South Korea was a model for other developing countries.

To make it easier for firms such as Hyundai to export to the United States and to protect firms that had taken out dollar loans, the South Korean government pegged the value of its currency, the won, to the U.S. dollar. Following Thailand's decision in July 1997 to abandon its peg, large-scale destabilizing speculation took place against the won. Foreign investors scrambled to sell their investments in Korea and to convert their won into dollars. South Korea was unable to defend the peg and allowed the won to float in October 1997.

Like other countries that underwent exchange rate crises, South Korea had attempted to maintain the value of the won by raising domestic interest rates. The result was a sharp decline in aggregate demand and a severe recession. However, unlike other East Asian countries—particularly Thailand and Indonesia—that made only slow progress in recovering from exchange rate crises, South Korea bounced back rapidly. The figure on the next page shows that after experiencing falling real GDP through 1999, South Korea quickly returned to high rates of growth.

Why was the performance of South Korea so much better than that of other East Asian countries? Jahyeong Koo and Sherry L. Kiser, economists at the Federal Reserve Bank of Dallas, cite several factors:

- South Korea benefited from a $21 billion loan from the IMF in December 1997. This loan helped stabilize the value of the won.

- Even though South Korean banks were badly hurt in the crisis and cut back their loans, South Korean firms were able to obtain financing for investment projects from the stock and bond markets.

- The South Korean labor market was flexible enough to allow wage reductions, which offset some of the negative effect of the crisis on corporate profits.

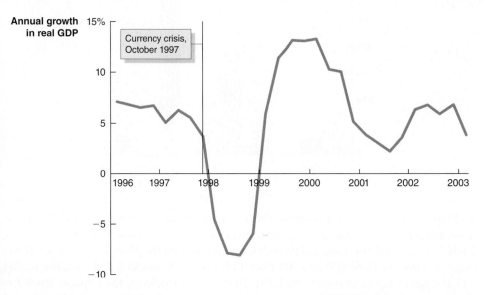

In 2011, some South Korean firms were still paying off debts originally incurred in the late 1990s, and the Korean banking system had yet to fully recover. But South Korea was able to emerge from its exchange rate crisis without suffering the political and social upheavals that occurred in countries such as Indonesia.

Based on Korea National Statistical Office; and Jahyeong Koo and Sherry L. Kiser, "Recovery from a Financial Crisis: The Case of South Korea," *Federal Reserve Bank of Dallas, Economic and Financial Review*, Fourth Quarter 2001.

**Your Turn:** Test your understanding by doing related problem 2.25 on page 1035 at the end of this chapter.

MyEconLab

---

# International Capital Markets

One important reason exchange rates fluctuate is that investors seek out the best investments they can find anywhere in the world. For instance, if Chinese investors increase their demand for U.S. Treasury bills, the demand for dollars will increase, and the value of the dollar will rise. But if interest rates in the United States decline, foreign investors may sell U.S. investments, and the value of the dollar will fall.

Shares of stock and long-term debt, including corporate and government bonds and bank loans, are bought and sold on *capital markets*. Before 1980, most U.S. corporations raised funds only in U.S. stock and bond markets or from U.S. banks. U.S. investors rarely invested in foreign capital markets. In the 1980s and 1990s, European governments removed many restrictions on foreign investments in their financial markets. It became possible for U.S. and other foreign investors to freely invest in Europe and for European investors to freely invest in foreign markets. Improvements in communications and computer technology made it possible for U.S. investors to receive better and more timely information about foreign firms and for foreign investors to receive better information about U.S. firms. The growth in economies around the world also made more savings available to be invested.

Although at one time the U.S. capital market was larger than all other capital markets combined, this is no longer true. Today there are large capital markets in Europe

**30.3 LEARNING** OBJECTIVE

Discuss the growth of international capital markets.

## Figure 30.5

### Growth of Foreign Portfolio Investment in the United States

Between 1995 and 2007, there was a large increase in foreign purchases of stocks and bonds issued by U.S. corporations and of bonds issued by the federal government. In 2010, the slow recovery in the United States from the 2007–2009 recession increased the degree of risk that foreign investors saw in holding these securities. Foreign purchases of U.S. government bonds soared, however.

Data from International Monetary Fund, *International Capital Markets*, August 2001; and U.S. Department of the Treasury, Treasury Bulletin, September 2011.

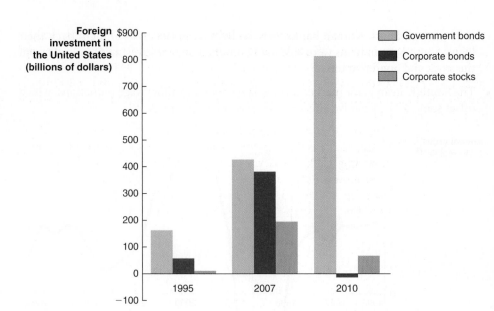

and Japan, and there are smaller markets in Latin America and East Asia. The three most important international financial centers today are New York, London, and Tokyo. Each day, the *Wall Street Journal* provides data not just on the Dow Jones Industrial Average and the Standard & Poor's 500 stock indexes of U.S. stocks but also on the Nikkei 225 average of Japanese stocks, the FTSE 100 index of stocks on the London Stock Exchange, and the DJ STOXX 50 index of European stocks. By 2011, corporations, banks, and governments had raised more than $1 trillion in funds on global financial markets.

Beginning in the 1990s, the flow of foreign funds into U.S. stocks and bonds—or *portfolio investments*—increased substantially. As Figure 30.5 shows, foreign purchases of stocks and bonds issued by corporations and bonds issued by the federal government increased dramatically between 1995 and 2007. In 2010, however, foreign purchases of U.S. corporate stocks and bonds declined sharply, as the slow recovery in the United States from the recession of 2007–2009 increased the degree of risk foreign investors saw in holding these securities. Foreign purchases of U.S. government bonds soared, however, as fears that some European governments might default on their bonds led investors to a *flight to safety*, in which they sold other investments to buy U.S. government bonds. The fact that the United States continued to run large current account deficits also fueled some of the demand for U.S. government bonds. These current account deficits led to an accumulation of dollars by foreign central banks and foreign investors who used the dollars to purchase U.S. government bonds.

Figure 30.6 shows the distribution during 2010 of foreign portfolio investment in the United States by country. Investors in the United Kingdom accounted for about half of all foreign purchases of U.S. stocks and bonds. The two other countries with the largest shares of foreign purchases were Japan, with 18 percent, and China, with 7 percent.

## Figure 30.6

### The Distribution of Foreign Purchases of U.S. Stocks and Bonds by Country, 2010

Investors in the United Kingdom accounted for about half of all foreign purchases of U.S. stocks and bonds, while investors in Japan accounted for 18 percent, and investors in China accounted for 7 percent.

Data from U.S. Department of the Treasury, *Treasury Bulletin*, September 2011.

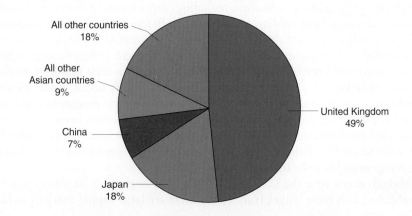

The globalization of financial markets has helped increase growth and efficiency in the world economy. Now it is possible for the savings of households around the world to be channeled to the best investments available. It is also possible for firms in nearly every country to tap the savings of foreign households to gain the funds needed for expansion. No longer are firms forced to rely only on the savings of domestic households to finance investment.

But the globalization of financial markets also has a downside, as the events of 2007–2009 showed. Because financial securities issued in one country are held by investors and firms in many other countries, if those securities decline in value, the financial pain will be widely distributed. For example, the sharp decline in the value of mortgage-backed securities issued in the United States hurt not only U.S. investors and financial firms but investors and financial firms in many other countries as well.

Continued from page 1013

## Economics in Your Life

### Exchange Rate Risk in Your Life

At the beginning of the chapter, we posed this question: If economists are correct about the relative rates of average productivity growth between Spain and the United States in the next decade, then, all else being equal, will the savings that you accumulate (in euros) be worth more or less in U.S. dollars than it would have been worth without the relative gains in Spanish productivity? To answer this question, we saw in this chapter that when the average productivity of firms in one country increases faster than the average productivity of firms in another country, the value of the faster-growing country's currency should—all else being equal—rise against the slower-growing country's currency. Of course, Spain is only 1 of the 17 countries using the euro, so the impact of productivity increases in Spain on the value of the euro may not be large. But the savings that you accumulate in euros while you are in Spain are likely to be worth more in U.S. dollars than they would have been worth without the gains in Spanish productivity.

# Conclusion

Fluctuations in exchange rates continue to cause difficulties for firms and governments. From the gold standard to the Bretton Woods system to currency pegging, governments have attempted to find a workable system of fixed exchange rates. Fixing exchange rates runs into the same problems as fixing any other price: As demand and supply shift, surpluses and shortages will occur unless the price adjusts. Seventeen countries in Europe are attempting to avoid this problem by using a single currency. Economists are looking closely at the results of that experiment.

Read *An Inside Look at Policy* on the next page for a discussion of a Senate bill aimed at raising tariffs on goods from China in response to claims that country's currency was undervalued.

# Can Tariffs Offset the Effect of Overvaluation?

## *ASSOCIATED PRESS*

## China Slams U.S. Currency Bill as Threat to Trade

China criticized an American currency bill as a threat to a shaky global economic recovery and warned Wednesday that trade ties will be "severely damaged" if it becomes law.

Beijing rejected the measure passed Tuesday by the Senate as a form of damaging protectionism at a time when other nations are trying to sustain free trade. The bill would allow Washington to raise tariffs on Chinese imports that critics say are unfairly cheap due to Beijing's exchange-rate controls and are destroying U.S. jobs.

"It is completely harmful and unbeneficial," said Foreign Ministry spokesman Ma Zhaoxu in a statement. Ma said it would do nothing to reduce U.S. unemployment and would disrupt global efforts to revive economic growth.

Tuesday's 63–35 Senate vote showed a bipartisan consensus in favor of tougher action against Beijing after years of diplomatic pressure and a gradual rise in China's currency, the yuan, that critics say is inadequate.

Still, the bill is unlikely to become law because it lacks the support of the majority Republican leadership in the lower House of Representatives, who are reluctant to take up the measure. The White House and President Barack Obama have not come out against the bill but have shown they are uncomfortable with it.

U.S. manufacturers complain that Beijing's controls keep the yuan undervalued by up to 40 percent. They say that gives China's exporters an unfair price advantage and hurts foreign competitors, eroding American employment. The currency bill's supporters say it would support creation of 1 million jobs in the United States.

American critics of the bill have warned Beijing might retaliate, hurting U.S. companies in China's relatively robust markets, which are a rare bright spot for exporters amid weak demand elsewhere.

If it becomes law, "Sino–U.S. economic and trade relations will inevitably be severely damaged," Commerce Ministry spokesman Shen Dayang said in a statement.

Some opponents of the measure argue that currency sanctions would do little to help the U.S. job market because Chinese goods would simply be replaced by goods from other low-wage countries such as Vietnam and Bangladesh.

Ma, the Foreign Ministry spokesman, said the measure violates World Trade Organization rules.

"It not only cannot solve the problems in the U.S. economy or unemployment, but will seriously impede Sino–U.S. economic and trade ties and impede the joint efforts that China, the U.S. and the international community have made to enable a strong recovery and the growth of the global economy," Ma said.

The officials gave no details of a possible response but have warned in the past that unilateral trade action could damage the full array of U.S.–Chinese cooperation. That ranges from efforts to protect U.S. intellectual property rights in China to assuring the security of Taiwan and keeping the Korean Peninsula peaceful. . . .

The currency legislation would set in motion the imposition of higher tariffs on a country if the U.S. Treasury Department decides its currency is "misaligned" and the country does not act to correct it. Currently, Treasury must resolve that a country is willfully manipulating its currency, a higher bar to reach, before sanctions can be considered.

The bill also makes it easier for specific industries to petition the Commerce Department for redress if they believe an exchange rate is giving a foreign competitor the equivalent of an export subsidy.

Beijing has said repeatedly it is pushing ahead reforms of its exchange rate controls but says it will set the pace. Chinese leaders have warned that an abrupt rise in the yuan could lead to job losses and fuel unrest.

The yuan's value has been allowed to rise by about 5 percent against the dollar over the past year in tightly controlled trading. The rise has quickened in recent weeks.

On Wednesday, China's central bank issued a statement defending its currency controls as an "important contribution" to international financial stability.

*Source:* "China Slams U.S. Currency Bill as Threat to Trade," by Joe McDonald from the *Associated Press*, October 12, 2011. Copyright © 2005 by the Associated Press. Reproduced with permission of the YGS Group.

## Key Points in the Article

China was the main target of a U.S. Senate bill to raise tariffs. Many politicians claimed that China had manipulated its currency to give Chinese exporters an unfair advantage over U.S. companies. Politicians and U.S. manufacturers supporting the bill argued that the Chinese yuan was undervalued by up to 40 percent, leading to job losses in the United States. Some opponents of the bill claimed that the sanctions would do little to help employment in the United States because the targeted Chinese products would just be replaced by goods from other countries. China said that the bill violates World Trade Organization rules and might retaliate should the bill become law. However, the bill was not expected to pass in the House of Representatives, nor did it get support from the Obama White House.

## Analyzing the News

(a) In October 2011, the U.S. Senate passed a bill that would allow U.S. companies to apply for tariffs on imports from countries that deliberately undervalued their currencies in order to become more competitive. As you read in this chapter, a currency is said to be *undervalued* if it is pegged at a value below the market equilibrium exchange rate. Many politicians claimed that China kept its currency

undervalued in order to keep the prices of its exports low. The figure below shows the value of the yuan against the U.S. dollar. After 2005, the appreciation of the yuan against the dollar was relatively modest in comparison with the growing U.S. trade deficits with China. As you read in this chapter, the Chinese central bank has managed to keep the yuan at relatively low levels by buying large amounts of U.S. dollars with yuan. An increase in the U.S. trade deficit with China caused an increase in the supply of dollars in the foreign exchange market. Without any government intervention, the exchange rate between the U.S. dollar and the yuan might have dropped below 6 yuan per dollar. By increasing the demand for dollars in exchange for yuan, the Chinese government was able to keep the exchange rate between 6 and 7 yuan per dollar.

(b) U.S. manufacturers supporting the tariff bill claim that the Chinese yuan is undervalued by up to 40 percent, and this has given Chinese exporters an unfair advantage in competing with U.S. firms, leading to job losses. Supporters of the bill claim it would help create 1 million jobs in the United States. Critics have warned that Chinese retaliation could hurt U.S. companies that currently export to China and lead to unemployment in those exporting industries.

(c) The U.S. Treasury is required by law to investigate whether any country unfairly manipulates its currency. If it became law, the Senate bill would impose higher tariffs on countries if the Treasury Department determined that a currency is "misaligned" and the country took no corrective action. The bill also would make it easier for manufacturing firms to petition for sanctions if they believe a country is undervaluing its currency and giving foreign manufacturers what amounts to an export subsidy. China is the largest creditor of the United States, with holdings of more than $1.1 trillion in Treasury securities as of August 2011.

## Thinking Critically about Policy

1. Supporters of the tariff bill discussed in this article claim that the yuan is undervalued, and tariffs on Chinese products would save jobs in the United States. Would passage of the bill hurt anyone in the United States? Briefly explain.

2. China is currently the largest creditor of the United States, with holdings of more than $1 trillion in U.S. Treasury securities in 2011. Suppose the Senate tariff bill were signed into law and China retaliated by selling all of its holdings of U.S. Treasury securities. How would interest rates in the United States be affected? How would the exchange rate of the U.S. dollar be affected? Briefly explain.

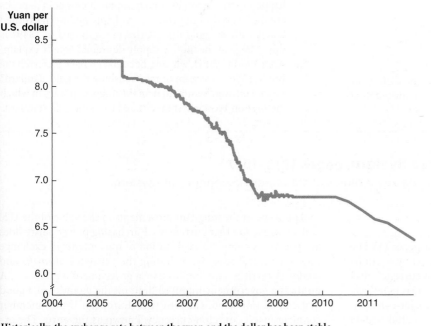

**Historically, the exchange rate between the yuan and the dollar has been stable.**
Data from Federal Reserve Bank of St. Louis.

# Chapter Summary and Problems

## Key Terms

Euro, p. 1015

Exchange rate system, p. 1014

Fixed exchange rate system, p. 1014

Floating currency, p. 1014

Managed float exchange rate system, p. 1014

Pegging, p. 1023

Purchasing power parity, p. 1017

Quota, p. 1018

Tariff, p. 1018

 **30.1** **Exchange Rate Systems, pages 1014–1015**
LEARNING OBJECTIVE: Understand how different exchange rate systems operate.

## Summary

When countries agree on how exchange rates should be determined, economists say that there is an **exchange rate system**. A **floating currency** is the outcome of a country allowing its currency's exchange rate to be determined by demand and supply. The current exchange rate system is a **managed float exchange rate system**, under which the value of most currencies is determined by demand and supply, with occasional government intervention. A **fixed exchange rate system** is a system under which countries agree to keep the exchange rates among their currencies fixed. Under the gold standard, the exchange rate between two currencies was automatically determined by the quantity of gold in each currency. By the end of the Great Depression of the 1930s, every country had abandoned the gold standard. Under the Bretton Woods system, which was in place between 1944 and the early 1970s, the United States agreed to exchange dollars for gold at a price of $35 per ounce. The central banks of all other members of the system pledged to buy and sell their currencies at a fixed rate against the dollar.

 MyEconLab    Visit www.myeconlab.com to complete these exercises online and get instant feedback.

## Review Questions

1.1 What is an exchange rate system? What is the difference between a fixed exchange rate system and a managed float exchange rate system?

1.2 How were exchange rates determined under the gold standard? How did the Bretton Woods system differ from the gold standard?

## Problems and Applications

1.3 **[Related to the** Don't Let This Happen to You **on page 1015]** Briefly explain whether you agree with the following statement: "The Federal Reserve is limited in its ability to issue paper currency by the amount of gold the federal government has in Fort Knox. To issue more paper currency, the government first has to buy more gold."

1.4 The United States and most other countries abandoned the gold standard during the 1930s. Why would the 1930s have been a particularly difficult time for countries to have remained on the gold standard? (*Hint*: Think about the macroeconomic events of the 1930s and about the possible problems with carrying out an expansionary monetary policy while remaining on the gold standard.)

1.5 If a country is using the gold standard, what is likely to happen to the country's money supply if new gold deposits are discovered in the country, as happened in the United States with the gold discoveries in California in 1849? Is this change in the money supply desirable? Briefly explain.

1.6 After World War II, why might countries have preferred the Bretton Woods system to reestablishing the gold standard? In your answer, be sure to note the important ways in which the Bretton Woods system differed from the gold standard.

**30.2** **The Current Exchange Rate System, pages 1015–1027**
LEARNING OBJECTIVE: Discuss the three key features of the current exchange rate system.

## Summary

The current exchange rate system has three key aspects: (1) The U.S. dollar floats against other major currencies, (2) most countries in Western Europe have adopted a common currency, and (3) some developing countries have fixed their currencies' exchange rates against the dollar or against another major currency. Since 1973, the value of the U.S. dollar has fluctuated widely against other major currencies. The theory of **purchasing power parity** states that in the long run, exchange rates move to equalize the purchasing power of different currencies. This theory helps to explain some of the long-run movements in the value of the U.S. dollar relative to other currencies. Purchasing power parity does not provide a complete explanation of movements in exchange rates for several reasons, including the existence of *tariffs* and *quotas*. A **tariff** is a tax imposed by a government on imports. A **quota** is a government-imposed limit on the quantity of a good that can be imported. Currently, 17 European Union member countries use a common currency, known as the **euro**. The experience of the countries using the euro will provide economists with information on the costs and benefits to countries of using the same currency.

When a country keeps its currency's exchange rate fixed against another country's currency, it is **pegging** its currency. Pegging can result in problems similar to the problems countries encountered with fixed exchange rates under the Bretton Woods system. If investors become convinced that a country pegging its exchange rate will eventually allow the exchange rate to decline to a lower level, the demand curve for the currency will shift to the left. This illustrates the difficulty of maintaining a fixed exchange rate in the face of destabilizing speculation.

**MyEconLab**  Visit **www.myeconlab.com** to complete these exercises online and get instant feedback.

## Review Questions

**2.1** What is the theory of purchasing power parity? Does the theory give a complete explanation for movements in exchange rates in the long run? Briefly explain.

**2.2** Briefly describe the four determinants of exchange rates in the long run.

**2.3** Which European countries currently use the euro as their currency? Why did these countries agree to replace their previous currencies with the euro?

**2.4** What does it mean when one currency is "pegged" against another currency? Why do countries peg their currencies? What problems can result from pegging?

**2.5** Briefly describe the Chinese experience with pegging the yuan.

## Problems and Applications

**2.6** [Related to the Making the Connection **on page 1016**] In the *Toronto Sun*, columnist Bob Elliot wrote: "Is there advantage to playing for the [Toronto] Blue Jays over the Boston Red Sox or New York Yankees? . . . The exchange numbers say it's better to play for the Jays—as long as you are paid in Canadian funds." Why would it be better for a baseball player on a Canadian team to be paid in Canadian dollars rather than U.S. dollars? What do the "exchange numbers" have to do with your answer? Does it matter whether the player lives in Canada or in the United States? Briefly explain.

From Bob Elliott, "Jays Wishing They Signed for Canadian Coin?" *Toronto Sun*, May 11, 2011.

**2.7** Consider the following headline from an article in the *Wall Street Journal*: "Strong Franc Hurts Swiss Business." What does the article mean by a "strong franc"? Why would a strong Swiss franc be bad for Swiss businesses?

From Goran Mijuk, "Strong Franc Hurts Swiss Business," *Wall Street Journal*, October 20, 2011.

**2.8** Consider this statement:

It usually takes more than 75 yen to buy 1 U.S. dollar and more than 1.5 dollars to buy 1 British pound. These values show that the United States must be a much wealthier country than Japan and that the United Kingdom must be wealthier than the United States.

Do you agree with this reasoning? Briefly explain.

**2.9** The following is from an article in the *Wall Street Journal*:

Honda said its profit fell to ¥60.4 billion ($796.5 million) in the three months ended Sept. 30 [2011]. . . . Troubles related to the yen . . . come as both Honda and Toyota are working to get back to normal operations in the wake of the March 11 earthquake in Japan.

**a.** According to the information in this article, what was the exchange rate between the yen and the dollar in September 2011? If Honda was experiencing troubles related to the yen, was it likely that the yen had been rising in value in exchange for the U.S. dollar or falling in value in exchange for the U.S. dollar? Briefly explain.

**b.** Was the change in the yen–dollar exchange rate that you indicated was happening in part a. good news or bad news for U.S. consumers who buy goods imported from Japan? Briefly explain.

From Mike Ramsey and Yoshio Takahashi, "Car Wreck: Honda and Toyota," *Wall Street Journal*, November 1, 2011.

**2.10** According to the theory of purchasing power parity, if the inflation rate in Australia is higher than the inflation rate in New Zealand, what should happen to the exchange rate between the Australian dollar and the New Zealand dollar? Briefly explain.

**2.11** [Related to the Making the Connection **on page 1018**] Look again at the table on page 1018 that shows the prices of Big Macs and the implied and actual exchange rates. Indicate which countries listed in the table have undervalued currencies versus the U.S. dollar and which have overvalued currencies.

**2.12** [Related to the Solved Problem 30.2 **on page 1019**] Fill in the missing values in the following table. Assume that the Big Mac is selling for $4.07 in the United States. Explain whether the U.S. dollar is overvalued or undervalued relative to each of the other currencies and predict what will happen in the future to each exchange rate. Finally, calculate the implied exchange rate between the Russian ruble and the New Zealand dollar and explain which currency is overvalued in terms of Big Mac purchasing power parity.

| Country | Big Mac Price | Implied Exchange Rate | Actual Exchange Rate |
|---|---|---|---|
| Chile | 1,850 pesos | | 463 pesos per dollar |
| Israel | 15.9 shekels | | 3.40 shekels per dollar |
| Russia | 75.0 rubles | | 27.8 rubles per dollar |
| New Zealand | 5.10 New Zealand dollars | | 1.16 New Zealand dollars per U.S. dollar |

Data from "Currency Comparisons, to Go," *Economist*, July 28, 2011.

**2.13** Britain decided not to join other European Union countries in using the euro as its currency. One British opponent of adopting the euro argued, "It comes down to economics. We just don't believe that it's possible to manage the entire economy of Europe with just one interest rate policy. How do you alleviate recession in Germany and curb inflation in Ireland?" What interest-rate policy would be used to alleviate recession in Germany? What interest-rate policy would be used to curb inflation in Ireland? What does adopting the euro have to do with interest-rate policy?

From Alan Cowell, "Nuanced Conflict over Euro in Britain," *New York Times*, June 22, 2001.

**2.14** When the euro was introduced in January 1999, the exchange rate was $1.19 per euro. In October 2011, the exchange rate was $1.38 per euro. Was this change in the dollar–euro exchange rate good news or bad news for U.S. firms exporting goods and services to Europe? Was it good news or bad news for European consumers buying goods and services imported from the United States? Briefly explain.

**2.15** **[Related to the** Making the Connection **on page 1021]** Jordi Galí, an economist at the Universitat Pompeu Fabra in Spain, notes that the Spanish economy was in recession during the early 1990s, but that "in 1992 and 1993 a series of [exchange rate] devaluations got us out of trouble." Was Spain able to use exchange rate devaluations to deal with the recession of 2007–2009? Briefly explain.

From "One Size Fits None," *Economist*, June 11, 2009.

**2.16** Construct a numerical example that shows how an investor could have made a profit by selling Thai baht for dollars in 1997.

**2.17** **[Related to the** Chapter Opener **on page 1013]** When Airbus, a subsidiary of a company located in France, sold A380 super-jumbo jetliners to Air France, the transaction was made in dollars, rather than euros. What advantages are there to aerospace firms in different countries in agreeing to carry out all transactions in a single currency? What disadvantages are there?

**2.18** Use the graph to answer the following questions.

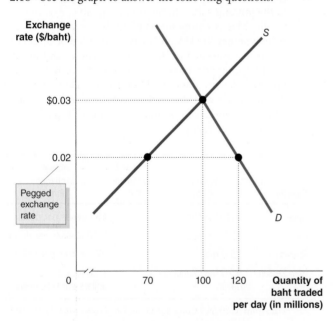

**a.** According to the graph, is there a surplus or a shortage of baht in exchange for U.S. dollars? Briefly explain.

**b.** To maintain the pegged exchange rate, will the Thai central bank need to buy baht in exchange for dollars or sell baht in exchange for dollars? How many baht will the Thai central bank need to buy or sell?

**2.19** For many years, Argentina suffered from high rates of inflation. As part of its program to fight inflation, in the 1990s, the Argentine government pegged the value of the Argentine peso to the U.S. dollar at a rate of one peso per dollar. In January 2002, the government decided to abandon the peg and allow the peso to float. Just before the peg was abandoned, firms in Buenos Aires posted signs urging customers to come in and shop and take advantage of the "Last 72 Hours of One to One." What was likely to happen to the exchange rate between the dollar and the peso when Argentina abandoned the peg? Why would customers find it better to shop before the peg ended than after?

Based on Larry Rohter, "Argentina Unlinks Peso from Dollar, Bracing for Devaluation," *New York Times*, January 7, 2002.

**2.20** The *Economist* observed the following: "In Argentina, many loans were taken out in dollars: this had catastrophic consequences for borrowers once the peg collapsed." What does it mean that Argentina's "peg collapsed"? Why was this catastrophic for borrowers in Argentina who had taken out dollar loans?

From "Spoilt for Choice," *Economist*, June 3, 2002.

**2.21** In a column in the *New York Times*, by Christina Romer, former chair of President Barack Obama's Council of Economic Advisers, made the following observations:

**a.** "Our exchange rate is just a price—the price of the dollar in terms of other currencies. It is not controlled by anyone."

**b.** ". . . a high price for the dollar, which is what we mean by a strong dollar, is not always desirable."

Briefly explain whether you agree with these two observations.

From Christina D. Romer, "Needed: Plain Talk about the Dollar," *New York Times*, May 21, 2011.

**2.22** Suppose that a developing country pegs the value of its currency against the U.S. dollar. Further, suppose that the dollar appreciates against the yen and against the euro. What will be the impact on the ability of the developing country to export goods and services to Japan and Europe? Briefly explain.

**2.23** Graph the demand and supply of Chinese yuan for U.S. dollars and label each axis. To maintain its pegged exchange rate, the Chinese central bank used yuan to buy large quantities of U.S. dollars. Indicate whether the pegged exchange rate was above or below the market equilibrium exchange rate and show on the graph the quantity of yuan the Chinese central bank would have to supply each trading period.

**2.24** According to an article in the *Wall Street Journal* on a trip by U.S. Treasury Secretary Timothy Geithner to China:

> The message signals that [the] Treasury is beginning to look . . . toward preventing a return to ever-mounting trade deficits and the constant political tensions they generate between the U.S. and China. . . . The issue has long been a sensitive one, with U.S. manufacturers and their political allies accusing China of manipulating its currency to get an unfair edge in foreign trade.

How would a government manipulate its currency to get an "unfair" advantage in trade? Why would U.S. manufacturers be concerned about U.S. trade deficits with China?

From "U.S. to Urge China to Shop, Not Save," *Wall Street Journal,* May 29, 2009.

2.25 **[Related to the** Making the Connection **on page 1026]** The following is from an article in the *Wall Street Journal* on changes in the Korean economy:

> The biggest is a change in where Korean companies are finding growth. It is no longer just the U.S. and Europe, markets where Samsung,

Hyundai and other big exporters have long focused on. Instead, it is in places like China, central Asia and the Middle East. . . . The broader trend is that global economic growth is less tied to the U.S., a phenomenon that has been called "decoupling."

If the trend identified in this article is correct, what are the implications for the policy of the Korean government with respect to the dollar–won exchange rate?

From "Korean Stock Rally Shows a Different Picture," *Wall Street Journal,* June 19, 2007, p. C3.

---

**30.3** **International Capital Markets,** pages 1027–1029

LEARNING OBJECTIVE: Discuss the growth of international capital markets.

## Summary

A key reason exchange rates fluctuate is that investors seek out the best investments they can find anywhere in the world. Since 1980, the markets for stocks and bonds have become global. Foreign purchases of U.S. corporate bonds and stocks and U.S. government bonds have increased greatly in the period since 1995. As a result, firms around the world are no longer forced to rely only on the savings of domestic households for funds.

 Visit **www.myeconlab.com** to complete these exercises online and get instant feedback.

## Review Questions

3.1 What were the main factors behind the globalization of capital markets in the 1980s and 1990s?

3.2 Briefly describe the pattern of foreign investments in U.S. securities between 1995 and 2010.

## Problems and Applications

3.3 Why are foreign investors more likely to invest in U.S. government bonds than in U.S. corporate stocks and bonds?

3.4 The text states that "the globalization of financial markets has helped increase growth and efficiency in the world economy." Briefly explain which aspects of globalization help to increase growth in the world economy.

3.5 The global financial crisis of 2007–2009 led some economists and policymakers to suggest the reinstitution of capital controls—or limits on the flow of foreign exchange and financial investments across countries—which existed in many European countries prior to the 1960s. Why would a financial crisis lead to a reconsideration of using capital controls? What problems might result from reinstituting capital controls?

# Appendix

**LEARNING** OBJECTIVE

Explain the gold standard and the Bretton Woods system.

## The Gold Standard and the Bretton Woods System

### The Gold Standard and the Bretton Woods System

It is easier to understand the current exchange rate system by considering further two earlier systems, the gold standard and the Bretton Woods system, which together lasted from the early nineteenth century through the early 1970s.

### The Gold Standard

As we saw in this chapter, under the gold standard, the currency of a country consisted of gold coins and paper currency that could be redeemed for gold. Great Britain adopted the gold standard in 1816, but as late as 1870, only a few nations had followed. In the late nineteenth century, however, Great Britain's share of world trade had increased, as had its overseas investments. The dominant position of Great Britain in the world economy motivated other countries to adopt the gold standard. By 1913, every country in Europe, except Spain and Bulgaria, and most countries in the Western Hemisphere had adopted the gold standard.

Under the gold standard, the exchange rate between two currencies was automatically determined by the quantity of gold in each currency. If there was 1/5 ounce of gold in a U.S. dollar and 1 ounce of gold in a British pound, the price of gold in the United States would be $5 per ounce, and the price of gold in Britain would be £1 per ounce. The exchange rate would therefore be $5 = £1.

### The End of the Gold Standard

From a modern point of view, the greatest drawback to the gold standard was that the central bank lacked control of the money supply. The size of a country's money supply depended on its gold supply, which could be greatly affected by chance discoveries of gold or by technological change in gold mining. For example, the gold discoveries in California in 1849 and Alaska in the 1890s caused rapid increases in the U.S. money supply. Because the central bank cannot determine how much gold will be discovered, it lacks the control of the money supply necessary to pursue an active monetary policy. During wartime, countries usually went off the gold standard to allow their central banks to expand the money supply as rapidly as was necessary to pay for the war. Britain abandoned the gold standard at the beginning of World War I in 1914 and did not resume redeeming its paper currency for gold until 1925.

When the Great Depression began in 1929, governments came under pressure to abandon the gold standard to allow their central banks to pursue active monetary policies. In 1931, Great Britain became the first major country to abandon the gold standard. A number of other countries also went off the gold standard that year. The United States remained on the gold standard until 1933, and a few countries, including France, Italy, and Belgium, stayed on even longer. By the late 1930s, the gold standard had collapsed.

The earlier a country abandoned the gold standard, the easier time it had fighting the Depression with expansionary monetary policies. The countries that abandoned the gold standard by 1932 suffered an average decline in production of only 3 percent between 1929 and 1934. The countries that stayed on the gold standard until 1933 or later suffered an average decline of more than 30 percent. The devastating economic performance of the countries that stayed on the gold standard the longest during the 1930s is the key reason no attempt was made to bring back the gold standard in later years.

## The Bretton Woods System

In addition to the collapse of the gold standard, the global economy suffered during the 1930s from tariff wars. The United States had started the tariff wars in June 1930 by enacting the Smoot–Hawley Tariff, which raised the average U.S. tariff rate to more than 50 percent. Many other countries raised tariffs during the next few years, leading to a collapse in world trade.

As World War II was coming to an end, economists and government officials in the United States and Europe concluded that they needed to restore the international economic system to avoid another depression. In 1947, the United States and most other major countries, apart from the Soviet Union, began participating in the General Agreement on Tariffs and Trade (GATT), under which they worked to reduce trade barriers. The GATT was very successful in sponsoring rounds of negotiations among countries, which led to sharp declines in tariffs. U.S. tariffs dropped from an average rate of more than 50 percent in the early 1930s to an average rate of less than 2 percent in 2011. In 1995, the GATT was replaced by the World Trade Organization (WTO), which has similar objectives.

The effort to develop a new exchange rate system to replace the gold standard was more complicated than establishing the GATT. A conference held in Bretton Woods, New Hampshire, in 1944 set up a system in which the United States pledged to buy or sell gold at a fixed price of $35 per ounce. The central banks of all other members of the new **Bretton Woods system** pledged to buy and sell their currencies at a fixed rate against the dollar. By fixing their exchange rates against the dollar, these countries were fixing the exchange rates among their currencies as well. Unlike under the gold standard, neither the United States nor any other country was willing to redeem its paper currency for gold domestically. The United States would redeem dollars for gold only if they were presented by a foreign central bank. The United States continued the prohibition, first enacted in the early 1930s, against private citizens owning gold, unless they were jewelers or rare coin collectors. The prohibition was not lifted until the 1970s, when it again became possible for Americans to own gold as an investment.

> **Bretton Woods system** An exchange rate system that lasted from 1944 to 1973, under which countries pledged to buy and sell their currencies at a fixed rate against the dollar.

Under the Bretton Woods system, central banks were committed to selling dollars in exchange for their own currencies. This commitment required them to hold *dollar reserves*. If a central bank ran out of dollar reserves, it could borrow them from the newly created **International Monetary Fund (IMF)**. In addition to providing loans to central banks that were short of dollar reserves, the IMF would oversee the operation of the system and approve adjustments to the agreed-on fixed exchange rates.

> **International Monetary Fund (IMF)** An international organization that provides foreign currency loans to central banks and oversees the operation of the international monetary system.

Under the Bretton Woods system, a fixed exchange rate was known as a *par exchange rate*. If the par exchange rate was not the same as the exchange rate that would have been determined in the market, the result would be a surplus or a shortage. For example, Figure 30A.1 shows the exchange rate between the dollar and the British pound. The figure is drawn from the British point of view, so we measure the exchange rate on the vertical axis as dollars per pound. In this case, the par exchange rate between the dollar and the pound is above the equilibrium exchange rate as determined by supply and demand.

In this example, at the par exchange rate of $4 per pound, the quantity of pounds demanded by people who want to buy British goods and services or who want to invest in British assets is smaller than the quantity of pounds supplied by people who would like to exchange them for dollars. As a result, the Bank of England must use dollars to buy the surplus of £1 million per day. Only at an exchange rate of $2.80 per pound would the surplus be eliminated. If the par exchange rate was below the equilibrium

**Figure 30A.1**

**A Fixed Exchange Rate above Equilibrium Results in a Surplus of Pounds**

Under the Bretton Woods system, if the par exchange rate was above equilibrium, the result would be a surplus of domestic currency in the foreign exchange market. If the par exchange rate was below equilibrium, the result would be a shortage of domestic currency. In the figure, the par exchange rate between the pound and the dollar is $4 = £1, whereas the equilibrium exchange rate is $2.80 = £1. This gap forces the Bank of England to buy £1 million per day in exchange for dollars.

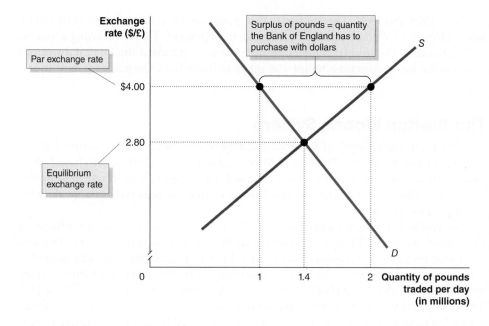

**Devaluation** A reduction in a fixed exchange rate.

**Revaluation** An increase in a fixed exchange rate.

exchange rate, there would be a shortage of domestic currency in the foreign exchange market.

A persistent shortage or surplus of a currency under the Bretton Woods system was seen as evidence of a *fundamental disequilibrium* in a country's exchange rate. After consulting with the IMF, countries in this position were allowed to adjust their exchange rates. In the early years of the Bretton Woods system, many countries found that their currencies were *overvalued* versus the dollar, meaning that their par exchange rates were too high. A reduction in a fixed exchange rate is a **devaluation**. An increase in a fixed exchange rate is a **revaluation**. In 1949, there was a devaluation of several currencies, including the British pound, reflecting the fact that those currencies had been overvalued against the dollar.

## The Collapse of the Bretton Woods System

By the late 1960s, the Bretton Woods system faced two severe problems. The first was that after 1963, the total number of dollars held by foreign central banks was larger than the gold reserves of the United States. In practice, most central banks—with the Bank of France being the main exception—rarely redeemed dollars for gold. But the basis of the system was a credible promise by the United States to redeem dollars for gold if called upon to do so. By the late 1960s, as the gap between the dollars held by foreign central banks and the gold reserves of the United States grew larger and larger, the credibility of the U.S. promise to redeem dollars for gold was called into question.

The second problem the Bretton Woods system faced was that some countries with undervalued currencies, particularly West Germany, were unwilling to revalue their currencies. Governments resisted revaluation because it would have increased the prices of their countries' exports. Many German firms, such as Volkswagen, put pressure on the government not to endanger their sales in the U.S. market by raising the exchange rate of the deutsche mark against the dollar. Figure 30A.2 shows the situation faced by the German government in 1971. The figure takes the German point of view, so the exchange rate is expressed in terms of dollars per deutsche mark.

Under the Bretton Woods system, the Bundesbank, the German central bank, was required to buy and sell deutsche marks for dollars at a rate of $0.27 per deutsche mark. The equilibrium that would have prevailed in the foreign exchange market if the Bundesbank had not intervened was about $0.35 per deutsche mark. Because the par exchange rate was below the equilibrium exchange rate, the quantity of deutsche marks demanded by people wanting to buy German goods and services or wanting to invest

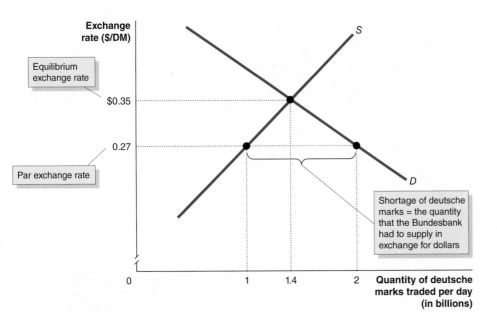

**West Germany's Undervalued Exchange Rate**

The Bundesbank, the German central bank, was committed under the Bretton Woods system to defending a par exchange rate of $0.27 per deutsche mark (DM). Because this exchange rate was lower than what the equilibrium market exchange rate would have been, there was a shortage of DMs in the foreign exchange market. The Bundesbank had to supply DMs equal to the shortage in exchange for dollars. The shortage in the figure is equal to 1 billion DMs per day.

in German assets was greater than the quantity of deutsche marks supplied by people who wanted to exchange them for dollars. To maintain the exchange rate at $0.27 per deutsche mark, the Bundesbank had to buy dollars and sell deutsche marks. The number of deutsche marks supplied by the Bundesbank was equal to the shortage of deutsche marks at the par exchange rate.

By selling deutsche marks and buying dollars to defend the par exchange rate, the Bundesbank was increasing the West German money supply, risking an increase in the inflation rate. Because Germany had suffered a devastating hyperinflation during the 1920s, the fear of inflation was greater in Germany than in any other industrial country. No German government could survive politically if it allowed a significant increase in inflation. Knowing this fact, many investors in Germany and elsewhere became convinced that eventually, the German government would have to allow a revaluation of the mark.

During the 1960s, most European countries, including Germany, relaxed their *capital controls*. **Capital controls** are limits on the flow of foreign exchange and financial investment across countries. The loosening of capital controls made it easier for investors to speculate on changes in exchange rates. For instance, an investor in the United States could sell $1 million and receive about 3.7 million deutsche marks at the par exchange rate of $0.27 per deutsche mark. If the exchange rate rose to $0.35 per deutsche mark, the investor could then exchange deutsche marks for dollars, receiving $1.3 million at the new exchange rate: a return of 30 percent on an initial $1 million investment. The more convinced investors became that Germany would have to allow a revaluation, the more dollars they exchanged for deutsche marks. Figure 30A.3 shows the results.

The increased demand for deutsche marks by investors hoping to make a profit from the expected revaluation of the mark shifted the demand curve for marks to the right, from $D_1$ to $D_2$. Because of this expectation, the Bundesbank had to increase the marks it supplied in exchange for dollars, raising further the risk of inflation in Germany. As we saw in the chapter, because these actions by investors make it more difficult to maintain a fixed exchange rate, they are referred to as *destabilizing speculation*. By May 1971, the Bundesbank had to buy more than $250 million per day to support the fixed exchange rate against the dollar. Finally, on May 5, the West German government decided to allow the mark to float. In August, President Richard Nixon decided to abandon the U.S. commitment to redeem dollars for gold. Attempts were made over the next two years to reach a compromise that would restore a fixed exchange rate system, but by 1973, the Bretton Woods system was effectively dead.

**Capital controls** Limits on the flow of foreign exchange and financial investment across countries.

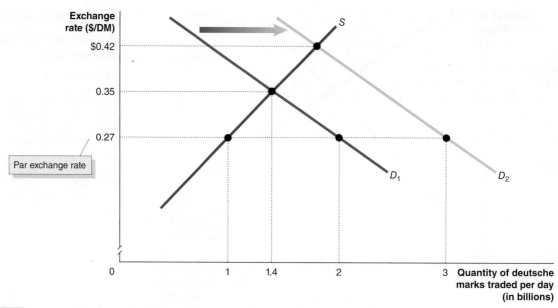

**Figure 30A.3    Destabilizing Speculation against the Deutsche Mark, 1971**

In 1971, the par exchange rate of $0.27 = 1 deutsche mark was below the equilibrium exchange rate of $0.35 = 1 deutsche mark. As investors became convinced that West Germany would have to revalue the deutsche mark, they increased their demand for marks, shifting the demand curve from $D_1$ to $D_2$. The new equilibrium exchange rate became $0.42 = 1 deutsche mark. This increase in demand raised the quantity of marks the Bundesbank had to supply in exchange for dollars to defend the par exchange rate from 1 billion deutsche marks to 2 billion deutsche marks per day.

## Key Terms

Bretton Woods system, p. 1037

Capital controls, p. 1039

Devaluation, p. 1038

International Monetary Fund (IMF), p. 1037

Revaluation, p. 1038

---

**30A**  **The Gold Standard and the Bretton Woods System, pages 1036–1040**
LEARNING OBJECTIVE: Explain the gold standard and the Bretton Woods system.

 MyEconLab    Visit www.myeconlab.com to complete these exercises online and get instant feedback.

## Review Questions

**30A.1** What determined the exchange rates among currencies under the gold standard? Why did the gold standard collapse?

**30A.2** Briefly describe how the Bretton Woods system operated.

**30A.3** What is the difference between a devaluation and a revaluation?

**30A.4** What are capital controls?

**30A.5** What role did the International Monetary Fund play in the Bretton Woods system?

**30A.6** What is destabilizing speculation? What role did it play in the collapse of the Bretton Woods system?

## Problems and Applications

**30A.7** Suppose that under the gold standard, there was 1/5 ounce of gold in a U.S. dollar and 1 ounce of gold in a British pound. Demonstrate that if the exchange rate between the dollar and the pound was $4 = £1, rather

than $5 = £1, you could make unlimited profits by buying gold in one country and selling it in the other. If the exchange rate was $6 = £1, how would your strategy change? For simplicity, assume that there was no cost to shipping gold from one country to the other.

**30A.8** An article in the *Economist* observes, "When the Depression [of the 1930s] struck, this gold standard became a noose around the necks of struggling economies." In what sense was the gold standard a "noose around the necks of struggling economies" during the 1930s?

From "A Brief Post on Competitive Devaluation," *Economist*, October 31, 2011.

**30A.9** According to an article in the *Economist*, when most countries left the gold standard in the 1930s, in South Africa "the mining industry flourished." Briefly explain why the end of the gold standard might be good news for the owners of gold mines.

From "Johannesburg," *Economist*, August 18, 2004.

**30A.10** By the mid-1960s, the price of gold on the London market had increased to more than $35 per ounce. (Remember that it was not legal during these years for investors in the United States to own gold.) Would this have happened if foreign investors had believed that the U.S. commitment to buy and sell gold at $35 per ounce under the Bretton Woods system would continue indefinitely? Briefly explain.

**30A.11** An article in the *New York Times* states that, "On Aug. 15, 1971, President Nixon unhitched the value of the dollar from the gold standard." Is the author of this article correct that the United States abandoned the gold standard in 1971? What led President Nixon to take the action described in the article?

From "Bretton Woods System" *New York Times*, October 31, 2011.

**30A.12** Barry Eichengreen, an economist at the University of California, Berkeley, describes actions taken by the Federal Reserve in 1931 to try to keep the United States on the gold standard: "[T]he New York Fed raised its discount rate by a full percentage point to defend the dollar. A week later it raised the discount rate a second time, again by a full percentage point." Why would an increase in interest rates help the United States stay on the gold standard?

From Barry Eichengreen, *Exorbitant Privlege*, (Oxford: Oxford University Press, 2011), p. 36.

**30A.13** One economist has argued that the East Asian exchange rate crisis of the late 1990s was due to "the simple failure of governments to remember the lessons from the breakdown of the Bretton Woods System." What are these lessons? In what sense did the East Asian governments fail to learn these lessons?

From Thomas D. Willett, "Crying for Argentina," *Milken Institute Review*, Second Quarter 2002.

**30A.14** An article in the *Wall Street Journal* argues that, "The Bretton Woods system ran into trouble in the 1960s, in part because U.S. trade deficits mounted." Why would increases in the U.S. trade deficit cause problems for the Bretton Woods system?

From Jon E. Hilsenrath and Mary Kissel, "Currency Decision Marks Small Shift toward Flexibility," *Wall Street Journal*, July 22, 2005.

**30A.15** An article in the *Economist* notes that after the end of the Bretton Woods system, "The Europeans did not like leaving their currencies to the whims of the markets. . . ." What does it mean for a country to leave its currency to the "whims of the markets"? What problems might a country experience as a result? What exchange rate system did most European countries ultimately adopt?

From "Forty Years On," *Economist*, August 13, 2011.

# GLOSSARY

## A

**Absolute advantage** The ability of an individual, a firm, or a country to produce more of a good or service than competitors, using the same amount of resources.

**Accounting profit** A firm's net income, measured as revenue minus operating expenses and taxes paid.

**Adverse selection** The situation in which one party to a transaction takes advantage of knowing more than the other party to the transaction.

**Aggregate demand (*AD*) curve** A curve that shows the relationship between the price level and the quantity of real GDP demanded by households, firms, and the government.

**Aggregate demand and aggregate supply model** A model that explains short-run fluctuations in real GDP and the price level.

**Aggregate expenditure (*AE*)** Total spending in the economy: the sum of consumption, planned investment, government purchases, and net exports.

**Aggregate expenditure model** A macroeconomic model that focuses on the short-run relationship between total spending and real GDP, assuming that the price level is constant.

**Allocative efficiency** A state of the economy in which production is in accordance with consumer preferences; in particular, every good or service is produced up to the point where the last unit provides a marginal benefit to society equal to the marginal cost of producing it.

**Antitrust laws** Laws aimed at eliminating collusion and promoting competition among firms.

**Arrow impossibility theorem** A mathematical theorem that holds that no system of voting can be devised that will consistently represent the underlying preferences of voters.

**Asset** Anything of value owned by a person or a firm.

**Asymmetric information** A situation in which one party to an economic transaction has less information than the other party.

**Autarky** A situation in which a country does not trade with other countries.

**Automatic stabilizers** Government spending and taxes that automatically increase or decrease along with the business cycle.

**Autonomous expenditure** An expenditure that does not depend on the level of GDP.

**Average fixed cost** Fixed cost divided by the quantity of output produced.

**Average product of labor** The total output produced by a firm divided by the quantity of workers.

**Average revenue (*AR*)** Total revenue divided by the quantity of the product sold.

**Average tax rate** Total tax paid divided by total income.

**Average total cost** Total cost divided by the quantity of output produced.

**Average variable cost** Variable cost divided by the quantity of output produced.

## B

**Balance of payments** The record of a country's trade with other countries in goods, services, and assets.

**Balance of trade** The difference between the value of the goods a country exports and the value of the goods a country imports.

**Balance sheet** A financial statement that sums up a firm's financial position on a particular day, usually the end of a quarter or year.

**Bank panic** A situation in which many banks experience runs at the same time.

**Bank run** A situation in which many depositors simultaneously decide to withdraw money from a bank.

**Barrier to entry** Anything that keeps new firms from entering an industry in which firms are earning economic profits.

**Behavioral economics** The study of situations in which people make choices that do not appear to be economically rational.

**Black market** A market in which buying and selling take place at prices that violate government price regulations.

**Bond** A financial security that represents a promise to repay a fixed amount of funds.

**Brand management** The actions of a firm intended to maintain the differentiation of a product over time.

**Bretton Woods system** An exchange rate system that lasted from 1944 to 1973, under which countries pledged to buy and sell their currencies at a fixed rate against the dollar.

**Budget constraint** The limited amount of income available to consumers to spend on goods and services.

**Budget deficit** The situation in which the government's expenditures are greater than its tax revenue.

**Budget surplus** The situation in which the government's expenditures are less than its tax revenue.

**Business cycle** Alternating periods of economic expansion and economic recession.

**Business strategy** Actions that a firm takes to achieve a goal, such as maximizing profits.

## C

**Capital** Manufactured goods that are used to produce other goods and services.

**Capital account** The part of the balance of payments that records relatively minor transactions, such as migrants' transfers and sales and purchases of nonproduced, nonfinancial assets.

**Capital controls** Limits on the flow of foreign exchange and financial investment across countries.

**Cartel** A group of firms that collude by agreeing to restrict output to increase prices and profits.

**Cash flow** The difference between the cash revenues received by a firm and the cash spending by the firm.

**Catch-up** The prediction that the level of GDP per capita (or income per capita) in poor countries will grow faster than in rich countries.

**Centrally planned economy** An economy in which the government decides how economic resources will be allocated.

***Ceteris paribus* ("all else equal") condition** The requirement that when analyzing the relationship between two variables—such as price and quantity demanded—other variables must be held constant.

**Circular-flow diagram** A model that illustrates how participants in markets are linked.

**Closed economy** An economy that has no interactions in trade or finance with other countries.

**Coase theorem** The argument of economist Ronald Coase that if transactions costs are low, private bargaining will result in an efficient solution to the problem of externalities.

**Collusion** An agreement among firms to charge the same price or otherwise not to compete.

**Command-and-control approach**  An approach that involves the government imposing quantitative limits on the amount of pollution firms are allowed to emit or requiring firms to install specific pollution control devices.

**Commodity money**  A good used as money that also has value independent of its use as money.

**Common resource**  A good that is rival but not excludable.

**Comparative advantage**  The ability of an individual, a firm, or a country to produce a good or service at a lower opportunity cost than competitors.

**Compensating differentials**  Higher wages that compensate workers for unpleasant aspects of a job.

**Competitive market equilibrium**  A market equilibrium with many buyers and many sellers.

**Complements**  Goods and services that are used together.

**Constant returns to scale**  The situation in which a firm's long-run average costs remain unchanged as it increases output.

**Consumer price index (CPI)**  An average of the prices of the goods and services purchased by the typical urban family of four.

**Consumer surplus**  The difference between the highest price a consumer is willing to pay for a good or service and the price the consumer actually pays.

**Consumption**  Spending by households on goods and services, not including spending on new houses.

**Consumption function**  The relationship between consumption spending and disposable income.

**Contractionary monetary policy**  The Federal Reserve's increasing interest rates to reduce inflation.

**Cooperative equilibrium**  An equilibrium in a game in which players cooperate to increase their mutual payoff.

**Copyright**  A government-granted exclusive right to produce and sell a creation.

**Corporate governance**  The way in which a corporation is structured and the effect that structure has on the corporation's behavior.

**Corporation**  A legal form of business that provides owners with protection from losing more than their investment should the business fail.

**Coupon payment**  An interest payment on a bond.

**Cross-price elasticity of demand**  The percentage change in quantity demanded of one good divided by the percentage change in the price of another good.

**Crowding out**  A decline in private expenditures as a result of an increase in government purchases.

**Currency appreciation**  An increase in the market value of one currency relative to another currency.

**Currency depreciation**  A decrease in the market value of one currency relative to another currency.

**Current account**  The part of the balance of payments that records a country's net exports, net income on investments, and net transfers.

**Cyclically adjusted budget deficit or surplus**  The deficit or surplus in the federal government's budget if the economy were at potential GDP.

**Cyclical unemployment**  Unemployment caused by a business cycle recession.

## D

**Deadweight loss**  The reduction in economic surplus resulting from a market not being in competitive equilibrium.

**Deflation**  A decline in the price level.

**Demand curve**  A curve that shows the relationship between the price of a product and the quantity of the product demanded.

**Demand schedule**  A table that shows the relationship between the price of a product and the quantity of the product demanded.

**Demographics**  The characteristics of a population with respect to age, race, and gender.

**Derived demand**  The demand for a factor of production; it depends on the demand for the good the factor produces.

**Devaluation**  A reduction in a fixed exchange rate.

**Direct finance**  A flow of funds from savers to firms through financial markets, such as the New York Stock Exchange.

**Discount loans**  Loans the Federal Reserve makes to banks.

**Discount rate**  The interest rate the Federal Reserve charges on discount loans.

**Discouraged workers**  People who are available for work but have not looked for a job during the previous four weeks because they believe no jobs are available for them.

**Diseconomies of scale**  The situation in which a firm's long-run average costs rise as the firm increases output.

**Disinflation**  A significant reduction in the inflation rate.

**Dividends**  Payments by a corporation to its shareholders.

**Dominant strategy**  A strategy that is the best for a firm, no matter what strategies other firms use.

**Dumping**  Selling a product for a price below its cost of production.

## E

**Economic discrimination**  Paying a person a lower wage or excluding a person from an occupation on the basis of an irrelevant characteristic such as race or gender.

**Economic efficiency**  A market outcome in which the marginal benefit to consumers of the last unit produced is equal to its marginal cost of production and in which the sum of consumer surplus and producer surplus is at a maximum.

**Economic growth**  The ability of the economy to increase the production of goods and services.

**Economic growth model**  A model that explains growth rates in real GDP per capita over the long run.

**Economic loss**  The situation in which a firm's total revenue is less than its total cost, including all implicit costs.

**Economic model**  A simplified version of reality used to analyze real-world economic situations.

**Economic profit**  A firm's revenues minus all its costs, implicit and explicit.

**Economic rent (or pure rent)**  The price of a factor of production that is in fixed supply.

**Economics**  The study of the choices people make to attain their goals, given their scarce resources.

**Economic surplus**  The sum of consumer surplus and producer surplus.

**Economic variable**  Something measurable that can have different values, such as the incomes of doctors.

**Economies of scale**  The situation when a firm's long-run average costs fall as the firm increases output.

**Efficiency wage**  A higher-than-market wage that a firm pays to increase worker productivity.

**Elastic demand**  Demand is elastic when the percentage change in quantity demanded is *greater* than the percentage change in price, so the price elasticity is *greater* than 1 in absolute value.

**Elasticity**  A measure of how much one economic variable responds to changes in another economic variable.

**Endowment effect**  The tendency of people to be unwilling to sell a good they already own even if they are offered a price that is greater than the price they would be willing to pay to buy the good if they didn't already own it.

**Entrepreneur** Someone who operates a business, bringing together the factors of production—labor, capital, and natural resources—to produce goods and services.

**Equity** The fair distribution of economic benefits.

**Euro** The common currency of many European countries.

**Excess burden** A measure of the efficiency loss to the economy that results from a tax having reduced the quantity of a good produced; also known as the deadweight loss.

**Excess reserves** Reserves that banks hold over and above the legal requirement.

**Exchange rate system** An agreement among countries about how exchange rates should be determined.

**Excludability** The situation in which anyone who does not pay for a good cannot consume it.

**Expansion** The period of a business cycle during which total production and total employment are increasing.

**Expansionary monetary policy** The Federal Reserve's decreasing interest rates to increase real GDP.

**Expansion path** A curve that shows a firm's cost-minimizing combination of inputs for every level of output.

**Explicit cost** A cost that involves spending money.

**Exports** Goods and services produced domestically but sold in other countries.

**External economies** Reductions in a firm's costs that result from an increase in the size of an industry.

**Externality** A benefit or cost that affects someone who is not directly involved in the production or consumption of a good or service.

**F**

**Factor market** A market for the factors of production, such as labor, capital, natural resources, and entrepreneurial ability.

**Factors of production** Labor, capital, natural resources, and other inputs used to produce goods and services.

**Federal funds rate** The interest rate banks charge each other for overnight loans.

**Federal Open Market Committee (FOMC)** The Federal Reserve committee responsible for open market operations and managing the money supply in the United States.

**Federal Reserve** The central bank of the United States.

**Fee-for-service** A system under which doctors and hospitals receive a separate payment for each service that they provide.

**Fiat money** Money, such as paper currency, that is authorized by a central bank or governmental body and that does not have to be exchanged by the central bank for gold or some other commodity money.

**Final good or service** A good or service purchased by a final user.

**Financial account** The part of the balance of payments that records purchases of assets a country has made abroad and foreign purchases of assets in the country.

**Financial intermediaries** Firms, such as banks, mutual funds, pension funds, and insurance companies, that borrow funds from savers and lend them to borrowers.

**Financial markets** Markets where financial securities, such as stocks and bonds, are bought and sold.

**Financial system** The system of financial markets and financial intermediaries through which firms acquire funds from households.

**Fiscal policy** Changes in federal taxes and purchases that are intended to achieve macroeconomic policy objectives.

**Fixed costs** Costs that remain constant as output changes.

**Fixed exchange rate system** A system under which countries agree to keep the exchange rates among their currencies fixed.

**Floating currency** The outcome of a country allowing its currency's exchange rate to be determined by demand and supply.

**Foreign direct investment (FDI)** The purchase or building by a corporation of a facility in a foreign country.

**Foreign portfolio investment** The purchase by an individual or a firm of stocks or bonds issued in another country.

**Fractional reserve banking system** A banking system in which banks keep less than 100 percent of deposits as reserves.

**Free market** A market with few government restrictions on how a good or service can be produced or sold or on how a factor of production can be employed.

**Free riding** Benefiting from a good without paying for it.

**Free trade** Trade between countries that is without government restrictions.

**Frictional unemployment** Short-term unemployment that arises from the process of matching workers with jobs.

**G**

**Game theory** The study of how people make decisions in situations in which attaining their goals depends on their interactions with others; in economics, the study of the decisions of firms in industries where the profits of a firm depend on its interactions with other firms.

**GDP deflator** A measure of the price level, calculated by dividing nominal GDP by real GDP and multiplying by 100.

**Globalization** The process of countries becoming more open to foreign trade and investment.

**Government purchases** Spending by federal, state, and local governments on goods and services.

**Gross domestic product (GDP)** The market value of all final goods and services produced in a country during a period of time, typically one year.

**H**

**Health care** The goods and services, such as prescription drugs and consultations with a doctor, that are intended to maintain or improve a person's health.

**Health insurance** A contract under which a buyer agrees to make payments, or *premiums*, in exchange for the provider's agreeing to pay some or all of the buyer's medical bills.

**Horizontal merger** A merger between firms in the same industry.

**Human capital** The accumulated knowledge and skills that workers acquire from education and training or from their life experiences.

**I**

**Implicit cost** A nonmonetary opportunity cost.

**Imports** Goods and services bought domestically but produced in other countries.

**Income effect** The change in the quantity demanded of a good that results from the effect of a change in the good's price on consumers' purchasing power.

**Income elasticity of demand** A measure of the responsiveness of quantity demanded to changes in income, measured by the percentage change in quantity demanded divided by the percentage change in income.

**Income statement** A financial statement that sums up a firm's revenues, costs, and profit over a period of time.

**Indifference curve** A curve that shows the combinations of consumption bundles that give the consumer the same utility.

**Indirect finance** A flow of funds from savers to borrowers through financial intermediaries such as banks. Intermediaries raise funds from savers to lend to firms (and other borrowers).

**Industrial Revolution** The application of mechanical power to the production of goods, beginning in England around 1750.

**Inelastic demand**   Demand is inelastic when the percentage change in quantity demanded is *less* than the percentage change in price, so the price elasticity is *less* than 1 in absolute value.

**Inferior good**   A good for which the demand increases as income falls and decreases as income rises.

**Inflation rate**   The percentage increase in the price level from one year to the next.

**Inflation targeting**   Conducting monetary policy so as to commit the central bank to achieving a publicly announced level of inflation.

**Interest rate**   The cost of borrowing funds, usually expressed as a percentage of the amount borrowed.

**Intermediate good or service**   A good or service that is an input into another good or service, such as a tire on a truck.

**International Monetary Fund (IMF)**   An international organization that provides foreign currency loans to central banks and oversees the operation of the international monetary system.

**Inventories**   Goods that have been produced but not yet sold.

**Investment**   Spending by firms on new factories, office buildings, machinery, and additions to inventories, plus spending by households and firms on new houses.

**Isocost line**   All the combinations of two inputs, such as capital and labor, that have the same total cost.

**Isoquant**   A curve that shows all the combinations of two inputs, such as capital and labor, that will produce the same level of output.

## K

**Keynesian revolution**   The name given to the widespread acceptance during the 1930s and 1940s of John Maynard Keynes's macroeconomic model.

## L

**Labor force**   The sum of employed and unemployed workers in the economy.

**Labor force participation rate**   The percentage of the working-age population in the labor force.

**Labor productivity**   The quantity of goods and services that can be produced by one worker or by one hour of work.

**Labor union**   An organization of employees that has a legal right to bargain with employers about wages and working conditions.

**Law of demand**   The rule that, holding everything else constant, when the price of a product falls, the quantity demanded of the product will increase, and when the price of a product rises, the quantity demanded of the product will decrease.

**Law of diminishing marginal utility**   The principle that consumers experience diminishing additional satisfaction as they consume more of a good or service during a given period of time.

**Law of diminishing returns**   The principle that, at some point, adding more of a variable input, such as labor, to the same amount of a fixed input, such as capital, will cause the marginal product of the variable input to decline.

**Law of supply**   The rule that, holding everything else constant, increases in price cause increases in the quantity supplied, and decreases in price cause decreases in the quantity supplied.

**Liability**   Anything owed by a person or a firm.

**Limited liability**   The legal provision that shields owners of a corporation from losing more than they have invested in the firm.

**Long run**   The period of time in which a firm can vary all its inputs, adopt new technology, and increase or decrease the size of its physical plant.

**Long-run aggregate supply (LRAS) curve**   A curve that shows the relationship in the long run between the price level and the quantity of real GDP supplied.

**Long-run average cost curve**   A curve that shows the lowest cost at which a firm is able to produce a given quantity of output in the

long run, when no inputs are fixed.

**Long-run competitive equilibrium**   The situation in which the entry and exit of firms has resulted in the typical firm breaking even.

**Long-run economic growth**   The process by which rising productivity increases the average standard of living.

**Long-run supply curve**   A curve that shows the relationship in the long run between market price and the quantity supplied.

**Lorenz curve**   A curve that shows the distribution of income by arraying incomes from lowest to highest on the horizontal axis and indicating the cumulative fraction of income earned by each fraction of households on the vertical axis.

## M

**M1**   The narrowest definition of the money supply: The sum of currency in circulation, checking account deposits in banks, and holdings of traveler's checks.

**M2**   A broader definition of the money supply: It includes M1 plus savings account balances, small-denomination time deposits, balances in money market deposit accounts in banks, and noninstitutional money market fund shares.

**Macroeconomics**   The study of the economy as a whole, including topics such as inflation, unemployment, and economic growth.

**Managed float exchange rate system**   The current exchange rate system, under which the value of most currencies is determined by demand and supply, with occasional government intervention.

**Marginal analysis**   Analysis that involves comparing marginal benefits and marginal costs.

**Marginal benefit**   The additional benefit to a consumer from consuming one more unit of a good or service.

**Marginal cost**   The additional cost to a firm of producing one more unit of a good or service.

**Marginal productivity theory of income distribution**   The theory that the distribution of income is determined by the marginal productivity of the factors of production that individuals own.

**Marginal product of labor**   The additional output a firm produces as a result of hiring one more worker.

**Marginal propensity to consume (MPC)**   The slope of the consumption function: The amount by which consumption spending changes when disposable income changes.

**Marginal propensity to save (MPS)**   The amount by which saving changes when disposable income changes.

**Marginal rate of substitution (MRS)**   The rate at which a consumer would be willing to trade off one good for another.

**Marginal rate of technical substitution (MRTS)**   The rate at which a firm is able to substitute one input for another while keeping the level of output constant.

**Marginal revenue (MR)**   The change in total revenue from selling one more unit of a product.

**Marginal revenue product of labor (MRP)**   The change in a firm's revenue as a result of hiring one more worker.

**Marginal tax rate**   The fraction of each additional dollar of income that must be paid in taxes.

**Marginal utility (MU)**   The change in total utility a person receives from consuming one additional unit of a good or service.

**Market**   A group of buyers and sellers of a good or service and the institution or arrangement by which they come together to trade.

**Market-based reforms**   Changes in the market for health care that would make it more like the markets for other goods and services.

**Market demand**   The demand by all the consumers of a given good or service.

**Market economy** An economy in which the decisions of households and firms interacting in markets allocate economic resources.

**Market equilibrium** A situation in which quantity demanded equals quantity supplied.

**Market failure** A situation in which the market fails to produce the efficient level of output.

**Market for loanable funds** The interaction of borrowers and lenders that determines the market interest rate and the quantity of loanable funds exchanged.

**Marketing** All the activities necessary for a firm to sell a product to a consumer.

**Market power** The ability of a firm to charge a price greater than marginal cost.

**Median voter theorem** The proposition that the outcome of a majority vote is likely to represent the preferences of the voter who is in the political middle.

**Menu costs** The costs to firms of changing prices.

**Microeconomics** The study of how households and firms make choices, how they interact in markets, and how the government attempts to influence their choices.

**Minimum efficient scale** The level of output at which all economies of scale are exhausted.

**Mixed economy** An economy in which most economic decisions result from the interaction of buyers and sellers in markets but in which the government plays a significant role in the allocation of resources.

**Monetarism** The macroeconomic theories of Milton Friedman and his followers, particularly the idea that the quantity of money should be increased at a constant rate.

**Monetary growth rule** A plan for increasing the quantity of money at a fixed rate that does not respond to changes in economic conditions.

**Monetary policy** The actions the Federal Reserve takes to manage the money supply and interest rates to pursue macroeconomic policy objectives.

**Money** Assets that people are generally willing to accept in exchange for goods and services or for payment of debts.

**Monopolistic competition** A market structure in which barriers to entry are low and many firms compete by selling similar, but not identical, products.

**Monopoly** A firm that is the only seller of a good or service that does not have a close substitute.

**Monopsony** The sole buyer of a factor of production.

**Moral hazard** The actions people take after they have entered into a transaction that make the other party to the transaction worse off.

**Multiplier** The increase in equilibrium real GDP divided by the increase in autonomous expenditure.

**Multiplier effect** The series of induced increases in consumption spending that results from an initial increase in autonomous expenditures.

## N

**Nash equilibrium** A situation in which each firm chooses the best strategy, given the strategies chosen by other firms.

**Natural monopoly** A situation in which economies of scale are so large that one firm can supply the entire market at a lower average total cost than can two or more firms.

**Natural rate of unemployment** The normal rate of unemployment, consisting of frictional unemployment plus structural unemployment.

**Net exports** Exports minus imports.

**Net foreign investment** The difference between capital outflows from a country and capital inflows, also equal to net foreign direct investment plus net foreign portfolio investment.

**Network externalities** A situation in which the usefulness of a product increases with the number of consumers who use it.

**New classical macroeconomics** The macroeconomic theories of Robert Lucas and others, particularly the idea that workers and firms have rational expectations.

**New growth theory** A model of long-run economic growth that emphasizes that technological change is influenced by economic incentives and so is determined by the working of the market system.

**Nominal exchange rate** The value of one country's currency in terms of another country's currency.

**Nominal GDP** The value of final goods and services evaluated at current-year prices.

**Nominal interest rate** The stated interest rate on a loan.

**Nonaccelerating inflation rate of unemployment (NAIRU)** The unemployment rate at which the inflation rate has no tendency to increase or decrease.

**Noncooperative equilibrium** An equilibrium in a game in which players do not cooperate but pursue their own self-interest.

**Normal good** A good for which the demand increases as income rises and decreases as income falls.

**Normative analysis** Analysis concerned with what ought to be.

## O

**Oligopoly** A market structure in which a small number of interdependent firms compete.

**Open economy** An economy that has interactions in trade or finance with other countries.

**Open market operations** The buying and selling of Treasury securities by the Federal Reserve in order to control the money supply.

**Opportunity cost** The highest-valued alternative that must be given up to engage in an activity.

## P

**Partnership** A firm owned jointly by two or more persons and not organized as a corporation.

**Patent** The exclusive right to a product for a period of 20 years from the date the patent is filed with the government.

**Patient Protection and Affordable Care Act (PPACA)** Health care reform legislation passed by Congress and signed by President Barack Obama in 2010.

**Payoff matrix** A table that shows the payoffs that each firm earns from every combination of strategies by the firms.

**Pegging** The decision by a country to keep the exchange rate fixed between its currency and another country's currency.

**Perfectly competitive market** A market that meets the conditions of (1) many buyers and sellers, (2) all firms selling identical products, and (3) no barriers to new firms entering the market.

**Perfectly elastic demand** The case where the quantity demanded is infinitely responsive to price, and the price elasticity of demand equals infinity.

**Perfectly inelastic demand** The case where the quantity demanded is completely unresponsive to price and the price elasticity of demand equals zero.

**Personnel economics** The application of economic analysis to human resources issues.

**Per-worker production function** The relationship between real GDP per hour worked and capital per hour worked, holding the level of technology constant.

**Phillips curve** A curve showing the short-run relationship between the unemployment rate and the inflation rate.

**Pigovian taxes and subsidies** Government taxes and subsidies intended to bring about an efficient level of output in the presence of externalities.

**Positive analysis** Analysis concerned with what is.

**Potential GDP** The level of real GDP attained when all firms are producing at capacity.

**Poverty line** A level of annual income equal to three times the amount of money necessary to purchase the minimum quantity of food required for adequate nutrition.

**Poverty rate** The percentage of the population that is poor according to the federal government's definition.

**Present value** The value in today's dollars of funds to be paid or received in the future.

**Price ceiling** A legally determined maximum price that sellers may charge.

**Price discrimination** Charging different prices to different customers for the same product when the price differences are not due to differences in cost.

**Price elasticity of demand** The responsiveness of the quantity demanded to a change in price, measured by dividing the percentage change in the quantity demanded of a product by the percentage change in the product's price.

**Price elasticity of supply** The responsiveness of the quantity supplied to a change in price, measured by dividing the percentage change in the quantity supplied of a product by the percentage change in the product's price.

**Price floor** A legally determined minimum price that sellers may receive.

**Price leadership** A form of implicit collusion in which one firm in an oligopoly announces a price change and the other firms in the industry match the change.

**Price level** A measure of the average prices of goods and services in the economy.

**Price taker** A buyer or seller that is unable to affect the market price.

**Principal–agent problem** A problem caused by agents pursuing their own interests rather than the interests of the principals who hired them.

**Prisoner's dilemma** A game in which pursuing dominant strategies results in noncooperation that leaves everyone worse off.

**Private benefit** The benefit received by the consumer of a good or service.

**Private cost** The cost borne by the producer of a good or service.

**Private good** A good that is both rival and excludable.

**Producer price index (PPI)** An average of the prices received by producers of goods and services at all stages of the production process.

**Producer surplus** The difference between the lowest price a firm would be willing to accept for a good or service and the price it actually receives.

**Production function** The relationship between the inputs employed by a firm and the maximum output it can produce with those inputs.

**Production possibilities frontier (PPF)** A curve showing the maximum attainable combinations of two products that may be produced with available resources and current technology.

**Productive efficiency** A situation in which a good or service is produced at the lowest possible cost.

**Product market** A market for goods—such as computers—or services—such as medical treatment.

**Profit** Total revenue minus total cost.

**Progressive tax** A tax for which people with lower incomes pay a lower percentage of their income in tax than do people with higher incomes.

**Property rights** The rights individuals or firms have to the exclusive use of their property, including the right to buy or sell it.

**Protectionism** The use of trade barriers to shield domestic firms from foreign competition.

**Public choice model** A model that applies economic analysis to government decision making.

**Public franchise** A government designation that a firm is the only legal provider of a good or service.

**Public good** A good that is both nonrival and nonexcludable.

**Purchasing power parity** The theory that in the long run, exchange rates move to equalize the purchasing powers of different currencies.

## Q

**Quantity demanded** The amount of a good or service that a consumer is willing and able to purchase at a given price.

**Quantity supplied** The amount of a good or service that a firm is willing and able to supply at a given price.

**Quantity theory of money** A theory about the connection between money and prices that assumes that the velocity of money is constant.

**Quota** A numerical limit a government imposes on the quantity of a good that can be imported into the country.

## R

**Rational expectations** Expectations formed by using all available information about an economic variable.

**Real business cycle model** A macroeconomic model that focuses on real, rather than monetary, causes of the business cycle.

**Real exchange rate** The price of domestic goods in terms of foreign goods.

**Real GDP** The value of final goods and services evaluated at base-year prices.

**Real interest rate** The nominal interest rate minus the inflation rate.

**Recession** The period of a business cycle during which total production and total employment are decreasing.

**Regressive tax** A tax for which people with lower incomes pay a higher percentage of their income in tax than do people with higher incomes.

**Rent seeking** Attempts by individuals and firms to use government action to make themselves better off at the expense of others.

**Required reserve ratio** The minimum fraction of deposits banks are required by law to keep as reserves.

**Required reserves** Reserves that a bank is legally required to hold,

based on its checking account deposits.

**Reserves** Deposits that a bank keeps as cash in its vault or on deposit with the Federal Reserve.

**Revaluation** An increase in a fixed exchange rate.

**Rivalry** The situation that occurs when one person's consuming a unit of a good means no one else can consume it.

**Rule of law** The ability of a government to enforce the laws of the country, particularly with respect to protecting private property and enforcing contracts.

## S

**Saving and investment equation** An equation that shows that national saving is equal to domestic investment plus net foreign investment.

**Scarcity** A situation in which unlimited wants exceed the limited resources available to fulfill those wants.

**Securitization** The process of transforming loans or other financial assets into securities.

**Security** A financial asset—such as a stock or a bond—that can be bought and sold in a financial market.

**Separation of ownership from control** A situation in a corporation in which the top management, rather than the shareholders, control day-to-day operations.

**Shortage** A situation in which the quantity demanded is greater than the quantity supplied.

**Short run** The period of time during which at least one of a firm's inputs is fixed.

**Short-run aggregate supply (SRAS) curve** A curve that shows the relationship in the short run between the price level and the quantity of real GDP supplied by firms.

**Shutdown point** The minimum point on a firm's average variable cost curve; if the price falls below this point, the firm shuts down production in the short run.

**Simple deposit multiplier** The ratio of the amount of deposits created by banks to the amount of new reserves.

**Single-payer health care system** A system, such as the one in Canada, in which the government provides health insurance to all of the country's residents.

**Social benefit** The total benefit from consuming a good or service, including both the private benefit and any external benefit.

**Social cost** The total cost of producing a good or service, including both the private cost and any external cost.

**Socialized medicine** A health care system under which the government owns most of the hospitals and employs most of the doctors.

**Sole proprietorship** A firm owned by a single individual and not organized as a corporation.

**Speculators** Currency traders who buy and sell foreign exchange in an attempt to profit from changes in exchange rates.

**Stagflation** A combination of inflation and recession, usually resulting from a supply shock.

**Stock** A financial security that represents partial ownership of a firm.

**Stockholders' equity** The difference between the value of a corporation's assets and the value of its liabilities; also known as *net worth*.

**Structural relationship** A relationship that depends on the basic behavior of consumers and firms and that remains unchanged over long periods.

**Structural unemployment** Unemployment that arises from a persistent mismatch between the skills and attributes of workers and the requirements of jobs.

**Substitutes** Goods and services that can be used for the same purpose.

**Substitution effect** The change in the quantity demanded of a good that results from a change in price, making the good more or less expensive relative to other goods that are substitutes.

**Sunk cost** A cost that has already been paid and cannot be recovered.

**Supply curve** A curve that shows the relationship between the price of a product and the quantity of the product supplied.

**Supply schedule** A table that shows the relationship between the price of a product and the quantity of the product supplied.

**Supply shock** An unexpected event that causes the short-run aggregate supply curve to shift.

**Surplus** A situation in which the quantity supplied is greater than the quantity demanded.

**T**

**Tariff** A tax imposed by a government on imports.

**Tax incidence** The actual division of the burden of a tax between buyers and sellers in a market.

**Tax wedge** The difference between the pretax and posttax return to an economic activity.

**Taylor rule** A rule developed by John Taylor that links the Fed's target for the federal funds rate to economic variables.

**Technological change** A change in the ability of a firm to produce a given level of output with a given quantity of inputs.

**Technology** The processes a firm uses to turn inputs into outputs of goods and services.

**Terms of trade** The ratio at which a country can trade its exports for imports from other countries.

**Total cost** The cost of all the inputs a firm uses in production.

**Total revenue** The total amount of funds received by a seller of a good or service, calculated by multiplying price per unit by the number of units sold.

**Trade** The act of buying and selling.

**Trade-off** The idea that because of scarcity, producing more of one good or service means producing less of another good or service.

**Tragedy of the commons** The tendency for a common resource to be overused.

**Transactions costs** The costs in time and other resources that parties incur in the process of agreeing to and carrying out an exchange of goods or services.

**Transfer payments** Payments by the government to households for which the government does not receive a new good or service in return.

**Two-part tariff** A situation in which consumers pay one price (or tariff) for the right to buy as much of a related good as they want at a second price.

**U**

**Underground economy** Buying and selling of goods and services that is concealed from the government to avoid taxes or regulations or because the goods and services are illegal.

**Unemployment rate** The percentage of the labor force that is unemployed.

**Unit-elastic demand** Demand is unit elastic when the percentage change in quantity demanded is *equal to* the percentage change in price, so the price elasticity is equal to 1 in absolute value.

**Utility** The enjoyment or satisfaction people receive from consuming goods and services.

**V**

**Value added** The market value a firm adds to a product.

**Variable costs** Costs that change as output changes.

**Velocity of money** The average number of times each dollar in the money supply is used to purchase goods and services included in GDP.

**Vertical merger** A merger between firms at different stages of production of a good.

**Voluntary exchange** A situation that occurs in markets when both the buyer and seller of a product are made better off by the transaction.

**Voluntary export restraint (VER)** An agreement negotiated between two countries that places a numerical limit on the quantity of a good that can be imported by one country from the other country.

**Voting paradox** The failure of majority voting to always result in consistent choices.

**W**

**Wall Street Reform and Consumer Protection Act (Dodd-Frank Act)** Legislation passed during 2010 that was intended to reform regulation of the financial system.

**World Trade Organization (WTO)** An international organization that oversees international trade agreements.

Key terms and the page on which they are defined appear in **boldface**.

# CREDITS

## Photo

**Front matter**, *page vii*, Courtesy of the authors; *page xxxvii*, Wavebreakmedia, Ltd./Shutterstock; *page xl*, MCT/Getty Images.

**Chapter 1**, *page 2*, Getty Images; *page 15*, Ocean/Corbis.

**Chapter 2**, *page 38*, Bloomberg/Getty Images; *page 43*, Caro/Alamy; *page 53*, JupiterImages; *page 53*, MBI/Alamy; *page 53*, Mikael Damkier/Shutterstock; *page 53*, Elena Elisseeva/Shutterstock; *page 55*, Brooks Kraft/Corbis.

**Chapter 3**, *page 68*, Wavebreakmedia, Ltd./Shutterstock; *page 73*, British Retail Photography/Alamy; *page 77*, MCT/Getty Images.

**Chapter 4**, *page 100*, Janine Wiedel Photolibrary/Alamy.

**Chapter 5**, *page 136*, James Schwabel/Alamy; *page 145*, Natacha Pisarenko/AP Images.

**Chapter 6**, *page 170*, Tom Merton/Getty Images; *page 185*, Yonhap News Agency/EPA/Newscom.

**Chapter 7**, *page 204*, StockbrokerXtra/Glow Images; *page 219*, Official White House Photo by Pete Souza; *page 228*, Jim West/Alamy.

**Chapter 8**, *page 236*, Bloomberg/Getty Images; *page 240*, Mangostock/Shutterstock; *page 254*, Getty Images.

**Chapter 9**, *page 272*, Charles Rex Arbogast/AP Images; *page 284*, Sean Pavone Photo/Shutterstock; *page 291*, Robert F. Bukaty/AP Images; *page 294*, Joerg Boethling/Alamy.

**Chapter 10**, *page 308*, Christopher Polk/Getty Images Entertainment/Getty Images; *page 320*, Tiziana and Gianni Baldizzone/Corbis; *page 321*, Chelsea Matiash/AP Images; *page 328*, Jay Paul/The New York Times/Redux; *page 329*, Larry Kolvoord/The Image Works.

**Chapter 11**, *page 352*, TWPhoto/Corbis; *page 355*, Washington Post/Getty Images; *page 356*, Martin Black/PhotoLibrary; *page 361*, Ria Novosti/Alamy; *page 371*, Everett Collection, Inc./Alamy; *page 390*, Tomasso DeRosa/Corbis.

**Chapter 12**, *page 394*, Gary Kazanjian/AP Images; *page 416*, Alex Segre/Alamy.

**Chapter 13**, *page 430*, Michele Falzone/Alamy; *page 440*, Lou Linwei/Alamy; *page 445*, Ian Dagnall/Alamy; *page 447*, Studiomode/Alamy.

**Chapter 14**, *page 458*, Diana Bier/British Library, London/Alamy; *page 466*, Vicki Beaver/Alamy; *page 469*, David Butow/Corbis; *page 476*, Damian Dovarganes/AP Images.

**Chapter 15**, *page 486*, AP Images; *page 489*, Paul Sakuma/AP Images; *page 491*, AP Images; *page 492*, Niall McDiarmid/Alamy; *page 507*, Dick Blume/The Post-Standard /Landov.

**Chapter 16**, *page 518*, Yvette Cardozo/Alamy; *page 527*, Bruce Newman/Oxford Eagle/AP Images; *page 530*, David Young-Wolff/PhotoEdit, Inc.

**Chapter 17**, *page 544*, Getty Images; *page 557*, Left Eyed Photography/Shutterstock; *page 559*, AP Images; *page 563*, Ariel Skelley/Blend Images/Corbis; *page 567*, Safelite Group.

**Chapter 18**, *page 580*, Kristoffer Tripplaar/Alamy; *page 592*, Spencer Grant/PhotoEdit, Inc.; *page 595*, Amy Sussman/Corbis.

**Chapter 19**, *page 614*, Jeff Kowalsky/Bloomberg/Getty Images; *page 619*, Mikael Damkier/Shutterstock; *page 619*, Eric Gevaert/Shutterstock; *page 619*, Bill Aron/PhotoEdit, Inc.; *page 619*, JupiterImages; *page 619*, Yoshio Tomii/SuperStock; *page 625*, Mohamed Nureldin Abdallah/Reuters.

**Chapter 20**, *page 640*, Richard Levine/Alamy; *page 654*, Chris Keane/Reuters.

**Chapter 21**, *page 676*, Stephen Brashear/Getty Images; *page 690*, Everett Collection; *page 696*, Paul Sakuma/AP Images.

**Chapter 22**, *page 710*, Zuma Press/Newscom; *page 713*, Author's Image Ltd/Alamy; *page 716*, Grant Neuenburg/Reuters/Corbis; *page 720*, Lionel Cironneau/AP Images; *page 736*, Claro Cortes IV/Reuters/Corbis.

**Chapter 23**, *page 748*, Justin Sullivan/Staff/Getty Images; *page 775*, Everett Collection/SuperStock.

**Chapter 24**, *page 792*, AGE Fotostock/SuperStock; *page 808*, Kimberly White/Corbis; *page 811*, Kevin Dietsch/UPI/Newscom; *page 827*, Lebrecht Music and Arts/Photo Library/Alamy.

**Chapter 25**, *page 828*, Marco Di Lauro/Getty Images; *page 833*, Brooks Kraft/Corbis; *page 835*, James L. Amos/Photo Researchers, Inc.; *page 848 (far left and third from right)*, Lynne Sladky/AP Images; *page 848 (center left and center right)*, Ezio Petersen/UPI/Landov; *page 848 (third from left and far right)*, Eightfish/Alamy; *page 848 (bottom left)*, Imagebroker/Alamy; *page 853*, Bettmann/Corbis.

**Chapter 26**, *page 864*, Matt Nager/Bloomberg/Getty Images; *page 877*, NetPhotos/Alamy; *page 888*, Iofoto/Shutterstock; *page 892*, Rebecca Cook/Reuters/Corbis.

**Chapter 27**, *page 904*, Justin Sullivan/Getty Images; *page 909*, Tom Grill/Corbis Super RF/Alamy; *page 924*, David Banks/EPA/Corbis; *page 928*, AP Images.

**Chapter 28**, *page 950*, Bloomberg/Getty Images; *page 956*, Corbis Super RF/Alamy; *page 960*, David J. Green-Lifestyle/Alamy.

**Chapter 29**, *page 982*, Imaginechina/Corbis; *page 989*, Iain Masterton/Alamy.

**Chapter 30**, *page 1012*, Meigneux/SIPA/AP Images; *page 1016*, Thomas Barwick/Getty Images; *page 1018*, Bloomberg/Getty Images; *page 1022*, Yves Logghe/AP Images.

We use **business examples** to explain economic concepts. This table highlights the topic and **real-world** company introduced in the chapter-opening vignette and revisited throughout the chapter. This table also lists the companies that appear in our *Making the Connection* and *An Inside Look* features.